GAY &
LESBIAN
LITERATURE

VOLUME 2

GAY & LESBIAN LITERATURE

VOLUME 2

INTRODUCTION TO GAY MALE LITERATURE
JIM MARKS

INTRODUCTION TO LESBIAN LITERATURE
LORALEE MACPIKE

EDITORS
TOM PENDERGAST
&
SARA PENDERGAST

ENDORSED BY THE GAY, LESBIAN, AND BISEXUAL LIBRARIANS TASK FORCE
AMERICAN LIBRARY ASSOCIATION

THE GAY, LESBIAN, AND BISEXUAL LIBRARIANS TASK FORCE
IS THE NATION'S FIRST GAY, LESBIAN, AND BISEXUAL
PROFESSIONAL ORGANIZATION

ST. JAMES PRESS

AN IMPRINT OF GALE

DETROIT • NEW YORK • TORONTO • LONDON

Tom Pendergast and Sara Pendergast, *Editors*

Sharon Malinowski, David Collins
Project Coordinators

Laura Standley Berger, Joann Cerrito, Nicolet V. Elert, Miranda Ferrara,
Kristin Hart, Janice Jorgensen, Margaret Mazurkiewicz, Michael J. Tyrkus
St. James Press Staff

Peter M. Gareffa, *Managing Editor, St. James Press*

Mary Beth Trimper, *Production Director*
Shanna Heilveil, *Production Assistant*

Cynthia Baldwin, *Product Design Manager*
Gary Leach, *Art Director*

The paper used in this publication meets the minimum
requirements of American National Standard for Information Sciences—
Permanence Paper for Printed Library Materials, ANSI Z39.48-1984.

A CIP record is available from the British Library
ISBN 1-55862-350-7

Printed in the United States of America
Published simultaneously in the United Kingdom

St. James Press is an imprint of Gale
10 9 8 7 6 5 4 3 2 1

Contents

Preface

In 1994, St. James Press published the first volume of *Gay and Lesbian Literature* to fill a need for reference sources on homosexuality in both academic and public libraries. Since that time interest in the fields of gay, lesbian, bisexual, and transgender literature has continued to increase, meriting a second volume of *Gay and Lesbian Literature.* With the endorsement of the Gay, Lesbian, and Bisexual Librarians Task Force of the American Library Association's Social Responsibilities Round Table, St. James Press introduces this extensive compilation of biographical, bibliographical, and critical information on nearly 200 authors who have figured prominently in gay and lesbian literature and culture since 1900.

Scope

International in scope, *Gay & Lesbian Literature* includes novelists, poets, short story writers, dramatists, journalists, editors, filmmakers, performance artists, and writers of nonfiction, including scholars whose work has contributed significantly to the field, in addition to authors known predominantly for their work in social and political arenas. Inclusion is based upon the gay and lesbian thematic content of a writer's work and not upon sexual identity. Although the emphasis of this collection focuses upon the most eminent and frequently studied authors of gay and lesbian literature writing today, significant deceased authors from the earlier portion of the century who have exerted a major influence on contemporary gay and lesbian literature are also included, as are younger writers whose work promises to generate a lasting contribution to the field.

Preparation

The editor of the first volume of *Gay & Lesbian Literature* passed on to us a list of over one thousand writers for consideration for this volume. Working with our advisory board, several members of whom are or have been active in the Gay, Lesbian, and Bisexual Librarians Task Force of the American Library Association, we added to this list and then selected some 250 authors for potential inclusion. Mailings were made to all living authors so that information might be as complete and accurate as possible.

Entry Format

Entries in *Gay & Lesbian Literature* provide in-depth biographical, bibliographical, and critical information that is unavailable in any other single reference source. The format of each entry is designed for ease of use by students, teachers, scholars, librarians, and the general public. Entries in *Gay & Lesbian Literature* provide all available information under the appropriate headings and are arranged as follows:

- Author is featured under name by which he/she is best known—if a pseudonym or variation, the author's given name follows. Any pseudonyms or name variations used for writing are also listed and cross-references appear throughout the text.

- Personal information about the author, including date and place of birth, country of residence or citizenship, and educational background, plus marriage and/or companion information.

- Summary of author's career, including employers, positions, and dates held for each career post, vocational achievements, and military service.

- Summary of professional, civic, and other affiliations, plus any official posts held.

- Awards: List of major prizes and nominations, fellowships, and grants, honoring the author and his/her work.

- Agent/Addresses: Address at which author or his/her agent may be contacted.

- If author is deceased, the place, cause, and date of his/her death.

- A comprehensive list of titles, publishers, dates of original publication and revised editions, and production information for plays, televised scripts, and screenplays by the featured author are typically arranged by genre and include uncollected short fiction and nonfiction, where available. Also included is a list of recorded versions made by the author of his/her work.

- Adaptations: Films, plays, and other media adaptations based upon the author's work, includes stage plays, musicals, operas, teleplays.

- Manuscript Collections: A listing of the institutions which house significant collections of manuscripts relating to the featured author.

- Biography: Biographical sources on the featured author in both books and articles.

- Interviews: Major interviews with the featured author.

- Bibliography: A listing of bibliographies that have been compiled on the featured author.

- Critical Sources: A selected list of sources that combines the major scholarship existing on the featured author, with an emphasis on the gay and lesbian scholarship extant, plus a list of sources used in preparing the critical essay, including citations culled from scholarly, mainstream, and alternative press indexes.

- Author Comment: A statement made by the featured author concerning his/her own work.

- Signed critical essays commissioned from a diverse group of scholars, librarians, and free-lance writers in the area of gay and lesbian literature discuss the gay and lesbian content of the work of the featured authors. The approach taken with each essay varies, but the emphasis is on that which makes the author's work important to his/her own literary canon specifically and to the gay and lesbian literary or historical world generally.

Indexes

This edition of *Gay & Lesbian Literature* provides the following indexing to the featured entries:

- General Index: Alphabetically lists the names, name variations, and pseudonyms of featured authors in *both* the first and second volumes of *Gay & Lesbian Literature*, along with the volume in which the author's entry appears.

- Nationality Index: Alphabetically lists featured authors according to country of origin, lengthy residence, and/or country of citizenship; this is also a cumulative index featuring authors from both volumes.

- General Subject and Genre Index: Alphabetically lists featured authors according to genres in which their work appears, and refers readers to subjects relevant to the study of gay and lesbian literature. This index is not cumulative.

Highlights

In an effort to make this volume as useful as possible, and with the assistance of the advisory board, the editors have provided the following lists or appendices which may assist readers in securing additional information and may serve as an acquisitions tool for libraries seeking to augment their collections in this burgeoning field.

- Selected Critical Works: A selective list of important critical works on various genres of writing about gay and lesbian themes.

- Awards Listing: Lists recipients of gay and lesbian literary awards.

Acknowledgments

The editors gratefully acknowledge the members of the advisory board for their generous expertise, valuable suggestions and assistance, and general collaboration; Rob Ridinger, Patti Capel Swartz, Francesca Canadé Sautman, Tina Gianoulis, tova, and Loralee MacPike for their useful suggestions and encouragement along the way; the many entrants who contributed comments and corrected errors; the contributors of critical essays for their intelligence; Tim Seul for his careful copyediting; Sharon

Malinowski for helping us get this project going and providing sage advice; and Dave Collins for shepherding this manuscript through the publication process.

Suggestions Are Welcome

The editor hopes that you find *Gay & Lesbian Literature* a useful reference tool and welcomes comments and suggestions on any aspects of this work. We have made every effort to ensure the accuracy of the material in this publication, but if an error is brought to our attention we would be pleased to verify it and make the corrections in future editions. Please send comments to: The Editors, *Gay & Lesbian Literature,* St. James Press, 835 Penobscot Building, 645 Griswold St., Detroit, MI 48226-4094; or call toll-free at 800-347-GALE; or fax to 313-961-6347.

Advisory Board

Lesbian Writing in the Golden Age

by Loralee MacPike

The book you hold in your hands is a monument to a singular moment in history: a Golden Age of lesbian and gay literature, an age that will take its place among the other Golden Ages of literature as an exemplar of the best of its kind. Periclean Athens, which flourished between 460 and 430 b.c.e., developed the "public" arts of drama, history, philosophy. Augustan Rome's great literary period, within a century either way of 100 c.e., reinvented the epic in the Latin language. The best of Heian Japanese literature (*The Tale of Genji, The Pillow Book*), produced by women around 1000, far surpassed the elegant derivatives of Chinese writing which "real" poets were writing at the time. Between 1360 and 1400, Chaucer led the first great flowering of literature in English. The English Renaissance, dating roughly 1530 to 1620, is arguably the most significant single literary Golden Age yet.

We are now witnessing the development of another Golden Age of literature, a Golden Age of lesbian and gay writing. And it seems to me there are some reasons why we are in such a period. It has been said that literature both grows out of and creates the society that produces it, and that is nowhere more true than with the lesbian literature of the 1990s. The first volume of *Gay and Lesbian Literature,* edited in 1994 by Sharon Malinowski with introductory essays by Wayne R. Dynes and Barbara G. Grier, chronicled 94 years during which many things were written but few were publicly successful, acclaimed, or influential beyond their scattered lesbian and gay readership, and none cohered to form something we could call a literary movement. This second volume focuses on a much smaller time span: over 75% of the lesbian writers in this book were writing in the 1990s, and a great number of them are currently producing their best work. Never before have we seen so many lesbian writers, such good lesbian writers, writing about so many things—including but by no means limited to "lesbian" things.

Why such an outpouring of lesbian literature and literature by lesbians? I'm convinced we are living in a time whose cultural values and social configurations and conflicts make it possible. If we look back at earlier Golden Ages, we can see that they share certain features and occur when certain circumstances coincide. Golden Ages usually occur during times of social, political, scientific, and military upheaval. They usually grow out of urban areas which contain a critical mass of population. They occur in cultures in which literature is one of the major means of discussion, in which literature *matters.* Golden Age writers discover something new and important to write about; they have a sense that it matters if—and what—they write. Finally, a Golden Age culture values literature as an important mode of expression and finds ways of rewarding it. When all these circumstances combine, as they have for lesbian and gay writing at the end of the twentieth century, we may see a Golden Age, a flowering of literary thought and form and variety hitherto unexperienced in human history. This is where we now stand.

Golden Ages occur during times of social or political turmoil. It may be that we are blessed by living at the end of a century. The most cursory study of history will show that the final decade of a century is often a time of great upheaval, great uncertainty, and also great events which move history forward by giant steps. The end of the sixteenth century saw Britain's historic defeat of the Spanish Armada, the creation of modern science, the birth of the British Empire—and the English Renaissance, with its brilliant statesmanship and literature. The end of the eighteenth century brought the French Revolution, the invention of modern medicine, the start of the Industrial Revolution, and the birth of Romanticism and its great literature. The end of the nineteenth century witnessed the Art Nouveau movement; Modernist literature; the birth of abstract art and surrealism; the Boer War; the Spanish-American war, the first Russian Revolution; the advent of our technical and nuclear age; the "invention" of homosexuality; and the first explicit writings by women-identified women.

Historically speaking, then, it's not surprising that there's something afoot literarily during the final decade of the twentieth century as well and that that something is linked with cultural, social, political, scientific, and military activities. Wars in Bosnia, Afghanistan, Kuwait, Rwanda, Zaire, and Albania have peppered the decade. The uprising at Tienanmen Square and the fall of the Soviet Union epitomize the vast political shifts we are witnessing. In America, we live our individual lives amid political scandals, gang activity and drive-by shootings, the dismantling of the social safety net, a nationwide repudiation of our historic welcoming of immigrants, and a disaffected middle class which increasingly just wants to be left alone in its gated communities to accumulate money. Even a cursory comparison of a week's worth of 1997 newspapers with a week's worth of 1957 newspapers suggests that we are in a particularly troubled—and troubling—period.

One of the things that troubles many people today, openly and explicitly, is homosexuality. The attention given homosexuality nowadays is related to other identity issues which permeate our culture—racial identity, ethnic identity, gender identity—as well as value issues such as the contested demarcation of the family. Our notions of individual and collective identity have changed radically in the postwar period, and these changes have, I believe, provided one necessary backdrop for our current preoccupation with issues of identity, among them sexual identity, and what sexual identity might mean in a postmodern world. The constellation of personal, sexual, racial, familial, gender, and ethnic identity issues freights homosexuality with larger-than-life significance. Of course homosexuality (and the other currently "hot" issues as well) has always seemed significant and troublesome, but in the past it has been covertly and implicitly troublesome. Today its public conjunction with other issues of identity and relationship makes lesbians one of the visible and acknowledged "troubles" of our times. But this curse is also a blessing, because it provides a space for dialogue and argument and persuasion and deep emotions. We are gifted with a provocative, moiling space in which to write.

Golden Ages are usually focused in urban areas which contain a homogenous social unit with a critical mass of people. Elizabethan England during the Renaissance had a population of about 200,000. Athens in the fifth century b.c.e. had a population of about 400,000, of whom about 100,000 were citizens. Japan during the Heian period had a sizable urban population and a very small literate elite. I am convinced that one reason we have had such a strong, positive, multitongued lesbian voice in the 1990s is that lesbianism has grown up through small, "specialized" communities within larger urban areas. We believe that we have a lot in common and that we will benefit from mutual support and encouragement and understanding. In fact, we began by talking to ourselves, and the conversation became so compelling that everyone else suddenly and desperately wanted to listen in, to become a virtual, if not a real, part of our community. It's still possible in 1997—just barely—to speak of "the lesbian community," although that possibility is about to move beyond our grasp as we fully flower into our maturity; but in 1990 "lesbian community" was a well-understood (if somewhat unbounded) concept. It couldn't be authoritatively defined or delineated, but we all knew what it was: it was *us* acknowledging—and indeed creating through that acknowledgment—a sharing of something profound, something absolutely basic to our identities as people. And that something basic was what we variously called our "sexual preference," or, later, our "sexual orientation," or simply "the Life." We knew who we were, and we knew who wasn't us.

This community first found communal public voice in 1969 during Stonewall, in a city large enough to house a sizable group of lesbian and gay people. It grew as a series of enclaves in large cities—New York, San Francisco, Los Angeles, Seattle. It became visible as part of the ongoing life of these urban areas, in which it was possible both to find numbers of people like yourself and at the same time preserve a sort of privacy that's largely impossible in small towns. In a city you can choose to spend your time with people whose interests you share but whose neighborhood you don't. Cities offer the unity and anonymity that make it possible to speak out. We must speak to an Other, a listener, and we can speak most truly when we believe we will be heard directly, not filtered through "interpretation" or "values." But we must also feel relative safety in order to speak, and that safety is often gained through *not* being known by *everyone*. These are precisely the circumstances out of which Stonewall erupted and within which lesbian writers have been blooming.

The formation of a community is absolutely vital as a first step in claiming an identity. Before Stonewall, broadly speaking, lesbian culture lacked an adequate set of culture-wide referents against which lesbians could measure and name their lives. Through the process of speaking to one another, first in person and then through literature, lesbians have created an abundance of such referents. The resulting lesbian literature has extended the lesbian community beyond its urban origins.

One of the early ramifications of this extension is what has been called the Women in Print movement of the 1970s, when women, many of them lesbians, began publishing their own and other women's writings and feminist bookstores sprang up to sell those books. The conjunction of the feminist movement and the lesbian and gay movement provided the critical mass (and readership) for a genuinely new movement in which our voices spoke, first to our community, and then to a wider audience.

Now in 1997 the community which became visible with Stonewall and Women in Print is reaching a maturity which is part of our Golden Age of lesbian literature. One manifestation of that maturity is a certainty that there are people who will read and understand what we write. Surely another is a new fragmentation as we begin to be able to look at ourselves beyond simply our lesbianism and to define individual lives within, rather than by means of, a lesbian context. We no longer need to assert that we exist; we are now asking what it means to be a lesbian, a butch or femme, a bisexual dyke, a lesbian married to a man, a heterosexual woman who sleeps with women. This shift away from a unified, if indefinable and always arguable, "lesbian" community and toward a more polyglot identity politics with its corresponding literature is yet another mark of our Golden Age.

The culture values and rewards literary achievement. Despite the rapid increase in on-line activities which make hard copy less central to reading, research, the dissemination of knowledge, and the building of a literature, American culture is currently in a period of the expansion of the traditional written word in such forms as books, chapbooks, magazines, newspapers, and broadsheets. More writers are getting published; more people are reading books; there is more written *about* books; there are more awards for books and for writing in general. The end of the twentieth century is indisputably a word-focused time in the history of literature. And I would argue that it is even more so for lesbian writers, for a number of reasons related to a valuing of our words, a linked system of rewards, and an ever more finely honed series of procedures and venues for distinguishing good from bad.

For one thing, it is now possible for some lesbians to earn their livings through writing g/l/b/t materials. Even the casual reader of lesbian and gay literature can name writers who support themselves through writing or writing-related activities, Americans like Lisa Alther, June Jordan, Sarah Schulman, Jacqueline Woodson, Cheryl Clarke, Chrystos, Minnie Bruce Pratt, or Swede Gerd Brantenberg or Briton Jeannette Winterson. Acclaimed scholars of lesbianism include Gloria Anzaldua, Judith Butler, Ana Castillo, Teresa de Lauretis. There are others who earn a living in ancillary ways—publisher and critic Barbara Smith, Susan Horwitz of the National Women's Mailing List, Patricia Ireland of NOW, lesbian sexuality guru Jo Ann Loulan, filmmaker

Parmar Pratibha, teacher and writer Paula Gunn Allen—as well as the many people supported by such publications as Seattle's *Just Out,* Boulder's *Out Front Colorado,* Washington D.C.'s *Lambda Book Report* and *Washington Blade,* New York's *The Advocate,* Boston's *Bay Windows* and *Harvard Gay and Lesbian Review,* and Southern California's *The Lesbian Review of Books* and *The Lesbian News,* to name just a few. It is true that writing alone does not yet support most of our writers—nor most mainstream heterosexual writers. Still, twenty years ago it would have been difficult to compile a list like this; today it barely skims the surface of the people who gain employment through lesbian and gay writing.

A second indicator here is the startling increase in bookstore square footage, oftentimes in unlikely places, and the concurrent increase in shelf space devoted to g/l/b/t books. I mourn the demise of so many small independent bookstores and feel wary about the ascendancy of large chains whose apparent willingness to carry g/l/b/t materials may be ephemeral; but at the same time I can't help but notice that these corporate behemoths are filled with people—people reading books, people buying books, people intimately, regularly, eagerly, thoughtfully, fiscally engaging with written words. And more and more of those words were written by us.

Third, each year I see more publishers publishing lesbian and gay material. Our traditional presses—presses like Beacon, Alyson, Naiad, Seal, Firebrand, Cleis, New Victoria—continue to exist even in these parlous financial times. Previously languid presses like Spinsters Ink gain renewed vitality (and sales). New presses spring up—Rising Tide, Serpent's Tail, Paradigm. Lesbian-run presses outside the United States, like Press Gang and gynergy and Sister Vision in Canada, Spinifex in Australia, and Onlywomen in Britain, add riches to our bookshelves. Despite market fluctuations and the uncertain state of many feminist bookstores, lesbian publishing has proven itself tenacious and ingenious, and the lesbian publishing industry is well enough established that it's unlikely to disappear.

Several important academic presses have established g/l/b/t series: Columbia University Press with its "Between Women/ Between Men" and "Gender and Culture" series, New York University Press with "The Cutting Edge: Lesbian Life and Literature." St. Martin's Press has just put out a "Gay and Lesbian Titles" catalog. Others—Indiana University Press, University of California Press, Temple University Press—devote a larger share of their pages than ever before to lesbian- and gay-themed books. British publishers Cassell and Routledge and Canadian University of Toronto Press publish lesbian titles. Non-lesbian feminist presses like the Feminist Press and Crossing Press devote an ever-larger share of their list to lesbian titles. And, perhaps most astonishing of all, in the past decade, mainstream popular presses have "discovered" lesbian and gay writing. It sells, and so they seek it out. Plume, Dutton, Simon & Schuster, Viking, Harper, Norton, Knopf all regularly offer writing by lesbians. For all our (deserved) scorn of the hegemony of market forces, they can work in our favor. And we are in a period in which they *are* working in our favor. Because we are "hot," our books get published. It is evident, then, that we are in a cultural period which values books in general and lesbian books in particular and financially rewards the production of them.

Fourth is the almost unimaginable boom in lesbian and gay and queer scholarship. In the disciplines of literature, history, anthropology, psychology, and sociology there exist established sub-disciplines of lesbian and gay studies, with the resulting spate of publications by academics. The growth of lesbian studies programs and queer studies programs across the country suggests that we are the latest trend in the academic industry. Just as the social sciences grew out of cultural developments at the end of the nineteenth century, when people began to explore the psychological and social arrangements of human beings as an outgrowth of the century's interest in evolution, so today the centrality of the questions lesbianism (and homosexuality in general) raises about the nature of human identity is being translated into specific academic fields of study. And academic disciplines produce academic writings which highlight, among other things, lesbian literary works. To be studied by a scholar and written about in a scholarly volume is one sign of having "arrived"—a sign unavailable to lesbian writers until the 1990s. Journals such as the new *Journal of Lesbian Studies,* and academic societies which study non-canonical writings (e.g., MELUS, devoted to writers of color, including lesbian writers), are yet another sign of the academic reward for lesbian writing.

A fifth sort of reward, one that could scarcely exist in the absence of a financially remunerative market, is the establishment of official and public awards for lesbian and gay writing. The Lammys, established in 1989 by the *Lambda Book Report,* are the best known, although the American Library Association's Gay/Lesbian/Bisexual Task Force gave the first awards for gay and lesbian literature back in 1971. The establishment of the ALA and Lammy awards legitimized lesbian and gay writing in the eyes of the mainstream reading public. Most of the recipients of these awards don't yet support themselves by their writing, but the award makes writers more marketable. And, probably more important, these awards encourage writers; they create a standard of excellence toward which lesbian writers can strive. Recently both the Lammys and the ALA awards expanded to include lesbian and gay young adult literature; such specialized awards are yet another sign of a Golden Age.

Literary awards are a major factor in the establishment of a system of differentiating between good and less good lesbian writing. Another factor is book reviewing. Until recently the lesbian writing community didn't have a major book review outlet to analyze, critique, and publicize its writing. *The Lambda Book Report,* established in 1988, regularly publicizes both lesbian and gay writing, but its reviews are very short and it has been weighted toward a gay rather than a lesbian readership. Virtually all lesbian and gay newspapers carry book reviews, but these constitute a small portion of the paper and tend to be summative in nature rather than evaluative.

One sign of a major literary movement is that it generates a variety of review outlets. And indeed, in the summer of 1994 two such outlets appeared, entirely independently of each other and yet not coincidentally, for they were the logical next step in the establishment of a Golden Age of lesbian and gay literature. These were *The Lesbian Review of Books,* the first full-length, international journal devoted exclusively to reviewing books by, for, and about lesbians; and *The Harvard Gay and Lesbian Review,* which features both lesbian and gay writing and includes politically- and philosophically-oriented essays along with book reviews. Both are flourishing and growing in their fourth year of publication, in response to a hunger on the part of lesbian and gay readers for information about our writing and to the steady increase in the number of books focusing on lesbian issues which need to be reviewed and publicized. And both give voice to new critical thinking about the nature, intent, result, and ethics of lesbian writing. As they evolve, they establish new evaluative criteria which in turn refine and direct writing, creating a tension and a dialogue between writers and readers which shapes literary movements.

Literature needs to matter *culturally. And it needs to matter to the* whole *culture, not just to part of it.* In some eras, literature can be said to be decorative or entertaining but may fail to achieve what we would call "importance"—a standing as one of the central spokesforms of its era. There seem to be no intrinsic reasons why any given era might be one in which literature matters culturally, but we can often tell by the forms in which literature appears the extent to which it matters. We happen to be in a period of unprecedented expansion of ways in which literature can be disseminated, due to a series of (probably) related phenomena: increasing education and literacy which promotes both the writing and the reading of literature; increased publishing, marketing, and publicity of writing within traditional venues; and new forms and venues (such as the Internet) for dispersing works once they've been written. Together these provide at least the foundations for making literature matter.

People have always written, of course. But many who wrote didn't consider themselves "writers," didn't expect or seek publication, and would not, even had they published their writings, have aspired to join the ranks of the literary because—in part at least—there was little sense that *their* words and *their* lives fit into the current literary formulations. This has been especially true for lesbian writers, of course, because "the love that dared not speak its name" could hardly hope to have that name blazoned across the cover of a book the public would see. The growing assumption that virtually everyone should be educated beyond secondary school gives many more people some exposure to literature and some practice in writing. Job advertisements tell prospective employees that communications skills are critical. Therapists try to get clients to create coherent stories of their lives. Our fascination with genealogy draws us to the histories of our families. Even holiday cards call for a coherent recounting of our days and doings. In these and dozens of other ways, we live in a time when the telling of our individual stories, often in written form, is valued as a path to self-knowledge, relationships, happiness, and meaning. And we seek out others' stories—to measure our own against, to supplement those we already know, to reinforce what we want to believe or understand. Literature comes to matter as it becomes more necessary and more accessible. I don't for a moment think I've "explained" why, in any given era, literature might matter intensely. But I do think it's possible to trace at least a few of the things that make it matter for us, now.

The expansion of publishers and bookstores is both a result of our increased valuation of literature and one of the causes of it. We see people feeling welcome in bookstore cafes, so we enter them with anticipation of welcome. Our friends talk about books they've read, and we think Hmm, maybe I'll read that book too. People begin to want to hear what other people—those other people so comfortable within the new welcoming space that literature provides—have to say.

The Internet gives virtually everyone potential access to all types of information and images. Some Internet journals retain traditional features of publisher selection, peer review, and editing; but the Internet has also created an increasing number of non-standard ways to publish. People who wouldn't buy a book will browse the Internet for hours, reading whatever comes up. Far from making us a nation of illiterates, the Internet will force literacy on a far broader range of people than ever before.

The world has gotten smaller and our need for words and information has gotten larger. It may well be that writing will soon be superseded by new forms of communication that don't require writing and publishing, but those forms don't yet exist. Only writing, in whatever form it gets transmitted to the reader, will satisfy the need for growth and knowledge which life at the very end of the twentieth century has generated. And so we are in a period when literature—writing—matters immensely, and matters to all of us, lesbian or gay or straight.

Writers need to feel that they can do something both important and new. One of the strikingly similar features of Periclean Athens, Augustan Rome, Heian Japan, and Renaissance England was that what they produced was in a very real sense *new.* Not that no English writer had encountered the Petrarchan sonnet before; not that no one in Augustan Rome had read an epic. But something changed the forms to make them new—an *English,* as opposed to an Italian, sonnet; a *Latin,* as opposed to a Greek, epic.

Transmutation suddenly becomes possible in a Golden Age; new forms, new ideas, new functions of literature, a newly empowered group of writers, a new readership can spark a Golden Age. I see many of these things happening today. Once, as I've noted, lesbian love "dared not speak its name." But that time has passed. Since the start of the twentieth century, when lesbian and gay writers began to publish—often somewhat timidly but increasingly with celebration and nowadays to applause—we have been speaking new truths. Of course, Radclyffe Hall was doing so too when she published *The Well of Loneliness* in 1928. But what Hall saw as important and new was rejected by the culture she was speaking to; it was indeed new, but it wasn't important—to them—and therefore it remained an isolated instance. Mary Casal was saying something new and important when she published the autobiographical *Stone Wall* in 1930. Jeannette Foster was breaking new ground with *Sex Variant Women in Literature* in 1956. May Sarton was writing about deep lesbian emotional support in *Mrs. Stevens Hears the Mermaids Singing* in 1974 (the same year Arno Press initiated its short-lived gay and lesbian reprint series). None of these initiated a Golden Age. Perhaps the time wasn't right. Perhaps not enough of the other features of Golden Ages were occurring—or perhaps too many. England in 1928 and America in 1930 were between wars and believed that permanent peace was possible, or Modernism might have foreclosed certain ways of "saying it new" which might have empowered Hall or Casal. Perhaps Foster's audience lacked that critical mass. Perhaps there wasn't enough social turmoil in 1974, or perhaps literature didn't matter to enough people in the same way it does now. For whatever concatenation of reasons, the sparks struck by Hall and Casal and Foster and Sarton and Arno Press didn't catch fire. The sparks being generated now do.

So although writing about lesbianism isn't new, the depth and intensity of the lesbian writing of the 1990s is. Hall took on the whole of lesbian life and as a result could only touch its surface, draw its outlines. Now we are filling in the outlines—and they're outlines that *have never, in the history of written communication,* been filled in. There is simply no equivalent to the outpouring of fiction, poetry, drama, biography and autobiography, memoir, mystery, romance, and essay that we are in the midst of. Most of what has been written has no predecessor. Ruthann Robson's *Another Mother* tells a new story of lesbian parenting. Israeli lesbians tell their stories for the first time in *Lesbiot*. Ellen Galford has created the first dybbuk in lesbian literature in *The Dyke and the Dybbuk*. In *Push* Sapphire tells the first story of an abused, illiterate inner-city lesbian girl. Julia Penelope has published the first lesbian crosswords ever. We meet our first Cuban lesbians in Achy Obejas's pages. Mary Wing's postmodern explorations of the mystery genre have never been done before. Kitty Tsui's erotic Asian-American butch is newly born. Indeed, the newness of lesbian literature is so self-evident that it seems almost redundant to mention it, except for those readers half a century from now who will be looking back on our Golden Age with wise old eyes that have seen a dozen lesbian dybbuks, shelves of lesbian crossword puzzles, three generations of Cuban lesbians. Yes, back in the 1990s we *were* doing something new. Something so new that virtually every book, every poem, every essay was a first, bursting upon a world eager to snatch it up because we were convinced it was important.

The impetus for the work of a Golden Age must come from a culture's willingness to examine its values and must represent a genuine change. Here is the key to our current Golden Age of lesbian literature. The impetus for our literature comes from our willingness—indeed our need—to examine our lives, and the willingness of our culture to hear and see and read our examinations. It comes from the politics we inhabit. It comes from the identities we seek to slough off or assume or create. It comes from the dailiness of our inventions of structures within which to be partners, parents, human beings. It comes from the meanings we have created, from the theories that fuel our choices and actions, from the chemistry of our desires and the physics of our collisions with a culture that would just as soon do away with us. We do not live amidst a finishing school for girls on the island of Lesbos, nor within the moneyed enclave of Paris in the 'teens of this century, where we can be seen by others—and see ourselves—as an isolated group, an Other. Some of us have thrust ourselves into the world of the 1990s, others have been pulled resisting into it, but however we got here, we are part of a movement. Whether we have sought it or not, whether we have chosen to be active within it, we are living in an era in which the public's eye is newly opened and fastened upon us, trying to understand what it sees.

In such a climate we have been given an impetus never before experienced; we have become empowered to speak out for ourselves at last. In the 1980s, it was still possible for me to edit the *first* book about lesbian and gay parents coming out to their children (*There's Something I've Been Meaning to Tell You,* Naiad), for someone to produce the *first* Broadway play about gay life, for someone else to win the *first* lesbian Lammy. In less than a decade we have moved into a space where it's possible to write a book as specialized as *Lesbians Raising Sons* (ed. Jess Wells; Alyson, 1997), to have three lesbian first-run movies running at the same time, to have lesbian books win non-lesbian book awards. These are heady times to live in precisely because we have seized the external dialogue *about* us and turned it into a dialogue *by* us. There is no mistaking the fact that this is a genuine change. We are writing words and works that have never been written before, that indeed could not have been written before.

The world in which we live has given us the gift of a Golden Age, and we are filling it with our words. The reader who holds this volume in her hands hot off the presses in 1997 is connected to the reader who uses the volume for historical research in 2047 through their shared experience of the Golden Age of lesbian literature recorded in these pages. Confucius notwithstanding, blessed is she who lives in interesting times.

Outing and Identity

by Jim Marks

Although it is obviously presumptuous, and inflates the present moment, there is yet a case to be made that the history of gay male literature can be divided into two periods: everything before 1969, and everything after.

There is a strong tradition of writing that details erotic and affectionate relationships between males that goes back at least to the ancient Greeks and continues, like a stream that periodically goes underground only to reemerge miles later, through much of the literature of the West. Although a major element in this writing focuses on the affection of friends—Jonathan and David, for instance, the Babylonian heroes Gilgamesh and Inkidu or, perhaps most beautifully and clearly, in Plato's Symposium—by far the greater proportion of gay male writing before the twentieth century construes homoerotic relationships through the lens of a hierarchical society in which men have the dominant roles and women and children are subservient. Because these writings assume male dominance, they do not violate the norms of their culture and have frequently been allowed a quite considerable, if relative, freedom of expression. Thus, the most typical homoerotic relationship in past literature is what we would now call pederastic, an attitude summarized by Christopher Marlowe in his declaration that "he that does not love tobacco and boies is a fool."

When a different kind of gay sensibility began to emerge in the writings of Edward Carpenter and others toward the end of the nineteenth and and the beginning of the twentieth century, this writing was interpreted in ways that surely misrepresented the history of same-sex affections and which continue to make it difficult to get a truer picture of the past. Carpenter and others in the "Uranian" movement were looking for an Eden, a past in which homosexuality was permitted and even approved. To their eyes, the Classical Greeks and the Renaissance—Socrates, Plato and Alexander the Great; Michelangelo, Montaigne and Shakespeare—provided just such an Eden, a period with high public prestige whose example could be used as a wedge to pry apart the doors of Victorian repression.

In a sense, what these gay pioneers were trying to do was "out" the past by identifying prototypical historical homosexuals. Where this approach surely falsifies the past is in attributing to these personages a sense of identity based on their sexual inclinations. Although we can be reasonably certain that Shakespeare, for instance, had strong emotional feelings toward other men which included some measure of physical attraction, it is ultimately absurd to talk about him, for better or worse, as a "gay" author. What immediately strikes those who read Shakespeare or see the many incarnations of his works is Shakespeare's "universality." It makes no sense to discuss his plays as if they were elaborately encoded exposes of the dynamics of male-male relationships and affections. Perhaps only a homosexual totally gifted in the art of survival in a hostile world, a homosexual capable of completely hiding his own identity and taking on that of others, could have written the plays, but the plays themselves are about nothing more, or less, than human life. Shakespeare has no identity, gay or otherwise; he has only his works.

The homoerotic literature of the twentieth century, and particularly since that rather arbitrary date of the Stonewall riot in the summer of 1969, is about, first and foremost, identity. It's central trope is the coming to terms with who one really is, the discovery of a true self hidden from the world and oneself. The central struggle of this literature is the struggle with oneself and only then, with the world. If the gay novel is, as some have suggested, the last refuge of the middle brow novel, then that is because it is the one place where the Freudian quests continue to have resonance. For what, after all, is the "gay" hero but a latter day Oedipus, ever striving to learn who he is, and forever punished both for his knowledge, and for learning it too late?

Two other elements have to be added to the equation if we are to understand "gay" literature as it developed in the post-Stonewall world. The struggle to attain and affirm identity supplied contemporary literature with its underlying ideology. But it took the development of a market to unleash the torrent of books that have spilled out of the closet and onto the shelves.

In the late 1970s and early 1980s, the book publishing and selling industry, which itself has been undergoing almost constant change since the 1950s, discovered gay books as one potential "niche" market. Although the numbers were small—typically, anywhere from 8,000-12,000 copies of a first novel would sell—there was a dependable enough market that made it possible for mainstream book publishers to produce books for that market. As the 1980s progressed, all the different components of this market came together: a network of gay and lesbian (and feminist) bookstores across the country that formed the primary core of the market, gay and lesbian newspapers and magazines that could provide reviews, author interviews, and other publicity, and "out" corporate officials who were willing to take on the still risky projects and see them through to completion. Although there were a number of figures who played important roles in this development, it was two editors—Bill Whitehead at E. P. Dutton, and Michael Denneny at St. Martin's Press—who are generally credited with realizing that gay books could succeed in this corporate world.

This niche market was markedly different from what had preceded it. These were not small presses which would produce one or two authors, or "high art" presses (one thinks of Virginia and Leonard Woolf's Hogarth Press) working more for the love of literature than lucre, or even feminist presses dedicated to make sure that books with a certain viewpoint saw print. The creation of a niche market involved large corporate entities (which, as the 1980s progressed and the publishing business was incorporated in the general media/entertainment business, became ever larger entities) with extensive corporate hierarchies and shrewd marketing professionals and programs and teams of sales persons. Although profit was the driving motive, throughout the 1980s and early 1990s, sales of gay books were never so large as to make the hope of big payoffs the driving force in this business. Instead, what kept the gay book business afloat was its reliability, and to keep the income flowing, the market proliferated into seemingly endless genres and subgenres. The gay market, in short, became a kind of shadow of the straight market, producing romances and mysteries, joke books and self help titles, biographies, histories, and novels. As the market became more self defined, and as the university publishing business came more to resemble its mainstream siblings, university presses began producing gay titles (most conspicuously, John Boswell's *Christianity, Homosexuality and Social Tolerance*) and even developing their own gay and lesbian book lines.

One consequence of the success of the gay male book in mainstream publishing was the relative failure of a gay small press industry to develop. Lesbian books had a harder time selling and getting sold to marketing directors, resulting in a thriving, varied lesbian small press cottage industry (Naiad Press specializing in romances, Firebrand in artistic titles, Cleis in "cutting edge" fiction and non-fiction). No such gay male industry was created. Only Alyson Press, headquartered in Boston, was able to develop and maintain a line of books, and it had to live with the fact of life that its major talents (novelist Larry Duplechan, mystery writer Michael Nava) were always susceptible to being picked up by larger houses with bigger budgets and more enticing ad campaigns.

Although there were the beginnings of a gay book industry as the 1980s dawned, it is questionable whether the market would have seen the explosion of titles that was to occur had it not been for the AIDS epidemic. AIDS (Acquired Immune Deficiency Syndrome) first appeared as a cluster of cases of unusual cancers and pneumonia in a small group of gay men. At first it appeared that the men had nothing in common but their sexual preference, but when their histories were tracked and compared, they also were discovered to have frequented one gay Los Angeles bathhouse, or had sex with someone who had frequented that bathhouse. Because the syndrome first presented itself almost exclusively in gay men, it quickly became associated with homosexuality, and in fact one of the early names proposed for the disease was GRID—gay related immune deficiency.

AIDS was—and still is—a very scary disease. It has a long incubation period, perhaps ten years, during which the person infected with the virus causing the disease appears entirely normal and healthy. Once the virus destroys the immune system, however, it's consequences are swift, visible, and horrible. People with AIDS frequently suffer from wasting syndromes, which make them look like Auschwitz survivors. One of the most common diseases associated with AIDS, Kaposi's Sarcoma, produces horrible, dried-blood colored lesions all over the body. The list of diseases that can follow include pneumonia, rare forms of tuberculosis, yeast infections of the throat, and bizarre brain infections like toxoplasmosis.

On the individual level, AIDS was a terrible tragedy. But on the mass cultural level, it turned out to be the single most energizing and mobilizing force ever to hit the gay community.

While there was a compelling logic to the ideology of gay identity, in practice it proved difficult to turn that ideology into a mass movement. Gay men had lived dual lives for millennia; why risk the comfort and power that many of them had attained by coming out of the closet? The Civil Rights movement made progress in part because racial discrimination was something everyone could see; how make an argument for a class of people who were, for all intents and purposes, invisible?

AIDS turned the theory of identity into a reality. The closet provided no protection from the disease. "We are everywhere!" the slogan went, and when people everywhere started to sicken and die, denial became impossible. Children discovered their fathers were gay; wives discovered their husbands were harboring potentially deadly secrets; and parents everywhere had long lonely vigils by the bedsides of sons they thought they had known. When Rock Hudson, the 1950s epitome of masculinity, became sick with AIDS in 1985, the popular media went into a frenzy. Suddenly, gay people were not in the shadows any more, and there were books available or soon to appear to provide a guide to this hidden world.

Contemporary gay literature, then, is a quest, conditioned by the market place, and accentuated by disease. The *Men on Men* short story anthology series, first edited by the late George Stambolian and, after his death from AIDS, by David Bergman, perhaps best captures the trajectory of this emerging movement. These collections of short stories quite consciously seek to assemble the best and most interesting gay writers and, while they reject any claims of being definitive, the series often has marked a writer's first major appearance on the public stage and has led to the production of many writer's first, full-length novel or collection of short stories. (It is another defining characteristic of contemporary homosexuality that it is not just an identity, but a career.) The first book in this massive project of self-discovery was set at ground zero: New York in the aftermath of the Stonewall riot, where urban gay men congregated in bars and looked for love. With each succeeding volume, the focus has widened: from New York to gay meccas like Key West and from the hunky gay male to the impassioned ranting of drag queens re-conceived as performance artists (*Men on Men 2*). The next volume moved to explore the relationship between gay men and their families, and the impact of the Plague, AIDS, which, as Edmund White has observed, has brought to gay writing the full panoply of human interests—sex, death, panic—and, in a perverse and extremely cruel irony, in a sense completed the community's movement out of the closet begun a scant dozen years before. *Men on Men 4* continued to broaden the scope, especially by adding ethnic identities with, for instance, stories of gay Cuban Americans, gay Chinese Americans, gay African-Americans. Five and six have now appeared, each adding an element to the mosaic—southern gothic and southwestern trailer trash—while the voices of those who were just born in 1969 are entering their maturity, commenting on growing up in a world where sex was always liberated, but never safe.

While the fiction of the *Men on Men* series (and the numerous novels and other collections those published in the series have produced) most fits the paradigm of a literature of identity—where the question "who am I?" comes first—it hardly exhausts the gay male writing produced since Stonewall. Edmund White's *States of Desire* stands as a kind of paradigm for what has become a whole genre. Identity is never purely personal: one doesn't just "come out," one comes out into a steadily evolving subculture. White, along with Felice Picano, Andrew Holleran, and the late Robert Ferro, Michael Grumley, and George Whitmore, was a leader in the most important post-Stonewall New York literary salon. His novels, from *Forgetting Elena* on, have been set in the heart of the emerging international gay culture. The voyage his hero takes in the autobiographical trilogy that begins with *A Boy's Own Story* and continues in *The Beautiful Room is Empty* (the final volume is scheduled for publication in the fall of 1997) is that journey from midwest innocence to New York sophistication (with not a little sex along the way). Once arrived in the gay scene, White traveled across the country to document and describe it, a latter-day de Tocqueville of the America subculture. Frank Browning's *Culture of Desire* provides a new take on the subject some 15 years later. The form blends travel guide anecdotes with amateur sociology/anthropology in an entertaining package meant for a general reader. This is just the tip of a non-fiction iceberg, most of it decidedly not amateur, starting with John Boswell and gay historian Jonathan Ned Katz, whose work is continuing to chart the dimensions of male-male sexuality throughout time and space and has sparked a lively and fruitful debate about the extent to which current and past sexual practices can be construed to be the same; one camp (Boswell their leading proponent) argues that gay identity is essentially the same over time, while Katz and others argue that the way sexuality is constructed in any one society makes male sexuality fundamentally different at different times and places, no matter how much the genitals and sex acts may remain the same.

If gay non-fiction exists at the point where literature and knowledge blur, gay male writing has flourished in the areas of drama and poetry as well. In a sense, the poets have not had to struggle to gain acceptance within the circle of their peers in the way that gay male fiction writers have. Poetry is itself so "queer"—that is, outside the mainstream of America life—that the sexuality of any individual poet has not been a determining factor. Gay male poets have participated in all levels of contemporary American poetry, from Ginsberg's "Howl" marking a style of avant-garde poet/prophet on one side, and his near contemporary, James Merrill, marking the formalist polish of a professional on the other side (with the two sides perhaps arriving at a sort of common ground in Merrill's visionary epic *The Changing Light at Sandover*).

Finally, because of its uniquely public, performative nature, gay drama seemed for many years to languish. Although small theater groups (notably, the Glines in New York) existed to present gay plays (and Charles Ludlum's Theater of the Ridiculous created a distinctly original style of play and acting) the works of early gay theater seemed for the most part destined to be a kind of closet drama, seen only by tiny audiences and known only in circles so small they might as well be coteries.

All that changed with AIDS. ACT-UP, the protest group that began in New York, saw its work as a kind of street theater and its demonstrations, on New York's Wall Street or at the Federal Drug Administration offices in suburban Washington, D.C., were staged with an eye toward catching the roving, jaded media eye with the most outrageous costuming and dramatically simplified message. It was this spirit that motivated Tony Kushner's award-winning *Angels in America,* which finally put the "Gay Play" front and center on the Broadway stage, combining the anger of the streets and the experimentation of the post-1960s dramatic world in an unique and entertaining drama whose deepest roots, surely, go back to the melodramatic stagings of Uncle Tom's Cabin.

(One wonders whether there are not many gay plays circulating in the fragmented world of regional theater, which has encouraged and created a lively theatrical tradition that simply goes unrecognized by those who don't make theater their chief field of study and interest. One thinks of two brilliant, if dissimilar, playwrights, Jim Grimsley—before his fiction was published, mostly associated with Atlanta's Seven Stages—and Nicky Silver, whose work frequently premiers at Washington's Woolly Mammoth theater and off-Broadway. Silver's recent "Raised in Captivity" practically reinvents the AIDS play; recasting it as an hysterical "Glass Menagerie" in which the alienated children—brother and sister—realize their heart's desire, which is to throw off the world of adult sexuality entirely and live together in the nursery of eternal innocence.)

There is some evidence that the publishing situation that prevailed in the late 1970s and 1980s became seriously destabilized in the middle of the 1990s. Among the many ironies in gay literature is that a movement that began out of the left of center politics of the late 1960s should have prospered so much because of market forces in the Reagan 1980s and now seems threatened by a classic market collapse. The peak of the speculative bubble (if that is what it is) was reached around 1994. The gay march on Washington in the spring of 1993 and the celebrations marking the 25th anniversary of the Stonewall riot in the summer of 1994 in New York, which included the fourth quadrennial Gay Games international athletic competition, caught the attention of the New York-based publishing industry. In late 1993, gay author Paul Monette won the prestigious National Book Award, and he was joined that year by a lesbian poet, Mary Oliver, who won the National Book Award for poetry, and by National Book Award finalist Dorothy Allison, whose book, *Bastard Out of Carolina,* was propelled by a glowing *New York Times* review into a best seller. The trade press was swept by reports of gay authors signing six figure deals.

This, sage heads like Michael Denneny wagged, was madness, and by the time the first wave of these books had appeared and been remaindered, it appeared that he had been right, as most of these books came nowhere close to earning back their advances.

Deepening the crisis within the gay book industry was the collapse—the word is not too strong—of the book industry in general in the summer of 1996. That summer, publishers were reporting staggering drops in sales—40 and 50 percent less than the previous year—and as sales dropped, publishers found themselves awash in book returns—again, at unheard of rates, at times equaling 70 percent. One theory is that book publishers gambled on the chain stores and lost: that books are not like tomatoes or loose-leaf binders, and it takes some one who reads them and loves them to sell them.

There is a weird "best of times, worst of times" aura to the gay book business these days, as gay books continue to come from the presses—there could easily be a thousand new gay and lesbian titles published in 1997—while there are fears that almost all the lesbian presses will go under financially, and rumors of previously successful authors sitting with two or three completed novels unsold.

Thus, just as the history of gay literature is beginning to come into something like clear focus, its future is uncertain. A literature that has existed in one form or another for at least 2000 years is unlikely to go away. But what shape will it take? Will it retreat to the ivory tower, and become the preserve of academics? Will it diffuse into the general culture, only to appear as heavily encoded missives whose "true" identity is only manifest in a certain, undefinable but unmistakable excess of style? More likely, as the great gay novelist E. M. Forster would have it, gay authors will continue to muddle through, looking back wistfully, perhaps, at the days of big money advances and all expense paid author tours, as they go back to their battered word processors and add one more page to the literature that they, at least, must have.

Featured Authors

AKHMATOVA, Anna Andreevna. Russian poet whose concrete and powerful portrayal of the difficulties facing women in revolutionary Russia and later the Soviet Union brought her the condemnation of the state.

ALLEN, Jeffner M. American writer and philosopher whose activism inspired her radical feminist poetics.

ALTHER, Lisa. American novelist and author of short stories whose work explores the human realities dismissed by stereotypes of women and homosexuals.

ANDERSON, Margaret C(aroline). American editor and autobiographer whose accounts of her life with lesbian companions offer insights into the literary and cultural life of the American avant-garde.

ANDERSON, Sherwood. American writer who was one of the first modernist writers who was not a homosexual to explore the complexities of homosexual identity and the homoerotic, as well as the first to present homosexual characters with sympathy and compassion.

ARAGON, Louis. French poet, novelist, and journalist who co-founded (and later rejected) the Surrealist movement, led the literary resistance during World War II, and was an early defender of sexual liberty.

ARENAS, Reinaldo. Cuban novelist, poet, lecturer, and journalist whose works detail the torment of living in Cuba as a gay dissident and his subsequent exile.

ASCH, Sholem. Polish, American, and Jewish playwright and novelist whose play *God of Vengeance* was the first play produced in the United States to deal with lesbian themes; the play met with widespread controversy and legal action.

BAILEY, Paul. British novelist and playwright whose work deals with the feelings of loneliness, isolation, and desperation of those who feel they are or actually are different from those around them.

BARR, James. American novelist and short story writer whose works present the full spectrum of possible literary and social images of homosexuality extant prior to the emergence of the gay liberation movement in 1969.

BATES, Katherine Lee. American poet and educator best known for writing "America the Beautiful"; her ode to companion Katherine Coman, titled *Yellow Clover* (1922), is a significant contribution to early 20th century lesbian literature.

BEAM, Joseph. American writer and editor whose *In the Life: A Black Gay Anthology* is generally acknowledged as the first literary anthology written exclusively by, for, and about gay African-American men.

BECHDEL, Alison. American cartoonist whose award-winning, bi-weekly comic strip deals with current events through the eyes of a semi-utopian lesbian community.

BELL, Arthur. American journalist, activist, and author of nonfiction whose *Dancing the Gay Lib Blues: A Year in the Homosexual Liberation Movement* was one of the first books about the gay liberation movement published by a mainstream American publisher.

BENAVENTE (y MARTINEZ), Jacinto. Spanish playwright, poet, and lecturer whose oblique references to the difficulties of living outside the norms of turn-of-the-century Spanish society are thought to have sprung from his own experience as a gay man.

BISHOP, Elizabeth. American poet whose poems, long considered among the best of the century, have recently been re-examined in light of her concealed lesbian identity.

BLAMAN, Anna. Dutch novelist and short story writer whose portrayals of homosexual love and existential questioning brought criticism from an intolerant European literary community.

BLOCH, Alice. Jewish American writer whose work deals with multicultural issues and especially the marginalization of Jewish lesbians.

BLOCK, Francesca L. American young adult author whose works illustrate the necessity of love and celebrate racial and sexual difference.

BOGUS, SDiane A. American writer and publisher who writes about defining herself in light of her multi-faceted identities as lesbian and racial minority in America.

BOYE, Karin. Swedish poet, novelist, and essayist whose poetry is considered among her country's finest and whose writings contributed to the liberalization of laws regarding homosexuals.

BRAND, Adolf. German book dealer, gay activist, writer, and publisher whose work to legitimize homosexual behavior in the first half of the twentieth century makes him an intellectual forefather of gay liberation theorists.

BRANTENBERG, Gerd. Norwegian novelist and critic whose work deals with the right of homosexuals to be loved and respected; best known for her satirical *Egalia's Daughters*.

BRIGHT, Susie. American sex educator and editor whose contribution to lesbian culture has been to bring lesbianism and sex together.

BRITE, Poppy Z. American horror writer who has earned her distinction by writing from the fringes of modern experience; her gay characters deal with addiction, sexuality, AIDS, technology, and cyberspace, as well as the expected amounts of gore.

BRONSKI, Michael. American cultural critic and essayist whose work focuses on gay and lesbian culture, especially sexuality, AIDS, politics, and social issues.

BROOKE, Rupert. British poet whose poems written during World War I indicate a dawning awareness of his gay sensibility.

BROSSARD, Nicole. Canadian poet and novelist whose work subverts conventional deployments of syntax, grammar, punctuation, spelling, typography, and genre in an effort to undermine, restore, and reinvent language.

BROUMAS, Olga. Greek poet and translator whose work synthesizes the Greek and English languages, the Greek and American cultures, the physical and the verbal, the inner and outer landscapes, the erotic and the academic.

BROWN, Rebecca. American novelist and author of short stories and nonfiction whose *Gifts of the Body* received acclaim for its treatment of the relationships between homecare workers and AIDS patients.

BUNCH, Charlotte (Anne). American author widely regarded as one of the foremost organizers and theorists of the lesbian and global feminist movements.

BUSCH, Charles. American playwright and actor who has often starred, in drag, in his own productions, which include *Vampire Lesbians of Sodom* and *Psycho Beach Party*.

BUTLER, Judith. American theorist whose work exposes the unexamined assumptions behind taken-for-granted classifications such as "lesbian" and "gay."

CALDERON, Sara Levi. Mexican author and scholar whose semi-autobiographical novel, *Dos Mujeres*, achieved unexpected bestseller status in Mexico.

CALLEN, Michael. American writer, musician, and activist who played a major role in shaping America's response to the AIDS epidemic.

CAMERON, Peter. American novelist and short story writer whose writings focus on gay people as they negotiate the broader worlds of their families, their lovers' families, and places of work.

CAMINHA, Adolfo. Brazilian novelist and poet whose *Bom Crioulo: The Black Man and the Cabin Boy* is one of the first explicitly gay works in Latin American literature.

CAMPO, Rafael. Cuban American poet and essayist whose work ponders both his role as a doctor treating those on the edge of death and the alienation he feels as a queer man of color.

CARDENAS, Nancy. Mexican playwright and poet whose life work was to humanize and celebrate the lesbian experience.

CARR, Emily. Canadian painter, novelist, and diarist whose autobiographical writings about her career as an opinionated unmarried woman with a powerful vocation serve as a model for how to live a life outside accepted gender norms.

CART, Michael. American critic, literary journalist, and novelist who has called for the incorporation of culturally diverse voices and the lifting of taboos about sexuality, especially homosexuality, in fiction for young adults.

CASAL, Mary. American autobiographer whose book *The Stone Wall* is one of the more puzzling works in lesbian literature because of the combination of professional regard and critical neglect it garnered.

CASEMENT, Roger. Irish patriot and essayist whose "Black Diaries," first circulated by the British government as evidence that led to his hanging, now serve as an early record of homosexual life.

CHRYSTOS. American poet, essayist, and short story writer whose work explores the lives of First Nations people in contemporary America and the lives of lesbians within a heterosexual culture.

CIXOUS, Helene. French theorist and literary critic whose work has contributed significantly to gay and lesbian studies, but whose writings about a history of change, of exploration, of social androgyny and personal passion defy categorization.

CLARKE, Cheryl. American poet and higher education administrator best known for her narrative poetry written from the perspective of a black lesbian feminist.

CLIFF, Michelle. Jamaican novelist, poet, and author of short stories and nonfiction whose works attempt to retrace and reclaim a repressed Afro-Caribbean past, and are sometimes concerned with lesbian themes.

CLUTHA, Janet Paterson Frame. New Zealand novelist and author of short stories, poetry, and essays whose work explores the ponderous and woman-negating influences of a patriarchal world.

COLLARD, Cyril. French author and film director whose novel-turned-movie *Savage Nights* dramatically increased the visibility of AIDs in contemporary France.

CORNWELL, Anita. American essayist and short story writer who became an early spokeswomen of feminist theory in her essays about black women.

CREVEL, René. French poet, novelist, and art critic whose contribution to gay and lesbian literature stems from his writings about his involvement with the emerging surrealist movement of the 1920s.

CULLEN, Countee. African American poet and editor whose poems have been used to understand the black gay subculture of the Harlem Renaissance.

CUNNINGHAM, Michael. American novelist who places his gay and bisexual characters in the mainstream of American life.

D'ANNUNZIO, Gabriele. Italian novelist, dramatist, poet, short story writer, and journalist whose romantic novels and plays dramatized the lifestyle of the turn-of-the-century hedonist.

DELANY, Samuel R. American science fiction writer who was among the first to introduce homosexuality into the genre.

DELARUE-MARDRUS, Lucie. French poet and novelist whose autobiographical works explore her various relations with women and comment on the social atmosphere of her time.

de LAURETIS, Teresa. Italian and American essayist, feminist critic, and scholar whose prolific body of writing has helped to shape the current theoretical directions of feminist film theory, feminist literary criticism, and the emerging academic field of gay and lesbian studies.

DeLYNN, Jane. American novelist whose satirical stories, especially *Don Juan in the Village,* have spurred controversy in the lesbian community.

DEMING, Barbara. American essayist, journalist, poet, novelist, and author of short stories who first became known for her political activism and later confronted her lesbianism in poetry, fiction, and essays.

DE VEAUX, Alexis. African-American poet, playwright, and fiction writer whose works explore the dynamics of exclusion and marginalization and the joys of lesbian love.

DONOGHUE, Emma. Irish novelist, playwright, and historian who, by firmly anchoring her novels in the lesbian experience, has changed the Irish literary landscape.

DOTY, Mark. American poet, memoirist, and educator whose poetry and prose explores the erotics of life, love, and the significance of death, from a perspective that is at once gay and profoundly universal.

DOWELL, Coleman. American novelist and short story writer best known for his penetrating treatments of the divided nature of the individual consciousness.

DREHER, Sarah. American novelist and playwright whose popular works include the character Stoner McTavish, an unassuming, lesbian travel agent.

DUNYE, Cheryl. American filmmaker whose works explore the intersections of race, gender, and sexuality in the contemporary United States.

DUPLECHAN, Larry. American novelist whose work depicts the trials and tribulations of life as a black gay male.

DYKEWOMON, Elena. American novelist, poet, fiction writer, editor, and activist who wrote one of the first specifically feminist-oriented lesbian novels.

FEINBERG, Leslie. American author who has contributed to lesbian and gay literature by representing in fiction and nonfiction the ways in which lesbian and gay culture is thoroughly interwoven with cross-gendered threads.

FREEDMAN, Estelle. American professor, historian, and writer who is best known for her history of sexuality in the United States, *Intimate Matters: A History of Sexuality in America,* which she co-wrote with John D'Emilio.

FRICKE, Aaron. American author whose autobiographical account of his childhood in a small town in Rhode Island, *Reflections of a Rock Lobster,* detailed his decision to ask for permission to take a male date to his senior prom and the subsequent backlash in the community.

FRYE, Marilyn. American scholar whose writings exploring the ways that gender organizes culture have clarified the issues facing the academic fields of women's studies and gay and lesbian studies.

GALFORD, Ellen. Scottish novelist who writes in a witty and humorous style of her deep commitment to feminism, to women, and to lesbian history through the ages.

GARBER, Marjorie. American scholar and cultural critic whose works have explored the cultural meanings of cross-dressing and bisexuality.

GARNER, Helen. Australian fiction writer whose work explores feminism and its influence on her characters and the "other," the outsider in society.

GEARHART, Sally Miller. American novelist, educator, and author whose book *The Wanderground* has gained virtual cult status among lesbian readers.

GLICKMAN, Gary. American novelist, short story writer, and librettist whose work is influenced by his identities as a Jew and a gay person.

GOOCH, Brad. American poet, novelist, and short story author whose fiction links humanity to community, and illustrates one of the greatest challenges facing gay American culture: the lack of vital communal connection.

GOODMAN, Melinda. American poet whose work explores neglect, destructive families, unloved adolescents, abuse, the sinister side of children, coming out, loving women, being misloved by women, sex, butch-femme relations, loss, community, isolation, racism, and social injustice.

GOYEN, William. American novelist, playwright, and author of short stories who crossed the boundaries of sexuality in both his life and work; his *House of Breath* explores same-sex desire within an extended Texas family.

GOYTISOLO, Juan. Spanish novelist, short story writer, literary critic, and editor whose works probe the depths of alienation: of being homeless in a world that threatens to destroy family, oppressed through language that reinforces what a dominant group terms "reality," and marginalized because of one's sexual preference.

GREENBERG, David F. American professor of sociology whose activism led him to explore the processes by which some behaviors came to be regarded as deviant.

GRIMSLEY, Jim. American playwright and novelist whose work explores the affects of the AIDS epidemic from various perspectives.

GUIBERT, Herve. French novelist and photographer whose daring and forthright novels about his experience with AIDS earned him great admiration.

HACKER, Marilyn. American poet and editor whose poetry has been hailed as some of the most important of the twentieth century.

HANSCOMBE, Gillian. Australian poet, novelist, and commentator whose book *Hecate's Charms* won her international recognition as a writer and whose work has been strongly influenced by her activism in the feminist movement of the 1960s and 1970s.

HARRIS, Bertha. American novelist whose works explore the lesbian sensibility, and whose novel, *Lover,* has become a lesbian classic.

HARTLEY, Marsden. American painter, poet, and art critic whose homosexuality emerges from the margins of both his painting and his poetry.

HOFFMAN, William M(oses). American playwright, critic, and editor who has contributed to the literature on AIDS and has especially shaped understandings of what theatrical representations of AIDS can do.

HOME, William Douglas. British playwright whose plays and characters continuously question sexual roles and attitudes.

HUGHES, Holly. American author and performance artist whose is best known as one of the "NEA Four" who lost National Endowment for the Arts fellowships because of the gay, lesbian, or nude content of their work; she is also credited with inventing dyke noire plays.

HWANG, David Henry. American playwright whose work examines stereotypes and the powerful ways in which stereotypes are used to continue prejudices and to keep power in place.

INGE, William. American playwright, screenwriter, and novelist whose homosexuality never emerged in such noted plays as *Come Back, Little Sheba, Picnic,* and *Bus Stop.*

JACOB, Max. French poet, painter, critic, and writer considered among the literary giants of his day, whose works both mask and reveal his homosexual identity.

JEWETT, (Theodora) Sarah Orne. American fiction writer whose early treatments of same-sex female relationships in such novels as *Deephaven* and *The Country of the Pointed Firs* stand as predecessors to contemporary lesbian writings.

JORDAN, June. American poet, essayist, playwright, and professor of African American Studies whose lyrical work explores the revolutionary power of love.

JORDAN, Neil. Irish fiction and screenplay writer who is best known for breaking down the binaries of gender, class, race, and nationality in his analysis of the intricacy of humanity. His screenplay, *The Crying Game,* won an Academy Award.

KARLINSKY, Simon. American scholar who pioneered the study of Russian gay and lesbian culture.

KAYE/KANTROWITZ, Melanie. Jewish American essayist, poet, short story writer, editor, professor, and activist whose work reflects her attempts to interweave her identities as woman, Jew, lesbian, feminist, and activist.

KEENAN, Joe. American fiction writer whose comedic work is sometimes labeled as insensitive or politically incorrect.

KHARITONOV, Evgeny Vladimirovich. Russian poet and fiction writer whose homosexuality delayed his recognition as one of his country's great writers.

KIM, Willyce. Novelist and poet who is one of the only Asian-American lesbian writers in print, and whose contribution to our understanding of lesbian literature comes through her depiction of lesbians as fully functional, multi-faced human beings.

KIRKWOOD, James. American actor turned playwright and novelist whose *Chorus Line,* written with Nicholas Dante, explored the hopes and aspirations of gay actors.

KLEPFISZ, Irena. American poet, essayist, editor, and activist whose work highlights the struggles involved in immigration, loss, destruction, economics, community, and acts of resistance and courage.

KLIUEV, Nikolai. Russian poet whose work contributed to the "Silver Age" in Russia, a time when homosexual themes began to appear in literature.

KOTZ, Cappy. American novelist, playwright, and author of short erotic fiction whose work explores issues central to lesbian life, including fat oppression, non-monogamy, butch-femme roles, sex, and the search for heritage.

KUREISHI, Hanif. British/Pakistani author, director, and playwright whose work explores issues of cultural and racial integration; best known for his screenplay *My Beautiful Laundrette.*

LAGERLOEF, Selma. Swedish novelist and short story writer who was the first female to win the Nobel Prize in 1909, and whose novel differentiation of male and female roles is claimed as a precursor to modern feminism.

LASSELL, Michael. American poet, essayist, theater critic, and editor whose work explores issues central to gay culture, including marginalization and AIDS.

LEYLAND, Winston. American publisher, editor, and author of gay literature who began the first gay publishing house, Gay Sunshine Press, which focuses on gay literature and non-fiction, and later Leyland Publications, which features books on gay erotica and fiction.

LIVIA, Anna. Irish/British writer of fiction, science fiction, and nonfiction whose work explores lesbianism and the relationship between gender and language.

LOCKE, Alain. American essayist and educator whose writings about African-American art and literature were influential in drawing attention to several gay writers of the Harlem Renaissance.

LOULAN, Jo Ann. American psychotherapist and lecturer who has been called the "Dr. Ruth of lesbian sex" and is the author of the best-selling book *Lesbian Sex.*

LUCAS, Craig. American playwright, screenwriter, and essayist whose work comments on the personal and social tolls taken by materialism, racism, and homophobia.

LYNCH, Lee. American novelist, author of short stories, and columnist whose work celebrates the qualities of queer culture: the diversity, unity, togetherness, perseverance, and strength of the greater gay and lesbian community.

MACKAY, John Henry. German novelist, poet, author of short stories, and essayist whose writings under the pseudonym Sagitta attempted to legitimate man-boy love in early twentieth century Germany.

MADDY, Yulisa Amadu. Sierra Leonean playwright and novelist whose works offer the rare instance of a positive portrayal of homosexuality in African literature.

MALOUF, David. Australian novelist, poet, and literary critic whose novels detailing intimate relationships among men border on but do not directly confront homosexuality.

MANNING, Rosemary (Joy). British novelist and educator whose novels and autobiographies shed light on the life of a closeted lesbian in mid-century England.

MARCUS, Eric. American journalist and author who has compiled oral histories, compilations of possible answers to frequently asked questions, and "how to" manuals to help others understand what he and many other gays and lesbians must face on a day to day basis.

MASO, Carole. American novelist whose work emphasizes language and the body and is often autobiographical.

McCAULEY, Stephen. American novelist who explores the relationships between gay men and their friends and families in such novels as *A Man in the House.*

McKAY, Festus Claudius. American writer associated with the Harlem Renaissance whose poetry and prose explore issues of race, class, gender, and sexuality.

MERRICK, Gordon. American novelist whose romances probe the difficulties of embracing a gay identity within a culture determined to rule homosexuality out of bounds.

MINER, Valerie. American novelist, author of short stories, and essayist whose feminist and lesbian writing is marked by her ef-fort to engage women's concerns across cultural, sexual, and socio-economic boundaries.

MOHR, Richard D. American philosopher, gay pundit, and social critic who has contributed to gay and lesbian literature by adding to the definition, formulation, and articulation of the philosophy of contemporary gay and lesbian politics.

MOLLOY, Sylvia. Argentinian author whose novel, *Certificate of Absence,* is one of the first Latin American novels centered on lesbian experiences.

MORGAN, Robin. American journalist, poet, and essayist whose *Sisterhood Is Powerful* is considered one of the most influential texts on feminism.

MORROW, Bruce. American author of fiction and nonfiction who has helped to broaden the view of African-American gay fiction with his anthology, *Shade: An Anthology of Fiction by Gay Men of African Descent,* and with fiction which acknowledges the race and sexuality of the characters but focuses on other central issues.

MUHANJI, Cherry. American poet, novelist, and author of short stories whose work investigates the racial, ethnic, and sexual personae of her characters.

NAMJOSHI, Suniti. Indian poet and fabulist whose work is written from a feminist and lesbian perspective and grapples with the alienation that those identities create.

NAVA, Michael. American author of mystery novels and nonfiction whose work has been at the forefront of the explosion of publication of mysteries with a gay protagonist.

NIN, Anais. French diarist and writer whose erotica depicts both homosexuality and heterosexuality freely and openly.

NUGENT, Richard Bruce. American poet, illustrator, and short story writer whose prose work "Smoke, Lilies and Jade" is regarded as the most forthright statement of homosexual love to come out of the Harlem Renaissance.

OBEJAS, Achy. Cuban-American novelist, short story writer, and journalist best known for her syndicated column and her first novel, *We Came All the Way from Cuba so You Could Dress Like This?*

PAGLIA, Camille. American scholar whose book *Sexual Personae: Art and Decadence From Nefertiti to Emily Dickinson* prompted a stir within the intellectual, feminist, and gay communities, causing some to hail her as a great thinker and others to question her intellectual ability.

PARMAR, Pratibha. British filmmaker who explores the circumstances of lesbians and women caught in the snares of culturally-sanctioned violence and bigotry.

PASTRE, Genevieve. French poet, philosopher, essayist, publisher, and playwright who has been a leading force in the modern lesbian and gay movement in France, and who has produced an original and versatile body of poetry, fiction, and essays in which her interests as an artist and her advocacy role complement each other.

PECK, Dale. American novelist whose first novel, *Martin and John,* has been called the gay novel of the 1990s.

PENELOPE, Julia. American theorist, essayist, editor, and linguist who first wrote on lesbian and gay literature in the late 1950s and early 1960s under the pseudonym J. Seeley and whose later work included humorous yet clear analyses of a patriarchal and heterosexist society.

PERELESHIN, Valery. Russian and Brazilian poet whose works, written in exile, are only now gaining critical recognition.

PERRY, Troy. American minister, activist, and author of nonfiction whose autobiographical work, including *The Lord Is My Shepherd and He Knows I'm Gay,* ranks as a landmark testimonial to the power of gay liberation after the watershed Stonewall Riots of 1969.

PETERS, Fritz. American novelist whose anguished embrace of his own homosexuality produced two powerful novels, *The World Next Door* (1949) and *Finistère* (1951).

PHILLIPS, Thomas Hal. American novelist whose work foregrounds the intricacies of class and race in the American South, as well as the anxieties arising in men who love other men within a homophobic culture.

PORTER, Cole. American composer and lyricist whose unabashedly bold references to sex, his critique and disavowal of heterosexual romance, and the presence of same-sex desire in his lyrics, underscored by his pulsing, aggressively rhythmic music, made his work stand apart from that of his contemporaries from the 1920s to the 1950s.

PRICE, Deb. American journalist and columnist whose weekly column was the first to deal exclusively with gay and lesbian issues for a mainstream publication.

RACHID O. Moroccan author who wrote the first Maghrebian book about homosexuality as a self-confessed gay Maghrebian writer.

REINIG, Christa. German novelist, poet, and author of short stories and radio plays whose work deconstructs patriarchy and promotes lesbian culture and identity in novels such as *The Woman in the Well.*

RICE, Anne. American novelist whose work in contemporary horror literature, which includes her collection "The Vampire Chronicles," is replete with gay and lesbian characters.

RICHARDSON, Henry Handel. Pseudonym for Ethel Florence Lindsay Richardson; Australian novelist and author of short stories whose works intimated at attractions toward women before such views could be expressed.

RIGGS, Marlon. American film director whose documentaries explored the dynamics with the African American gay community.

RILKE, Rainer Maria. Austrian poet, novelist, author of short stories, and playwright who is the best-known poet in the German language and one of the premiere poets of the twentieth century in any language, and who left behind a body of work that has become synonymous with the modern quest for the true self in the face of social disintegration.

ROBSON, Ruthann. American short story writer, novelist, and legal scholar whose fiction and legal writing probes the impact of legal statutes and systems upon lesbian existence.

ROCHEFORT, Christiana. French novelist whose work contributes to a lesbian and gay aesthetic because of its relentless challenge to normativity.

RODI, Robert. American novelist and short story writer whose satires of contemporary gay life have won him wide acclaim as a comic.

ROSCOE, Will. American anthropologist and historian whose work explores the historic role of gay people as mediators between the genders in American Indian tribes.

ROSS, Martin. A pseudonym for Violet Florence Martin, an Irish novelist, author of short stories, and essayist, who, with her first cousin, Edith Somerville, wrote works that discussed the ineffectuality of heterosexual marriage and love relationships.

ROZANOV, Vasily Vasilievich. Russian essayist, philosopher, and literary critic whose writings about sexuality at the turn of the century were without precedent in Russia; his *People of the Moonlight* is the only influential book-length study of the topic of homosexuality in Russia.

RUKEYSER, Muriel. American poet, biographer, translator, literary critic, novelist, and author of children's stories whose contribution to gay and lesbian literature is anchored in her feminist poetry.

SAINT, Assoto. American poet, dramatist, and dancer who was one of the first to write about the lives of gay African-American men.

SARGESON, Frank. New Zealand short story writer and novelist who is considered one of his country's greatest writers, and whose early works explore--in coded terms--the lives of homosexual men.

SEGREST, Mab. American essayist and poet whose work weaves personal history and experiences with journalistic chronicles of acts of racist, religious, and homophobic violence, mostly in North Carolina during the 1980s.

SHOWALTER, Elaine. American educator and author best known for her ground-breaking publication *A Literature of Their Own,* in which she introduced the concept of a literary tradition for women.

SILVERA, Makeda. African-Caribbean-Canadian short story writer and editor who is as well known for her publishing and her activism as she is for her well-crafted short stories.

SMITH, Lillian. American novelist and author of nonfiction whose well-known literary works defending civil rights and attacking American racism also contain significant references to the rights of lesbians.

STAMBOLIAN, George. American educator, author, and editor who pioneered the field of gay literary studies in the university and edited the influential *Men on Men* anthologies.

STEAKLEY, James D. American scholar whose works explore the early-twentieth century German gay liberation movement.

STEFAN, Verena. German novelist whose *Häutungen* (*Shedding*), which traces the unfolding of a woman's sexual and individual identity in the 1970s in Germany, became a cult phenomenon and marked the definitive entrance of German feminism into the public literary arena.

STRACHEY, Lytton. British essayist, critic, biographer, and historian whose works, written at the turn of the century, challenged Victorian sexual repression and reflected the writer's own homosexuality.

SWENSON, May. American poet whose poetry explores, from the distance demanded by homophobia, the delicate turns of lesbian love, among other themes.

TAKAHASHI, Mutsuo. Japanese poet, novelist, and critic whose work features poetic expressions of graphic sexuality and employs the language of metaphysics to explore the relationship between homosexuality and the divine.

TERRY, Megan. American playwright who has been called the "mother of feminist drama" and is credited with developing transformational theatre, a style in which actors transform from one character to another in response to a change in the given circumstances.

THURMAN, Wallace. American novelist, playwright, essayist and editor who may have included coded references to the problems facing homosexuals within his works dealing with the plight of African Americans in the first half of the century.

TRIFONOV, Gennady. Russian poet, essayist, and critic who presented one of the sharpest postwar challenges to Article 121 of the Soviet Union's criminal code, which not only prohibited the committing of any homosexual acts, but defined the condition of being homosexual out of legal existence.

TRINIDAD, David. American poet whose writings chronicle his search for and eventual discovery of meaningful love.

TSUI, Kitty. American poet, short story writer, novelist, essayist, and performance artist whose work exists to overcome invisibility and gain a voice for Asian American lesbians.

TSVETAEVA, Marina (Ivanovna). Russian writer and poet considered one of Russia's greatest poets of the 20th century, who often wrote poetry detailing her lesbian love affairs.

TUSQUETS, Esther. Spanish novelist and author of short stories whose work depicts lesbian relationships as shadows of a more mature, heterosexual love.

URBANITZKY, Grete von. Austrian author whose novel *Wild Garden* (1927) is regarded as "the best-known Austrian lesbian novel" between World Wars I and II.

VAID, Urvashi. American memoirist who surveyed the progress that the lesbian, gay, bisexual, and transgender communities have made in securing greater access to social equality in the United States in her book *Virtual Equality: The Mainstreaming of Gay and Lesbian Liberation.*

VINING, Donald. American diarist and advocate for older gays and lesbians who is best known for his book, *A Gay Diary,* which was among the first upbeat, hopeful depictions of gay life in America.

WALKER, Alice. American novelist whose work has contributed to the stripping away of coding and silence in African American literature.

WATNEY, Simon. British AIDS activist and author of essays whose work explores the political, cultural, and personal meanings of AIDS in the 1980s and 1990s.

WEIRAUCH, Anna Elisabet. German novelist who wrote the widely read and influential lesbian novel *The Scorpion* (1919), along with dozens of other works.

WESCOTT, Glenway. American novelist, essayist, and critic whose work is associated with the Midwest regional writers, the Paris expatriate writers, and the New York literary scene of the 1920s, and whose friendship and work with Doctor Alfred C. Kinsey contributed to the breakthrough work of the Institute for Sex Research.

WILHELM, Gale. American novelist and short story writer whose open treatment of lesbianism in *We Too Are Drifting* (1935) and *Torchlight to Valhalla* (1938) was rare for the time.

WILLHOITE, Michael. American illustrator and author of children's fiction and cartoons whose book *Daddy's Roommate* explores issues of gay identity and fatherhood.

WINANT, Fran. American poet and activist who is best known for her poem "Christopher St. Liberation Day, June 28, 1970," which captured the mood of the first gay liberation march.

WINGS, Mary. American novelist and short story writer who is best known for her mystery series featuring the lesbian sleuth Emma Victor.

WOLVERTON, Terry. American poet, novelist, and short story writer whose work has been a primary force in creating visibility for artists and writers, and in forging cohesion and creativity within queer communities.

WONG, Norman. Chinese-American short story writer whose work interweaves the assimilation of successive generations of an immigrant family to post-war America with the definition of a central character's sexual identity.

WOODSON, Jacqueline. American novelist and short story writer whose work for young adults integrates multiculturalism with the marginality felt by oppressed communities.

ZAPATA, Luis. Mexican author whose work explores the struggles of those forced to restrict their sexuality to codes of behavior specifically organized for increased biological and material productivity.

ZINOVIEVA-ANNIBAL, Lydia. Russian novelist, playwright, and author of short stories whose *Thirty-Three Abominations* (1907) is the first Russian novel to feature lesbian love.

A

AKHMATOVA, Anna Andreyevna

Nationality: Russian poet, translator, and author of critical studies. **Born:** Anna Andreyevna Gorenko near Odessa, Russia, 23 June 1888; took great grandmother's name. **Education:** Carskoe Selo and the Smolny Institute, St. Petersburg (Leningrad); completed secondary education in Kiev; attended colleges in Kiev and St. Petersburg, including Zhenskie Kursy; studied literature at Oxford University, Ph.D. 1965. **Family:** Married four times; lived with other companions. **Career:** Lived in Paris 1910-11; toured Italy in 1924 and 1964. **Member:** Member of Union of Soviet Writers (expelled in 1946); Writers' Union (honorary, elected to presidency, 1965). **Awards:** Candidate for the Nobel Prize, 1958 and 1965; Taormina Prize for Poetry, 1964; D. Litt.: Oxford University, 1965. **Died:** 5 March 1966.

WRITINGS

Poetry

Vecher ("Evening"). St. Petersburg, Poets' Guild, 1912.
Cetki ("Rosary"). St. Petersburg, Giperborey (organ of Poets' Guild), 1914.
Belaia Staia ("The White Flock"). St. Petersburg, Giperborey, 1917.
Skrizhal: Sbornik ("Scratchy collection"). Petrograd, Tipographiia "Dom Pechati," 1918.
U Samogo Moria ("At the Seaside"). St. Petersburg, Alkonost, 1921.
Podorozhnik ("Buck-thorn"). St. Petersburg, Petropolis Printers, 1921.
Anno Domini MCMXXI. St. Petersburg, Petropolis Printers, 1922.
Anno Domini. St. Petersburg, Petropolis Printers-Alkonost, 1923.
Stikhi ("Poems"). Russia, 1940.
Iz Shesti Knig: Stikhotvoreniia ("From Six Books"). Moscow, Sovetskii Pisatel, 1940.
Izbrannoe: Stikhi ("Selected Poems"). Tashkent(?), Sovetskii Pisatel, 1943.
Izbrannye Stikhi. Moscow, n.p., 1946.
Stikhotvoreniia 1909-1957 ("Poems 1909-1957"), edited by A.A. Surkov. Moscow, Khudozhestvennaia Literatura, 1958.
Poema Bez Geroia: Tryptykh ("Poem without a Hero: A Triptych"), in *Vozdushnye puti* ("Airways"); published privately, New York, R. N. Grinberg(?), 1959(?).
Stikhotvoreniia 1909-1960 ("Poems 1909-1960"). Moscow, Khudozhestvennaia Literatura, 1961.
Collected Poems: 1912-1963, edited by Virginia E. Van Wynen. Privately printed, 1963.
Rekviem ("Requiem"). Munich, T-vo Zarubezhnykh Pisatelei, 1963.
Beg Vremeni ("Race of Time"). Moscow, Sovetskii Pisatel, 1965.

Translator

Korethiskaia Klassicheskaia Poeziia ("Korean Classical Poetry"). Moscow, Khudozhestvennaia Literatura, 1958.

Lirika drevnego Egipta ("Ancient Egyptian Lyrics"). Moscow, Khudozhestvennaia Literatura, 1965.
Golosa Poetov ("Voices of the Poets"). Moscow, Progress, 1965.
Klassicheskaia poeziia Vostoka ("Classical Poetry of the East"). Moscow, Khudozestvennaia Literatura, 1969.

Collected Works

Sochineniia. Volumes 1 and 2, edited by G. P. Struve and B. A. Filippov, Munich, Inter-Language Literary Associates, 1967, 1968; Volume 3, edited by G. P. Struve, N. A. Struve, and B. A. Filippov, Paris, YMCA-Press, 1983.
Poems of Akhmatova, translated by Stanley Kunitz and Max Hayward. Boston, Little, Brown-Collins, 1973.
Anna Akhmatova: Selected Poems, edited and translated by Walter Arndt. Ardis, Ann Arbor, 1976.
Sochineniia. Volume 1, edited by V. A. Chernykh with an introduction by Mikhail Dudin, Moscow, Khudozhestvennaia Literatura, 1986; Volume 2, edited by G. Gershtein, A. A. Mandykina, V. A. Chernykh, and N. N. Glen, Moscow, Khudozhestvennaia Literatura, 1986.
The Complete Poems of Anna Akhmatova, translated by Judith Hemschemeyer, edited by Roberta Reeder. Boston, Zephyr, 1990.

Other

My Half Century: Selected Prose, edited by Ronald Meyer. Ann Arbor, Michigan, Ardis, 1992.

*

Biography: *Anna Akhmatova: A Poetic Pilgrimage* by Amanda Haight, New York, Oxford University Press, 1976; *Remembering Anna Akhmatova* by Anatoly Nayman, New York, Henry Holt, 1989; *The Akhmatova Journals* by Lidiia Chukovskaia, New York, Farrar, Straus & Giroux, 1993; *Anna Akhmatova* by Roberta Reeder, New York, St. Martin's Press, 1994.

Bibliography: *Anna Akhmatova in English: A Bibliography 1889—1966—1989* by Garth M. Terry, Nottingham, United Kingdom, Astra Press, 1989.

Critical Sources: *Anna Akhmatova* by Sam Driver, Boston, Twayne, 1972; *Anna Akhmatova: A Poetic Pilgrimage* by Amanda Haight, Oxford University Press, 1976; "Anna Akhmatova" by David McDuff, in *Parnassus* (New York), Vol. 11, No. 2, 1984, 51-82; "The Keening Muse" by Joseph Brodsky, in *Less Than One: Selected Essays,* New York, Farrar, Straus, & Giroux, 1986, 34-53; *In a Shattered Mirror: The Later Poetry of Anna Akhmatova* by Susan Amert, Stanford, California, Stanford University Press, 1992; "Anna Akhmatova's Requiem: A Retrospective of the Love Lyric and Epos" by Anna Ljunggren, and "On a Poem without a Hero" by Vitalii Vilenkin, in *Anna Akhmatova 1989-1989: Papers from the Akhmatova Centennial Conference,* edited by Sonia I. Ketchian, Oakland, California, Berkeley Slavic Specialties, 1993; "Tsvetaeva and the Feminine Tradition in Russian Poetry" by Jane

A. Taubman, in *Marina Tsvetaeva: One Hundred Years,* compiled and edited by Jane A. Taubman et al., Oakland, California, Berkeley Slavic Specialties, 1994; "Anna Akhmatova" by John Simon, in *New Criterion* (New York), Vol. 12, No. 9, May 1994, 29-39; "The Death of the Book a la russe: The Acmeists under Stalin" by Clare Cavanagh, in *Slavic Review,* Vol. 55, No. 1, spring 1996, 125-135.

*   *   *

Anna Akhmatova holds a legendary place among Russian poets. Writing for over half a century between 1910 and 1966 on a diverse range of subjects, Akhmatova endured the Stalinist purges, repeated sanctions against her work, and destitute poverty. She is hailed first and foremost as a poet of erotic love whose crisp, compact forms helped inaugurate a new literary style working against the vague, embellished verse of traditional Russian Symbolism. Although these love poems are nearly always read from a heterosexual perspective, owing perhaps to the abundant documentation on Akhmatova's sexual life as wife or companion to many men, rumor has it that KGB files report a female agent's amorous encounter with Akhmatova, who, after drinking vodka, begins to kiss and touch the agent, attempting to unfasten her dress.

Due to the social upheaval afflicting post-Revolutionary Russia from the 1920s onward, Akhmatova shared quarters with many women with whom she often formed profound, life-long attachments. The nature of her relationships with these women is certainly ambiguous, but we know that Akhmatova traveled (usually in homeless, impoverished exile) with different women and possibly formed "love triangles" with some of the couples who took her in. More importantly, the women surrounding Akhmatova were frequently entrusted with the great responsibility of recording the poet's daily life and poetic fragments at times when her poetry was forbidden and when association with her could be dangerous.

Under the influence of her first husband, celebrated poet Nikolay Gumilyov, Akhmatova became involved with the Poets' Guild, a small coterie of writers who rejected Symbolism and its emphasis on mystical, abstract principals in favor of Acmeism, a movement the group founded which attempted to capture, through clarity and directness, the concrete realities of the present world. Out of this literary environment Akhmatova's first published collections, "Evening" (1912) and "Rosary" (1914), appeared, receiving accolades from critics and audiences which gained her wide notoriety at an early age and established her in the eyes of many as a master of Acmeist tenets, despite Symbolist traces in her work.

These youthful efforts have been described as confessional and intensely lyrical, since their prominent motif centers on the trials of passionate love typically found in the exclusively female genre of Russian lyrical folk song. Diverse female characters appear in conjunction with a distinctly feminine, authorial "I" in these poems where Akhmatova often constructs her poetic settings out of women's artifacts and bodies, especially accessories, faces, lips, and hands. While social themes as well as reflections on poetic consciousness draw greater attention from Akhmatova in "White Flock" (1917), published after the Russian Revolution began, her contemporaries continued to refract her work through a lens of heterosexual love and speculations on her romantic life. Yet David McDuff points out in *Parnassus* that the young poet's "purpose is not to provide an open diary of her private emotional life," suggesting instead that the first-person pronoun represents "a fusion of identities that includes all "I's." Ironically, her famed ability to conjure poignant human emotions and her popularity with working women would soon lead to the State's complete suppression of her poetry.

If Akhmatova enjoyed the privilege of the literary elite early on, the Revolution ushered in lengthy periods of personal and political deprivation for the poet. During the same years that "Plantain" and *Anno Domini MCMXXI* were written (1916-22), her first husband was executed on charges of anti-Soviet conspiracy, her friends and relations were dying around her, a second marriage had ended, and her health was deteriorating. Hence, her poetry began to resonate with tones of fear and despair. Speaking of Russia, nature, remembrance, and religion, the poet weaves these "public" subjects into her repertoire of private experiences, and from this time onward memory becomes a "moral imperative" for her, according to Roberta Reeder in *Anna Akhmatova.* In "Lot's wife" Akhmatova writes: "Who will weep for this woman? / Isn't her death the least significant? / But my heart will never forget the one / Who gave her life for a single glance."

Akhmatova would be barred from publishing another volume of poetry until 1940, but her work surfaced sporadically in various magazines over the next few years, thanks to the relatively relaxed cultural atmosphere of the newly-born Soviet State. With Stalin's ascension to power in the mid-1920s, however, Akhmatova became an open target for attack. Numerous male critics had already disparaged her poems on the grounds of their feminine qualities, thus her deceptively quiet, thoughtful poems eventually came to signify all that threatened the authoritarian, paternalistic values of the Revolution. Although the famous Bolshevik, Aleksandra Kollontay (the world's first woman ambassador), noted that Akhmatova expressed important socialist values for women, including sexual freedom and self-fulfillment, this view was subsequently quashed by accusations of a decadent, coquettish element in her poetic voice which threatened the new regime's propagandized vision of womanhood.

In 1925, thirty-two of Akhmatova's poems were featured in a large anthology, but that same year introduced an unofficial ban on her poetry. so she began work on various critical studies in addition to translations. The early thirties found the poet poverty-stricken, frequently ill, and with no apartment of her own, yet she describes this period as the "vegetarian years" because they were mild compared to the coming decades. In 1938 her son, Lev Gumilyov, was arrested. Standing on the long prison queues, she waited for hours each day along with hundreds of Russian women. Her well-known poem, "Requiem," was inspired by these women—by the disruption of their lives and the suffering imposed on all of them, and by the love they shared for one another. This collision with political forces was to transform Akhmatova as a poet. Her use of the feminine, lyrical voice to convey her thoughts was no longer possible in this devastated world where multiple references to lifeless, silenced women abound: "Already she is cut off from the rest / As if they painfully wrenched life from her heart, / As if they brutally knocked her flat."

Akhmatova's life had always been tightly intertwined with various women, and in 1940 she met Russia's renowned lesbian/bisexual poet, Marina Tsvetaeva. Tsvetaeva had written several erotically-charged poems to Akhmatova, which Akhmatova kept on her person until the papers literally disintegrated. In 1941 Hitler invaded, and Akhmatova was briefly restored to her role as speaker of the people when she delivered a commanding radio address to the "wives, mothers, and sisters" of Leningrad. Shortly after, she was evacuated to the central Asian town of Tashkent where she wrote much of the monumental "Poem without a Hero." Here a mature Akhmatova tries to reconcile the historical realities of her beloved Russia through a series of complex digressions and allusions. The poem requires an intense reading to decipher the text, and the author admits: "But I confess that I used / Invisible ink.../ I write in mirror writing," anticipating the difficulties of this task. Yet in other passages, her purpose rings clearly: "Just ask my contemporaries: / Camp women, prison women, martyrs / And we will tell you of numb terror, / Of raising children for execution." Since she has experienced first hand the horrors of twentieth-century Russian life, her poem resounds with anguish for the dead and the survivors as she meditates on the past's relationship to the future and her role as a civic poet. Despite repeated silencing by the State, this poetry haunts the Russian word and cries out against the life-crushing, official apparatuses which continue to plague the poet's spirit.

In 1946, the Central Committee of the Communist Party passed a resolution against Akhmatova, expelling her from the Union of Soviet Writers. With her son in prison again, Akhmatova attempted to appease Stalin by writing a cycle of poems titled "In Praise of Peace," generally regarded as inferior work. After Stalin's death in 1953, many—though not all—of Akhmatova's poems were published in Russia and she traveled to receive national and international honors. Her late poetry still speaks strongly in the feminine, and her poems often address a lover or companion whose gender is unknown. Akhmatova undoubtedly possesses a sensual, erotic conception of woman in all her work even when she writes of pain, loss, or history's mistakes.

—Sioban Dillon

———

ALDRICH, Ann. *See* **MEAKER, Marijane.**

———

ALLEN, Jeffner

Nationality: American philosopher and poet. **Born:** San Diego, California, 11 October 1947. **Education:** University of California, San Diego, M.A. 1971; Duquesne University, Pennsylvania, Ph.D. 1973. **Career:** Assistant professor of Philosophy, University of Florida, Gainsville, 1974-79; associate professor of Philosophy, DePaul University, Chicago, Illinois, 1979-83; visiting scholar, Center for Research on Women, Stanford, California, 1982; visiting associate professor of Women's Studies, California State University, Fresno, 1983-84, and Eastern Montana State College, Billings, 1986-87; visiting associate professor of Philosophy, California State University, Chico, California, 1984-85, and California State University, Hayward, California, 1985-86; associate professor, then professor of Philosophy and Women's Studies, State University of New York, Binghamton, Binghamton, New York, 1987-93. **Address:** c/o Department of Philosophy, State University of New York, Binghamton, Binghamton, New York 13902, U.S.A.

WRITINGS

Nonfiction

Remembering: A Time I Will Be My Own Beginning. Berkeley, California, Acacia Press, 1984.
Lesbian Philosophy: Explorations. Palo Alto, California, Institute of Lesbian Studies, 1986.
Editor, with Iris Young, *The Thinking Muse: Feminism and Recent French Thought.* Bloomington, Indiana University Press, 1989.
Editor, *Lesbian Philosophies and Cultures.* Albany, State University of New York Press, 1990.
r e v e r b e r a t i o n s Across the Shimmering *CASCADAS,* Albany, State University of New York Press, 1994.
Sinuosities, Lesbian Poetic Politics. Bloomington: Indiana University Press, 1996.

Uncollected Nonfiction

"Doing Gender: An Ethnomethodological Approach," in *Human Studies,* Vol. 3, 1980, 107-15.
"An Introduction to Patriarchal Existentialism: Accompanied by a Proposal for a Way Out of Existential Patriarchy," in *Philosophy and Social Criticism,* Vol. 9, 1982, 450-65.
"Women and Food," in *Journal of Social Philosophy,* Vol. 15, No. 2, 1984, 34-41.
"Motherhood: The Annihilation of Women," in *Mothering: Essays in Feminist Theory,* edited by Joyce Trebilcot. Totowa, New Jersey, Littlefield, Adams, 1984; as "La Maternité: Annihilation des Femmes," translation by D. Vielleux, in *Amazones d'Hier,* Vol. 2, 1988, 65-87.
"Looking at Our Blood: A Lesbian Response to Men's Terrorization of Women," in *Trivia,* Vol. 4, 1984, 11-38.
"Une Economie Lesbienne," in *Amazones d'Hier,* Vol. 4, 1985, 16-27; as "Lesbian Economics," in *Trivia,* Vol. 8, 1986, 37-53.
"Through the Wild Region: An Essay in Phenomenological Feminism," in *Review of Existential Psychology and Psychiatry,* Vol. 18, 1986, 241-56.
"Women Who Beget Women Must Thwart Major Sophisms," in *Philosophy and Social Criticism,* Vol. 13, No. 4, 1987, 315-25.
"The Economy of the Body in a Post-Nietzschean Era," in *The Collegium Phaenomenologicum: The First Decade,* edited by John Sallis, G. Moneta, and J. Taminiaux. The Hague, Kluwer, 1988, 289-308.
"Poetic Politics, How the Amazons Took the Acropolis," in *Hypatia,* Vol. 3, No. 2, 1988, 107-122.
"Passion in the Gardens of Delight," in *Woman of Power,* Vol. 13, 1989, 26-27.
"Julie Velton Fauve" and "Clarisse Gauthier Coignet," in *A History of Women in Philosophy,* Vol. 3, edited by Mary Ellen Waithe. The Hague, Kluwer, 1991.
"Simone de Beauvoir," in *A History of Women in Philosophy,* Vol. 4, edited by Mary Ellen Waithe. The Hague, Kluwer, 1995.
"A Response to a Letter from Peg Simons, December 1993," in *Feminist Interpretations of Simone de Beauvoir,* edited by Margaret A. Simons. University Park, Pennsylvania University Press, 1995.

*

Critical Sources: "Jeffner Allen: A Lesbian Portrait" by Jacqueline Zita, in *Hypatia,* Vol. 7, No. 4, 1992, 6-13; "Amazon Intertextualities and Sinuosity in Sandra Shotlander's *Angels of Power*" by Rosemary Keefe Curb, in *Hypatia,* Vol. 10, No. 4, 1995, 90-103.

                    *   *   *

In an autobiographical moment of *Sinuosities,* Jeffner Allen remarks of her own work that it was initially inspired by her activism with the American radical feminist movement of the late sixties and early seventies, rather than by her formal education in continental philosophy. The spirit of radical feminism—that women could and would overthrow patriarchal oppression—is in few other instances developed into a social philosophy as it in Allen's poetic politics. Formulated in the lacuna between philosophy and poetry, poetic politics includes philosophical, poetical, autobiographical, and historical moments. The aggregate result of various reading and writing strategies, it is meant to embody the diversity and abundance of women's experiences and aspirations. In short, poetic politics is a writing of abundance which exceeds patriarchal narratives.

A sampling of Allen's strategies may be gathered from "A Response to a Letter from Peg Simons, December 1993," where Allen responds to Simons' question of how her views on Simone de Beauvoir's existential philosophy have changed in light of the posthumous publication of Beauvoir's personal letters and notebooks. Allen here performs a reading of Beauvoir not as a secondary figure in the existential movement but as its founding matriarch. In this transgressive reading, Sartre's philosophy is regarded as an appropriation and alteration of Beauvoir's theories, as well as a denigration of those ideas which he could not translate into his patriarchal existentialism. Also transgressive is the form which Allen's reading takes. Neither philosophy, nor poetry, nor any one form properly speaking, her writing interweaves different strategies and modes of writing, challenging the boundaries drawn between "thinker" and "literary writer."

Jeffner Allen's reading of Beauvoir and existentialism reveals the importance of Beauvoir's relations with other women, both emotionally and physically. At the heart of Allen's radical poetic politics are the patterns of women's lived experiences and the dynamic structures of the connections between women—what she calls sinuosities. The sinew, or tendon, is where both anger and strength are stored in the body. Sinuosity is, therefore, the unleashing of women's rage which leads to the discovery of new resources for strength. Also a turning of women to women, sinuosity requires that women come to trust and befriend each other, and come to care for each other's emotional and physical needs. The turn is also simultaneously a move by which women come to take back, from patriarchal institutions, their bodies—as ends and sources in themselves. Thus, in "Motherhood: The Annihilation of Women," Allen argues for the evacuation of motherhood, of being a man's wife or "womb," so that women may attend to each other's needs—that is, that they may conserve their energy sources and supplies, feed their hungers, and develop their literacy. In order to attend to their needs, women may create a "Lesbian Economics," an economy outside of the patriarchy which values women's work for itself, and in which women stand in relation to other women.

In "Poetic Politics, How the Amazons Took the Acropolis," the politically radical aspect of Jeffner Allen's poetics is symbolically depicted as the seizure of the Acropolis, the sacred high ground upon which the city of Athens was founded, by Amazon women. Athena, the ancient Libyan Amazon after whom the city of Athens is named and not the mythical Athena born from the head of Zeus, leads the attack. It is by this textual violence, and in the field of Amazon intertextuality, that a poetic politics can arise and be sustained. In addition, Allen explains how unlike a postmodern "politics of difference" where the feminine is elevated to status of Other but denied the specificities of her lived experiences, poetic politics allows her to speak herself for herself, in all of her incarnations. The experimental piece "r e v e r b e r a t i o n s moonflowers estrellas fugaces, r e v e r b e r a c i o n e s flores lunares falling stars" is a spoken song meant to be read out loud by two women fluent in both English and Spanish. In this piece of erotic lesbian poetry, the voices of two women lovers are heard overlapping, each in her own rhythm and tone. Here, women are not simply "the Other," but embodied, living, and speaking for themselves and to each other. Not assuming that there is or ever could be one woman who can speak for, and stand in for, all women, poetic politics embodies and expresses the differences between women, as they address each other with trust and care.

In "Jeffner Allen: A Lesbian Portrait," Jacqueline Zita well notes a progression in Jeffner Allen's writings from a militant radical feminist tone towards a poetic and sensuous tone; this can be evidenced in her most recent endeavors. The collection *r e v e r b e r a t i o n s* Across the Shimmering *CASCADAS* is in its entirety a celebration of experimental lesbian poetics, but these pieces should also be read as a political manifesto, one that asserts that women can and should challenge the patriarchal narrative which reduces writing to an instrument of precision, knowledge to that which can be possessed, and economy to laws of scarcity. The imagery of "On the Seashore, A Writing of Abundance," which is found in this collection, is that of combing the sea shore for rubble; it calls for women to gather what has been expelled by the patriarchal sea of knowledge, and to find in their memories the sources and resources for another economy, an economy of abundance. It is a call for women to write, and to write that which exceeds, and therefore escapes, patriarchal narratives.

—Rita Alfonso

ALTHER, Lisa

Nationality: American novelist and author of short stories. **Born:** Lisa Reed in Tennessee, 23 July 1944. **Education:** Wellesley College, B.A. **Family:** Married Richard Philip Alther, 26 August 1966; one daughter. **Career:** Secretary and editorial assistant, Atheneum Publishers, 1967; freelance writer, from 1967; writer, Garden Way, Inc., 1970-71; contributor of articles and short stories to periodicals including *Boston Globe, Cosmopolitan, Los Angeles Times, Natural History, New Englander, New Society, New York Times Book Review, New York Times Magazine, San Francisco Chronicle, Vermont Freeman, Vogue, Washington Post, Women's Review of Books,* and *Yankee.* Board of directors, Planned Parenthood of Champlain Valley, 1972. **Address:** c/o Watkins-Loomis, Inc., 133 East 35th St., New York, New York 10016, U.S.A.

WRITINGS

Novels

Kinflicks. New York, Knopf, 1976.
Original Sins. New York, Knopf, 1981.
Other Women. New York, Knopf, 1984.
Bedrock. New York, Knopf, 1990.
Five Minutes in Heaven. New York, Dutton, 1995.

Short Stories

"Encounter," in *McCall's,* August 1976.
"Termites," in *Homewords,* edited by Douglas Paschell and Alice Swanson. Knoxville, University of Tennessee Press, 1986.
"The Politics of Paradise," in *Louder Than Words,* edited by William Shore. New York, Random House, 1989.
"Silver Moon Bay," in *By the Light of the Silvery Moon,* edited by Ruth Petrie. London, Virago Press, 1994.

Essays

"They Shall Take Up Serpents," in *New York Times Sunday Magazine,* 6 June 1976.
"Into the Melting Pot," in *Mankind,* Vol. 5, No. 9, October 1976.
"Will the South Rise Again?," in *New York Times Book Review,* 16 December 1979.
"Introduction," in *A Good Man Is Hard to Find* by Flannery O'Connor. London, Women's Press, 1980.
"What I Do When I Write...," in *Women's Review of Books,* July 1989.
"Dear Old House: Sarah Orne Jewett," in *Art & Antiques,* December 1991.
"Growing Up a Southern Writer," in *Southern Living,* April 1996.

*

Interviews: "Interviews with Seven Contemporary Writers" by Laurie L. Brown, in *Women Writers of the Contemporary South,* edited by Peggy Whitman Prenshaw, Jackson, University Press of Mississippi, 1984.

Critical Sources: By Carol Edwards, in *Turnstile,* Vol. 4, No. 1, 34-50; by Lena Svanberg, in *Guardian,* 24 November 1977, 11; by A. S. Byatt, in *Harper's and Queen,* July 1978, 58; "Alther, Atwood, Ballantyne and Gray: Secular Salvation in the Contemporary Feminist Bildungsroman" by Bonnie Hoover Braendlin, in *Frontiers,* Vol. 1, No. 1, 1979; "The Next of *Kinflicks*" by Cathy Peake, in *Melbourne Age,* 1 February 1980; "Condemned to Survival: The Comic Unsuccessful Suicide" by Marilyn J. Smith, in *Comparative Literature Studies,* Vol. 17, No. 1, March 1980; "*Kinflicks* Author Is Back," by Michiko Kakutani, in *New York Times,* 19 December 1980; "New Directions in the Contemporary Bildungsroman: Lisa Alther's *Kinflicks*" by Hoover, in *Gender and Literary Voice,* edited by Janet Todd, New York, Holmes and Meier, 1980, 160-171; in *Avenue,* April 1981, 110; "Vermont's Ambivalent Southerner" by Andrew Feinburg, in *Horizon,* Vol. 24, No. 5, May 1981; by Pat William, in *Daily Mail,* 27 May 1981, 36; "Ms. Alther's North and South" by Polly Pattullo, in *London Observer Magazine,* 31 May 1981; "Lost Times Down Home" by Sandra McGrath, in *Weekend Australian Magazine,* 8 May 1982; "Symbiosis and Separation in Lisa Alther's *Kinflicks*" by Joan Lord Hall, in *Arizona Quarterly,* No. 38, 1982, 336-346; "The Female Novel of Development and the Myth of Psyche" by Mary Anne Ferguson, in *Denver Quarterly,* No. 17, 1983, 58-74; *American Fictions 1940-1980: A Comprehensive History and Critical Evaluation* by Frederick R. Karl, New York, 1983, 427; review of *Other Women,* in *People Weekly,* Vol. 22, 12 November 1984, 24; "Lisa Alther: The Irony of Return?" by Mary Anne Ferguson, in *Women Writers of the Contemporary South,* edited by Prenshaw, Oxford, University Press of Mississippi, 1984; "Female Stereotypes as Satiric Metaphors in Lisa Alther's *Kinflicks*" by Carey Kaplan, in *Whimsy II,* Tempe, Arizona State University Press, 1984; "*Kinflicks:* Sad Laughter and Satire" by J. Leo Harris, in *Whimsy III,* Tempe, Arizona State University Press, 1985; "Lisa Alther's Novel *Original Sins*" by Jochen Barkhausen, in *German Yearbook of American Studies,* Vol. 33, 1986; "Alther and Dillard: The Appalachian Universe" by Frederick O. Waage, in *Appalachia/America: Proceedings of the Third Appalachian Studies Conference,* 1986; "You Might as Well Laugh: Lisa Alther's Funny, Befuddled, Courageous Heroes" by Jane S. Bakerman, in *Whimsy V,* Tempe, Arizona State University Press, 1987; "Self-Assertive Humor in Recent Women's Comedy" by Charlotte Templin, in *Whimsy VI,* Tempe, Arizona State University Press, 1988; *Subjugation and Emancipation in the Fiction of Lisa Alther* by Gwendolyn Hale White, Murphreesboro, University of Middle Tennessee Press, 1988; "Sex, Truth and Rejection Slips" by Jane Sullivan, in *Melbourne Age,* 17 March 1990; "*Kinflicks* Meets Crowsfeet" by Shona Martyn, in *Australian Good Housekeeping,* July 1990; "Hot Property" by John Linklater, in *Glasgow Herald,* 5 August 1990; "Talking Dirty" by Susan Jeffreys, in *London Observer Magazine,* 12 August 1990; "Of Human Bondage" by Linda Grant, in *London Listener,* 16 August 1990; review of *Bedrock* by Jane Marcus, in *Nation* (New York), Vol. 251, No. 6, 27 August 1990, 212; "Twelve Years of Rejection Slips" by Marion McLeod, in *New Zealand Listener Magazine,* 26 August 1991; review of *Five Minutes in Heaven* by Hilary Mullins, in *Lambda Book Report* (Washington, D.C.), Vol. 4, No. 10, May-June 1995, 18; review of *Five Minutes in Heaven* by Elaine Kahn, in *People Weekly* (New York), Vol. 44, No. 4, 24 July 1995, 27; review of *Five Minutes in Heaven* by Julie Wheelwright, in *New Statesman and Society* (London), Vol. 8, No. 363, 28 July 1995, 38; "Growing Up a Southern Writer" by Lisa Alther, in *Southern Living* (Birmingham, Alabama), April 1996.

Lisa Alther comments:

What I've been trying to do in all my fiction is to get at the human reality behind our society's stereotypes, particularly those regarding women and homosexuals. My goal has been to portray members of such eternally stigmatized groups as unique and complex individuals, apart from the caricatures fostered by our culture, and sometimes by those groups themselves.

Sexual expression is of course one aspect to being homosexual, but it's not the only thing, any more than it is for heterosexuals. I attempt to give my gay and lesbian characters full, complicated lives involving work, households, politics, children, friends, spiritual struggles, etc. And one important facet to their lives is that their partners are the same sex as themselves.

This is exciting and satisfying work because it's a topic that wasn't written about much prior to the 1970s. And when it was, it was disguised in various ways, and hence distorted. To be in a position to write openly about gay and lesbian characters is very challenging—and not just about lesbians, but also about women in general. The female psyche is the great unexplored continent, in my opinion.

For centuries we've all read novels about the heterosexual experience of life and love. Gays and lesbians can and do relate to them, so I don't see why the opposite shouldn't be true. Life is a confusing and mysterious experience, so whatever light anybody can shed on it, from whatever their minority perspective, ought to be valued. But of course it often isn't.

*   *   *

"I can't decide whether to have my novel be a comedy or a tragedy," boasts the male lover of Lisa Alther's first heroine, the now legendary Ginny Babcock in *Kinflicks*. Terminally weary of male pretensions, she retorts, "Does it make any difference?" "Of course it does. It determines the whole structure. The essence of comedy is that life goes on; the main characters are survivors. They keep popping back up whenever they're knocked down. In tragedy, though, the heroes usually die and drag kingdoms down with them." In this rare moment of reflexive poetics, the young man is as wrong about Ginnie's sexuality as he is about Alther's own novelistic art. In Alther's comic novels, it is heroines who are knocked down and drag male kingdoms with them, only to pop back up and look around, ready to take on another one, optimally in the loving company of another woman.

Wars, rapes, tortures, treacheries, grisly maimings—our modern tragedies—proliferate. They change the rhythm of life but they cannot stop the protagonists' serio-comic, poignant quest for clarity and conviction. Social and political ideologies, indeed any inflexible system of knowledge, turns out to be pseudo-heroic posturing, just so much macho impedimenta. Along the way to that discovery Alther's comic heroines get themselves into hilarious dilemmas and do battle with some of America's most cherished cultural assumptions about social justice, personal identity, dignity, and love.

Her first novel, the best-selling *Kinflicks,* won Alther a wide audience in 1975, when reviewers at the *New York Times Book Review* and the *NatioN* hailed her "comic genius" and welcomed this new voice in American literature. Four subsequent novels, a novella, and four stories have strengthened that voice and extended its range, as Alther has continued exploring the lives and deaths of her generation of Americans. In 1996, recognizing Alther's prominent place in American letters, Penguin reissued the five novels in new editions. Regularly translated into many languages, Alther is one of few American lesbian novelists who have achieved mainstream readership and an international audience.

In addition to the appeal of madcap comic characters and deft social satire, one of the reasons for such steady success may be that, in an age when gay writers can deluge readers with explicit sexual detail, Alther is more concerned with the emotional impact of sex and sexualities. She takes a biographical approach to character (each protagonist is rooted in a rural Southern childhood before being loosed into the laboratory of the world) and she keeps her focus trained on the single, manifold problem of making sense of things—sex included. In an Alther fiction, sexuality begins straight (a Southern duty) only to turn wildly experimental in gay and lesbian follies, before settling into patterns of lesbian courtship, mechanical misfittings, spiritual misfirings, and other comic couplings that leave Alther's women ecstatic for a time, but increasingly bemused by the strange incompatibility of human desires. Alther's lesbians are born asking impertinent questions about the world and, all their lives, rejecting facile answers outright. Comedy occurs in the collisions with authority and the brutal tyrannies by "experts" of all sorts. Alther's people must strike out on their own, working their way through gender stereotypes and discarding conventional wisdom. One of Alther's distinctions is that her women must think their way forward, and so Alther's "comitragedies" (to borrow Beckett's term) resonate with rollicking debates about the nature of the individual in a swiftly changing culture.

Alther favors the *Bildungsroman,* or novel of education, tracking gay or androgynous characters from infancy forward, and charting both their inexhaustible sensuality and their increasing clarity of mind. Emily in *Original Sins* has "difficulty thinking in categories," and certainly cannot fit into any of them, until she realizes that most social categories are themselves manipulative, faintly absurd conventions. The most tenacious convention for Alther's people is the ideal of romantic love, which they keep rejecting and ridiculing—and reenacting. They all come to realize, like Jude in *Five Minutes in Heaven,* that "everyone is a house of mirrors," flashings of different heritages, social contexts, sensualities, which can combine now this way, now that, in a dynamic kaleidoscope of cultural icons and contradictory possibilities. Soulmates are a long shot.

Alther works with two primary forms, the multi-character epic or the duologue of two women in alternating states of consonance and dissonance. *Kinflicks* and *Five Minutes in Heaven* track one young woman through a lifetime's relations and acquaintances, flashing back repeatedly to past actions and origins of present reflections, and *Original Sins* fans out prismatically into alternating monologues of five different characters in successive stages of life. *Other Women* rotates two monologues, each riven with flashbacks, to weave the friendship that eventuates between a young lesbian mother and her psychotherapist, session by session. Alther once interlaced both forms in vigorous, tensile balance in *Bedrock,* where two women lovers try to comprehend an entire New England town. Whether the structure is prismatic or dual, the Alther novel uses monologues to alternate viewpoints and to weave the past (of American social history as well as main characters) into the present. Frequent flashbacks (Alther's people *are* their past-in-the-present) function both comically and tragically, revealing, for instance, the ludicrous hubris of youth and the grotesque mortality of a generation organizing Freedom Rides, discovering drugs and contraceptives, fighting in Vietnam, smashing color lines and gender ceilings, dying of cancer, and gay-bashing.

Alther's rebellious lesbians begin as gentle iconoclasts, wondering about the nature of stereotypes while enduring each one like a hair shirt. Ginny Babcock's uproarious escapades as a Southern tomboy, a Spinoza-spouting ivy-leaguer, a lesbian communer, a frantic New England housewife and mother, an angry adulteress, fuse into facets of the disillusioned young woman in the present. The hilarity of the heroines' predicaments derives both from the eccentricities of the people around them, a comic cast of Americana, and from their own (Southern) impulse to please them all. Minor characters in the margins furiously debate the novels' major issues—free will, medical ethics, human cruelty—like a satiric chorus to the heroine's epic endeavors on the main stage. Great ideas collide around them, and regional cultures clash within them, as they navigate the American landscape of 1950 through 1990, pot-holed with racism and bigotry, colonial war guilts, and liberation movements.

In taut prose of sure precision and figurative power, shot with deft comic timing and crackling dialogue, Alther fluidly shifts between several registers, from lyric to broad farce. She is primarily known as a social satirist, and she uses satire both to critique the sorry state of America's ideals and to celebrate the comical optimism that always surfaces again, if only in disenchanted burlesque.

Although the thematic territory differs in each novel, the Alther heroine stumbles like Candide through fake truths and phony promises. What begins in hapless earnest ends in the heroine comically discarding the savior *du jour* (evangelical religion, paternalistic capitalism, revolutionary politics), always including sexual correctness (sex is sport, sex is sacred) and manipulative lovers. In the end she throws up her hands and begins using honest candor as a way of living. Alther's implication seems to be that, where knowledge and the knowers are corrupt, aggressive naivete is the best self-defense—and may be an epistemological tool for the bare beginnings of understanding oneself and the world.

In early Alther, however, that is a lonely bargain, clarity at the cost of social connection. As the later novels center upon two women, in more nuanced "spelunking in the caverns of the psyche," as she puts it in *Other Women,* Alther's practice of constructing characters from their successive roles or incarnations is interiorized into the women's own reflections on their experience. Like Caroline in *Other Women,* they learn to see their own "reruns" and to discern, like Clea in *Bedrock,* their "connectedness" in a world without peace or perhaps even sanity.

Horrific scenes of cultural violence (white on black, black on black, liberal Yankee on conservative Southern, male on female) are riddled with Alther's irascible humor. In *Original Sins,* women are just orifices for black and white male sympathy (especially "the Great Ear"). Cinematic techniques of scene-splitting mock heroic pretensions (idealists quarrel against the background dialogue of *American Bandstand,* feminists couple to the strains of "Stand by your man/ Give him two arms to cling to"), and background TVs superimpose images of carnage, displaying Freedom Riders being hosed down in the barbaric South while Black Power leaders abuse "their" women in Manhattan. The novels are slashed or spliced with such comic and sarcastic fragments of their englobing cultural contexts in Alther's electronic fantasia of irreverence.

Such quicksilver slippage between viewpoints is more than just a comic technique, for it manifests the instability of perception and identity in the carnivalesque confusions of personal aspirations and cultural realities. Increasingly in the later novels, cultural lunacy extends its compass, and Alther focuses on the concomitant problem of whether love without erotics, even for two women who love each other intensely, can suffice in such a world. The answer, in the self-mocking flourish of fairy tale in *Bedrock* and in the uproarious mock-heroics in *Five Minutes in Heaven,* is probably laughter, an Erasmian hoot at the folly of such questions, in such a world.

Many readers have noted that they can trace the changes in contemporary American culture by charting the shifts in Alther's social landscape of America. But however turbulent the setting, Alther always measures politics—social and sexual—against a high standard of humane value; laughing travesty can swiftly soar into dark anger. In Manhattan Emily watches Civil Rights leaders exploit the women's movement: "And next week the sisters would be stacked in someone's attic like cast-off hulahoops. Political consumerism. Fuck it." In *Other Women,* Hannah is Alther's first authority figure worthy of affection, indeed honor, as a scarred and humane healer, and a woman. In *Five Minutes in Heaven,* following one of the finest sagas of Southern childhood since *Huckleberry Finn* (now with tomboys), and after the serial deaths of three beloveds, Jude flees to Paris—straight into Alther's first cross-cultural comedy of the not-so-innocent lesbian abroad, who trips over French social and sexual values with panache. Like several late Alther heroines, though more intensely, Jude ponders the nature of evil. Alther leaves her still thinking through it, and still learning to laugh.

—Jan Hokenson

ANDERSON, Margaret C(arolyn)

Nationality: American editor and autobiographer. **Born:** Indianapolis, Indiana, 24 November 1886. **Education:** Public schools in Indiana; Western College, Miami, Ohio, 1905-06. **Family:** Lived with Jane Heap, 1916-22; with Georgette Leblanc, 1923-41; and with Dorothy Caruso, 1942-55. **Career:** Book reviewer, *Interior* and *Chicago Evening Post,* Chicago, c. 1908-13; staff member, *Dial,* Chicago, c. 1910; literary editor, *Continent* (formerly *Interior*), Chicago, 1912-13; editor, *Little Review,* Chicago, San Francisco, New York City, and Paris, 1914-23; writer, in France and New York City, 1929-68. **Died:** Le Cannet, France, 1973.

WRITINGS

Autobiographies

My Thirty Years' War. New York, Covici Friede, and London, Knopf, 1930; with new preface by the author, New York, Horizon, 1969.
The Fiery Fountains. New York, Hermitage House, 1951; London, Rider, 1953; with foreword by Gorham Munson and "A Partial Portrait" by Janet Flanner, New York, Horizon, 1969.
The Strange Necessity. New York, Horizon, 1969.

Other

Editor, *The Little Review Anthology* (journal selections). New York, Horizon, and Heritage House, 1953.
The Unknowable Gurdjieff (philosophy). London, Routledge and Paul, 1962.

*

Manuscript Collections: Golda Meir Library, University of Wisconsin, Milwaukee.

Critical Sources: *A Trial Track for Racers: Margaret Anderson and the Little Review* by Jackson Robert Bryer (dissertation), University of Wisconsin, 1965; "The Personal Magazine: Margaret C. Anderson and the *Little Review,* 1914-1929" by Abby Ann Arthur Johnson, in *South Atlantic Quarterly* (Durham, North Carolina), Vol. 75, No. 3, 1976, 351-63; "The *Little Review:* Early Years and Avant Garde Ideas" by Susan Noyes Platt, in *The Old Guard and the Avant Garde: Modernism in Chicago, 1910-1940,* edited by Sue Ann Prince, Chicago, University of Chicago, 1990, 139-54; *"I Know Why I Say What I Do Say": Women Editors and Critics in the Little Magazines* by Jayne E. Marek (dissertation), University of Wisconsin-Madison, 1991; *The Passionate Years: Memoirs of Expatriate Women on the Left Bank, 1920-1940* by Pamelyn Nance Dane (dissertation), University of Oregon, 1992.

*　　*　　*

Early in *The Fiery Fountains* Margaret Anderson announces, "I always thought of myself as the happiest person in the world." As the three volumes of her autobiography make clear, Anderson can express that sentiment because, not in spite of, her lesbianism. In an era when lesbians were commonly regarded as tormented "inverts," Anderson presented her rejection of heterosexist norms as an act of liberatory self-determination.

Volume one of the autobiography *My Thirty Years' War* recounts Anderson's years at the helm of the *Little Review,* the lively journal which she founded in 1914 and which she and co-editor Jane Heap fashioned into a leading forum for avant-garde art and literature. Having at an early age dismissed the "higher joys of country clubs and bridge" favored by her bourgeois parents, she embraced instead Chicago's vibrant artistic community. Of her encounter with Heap in 1916, she notes, "This was what I had been waiting for, searching for, all my life." The following six years were spent publishing the journal in the face of a chronic shortage of funds, an enterprise which led them to San Francisco, New York, and eventually Paris.

Although Anderson does not explicitly identify her relationship with Heap as a lesbian one, neither did she disguise it as anything but. She underscored the mental stimulation she derived from Heap's conversation, but described that stimulation in sexually charged language. As the autobiography progresses, the relationship becomes increasingly strained, and the once exhilarating verbal jousts become the battles to which the title metaphorically alludes. When Anderson eventually renounced her claims to the *Little Review,* the passage's fractured typography hints at the agitation provoking and provoked by that decision (Heap would continue to publish the *Little Review* until 1929, when she and Anderson co-edited the final issue). *My Thirty Years' War* provides a disjointed and incomplete account of this time, a period complicated by Anderson's meeting and falling in love with the singer Georgette Leblanc.

The Fiery Fountains, the second volume of Anderson's autobiography, is a lyrical celebration of her love for Leblanc. Though Leblanc is 20 years Anderson's senior, the women shared a rare harmony. In marked contrast to Heap's theatricality, Leblanc was horrified by displays of temper and firm in her belief that there is no conflict "which couldn't be resolved by a glance between understanding eyes." *The Fiery Fountains* is far less oblique than its prequel regarding the nature of the relationship; Anderson writes that she knew immediately upon meeting Leblanc that "we were to join hands and advance through life together."

For two decades, the couple resided in France, Leblanc's native country. Leblanc performed concerts in the United States and Italy, and the women supplemented their meager income by writing, Anderson her autobiography and Leblanc a memoir of her marriage to Maeterlinck, the Belgian poet. Central to this period too were their studies with the cosmic philosopher George Gurdjieff, described more extensively in Anderson's book *The Unknowable Gurdjieff.* In 1939, their idyll was shattered when Leblanc was diagnosed with cancer. Their desperate battle against the disease was waged against the backdrop of Hitler's invasion of France—the women traversed the country in an attempt to procure medical attention for Leblanc and documents required to flee to the United States. The description of Leblanc's final months is delivered in tones of heart-rending poignancy. *The Fiery Fountains* concludes with her death, in France, in 1941.

The Strange Necessity, the most introspective of the three volumes, is a meditation upon a life dedicated to the pursuit of "Art as a state." Only late in the book does Anderson provide concrete details of the events which followed Leblanc's death—how while returning to New York she befriended Dorothy Caruso, a "femme du monde with visionary eyes" and widow of the famed Italian tenor. The women lived together in New York until Dorothy's death in 1955, but Anderson offers little information about her "last great friendship." Highlighting the similarities between Leblanc and Caruso—how, for example, both display the same fortitude in their fight against cancer—Anderson presents her relationship with the latter as somehow an extension of that she had shared with the former.

Following Caruso's death, Anderson returned to the south of France, to the villa where Leblanc had died. *The Strange Necessity,* published shortly before her death in 1973, offers an apt evaluation of Anderson's life: "so different, so special, and so blessed as to be unique."

—Nina van Gessel

ANDERSON, Sherwood

Nationality: American novelist, journalist, playwright, poet, and author of short stories. **Born:** Camden, Ohio, 13 September 1876. **Education:** Various Chicago public schools, 1884-1897; Wittenburg Academy, Chicago, 1899. **Military Service:** Served in the United States Army, Spanish American War, 1898. **Family:** Married 1) Cornelia Platt Lane in 1904 (divorced 27 July 1916); two sons and one daughter; 2) Tennessee Mitchell, 31 July 1916 (divorced 1924); 3) Elizabeth Prall in 1924 (divorced 1932); 4) Eleanor Copenhaver in 1933. **Career:** Held a variety of jobs in advertising, manufacturing, and publishing including advertiser for Crowell Publishing Co., Chicago; advertiser, Frank B. White Co., Chicago; president, United Factories Co., Cleveland, Ohio, 1906; president, Anderson Manufacturing Co., 1907-1912; advertiser, Taylor-Critchfield Co., Chicago; publisher and editor, *Marion Democrat* and *Smyth County News,* Marion, Virginia, 1927-29. Regular contributor, *Agricultural Advertising* (Frank B. White Agency, Chicago), 1903-04; frequent contributor to periodicals, including *Harpers, The Little Review, The Smart Set, Dial.* **Awards:** Dial award, 1921; National Institute of Arts and Letters, 1931. **Died:** Of peritonitis at Colon, Panama Canal Zone, 8 March 1941.

WRITINGS

Novels

Windy McPherson's Son. New York and London, John Lane, The Bodley Head, 1916; revised, New York, B. W. Huebsch, 1922.

Marching Men. New York and London, John Lane, The Bodley Head, 1917; as *Marching Men: A Critical Text,* edited by Ray Lewis White. Cleveland, Ohio, The Press of Case Western Reserve University, 1972.
Poor White. New York, B. W. Huebsch, 1920.
Many Marriages. New York, B. W. Huebsch, 1923.
Dark Laughter. New York, Boni & Liveright, 1925.
Beyond Desire. New York, Liveright, 1932.
Kit Branden: A Portrait. New York, Charles Scribner's Sons, 1936.

Short Story Collections

Winesburg, Ohio. New York, B. W. Huebsch, 1919; New York, Modern Library, [1919]; New York, New American Library, 1956; edited with an introduction by Malcolm Cowley, New York, Viking Press, 1958.
The Triumph of the Egg: A Book of Impressions from American Life in Tales and Poems. New York, B. W. Huebsch, 1921.
Horses and Men: Tales, Long and Short, from Our American Life. New York: B. W. Huebsch, 1923.
Alice and the Lost Novel. London, Elkin Mathews and Marrot, 1929.
Death in the Woods and Other Stories. New York, Liveright, 1933.
Sherwood Anderson: Short Stories, edited by Maxwell Geismar. New York, Hill & Wang, 1962.

Nonfiction

The Modern Writer. San Francisco, Lantern Press, 1925.
Hello Towns! New York, Liveright, 1929.
Perhaps Women. New York, Liveright, 1931.
No Swank. Philadelphia, Centaur Press, 1934.
Puzzled America. New York, Charles Scribner's Sons, 1935.
Home Town. New York, Alliance Book Corporation, 1940.
Return to Winesburg: Selections from Four Years of Writing for a Country Newspaper, edited by Ray Lewis White. Chapel Hill, University of North Carolina Press, 1967.
The Buck Fever Papers, edited by Wilford Dunaway Taylor. Charlottesville, University Press of Virginia, 1971.
The "Writer's Book" by Sherwood Anderson: A Critical Edition, edited by Martha Mulray Curry. Metuchen, New Jersey, Scarecrow Press, 1975.
Sherwood Anderson: Early Writings, edited by Ray Lewis White. Kent, Ohio, Kent State University Press, 1989.

Letters

Letters of Sherwood Anderson, edited by Howard Mumford Jones and Walter B. Rideout. Boston, Little, Brown, 1953.
Sherwood Anderson/Gertrude Stein: Correspondence and Personal Essays, edited by Ray Lewis White. Chapel Hill, University of North Carolina Press, 1972.
Sherwood Anderson: Selected Letters, edited by Charles E. Modlin. Knoxville, University of Tennessee Press, 1984.
Letters to Bab: Sherwood Anderson to Marietta D. Finley, 1919-1933, edited by William A. Sutton. Urbana, University of Illinois Press, 1985.
Sherwood Anderson's Love Letters to Eleanor Copenhaver Anderson, edited by Charles E. Modlin. Athens, University of Georgia Press, 1990.
Sherwood Anderson's Love Letters: For Eleanor, a Letter a Day, edited by Ray Lewis White. Baton Rouge, Louisiana State University Press, 1991.

Stage Plays

Plays, Winesburg and Others. New York, Charles Scribner's Sons, 1937.

Poetry

Mid-American Chants. New York and London, John Lane, The Bodley Head, 1918.
A New Testament. New York, Boni & Liveright, 1927.

Collected Works

The Sherwood Anderson Reader, edited by Paul Rosenfeld. New York, Houghton Mifflin Co., 1947.
The Portable Sherwood Anderson, edited by Howard Mumford Jones and Walter B. Rideout. New York, Viking Press, 1949.
The Complete Works of Sherwood Anderson, 21 Volumes, edited by Kichinosuke Ohasi. Kyoto, Japan, 1982.

Autobiography

A Story Teller's Story. New York, B. W. Huebsch, 1924; New York, Grove Press, 1958; as *A Story Teller's Story: A Critical Text,* edited by Ray Lewis White. Cleveland, Ohio, Press of Case Western Reserve University, 1968.
Sherwood Anderson's Notebook. New York, Boni & Liveright, 1926.
Tar: A Midwest Childhood. New York, Boni & Liveright, 1926.
Nearer the Grass Roots. San Francisco, The Westgate Press, 1929.
The American County Fair. New York, Random House, 1930.
A Writer's Conception of Realism. Olivet, Michigan, Olivet College, 1939.
Sherwood Anderson's Memoirs, edited by Paul Rosenfeld. New York, Harcourt, Brace, 1942; as *Sherwood Anderson's Memoirs: A Critical Edition,* edited by Ray Lewis White, Chapel Hill, University of North Carolina Press, 1969.
France and Sherwood Anderson: Paris Notebook, 1921, edited by Michael Fanning. Baton Rouge, Louisiana State University Press, 1976.
The Sherwood Anderson Diaries, 1936-1941, edited by Hilbert H. Campbell. Athens, University of Georgia Press, 1987.

*

Manuscript Collections: The Newberry Library, Chicago

Biography: *Sherwood Anderson* by Cleveland B. Chase, New York, Robert M. McBride & Co., 1927; *The Phenomenon of Sherwood Anderson: A Study in American Life and Letters* by N. Bryllion Fagin, Baltimore, Maryland, The Rossi-Bryn Co., 1927; "My Brother, Sherwood Anderson" by Karl James Anderson, in *Saturday Review of Literature,* Vol. 31, September 1948, 6-7; *Sherwood Anderson* by Irving Howe, New York, William Sloane Associates, 1951; *Sherwood Anderson* by James Schevill, Denver, University of Denver Press, 1951; *Sherwood Anderson* by Rex Burbank, New York, Twayne, 1964; *Sherwood Anderson* by Brom Weber, Minneapolis, University of Minnesota Press, 1964; *Sherwood Anderson: An Introduction and Interpretation* by David D. Anderson, New York, Holt, Rinehart & Winston, 1967; *Exit to Elsinore* by William A. Sutton, Muncie, Indiana, Ball State University Press, 1967; *The Road to Winesburg: A Mosaic of the Imaginative Life of Sherwood Anderson* by William A. Sutton, Metuchen, New Jersey, The Scarecrow Press, 1972; *Sherwood Anderson* by Wilford Dunaway Taylor, New York, Frederick Ungar, 1977; *Sherwood Anderson* by Kim Townsend, Boston, Houghton Mifflin, 1987; *A Storyteller and a City: Sherwood Anderson's Chicago,* Dekalb, Northern Illinois University Press, 1988.

Bibliography: "A Checklist of the Writings of Sherwood Anderson" by Mary E. Jessup, in *American Collector,* Vol. 5, 1928, 157-58; "A Bibliography of Sherwood Anderson's Contributions to Periodicals, 1914-1946" by Raymond D. Gozzi, in *Newberry Library Bulletin,* Second Series, No. 2, December 1948; *Sherwood Anderson: A Bibliography* by Eugene P. Sheehey and Kenneth A. Lohf, Los Gatos, California, The Talisman Press, 1960; "Additional Reviews of Sherwood Anderson's Work," by G. Thomas Tanselle, in *Papers of the Bibliographic Society of America* (Austin, Texas), Vol. 56, 1962, 358-65; *Checklist of Sherwood Anderson* by Ray Lewis White, Columbus, Ohio, Charles E. Merrill, 1969; *Sherwood Anderson: A Selective, Annotated Bibliography* by Douglas G. Rogers, Metuchen, New Jersey, The Scarecrow Press, 1976; *Sherwood Anderson: A Reference Guide* by Ray Lewis White, Boston, G. K. Hall, 1977; "Addenda to Sheehy and Lohf's Bibliography of Sherwood Anderson" by Richard C. Johnson, in *Papers of the Bibliographic Society of America* (Austin, Texas), Vol. 66, 61.

Critical Sources: "Sherwood Anderson" by Hart Crane, in *Double-Dealer,* Vol. 2, 1921, 42-45; "Hawthorne, Anderson, and Frost" by Robert Penn Warren, in *The New Republic,* Vol. 54, 1928, 399-401; "Homage to Sherwood Anderson," special issue of *Story,* Vol. 19, September-October, 1941; "Sherwood Anderson: An Appreciation" by William Faulkner, in *The Atlantic Monthly,* Vol. 191, 1953, 27-29; "A Reading of Sherwood Anderson's 'The Man Who Became a Woman'" by Howard S. Babb, in *PMLA* (New York), Vol. 80, 1965, 432-435; "Sherwood Anderson, Winesburg, Ohio" by Irving Howe, in *The American Novel from James Fenimore Cooper to William Faulkner,* edited by Wallace Stegner, New York, Basic Books, 1965, 154-165; "Freudianism and the Literary Mind" by Frederick J. Hoffman, in *The Achievement of Sherwood Anderson: Essays in Criticism,* edited with and introduction by Ray Lewis White, Chapel Hill, University of North Carolina Press, 1966, 173-192; "Sherwood Anderson" by Walter B. Rideout, in *Fifteen Modern American Authors: A Survey of Research and Criticism,* edited by Jackson R. Bryer, Durham, North Carolina, Duke University Press, 1969, 3-22; "Sherwood Anderson: American Mythopoeist" by Benjamin T. Spenser, in *American Literature* (Durham, North Carolina), Vol. 41, 1969, 1-18; "Earth-Mothers, Succubi, and Other Ectoplasmic Spirits: The Women in Sherwood Anderson's Short Stories" by William V. Miller, in *MidAmerica* (East Lansing, Michigan), 1974, 64-81, reprinted in *Critical Essays on Sherwood Anderson,* edited by David D. Anderson, Boston, G. K. Hall, 1981, 196-209; *Sherwood Anderson: A Collection of Critical Essays,* edited by Walter B. Rideout, Englewoods Cliffs, New Jersey, Prentice-Hall, 1974; "Horses or Men: Primitive and Pastoral Elements in Sherwood Anderson" by Glen A. Love, in *Sherwood Anderson: Centennial Studies,* edited by Hilbert H. Campbell, Troy, New York, Whitson, 1976, 235-248; "The Warmth of Desire: Sex in Anderson's Novels" by Ray Lewis White, in *Sherwood Ander-*

son: Dimensions of His Literary Art: A Collection of Critical Essays, edited by David D. Anderson, East Lansing, Michigan State University Press, 1976, 24-40; "Sexuality in Windy McPherson's Son" by J. R. Scafidel, in *Twentieth Century Literature* (Hempstead, New York), Vol. 23, 1977, 94-101; "'From East-Side to South-Side with Love': The Friendship of Sherwood Anderson and Paul Rosenfeld" by David D. Anderson, in *Midwestern Miscellany* (East Lansing, Michigan), Vol. 7, 1979, 41-55; "Gender Reconsiderations in Three of Sherwood Anderson's Novels" by Joyce R. Ladenson, *Massachusetts Studies in English* (Amherst), Vol. 6, Nos. 1-2, 90-102; "Sexual Metaphor and Social Criticism in Anderson's 'The Man Who Became a Woman'" by Lonna M. Malmsheimer, in *Studies in American Fiction* (Boston), Vol. 7, 1979, 17-26; "Sexuality and Human Development in Winesburg, Ohio" by Jurgen Michael Shawver, in *Dissertation Abstracts International* (Ann Arbor, Michigan), Vol. 39, 1979, 6767A; "The Feminine in Winesburg, Ohio" by Sally Adair Rigsbee, in *Studies in American Fiction* (Boston), Vol. 9, No. 2, 1981, 233-244; "Women in Sherwood Anderson's Fiction" by Nancy Bunge, in *Critical Essays on Sherwood Anderson,* edited by David D. Anderson, Boston, G. K. Hall, 1981, 242-249; "Sherwood Anderson and the Women of Winesburg" by Marilyn Judith Atlas, in *Critical Essays on Sherwood Anderson,* edited by David D. Anderson, Boston, G. K. Hall, 1981, 250-266; "'Implications of Obscenity': The English Trial of *Many Marriages*" by Ray Lewis White, in *Journal of Modern Literature* (Philadelphia), Vol. 10, No. 1, 1983, 153-158; "The Implied Community of Winesburg, Ohio" by Stephen C. Enniss, in *The Old Northwest* (Oxford, Ohio), Vol. 11, Nos. 1-2, 51-60; "Sherwood Anderson and the Postmodern Novel" by David Stouck, in *Contemporary Literature* (Madison, Wisconsin), Vol. 26, 1985, 302-316; "Sherwood Anderson's Use of Setting and Sexual Symbolism in 'The Mother'" by Margaret Nims, in *Journal of Evolutionary Psychology* (Pittsburgh, Pennsylvania), Vol. 8, August 1987, 219-222; "Anderson and the Androgyne: 'Something More than Man or Woman'" by Martin Bidney, in *Studies in Short Fiction* (Newberry, South Carolina), Vol. 25, Summer 1988, 261-273; "Anderson's 'Hands'" by Gwendolyn Morgan, in *Explicator* (Washington, D. C.), Vol. 48, No. 1, Fall 1989, 46-47; "Winesburg, Ohio and the End of Collective Experience" by Thomas Yingling, in *New Essays on Winesburg, Ohio,* edited by John W. Crowley, Cambridge, Cambridge University Press, 1990, 99-128; "Anderson's Wing Biddlebaum and Freeman's Louisa Ellis" by Lynda Brown, in *Studies in Short Fiction* (Newberry, South Carolina), Vol. 27, Summer 1990, 413-414; "Thinking about Walt and Melville in a Sherwood Anderson Tale: An Independent Woman's Transcendental Quest" by Martin Bidney, in *Studies in Short Fiction* (Newberry, South Carolina), Vol. 29, Fall 1992, 517-530; "Sherwood Anderson and Waldo Frank" by Charles E. Modlin, in *The Old Northwest* (Oxford, Ohio), Vol. 15, Winter 1991-92, 273-280; *Sherwood Anderson: A Study of the Short Fiction* by Robert Allen Papinchak, New York, Twayne, 1992; "Sherwood Anderson's Fear of Sexuality: Horses, Men, and Homosexuality" by James Ellis, in *Studies in Short Fiction* (Newberry, South Carolina), Vol. 30, Fall 1993, 595-601; "The Heritage of the Fathers in Sherwood Anderson's 'The Man Who Became a Woman'" by Christopher MacGowan, in *Journal of the Short Story in English* (Nashville, Tennessee), Vol. 21, Autumn 1993, 29-37; *A Reader's Guide to the Short Stories of Sherwood Anderson* by Judy Jo Small, New York, G. K. Hall, 1994.

*　　*　　*

Of the hundreds of scholarly essays and book-length studies of Sherwood Anderson's work, only a relative few focus on Anderson's interest in the rich complexity of human sexuality. Of those that do, most take a rather clinical approach, especially when dealing with his exploration of homosexuality. Although the ambiguity of his own statements about his sexuality might easily lead some to believe otherwise, Sherwood Anderson was not gay. Indeed, a large part of Anderson's work deals with the vagaries of heterosexual experience. In "The Rabbit-Pen," for example, readers encounter what might be called the archetypal Andersonian man: a heterosexual with an overly idealistic vision of women, who are usually seen as so many embodiments of one's mother, and hence beyond sexual desire. But Anderson certainly deserves acknowledgment for playing an important role in the history of twentieth-century gay and lesbian literature as he was one of the first modernist writers who was not a homosexual to explore the complexities of homosexual identity and the homoerotic, as well as the first to present homosexual characters with sympathy and compassion.

For Anderson, sex is not a question of those acts that are inherently sinful and those which are inherently "natural," or, in other words, with what is deviant and unacceptable desire and what is not. Sex and sexuality are ultimately a mystery to be resolved not within the discrete moments of the individual's physical and psychological experience, but over the course of a lifetime's experience. Sometimes, as in "Hands," that experience ultimately leads to tragedy, usually because of society's violent rejection of sexual difference; or, as in "The Man Who Became a Woman," it may lead to psychological conflict because of one's inability to understand one's own sexual identity and desires.

The short story "Hands," the first one in *Winesburg, Ohio,* presents the tragic results that arise from society's attempts to repress what it deems to be "deviant" sexuality. Wing Biddlebaum's tale thus serves as the standard—against which the novel's large cast of other "grotesques"—as the central consciousness of the novel, the Writer, calls them in his prologue—are measured. A twenty-year resident of Winesburg, Biddlebaum originally lived in Pennsylvania as the school teacher, Adolf Myers. Deeply fond of his pupils, his affection was often expressed through platonic caresses that are ultimately interpreted by the townspeople as actions pointing to "unspeakable things." The result is that "hidden, shadowy doubts that had been in men's minds...were galvanized into beliefs," and a vigilante group, intent on hanging him, finally forces Myers out of town. Though the story clearly implies that Biddlebaum's attraction to young men was at least partly erotic, the narrator cannot justify the cruelty of the Pennsylvania townspeople, whose actions have crippled Biddlebaum's soul and left him with a fear of his hands so paralyzing that he can no longer control their movements.

The story "The Man Who Became a Woman," from Anderson's third collection of stories, *Horses and Men,* explores the psychological complexities of sexual identity as it begins to emerge in adolescence. Here Herman Dudley retrospectively describes a puzzling experience in his youth, one that, he says, "I am forced, by some feeling inside myself, to tell." His story is about his love for race horses, associated in many of Anderson's short stories with masculine sexuality, and a horse groomer and aspiring writer named Tom Means. His love for Tom was strongly tinged by homoeroticism, and Herman wants his listeners to understand that his problem in dealing with this love arises in part because "Americans are shy and timid about saying things like that and a man

here don't dare own up he loves another man, I've found out, and they are afraid to admit such feelings to themselves even." Thus as a young man he unconsciously realized the problematic nature of his desire for Tom and that desire was then displaced onto the horses. Speaking of one horse in particular, named Pick-it-boy, the narrator says "I wished he was a girl sometimes or that I was a girl and he was a man." That "wish" was eventually fulfilled in the central episode of the story, when Herman visited a seedy bar in the town near the race track. While looking into a mirror behind the bar, he saw, instead of his own face, the reflection of a girl, "and a lonesome and scared girl too." Back at the horse track, he was then mistaken by the black stable hands as a being a young girl from the town who had been brought up by another worker. As they made their advances, Herman found himself unable to "say anything, not even a word." He once more became a woman, one who is "shy and afraid." He was eventually able to escape, but the events of that night have followed him throughout the rest of his life, even into what he calls a happy marriage. What troubles him in the subsequent years is not necessarily a fear of his inner femininity—and the possibility that it points to homosexuality; though he does remind readers that "I'm not any fairy," it seems clear that Herman does not experience a need to suppress his femininity in order to reach his masculinity. Instead, what seems to trouble him more is the question of why he could not bring himself "to save my life, scream or make any sound." "Could it be," he asks, "because at the time I was a woman, while at the same time I wasn't a woman? It may be that I was too ashamed of having turned into a girl and being afraid of a man to make any sound." It is having to be afraid of a man—especially when you are a man who has become a woman—that appears to be the central issue here. Because American culture provides no positively-valued outlet for the expression of love between men, Anderson seems to be arguing, the only psychological alternative for such expression is for one to become a woman, which is in itself a position defined by culture as negative.

Anderson himself made several personal statements regarding homosexuality, all of which may be readily found in the critical edition of his *Memoirs.* For instance, in recounting his close friendship with John Emerson (the pseudonym assigned by Anderson to Clifton Paden, with whose family Anderson and his brother Karl lived when they first arrived in Chicago in 1896), Anderson notes the stares from passersby he and John received when walking down the street "with John's arm about my shoulder." "I know now that they thought we were two fairies," writes Anderson, "but, at that time, I had never heard of homosexuality. I was a little embarrassed when we walked thus, feeling perhaps something in the eyes of the people we passed, something in their thoughts of us walking so, that made me uncomfortable. There was nothing of homosexuality in the feeling we had for each other. Of that I am sure." It is the act of labeling created by other's eyes that interests Anderson here, more so than an attempt to establish his sexual "normality."

Writing of a friend from the late 1910s, pseudonymously presented in the *Memoirs* as Luther Pawsey, Anderson begins to examine the ambiguity of his own same-sex attractions more fully. Concerned that Luther is sexually attracted to him, Anderson writes that "The idea that love could grow as between man and man, a thing outside sex, a feeling perhaps founded upon brotherhood, realization of self in another man, your own curious loneliness in life in him too, understanding of self a little got at perhaps through understanding of another, all of this was, at the time of which I am now speaking, new to me." Later he recalls an early encounter with a man that for Anderson was "the first time [he had] seen homosexuality that was unashamed." He is accosted by one of the local "sissies," the aftermath of which, Anderson reports, gave him the feeling that "a kind of door opened, as though I looked down through the door into a kind of dark pit, a place of monstrous shapes, a world of strange unhealth." But, much like Herman Dudley, instead of simply giving in to a homophobic urge for violent repression, Anderson begins to explore his reaction, which leads him to a position of empathy, for, as he writes, "Why, I was myself, unconsciously, one of them. The thing was in me too and the fear I had expressed was a sure sign of its presence." That arrival at a position of empathy, supported perhaps by a belief in the inherent bisexuality of adolescence as theorized by the psychologist Sigmund Freud, ultimately culminates, as Anderson reports, in both "Hands" and "The Man Who became a Woman."

For Anderson, one's sexuality and sexual identity often places the self in conflict with society, which in turn frustrates the already difficult struggle to find one's place within the community. This is especially so when one's sexual desires fall outside the communal "norms." In the end, there are no guide posts to lead the individual through the labyrinth of sexual identity, especially when that identity appears to be in conflict with more than simply desiring heterosexual intercourse in a repressive society. It is Anderson's awareness of the intensity of the conflict for emerging gay identities, and his sensitive treatment of these individuals, that commands the gay reader's attention.

—David Peterson

ARAGON, Louis

Pseudonym: Also wrote as Arnaud de Saint Roman, Albert de Routisie, and François la Colère. **Nationality:** French poet, novelist, and journalist. **Born:** Louis Andrieux in Paris, 3 October 1897. **Education:** Lycée Carnot in Paris, 1914-16; received Baccalauréat examinations in Latin, sciences, and philosophy, 1916; medical studies at preparatory school, 1916. **Military Service:** Served in the French infantry, 1917-19; auxiliary doctor; received *Croix de Guerre*, 1918; mobilized, 1939-40; received *Croix de Guerre* and *Medaille Militaire*, 1940. **Family:** Companion of Elsa Triolet, 1928-70 (married in 1939). **Career:** Founder and co-editor, with André Breton and Philippe Soupault, *Littérature*, 1919; newspaperman, *L'Humanité*, 1933-34; secretary, International Association of Writers for the Defense of Culture, 1935; co-director and editor, *Ce Soir*, 1937-53; co-founder, National Committee of Writers, 1941; editor, *Les Lettres Françaises*, 1949-72. **Awards:** Awarded Prix Renaudot for *Les Beaux Quartiers*, 1936; Lenin Peace Prize, 1957; H.D.: University of Prague, 1963; University of Moscow, 1965. **Died:** Paris, France, 24 December 1982.

WRITINGS

Novels

Anicet ou Le Panorama. Paris, Gallimard, 1921.

Les Aventures de Télémaque. Paris, Gallimard, 1922.
Le Libertinage. Paris, Gallimard, 1924; translated by John Calder as *The Libertine,* London, 1987.
Le Paysan de Paris. Paris, Gallimard, 1926; translated by Frederick Brown as *Nightwalker,* Englewood Cliffs, New Jersey, Prentice-Hall, 1970; translated by Simon Watson Taylor as *Paris Peasant,* London, Cape, 1971.
Le Con d'Irène (as Albert de Routisie). 1928; published under real name, J.J. Pauvert, 1968.
Les Cloches de Bâle. Paris, Denoël & Steele, 1934; translated by Haakon M. Chevalier as *The Bells of Basel,* New York, Harcourt, Brace, 1936; London, Peter Davies/Lovat Dickson, 1937.
Les Beaux Quartiers. Paris, Denoël & Steele, 1936; translated by Haakon M. Chevalier as *Residential Quarter,* New York, Harcourt, Brace, 1938.
The Century Was Young. Translated by Hannah Josephson, New York, Duell, Sloan & Pearce, 1941; as *Les Voyageurs de l'impériale,* Paris, Gallimard, 1942; as *Passengers of Destiny,* London, Pilot Press, 1946.
Aurélien, 2 Vols. Fribourg, Librairie de l'Université Egloff, 1944; 1 Vol., Paris, Gallimard, 1944; translated by Eithne Wilkins, London, Pilot Press, 1946; New York, Duell, Sloan & Pearce, 1947.
Les Communistes, 6 Vols. Paris, Bibliothèque Française, 1949-1951; revised in *Oeuvres romanesques croisées d'Elsa Triolet et Aragon,* 1964-1974.
La Semaine Sainte. Paris, Gallimard, 1958; translated by Haakon M. Chevalier as *Holy Week,* New York, Putnam's, 1961; London, Hamilton, 1961.
La Mise à Mort. Paris, Gallimard, 1965.
Blanche ou l'oubli. Paris, Gallimard, 1967.
Henri Matisse, roman, 2 Vols. Paris, Gallimard, 1971; translated by Jean Stewart as *Henri Matisse: A Novel,* 2 Vols., London, Collins, 1972; New York, Harcourt Brace Jovanovich, 1972.
Théâtre/Roman. Paris, Gallimard, 1974.

Short Stories

Le Mentir-vrai. Paris, Gallimard, 1980.

Nonfiction

Les Plaisirs de la capitale. Berlin, 1923.
Traité du style. Paris, Gallimard, 1928.
La Peinture au défi. Editions Surréalistes, J. Corti, 1930.
Pour un réalisme socialiste. Paris, Denoël & Steele, 1935.
Les Bons Voisins (as Arnaud de Saint Roman). Paris, Editions de Minuit, 1942.
Matisse en France. Paris, Martin Fabiani, 1943.
Neuf Chansons interdites, 1942-44 (as François la Colère). Paris, Bibliothéque Française, 1944.
Saint Pol Roux ou L'Espoir. Paris, Seghers, 1945.
Servitude et grandeur des Français: Scènes des années terribles. Paris, Bibliothéque Française, 1945.
Apologie du luxe. Geneva, Skira, 1946.
L'Homme Communiste. Volume 1, Paris, Gallimard, 1946.
La Culture et les hommes. Paris, Editions Sociales, 1947.
Chroniques du Bel Canto. Geneva, Skira, 1947.
La Naissance de la Paix. Paris, Bibliothéque Française, 1949.
Les Communistes, 6 Vols. Paris, Bibliothéque Française, 1949-1951.
La Lumière et la paix. Paris, Lettres Françaises, 1950.
L'Exemple de Courbet. Paris, Editions Cercle d'Art, 1952.

Hugo, poète réaliste. Editions Sociales, 1952.
La Vraie Liberté de la culture, réduire notre train de mort pour accroître notre train de vie. Paris, Lettres Françaises, 1952.
Les Egmont d'aujourd'hui s'appellent André Stil. Paris, Lettres Françaises, 1952.
L'Homme Communiste. Volume 2, Paris, Gallimard, 1953.
Le Neveu de Monsieur Duval. Editeurs Français Réunis, 1953.
Journal d'une poésie nationale. Lyons, Les Ecrivains Réunis, 1954.
La Lumière de Stendhal. Paris, Denoël, 1954.
L'un ne va pas sans l'autre. Lyons, Les Ecrivains Réunis, 1954.
Littératures soviétiques. Paris, Denoël, 1955.
With Jean Cocteau, *Entretiens sur le musée de Dresde.* Paris, Editions Cercle d'Art, 1957.
J'abats mon jeu. Paris, Editeurs Français Réunis, 1959.
With André Maurois, *Histoire parallèle des Etats-Unis et de l'U.R.S.S.,* 4 Vols. Paris, Presses de la Cité, 1962; revised as *Les Deux Géants: Histoire des Etats Unis et de l'U.R.S.S., de 1917 à nos jours,* 5 Vols., Paris, Editions du Pont Royal, 1962-1964; volumes 1 and 2 translated by Patrick O'Brien as *A History of the USSR from Lenin to Khrushchev,* New York, McKay, 1961; London, Weidenfeld & Nicolson, 1964.
Entretiens avec Francis Crémieux. Paris, Gallimard, 1964.
Les Collages. Hermann, 1965.
Aragon parle avec Dominique Arban. Paris, Seghers, 1968.
Je n'ai jamais appris à écrire ou Les Incipit. Geneva, Skira, 1969.

Poetry

Feu de joie. Paris, Sans Pareil, 1920.
Le Mouvement perpétuel. Paris, Gallimard, 1926.
La Grande Gaîté. Paris, Gallimard, 1929.
Persécuté persécuteur. Paris, Editions Surréalistes, 1931.
Aux Enfants Rouges. Bureau d'Editions et de Diffusion, 1932.
Hourra l'Oural. Paris, Denoël & Steele, 1934.
Le Crève-coeur. Paris, Gallimard, 1941.
Les Yeux d'Elsa. Neuchâtel, Editions de la Baconnière, 1942.
Brocéliande. Neuchâtel, Editions de la Baconnière, 1942.
En français dans le texte. Neuchâtel, Ides et Calendes, 1943.
Le Musée Grévin. Under the name François la Colère, Paris, Bibliothèque Française, 1943.
En étrange pays dans mon pays lui-même. Monaco, A la Voile latine, 1945.
La Diane française. Paris, Seghers, 1945; Bibliotèque Française, 1946.
Le Nouveau Crève-Coeur. Paris, Gallimard, 1948.
Mes Caravanes. Paris, Seghers, 1954.
Les Yeux et la mémoire. Paris, Gallimard, 1954.
Le Roman inachevé. Paris, Gallimard, 1956.
Elsa. Paris, Gallimard, 1959.
Les Poètes. Paris, 1960.
Le Fou d'Elsa. Paris, Gallimard, 1963.
Le Voyage de Hollande. Paris, Seghers, 1964.
Il ne m'est Paris que d'Elsa. Robert Laffont, 1964.
Elégie à Pablo Neruda. Paris, Gallimard, 1966.
Les Chambres. Paris, Editeurs Français Réunis, 1969.
Les Adieux. Messidor/Temps Actuels, 1982.

Collected Works

Oeuvres romanesques croisées d'Elsa Triolet et Aragon, 42 Vols. Paris, Laffont, 1964-1974.
Oeuvre poétique, 15 Vols. Paris, Livre Club Diderot, 1974-1981.

Editor

Avez-vous lu Victor Hugo? Editeurs Français Réunis, 1952.
Introduction aux littératures soviétiques. Paris, Gallimard, 1956.
Elsa Triolet choisie par Aragon. Paris, Gallimard, 1960.

*

Manuscript Collections: Fonds Doucet, Bibliotèque Sainte-Geneviève, Paris; Centre National de la Recherche Scientifique, Paris.

Biography: *Aragon: Une vie à changer* by Pierre Daix, Paris, Seuil, 1975; *Les Clés d'Elsa* by Dominique Desanti, Ramsay, 1983.

Bibliography: *Louis Aragon: Essai de Bibliographie. Oeuvres d' Aragon* by Crispin Geoghegan, London, Grant & Cutler, 1979, 1980; *Louis Aragon: bibliographie Analytique* by Marie Lemaître, Paris, Centre National de Documentation Pédagogique, 1983.

Critical Sources: "Recherches Sur La Sexualité Part d'Objectivité, Déterminations Individuelles, Degré de Conscience," in *La Révolution Surréaliste II* (Paris), 1928, 32-40; *Louis Aragon* by Lucille F. Becker, New York, Twayne World Authors, No. 114, 1971; *The Left Bank: Writers, Artists, and Politics from the Popular Front to the Cold War* by Herbert R. Lottman, Boston, Houghton Mifflin Company, 1982; "Canonical Criminalizations: Homosexuality, Art History, Surrealism, and Abjection" by Richard Easton, in *differences: A Journal of Feminist Cultural Studies,* Vol. 4, No. 3, fall 1992, 133-175; *Elsa Triolet and Louis Aragon: An Introduction to Their Interwoven Lives and Works* by Max Adereth, Lewiston/Queenston/Lampeter, The Edwin Mellen Press, Studies in French Literature, Vol. 17, 1994; "Marked Men, Numbered Days: French 'Collabo' Writers" by Jim Tuck, in *New Criterion,* Vol. 14, 1996, 25-28.

*　　*　　*

In January of 1928, Louis Aragon, co-founder of the Surrealist movement, participated in a two-day conference on sexuality. Others in attendance included André Breton, Man Ray, Yves Tanguy, Jacques Prévert, and Philippe Soupault. Aragon found himself in the center of a heated debate. The proceedings of the conference, published in the journal *La Révolution Surréaliste* under the title "Recherches Sur La Sexualité," focused on such topics as onanism, masturbation, and sexual equality. André Breton, an avid homophobe, returned again and again to the issue of "pédérasatie." He accused pederasts of "proposing to human tolerance for a mental and moral deficit which tends to systematically erect itself and to paralyze all the undertakings that I respect." When asked his own opinion, Aragon responded, "To me, pederasty appears to be just the same as other sexual habits, a sexual habit. In my mind it does not merit moral condemnation, and I do not think this is the moment to make restrictions against certain pederasts unless I make them as well against men with women."

The Surrealist movement had its beginnings in 1917 when Louis Aragon met André Breton during their recruitment in the French medical corps at Val-de-Grâce. The two men became friends and founded the journal *Littérature* soon after the first World War. Borrowing a term coined by Apollinaire, they named their movement "Surrealism." Breton, himself a psychoanalyst, brought Freud's ideas to the forefront of the movement. The writers sought ways to depict the conscious and unconscious through techniques of automatic writing and the juxtaposition of conflicting images.

Aragon broke with the surrealists shortly after joining the communist party in 1927. In 1930, he published a poem entitled "Rouge Front" in the magazine *Literature of the World Revolution.* The subversive tone of the poem condemned the French government and led to an indictment against Aragon for inciting French soldiers to mutiny. The writer was convicted in January, 1932. Although the surrealists came to his assistance, Aragon denounced them.

Although Aragon's chief texts focused on politics for the next 35 years, throughout his life the writer remained fascinated with the idea of romantic love. In *Le Pasan de Paris,* a novel which provokes the dream-like ambience characteristic of Surrealism, Aragon depicts amorous couples of all sorts meeting in the Buttes-Chaumont park. A later novel, *Aurélien,* contains scenes suggesting lesbian passion. His works are particularly concerned with social inequality. He was considered France's leading Resistance poet during World War II. The Nazi occupation led Aragon to compose poems of a more lyrical nature, ranging in theme from politics to Aragon's love for Elsa Triolet.

Contemporaries and later critics return again and again to the question of Aragon's sexuality. Tuck points out that a work by Louis-Ferdinand Céline, *D'un chateau l'autre,* presents Aragon as a man who enjoyed "a little fun in the urinals." According to Max Adereth, evidence supporting such accusations stemmed from gossip and from "some provocative statements and attitudes on the part of Aragon himself, both in his youth and his old age (caused, no doubt, by the wish to shock people)."

After Elsa Triolet's death in 1970, rumors about Aragon's supposed return to a homosexual lifestyle quickly spread. According to Jim Tuck, Aragon "openly embraced a gay lifestyle." He was often seen in the company of young men, and his elaborate manner of dress provoked critical commentary.

Although questions surrounding Aragon's alleged bisexuality may never be resolved, we can be certain that the author left behind an oeuvre which has yet to be fully scrutinized. In addition to composing 16 novels and over 25 books of poetry, Aragon authored books on literature, painting, culture, and politics. His literary career spanned two world wars, and he associated with many of the leading figures of French culture, including Picasso, Gide, Sartre, and Eluard.

—Gene Hayworth

ARENAS, Reinaldo

Nationality: Cuban novelist, poet, lecturer, and journalist. **Born:** Holguin, Oriente, Cuba, 16 July 1943; emigrated to the United States in 1990. **Education:** Universidad de la Habana, 1966-68; attended Columbia University, New York. **Career:** Researcher, Jose Marti Library, Havana, Cuba, 1963-68; editor, Instituto Cubano del Libro (Cuban Book Institute), Havana, 1967-68; journalist and editor, *La Gaceta de Cuba,* Havana, 1968-74; visiting professor of Cuban literature, Florida International University, 1981, Center for Inter-American Relations, 1982, and Cornell University, 1985; guest lecturer at Princeton University, Georgetown University, Washington University (St. Louis), Stockholm Universitet, Cornell University, University of Kansas, University of Miami, and University of Puerto Rico. **Awards:** First mention, Cirilo Villaverde contest for best novel, Cuba Writer's Union, 1965; *Le Monde* Prix Medici, for best novelist published in France, 1969; Cintas Foundation fellowship, 1980; John Guggenheim Memorial Foundation fellowship, 1982; Wilson Center Foundation fellowship, 1988. **Died:** Of drug and alcohol overdose, 7 December 1990.

WRITINGS

Novels

Celestino Antes del Albe. Havana, Cuba, Union de Escritores, 1967; as *Singing from the Wall,* translated by Andrew Hurley, New York, Viking, 1987.
El Mundo Aluciante. Mexico, Editorial Diogenes, 1969; as *Hallucinations: Being an Account of the Life and Adventures of Friar Servando Teresa de Mier,* translated by Gordon Brotherston, Harper, 1971; as *The Ill-Fated Peregrinations of Fray Servando,* translated by Andrew Hurley, New York, Avon, 1987.
El Palacio de las Blanqquisimas Mofetas. Paris, France, Editions du Seuil, 1975; as *Palace of the White Skunks,* translated by Andrew Hurley, New York, Viking 1990.
La Vieja Rosa. Caracas, Venezuela, Libreria Cruz del Sur, 1980; as *Old Rosa,* translated by Andrew Hurley, New York, Viking, 1989.
Otra Vez el Mar. Barcelona, Spain, Argos Vergara, 1982; as *Farewell to the Sea,* translated by Andrew Hurley, New York, Viking, 1986.
Graveyard of the Angels, translated by Alfred MacAdam. New York, Avon, 1987.
El Portero. Paris, France, Presses de la Renaissance, 1988; as *The Doorman,* translated by Dolores Koch, New York, Grove Weidenfeld, 1991.
El Asalto. Miami, Ediciones Universal, 1990; as *The Assault,* translated by Andrew Hurley, New York, Viking, 1994.
Viaje a la Habana. Miami, Ediciones Universal, c. 1990.

Poetry

El Central. Barcelona, Spain, Seix Barrel, 1981; as *El Central: A Cuban Sugar Mill,* translated by Anthony Kerrigan, New York, Avon, 1984.
Homenaje a Angel Cuadra. Miami, Solar, 1981.
Voluntad de Vivir Manifestandose. Madrid, Spain, Editorial Betania, c. 1989.

Other

Con los Ojos Cerrados (short stories). Montevideo, Arca, 1972.
Necesidad de Libertad. Argentina, Kosmos-Editorial, 1986.
Persecucion: Cinco Pezas de Teatro Experimental (play). Miami, Ediciones Universal, 1986.
Un Plebiscito a Fidel Castro. Madrid, Spain, Editorial Betania, 1990.
Antes que Anochezca (autobiography). Barcelona, Spain, Tusquets, 1992; as *Before Night Falls,* translated by Dolores Koch, New York, Viking, 1993.

*

Biography: *Before Night Falls* by Reinaldo Arenas, translated by Dolores Koch, New York, Viking, 1993; "Gay Lifewriting of Reinaldo Arenas" by Timothy Dow Adams and Barry N. Olshen, in *Auto/biography Studies* (Lawrence, Kansas), Vol. 10, No. 1, spring 1995, 126-44.

Critical Sources: "Dangerous Manuscripts: A Conversation With Reinaldo Arenas" by F.O. Giesbert, in *Encounter* (London), Vol. 58, No. 1, January 1982, 60-67; *The Work of Reinaldo Arenas* by Perla Rozencvaig, Mexico, 1986; *Reinaldo Arenas: Alucinaciones, Fantasias y Realidades,* 1990; "Last Interview Reinaldo Arenas" by Perla Rozencvaig, in *Review: Latin American Literature and Arts* (New York), Vol. 44, January-June 1991, 78-83; "Sentenced to Tell the Truth" by Clemmer Mayhew, in *Christopher Street* (New York), No. 210, February 1994, 13-16; "Call My Son Ishmael: Exiled Paternity and Father/Son Eroticism in Reinaldo Arenas and Jose Marti" by Benigno Sanchez-Eppler, in *Differences: A Journal of Feminist Cultural Studies* (Bloomington, Indiana), Vol. 6, No. 1, spring 1994, 69-97; "Between Nightfall and Vengeance: Remembering Reinaldo Arenas (Bridges to Cuba/Puentes a Cuba, part 2)" by Abilio Estevez and David Frye, in *Michigan Quarterly Review* (Ann Arbor, Michigan), Vol. 33, No. 4, fall 1994, 859-67; "Where We Stand: An Essay Review" by Alfred Corn, in *Kenyon Review* (Gambier, Ohio), Vol. 16, No. 4, fall 1994, 153-60.

*   *   *

Arenas' internationally acclaimed surrealistic novels were considered counter-revolutionary and insurrectionary to the Cuban regime of Fidel Castro. He was severely persecuted in his native country due to his homosexuality. Arenas admitted that because he was a writer and a homosexual he was considered an enemy of the state. Early in his career Arenas had to smuggle his manuscripts out of the country to be published. He was subsequently charged for disrespecting the "official rules of the literature" and unconventional morality (homosexuality), charges which resulted in imprisonment. Arenas was an avowed homosexual living in a hostile country; cognizant of being different where it was a crime and where nonconformity was to be abolished. Arenas fled his Latin American homeland when the government allowed over 140,000 dissidents, felons, and personas non grata to emigrate to the United States during the Mariel boatlift in 1980. Before departing, all of his manuscripts were confiscated by the Cuban government. He arrived in the United States on 5 May 1980 with little more than the possessions he carried. Arenas spent his remaining years living in New York in poverty, giving university lectures and rewriting the manuscripts seized in Cuba.

Arenas was born on a small farm in the rural province of Oriente, Cuba. His family was poor and illiterate. Arenas' father abandoned his mother shortly after their marriage, leaving the boy to be raised by his grandmother and several aunts. The home had a dirt floor in which his grandmother dug a playpen for the little boy to romp. His first sexual feelings were aroused at age five when he visited the local swimming hole where the boys swam in the nude. Living in the country, Arenas' life was filled with sexuality not only from the natural world, but also from family and peers. At age six Arenas declared he discovered masturbation, and by age eight was having sex with other boys. Eroticism became a driving force in the psyche of Arenas as a young man. His mother

viewed him as a constant reminder of her failed relationship with his father and her status as an abandoned woman. She remained distant and aloof, not giving Arenas the mother's warmth and nurturing which he desired. His grandmother, though uneducated, acted as an earthy, mystical figure giving Arenas access to knowledge which he instinctively valued.

When his grandfather sold the family farm and moved them to Holguin, Arenas' life passed from childhood to adolescence. He quickly discovered sexuality was not as fluid or frequent as in the countryside, but segregated to specific locations, such as houses of prostitution. While on a bus one day he met a young man named Raul, who soon became his first lover. They often frequented a local gay bar and hotel in Holguin, which would disappear with the arrival of the Communist regime in Cuba. While Arenas fell in love with Raul, Raul viewed him as a furtive affair and he soon ended the relationship.

Arenas joined the anti-Batista guerrillas in the hills of Cuba at age 15. Without a gun he was considered of little use to the insurrectionists, but was put to work doing odd jobs around the encampment. When Castro took over leadership of the Cuban government, Arenas was recruited for training in an agricultural accountancy program. He was assigned to a state-run farm in the southern part of Oriente province. After several sexual relationships, he soon settled into a pattern of preferring straight men or boys for sex. Traditional Cuban society made no allowances for same sex couples, and with a strong tradition of machismo, brief sexual encounters were the best a gay man could achieve.

During the course of several years Arenas worked in a guava paste factory, a poultry farm, a bank, and a sugar cane cooperative. Following a failed sugar cane harvest he was permitted to return to Havana. With Castro's police state in power, sexual repression became more stringent. Arenas befriended several workers at the National Library and with their influence had himself transferred there. He was sexually active and lived a bohemian lifestyle. Working in an environment of virulent political and social scrutiny, Arenas wrote his first novel *Celestino Antes del Alba,* which was awarded first mention in the Cirilo Villaverde contest for best novel, in 1965.

The book, translated in 1987 as *Singing from the Well,* conjures up fantastic visions of a mentally impaired boy growing up poor in rural Cuba. Reared by harsh grandparents in a household teeming with quarrels and cruelty, the boy has difficulty distinguishing reality from fantasy. To escape his predicament he has visions of flying into the clouds when threatened by his grandparents. He also seeks comfort in his cousin Celestino, who also portrays his alter ego. Arenas depicted the story as the revolt of a poet who wanted to work in a totally violent medium.

Arenas' second novel, *El Mundo Aluciante,* again blended a mixture of fantasy and reality. The fictionalized biography of nineteenth-century Mexican monk Fray Servando Teresa de Mier was translated in 1987 as *Hallucinations.* Paralleling many of Arenas' life experiences, Fray Servando is also depicted as a person suffering persecution from the government and struggling for independence. Arenas believed his depiction of Fray Servando could only be accomplished in his mind by the weaving of history and fantasy. The anti-revolutionary theme dispersed throughout *Hallucinations* led the book to be banned by Castro. While Arenas' writings were declared criminal by Castro, his gay lifestyle represented anarchy. Eventually, both manuscripts were smuggled out of Cuba and published in Paris without official permission. Soon afterward, Arenas was blacklisted by the Castro government.

Arenas witnessed, along with other young writers, the "Padilla Affair" and the completion of Stalinization on the island of Cuba. Many writers were forced to renounce their anti-revolutionary leanings, publicly denouncing both their activities and many fellow writers. It was observed that every gay writer, artist, and dramatist received a telegram informing them that their sexual behavior did not fall into the parameters of their jobs and were subsequently terminated or placed into forced labor camps. This marked the beginning of the dark passage of Arenas into the prisons of Cuba and the demise of intellectual life in the nation. It also signified the regime's heightened repression and persecution of gay persons within the island nation.

Arenas refused to apologize for having sex with his estimated 5,000 or more men and was subsequently arrested on morals charges. But Arenas made it quite clear that sexual repression cast out by the Cuban government was responsible for more sexual activity not only among gay men, but also among policemen, soldiers, and government officials operating under Castro.

Following a dramatic escape from the police, and after living a fugitive's life on the streets and parks of Havana, Arenas was recaptured and incarcerated in El Morro prison, one of the worst prisons in Cuba. He quickly realized his good luck in not being assigned to the section of the prison designated for gay prisoners, which was one of the most inhumane cell blocks in the complex. In this prison section gay inmates were brutally treated, tortured, and subjected to the most horrendous conditions. Arenas observed, though, a degree of authenticity and revolt in gay inmates' reactions because of their placement at the bottom of the prison social order.

Later Arenas was sent to Villa Marista for questioning, a site frequently used by the government for interrogation of political prisoners. After three months he agreed to sign a statement repudiating his counter-revolutionary life and sexual orientation. Furthermore, he disavowed his writings and denied his whole past, which had catastrophic personal effects. Following release from prison Arenas was shunned by the intellectual and cultural circles in Cuban society. He was viewed with the same disrepute as the informers, do-nothings, and cowards who turned their backs on the dissidents and allowed them to be tracked down and silenced by the government. Returning to his room one day Arenas noticed a sign placed near the door stating: "QUE SE VAYAN LOS HOMOSEXUALES. QUE SE VAYA LA ESCORIA" (Homosexuals get out, scum of the earth get out).

Acting upon the anti-gay sentiment in Cuba Arenas petitioned to emigrate to the United States, and identified himself as a passive homosexual man, someone beyond social redemption. Cuban officials handling his case were unaware of his stature as an internationally acclaimed dissident writer, since most of his books were published outside Cuba. Due to their ignorance he was permitted to leave Cuba. In May 1980, with 125,000 fellow citizens, Arenas departed from his Cuban homeland in the Mariel evacuation—leaving behind a bitter existence and his manuscripts, which were seized by the government.

After arriving in the United States Arenas lectured on Cuban literature on the university circuit, and continued his writing career. His novel Otra Vez el Mar, translated as Farewell to the Sea, was finally published after being confiscated twice by the Cuban government, and rewritten a third time following his immigration to the United States. The book, set at a resort outside of Havana, detailed the political upheaval in Cuba, and the impact on its citizens.

In 1988, while travelling in Spain, Arenas met with painter Jorge Camacho. The two, along with Jorge's wife, Margarita, composed a blunt letter to Fidel Castro requesting that he hold a plebiscite on his government. Knowing full well it would not proceed, copies were sent out to distinguished intellectuals and writers such as Vargas Llosa and Octavio Paz. Within several months the letter had garnered hundreds of signatures, include those of ten Nobel laureates. The letter appeared in over 50 newspapers, including the New York Times. The letter and its related documents, published as Un Plebiscito a Fidel Castro, became one of the most powerful political weapons against Fidel Castro and his government.

Arenas also took part in another anti-Castro protest, the documentary film Havana by Czech filmmaker Jana Bukova. The film, which portrays the dire living conditions of Castro's Cuba, was structured around the writings of Arenas and several other Cuban authors. The film opens with Arenas' "Empieza el Desfile" (The Parade Begins) and closes with "Termina el Desfile" (The Parade Is Over).

Living in New York meant that Arenas would be able to complete some of the writings which he had started in Cuba. His pentagonia, which started with Singing from the Well, Palace of the White Skunks, and Farewell to the Sea, would come full circle with the completion of El Color del Verano (The Color of Summer) and El Asalto (The Assault). Each of the stories contained strong autobiographical elements from Arenas' life, whether political or personal. Celestino, in Singing From the Well, portrays Arenas' childhood; Fortunato in The Palace is his adolescence, Hector in Farewell to the Sea is Arenas as a young man, and the gloomy skunk Gabriel in The Color of Summer is the mature man. The two books which Arenas defined as his New York cycle, El Portero (The Doorman) and Viaje a la Habana (Journey to Havana) were also finished. The books depict a quest for life and meaning in exile from Cuba.

Ironically, it was in New York that Arenas had the opportunity to finish his autobiography Antes Que Anochezca (Before Night Falls), which he started while eluding police in Havana. Most of his writing had to take place while on the run during daylight and before night fell. The book, which was published posthumously, documented not only the people, places, and events which shaped his life in Cuba but also his life as a person with AIDS in New York City. Arenas meticulously describes the horrible treatment AIDS patients without insurance receive from the American medical system. He reflects upon the stages of the disease he passed through, from the lesions of Karposi Sarcoma to toxoplasmosis. One night a glass sitting next to his bed mysteriously exploded, which symbolized to him the end of his luck in surviving AIDS.

Suffering from chronic bouts of neuropathy, pancreatitis, and AIDS-related afflictions, Arenas took a lethal dose of sleeping pills to end his pain and died on 7 December 1990. In his suicide note, which served as an epilogue to Before Night Falls, he blamed Castro for his emigration from Cuba and subsequent death from AIDS. Arenas stated in the note that "There is only one person I hold accountable: Fidel Castro. The sufferings of exile, the pain of being banished from my country, the loneliness, and the disease contracted in exile would probably never have happened if I had been able to enjoy freedom in my country."

Arenas' search for freedom would take him from the sugar cane fields of his native Oriente province in Cuba, to the dank inhuman jail blocks of El Morro prison, and finally to the literary circuits of the United States. He survived the persecution and torment of being gay in Cuba, only to succumb to the ravages of AIDS in the United States.

—Michael A. Lutes

ASCH, Sholem

Pseudonyms: Also known as Scholem Ash. **Nationality:** Polish, American, and Jewish playwright and novelist. **Born:** Kutno, Poland, 1 January 1880; came to the United States, 1914; became citizen, 1920. **Education:** Local *cheder* and *bet ha-midrash* until age 17; protege of Y. L. Peretz. **Family:** Married Matilda ("Madja") Spiro in 1901; three sons and one daughter. **Awards:** Honorary presidency, Yiddish PEN Club, 1932; Polish Republic's *Polonia Restituta* decoration, 1932; Nobel Prize nomination, 1933; H.D. (Hebrew Letters): Jewish Theological Seminary, 1937. **Died:** London, England, 1957.

WRITINGS

Novels in English

Kiddush Ha-Shem: An Epic of 1648, translated by Rufus Learsi (Isaac Goldberg). Philadelphia, Jewish Publication Society of America, 1912.
Mottke the Vagabond, translated by Isaac Goldberg. Boston, J. W. Luce, 1917.
America, translated by James Fuchs. New York, Alpha Omega Publishing Company, 1918.
Uncle Moses, translated by Isaac Goldberg. New York, E. P. Dutton, 1920; London, Fisher Unwin, 1922.
The Mother, translated by Nathan Ausubel. New York, Horace Liveright, 1930; London, G. Routledge, 1937.
Three Cities: A Trilogy, translated by Willa and Edwin Muir. New York, Putnam's, 1933; London, V. Gollancz, 1933.
Salvation, translated by Willa and Edwin Muir. New York, Putnam's, 1934; London, V. Gollancz, 1934.
Mottke the Thief, translated by Willa and Edwin Muir. New York and London, Putnam's, 1935.
The War Goes On, translated by Will and Edwin Muir. New York, Putnam's, 1936; translated into English as *The Calf of Paper,* by Edwin and Willa Muir. London, V. Gollancz, 1936.
Three Novels: Uncle Moses, Chaim Lederer's Return, Judge Not—, translated by Elsa Krauch. New York, Putnam's, and London, G. Routledge, 1938.
Song of the Valley, translated by Elsa Krauch. New York, Putnam's, and London, G. Routledge, 1939.
The Nazarene, translated by Maurice Samuel. New York, Putnam's, Toronto, G. Allen, and London, G. Routledge, 1939.
The Apostle, translated by Maurice Samuel. New York, Putnam's, and Toronto, G. Allen, 1943; London, Macdonald, 1949.
East River, translated by A. H. Gross. New York, Putnam's, and Toronto, G. Allen, 1946; London, Macdonald, 1948.
Mary, translated by Leo Steinberg. London, Macdonald, and Toronto, G. Allen, 1950; New York, Putnam's, 1951.
Moses, translated by Maurice Samuel. New York, Putnam's, 1951; London, Macdonald, 1952.

A Passage in the Night, translated by Maurice Samuel. New York, Putnam's, and Toronto, G. Allen, 1953; London, Macdonald, 1954.
The Prophet, translated by Arthur Saul Super. New York, Putnam's, 1955; London, Macdonald, 1956.

Plays in English

"The Sinner," translated by Isaac Goldberg. Included in *Six Plays of the Yiddish Theatre,* edited by Isaac Goldberg. Boston, J.W. Luce, 1916, 151-75.
"Winter," translated by Isaac Goldberg. Included in *Six Plays of the Yiddish Theatre,* edited by Isaac Goldberg. Boston, J. W. Luce, 1916, 123-49.
The God of Vengeance: Drama in Three Acts, translated by Isaac Goldberg. Boston, The Stratford Company, 1918.
"Night," translated by Jack Robbins. Included in *Fifty Contemporary One-Act Plays,* edited by Frank Shay and Pierre Loving. Cincinnati, Stewart & Kidd, 1920, 537-44.
Sabbatai Zevi: A Tragedy in 3 Acts and 6 Scenes, translated by Florence Whyte and George Rapall Noyes. Philadelphia, Jewish Publication Society of America, 1930.

Short Stories in English

In the Beginning, translated by Caroline Cunningham. New York, Putnam's, 1935.
Children of Abraham: The Short Stories of Sholem Asch, translated by Maurice Samuel. New York, Putnam's, 1942.
Tales of My People, translated by Meyer Levin. New York, Putnam's, 1948.
From Many Countries: The Collected Short Stories of Sholem Asch, translated by Maurice Samuel and Meyer Levin. London, Macdonald, 1958.

Uncollected Short Stories in English

"Through the Wall," translated by Isabel Shostac, in *Current Literature,* Vol. 49, October 1910, 461-63.
"A Simple Story," translated by Helena Frank, in *Yiddish Tales,* edited by Helena Frank. Philadelphia, Jewish Publication Society of America, 1912, 493-505.
"The Sinner," translated by Helena Frank, in *Yiddish Tales,* edited by Helena Frank. Philadelphia, Jewish Publication Society of America, 1912, 529-39.
"Abandoned," in *Great Short Stories of the World: A Collection of Complete Short Stories Chosen from the Literature of All Periods and Countries,* edited by Barrett H. Clark and Maxim Lieber. New York, Robert M. McBride, 1928, 740-43.
"The Red Hat," in *Esquire,* Vol. 1, April 1934, 48-49, 100.
"A Village Tsaddik," translated by Shifra Natanson and N. B. Jopson, in *Slavonic Review,* Vol. 13, July 1934, 41-45.
"I Adopt an Ancestor: A Fable," in *American Mercury,* Vol. 56, January 1943, 47-53.
"Katie Stieglitz," in *Common Ground,* Vol. 3, spring 1943, 19-23.
"Kola Street," translated by Norbert Guterman, in *A Treasury of Yiddish Stories,* edited by Irving Howe and Eliezer Greenberg. New York, Meridian Books, 1958, 260-75.
"Kola Road," translated by Joseph Leftwich, in *Yisroel: The First Jewish Omnibus,* revised edition, edited by Joseph Leftwich. New York, Thomas Yoseloff, 1963, 456-70.

Nonfiction in English

What I Believe, translated by Maurice Samuel. New York, Putnam's, 1941; as *My Personal Faith,* translated by Maurice Samuel, London, G. Routledge, 1942.
One Destiny: An Epistle to the Christians, translated by Milton Hindus. New York, Putnam's, 1945.

*

Biography: *The Controversial Sholem Asch* by Ben Siegel, Bowling Green, Ohio, Bowling Green University Popular Press, 1976.

Critical Sources: "'The God of Vengeance' Is the Play Immoral?—Is it a Great Drama?," in file, "*God of Vengeance:* Programmes," Lincoln Center Library for the Performing Arts, Lincoln Center, New York; "Drama and Detectives," in *Nation,* Vol. 116, 6 June 1923, 646; *The Yiddish Theatre in America* by David S. Lifson, New York and London, Thomas Yoseloff, 1965; "Speaking to Our Dust: Directing Asch's *God of Vengeance*" by Robert Skloot, in *Yiddish,* Vol. 5, Fall 1982, 22-34; *"We Can Always Call Them Bulgarians": The Emergence of Lesbians and Gay Men on the American Stage* by Kaier Curtin, Boston, Alyson Publications, 1987; "SMUT! How the Society for the Suppression of Vice Imposed Censorship on the Legitimate Theatre in New York City" by Robin Bernstein (M.A. thesis), University of Maryland, 1995.

*   *   *

In 1907, at the age of 21, writer Sholem Asch showed his new playscript to his mentor, Y. L. Peretz, Yiddish literature's most prominent author. Peretz, scandalized by the play's depiction of Jewish lesbians and prostitutes, handed the play back to Asch with a single recommendation: "Burn it."

Asch, however, did not discard the script, and the play *God of Vengeance* subsequently enjoyed translation from Yiddish into over 15 languages; it was produced in dozens of cities around the world and continues to be revived until this day. The play is generally recognized as a masterpiece. After its world-wide success, even Peretz reversed his opinion and declared, "Asch has given the stage...a poem." In 1922, it became the first play with lesbian characters ever performed in English. Also during the 1920s, *God of Vengeance* became the center of one of the most important theatrical censorship controversies in the history of the United States.

God of Vengeance depicts a Jewish brothel-keeper who purchases a *Torah* (Judaism's holiest ritual object) in a superstitious belief that it will protect the purity of his daughter Rivkele, who, unknown to him, is romantically involved with Manke, one of the prostitutes. The second act closes with a delicately erotic (and non-homophobic) seduction in which Rivkele and Manke pretend to be a bride and groom on their wedding night.

> MANKE. Your father and mother have gone to bed. Bride and groom have met at the table. We're embarrassed. Right?
>
> RIVKELE (nodding her head). Yes, Manke.
>
> MANKE. Then we draw close to each other: you're my bride and I'm your bridegroom. We embrace. (She puts her arms around her). We're pressed together and we kiss

very quietly, like this. (They kiss). We blush, we're so embarrassed. It's good, isn't it, Rivkele?

> RIVKELE. Yes, Manke, it is.
>
> MANKE (lowers her voice, whispering in her ear). And then we go to sleep in the same bed. No one sees; no one knows, just the two of us, like this. (She presses RIVKELE to her). Would you like to sleep the whole night through with me, Rivkele, in the same bed?
>
> RIVKELE (embracing her). I would, I would.

God of Vengeance played in Berlin, St. Petersburg, and other cities with little opposition. When it opened in Yiddish in New York, however, audiences were outraged at what they considered to be the sacrilegious treatment of the *Torah.* One production endured a hail of rotten eggs from the audience; a few Yiddish publications demanded Asch's "excommunication" (which is impossible in Judaism). Although controversy raged in the Yiddish newspapers, non-Jewish authorities did not become involved. New York's Yiddish productions of *God of Vengeance* ran sporadically for 15 years without legal intervention.

On December 20, 1922, New York's Provincetown Playhouse opened the world premier of *God of Vengeance* in English—and thus brought lesbian characters to an English-language stage for the first time. The production received overwhelmingly negative reviews. Although many critics hailed the performance of Rudolph Schildkraut in the role of the brothel-keeper, almost all splattered their reviews with adjectives such as "irregular," "nasty," "offensive," "ugly," "sordid," "repellent," "horrible," "repulsive," "perverted," and "nauseating."

Nearly all the critics understood but deliberately avoided mentioning the play's lesbian content. A few, however, did mention the lesbian aspects. For example, the reviewer for the *New York Evening Post* reported that "the girl falls victim to a lesbian." And Maida Castellun—probably the only woman to review the play—reported in the *Call* that the Rivkele's "perverted curiosity makes her the easy victim of her sex, and she escapes with Manke, a Lesbian companion, to her predestined fate."

Many members of the audience and at least one member of the cast, however, failed to recognize the lesbian eroticism as such. For example, Morris Carnovsky, a member of the original cast, told historian Kaier Curtin that the lesbian content never "even occurred to me until some reviewers mentioned it."

Despite the critics' invectives, the police did not interfere with the Provincetown production of *God of Vengeance.* In February 1923, however, producer Harry Weinberger moved Provincetown's production to the Apollo Theatre on Broadway. In such a prominent, mainstream venue, the play garnered complaints that it was obscene and anti-Semitic (the charge of anti-Semitism centered on the sacrilege of a *Torah* in a brothel and on the negative depictions of many Jewish characters). Weinberger, the manager, and all 12 members of the cast were indicted by the grand jury; they stood accused of violating the penal code which forbade "indecent, immoral and impure theatrical performance." The accused pled not guilty and were released on $300 bail apiece.

In response to the attempt at censorship, Weinberger published "'The God of Vengeance' Is the Play Immoral?—Is it a Great Drama?," a souvenir program consisting almost entirely of endorsements by prominent men and women. Abraham Cahan of the *Jew-*

ish Daily Forward, Elmer Rice, Constantin Stanislavsky, Eugene O'Neill, and many others rushed to defend the play as moral. Before the trial began, however, the show closed.

On May 23, 1923, after only 90 minutes' deliberation, a jury convicted Weinberger and all 12 members of the cast (the manager was tried separately). They faced a maximum penalty of three years imprisonment and a fine of $500 apiece. On May 28, McIntyre sentenced Schildkraut and Weinberger each to pay a fine of $200; the other members of the cast received suspended sentences. As the *New York Times* noted, this case was the first in which a jury convicted a cast or manager for "giving an immoral performance." The only similar case—the prosecution of *Orange Blossoms* in 1896—was decided by a judge.

Of the controversy, Asch wrote in Weinberger's souvenier program:

> I was not concerned whether I wrote a moral or immoral play. What I wanted to write was an artistic play and a true one.... As to the scenes between Manka [sic] and Rifkele [sic], on every European stage, especially the Russian, they were the most poetic of all, and the critics

of those countries appreciated this poetic view. This love between the two girls is not only an erotic one. It is the unconscious mother love of which they are deprived... As to the comment that the play is a reflection on the Jewish race, I want to say that I resent the statement that "The God of Vengeance" is a play against the Jews.... Jews do not need to clear themselves before any one. They are as good and as bad as any race.

Asch was conscious, however, of the possibility that his negative portrayal of Jews (particularly his characterization of the brothel-keeper) might arouse anti-Semitism. During the Holocaust, he refused to allow the play to be performed anywhere in the world.

The *God of Vengeance* controversy was but one of many in Asch's career. Later in his life, he wrote epic novels on Christian themes, which angered some segments of the Jewish community. He remains, however, an acknowledged giant of Yiddish literature and theatre—and a pioneer for his sensitive and early portrayal of lesbians.

—Robin Bernstein

B

BAILEY, Paul

Nationality: British actor, playwright, and novelist. **Born:** Peter Harry Bailey in Battersea, London, 16 February 1937. **Education:** Sir Walter St. John's School, London, 1948-53; Central School of Speech and Drama, London, 1953-56. **Career:** Actor, 1956-63; Literary Fellow, University of Newcastle-upon-Tyne and University of Durham, 1972-74; visiting lecturer, North Dakota State University, Fargo, 1977-79; contributor to periodicals, including *Daily Telegraph, Listener, London Magazine, New Statesman,* and *Observer.* **Awards:** Somerset Maugham Award, 1968; Arts Council Award, 1968; Author's Club Award, 1970; E.M. Forster Award, National Institute of Arts and Letters Awards, 1974; Bicentennial Arts Fellowship, 1976; George Orwell Memorial Prize, 1978. **Address:** 79 Davisville Road, London W12 9SH, England.

WRITINGS

Novels

At the Jerusalem. London, Cape, and New York, Atheneum, 1967.
Trespasses. London, Cape, and New York, Harper, 1970.
A Distant Likeness. London, Cape, 1973.
Peter Smart's Confessions. London, Cape, 1977.
Old Soldiers. London, Cape, 1980.
Gabriel's Lament. London, Cape, 1986; New York, Viking, 1987.
Sugar Cane. London, Bloomsbury, 1993, New York, Penguin, 1994.

Plays

At Cousin Henry's (radio play). 1964.
A Worthy Guest (produced Newcastle-upon-Tyne, 1973; London, 1974).
Alice (produced Newcastle-upon-Tyne, 1975).
Crime and Punishment (produced Manchester, 1978; adaptation of novel by Dostoevsky).
With Tristram Powell, *We Think The World of You* (television play). 1980.

Other

"Living in London," in *London Magazine Editions,* 1974.
An English Madam: The Life and Work of Cynthia Payne. London, Cape, 1982.
An Immaculate Mistake: Scenes from Childhood and Beyond (autobiography). London, Bloomsbury, 1990; New York, Dutton, 1991.

Editor, *The Oxford Book of London.* Oxford, New York, Oxford University Press, 1995.

*

Critical Sources: *Contemporary Literary Criticism,* Vol. 45, Detroit, Gale Research, 1990; *An Immaculate Mistake: Scenes from Childhood and Beyond* by Paul Bailey, New York, Dutton, 1991.

*   *   *

From his earliest writing—the short story he wrote in France in 1951 about a lad of 20 who detests his own body, indeed himself, and seeks the freedom of nakedness by running out into Paris's busy Champs-Elysees, only to be arrested for his boldness, and who returns to his room and in despair commits suicide—to his latest—his memoir, *An Immaculate Mistake,* published in 1991, in which he is forthright about both his homosexuality and his early wishes to commit suicide—Paul Bailey is not writing so much about homosexuality as he is writing about loneliness, feelings of being and actually being different, isolated, and desperate. In these works, that sense of hopelessness looms, and all too frequently prevails.

His novels, such as *At the Jerusalem,* illustrate precisely how human beings who are different, in this case aged and infirm, are denied the basics of human compassion, fellowship, even love. While Bailey doesn't explicitly address homosexuality until his 1991 memoir, his life is dedicated to shedding light on the emotional isolation, suffering, and despair that plague many who are in his understanding really no different from himself. Bailey has profound sympathy for those who, because they are physically or emotionally different, are made fun of, separated out, and, in the extreme, locked away and ostracized. Bailey, who left a position in sales at Harrod's to act, found in acting a way to hide his real self, to become someone else. Yet he was confident enough in his acting to change his name to Paul to avoid confusion with another Peter Bailey who was active in the British theatre.

As a child Bailey pretended to have an identical twin, Paul. "It was fun," his writes in his memoir, "being someone else, escaping from the Peter that I was into the Paul of my imagination, giving him different characteristics.... Paul was a livelier creature than his dull impersonator." Later, onstage, he found acting "was a release into the nature of others. It was a wonderful way of not being Peter." At home, however, he was always as his mother unwittingly accused him of being, something "unnatural," a "pansy, wary of displaying his true colors in the sunlight, as did so many others of the same peculiar genus, in the shade. That is where we had to function, if at all, in the days when we were accounted criminals."

The emotional trauma of such an upbringing informed his first novel, written when he was just 30 years old. The story of the elderly people living at a home for the aged, *At the Jerusalem* evinces a genuine sympathy for those who feel a keen sense of hopelessness about the future. It is a hopelessness that Bailey understood and sensed within himself.

—Andrea L.T. Peterson

BARR, James

Pseudonyms: James Fugate. **Nationality:** American novelist and short story writer. **Born:** 13 February 1922 in Texas (some sources say Oklahoma). **Military Service:** Served in the United States Navy, c. 1941-45. **Died:** Claremore, Texas, 28 March 1995.

WRITINGS

Fiction

Quatrefoil: A Modern Novel. New York, Greenberg, 1950.
The Occasional Man. New York, Paperback Library, 1966.

Nonfiction (as James Barr Fugate)

"Release from the Navy under Honorable Conditions," in
    Mattachine Review, Vol. 3, May-June 1955, 6-9, 39-42.
"Homosexuality and the Liberal Mind," in *Mattachine Review,* Vol.
    5, September-October 1955, 18-21.
"Hold That Curtain—Juliet's Still Shaving," in *Mattachine Review,*
    Vol. 1, No. 7, Christmas 1955, 5-7.
"Homosexuality and the Child Molesters," in *Mattachine Review,*
    Vol. 2, No. 2, April 1956, 6-10.

Other

Derricks (short stories). New York, Greenberg, 1951; Pan Books,
    1957.
*Game of Fools: A Play of Those Fools, By Those Fools, and For
    Those Fools, Who Stubbornly Refuse to Perish from this Earth*
    (play). Los Angeles, One, Inc., 1955.
"Facing Friends in a Small Town" (nonfiction), in *Mattachine Re-
    view,* Vol. 1, January-February 1955, 9-12.
"Her Son, Her Son" (as James Barr Fugate; letters), in *Mattachine
    Review,* Vol. 2, No. 6a, November 1956, 9-12.

*

Critical Sources: "Quatrefoil" by Hubert Kennedy, in *Advocate,*
Vol. 344, 10 June 1982, 43; "Quatrefoil Broke New Ground" by
Hubert Kennedy, in *Harvard Gay and Lesbian Review,* winter
1996, 22-24.

*   *   *

The power of literary depiction to shape the hopes, dreams,
and possibilities for a particular audience and give voice to the
nebulous idea of community has been demonstrated in many contexts during the twentieth century. Expressing the experience of
membership in a particular minority group (however defined) pre-
supposes that the existence of its members is treated as a recognized and accepted fact by the majority of the mainstream culture. While this premise underlies the rich explosion of narratives,
fiction, poetry, and theater produced by African American, Latino,
and Asian American authors and writers who identify themselves
with the women's community, its construction for the United
States gay and lesbian community has received less analysis. The
beginnings of what was to become the movement for contemporary gay and lesbian social and legal equality lie in the years immediately following World War II, when the only safe means of
depicting homosexuals in literature was as foredoomed tragic figures who could be (and nearly always were) safely disposed of
by the final paragraph through suicide, mental breakdown, or some
type of fatal accident. Their portrayal as completely human figures capable of a full range of emotions, each with its own complexity and integrity, would have been considered only within the
contexts of the disciplines of psychology and psychiatry.

Awareness and resentment of the uniformly negative images of
homosexuals presented to the public by literary genres and the
media (and internalized by many individuals, raising further obstacles to their acceptance of their sexual identities and needs) is
a recurrent theme in the pages of the earliest successful periodicals catering to this audience and produced during this era, *The
Mattachine Review* and *ONE.* The latter also provided the first
test case of the legality of distributing homosexually oriented materials through the mails with a lawsuit successfully argued before
the United States Supreme Court in 1958. While many of the books
dealing with homosexuality at this time were either apologetic in
tone, urging understanding and acceptance of people who had not
chosen to be attracted to their own gender, or frankly clinical
analyses of such behavior as a pathology, both of these viewpoints
were often utilized by writers seeking to create fiction. It is within
this context that the impact and importance of the writing of James
Barr Fugate must be considered.

In many ways, Barr was a typical son of his times, attending
college (where he discovered his preference for his own gender
with a fellow fraternity member), then entering the United States
Navy following the attack on Pearl Harbor in 1941. During his
military service, he met up once again with his friend, whose post-
war life would later contribute significant elements to the plot of
his first novel. Upon being discharged in 1945, Barr returned to
university to study writing with the intention of completing his
bachelor's degree. News of his friend's suicide in Oklahoma made
life on campus intolerable, and he left to write advertising copy
for television in New York City. As he later wrote in an epilogue
for *Quatrefoil,* "tired of pretty little boys with their...toys in their
velvet-lined worlds...I wanted to get down among the men who
lived and fought with the ugliness of life." He subsequently carried out his wish, living and working as a roustabout in the oil
fields, where he met many of the strong basic men whose ana-
logues were to appear in his collection of seven stories set in their
world, *Derricks.*

The major work for which Barr is most generally known, *Quatrefoil,* first appeared in print in 1950. For its time, it was one of
the first twentieth-century works to frankly explore the dimensions of love between two men, and to do so with careful attention to creating fully realized characters whose behavior and actions challenged the prevailing stereotypes. It is in many ways
the forerunner of what would become known as "coming out" literature, as one of the themes is the gradual acceptance of a homosexual identity and its affirmation (albeit in secret) as a positive
thing. Barr drew heavily upon his wartime experiences to trace
out the details of the military world, an environment where homosexuality had always been officially condemned although tacitly present. The basic plot revolves around the romance between
Ensign Philip Froelich and an older married officer, Commander
Timothy Danelaw, their successful concealment of their relationship, and the eventual decision by Froelich to repudiate suicide
following his lover's death in a plane crash. When the novel was
published, the publisher was immediately subjected to unsuccessful
pressure from military authorities seeking to learn the identity of
the author.

Turning from the novel form, Barr's next literary creations were
a series of short stories, published in 1951 under the title *Derricks.* In the preface, he clarifies the term as meaning "the situations by which men and women here and there rise up above the
mundane sweep of their lives for a short while to stand against
that which eternally surrounds them." The stories convey the full

range of attitudes held by society towards homosexuality in the 1940s and 1950s, ranging from the clinical approach of the medical and psychiatric professions through the potential for blackmail attempts by criminals. Perhaps the most important thread in some of these stories is Barr's challenging of the then-prevalent belief that inevitable melancholy, absence of masculinity, bitterness, loneliness, and disaster accompanied the condition of being homosexual. For their time, these stories both presented and dared to question forbidden sexual subjects in much the same fashion as the controversial 1948 Kinsey Report.

At the beginning of the Korean War, Barr volunteered for service as a reserve officer and was assigned to a naval base in Alaska. Shortly after his arrival, his identity as the author of *Quatrefoil* and *Derricks* was discovered, resulting in an eight-month investigation by the Office of Naval Intelligence. Upon its completion, he was separated from the Navy with a discharge under honorable conditions, an unusual result for the time and one which politicized him to become active in the fledgling homosexual rights movement. He resumed writing, contributing several pieces to the *Mattachine Review,* including his own "coming-out" essay on his expulsion from the Navy in which he identified himself as the author of *Quatrefoil.* His courage in taking this step was applauded by the *Review*'s readers, as were his explorations of popular misconceptions such as the idea that homosexuals were child molesters. Of a planned five-play cycle, only the openly propagandistic *Game of Fools* was ever written, with his literary work concluding in 1966 with the publication of his final novel, *An Occasional Man.* In the latter, the noble philosophical ideas expressed in *Quatrefoil* and *Derricks* had faded, while, as noted by Hubert Kennedy, "the height of high-minded thinking for its protagonist is not to initiate anyone into homosexuality." Following his discharge, he returned to his family in Kansas, where he became a newspaper reporter and photographer and remained there until his foster mother's death in the early 1970s. A brief return to New York was succeeded by a ten-year stint working in the emergency room of a large hospital, from which he retired.

Barr's work thus portrays the full spectrum of possible literary and social fixed images of homosexuality extant prior to the emergence of the gay liberation movement in 1969. The clear masculinity, sanity, and integrity of the lovers in *Quatrefoil,* however, also point the way to contemporary gay fiction's realistic depiction of relationships between men.

—Robert B. Marks Ridinger

BATES, Katharine Lee

Pseudonyms: Also wrote as James Lincoln. **Nationality:** American poet and educator. **Born:** Falmouth, Massachusetts, 12 August 1859. **Education:** Wellesley (then Grantville) High School, Massachusetts, 1870-74; Newton High School, Massachusetts, 1874-76; Wellesley College, Wellesley, Massachusetts (Phi Sigma, Class Poet, 1880), 1876-80, A.B. 1880, A.M. 1891; Oxford, 1889-90. **Family:** Companion of Wellesley professor Katharine Coman, 1890-1915 (died of breast cancer). **Career:** Teacher, Natick High School, Massachusetts, 1880-81, and Dana Hall School, Wellesley, Massachusetts, 1881-85; instructor of English literature, 1886-88, associate professor, 1888-91, professor, 1891-25, head of English literature department, 1891-1920, Wellesley College. Director, International Institute for Girls in Spain, intermittently, 1904-20; frequent contributor to a variety of popular, religious, scholarly, and children's magazines. **Member:** Founding member, Boston Authors Club, 1900; founder, New England Poetry Club, 1915. **Awards:** Congregational Publishing Society first prize, for juvenile fiction, 1889; L.H.D.: Middlebury College, 1914; Oberlin College, 1916; Wellesley College, 1925. **Died:** Wellesley, Massachusetts, of pneumonia, 28 March 1929.

WRITINGS

Nonfiction

The English Religious Drama. New York, Macmillan and Co., 1893.
American Literature. New York, Macmillan and Co., 1897.
Sigurd our Golden Collie and Other Comrades of the Road. New York, E. P. Dutton and Co., 1919; London, J. M. Dent, 1921.

Travel Sketches

"Cape Cod Towns," in *Historic Towns of New England,* edited by Lyman P. Powell. New York, G. P. Putnam's Sons, 1898.
Spanish Highways and Byways. New York, Macmillan and Co., 1900; London, Macmillan and Co., Ltd., 1901.
From Gretna Green to Land's End: A Literary Journey in England. New York, Thomas Y. Crowell Co., 1907; London, Grant Richards, 1908.

Children's Fiction

Rose and Thorn. Boston, The Congregational Sunday-School and Publishing Society, 1889.
Hermit Island. Boston, D. Lathrop Company, 1890.
In Sunny Spain with Pilarica and Rafael. New York, E. P. Dutton and Co., 1913; London, J. M. Dent, 1913.

Poetry

The College Beautiful and Other Poems. Cambridge, H. O. Houghton, 1887.
Relishes of Rhyme (as James Lincoln). Boston, Richard G. Badger, 1903.
America the Beautiful and Other Poems. New York, Thomas Y. Crowell and Co., 1911.
The Retinue and Other Poems. New York, E. P. Dutton and Co., 1918.
Yellow Clover: A Book of Remembrance. New York, E. P. Dutton and Co., 1922.
The Pilgrim Ship. New York, The Woman's Press, 1926.
America the Dream. New York, Thomas Y. Crowell Co., 1930.
Selected Poems of Katharine Lee Bates. Boston, Houghton Mifflin Co., 1930.

Poetry for Children

Sunshine and Other Verses. Wellesley Alumnae, 1890.
The Story of Chaucer's Canterbury Pilgrims. New York, Rand, McNally and Co., 1909.

Fairy Gold. New York, E. P. Dutton and Co., 1916.
Little Robin Stay-Behind and Other Plays in Verse for Children.
New York, The Women's Press, 1923.

Editor

The Wedding-Day Book, with the Congratulations of the Poets.
Boston, Lothrop Publishing Co., 1895.
With Lydia Bowker Godfrey, *English Drama, A Working Basis.*
Boston, Press of S. G. Robinson, 1896.

Other

Translator, with Cornelia Frances Bates, *Romantic Legends of
Spain* by Gustavo Adolfo Becquer. New York, Thomas Y.
Crowell and Company, 1909.
An Autobiography in Brief of Katharine Lee Bates (autobiography).
Falmouth, Mass., Enterprise Press, 1930.

*

Manuscript Collections: Arthur and Elizabeth Schlesinger Library on the History of Women in America, Radcliffe College, Cambridge, Massachusetts; Falmouth Historical Society, Massachusetts; Houghton Library, Harvard University, Cambridge, Massachusetts; Wellesley College Archives, Massachusetts.

Biography: *Katharine Lee Bates, Poet and Professor* by Dorothea Lawrance Mann, reprinted from *Boston Evening Transcript,* 1931; *On Journey* by Vida Dutton Scudder, New York, E. P. Dutton and Co., 1937; *Dream and Deed: The Story of Katharine Lee Bates* by Dorothy Whittemore Bates Burgess, Norman, University of Oklahoma Press, 1952; *In Adamless Eden: The Community of Women Faculty at Wellesley* by Patricia Ann Palmieri, New Haven, Yale University Press, 1995.

Critical Sources: *"Yellow Clover:* Katharine Lee Bates and Katharine Coman" by Judith Schwarz, in *Frontiers: A Journal of Women's Studies* (Boulder), Vol. 4, No. 1, spring 1979, 59-67; "Katharine Lee Bates" by Lillian Faderman, in *Chloe Plus Olivia: An Anthology of Lesbian Literature from the Seventeenth Century to the Present* (New York), Viking, 1994.

*   *   *

When Katharine Lee Bates is remembered today, it is usually due to her poem "America the Beautiful," often referred to by its first line, "O beautiful for spacious skies." First published in the religious magazine the *Congregationalist* on 4 July 1885, and later set to music, it was inspired by Bates' view from atop Pikes Peak in Colorado during a trip there in 1893, while teaching a summer session at Colorado College.

It is her collection of poems, *Yellow Clover: A Book of Remembrance,* for which Bates must be seen as a significant contributor to early 20th century American lesbian writing. Judith Schwarz, in her 1979 essay, *"Yellow Clover:* Katharine Lee Bates and Katharine Coman," opens by stating that "Bates wrote one of the most anguished memorials to the love and comradeship between two women that has ever been written...." Wellesley professor Vida Dutton Scudder, in her 1937 memoir *On Journey,* stated that *Yellow Clover* contains Bates' "[m]ost poignant and distinguished

verse..." Scudder continues, "Some day we shall have an 'In Memoriam' or a sonnet-cycle...written by a woman of a woman. [Alfred Tennyson had written 'In Memoriam' some 70 years previously to commemorate the death of his intimate friend Arthur H. Hallam.] Katharine Lee Bates' poems in memory of Katharine Coman...are the nearest approach I know."

Bates dedicated *Yellow Clover* to Coman, and her portrait served as frontispiece; the book itself is decorated with a strip of yellow clover design, and was printed in 1922, in a limited edition of 750, as an Easter gift to Bates' colleagues and friends. As her niece Dorothy Burgess wrote in *Dream and Deed,* it was "the climax of her poetic aspirations. She had realized her deepest desire—to memorialize the dearest companion of her life."

"In Bohemia: A Corona of Sonnets," which constitutes about half of *Yellow Clover,* was, said Burgess, "unique in poetry" in that "no series of poems had ever been written celebrating the friendship of women—not necessarily a 'new type of friendship,' as Jane Addams [an old friend of Coman's, and 1931 Nobel Peace Prize recipient] called it in a letter [to Bates] but a relationship developing naturally in the community life of a woman's college." "In Bohemia" was named for Coman's room in the home she and Bates shared with Bates' mother and sister. Bates had a penchant for naming everything in their lives, and it was in Bohemia where Bates wrote after Coman's death.

Throughout their lives, Bates called Coman her "Joy-of-Life." "In Bohemia" contains over 40 repetitions of the word joy. Sonnett II begins: "Our word shall still be Joy, shall still be Joy. / Death shall not be a frost that blackens all / The blossoms in our garden...." The sobriquet "Joy-of-Life" also appears throughout *Sigurd our Golden Collie,* which was published three years before *Yellow Clover.* Coman (and Sigurd) served as frontispiece for this celebration of their domestic life.

"Partly to amuse herself," says Burgess, Bates had written a handful of poems under the name of James Lincoln, which appeared in the *Atlantic Monthly,* among other magazines and newspapers. *Relishes of Rhyme,* a collection of these poems published in 1903, was dedicated to "Janet." This is possibly Bates' sister Jane, her sole typist. The poems were, says the foreword, suggested "by cablegrams from South Africa as given to the American press during the Boer War [of 1899-1902]." One senses that Bates greatly enjoyed her pseudonymic freedom, in which she allowed herself to be sarcastic, though love always triumphed. Even foes can "Drink to the immortal / Joy of love"—her only (veiled) reference in that collection to her Joy-of-Life.

Bates had begun to write poetry as a child; her diaries, reproduced in part in *Dream and Deed,* describe a budding, insightful feminist and prolific poet. While a Wellesley sophomore, her poem "Sleep" was published in *Atlantic Monthly,* and Henry Longfellow spoke of it approvingly. All of Bates' poetry is thoroughly reflective of the Victorian era; she was not influenced by the Imagists, a movement led by her contemporary, Boston lesbian poet Amy Lowell.

Much of Bates' prolific output was due to the need to supplement her salary. The low wages paid to college faculty did not allow for any extras. Most of her writings grew out of her holiday or sabbatical experiences. She travelled extensively through Europe and the Near East, either with Coman or other Wellesley colleagues. Burgess quotes Bates' letters to her mother, written during her first sabbatical at Oxford, stating that she had met many young men, whom she called "brothers," but she "sternly nip[ped] these frivolities in the bud."

Though *Yellow Clover* is written in highly coded language filled with Christian iconography and overlaid by proper Bostonian morals and sensibilities, there is no doubt about Bates' deep and enduring love for Coman, regardless of the form in which it appeared.

—Martha E. Stone

BEAM, Joseph Fairchild

Nationality: American writer and editor. **Born:** Philadelphia, Pennsylvania, 30 December 1954. **Education:** St. Joseph School for Boys, Clayton, Delaware; Malvern Preparatory School, Paoli, Pennsylvania; St. Thomas More High School, Philadelphia; Franklin College, Franklin, Indiana (Omega Psi Phi Fraternity Award for Broadcasting, 1974), B.A. 1976. **Career:** Held a variety of jobs including waiter and bookseller; founding editor, *Black/Out;* contributing editor, *Blacklight;* columnist, *Au Courant.* Contributor to periodicals, including the *Advocate, Blackheart, Gay Community News, New York Native, Painted Bride Quarterly, Philadelphia Gay News,* and *Windy City Times;* member of the Board of Directors, National Coalition of Black Lesbians and Gays. **Awards:** *Philadelphia Gay News* Lambda Award for Outstanding Achievement, 1985. **Died:** Philadelphia, Pennsylvania, of complications from AIDS, 27 December 1988.

WRITINGS

Editor and author of introduction, *In the Life: A Black Gay Anthology.* Boston, Alyson Publications, 1986.
"Brother to Brother: Words from the Heart," in *In the Life: A Black Gay Anthology.* Boston, Alyson Publications, 1986.

*

Manuscript Collections: Schomburg Center for Research in Black Culture, New York City.

Biography: "Joseph Beam, Writer and Gay Activist" by Donna St. George, in the *Philadelphia Inquirer,* 31 December 1988, B5; "A Son's Work and a Mother's Love" by Carol Horner, in the *Philadelphia Inquirer,* 4 February 1992, C1, 7; "Joseph Beam" by Joseph M. Eagan, in *Gay & Lesbian Biography,* edited by Michael J. Tyrkus, Detroit, Michigan, St. James Press, 1996, 54.

Critical Sources: Review of *In the Life: A Black Gay Anthology* by Larry Duplechan, in the *Advocate* (Los Angeles), No. 460, November 1986, 55; review of *Brother to Brother: New Writings by Black Gay Men* by Phil Harper, in *Gay Community News* (Boston), Vol. 18, No. 45, 9-15 June 1991, 26; "Gay Voices, Gay Lives" by Don Belton, in the *Philadelphia Inquirer,* 25 August 1991, C1, 2; "African-American Literature, Gay Male" by Emmanuel S. Nelson, in *The Gay and Lesbian Literary Heritage,* edited by Claude J. Summers, New York, Henry Holt, 1995, 8-12.

*   *   *

Joseph Beam's life and work exemplifies the influence that one unknown writer could have on gay male literature in the 1980s.

Beam's greatest accomplishment was conceiving and editing *In the Life: A Black Gay Anthology,* which was published in 1986 by Alyson Publications. This collection is generally acknowledged as the first literary anthology written exclusively by, for, and about gay African-American men.

Born and raised in Philadelphia, Beam remained close to his parents and his hometown roots throughout his life. In his essay from *In the Life* entitled "Brother to Brother: Words from the Heart," he explained his relationship with his father, Sun Fairchild Beam, in this way: "We are not friends: he is my father, I am his son. We are silent when alone together...Yet we are connected: his past is my present, our present a foundation for the future." Dorothy Saunders Beam, a teacher and counselor in the Philadelphia public schools, was supportive of her son when he came out as a gay man while in college. After earning a B.A. from Franklin College in Franklin, Indiana, in 1976, Beam returned to Philadelphia. Until his death in 1988, he held a variety of jobs, including that of bookseller at Giovanni's Room, a Philadelphia gay, lesbian, and feminist bookstore.

Beam's writing focused on two major themes in late twentieth-century black gay literature: racism and the role of the black gay male in the African-American community. He became acutely aware of racism in the white gay community and consequently felt alienated from the mainstream gay culture of the late 1970s and early 1980s. In "Leaving the Shadows Behind," his introduction to *In the Life,* he decried the invisibility of black gay men in contemporary gay male literature: "By mid 1983 I had grown weary of reading literature by white gay men.... None of them spoke to me as a Black gay man." Beam, already strongly influenced by the writings of James Baldwin, drew further inspiration from lesbian and black feminist authors such as Audre Lorde, Barbara Smith, Cherrie Moraga, and Barbara Deming. Although he viewed the black community as an extension of his home life, he expressed frustration and anger at the invisibility of black gays and lesbians in the African-American community. In "Brother to Brother" he wrote: "When I speak of home, I mean not only the familial constellation from which I grew, but the entire Black community...Where is my reflection? I am most often rendered invisible, perceived as a threat to the family, or am tolerated if I am silent and inconspicuous. I cannot go home as who I am and that hurts me deeply."

In April of 1984 Beam presented Alyson Publications, a gay and lesbian press, with his idea for a black gay anthology to fill the void that he recognized in both gay and African-American literature. Although the manuscripts initially arrived slowly, Beam was eventually inundated with contributions. *In the Life,* which was published in October of 1986, contained 38 literary works by 24 authors. The selections included autobiographical pieces, essays, interviews, poems, and short fiction by a diverse group of contributors. The science fiction writer Samuel R. Delany was one of the few widely known contributors. But many contributors, including Melvin Dixon, Essex Hemphill, and Assotto Saint, would gain widespread praise for their literary works within a few years of publication of *In the Life.*

Several critics have noted the groundbreaking nature of *In the Life,* as well as its significance to gay literature. Phil Harper, reviewing *Brother to Brother: New Writings by Black Gay Men* in *Gay Community News* in 1991, acknowledged the significance of Beam's anthology: "The major achievement of *In the Life,* then, was to affirm for its readers that there exists a critical mass of black gay men who are engaged in important political and cultural work, and to present that work not as the independent efforts of isolated individuals, but rather as integrally related elements in a larger movement." Writing in the *Philadelphia Inquirer,* Don Belton explained, "Beam and *In the Life* helped open new areas of discussion, and, through that discussion, the experience of being black and gay in a racist and anti-sexual society richly contributed to the literature of the human spirit. *In the Life* was welcome evidence that the meaning of the often-lone witness of James Baldwin...had not been lost on a new generation."

At the time of his death on 27 December 1988, Beam was compiling material for a second literary collection by black gay men. His friend, Essex Hemphill, the writer and poet, took over the task of editing the anthology, which was published by Alyson Publications in 1991 under the title, *Brother to Brother: New Writings by Black Gay Men.* Dorothy Saunders Beam, who served as project manager for the second anthology, has worked to preserve her son's memory. Largely through her efforts, Joseph Beam's personal papers are held by the Schomburg Center for Research in Black Culture in New York City.

—Joseph M. Eagan

BECHDEL, Alison

Nationality: American cartoonist. **Born:** Lock Haven, Pennsylvania, 10 September 1960. **Education:** Simon's Rock, Great Barrington, Massachusetts, 1977-79; Oberlin College, Oberlin, Ohio, 1979-81, B.A. in studio arts and art history 1981. **Family:** Companion of Amy Rubin. **Career:** Proofreader, word processor, and volunteer for *Womanews,* 1981-85; full-time cartoonist, from 1985. **Awards:** Lambda Literary Award, for lesbian and gay humor, 1991, 1993, 1994. **Address:** P.O. Box 215, Jonesville, Vermont 05466, U.S.A.

WRITINGS

Cartoon Collections

Dykes to Watch Out For. Ithaca, New York, Firebrand Books, 1986.
More Dykes to Watch Out For. Ithaca, New York, Firebrand Books, 1988.
New, Improved! Dykes to Watch Out For. Ithaca, New York, Firebrand Books, 1990.
Dykes to Watch Out For: The Sequel. Ithaca, New York, Firebrand Books, 1992.
Gay Comics #19, edited by Andy Mangels. Portland, Oregon, Gay Comics, 1993.
Spawn of Dykes to Watch Out For. Ithaca, New York, Firebrand Books, 1993.
Unnatural Dykes to Watch Out For. Ithaca, New York, Firebrand Books, 1995.

Uncollected Cartoons

"Ms. Visits the Twenty-One-Year Reunion of a Consciousness-Raising Group," in *Ms.,* No. 4, July/August 1993.
"My Own Private Michigan Hell," in *Strange-Looking Exile #5,* edited by Robert Kirby. New Haven, Connecticut, Giant Ass Publishing, 1994.

"A Few Things Gay Men Have Always Wanted to Know about Lesbians," in *Long Road to Freedom: The Advocate History of the Gay and Lesbian Movement,* edited by Mark Thompson. New York, St. Martin's Press, 1994.

Other

Dykes to Watch Out For (annual calendar). Ithaca, New York, Firebrand Books, from 1990.

*

Critical Sources: "Dyke to Watch Out For: Talking to Cartoonist Alison Bechdel," in *Coming Up!,* December 1987, 7, 54; "A Cartoonist to Watch Out For" by Evan Kerr, in *Twin Cities Reader,* 17-23 August 1988; "Drawing on the Lesbian Community" by June Thomas, in *off our backs,* August/September 1988, 1, 14; "A Dyke to Watch Out For" by Ann Klauda, in *Advocate,* 13 September 1988, 50-51; "Cartoonist with a Cause" by Dave Matheny, in *Star Tribune,* 22 March 1990, 1, 7; "Not Playing it Straight" by Rob Walker, in *Images,* 19 July 1990, 18-19; "Alison Bechdel: A Cartoonist to Watch Out For" by Susan Denelsbeck, in *Utne Reader,* July/August 1990, 36; "Two Women to Watch Out For: Holly Tuttle and Alison Bechdel" by Harvey Pekar, in *Comics Journal,* No. 138, October 1990, 129-132; "Alison Bechdel: Cartoonist to Watch Out For" by Christopher Seymour, in *Guardian,* 29 May 1991, 20; "A Talk with Alison Bechdel" by Sage Russell, in *Out in the Mountains,* June 1991, 12-14; "A Cartoonist on the Brink" by Paula Routly, in *Vermont Times,* 9 January 1992, 11-12, 17; "Watch Out for Alison Bechdel" by Lyn Stoesen, in *Washington Blade,* 15 May 1992, 53, 55; "A Dyke to Watch Out For: Alison Bechdel" by Katie Brown, in *Deneuve,* January/February 1993, 35-39; "Strip Artist" by Dwight Garner, in *Boston Globe Magazine,* 15 August 1993, 15-17, 20-25; "Mutual Admiration Society" by Robin Bernstein, in *Washington Blade,* 18 February 1994, 43-44; "Where Women Rule" by Robin Bernstein, in *Harvard Gay and Lesbian Review,* September 1994, 20-23; "Alison Bechdel: I Would Love to Be the Lesbian Norman Rockwell" by Heather Stephenson, in *Vermont Sunday Magazine,* 4 June 1995, 4-6, 12-13; "Alison Bechdel" by Anne Rubenstein, in *Comics Journal,* No. 179, August 1995, 112-121; "Fire and Nice" by Heather Joslyn, in *City Paper,* 8 November 1995.

*   *   *

In 1994, a cartoonist's dream came true for Alison Bechdel. The Universal Press Syndicate, which manages cartoons for most of the major newspapers in the United States, invited her to create a daily strip. Most cartoonists spend years begging the Universal Press Syndicate even to glance at their work. For the Syndicate to call a cartoonist is almost unheard of—and for the press to approach an openly lesbian artist was nothing short of miraculous. But times were changing: a character had recently come out in Lynn Johnston's strip, *For Better or Worse,* and the Syndicate felt the mainstream was ready for a gay comic.

Bechdel considered the offer for several weeks, then turned the Syndicate down. "It's a wasteland, the daily funnies, a wasteland," Bechdel told Heather Stephenson in the *Vermont Sunday Magazine.* "And I'm not interested in speaking to the mainstream. What can you say?" With that decision, Bechdel re-affirmed her commitment to her chosen audience: the readers of the almost fifty gay and alternative papers which carry her highly successful bi-weekly comic, *Dykes to Watch Out For.*

When she was 11, Bechdel filled out a questionnaire that asked what she imagined she would be doing in 20 years. Bechdel wrote that she would be a cartoonist. Bechdel's parents, Helen Fontana Bechdel and Bruce Bechdel, both high school English teachers, encouraged their daughter's artistic talents. Bechdel's early influences included Edward Gorey, Norman Rockwell, *Mad Magazine,* and such illustrators of children's books as Hillary Knight, Dr. Seuss, and Richard Scarry.

As a child and young adult, Bechdel drew men exclusively. This focus worried Bechdel. "I thought I had some kind of weird psycho-sexual disorder," she told Katie Brown in *Deneuve.* "Ultimately, the reason I was only drawing men *was* because of a psycho-sexual disorder...Not mine...but our culture's." In mainstream comics, Bechdel told Anne Rubenstein in the *Comics Journal,* "Men get represented as 'universal' and women get represented as a sexualized subset, an aberration. [As a child,] I didn't want that. I wanted to be a regular human, I wanted to be a whole person, I wanted to be a subject in the world, not an object."

As a child, Bechdel reacted to misogyny by refusing to consider herself a girl. "To be a girl seemed like the worst, most humiliating thing in the world," she told Brown. "I thought of myself as something else—neither a boy nor a girl." At the age of 19, when she was a junior at Oberlin College in Ohio, Bechdel came out as a lesbian. According to Brown, that realization "awakened her to a greater truth: 'That must mean I'm a woman, then,'" Bechdel "acknowledged with surprise."

After Bechdel came out, her feminist consciousness impelled her to draw women. When she tried to do so, however, she "felt as though I was drawing with someone else's hand. It was awkward and alien for me, and I went through this period of not drawing much," she told Louise Rafkin in *Coming Up!* "I was ideologically opposed to drawing men, but I couldn't draw women," she told Brown. Then one day, Bechdel got the idea to try to draw lesbians rather than generic women. After some initial awkwardness, Bechdel found she could do it. As she told Rafkin, "After I drew a lesbian I really found my own hand."

Soon after that, Bechdel mailed a letter to a friend with a doodle in the margin. As she told Rubenstein, the doodle depicted "this whacked-out lesbian holding a coffee pot, and [I] called it 'Marianne, dissatisfied with the breakfast brew: Dykes To Watch Out For, plate number 27.' Even though this was the first one I ever drew. But something about it really held my interest, and I started doing a series of drawings of these whacked-out lesbians."

In 1983, New York's *Womanews,* for which Bechdel volunteered, ran two of Bechdel's cartoons in their Lesbian Pride issue. The experience thrilled Bechdel, and she drew many more single-panel comics. Soon after that, Bechdel received a fan letter from Nancy Bereano, who had just left her editing job at the Crossing Press to begin her own feminist press, Firebrand Books. Firebrand published Bechdel's first collection, *Dykes To Watch Out For,* in 1986, as well as the subsequent compilations and calendars.

Dykes To Watch Out For centers on a semi-utopian, multicultural lesbian community in a college town. Bechdel typically maintains several simultaneous plot lines. Although threads often focus on the personal lives of the characters, Bechdel consistently includes a broader political commentary. The strip advances in real time; the characters age and react to real events such as Audre Lorde's death and the confirmation of Supreme Court Justice Clarence Thomas. Bechdel's central character is Mo, whom Bechdel de-

scribed to Rubenstein as a "young white middle-class dyke, vaguely based on me.... Mo is the extreme embodiment of the lesbian-feminist social conscience." Bechdel described Mo to Brown as "guilt-ridden, anxious, judgmental, very critical and [possessing] very high standards."

Bereano described Bechdel to Brown as a "very loving critic of the lesbian community.... She's not sentimental. She's a real observer." Bechdel's style has been hailed by both readers and critics. Susan Denelsbeck wrote in *Utne Reader,* "Regular readers know to look carefully at each panel—background activity, conversations off to the side of the main story line, the book titles on Mo's nightstand are all apt to offer a hilarious subtext. Bechdel's drawings are so fluid, her mastery of facial expressions and body movements so complete, that her characters almost appear to be about to move."

In the *Boston Globe,* Dwight Garner praised Bechdel's work as "on par with anything Garry Trudeau has done; in terms of depicting sheer human complexity, it may be in a league with Art Speigelman's *Maus* books." And highly respected fellow comics writer Harvey Pekar called Bechdel "good at differentiating people visually in her unpretentious, economical drawings; she has a sharp eye for what's essential and a good memory and uses them to make her characters come alive." Pekar further described *Dykes To Watch Out For* as "entertaining and, unlike most comic strips, edifying and substantive. She refuses to dilute her message to gain popularity, which is one reason she deserves to be popular."

And popular Bechdel is. Her books and calendars have sold over 150,000 copies; her side business selling *Dykes To Watch Out For* t-shirts, mugs, and other items helps support her. She regularly lectures and presents a slide show on her work at various universities. Her strip runs in almost 50 newspapers in the United States, United Kingdom, and Canada; it has been officially translated into French and German, and bootleg copies have surfaced in Danish, Finnish, Italian, and Japanese. Bechdel has won three prestigious Lambda Literary Awards in the category of lesbian and gay humor.

Bechdel starts the process of creating each strip by reading magazines and newspapers to see what issues are affecting the community, and what people are wearing. She then consults a chart on which she tracks the events in her characters' lives, to see whose plot needs attention. Next, she writes a complete script for the strip. She then draws a rough sketch, which she traces and refines. She uses herself or others as models, frequently utilizing mirrors or polaroids. After she goes over the sketch again, she traces it with a light box onto bristol board. Finally, she inks the cartoon.

In addition to *Dykes To Watch Out For,* Bechdel has completed several autobiographical stories which can be found in *Strange-Looking Exile #5, Gay Comics #19,* and *Dykes To Watch Out For: The Sequel.* From 1988 to 1990, the *Advocate* commissioned her to create *Servants to the Cause,* a strip about a six-member collective of a gay and lesbian newspaper.

Bechdel has also contributed to the development of Diane DiMassa's comic book, *Hothead Paisan: Homicidal Lesbian Terrorist.* DiMassa, who calls Bechdel "Your Majesty," told Robin Bernstein in the *Washington Blade,* "I saw Bechdel's slide show at Yale...before I ever started doing *Hothead.* I had already been a fan of her work, and I went up to her and told her I was doing these recovery greeting cards. She said, 'Oh, I'd love to see your stuff. Send it to me!' So I did. And she sent me back the greatest letter. It was really encouraging to me, and at that point in my life, it kind of meant everything. It wasn't long after that I started *Hothead*."

Dykes To Watch Out For and *Hothead Paisan* remain linked: the artists regularly nod to each other in their strips (for example, a character in *Dykes* buys a copy of *Hothead*), and they often inadvertently introduce similar topics, such as transgenderism, simultaneously. Bechdel told Heather Joslyn in the *City Paper* that DiMassa "keeps me on my toes.... I might be the superego of the lesbian community, but DiMassa is the id."

The balance and thoughtfulness in *Dykes To Watch Out For,* however, suggests more ego than either superego or id. Bechdel's work provides a beautiful, intelligent, and witty mirror for the lesbian community. In her own way, Bechdel is writing history as she is making it.

—Robin Bernstein

BELL, Arthur (Irving)

Pseudonyms: Wrote as Arthur Irving for *Gay Power.* **Nationality:** American journalist, activist, and author of nonfiction. **Born:** Brooklyn, New York, 14 November 1939. **Education:** Attended a commercial high school in Montreal, Quebec. **Family:** Companion of Arthur Evans, 1964-70. **Career:** Worked in publicity, for children's books, Viking Press, Inc., 1960-68, and Random House, Inc., 1968-70; reporter, *Village Voice,* 1970-84. Co-founder, Gay Activists Alliance, 1969; frequent contributor, *Cosmopolitan, Esquire, Gay, Gay Power,* and *Playboy.* **Died:** New York City, of complications from diabetes, 2 June 1984.

Writings

Nonfiction

Dancing the Gay Lib Blues: A Year in the Homosexual Liberation Movement. New York, Simon and Schuster, 1971.
"The Baths Life Gets Respectability," in *Gay Source: A Catalog for Men,* edited by Dennis Sanders. New York, Coward, McCann, and Geoghegan, 1977.
Kings Don't Mean a Thing: The John Knight Murder Case. New York, William Morrow, 1978.

*

Biography: *The Gay Militants* by Donn Teal, New York, Stein and Day, 1971; "Bell, Arthur," in *Contemporary Authors,* Vols. 85-88, edited by Frances Carol Locher, Detroit, Gale, 1980, 48-49; "Arthur Bell, 51, a Columnist, Homosexual Rights Activist," in *New York Times* (New York), 4 June 1984; "A Death in the Family" by David Schneiderman, in *The Village Voice,* 12 June 1984, 3; "Arthur Bell: Two or Three Things We Loved About Him" in *The Village Voice,* 26 June 1984, 10-11; "Bell, Arthur" in *Contemporary Authors,* Vol. 112, edited by Hal May, Detroit, Gale, 1985, 54; *Stonewall* by Martin Duberman, New York, Dutton, 1993.

Interviews: "Arthur Bell" by Charles Ortleb, in *Christopher Street* (New York), Vol. 3, No. 7, February 1979, 61-63.

Critical Sources: Review of *Dancing the Gay Lib Blues* by Gene D. Phillips, in *America* (New York), Vol. 126, No. 1, 8 January 1972, 26; "Lesbians Are Homosexuals Too" by Jill Johnston, in *New York Times Book Review* (New York), 20 February 1972, 5, 10, 12, 14; review of *Dancing the Gay Lib Blues* by Joan K. Marshall, in *Library Journal* (New York), Vol. 97, No. 11, 1 June 1972, 2109-2110; review of *Kings Don't Mean a Thing* by Stephen H. Wolf, in *Library Journal* (New York), Vol. 103, No. 16, 15 September 1978, 1761; "Homicide" by Evan Hunter, in *New York Times Book Review* (New York), 17 December 1978, 20-21; review of *Kings Don't Mean a Thing* by Martin Duberman, in *New Republic* (Washington, D.C.), Vol. 180, No. 1, 6 January 1979, 30-32.

*   *   *

Arthur Bell was a prominent New York City journalist and gay political activist from the aftermath of the 1969 Stonewall riots until his death in 1984. He was a co-founder of the Gay Activists Alliance (GAA) and one of the first openly gay men to be featured on a full-length television program in the United States. Through his writings for *Gay Power* and *The Village Voice,* he helped to publicize the politics and culture of the emerging gay liberation movement that emanated from the Greenwich Village neighborhood of New York City. His account of his first year as a gay political radical, *Dancing the Gay Lib Blues: A Year in the Homosexual Liberation Movement,* was one of the first books about the gay liberation movement published by a mainstream American publisher.

Bell was born on 14 November 1939, in Brooklyn, New York. His father was a successful clothing manufacturer, and his mother was a designer. The family moved to Montreal when Arthur was in junior high school. At age 17, he had his initial homosexual experience in a Montreal movie theater. While visiting his grandparents in Brooklyn shortly thereafter, he discovered some of the Manhattan bathhouses and bars where homosexual men gathered in the 1950s. He moved to New York City in 1960 and worked in publicity for children's books for Viking Press, Inc., and later Random House, Inc., for the next decade. In 1964 he began a relationship with Arthur Evans, a film distributor who eventually pursued a Ph.D. in philosophy at Columbia University.

In the aftermath of the Stonewall riots of June 1969, Bell and Evans joined the Gay Liberation Front (GLF), a radical homosexual organization committed to a variety of leftist causes. Both men, however, quickly became dissatisfied with GLF's mission and tactics. A group of local gay activists joined Evans and Bell at the latter's Greenwich Village apartment on 21 December 1969, where they formally adopted a charter and elected officers for a new group, the Gay Activists Alliance (GAA). Like many American homophile organizations of the 1950s and 1960s, GAA focused exclusively on homosexual issues. But, it had an open membership, a militant agenda, and a confrontational style that differentiated it from many earlier homophile groups. As GAA's first publicity chair, Bell used the skills and contacts that he had developed in publishing to promote the organization in the media. Using the pseudonym "Arthur Irving," he wrote a column publicizing GAA activities in the New York City biweekly newspaper *Gay Power.* New York television station WOR-TV televised a three-part feature presentation in November 1970 on Bell's life and work as a gay activist.

The year 1970 was a turning point in Bell's life. He resigned his Random House position to devote himself full-time to the gay liberation movement and to writing. His first *Village Voice* piece, "Gay Is Political and Democrats Agree," appeared on 13 August 1970. He eventually wrote 179 articles for *The Village Voice* covering a variety of topics, including gay liberation, New York's gay community, entertainment, and the arts. He became best known, however, for his coverage of murder in the American gay male community. The most sensational case that Bell wrote about was the brutal 1975 murder in Philadelphia of John Knight III, the heir-apparent to the Knight media empire, by his lover, Felix Melendez, a hustler who was subsequently murdered by one of his own accomplices. Beginning in 1976, Bell also wrote a weekly *Village Voice* column, "Bell Tells," that focused on crime, entertainment, nightlife, and gossip. He contributed articles to several periodicals, including *Cosmopolitan, Esquire, Gay* (New York), *Playboy*, and the *New York Times*. He also wrote a chapter entitled "The Baths Life Gets Respectability" for a 1977 gay anthology, *Gay Source: A Catalog For Men*. By the late 1970s, however, Bell had become a controversial figure among lesbians and gays because of his fascination with the sordid gay netherworld of street hustlers, bathhouses, and bars.

Bell wrote two nonfiction books in the 1970s. *Dancing the Gay Lib Blues: A Year in the Homosexual Liberation Movement* was an autobiographical work that provided Bell's personal insights into the GAA's early history. Reviewing the book in the *New York Times Book Review*, Jill Johnston commented, "Bell as reporter and activist blends the story of the civil-libertarian radical homosexual organization he helped to found with the tale of his hairy romance with one of the other leaders." *Dancing the Gay Lib Blues* remains one of the most important documents written by a gay male about the post-Stonewall gay liberation movement in America. It has often been compared with three other titles published in 1971: Donn Teal's *The Gay Militants*, John Murphy's *Homosexual Liberation: A Personal View*, and *Homosexual: Oppression and Liberation*, by Dennis Altman. Bell's second book, *Kings Don't Mean a Thing: The John Knight Murder Case*, amplifies his *Village Voice* pieces on the Knight and Melendez murders. Writing in *The New Republic*, Martin Duberman commented, "The book should be valued for what it is: the proverbial 'good read,' stylish and titillating."

Arthur Bell died of complications from diabetes in New York City on 2 June 1984. His writings will be remembered as a chronicle of New York's gay community from the aftermath of the Stonewall riots to the onset of the AIDS epidemic.

—Joseph M. Eagan

BENAVENTE, Jacinto

Nationality: Spanish playwright, poet, and lecturer. **Born:** Madrid, 12 August 1866; son of the pediatric disease specialist Mariano Benavente. **Education:** Colegio de San José and Instituto de San Isidro, 1871-82; Universidad Central de Madrid, 1882-85. **Career:** Actor, in the company of María Tubau, 1890; editor of *Vida literaria* and *Madrid Cómico*; contributor to periodicals, including *Alma española, El arte del teatro, Ilustración española, El imparcial, La lectura, Helios,* and *Revista contemporánea español*;

touring director, Teatro español. **Awards:** Nobel Prize in Literature, 1922; Great Cross of Alfonso el Sabio, and Madrid City Council's Favorite Son, 1924; honorary member, Spanish Royal Academy, 1946; Mariano de Cavia Prize for journalism, 1948. **Died:** Madrid, of complications from a heart condition, 14 July 1954.

WRITINGS

Selected Plays (produced in Madrid, unless otherwise noted)

El nido ajeno (1894).
Gente conocida (1896).
La comida de las fieras (1898).
El hombrecito (1903).
Rosas de otoño (1905).
Los intereses creados (1907).
La malquerida (1913).
La ciudad alegre y confiada (1916).
El mal que nos hacen (1917).
La vestal de Occidente (1919).
Una señora (1920).
De muy buena familia (1931).
El rival de su mujer (produced Buenos Aires, 1933).
Por salvar el amor (1954).

Selected Nonfiction

Cartas de mujeres. Madrid, T. Franco-Española, 1893.
Teatro del pueblo. Madrid, Fernando Fe, 1909.
De sobremesa. Madrid, Hernando, 1910-16.
Recuerdos y olvidos: Memorias. Madrid, Aguilar, 1962.

Other

Versos (poetry). Madrid, T. Franco-Española, 1893.
Vilanos (short story). Madrid, I. Fortanet, 1905.

*

Critical Sources: *Teatro Español Contemporáneo* by Manuel Bueno, Madrid, 1909; *Plays* by Jacinto Benavente, introduction by John Garrett Underhill, Scribner's, 1917, vii-xxv; *Tres Comedias* by Jacinto Benavente, introduction by John Van Horne, Heath, 1918, xi-xxxi; "Benaventiana" by John Garrett Underhill, in *Plays* by Jacinto Benavente, Scribner's, second series, 1919, vii-xviii; *Jacinto Benavente* by Federico de Onís, New York, Instituto de las Españas, 1923; *Jacinto Benavente* by Walter Starkie, London, Oxford University Press, 1924; *De su vida y de su obra* by ángel Lázaro, Paris, Agencia Mundial de Librería, 1925; "Modernists: Benavente" by L.A. Warren, in *Modern Spanish Literature: A Comprehensive Survey of the Novelists, Poets, Dramatists, and Essayists from the Eighteenth Century to the Present Day* by L.A. Warren, Vol. 2, Brentano's Ltd., 1929, 556-65; *The Modernismo of Jacinto Benavente* by Marcia Simpson Lewis, Urbana, University of Illinois, 1962; *Jacinto Benavente* by Marcelino C. Peñuelas, New York, Twayne Publishers, 1968; "A Century of Spanish Theatre" by Alfredo Marquerie, in *Topic* (Washington and Jefferson College), Vol. 8, No. 15, spring 1968, 30-8; *Las mejores novelas contemporáneas* by Joaquín de Entrambasaguas, Barcelona,

Planeta, 1970, 547; *The Social, Moral, and Political Thought of Jacinto Benavente* by Glafyra Rangel Fernández Ennis, University of Michigan, 1974; *Benavente and the Spanish Panorama* by Robert Louis Sheehan, Valencia, 1976; *Una temprana guía gay: Granada (Guía emocional), de Gregorio Martínez Sierra (1911)* by Daniel Eisenberg, in *Erotismo en las letras hispánicas. Aspectos, Modos y Fronteras,* edited by Luce López-Baralt and Francisco Márquez Villanueva, Mexico, El Colegio de México, 1995, 111-20.

*   *   *

Jacinto Benavente emerged from the upper strata of twentieth-century Spanish society to be both its quintessential member and greatest critic. Primarily focusing on drama to express his motivations, Benavente developed what is known as the "theater of ideas," which emphasized character development and dialogue over plot. Benavente's drama is a firsthand account of the profound conflicts and ambiguities regarding the evolving social issues of his society. Despite a lack of explicit homosexual references in his work, Benavente deals with the complexities of early twentieth-century gay culture through a subversive language of steadily intensifying suggestions. In his own way, Benavente was able to move to the forefront of modernist thinking and lead in the primary phase of gay literary expression.

It has been said that Benavente's main qualifying achievement for the 1922 Nobel Prize in Literature was his schism from the work of his famous predecessor, Jose Echegaray. Benavente moved away from the artificiality and melodrama of Echegaray toward more direct social criticisms, which were brought to life by characters who were neither inherently good nor evil. He invented his own form of dramatic expression which was unique in the diminished role of exterior action, and redirected energy toward subtle psychological developments in dialogue. Benavente's dialogue displayed a sense of intimate yet satirical conversation, thereby creating a more realistic picture of modern life. It is important to note that Benavente's uniquely intimate characterizations are made possible mostly because of his own ties to the society upon which his writings focus. Perhaps indicative of his own internal struggles, and relevant to gay thought of his time, Benavente's principal characters share a common search for identity and a place in the world. They are usually depicted as struggling between individual reality and the social mores of a dominant culture, whose hypocrisy is an equally prevailing theme.

There is much debate as to whether Benavente was attempting to reform or support the social issues of dominant early twentieth- century culture, but the former is more widely accepted. He frequently satirized traditional upper middle-class values, though he was considered by many to be its most representative member. Benavente exemplified the typical Madrid gentleman, a figure which appears to be the basis for many of his male characters. He was known to have been elegant, well-dressed, and courteous. Benavente frequented theaters and cafés, where he socialized with the Spanish elite and contemporary artists, both invaluable sources of inspiration for his work. Benavente's critics frequently attacked his personal indulgences and wealth as manifestations of moral depravity. It was a popular thought of his period that one who wrote of immorality, was him or herself lacking in morals.

Though many criticized Benavente's aristocratic associations, it was in fact his own relatively wealthy upbringing which gave him the proper perspective for writing comedies in which emotional and not economic problems were central. His father's professional and personal contacts initially gained Benavente access to the theatrical world. But this help came only after his father's death. While alive, Benavente's father tried to redirect his energy away from drama, and was depicted by his son as being somewhat cold and unsentimental. Ángel Lázaro, an expert on Benavente's drama, stated in his *De su vida y de su obra* that Benavente's frequent depictions of children who suffer because of adult indifference reflect his own memories. Benavente's father died when the writer was 19 years old, leaving him enough money and freedom to dedicate himself completely to his literary work, and develop socially as a young man of the early twentieth century.

Central to Benavente's literary maturity and unique social awareness was his participation in the "tertulias," or conversation groups of his time period. He was the best known and most regular member of the "tertulias" of writers who met at urban cafés. While together, they debated important social issues, tested creative ideas, and honed their rhetorical skills. It was at these intellectual meetings that Benavente developed the intimate conversation and intense dialogues which became a focal point in the structure of his work. One early critic of Benavente's drama, Walter Starkie, in his *Jacinto Benavente* compares him to other early modern gay writers such as Oscar Wilde in his "mastery of aphorisms and basic ability to comprehend the nature of the art of conversation." This skill was useful to Benavente in the development of a conscious rhetorical strategy, which expressed his complex social observations without the need for direct explanation.

Benavente brought to Spain a more liberal and realistic drama that sharply contrasted with the typical romantic literature which preceded it. He studied European trends and translated them into the context of modern Spain. Benavente introduced innovative humor into Spanish theater, helping it to evolve along with the rest of the continent. There was much more to his humor than entertainment, however; as stated by Manuel Bueno in *Teatro Español Contemporáneo,* "laughing at social fallacies combats them better than sermons." Humor was a powerful tool for Benavente in bringing to light the ills of his society.

Benavente's drama has, as its principle goal, both the probing into and development of an individual character in relation to the world around it. He achieves this effect by conveying a series of implicit suggestions regarding the underlying motivations of an individual, which seldomly end with any definitive conclusion. The pains and tragedies within his portrayals, both implied and explicit, helped to awaken his readers to the need for liberation from the confines of traditional Spanish society. Benavente pushed for the freedom to choose one's individual relationship to society. This concept made his work important to the newly emerging homosexual community of the twentieth century, struggling for its place in literary culture.

Though explicit homosexuality was largely absent from Benavente's plays, nontraditional love and relationships can be seen at the center of almost all of his works. These relationships presented readers and audiences with a constant struggle between the artifice of early twentieth century morality and individual experience. Benavente emphasizes tolerance at the comic expense of notably inflexible foil characters. In Benavente's *El nido ajeno,* he bewilders readers with the oblique suggestion of a secret love between a brother-in-law and sister-in-law. This relationship is implied to the reader, and suspected by the very traditional husband, but is only realized by the principle characters at the end.

Of greater importance is the shroud of sexual ambiguity surrounding the character of the brother-in-law. He is depicted as an exemplary gentleman of the twentieth century, wealthy, well dressed, and favored by many ladies. Only the crucial question of sexual partnership remains ambiguous. Possibly more than coincidence, the intimacies of Benavente's own life were known but seldomly written about. Benavente was the subject of continual rumors regarding his homosexuality. He responded to frequent comments regarding his sexuality with little affect. Marcia Simpson Lewis, in *The Modernismo of Jacinto Benavente,* quotes him as once saying that "men should be judged from above, from the forehead to the heart."

Benavente suppressed the tension of sexual innuendo in his writings, possibly in an attempt to shelter his audience and thereby his career. He was cautious not to directly provoke controversy, by promoting a sense of skepticism in his characterizations, but nothing more. Yet the insinuation of homosexuality is easily derived from his play *De muy buena familia.* Covered in the sexual ambiguity of the character Manolo's relationship with a secret circle of friends, suggestions of some hidden misunderstood reality escalate almost to the point of bursting into the text. His observations of human nature were critical, yet he made no attempt to make any definitive moral judgments. Benavente's subversive techniques were crucial during the early twentieth-century when behavior conventionally thought of as immoral, such as homosexuality, was persecuted by both the Spanish church and legal sectors. In fact, the literary world of early twentieth century Spain is now quite noted for its hidden allusions to homosexuality. Benavente himself not only was active in this practice, but also supported the works of others such as Gregorio Martínez Sierra, with whom he was known to have had an intimate relationship, who published the first known "coded" homosexual touristic guide. At the turn of the century, concerns of censorship in predominantly Roman Catholic Spain could have easily become threatening if dramatic depictions were deemed too true to life.

Benavente's writings placed him at the threshold of early twentieth century literary movements, and thereby were secured among the initial steps towards a definitive gay literary culture. His drama is important in that through his "theater of ideas" he was able to express the need for a cultural and moral revolution in his society. Benavente's ingenious use of innuendo gave him the freedom to promote deep social criticisms in what was one of Europe's most morally conservative nations and time periods.

—Alberto Romero, Jr.

BISHOP, Elizabeth

Nationality: American poet. **Born:** Worcester, Massachusetts, 8 February 1911. **Education:** Walnut Hill boarding school, Natick, Massachusetts, 1927-30; Vassar College, Poughkeepsie, New York, 1930-1934. **Family:** Companions included Louise Crane, Marjorie Carr Stevens, Lota de Macedo Soares, and Alice Methfessel. **Career:** Consultant in Poetry, Library of Congress, 1949-1950; instructor. University of Washington, Seattle, Washington, 1966, and Harvard University, Cambridge, Massachusetts, 1971-75; visiting professor, New York University, 1977. **Awards:** Houghton Mifflin Poetry Prize Fellowship, for *North & South,* 1945; Guggenheim

fellowship, 1947; American Academy of Arts and Letters award, 1950; Lucy Martin Donnelly Fellowship, Bryn Mawr College, 1951; Shelley Memorial Award, 1952; inducted into National Institute of Arts and Letters, 1954; Pulitzer Prize, for *North & South/ A Cold Spring,* 1955; Partisan Review Fellowship, 1956; Amy Lowell Travelling Fellowship, 1957; Academy of American Poets Fellowship, 1964; Merrill-Ingram Award, 1968-69; National Book Award, for *The Complete Poems,* 1969; St. Botolph Club Arts Award, Boston, 1975; Neustadt International Prize for Literature, 1976; National Book Critics Circle Award, for *Geography III,* 1977. **Died:** Boston, Massachusetts, 6 October 1979.

WRITINGS

Poetry

North & South. Boston, Houghton Mifflin, 1946.
Poems: North & South—A Cold Spring. Boston, Houghton Mifflin, 1955.
Poems. London, Chatto and Windus, 1956.
Questions of Travel. New York, Farrar, Strauss, and Giroux, 1965.
Selected Poems. London, Chatto and Windus, 1967.
The Ballad of the Burglar of Babylon. New York, Farrar, Strauss, and Giroux, 1968.
The Complete Poems. New York, Farrar, Strauss, and Giroux, 1969.
Geography III. New York, Farrar, Strauss, and Giroux, 1976.

Collected Works

Collected Poems: 1972-1979. New York, Farrar, Strauss, and Giroux, 1983.
The Collected Prose. New York, Farrar, Strauss, and Giroux, 1984.

Editor and Translator

The Diary of "Helena Morley." New York, Farrar, Strauss, and Cudahy, 1957; with additional foreword, New York, The Ecco Press, 1977.
With Emanuel Brasil, *An Anthology of Twentieth-Century Brazilian Poetry.* Middletown, Connecticut, Wesleyan University Press, 1972.

Other

With the editors of *Life, Brazil* (nonfiction). Life World Library, New York, Time Incorporated, 1962.
One Art: Letters by Elizabeth Bishop, edited by Robert Giroux. New York, Farrar, Strauss, and Giroux, 1994.

*

Manuscript Collections: Vassar College Library, Poughkeepsie, New York.

Biography: *Elizabeth Bishop: The Biography of a Poetry* by Lorrie Goldensohn, New York, Columbia University Press, 1992; *Elizabeth Bishop: Life and the Memory of It* by Brett Millier, Berkeley, University of California Press, 1993; *Remembering Elizabeth Bishop: An Oral Biography* by Gary Fountain and Peter Brazeau, Amherst, University of Massachusetts Press, 1994.

Interviews: Interview by Ashley Brown, in *Shenandoah,* winter 1966, 3-19; "Poets," in *Time,* 2 June 1967; interview by Eileen Farley, in *University of Washington Daily* (Seattle), 28 May 1974; interview by Anna Quindlen, in *New York Post,* 3 April 1976; interview by Jim Bross, in *Norman Transcript* (Oklahoma), 11 April 1976; interview by Margo Jefferson, in *Newsweek,* 31 January 1977; interview by Leslie Hanscom, in *Newsday,* 6 February 1977; interview by David W. McCullough, in *Book-of-the-Month Club News,* May 1977, reprinted in *People, Books, and Book People,* New York, Harmony Books, 1981, 20-24; interview by George Starbuck, in *Ploughshares,* Vol. 3, Nos. 3 and 4, 1977, 11-29; interview by Elizabeth Spires, in *Vassar Quarterly,* winter 1979, reprinted in a different form, in *Paris Review,* summer 1981.

Bibliography: *Elizabeth Bishop: A Bibliography 1927-1979* by Candace W. MacMahon, Charlottesville, University Press of Virginia, 1980.

Critical Sources: "Elizabeth Bishop: Questions of Memory" by David Kalstone, in *Five Temperaments,* New York, Oxford University Press, 1977; *Elizabeth Bishop and Her Art,* edited by Lloyd Schwartz and Sybil P. Estess, Ann Arbor, University of Michigan Press, 1983; "The Eye of the Outsider: Elizabeth Bishop's *Complete Poems, 1927-1979*" by Adrienne Rich, in *Blood, Bread, and Poetry: Selected Prose 1979-1985,* New York, Norton, 1986; *Becoming a Poet: Elizabeth Bishop with Marianne Moore and Robert Lowell* by David Kalstone, edited by Robert Hemenway, New York, Farrar, Strauss, and Giroux, 1989; "Elizabeth Bishop and Brazil" by Lloyd Schwartz, in *New Yorker,* Vol. 67, No. 32, 30 September 1991, 85; "The Points of Her Compass" by Anthony Hecht, in *Washington Post Book World,* 21 March 1993, 9; "A Slight Transvestite Twist: Elizabeth Biship's Lifetime 'Impersonation of an Ordinary Woman'" by Sue Russell, in *Lambda Book Report,* Vol. 3, No. 10, May/June 1993, 8-10; "Elizabeth Bishop" by Frank Bidart, in *Threepenny Review,* No. 58, summer 1994, 6-7; "Elizabeth Bishop's Extraterrestriality" by Vijay Seshadri, in *Threepenny Review,* No. 60, winter 1995, 18-19; "Elizabeth Bishop" by Meg Schoerke, in *The Gay and Lesbian Literary Heritage,* edited by Claude J. Summers, New York, Henry Holt, 1995, 105-107.

*   *   *

"The art of losing isn't hard to master," wrote Elizabeth Bishop in the villanelle "One Art," which appeared in her last book, *Geography III* (1976). The losses the poem documents range from familiar objects (keys, watch) to places (three houses, two cities, two rivers, a continent) and finally to people. The "you" whose loss would be a "disaster" was Alice Methfessel, Bishop's lover and companion in the last years of her life. Looking back through the lens of this little poem, one sees a life marked not only by loss but also by the ability to frame it with such clarity and precision that the words themselves remain when everything else is gone.

In the years since her death in 1979, the poetry of Elizabeth Bishop has gained more attention than it did in her lifetime. A "poet's poet" admired by her peers, she won all the major awards but was only known to a handful of discriminating readers. This resurgence of interest has occurred with the details of her life as well, adding a certain irony for a poet who was famous for her reticence. Elizabeth Bishop was born in Worcester, Massachusetts, in 1911. Her father died of Bright's disease when she was eight months old, and her mother, Gertrude Boomer Bishop, was institutionalized for mental illness when Bishop was only five. Bishop spent her early years in Great Village, Nova Scotia, among her relatives from the Boomer family. After the hospitalization, the young girl never saw her mother again, but she could not escape the memory of this woman's raging presence, nor can any reader of her autobiographical short story, which begins: "A scream, the echo of a scream, hangs over that Nova Scotian Village. No one hears it; it hangs there forever..." ("In the Village").

Bishop spent her remaining childhood years shuttling between relatives in Canada and Massachusetts. Later, while she attended Vassar College, she would pass the hospital where her mother was committed each time she took the train back to school. It is not surprising that someone with so little security of person or place in her early life would come to value her own privacy to such a high degree, nor is it strange that those who knew her would be equally protective, even after her death. The gay poet Frank Bidart, a close friend and confidant in Bishop's later years, expressed what others must feel in the face of recent biographical disclosures:

> ...almost nothing I've said about Elizabeth's life would she want said. That's why, after her death, I decided I didn't want to be the source of anything that appeared in print about her drinking, sexual life, etc. But the intensity of interest in her work, and the nature of contemporary biography, made revelations that she would have found intolerable in her lifetime inevitable. I just don't want to be their source. What I *could* do was treat these subjects in as un-flamboyant, adequate a way as I was capable, once they had already become part of the record. At this point, Elizabeth would gain nothing from my silence.

This poet, who once said there could never be enough closets, has now been exposed for all to see. We know at least a few of the details about her sexual life. Some of the names and faces have entered the public record, while other pieces of information remain in the realm of innuendo or rumor. Was Bishop the model for the lesbian character in her Vassar friend Mary McCarthy's novel a clèf, *The Group*? Was she an alcoholic, or did she simply drink a little too much? When did she have her first sexual experience with a woman? Did she occasionally sleep with men after her early twenties? Biographers, scholars, fans, and Bishop's acquaintances continue to debate these issues and others.

What we do know is that she moved around a lot, first to New York after graduating from Vassar, and, after a period of extended European travel, to Key West, the site of one of her three lost houses from "One Art." In 1951, with money obtained through a fellowship from Bryn Mawr, she planned to tour Brazil but an allergic reaction to the cashew fruit soon after her arrival left her ailing and under the care of Lota de Macedo Soares, a friend whom she had met earlier in New York. When Lota invited her to stay indefinitely at her home near Petropolis, called Samambaia, Bishop was taken by the generosity of the offer. For Lota, the attraction seemed to be immediate, but for Bishop, that sense of gratitude later grew into love.

The years in Brazil were productive for Bishop, who was known for her perfectionism and deliberation. Between 1951 and 1965 she published two books of poetry, two important autobiographical stories, a translation from the Portuguese of *The Diary of "Helena Morley,"* and a Time/Life book on Brazil. Among the poems from this period found in her book of *Collected Poems* is "The Shampoo," a love poem for Lota, which ends with these lines:

The shooting stars in your black hair
in bright formation
are flocking where,
so straight, so soon?
—Come, let me wash it in this big tin basin,
battered and shiny like the moon.

Unfortunately, this happy period ended in tragedy, when Lota, suffering from ill health and exhaustion after an extended work assignment in Brazil, committed suicide in 1967. Bishop kept a home in Ouro Prêto, Brazil, named Casa Mariana, after the poet Marianne Moore, and lived there for short periods from Lota's death until 1971. Samambaia and Casa Mariana are the second and third of Bishop's lost houses, and South America presumably the lost continent.

For a good deal of her life, Bishop was able to live on an inheritance from the father she never knew. Toward the end of her time in Brazil, however, the money grew scarce, and she was more dependent on funding from grants and fellowships. Eventually, she began to accept teaching offers, starting at the University of Washington in Seattle, and later at Harvard. It was there that she met Alice Methfessel, a young woman who managed student housing where Bishop first resided in Cambridge. Although their relationship hit some trouble spots in the period between 1970 up until Bishop's death in 1979, Methfessel, like Bishop, was an adventurous traveller, and the two enjoyed several memorable trips together, including one to the Galapagos Islands.

Bishop held staunchly to her position against "segregated" anthologies during her lifetime, feeling that they were inevitably patronizing toward women. Literature was literature, she argued, and should not be divided into sub-groups. Because her estate continues to honor her wishes, Bishop's poems will not be found in popular anthologies such as *No More Masks* or *Gay and Lesbian Poetry in Our Times.* Nevertheless, the word about her lesbian relationships is available in biography and criticism, allowing intrepid readers the opportunity to read her poems in the context of this new information.

The revisionist view of Bishop concentrates primarily on the dark edges behind the seemingly polite and manicured poems of the white-gloved "lady poet" (known always as Miss Bishop) who wrote them. Writers like Adrienne Rich, in her landmark essay, "The Eye of the Outsider," argued that as a narrator Bishop characteristically places herself on the outside looking in as a gesture of affinity with the disenfranchised, which would, in turn, include herself as a lesbian. One poem where this stance is evident is "Pink Dog," written in 1979 and published posthumously in *Collected Poems,* in which Bishop deftly focuses the reader's attention on a lone, hairless dog amid the Carnival festivities in Rio de Janeiro:

Oh, never have I seen a dog so bare!
Naked and pink, without a single hair...
Startled, the passersby draw back and stare.
Of course they're mortally afraid of rabies.
You are not mad; you have a case of scabies
but look intelligent. Where are your babies?

Another lesbian-oriented approach to the work of Elizabeth Bishop is to look closely at her direct influences among other women poets, especially Marianne Moore. The mentor relationship can thus be seen as a kind of courtship dance in which each personal gift or piece of advice contributes to the dynamic of the whole. Indeed, Bishop offers an inventory of those real-life gifts from herself to Moore in the essay, "Efforts of Affection." Likewise, Bishop's "mentoring" of the slightly younger poet, May Swenson, has a similar aspect, as evidenced in Swenson's poem, "Dear Elizabeth."

Readers have also taken an interest in finding unpublished poems or drafts in which lesbian sex and identity are more clearly presented. Biographer and critic Lorrie Goldensohn, for example, has looked at a sheaf of papers Bishop carried with her to Brazil, which included love poems apparently written in Key West, including one that begins, "It is marvellous to wake up together / At the same minute..." Even in this poem, however, the dominant pronoun is "you," and no physical hints are provided related to the sex of the lovers. Goldensohn wisely notes, as do other critics, that it is not so much that Bishop did not write lesbian love poems as that she seldom wrote any love poems at all. As a traditionally female genre, the love poem was suspect and limiting, especially for poets like Bishop, Moore, and Swenson, with a broad range of interests in science and art.

Consequently, we must look for more subtle instances of a lesbian presence. They can be found in dramatic monologues like "Crusoe in England," where the male speaker has the opportunity to express his affection for his deceased male companion, Friday, and in other poems in *Collected Poems* that contain elements of the gay male sensibility, like "Exchanging Hats," which begins:

Unfunny uncles who insist
in trying on a lady's hat,
—oh, even if the joke falls flat,
we share your slight transvestite twist

Poems such as this make it clear that, although Bishop might have been reticent about announcing her lesbian status to the world, she was in no way unfamiliar with the lingo. Bishop's poetry, and her qualities as a friend, have been especially important to such gay male poets as James Merrill, who uttered perhaps the most frequently quoted words about Bishop regarding her "instinctive, modest life-long impersonations of an ordinary woman." Likewise, allusions to Bishop show up in the work of other contemporary gay writers, such as John Weir's novel *The Irreversible Decline of Eddie Sockett.*

Bishop's poems appeal to readers who themselves have nothing much in common. Thus the post-Modern Ashbery can, figuratively speaking, rub shoulders with the narrative family dramatist Robert Lowell. Explaining his selection of Bishop for the Neustadt International Prize for Literature, John Ashbery remarked, "I chose her because she's my favorite living poet." The appeal of Bishop's work lies in the perfection of tone and nuance in evoking a particular emotional response. Without preaching or intellectualizing, Bishop gives substance to that existential moment that binds us together as human, so that we are on the bus with her spotting "The Moose" in the wilds of Canada or looking out from the boat in "Arrival at Santos." Our own experiences of these moments become memorable through the clarity of her language.

Although her poetic output was relatively small (she only published 95 poems in her lifetime), Elizabeth Bishop is unquestionably one of the major poets to emerge from the twentieth-century. The poet William Meredith had this to say about quantity and quality with regard to Bishop's life work: "The two kinds of poetry are, Excellent and Other.... They cannot lie down together because somebody always gets squashed. Elizabeth Bishop, so far as we know, writes only the one kind. Most other poets show off, in print, their greater versatility." As Robert Giroux, the editor of Bishop's letters, has noted, the "one art" referred to in the poem of the same name is clearly poetry itself, or at least the poetry of Elizabeth Bishop, which stands up against all the other losses and proves that, indeed, she was a master.

—Sue Russell

BLAMAN, Anna

Pseudonyms: Johanna Petronella Vrugt. **Nationality:** Dutch novelist and short story writer. **Born:** Rotterdam, Netherlands, 31 January 1905. **Education:** Primary school teaching certificate, Rotterdam; secondary school teaching certificate in French, The Hague, 1945. **Family:** Life-long, interrupted relationship with "Nurse B" (Alie Bosch). **Career:** Held a variety of teaching and administrative jobs; wrote reviews for several newspapers and magazines; wrote minor pageant-plays for open-air events in Rotterdam; helped establish the "Rotterdam Circle of Authors"; dramaturge for the Rotterdam Theatre. **Awards:** Lucy B. and C.W. van der Hoogtprijs, for *Eenzaam Avontuur,* 1949; Literatuurprijs, awarded by the City of Amsterdam, for *Eenzaam Avontuur,* 1950, and for *Op Leven en Dood,* 1956; P.C. Hooftprijs, for body of work, 1957. **Died:** Rotterdam, 13 July 1960.

WRITINGS

Fiction

Vrouw en vriend. Amsterdam, Meulenhoff, 1941.
Eenzaam avontuur. Amsterdam, Meulenhoff, 1948.
De Kruisvaarder. Amsterdam, Meulenhoff, 1950.
De doolhof. Roman door Anna Blaman, Antoon Coolen (e.a.) (novel in multi-author edition). Amsterdam, het Wereldvenster, 1951.
Op leven en dood. Amsterdam, Meulenhoff, 1954.
De verliezers. Amsterdam, Meulenhoff, 1960.

Short Stories

Ontmoeting met Selma. Utrecht, Jac. P. Romijn, 1943.
Ram Horna en andere verhalen. Amsterdam, Meulenhoff, 1951.
Overdag en andere verhalen. Amsterdam, Meulenhoff, 1957.
Verhalen. Amsterdam, Meulenhoff, 1963.

Plays

In duizend vrezen (pageant-play). 1956.
Het Costerman-oproer (pageant-play). 1957.
Het De Vletter-oproer (pageant-play). 1959.

Other

Anna Blaman over zichzelf en anderen. Poëzie, artikelen en lezingen (miscellaneous poetry, articles, and lectures; collected by A. Kossmann and C. Lührs). Amsterdam, Meulenhoff, 1963.
Spelen of sterven (miscellaneous prose; collected by A. Kossmann). Amsterdam, Meulenhoff, 1974.
Anna Blaman Fragmentarisch. Nagelaten proza, bijeengebracht, ingeleid en van toelichtingen voorzien door Henk Struyker Boudier (collected and annotated prose fragments). Amsterdam, Meulenhoff, 1978.

Recordings: *Fragment uit: De Verliezers* (gramophone recording; with text and bibliographical details), Den Haag/Amsterdam, Nederlands Letterkundig Museum, Querido, 1960.

*

Adaptations: *Hotel Bonheur* (theatre adaptation of short story "Hotel Bonheur" by Bonheur Theatre Company; performed Rotterdam, 1984); *Affaire B* (theatre adaptation of *Eenzaam Avontuur* by Matin van Veldhuizen, for RO-Theatre; performed Rotterdam, 1985-86).

Biography: *Mijn zuster Anna Blaman* by Corrie Lührs, Amsterdam, Meulenhoff, 1976.

Critical Sources: *Anna Blaman. Twee Lezingen* by H. Haasse and A. Kossmann, Amsterdam, Meulenhoff, 1961; *Speurtocht naar een onbekende. Anna Blaman en haar Eenzaam avontuur* by Henk Struyker Boudier (dissertation), Amsterdam, 1973.

*   *   *

Anna Blaman's work is characterized by a relentless honesty about the human failure to love unconditionally, resulting in an existentialist loneliness, a theme characteristic of much post-war literature. Yet, whereas her work shares the same thematics found in Jean-Paul Sartre and Simone de Beauvoir's work, her novels and short stories remain free from any philosophical, and therefore, detached analysis of the spiritual death of the heart. With a degree in French, Blaman was well-acquainted with the work of the French existentialists, whom she greatly admired. Yet, in her short story, "Feestavond" ("The Party"), she is capable, in admirably lucid and purely literary terms, of outlining the difference between a philosophical notion and the searing pain of the living human being.

In this story, a writer, Erica Hart, presents a literary gathering with a philosophical dilemma between the dictates of genius and that of human sympathy. She wraps it up in a short narrative about a simple shop assistant who discovers and develops his musical talents, neglecting his common wife who takes in menial jobs to pay for the family's upkeep. Completely engrossed in his own world, he no longer partakes of a life with his family. Only after the lonely death of his self-sacrificing wife, does he become engulfed in a helpless sense of guilt. The audience present overindulges in the kind of literary criticism typical of such self-congratulatory companies. Yet, it is the relative outsider, Daniël de Leeuw, who in the short scope of the story, develops from a rather cynical doctor, to an "angry and sad angel," who formulates the major issue:

...[Y]ou've got to do everything, not only what's humanly possible, but also what's impossible, whether it concerns your own life or someone else's. So this composer was in fact rather a strong character. The only thing is, he shouldn't have lamented his fate...A decision is a decision...But you've talked about this dilemma as if you're used to deciding whether to do the one or the other every day in your life...In reality you have nothing to decide, life, circumstances do it for you. And you know the only thing left of yourself in your decisions is your futility, your cowardliness, nothing else!

The theme of cowardliness and impotence echoes through all of Blaman's work. All human relations fall short of the real desire or courage to love unconditionally. Blaman's novel, *Eenzaam Avontuur* ("Lonely Adventure"), published in 1948, epitomizes the tortuous relationships between characters who can not but hurt each other with an almost unnatural intensity. Alide betrays her husband Kosta—who loves her to the point of obsession—with a character Peps, about whom many readers have puzzled as Blaman chose to depict him in such despicable terms. Alide blames the circumstances for her own failure, this time defined as psychological determinism: "And he [Kosta] would never understand that she was just as loyal to herself now, as she was before. She was herself with Kosta, owing to her love for him, and she was herself with Peps, owing to things other and more inevitable than love." This adulterous relation is repeated in the love-hate relationship between detective King and the poisoner Juliette in the novel-within-the-novel, a detective story written by Kosta, in which he works out his own obsessions. Only the minor character Berthe, a young woman secretly in love with Alide, searches for her own moral codes. Hurt after a far from sincere encounter with the "vamp" Anne, she suffers, not only from the loneliness which marks all the characters in this book, but also "because she would like to be convinced that it is natural and moral, that kind of love." Upon which she receives the answer: "Love is self-evidently natural and moral...No single prejudice can ever prevent you from loving and finding your love answered. So what is the problem?"

In Dutch literary circles in the 1940s and 1950s, literary critics fought over the question whether the theme of "moral love" related to the writer's own homosexuality and the representation of gay characters in her work, or whether it claimed a more universal condition, as the writer herself advocated. These critical positions were themselves derived from the two dominant critical approaches at the time—the biographical approach which claimed that the text was nothing but the personal outpouring of the author's emotional life in literary disguise, and the new critical approach which looked upon the work of art as an autonomous whole. Critics of the first category blamed Blaman for idealizing lesbian love at the expense of heterosexual relationships, while critics of the second either praised the book's persistent honesty in dissecting the hypocrisy underlying practically all forms of love, or hated it because they saw it as a "monstrosity of moral decay." The debate finally ended in a particularly nasty form of character bashing. A "tribunal" was organized—partly as a publicity stunt—in which the novel was going to be put on trial. Yet, not the book itself, but the author was summoned. What she was being summoned for was "a series of considerable failures in the field of literature, blatant and guilty ignorance of the novelist's metier, deliberate misleading of the reading public." Anna Blaman never went, so her first book was judged

and acquitted in her absence. Many journalists condemned this example of cultural vandalism, and the incident is still remembered as one of the more deplorable cases of cultural intolerance.

Not Anna Blaman's would-be critics, but the author herself would prove to be the best judge of her "failures": "I catch myself at human failures all the time, and if this stems from my human imperfection, I am conscious of a continuous fiasco...and this means that my human failures also constitute my human guilt."

—Tonie van Marle

BLOCH, Alice

Nationality: Jewish-American writer. **Born:** Youngstown, Ohio, 1947. **Education:** University of Michigan, Cornell University, and the Hebrew University of Jerusalem. **Career:** Has worked as an editor and technical writer; columnist, "Out of the Closet," *The Jewish Newspaper,* Los Angeles, 1985-86. Contributor of articles and reviews to feminist and lesbian periodicals; editorial board member, *Lesbian Review of Books.* **Address:** 4055 S. W. Henderson St., Seattle, Washington 98136, U.S.A.

WRITINGS

"Six Years," "Fuel," and "To Eddie" (poems), in *rara avis,* December 1978.
"Naturally Occurring Phenomena" (nonfiction), in *Bachy 16,* winter 1980.
Lifetime Guarantee: A Journey Through Loss and Survival (memoir). Boston, Alyson Publications, 1981.
The Law of Return (novel). Boston, Alyson Publications, 1983.
"Learning the Hula" (nonfiction), in *Hers 2,* edited by Terry Wolverton and Robert Drake. Boston, Faber & Faber, 1997.

*

Critical Sources: *"Lifetime Guarantee:* An Intense, Intimate Odyssey" by Bob Freitag, in *Out Magazine,* 22 October 1981; "Moving Through Loss and Survival" by Andrea Lowenstein, in *Gay Community News,* 7 November 1981; "A Journey Through Loss and Survival" by Diane Bertram, in *Womansight,* Vol. 2, No. 5, November 1981; *Lammas Little Review,* November 1981; review of *Lifetime Guarantee* by Judi Hernandez, in *Lesbian News,* December 1981; review of *Lifetime Guarantee* by Susanna J. Sturgis, in *off our backs,* December 1981; review of *Lifetime Guarantee* by Felice Newman, in *Motheroot Journal,* winter 1981; "Survivor's Story" by Elizabeth M. Bounds, in *Sojourner,* February 1982; "Sisters" by Elaine Starkman, in *Small Press Review,* May 1983; "Lesbian Understanding of Israel and Judaism" by Felice Newman, in *off our backs,* June 1983; *Publishers Weekly,* 29 July 1983; review of *The Law of Return* by Rebecca Sue Taylor, in *Library Journal,* 1 September 1983, 1719; *This Week in Mississippi,* 8 December 1983; review of *The Law of Return* by Eve Goldberg, in *Lesbian News,* January 1984; review of *The Law of Return* by Jesse Monteagudo, in *Connection,* February 1984; "Zion and Her Daughters" by Mary Ann Daly, in *Washington Blade,* 9 March 1984; review of *The Law of Return,* in *Lesbian Resource,* spring

1984; review of *The Law of Return* by Yvonne Klein, in *New Women's Times,* May/June 1984; "Lesbian Jews' Dilemma" by Diane Gregory, in *Bay Area Reporter,* 5 July 1984; "Instant Citizenship: Delayed Lesbianism" by Jackie Goodwin, in *Body Politic,* September 1984; "Jewish Feminists Claim Their Identity" by Bettina Aptheker, in *Demeter* (Monterey, California), February 1985; review of *The Law of Return* by Evelyn Torton Beck, in *News* (Los Angeles), 11 December 1987; review of *The Law of Return* by Sarah Craig, in *Windy City Times,* 17 December 1987; review of *The Law of Return* by Katherine V. Forrest, in *Advocate,* February 1988.

*   *   *

Like any talented writer whose books explore and reveal more than one culture, Alice Bloch receives attention and admiration from many different groups. People struggling with a terminal disease draw comfort from Bloch's narrative of her sister's cancer; American Jews appreciate seeing Israel and Orthodoxy through Bloch's Western eyes; and lesbians and gays, especially intellectuals, identify with Bloch as queer narrator of her own life. Both *Lifetime Guarantee: A Journey Through Loss and Survival* and *The Law of Return* are coming-out stories, though they describe a coming-out that involves more than sexuality.

Feminists note that, especially in *The Law of Return,* the political always becomes personal. The book describes how a young woman who goes to Israel to find "her people" and herself fits in well, despite uncertainty about her sexual orientation, until social and religious pressure to marry drives her back to the United States, where she gets engaged to a closeted male friend. The resulting misery shows the effects of patriarchal religion and rules on the human being. How can homosexuals, even the most devout, fit in to an Orthodox Judaism that demands, among "umpteen little laws," that, on Friday nights, a husband lie with his wife? Even after finding a woman lover, the narrator struggles with the homelessness and statelessness of lesbian Jews. Not only Jewish dykes but all gays must create community, and the chronicle of the narrator's thoughts and feelings, the record of her discussions, arguments, and actions, serves as both map and memory.

While *The Law of Return* is a novel, *Lifetime Guarantee* is a memoir of Bloch's experiences dealing with her sister's impending death from cancer. Because of the writing's emotional depth, reading it is like peeking into a diary. In fact, *Lifetime Guarantee* incorporates the sisters' letters, journal entries, and poems. In each book the writer chronicles the effects of trauma, growth, and change on the individual sensibility, writing with much feeling but without sentimentality or cliche.

As Kate Millett does in autobiographical works, Bloch shows her education and intellect in constant questioning and, also like Millett, she revolutionizes the first-person narrative stance. In *The Law of Return,* Bloch's narrator speaks in the first person (the "I" is the American "Ellen") and the third person ("she" being the Israeli "Elisheva"); the story is told sometimes as straightforward scene, sometimes as stream-of-consciousness. Hebrew and English weave together, while the language of music permeates Bloch's work both as subject matter and in the rhythms of the prose.

At the heart of both books is the writer-as-narrator, who seems plucky, intelligent, and strong. Her dyke development is fascinating: the narrator evolves from a young girl confused by her dreams to a mature woman who leaves her first lover confident of her ability to develop another close relationship. "I feel hurt and abandoned by Denise, but still I feel a basic confidence about forming relationships with women, a confidence I never felt with men," writes Bloch in *Lifetime Guarantee.* She records long, interesting conversations about being gay, being Jewish, being a daughter and a sister. Like many contemporary lesbian authors Bloch writes of an aware, intelligent, and unselfish young adult in extraordinary situations, of talk and dancing and sex and love between women, but Bloch's concerns bear no similarity to lesser writers' obsession with prurience or trivial social fads. Finally Bloch's work is more about family and history than romance, more about touching than sex, and more about language—in all its forms, especially music—than mere conversation.

—Gillian Kendall

BLOCK, Francesca Lia

Nationality: American novelist, poet, and author of short stories. **Born:** Hollywood, California, 3 December 1962; daughter of artist Irving A. Block and poet Gilda Klein Block. **Education:** University of California, Berkeley (Phi Beta Kappa; Shrout Fiction Award, University of California, Berkeley, 1986; Emily Chamberlain Cook Poetry Award, University of California, Los Angeles, 1986), B.A. 1986. **Career:** Cataloger, Ankrum Gallery, Los Angeles, 1989; instructor of writing workshops, Berkeley and Los Angeles; contributor of articles and short stories to *Berkeley Fiction Review, Los Angeles Times Book Review, New York Times Book Review,* and *SPIN;* contributor of poetry to *Artline* (UCLA campus publication), *Berkeley Poetry Review* and *Westwind* (UCLA campus publication). **Awards:** American Library Association Best Books for Young Adults 1989, 1992, 1993, 1995; Book of the Year shortlist, American Library Association, 1989; *Booklist* Editor's Choice, 1989; *Booklist* Best of the 1980s list; YASD Best Book Award 1989; Recommended Book for Reluctant Young Readers 1989, 1990, 1992, 1993, 1994; Recommended Book for Young Readers, 1994; Best Books citation, *School Library Journal,* 1991; Best Books citation, *New York Times,* 1992; Best Books citation, *Publisher's Weekly,* 1992; American Library Association Gay, Lesbian & Bisexual Book Award, 1995; American Library Association Gay and Lesbian Task Force Book Award nomination, for fiction, 1996. **Agents:** Lydia Wills, Artist's Agency, 230 W. 55th Street, suite 29D, New York, New York 10019, U.S.A.; Julie Fallowfield, McIntosh & Otis, 310 Madison Ave., New York, New York 10017, U.S.A.

WRITINGS

Young Adult Fiction

Weetzie Bat. New York, HarperCollins, 1989.
Witch Baby. New York, HarperCollins, 1990.
Cherokee Bat and the Goat Guys. New York, HarperCollins, 1991.
Missing Angel Juan. New York, HarperCollins, 1993.
The Hanged Man. New York, HarperCollins, 1994.
Baby Be-Bop. New York, HarperCollins, 1995.
Girl Goddess #9: Nine Stories. New York, HarperCollins, 1996.

Novels

Ecstasia. New York, New American Library, 1993.
Primavera. New York, New American Library, 1994.

Poetry

Moon Harvest, illustrated by Irving Block. Los Angeles, Santa
    Susana Press, 1978.
Season of Green, illustrated by Irving Block. Los Angeles, Santa
    Susana Press, 1979.

Short Stories

"Winnie and Tommie," in *Am I Blue? Coming Out from the Si-
    lence,* edited by Maria Dane Bauer, New York, Harper, 1994.
"Blue," in *When I Was Your Age,* edited by Amy Erlich. Candlewick
    Press, 1994.
Also author of "Tweetie Sweetie Pea," in *Soft Tar,* and "Blood
    Oranges," in *Dark Carnival Barker.*

Recordings: Cherokee Bat and the Goat Guys, Talking Books;
    Baby Be-Bop, Talking Books.

*

Adaptations: *Weetzie Bat* by Ann Bayd and Julia Neary
(stageplay; produced Chicago); *Missing Angel Juan* by Ann Bayd
and Julia Neary (stageplay; produced Chicago); *Witch Baby* by
Julia Hickson (screenplay; for Storyopolis).

Critical Sources: "People Are Talking About . . . Francesca Lia
Block" by Patrick Jones, in *Horn Book Magazine* (Boston), Vol.
LXVIII, No. 6, November-December 1992, 697-701; "Block,
Francesca Lia. *Ecstasia,*" in *Library Journal,* May 15, 1993, 100;
"People Are Talking About . . . Francesca Lia Block" by Patricia
J. Campbell, in *Horn Book Magazine* (Boston), Vol. LXIX, No.
1, January-February 1993, 57-63; "The Hanged Man," in *The Bul-
letin of the Center for Children's Books,* Vol. 48, September 1994,
6; "Francesca Lia Block," in *Something About the Author Autobiography Series.* Detroit, Gale Research, Vol. 21, 1996.

Francesca Lia Block comments:
    I hope that you are all able to set your stories free.

*   *   *

The major themes in Francesca Lia Block's books include the
necessity of love and the acceptance of and celebration of racial
and sexual difference. The importance of story is foregrounded in
her work, for it is the individual stories that her characters narrate
to themselves and to the reader that "set us free." Her novel *Baby
Be-Bop* ends with the words: "Our stories can set us free.... When
we set them free." Block's books incorporate people's need to
love each other and their environment as they highlight the beauty
and magic in the everyday and illustrate the magic of finding oneself. Block allows the heros in her stories to discover what is truly
important to them and to accept themselves, as Dirk in *Baby Be-
Bop* accepts himself as gay and her character Cubby discovers that
"The most beautiful people are the ones that don't look like one
race or even one sex" in "Winnie and Cubby" from the collection
Girl Goddess #9.

Block's work goes beyond the "coming out" story of most Young
Adult fiction that discusses lesbian, gay, or bi-sexual themes. Being gay, lesbian, bi-sexual or trans is as natural in Block's books
as heterosexuality. As Gazelle in *Baby Be-Bop* says, "Any love
that is love is right." This does not mean, however, that acceptance of the self comes without pain, for the social pressures that
impinge on Block's characters are as real as those of the world
she lives in. Dirk and Duck of the Weetzie series of books struggle
with acceptance of themselves, with fears of family disapproval,
with social disapproval, and with hatred as they come to know
who it is that they are and help to create and live in a family in
which all sexualities are accepted.

Dirk and Duck are enduring characters in Block's fiction and
appear, at least in mention, in not only *Weetzie Bat* where they
find each other, but also in *Witch Baby* where Duck comes out
and finds acceptance from his family, in *Cherokee Bat and the
Goat Guys* as family members who are away shooting a film, in
Missing Angel Juan as concerned about Witch Baby finding herself as she looks for lost love, and in *Baby Be-Bop,* the story of
their lives prior to Dirk's meeting either Weetzie or Duck and forming a family. Block's treatment of Dirk and Duck's hopes for finding love and fears about their sexuality in an age of AIDS make
these books particularly appealing to gay, lesbian, bi-sexual, and
trans readers.

Sexuality is not confined to the discovery or "coming out" period in Block's books. She sets her characters in situations that
also explore mature same sex relationships. Her characters Mal-
lard and Meadows, an older gay couple, help Witch Baby to find
herself, care for her, and provide a family for her, as she searches
for both herself and Angel Juan in New York in *Missing Angel
Juan.* In addition, Block personifies the issue of AIDS, the disease that Dirk and Duck cannot mention to each other, in Duck's
friend Bam-Bam in *Weetzie Bat.*

Block creates bi-sexual and gay male characters in her fantasy
fiction for adults as well. Rafe first loves Lily in Block's *Ecstasia,*
but the love Paul and Rafe share is crucial to the creation of a
kinder, pristine world of bloom created in the desert in both
Ecstasia and in that book's sequel, *Primavera.* These books have
regeneration and reproduction as major themes. They focus on
the dark myths of Orpheus, Eurydice, and of Calliope and
Persephone, retelling myths in current terms of environmental con-
tamination, hatred of difference, racism, glorification of youth culture, and the immediate gratification of pleasures endemic not only
in Los Angeles, the city where one can enter the underworld to
which the elders are banished to die, but also in so many parts of
the United States. Block does not remove gays from a regenera-
tive world order. In fact, as Paul realizes in *Primavera,* "you, Rafe,
are my child, and I yours...and our child is this love we have made
palpable as if a third heart beat between our hard chests."

Lesbians and trans people are present in Block's short stories
in *Girl Goddess # 9.* In "Blue," a story that focuses on being
different, La is more attracted to females than to males and her
friend Blue is part male, part female. As Block's characters so
often are, La is set free by telling her story. In "Dragons in Manhattan" Tuck reunites her grandparents with Izzy, one of her mothers, after searching for her father Irving, a woman who had lived
inside a male body before her operation. Not only are Izzy and
her parents reunited, but Anastasia, Tuck's other mother, finds
her voice, a voice that had nearly been silent from trying to protect Izzy's story, and her own. Tuck realizes that she loves them
all: "Anastasia and Izzy and Irving, too."

"Girl Goddess # 9" more than hints at same sex desire as the 'zine creators cry because they "want to touch the [white goddess's] hair and skin and toenails" more than her partner, nick agate's whom they thought they adored. They realize there will always be a "Girl Goddess # 9." Important relationships between women are shown in "Pixie and Pony," where Pony is Pixie's wished for best friend and, as Pony states to Pixie, the two "are sisters." Friendship as a form of love as necessary and as strong as sexual desire is explored in "Winnie and Cubby." Winnie loves Cubby, and desires him, yet she sees men/women in the bars as "more beautiful than men or women," as though "they are from another world." When she learns that Cubby is gay, at first she is hurt and hates herself. She realizes, however, that the friendship she and Cubby share "will just be a different thing," as important as sexual love.

Block's *The Hanged Man* is an exploration of a different kind: coming to love oneself and accept sexuality after sexual abuse by a parent. The title is taken from a Tarot card, and illustrations from and instructions for the Rider-Waite Tarot deck delineate events in the chapter and the experiences of the hero, Laurel. In the hospital waiting room during the time that her father is dying, Laurel meets Jack who, after the death of her father, becomes her demon lover, releasing her from the pain and fear that her father's abuse has caused, and from her anorexia. Jack also makes her realize the importance of female friendship, and that, as she becomes stronger, she will be able to help her friends, Claudia and Perdita. Laurel recognizes not only her need for friends, but also her desire for Claudia as she reconciles with her mother, begins eating, and returns to life. She hears "Jack's voice: Let go of it, let go. And I go to her." As the review of this book in *The Bulletin of the Center for Children's Books* pointed out, "Kids may not pick up the clues to the source of Laurel's pain...but the poetic style and mystical narration will hold the attention of Block fans and those with a taste for shadows."

Block is a prolific writer. Since the publication of her first novel, *Weetzie Bat,* in 1989 she has produced at least a book a year and has become one of the most loved and prestigious writers of Young Adult fiction, winning awards for almost everything she has published. Her books are not necessarily mainstream Young Adult fiction and have been criticized for the controversial content they contain: gays, punkers, magic, mythos, "differently" constructed families, sexuality, and AIDS. However, her approach to difference fills a great need in the lives of young people who need to see that difference does not make one "bad." As Patricia J. Campbell noted in *Horn Book Magazine,* that she agreed with Patrick Jones "that 'there are still lines to cross in young-adult literature and that the journey is well worth it'—and that it would be a great shame if the extraordinary books of Francesca Lia Block were kept from young people by even one librarian's fear of the unfamiliar."

Perhaps the most controversial characters are the gay characters of Block's books who are presented simply as being in need of becoming who they are. Block wrote in *Something About the Author Autobiography Series,* that writing is a genie: "It is the wise, benevolent, illuminating spirit that helps me get in touch with the love inside of me. And out of that comes healing." Her books are also healing for "different" heterosexual readers, and especially for gay, lesbian, bi-sexual, and transgendered people who find representations of themselves told with love.

—Patti Capel Swartz

BOGUS, SDiane Adams

Nationality: American poet, author of short stories, playwright, and essayist. **Born:** Chicago, Illinois, 22 January 1946; after her mother's death moved to Birmingham, Alabama, 1960. **Education:** A.H. Parker High School, Birmingham, Alabama; Stillman College, Tuscaloosa, Alabama (cum laude), B.A. in English and Spanish 1968; Syracuse University, New York, M.A. in English 1969; Miami University, Oxford, Ohio (Walser fellow), Ph.D. in American Literature 1988. **Career:** Teacher, Miles College, Birmingham, Alabama, 1969-71; supervisor of student teaching, Master of Arts Teaching Program, Northwestern University, Chicago, Illinois, 1972; instructor, English Department, Los Angeles Southwest Community College, 1976-81; teaching fellow, English Department, Miami University, Oxford, Ohio, 1981-84; instructor, City College of San Francisco, California, 1985-86; faculty adviser, 1987-88, faculty mentor, 1988-89, California State University, Stanislaus; visiting lecturer, English, Foreign Language, and Philosophy Department, California State University, Stanislaus, 1987-89; professor of Composition and Literature, De Anza College, Cupertino, California, from 1990. Founder, Woman in the Moon (WIM) Publications, Cupertino, California; editor, *The Spirit* newsletter, WIM Publications; board member, Multicultural Publishers Exchange, 1991-93; contributor of articles and reviews to periodicals, including *Black American Literature Forum, Black Scholar, Black Thought, Catalyst, Dickinson Studies, Sinister Wisdom,* and *Women's Review of Books.* **Awards:** Poetry Arts Project finalist, 1989; Innovator of the Year Award, League of Innovation, 1991-92, 1993-94; Black Writer's Award, Peninsula Book Club, 1992. **Address:** Woman in the Moon Publications, P. O. Box 2087, Cupertino, California 95015-2087, U.S.A.

WRITINGS

Poetry

I'm Off to See the Goddam Wizard, Alright! Inglewood, California, Woman in the Moon Publications, 1971.
Woman in the Moon. Stamford, Connecticut, Soap Box Publishing, 1977.
Her Poems: An Anniversaric Chronology. Inglewood, California, Woman in the Moon Publications, 1979.
Sapphire's Sampler. Inglewood, California, Woman in the Moon Publications, 1982.
Dykehands and Sutras Erotic and Lyric. San Francisco, California, Woman in the Moon Publications, 1988.
The Chant of the Women of Magdalena and the Magdalena Poems. San Francisco, California, Woman in the Moon Publications, 1990.
For the Love of Men: Shikata Gai Nai. San Francisco, California, Woman in the Moon Publications, 1992.

Fiction

"Dreams of Sapphira," in *Intricate Passions Banned Books.* 1989.
"Mom De Plume," and "To My Mother's Vision," in *Double Stitch.* New York, HarperCollins, 1991.
"The Joy and Power of Celibacy," in *Piece of My Heart: A Lesbian of Color Anthology.* Sister Vision Press, 1991.

"Greystroke," "Dykehands," and "Making Whoopi," in *Erotique Noir/Black Erotica*. New York, Doubleday, 1992.
"Down Home Blues," in *Dagger*. Pittsburgh, Pennsylvania, Cleis Press, 1994.

Other

"My Writing Life" (autobiography), in *Happy Endings*. Tallahassee, Florida, Naiad Press, 1993.
Editor, *Poetry Workbook*. San Francisco, California, Woman in the Moon Publications, 1995.
Editor, *The Studenthood Reader: a New Age Educational Collection with Supplements*. New York, Simon and Schuster, 1995.

Recordings: *SDiane Bogus Creativity* (video; directed by Tee Corinne), San Francisco, California, Woman in the Moon Publications, 1990; *SDiane Reading the Chant of the Women of Magdalena and Selected Magdalena Poems* (video), San Francisco, California, Woman in the Moon Publications, 1992.

                                        *

Critical Sources: "Celebrating Themselves: Four Self-Published Black Lesbian Authors" by Becky Birtha, in *Off Our Backs* (Washington, D.C.), Vol. 15, August/September 1985, 19-21; "*Dykehands and Sutras Erotic and Lyric*: Poems and Lyrics by SDiane Bogus" by Terri Jewell, in *Womenwise*, Vol. 12, No. 4, winter 1990, 12; "We're Moonstruck over SDiane Bogus," in *Womyn's Words,* July 1990, 1; "Every Which Way but Easy: Poet SDiane Bogus Comes Out on Top" by Karen Dale Wolman, in *Advocate,* Vol. 14, August 1990, 73; "A Farewell to Harms: Women Reclaim the Sea," in *Lambda Book Report,* Vol. 2, No. 10, May/June 1991, 29; "SDiane Adams Bogus" by Rita B. Dandridge, in *Contemporary Lesbian Writers of the United States: a Bio-bibliographical Critical Sourcebook,* Westport, Connecticut, Greenwood Press, 1993.

SDiane Bogus comments:

The single question of my life has been "Who am I?" And I ask it daily. One of my poems—"A.P.B." in *Dykehands*—attempts to explore how I seek myself. It appears that I grow large with each passing year and broader each passing day. My work has covered all the genres and I still find myself reaching for expression. I am a poet and writer, but I am an actor, a singer, a healer, and a teacher. I began to understand because I chose to live my lesbian/bulldagger's life without compromise of children or side lines with men, I have given myself limitless opportunity to be a shape shifter. I find it disconcerting to change and grow at such a pace, but it is my power and strength.

My new work in progress, *Hatshipsut's Legacy,* attempts to trace Black lesbian herstory in fiction and show the faces of our love in various uncommon settings beginning at Egypt and ending at the modern rodeo. I see myself as a transition writer for the new age and I hope my work survives me. My papers and journals will be deposited with the Lesbian Herstory archives at the end of my life.

                        *   *   *

SDiane Bogus began loving women at an early age, and from the beginning, she made it a visible and intrinsic part of her life and her writing. She lost an early teaching job at Miles College in Birmingham, Alabama, because she did not hide her relationship with a young woman there, and, almost 20 years later, settled out of court with California State College at Stanislaus, charging that she lost her job there as a result of discrimination based on race and sexual orientation.

Growing up African-American, first in the urban center of Chicago, then in segregated Birmingham, Alabama, and discovering sexual feelings for other girls at the age of eight insured that Bogus would grow up no stranger to struggle. She was 14 when her mother "died of cancer, died of overwork and worry and Blackness in an underpaid, poor person's factory job," as Bogus stated in "To My Mother's Vision," and that loss is felt deeply throughout her work. Though she had written poetry since early adolescence, there was little support for budding black writers in the pre-civil rights movement South. She started her own literary magazine at Stillman College in Tuscaloosa, a largely black institution, but it was there that she first had the epithet "bulldagger" directed at her. It was one of many indications that there might always be parts of her that were not acceptable to someone.

Though the atmosphere of struggle is certainly present in her work, it is not pain or difficulty that most overwhelms the reader of Bogus' writing, but joy and strength. She is a woman who has created a space for herself. From the very concrete—when publishing houses turned her down, she founded her own—to the poetic, Bogus' career has been very much about defining herself and demanding the same of her readers.

In the introduction to *Dykehands and Sutras Erotic and Lyric,* Bogus writes, "This collection of my work will offend some because it walks the line between crude and refined, reverence and disrespect, between the secular and the spiritual, sexual repression and sexual expression, but it is that very line that lesbians tightrope walk everyday of their lives." Though she is only writing about one collection, this sentence describes fairly accurately what is often controversial in all of Bogus' work, the constant work of self-definition when the self is so complex and ever-changing.

Bogus' earliest publications were what she called "Black poems," poetry inspired by the anger and activism of the civil rights struggle. But they were also inspired by the events of her own life, and so they necessarily included lesbian content. Her insistence on writing about all parts of her life and struggle, and on seeing the lives and struggles of all women reflected in them, has prevented Bogus from being accepted by either the mainstream white press or the black press. Stubbornly self-reliant, she saved the money to publish her poems herself, and Woman in the Moon Publications was on the way to being born.

With the rise of feminism and gay liberation in the early 1970s, Bogus began to find a community of lesbians, and to move out of the isolation that comes from being something that is not supposed to exist. She never, however, naively accepts any doctrine for long, and her ambitious *Sapphire's Sampler* illustrates the many facets of her person and her politics. *The Chant of the Women of Magdalena and the Magdalena Poems* is the story of 32 women inmates who escape an English prison and ultimately triumph, settling together in the Pyrenees mountains. In this stark and extreme vision of women making a place for themselves against all odds, Bogus uses imagery of nature and great universal themes, making them deeply personal. She also recorded herself reading these poems, which exemplifies another aspect of her career. Bogus has developed a one-woman show where she dynamically recreates portions of her written work.

Another side of Bogus's writing is her academic work. Though superficially quite different in tone and language from her poetic and fiction writing, even in these the reader sees the black lesbian author winking at us from behind the erudite phrasing, saving it from dryness, and making the academic research her own. In "Not So Disparate: An Investigation of the Influence of E.B.B. on the Work of E.D.," Bogus focuses on Elizabeth Barrett Browning and her importance to the writing of Emily Dickenson, both writers long read and claimed, in a subtle, underground way, by lesbians. When Bogus writes, "E.D. sought to edify Browning out of her love and respect for her as a woman and a writer," it is very satisfying for those of us concerned with lesbian history and culture, not because we believe these two women were necessarily having sex with other women, but because the history of women's love and respect for each other is a radical and intrinsically lesbian subject.

Likewise in the article, "The 'Queen B' figure in Black Literature," Bogus argues the existence of an archetypal figure of "woman-loving royalty," the bulldagger or queen B. In this way, and in a serious academic format, she explores the roots of a word that has no doubt been used against her many times, with the intention of reclaiming it as a powerful archetype.

Bogus' writing is a diverse blend of her experiences, having been published everywhere from science fiction magazines to mainstream family journals to lesbian periodicals. Her influences are white English and American writers, black literature and politics, feminist dialectic, lesbian vision, spiritual quest, and more. Her writing and her life have been characterized by both a refusal to be pigeonholed as only one kind of person or writer and a refusal to deny any of the controversial aspects of her identity.

—Tina Gianoulis

BOYE, Karin

Nationality: Swedish poet, novelist, and essayist. **Born:** Göteborg, 26 October 1900. **Education:** Junior schools in Göteborg and Stockholm; Uppsala University, 1920-28. **Family:** Married Leif Björk in 1929 (divorced 1931); companion of Margot Hanel, 1932-41. **Career:** Editor, *Spektrum* (literary magazine), Berlin, 1931-33; teacher, Viggbyholm boarding school, Sweden, 1936-39. **Died:** Alingsås, of exposure, 23 April 1941.

WRITINGS

Poetry

Moln ("Clouds"). Stockholm, Bonnier, 1922.
Gömda land ("Hidden Country"). Stockholm, Bonnier, 1924.
Härdarna ("Hearths"). Stockholm, Bonnier, 1927.
För trädets skull ("For the Tree's Sake"). Stockholm, Bonnier, 1935.
De sju dödssynderna ("The Seven Deadly Sins"). Stockholm, Bonnier, 1941.

Dikter ("Poems"). Stockholm, Bonnier, 1942.
Till dig ("To You"). Stockholm, Bonnier, 1963.
Karin Boye: Complete poems, translated by David McDuff. Newcastle upon Tyne, Bloodaxe Books, 1994.

Novels

Astarte ("Astarte"). Stockholm, Bonnier, 1931.
Merit vaknar ("Merit Wakens"). Stockholm, Bonnier, 1933.
Kris ("Crisis"). Stockholm, Bonnier, 1934.
För lite ("Too Little"). Stockholm, Bonnier, 1936.
Kallocain. Stockholm, Bonnier, 1940; translated by Gustaf Lannestock as *Kallocain,* with an introduction by Richard C. Vowels, Madison, University of Wisconsin Press, 1966.

Short Stories

Uppgörelser ("Reckonings"). Stockholm, Bonnier, 1934.
Ur funktion ("Out of Commission"). Stockholm, Bonnier, 1940.
Bebådelse ("Annunciation"). Stockholm, Bonnier, 1941.

Translator

Strindberg och hans andra hustra (translation of Frida Ulh's *Married to Genius*). Stockholm, Bonnier, 1933-34.
With Erik Mesterton, "Det öde landet" (translation of T.S. Eliot's *The Waste Land*), in *Dikter i urval,* edited by Ronald Bottrall and Erik Mesterton. Stockholm, Bonnier, 1942.
With Ake Thulstrup, *Brev till min dotter Kerstin* (translation of August Strindberg's *Letters to my Daughter Kersten*). Stockholm, Bonnier, 1961.

Other

Samlade skrifter (collected works). Stockholm, Bonnier, 1948-49.

*

Manuscript Collections: Huddinge Bibliotek, Sweden.

Biography: *Drabbad av renhet* ("Stricken with Purity") by Margit Abenius, Stockholm, Bonnier, 1950, reprinted as *Karin Boye,* Stockholm, Bonnier, 1965.

Critical Sources: "Karin Boye" by Sven Stolpe, in *Kämpande dikt,* Stockholm, Kooperativa förbunets bokförlag, 1938, 19-29; "Karen Boye" by Knut Jaensson, in *Nio moderna svenska prosaförfattare,* Stockholm, Bonnier, 1941; *Karin Boye: minnen och studier,* edited by Margit Abenius and Olof Lagercrantz, Stockholm, Bonnier, 1942; "De sju dödssynderna" by Margit Abenius, in *Kontakter,* Stockholm, Bonnier, 1944, 207-33; "Ripeness is All: A Study of Karin Boye's Poetry" by Richard B. Vowles, in *Bulletin of the American Swedish Institute,* Vol. 7, 1952, 3-8; "Ny ton i svensk poesi" by Hagar Olsson, in *Tidiga fanfarer,* Helsingfors, 1953; "Havssymbolik hos Karin Boye: en utvecklingslinje i hennes 20-talsdiktning" by Alf Kjellén, in *Studie tillägnade Henry Olsson,* Stockholm, 1956, 296-313; *A History of Swedish Literature* by Alrik Gustafson, Minneapolis, University of Minnesota Press, 1961; *Ny illustrerad svensk litteraturhistoria* by Erik Hjalmar Linder, Stockholm, Natur och Kultur, 1966; "I oss ä en mångfald levande: Karin Boye som kritiker och prosamodernist" by Gunilla Domellof (dissertation), 1986; *Karen Boyes liv och diktning,* 7 Vols. (memorial essays and other compositions by the Karen Boye Society), Huddinge, Karen Boye sällskapet, 1983-1993.

*   *   *

The title of Karin Boye's biography, "Stricken with Purity," is a line from one of her poems. Boye's quest for the ideal, whether in love, religion, politics, or art, was a constant struggle. The biography, written by her close friend Margaret Abenius, describes the inner conflict of Sweden's greatest female poet. Despite the melancholic tone of much of her poetry, the beauty of her lyrics is unquestioned and her verse patterns well-crafted. Many of the poems reflect her religious struggle as well as her desire for earthly pleasures. Boye was unable to resolve her personal and creative conflicts and took her own life by walking out into the freezing countryside with a bottle of sleeping pills. Her body was found in a sitting position, several days later.

Boye was born in the industrial city of Göteborg. She was brought up in a household that was both religious and intellectual due to her mother's interest in European literature and oriental religions. In 1909, the family moved to Stockholm. During this time, Boye's father was affected by a "nervous debility" and retired early. While in school, Boye studied and followed Buddhism until she eventually moved to Christianity. In Christian summer camp Boye met Anita Nathorst, a student from Uppsala University. Boye was clearly smitten with Nathorst and maintained a friendship with her that would last the rest of Boye's life.

In 1920, Boye enrolled in Uppsala University. She originally studied theology but changed her focus to psychology and teaching. Her decision may have had to do with her awakening sexuality and the growing awareness that her orientation was towards women. Later, she would write of these experiences in a series of Socratic dialogues called *Kris* ("Crisis"). The book was published in 1933, and as there was much discussion at the time of Sweden's liberalization of homosexuality laws, *Kris* was widely read and contributed to public debate.

Her first book of poems, *Moln* ("Clouds"), published in 1922, was well-received by the public and critics. Boye studied Greek in order to read Plato in the original, as well as the Nordic languages. Boye and Nathorst were still close and became interested in Freud's works. This would have a profound effect on Boye, who became enthusiastic about psychoanalysis. Her explorations into the realm of the unconscious and dream interpretations influenced her future writing. During her last year at Uppsala, Boye joined the Clarté followers. The Clarté group was a Swedish branch of the international organization dedicated to radical political socialism. Some felt that this move on Boye's part was prompted by her desire to become a "normal" woman, involved with a popular student movement. Encouraged by her mother, she married one of its members, a poet named Leif Björk. But the marriage did not last long. Boye was already deeply involved with psychoanalysis in an attempt to piece together what she felt was missing in her life. Psychoanalysis, however, did not alleviate her bouts of depression (which may have been inherited from her father) or thoughts of suicide.

A 1928 visit to Russia with her fellow Clarté members caused Boye to question the group's enthusiasm for Communism. She would later write of the effects of a totalitarian society on the individual in her greatest novel, *Kallocain,* published shortly before her death. The title of the novel comes from a green serum that when injected into the bloodstream of an individual, causes them to reveal their innermost thoughts. Boye was deeply concerned about the larger implications of thought control in such a dystopia, but probably had something more personal in mind when she described the incident where the creator of the drug injects it into his wife, thereby gaining access to her secret thoughts. Although married, Boye still thought about women.

In 1932, Boye moved to Berlin and continued psychoanalysis. She worked as a literary translator and was editor of the Swedish avant-garde magazine *Spektrum,* which published the early work of Swedish modernist Gunnar Ekelöf, among others. It was around this time that Boye began a relationship with Margot Hanel, a German woman 12 years younger than Boye. The relationship did not seem to be a healthy one. Hanel was demanding and jealous and ever since her days at Christian camp, Boye needed to feel she was sacrificing herself to something or someone. Both women fulfilled a need in one another, so much so that one month after Boye's death, Hanel committed suicide as well. Lines from Boye's poem "You are the Seed" indicate Boye was well-aware of the symbiotic nature of their relationship:

> You are the seed and I your soil.
> You lie in me and grow.
> You are the child expected.
> I am your mother now...
> That is why it hurts to the living quick
> inside me now:
> something is growing and breaking me—
> my love, it is you!

Between 1936 and 1939, Boye taught at Viggbyholm boarding school, near Stockholm. Hanel had moved to Stockholm in 1934 at Boye's request. Although Boye was a popular teacher, she could not escape her inner torments and once, during a class, she broke down crying while reading a poem. She made several male friends at Viggbyholm and one may have been romantic, but Boye ended it after an encounter with Hanel.

After 1939, Boye began corresponding again with Anita Nathorst. Nathorst had cancer and Boye traveled to Alingsås, a city near Göteborg, to take care of her. While in Alingsås, Boye wrote letters to Hanel to reassure her of her affection but now Boye had Nathorst to fulfill her constant need for self-sacrifice. The great love Boye felt for Nathorst, however, was not reciprocated in the same way and when Nathorst moved from Alingsås to Malmö, it may not have been entirely due to medical reasons. In spite of the enthusiastic reception of *Kallocain,* and an invitation to meet the Danish royal family, Boye fell into a depression from which she would never recover.

Karin Boye is widely considered among the greatest Swedish poets of all time. Critics are divided on whether or not her work is "modernist," as is the work of the next generation of Swedish poets such as Gunnar Ekelöf, Erik Asklund, and Artur Lundkvist, to name but a few. If not especially modern in form, Boye's poetry shows a modernity in spirit with its vacillations between religious and earthly desires and her delving into the realm of the unconscious. In her 1986 dissertation, Gunilla Domellöf asserts that Karin Boye's role in the influence and development of modernism in Swedish letters has never been reevaluated since her reception by male Swedish critics between 1931 and 1934. Domellöf feels that, as a female intellectual, Karin Boye has not been given the recognition for her modernist attempts that she rightly deserves.

—Robin Imhof

BRAND, Adolf

Nationality: German book dealer, gay activist, writer, and publisher. **Born:** 1874. **Career:** Publisher, *Der Eigene*, 1896-31, *Freundschaft und Freiheit*, 1921, and *Rasse und Schonheit*, 1926-(?); co-founder, *Gemeinschaft der Eigenen*. **Died:** Berlin, Germany, in an Allied bombing raid, 1945.

WRITINGS

Editor

Eros: Zeitschrift fur Freundschaft und Freiheit. Berlin-Wilhlemslagen, Kunst-Verlag, 19(?)-(?).
Die Gemeinschaft der Eigenen. Wilhlemslagen bei Berlin, 19(?)-(?).
Extrapost des Eigenen. Wilhelmshagen, 1911.
Rasse und Schonheit. Berlin, Blatter fur Nacktkultur, 1926-(?).

Other

"Was wir wollen" ("What We Want"), in *Journal of Homosexuality*, Vol. 22, No. 1/2, 1991, 155-66.

*

Critical Sources: *Eldorado: Homosexuelle Frauen und Manner in Berlin 1850-1950; Geschichte, Alltag und Kultur,* Berlin, Frolich und Kaufmann, 1984; "Homosexual Emancipation In Germany Before 1933: Two Traditions" by Harry Oosterhuis, in *Journal of Homosexuality*, Vol. 22, 1991, 1-27.

*   *   *

One of the earliest problems facing those individuals who believed in social, civil, and legal equality for persons attracted to their own gender was the limited means available to circulate this new philosophy to the general public. The series of pamphlets, written by Karl Heinrich Ulrichs beginning in 1864, promulgating the idea that such people constituted a separate unique class of beings, were privately printed and issued in very small numbers. Their readership, at least initially, consisted chiefly of individuals who were homosexual or sympathetic to their situation. Although Ulrichs himself envisioned a public organization, the "Urning Union," and drafted its bylaws in September 1865, no such body was ever organized during his lifetime. He also proposed a periodical for homosexuals, and the first and only issue appeared in January 1870 under the title *Uranus*. The creation of such formal groups of homosexuals and their allies would not occur until the 1890s, when two separate organizations emerged in Berlin—the

"Scientific Humanitarian Committee" (founded by Dr. Magnus Hirschfeld in 1897) and the *Gemeinschaft der Eigenen,* the "Community of the Special," among whose leaders and chief writers was Adolf Brand.

Originally a teacher by profession, Adolf Brand abandoned that field due to problems arising from his anarchist-leanings and his associations with freethinkers. After founding a bookshop and publishing firm in 1896, he met the prominent physician Dr. Magnus Hirschfeld, with whom he briefly worked planning a political campaign against the classification of homosexuality as criminal behavior under Paragraph 175 of the German legal code. It was Hirschfeld's first book on homosexuality, *Sappho und Sokrates,* that introduced Brand to this field of activism. Due to sharp philosophical differences, however, Brand and Hirschfeld quickly parted company. Later in 1896 the first issue of *Der Eigene* appeared. The title of this periodical (which was to become the mouthpiece for a view of homosexuality challenging the medical approach advocated by Hirschfeld's Scientific Humanitarian Committee) was drawn from the writings of the anarchist Max Stirner, who strongly opposed the subordination of individuals to any type of authority, whether legal, spiritual, or moral. In 1898, *Der Eigene* shifted subject matter from anarchism to a literary and artistic exploration of male eroticism among youths and young men, the rationale being that the self-determination of anarchism should also be extended to one's mind and body and the uses of sexuality.

Following a three-year absence due to insufficient funds, in 1903 *Der Eigene* became a journal for "male culture, art, and literature." By this time Brand had also begun to publish more specialized periodicals rooted in the then-contemporary *Freikorperkultur* nudist movement. To further stabilize his situation and gain greater public acceptance, in the same year he and a few friends founded a formal organization, the *Gemeinschaft der Eigenen* (most commonly translated as the "Community of the Special," whose stated purpose was "for friendship and freedom." This phrase would later be adopted by an American gay veteran of World War I, Henry Gerber, and become the title of the first short-lived gay newspaper in the United States, published in Chicago from 1924 to 1925. The *Gemeinschaft* met weekly at Brand's home in Wilhelmshagen, a Berlin suburb, where poetry and essays were read and subjects related to male homosexuality debated.

Brand first came to widespread public notice outside Germany in 1907 after authoring a pamphlet attacking the prime minister, Bernard von Bulow, one of the figures involved in the sensational Harden-Eulenburg scandal. In his text, Brand objected to Bulow's role in the then-ongoing investigation into the alleged homosexuality of two noblemen closely connected to Kaiser Wilhelm II. Brand also charged Bulow with having an affair with one of his male aides. He was immediately sued by the outraged Bulow for libel. He was convicted and sentenced to 18 months imprisonment. This extreme course of action fits with his belief (shared by some other German activists of the time) that exposing homosexual relationships among high-ranking individuals would lead to the abolition of Paragraph 175, an attitude not unlike the practice of "outing" prominent figures in the early 1990s. The refusal of Magnus Hirschfeld and the Scientific Humanitarian Committee to support him at this time was a longstanding grievance.

After the first World War, the heady atmosphere of change brought about by the Weimar Republic offered a better chance for actual repeal of Paragraph 175. The *Gemeinschaft* collaborated with Hirschfeld's group in an alliance that lasted until 1925. In that year, Brand published a book by a regular contributor to *Der*

Eigene, Ewald Tscheck, stating that the Scientific Humanitarian Committee ought to be opposed since its actions were harmful to the German people. Another publication by Brand, "What We Want" ("Was wir wollen"), is essential to any study of the German homosexual movement. Its 20 sections set out the areas of interest and purposes of the *Gemeinschaft Der Eigenen,* ranging from bisexuality, prostitution, and nudism to opposition to "population politics."

By 1929, Brand's optimistic hopes for the new democracy had faded, leading him to declare that legal reform was only a minor goal of his organization. He concluded that the sensual activities banned by Paragraph 175 were unrelated to the more refined concepts of same-gender love espoused by the *Gemeinschaft.* The intellectual tone of *Der Eigene* limited its appeal, and its total readership remained small in comparison to more widely circulated homosexual-oriented periodicals. In the early 1930s, Brand announced plans to write his memoirs but the ascension to power of the National Socialists prevented their publication. The *Gemeinschaft* and its writings were banned and Brand's home was raided five times, with his books, photos, and journals being seized. Despite this, Brand himself was never arrested by the Nazis. He survived the war with his wife until an Allied bombing raid on Berlin killed them in their home in 1945.

Brand's legacy lived on in the person of his assistant Karl Meier, who salvaged a portion of his works and fled to Switzerland where he founded *Der Kreis* in 1932, the most important European gay journal until 1968 and the only one of the pre-war homosexual periodicals to survive World War II. His radical approaches to the ideas of individuality, unrestrained sensuality, and political freedoms and their relationship to classical same-sex love, place him as the intellectual forefather of the gay liberation theorists of the post-Stonewall years and the frank declaration that "Gay is Good."

—Robert B. Marks Ridinger

BRANTENBERG, Gerd

Nationality: Norwegian novelist and critic. **Born:** Oslo, Norway, 27 October 1941; grew up in Fredrikstad. **Education:** Schools in Fredrikstad; University of Oslo, cand. philol. (arts degree in English language and literature, history, and political science) 1970. **Career:** High school teacher, St. Hallvard Gymnasium, Drammen, 1971, Tarnby Gymnasium, Copenhagen, 1971-74, and Sinsen Gymnasium, Oslo, 1974-82; freelance writer, from 1982; columnist, *Fredriksstad Blad* and *Blikk,* Oslo. Activist, Women's Houses, Copenhagen and Oslo, 1972-83; co-founder and administrator, Literary Women's Forum, 1978-91; co-organizer, International Feminist Book Fairs, London, 1984, Oslo, 1986, Barcelona, 1990, and Amsterdam, 1992. **Member:** Board member, Union of 1948 (gay organization), Denmark, 1972-73, Norwegian Union of 1948, 1975-76, and the Norwegian Writer's Union, 1981-83; member, Norwegian Society of Authors, Norwegian Author's Centre, Norwegian Society of Playwrights, and Literary Forum for Women. **Awards:** State Scholarship for Artists and Writers. **Addresses:** c/o Women in Translation, 3131 Western Avenue, Suite 410, Seattle, Washington 98121, U.S.A.; c/o Rebecca Engrav, Seal Press, 3131 Western Avenue #410, Seattle, Washington 98121, U.S.A.

WRITINGS

Novels

Opp alle jordens homofile. Oslo, Gyldendal, 1973; translated by Brantenberg as *What Comes Naturally,* London, Women's Press, 1986.
Egalias døtre. Oslo, Pax, 1977; translated by Louis Mackay with Brantenberg as *Egalia's Daughters,* Seattle, Washington, Seal Press/Women in Translation, 1985.
Ja, vi slutter (Yes, We Stop). Oslo, Asch., 1978.
Sangen om St. Croix (The Song of St. Croix). Oslo, Asch., 1979.
Ved fergestedet (The Ferry Landing: Student Lives 1955-60). Oslo, Asch., 1985.
Favntak (Embraces). Oslo, Pax, 1985.
For alle vinder. Oslo, Asch., 1989; translated by Margaret Hayford O'Leary as *The Four Winds.* Seattle, Washington, Women in Translation, 1996.

Other

"'Anne og Anne Kommer hjem til jul'—en historie fra uvirkeligheten" (short story), in *Kjaerlightet i rosebedet.* Oslo, n.p., 1981.
Egalia (play; produced Scene 7, Oslo, 1982/83).
With others, *På Sporet av den tapte lyst (In Remembrance of Lusts Past;* literary motif study). Oslo, Pax, 1986.
Nattradio (play), in *Voksende fjell av trass.* Oslo, n.p., 1987.
"Barnet som elsket fru Samuelsen" (short story), in *Den sommeren.* Oslo, n.p., 1991.
"Frøken Detektiv og de mystiske menn" (short story), in *Byen som sluttet å plystre.* Fredrikstad, n.p., 1991.
Eremitt & entertainer (Hermit and Entertainer; essays). Oslo, Pax, 1992.
Ompadorastedet (The Ompadora Place; children's book). Oslo, Pax, 1992.

*

Adaptations: *Egalia's Daughters* adapted as a play in Sweden and Denmark.

Interviews: Interview with Verne Moberg, 30 June 1984; interview with Barbara Wilson, 1986.

Critical Sources: "A Norwegian Women's Fantasy: Gerd Brantenberg's *Egalias Døtre* as *Kvinneskelig* Utopia" by Verne Moberg, in *Scandinavian Studies,* No. 57, 1985, 325-332; "'Laughing in a Liberating Defiance': *Egalia's Daughters* and Feminist Tendentious Humor" by Marleen S. Barr, in *Discontented Discourses,* Chicago, Illinois, University of Illinois Press, 1989, 87-89; "*Egalia's Daughters*: A Satire of the Sexes" by Ann Goetting, in *Journal of Comparative Family Studies,* Vol. XXIV, No. 2, summer 1993, 264; "Molding Mothers' Maxims, Memwim's Lib, and the Great Peho Burning" by Janet Palmer Mullaney, in *Belle Lettres,* summer 1995; "Fighting Against Joy" by Lisa Alther, in *Women's Review of Books,* Vol. XIII, No. 10/11, July 1996, 35; "Introduction" by Margaret Hayford O'Leary, in *The Four Winds,* Seattle, Washington, Women in Translation, 1996; "Alternative Antisexiste—Groupe mixte Õtudiant europoen antisexiste," http://www-users.informatik.rwth-aachen.de/~florath/Mixture/

Franzoesich/Mixture.html; "Book Review: The Four Winds," http://www.norway.org/arp96/review/htm; "Gendered Communication and Language," http://www.intac.com/manfaq/feminism/refs1.; "The Light of the Midnight Sun" by Shelagh Cox, http:www.massey.ac.nz/~NZSRDA/nzssreps/journals/sites/cox14.htm; "Norwaves: News from Norway," http://rosa.nbr.no/etids/norwaves; "Norwegian Literature in English Translation," http://www.norway.org.englist.htm; "Trends in Contemporary Norwegian Literature" by Janneken Øverland, Ministry of Foreign Affairs, http://odin.dep.no/ud/nornytt/uda-424.html; interview with Gerd Brantenberg by Patti Capel Swartz, October 1996.

Gerd Brantenberg comments:

Much has changed since the 1950s. There is so much more attention on media today. I do think that *Egalia's Daughters* has had an effect on feminist consciousness raising and in changes, particularly in language, in the ways in which language is used, but language is sometimes a double edged sword.

*   *   *

Gerd Brantenberg is one of the most translated Norwegian writers. Brantenberg has "at least one clear message; the right of homosexuals to be loved and respected," Janneken Øverland wrote in "Trends in Contemporary Norwegian Literature." Brantenberg is best known for her satire of the sexes, *Egalia's Daughter,* as witnessed by the declaration of the Antisexist Alternative—European Mixed Group of Students Against Sexism that Gerd Brantenberg's *Egalia's Daughters* is among the most important anti-sexist books published. In addition, Brantenberg's other works have been well received. Her critical assessment of Scandinavian lesbian women's literature, *På Sporet av den tapte lyst,* is an important recovery of lesbian writing and precedents for current writing. A lesbian novel, *Embraces,* a collection of essays, *Hermit and Entertainer,* and *Ompadorastedet,* a children's fantasy are also important. And *What Comes Naturally, The Song of St. Croix,* and *The Four Winds* make up a semi-autobiographical trilogy of life in a small Norwegian town, exploring relationships between men and women and coming of age as a lesbian.

What Comes Naturally was Brantenberg's first published novel, but she had started years before working on the book that was to become her most famous and influential novel, *Egalia's Daughters.* As Cindy Tittle Moore noted, *Egalia's Daughters* "turns the language and social stereotypes upside down. It is really interesting to see how easily one, as reader, gets used to the 'unusual' language. This also illustrates how powerful the sexism of the language is." The condition of women and the construction of language are reversed, pointing out how women's secondary status and condition permeates patriarchal cultures. In Egalia, women rule. The care of children is undertaken by the "housebound" mafele (man) a wom (woman) has chosen, or by mafeles who must act as single parents. At the book's opening, we are introduced to the main character, Petronius. Petronius is coming of age and hopes to find a wom who will support him. To his horror, Petronius must begin wearing a peho (the counterpart of a brassiere), a contrivance that holds up and displays his penis. Pehoes are required attire, along with skirts, ruffles, and beard ribbons, for all mafeles in Egalia.

Initially, receiving protection as a "housebound" is Petronius' greatest dream. However, his attitudes change, partly as a result of a gift—a deep sea diving suit with a built-in peho—and be-

cause of a rape by three women in the dark wood one night. His reaction, and prevailing attitudes to burgeoning mafele sexuality, provide a most insightful commentary on women's roles in the patriarchal culture.

Egalia has problems. The birthrate is falling. Mafeles are becoming increasingly sexually unresponsive and restless. Isolated in their homes, mafeles, like Petronius' father, often tell their sons to attempt to avoid becoming housebounds. These housebounds become old early from the responsibilities of child care, their duty to serve their wim as often ridiculed servants and as sexual slaves. Petronius looks for alternatives. At first he feels that the wom Gro can provide answers through the economic philosophy of Clara Sparks and a group of mafeles begin to meet at Gro's home. However, she wants too much control, and when Petronius tells her he will not be her housebound although he will raise the child she is carrying, she beats and nearly drowns him. Meanwhile Petronius has realized he is truly in love with his mafele friend Baldrian. With a group of other mafeles, Petronius and Baldrian learn about past uprisings, patriarchal cultures, and the group plans political activities like public burning of pehoes and a coup of the parliament.

The message of *Egalia's Daughters* is that all people should be accepted on equal terms. Through delightful role reversals and uproarious satire, Brantenberg makes the condition of women clear. Janet Palmer Mullaney quoted an interview with Brantenberg in which she discussed the importance of language as "part of the whole setup of the kind of things for the oppressive patriarchal culture that you don't think about, like battering or rape, or lower pay.... Most of the things concerned with women's oppressions are things you never think about because they're just there. And I think that's probably where *Egalia's Daughters* has its mission, because it forces you into situations where you have to think 'Is it really as bad as that...' Then you find out, yes, it is as bad as that."

Brantenberg delights in playing with multiple meanings. As Margaret O'Leary pointed out, *The Four Winds* contains the same "exuberance and sense of humor" as *Egalia's Daughters,* but it "strikes a deeper chord, underscoring the emotional and psychological range of this versatile and talented writer." Certainly, the hero of this book and the other members of this trilogy deserve kindness. "Anyone who recalls the bad old days when same-sex love was a silent and lonely pursuit will want to read *The Four Winds,*" noted Lisa Alther in *Women's Review of Books* review.

It is easy to think that the "bad old days" are gone. They are not. As so much autobiographical writing about teenagers indicates, "same-sex love" can still be a "silent and lonely pursuit," writes Branterberg in *The Four Winds.* Brantenberg's book can help to take away that silence and some of that loneliness, helping young people to realize that they are not alone. This book, then, serves a double purpose: it is both a tale of the way things were for those fortunate enough not to have lived through these lonely times, and a book that speaks to the loneliness some still encounter. As Lisa Alther pointed out, "*The Four Winds* is a deeply moving and a very funny book. Every lesbian under 35 ought to read it."

The Four Winds follows Inger Holm from her high school graduation in Fredrikstad to work as an *au pair* in Edinburgh, Scotland, and on a sea voyage to the University at Oslo with a man who wants to marry her. Inger realizes that she is attracted to women, not to men. Her self-condemnation reflects the social condemnation of the time, and medical and psychological attitudes toward lesbianism. Inger's sense of isolation lessens through the novel. From her unspoken crush on the daughter of the Scottish household in which she works (unspoken despite that daughter's hand on her leg almost daily) to her beginning of an affair while at the university with a classmate from Fredrikstad, Inger searches for acceptance of herself. For the first time in Ingmar Bergman's *The Silence* Inger hears one woman tell another "I love you." At the time, Inger was in love with a heterosexual woman, Rose Mary, who asked her to explain the film. She wants to say "That's you and me, Rose Mary. How could it be possible that you didn't see it?" but she realizes that "the fact she didn't see it—was exactly what the film was about."

After Rose Mary leaves for her home in England, Inger discovers Marit, an old friend is also a lesbian, and the two begin a relationship. Once they start making love, they never get enough. Despite their own questions about their relationship and whether or not it could last, Inger realizes that although "she didn't know if they could stay together, and if there would even be a world for them to stay together in, and if it was possible to create such a world...she had an intense feeling of future." Lisa Alther pointed out, she "begins to foresee a time when women who love each other can stop 'fighting against joy'; as Alther indicated, "the time may not be yet, but *The Four Winds* is a valuable contribution to that inevitable meltdown."

The Four Winds is a family's story as well. Inger's life is interwoven with that of her grandmother's, and with that of her often brutal, alcoholic father and the mother whose acceptance she treasures. It is the story of sisters, one of whom dies, and one who is born much later as an attempt to replace the lost daughter. Despite the loneliness and brutality of this book, however, it contains a tenderness and humor that heal both the writer and the reader.

Brantenberg's *What Comes Naturally,* is another part of the trilogy of Inger Holm. Shelagh Cox, in her review "The Light of the Midnight Sun," claimed that it has become "a cult book in Scandinavia." Set in Oslo in the 1960s, *What Comes Naturally* describes the absurdities of lesbian clandestine life. Cox noted that it "takes us into the absurd situations that arise when women with strong and forthright natures have to dissemble in a society in which they cannot say who they are." The comic elements of this book make the "serious portrayal of the life of a lesbian woman" more effective than some wholly serious books, and the book is "profoundly feminist in...acknowledg[ing] and tak[ing] on the struggle women must engage in with themselves," according to Cox.

—Patti Capel Swartz

BRIGHT, Susie

Nationality: American sex writer, editor, and performer. **Born:** Arlington, Virginia, 25 March 1958. **Education:** California State University, Long Beach; University of California, Santa Cruz, B.A. in Community Studies 1981. **Family:** One daughter. **Career:** Writer and educator on lesbian sex and lifestyle issues. Staffer and manager, Good Vibrations erotic supplies store, San Francisco, California, 1981-86; editor, *On Our Backs: Entertainment for Adventurous Lesbians,* San Francisco, California, 1984-91; contributing editor and film consultant, *Penthouse Forum,* 1987-89; appeared as the character Susie Sexpert in Monica Treut's film *The Virgin Machine,* 1988; columnist, *San Francisco Review of Books,* 1992-94; advisory board member, *OUT!,* 1995; contributing fiction editor, *Penthouse,* 1995-96; "technical consultant" for sexual scenes in the film *Bound,* 1996; contributor of essays and reviews to periodicals, including *Advocate, Elle, Esquire, Future Sex Magazine, New York Times Book Review, Playboy, San Francisco Erotic Dancer, Utne Reader, Village Voice,* and *Whole Earth Review.* **Agent:** Worley/Shoemaker Management, 215 West 53rd Street, Kansas City, Missouri 64112, U.S.A.

WRITINGS

Nonfiction

Susie Sexpert's Lesbian Sex World. New York, Cleis Press, 1990.
Susie Bright's Sexual Reality: A Virtual Sex World Reader. New York, Cleis Press, 1992.
Susie Bright's Sexwise: America's Favorite X-rated Intellectual Does Dan Quayle, Catherine MacKinnon, Stephen King, Camille Paglia. New York, Cleis Press, 1995.
And co-editor, with Jill Posener, *Nothing but the Girl: The Blatant Lesbian Image,* Cassell, 1996.
Sexual State of the Union, New York, Simon & Schuster, 1997.

Editor

Herotica: A Collection of Women's Erotic Writing. San Francisco, Down There Press, 1988.
With Joani Blank, *Herotica II: A Collection of Women's Erotic Fiction.* New York, Plume, 1992.
Series editor, *The Best American Erotica.* New York, Colliers-MacMillan, 1993-97.
Herotica III: A Collection of Women's Erotic Fiction. New York, Plume, 1994.
Totally Herotica, Book-of-the-Month Club, 1995.

Other

The Virgin Machine (screenplay), directed by Monica Treut. 1988.
"Safe Sex for Sex Maniacs" (lecture; delivered at Smith College, March 1993).
"Covering Sex: Sex in the Media" (lecture; delivered at Lesbian/Gay Media Conference, New York, 1993).
"Porn I've Known and Loved and Even Been Offended By" (performance; produced at Roxie Theater, 1993, 1995).
Erotique (screenplay). Group 1 Films, 1994.

Recordings: Cyborgasm (produced by Lisa Palac and Ron Gommpertz), Heydey/Time Warner, 1994; The Edge of the Bed (produced by Palac), Heydey/Time Warner, 1995; with Molly Katzen and Harriet Lerner, Food, Sex, and Relationships (audio book), Sounds True, 1996.

*

Interviews: By Andrea Juno in *Angry Women,* San Francisco, Re/Search Publications, 1991, 194-221; "Susie Bright: On Girl Jocks" by Roxxie, in *Girljock,* summer 1991; "An Interview with Susie Bright" by Margaret Maree, in *Impact: New Orleans,* September

1995; "Amazon.com talks to Susie Bright," at *www.Amazon.com*, 1996; "Laura Post Chats with Susie Bright," in *Harvard Gay & Lesbian Review*, winter 1996; "Interview with Susie Bright" by Brian Plattoff, in *School of the Art Institute Newspaper*, April 1996.

Critical Sources: "Feminist Pornography" by Laura Frazier, in *Mother Jones,* February/March 1990; "Gay and Lesbian Erotica in the US" (documentary), London, BBC, 1991; "Walk on the Bright Side" by Jenny Jedekin, in *Rolling Stone*, January 1991; "Increasing Our Dirty Word Power: Why Yesterday's Smut Is Today's Erotica" by Walter Kendrick, in *New York Times Book Review,* May 1992; "Sex in the 90s: There's More Going On—Straight and Gay, Safe and Unsafe—Than You'd Think" by Michael Gross, in *New York,* June 1992; "That Girl by the Stage, and Why She's There" by Ann Powers, in *New York Times,* December 1992; "Gay Clout: The New Power Brokers," in *Newsweek,* 3 May 1993; "The Rise of 'Do Me' Feminism," in *Esquire,* February 1994; "The Prime of Ms. Susie Bright," in *Windy City Times,* 30 June 1994; "A Primer on Erotic Prose" by Alistair Williamson, in *Harvard Gay & Lesbian Review,* winter 1995; "Briefly, Susie Bright" by George Kalogerakis, in *Vanity Fair* (New York), February 1995, 68; "The X-rated Intellectual" by Chris Watson, in *Santa Cruz Sentinel,* 11 June 1995; "Lesbian Chic" by Brendan Baber and Eric Spitznagel, in *Playboy,* August 1995; "An Erotica of Our Own" by Eric Alterman, in *Elle,* August 1995; "Slap Shots" by Jack Boulware, in *San Francisco Weekly,* 2 August 1995; "Too Sexy for Her Shirt" by Louise Carolin, in *Diva,* January 1996; "Pornography: Does it Suck?" by Cynthia Heimel, in *Playboy,* May 1996; "How to Succeed in Sex without Really Trying" by Adam Begley, in *New York Observer,* 21 October 1996; "Susie Bright" by Denise Sullivan, in *Speak,* fall 1996.

Susie Bright comments:

My first public writing began because I put out an underground high school newspaper with my friends in the mid 1970s. I wrote articles about narcs on campus, how to get free birth control, and socialism in our lifetime! A lot of this writing was radical-hack-rhetoric, but I was also learning, in my fashion, how to express myself. In the early 1980s, I started putting out small press magazines and books about women's sexuality, and they caused a bit of a sensation. My friends teased me, calling me "Susie Sexpert"—and the name stuck. I probably do know more about porn, lesbianism, feminism, and sexual politics than any life form ought to. I've always thought that the most intriguing part of politics is in the personal details. Sexuality is often at the center of that intersection! (From an interview with Susie Bright on *www.Amazon.com,* used with permission of the author.)

*   *   *

One's first encounter with Susie Bright is as likely to occur in a cinema as in a bookstore. In Monica Treut's *The Virgin Machine*, released in 1988, a naive young German woman is exploring the San Francisco underground lesbian scene, which is much wilder and stranger than she expected. One of her mentors is a voluptuous, bespectacled, slyly grinning woman known as Susie Sexpert who opens a doctor's bag to reveal a bewildering array of dildoes to the stunned main character and by extension to us, the equally "inexperienced," shockable audience.

The playfulness and boldness of Susie Bright's screen character captures her own personality: she has played the role of lesbian "sexpert" for many years, delighting audiences both in her home base of San Francisco and around the country with her lesbian erotica film/lecture presentations "How to Read a Dirty Movie," and "All Girl Action." Yet Bright seems in some ways an elusive figure, a multi-faceted renaissance woman of sex in a conservative era when feminist consciousness-raising had become a thing of the past. It is Susie Bright's insistence on playing many roles and appealing to mixed audiences, yet staying grounded in the lesbian community, that makes her work so compelling, original, and provocative.

Bright's background explains a little of this crusading spirit of hers. As she writes in *Susie Sexpert's Lesbian Sex World,* she "went to high school in West L.A., which during the mid-seventies was a beehive of teenage lesbian feminists, hippie bisexuals and proto-punk anarchists. In 1974 I would have thought you had a screw loose if you weren't politically and sexually committed to women." She was involved in intense socialist activism during this time, leaving school at age 17 to join a youth group in the Midwest. Her first sexual experience had come at the age of 16 in a threesome with a man and a woman. She never looked back. Sexual liberation was always on her agenda, always an integral part of her feminism. She writes lyrically about her early days as a teenage lesbian, yet implies that her true sexual awakening came later, when she discovered vibrators, sex toys, the butch-femme community, and porn.

Susie Bright began working in Good Vibrations, the feminist erotic supplies store, in 1981. "Every day in the guise of selling vibrators, dildoes, erotic books and lubricants, I talked to women in detail about their sexual lives," she writes in *Lesbian Sex World.* What she discovered was that even the fairly liberated and sexually-aware customers were filled with shame about their bodies, often did not know how to orgasm, and were unaware of basic anatomical facts. Her years as a sex educator were put to good use when she became editor of *On Our Backs* magazine, which styled itself as "entertainment for the adventurous lesbian." *On Our Backs* was a magazine of lesbian erotica which featured graphic stories and pictures, along with Susie Bright's "Toys for Us" column. The mixture of sex education and entertainment was pure Susie Bright. When she published a collection of these columns as *Susie Bright's Lesbian Sex World* in 1990, astonished and eager readers were presented with a wonderful treasure trove of essays on such topics as the G-Spot, fisting, safe sex, vibrators, dildoes, anal sex, the butch-femme dynamic, porn, masturbation, even pre-natal lesbian sex.

What was new about these essays is that sexual information was presented frankly, playfully, stylishly, yet never less than explicitly. Susie Bright's "sex writing" is not sleazy; instead, it seems that she truly cares about the quality of her readers' lives. She brings a worldliness and a sophistication to the lesbian canon. It is as if she is bringing the world of sex and the world of lesbianism together, and showing both the world and the lesbian community that lesbians are sexual, diverse, and beautiful. Her writing can be slick, but it is often intensely physical and earthy, as when she describes the heretofore obscure practice of fisting in *Lesbian Sex World*:

> "The intimacy is unbelievable. You are all the way inside of your lover; her body is wrapped around your fist like a cocoon....If this sounds romantic, you're right. Fisting is incredibly romantic."

With writing like this, she convinces us that it is.

Susie Bright's later books, *Susie Bright's Sexual Reality* and *Sexwise,* are also in the same vein: collections of essays that combine the titillating, the intellectual, and the practical. Bright participated in another struggle, however, which underlines another important part of her life: the pro/anti porn debate, which simmered and exploded in the mid 1980s around the time the Reagan administration produced the Meese Commission report on pornography. Here Bright stepped outside of the gay community to champion straight porn's right to exist, opposing such "anti-porn feminists" as Catharine MacKinnon and Andrea Dworkin. This struggle had a potentially serious side: Dworkin and MacKinnon wanted to ban all pornography as dangerous to women, which would presumably have included feminist erotica and authors like Bright herself and Pat Califia. In her introduction to one of the excellent collections of erotica she edited, *Herotica 3*, Bright decries this "anti-erotic lock on feminist ideology." This is not *her* feminism, and she was horrified to find herself suddenly demonized and dismissed as a dupe of the porn industry.

Herotica 1, 2, and *3* are collections which brought women's erotica to a new and fascinating level. Susie Bright's love of the nitty-gritty of sex, of telling it like it is, make her her ideal editor. These are mixed stories: women of all sexual orientations contributed. The smorgasbord of sexual activities described all have one thing in common: the woman's sexual desire is never in question, *her* orgasm is the goal, and none of the stories are "politically correct." This emphasis on sexual variety, on tenderness and roughness, on the blurring of sexual orientation, is presented as a healthy and vital thing. Susie Bright herself writes frequently about choosing to call herself a lesbian, yet practicing bisexuality; this is not a contradiction for her, nor to many women in the lesbian community who are grateful for her candor and for whom labels have become increasingly meaningless. Her goal is to "shatter stereotypes and misleading information," she told *Angry Women*.

Bright also understands, and writes about, sexuality's dark side, acknowledging that the fantasies that get people off best are often the least palatable ones. This truth is often ignored by the feminist "moral majority," who believe that every fantasy can potentially become reality and harm women. Bright writes eloquently in her introduction to *Herotica 3* about the middle-class habit of deferring sexual gratification so as to ensure a secure future, as opposed to the working class concept of enjoying pleasure now and living for the moment. She concludes: "I won't turn my back on sexual exploration even when I sense darkness there. That's exactly what keeps me pushing. I am making a different kind of investment in the future, one with such intimate rites that it cannot be deferred ultimately; one that we cannot hold back, disguise or deny."

The very real bravery in her self-disclosure should not be minimized. It is rare that women writers are comfortable enough with themselves to approach sexuality in the no-holds-barred way that Susie Bright has done. She has given all of us a clearer idea of our choices, and showed us that we have nothing to gain by deferring our pleasures.

—Gabriella West

BRITE, Poppy Z.

Nationality: American novelist and short story writer. **Born:** New Orleans, 25 May 1967. **Education:** Briefly attended University of North Carolina, Chapel Hill. **Family:** Married to Christopher DeBarr. **Career:** Has worked as a gourmet candymaker, mouse caretaker, artist's model, and exotic dancer; writer, from 1991. **Awards:** *Lambda* Literary Award nominations, 1991, 1993; Bram Stoker Award nomination, 1991; World Fantasy Award nomination, 1993; British Fantasy Society Best Newcomer Award, 1994; International Critics' Award, World Horror Convention, for best anthology, 1994. **Address:** P.O. Box 750151, New Orleans, Louisiana 70125, U.S.A.

WRITINGS

Novels

Lost Souls. New York, Delacorte Press, 1992; London, Penguin Books, 1993.
Drawing Blood. California, Cahill Publishing, 1993; New York, Delacorte Press 1993; London, Penguin Books, 1994.
Exquisite Corpse. London, Orion Books 1996; New York, Simon & Schuster, 1996.

Short Stories

"Optional Music for Voice and Piano," in *Horror Show*, 1985.
"Missing," in *Horror Show*, Vol. 4, No. 4, 1986.
"The Elder," in *Horror Show*, Vol. 5, No. 1, 1987.
"Love (Ash 1)," in *Horror Show*, Vol. 5, No. 4, 1987.
"Angels," in *Horror Show*, Vol. 5, No. 4, 1987.
"A Taste of Blood and Altars," in *Horror Show*, Vol. 6, No. 2, summer 1988.
"Footprints in the Water," in *Women of Darkness 2*, edited by Kathryn Ptacek. New York, Tor Books, 1990.
"His Mouth Will Taste of Wormwood," in *Borderlands 1*, edited by Thomas F. Monteleone. Baltimore, Borderlands Press, 1990.
"Xenophobia," in *Horror Show*, Vol. 8, No. 1, 1990.
"The Ash of Memory, the Dust of Desire," in *Dead End: City Limits*, edited by David Silva and Paul F. Olsen. New York, St. Martin's Press, 1991.
"Calcutta, Lord of Nerves," in *Book of the Dead 2: Still Dead*, edited by John Skipp Bantam and Craig Spector. California, Zeising Books, 1992.
"How To Get Ahead In New York," in *Gauntlet*, No. 4, 1992.
"The Sixth Sentinel," in *Borderlands 3*, edited by Thomas F. Monteleone. Baltimore, Borderlands Press, 1993.
"Toxic Wastrels," in *The Earth Strikes Back*, edited by Richard Chizmar. California, Ziesing Books, 1994.
With Christa Faust, "Saved," in *Young Blood*, edited by Mike Baker. New York, Zebra Books, 1994.
"Exquisite Creep," in *South from Midnight*, edited by Richard Gilliam. Southern Fried Press, 1994.
His Mouth Will Taste of Wormwood (limited edition). London, Penguin Books, 1994.
Swamp Foetus. Baltimore, Borderlands Press, 1994; London, Penguin Books, 1995; reprinted as *Wormwood*, New York, Dell, 1996.
"Mussolini and the Axeman's Jazz," in *Dark Destiny: Proprietors of Fate*, edited by Edward E. Kramer. Atlanta, White Wolf Books, 1995.
"Becoming the Monster," in *Weird Business*, edited by Joe R. Lansdale and Richard Klaw. Austin, Mojo Press, 1995.

With David Ferguson, "The Poor Miller's Apprentice and the Cat" (short story), in *Happily Ever After: Fairy Tales for Gay Men.* New York, Richard Kasak Books, 1996.

With Christa Faust, "Triads" (novella), in *Revelations,* edited by Douglas E. Winter. New York, HarperPrism, 1997.

"Self-Made Man," in *Dark Terrors 3: The Gollancz Book of Horror,* edited by Stephen Jones and David Sutton. London, Gollancz, 1997.

"Entertaining Mr. Orton," in *Grave Passions,* forthcoming.

"Pin Money," in *Rage,* forthcoming.

Other

Editor, *Love In Vein* (anthology). New York, HarperPrism, 1994.

"Untitled" (nonfiction), in *Dick for a Day.* New York, Villard Books, 1996.

"Sur le Decadence" (nonfiction), in *Tribe* (New Orleans), October 1996.

"The Poetry of Violence" (nonfiction), in *Screen Violence: An Anthology.* London, Bloomsbury Books, 1996.

"Sinsemilla and Sensibility" (nonfiction), in *Rage* (Beverly Hills, California), No. 1, 1996.

"Depraved in Dublin" (nonfiction), in *Rage,* December 1996.

Editor, *Love In Vein 2* (anthology). New York, HarperPrism, 1997.

"Reviving the Oval Offspring" (nonfiction), in *Spy,* 1997.

Courtney Love: The Real Story (biography). New York, Simon & Schuster, 1997.

*

Interviews: *Horror Show,* Vol. 5, No. 4, 1987; *Cemetery Dance,* Vol. 5, No. 3-4, fall 1993; "Poppy Z. Brite" by Nancy Kilpatrick, in *Horror,* No. 1, January 1994; *Independent on Sunday* (London), 13 March 1994; *Time Out* (London), 1994; *Mondo 2000,* No. 14, 1995; *Washington Post,* 29 August 1994; *Out,* September 1996.

Bibliography: "Poppy Z. Brite Bibliography," at http://www.negia.net/~pandora/pzbbiblio.html.

Critical Sources: "The Top 10 Books That Suck" by Linda Marotta, in *Fangoria,* No. 116, September 1992; "Poppy Z. Brite: A Fact Sheet" by Bill Evans, at http://sflovers.rutgers.edu/pub/sf-lovers/FAQs/brite.faq, 1 May 1995; review of *Exquisite Corpse,* in *Kirkus Reviews,* 15 May 1996; review of *Exquisite Corpse,* in *Publishers' Weekly,* 24 June 1996.

Poppy Z. Brite comments:

I'm often asked if my work is intended to have a "liberating" effect on gay readers, especially younger ones. While I love the idea of having a liberating effect on anyone, I don't write with any sort of agenda—I write what I have to write. If the reader finds something he can use, something to inspire him, that's wonderful—nothing makes me happier than a fan letter saying "You gave me the courage to come out"—but when it comes to their work, writers are a lonely, selfish bunch. First and foremost, I write this stuff for myself, because I don't have a choice.

If I spent time worrying about what straight readers were going to think of my work, I'd never get anything done. I haven't received much negative feedback toward my sexual situations except for being called "amoral," which I choose to take as a compliment. One reviewer pointed out that I was limiting my audience by my affinity for male homosexuals. And that's probably true. But I would limit my audience in some way no matter who I wrote about, unless I chose only bland, featureless characters with no lives whatsoever. I write about the people I love.

And I don't especially *want* homophobes for my audience, any more than I would want, say, racists. If they want to ready my books, great. They don't *have* to, and if they do and find something that makes them squirm, I offer no apology for that. It's good for them.

*   *   *

Essentially a horror writer, Poppy Z. Brite has earned her distinction by writing from the fringes of modern experience. Her fiction is informed by a fusion of cyberpunk, Goth, underground comics, and more than a few drugs. She has confidently claimed her fictional territory by re-inventing an often repetitive genre as a mode of contemporary expression. Her characters deal with addiction, sexuality, AIDS, technology, cyberspace, as well as the expected amounts of gore. Like Anne Rice, who brought the homosexual undertones of vampirism to the surface in her popular novels, Brite creates characters who are almost always gay men.

Her first novel, *Lost Souls,* which was written in 1987-88 and published after revisions in 1992, focuses on the familiar horror device of vampires. But Brite's are no traditional vampires. Molochai, Twig, and their leader Zillah, with their "dark blots of makeup," are more like immortal Goths as they travel around America in their black van, listening to rock music, and satisfying themselves with blood, torture, and a vast array of drugs. The complications arise when Nothing, Zillah's half-vampire son, tracks down his father and finds himself sexually drawn to him. The book is ripe—perhaps overripe—with decadence and corruption, and the language is sometimes adolescently purple. Brite herself refers to this as a "young" novel, acknowledging that in the time lapse between writing and publication she had written several short stories and most of another novel. What is interesting is the way that the themes she sets out here—of death and sex and homosexual attraction—become stronger and more controlled as her fictional experience increases.

In her second novel, *Drawing Blood,* Brite again mixes the modern with the traditional. Her protagonist, Zachary Bosch, is a computer hacker on the run from New Orleans after cracking one code too many. He encounters Trevor McGee, a misfit with a bloody family history, in a North Carolina Bible Belt town called Missing Mile. Having set up a home with Zach, the past comes back to haunt Trevor and the tender descriptions of love and sex contrast starkly with the gory goings-on at the house: taps that spout blood, mirrors that reflect decaying faces. Brite makes some thoughtful connections between cyberspace and hauntings and, in the process, cleverly remixes her genre. Where *Drawing Blood* most succeeds, however, is in its portrayal of Trevor and Zach's relationship. Trevor, damaged and then haunted by a violent and murderous father, learns to love Zach, realizing that lovemaking can be as "raw as holding someone's heart in his hands." Despite what some critics have called an unnecessarily sloppy ending, Brite raises pertinent emotional issues, giving credence to her claim to be a gay man within a woman's body.

Exquisite Corpse, her strongest work in terms of theme and gory content, tells the story of two serial killers, Andrew Compton and Jay Byrne. Compton is a notorious English psychopath whom we first encounter in his cell in Painswick Prison. By successfully faking his own death he flees England to New Orleans, where he meets Jay Burne, his American counterpart, who has for years been trawling the French Quarter to find boys to torture and mutilate. Their meeting is one of like minds and together they search New Orleans for the perfect victim.

With *Exquisite Corpse,* Brite takes the Gothic thriller genre back to its origins as a "fantastic" vehicle for the expression of our fear of dystopia, a means of saying in fiction what we dare not say in real terms. She portrays the serial killers as modern vampires, hungry for flesh in order to gain emotional fulfillment. Until their meeting both Burne and Compton are unable to enjoy sex unless it is with a corpse, or parts of corpses. Theirs is a need to posses and control not only metaphorically, but actually, literally, by being able to take a body apart and reduce it to "manageable pieces." This vision of emotional dystopia is particularly relevant to fin-de-siecle neurosis. Brite portrays a world where love can only be satisfied through death and where complete control of the love object is paramount in the sexual experience.

Some of the book's strongest writing comes from the sub-plot concerning Luke Ransom and his ex-lover, a Vietnamese American named Tran Vinh. Ransom is a cult novelist, struggling to come to terms with his HIV-positive status and the consequent loss of Tran. He broadcasts on the pirate radio station WHIV, spouting vitriol and playing loud music to New Orleans under the pseudonym of Lush Rimbaud. Through this story Brite romanticizes AIDS in the same way Gothic novelists once romanticized consumption. Luke takes on the personae of a suffering anti-hero railing against the world, and is ultimately more heroic than the two "superhuman" serial killers who see their HIV status as another excuse to continue their killing spree. Brite manages to write about AIDS and HIV without campaigning or moralizing; she has found a fresh way to fictionalize a disease that has haunted the late twentieth-century consciousness.

—Julia Bell

BRONSKI, Michael Allen

Nationality: American writer, cultural critic, and activist. **Born:** Queens, New York, 12 May 1949; moved to Union, New Jersey, 1955. **Education:** Rutgers University, Newark, New Jersey; Brandeis University, Waltham, Massachusetts, M.F.A. in playwriting 1973. **Family:** Companion of poet and writer Walta Borawski, from 1975 until Borawski's death from AIDS related complications in 1994. **Career:** Freelance writer, Cambridge, Massachusetts, from 1973; consulting editor, *Gay Community News,* from 1985; book review co-editor, *Z Magazine,* from 1986; book review columnist, "First Hand" and "Between the Lines," in *The Guide*; film review columnist, "Flickers," in *The Guide,* and "Reel Politic," in *Z Magazine*; gay history columnist, "Great Gay Guys," in *Guys*; political opinion columnist, "One-in-Ten," in *Boston Phoenix,* and "Bronski Beat," in *In Newsweekly,* 1992-95; contributor of reviews and articles to periodicals, including *Advocate* and *Radical America,* from 1985, *South End News,* 1985-93, *Lambda Book Report,* from 1986. Publisher, *Good Gay Poets* and Fag Rag Books; program coordinator, for OutWrite: Lesbian and Gay Literary Conference (a project of the Bromfield Street School Educational Foun-

dation), 1992, 1993, 1995, 1996, and 1998; **Member:** Board member, Bromfield Street School Educational Foundation; curator, with writer Michael Lowenthal, GCN-off-the-Page Reading Series, from 1994. Founding member, Fag Rag Collective, from 1971, *Boston Gay Review,* 1978-84, and Good Gay Poets Collective. **Agent:** Jed Mattes, 2095 Broadway #302, New York, New York 10023, U.S.A.

WRITINGS

Nonfiction

Culture Clash: The Making of Gay Sensibility. Boston, South End Press, 1984.
Editor, *Taking Liberties: Gay Men's Essays on Politics, Culture, and Sex.* New York, Masquerade Books, 1996.
Editor, *Flashpoint: Gay Male Sexual Writing.* New York, Masquerade Books, 1996.
The Pleasure Impulse: Culture, Backlash and the Struggle for Gay Freedom. New York, St Martin's Press, 1997.
Gay and Lesbian Culture, New York, Chelsea House, 1997.

Essays

"Judy Garland and Others: Notes on Idolization and Derision," in *Lavender Culture,* edited by Karla Jay and A. Young. New York, Harcourt, Brace Jovanovich, 1978.
"Gay Men and Movies: Reel to Real," in *Gay Life: Leisure, Love and Living for the Contemporary Gay Male,* edited by E. Rofes. New York, Doubleday, 1986.
"Reform of Revolution? The Challenge of Creating a Gay Sensibility," in *Gay Spirit: Myth and Meaning,* edited by Mark Thompson. New York, St. Martin's Press, 1987.
"AIDS, Art and Obits," in *Personal Dispatches: Writers Confront AIDS,* edited by John Preston. New York, St. Martin's Press, 1989.
"Death and the Erotic Imagination," in *Taking Liberties,* edited by E. Carter and S. Watney. London, Serpent's Tail, 1989.
"A Dream Is a Wish Your Heart Makes: Notes on the Materialization of Sexual Fantasy," in *Leatherfolk,* edited by Mark Thompson. Boston, Alyson Publications, 1991.
"All That Jazz: Gay Men and Pop Divas," in *The Big Gay Book: A Gay Man's Survival Guide for the '90s,* edited by John Preston. New York, New American Library/Plume, 1991.
"Seduced and Abandoned: Fantasies and Fallacies of Harvard Square," in *Hometowns: Gay Men Write About Where They Belong,* edited by John Preston. New York, New American Library/Dutton, 1991.
"The Brother, the Turtle, the Crackers, the Glasses," in *A Member of the Family,* edited by John Preston. New York, Dutton, 1992.
"How Sweet (and Sticky) It Was: Public Sex and Private Memories," in *Flesh and the Word 2,* edited by John Preston. New York, Dutton, 1993.
"How to Meet Men in a World that Is Falling Apart," in *Positively Gay,* edited by Betty Berzon. San Francisco, Celestial Arts, San Francisco, 1993.
"Magic and AIDS: Presumed Innocent," in *Our Time 3: Readings From Recent Periodicals,* edited by R. Atwan. New York, St. Martin's Press, 1993.

"War Culture: War Language, Rape and AIDS," in *A Certain Terror: Heterosexism, Militarism, Violence & Change,* edited by R. Cleaver. Ann Arbor, Michigan, American Friends Service Committee, 1993.

"Culture Clash," in *The Long Road to Freedom,* edited by Mark Thompson. New York, St. Martin's Press, 1994.

"I'll Call Tomorrow: Susan Hayward, Summer Nights, and the Scent of Memory," in *Friends and Lovers: Gay Men Write About Their Chosen Families,* edited by John Preston. New York, Dutton, 1994.

"Why Gay Men Can't Talk About Sex," in *Flesh and the Word 3,* edited by John Preston. New York, Dutton, 1994.

Contributor, *The Gay Almanac,* edited by L. Witt, S. Thomas, and E. Marcus. New York, Warner, 1995.

Contributor, *Gay and Lesbian Literature,* Vol. 1, edited by Sharon Malinowski. Detroit, Gale Research, 1995.

"Meditation and Litany 1995," in *Queer View Mirror: Lesbian and Gay Short, Short Fiction,* edited by James C. Johnstone and Karen X. Tulchinsky. Arsenal Pulp Press, 1996.

With Michael Lowenthal, "Doctor Fell," in *Flesh and the Word 4.* New York, Dutton, 1997.

"Death and the Erotic Imagination," in *Personal Dispatches: Writers Confront AIDS.*

*

Critical Sources: Unpublished interview with Michael Bronski by Andrea L.T. Peterson, October 1996.

*   *   *

Writer and activist Michael Bronski, who learned through "social change" movements that "the fight for personal freedom is inseparable from that of social freedom," has been politically active since the 1960s. His involvement with Students for Democratic Society (SDS) and the Gay Liberation Front profoundly influenced him. Lesbian/feminist writers as well as such social critics as Norman O. Brown and Herbert Marcuse "helped form" his critical thinking. In an interview with Andrea L.T. Peterson, Bronski said that the Gay Liberation Movement "and its connection to broader political and social change movements helped shape how I view my life, work, politics, and sex." Though the movements and writings of the 1960s influenced Bronski, he has long had a strong sense of himself. He knew he was gay from around age 8 and actually came out at 18 in 1967.

As a cultural critic, Bronski has written about all aspects of gay and lesbian culture and politics and reviewed film, books, theater, performance art, and the visual arts. In addition, Bronski has written extensively about sexuality, AIDS, politics, and social issues—often in an attempt to explain to himself "why I like or respond to a piece of art or culture." "It is impossible," he commented, "to talk about any aspects of culture or politics without factoring in people's relationship to/with sexuality and eroticism. The basis for all of gay and lesbian culture," he declared, "is gay people's specific relationship to sexuality and the importance of that sexuality in gay people's lives." Bronski noted that sexuality "divorced from reproduction is a radical idea in Western culture and it places gay people in an outsider position that allows them to be critical observers of mainstream culture as well as offering alternatives and options for that culture."

Bronski not only comments on culture but also writes to explain "how culture works." "Culture doesn't just happen," Bronski told Peterson; there are "political and psychological factors that go into different phenomena in our culture." Bronski writes about culture as a "complex response to sexual, political, economic, and social factors. When we understand that," he continued, "we will understand how we respond to culture, and how we can use culture to our advantage politically."

Bronski elaborated on some of the complexities of his own responses to Peterson. "Ironically," he said, "although I am now overtly critical of the Catholic Church and its social policies, being raised Roman Catholic has been an enormous influence on my thinking and writing." The idea of the "mystical body of Christ," he adds, "which connects all humans in a seamless web of responsibility and commune-ship, can easily be translated into progressive political terms." The virtual fear of the body and unmasked homophobia expressed in the teachings of the Church have been tempered for Bronski by the "emphasis placed on the body in the works of such mystics as Julian of Norwich, Margery Kemp, St. Theresa of Avila, and St. John of the Cross." Through these writings Bronski has grasped how important the human body is "in understanding our relationship to others as well as a larger community."

As an extremely vocal cultural critic, Bronski's strong opinions and insistence on the interconnectedness of culture have helped to encourage and to form the critical thinking of a new generation of gay men and lesbians. His *Culture Clash* "attempted to place gay male culture and sensibility into a larger and broader historical and theoretical framework." No other books had yet attempted to do this. The book continued to be a popular contribution to the understanding of gay and lesbian culture into the 1990s. Bronski planned to elaborate on *Culture Clash* with the publication of his book *The Pleasure Impulse.*

—Andrea L.T. Peterson

BROOKE, Rupert

Nationality: British poet. **Born:** Rugby, 3 August 1887. **Education:** Highbrow Preparatory School; Rugby, 1901-06; Kings College, Cambridge, 1906-10. **Military Service:** Served in the Royal Navy, 1914-15; Sub-Lieutenant. **Died:** The Aegean Sea on the hospital ship Duguay-Trouin, of blood poisoning, 23 April 1915 (buried on the Greek island of Skyros).

Writings

Poems. London, Sidgwick & Jackson, 1911.

Lithuania: A Drama in One Act. Chicago, The Chicago Little Theatre, 1915.

1914 and Other Poems. London, Sidgwick & Jackson, 1915.

The Collected Poems of Rupert Brooke: With an Introduction by George Edward Woodberry, and Biographical Note by Margaret Lavington. New York, John Lane, 1915.

John Webster and the Elizabethan Drama. London, Sidgwick & Jackson, 1916.

Letters from America. London, Sidgwick & Jackson, 1916.

The Collected Poems: With a Memoir by Edward Marsh. London, Sidgwick & Jackson, 1918.
Democracy and the Arts. London, Rupert Hart-Davis, 1946.
The Poetical Works of Rupert Brooke, edited by Geoffrey Keynes. London, Faber & Faber, 1946.
The Prose of Rupert Brooke, edited by Christopher Hassall. London, Sidgwick & Jackson, 1956.
The Letters of Rupert Brooke, edited by Geoffrey Keynes. London, Faber and Faber, 1968.
Letters from Rupert Brooke to His Publisher, 1911-1914. New York, Octagon Books, 1975.
Song of Love: The Letters of Rupert Brooke and Noel Olivier, 1909-1915, edited by Pippa Harris. London, Bloomsbury, 1991.

*

Adaptations: "The Dead" and "The Soldier" were both adapted for voice, violoncello, and piano by Theodore Chanler in 1917; "The Soldier" was adapted as a song by John Ireland in 1917, and again the same year for mezzo-soprano or baritone and piano, by Matthijs Vermeulen; poems from *1914 & Other Poems* were adapted as *Spring Sorrow* and *Blow Out, You Bugles* by John Ireland, 1918; "Waikiki" was adapted as one part of *Three Poems for Voice and Piano, Op. 9* by Charles Tomlinson Griffes, 1918; "The Clouds" and "The Dead" were both adapted for bass or baritone and piano by Reginald C. Robbins, 1927; "The Clouds" was again adapted for high voice and piano by Godfrey Turner, 1934; "The Dead" was adapted for chorus and orchestra with soprano, alto, or tenor solo, by Orvis Ross, 1942; "Jealousy" was adapted as one part of *Four Orchestral Songs* by Quinto Maganini, 1943; "Sonnet," "The Wayfarers," and "Springtime" were adapted as *3 Poems: Op. 123, for Tenor, Flute, Oboe, Clarinet, and French Horn* by Siegfried Borris, 1976; "The Way That Lovers Use" was adapted by Ethel Glenn Hier (1889-1971) for voice and piano in an undated holograph score; six poems ("Song," "Colloquial," "Travel," "The Way That Lovers Use," "Beauty and Beauty," and "The Young Man in April") were adapted as *After: Six Songs of Poems by Rupert Brooke* by Marjo Tal, 1978; "The Dead" was adapted as one section of *Time for Remembrance: A Peace Cantata for Soprano or Mezzo-Soprano, Speaker and Orchestra* by John Duffy, 1991.

Manuscript Collections: British Library, Department of Manuscripts, London; King's College, Library, Cambridge; Imperial War Museum, Department of Documents, London; Rugby School, Temple Library, Rugby; University of Cambridge, Library, Department of Rare Books, Cambridge; University of Oxford, Bodleian Library, Oxford; Temple University Libraries, Special Collections, Philadelphia.

Biography: *Rupert Brooke, a Memoir* by Edward Marsh, London, Sidgwick & Jackson, 1918; *Red Wine of Youth: A Life of Rupert Brooke* by Arthur Stringer, Indianapolis, Bobbs-Merrill, 1948; *Rupert Brooke: A Biography* by Christopher Hassall, London, Faber and Faber, 1964; *The Handsomest Young Man in England: Rupert Brooke* by Michael Hastings, London, Joseph, 1967; *Rupert Brooke: The Man and Poet* by Robert Brainard Pearsall, Amsterdam, Rodopi, 1974; *Rupert Brooke, His Life and His Legend* by John Lehmann, London, Weidenfeld & Nicolson, 1980, also published as *The Strange Destiny of Rupert Brooke,* New York, Holt, Rinehart, and Winston, 1980; *The Neo-Pagans: Friendship*

and Love in the Rupert Brooke Circle by Paul Delany, London, Macmillan, 1987, also published as *The Neo-Pagans: Rupert Brooke and the Ordeal of Youth,* New York, Free Press, 1987; *The Muse Colony: Rupert Brooke, Edward Thomas, Robert Frost, and Friends, Dymock, 1914* by Keith Clark, Bristol, Redcliffe, 1992; *Rupert Brooke: The Splendour and the Pain* by John Frayn Turner, London, Breese Books, 1992; *Rupert Brooke* by William E. Laskowski, New York, Twayne, 1994.

Bibliography: *Rupert Brooke: A Bibliographical Note on His Works Published in Book Form, 1911-1919* by Richard Montgomery Gilchrist Potter, Hartford, Finlay, 1923; *A Bibliography of Rupert Brooke* by Geoffrey Keynes, London, R. Hart-Davis, 1964; *Catalogue of Books and Manuscripts by Rupert Brooke, Edward Marsh, and Christopher Hassall,* collected, compiled, and annotated by John Schroder, Cambridge, Rampant Lions Press, 1970; *Collecting Rupert Brooke* by John Schroder, Cambridge, Rampant Lions Press, 1992.

Critical Sources: "Some Recent Verses," in *Times Literary Supplement,* (London), Vol. 11, 1912, 337; *Rupert Brooke and the Intellectual Imagination: A Lecture* by Walter de la Mare, London, Sidgwick and Jackson, 1919; *War Poets, 1914-1918* by Edmund Blunden, London, Longmans, Green, 1958; "Bugles, Trumpets, and Drums: English Poetry and the Wars" by W. R. Martin, in *Mosaic: A Journal for the Interdisciplinary Study of Literature* (Winnepeg, Manitoba), Vol. 13, No. 1, 1979, 31-48; *The War Poets* by Robert Giddings, London, Bloomsbury, 1988; "Virginia Woolf and Rupert Brooke: Poised Between Olympus and the 'Real World'" by Karen L. Levenback, in *Virginia Woolf Miscellany* (Rohnert Park, California) Vol. 33, 1989, 5-6; *Taking It Like a Man: Suffering, Sexuality, and the War Poets: Brooke, Sassoon, Owen, Graves* by Adrian Caesar, Manchester, Manchester University Press, 1993; "The Falling House That Never Falls: Rupert Brooke and Literary Taste" by Clive Bloom, in *British Poetry, 1900-50: Aspects of Tradition,* edited by Gary Day, New York, St. Martin's Press, 1995.

*   *   *

The contradictions between the life and the legend of Rupert Brooke are perhaps the most intriguing aspect of the man. His fame during his lifetime was based not so much upon his literary achievements as upon his physical beauty. Although the posthumous molders of his reputation made much of his brief relationships with a number of well-bred Edwardian women, at least two later biographers quote Brooke's own graphic description of his homosexual seduction of a former classmate, and his poems reveal both an aversion to female sexuality and an obsession with the physicality of manhood. After his death in the First World War, Brooke came to symbolize the tragic slaughter of the best of Britain's young men among the barbed wire and phosgene gas of Ypres and the Somme, and yet he died of an infected insect bite on a ship in the Aegean, never having fired a gun in actual combat.

Clearly, Rupert Brooke's face was both his curse and his ticket to immortality. After a somewhat typical English schoolboy career at Hillbrow and Rugby, in 1906 he went up to King's College, Cambridge, where he made his university debut in the nonspeaking role of a Herald in a student production of *Eumenides,* in which he was required only to look alluring and pretend to blow a prop trumpet. He was an immediate sensation among the Cambridge intellectual elite. Nearly all reminiscences of Brooke, by both males and females, begin with an exclamation about his physical appearance, and stress that surviving photographs do not begin to capture the luminescent, almost Olympian quality of his beauty, or to reveal his dazzling personality, which combined a radiant innocence with a calculated affability. He was perhaps best captured in Frances Cornford's word portrait of him: "A young Apollo, golden-haired, / Stands dreaming on the verge of strife, / Magnificently unprepared / For the long littleness of life."

Brooke was spared the long littleness of life, but in death his literary reputation struggles against the attractiveness of his frontispiece portraits. Like many beautiful women, Brooke found it difficult as a student—and later as a poet and a soldier—to be taken seriously by those who could not see beyond his good looks. His true talent as a poet is now difficult to judge, swamped as it is by The Myth: romantic icon, doomed youth, Empire, patriotism, and "some corner of a foreign field that is forever England."

Biographers have noted with curiosity that Brooke's father, though he was his housemaster at Rugby during Rupert's years there, seems to have exerted only a minor influence on him. The overwhelming figure during his boyhood and adolescence was his mother, whose fervent Evangelicalism instilled in her son both high standards of Christian conduct and an ambivalence about the power and seductiveness of women. His mother's worldview is reflected in one of the major dichotomies of Brooke's poems: the opposition of "clean" and "dirty." Clean is everything godly, high-minded, and pure; dirty is everything bestial, erotic, and morally complex.

At Cambridge, Brooke gathered around him a group of young men and women that writer Virginia Woolf named the "Neo-Pagans." The term was intentionally ironic, pointing to their throwing off of drawing-room conventions in favor of vigorous hikes, outdoor camping, frank discussions, and inter-gender nude bathing. Yet, compared to the polysexual amorous entanglements of Woolf's own Bloomsbury set, the Neo-Pagans were almost puritanical. Brooke flirted and posed, but avoided sexual intimacy. His poem "The Voice," written during this period, frankly describes his ambivalence. The poet sits in a darkening wood and imagines that he will soon uncover the mystery of why the night and the forest and his thoughts of the woman he loves are moving him so deeply. But then with quacking voice and swishing skirt the woman herself comes clumsily crashing through the underbrush, interrupting his ethereal meditation: "The spell was broken, the key denied me / And at length your flat clear voice beside me / Mouthed cheerful clear flat platitudes. / ...By God! I wish—I wish that you were dead!" The misogyny is palpable.

At the close of 1910, in an attempt both to improve his German and to escape his mother's watchful eye, Brooke went abroad for three months. While in Munich, he pursued an unconsummated affair with Elisabeth van Rysselberghe, the daughter of a Belgian painter. Though she was passionately in love with him, and he obsessed with the idea of having sex with her, Brooke was unable to bring himself to move obsession to action. Out of this frustration came the poem originally titled "Lust" (on the insistence of his editor he changed the title to "Libido" before including it in his first collection of poems). In the poem, the narrator describes the "enormous wheels of will" that drove him to his beloved, and his sudden change of heart when her eager response to his sexual overtures made conquest an unexpected possibility. Taken aback by her acquiescence, he reconsiders: "My conqueror's blood was cold as a deep river / In shadow; and my heart beneath your hand / Quieter than a dead man on a bed."

In 1911, though nominally engaged to Noel Olivier, the youngest and most boyish of the four bohemian Olivier sisters, Brooke conceived a passion for Katherine ("Ka") Cox, who had been a student at Newnham when he was at King's College. His infatuation appears to have been inflamed by her ambivalence (she was in love with another man). Brooke pursued her with a frenzy and, near prostration from a nervous breakdown, collapsed under his mother's care at a villa in Cannes. Cox, who was in Munich at the time, became alarmed by the desperate tone of his letters, and made plans to visit him in France. Unwilling to risk his mother's disapproval of the affair, Brooke arranged instead to rendezvous in Verona, and then travelled on to Germany, where he at last lost his heterosexual virginity to a confused but maternal Cox. True to form, no sooner had Brooke's obsession been consummated than he lost interest. Biographer John Lehmann quotes a letter from Brooke to a friend in which he confesses, "I've a sort of dim, reflected, affection for something in her. But it's all sufficiently dreary...I've a sort of hunger for cleanness."

Brooke began writing poetry at an early age, and won several minor awards for his early efforts. At college he contributed poetry to Cambridge literary journals, and in September 1909, four of his poems appeared in the *English Review*. A book of his verses was published by Sidgwick and Jackson in December 1911 (Brooke's mother paid the publishing costs). Besides the poem "Lust" this volume included "A Channel Passage," in which the narrator's seasickness is intertwined with memories of a failed love affair: "Do I forget you? Retchings twist and tie me / Old meat, good meals, brown gobbets, up I throw, / Do I remember? Acrid return and slimy / The sobs and slobber of a last year's woe." While grudgingly admiring his "swagger and brutality," the *Times Literary Supplement* in their review took particular objection to this poem. "His disgusting sonnet on love and sea-sickness ought never to have been printed; but we are tempted to like him for writing it. Most people pass through some such strange nausea as this on their stormy way from romance to reality...here is clearly a rich nature—sensuous, eager, brave—fighting eagerly towards the truth."

The truth that Rupert Brooke was fighting towards, the truth that he perhaps never fully reached before his death, was that he was emotionally and erotically drawn to men. His later poems, which focus on his experiences at war, show that his inner turmoil was calmed by his identification with a cause that was purposeful, morally unambiguous, and overwhelmingly male. Compare the violent nausea of "A Channel Crossing" with the quiet glow of "Fragment." The poet stands on the deck of a troop ship and "peeps" through the window at his fellow soldiers playing cards. "I would have thought of them / —Heedless, within a week of battle—in pity, / Pride in their strength and in the weight and firmness / And link'd beauty of bodies, and pity that / This gay machine of splendour 'ld soon be broken..."

Clearer still is the message of the poem tellingly titled "Peace," one of the War Sonnets that secured Brooke's reputation as the leading War Poet of the day. Here the poet/soldier rejoices that the call to combat has shaken awake Britain's young men, who are now glad to "Leave the sick hearts that honour could not move, / And half-men, and their dirty songs and dreary, / And all the little emptiness of love!" The dirty emptiness of Brooke's frustrated relations with women and effete intellectuals was replaced by an erotically-charged fellowship with his fellow soldiers. He is filled with awe and longs to join them as they "With hand made sure, clear eye, and sharpened power, / ...turn, as swimmers into cleanness leaping."

While on leave in Port Said, Egypt, Brooke was troubled by sunstroke and by a sore on his upper lip, diagnosed as a mosquito bite, which quickly developed into blood poisoning. He evidently suffered from a weak immune system: for years he had from time to time developed serious infections from relatively minor cuts and scrapes. The illness left him weak and feverish, but he rejoined his ship when it sailed. As his condition worsened, he was transferred to a hospital ship, and on 23 April 1914 he died. He was buried on the Greek island of Skyros.

—William Benemann

BROSSARD, Nicole

Nationality: Canadian poet and novelist. **Born:** Montréal, Québec, 27 November 1943. **Education:** Collège Marguerite-Bourgeois, Montréal, 1956-60; Notre-Dame Secretarial School, Montréal, 1961; Université de Montréal, B.A. in Literature 1968. **Family:** One daughter. **Career:** Worked as a secretary for an insurance company, 1961-63; high school teacher, Regina Mundi School, Ville Saint-Laurent, 1968-69, 1972-73; co-founder, *La Barre du jour* journal, 1965 (became *La Nouvelle Barre du jour*, 1977); co-founder, *Les Têtes de Pioche* feminist magazine, 1976; co-director and co-researcher, *Some American Feminists* (film), 1976; founder and director, L'Intégrale publishing house, Montréal, from 1982; visiting professor, Queen's University, Kingston, Ontario, 1982, 1984. Member of board of directors, 1977-79, vice-president, 1983-85, L'Union des Écrivains Québécois. **Awards:** Governor General Awards for poetry, Canada Council, 1974, 1984; Grand Prix de Poésie, La Foundation Les Forges, 1989; Harbourfront Festival Prize, 1991; Prix Athanase-David, 1991; Doctorat Honoris Causa: University of Western Ontario, 1991. **Address:** 34 avenue Robert, Outrement, Québec H3S 2P2, Canada.

WRITINGS

Poetry

Aube à la saison, in *Trois,* A.G.E.U.M., 1965.
Mordre en sa chair. Montréal, Québec, Estérel, 1966.
L'Écho bouge beau. Montréal, Québec, Estérel, 1968.
Suite Logique. Montréal, Québec, Editions de l'Hexagone, 1970.
Le Centre blanc. Montréal, Québec, Editions d'Orphée, 1970; with additions as *Le Centre blanc: poèmes 1965-1975,* Montréal, Québec, Editions de l'Hexagone, 1978.
Mécanique jongleuse. Colombes, France, Génération, 1973; revised as *Mécanique jongleuse suivi de Masculin grammaticale,* Montréal, Québec, Editions de l'Hexagone, 1974; translated by Larry Shouldice as *Daydream Mechanics,* Toronto, Ontario, Coach House Press, 1980.
La Partie pour le tout. Montréal, Québec, L'Aurore, 1975.
D'Arcs de cycle la dérive (etchings by Francine Simonin), Editions de la Maison, 1979.
Amantes. Montréal, Québec, Quinze, 1980; translated by Barbara Godard as *Lovhers,* Guernica Editions, 1986.
Double Impression: poèmes et textes 1967- 1984. Montréal, Québec, Editions de l'Hexagone, 1984.

L'Aviva. Montréal, Québec, Editions NBJ, 1985.
Domaine d'écriture. Montréal, Québec, Editions NBJ, 1985.
With Daphne Marlatt, *Mauve.* Montréal, Québec, Editions NBJ, 1986.
With Marlatt, *Character/Jeu de lettres.* Montréal, Québec, Editions NBJ, 1986.
Sous la langue/Under Tongue. Translation by Susanne de Lotbinière-Harwood, L'Essentielle éditrices/Gynergy Books, 1987.
Installations. Ecrits des Forges, 1989.
à tout regard. Montréal, Québec, Editions NBJ, 1989.
La Subjectivité des Lionnes. L'arbre à paroles, 1990.
Typhon Dru, with photographs by Christine Davis. Collectif Génération, 1990.
Langues Obscures, Montréal, Québec, Editions de l'Hexagone, 1992.
La Nuit verte du Parc Labyrinthe. Trois, 1992.
Vertige de l'avant-scène. Ecrits des Forges, 1997.

Novels

Un Livre. Editions du Jour, 1970; translated by Larry Shouldice as *A Book,* Toronto, Coach House Press, 1976.
Sold-out: Etreinte/illustration. Editions du Jour, 1973; translated by Patricia Claxton as *Turn of a Pang,* Toronto, Coach House Press, 1976.
French Kiss: Etreinte/exploration. Editions du Jour, 1974; translated by Patricia Claxton as *French Kiss; or, a Pang's Progress,* Toronto, Coach House Press, 1986.
L'Amèr ou le Chapitre Effrité: Fiction Théorique. Montréal, Québec, Quinze, 1977; translated by Barbara Godard as *These Our Mothers; or, the Disintegrating Chapter,* Toronto, Coach House Press, 1983.
Le Sens apparent. Flammarion, 1980; translated by Fiona Strachan as *Surfaces of Sense,* Toronto, Coach House Press, 1989.
Picture Theory. Nouvelle Optique, 1982; translated by Barbara Godard, Guernica Editions, 1991, New York, Roof Press, 1991.
Journal Intime. Les Herbes rouges, 1984.
Le Désert Mauve. Montréal, Québec, Editions de l'Hexagone, 1987; translated by Susanne de Lotbinière-Harwood as *Mauve Desert,* Toronto, Coach House Press, 1990.
Baroque d'aube. Montréal, Québec, Editions de l'Hexagone, 1995; translated by Patricia Claxton as *Baroque at Dawn,* McClelland & Stewart Inc., 1997.

Radio Plays

Narrateur et personnages (first aired by Radio-Canada, 1971).
Une Impression de fiction dans le rétroviseur (first aired by Radio-Canada, 1978).
La Falaise (first aired by Radio-Canada, 1985).
Souvenirs d'enfance et de jeunesse (first aired by Radio-Canada, 1986).
With Michèle Causse, *Correspondence* (first aired by Radio-Canada, 1987).

Other

"L'Écrivain" (monologue; first produced Montréal, Québec, Le Théâtre du nouveau monde, 1976). Published in *La Nef des sorcières,* Montréal, Québec, Quinze, 1976; translated by Linda Gaboriau as *Clash of Symbols,* Toronto, Coach House Press, 1979.

Editor, *The Story So Far: 6/Les Stratégies du réel* (anthology). Toronto, Coach House Press, 1979.

La Lettre aérienne (essays). Montréal, Québec, Editions du remue-ménage, 1985; translated by Marlene Wildeman as *The Aerial Letter,* Toronto, Women's Press, 1988.

Editor, with Lisette Girouard, *Anthologie de la poésie des femmes au Québec (1677-1988).* Montréal, Québec, Editions du remue-ménage, 1991.

*

Interviews: "'Before I became a feminist, I suppose I was an angel, a poet, a revolutionary...'" by Janice Williamson, in *Sounding Differences: Conversations with Seventeen Canadian Women Writers,* Toronto, University of Toronto Press, 1993.

Critical Sources: "Poetic Politics" by Nicole Brossard, in *The Politics of Poetic Form: Poetry and Public Policy,* edited by Charles Bernstein, New York, Roof Books, 1990, 73-86; "Nicole Brossard: Beyond Modernity or Writing in the Third Dimension," in *Writing in the Feminine* by Karen Gould, Carbondale, Southern Illinois University Press, 1990, 52-107; "Nicole Brossard" by Nicole Brossard, in *Contemporary Authors Autobiography Series,* Vol. 16, 1992, 39-57; *Resurgent: New Writing by Women* edited by Lou Robinson and Camille Norton, Champaign-Urbana, University of Illinois Press, 1992, 20-32; "Reading Nicole Brossard" by Susan Knutson, in *Ellipse* (Sherbrooke, Québec), Vol. 53, 1995, 9-21.

Nicole Brossard comments:

Once you have felt the presence of the other woman as vital in your life, the body has wings to meet her, arms, knees, and thighs to embrace her. It even develops a skin so soft that it almost becomes a personal proof of faith in each woman.

Once desire takes over, the whole soul follows and the body acquires an incredible lightness, sometimes even becomes transparent and aerial. Always travelling, where the lovher's song brings it, it can spend entire days dreaming of utopia. Its ardour and certitude intertwined with passion and rapture. In short, life is at a very high level of consciousness and exuberance. It is the thought of emotion and the emotion of thought working their way in language as a poignant voice. The skin suddenly appears as a little marvel of singularity and integrity.

The lesbian body transforms everything on its passage: thoughts, images. It navigates in the language with the ability of a radiant subject. Good for it. Harmonious body.

Where there is a happy body, she can relax in the abundance of abstraction and enjoy audacity and the overflowing of meaning.

I cannot do anything about it. I associate the lesbian body with an intelligent body, with an inclination for utopia and hope. I cannot do anything about it and indeed I like to repeat that it is my lesbian body which gave me the best ideas, which inspired in me the greatest drift and transformed my gaze into a vision.

The lesbian body nourishes fantasies yet with no name, brings *she* closer to the poem, situates her straightaway on the side of *insoumission*. The lesbian body constantly moves her toward the other woman.

*   *   *

In "Poetic Politics," Québécoise poet Nicole Brossard describes the launch of her writing career in the 1960s, recalling that her "'basic intention' was to make trouble, to be a troublemaker in regard to language." This trouble-making has proven to be the inexorable engine of her poetics, driving early formalist works such as *Suite Logique* and *Un Livre* as well as the more recent corpus of poetry and novels embraced by lesbian readers and writers. Brossard's early efforts to challenge, through textual innovation, the cultural, economic, and ideological colonizations associated variously with English Canadian politics, American multinationals, Roman Catholicism, and French literature, prepared the way for a woman-focused writing which is profoundly engaged with the materiality of language. Brossard subverts conventional deployments of syntax, grammar, punctuation, spelling, typography, and genre in an effort to undermine, restore, and reinvent a language invested, as she states in "Poetic Politics," with "male sexual and psychic energies."

Brossard began to infuse her writing with this lesbian-feminist motive in 1974, a year of momentous firsts: that was the year she became a mother and fell in love with a woman for the first time. It was then, she has said, that her writing "became more fluid." Her shifting focus can be marked in the notable difference between the 1973 publication of *Mécanique jongleuse* and its reappearance a year later as *Mécanique jongleuse suivi de masculin grammaticale.* The added *masculin grammaticale* signals, even through the errant, feminizing "e" of its title, Brossard's new, explicit focus on women's relationship to language. This poetic sequence, beginning "son désir l'explore" ("her desire explores her"), reflects the translation of her persistent interest in textual erotics into an articulation of a specifically lesbian sexuality.

Throughout her career Brossard has maintained, along with a commitment to textual innovation, an ethic of collaboration. Her interest in connecting with other writers and thinkers has resulted in numerous significant cultural events, anthologies, conferences, works of poetry, even periodicals. Sparked by the need for a feminist newspaper in Montréal, she co-founded *Les Têtes de Pioche* just as, ten years earlier, a passion for Québec literature led her to co-found the influential literary journal *La Barre du jour.* She has either organized or participated in many national and international conferences which have brought women writers together, among them "Recontre Québécoise/Internationale des Ecrivains," "Women and Words/Les femmes et les mots," and the Third International Fair of Feminist Books. Through collaboration with other cultural workers, Brossard produced the film *Some American Feminists* and the play *La Nef des sorcières.* Works such as *Amantes* and *Picture Theory* thematize the physical and intellectual connections between women and explicitly invite, as well, the productive collaboration of readers.

Perhaps Brossard's most impressive works are those which have been informed by her exposure to the undeniably collaborative practice of translation. English Canada's interest in her work has propelled a number of projects for translators (including Patricia Claxton, Barbara Godard, Marlene Wildeman, Susanne de Lotbinière-Harwood) with whom Brossard has fostered close working relationships. Inspired by what translation reveals about linguistic differences, noting both the evaporation and sudden clustering of meaning which occurs when a text moves into another language, Brossard embarked on two translative projects with West Coast writer Daphne Marlatt, *Mauve* and *Character/Jeu de Lettres.* These works shimmer with the energy of connection between lesbian poets, the energy of gaps and gifts between English and French, the energy of each writer inspired to open gaps and gifts in her own language. This last translation-effect compelled Brossard to write the poetic sequence *l'Aviva,* comprised of ten poems and their revisions, a self-translation from French into French.

The influential novel *Le Désert mauve* (translated by Susanne de Lotbinière-Harwood as *Mauve Desert*) takes translation as both its subject and its compositional principle. Offering us two versions of one novel in this book, Brossard is able to explore differences within one language; *l'Aviva* and *Le Désert mauve* both perform the subtle syntactic, grammatical, and stylistic shifts which excite and motivate an experimental poet intent on shifting current realities. Susan Knutson has identified in this reflexive practice a "drive to reach the internal horizons of meaning and the consciousness or construction of reality." The two lesbian novels in *Le Désert mauve* are cross-stitched by the section entitled "Un Livre à traduire" ("A Book to Translate"), an articulation of the intimate process carried out between fictional female author and fictional female translator. Translation, for Brossard, proves both a productive figure through which to elaborate lesbian erotics and a compositional practice which promises to extend the "internal horizons" of a language which has yet to render lesbians fully visible.

—Susan Holbrook

BROUMAS, Olga

Nationality: Greek poet and translator. **Born:** Syros, May, 1949; came to the United States in 1967. **Education:** University of Pennsylvania, B.A. in Architecture 1970; University of Oregon, M.F.A. in Creative Writing 1973. **Career:** Instructor of creative writing, 1972-74, and Women's Studies Co-ordinator and instructor, 1974-76, University of Oregon; visiting associate faculty, University of Idaho, 1978; associate faculty, Goddard College, 1979-81; poet in residence, Women Writers' Center, 1981-82, University of Alabama, 1988, Vassar College, 1989; co-founder and teacher, Freehand Inc. residential fine arts program, Provincetown, Massachusetts, 1982-87; consultant, Wesleyan University Press Poetry Program, 1983-90; co-founder, with T. Begley, of *Body, Sound and Text,* educational workplace and training sessions for women, Brewster, Massachusetts, from 1989; Fannie Hurst Professor, 1990-92, poet-in-residence, from 1993, and director of Creative Writing program, from 1995, Brandeis University, Waltham, Massachusetts. Massage therapist; contributor of articles and reviews to periodicals; frequent lecturer at conferences and meetings, from 1992. **Awards:** Fulbright Travel Grant, 1967; Yale Younger Poets Award, 1977; Oregon Arts Council Grant, 1978; National Endowment for the Arts Fellowship, 1979; Vermont Arts Council Grant, 1980; Guggenheim Fellowship, 1981; Witter Bynner Translation Grant, with T. Begley, 1991. **Address:** Creative Writing Program, Brandeis University, Waltham, Massachusetts 02254-9110, U.S.A.

WRITINGS

Poetry

Restlessness. Athens, Greece, Alvin Redman Hellas, 1967.
Caritas (chapbook). Jackrabbit Press, 1976.
Beginning with O. New Haven and London, Yale University Press, 1977.

From Caritas: Poem 3. Brooklyn, New York, Out and Out Books, 1978.
Soie Sauvage. Port Townsend, Washington, Copper Canyon Press, 1979.
Pastoral Jazz. Port Townsend, Copper Canyon Press, 1983.
With Jane Miller, *Black Holes, Black Stockings.* Middletown, Connecticut, Wesleyan University Press, 1985.
Perpetua. Port Townsend, Copper Canyon Press, 1989.
With T. Begley, *Sappho's Gymnasium.* Port Townsend, Copper Canyon Press, 1994.
With Begley, *Helen Groves.* Kore Press, 1994.
With Begley, *Unfolding the Tablecloth of God* (chapbook). Red Hydra Press, 1995.
With Begley, *Ithaca: Little Summer in Winter* (chapbook). Radiolarian Press, 1996.

Translator

What I Love: Selected Poems of Odysseas Elytis. Port Townsend, Copper Canyon Press, 1986.
The Little Mariner by Odysseas Elytis. Port Townsend, Copper Canyon Press, 1988.
With Begley, *Open Papers: Selected Essays of Odysseas Elytis.* Port Townsend, Copper Canyon Press, 1995.
Odysseas Elytis: Poems, Selected and Last. Port Townsend, Copper Canyon Press, 1997.

Other

Vocal score, with music by Robert Kosse, *Portraits in Concert: A Song Cycle for Women's Chorus and Chamber Ensemble.* Holograph, New York Public Library, 1978.

Recordings: *If I Yes.* Washington, D.C., Watershed Tapes, 1981.

*

Critical Sources: "Forward" by Stanley Kunitz, in *Beginning With O* by Olga Broumas, New Haven, Connecticut, Yale University Press, 1977, iv-xii; review of *Beginning with O* by Ellen Frye, in *Off Our Backs,* January 1978, 20-21; "The Importance of *Beginning With O*: A Reflection on Olga Broumas" by Toni McNaron, in *Sinister Wisdom,* winter 1979, 77-85; "The ReVision of the Muse: Adrienne Rich, Audre Lorde, Judy Grahn, Olga Broumas" by Mary J. Carruthers, in *Hudson Review,* summer 1983, 293-327; *(Sem)erotics Theorizing Lesbian: Writing* by Elizabeth A. Meese, New York and London, New York University Press, 1992; "Olga Broumas" by Kate Carter, in *Contemporary Lesbian Writers of the United States: A Bio-Bibliographical Sourcebook,* edited by Sandra Pollack and Denise D. Knight, Westport, Connecticut, Greenwood Press, 1993, 89-93.

*　　*　　*

Synthesis is the word that comes closest to explaining the complex movement one feels underneath the surface of the words reading the poems of Olga Broumas. Synthesis—the bringing together of individual components resulting in the creation of an entirely new entity. Broumas is a Greek lesbian who moved to the United States when she was 18. Now she writes mostly in English, her adopted language, but her Greek consciousness and, occasionally, Greek words and quotes ripple through her lines.

The Greek and English languages, the Greek and American cultures, the physical and the verbal, the inner and outer landscapes, the erotic and the academic, these are some of the elements synthesized in poems such as "The Bite":

>...I am wrapped
>in myself as the smell of night
>wraps round my sleep when I sleep
>outside. By the time
>I get to the corner
>bar, corner store, corner construction
>site, I become divine. I turn
>men into swine. Leave
>them behind me whistling, grunting, wild.

Such lines are so sensual that the reader can almost feel the tearing of the disparate parts straining, not against, but toward unity.

Broumas was recognized by the academic establishment when she was not only quite young but also quite new to living in the United States. She was the first non-native speaker of English to receive the Yale Series of Younger Poets Award in 1977. Reviewing her *Beginning With O* in *Off Our Backs* shortly after it received the award, Ellen Frye welcomed Broumas as a woman speaking to women in a lesbian language, with a clear and incisive perception of the dangers of accolades from the powerful, as expressed in the poem "Leda and her Swan": "The fathers are nodding like / overdosed lechers, the fathers approve / with authority.../ I dream."

It can be argued that the very nature of lesbian language and culture is synthesis. Synthesis of erotic, political, and spiritual identity, and synthesis of many cultures, ethnicities, and traditions. Broumas's poetry is rich with powerful and sensual imagery from her differing cultural perspectives—homely: "The Px wives who smuggled the dinette / set for my mother on Stadiou Street in 1956" ("After Lunch"); cosmic: "Chafed ocean, a chadored moon / fluting the supple acres" ("Walk on the Water"); political: "the venom of the dispossessed inoculates me" ("Evensong"); and erotic: "Tongues / sleepwalking in caves" ("Rumplestiltskin").

She shows us the passion of motherhood, daughterhood, the heart and brain of an animal of the earth. Her poems often rage, particularly the early ones, and through the progression of her work, as Elizabeth A. Meese says in *(Sem)erotics Theorizing Lesbian: Writing,* she seems to move from a raw "pain of exposure" to a deeper acceptance and clearer vision of all of her selves. Meese quotes Broumas, "A poem begins for me as a somatic reality," and this is the purest synthesis of all, the connection of mind and body. A body worker herself, as well as an architect, Broumas uses her words to create a physical effect in the reader, communicating the inseparable passion of the mind and intellect of the body. Much of her work as an educator has come back to this connection, writing out of the body.

Another level of fusion in Broumas's work is found in her collaborations and translations, which are, after all, another kind of synthesis. In *Black Holes, Black Stockings* and *Sappho's Gymnasium,* as well as her translations of the poetry of Odysseas Elytis, one finds a blending of emotion, perception, and language that is rich and unique. Each volume has its own voice and that voice is neither the voice of one writer or the other, but a third voice that is the creation of the blending.

Olga Broumas came to the United States to study, teach, and write at a time when the second wave of U.S. feminism was changing women's perceptions of their lives, bodies, emotions, language, and possibilities. Her teaching work reflects her participation in this tremendous upheaval, from helping create the Women's Studies Program at the University of Oregon to the innovative programs at Freehand and *Body, Sound and Text.* Her poetry also places her as an agent as well as a recipient of the changes of her time. In *Writing Poetry,* Marie Gilchrist said, "The life of poetry lies in fresh relationships between words." One could expand this to include fresh relationships between emotions, ideas, and identities, and by that explain much of the life and movement in the writing of Olga Broumas.

—Tina Gianoulis

BROWN, Rebecca (Susan)

Nationality: American novelist and author of short stories and nonfiction. **Born:** San Diego, California, 27 March 1956. Moved as a child to Florida, Texas, Oklahoma, and Spain due to father's military career. **Family:** Companion of Chris Galloway. **Education:** George Washington University, Washington, D.C. (Phi Beta Kappa), B.A. in English Literature 1978; University of Virginia, Charlottesville, M.F.A. in writing 1981. **Career:** Creative writing teacher, University of Washington Extension, Seattle; has worked as copy editor, carpenter, homecare worker, bartender, coffee cart girl, xerox girl, "out" lesbian rock music critic, and tour guide of Robert and Elizabeth Barrett Browning's home in Florence, Italy. **Awards:** Artist in Residence, Haffington Castle, Scotland, 1988; McDowell Artist Colony fellowship, 1993, 1995; *Lambda* Literary Award, for fiction, 1994; *Boston Book Review* Award, for fiction; Pacific Northwest Bookseller's Association Award; Governor's Award, State of Washington. **Agent:** Harold Schmidt, 343 W. 12th St., Suite 1B, New York, New York 10014, U.S.A.

WRITINGS

Novels

The Haunted House. London, Picador, 1986; New York, Viking Penguin, 1987.
The Children's Crusade. London, Picador (Pan Books), 1989; Seattle, Seal Press, 1991.
The Terrible Girls. London, Picador, 1990; San Francisco, California, City Lights, 1992.
The Gifts of the Body. New York, HarperCollins, 1994.

Short Story Collections

The Evolution of Darkness. London, Brilliance Books, 1984.
Annie Oakley's Girl. San Francisco, California, City Lights, 1993.
Keeps Me Here. New York, HarperCollins, 1996.

Recordings: *The Gifts of the Body,* Seattle, Washington, Hall Audio Tapes.

*

Interviews: By Patrick McRoberts, in *Point No Point* (Seattle, Washington), No. 4, spring/summer 1996.

Critical Sources: Review of *The Children's Crusade* by Sue Roe, in *Times Literary Supplement,* No. 4514, 6 October 1989, 1104; review of *The Terrible Girls* by Kay Parris, in *New Statesman and Society,* 7 September 1990, 44; review of *The Terrible Girls* by Sue Roe, in *Times Literary Supplement,* No. 4576, 14 December 1990, 1359; review of *The Children's Crusade* by Penny Kaganoff, in *Publisher's Weekly,* 15 February 1991, 86; review of *The Terrible Girls,* in *Publisher's Weekly,* 4 May 1992, 53-54; review of *The Terrible Girls* by Victoria A. Brownworth, in *Lambda Book Report,* Vol. 3, No. 5, July/August 1992, 22; review of *Annie Oakley's Girl,* in *Publisher's Weekly,* 26 April 1993, 70; review of *Annie Oakley's Girl* by Stephanie Furtsch, in *Library Journal,* 1 May 1993, 119; review of *Annie Oakley's Girl* by Charlotte Innes, in *Lambda Book Report,* Vol. 3, No. 12, September/October 1993, 20-21; review of *Annie Oakley's Girl* by Gail Shepherd, in *Belles Lettres: A Review of Books by Women,* Vol. 9, No. 2, Winter 1993, 58-62; review of *The Gifts of the Body,* in *Publisher's Weekly,* 15 August 1994, 85; review of *The Gifts of the Body* by Lisa Meyer, in *Ms. Magazine,* Vol. 5, No. 3, November/December 1994, 76; review of *The Gifts of the Body* by Bia Lowe, in *Lambda Book Report,* Vol. 4, No. 8, January/February 1995, 24-25; review of *The Gifts of the Body* by Rebecca Pope, in *Belles Lettres: A Review of Books by Women,* Vol. 10, No. 2, Spring 1995, 50; review of *Annie Oakley's Girl* by Sara McAulay, in *Studies in Short Fiction,* Vol. 12, No. 7, Spring 1995, 243-244; review of *The Gifts of the Body* by Valerie Miner, in *Women's Review of Books,* Vol. 12, No. 7, April 1995, 14-15; review of *What Keeps Me Here,* in *Publishers Weekly,* 12 August 1996, 66; "Rebecca Brown: The Erotics of Excess and the Difficulties of Difference" by Carolyn Allen, in *Following Djuna: Women Lovers and the Erotics of Loss,* Bloomington, Indiana University Press, 1996.

*   *   *

Rebecca Brown's fiction provides texture, surreal imagery, and allegory to the invisible worlds of love, loss, obsession and betrayal, especially between women relating intimately to one another. She also writes with precision and intensely-controlled passion about caring for people dying of AIDS. "She is a surgeon of emotion, carving up the mind without a touch of sentiment," writes Charlotte Innes in the *Lambda Book Report.*

Because her unique and original voice defies categorization within genres common to lesbian novels, and to fiction in general, Brown spent many frustrating years searching for a U.S. publisher. Her break came when "Annie," eventually the title piece for *Annie Oakley's Girl,* was included in a 1983 Faber and Faber anthology, *Mae West is Dead: Recent Lesbian and Gay Fiction,* and came to the attention of Adam Mars-Jones of Brilliance Books. *The Evolution of Darkness,* which was purchased by acquisitions editor Jeanette Winterson, met with wide critical acclaim in England, and her career was launched.

After her novel *The Haunted House* was picked up in 1986 by prestigious Picador, which publishes the likes of Carlos Fuentes and Gabriel Garcia Marquez, she moved to London and stayed there for several years, she explained in an interview in *Point No Point*: "I moved to Europe, because: why stay here when they loved my book over there and were willing to pay me for it?" She

managed to stay in England and Florence, Italy, for several years working on her next novels. "It still has been only in the last couple of years that I, as a lesbian writing about characters who are lesbians, have been embraced by the mainstream. But over there it's not so categorized or ghettoized."

When City Lights Books in San Francisco began publishing her work in the early 1990s, reviews became more frequent in the U.S. press. She was accepted for two McDowell Fellowships so she could, temporarily, "quit her day job" and focus on the next novels.

Her award-winning novel *The Gifts of the Body,* written from the point of view of an AIDS homecare worker, received steady praise from a wide range of readers in the gay and lesbian and mainstream presses. While not completely typical of her earlier works, it exhibits the invisible, no-frills language she utilizes in her fiction writing. Each of the 11 accounts focuses on a different character. The homecare worker is a quiet, unnamed "I," who describes her physical actions in relation to her patients and shows how we, as human beings, care for the dying. Rather than sentimentalizing these last weeks and hours, Brown gives her readers the gift of clarity, a way to see people with AIDS as individuals. Scott Heim called *The Gifts of the Body* "the best book about AIDS I've ever read."

Brown describes her writing process as deliberate and crafted. She has learned to rewrite "40 times," cutting as she goes, walking the rhythm of every sentence. She is interested in the human desire to connect and in finding new metaphors which depict the yearning and savagery in unexpressed feelings. Generally, her books are constructed as loosely-connected "novels of stories," held together by the narrators' moment-to-moment emotions. She embraces the "I-thou" mode, revealing how the merest change of body language can alter intimate relations forever.

Brown also shows how children's emotional habits are formed in relation to the unconscious, habitual behavior of their parents, and how these versions of reality haunt their future relations with others. In part 3 of *The Haunted House,* for example, she depicts two women enmeshed in a merged relationship. Everything appears perfect in the home they've remodeled together until mysterious, invisible spirits (ghosts from childhood, perhaps) come between them and eventually flood and wreck what they've built. Brown calls her work "emotionally autobiographical," and compares her writing to medieval religious mystics, especially St. Catherine of Siena, Julian of Norwich, and St. Theresa of Avila. In some of her stark portrayals, she uses blood, self-mutilation, torture, and the rich experiences of the visionary to tell her tales. Alternately, her work is often peppered with irony as well as a quirky sense of the absurd. She says her ideas come as images or aural lines of text, and then she explores their meaning as the writing progresses.

In her book *What Keeps Me Here,* Brown produces a masterpiece of revolving perceptions in the story "A Relationship." She creates three compelling first-person accounts of the same incident such that the reader begins to see the incident in 3-D from outside the door, inside the door, moving toward the door. The transitions from one "I" to another are so masterful that they impart a delightful surprise when they occur.

Brown's works have earned the accolades of reviewers. Joan Nestle says of *The Terrible Girls*: "Its subversive and passionate transformations carry the lesbian literary voice into the 21st century." Dorothy Allison says: "I read everything Rebecca Brown writes, watch for her books and short stories. She is simply one of the best contemporary lesbian writers."

—Ellen Farmer

————

BRUCE, Richard. *See* **NUGENT, Richard Bruce.**

————

BUNCH-WEEKS, Charlotte. *See* **Bunch, Charlotte.**

————

BUNCH, Charlotte (Anne)

Pseudonym: Wrote as Charlotte Bunch-Weeks, 1968-70. **Nationality:** American feminist political organizer and theorist, nonfiction writer, editor, lecturer, and educator. **Born:** West Jefferson, North Carolina, 13 October 1944; grew up in Artesia, New Mexico. **Education:** Duke University, Durham, North Carolina, B.A. in history 1966 (magna cum laude); Institute for Policy Studies, 1967-68. **Family:** Married James L. Weeks in 1967 (divorced 1971). **Career:** Fellow, Institute for Policy Studies, Washington, District of Columbia, 1969-77; founder and director, Public Resource Center, Washington, District of Columbia, 1977-81; founder, director, and consultant, Interfem Consultants, New York City, 1979-87; Laurie New Jersey Chair in Women's Studies, Douglass College, Rutgers University, New Brunswick, New Jersey, 1987-89; founder and director, Center for Women's Global Leadership, Douglass College, Rutgers University, from 1989; professor, Bloustein School of Planning and Public Policy, Rutgers University, from 1991. Co-founder and national president, University Christian Movement, New York City, 1966-67; member of editorial board, *Motive,* 1967-73; member of campus ministry staff, Case Western Reserve University, Cleveland, Ohio, 1968-69; co-founder and editor, *The Furies,* 1972-73; co-founder and editor, *Quest: A Feminist Quarterly,* 1974-79; member of board of directors, National Gay and Lesbian Task Force, 1974-81, and of the executive committee, 1976-78; consultant to Daughters, Inc. (feminist publishing company), 1976-78; associate, Women's Institute for Freedom of the Press, 1978-86; co-chair of United Nations Decade Committee, New York City Commission on the Status of Women, 1982-86; associate, Isis International, from 1985; visiting lecturer and organizer of conferences and seminars throughout the United States, Africa, Asia, Europe, Latin America, and the Pacific. **Awards:** Community service award, Lambda Legal Defense Fund, 1982; community service award, National Lesbian and Gay Health Foundation, 1986; Wise Woman Award, Center for Women's Policy Studies, 1989; Lesbian Rights Award, Southern California Women for Understanding, 1991; Resourceful Woman Award, 1992; inducted into National Women's Hall of Fame, Seneca Falls, New York, 1996. **Address:** c/o Center for Women's Glo-

bal Leadership, Douglass College, 27 Clifton Avenue, New Brunswick, New Jersey 08903, U.S.A.

WRITINGS

Nonfiction

A Broom of One's Own (as Charlotte Bunch-Weeks). Washington, District of Columbia, Washington Women's Liberation, 1970.
With Shirley Castley, *Developing Strategies for the Future: Feminist Perspectives—Report of the International Feminist Workshop held at Stony Point, New York, April 20-25, 1980.* New York, International Women's Tribune Centre, 1980.
Feminism in the '80s (pamphlet series). Denver, Colorado, Antelope Publications. Book 1, *Facing Down the Right,* 1981; Book 2, *Going Public With Our Vision,* 1983; Book 3, *Bringing the Global Home,* 1985.
Passionate Politics: Feminist Theory in Action—Essays, 1968-1986 (collected works). New York, St. Martin's, 1987.
With Roxanna Carrillo, *Gender Violence: A Development and Human Rights Issue.* New Brunswick, New Jersey, Center for Women's Global Leadership, 1991.
With Niamh Reilly, *Demanding Accountability: The Global Campaign and Vienna Tribunal for Women's Human Rights.* New Brunswick, New Jersey, Center for Women's Global Leadership, and New York, United Nation's Development Fund for Women, 1994.

Editor

With Joanne Cooke and Robin Morgan, *The New Women: A Motive Anthology on Women's Liberation* (as Charlotte Bunch-Weeks). Indianapolis, Bobbs-Merrill, 1970.
With Nancy Myron, *Class and Feminism: A Collection of Essays from The Furies.* Baltimore, Maryland, Diana Press, 1974.
With Nancy Myron, *Women Remembered: A Collection of Biographies from The Furies.* Baltimore, Maryland, Diana Press, 1974.
With Nancy Myron, *Lesbianism and the Women's Movement.* Baltimore, Maryland, Diana Press, 1975.
With Jane Flax and others, *Building Feminist Theory: Essays from Quest, A Feminist Quarterly.* New York, Longman, 1981.
With Sandra Pollack, *Learning Our Way: Essays in Feminist Education.* Trumansburg, New York, Crossing Press, 1983.
With Kathleen Barry and Shirley Castley, *International Feminism: Networking Against Female Sexual Slavery: Report of the Global Feminist Workshop to Organize Against Traffic in Women, Rotterdam, the Netherlands, April 6-15, 1983.* New York, International Women's Tribune Centre, 1984.

Selected Essays

"Asian Women in Revolution" (as Charlotte Bunch-Weeks), in *Liberation Now! Writings from the Women's Liberation Movement,* edited by Deborah Babcox and Madeline Belkin. New York, Dell, 1971.
"Perseverance Furthers: Separatism and Our Future," in *The Furies* (Washington, D.C.), fall 1972.
"Perseverance Furthers: Woman's Sense of Self," in *The Furies* (Washington, D.C.), January/February 1973.

"Lesbian Feminist Politics," in *Off Our Backs* (Washington, D.C.), April 1973.

"Self Definition and Political Survival," in *Quest: A Feminist Quarterly* (Washington, D.C.), winter 1975.

"Election Year: Gay Perspectives," in *Christopher Street* (New York), July 1976.

"Learning from Lesbian Separatism," in *Ms.,* November 1976; *Lavender Culture,* edited by Karla Jay and Allen Young. New York, Harcourt Brace, 1978.

"ERA Debate: A Tendency to Blame the Victim," in *Washington Post,* 5 August 1978.

"Lesbian-Feminist Theory," in *Our Right to Love: A Lesbian Resource Book,* edited by Ginny Vida. Englewood Cliffs, New Jersey, Prentice-Hall, 1978.

"Lesbians in Revolt," in *Feminist Frameworks: Alternative Theoretical Accounts of the Relations Between Women and Men,* edited by Alison M. Jaggar and Paula Rothenberg Struhl. New York, McGraw-Hill, 1978; second edition, 1984.

"Not for Lesbians Only," in *The Women Say, The Men Say: Women's Liberation and Men's Consciousness,* edited by Evelyn Shapiro and Barry M. Shapiro. New York, Dell, 1979.

"Personal Statement," in *What Women Want: From the Official Report to the President, the Congress, and the People of the United States,* by Caroline Bird and others. New York, Simon and Schuster, 1979.

"Lesbianism and Erotica in Pornographic America," in *Take Back the Night: Women on Pornography,* edited by Laura Lederer. New York, Morrow, 1980.

"Feminist Journals: Writing for a Feminist Future," in *Women in Print II,* edited by Joan E. Hartman and Ellen Messer-Davidow. New York, Modern Language Association, 1982.

"Global Feminism," in *ISIS Women's International Journal* (Rome, Italy), December 1983.

"The Reform Tool Kit," in *First Harvest: The Institute for Policy Studies, 1963-1983,* edited by John S. Friedman. New York, Grove, 1983.

"Woman Power: The Courage to Lead, the Strength to Follow, and the Sense to Know the Difference," in *Current Issues in Organizational Leadership,* edited by William V. Burgess. Lexington, Massachusetts, Ginn, 1983.

"New Introduction to the Reprint Edition," in *Crimes Against Women: Proceedings of the International Tribunal,* edited by Diana E.H. Russell and Nicole Van de Ven. East Palo Alto, California, Frog in the Well, 1984.

With Roxanna Carrillo and Ied Guinee, "Feminist Perspectives: Report of the Feminist Perspectives Working Group to the Closing Plenary," in *Women's Studies International Forum* (Oxford, England), 1985.

"Making Common Cause: Diversity and Coalitions," in *IKON* (New York), No. 7, 1987; in *Out the Other Side,* edited by McEwen and O'Sullivan, London, Virago Press, 1988.

"International Feminism: A Passionate Politics," in *Woman of Power* (Boston), summer 1987.

"Against All Forms of Domination," in *The Progressive* (Madison, Wisconsin), November 1990.

"The Politics of Violence," in *On the Issues* (Forest Hills, New York), fall 1990.

With Roxanna Carrillo, "Feminist Perspectives on Women in Development," in *Persistent Inequalities: Women and World Development,* edited by Irene Tinker. New York, Oxford, 1990.

"Global Feminism and Diversity," in *Women and Development: Challenges for the Future.* Ottawa, Ontario, Spirals/Spirales (Women's Studies Programme, University of Ottawa), 1992.

"A Global Perspective on Feminist Ethics and Diversity," in *Explorations in Feminist Ethics: Theory and Practice,* edited by Eve Browning Cole and Susan Coultrap-McQuin. Bloomington, Indiana University Press, 1992.

"Feminist Visions of Human Rights in the 21st Century," in *Human Rights in the 21st Century: A Global Challenge,* edited by Kathleen and Paul Mahoney. Canada, Caswell Publications, 1992.

"Feminism," in *Oxford Companion to Politics of the World.* London, Oxford University Press, 1992.

"Organizing for Women's Human Rights Globally," in *Ours by Right: Women's Rights as Human Rights,* edited by Joanna Kerr. London, Zed Books in association with The North-South Institute, 1993.

With Roxanna Carrillo, "Global Violence Against Women: The Challenge to Human Rights and Development," in *World Security: Challenges for a New Century,* 2nd edition, edited by Michael T. Klare and Daniel C. Thomas. New York, St. Martin's, 1994.

"Transforming Human Rights from a Feminist Perspective," in *Women's Rights, Human Rights: International Feminist Perspectives,* edited by Julie Peters and Andrea Wolper. New York, Routledge, 1995.

"Foreword, in *Unspoken Rules: Sexual Orientation and Women's Human Rights,* edited by Rachel Rosenbloom. San Francisco, International Gay and Lesbian Human Rights Commission, 1995.

"On Globalizing Gender Justice," in *Nation,* 11 September 1995.

*

Biography: "Introduction" by Charlotte Bunch, in *Passionate Politics,* New York, St. Martin's, 1987; "Bunch, Charlotte (Anne), 1944—" by Christa Brelin, in *Contemporary Authors,* Vol. 126, Detroit, Michigan, Gale, 1989; "Bunch, Charlotte, Feminist Writer, Activist," in *Biographic Supplement and Index, The Young Oxford History of Women in the United States,* by Harriet Sigerman, New York, Oxford, 1995.

Interviews: "Profile: Charlotte Bunch, Hustling Theoretician" by Jeanne Cordova, in *Lesbian Tide* (Los Angeles, California), Vol. 6, No. 6, May/June 1977, 3, 38-39; "Two Feminists Tell How They Work Outside the System: Charlotte Bunch" by Gloria Steinem, in *Ms.* (New York), Vol. 6, No. 1, July 1977, 53, 92; "Charlotte Bunch: Global Feminist and Bridge Builder" by Karla Dobinski, in *Feminist Connection* (Madison, Wisconsin), March 1983, 5; "Charlotte Bunch on Global Feminism" by Carol Anne Douglas, in *Off Our Backs* (Washington, D.C.), Vol. 17, No. 9, October 1987, 10-12; "Bringing Together Feminist Theory and Practice: A Collective Interview" by Heidi Hartmann, Charlotte Bunch, and others, in *Signs* (Chicago, Illinois), Vol. 21, No. 4, 1996, 917-951.

Critical Sources: "Live and Learn" by Helene V. Wenzel, in *Women's Review of Books* (Wellesley, Massachusetts), Vol. 2, No. 1, October 1984, 13-14; "Bunch, One Woman Coalition" by Debra Schultz, in *New Directions for Women* (Dover, New Jersey), Vol. 16, No. 6, November/December 1987, 4-5; "Thinking Globally, Acting Locally" by Blanche Wiesen Cook, in *Women's Review of Books* (Wellesley, Massachusetts), Vol. 5, No. 2, November 1987,

5-6; *Love and Politics: Radical Feminist and Lesbian Theories,* by Carol Anne Douglas, San Francisco, California, Ism Press, 1990.

*   *   *

Regarded as one of the foremost organizers and theorists of the lesbian and global feminist movements, Charlotte Bunch began her careers as activist and writer in the 1960s. The daughter of a white middle-class family, she put her background in Social Gospel Methodism to work in the civil rights and other justice movements as soon as she entered Duke University. After graduating in 1966, she married a fellow activist and moved to Washington, D.C. There she was a founder of Women's Liberation and helped organize the first national women's liberation conference, held outside Chicago in 1968. While her earliest publications, appearing under the name Charlotte Bunch-Weeks, analyzed the emerging feminist movement and introduced many of the continuing themes of her work—women's control over their own bodies and sexualities, leadership without elites, coalitions—they included no explicitly lesbian content.

Charlotte Bunch discovered her lesbianism in the context of the feminist movement and, following a very public "coming out" in 1971, immediately experienced the movement's traumatic "gay-straight" split. Believing there was no hospitable space within the existing women's movement to develop a lesbian feminist politics and culture, Charlotte Bunch, Rita Mae Brown, and several others formed a small lesbian separatist community. In 1972, they began publishing *The Furies,* a periodical named for their collective.

As a member of The Furies, Charlotte Bunch learned that she "could be a writer and theorist," as she later told Gloria Steinem; and she produced some of the first documents of lesbian feminism. "The development of a political analysis encompassing lesbianism and heterosexuality not only fascinated me intellectually but became integral to my survival," she recalled in *Passionate Politics.* In learning to understand the ways fear and persecution of lesbians contributed to the oppression of all women, she also discovered that political theory could serve practical uses, as an aid in identifying appropriate strategies.

The Furies collective disbanded in 1972 and ceased publishing in 1973. But their writings received wider distribution when, with Nancy Myron, Bunch edited three volumes of *Furies* articles. *Women Remembered,* a collection of biographical sketches, suffered from some poor writing and inexpert research. *Class and Feminism,* though uneven, presented early and often insightful analysis of the complex interactions of gender, class, and sexual preference. *Lesbianism and the Women's Movement* included important contributions to developing feminist theory, among them Bunch's article from January 1972, "Lesbians in Revolt," a discussion of the political nature of lesbianism and rationale for lesbian separatist politics.

Bunch began moving away from separatism in 1973. In 1974, she was a founder of *Quest: A Feminist Quarterly,* which operated from her office at the Institute for Policy Studies, a progressive Washington think tank, for several years. Among *Quest*'s goals was the integration of lesbian feminist analysis into the women's movement. Bunch resigned from the *Quest* staff in 1979, but later returned as editor of a collection of *Quest* articles; the aptly-titled *Building Feminist Theory* reprinted her essays, "The Reform Tool Kit," a discussion of radical reform, and "Not for Lesbians Only," a lesbian feminist analysis of the economic and other functions of compulsory heterosexuality. "Socialism had Marx, black power had Malcolm X...and lesbian feminism has Charlotte Bunch as one of its most gifted thinkers," wrote Jeanne Cordova in 1977.

In the late 1970s, Bunch began organizing and consulting internationally around events related to the United Nations' Decade for Women. Much of her writing shifted to topics in global feminism, which she described in a 1983 *Isis* article as "a transformational politics [that] addresses every area of life from the perspective of women's oppression, and goes on to challenge domination in any form (sex, race, sexual preference, class, religion, nation ...)." She continued her editing activities with *Learning Our Way,* the first anthology of essays on feminist teaching, and with *International Feminism: Networking Against Female Sexual Slavery,* both of which included some lesbian-related content.

In 1987, *Passionate Politics: Feminist Theory in Action—Essays, 1968-1986,* a collection of Bunch's articles and speeches, appeared to praise from reviewers in feminist and women's studies journals, who applauded her integrity, consistency, and ability to connect theory with activism. *Passionate Politics* divided her work into several thematic sections, with only one specifically identified as "Lesbian Feminism." But lesbian feminism served as a lens for viewing other issues as well. "While I am out of the closet and concerned about homophobia, there are many other topics that I want to address besides lesbianism," she wrote in a 1986 article reprinted in *Passionate Politics.* "I decided in the late 1970s that I would not write any more only about lesbianism, but instead I would address other subjects and incorporate my lesbian feminist analysis within them."

In 1989, Bunch founded the Center for Women's Global Leadership at Rutgers University. *Gender Violence: A Development and Human Rights Issue,* the first of the Center's working papers, reprinted her influential 1990 article, "Women's Rights as Human Rights." Positing that abuse of women was political in nature (rather than solely personal or cultural) and extending the framework of human rights beyond the traditional perspective of civil liberties, this essay proposed a feminist transformation of human rights concepts, and placed lesbian rights within the context of women's rights to freedom of sexuality and bodily integrity.

Demanding Accountability described the successful organizing activities of women's non-governmental organizations to ensure that gender-based violence would have a central place in the United Nations World Conference on Human Rights held in Vienna in 1993. Included among the powerful testimonies presented by women from 25 countries were accounts by lesbians. "While enforced heterosexuality is used to control women of all sexual orientations," noted Bunch and her co-author, "lesbians pose the most visible and profound challenge to their coercion and are therefore often explicitly and legally persecuted by their families and communities, in work places, and as part of state policy."

Charlotte Bunch has written for a wide variety of feminist, popular, and academic journals; her essays have appeared in many anthologies on topics ranging from feminist ethics to organizational leadership to world security. "My recent work has not been primarily lesbian identified," Bunch observed in a 1996 *Signs* interview. But neither have her recent publications skirted or ignored the topic of lesbianism. Within her global feminist reconception of human rights, the writings of Charlotte Bunch continued to bring lesbian concerns to international fora, to advocate for the human rights of lesbians, and to identify compulsory heterosexuality as a powerful means of controlling and limiting the lives of all women.

— Carolynne Myall

BUSCH, Charles

Nationality: American actor and playwright. **Born:** New York, New York, 23 August 1954. **Education:** Northwestern University, Evanston, Illinois, B.S. 1976. **Career:** Has held a variety of jobs including portrait artist, encyclopedia salesperson, memorabilia shop manager; playwright and actor. Frequent contributor to periodicals, including *Advocate, Interview, New York,* and *New York Times Book Review.* **Awards:** Charlie Local and National Comedy Award, Association of Comedy Artists, for special contribution to the art of comedy, 1985; Manhattan Academy of Cabaret Award, 1985, 1993. **Address:** c/o attorney Marc Glick, Glick and Weintraub, 1501 Broadway, Suite 2401, New York, New York 10036, U.S.A.

WRITINGS

Plays

Hollywood Confidential (one-person show; produced at One Sheridan Square Theatre, New York City, 1978).
Alone with a Cast of Thousands (one-person show; produced at the Source Theatre, Washington, D. C., 1980).
Theodora, She-Bitch of Byzantium (produced at the Limbo Lounge, New York City, 1984).
Vampire Lesbians of Sodom (produced at the Limbo Lounge, New York City, 1984; Provincetown Playhouse, New York City, 1985-90; Coronet Theatre, Los Angeles, 1990). Published as *Vampire Lesbians of Sodom, and Sleeping Beauty or Coma,* New York, Samuel French, 1985.
Times Square Angel (produced at the Provincetown Playhouse, 1985-86). New York, Samuel French, 1985.
Pardon My Inquisition, or Kiss the Blood Off My Castanets (produced at the Limbo Lounge, 1986).
Psycho Beach Party (produced at the Players Theatre, New York City, 1987-88). New York, Samuel French, 1987.
Four Plays. Garden City, New York, Fireside Theatre, 1988.
The Lady in Question (two act; produced at the WPA Theatre, New York City, 1988; Orpheum Theatre, New York City, 1989). New York, Samuel French, 1989.
Red Scare on Sunset (produced at the WPA Theatre, 1991). New York, Samuel French, 1991.
Charles Busch Review (produced at the Ballroom Theatre, New York City, 1993).
With Linda Thorsen Bond and William Repicci, *Swingtime Canteen* (produced at the Blue Angel Supper Club, New York City, 1995).

Other

Whores of Lost Atlantis (novel), New York, Hyperion, 1993.
"The New Feminine Mystique," in *New York,* 17 July 1995, 24-32.
Call Me a Vampire Lesbian, New York, HarperCollins, forthcoming.

*

Critical Sources: "The Dresser" by Howard Karren, in *New York,* 3 March 1986, 42; "Reviews" by Mimi Kramer, in *New Yorker,* 10 August 1987, 60; "East Village, West Bank" by John Simon, in *New York,* 7 August 1989, 44-45; "On the Edge" by Mimi Kramer, in *New Yorker,* 5 August 1991, 67; "Charles Busch: Some Kind of Diva" by Daniel Mendelsohn, in *American Theatre,* Vol. 10, No. 12, 1993, 44-46; "Swingtime Canteen" by Richard Corliss, in *Time,* 4 September 1995, 72.

*   *   *

That playwright Charles Busch is a gay man who draws on the experience of being homosexual in twentieth-century America is no surprise to anyone familiar with his work. After all, his first off-Broadway hit was *Vampire Lesbians of Sodom,* and he appeared, in drag, as the female lead. In fact, Busch usually plays the female lead in his productions and has gone so far as to tell Howard Karren, writing in *New York,* that he "felt the public would discover me in a dress." His only published novel, the admittedly autobiographical *Whores of Lost Atlantis,* reinforces this point. In the book the protagonist, Julian, is—like Busch in real life—a performance artist and playwright. And the antics of Julian and his strange assortment of friends as they attempt to produce his play in a small venue in the East Village of New York City are described in the camp tones that mark much recent humorous fiction written by gay men.

But with the exception of Julian, his friends, and the Vampire Lesbians, Busch's plays are not over-populated with lesbian and gay characters. There are Yo Yo and Provoloney, two surfers who finally admit their love for one another to themselves and to their friends in *Psycho Beach Party.* But if casual readers ignore the cast list of the off-Broadway productions of his plays, such as *The Lady in Question,* they may not realize that the author is a gay man nor see the play as being particularly "gay" in any way. In fact, Busch adds to this impression by asserting in the "Author's Note" that precedes each play that the production will not be harmed if the female lead is played by an actual woman.

It is clear, however, that much of what makes Busch's plays so funny and, ultimately, so serious, are the elements of gay urban culture that he combines in their crafting. The camp settings of his plays and the camp tones of his characters clearly connect with many of the gay men who see his productions. John Simon, writing in *New York,* points out that the audience who shared *The Lady in Question* with him, "mostly men with other men," were "moved by that emotional unison Jules Romains called *unanimisme.*" While Busch claims that his plays do not need drag performers, it is obvious that drag performance is very important to him as an individual as well as a writer. And while the humor of his plays may seem anything but serious, he repeatedly turns to topics that are important to lesbians and gay men.

If camp is characterized by over-exaggeration, Busch begins with genres which are a bit overblown already and then takes them over the top. *The Lady in Question* is, as John Simon points out in *New York,* "a takeoff on old Hollywood melodramas about Nazism." There is a typical plot: a famous American actress is imprisoned by Nazis for a courageous performance in an anti-Hitler play; her son and two German allies have plans to rescue her. The Nazis are evil—they include a doctor with a penchant for experimentation on human subjects, a cigar smoking grandmother, and a sexually precocious, manipulative 12-year-old girl in dirndl. The Americans are brave and appropriately contemptuous of the Nazis' plans for world domination. Busch introduces into this mix an old vaudevillian-turned-concert-pianist, Gertrude Garnet (pronounced Garnay, as she frequently points out), who is after the evil Baron for his money and sophistication. The plot develops as she changes from a selfish would-be European into plain Gertie Garnet (with a hard t) from Brooklyn, New York, who does not hesitate to proclaim, "This whole set-up in Germany stinks. And your Fuhrer, Herr Hitler, has only one nut to his name."

In *Psycho Beach Party* Busch performs a similar operation on early-nineteen-sixties beach movies. Instead of Gidget pestering the great Kahuna, we are given Chicklet, a would be surfer with, as Mimi Kramer puts it in the *New Yorker,* a mother "like the mother in Hitchcock's 'Marnie,'" multiple personalities, and a penchant for shaving off other people's hair. All of it. But, just as in the Sandra Dee movies, all turns out for the best in the end. One of the surf bums, Star Cat, just happens to be a drop out from a psychiatry training program, and he is able to guide Chicklet through her problems and into wearing his fraternity pin.

Busch claims that he gained his artistic sensibility at an early age. Daniel Mendelsohn, in *American Theatre,* recounts the playwright telling him his life's course had been set when his father took him, at eight years of age, to see Joan Sutherland perform at the old Metropolitan Opera House.

> "The theatre itself, the gilt on the ceiling—I'd never seen anything more fantastic," Busch recalls some 30 years later. "And then—there she was, with this red hair and this pale green dress. Just huge." He pauses. "I've been recreating that ever since."

And he has been enormously successful. It is the plays that have, as Mendelsohn puts it, "taken the form of benzedrinelaced [sic] send-ups of Hollywood and Broadway leading-lady vehicles that have made Busch famous." And while some critics found his early work, particularly *Vampire Lesbians of Sodom,* a bit too much, most agree that he has become more subtle over time. Mimi Kramer points out in "On the Edge," her *New Yorker* review of *Red Scare on Sunset,* that "in this country, where drag tends to be about celebrating excess, Mr. Busch is an anomaly in a number of ways. He pretty much introduced downtown drag and subtlety to each other. He resists playing to an audience. Nor does he overpopulate his work with drag characters."

But drag is important for Busch. In an article on the rising popularity of drag he wrote for *New York,* he states, "drag to many performers is intrinsically linked to their identities as gay men. It's our sense of humor, our sense of aesthetics.... We worship outrageous female performers and long to recreate some of that magic in ourselves." It is the performance that is important here. Busch makes it clear that most drag performers are neither transsexuals nor transvestites. And while he may "worship outrageous female performers," his performances are anything but outrageous. Mimi Kramer goes so far as to say, in "On the Edge," that the drag in *Red Scare on Sunset* "is gentle, and acts as a kind of signature or flourish, almost like the couplets in Shakespeare."

Busch brings the same talent to his performance in *Swingtime Canteen,* a play that depicts an all-girl band entertaining the Eighth Air Force during World War Two. Richard Corliss, writing in *Time,* describes his performance by asking the reader to "imagine Tallulah Bankhead working the low notes and Shirley Temple the high ones on the Johnny Mercer-Harold Arlen 'Ac-cent-tchu-ate the Positive,' and you have an idea of the suave campery at which Busch excels." But Busch, of course, is not the first gay man to dress in drag and entertain the troops. Gay GIs did the same thing during the war, most notably in Irving Berlin's all-soldier show, *You're in the Army.*

So just as Busch's use of drag helps to reinforce some gay men's sense of identity, his choice of themes strikes a resonance with others. In *Vampire Lesbians of Sodom* it isn't just the hilarity of two women surviving from ancient Palestine, where they were worshipped, to find work on a chorus line at Caesar's Palace in Las Vegas that makes the play so successful. It is also the fact that the play works to undercut the biblical story that is still used to make so many lesbian and gay men's lives uncomfortable. *The Lady in Question* is set in Nazi Germany where, as every gay man and lesbian knows, not only brave American actresses, but Jews and Gypsies and, yes, homosexuals, were threatened with the final solution. Part of the reaction to the play that John Simon witnessed is due, I suspect, not only to the joy of seeing evil defeated, but to seeing evil defeated by a gay man in drag using all the toughness and extravagance of his ex-vaudevillian character to destroy the overbearing Nazi family.

Red Scare on Sunset works in much the same way. Set at the height of the anti-Communist fervor of the 1950s, the play depicts a radio personality, Pat Pilford, who believes that everyone she knows is involved in a Communist plot to take over the film industry. Her friend, Mary Dale (who is staring in a musical version of Lady Godiva and who is played by Busch in the original production) discovers that it is true, that everyone she knows is a Communist. But equipped with the knowledge that the McCarthy era cost more homosexuals their jobs than actual Reds, the reader can make a quick substitution and experience the play from a different angle. And Cricket's transformation from a troubled teen suffering from a split personality to a whole individual who gets pinned by her fraternity man in *Psycho Beach Party* parallels the fantasy coming-out of more than one gay man.

Most critics agree that Charles Busch's work develops from the maniacal, over-the-top intensity of *Vampire Lesbians of Sodom* to the more subtle writing and acting of his later plays. But his combined works present at least one version of an urban gay male sensibility. His use of camp, his dedication to drag, and his treatment of significant themes all contribute to make his work important for both gay people and the wider literary community.

—C. Steven Douglas

BUTLER, Judith (Pamela)

Nationality: American philosopher, rhetorician, and theorist. **Born:** Cleveland, Ohio, 24 February 1956. **Education:** Yale University, New Haven, Connecticut, B.A. 1978, M.A. 1982, Ph.D. 1984. **Career:** Professor, Humanities Center, Johns Hopkins University, Baltimore, Maryland, 1984-92; Chancellor's Professor of Rhetoric and Comparative Literature, University of California, Berkeley, from 1993. **Address:** Department of Rhetoric, University of California, Berkeley, California 94720-2670, U.S.A.

WRITINGS

Nonfiction

Subjects of Desire: Hegelian Reflections in Twentieth-century France. New York, Columbia University Press, 1987.
Gender Trouble: Feminism and the Subversion of Identity. New York and London, Routledge, 1990.

Editor, with Joan W. Scott, *Feminists Theorize the Political.* New York, Routledge, 1992.
Bodies That Matter: On the Discursive Limits of Sex. New York and London, Routledge, 1993.
Exitable Speech: A Politics of the Performative. New York and London, Routledge, 1997.
The Psychic Life of Power: Theories in Subjection. Stanford, California, Stanford University Press, 1997.

Essays

"Sex and Gender in Simone de Beauvoir's *Second Sex,*" in *Yale French Studies* (New Haven, Connecticut), Vol. 72, 1986.
"Sexual Ideology and Phenomenological Description: A Feminist Critique of Merleau-Ponty's *Phenomenology of Perception,*" in *The Thinking Muse: Feminism and Modern French Philosophy,* edited by Jeffner Allen and Marion Young. Bloomington, Indiana University Press, 1989.
"Lana's 'Imitation': Melodramatic Repetition and the Gender Performative," in *Genders* (New York), Vol. 9, 1990.
"The Nothing That Is: Wallace Stevens' Hegelian Affinities," in *Theorizing American Literature: Hegel, the Sign, and History,* edited by Bainard Cowan and Joseph G. Kronick. Baton Rouge, Louisiana State University Press, 1991.
"Imitation and Gender Insubordination," in *Inside/Out: Lesbian Theories, Gay Theories,* edited by Diana Fuss. New York, Routledge, 1991.
"Sexual Inversions," in *Discourses of Sexuality: From Aristotle to AIDS,* edited by Domna C. Stanton. Ann Arbor, University of Michigan Press, 1992.
"Response to Bordo's 'Feminist Skepticism and the Maleness of Philosophy,'" in *Hypatia* (Tampa, Florida), Vol. 7, No. 3, 1992.
"Poststructuralism and Postmarxism," in *Diacritics* (Baltimore, Maryland), Vol. 23, No. 4, 1993.
"A Skeptical Feminist Postscript to the Postmodern," in *Postmodernism Across the Ages,* edited by Bill Readings and Bennet Schaber. Syracuse, New York, Syracuse University Press, 1993.
"The Body Politics of Julia Kristeva," in *Ethics, Politics, and Difference in Julia Kristeva's Writing,* edited by Kelly Oliver. New York, Routledge, 1993.
"Feminism By Any Other Name," "Against Proper Objects," and "Sexual Traffic," in *Differences: A Journal of Feminist Cultural Studies* (Providence, Rhode Island), Vol. 6, No. 2/3, 1994.
"Kantians in Every Culture?," in *Boston Review,* Vol. 19, No. 5, 1994.
"Contingent Foundations: Feminism and the Question of 'Postmodernism,'" in *Critical Encounters: Reference and Responsibility in Deconstructive Writing,* edited by Cathy Caruth and Deborah Esch. New Brunswick, New Jersey, Rutgers University Press, 1994.
"Bodies That Matter," in *Engaging With Irigaray: Feminist Philosophy and Modern European Thought,* edited by Carolyn Burke and Naomi Schor. New York, Columbia University Press, 1994.
"Conscience Doth Make Subjects of Us All," in *Yale French Studies* (New Haven, Connecticut), Vol. 88, 1995.
"Burning Acts: Injurious Speech," in *Deconstruction Is/In America: A New Sense of the Political,* edited by Anselm Haverkamp. New York City, New York University Press, 1995.

"An Affirmative View," in *Representations* (Berkeley, California), Vol. 55, 1996.

*

Interviews: "An Interview with Judith Butler" by Patrick Greaney and Emily O. Wittman, in *Yale Literary Magazine,* Vol. 4, No. 2, 1993, 46-54.

Critical Sources: "Review of *Gender Trouble*" by Margaret Nash, in *Hypatia* (Tampa, Florida), Vol. 5, No. 3, 1990, 171-174; "Review of *Gender Trouble*" by E. Ann Kaplan, in *Signs: Journal of Women In Culture and Society* (Seattle, Washington), Vol. 17, No. 4, 1992, 843-847; "Bodies That Mutter: Rhetoric and Sexuality" by Tim Dean, in *Pre/Text: A Journal of Rhetorical Theory,* Vol. 15, No. 1/2, 1994, 80-117; "Theory That Matters" by Jeffrey Nealon, in *Postmodern Culture,* Vol. 5, No. 1, 1994, 1-12; "Review of *Bodies That Matter*" by Jacquelyn Zita, in *Signs: Journal of Women In Culture and Society* (Seattle, Washington), Vol. 21, No. 3, 1996, 786-794; "Mattering" by Pheng Cheah, in *Diacritics* (Baltimore, Maryland), Vol. 26, No. 1, 1996, 108-139.

*   *   *

In her contribution to Diana Fuss's seminal collection of essays on gay and lesbian theory, *Inside/Out: Lesbian Theories, Gay Theories,* Judith Butler announced her reluctance to appear in such an anthology under the banner of "lesbian": "I'm not at ease with 'lesbian theories, gay theories,' for as I've argued elsewhere, identity categories tend to be instruments of regulatory regimes.... This is not to say that I will not appear at political occasions under the sign of lesbian, but that I would like to have it permanently unclear what precisely that sign signifies." As this statement suggests, a recurring theoretical theme in Butler's work is her desire to expose the unexamined assumptions behind taken-for-granted classifications such as "lesbian" and "gay." Building on the theoretical frameworks of twentieth-century deconstruction and postmodernism—contemporary movements that question the stability or innateness of the self—Butler reveals the coercive and limiting aspects of identity categories.

For Butler, identity categories are never simply rallying points or organizing principles for liberationist goals such as the recognition of same-sex marriages, anti-discrimination laws, or the publication of gay and lesbian anthologies. Rather, beginning with her influential 1990 book *Gender Trouble,* Butler argues that identity categories are also regulatory tools that rigidly delineate not only who is or is not a member of the category at hand, but also prescribe how that member must act, think, and write. Butler's work does not, however, suggest that classifications like "gay" and "lesbian" should be, or even could be, finally dispensed with. In one of her most important contributions to the ongoing discussion of gay and lesbian identities, Butler reminds activists and academics alike that categories and theories construct and constrict us even as we construct and shape them. Butler cautions that we must be aware of who is excluded from identity categories and seek to understand how that exclusion is maintained. According to Butler, coalition politics which emphasize unity risk settling in advance on priorities and dominant views that set up exclusionary boundaries.

In opposition to conventional identity politics, Butler disputes the presumption that a stable subject or identity "must" exist in order to have an effective politics. She advocates, instead, a constant interrogation of the categories themselves. Identity categories, then, are at once a hindrance and also a necessary starting point of resistance and opposition. Or, as Butler succinctly states in "Imitation and Gender Insubordination": "I'm permanently troubled by identity categories, consider them to be invariable stumbling-blocks, and understand them, even promote them, as sites of necessary trouble." Rethinking this notion of "trouble," Butler challenges readers of *Gender Trouble* to accompany her along a theoretical path that encompasses Simone de Beauvoir, Michel Foucault, Sigmund Freud, Luce Irigaray, Julia Kristeva, and Monique Wittig, and insists on pursuing the continual critique of all foundational categories of identity.

Central to Butler's continual critique of identity categories is her ongoing analysis of the performance-based nature of all identities. *Gender Trouble* examines how parodic practices, especially drag performances, may disrupt cultural constructions of gender and sexual norms by revealing the codes and assumptions by which these identities proceed. Butler's understanding of the performance-oriented nature of identity has made a significant impact on gay and lesbian studies within the academy. As E. Ann Kaplan points out in her review in *Signs,* "*Gender Trouble* may be seen as a much-needed attempt to theorize and affirm the value of gay/lesbian practices (play with dress, ways of living) that have long been carried out in hidden, marginalized ways." Butler foregrounds specific performances in her work not just as a means of affirming lesbian and gay activities but, more importantly, as a tool for reconceptualizing identity as a series of stylized acts that, repeated over time, establish the illusion of a coherent subject.

Butler's rigorous scrutiny of identity categories and their performances continues in her 1993 book, *Bodies That Matter: On the Discursive Limits of Sex.* As the title suggests, this text pushes another step beyond an examination of gender performances to consider the "performative" nature of sex and the body itself. In foregrounding the concept of the "performative," Butler corrects many of the critical (mis)readings of her earlier work on performance in *Gender Trouble.* Butler instructs readers of *Bodies That Matter* that, in opposition to these previous (mis)readings, her theory of gender performativity does not simply mean that "one woke in the morning, perused the closet or some more open space for the gender of choice, donned that gender for the day, and then restored the garment to its place at night." Performativity, then, cannot be reduced to performance. Understanding Butler's distinction between performance and performativity is crucial in comprehending many of the key concepts in her work, especially those of "reiteration" and "resignification."

Drawing from philosopher Michel Foucault, literary theorist Jacques Derrida, and linguistic theorist J.L. Austin's speech act theory and notion of iterability, as well as literary and queer theorist Eve Kosofsky Sedgwick's work on performativity, Butler constructs a notion of performative identity that "must be understood not as a singular or deliberate 'act,' but, rather, as the reiterative and citational practice by which discourse produces the effects it names." According to Butler, we cannot simply choose our gender as actors pick parts in plays because identity is the product of specific constraining normative frames. But, at the same time, these compulsory normative frames never merely determine our identities without simultaneously opening spaces of resistance. Butler argues that the power of identity categories and their accompanying restrictions is established in the process of endless reiteration or repetition of those identities, and that it is precisely

within this process of reiteration, within the gaps between repetitions, that places of resistance are made possible. What is useful for gay and lesbian theory and politics in this complex discussion of identity production is that the hope of counteracting prescriptive or "normal" ways of being already exists within the dominant norms themselves: "[s]ince the law must be repeated to remain an authoritative law, the law perpetually reinstitutes the possibility of its own failure." If these norms must be constantly repeated in order to maintain their power, then lesbians and gays can intervene at the moment of repetition and refashion the constraining framework. The subversion of identities, in Butler's theoretical work, is a subversion from within. Even as we oppose dominant norms we are implicated and constrained by them, but we may resignify the meanings of these categories by inhabiting that space of resistance that is opened up in the process of reiteration.

In *Bodies That Matter,* Butler sets out to demolish the sex/gender binary and the accompanying notion that gender is a cultural construct while biological sex is a given. Through essays on Willa Cather, Jacques Lacan, Nella Larsen, "Paris is Burning," and Plato, among others, *Bodies That Matter* denaturalizes sex and questions the materiality of the body by rethinking biological sex as a discursive production. Employing her understanding of performativity once again, Butler argues that even the body is produced through a perpetual repetition of cultural norms. Butler's work on the performative nature of gender, sexuality, and even biological sex is a vital and necessary addition to feminist as well as gay and lesbian understandings of identity formation. *Bodies That Matter* allows its readers to see past the limiting binary categories of conventional identities (i.e. gay or straight; male or female; man or woman; etc.) and calls for a continual democratization of these terms. Indeed, Butler's ongoing critique of identity categories initiates a "self-critical dimension within activism" that requires we question who is represented by which use of the term and who is excluded.

In the tradition of gay and lesbian recuperations of historically-freighted terminology, Butler's work embraces "queer" as a useful political and theoretical rallying point. This does not mean, however, that readers of her work may set down Butler's books or articles secure in the permanence of this alternative identity category. Butler instructs that any term of identification, including gay, lesbian, and queer, must "remain that which is, in the present, never fully owned, but always and only redeployed, twisted, queered from a prior usage and in the direction of urgent and expanding political purposes." For Butler this means that a term or an identity category may need to be given up once it becomes restrictive or limiting; for gay and lesbian activists this means that the contours of a queer political movement can never be fully anticipated and are constantly redrawn. The continual critique of conventional terms of identity, according to Butler, potentially extends the range of gay and lesbian identity categories and insists that we consider at what expense and for what purposes the terms are used.

The prominence of Butler's work in gay and lesbian as well as queer studies programs across North America has led at least one critic, Robyn Wiegman, to designate Butler and American literary theorist Eve Kosofsky Sedgwick "queer theory's diva couple." The accuracy of this nomination is borne out time and time again at North American gay and lesbian academic conferences where the citation of Butler's theories is a favorite pastime. Perhaps more than the work of any other contemporary theorist, Butler's texts map out the terrain of queer theory and provide the tools necessary for rethinking all identity categories. Butler's work persuasively opens up to debate previously established identity boundaries, and provides for a rethinking of what gay and lesbian identities might come to mean.

—B.J. Wray

C

CALDERON, Sara Levi

Nationality: Mexican writer and scholar. **Born:** 29 November 1941, in Mexico City; lives in Mexico and San Francisco, California. **Family:** Married and had two sons; divorced. **Education:** University of Mexico, B.A. in Sociology, 1980. **Career:** Teacher of communications, University of Mexico, 1982-84. **Address:** c/o Aunt Lute Books, P.O. Box 410687, San Francisco, California 94141-0687, U.S.A.

WRITINGS

Fiction

Dos Mujeres. Mexico City, Diana, 1990; translation by Gina Kaufer with revisions by the author as *The Two Mujeres,* San Francisco, Aunt Lute Books, 1991.
Hija de Buena Familia. Forthcoming.

*

Critical Sources: "Monobodies, Antibodies and the Body Politic: Sara Levi Calderon's *Dos Mujeres,*" in *Danger Zones: Homosexuality, National Identity, and Mexican Culture* by Claudia Schaefer, Tucson, University of Arizona Press, 1996.

*   *   *

The cohesion of a national culture relies upon the notion of a homogenous national identity, which exerts control on a society by establishing limits on the behavior of its members. In Sara Levi Calderon's *The Two Mujeres,* the character Valeria symbolizes the element in society that destabilizes this assumption of uniformity. Valeria is a divorced mother, a wealthy woman from a prominent Mexico City family, the daughter of Jewish refugees, and a lesbian. These multiple identities illustrate the many differences that thrive behind the illusion of sameness. Valeria also serves as a reminder of the paradox of vulnerability and strength that a person living outside the mainstream experiences.

Valeria's family is at the center of her struggle to live out her life as a lesbian and an individual on her own terms. Her father gradually amassed a fortune in the cement business, and the family soon became one of the most wealthy and prominent in Mexico City. Valeria resisted the constraints that came with this status, and violence was the means through which conformity was physically imposed upon her, at the hands of her father, brother, husband, and even her own sons. Still, Valeria was able to fight for her own needs: she divorced her abusive husband and went to school to pursue a degree in Sociology.

As a university student and divorcée, Valeria's lifestyle was unacceptable to her family, and the shadow of her family's disapproval loomed over her apparent freedom. The conclusive break from the family's social paradigm comes when Valeria meets Genovesa, the cousin of her friend Morena. Genovesa is 14 years younger than Valeria and is an unemployed artist, yet despite these substantial differences, the two women fall in love. When they kiss for the first time, Valeria experiences a new freedom she could never have dreamed of if she had continued to live her prescribed role of wife and mother. After the kiss, however, the gravity of their transgression is already painfully clear: "It's not easy to shun our ancestral ghosts," Valeria says to Genovesa. "What we are doing means that the oldest symbols, the ones we were given even before birth, have to be replaced...and we must find new ones."

At first, Valeria and Genovesa are able to live out their relationship in seclusion and secrecy, stealing romantic moments only in their private domains. However, this avoidance of others cannot last forever. When the two go into town after several days without leaving the house, they suddenly feel the weight of their outsider status: "Genovesa took my hand but let it drop immediately. We were out on the streets now for the first time, and we sensed the *gran familia,* the extended Mexican family traveling with us. Some were sitting on the trunk, others were hanging from the doors. They all pointed at us with their tiny fingers. 'You've gone too far,' they seemed to say."

Valeria's family disapproves of her new female friend, and they put increasing financial pressure on her to attend to her responsibilities as a representative of the family. This exertion of power is often physical as well as emotional and financial. One incident in particular symbolizes how threatening Valeria's defiance truly is: her son beats her over the head with a precious family menorah. This action illustrates the powerful dynamics she is struggling against, including her obligations to her ancestors, and in the image of the menorah, the formidable authority of the patriarchal Jewish religious system.

Although Valeria suffers under the brutality of her family, she continues to fight on their terms, hoping for a resolution that will allow her to maintain her financial security. Her father offers to buy her an apartment in the United States, a thinly veiled attempt to lure her away from Genovesa through money. Valeria naively considers his offer, believing that she will be able to maneuver around her father's plans and live on her inheritance money with Genovesa in San Francisco. While she and Genovesa are abroad looking at houses, the family invades Valeria's home and discovers her journals and intimate records of their relationship. They cancel her credit cards and empty her bank accounts, and her sons' threats of violence make it unsafe for Valeria to enter her own house alone. Disinherited and robbed of her personal freedom, Valeria is forced to stay in Genovesa's house, and suddenly experiences the loss of her class identity along with the loss of her family. She is disoriented: "Genovesa's apartment became the symbol of the break with my family. I used to go out walking around the streets of her neighborhood. Everything was so unfamiliar; none of the coordinates in my memory helped me locate myself. I felt as if I were living in exile."

Nevertheless, Valeria stays with Genovesa in Mexico City for several years, believing that somehow her family will learn to treat her with tolerance if not acceptance. In the end, however, she realizes that this is not possible. She cannot live openly as a lesbian and maintain her upper-class status in Mexican society. The family refuses to endanger their social prestige for the sake of their daughter, and they continue to threaten and malign her and to place the blame for the family's problems on her shoulders.

In the last chapter, Valeria and Genovesa are living in an idyllic spot on the Aegean Sea, far from the pain and trauma of Mexico City. Now both in exile, they have found the peace that will allow them to live out their love without restrictions and free from violence. Freedom comes, however, at the price of leaving behind the security and familiarity of their culture.

Despite her failure to withstand her family's attacks, Valeria discovers a new source of strength and power that is entirely her own: her voice. She writes down the story of their love, the story of *dos mujeres,* and in so doing frees herself from the burden of silence she has lived with for so long. Critic Claudia Schaefer has commented that this semi-autobiographical novel achieved unexpected bestseller status in Mexico when it was published, and the author's father attempted to prevent the book's distribution by buying all the copies he could find. Ironically, in this instance, money and prestige could not triumph over the power of one woman's words. The conclusion of the novel is thus both sobering and encouraging. Valeria and Genovesa have to live in exile in order to remain together, but in their struggle they have won a much larger battle. Their story provides an example of how it is possible, even in the face of seemingly insurmountable odds, to transform silence into strength.

—Caitlin L. Gannon

CALLEN, Michael Lane

Nationality: American writer, musician, and activist. **Born:** Rising Sun, Indiana, 11 April 1955; grew up in Hamilton, Ohio. **Education:** Taft High School, Hamilton, Ohio, 1973; Boston University, B.A. in English Literature 1977. **Family:** Companion of Richard Dworkin. **Career:** Worked as a certified paralegal and legal secretary, 1975-84; founding member and first editor, PWA (People With AIDS) Coalition Newsline, 1984-88; founding member and singer, The Flirtations, an a cappella group, 1988-93. Founding member, People With AIDS, People With AIDS Coalition, New York, National Association of People With AIDS, People With AIDS Health Group, the Mayor's Interagency Task Force on AIDS, and the AIDS Medical Foundation (now known as AmFar) Institutional Review; founding board member, Community Research Initiative, New York Gay & Lesbian Community Center, and the New York State AIDS Advisory Council. Co-hosted PWA Coalition cable show, 1985; contributor to *Village Voice, New York Native, Medical Month, Hastings Center Review, QW, NYQ, Genre,* and *Advocate.* **Awards:** First Annual Gay/Lesbian American Music Awards, for Male Artist, Duo/Group, Choral Group, and Album of the Year, 1996. **Died:** Los Angeles, California, from complications associated with AIDS, 27 December 1993.

WRITINGS

Nonfiction

With Richard Berkowitz, *How to Have Sex in an Epidemic: One Approach* (booklet). News from the Front Press, 1983.
Editor, *Surviving and Thriving with AIDS: Hints for the Newly Diagnosed.* New York, PWA Coalition, 1987.

Editor, *Surviving and Thriving with AIDS: Collected Wisdom.* Volume 2, New York, PWA Coalition, 1988.
Contributor, *You Can Do Something About AIDS.* Stop AIDS Project, 1988.
"AIDS: The Linguistic Battlefield," in *The State of the Language,* edited by L. Michaels and C. Ricks. Berkeley, University of California Press, 1990.
Surviving AIDS. New York, HarperCollins, 1990.

Recordings: *Purple Heart,* Significant Other Records, 1988; *The Flirtations,* Significant Other Records, 1990; *Out on the Road,* Flirt Records, 1992; *Legacy,* Significant Other Records, 1996.

*

Critical Sources: *Surviving AIDS* by Michael Callen. New York, HarperCollins, 1990; unpublished interview with Richard Dworkin by Andrea L. T. Peterson, October/November 1996.

*   *   *

Michael Callen "was one of the omnipresent, one of the titans," said playwright Tony Kushner. As a composer, singer, writer, and AIDS activist Callen played a major part in shaping America's response to the AIDS epidemic. An AIDS activist before there was an AIDS movement, he was involved in virtually all of the "positive" responses to the epidemic since his own diagnosis of Gay Related Immune Deficiency (GRID) in 1982, according to Richard Dworkin, Callen's companion for more than a decade.

Callen first heard the word "homosexual" when he was 14 and "broke out in a cold sweat," he recalled in *Surviving AIDS.* He "instinctively" knew that being homosexual must be something truly horrible and that he was homosexual. By the time he was 27 he was diagnosed with GRID. Callen endeavored to combat the hopelessness that surrounded most of the reports and media presentations of the disease that came to be called AIDS. In an effort to change the view of people with AIDS as victims, Callen coined the term People With Aids (PWAs) and fought to emphasize that PWAs could live with AIDS and continue to make significant contributions to society. He used his life, his song lyrics, his essays, his articles, and his books to serve as proof of his convictions.

Callen's clear, precise descriptions and guidelines for living with AIDS or the threat of contracting AIDS served his community well. "We Know Who We Are: Two Gay Men Declare War on Promiscuity," one of his earliest writings, warned other gay men that some of their sexual practices put them at higher risk for AIDS. He was involved in the self-empowerment of PWAs, the development of the concept and practice of safer sex, the community-based research movement, and the development of prophylaxis for major opportunistic infections. He facilitated the establishment of buyers' clubs providing low-cost access to both experimental and approved AIDS treatments.

Callen was a vocal and proud spokesperson for his communities: the gay and lesbian community as well as the smaller community of People With AIDS. He founded a handful of advocacy groups for people with AIDS and he was instrumental in organizing the first national gathering of people with AIDS at at a health care conference held in Denver in 1983. He provided testimony before every legislative body from New York City Council sub-committees up to the President's Commission on AIDS. And he appeared on numerous television specials, documentaries, and talk shows, and was featured in the Oscar-winning movie *Philadelphia* and in the HBO documentary *Why Am I Gay?*

Especially interesting are the lyrics to his moving songs, including "Love Don't Need a Reason" (written with Peter Allen and Marsha Malamet), "Healing Power of Love," "How to Have Safe Sex in an Epidemic," and "Living in Wartime." In the year before his death on December 27, 1993, he recorded the vocals for more than fifty songs, 29 of which were posthumously released on the album *Legacy*. A sample of Callen's passionate feelings are found in the song, written with Marsha Malamet, called "Love Worth Fighting For":

> It's a crazy world
> We shouldn't have to hide
> All love's good and should be welcomed!
> So I refuse to lie anymore
> Who are they to say?
> Who says it's not okay?
> Their rules just don't apply
> Who are they anyway?
> There's more than just one way

As an independent thinker, a determined activist and advocate, and a creative optimist who looked AIDS in the face when turning inward might have been easier, Callen educated, served as a role model, and offered himself as living proof of the ideas and ideals embodied in his work. Perhaps his proudest accomplishment is that against the odds, and contrary to conventional wisdom, he thrived for 12 years with AIDS.

—Andrea L.T. Peterson

CAMERON, Peter

Nationality: American novelist and short story writer. **Born:** Pompton Plains, New Jersey, 29 November 1959. **Education:** Hamilton College, B.A. 1982. **Career:** Instructor, Unterberg Poetry Center, 92nd Street Y, New York, 1989-93; executive assistant, Lambda Legal Defense and Education Fund, New York, from 1990; adjunct assistant professor, Columbia University, New York, 1991-96; visiting professor of writing, Hamilton College and Oberlin College. Contributor of stories to periodicals, including *Antioch Review, Bostonia, Grand Street, Kenyon Review, Mademoiselle, Mississippi Review, New Yorker, Paris Review, Quarterly (Q), Rolling Stone,* and *Yale Review*. **Awards:** MacDowell Colony Residencies, 1984, 1986, 1988, 1990, 1992; O. Henry Awards, 1985, 1986, 1995; National Endowment for the Arts Grant, 1987; Ernest Hemingway Foundation/PEN America Award for First Book of Fiction, Special Citation, 1987; Yaddo Residency, 1987, 1996. **Address:** c/o Farrar Straus Giroux, 19 Union Square West, New York, New York 10003, U.S.A.

Writings

Novels

Leap Year. New York, Harper & Row, 1990.
The Weekend. New York, Farrar Straus Giroux, 1994.
Andorra. New York, Farrar Straus Giroux, 1997.

Short Stories

One Way or Another. New York, Harper & Row, 1986.
Far-flung. New York, HarperCollins, 1991.
"Jump or Dive," in *The Penguin Book of Gay Short Stories,* edited by David Leavitt and Mark Mitchell. New York, Viking, 1994.
"Departing," in *Yale Review* (New Haven, Connecticut), Vol. 82, No. 1, January 1994, 88-103.
"Aria," in *Yale Review,* Vol. 83, No. 2, April 1995, 100-106.
The Half You Don't Know: Selected Stories. New York, NAL/ Dutton, 1997.

*

Critical Sources: "Between Jumping and Diving" by Victor Kantor Burg, in *New York Times Book Review,* 22 June 1986, 11; "Peter Cameron," in *Contemporary Literary Criticism,* Vol. 44, Detroit, Gale Research Company, 1987; "Cameron, Peter," in *Contemporary Authors,* Vol. 125, Detroit, Gale Research Company, 1989; "Simple Truths Are Hard to Know" by Joyce Reiser Kornblatt, in *New York Times Book Review,* 29 May 1994, 16; "The Weekend" by Brian Kenney, in *Library Journal,* Vol. 119, July 1994, 124.

*   *   *

Peter Cameron writes not about the gay world, nor exclusively about gay characters, but rather about gay people who negotiate the broader worlds of their families, their lovers' families, and places of work. His stories are about educated people, often of independent means, whose privilege, material resources, and opportunities exceed their emotional resources. Since the publication of his story "Memorial Day" in the *New Yorker* in 1983, about an adolescent whose only means of expressing his anger toward his mother is to stop speaking altogether, Cameron's writing has been recognized for its lyricism, understatement, and distinct ability to portray the anomie of undirected adolescent or twenty- and thirty-something characters.

Born in New Jersey in 1959, Cameron attended Hamilton College, where he became attentive to story writing. He received considerable critical acclaim with the publication of *One Way or Another* in 1986. With stories published in *Prize Stories: The O. Henry Awards,* he earned several grants and residences in successive years. He has taught in several writing programs in New York, was a visiting professor of creative writing at Hamilton and Oberlin Colleges, and serves as a judge for several writing awards.

Cameron's early work was often favorably compared with the laconic, muted prose of Ann Beattie and Raymond Carver. Like Beattie's characters, Cameron's are often young, educated, well-travelled, propertied, and of comfortable means, while many are also emotionally inarticulate and mildly aimless. Some are adolescents whose sexuality is not fully defined, but who express their ambiguity indirectly through their tentativeness, ambivalence, and introspection. In "Jump or Dive," Evan, a high-school sophomore, delays a visit with his parents to spend time with his gay Uncle Walter and his married lover Jason. Evan plays a game with Jason, to whom he feels simultaneously attuned and resistant: he leaps from the diving board waiting to be told whether to dive or jump. He cannot decide; neither can he decide whether to leave with his parents or to risk staying on for a few days in the vaguely attractive homosexual domestic setting. Freddie, the main character in "Freddie's Haircut," plagued by others' concerns that his new earring indicates he is gay, is brought to tears by an unflattering haircut and an unearned dismissal from his job. Cameron reveals Freddie's distress to the reader through a third-person narrator; the result is an empathic voice that distills the character's uncertainty and disappointment as mundane events unfold.

First published as a serial novel by the magazine *7 Days, Leap Year* is a comic novel about ten months in the lives of a group of people living in New York. At the center of the constellation is David Parish, recently divorced and pursuing a romantic relation with Heath. Revolving around them are Loren, David's former wife, her new beau, Gregory, and Lillian, David's unmarried friend. Their lives are interrupted by a murder, a kidnapping, and an earthquake. Admired for its social satire of tony Manhattan environments in the late 1980s, *Leap Year* was also praised for the affection the author showed his characters.

With *Far-flung* Cameron's voice found its most audible register and developed greater resonance. In "What?," Ruth and Joanna, both academics, have recently ended their relationship. They display their melancholy within a domestic context: preparing familiar recipes, polishing furniture, and, most poignantly, caring for Virgil, the dog. In "The Café Hysteria" we meet the endearing narrator Lillian, who interacts with the other characters developed further in *Leap Year.* Tom, the narrator of "Slowly," debates whether to follow Charles to his diplomatic post in Africa. In "The Meeting and Greeting Area," Charles has his turn to narrate and tells Tom, from whom he has separated to take the post, that he still loves him. Here the acutely observed details of sharing a bed evoke with poignancy the complexity of a dissolving relation: "And then he did touch me; his fingers slid up and gently clasped my arm right below my elbow. It was an odd, unerotic place to hold someone. It was where you'd hold someone to pull him back from traffic, or other sudden dangers."

In his second novel, *The Weekend,* Cameron assembles five people at a house in upstate New York: John and Marian, who own the house; their infant son Roland; Lyle, whose late lover Tony was John's half-brother; and Robert, Lyle's new romantic interest. The elegiac tone of the novel fits the sorrowful mood of the characters; each seeks to nurture something, whether it is the serpentine stone wall that John is building, the infant Roland about whom Marian worries, or Robert's vain effort to kindle a suitable romantic relation with Lyle. Cameron excels at the metaphoric language of small gestures; as Lyle and his companion travel north by train, we read that "Robert was unswaddling the Danish." Lyle is the only satirical character in the novel; he seems to sense few limits to the use of art historical jargon and pretentious critical statements.

Andorra moves into another genre. Its atmospheric quality evokes Orson Welles's *The Third Man,* and this story of the relocation of a young widower, the mysterious Alex Fox, to the romantic principality of Andorra introduces only tangential gay characters: the sexually ambiguous and tormented Ricky Dent and Vere, who was romantically linked with Alex's brother-in-law Philip. Unspecific in time, but highly exacting about details of place, *Andorra,* with its dislocated characters and quiet pace, echoes the novels of Anita Brookner.

While Cameron's characters remain befuddled by the complexities of love, they are usually people aspiring to be good, unconvinced, however, that they possess fundamental goodness.

In the course of inventing characters who sound real, Peter Cameron examines with insight and precision the moral ambiguities of members of his generation.

—Paul Glassman

CAMINHA, Adolpho (Ferreira)

Nationality: Brazilian novelist and poet. Name modernized as Adolfo Caminha. **Born:** Aracati, province of Ceará (now state of Ceará), 29 May 1867. **Education:** At home in Fortaleza, Ceará; Escola de Marinha, Rio de Janeiro, 1883-86, graduated 1886. **Military Service:** Served in the Brazilian Navy, 1886-90; Second Lieutenant. **Family:** Companion of Isabel Jata de Paula Barros (a married woman). **Career:** Clerk in Treasury of Agriculture, Fortaleza, Ceará 1890-92; founder of magazines *Revista Moderna,* 1892, and *Nova Revista,* 1896; official of the Federal Treasury, 1892-97. **Died:** Rio de Janeiro, of tuberculosis, 1 January 1897.

WRITINGS

Fiction

Judite e Lágrimas de um crente ("Judith and Tears of a Believer"; short stories). Rio de Janeiro, Tipografia da Escola Serafim José Alves, 1887.
A normalista ("The Schoolgirl"; novel). Rio de Janeiro, Domingos de Magalhães Editor, 1893.
Bom Crioulo (novel). Rio de Janeiro, Domingos de Magalhães Editor, 1895; as *Bom Crioulo: The Black Man and the Cabin Boy,* translated by E. A. Lacey, San Francisco, Gay Sunshine Press, 1982.
Tentação ("Temptation"; novel). Rio de Janeiro, Laemmert & Companhia, 1896; as *Tentação: No país dos Ianques* ("Temptation: In the Land of the Yankees"), with critical introduction by Sânzio de Azevedo, Rio de Janeiro, Livraria José Olympio Editora, 1979.

Other

Vôos incertos ("Uncertain Flights"; poems). Rio de Janeiro, Tipografia da Escola Serafim José Alves, 1886.
No paíz dos Yankees ("In the Land of the Yankees"; travel sketches). Rio de Janeiro, Domingos de Magalhães Editor, 1894; as *Tentação: No país dos Ianques* ("Temptation: In the Land of the Yankees"), with critical introduction by Sânzio de Azevedo, Rio de Janeiro, Livraria José Olympio Editora, 1979.
Cartas litterárias (modernized as *Cartas literárias*; "Literary Letters"; literary criticism). Rio de Janeiro, Tipografia Aldina, 1895.

*

Biography: *Roteiro de Adolfo Caminha* by João Felipe de Sabia Ribeiro, Rio Janeiro, Livraria São José, 1957; *Alguns aspectos de Adolfo Caminha (à margem de sua obra e vida)* by João Felipe de Sabia Ribeiro, Rio de Janeiro, Tupy, 1964; *O romanicista Adolfo Caminha, 1867-1897: em comemoração do seu centenário* by João Felipe de Sabia Ribeiro, Rio de Janeiro, Editora Pongetti, 1967.

Critical Sources: *Now the Volcano: An Anthology of Latin American Gay Literature,* edited by Winston Leyland, translated by Erskine Lane, Franklin D. Blanton, and Simon Karlinsky, San Francisco, Gay Sunshine Press, 1979; "Adolfo Caminha's *Bom Crioulo*" by Robert Howes, in *Bom Crioulo: The Black Man and the Cabin Boy,* translated by E. A. Lacey, San Francisco, Gay Sunshine Press, 1982, 11-21; *Race and Color in Brazilian Literature* by David Brookshaw, Metuchen, New Jersey, Scarecrow Press, 1986; "Adolfo Caminha's *Bom Crioulo*: A Founding Text of Brazilian Gay Literature," in *Gay and Lesbian Themes in Latin American Writing* by David William Foster, Austin, Texas, University of Texas Press, 1991, 9-22; "Uma subjetividade outra" by Francisco Caetano Lopes Júnior, in *Toward Socio-Criticism: Selected Proceedings of the Conference "Luso-Brazilian Literatures,* edited by Roberto Reis, Tempe, Arizona, Center for Latin American Studies, Arizona State University, 1991, 67-75.

*　　*　　*

Adolfo Caminha (1867-1897) had a short but intense publishing career. Its highlight, *Bom Crioulo: The Black Man and the Cabin Boy* (1895), has been praised by critics for its objective portrayal of homosexuality and is identified by Winston Leyland in *Now the Volcano: An Anthology of Latin American Gay Literature* as one of the first explicitly gay works in Latin American literature. Set in Caminha's native Brazil, the novel examines the relationship between an Afro-Brazilian sailor (the ex-slave Amaro or "Bom Crioulo") and a white cabin boy (Aleixo) shortly after the abolition of slavery in 1888.

What we know of Caminha's life suggests that he often incited controversy. In 1885, while a student at naval school, he delivered a speech on the occasion of the death of Victor Hugo. In the presence of the Brazilian Emperor, Dom Pedro II, the upstart Caminha praised Hugo's republicanism and called for the abolition of slavery. In 1890, Caminha was forced out of the Navy by the scandal surrounding his companion, Isabel Jata de Barros, who had left her husband, a military officer, to live with the author. His attitude of defiance toward social norms is equally apparent in Caminha's writings, which include novels centered around the taboo subjects of incest in *A normalista* ("The Schoolgirl"; 1893) and adultery in *Tentação* ("Temptation"; 1896).

With a poor, Afro-Brazilian homosexual as its protagonist, *Bom Crioulo* is Caminha's most provocative work. Previous naturalist novels in Brazil had predominantly focused on white elite families. In addition to his daring choice of protagonist, Caminha's novel offers a biting critique of the Brazilian Navy and its inhumane disciplinary measures, particularly the use of the lash.

Despite its liberating elements, its denunciation of corporal punishment, and its remarkably direct treatment of homosexuality, Caminha's novel is enmeshed in the scientific determinism of its day. This complicates any appreciation for *Bom Crioulo*. By transposing the theme of emancipation from slavery to a theme of sexual emancipation, the novel indicates that freedom for individuals naturally inclined to animal-like conduct will invariably lead to dismal ends. The promise of emancipation due to Amaro's escape from slavery and from sexual strictures is proven false as his "animal" nature drives him to kill his lover Aleixo in a fit of jealousy.

Critics have read *Bom Crioulo* as part of an attempt to reestablish social order during a critical moment of social transition. Brazilian intellectuals were anxious about the social place and power of the newly liberated Afro-Brazilian population. "Natural" ten-dencies and forces were used to prove the inferiority of Afro-Brazilians and to justify the stratification of Brazilian society. Amaro, for example, can expect nothing more from his liberation than hard physical labor. He is often described in purely physical terms; "A real animal, whole and hale, that's what he is!" says a fellow sailor. Race-marked descriptions of Amaro's out-of-control behavior support the myth of pathological violence as inherent to Afro-Brazilians. As the novel progresses, Amaro is pathologized both for his race and for his homosexuality.

What distinguishes *Bom Crioulo* from other naturalist novels is that the laws of heredity provide the basis for a "scientific domination," justifying the economic exploitation of Afro-Brazilian labor. As *Bom Crioulo* shows, applying European scientific theories to Brazilian society via naturalism helped reinforce preexisting prejudices concerning class, race, and sexuality in Brazil.

Still, there is a contradiction within *Bom Crioulo* that may account for its attraction for readers over the past century. Amaro is at times presented as a romantic figure, a noble savage. Both good and evil, he is impelled by forces beyond his control:

> Bom Crioulo had one of those terrible fits that attacked him from time to time. He groaned a hoarse, long, low 'ah!', and, light-footed, furious, beside himself with anger, without losing a second, he raced like an arrow into the street. He could see nothing, he could distinguish nothing, in his rage, as if suddenly his sight and his reason had abandoned him.

Though we see him moving toward his biological destiny—extinction—through the lens of naturalism, Amaro is presented as a victim. The reader is left with the puzzle of Amaro's homosexuality; is it heroic or is it unnatural? As David William Foster has recognized in *Gay and Lesbian Themes in Latin American Writing,* this question itself points to a contradiction in naturalist thinking, for how can homosexuality be both against nature and natural?

The ambiguities of *Bom Crioulo* stem both from the contradictions of naturalism and from the complex intersection of race, sexuality, and gender it portrays. Amaro can resist tremendous corporal punishment, but he is brought to his destruction by a white female prostitute who seduces Aleixo away from him. Certainly in his own time Caminha's work raised hackles for its direct treatment of sexuality. Some Brazilian critics claim that all of his writing has been deliberately ignored for this reason. In "Uma Subjetividade Outra" ("An Other Subjectivity"), Francisco Lopes Caetano Júnior calls *Bom Crioulo* a minority text, one that flees from traditional models forged in a closed and highly hierarchical community. This view is representative of the renewed interest we see in Caminha's work as a frank, if not wholly positive, treatment of racial and sexual identities.

—Elizabeth A. Marchant

CAMPO, Rafael

Nationality: Cuban American poet and essayist. **Born:** 24 November 1964. **Education:** Amherst College, B.A. 1987; Boston University, M.A. 1991; Harvard Medical School, M.D. 1992. **Ca-**

reer: Practicing physician, Harvard Medical School and Beth Is-rael Hospital, Boston. Contributor of reviews to periodicals, including *Ploughshares* and the *Nation*. **Awards:** Rolfe Humphries Poetry Prize, 1986-87; George Starbuck Writing Fellowship, 1990; Boston Literary Guild Prize, for AIDS-related Writing, 1991; *Agni* Poetry Prize, 1991; *Kenyon Review* Emerging Writer of the Year, 1992; National Poetry Series Open Competition, 1993; echoing green Award, for literary nonfiction, 1995; Guggenheim Fellowship, 1997. **Address:** 22 Thomas St., Boston, Massachusetts 02130, U.S.A.

WRITINGS

Poetry

The Other Man Was Me: A Voyage to the New World. Houston, Arte Público Press, 1994.
What the Body Told. Durham, Duke University Press, 1996.
Things Shaped in Passing: Poets for Life II. New York, Persea Books, forthcoming.

Essays

"The Emanation of Pain," in *Parnassus: Poetry in Review* (New York), spring-fall 1995.
"A Case of Mistaken Identities: The Human Body," in *Currents from the Dancing River: Contemporary Latino Fiction, Nonfiction, and Poetry,* edited by Ray Gonzalez. New York, San Diego, London, Harcourt Brace and Company, 1994.
"About Marilyn Hacker," in *Ploughshares,* spring 1996.
The Poetry of Healing: A Doctor's Education in Empathy, Identity, and Desire. New York, W.W. Norton, 1997.

*   *   *

Physician and poet Rafael Campo brings a powerful new voice to the pantheon of Latino gay writers. Although the themes and settings of many of his poems are a familiar part of the American literary landscape—for example, one angst-ridden character hits the highway in order to escape "it all"—Campo's focus is uniquely his own. He often ponders both his role as a doctor treating those on the edge of death and the alienation he feels as a queer man of color. In his essay "A Case of Mistaken Identities: The Human Body," he writes of coming to terms with his conflicted identity: "It is the surgery I have been performing on myself since I began writing poems, as if I too required assisted breathing the way a patient undergoing an operation to remove a malignant tumor requires the temporary artificial imposition of the innate breathing rhythms."

His poems are highly structured, usually sonnets in iambic pentameter; he uses the security of form as a position from which to delve deep into the heart of his own feelings—feelings for his AIDS and cancer patients and for emergency room arrivals who have suffered from brutal encounters with an overwhelmingly homophobic and racist American society. In "A Case of Mistaken Identities" he tells us, "Writing iambic pentameter feels like putting stitches into the anonymous, eternally gaping wound of being human, and rhymes can be intertwined like surgical knots. To write formal poetry is sometimes even a way of sewing myself into the body of tradition from which I feel excluded, as if I were

an amputated clubfoot yearning to have its blood supply restored." A poem called "In the Form," featured in his first collection, *The Other Man Was Me: A Voyage to the New World,* reads: "A sonnet? Tension. Words withheld. A rhyme / Where memory has left its watermark, / A turn of phrase that brings another time."

Campo grew up culturally and sexually conflicted. As a child he was keenly aware of ethnic difference, for his mother was Italian and his father Cuban. Fleeing Castro's reign, the family moved to a predominantly white New Jersey suburb, where, he tells us, "I was the darkest note in the white harmony of an antiseptic classroom." Even stolen moments of privacy offered only a limited sense of freedom: In "My Mother's Closet," he wishes he "could wear it all— / Except my mom was tall and thin, while I / Was built like a man." His father, an engineer turned factory worker, saw his own dreams die in New Jersey. So it was left to Rafael to free himself of Cuban baggage and pursue the American Dream. Finding the strength to discard the old culture was necessary for the liberation of the boy's sexual identity; he calls his father his "homonym: he gave to me his name.... I was afraid he'd be ashamed his son, / On whom he'd practiced so much strength, was gay."

Thus, as an adult, Campo turned to poetry as a way of revisiting and revising his family history, ultimately liberating himself from the past. In many of his autobiographical poems, Campo presents the overabundance of his family's memories (repeated to him endlessly during his childhood), his father's machismo, and even the Spanish language as heavy and oppressive elements alienating him from the world in which he found himself. Through poetry he tried to see the past clearly, refusing to repeat it. Of his grandfather's death, Campo wrote, "What I saw / Was skin falling from bones; the scars I saw / made me wince. I said, 'this reflection / Is not of me.'" The new homeland and new language offer a measure of release. In "San Fernando" Campo notes, "I write to you in English, Father, / Because I am evolving. I'm freer / Than I was before." Therefore, unlike many Latino poets who make politically liberating gestures by introducing the thrum of Spanish-language rhythm and syntax into their verse, Campo chooses to write exclusively in English.

Many of the poems that make up *The Other Man Was Me* examine Campo's adulthood and feelings of alienation as a gay man. In an homophobic culture, outward signs of love and affection have to take place surreptitiously, on roads less traveled. Campo captured the sense of outsider-ness when he used the third person in the poem "Finally," which begins:

> Two lovers met. It wasn't lovers' lane,
> But a lesser traveled road. No others came.
> One lover held the other's hand. The other
> Man was me. I watched as if I hovered
> Far above the scene.

It is largely as a doctor treating those at the edge of death that Campo is able to make connections with his fellow human beings. In his collection, *What the Body Told,* he focuses on encounters with people admitted to an emergency room. Here his poems are short and succinct, assuming the form of the doctor's rapid diagnosis and notetaking. In "The Doctor" he writes, "I watch as blood pressures ascend, hearts stop; / A cancer dimpling a woman's breast, / As if to pull her in, inside herself. / On certain days I want to die myself." Comparison to physician-poet William Carlos Williams, who used a similar technique in his poem "Paterson" in the 1930s, might seem inevitable, but there is more at stake in Campo's work. Because he writes as a gay doctor who treats AIDS patients, his poems gain extra layers of significance: In "Safe Sex Revisited" he writes:

> I've learned
> A power to protect myself from AIDS.
> I call it 'Poetry of the Absurd.'
> ...The virus tries
> To penetrate, but I write poetry
> And so it finds no place to multiply—
> My blood cells are replaced by words for "bleed,"
> My penis is a pen with which I write
> These contradictions.

So although Campo discovers that he can channel his desire to outwardly and freely express same-sex love through his work as a doctor, he must, in the era of AIDS, protect himself. His poetry acts both as a way to get nearer to his patients, himself, and his sexual identity, and as a prophylactic that allows him safely "to touch my patients without the protective barrier of latex." Rafael Campo, then, is a physician whose poetry attempts to cure himself and those he encounters in the hospital; with the curative powers of the poem's "sublingual nitroglycerin" he hopes "each one of us might survive."

—Frederick Luis Aldama

CÁRDENAS, Nancy

Nationality: Mexican playwright, poet, and film and theater critic. **Born:** Parras, Coahuila, 29 May 1934. **Education:** Universidad Nacional Autonoma de Mexico, Ph.D. in dramatic arts; film and theater scholar at Yale University, 1960-61; studied Polish literature and language in Lodz, Poland, 1961. **Career:** Production coordinator of radio station and television station consultant, Universidad Nacional Autonoma de Mexico (UNAM). **Awards:** Asociacion de Criticos de Teatro prize, 1970; "El Heraldo" prize, 1980. **Died:** Mexico City, 22 March 1994.

Writings

Stage Plays

El cántaro seco ("The Empty Pitcher"; produced Mexico, Universidad Nacional Autonoma de Mexico, 1960).
La vida privada del profesor Kabela ("The Private Life of Professor Kabela"; broadcast on the Serie Nuevo Teatro de Radio Universidad, Mexico, 1963).
El d a que pisamos la luna ("The Day We Stepped on the Moon"; broadcast on Serie Nuevo Teatro de Radio Universidad, Mexico, 1981).
Las hermanitas de Acámbaro ("The Sisters of Acámbaro"; broadcast on Serie Nuevo Teatro de Radio Universidad, Mexico, 1983).
With Gilberto Flores Alavez, *Sangre de mi sangre* ("Blood of my Blood"), 1984-85.

Sexualidades I ("Sexualities I"), 1992.
Sexualidades II ("Sexualities II"), 1993.

Poetry

"Ahora un poco de flores para ti" ("Now a Few Flowers for You"), in *El Gallo Ilustrado* (Mexico City), Vol. 421, 19 July 1970.
"Vuelo acordado" ("Agreed Flight"), in *Tarjetas de Tabajo* (Mexico City), 1971.
"Amor de verano" ("Summer Love") in *Katún* (Mexico City), 1985.

Other

"El cine polaco" ("Polish Cinema"). *Cuadernos de Cine,* Direccion General de Difusion Cultural, Mexico City, 1962.
"Aproximaciones al teatro de vanguardia" ("Approaches to the Vanguard Theater"; master's thesis), UNAM, Mexico, 1965.
"Locura y libertad: sobre Antonin Artaud" ("Madness and Freedom: On Antonin Artaud"), in *Plural,* Vol. 8, No. 93, June 1979, 55-58.
With Carlos Monsiváis, "Mexico de mis Amores" ("Mexico my Love"; screenplay), 1979.

Cardenas was involved in adapting, translating, and/or directing a number of plays, including: *El difunto y Picnic en el campo de batalla* ("The Dead One and Picnic in the Battlefield"), 1961; *El efecto de los rayos gamma sobre las caléndulas* ("The Effect of Gamma Rays on the Marigolds"; Mexico City, 1970); *Aquelarre* ("Witches Sabbath"; Mexico City, 1972); *Cuarteto* ("Quartet"; Mexico City, 1974); *Diálogos de refugiados* ("Dialogues of Refugees"; Mexico City, 1978); *La Dorotea* ("Dorothy"; Mexico City, 1978); *Las locas abuelas* ("The Crazy Grandmothers"; Mexico City, 1978); *Misterio Bufo* ("Mystery Play", 1978; revised and enlarged adaptation, 1989); *Claudine en la escuela* ("Claudine in School"; Mexico City, 1979); *La hiedra* ("The Ivy"; Mexico City, 1979); *Los soles truncos* ("The Mutilated Suns"; Mexico City, 1979); *Pedro Páramo* (Mexico City, 1979); *Pigmalion* (Mexico City, 1979); *Las amargas lágrimas de Petra von Kant* ("The Bitter Tears of Petra von Kant"; Mexico City, 1980); *Aprendiendo a ser senora* ("Learning to Be a Lady"; Mexico City, 1982); *El pozo de la soledad* ("The Well of Loneliness"; Mexico City, 1985); *Sida, asi es la vida* ("AIDS, That's the Way Life Goes"; Mexico City, 1988); *Quisiera arrancarme el corazon* ("I Would Want to Wrench My Heart Out"; Mexico City, 1992); *Los chicos de la banda* ("The Guys of the Gang"; Mexico City, 1982).

*

Interviews: "Nancy Cárdenas: una múltiple vocacion" by Andrés de Luna and Olga Cáceres, in *Sumario,* Vol. 32, No. 11, July 1978, 16-19; "Crear una memoria: Nancy Cárdenas habla de la critica teatral" by Ignacio Hernández, in *Sumario,* Vol. 33, Nos. 2-3, October/November 1978, 59; "Pais que ataca a sus minorias, es un pais emponzo–ado por el fascismo" by Patricia Ruiz Manjarrez, in *Siempre!,* No. 1937, August 1990.

Critical Sources: *Bibliografia del teatro mexicano del siglo XX* by Ruth S. Lamb, Mexico, Edicion de Andrea, 1962; *Diccionario de escritores mexicanos,* edited by Aurora Ocampo de Gomez, Mexico, UNAM, 1967; *Dictionary of Mexican Literature,* edited by Eladio Cortés, Connecticut, Greenwood Press, 1992; *Latin American Writers on Gay and Lesbian Themes: A Biocritical Source Book,* edited by David William Foster, Connecticut, Greenwood Press, 1994.

* * *

"Sex" is a dirty word in Mexican culture. "Lesbian" and "queer" sexuality are even dirtier. Refusing to be silenced, Mexican dramatist and poet Nancy Cárdenas struggled over the last three decades to make public her lesbian voice. After stumbling across a poster from Europe which read, "I am Lesbian. I am Beautiful," in the early 1970s, Cárdenas set out to humanize and celebrate what was perceived by the masses to be sexually "perverse." For Cárdenas, such public celebration—art, literature, drama, journalism—of lesbian sexuality would counter the abundance of negative images circulated by the tabloids and church. In 1990, she told Patricia Ruiz Manjarrez about meetings with other lesbian and gay writers at her house, where one of the goals was to look "into who we were [...] it was marvelous, since we had heard about homosexuals only from writings by heterosexuals or from psychologists or other practitioners who give the point of view of homosexuals who have fallen ill."

In the years before turning her energies toward creating a lesbian poetic, Cárdenas wanted to become a role model for those afraid to come out. She told Manjarrez, "In 1973 I was invited to participate in a television discussion directed by Jacobo Zabludovsky in his program called *24 horas,* seen all over the country. I had to make myself brave to decide to participate in that program that could be seen in Parras, where my parents lived and where they could be harassed." In spite of the ensuing verbal and physical abuse inflicted on Cárdenas and those around her, this move provided her with the springboard to send her into a life dedicated to extending the nation's heterosexist, macho-based cultural boundaries to include those voices at the margins. Her poetry and plays openly explore the complex web of what it means to be lesbian in a society so violently opposed to difference.

Like other Latin American writers such as Manual Puig, Darcy Penteado, and Adolfo Caminha, Cárdenas foregrounds the importance of asserting one's sexuality, as lesbian, gay, or as "straight" women, in a society that uses sexuality to oppress and censor voices of dissent. Resistance to sexual "norms" becomes a political act itself. Such resistance becomes doubly significant for Cárdenas, as lesbians are oppressed both as women and as sexually "deviant." Although Cárdenas claims certain allegiances with these other writers, she announces, "I thought that gays or heterosexual men could speak about homosexuality. I thought it my task to talk about women homosexuals."

Cárdenas charts the full range of human experience in her gay-oriented play *Sexualidades* (1993). The four characters' interlocking perspectives—one man is bisexual, another gay, one woman is heterosexual and another is celibate—play out the different forms of oppression that come out of patriarchal control of their bodies. Such a system leaves no room for emancipation—they are ostracized one way or another for not conforming to the macho behavioral codes of conduct. After the straight is brutally victimized, she is no longer valuable. Both the bisexual and gay men are completely destroyed over the course of the action. Interestingly, Cárdenas invests her characters' difference with a certain power. She gives them the strength to speak out and resist tyrannical powers, even if their actions result in their ultimate annihilation.

Unlike her dramatic productions, which make explicit links between a society that destroys any forms of queer love and eroticism, her poems suggest a more life-affirming space for those sexually outlawed. In her long poem "Cuaderno de amor y de desamor" ("Notebook on Love and Non-Love"), she revises the story of the Fall. Here, the self-acclaimed lesbian poet-narrator takes Adam's place. Cárdenas revises and subverts the heterosexual archetype through her poet-narrator's play with language (puns, pronominal mixes, and use of Mexico's popular love songs) and theme (both the lesbian characters are equally mischievous and responsible for their Fall). Same-sex love gives an affirmative spin to the otherwise guilt-laden Fall.

In this work, Cárdenas celebrates the lesbian body in all of its physical and spiritual vitality. Before and after the Fall, both remain spiritually and physically strong. In such a world void of the presence of heterosexual love, the lovers exist in harmony with the world. The poem's cyclical structure, beginning and ending with the same stanza, emphasize the lovers' peaceful existence outside of heterosexual-based drives to dominate the environment through biological and material production. She bases her vision of romantic love and eroticism on self-containment outside of heterosexual social systems and suggests such love can be far more fulfilling than any other. She celebrates, in Cárdenas's words, what it means "to be different (peculiar) and at the same time possess the beauty of any other human being."

Restricted by the amount of magazines, theaters, and publishing houses receptive to queer voices, Cárdenas spent much of her time making ends meet by producing and directing mainstream plays. As a result, she told Manjarrez, "only one-third of my theatrical production is gay. The rest is made of different cultural subjects with plays by writers such as Lope de Vega, Dario Fo, Chekov, Bertolt Brecht and many others." By the 1990s, however, Cárdenas is identified by "critics, news reporters, and audience [...] with gay theater."

As much as she is celebrated today for extending Mexico's cultural canon, her work remains largely unpublished and untranslated. Mexico has come a long way since the seventies when she first set out on her mission to revolutionize her cultural canon, but many there continue to resist difference, especially where women are concerned. Her plays, journalism, and poems have, however, had a tremendous impact on Mexican society. Mexico owes much of the public presence of gay and lesbian writers to Cárdenas' unremitting dedication to celebrating and giving human contours to gay identity in general, and to lesbianism in particular.

—Frederick Luis Aldama

CARR, Emily

Nationality: Canadian painter, novelist, author of short stories, and diarist. **Born:** Victoria, British Columbia, 3 December 1871. **Education:** Mrs. Fraser's Private School, Victoria, 1879-87; Victoria High School, 1888; California School of Design, San Francisco, 1890-93; Westminister School of Art, London, 1899-03; Academie Colarossi, Paris, 1910; also studied privately with artists John Duncan Fergusson, Henry Gibb, and Frances Hodgkins. **Career:** Founding member, British Columbia Society of Fine Arts; teacher, children's art classes, Victoria, 1893, Vancouver Studio Club and School of Art, 1906, and of children's art lessons, Vancouver; cartoonist, for the Victoria *Week,* 1905; landlady of a small apartment house in Vancouver for many years. **Awards:** Governor General's Award for Non-Fiction, for *Klee Wyck,* 1942. **Died:** Victoria, British Columbia, of a stroke, 2 March 1945.

WRITINGS

Klee Wyck. New York, Toronto, Farrar and Rinehart, 1942.
The Book of Small. Toronto, Oxford University Press, 1942.
The House of All Sorts. Toronto, Oxford University Press, 1944.
Growing Pains. Toronto, Oxford University Press, 1946.
The Heart of a Peacock (with line drawings by the author). Toronto, Oxford University Press, 1953.
Pause, a Sketch Book. Toronto, Clarke, Irwin, 1953.
Hundreds and Thousands: The Journals of Emily Carr. Toronto, Clarke, Irwin, 1966.
Fresh Seeing: Two Addresses by Emily Carr. Toronto, Clarke, Irwin, 1972.
Dear Nan: Letters of Emily Carr, Nan Cheney, and Humphrey Toms, edited by Doreen Walker. Vancouver, University of British Columbia Press, 1990.
The Emily Carr Omnibus. Vancouver, Douglas and McIntyre, and Seattle, University of Washington Press, 1993.

*

Biography: *Emily Carr: The Untold Story* by Edythe Hembroff Scheleicher, Saanichton, British Columbia, Hancock House, 1978; *Emily Carr: A Biography* by Maria Tippett, Toronto, Oxford, and New York, Oxford University Press, 1979; *Emily Carr* by Doris Shadbolt, Vancouver and Toronto, Douglas and McIntyre, and Seattle, University of Washington Press, 1979.

Bibliography: *The Life and Work of Emily Carr, 1871-1945: A Selected Bibliography* by Marguerite Turpin, Vancouver, School of Librarianship, University of British Columbia, 1965.

Critical Sources: *M.E.: A Portrayal of Emily Carr* by Edythe Hembroff-Schleicher, Toronto, Clarke, Irwin, 1969; *The Art of Emily Carr* by Doris Shadbolt, Toronto, Clarke, Irwin, Vancouver, Douglas and McIntyre, and Seattle, University of Washington Press, 1979; *The Emily Carr Omnibus* by Doris Shadbolt, Vancouver, Douglas and McIntyre, and Seattle, University of Washington Press, 1993.

*   *   *

Though Emily Carr was in many ways the archetype of a simple and direct woman, her life and her work are full of contradictions, ranging from the whimsical to the painful. One of the foremost Canadian painters of all time, she was first widely known and loved for her writing. It was not until after her death that her paintings were popularly acclaimed. Both in her writing and in her painting, Carr employs a deceptive and carefully crafted simplicity to convey a wealth of complexity.

Though Carr wrote all her life—creating poetry, songs, and little stories she called her "scribblings"—most of her published work was written between the ages of 63 and 71. In failing health, and no longer able to go on her solitary painting rambles, indeed, no longer able to even exert the energy required to stand and paint, she wrote, and, in writing, revisited the whole of her life. She immersed herself in her past to assuage her pain at the art that was lost to her. In doing so, she created another art, and recreated the world she had experienced to leave behind as a legacy. Though she took many liberties with fact, even in her autobiography, Carr's books paint a compelling picture of her life and her Canada.

Emily Carr was, perhaps above all other things, a misfit. She grew up in a Victorian household with her sisters, her mother, and her authoritarian father. As a child she was close to her father, but at puberty had a traumatic experience with him, after which she hated him. She kept all this secret until a few years before her death, when she still referred only vaguely to the event and to her father as "a cross gouty sexy old man who hurt and disgusted" her. All her life in her writing, Carr would rail at hypocrisy and falseness. All her life she would apparently remain celibate, receiving the epithet "frigid" from some of her biographers, but seeming simply like an extremely vital and vibrant woman who was damaged at an early age.

Deeply Canadian, not by virtue of patriotism, but by a profound love for the trees, water, and land of her native country, Carr spent many years in her youth and young adulthood travelling out into the forests and islands to paint. Here she lived among the native people for whom she developed a lasting attachment. Her depictions of them are often over-sentimental and are full of the racist assumptions that were unquestioned by most whites of her time, but even so, the deep bond she felt with the people she lived among is evident. A misfit in her own white Victorian world, she felt a passionate connection with others who were excluded from that world. With native people she also felt free of the social and religious hypocrisy that she thought dominated the life of middle-class white Canadian society.

It is here that lesbians and gays find their first point of identification in Carr's writing. The protagonist of her stories, whether Small, or Klee Wyck, or simply "I," is always a curmudgeonly figure, isolated and cast off by cultivated society because of her refusal to be other than herself. That self is a strong minded, even eccentric girl-woman with decided opinions and values and a no-nonsense way of expressing them. There is kindness in the character of these women and capacity for deep connection, especially with other people who have left or been thrust from society, and with animals.

Modern readers reading Carr's works find much that still speaks to current issues. Her observations of native life and her criticisms of the treatment the native people as well as other minorities, such as the Chinese, received at the hands of whites are still unfortunately quite relevant today. The love she felt for the forests of British Columbia and the anguish she experienced over their destruction seems remarkably modern. And any lesbian or feminist reading of Carr's struggle to exist as an opinionated unmarried woman with a powerful vocation will resonate with sister-feeling. Just looking at a picture of Carr, a husky, imposing woman dressed in practical and unconventional clothes, hunkered in front of the caravan she took to go painting in the wilderness and surrounded by the menagerie of animals she loved, is enough to warm many a lesbian heart.

As a young woman, Carr spent several years studying in San Francisco, where she had happy social times as well as learning and sharing more about her painting. She delighted in parties and picnics with her friends and was a mentor to many of the younger students. Life was harder when she went to London to study, because she not only missed her home, but found few friends there to help with that pain. In Paris, she studied and made friendships with artists who were in the social circle of Gertrude Stein and her friends, but there is little evidence that Carr herself connected to the lesbian social life of Paris.

In 1927, Carr made the acquaintance of the Toronto artists of the Group of Seven, beginning an intense time of renewal for both her painting and her social life. Once again she felt inspired by friends, and once again she felt tormented by homesickness for her "gracious great pines."

This was always another major conflict in Carr's life, with which gays and lesbians can often sympathize, the constant tug of war between isolation and connection. At various times in her life, she found deep and meaningful friendships and artistic associations, but these were always during those times that she left British Columbia to study or work in cultural centers like San Francisco, London, Paris, and Toronto. Carr often agonized over the impossible choice between living in the land she loved— the untamed country but conventional society of the west—and being among friends and artists with whom she could communicate. It is a choice gays and lesbians often face, if they come from rural areas or conservative urban centers. Any attachment they feel towards "home" must be weighed against the pain and isolation of not having gay society around them. Moving to more welcoming urban areas, such as San Francisco, fulfills that need, but can often feel like exile to the individual who truly loves the area they grew up in.

Speaking of Carr's life is, in fact, to speak of her writing, because her writing is so thoroughly a retelling of her life. *The Book of Small* is filled with the stories of her childhood, and *The House of All Sorts* is the humorous, if often scathing, account of the bitter years when she earned her living as a landlady. *Hundreds and Thousands* is made up of edited journal entries from 1927 through 1941, and is named for the candies Carr was treated to on occasion as a child, when she was allowed to put her hand in the jar and get a handful of the tiny sweets. The reader of her writing often feels just this way. Because of her style of filling a book with separate little stories, like sketches, one can open one of them anywhere and be treated to a tiny piece of Carr's life presented simple and complete.

Hundreds and Thousands, because it is directly a journal, is one of the most personal of Carr's works. In it she describes her daily thoughts about her art, her writing, her friends, and her animals, with whom she was perhaps closest of all. Most revealing are her agonies of insecurity about her writing, coupled with her fierce defense of her own expression. On 8 August 1934, she wrote in excitement, "My story has been selected by class vote as the one to be read at the closing assembly...I was stricken with horror when I found I had to read it *myself,* and wished they'd chosen someone else's." But when the teacher of her short story class criticized her story and volunteered to help "fix it up," Carr exploded, "I don't want Mrs. S. to fix it. I don't want it to have a darn magazine story plot and set people worrying to unravel it. I just want it to be the 'Cow Yard' and make people feel and smell and see and love it like I did as I wrote it—blessed old haven of refuge for a troubled child and a place of bursting joy for a happy one."

One of the most radical aspects of Carr's writing is the intensity with which she inspects her own life. The innermost thoughts and daily exertions of a single woman were often not considered of great importance, but because Carr herself gave them importance, we now have invaluable information about just what her life and thoughts were like, and it gives us insight into the lives of other such women who remain undocumented.

Because of Carr's willingness to be self-revealing, even of her faults and her most painful thoughts, she has left us with a rich legacy. Her paintings are a loving document of a landscape and a native culture that has been changed beyond recognition by the invasion of white European culture. Her writing is also a loving document, because even through her self-deprecation, Emily Carr is an irrepressible self-loving woman. This is the legacy she has left, the history of an unconventional woman who was a shrewd observer of simple truths.

—Tina Gianoulis

CART, Michael

Nationality: American critic, literary journalist, and novelist. **Born:** Logansport, Indiana, 6 March 1941. **Education:** Attended public schools in Logansport, Indiana; Northwestern University, Evanston, Illinois (McCormick Scholar), B.S. in Journalism 1963; Columbia University, New York City (honors), M.S. in Library Science, 1964. **Military Service:** Served in the United States Army, 1964-67; Specialist 5th Class; received Army Commendation Medal. **Family:** Partner of John V. Ledwith, Jr., 1980-92. **Career:** Director, Logansport-Cass County Public Library, Indiana, 1967-73; director of public services, Pomona Public Library, California, 1973-76; assistant director, Beverly Hills Public Library, California, 1976-79; director of library and community services, Beverly Hills, California, 1979-91; writer, from 1991; Bradshaw Professor, School of Library and Information Service, Texas Women's University, 1992. Regular contributor, *School Library Journal,* 1963-93; host/co-producer, "In Print" nationally syndicated cable television author interview program, 1981-91, and from 1996; author of "Carte Blanche" column, *Booklist,* from 1994; author of "Children's Bookshelf" column, *Los Angeles Times Book Review,* from 1994; children's book editor, *Parents,* from 1997; contributor to periodicals, including *New York Times Book Review, Library Journal,* and *American Libraries.* **Member:** Best Books for Young Adults Committee, American Library Association (ALA), 1988-89; member, Caldecott Medal Committee, ALA, 1990-91; member of advisory committee, *Senior High School Library Catalog,* 14th and 15th editions, 1991, 1996; member, Notable Children's Books Committee, ALA, 1992-95; member, USBBY Hans Christian Andersen Medal Committee, 1993; board of directors, Young Adult Library Service Association, 1994-96; vice-president/president-elect, Young Adult Library Service Association, 1996-97. **Awards:** John Cotton Dana Award, 1975, 1976; Dorothy C. McKenzie Award for Service to Children and Literature, 1983; Allie Beth Martin Award Nominee, 1989, 1990; *City Hall Digest* Grand Award, 1990; Educational Press Association of America Distinguished Achievement Award, 1994; National Association of Television Officials and Administrators Award, 1990, 1996; Best Book for Young Adults, American Library Association, 1997. **Agent:** Sterling Lord Literistic, Inc., 65 Bleecker

Street, New York, New York 10012, U.S.A. **Address:** 4220 Arch Drive, #10, Studio City, California 91604, U.S.A.

WRITINGS

Nonfiction

Presenting Robert Lipsyte. New York, Twayne, 1995.
What's So Funny?: Wit and Humor in American Children's Literature. New York, HarperCollins, 1995.
From Romance to Realism: 50 Years of Growth and Change in Young Adult Literature. New York, HarperCollins, 1996.
Presenting Francesca Lia Block. New York, Twayne (forthcoming, 1998).

Young Adult Novel

My Father's Scar. New York: Simon & Schuster, 1996.

Critical Sources: "Two Great Books" by Dorothy Broderick, in *VOYA,* December 1996, 253; review of *My Father's Scar* by Eden Ross Lipson, in *New York Times Book Review,* 28 July 1996, 21; review of *My Father's Scar* by Claudia Morrow, in *School Livbrary Journal,* March 1996, 132; review of *My Father's Scar,* in *Publishers Weekly,* 27 May 1996, 79-80; review of *My Father's Scar* by Linda Roberts, in *VOYA,* August 1996, 154-55; review of *My Father's Scar* by Roger Sutton, in *Bulletin of the Center for Children's Books,* April 1996; review of *My Father's Scar* by Susan Marie Swanson, in *Five Owls,* May/June 1996, 115.

Michael Cart comments:

In a wired age that demands instant, on-line gratification, I stubbornly cling to my old-fashioned belief that books are important and *relevant* to today's lives. Why? Well, because they offer the entertainment of story and the enjoyment of art, of course, but more importantly because they offer engagement and enlightenment—first for the mind by stimulating thought but then for the spirit, too, since by giving readers the opportunity to eavesdrop on the hearts of others, books stimulate empathy and sympathy. In short, books are important because they have the power to enlarge and change both minds and lives.

This is why it is so important to have books for and about gay and lesbian young adults. Not only so that homosexual youth can see themselves positively represented in literature (there were no gay role models in books when I was growing up in the 1950s) but also so that heterosexual teenagers can read about the homosexual experience and, accordingly, educate and expand their own hearts and minds.

To make that possible, of course, there must be good books that present, with art and authenticity, the experience of growing up gay or lesbian. Unfortunately there are not enough such books. Silence equals death—not only of the body but of the spirit. That is why, as a critic, I began writing about the literature—and the lack thereof—and why, as a novelist, I write fiction with homosexual themes and characters.

*   *   *

Until recently, Michael Cart has been best known within the small community of children's and young adult specialists in the library world. Active in the American Library Association, Cart has been a frequent speaker and writer on these topics and is well known for his wide-ranging erudition and acerbic wit. Since his early retirement from the directorship of the Beverly Hills Public Library in 1991, he has been a full-time writer and his sphere of influence has widened considerably.

Cart's first two books were published in 1995. In *What's So Funny?: Wit and Humor in American Children's Literature,* he takes a look at some of the books that have made children laugh. Not surprisingly, Cart, a past president of Friends of Freddy, devotes one chapter to a discussion of the novels by Walter R. Brooks about that amiable pig. *Presenting Robert Lipsyte* is a literary biography of a writer best known for the wrenching realism of his 1967 novel about a struggling young African-American boxer, *The Contender.*

From Romance to Realism: 50 Years of Growth and Change in Young Adult Literature is an overview of the young adult novel in America. Cart approaches this genre by way of an historical overview before moving to an analysis of the contemporary young adult novel. Throughout, he consistently transmits his belief in the power of young adult fiction to offer teenagers what T.S. Eliot called the true value of literature: the acquisition of wisdom, the enjoyment of art, and the pleasure of entertainment. Nonetheless, Cart acknowledges that the young adult novel's lack of visibility, its lack of market power, and its lack of status in the world at large make it as endangered and at risk as many of its intended readers. He issues a manifesto for the inclusion of topics that are relevant, immediate, and important in the lives of young people. He is particularly eloquent in his call for the incorporation of culturally diverse voices and the lifting of taboos about sexuality in fiction for young adults. He notes, for example, that AIDS is almost unacknowledged in young adult literature in spite of the fact that young people are contracting and dying of this disease in alarming numbers.

Cart writes at length about the inadequacy of the treatment of homosexuality in young adult literature. He observes that there have only been 67 young adult novels with gay themes or characters since the first, John Donovan's *I'll Get There: It Better Be Worth the Trip,* appeared in 1969. Furthermore, Cart gives evidence that many titles fail to present life-affirming gay characters or to rise above the limitations of the problem novel to succeed as literature. The result, he says, is the perpetuation of ignorance and fear, which in turn results in homophobia. Gay and lesbian adolescents suffer the consequences; at an age when they are struggling hardest to define themselves, they are likely to find little social or literary acknowledgment and acceptance of their own sexual identity. "Gay kids, like any others," he writes, "need to see themselves represented in literature; they need positive role models too, just like any other kids." Cart is quite specific about his criteria for a good gay-themed young adult novel: he looks for general literary quality; for characters that are defined by their actions and their social world, not just by their sexual preference; and for honesty and candor. And perhaps most significantly, he cites Francesca Lia Block's *Weetzie Bat* as an example of a novel which exemplifies what makes a book about homosexuality successful and satisfying, presenting sexual preference in the context of love, acceptance, and respect.

At bottom, then, Michael Cart is advocating that gay-themed novels be both literary and romantic. As it happens, he has written just such a novel. Cart has drawn on the pain and the promise of his own life experiences to create *My Father's Scar,* a gay coming-of-age novel about Andy Logan, an introverted, bright college freshman. Flashbacks tell the story of his early adolescence, in which his alcoholic father's brutality and lack of understanding for his bookish, fat son produce confusion and self-loathing in the 11-year-old boy. Andy begins to run obsessively, shedding pounds but retaining a conviction that he is fat and unloved. The attentions of a book-loving, gay but closeted uncle and a loving friendship with an older gay boy lead Andy to suspect his own homosexuality. An affair in his senior year of high school confirms Andy's sexual identity; but when he comes out to his parents on the morning after graduation, his father throws him out of the house. Now Andy is on his own, isolating himself in a world of books and ideas at the university, where he suffers an ill-fated crush on an English teacher before discovering true love with the professor's teaching assistant.

Cart succeeds in creating a young gay character who has interests and relationships, dreams and ideas, conflicts and desires that have nothing and everything to do with his sexual identity. Andy Logan is placed in a concrete and evocative social context, moving from the church and family-oriented small town of his high school years to life in a freshman college dormitory. *My Father's Scar* is a romantic, complex, richly-textured novel which both gay and straight teenagers can read with appreciation for its insights into sexual awakening, first love, and dysfunctional families.

—Virginia A. Walter

CASAL, Mary

Nationality: American autobiographer. **Born:** New England, 1864. **Education:** Attended a midwestern university, B.A. **Career:** Held a variety of jobs including teacher, inventor, and traveling saleswoman. **Died:** After 1930.

WRITINGS

The Stone Wall (autobiography). Chicago, Eyncourt Press, 1930; New York, Arno Press, 1975.

*

Critical Sources: "Casal, Mary" by Gene Damon, in *The Lesbian in Literature: A Bibliography.* Reno, Nevada, The Ladder, 1975, 21.

*   *   *

Mary Casal wrote, so far as we know, only one book, *The Stone Wall.* She has received no attention from critics. And yet *The Stone Wall* received the highest rating in Gene Damon's exhaustive compilation, *The Lesbian in Literature: A Bibliography,* and was said to "[stand] alone as a classic of its kind" in the *1960 Checklist* by Marion Bradley and Gene Damon. Arno Press included *The Stone Wall* as one of the 56 items in its 1975 reprint series "Homosexuality: Lesbians and Gay Men in Society, History, and Literature."

This unusual combination of professional regard and critical neglect makes *The Stone Wall* one of the more puzzling works in lesbian literature.

The name Mary Casal was probably a pseudonym. The book's narrator aims to tell the story of her life as a homosexual woman. Born on a New England farm in 1864, the youngest of nine children, she chronicles 70 years of her life in order to bring to public attention its normality, its values, and its difficulties. Throughout, Casal is unapologetic about her sexuality, maintaining that hers was a valuable human life and that her sexuality was both normal and moral. In 1930, this was indeed an unusual stance. Stephen Gordon, the protagonist of Radclyffe Hall's notorious *The Well of Loneliness,* had burst upon the literary scene only two years earlier as what Blanche Wiesen Cook termed the "mythic, mannish lesbian." Her image had quickly become the archetype of the doomed "invert," her female body always at war with her male mind and soul in a world hostile to her very existence. The self Casal portrays in *The Stone Wall* is very different from Stephen Gordon, a powerful antidote to the deterministic unhappiness Hall painted. And yet her opposing portrait, which might have brought hope and even joy to many early surreptitious readers seeking their own images in literature, remains virtually unknown to this day, despite efforts such as Arno Press's to make it visible.

From her earliest memories Casal knew that she did not feel sexual attraction toward males. She identified as male in mind and spirit, preferring to play with her brothers and male cousins and disdaining girl toys and girl activities. In order to remain a member of the boys' play group, she learned to submit to sexual exploration and to "playing hen and rooster." At nine she was assaulted by a neighbor (whether this is a rape is unclear, but he does rupture her hymen). Her mother misunderstood the blood on her underclothes and said that this "happened to all little girls," leaving Casal convinced that she can never speak of her pain or outrage but must instead submit to sexual manipulation as part of her role as a female. The offending man did manage to achieve coitus with her, as did an 11 year-old male cousin. This established pattern of male predation continues throughout the first half of the book. Both her brothers-in-law forced her to have sex with them and enforce her silence by threatening to tell their wives. Casal finds this sex with males disgusting and decidedly unerotic; she decides that "my nature was normal from the beginning and...the dislike for men as males was inherent."

After she went away to school, Casal discovered her attraction to girls. She had several friends who permitted and returned her kisses and caresses. In college she had a long-term crush on the wife of one of her professors. These attachments became the pattern which would characterize her life. Nonetheless, at the age of 20 she married. The sex disgusted her, but she accepted it because she wanted to have children. Two babies were stillborn after difficult labors, and she was advised not to become pregnant again. With no reason to continue a heterosexual relationship, she left her husband and finally decided that "the masculine role was the one which appealed to me far more than that of the female." After successfully running a school for young children, she established herself financially by inventing and selling a popular toy. On one of her sales trips, she met Juno, whom she courted assiduously. They share a love of theater, music, and art. Having found her "mate," Casal gave up her travelling job, her fortune, and she settled down. She eventually established another school in order to earn a living.

Once settled, Casal and Juno began to meet other lesbians. At first, they were startled to learn that other women shared a passion for one another. Their first lesbian friends introduced them to lesbian bars in New York and later in Paris, but they were disgusted by lesbian sexual freedom and they firmly renounced it in favor of conservative monogamy. After many years of the equivalent of married bliss, Juno became involved with men. Numerous reconciliations failed; Juno ended up with a married man, and Casal remained devoted to the memory of her blissful life with Juno.

There are several features of Casal's story which are striking to the modern reader. For one thing, despite women's obvious attractions to and sexual activity with her, she "felt that I was the only girl who had the sex desire for woman, rather than the accepted one for men." This was true even during her long-term relationship with Juno. Such a belief is exactly consonant with sexological theory between 1880 and 1930, which differentiated the true invert from the woman who simply loved an invert but was presumed "normal." *The Stone Wall* echoes the aloneness many lesbians felt during a period when their sexuality dared not speak its name.

Second, Casal conforms to the pattern of butch/femme established early in the century in such works as *The Well of Loneliness.* She emphasized that she preferred the company of men and that masculine behaviors and roles were natural for her. After some years of dressing in feminine clothes, she switched to pants. (She convinced Juno to adopt her "tailor suit" attire, and the other lesbians in the book also wear male-style clothing.) She did not like women who courted her. She always preferred to be the initiator: "I preferred to be the one to woo when I became attracted to a girl."

Third, Casal took pain to emphasize that she was attractive to both males and females and thus was not a social outcast, or a woman reduced to female sexual partners because she was too unattractive to win a man's love. Casal loved to socialize, to dance, and to attend parties. She often repeated that she had had many opportunities to marry and was in fact quite attractive to a variety of men. Her lesbianism is depicted as fully and consciously chosen.

But Casal's ultimate purpose in writing *The Stone Wall* was to argue that human sexuality should be allowed to develop "normally." As she recounts her childhood, she is sure that if her mother had answered her questions truthfully and refrained from punishing her when she raised issues of sexuality, she would have been a more open and loving child and would have discovered her true sexual nature both earlier and in a healthier fashion. She conveyed a strong and direct message to her readers that children should be told the truth about sexuality and allowed to express it in whatever ways seem natural and pleasant for them. One reason she wrote the book, she says repeatedly, was to help parents understand that children's curiosity is natural and should be responded to openly. Only an open response will allow a child's sexuality to develop normally and to find its best and most natural expression, whether that expression be heterosexuality or homosexuality. In her own work with children, Casal models the behavior she describes, but she was forced to admit that the American public was not ready to accept her precepts, despite their obvious benefits to individual children.

She also believed that the time would come when same-sex attractions were viewed as normal and would be studied not to discredit them but to understand their dimensions and their benefits. This was not a popular attitude when the book was written. It is

yet another example of Casal's many-faceted attempt to normalize lesbian sexuality through her honest depiction of an actual lesbian life.

Perhaps the most uplifting message of *The Stone Wall* is Casal's firm belief that the emotional and physical relationship she shared with Juno "was the very highest type of human love...the purest and most ideal of any type of union known." The weight of the work rests on this belief. Unlike Stephen Gordon in *The Well of Loneliness,* who can only plead for acceptance because God made her as she was, Casal asserts not only the normality but the sacredness of her sexuality. The book should be much more widely read than it is; it is a genuine counterpart to *The Well of Loneliness,* showing a very different dimension of lesbian thought in the early decades of the twentieth century.

—Loralee MacPike

CASEMENT, Roger (David)

Pseudonyms: Also wrote as Sean Bhean Bhoct and Batha Mac Crainn. **Nationality:** Irish patriot, poet, and essayist. **Born:** Sandycove County, Dublin, 1 September 1864. **Education:** Ballymena Academy, 1873-81. **Career:** Held a number of jobs including purser, Elder Dempster shipping, Liverpool, 1881-87; volunteer, various exploring companies, Africa, 1887-92; travelling commissioner, Nigerian Protectorate for the British Colonial Office, 1892-95; British consul, Lourenco Marques, Portuguese East Africa, 1895-98, Luanda, Angola, 1898-00, Boma, Belgian Congo, 1901-04, and Brazil, 1906-11. Member, Irish National Volunteers, 1911-16. **Awards:** South African Medal, 1903; C.M.G., 1905; Knighthood, 1911. **Died:** By hanging in Pentonville Gaol, 3 August 1916.

WRITINGS

Collected Works

Some Poems of Roger Casement. Dublin, Talbot Press, 1918.
The Crime Against Europe, edited by Herbert O. Mackey. Dublin, C.J. Fallon Limited, 1958.

*

Manuscript Collections: National Library of Ireland, Dublin.

Biography: *The Black Diaries of Roger Casement* by Peter Singleton-Gates and Maurice Girodias, New York, Grove Press, 1959; *Roger Casement* by Brian Inglis, New York, Harcourt Brace Jovanovitch, 1973; *The Lives of Roger Casement* by B.L. Reid, New Haven, Yale University Press, 1976.

*   *   *

Roger Casement is probably best known for the role he played in Ireland's 1916 Easter Rising, but Casement was first known for the reports he wrote detailing the atrocities in the Belgian Congo

(1904) and against the Putayamo Indians in South America (1911). Casement's revelations of the horrors of colonial expansion won him acclaim from the general public and the British government, eventually earning him Knighthood in 1911. By the time he received his award from King George, Casement was a deeply divided man. Although he was working for the British government, Casement was defining himself more often as an Irishman. As an Irishman, Casement was beginning to see comparisons between the subjects of his reports and the British situation in Ireland. By 1911, Casement had decided to retire from service with the British government and devote himself to Irish causes.

Casement first became interested in the Irish language movement, contributing money to the Gaelic League. He then began to work for the Home Rule movement and then joined the Irish Volunteers in 1913. When Britain's promise of Home Rule was deferred by World War I, Casement became even more disillusioned with the British government. Casement saw World War I as Ireland's chance to win independence while Britain was distracted by the war. With this in mind, he went to Berlin in November of 1914 and tried to organize Irish prisoners of war into a brigade that could assist in the revolution. This crusade ultimately failed and Casement returned to Ireland, via a German submarine, to warn the leaders of the Easter Rising that no reinforcements would be coming. Both he and a load of arms were captured by the British in Tralee Bay. Casement was charged with treason and was sentenced to die. English and American audiences both cried for his release and the British government began to circulate diary entries that recorded Casement's homosexual activities. These "Black Diaries" succeeded in turning public opinion against Casement and he was hanged on 3 August 1916.

Casement's Black Diaries are probably his most important contribution to gay and lesbian history. When these records of his homosexual assignations were released in 1916, many questioned their veracity, suggesting that no true patriot could be a homosexual. The diaries were often considered a forgery produced by the British government for their own ends. In 1922, Peter Singleton-Gates came into possession of the diaries and, despite the protests of the British government, was able to publish portions of them in 1956. Since that time, the diaries have been considered to be authentic.

Historically, the diaries are a revealing memoir detailing the life of a homosexual man in the early 1900s. While the diaries are strangely coded in places, it is possible to see how Casement found his sexual partners, what class and race they were, where they met, and the sexual acts performed. Casement's enthusiasm and adulation for his lovers is also apparent throughout his diaries.

Casement also wrote a fair amount of poetry, some of which can be read to have homosexual subtexts. In these poems ("Love's Cares," "Love's Awakening," and "Fragment—Forgotten Music"), Casement expresses some unusual ideas about homosexuality for the time. For Casement, homosexuality was about men loving men, not about inversion (women trapped in men's bodies) or mental illness, typical explanations of homosexuality at the time. In the poems, Casement celebrates the physical beauty of men and asks why his love should be seen as destructive or evil. Just as Casement questioned why the natives of Africa and South America should be abused by colonizing nations, in his diaries and poetry, Casement questions why homosexuals should be held in contempt by a heterosexual society.

—Tanya Olson

CAUSSE, Michèle

Nationality: French and Canadian translator, essayist, playwright, poet, and "lovher." **Education:** Studied English and Italian in Paris and Chinese in Rome. **Career:** Contributor to *Masques;* co-founder, *Vlasta* journal, 1983; invited professor of lesbian literature, Québec; frequent speaker on lesbian issues at feminist cultural gatherings. **Address:** Parole de Lesbiennes, c/o Fovrest, 14 rue Saulnier, 75009 Paris, France.

WRITINGS

Fiction

L'Encontre: Fable Autobiographique. Paris, Editions des Femmes, 1975.
Petite Réflexion sur Bartleby: An Essay. Paris, Le Nouveau Commerce, 1976.
Stèle de Jane Bowles (essay and translations). Paris, Le Nouveau Commerce, 1976.
Lesbiana. Seven Portraits. Paris, Nouveau Commerce, 1980.
Lettres à Omphale. Paris, Denoël-Gonthier, 1984.
(Parenthèses) (original title consists of two ( ) and fifteen spaces). Laval, Québec, Trois, 1987.
"The World as Will and Representation," in *Lesbian Philosophies and Cultures,* edited by Jeffner Allen. Albany, State University of New York Press, 1990.
A Quelle Heure est la Levée dans le Désert? (play). Laval, Québec, Editions Trois, 1989.
"Femmes Versus Lesbiennes," in *La Parole Métèque.* Laval, Québec, Trois, 1991.
L'Interloquée. Les Oubliées de l'Oubli. Dé/générée (essays). Laval, Québec, Trois, 1991.
Voyages de la Grande Naine en Androssie. Laval, Québec, Trois, 1993.
Quelle lesbienne êtes-vous? Paris, Parole de Lesbiennes, 1996.

Editor

Ti-Grace Atkinson, Odyssée d'une Amazone. Paris, des Femmes, 1975.
And author of postface, *Journal d'une Femme Soumise* by Mara. Paris, Flammarion, 1979.
Berthe ou un Demi-siècle Auprès de L'Amazone. Souvenirs de Berthe Cleyrergue Recueillis et Précédés d'une Etude sur Natalie C. Barney (et Suivis d'un Dramatis personae). Paris, Editions Tierce, 1980.

Translator

With Nicole Monin, *L'Univers Fermé des Grandes Iles du Monde.* Paris, Hachette, 1963.
Si C'est un Homme by Primo Levi. Paris, Buchet-Chastel, 1964.
Une Jeune Fille de Catane by Ercole Patti. Paris, Stock, 1971.
With Maurice Muller-Strauss, *La Rivière des Castors* by Eric Collier. Paris, J'ai Lu, 1973.
La Fille Prodigue by Alice Ceresa. Paris, des Femmes, 1975.
Bartleby by Herman Melville. Paris, le Nouveau Commerce, 1976.
Femme en Guerre by Dacia Maraini. Paris, des Femmes, 1977.

With Catherine Erhel, *Histoire des Passions Françaises. 3. Goût et Corruption* by Theodore Zeldin. Paris, Recherches, 1979; 2d edition, Editions du Seuil, 1981.

Notes pour une ontologie du feminisme radical by Mary Daly. Montréal, L'essentielle, 1980.

With Jean-Paul Samson, *Fontamara* by Ignazio Silone. Paris, B. Grasset, 1981; revised 1995.

And author of postface, *L'Almanach des Dames* by Djuna Barnes. Paris, Flammarion, 1982.

Aux Abysses. (suivi de) La Colombe by Djuna Barnes. Marseille, Ed. Ryoan-ji, 1984.

Divagations Malicieuses by Djuna Barnes. Marseille, Ryoan-ji, 1985.

Q.E.D. by Gertrude Stein, Montreal, Remue Mènage, 1986.

Bartleby; les Iles Enchantées; le Campanile by Herman Melville. Paris, Flammarion, 1989.

Jane Bowles, une Femme Accompagnée: Biographie by Millicent Dillon. Paris, Deuxtemps Tierce, 1989.

Les Mots de la Tribu by Natalia Ginzburg. Paris, Grasset, 1992.

Destins Obscurs by Willa Cather. Paris, Deuxtemps-Tierce, 1992; second edition, Paris, Rivages, 1994.

Other

With Maryvonne Lapouge, *Ecrits: Voix d'Italie (Textes et Témoignages Traduits de l'Italien).* Paris, des Femmes, 1977.

"Natalie Clifford Barney," in *Masques,* No. 5, summer 1980, 113-115.

"Lettre à Suzette Triton," in *Masques,* No. 7, winter 1980-81, 69-71.

Ontmoeting met Djuna Barnes. Amsterdam, Funk, 1989.

"Le Bien Aimer" (interview of Geneviève Pastre), in *Lesbia Magazine,* No. 145, January 1996, 33-37.

*

Critical Sources: "L'Interloquée de Michèle Causse" by Françoise Armengaud, in *Nouvelles Questions Féministes,* Vol. 13, No. 1, 1992, 89-90; *La Commutation de Codes dans "Picture Theory" de Nicole Brossard et "[Parenthèses]" de Michèle Causse* by Catherine Anne Paul (dissertation), Queens University, Kingston, New York, 1993; "Le Voyage de la Grand Naine" by Françoise Armengaud, in *Nouvelles Questions Féministes,* Vol. 15, No. 1, 1994, 105-110; *Les Relations Amoureuses entre les Femmes* by Marie-Jo Bonnet, Paris, 1995.

Michèle Causse comments:

My writing's origins repose upon a paradox. My profound taste for a language—any language—and my no less profound distaste for language as a male construction. Whatever the subject gendered in the feminine, she can only be horrified by the treatment to which language submits her—a faithful translation, in truth, of the treatment concretely inflicted upon her in the real world. Many writers have pointed out their alienation in using words which are not theirs: from Jeanne Hyvrard and Clarice Lispector—authors well aware of the ravages of a language setting them up for their own eviction, all the way up to Monique Wittig, Adrienne Rich, Bertha Harris, Mary Daly, and Judy Grahn—authors who have known how to bend language to their glorification.

In my first work, *L'Encontre,* an allegorical figuration of a monosocial world system, I underlined—or rather denounced—

the asymmetrical status inflicted on human bodies in the *viriocratic system,* by naming them "superior anterior protuberances" and "inferior anterior protuberances," by making things symmetrical, in other words, in the feminine plural so as to evince the *coup de force* that permits the masculine ones to lord it over the feminine ones, by taking anatomy as the basis of this *coup de force,* but without ever mentioning it, indeed by removing it altogether. I showed how these clandestine or lesbian bodies—existing in a state of non-relation to the protagonist subjects of the system and rebellious before their physical and symbolic violence—were able to partially escape from the *viriocratic* forces that determine forms of living in this world through figurations recalling those of Beckett in *Le Dépeupleur.*

Always indignant about of the ubiquity of oppression, I present in my fable, *Adventures of the Great Dwarf in Androssia,* the players of the social world as Animals. Animality as an allegory functions to expose the cruelty presiding over social exchanges between animated beings. I forge new personal pronouns to show the difference existing between "ille," the female social construction of Man, and "elle," the resisting lesbian who invents her own world. Escapee from those prescriptions that make masculine and feminine the poles of a general human alienation.

My various essays have the goal of bringing out an invisible fact. The very language we speak is altogether *sexo-lectical* since it emanates from a subject gendered in the masculine and taking itself for universal: an *andro-lectical* language or androlecte dictating its law to the two sexes it defines and so condemns to either difference or similitude according to its own needs and desires. We are all of us victims of a retinal dogma: there exists but one good view or representation of the world.

Finally, in *Bréviaire des gorgones (The Gorgon's Breviary)* I try to show how male anatomy and physiology have become the reference of life and death on the planet, I show how the male subjects use Sex/cision to turn one part of the Sapiens species into inferior and use gender as sexage. The dictionary is denounced as being a place of maximum contention, the founding place of the hierarchy between the sexes, in short a repressive and prescriptive text that may be likened to holy scripture. I demonstrate that the archimorphemes of any language are always patriarchal, misogynist, unilobist, as much dictaters as dictators.

Yet, through her very praxis and refusal of bodily constraints, the realization of a new anatomy, a lesbian breaks linguistic looking mechanisms, denounces the same as fraudulent and gains access to a new language, the reflection of a new autonomy.

*   *   *

Michèle Causse is a forceful and versatile figure in the French and Canadian world of letters. She has written poetry, essays, philosophical fables, and a play, while maintaining a distinguished career as a translator. She has been a major force in constituting and transmitting to French readers a specifically lesbian corpus of texts, reflecting a cosmopolitan lesbian culture and feminist concerns, in particular through her translating and editing work.

Causse was translating texts from the English and the Italian beginning in the early 1970s; the texts covered a wide range from social novels to adventure narratives. Feminist texts were to follow in the mid 1970s, with works by Italian feminists in particular, including the leading feminist Italian writer, Dacia Maraini. Between 1982 and 1989, Causse translated four of Djuna Barnes' works, adding a postface to the *Ladies Almanack,* as well as

Millicent Dillon's famous biography of Jane Bowles. In the early 1980s she offered works by Natalia Ginzburg and Dacia Maraini to the French public, and in the 1990s she offered works by Willa Cather and Jane Bowles. In an interview with Geneviève Pastre, Causse deplored the lack of interest displayed by French publishing houses when she offered to translate other important lesbian texts, mostly from the United States. For Causse, this means that "A French woman is forced to live in ignorance of the most vivifying symbolic products of her time. It is a conscious lesbocide...." This creates an intolerable situation for the lesbian who constitutes such works as "the very origin of her definition and of her theoretical tools."

Providing the tools essential to forming a sense of self and past has been Causse's work as a careful editor of texts that are rare and novel in their category, to which she adds a theoretical postface or preface. She has brought to light texts that have a significant place in reconstituting lesbian history. Two such texts are Mara's *Diary of a Subjected Woman* (translation by contributor) and Berthe Cleyrergue's memoirs of her life with Natalie Barney. The postface to Mara's meditation on the workings of a woman's inner voice, as she painfully wills her coming out, picks up where Mara leaves off; rather than mere explicating Mara's work, Causse raises an entire new landscape of questions about language. Berthe Cleyrergue's memoirs provide readers with the autobiographical souvenirs of the woman who was Nathalie Barney's housekeeper for half a century, rich in details about the period and Barney's circle. However, it is not merely an intriguing document of the lives of famous lesbians, but also a narrative in its own right, where sexual identity and social class interact in subtle ways. In editing Berthe's recollections in her own words, Causse has insured the transmission of a fascinating page of social history.

In the early 1980s, Causse contributed briefly to *Masques,* the French journal of homosexual culture, which ceased publication in 1985. In 1983, she founded *Vlasta* with others. The journal took its name from an eighth century Czech heroine, and presented "amazon" fictions and utopias as a political position. The first issue defined the journal as a space for women who saw themselves as "guardians of a visionary perspective."

Michèle Causse often lives and works in Québec, at least in part a result of the frustration experienced by radical lesbians among "hetero-feminists" in France by the 1980s, according to Marie-Jo Bonnet in her *Les Relations Amoureuses entre les Femmes.* Her writing reflects debates around gender but systematically aims at uncovering and affirming a specifically lesbian ontology. Causse's essays thus espouse the belief, famously argued by Monique Wittig, that lesbians must be seen as separate from the category "women." "A woman is not born woman, she becomes one, she writes, through the experience of sexuality. And it is sexuality that determines gender and not the opposite," Causse states in her essay "Sexualité et Pouvoir" in *La Parole Métèque.* In her 1991 essay on gender and language, *Dé/générée,* she adds: "The word lesbian has been spoken but it has never been elaborated. Indeed one cannot 'construct' it outside of that moment when one deconstructs the concept of woman. The lesbian is she who has exercized—during her whole life—the greatest resistance to forced conscription into gender.... in fact, the lesbian is, for now, the only de-gendered [being]," as translated by Francesca Canadé Sautman.

Causse's work has relentlessly challenged the notion of authority embodied in language itself, and its responsibility for erasing the lesbian. Thus, decentering and fragmentation are crucial devices in Causse's own narrative or poetic writing. In *La Commu-*

tation de Codes, a partial study of Causse's writing, Catherine Anne Paul sees examples of "code-switching," in which Causse uses English words with thematic resonances as an instance of confronting the "myth of a pure language." The passage from one language to another is indeed crucial to Causse's project of destabilizing patriarchal logocentic power. In *Lettres à Omphale* (1980), four women, all of them protected by pseudonyms, write love letters that are actually translations to Omphale, a Francophone woman writer, of whom nothing is really said. In the same period, Causse published *Lesbiana. Seven Portraits* (1980) in English, although it is absolutely not her mother tongue, partially as an act of protest against French indifference to the ebullient field of lesbian writing in the Anglophone world, she explained in her "Lettre à Suzanne Triton".

Causse's play, *A Quelle Heure est la Levée dans le Désert* (1989), dedicated to the memory of Jane Bowles, reflects Causse's strong interest in Bowles but also in flight from home to distant lands. Bowles' loss of self in North Africa is the apparent theme of the play, but it competes with other female voices, particularly that of Cherifa, the Arab woman she loves. The orientalist gaze is turned around as the Algerian woman, coded by dress and manner as butch, reveals her dominance over the rich foreigner who "bought her." The play underscores the importance of race within difference itself. The dialogues between Bowles and Cherifa are filled with tension, as the wealthy American seeks oblivion and destruction at the hands of a woman who has fascinated her in every sense of the word. Cherifa, on the other hand, seeks to destroy and dominate, but also to seduce and be valued, ambivalent in her professed hate and contempt. Inscribing the left page of the text with brief poetic monologue, parallel to the dialogue and action of the play, Causse writes with an uncompromising awareness of complex differences within a struggling lesbian world and of their impact on the writer's craft.

Three essays from 1991 illustrate her lesbian-centered theoretical deconstruction, her working to create lesbian culture and lesbian space through dissident language. *L'interloquée* begins with a play on the word's original meaning of being amazed, caught short, now expanded to woman as banned, interrupted, bereft of true interlocutor, speaking one language only, one sexolect for both sexes: *androlect,* man's symbolical capture of the world through words. The second essay, *Les Oubliées de l'Oubli,* dissects the particular "a-memory" that has affected men in their "his/story," and claims a lesbian political will to undo history and gender itself. The third essay, *Dé/générée,* proposes lesbian theatre as "mutant," as autonomous lesbian culture, and plays on the word "degenerate," often applied to lesbians, and the new, active, meanings of "de-gendered" or "outside of gender." Her philosophical fable *Voyages de la Grande Naine en Androssie* (1993) sets lesbian resistance to being hunted down and eradicated in an imaginary world of animalized beings, where the "animales" (among whom we recognize Monique Wittig), become "anomales," that is, beyond the norm, refusing the norm, rather than "abnormal," notes Françoise Armengaud in her review of the text.

Causse has been a significant voice in the movement of French feminist deconstruction born out of the rebellious post-1968 climate. She has brought together a highly theoretical lesbian intellectual discourse, exacting in its calls for independent ontological discovery, with specific projects concerning feminist and lesbian history.

—Francesca Canadé Sautman

CHRYSTOS

Nationality: American poet, essayist, and short story writer. **Born:** Off-reservation, in San Francisco, California, 7 November 1946. **Education:** Self-educated. **Career:** Has held a variety of jobs, most often as a maid. Contributing editor, *Lesbian Review of Books*. **Awards:** Barbara Deming Memorial Grant, 1989; National Endowment for the Arts Grant, 1990; Lannan Foundation Grant for Poetry, 1991; Fund for Human Rights Freedom of Expression Award (with Minnie Bruce Pratt and Audre Lorde), 1992; Audre Lorde International Poetry Competition, 1994; Sappho Award of Distinction, Astraea National Lesbian Action Foundation, 1995. **Address:** P.O. Box 4663, Rolling Bay, Washington 98061, U.S.A.

WRITINGS

Poetry

Not Vanishing. Vancouver, British Columbia, Canada, Press Gang, 1988.
"Dancing on the Rim of the World," in *Dancing on the Rim of the World: An Anthology of Contemporary Northwest Native Writing,* edited by Andrea Lerner. Tucson, University of Arizona Press, 1990.
Dream On. Vancouver, Press Gang, 1991.
In Her I Am. Vancouver, Press Gang, 1993.
Fugitive Colors. Cleveland, Ohio, Cleveland Poetry Center, 1995.
Fire Power. Vancouver, Press Gang, 1995.

Essays

"Perhaps," in *Out the Other Side: Contemporary Lesbian Writing,* edited by Christian McEwan and Sue O'Sullivan. Freedom, California, Crossing Press, 1989.
"Not Editable," in *Making Face, Making Soul: Haciendo Caras, Creative and Critical Perspectives by Women of Color,* edited by Gloria Anzaldúa. San Francisco, California, Aunt Lute Foundation, 1990.
"Headaches and Ruminations," in *Out of the Class Closet: Lesbians Speak,* edited by Julia Penelope. Freedom, Crossing Press, 1994.

*

Interviews: "Chrystos: Not Vanishing and in Person" by Karen Claudia and Lorraine Sorrel, in *Off Our Backs* (Washington, D.C.), March 1989, 18-19.

Critical Sources: "Chrystos" by Barbara Dale May, in *Contemporary Lesbian Writers of the United States: A Bio-Bibliographical Critical Sourcebook,* edited by Sandra Pollack and Denise D. Knight, Westport, Connecticut, Greenwood Press, 1993, 118-121; "Voicing Another Nature" by Patrick D. Murphy, in *A Dialogue of Voices: Feminist Literary Theory and Bakhtin,* edited by Karen Kohne and Helen Wassow, Minneapolis, University of Minnesota Press, 1994, 59-82.

*   *   *

Chrystos's poetry interweaves and plays fugues upon two major themes: the lives of First Nations people in contemporary America and the lives of lesbians within a heterosexual culture. Taken as a whole, her work shines a powerful searchlight on the ways human life compounds identity and refuses our attempts to simplify or glorify the categories into which we place ourselves and are placed by others.

In her first collection, *Not Vanishing,* Chrystos focuses on the relationships between Native Americans and whites in order "to make it as clear and as inescapable as possible, what the actual, material conditions of our [Native American] lives are." Poem after poem creates an angry pentimento of the white reality painted over a Native American background: car dealerships sit atop cornfields, zoo denizens are buffalo herds in captivity. Even as she calls upon her readers to understand and honor tribal traditions, she refuses the role of spirit leader or educator and renounces allegiance to the treaties forced on her forebears. What she will give—and gives freely throughout the five volumes of her collected works—is a "give away poem for anyone who will listen"; for, in the end, "when my hands are empty / I will be full."

Anger and love interweave. As she writes about her own life and the lives of other First Nations people, she sears the reader with her justifiable fury, never for a moment letting drop the mental and physical curtain which would shield us all from the sight of what we do to the Other. But behind that curtain, healing also lives. Chrystos seeks to create a reader who, once seared with the truth, will step through the fire and, joining hands with others, will work toward the peace that only acceptance—of others, of ones own responsibilities, of what is truly of value in the world—can bring. For although "you think you live outside of my story," in fact "I'm part of the balance of the universe" and "you're part of me too," she writes in *Fugitive Colors.*

The delicate dialectic Chrystos creates between anger and love is lived out in her erotic poems. Just as in *Not Vanishing* she focuses on Native American lives, so in her third volume, *In Her I Am,* she creates a new—and specifically lesbian—erotic. In her characteristic free verse and prose poems, she explores ways to talk about lesbian erotic desire. She employs many of the same metaphors and images as do writers of mainstream lesbian romances—petals, cream, feathers, juices, wings—but they are transformed in these poems into a kind of naturalization of sexuality (in this case lesbian, but not necessarily), in which the sexual acts and desires Chrystos describes meld with the objects and living entities of nature. The result, for the reader, is that rare thing in erotic writing, an embodied union with the events of the poem. More perhaps than any poet since Adrienne Rich in "Floating Poem" from *Twenty-One Love Poems,* Chrystos unites poem with reader so that the erotic experience of the poem *becomes* the readers.

The experiences Chrystos describes are not, however, what readers of lesbian erotica have come to expect. There are feathers and wings and cream, but this is not vanilla poetry. There is role-playing; there are dildoes and fists, spanking and bondage and servitude, but these are not the erotics of sadomasochistic sex. And despite the poems' focus on the female body and its processes, this erotica is not detached from the world into which the bodies emerge when they arise from the lovers bed.

Chrystos has achieved the remarkable creation of a distinction between lesbian sexual activities/events themselves and the meanings our culture has placed upon them. As she says in her postscript essay from *In Her I Am,* "The Night Gown," "many of the behaviors I describe (fantasy play, use of dildoes, enjoyment of leather, bondage) are commonly considered s/m, although I disagree." In these poems she delineates the line between sadism and desire, between the erotic and the pornographic, as a distinction between power and equality rather than between control and consent. The mutuality of the experiences comes through a sharing of power which requires complete honesty about the body's responses, even when those are "politically incorrect."

Such honesty demands a high degree of self-knowledge. That self-knowledge, however, is not too distant from the self-knowledge Chrystos demands of her readers of the First Nations poems. In all five of her volumes, knowledge of our erotic selves must be integrated with what we know: that our "real enemies are colonization, warfare, exploitation, racism, and greed," she writes in *In Her I Am*. When Indians hate or exile lesbians, they are betraying their own ideals; Chrystos's longing for a home on the reservation is palpable. When gays demonize Indians, she sees, as in *Not Vanishing,* that "even in gay america / no place for Indian birds at the inn." When lesbians exploit one another sexually or seek such exploitation, even when it reflects a genuine "desire," we allow socially-constructed desire to make us complicitous in replicating our oppressions; we are, as Audre Lorde, one of Chrystos's mentors, has said, doing the work of our oppressors. Only complete acceptance and acknowledgment can untangle this tapestry of oppression. Chrystos believes strongly that lesbians' truest sexuality must be free of such unconscious social controllers, "decoding to a place where love isn't a wound," as she expresses it in *Fugitive Colors*. There is a place for dildoes and bondage in sexuality, but that place must be created through full consciousness of how rape and war and discrimination have given meanings to our acts and desires which we must deconstruct in order to avoid repeating.

These are difficult things to say. As with her Native American poetry, Chrystos takes the immense risk of saying what we do not want to hear. She calls her lesbian readers to responsibility, not just for their own sexual acts but for the historically-undergirded force those acts have against other women. None of us singlehandedly created the culture she describes, but we all perpetuate it; and Chrystos calls to us in one of today's clearest voices to become aware of who we are and what we do and then to take responsibility for change. She also acknowledges that we will all, in small ways or large, fail: "I want to be shown / the unlikely one person who / given our lives / hasn't sold something to get by" ("She Said They Say," from *Fugitive Colors*). And she indicts herself for the failures she taxes her readers with.

That the desired changes intertwine ethnic and sexual difference creates resonances which few writers offer lesbian readers. It is not enough, Chrystos tells us, to assert the validity of our own difference. Only when we come truly to respect and honor others' differences can we hope that ours too will be well treated. Only then will we have a just world. Lesbian rights are a metonymy for human rights, and lesbianism becomes a sacred burden.

This sacred burden, in turn, is sanctified through the nature imagery Chrystos uses to describe lesbian coupling. It isn't always beautiful: there is anger here too, anger at the ultimate failure of intimacy to heal, at the intractable isolation our bodies impose even as they are the agents of union. But always Chrystos's voice breaks through, "my breath a silver promise alive" that the painful magic of her incantations can, finally, heal us all.

—Loralee MacPike

CIXOUS, Hélène

Nationality: French theorist and literary critic. **Born:** Oran, Algeria, 5 June 1937; emigrated to France, 1955. **Education:** Received Agregation d'Anglais, 1959, and Docteur ès Lettres 1968. **Family:** Married 1955 (divorced, 1965); two children. **Career:** Assistante, Université of Bordeaux, France, 1962-65; maitre assistante, University of Paris (Sorbonne), 1965-67; maitre de conference, Univeristy of Paris X (Nanterre), 1967-68; founding member and later professor of English, Chargé de mission, Université de Paris VIII, from 1968; founder and director, Centre de Recherches en Études Féminines, from 1974. Cofounder, *Revue de Theorie et d'Analyse Litteraire: Poetique,* 1969; visiting professor and lecturer at numerous universities around the world. **Awards:** Prix Medicis, 1969; Southern Cross of Brazil, 1989; Legion d'Honneur, 1994; Prix des Critiques, for best theatrical work, 1994; honorary doctorate: Queen's University, Canada, 1991; Edmonton University, Canada, 1992; York University, England, 1993; Georgetown University, 1995; Northwestern University, 1996. **Address:** *Home:* 14-16 Villa Leblanc, 92120 Montrouge, France. *Office:* Université de Paris VIII, 2 rue de la Liberte, 93526 St. Denis, Cedex 02, France.

WRITINGS

Selected Literary Prose

Le Prénom de Dieu. Paris, Grasset et Fasquelle, 1967.
Dedans. Paris, Grasset et Fasquelle, 1968; translated by Carol Barko as *Inside,* New York, Schocken, 1986.
L'Exil de James Joyce; ou, L'Art du remplacement. Paris, Grasset et Fasquelle, 1968; translated by Sally A. J. Purcell as *The Exile of James Joyce,* New York, David Lewis, 1972.
Neutre. Paris, Grasset et Fasquelle, 1972.
With Catherine Clément, *La Jeune née.* Paris, Union Générale d'Éditions, 1975; translated by Betsy Wing as *The Newly Born Woman,* Minneapolis, University of Minnesota Press, 1986.
With Annie Leclerc and Madeleine Gagnon, *La Venue à l'écriture.* Paris, Union Générale d'Éditions, 1977; translated by Deborah Jenson as "Coming to Writing" in *Coming to Writing and Other Essays,* edited by Deborah Jenson, Cambridge, Massachusetts, Harvard University Press, 1991.
Vivre l'orange/To Live the Orange (bilingual edition), translated by Ann Liddle and Sarah Cornell. Paris, Des Femmes, 1979.
Illa. Paris, Des Femmes, 1980.
Limonade tout était si infini. Paris, Des Femmes, 1982.
Le Livre de Promethea. Paris, Gallimard, 1983; translated by Betsy Wing as *The Book of Promethea,* Lincoln and London, University of Nebraska Press, 1991.
La Bataille d'Arcachon. Laval, Quebec, Trois, 1987.
Manne aud Mandelstams aux Mandelas. Paris, Des Femmes, 1988; translated by Catherine MacGillivray as *Manna: For the Mandelstams for the Mandelas,* Minneapolis, University of Minnesota Press, 1993.
L'Ange au secret. Paris, Des Femmes, 1991.
With Mireille Calle-Grüber, *Hélène Cixous, Photos de Racine.* Paris, Des Femmes, 1994; translated by Eric Prenowitz as *Hélène Cixous, Rootprints,* London, Routledge, 1997.

Selected Theater

Portrait de Dora. Paris, Des Femmes, 1976.

La Prise de l'école de Madhubaï. Paris, Avant-scène, 1984; translated by Deborah Carpenter as *The Conquest of the School at Madhubaï,* in *Women and Performance 3,* 1986.

L'Histoire terrible mais inachevée de Norodom Sihanouk roi du Cambodge. Paris, Théâtre du Soleil, 1983; translated by Juliet Flower MacCannell, Judith Pike, and Lollie Groth as *The Terrible But Unfinished Story of Norodom Sihanouk, King of Cambodia,* Lincoln, University of Nebraska Press, 1994.

Théâtre. Paris, Des Femmes, 1986.

L'Indiade ou l'Inde de leurs rêves. Paris, Théâtre du Soleil, 1988.

On ne part pas, on ne revient pas. Paris, Des Femmes, 1991.

Selected Essays

"Le Rire de la Méduse," in *L'Arc,* Vol. 61, 1975, 39-54; translated by Keith Cohen and Paula Cohen as "The Laugh of the Medusa," in *New French Feminisms: An Anthology,* edited by Elaine Marks and Isabelle de Courtivron, New York, Schocken Books, 1981.

"Le Sexe ou la tête," in *Les Cahiers du GRIF,* Vol. 13, October 1976, 5-15; translated by Annette Kuhn as "Castration or Decapitation?," in *Signs,* Vol. 7, No. 1, Autumn 1981, 41-55.

"La Missexualité, où jouis-je?," in *Poétique,* Vol. 26, 1976, 240-249.

"Reaching the Point of Wheat, or a Portrait of the Artist as a Maturing Woman," in *New Literary History,* Vol. 19, Autumn 1987, 1-21.

"From the Scene of the Unconscious to the Scene of History," in *The Future of Literary Theory,* edited by Ralph Cohen. New York, Routledge, 1989.

*

Biography: "Hélène Cixous" by Verena Andermatt Conley, in *Dictionary of Literary Biography,* Vol. 83, *French Novelists since 1960,* Detroit, Gale Research, 1989, 52-61.

Interviews: "Rethinking Differences: An Interview" by Isabelle de Courtivron, in *Homosexualities and French Literature: Cultural Contexts/Critical Texts,* edited by George Stambolian and Elaine Marx, Ithaca, Cornell University Press, 1979; "An Exchange With Hélène Cixous" by Verena Andermatt Conley, in *Hélène Cixous: Writing the Feminine,* Lincoln, University of Nebraska Press, 1984; "Hélène Cixous" by Alice Jardine and Anne Menke, translated by Deborah Jenson and Leyla Rouhi, in *Shifting Scenes: Interviews on Women, Writing, and Politics in Post-68 France,* New York, Columbia University Press, 1994.

Bibliography: *French Feminist Theory: Luce Imigaray and Hélène Cixous: A Bibliography* by Joan Nordquist, Santa Cruz, California, Reference and Research Services, 1990.

Critical Sources: "Writing the Body: L'Écriture féminine" by Ann Rosalind Jones, in *The New Feminist Criticism: Essays on Women, Literature and Theory,* edited by Elaine Showalter, New York, Pantheon Books, 1985; "'I Want Vulva'! Cixous and the Poetics of the Body" by Vivian Kogan, in *L'Esprit Créateur* (Lexington, Kentucky), Vol. 25, No. 2, Summer 1985, 73-85; "Hélène

Cixous: An Imaginary Utopia" by Toril Moi, in *Sexual/Textual Politics: Feminist Literary Theory,* London, Methuen, 1985; *Writing Differences: Readings from the Seminar of Hélène Cixous,* edited by Susan Sellers, New York, St. Martin's Press, 1988; "L'Indiade: Ariane's and Hélène's Conjugate Dreams" by Anne-Marie Picard, in *Modern Drama* (Downsville, Ontario), Vol. 32, No. 1, March 1989, 73-88; *Hélène Cixous: A Politics of Writing* by Morag Shiach, London, Routledge, 1991; *Les fictions d'Hélène Cixous: Une autre langue de femme,* by Martine Motard-Noar, Lexington, Kentucky, French Forum, 1991; "'Body Presence': Cixous's Phenomenology of Theater" by Marc Silverstein, in *Theatre-Journal* (Baltimore, Maryland), Vol. 43, No. 4, December 1991, 507-516; "The Autobiographical Manifesto: Identities, Temporalities, Politics" by Sidonie Smith, in *Autobiography and Questions of Gender,* edited by Shirley Neuman, London, Cass, 1992; "Hysteria as Feminist Protest: Dora, Cixous, Acker" by Gabrielle Dane, in *Women's Studies,* Vol. 23, No. 3, July 1994; *On the Feminine,* edited by Mireille Calle-Grüber, Atlantic Highlands, New Jersey, Humanities Press, 1996; *Hélène Cixous,* by Lynn Penrod, New York, Twayne, 1996; *Hélène Cixous: Authorship, Autobiography, and Love,* by Susan Sellers, Cambridge, Massachusetts, Blackwell, 1996.

*　　　*　　　*

Hélène Cixous's contributions to what American academic culture categorizes as "gay and lesbian literature" are substantial. Of the hundreds of academic articles referring to her work, a sizable number interrogate gender and sexuality, or connect her writings to those of other women writers who have been appropriated for "queer studies," such as Gertrude Stein. But while Cixous's work is apparently useful to gay and lesbian studies, the notion of gay and lesbian studies as a category is not necessarily useful to the study of Cixous. Why? There are several paradigms which render sex and gender categories oblique and difficult to exploit in Cixous's writing. These include, first and foremost, poetry, and, concurrently or alternatively, psychoanalysis, theater, and history. Exploration of these paradigms aids in confronting the challenge of her often paradoxical categories of sex and gender.

How should one, for instance, interpret the following statements, culled from a variety of Cixous's texts and representative of the range of surprises in her work? The French male writer Jean Genet is in some sense "lesbian" in that for Cixous he is an example of "abundant, natural, pederastic femininity," she writes in "Sorties." We are all lesbians, she contends in "The Laugh of the Medusa": "The Americans remind us, 'We are all Lesbians'; that is, don't denigrate woman, don't make of her what men have made of you." "Bi-sexuality" is not a pre-disposition to sexual relationships with partners of both genders, but "each one's location in self (repérage en soi) of the presence...of both sexes, nonexclusion either of the difference or of one sex." And the line between sexual love and cannibalism, explored in *Le Livre de Promethea,* is happily indistinct: "[A]m I going to say that our cannibalism is a happy one? If there is such a thing as good cannibalism, than ours is it."

Same-sex representations may be inevitable for the writer of l'écriture féminine ("feminine writing")—"I have never dared create a real male character in fiction...I know nothing of his *jouissance* [pleasures]"— unless it is in writing for the theater, where actors "give us the whole body that we don't have to invent," she wrote in "From the Scene of the Unconscious to the Scene of History." And the Cixousian narrator's sexual anatomy, explored in "Coming to Writing," is diverse indeed: "I have an animale. It's a nannymale, a species of meowse, a he- or she-bird, i.e., a missbird. It lives in me, it makes its nest, it makes my shame in its nest. It's crazy, it's edgy. I'm deeply chagrined to admit it: it gives me the greatest pleasure."

Poetry

Some of Cixous's plays are actually written in verse, as in *The Terrible but Unfinished Story of Norodom Sihanouk, King of Cambodia.* But poetry is primarily evident in Cixous's work as operations within her prose, operations which differentiate her writing from the philosophical and human sciences texts which sometimes appear to be the models for hers. "I do not answer the calling of philosophy even if I am in duet with something 'philosophical,' yet all the while invoking all the liberties warranted or unwarranted of poetry," Cixous explained in a 1982 interview with Verena Andermatt Conley. The "liberties" of poetry in Cixous's apparently philosophical or theoretical texts give her writing the expressive brilliance that has made the short text "The Laugh of the Medusa" a classic of feminist thought. Its elliptical syntax and passionate images have made it both an enduring manifesto, a rallying call for change and emotion, and an example of innovations in the essay genre: "We the precocious, we the repressed of culture, our lovely mouths gagged with pollen, our wind knocked out of us, we the labyrinths, the ladders, the trampled spaces, the bevies—we are black and we are beautiful."

Cixous's poetry has also spawned controversies in which she is criticized for taking her "poetic liberties" too seriously and not representing a stable, coherent political position. Consider, for instance, her depictions of female sexuality in "The Laugh of the Medusa." She states on the one hand that "you can't talk about *a* female sexuality, uniform, homogeneous, classifiable into codes— any more than you can talk about one unconscious resembling another." But this insistence on multiplicity and difference does not prevent her from articulating a poetics of the sexual female body: "Her flesh speaks true. She lays herself bare. In fact, she physically materializes what she's thinking; she signifies it with her body." Rather than simply theorizing, Cixous makes the text sexual by arousing the sensuality of poetic language. She refuses to sidestep the experiential drama of sexuality just because she also has an abstract idea about it. In other words, the fact that "you can't talk about *a* female sexuality"—one monolithic and overdetermined female sexuality—doesn't literally mean for Cixous that "you can't talk about a female sexuality," and talk about it in ways that milk the unconscious as much as sexuality itself does. Even before Cixous's texts represent women loving women, her language loves women. The "liberties" that she takes with language are also liberties taken with the (depicted) body.

Anglo-American feminists have at times considered this poetry of sexuality (which of course also highlights the sensuality of poetry) to be "essentialist"—prescriptive of a basic or "essential" gendered nature. Thus for Ann Rosalind Jones in "Writing the Body: L'Écriture féminine," Cixous' poetry of the body, employing a corporeal lexicon that conforms to the basic characteristics of female and reproductive anatomy—womb, vulva, blood, milk— belies her emphasis on an endlessly generative difference: "her comparisons and lyricism suggest that she admires in women a sexuality that is remarkably constant...." And if Cixous's bodily po-

etry sins by being too specific and constant, it also sins in the other direction, by being too abstract in relation to the identity politics that are arguably "essential" to Anglo-American feminism, as in her rather awkward recapitulation of the formula of "queer" identity, cited above: "The Americans remind us, 'We are all Lesbians'; that is, don't denigrate woman, don't make of her what men have made of you."

Cixous is predictably unrepentant concerning what Toril Moi, in *Sexual/Textual Politics,* calls this "fundamentally contradictory" shift between "a Derridean emphasis on textuality as difference" and a "full-blown metaphysical account of writing as voice, presence and origin." In her interview with Conley, Cixous acknowledges that "If I were a philosopher, I could never allow myself to speak in terms of presence, essence, etc.... [But] I let myself be carried off by the poetic word." But as a poet, Cixous's gender and sexual politics are defined by the hybridity of the "poetically political" and the "politically poetic." She explains to Conley that faced with the two terms, "I must confess that I put the accent on poetic. I do it so that the political does not repress, because the political is something cruel and hard and so rigorously real." For Cixous, in other words, at some point on a continuum, even an emancipatory politics repress. The insertion of the poetry of the unconscious into theories of sexual politics deserves to be studied as a link between Cixous and the most important avant-garde movements of the twentieth-century, notably Surrealism.

Poetry, because it is typically structured around the cognitive passage between two terms, as in the linkage of two comparative terms in analogy, serves according to Cixous as a catalyst for movement, for metamorphosis, for translation, for the breaking down of boundaries—boundaries between discourses, for example. In an interview with Alice Jardine and Anne Menke in the volume called *Shifting Scenes,* Cixous notes, "What interests me is the passage into literature of a portion of philosophy, the passage into philosophy of a portion of psychoanalysis, etc." It is also clearly implicated in Cixous's "passage" from the nativism of "writing the body"—potentially delimited by the boundaries of the self—to her fictions of other cultures. This is evident, for instance, in her fiction *Manna,* in which the trope of manna is used to open the stories of the Mandelstams in Russia and the Mandelas in South Africa.

This idea of poetic passage is also central to one of Cixous's favorite "sexual" tropes, the trope of reproduction, the passage from life to life and body to body. In "The Laugh of the Medusa," she says that "In women there is always more or less of the mother who makes everything all right, who nourishes, and who stands up against separation." But "The mother, too, is a metaphor." The maternal metaphor describes the "desire to write": "a desire to live self from within, a desire for the swollen belly, for language, for blood." Does the dominance of the maternal metaphor mean that for Cixous, only mothers can "write the body"? One could just as well ask, since Cixous's language of love comes from a language which loves female bodies (reproductive organs and all), whether the poetry of maternity is "queer." It is certainly free to be so. It infuses Cixous's narratives of love even between women who are not identified as mothers.

Psychoanalysis

Psychoanalysis is also implicated in Cixous's ambiguous and discontinuous gender or sexual classifications. She exploits, of course, the psychoanalytic idea of the unconscious (crucial to her concept of poetry) and likewise the metaphors of psychoanalysis, such as Freud's sexual interpretation of the myth of the Medusa. These structures complicate and de-literalize sex and gender in her work. But it is her critique of psychoanalysis that most strongly destabilizes her presentation of sex and gender. In "Sorties" she attacks what she calls "the Freudian theses that make woman out to be a flawed man." Freud's notion of "woman" is grounded in anatomical differences between women and men, notably in the man's fear of the absence of male genitalia on woman's body, by which woman comes to represent the threat of castration for the man. Cixous avoids perpetuating such classifications by emphasizing the qualifiers "masculine" and "feminine" rather than the nouns "man" and "woman," and therefore renders concrete sexual difference indistinct: "I make a point of using the *qualifiers* of sexual difference here to avoid the confusion man/masculine, woman/feminine; for there are some men who do not repress their femininity, some women who, more or less strongly, inscribe their masculinity." Because Cixous's work on gender thus emphasizes a "femininity" not necessarily associated with the fact of being female, she passes up feminism as an unintentional position of complicity with anatomical models.

Cixous reinvents the notion of bisexuality as a less restrictive model of identity. It "does not annihilate differences but cheers them on, pursues them, adds more." Bisexuality could be contextualized equally well within the sexual practices of heterosexuality or homosexuality or bisexuality. Like the replacement of the nouns "male" and "female" with the qualifiers "masculine" and "feminine," Cixous's concept of bisexuality is a countertheme for the dominance of the castration complex in psychoanalytic accounts of personal development and its connections to the state of civilization. A parallel move to unhinge gender as a social construction from sexuality as a bodily experience is found in the notion of "missexuality," which Conley equates with "a feminist praxis of writing on the crease of alterity."

Theater

The theater for Cixous is "the *immediate* site of desire of the other, of desire of all the others.... And to get there, one must reach this state of '*démoïsation,*' this state of without me, of depossession of the self, that will make possible the *possession* of the author by the characters," she writes in "From the Scene of the Unconscious to the Scene of History." The loosening of identity experienced by the writer of theater is the ultimate form of poetry, or of bisexuality. Like metaphor, it sets the stage for transformation; like bisexuality, it is inclusive. The extension of authorial subjectivity through the actors' embodiment of fiction creates a phenomenology of sexual or gendered otherness. Cixous asserts that in fiction she has never dared to create a real male character "because I write with the body, and I am a woman, and a man is a man.... And a man without body and without pleasure, I can't do that." In the theater sexual pleasure eludes representation more than in fiction, but that "does not mean that characters are demicreatures who stop at the belt. No, our characters lack nothing, not penises, not breasts, not kidneys, not bellies.... The actor, the actress, give us the whole body." The performance of a writing of a body, in other words, allows the playwright to transcend the limitations and the specificity of the body from which she writes.

It is in the theater that writing about King Sihanouk of Cambodia, or Nelson Mandela of Africa, can equal "writing the body." The metaphorical body becomes a collective and politicized cite, in which the body's "actors" strive to represent, as a unified troupe, the tensions and passions that divide the cultural scene.

History

"And History? Terrible question that has haunted me without cease.... My path is escorted by the phantoms of peoples," writes Cixous in "From the Scene of the Unconscious to the Scene of History." History is particularly troublesome because Cixous doesn't know "which History is mine"—she belongs to several of the groups by which history is peopled. "My first people was the Jewish people, then the Algerian people, then the people of women, etc.," she muses in "Shifting Scenes" Because her history is that of different peoples, Cixous's narrator is not consistently or simply "feminine." History is a "theater" of diversity, in which different bodies play different roles. When Cixous takes on historical agency in her work, as in texts like *Manna,* she becomes an historical actor, one who plays men as well as women. History is also, for Cixous, a theater of possibility. History poses the question of how the self is constructed by context. In "Sorties," she queries, "And what would I have been? Who?" As a girl, history for Cixous was a means of departure from "the real, colonial space."

The changing categories of Cixous's own literal history also provide a catalyst for the indeterminacy of gender and sexual categories. In her interview in *Shifting Scenes,* she explains that although the women's movement in France began with the political and social upheavals of 1968, she was absorbed in literary analysis (notably of James Joyce and Shakespeare) at the foundation of her career as a scholar and a professor: "I was working there in my corner, on literary textuality." The chance to participate and figure in the historical development of questions of gender and sexuality came in 1975, through her association with Antoinette Fouque, the charismatic leader of the group *Psych et po* ("Psychoanalysis and Politics"), and later the founder and editor of the publishing house Des Femmes. Cixous recounts, "the opportunity didn't arise for me until 1975. The opportunity, which is to say the direct call, [came from] Antoinette Fouque.... I arrived at the movement that she had inaugurated seven years earlier."

During this period in which she wrote many important texts on gender and sexuality, including *Portrait of Dora* and "Coming to Writing," Cixous also discovered and became devoted to the writing of a deceased Brazilian woman writer, Clarice Lispector. This intensive and long-lasting intertextual relationship of one woman writer with the oeuvre of another is perhaps unique to the history of Western letters, and establishes an ethos of loving reading.

In the early 1980s Cixous's work took another major turn when she began writing "epic" plays for performance in the Théâtre du soleil ("Theater of the Sun") directed by Ariane Mnouchkine. While in her dramatic work she ventured further and further into an historical and in some ways "masculine" writing, in her fiction she plumbed the depths of the passionate feminine body. "The whole world was giving way before the pressure of her desire, caving in, letting itself be penetrated, opening up sweetly moist beneath her caressing, pressing fingers, [and] the world was not refusing her its sweet, moist, depths," she writes in *The Book of Promethea.*

Cixous's history is, therefore, a history of change, of exploration, of social androgyny and personal passion. In "Coming to Writing," her elusiveness in relation to categorization is presented as a problem for which she is admonished by the figure of a "capitalist-realist Superuncle," the "Anti-Other in papaperson": "The public wants to know what it's buying. The unknown just doesn't sell. Our customers demand simplicity. You're always full of doubles, we can't count on you, there is otherness in your sameness. Give us a homogeneous Cixous. You are requested to repeat yourself...Halt! At ease! Repetition!" This is advice which Cixous refuses to follow. When Alice Jardine, in *Shifting Scenes,* asks how her texts will be read in the twenty-first century, Cixous replies, "I have never asked myself that question. My question is: how 'I' shall read in the twenty-first century, i.e., the remaining unknown I."

—Deborah Jenson

CLARKE, Cheryl

Nationality: American poet and higher education administrator. **Born:** Washington, D.C., 16 May 1947. **Education:** Howard University, B.A. 1969; Rutgers University, M.A. 1974, M.S.W. 1980. **Career:** Co-chair of the board, Center for Gay and Lesbian Studies, City University of New York Graduate Center, New York City, 1990-92; Director of Diverse Community Affairs, Rutgers University, New Brunswick, New Jersey, from 1992; administrator, Office of the Provost, Rutgers University, New Brunswick, New Jersey; contributor to *Black Scholar, Callaloo, Conditions, Essence, Feminist Studies, Hellas, IKON Magazine, Outweek, Sinister Wisdom,* and *Sojourner.* **Member:** Member of editorial collective, *Conditions* magazine, 1981-90; member, New York Women Against Rape, 1985-88; member of steering committee, New Jersey Women and AIDS Network, 1988-91. **Address:** 165 1/2 Cole Street, Jersey City, New Jersey 07302, U.S.A.

Writings

Poetry

Narratives: Poems in the Tradition of Black Women. New Brunswick, New Jersey, Sister Books, 1982; Latham, New York, Kitchen Table—Women of Color Press, 1983; reprinted, with addition of "The johnny cake" and "Cantaloupe," Latham, New York, Kitchen Table—Women of Color Press, 1985.
"IV," in *Conditions* (Brooklyn, New York), No. 11, 1985.
Living as a Lesbian: Poetry. Ithaca, New York, Firebrand Books, 1986.
"Living as a Lesbian Underground: Futuristic Fantasy II" and other poems, in *Serious Pleasure: Lesbian Erotic Stories and Poetry,* edited by Sheba Collective. London, Sheba Feminist Publishers, 1989.
Humid Pitch: Narrative Poetry. Ithaca, New York, Firebrand Books, 1989.
"'Of Althea and Flaxie,' and Other Poems," in *Bluestones and Salt Hay: An Anthology of Contemporary New Jersey Poets,* edited by Joel Lewis. New Brunswick, Rutgers University Press, 1990.
"Hurricane Season," in *The Word,* New York, St. Mark's Poetry Project, 1992.

"The Turnstyle," in *Feminist Studies* (New York), fall 1992.
Experimental Love: Poetry. Ithaca, New York, Firebrand Books, 1993.
Chicago: A Manuscript of Poems (forthcoming).

Essays

"Lesbianism: An Act of Resistance," in *This Bridge Called My Back: Writings by Radical Women of Color,* edited by Cherríe Moraga and Gloria Anzaldúa. Watertown, Massachusetts, Persephone Press, 1981; reprinted by Kitchen Table—Women of Color Press, Latham, New York, 1984.
"The Failure to Transform: Homophobia in the Black Community" and "Women of Summer," in *Home Girls: A Black Feminist Anthology,* edited by Barbara Smith. Latham, New York, Kitchen Table—Women of Color Press, 1983.
"Creating Sexual Poetry," in *Gay Community News* (Boston), 20-26 December 1987.
"If You Black Get Back," in *Ain't I a Woman,* edited by Illona Linthwaite. London, Virago Press, 1987.
Contributor, "1988: Some Thoughts from 15 Artists" by Gary Indiana, in *The Village Voice* (New York), 19 January 1988.
"Silence and Invisibility: Costly Metaphors," in *Gay Community News* (Boston), 19-25 February 1989.
"Saying the Least Said, Telling the Least Told: The Voices of Black Lesbian Writers," in *Lesbian and Gay Studies Newsletters* (Toronto), February, 1990; in *Piece of My Heart: A Lesbian of Colour Anthology,* edited by Makeda Silvera. Toronto, Sister Vision, 1991.
Contributor, "'The Homoerotic Other,' Gay Voices, Black America: Essays from Twelve Black Gay and Lesbian Writers," in *Advocate* (Los Angeles), 12 February 1991.
"The Everyday Life of Black Lesbian Sexuality," in *InVersions: Writing by Dykes, Queers & Lesbians,* edited by Betsy Warland. Vancouver, Press Gang Publishers, 1991.
"Living the Texts Out," in *Theorizing Black Feminisms: the Visionary Pragmatism of Black Women,* edited by Stanlie M. James and Abena P. A. Busia. London, New York, Routledge, 1993.
"*Out* Outside the Classroom: The Co-Curricular Challenge," in *Radical Teacher* (New York), winter 1994.
"New Notes on Lesbianism," in *Frontline Feminism 1975-1995: Essays from Sojourner's First 20 Years,* edited by Karen Kahn. San Francisco, Aunt Lute Books, 1995.

Literary Criticism

"*Blue Heat* by Alexis DeVeaux," in *Conditions* (Brooklyn, New York), No. 13, 1986.
"Ann Petry and the Isolation of Being Other," in *Belles Lettres: A Review of Books by Women* (Arlington, Virginia), fall 1989.
"Knowing the Danger and Going There Anyway," in *Sojourner: The Women's Forum* (Cambridge, Massachusetts), September 1990.
"...She Still Wrote Out the Word Kotex on a Torn Piece of Paper Wrapped Up in a Dollar," in *Conversant Essays: Contemporary Poets on Poetry,* edited by James McCorkle. Detroit, Michigan, Wayne State University Press, 1990.
"'Making Face, Making Soul—Haciendo Caras: Creative and Critical Perspectives by Women of Color' by Gloria Anzaldúa," in *Bridges: A Journal for Jewish Feminists and Our Friends* (Eugene, Oregon), spring 1991.

"What Is Found There: Notebooks on Poetry and Politics," in *Belles Lettres: A Review of Books by Women* (Arlington, Virginia), fall 1994.

"Diaspora Legacy" and *The Marvelous Arithmetics of Distance: Poems 1987-1992 by Audre Lorde,*" in *Women's Review of Books* (Wellesley, Massachusetts), September 1994.

"The Loss of Lyric Space and the Critique of Traditions in Gwendolyn Brooks' *In the Mecca,*" in *Kenyon Review* (Syracuse, New York), winter 1995.

"Race, Homosocial Desire, and 'Mammon' in *Autobiography of an Ex-Colored Man,*" in *Professions of Desire: Lesbian and Gay Studies in Literature.* New York, Modern Language Association of America, 1995.

"Cheryl Clarke in Sapphire's Precious' World: An Identity of One's Own," in *Harvard Gay and Lesbian Review* (Cambridge, Massachusetts), fall 1996.

Other

"Narratives: A Dramatic Event" (play; adaptation of *Narratives: Poems in the Traditions of Black Women*; 133 W. 14th Street, New York, 1982; National Women's Theatre Festival, Santa Cruz, California, 1983; San Francisco Opera House, San Francisco, California, 1984).

"Women of Summer" (short story), in *Home Girls: A Black Feminist Anthology,* edited by Barbara Smith. Latham, New York, Kitchen Table—Women of Color Press, 1983.

"Leavings" (short story), in *Thirteenth Moon* (New York), 1984.

"Epic of Song" (play; Medicine Show Theatre Ensemble's Third Annual Carnival of the Spoken Word, New York, 1987).

"gothic tourism," in *Tourist Attractions* (Top Stories, #25-26), edited by Anne Turyn and Brian Wallis. New York, Top Stories, 1987.

"A Slave's Sacred Supper," in *Cookin' With Honey: What Literary Lesbians Eat,* edited by Amy Scholder. Ithaca, New York, Firebrand Books, 1996.

Recordings: *Narrative Poems in the Tradition of Black Women,* Pacifica Tape Library, 1983; *This Bridge Called My Back: Writings by Women of Color,* Los Angeles, Pacifica Tape Library, 1983; "Hell Divin' Women," in *Tiny & Ruby: Hell Divin' Women* (video documentary), directed by Greta Schiller. New York, Jezebel Productions, 1988.

*

Biography: "Cheryl Clarke," in *Black Writers: A Selection of Sketches from "Contemporary Authors,"* 2nd edition, Detroit, Gale Research, 1989; "Cheryl Clarke," in *Contemporary Authors,* Vol. 143, Detroit, Gale Research, 1995, 84-85.

Interviews: "Feminist Breakfast Set for New York: Poets Clarke and Pratt, Author Barbara Smith to Speak" by Madeleine Tainton and Deborah Turner, in *Women in Libraries: Newsletter of the American Library Association Feminist Task Force* (New York), Vol. 25, No. 4, June 1996, 1, 3-4; "Truth Be Told" by Synde Mahone, *Womanews,* May 1986, 15.

Critical Sources: "Black Women in Focus: Cheryl Clarke's Narrative Poetry" by Jewell Gomez, in *Womanews,* April 1983, 11; "Living as a Lesbian: Poetry" by D. Davenport, in *Black/Out* (Philadelphia, Pennsylvania), Vol. 1, No. 1, summer 1986, 21; "Hu-

mid Pitch: Narrative Poetry" by Jane Campbell, in *Belles Lettres: A Review of Books by Women* (Arlington, Virginia), fall 1990, 53; "Cheryl Clarke" by Elizabeth Randolph, in *Contemporary Lesbian Writers of the United States: A Bio-Bibliographical Critical Sourcebook,* edited by Sandra Pollack and Denise D. Knight, Westport, Connecticut, Greenwood Press, 1993, 122-127; "Speculative Fiction and Black Lesbians" by Jewelle Gomez, in *Signs* (Chicago), Vol. 18, No. 4, summer 1993, 948-955; "Experimental Love Poetry" by Terri L. Jewell, in *Lambda Book Report,* Vol. 4, No. 1, November-December 1993, 47.

Cheryl Clarke comments:

I write to educate and inspire whoever comes to my work. I have tried to place a black lesbian sensibility in the tradition of Afro-American literature as well as to mark a departure from conventional expectations of that literature.... 'Lesbian sensibility' [refers to] the idea that Black women achieve a sensual, cultural, and political solidarity in their identification with women.

*   *   *

Cheryl Clarke is best known for her narrative poetry written from the perspective of a black lesbian feminist. Yet her lesser-known essays and literary criticism also demonstrate her knowledge of literature and mastery of the pen. Her works weave stories, sexuality, and music into literature and "herstory." With emotion-filled clarity and brilliant complexity, she depicts homophobia in the black community and racism in the white-dominated lesbian community. Of considerable note is the way she uses historical images and language to provide context for current events. Clarke's writing not only builds upon the oral tradition, literary legacy, and theoretical analysis of black women writers like Zora Neale Hurston, June Jordan, and Audre Lorde; it also furthers efforts to expand the notion of black arts that flowered during the Harlem Renaissance of the 1920s and the Black Arts Movement of the 1970s. Ardel Thomas, writing in the *Oxford Companion to Women's Writings in the United States,* claims that Clarke has become one of the most influential black lesbian activists and writers in the United States.

Very early in her writing career, Clarke chose poetry as her medium. Poetry is a method by which she can take up a political discourse with peers, while essay writing is more of "a political responsibility," she has explained in two anthologized essays printed in *InVersions* and *A Piece of My Heart: A Lesbian of Colour Anthology.* Clarke writes primarily about the experiences of black lesbians and non-lesbians, confronting themes including lesbian relationships, identity formation, racism, homophobia, and double marginality.

Clarke's poetry moves from the humorous to the tragic, detailing experiences that come out of a black lesbian experience and yet resonate with a pathos that can be felt by anyone coming to understand their identity. In "Dykes Are Hard," a poem from the Lambda Book Award-nominated collection *Experimental Love,* the narrator complains about an unrealistic date who is ready to form a marriage-like union "all before the first show of flesh." And in "passing," from the same collection, Clarke explores the fluidity of gender identity when she writes: "I'll pass as a man today and take up space with my urges." At times such poetry is specifically rooted in time and place, as in the poem "April 4, 1968: Washington, D.C.," from *Narratives: Poems in the Tradition of Black Women.* In the wake of Martin Luther King, Jr.'s assassination, a young girl watches as her family struggles to cope with an environment tainted by racism and the lack of economic opportunity. Each family member clings to what they find important, and yet the outcome of the poem suggests that even some survival tactics can play a part in the destruction of the black community. "the layoff," from *Living as a Lesbian,* similarly depicts the weakening of coping mechanisms in the presence of economic and race-related obstacles: "Marijuana ain't what it used to be in this/era of the nuclear renaissance white boy."

In "The Failure to Transform: Homophobia in the Black Community," which is included in the pivotal anthology *Home Girls,* Clarke outlines some reasons for antagonism against homosexuality. Such homophobia is given poetic form in poems such as "The Day Sam Cooke Died," in *Humid Pitch,* where Clarke narrates the effects of homophobia in one family. In this poem, an adolescent woman's mother finds "it was easier not to meddle" in her daughter's budding lesbian relationship. Thus, the daughter, deprived of parental support, runs away from home to join her woman lover in New Jersey.

Sexuality has been a consistent concern of Clarke's, in both her poetry and her prose. Openly dealing with sexuality is politically important, maintains Clarke in her essay, "...She Still Wrote Out the Word Kotex..." Examining the works of earlier black women poets, Clarke asserts that discussions of sexuality are hidden behind homophobia, racism, and sexism, as well as behind literary devices like allusion, metaphor, and hyperbole. Clarke advocates that more black woman participate in the literature that discusses their sexuality in order to continue changing the stereotypes and misinformation which surround the topic. And Clarke is not afraid to take her own advice. In *Living,* Vicki, of "Vicki and Daphne," counteracts her lover's faithlessness and her own sexual need with "an odd object of comfort,...awaking at 6 a.m....without Daphne.../ ...pulls top sheet and comforter over passion and menses/stained sheets..." The narrator in "Committed Sex," from *Experimental Love,* suggests that there exist similarities between actively exploring good sex and engaging in radical political activism. One could begin to see why Terri L. Jewell, writing in *Lambda Book Review,* describes some of Clarke's poems as being from the perspective of a "sexual outlaw."

In one instance, Clarke seems to contradict her call to more openly discuss sexuality. She writes of the struggles lesbians endure, in the passionate, powerful, and informative essay "Lesbianism: An Act of Resistance," included in *This Bridge Called My Back.* Yet, she describes bisexuals as those taking advantage of "heterosexual presumption." Later in the same essay, Clarke rhetorically asks whether or not there has been enough harm caused by infighting within the black community. If one were to exchange the word "black" for the term "queer," the statement contradicts and slightly weakens the essay's ultimate conclusion—a call for greater alliances within the diverse lesbian community. It is essential, however, to realize that in the early 1980s, when the essay was published, bisexuality was chiefly viewed (and continues to be by many) as a way to "pass," or to be accepted, as heterosexual.

Clarke's works also enter into a passionate and imaginative engagement with history. The powerful "Bulletin," from *Pitch,* begins with an original, colonial-period poster advertising a reward for the capture of a runaway slave girl. In the fictionalized verse that follows, Clarke gives voice to the fugitive teen who encounters the posting for her capture: "I'm wearing a westcoat and pants/ left the petticoat in a cornfield." Focussing on information about the girl's identity that was excluded from the original posting and thus from history, the poem urges the reader to ponder the idea of lesbian slaves. By successfully utilizing such narrative poetry forms, Clarke blurs the line between fiction and history. In an interview with Deborah Turner, Clarke said that "in some instances, we have to create our own history in order to claim a visibility." The poet went on to stress that this is particularly true for lesbians.

Clarke often presents her readers with black lesbian and nonlesbian realities that are seldom recorded. In "Women of Summer," a short story in *Home Girls,* the narrator describes the United States Black Power Movement of the late 1960s and early 1970s from the perspective of two women outlaws. A host of criminal, revolutionary events are described by newscasters, men in the revolution, and supporters on the fringe of it. The marginalization of women in the movement is unveiled as their successes and concerns get little to no attention from the traditional media or from oral tradition. Clarke's storytelling focuses on information excluded from more mainstream newsbearing and historical accounting methods in both the dominant and black cultures.

Though "Bulletin," "Women of Summer," and other works directly address history, Clarke also uses historical concepts to draw parallels to the present as well as to provide points of reference. A few of her works compare experiences of light-skinned blacks "passing" as white to those of lesbians and gays posing as heterosexual, or being "in the closet." In "Lesbianism: An Act of Resistance," Clarke uses the phrase "nigger-in-the-woodpile" to describe the experience of being "outed," or discovered as being a lesbian without one's consent. Clarke's works also include a fair number of occasional poems, acknowledging times and events like "Miami: 1980" and "to Vanessa Williams: Miss America (black) 1984" both in *Living.*

Clarke's attention to marginalization is not limited to revisiting history. According to Jewelle Gomez in *Signs,* Clarke even begins to inform the future. Gomez claims that at least two of Clarke's poems could be categorized as speculative fiction, assuming a time and circumstance that has yet to be revealed. "Living as a Lesbian: Futuristic Fantasy II," Gomez writes, satisfies the genre in part because the hopelessness contained within it does not hide behind a utopian dream. Yet, the poem does envision a probable future replete with all the problematic characteristics—racism, homophobia, sexism, and the like—of the present.

Regardless of the era of Clarke's subject matter, she has an eloquent ability to lace music together with words. In her *Belles Lettres* review, Jane Campbell applauds the tribute *Pitch* pays to black music, especially the Blues. Its centerpiece work, "Epic of Song," winds through the trials and tribulations of an all-black band, the Road Temple Eagle Rockers. The main character and lead singer, Mean Candy Sweat (pronounced "sweet"), calls her prodigy Star to her with all that the Blues offers, "'Black gal / Black gal / Where you gone? / Git back here. / (I don't wanna face the dawn alone.)'" This loneliness and longing is repeated by various characters throughout the epic. Later, for example, a white Indian doctor tries a rhyme, "Hey, black gal, I want to swim in your sea. / Hey, black gal, I want to swim in your sea. / I'm just a po ship that been wandering long / lookin for a port to lay my anchor in." Also, Clarke echoes Blues legend Bessie Smith in "living as a lesbian underground: a futuristic fantasy" and "no more encomiums," in *Living.* Clarke told Sydne Mahone in an interview for *Womanews* that the music of Nona Hendrix, Joan Armatrading, and Dinah Washington influenced her poetry.

Clarke has not only added creative works to the African American literary cannon, she has also helped advance the standards of feminist literary criticism, taking on African American literary works that have too often been approached gingerly. Until very recently, prejudice and discrimination in the traditional United States publishing industries, as well as in society as a whole, created various obstacles and challenges for women writers, especially for lesbians of color. Thus it became somewhat customary to celebrate and praise those few whose works did get published. Critiquing them was considered a bold act from which a few, including Cheryl Clarke, have not shied away.

Clarke is not convinced by Alexis DeVeaux's politics in *Blue Heat,* which she reviewed in *Conditions.* She does, however, appreciate the seriousness with which DeVeaux approaches her writing. In "...And Still She Wrote...," Clarke unveils the coded descriptions of sexuality in works by black women since 1969, including Nikki Giovanni, Nzotake Shange, and Alice Walker. In that essay, she also critiques Claudia Tate's interviewing tactics in *Black Women Writers at Work.* Clarke claims that Tate fails to further question a link Sonia Sanchez makes between the act of writing and that of sex. Adrienne Rich's reflections on her own educational process receive applause, but Clark questions Rich's extensive cataloging of the black lesbian community's shortcomings in a *Belles Lettres* review. Clarke's evaluations of contemporary literature consistently contain more than simple praises. She furnishes honest feedback abundant with congratulations and criticism alike.

Cheryl Clarke's works offer vivid, complex treatments of sexuality, marginality, racism within the lesbian community, homophobia within the black community, and the search for identity. Part of Clarke's talent lies in her ability to sculpt poems that exhibit the random and varied textures of life. That is, a second or third reading of her verse tends to reveal nuances not apparent in an initial reading. It is no wonder Clarke's works have been so widely anthologized.

Clarke's emotionally charged, tell-it-like-it-is lyrical works have given momentum to the Gay Rights Movement of the late 20th century, a movement which has allowed for a proliferation of "out" lesbians and gays in almost all walks of life. Clarke also has a gift for recalling the past to help inform the present. She reframes well known historical events; by focusing on those erased from and forced into the margins of history, she openly integrates black lesbian identities into African American history. Her success in using historical events as reference points not only lies in commemorating those events, but also in naming what occasions are significant to blacks and black lesbians. Her descriptions, whether in her creative, lyrical poetry or her well-informed, poignant prose, educate readers from her black, lesbian, feminist perspective.

—Deborah Turner

CLIFF, Michelle

Nationality: Jamaican novelist, poet, and author of short stories and nonfiction. **Born:** Kingston, Jamaica, 2 November 1946; naturalized United States citizen. **Education:** Wagner College, New York, A.B. 1969; Warburg Institute, London, England, M. Phil. 1974. **Career:** Has held a variety of jobs including reporter and researcher for *Life* magazine, New York City, 1969-70; copy editor and then manuscript and production editor specializing in history, politics, and women's studies, W. W. Norton and Co., Inc., New York City, 1974-79; co-publisher and editor, *Sinister Wisdom,* Amherst, Massachusetts, 1981-83; faculty member, adult degree programs, Norwich University, Vermont College Campus, Montpelier, 1983-84; faculty member, New School for Social Research, 1974-76, Hampshire College, 1980-81, University of Massachusetts at Amherst, 1980, and Vista College, 1985; visiting faculty member, San Jose State, 1986, and University College of Santa Cruz, 1987; visiting lecturer, Stanford University, 1987-91; visiting writer, 1990, and Allan K. Smith Visiting Writer, 1992, Trinity College; contributor, *Feminist Review, Ms., Sojourner,* and *Village Voice.* **Awards:** MacDowell College fellowship, 1982; National Endowment for the Arts fellowship, 1982, 1989; Massachusetts Artists Foundation fellowship, 1984; Eli Kantor fellowship, Yaddo, 1984; Fulbright fellowship, New Zealand, 1988. **Agent:** Faith Childs Literary Agency, 275 West 96th St., No. 31B, New York, New York 10025, U.S.A.

WRITINGS

Novels

Abeng. Trumansburg, New York, Crossing Press, 1984.
No Telephone to Heaven. New York, Random House, 1987.
Free Enterprise. New York, Dutton, 1993.

Short Stories

Bodies of Water. New York, Dutton, 1990.
"Provenance," in *Ms. Magazine* (New York), 1992.
"History as Fiction, Fiction as History," in *Ploughshares,* 1994.
"A Public Woman," in *Southwest Review,* 1996.

Poetry

Claiming an Identity They Taught Me to Despise. Watertown, Massachusetts, Persephone Press, 1980.
The Land of Look Behind. Ithaca, New York, Firebrand Books, 1985.

Other

Editor, *The Winner Names the Age: A Collection of Writing by Lillian Smith.* New York, Norton, 1978.
"Sister/Outsider: Some Thoughts on Simone Weil," in *Between Women,* edited by Carol Anshaw, Louise DeSalvo, and Sara Ruddick. Boston, Beacon Press, 1984.
"Clare Savage as a Crossroads Character," in *Caribbean Women Writers: Essays From the First International Conference,* edited by Selwyn Cudjoe. Wellesley, Massachusetts, Calalou, 1990.

*

Interviews: "The Art of History: An Interview with Michelle Cliff" by Judith Raiskin, in *Kenyon Review,* Vol. 15, No. 1, 1993, 57-71; "Journey Into Speech—A Writer: An Interview with Michelle Cliff" by Opal Palmer Adisa, in *African American Review,* Vol. 28, No. 2, 1994, 273-281.

Critical Sources: "Narration and the Postcolonial Moment: History and Representation in *Abeng*" by Simon Gikandi, in *Writing in Limbo,* Ithaca, Cornell University Press, 1992, 231-251; "Race, Privilege, and the Politics of (Re)Writing History: An Analysis of the Novels of Michelle Cliff" by Belinda Edmondson, in *Callaloo,* Vol. 16, No. 1, 1993, 180-191; "Michelle Cliff" by Mary Pollock, in *Contemporary Lesbian Writers: A Bio-Bibliographical Sourcebook,* edited by Sandra Pollack and Denise Knight, Westport, Connecticut, Greenwood Press, 1993, 135-140; "Inverts and Hybrids: Lesbian Rewritings of Sexual and Racial Identities" by Judith Raiskin, in *The Lesbian Postmodern,* edited by Laura Doan, New York, Columbia University Press, 1994, 156-172; "After 'The Tempest': Shakespeare, Postcoloniality, and Michelle Cliff's New, New World Miranda" by Thomas Cartelli, in *Contemporary Literature,* Vol. 36, No. 1, 1995, 82-100.

*   *   *

In an essay about the autobiographical origins of her first fictional heroine, Clare Savage, Michelle Cliff describes herself as a writer of "Afro-Caribbean (Indian, African, and white) experience and heritage and Western experience and education (indoctrination)." Through her fiction, poetry, and autobiographical prose, Cliff struggles to understand the anglocentrism of British West Indian culture which she has inherited and to articulate a specifically Caribbean past which the culture of colonialism has attempted to annihilate. By writing about the ways in which Caribbean subjects strive to claim their identities, Cliff aims for wholeness from the fragmentation that characterizes the history of the Caribbean diaspora. Cliff depicts lesbian themes in her work, but her main focus returns always to the history of racism and colonialism in Western culture.

Although she has lived and studied extensively in England and the United States, Cliff writes in the preface to *The Land of Look Behind* that she travels "as a Jamaican" for it is Jamaica that "forms [her] writing for the most part." Yet, she considers herself not just a Caribbean writer, but also "an American writer in a certain way of being of the Americas, at least," she told interviewer Judith Raiskin. Cliff's major works are efforts to retrace and reclaim a repressed Afro-Caribbean and specifically Jamaican past, a goal which resonates with personal urgency for Cliff who, as a Jamaican with white ancestry, was urged to "pass." In the short prose poem "Passing," Cliff recounts the painful contradictions she faces as a "white creole woman": "Forget about your great-grandfather with the darkest skin.... Cultivate normalcy. Stress sameness. Blend in. For God's sake don't pile difference upon difference." Another poem, "The Laughing Mulatto (Formerly a Statue) Speaks," narrated by a mulatto woman ironically carved in white stone rather than "onyx, dark clay, or mahogany," extends the metaphor of "passing" to remember two women who "chose to live as ghosts." According to this poem, these two living women have been forced to disavow both their blackness and their lesbian identity to accommodate the racism and homophobia of Western culture. Here, Cliff articulates the intersections of race and sexuality, suggesting that one component of identity is intrinsically linked to all others.

Like the poem "The Laughing Mulatto," Cliff's novels draw connections among the histories and experiences of women and other colonized peoples, including those individuals marginalized because of their sexual orientation. Belinda Edmondson comments that the novels reflect Cliff's "search for an Afrocentric identity through her matrilineal ancestry while attempting to come to terms with her father's lineage of planters and slaveowners." Her first novel, *Abeng,* introduces an autobiographical heroine, the light-skinned Clare Savage, and traces her journey toward understanding her place in Jamaican society. Clare's quest to make meaning of her life is facilitated through interactions with her mulatto-born mother Kitty, her well-respected grandmother, her first love, a black girl named Zoe, and Miss Beatrice, a white woman who teaches Clare not to "act like a boy." As the novel presents the conflicts between the adolescent Clare and women of various racial and class backgrounds, Cliff also weaves in Jamaican history and culture, simultaneously questioning certain foundational narratives, such as the story of Christopher Columbus, that have erased the Caribbean past from the collective memory of its people. Cliff begins to recover a specifically female Jamaican history by rewriting the myth of Nanny, a Maroon fighter who led slave revolts and allegedly caught bullets between her buttocks, and by representing Mma Alli, a lesbian obeah woman who teaches women about their erotic power.

Cliff's second novel, *No Telephone to Heaven,* builds upon *Abeng* by chronicling Clare's adult life and her return to Jamaica after sojourns to North America and England. In her commentary on Clare Savage as a "crossroads character," Cliff remarks that the "theme of the grandmother" establishes continuity between the two novels. In this regard, Cliff continues to convey the significance of both real and symbolic female ancestors for Clare's development of her sense of self. Although Clare is murdered in an act of resistance against the imperialist powers who are destroying her native land, Cliff perceives this ending in positive terms for it emblazons Clare "into the landscape of Jamaica," fortifying her connections with her ancestors.

Free Enterprise, Cliff's third novel, is again concerned with the recovery of the Jamaican past and the history of resistance against slavery, colonization, and imperialism. This novel draws upon the lives of real historical figures including Lucy Parsons, a black female American revolutionary, and Mary Ellen Pleasant, a black woman who helped finance John Brown's raid on Harper's Ferry. Set primarily in the United States, *Free Enterprise* illustrates that the resistance against slavery embodied by the mythic figures of Nanny and Maroons is part of the complex historical record of rebellion and collaboration that links the United States with the global slave trade.

Two of Cliff's stories in her collection *Bodies of Water* are also historical fictions. Cliff based "A Hanged Man" on the life of Peg-leg Joe, a sailor who led slaves to freedom; another story, "A Woman Who Plays Trumpet Is Deported" is "an imagining" inspired by Valaida Snow, a trumpet player who escaped from a concentration camp. Other stories feature a black woman who bleaches her skin to perform in a circus sideshow and a young boy alienated from his family after the death of his father. The theme that links together the multiple narrative voices in this collection parallels the focus of Cliff's novels: the struggle for identity and wholeness in a fragmented, incomprehensible world shattered by racism, sexism, imperialism, and homophobia.

—Annmarie Pinarski

———

COCLES, Angelo. *See* **D'ANNUNZIO, Gabriele.**

———

COLLARD, Cyril

Nationality: French novelist and film director. **Born:** Paris, 19 December 1957. **Education:** Studied mathematics and physics before becoming an author, actor, and director. **Awards:** César Award, for Best Film of the Year and Best First Film of the Year, 1992. **Died:** Of AIDS in Versailles, France, 5 March 1993.

Writings

Novels

Condamné amour (Condemned to Love; novel). Paris, Flammarion, 1987.
Les nuits fauves. Paris, Flammarion, 1989; translated by William Rodarmor as *Savage Nights,* London, Quartet Books, Ltd., 1993, Woodstock, New York, The Overlook Press, 1994.

Other

L'ange sauvage (The Savage Angel; notebooks). Paris, Flammarion, 1993.
L'animal (The Animal; poetry). Paris, Flammarion, 1994.

*

Critical Sources: "The French Connection" by Simon Watney, in *Sight and Sound* (London), June 1993, 24-25; "*Blue* and the Outer Limits" by Paul Julian Smith, in *Sight and Sound* (London), October 1993, 18-19; *Le sida, combien de divisions?* by ACT UP-Paris, Paris, Dagorno, 1994.

*   *   *

France has been the European country with the highest rate of HIV (Human Immune-defiency Virus) and AIDS (Acquired Immune Deficiency Syndrome). After almost a decade of national denial about the seriousness of the epidemic, the late 1980s and early 1990s have seen a sharp rise in AIDS awareness. While many social and political factors must be credited for this reversal, authors with HIV or AIDS have played a crucial role in it.

In 1990, Hervé Guibert was the first young gay writer with AIDS to become a household name, and his autobiographical novels were received with great enthusiasm by critics and the public alike. In 1992, Cyril Collard's film adaptation of his own novel, *Savage Nights (Les nuits fauves),* was more than the most successful French film of the year, it was truly an extraordinary social and cultural event. As never before, AIDS was at the center of the public debate in France. Collard not only directed the film, but also wrote the script, played the main character, and wrote and performed most of the soundtrack. He died of AIDS on 5 March 1993, in the midst of national elections, one day before what was then the largest AIDS march in Paris, and three days before his film received four César awards (the French "Oscars"), including Best Picture of the year.

In addition, before his death Collard directed several music videos and television reports, and published two novels: *Condamné amour,* which has not yet been translated into English, and *Savage Nights,* his most important work. A collection of diaries and notebooks entitled *L'ange sauvage,* as well as an earlier, book-length poem entitled *L'animal* were published posthumously.

Collard's two novels share similar themes, styles, and obsessions: a young, artistically-minded, bisexual man as narrator; a raw, poetic style; an attraction for North African people, cultures, and politics; a taste for dark and violent sexual practices; and most of all, a vibrant and uncompromising quest for self-discovery through sexual desire. In terms of artistic influence, Collard claims the legacy of two French gay authors with strong poetic visions and rebellious personalities: the nineteenth-century poet Arthur Rimbaud and the twentieth-century author Jean Genet.

If the theme of AIDS remains implicit in Collard's first novel, it is at the heart of his second. *Savage Nights* tells the largely autobiographival story of Jean, a bisexual film and video director who has AIDS. Jean is torn by contradictory but equally powerful desires: his love for Laura, with whom he initially has sex without telling her about his HIV status, his relationship with Samy, the son of Spanish immigrants, his attraction for working-class Arab boys, and his taste for anonymous sexual encounters with men. As Jean laments: "I'm made up of pieces of myself that have been scattered about, then stuck together anyhow, because after all, you need some sort of body." Eventually, Jean will reconcile the pieces of his life, and reach a state of oneness with himself and the world.

The huge success of both the novel and film adaptation of *Savage Nights* among young people can be explained by many factors. First, Collard's charisma, good looks, and rebellious energy made him a perfect, if unconventional, youth hero. The storyline, involving a doomed love story and probable death, added popular, Romantic elements. But most of all, Collard's unique ability is to echo the confusion and anxieties of young people in France of the 1990s. His approach to homosexuality, for instance, represents a common French attitude. His character, Jean, never identifies as gay or bisexual. He simply tells Laura: "I like boys too." As Paul Julian Smith writes in an essay on several AIDS films, for Collard homosexuality "is something you do, not something you are." Indeed, this may be problematic for Anglo-saxon audiences, more accustomed to the notion of a gay identity. Collard, however, never shies away from this central aspect of the AIDS crisis, sexual desire—even and especially if it raises real and uncomfortable issues such as unprotected sex in the midst of sexual passion.

Savage Nights also replaces the epidemic within its broader social context of immigration, cultural diversity, racism, and unemployment. Although Collard has often been criticized for not establishing a clear link between homophobia and the spread of AIDS, and for being too concerned with his own image to offer any interesting political insight into the epidemic, his work remains a vibrant and powerful testimony of a bisexual man's fight for his dignity in the face of disease and death.

—David Caron

CORNWELL, Anita

Nationality: American essayist and short story writer. **Born:** Greenwood, South Carolina, 23 September 1923; moved to Philadelphia, Pennsylvania, 1939. **Education:** Temple University, Philadelphia, B.S. in journalism and social sciences, 1948. **Career:** Performed clerical work for federal, state, and city governments; caseworker, for two years at the Pennsylvania State Department of Welfare; newspaper reporter; free-lance writer; columnist, *Griot*, Philadelphia; judge, Lambda Book Awards, from 1990. **Member:** Lifetime member, Dramatists Guild. **Address:** c/o New Seed Press, P.O. Box 9488, Berkeley, California 94709-7556, U.S.A.

WRITINGS

Fiction

"Sound of Crying," in *Negro Digest* (Chicago), Vol. 13, June 1964, 53-61.

"Something To Look Forward To," in *Elegant Teen*, September 1965.

"The Rope on the Steps," in *Negro Digest*, Vol. 14, May 1965, 56-68.

"And Save a Round for Jamie Brown," in *Negro Digest*, Vol. 15, April 1966, 83-92.

"Between the Summers," in *Phylon*, fall 1966.

"Arlanda and Sarabell," in *Black Maria*, Vol. 3, No. 3, 1977.

The Girls of Summer (for young adults), Berkeley, California, New Seed Press, 1989.

Essays

"Why We May *Never* Overcome," in *Negro Digest*, Vol. 14, July 1965, 3-6.

"The Negro Woman: America's Unsung Heroine," in *Negro Digest*, Vol. 14, October 1965, 15-18.

"Memo to Nellie, the *Cullud* Maid," in *Negro Digest*, Vol. 15, November 1965, 30-32.

"Strapped on a Sinking Ship," in *Negro Digest*, Vol. 15, May 1966, 32-36.

"The Boy," in *Negro Digest*, Vol. 15, September 1966, 36-40.

"On Being Black," in *Liberator*, April 1967.

"Whither Goest the Battered Woman?" in *Hera*, April/May 1975.

"First Love and Other Sorrows," in *Gay Alternative*, Vol. 1, No. 9.

"The Black Lesbian in a Malevolent Society," *Dyke, A Quarterly*, No. 5, 1977.

"Stopping Traffic on the IRT," in *Format, Art and Society*, summer 1982.

"Backward Journey," in *Feminary*, Vol. 12, No. 1, 1982.

"To a Young Soul Sister," in *Philadelphia Gay News*, 8 September 1983.

"The Joys and Sorrows of Putting Pen to Paper," in *Azalea*, Vol. 5, No. 2, 1983.

"Is Vanessa Williams America's Newest Heroine?" in *Philadelphia Gay News*, 9 August 1984.

"Human Driftwood: A Welfare Worker's Story," in *Welcomat*, 19-26 November 1986.

"The Heroism of the Southern Black Teacher," in *Welcomat*, 18-24 February 1987.

"Mama's Low Road to Higher Education," in *Welcomat*, 16 March 1988.

"Mike Tyson and the Politics of Rape," in *Griot*, September 1992.

"Toni Morrison: Nobel Laureate in Literature, 1993," in *Griot*, December 1993.

"Why Such Abject Fear of Feminism?" in *Griot*, April 1994.

"The Montgomery Bus Boycott," in *Griot*, July/August 1995.

"Mary McLeod Bethune," in *Griot*, January/ February 1996.

Black Lesbian in White America. Tallahassee, Florida, Naiad Press, 1983.

Interviews

"Pat Parker, Poet from San Francisco," in *Hera*, Vol. 1, No. 4, fall 1975.

"So Who's Giving Guarantees? An Interview with Audre Lorde," in *Sinister Wisdom*, fall 1977.

"Attuned to the Energy: Sonia Sanchez," in *Essence*, July 1979.

"Writer/Activist, Barbara Smith at Bryn Mawr," in *Au Courant*, 13 May 1985.

"Angela Davis: Evolution of an Activist," in *Witness*, Vol. 73, January 1990.

"Maggie Kuhn: Rebel with Many Causes," in *Witness*, May 1990.

Other

Cornwell's writings have appeared in numerous anthologies, including: *The Lavender Herring, Lesbian Essays from the Ladder*, edited by Barbara Grier and Coletta Reid, Baltimore, Diana Press, 1976; *Lavender Culture*, edited by Karla Jay and Allen Young, New York, Jove/Harcourt Brace, 1979; *Top Ranking, An Anthology on Racism and Classism in the Lesbian Community*, edited by Joan Gibs and Sara Bennett, Brooklyn, February 3rd Press, 1980; *For Lesbians Only: A Separatist Anthology*, edited by Sarah L. Hoagland and Julia Penelope, London, Onlywomen Press, 1988; *The Romantic Naiad, Love Stories by Naiad Authors*, edited by Katherine V. Forrest and Barbara Grier, Tallahassee, Naiad Press, 1993; *Revolutionary Tales, African American Women's Short Stories, from the First Story to the Present*, edited by Bill Mullen, New York, Dell Publishing, 1995.

*

Critical Sources: "Foreword" by Becky Birtha, in *Black Lesbian in White America*, Tallahassee, Florida, Naiad Press, 1983; review of *Black Lesbian in White America* by Janet Mason, in *Off Our Backs* (Washington, D.C.), Vol. 13, No. 11, December 1983, 21.

Anita Cornwell comments:

As far as my work is concerned, I think it has provided a safety valve for me as there is so much unfairness, injustice, and violence in America, the bulk of it directed toward women, children, and minorities, that I would have gone insane if I weren't able to at least try to help bring a tiny measure of redress by putting pen to paper.

*   *   *

Anita Cornwell is no less than a pioneer of radical lesbian feminist thought. Many of her works were published in the *Ladder*, one of the first major lesbian publications in the United States. Another early "home" that Cornwell found for her writing was the journal *Negro Digest*, which was an important voice for black thought and politics. She began by publishing short stories there, powerfully written pieces on the effects of racism and the dignity that black people retained in spite of it. Her essays in *Negro Di-*

gest show a complex grasp of the many forces that made up American society in the mid 1960s. Cornwell examines the interaction of the United States' interventionist policies, sexism, racism, and classism in an unflinching style. Thirty years later, most of the essays still ring true.

Cornwell took her place as one of the early spokeswomen of feminist theory in her essays about black women, as in "The Negro Woman: America's Unsung Heroine," where she describes male supremacy as obsolete and ridicules so-called experts who see black women's lack of submissiveness as a problem to be solved. In "Memo to Nellie, the *Cullud* Maid" she describes how oppression is self-perpetuating: "Miss Ann, imprisoned in *her own place,* which is under The Liberal's big foot, is most certainly going to keep you reminded that *you* are under her foot."

In "Strapped on a Sinking Ship" she warns her readers against merely striving for a larger piece of American pie. The pie itself is poisoned, she states, by the United States' oppressive policies at home and abroad, and it is the entire system and its philosophy that must be changed for the good of all, white and black:

> "And one bright day these same insecure men, or men like them, are apt to find themselves in a situation involving The Bomb, and in order to 'save face and look strong' they may just as casually blow up the world. And won't those brainwashed white women be surprised when they find that, after all these years of proclaiming, "my place is the home," the home is going to be the first place blasted off the map when America's bombs come to roost?

As a black woman born in the deep south, Cornwell formed her radical opinions early, learning them in "'the school of hard knocks,' as my Mother is so fond of calling life in the raw," she once wrote. She was raised by a single mother and was first intrigued by journalism when she read the *True Stories* magazine that her mother brought home. Even then, she noticed that the stories given to the male reporters were much more interesting than what the women got to write. Journalism became her goal.

From her mother she learned how hard life can be for a dark-skinned woman alone with a child; she also learned how a woman's strength alone can be enough for her to survive. From her childhood on, she has loved and valued the qualities she has found in the women around her and has raged against the men that so often brutalize those women and hold them back. The dedication of *Black Lesbian in White America* states this credo simply: "To the Womyn of the World/ Who have done so much/ For so little."

Much of Cornwell's published work was written in the early years of the second wave of U.S. feminism and it bears the mark of that era of anger and idealism. Her judgements are forthright and powerful: "I can say without reservation that *any* womin sleeping with *any* man on a fairly regular basis is prostituting her mind, her body, and her spirit no matter what the relationship is called," according to her letter number "Two" in *black Lesbian in White America.* Even her spelling throughout—"womin" for "woman" and "womyn" for "women"—expresses her rejection of the idea that woman is derived from man. Reading her outspoken essays in the climate of the late 1990s is like taking a refreshing breath of air in a room stuffy with equivocation.

Cornwell dealt with being a black, a lesbian, and a woman by recognizing that these aspects of herself are inseparable in her identity, and by remaining just slightly outside each group, strongly loving, yet critical of each, and slightly alienated from each be-

cause of that criticism. In "Three for the Price of One: Notes From a Gay, Black, Feminist," which appeared in 1978 in *Lavender Culture,* she explores the complex interactions of racism within the women's movement, sexism and homophobia within the black community, and sexist role stereotyping among lesbians. Like her other essays, it is a strongly felt piece of writing, filled with courageous political analysis and underlaid with the deep pain that has been the growth medium for that analysis. Cornwell came out in print as a lesbian with the publication of "Letter to a Friend," that first appeared in *The Ladder* in December/January 1971/1972.

Nowhere is that pain more evident than in her writing about heterosexual women. "Lament for Two Bamboozled Sisters—A Sequence of Letters," which appeared in *Black Lesbian in White America,* is written as a series of six letters from a black lesbian, four to a straight woman friend and two to the friend's daughter after her mother's death. Into these letters Cornwell pours all the passion—love, anger and protectiveness—that she feels towards women who insist on continuing to relate to men even though it may damage or even kill them. After the death of her friend the letter writer rails:

> During the past ten years, I have spent many long hours pondering the behavior of womyn and I have yet to come up with little more than a long list of questions, recurring in my head with the frequency of one of my oldest and most disturbing nightmares is, How did men do it? That is, how did they ever manage to enslave womyn so completely while getting womyn to cherish that enslavement so dearly?

Though the first recipient of the letters, the writer's friend Bonnie, never manages to get away from the husband who abuses her, the letters end on a slightly hopeful note when Bonnie's daughter Chrisse continues the correspondence and finally does break up with her own abusive fiancé. The writer encourages her to continue in the alternate path she has chosen:

> My dear, please come to your senses and rejoice that freedom is now yours. And resolve to make the most of that freedom by working to show other Sisters that there *is* a way to live without being terrified of one's shadow twenty four hours each and every day. Now, on with the Revolution!

Perhaps Cornwell's greatest contributions to the body of lesbian feminist writing are her explorations of racism, especially as it occurs within the feminist and the lesbian communities. Alienated from straight men because of their treatment of women and from straight women because of their attachment to their men in spite of that treatment, connection to lesbians, and to a lesser extent to heterosexual feminist women, was extremely important to her. Finding the lesbian community had been like grasping a lifeline for Cornwell, but at the other end of that lifeline was a complex and often problematic group of allies. Almost everything she writes includes some analysis of the racism around her, in women's groups as well as in the larger world. She does not, however, merely repeat media cliches about a white and middle class women's movement. Instead, she chronicles in her down-to-earth style "the outrages I have faced on a daily basis because of the color of my skin." These can be as subtle as a fleeting frightened look on the face of a white feminist in a meeting or as extreme as the murder of George Jackson in prison, and all are confronted head-on with energy and vehemence.

Cornwell's style is direct and earthy. Her essays are not academic exercises, but emotional treatises. She takes liberties with the essay format, quoting her friends as she might quote accepted authorities and using an inexact conversational style, as in "The Black Lesbian in a Malevolent Society," where she says, "Finally, giving weight to my theory, I recalled reading that one Buddhist sect (or some such group) believes that men should spend all of their lives trying to purify their souls. And what about womyn? Well, they believe womyn are automatically in that state of grace or worthiness from the moment they are born." The reader is meant to *feel* these ideas, not try to look up the references.

Cornwell's skill as a theorist lies in large part in her ability and willingness to look at a broad picture of oppression and power and to continue to make it broader. Her own experience of surviving a complex mixture of bias, discrimination, and hate based on her identity as a black lesbian feminist and later as an older woman has given her a savvy grasp of where power lies and the ramifications of its misuse. She deals with issues like racism, homophobia, and sexism in a comprehensive way, including the complexities added by factors such as ageism. Her attention to these factors may be brief, but surgically perceptive: "...in a patriarchal society, the middle-aged womin is about as relevant as the square-earth theory, and even more ridiculed," she writes in "Three for the Price of One."

Another note which recurs throughout Cornwell's essays concerns the media and its influence on American life. As a disenfranchised person, she exhibits a clear mistrust of the major media, especially its reflection of feminism and gay politics. She mentions this in many different essays, but "On Watching a TV Special: Aw Womyn, Why Men?" is devoted to dissecting the mixed motives of network TV through a critique of a 1975 television special about sex roles. She points up the white male heterosexist bias of most mass media, and though her essays were written decades ago, her analysis seems alarmingly up to date. The point she makes repeatedly is that feminists and lesbians need access to their own media, and that reliance on the communications media of the status quo will only lead to misrepresentation and frustration.

The next generation of women and the lack of strong models for them in existing media is another matter of consequence to Cornwell. The feminist movement of the early 1970s ushered in a new way of looking at children's education and of beginning to create a non-sexist curriculum. Cornwell participated in this movement in essays such as "A Portrait of the Artist As a Young Black Dyke," that appeared in *New York Native,* writing:

> One of the most disturbing things I discovered while exploring the possibility of writing for children in the late 60s was the blatant sexism and racism that existed in the field. Perhaps even more disturbing was the open, blunt way writers and editors spoke about the sexism...All too often, I'd hear such statements as "The editor told me to *always* cater to boys and boy characters. Girls will read stories written for boys and with only boy characters, but boys will *never* read stories concerning girls. They really prefer to eliminate all girl characters entirely"...that practice still continues, but perhaps not quite as blatantly....

Cornwell attempted to provide role models for girls by writing

The Girls of Summer, an illustrated book about girls who form a baseball team. Though baseball might seem a traditional enough theme for a children's story, the multiracial aspect of Cornwell's book as well as the fact that it is girls who are gaining the experience of learning through teamwork and pushing the physical limits of their bodies make it quite a radical subject. *The Girls of Summer* was written in the mid 1970s but was not published until 1990, a clear indication of the continued timeliness of non-sexist educational tools.

And Cornwell has had experience with the difficulty of getting published in the mainstream markets. She wrote in "Portrait of the Artist As a Young Black Dyke," that "In 1950, Zora Neale Hurston, writing in *Negro Digest* about 'What White Publishers Won't Print,' stated that she was 'amazed by the Anglo-Saxon's lack of curiosity about the internal lives and emotions of...Negros, and for that matter, any non-Saxon Peoples...above the class of unskilled labor' ....Today...lesbians [especially Black lesbians] have experienced even greater difficulty in getting their lives or their work before the public. In an interview in *Lesbian Tide* some years ago, Gloria Steinem, a founding editor of *Ms.,* said that one reason they had not done an issue on lesbians was because they talked too much about the pain of coming out, and she found it boring...strange she doesn't find all those repetitive stories straight women keep reeling off about their men doing them wrong boring and at times sickening!"

An important section of *Black Lesbian in White America* is a directly autobiographical narrative titled, "First Love and Other Sorrows: Six Pieces from an Autobiography." In it Cornwell gives a lively and pointed third-person account of her early years as a lesbian. These six pieces vividly describe the divided life of closeted lesbians who must juggle family responsibilities (often with family members who do not know about their lesbianism), independence, and longing for romantic love and community. They are a dramatic chronicle of a significant time in lesbian history, perhaps a kind of tribute to the "true stories" which first inspired Cornwell to write.

All of Anita Cornwell's writing comes from deeply held beliefs. As a child struck by the unfairness that "men got all the good stories," she has written the stories of the disenfranchised, the blacks, the women, the lesbians. Her style is direct and down-to-earth, her tone, though angry and passionate, is hopeful. The end of her introduction to *Black Lesbian in White America,* expresses her overriding desire for unity:

> If I might be so bold as to express a heartfelt wish for the future, it would be that all Sisters of all races, creeds, colors, and sexual persuasions might realize the folly of fighting amongst ourselves and band together to confront our common enemy, who continues to wage an unrelenting war against all of us.

—Tina Gianoulis

CREVEL, René

Nationality: French poet, novelist, and art critic. **Born:** Paris, 10 August 1900. **Education:** Attended the Sorbonne and the Faculty of Law. **Career:** Cofounder, *Aventure.* **Died:** Committed suicide, 18 June 1935.

Writings

Novels

Détours (with a portrait of the author by Eugene McCown). Paris, Edition Nouvelle Française, 1924; new edition, preface by Michel Carassou, textes réunis par M. Carassou et Jean-Claude Zylberstein, Paris, Nouvelles Editions Pauvert, 1985.

Mon Corps et Moi. Paris, Editions du Sagittaire, Simon Kra, 1925.

La Mort difficile. Paris, Simon Kra, Coll. européenne, 1926; translated as *Difficult Death* by David Rattray, San Francisco, North Point Press, 1986.

Babylone, roman. Paris, Simon Kra, 1927; translation and afterword as *Babylon, a Novel* by Kay Boyle, illustrated by Max Ernst, San Francisco, North Point Press, 1985.

Etes-vous Fous? Paris, Editions de la Nouvelle Revue Française, 1929.

Le Clavecin de Diderot. Paris, Editions surréalistes, chez José Corti, 1932.

Les Pieds dans le Plat. Paris, Editions du Sagittaire, 1933; translated as *Putting My Foot in It* by Thomas Buckley, foreword by Edouard Roditi, Normal, Illinois, Dalkey Archive Press, 1992.

Le Roman cassé. Paris, Editions Jean-Jacques Pauvert, 1989.

Art Criticism and History

"Merci Paul Klee, Danke Paul Klee," in *Paul Klee.* Ostern, Editions Galerie Alfred Flechtheim, 18 May 1928.

"Préface," in *Max Ernst, ses oiseaux, ses fleurs nouvelles, ses forêts volantes, ses malédictions, ses satanas . . .* Paris, Editions Galerie Georges Bernheim, 1-15 December 1928.

Renée Sintenis. Paris, Edition de la Nouvelle Revue Française, 1930.

Paul Klee. Paris, Editions de la Nouvelle Revue Française, 1930.

Dali ou l'Anti-Obscurantisme. Paris, Editions Surréalistes, José Corti, 1932.

"L'Antitête," in "Bulletin de Souscription pour Tristan Tzara," *L'Antitête.* Paris, Edition des Cahiers Libres, 1933.

Collections

Feuilles éparses. Paris, Broder, Collection Archives 187, Vol. 1, 1965.

Révolution, surréalisme, spontanéité, preface by Jean-Michel Gautier. Paris, Plasma, 1978.

Other

"Acceuil" ("Welcome"; autobiographical essay), in *Dés* (Paris), April 1922.

1830. Englewood, New Jersey, The As Stable Publications (The As Stable Pamphlets), 1926.

With a portrait by Tchelitchew, *L'Esprit contre la raison et autres écrits surréalistes.* Marseille, Editions des Cahiers du Sud, 1927.

Les Soeurs Brontë, filles du vent, illustrated by Marie Laurencin. Paris, Editions des Quatre-Chemins, 1930.

Mr. Knife and Mrs. Fork, translated by Kay Boyle, illustrated by Max Ernst. Paris, The Black Sun Press, 1931.

"The Negress in the Bordel," in *Negro Anthology,* edited by Nancy Cunard. London, Nancy Cunard at Wishattand, 1934.

Accueil, with plates by Dorothea Tanning. Paris, J. Hugues, 1958.

Lettres de désir et de souffrance, preface by Julien Green, présentation par Eric le Bouvier. Paris, Fayard, 1996.

*

Biography: *René Crevel* by Michel Carassou, Paris, Fayard, 1989; *Crevel* by François Buot, Paris, Grasset, 1991.

Critical Sources: *René Crevel, une étude de Claude Courtot avec un choix de textes, cinquante illustrations et une chronologie bibliographique: René Crevel et son temps* by Claude Courtot, Paris, Seghers, 1969; "Analyse d'une interprétation," [on *Le Clavecin de Diderot*] by Jacques Chocheyras, in *Le Surréalisme dans le texte,* edited by Daniel Bougnoux and Jean-Charles Gateau, Grenoble, Publications de l'Université des Langues et Lettres de Grenoble, 1978, 175-183; *René Crevel: le pays des miroir absolus* by Myrna Bell Rochester, Saratoga, California, Anma Libri, 1978; "Theatre: René Crevel," in *Masques,* No. 9-10, summer 1981, 175; "Le Roman familial de René Crevel" by Michel Carassou, 51-58, and *"Les Pieds dans le Plat*: Histoire d'une Publication" by Edouard Roditi, 69-73, in "Dossier Crevel," *Masques,* No. 18, summer 1983; "Les Faces antithétiques de l'érotisme chez René Crevel" by Renée Linkhorn in *French Literary Series* (Amsterdam), Vol. 10, 1983, 80-87; "René Crevel: Rue du Taudis-des-Chômeurs" by Marie-Claire Dumas, in *Revue des Sciences Humaines,* Vol. 64, No. 193, January-March 1984, 129-152; "Epitaphe pour René Crevel par Wolfgang Cordan, témoin du surréalisme en Hollande" by Jose Vovelle, in *Pleine Marge,* 4 December 1986, 52-54; "René Crevel: Ecrire-Mourir: le drame de l'écriture" by Fabienne Cabelguenne, in *Littératures* (Toulouse), Vol. 18, spring 1988, 101-107; *René Crevel, o il surrealismo come revolta* by Paola Decina-Lombardi, Geneva, Slatkine, 1989; "The Identification of Difference: Raymond Roussel, René Crevel and the Colonial Exhibitions of Interwar France" by Elizabeth Rose Ezra (dissertation), Cornell University, 1992; *René Crevel et le roman* by Jean-Michel Devesa, Amsterdam, Rodopi, 1993; "On René Crevel: A French Writer in the Decade of Illusion" by Edouard Roditi, in *Anais: An International Journal,* Vol. 11, 1993, 109-18; "Tombeau de René Crevel et de Benjamin Péret" by Jean-Michel Devesa, in *Oeuvres et Critiques* (Tübingen), Vol. 18, Nos. 1-2, 1993, 83-90; *Alcibiades at the Door: Gay Discourses in French Literature* by Lawrence R. Schehr, Stanford University Press, 1995.

*   *   *

René Crevel was born in 1900, in a comfortable, middle-class family. His father was a printer of songbooks at the Porte-St-Denis, and the family lived on the very staid and bourgeois rue de la Pompe. When his son was 14, Crevel's father committed suicide by hanging, leaving no explanation for his gesture. Crevel's mother made the decision to expose her son to the dead man's body so he would be marked by the monstrous irresponsibility of the gesture. Marked he was, and biographers tend to discuss at great length Crevel's professed abhorrence of his stern, authoritarian mother, a sentiment which apparently never abated, even on her deathbed, as Carassou underscored in his essay in *Masques.* It has been a quick step from Crevel's unhappy family history to psychoanalytical efforts at "explaining" his homosexuality—he hated his mother and her lack of femininity, is one of the common "causes" advanced—and most significantly, his malaise with his sexual identity.

After successful secondary studies, early in his short life, Crevel formed vibrant networks of friends who, like him, were passionately devoted to the arts and to literature. Early on, he was in communication with many of the literary names of the time and he began a rather successful journalistic career, mostly as a critic, passionately interested in art. During this period of his life, Crevel was somewhat of a golden boy in artistic and elegant society circles, invited to opulent parties in aristocratic surroundings, and a constant guest of Robert and Sonia Delaunay, whose always generous hospitality provided him with the sense of home he lacked. He also was very close to Salvador Dali, and even more so, maybe, to Dali's companion, Gala, and wrote several of his works in their Spanish home of Port-Lligat. Marie Laurencin counted among his intimates, and they produced together a rare edition of a biography of the Brontës. He wrote on Klee, on Ernst, on Dali, befriended the Tchelitchews, strove to make the German woman artist Renée Sintenis known to the public, and his works were illustrated by several of these celebrated artists. In the early 1920s, he met the American artist Eugene McCown, who was already quite successful in Paris circles and became his lover; the somewhat tormented relationship only lasted a few years.

His first novel appeared when he was 20 years old, and was already deeply engaged with the emerging surrealist movement. After a rocky transition through Dada, shifting allegiances during the latent strife opposing Breton's new group to their former ally Tzara, to Cocteau—hated by the Breton, and eventually, by Crevel himself—and others considered insufficiently revolutionary, Crevel became a faithful advocate of the surrealist movement. He participated in some of the more flamboyant public actions, which, periodically, landed members of the group in the local police precinct. His loyalty, albeit at times strained, to its forceful and domineering leader, André Breton, whom he revered, remained complete until his death. Thus, from 1924 to 1933, Crevel added his signature to all the surrealist manifestos, even when he had doubts about some of the movement's aspects, and, in 1930, when Breton was attacked at Aragon's behest, he also signed the manifesto of loyalty to him. Crevel, who had in fact moved away from the surrealist group by then, in solidarity, broke with Aragon and the Communist Party. Yet, he still adhered to many of its principles during that crisis, and negotiated the compromise allowing the surrealist presence at the 1935 AEAR (Association of Revolutionary Writers and Artists) Congress.

Siding with Breton, Crevel, at the same time, was troubled by the isolation he foresaw for the surrealist movement, and truly believed in a broad united front of the left in these troubled times that witnessed the rise of fascism. The sacrifice he made to his admiration for Breton cannot be underestimated. In a naive, but sincere way, Crevel was enthusiastic about some of his Communist Party experiences, which put him, a middle-class intellectual, in contact with young workers he truly admired; for instance, when, in 1932 he volunteered as a proofreader for the periodical l'Humanité, correcting contributions from working class readers. At the same time, Crevel kept his independence of thought vis-a-vis the Communist Party's endorsement of socialist realism as the one viable artistic choice. He believed in organizing to better the lot of the working class, despised the bourgeoisie, and was sincerely anti-fascist, but also felt that intellectual freedom had to be safeguarded.

Crevel's independence from many other views is most evident in his last, and arguably, one of his richest works, the novel Les Pieds dans le Plat (translated as Putting my Foot in it), which he had great difficulty publishing. The work was praised by many people who did not understand Crevel's message. As Edouard Roditi pointed out, Pound, for instance, extolled it because it derided the family and the French Republic, not seeing that Crevel's novel was precisely an alarm bell against the Republic's inability to oppose the rise of fascism.

The last ten years of his short life (almost half) were marked by intense physical suffering under the effect of tuberculosis. From 1926 on, Crevel spent much of his time in and out of clinics, consigned to the sanatorium, mostly in Switzerland, where strictly enforced conditions of calm and isolation made him feel dead to the world and imprisoned. This was a long struggle for him, as he was used to the delights of Paris nightlife and art circles, and it took an enormous psychological toll on him, as his letters to his close friend and kindred spirit, Marcel Jouhandeau, attest. In the last three years of his life, intense physical pain was accompanied by a discouraging medical diagnostic, which gave him very little hope for the future.

Crevel had many friends, and he did socialize with other prominent lesbian and homosexual intellectuals and high society figures, like the Duchess, whom he comically calls "Comrade Clermont-Tonnerre," or, closer to him, Nancy Cunard. In Paris, he often saw Gertrude Stein and Max Jacob. Jacob in particular was very dear to him: "A whole evening with Max Jacob, almost a dream," he wrote to a common friend. Crevel's attitude towards homosexuality was at once ambiguous and very courageous. It would have been hard to find milieux less favorable to the serene expression of homosexuality than those he travelled. The surrealist creed, as expressed by Breton, was extraordinarily intolerant in that respect for a movement that made revolution and free love some of its dearest tenets. In a discussion of the subject—labeled "pederastie," as was and still is common in France—Queneau, for instance, was willing to be open-minded, but Breton cut the discussion short, peremptorily declaring that any perversion was acceptable for him, except "that one." This exchange was reproduced in the periodical La Révolution Surréaliste of 15 March 1928, and later, reproduced in the Masques special issue on Crevel.

The Communist Party was no less homophobic; Ehrenbourg's attack on the surrealists is an indication of the prevailing mood. Crevel was thus one of the only surrealists to dare diverge from heterosexuality in an open way—the other one, rarely mentioned in works on the movement, being the lesbian artist Claude Cahun—and one of the rare Communist Party sympathizers to be open about his sexuality. At the same time, it cannot be said that Crevel was happy to be a homosexual. Much of his writing on the subject, usually in the form of confessional fragments within his fictional works, reflects an anguished, tortured, and dissatisfied search for the self that would answer the troubling question of his sexual difference, perceived by him as a deficiency in virility. Crevel also was intimately and romantically involved with women. At the time of his death, he was living on and off with Tota Cuevas, who travelled freely on her own and came back unpredictably, also aware and tolerant of his numerous infidelities with men. Crevel's misgivings may have a lot to do with his profound affection for Jouhandeau, like him openly homosexual, but torn, as he remained married and deeply religious throughout his life. Whether "the mother is to be blamed" or not, it is clear that the poet suffered considerably over the awareness of this difference, while living fully homosexual desires and relationships.

On 18 June 1935, the preparation of the much awaited congress of the AEAR in Paris was interrupted by startling news; René Crevel had been found dead, apparently having taken his own life. All he left was a note to his friends, with these few enigmatic words: "Please cremate me. Disgust." To his companion, he left a longer note apologizing for his gesture. Crevel's dismayed friends and acquaintances tried to sort out the many threads that led to the 35 year old writer's suicide. For many of them, these led to dissent amongst the ranks of the surrealists to which Crevel had contributed so much activism, the continuous crisis between them and the Communist Party, and, it was assumed, Crevel's crushing disenchantment. Persons close to him, like his companion Tota Cuevas, insisted on Crevel's intermittent difficulties with André Breton, whom Crevel lionized, and the events around the AEAR Congress. The surrealists had been excluded from the proceedings, after Breton repeatedly slapped the Soviet delegate, Ilya Ehrenbourg, right in the street for having written, among other niceties, that the surrealists were a bunch of "pederasts and sodomites." Only Crevel's mediation and his friendship with organizers allowed a compromise, with Eluard reading the speech instead of Breton, a speech written by the then dying Crevel himself.

Cuevas and Valentine Hugo surmised that this was not a suicide but an assassination, because of Crevel's outspoken communist politics. And Breton's group threatened more upheaval, because Crevel was going to be buried by the Church, with a crucifix placed on his corpse by Elise Jouhandeau, wife of his close friend Marcel. The family backed down, the confrontation was avoided, and Crevel was buried. Yet, the mystery about the causes of his death was to remain entire, the object of much speculation for decades to come, providing fuel for biographical discussions. But suicide, as a daring act transcending the mediocrity of life, as Buot suggests in his biography, remained a major and constant theme in Crevel's work. Several of his works were blueprints for the final act of taking his own life, down to the method used; more importantly, Crevel had repeatedly signified his profound alienation from and rejection of all of life's little compromises and lost illusions.

René Crevel was a complex and accomplished artist and individual, and the story of his life and his work is infinitely richer than the one mystery of his death by suicide.

—Francesca Canadé Sautman

CULLEN, Countee P(orter)

Pseudonym: Also known as Countee Leroy Porter. **Nationality:** African American poet, editor, novelist, dramatist, and playwright. **Born:** New York City, 30 May 1903; adopted by Reverend Frederick A. Cullen in 1918. **Education:** DeWitt Clinton High School, New York City (accepted into Artista, the scholastic honor society; graduated with several honors), 1922; New York University, New York City (Phi Beta Kappa, 1925), B.A. 1925; Harvard University, Boston, Massachusetts, M.A. in Literature 1926; Sorboone, Paris, France (Guggenheim Fellowship), 1928-30. **Family:** Married Nina Yolande Du Bois (daughter of W. E. B. Du Bois) in 1928 (divorced in Paris, 1930); married Ida Mae Roberson in 1940 (died). **Career:** Held a variety of jobs including columnist

and teacher; editor, *Clinton News,* c. 1920-22, and *The Magpie,* DeWitt Clinton High School, New York City, c. 1921-22; columnist and assistant editor, writing "The Dark Tower" column, *Opportunity: The Journal of Negro Life,* New York, 1926-28; schoolteacher, Frederick Douglas Junior High School (P.S. 139), Harlem, New York City, 1934-46. Frequent contributor to periodicals, including *American Mercury, Bookman, Century, Crisis, Harper's, Nation, Palm, Phylon,* and *Poetry*; member, Alpha Delta Phi, and New York Civic Club. **Awards:** Inter-High School Poetry Contest, second prize, c. 1920; contest winner, Federation of Women's Clubs, 1921; Witter Bynner Undergraduate Poetry Contest, second prize, 1923, 1924, first prize, 1925; *Opportunity* Literary Contest, second prize, 1925; John Reed Memorial Prize, *Poetry,* 1925; Amy Spingarn Award, *Crisis,* 1925; *Palm* Poetry Contest, second prize, 1925; Poetry Contest winner, *Crisis,* 1926; Harmon Foundation Literary Award, from National Association for the Advancement of Colored People (NAACP), 1927. **Died:** New York City, 9 January 1946.

WRITINGS

Poetry

Color. New York, Harper & Brothers, 1925.
Copper Sun. New York and London, Harper & Brothers, 1927.
The Ballad of the Brown Girl, an Old Ballad Retold. New York and London, Harper & Brothers, 1927.
The Black Christ, and Other Poems. New York and London, Harper & Brothers, 1929.
The Medea, and Some Poems. New York and London, Harper & Brothers, 1935.
On These I Stand: An Anthology of the Best Poems of Countee Cullen (selections made by author; includes six poems never before published). New York and London, Harper & Brothers, 1947.
My Soul's High Song: The Collected Writings of Countee Cullen, Voice of the Harlem Renaissance, edited and with an introduction by Gerald Early. New York, Doubleday, 1991.

Collaborations

With Christopher Cat, *The Lost Zoo (A Rhyme for the Young, but Not Too Young).* New York and London, Harper & Brothers, 1940; illustrated by Brian Pinkney, Englewood Cliffs, New Jersey, Silver Burdett Press, 1992.
With Christopher Cat, *My Lives and How I Lost Them,* with drawings by Robert Reid Macguire. New York and London, Harper & Brothers, 1942.

Plays (unpublished)

With Walter Trupin, "Let the Day Perish."
"The Spirit of Peace."
With Harry Hamilton, "Heaven's My Home" (adaptation of *One Way to Heaven*).

Other

Editor, *Caroling Dusk: An Anthology Of Verse By Negro Poets.* New York and London, Harper & Brothers, 1927.

One Way to Heaven (novel). New York and London, Harper & Brothers, 1932.

"The Creative Negro," in *America as Americans See It,* edited by Fred J. Ringel. New York, The Literary Guild, 1932.

With Owen Dodson, "The Third Fourth of July: A One-Act Play," in *Theatre Arts,* Vol. 30, August 1946, 488-493.

*

Adaptations: *Anthology of Negro poetry* (sound recording), Folkways Records, 1954; *An Anthology of Negro Poetry For Young People* (sound recording), Folkways Records, 1958; *Poetry of the Negro* (sound recording), Glory Records, c. 1960; *Poetry of the Black Man* (sound recording), United Artists, 1969; *To Make a Poet Black: The Best Poems of Countee Cullen* (sound recording), Caedmon, 1971; *Anthology of Black Poets* (radio program), Pacifica Radio Archive, 1983; *The Spoken Arts Treasury of 100 Modern American Poets Reading Their Poems* (sound recording), Vol. 8, Spoken Arts, 1985; *Anthology of Negro Poets in the U.S.A. 200 Years* (sound recording), Smithsonian Folkways Records, 1992.

Manuscript Collections: Papers of Countée Cullen, 1921-1969, Amistead Research Center, Dillard University, New Orleans, Louisiana; Beinecke Rare Book and Manuscripts Library, Yale University, New Haven, Connecticut.

Biography: "Countee Cullen" by Arthur P. Davis, in *Dictionary of American Negro Biography,* edited by Rayford W. Logan and Michael R. Winston, New York, Norton, 1982, 148-52; "Countee Cullen" by Alan Shucard, in *Black Writers: A Selection of Sketches from Contemporary Authors,* edited by Linda Metzger, et al., Detroit, Michigan, Gale Research Inc., 1989, 124-28; "Countee Cullen's Uranian 'Soul Windows'" by Alden Reimonenq, in *Journal Of Homosexuality* (New York), Vol. 26, Nos. 2-3, 1993, 143-65.

Bibliography: *A Bio-Bibliography of Countee P. Cullen, 1903-1946* by Margaret Perry, Contributions in Afro-American and African Studies, No. 8, Westport, Connecticut, Greenwood Pub. Co., 1971; *Black American Writers Past and Present: A Biographical and Bibliographical Dictionary* by Theressa Gunnels Rush, et al., Metuchen, New Jersey, Scarecrow Press, 1975, 184-90; *Countee Cullen* by Alan R. Shucard, Twayne's United States Authors Series, Boston, Twayne, 1984.

Critical Sources: *A Many-Colored Coat of Dreams: The Poetry of Countee Cullen* by Houston A. Baker, Jr., Broadside Critics Series, No. 4, Detroit, Michigan, Broadside Press, 1974; *When Harlem Was in Vogue* by David Levering Lewis, New York, Knopf, 1981; "Countee Cullen: A Key to the Puzzle" by Michael L. Lomax, in *The Harlem Renaissance Re-Examined,* Vol. 2, edited by Victor A. Kramer, Georgia State Literary Studies, New York, AMS, 1987, 213-22; "A Spectacle in Color: The Lesbian and Gay Subculture of Jazz Age Harlem" by Eric Garber, in *Hidden From History: Reclaiming the Gay and Lesbian Past,* edited by Martin Bauml Duberman, et al., New York, New American Library, 1989, 318-31; "The Unreadable Black Body: 'Conventional' Poetic Form in the Harlem Renaissance" by Amitai F. Avi-Ram, in *Genders* (New York), 7 March 1990, 32-46; *Gaiety Transfigured: Gay Self-Representation in American Literature* by David Bergman, Madison, Wisconsin, University of Wisconsin Press,

1991; "'My Souls High Song'—The Collected Writings of Countee Cullen Voice of the Harlem Renaissance—Gerald Early" by Darryl Pinckney, in *New York Review of Books,* Vol. 39, No. 5, 5 March 1992, 14-18; "Gay Re-Readings of the Harlem Renaissance Poets" by Gregory Woods, in *Journal Of Homosexuality* (New York), Vol. 26, Nos. 2-3, 1993, 127-42; "Countee Cullen" by Alden Reimonenq, in *The Gay and Lesbian Literary Heritage: A Reader's Companion to the Writers and Their Works, From Antiquity to the Present,* edited by Claude J. Summers, New York, H. Holt, 1995, 185-86.

*   *   *

Countee Cullen was nicknamed the "Poet Laureate" of the Harlem Renaissance. Although his body of works include articles, plays, and reviews, he is famous for his poetry, especially those poems from early in his career. Cullen is also known for adhering to a nineteenth-century, English romantic writing style. Of the British poets, Keats seemed to have influenced Cullen the most. Some common themes found in Cullen's works concern universal human experiences such as love, death, nature, and beauty. His earnest efforts to be acknowledged simply as a poet, not a black poet, lead one to believe he would have shunned being referred to as a black gay poet. Nonetheless, a re-examination of Cullen's traditional writing style reveals poetic references to homosexual as well as racial homosexual relations.

Most critics of Cullen seem to agree that it is essential to understand aspects of the cultural and historical context during his lifetime in order to comprehend his works. During the 1920s and early 1930s, New York City's Harlem burgeoned with great numbers of blacks who migrated from the rural South to the urban North. As a result of this migratory phenomena, as well as other political and economical dynamics, black arts blossomed. This period is widely known as the Harlem Renaissance. Many efforts were made to showcase the richness of and eradicate stereotypes associated with black culture. In "A Spectacle in Color" Eric Garber depicts a thriving Harlem gay and lesbian subculture, yet clearly indicates the frequent, dire consequences of being openly or publicly "out" during this period.

Cullen is best known for highly structured, lyric poetry—though his poems include ballads, children's verse, epitaphs, and sonnets—and his universally accessible subject matter, including disillusionment with and loss of love, images of nature, conflicts with religion, and experiences surrounding friendships. Darryl Pinckney of the *New York Review of Books* states that Cullen's adherence to this structure sometimes compromises the content of his poems. Cullen's use of traditional British aesthetics and universal themes exemplify, in part, his attempts to be known for his humanity, rather than his race. Ironically, he was more often than not remembered as a famous black poet. Perhaps the most cited example of this paradox can be found in the poem "Yet Do I Marvel" in *Color,* Cullen's first—and arguably best—book. "Yet do I marvel at this curious thing / To make a poet black, and bid him sing!" Moreover, this contradiction is also exemplified in many of Cullen's works in which he depicts the social conditions of blacks. In an essay on Cullen, Alden Reimonenq claims that Cullen's conservative style not only contains depictions of the racial climate, but also masks themes prominent in same sex relationships.

Cullen's most concrete reference to homosexuality occurs in the epic poem "The Black Christ." It is poem set in the rural, southern United States and narrated by the brother of the main character, Jim. Jim is wrongfully accused of and lynched for the rape of a white woman, also a friend. In spite of this familial relationship, Gregory Woods notes the narrator's homo-erotic description of his brother in "Gay Re-Readings of the Harlem Renaissance Poets." Upon Jim's death, he is referred to as Lycidas, the beloved college friend of John Milton; Jonathan, the lover of David; and, Patrocles, or Patroclus, the lover of Achilles. Woods further adds that each of these characters had died prematurely and was mourned by the men who loved them. By comparing Jim to other gay characters in history, the narrator invites readers to assume that Jim might also be gay.

In re-reading works for gay content, Woods explicates the relevance Cullen's body of works has to gay literature. By viewing themes of racial oppression under the more general topic of oppression, Woods argues that one can begin to associate, at least on the surface, the similarities it has to topics of sexual oppression. For instance, in "Tableau" from *Color,* local townspeople react to a friendship between two boys; one black, the other white. "From lowered blinds the dark folk stare / And here the fair folk talk / Indignant that these two should dare / In unison to walk." In an associative, gay re-reading of the poem, the homosexual relationship becomes as apparent as the interracial relationship. Reimonenq adds that common interpretations of this poem are as much filled with heterosexism as racism. That is, readers too quickly assume that the two boys are not romantically inclined towards one another. Gays and lesbians who choose to remain abreast of both heterosexual and gay cultures also experience this sort of dual allegiance.

"Heritage," from *Color,* is heralded for its exploration of what Africa means to African-Americans. It is also an exploration of having an allegiance to more than one culture. At one point, the speaker in "Heritage" poignantly addresses Jesus, "With my mouth thus, in my heart / Do I play a double part."

Many of Cullen's poems lament the rejection of those who are considered inferior or different. Consider "Uncle Jim" and "From the Dark Tower," both in *Copper Sun.* Note here the invitation for the reader to consider equality: "The night whose sable breast relieves the stark / White stars is no less lovely being dark." Additionally, Woods remarks that the night time and day light imagery in the later poem can be read as a metaphor for being "closeted," or in the dark, and "coming out," or coming into the light.

Many of Cullen's verses with love themes lack a designation of gender. Examples of these can be found in "At a Parting," "Song in Spite of Myself," and "Therefore, Adieu," each from *The Black Christ and Other Poems,* and "Although I Name You Not..." in *The Medea and Some Poems.* The lack of clearly identified gender lines is consistent with Cullen's attempt to portray universal human experiences. It may seem over-zealous to analyze this seemingly superficial evidence. However, if one coupled a re-examination of Cullen's entire body of works as a whole together with the "closeted" social context in which he wrote, these gender-neutral love poems can be viewed as a significant codification of issues often encountered in homosexual relationships.

Much has been written on Countee Cullen. Most would agree that he wrote his best works at the start of his writing career. Many critics note that Cullen never wrote one great work, even though he personally selected the poems for inclusion in the posthumous volume, *On These I Stand.* Still, given the climate of the effervescent Harlem Renaissance, a gay re-reading of Cullen's works provides an opportunity to venture into parts of the gay

and lesbian subculture of that time period. To re-read Cullen's works for gay content neither diminishes his references to black culture, nor fully explains those to gay culture. Instead, it aids one in beginning to appreciate the intricate, multifaceted richness of Cullen's writings.

—Deborah Turner

CUNNINGHAM, Michael

Nationality: American novelist and author of short stories and nonfiction. **Born:** Cincinnati, Ohio, 6 November 1952. **Education:** Stanford University, B.A. in English 1975; University of Iowa, M.F.A. in writing 1980. **Family:** Companion of psychologist Ken Corbett, from 1988. **Career:** Employed by Carnegie Corporation in New York City, from 1986; contributor to periodicals, including *Atlantic, Los Angeles Times, Mother Jones, New Yorker, New York Times, Paris Review,* and *Redbook.* **Awards:** *Irish Times*-Aer Lingus International Fiction Prize nomination, 1991; Guggenheim Fellowship, 1993; *Lambda* Literary Award, for gay men's fiction, 1995. **Address:** c/o Bantam Books, Inc., 1540 Broadway, New York, NY 10036-4094, U.S.A.

WRITINGS

Novels

Golden States. New York, Crown, 1984.
A Home at the End of the World. New York, Farrar, Straus, and Giroux, 1990; London, Hamish Hamilton, 1991.
Flesh and Blood. New York, Farrar, Straus, and Giroux, and London, Hamish Hamilton, 1995.

Short Stories

"Cleaving," in *Atlantic* (Boston), January 1981.
"Bedrock," in *Redbook* (New York), April 1981.
"Pearls," in *Paris Review* (New York), Fall 1982.
"White Angel," in *New Yorker* (New York), 25 July 1988.
"Ghost Night," in *New Yorker* (New York), 24 July 1989.
"Ignorant Armies," in *The Penguin Book of Gay Short Stories,* edited by David Leavitt and Mark Mitchell. New York, Viking Penguin, 1994.
"Cassandra," in *Best American Gay Fiction, 1996,* edited by Brian Bouldrey. Boston, Little, Brown & Co., 1996 (excerpt from *A Home at the End of the World*).

Uncollected Nonfiction

"After AIDS, Gay Art Aims for a New Reality," in *New York Times* (New York), 26 April 1992.
"If You're Queer and You're Not Angry in 1992, You're Not Paying Attention," in *Mother Jones* (San Francisco), May 1992.
"Straight Arrows, Almost," in *New York Times* (New York), 7 May 1995.

"An Older, Wiser Bad Boy of Dance," in *New York Times* (New York), 10 September 1995.

*

Biography: "Real Writing" by Tracy Young, in *Vogue* (New York), January 1989, 62; "A Novel to Write Home About" by Kelli Pryor, in *New York* (New York), 12 November 1990, 30; "Cunningham's Happy Days" by Stephen Kory Friedman, in *10 Percent* (San Francisco), March/April 1995, 56-61.

Critical Sources: "Giving New Twists and Fresh Style to Time-less Coming-of-Age Theme" by Ruth Doan MacDougall, in *Christian Science Monitor* (Boston), 4 May 1984, 20; "Family Affair" by Elizabeth Royte, in *Village Voice* (New York), 4 September 1984, 52; "Michael Cunningham," in *Contemporary Literary Criticism Yearbook 1984*, edited by Sharon K. Hall, Vol. 34, Detroit, Michigan, Gale, 1985, 40-42; "*A Home at the End of the World*: A Novel by Michael Cunningham" by John Harris, in *Christopher Street* (New York), Vol. 13, No. 9, 1990, 4-5; "Such Good Friends" by Joyce Reiser Kornblatt, in *New York Times Book Review*, 11 November 1990, 12-13; "Menage a la Mode" by Patrick Gale, in *Washington Post Book World*, 9 December 1990, 7; "All in the Family" by David Kaufman, in *Nation* (New York), Vol. 253, No. 1, 1 July 1991, 21-25; "Cunningham, Michael" in *Contemporary Authors*, edited by Susan M. Trosky, Vol. 136, Gale, 1992, 96-97; "Michael Cunningham" by Reed Woodhouse, in *Contemporary Gay American Novelists: A Bio-bibliographical Critical Sourcebook*, edited by Emmanuel S. Nelson, Greenwood Press, 1993, 83-88; "Home Is Where the Hurt Is" by Jonathan Yardley, in *Washington Post Book World*, 2 April 1995, 3; "The Greater the Risk" by Richard Eder, in *Los Angeles Times Book Review*, 9 April 1995, 3, 7; "Brave New Melodrama" by Walter Kirn, in *New York*, Vol. 28, No. 15, 10 April 1995, 72-73; "Suburban Sprawl" by Meg Wolitzer, in *New York Times Book Review*, 16 April 1995, 13; "Revisiting Tolstoy's Formula" by Harlan Greene, in *Lambda Book Report* (Washington, D.C.), Vol. 4, No. 10, May/June 1995, 14; "Dark and Passionate" by Julian Ferraro, in *Times Literary Supplement* (London), No. 4819, 11 August 1995, 20; "Tacky Dress" by Dale Peck, in *London Review of Books*, Vol. 18, No. 4, 22 February 1996, 27-31.

*   *   *

Michael Cunningham emerged as a major gay American author in the early 1990s with the publication of his second novel, *A Home at the End of the World*. His three novels consistently explore the themes of family, friendship, commitment and identity. Cunningham has been widely praised for his prose, sense of place, use of imagery, and psychological insight into his characters. He has also been noted as an author who places his gay and bisexual characters in the mainstream of American life, but who views their homosexuality as only one aspect of their identity.

Golden States, Cunningham's first novel, charts a critical rite of passage in the coming of age of David Stark. Twelve-year old David lives in a single-parent household in a contemporary southern California suburb. Although beset by emotional problems, the Stark family is united by both love and vulnerability. Janet, David's older stepsister, has fled home from her fiancé. Bordering on an emotional collapse, she compulsively swims in the backyard pool at night. David's younger sister is obnoxious and eccentric. His

mother, already ashen and isolated in her forties, retains her wit and sensitivity despite her loneliness.

David Stark, a likeable but insecure protagonist, is unsure of his identity but anxious to protect his family. He frequently retreats into fantasy, where he imagines himself mastering situations that, in reality, he cannot cope with. Stunned by the sudden rejection of his only friend and alarmed by Janet's return to her fiancé in San Francisco, David impulsively embarks on a bizarre journey to rescue her. Symbolically, Cunningham arranges that a benign gay man, Warren, drives David into San Francisco. When Warren kisses David, the boy undergoes a catharsis. The reader, however, can only surmise David's homosexuality from this incident. He returns home without Janet, but proudly displays the Japanese paper umbrella that Warren has given him. Cunningham's treatment of homosexuality in *Golden States* is understated and ambiguous. While David Stark may remind some gay readers of themselves as children, this is not a gay "coming out" story.

A Home at the End of the World, Cunningham's second novel, amplifies the themes in his earlier work. Jonathan Glover, the main protagonist, grows up as an introverted child in 1950s and 1960s suburban Cleveland. In the seventh grade he is transformed when he meets Bobby Morrow, a wild boy who is traumatized by the successive deaths of his entire family. The friendship develops into an adolescent homosexual relationship, but Cunningham's characters are inarticulate and anxious about their sexuality.

Bobby, increasingly quiet and observant as the novel unfolds, becomes Cunningham's device for exploring alternative concepts of family and friendship. After Jonathan goes to college in New York City, Bobby moves into his bedroom and becomes a surrogate son to Alice and Ned Glover. A few years later he is sharing a New York City apartment with Jonathan and Clare, who have established a close but platonic friendship. Clare seduces Bobby and becomes pregnant. The three friends move to a rural home together and share the parenting of Clare's daughter Rebecca. The novel's ending finds the two men alone, now inseparable friends if not lovers, after Clare and Rebecca leave them.

In *A Home at the End of the World* Cunningham explores family and friendship from several perspectives, establishing some maxims along the way. Nuclear families in suburban America, as exemplified by the Glovers and the Morrows, are seen as destructive. Trapped in an unsatisfactory marriage, Alice and Ned Glover have only a distant, shallow connection with their only son. The Morrow family literally self-destructs, abetted by drugs, alcohol, and loneliness. Cunningham also portrays alternative family structures as untenable. Thus friendship is seen as a more enduring commitment than any family ties. However, Cunningham rejects the notion advanced by other contemporary gay writers, notably Ethan Mordden and Felice Picano, that friendships based on shared gay identities can supplant family. Indeed, Jonathan and his frequent sex partner, Erich, have no gay friends and few ties to the gay community.

The characters' struggle to develop positive identities becomes a central theme of *A Home at the End of the World*. The novel is replete with bored, disillusioned, and joyless people disconnected to society and unable to equate sex with love. Jonathan, for example, discovers his homosexuality at an early age, but never integrates it into his life. His relationship with Erich remains an erotic coupling between two lonely men. Fearing that he has contracted HIV from Erich, he keeps his anxieties to himself.

Although family, friendship, and identity are again predominant themes in Cunningham's third novel, *Flesh and Blood*, homosexuality and AIDS play a larger role than in his previous works. This intergenerational saga focuses on an ethnic family whose members struggle to achieve individual identities amidst strong family ties. Constantine Stassos, a poor Greek immigrant, marries Mary, a beautiful Italian-American, but the union is tense from the beginning. As Constantine strives for wealth in the 1950s New York suburbs, he becomes alienated from his wife and three children. His eldest daughter, Susan, escapes his sexual advances through a prestigious but unhappy marriage. She has a secret affair that produces a child, Benjamin. Constantine's only son, Billy, aggravates his father even as a child. Renamed Will while attending Harvard, he gradually accepts his homosexuality, overcomes his low self-esteem, and finds a career as an elementary school teacher in Boston. His relationship with a gentle gay doctor, Harry, is most enduring and loving union of the novel. Constantine's youngest child, Zoe, flees the comfortable suburbs for a squalid life of sex and drugs in New York City. She has an illegitimate child, Jamal, before she discovers that she is infected with HIV.

Zoe befriends a wise and witty transvestite, Cassandra, who embodies the limitless possibilities of family and friendship in *Flesh and Blood*. Cassandra acts as Jamal's mentor and surrogate mother when Zoe becomes sick with AIDS. Mary, now divorced from Constantine, is transformed into a more accepting and liberated person through her surprising friendship with Cassandra.

Constantine remarries, erects a gaudy Long Island mansion, and lavishes his attention on his grandson, Benjamin. But Benjamin tragically drowns after he mistakenly thinks that Constantine has discovered his infatuation with his cousin Jamal. By the novel's end, each surviving protagonist achieves a degree of self-knowledge and contentment, and the Stassos family is intact but forever altered.

Cunningham's treatment of gay characters, relationships, and themes in *Flesh and Blood* is more articulated, compassionate and realistic than in his previous novels. Cassandra, Will, and Harry are genuine characters who struggle to incorporate their sexual orientation into their identity. Will and Harry's contented life together, while subject to inevitable uncertainties and failings, is contrasted with the unhappy marriage of Susan. The theme of "coming out" is examined in two situations separated by a generation. Will overcomes psychological, societal, and family pressures as he gradually accepts his homosexuality in his twenties. The uncertainty, loneliness and eventual liberation that he undergoes is vividly portrayed for readers of all sexual orientations. In contrast, Benjamin's tragic death a generation later occurs because he cannot admit, even to himself, that he is gay.

Cunningham's second and third novels both enjoyed widespread critical acclaim in both the gay and mainstream press. Both works were also commercial successes that demonstrate the appeal of novels with gay themes and characters. With their publication Cunningham joins a generation of gay novelists, including David Leavitt, Christopher Bram, Lev Raphael, and Gale Patrick, who mesh gay themes and characters with the larger concerns of a straight world. For these writers, homosexuality is a lens through which the world is viewed, not a world unto itself. Cunningham's work, however, continues a gay literary heritage categorized by strong autobiographical elements, a preference for urban life and settings, and an ability to see the unusual as ordinary.

—Joseph M. Eagan

D

D'ANNUNZIO, Gabriele

Nationality: Italian novelist, dramatist, poet, short story writer, and journalist. **Pseudonym:** Also wrote as Il Duca Minimo, Bull Calf, Vere de Vere, Lila-Biscuit, Miching-Mallecho, Happermouche, Myr, Il Barone Cicogna, and Angelo Cocles. **Born:** Pescara (Abruzzi), 12 March 1863. **Education:** At home by private tutors; Reale Collegio Cicognini boarding school, Prato, 1874-81; University of Rome, 1881. **Military Service:** Served in Italian cavalry, 1889-90; active service 1915-18; Comandante of Fiume, 1919-21. **Family:** Companion of Elda Zucconi ("Lalla"), 1881-83; married Duchess Maria Hardouin di Gallese, 1883 (separated 1891); three sons; companion of Olga Ossani, 1884; companion of Barbara Leoni (Elvira), 1887-92; companion of Princess Maria Gravina Cruyllas di Romacca, 1890-96; one daughter and one son, Gabriele; companion of actress Eleanora Duse ("Ermione"), 1895-04; companion of Alessandra di Rudini ("Nike"), 1903-07; companion of Guiseppina Mancini ("Armaranta"), 1907-08; companion of Natalia de Goloubeff ("Donatella"), 1908-15; companion of Olga Levi ("Venturina"), 1916-38. **Career:** Freelance reporter and society columnist for fashionable newspapers in Rome, 1881-88; reporter, *Tribuna*, to 1888; Member of Parliament, 1898-90. Political activist during World War I; President, Italian Royal Academy, 1937. **Awards:** Named Prince of Montenevoso, by Benito Mussolini, 1924. **Died:** Of a cerebral hemorrhage at Il Vittoriale degli Italiani, in Gardone, Lake Garda, Italy, 1 March 1938.

WRITINGS

Novels

Giovanni Episcopo. Naples, 1892; as *Episcopo & Company,* translated by M.L. Jones, Chicago, 1896.
L'Innocente. Naples, 1892; as *The Intruder,* translated by A. Hornblow, Boston, 1897.
Il piacere. Milan, 1889; as *The Child of Pleasure,* translated by G.H. Harding, New York, 1898.
Trionfo della morte. Milan, 1894; as *Triumph of Death,* translated by A. Hornblow, Boston, 1896.
Le vergini delle rocce. Milan, 1896; as *Maidens of the Rocks,* translated by A. H. Antona and G. Antona, Boston, 1898.
Il fuoco. Milan, 1900; as *The Flame of Life,* translated by Gustavo Tosti, Boston, 1900.
Forse che si forse che no. Milan, 1910; revised, 1932.

Short Stories

Terra vergine. Rome, 1882; revised, 1884.
Il libro delle vergini. Rome, 1884.
San Pantaleone. Florence, 1886; revised and enlarged as *Le novelle della Pescara,* Milan, 1902; as *Tales of My Native Town,* translated by R. Mantalini, New York, 1920.
La Leda senza cigno (serial), in *Corriere della sera,* 1913.

Autobiographies

Contemplazione della morte. Milan, 1912.
Notturno. Milan, 1921.
Le faville del maglio:
Volume 1, *Il venturiero senza ventura e altri studii del vivere inimitabile.* Milan, 1924.
Volume 2, *Il compagno dagli occhi senza cigli e altri studii del vivere inimitabile.* Milan, 1928.
Cento e cento e cento e cento pagine del libro segreto di Gabriele D'Annunzio tentato di morire (as Angelo Cocles). Milan, 1935.

Stage Plays

Sogno d'un mattino di primavera. Rome, 1897.
La citta morta. Milan, 1898; as *The Dead City,* translated by A. Symons, London, 1900.
Sogno d'un tramonto d'autunno. Milan, 1898.
La Gioconda. Milan, 1899; as *Gioconda,* translated by A. Symons, New York, 1901.
La gloria. Milan, 1899.
Francesca da Rimini. Milan, 1902; translated by A. Symons, London, 1902.
La figlia di Iorio. Milan, 1904; as *The Daughter of Jorio,* translated by C. Porter, A. Henry, and P. Isola, Boston, 1907.
La fiaccola sotto il moggio. Milan, 1905.
Piu che l'amore. Milan, 1907.
La Nave. Milan, 1908.
Fedra. Milan, 1909.
Le martyre de Saint Sebastien. Paris, 1911.
La crociata degli innocenti. Milan, 1911.
La Parisina La Pisanelle ou la mort parfumee. Paris, 1913.
Cabiria (movie script). Turin, 1914.
Il ferro. Milan, 1914.

Poetry

Primo vere. Chieti, 1879; revised, Lanciano, 1880.
In memoriam. Pistoia, 1880.
Canto novo. Rome, 1882; revised, Milan, 1896.
Intermezzo di rime. Rome, 1884; revised as *Intermezzo,* Naples, 1894.
Isaotta Guttadauro ed altre poesie. Rome, 1886; revised as *L'Isotteo—La Chimera (1885-1888),* Milan, 1890.
Elegie romane (1887-1891). Bologna, 1892.
Odi navali. Naples, 1892; augmented edition published in *Poema paradisiaco,* Milan, 1893.
Poema paradisiaco—Odi navali—1891-1893 (includes augmented edition of *Odi navali*), Milan, 1893.
Laudi del cielo del mare della terra e degli eroi:
Volume 1, *Maia.* Milan, 1903.
Volume 2, *Elettra—Alcyone.* Milan, 1904.
Le canzoni della gesta d'oltremare. Laudi del cielo del mare della terra e degli eroi. Libro IV. Merope. Milan, 1912.

Other

Opera omnia, 49 Vols. Milan, 1927-1936.

Roma senza lupa: cronache mondane 1884-1888 (journalism). 1938.

Solus ad solam (journal entries, 8 September-5 October 1908). 1939.

Taccuini (notebooks). 1965.

Altri Taccuini (notebooks). 1976.

*

Manuscript Collections: *Il Vittoriale degli Italiani,* Gardone, Lake Garda, Italy.

Biography: *The Poet as Superman: A Life of Gabriele D'Annunzio* by Anthony Rhodes, London, 1959; "D'Annunzio, Gabriel" by Giuseppe Prezzolini, in *Columbia Dictionary of Modern European Literature,* edited by Jean Albert Bede and William B. Edgerton, New York, 1980; *D'Annunzio* by Paolo Altari, Turin, UTET, 1983; "D'Annunzio, Gabriel" by M. Carlino and P. Craveri, in *Dizionario Biografico degli Italiani* (Rome), Vol. 32, 1986, 626-655.

Critical Sources: *Twentieth Century Literary Criticism,* Vol. 6, 1982, Vol. 40, 1991, Detroit, Gale Research; *Gabriele D'Annunzio: Volti e maschere di un personaggio* edited by Simona Costa, Florence, Sansoni, 1988; *Gabriele D'Annunzio* by Charles Klopp, Boston, Twayne Publishers, 1988; "Gabriele D'Annunzio" by Charles Klopp, in *European Writers, Vol. 8: The Twentieth Century,* edited by George Stade, New York, Charles Scribner's Sons, 1989; *Gabriele D'Annunzio: The Dark Flame* by Paolo Valesio, translated by Marilyn Migiel, New Haven and London, Yale University Press, 1992; *D'Annunzio and the Great War* by Alfredo Bonadeo, Madison, New Jersey, Fairleigh Dickinson University Press, 1995.

*   *   *

Acknowledged as the most important figure in Italian literature of the late nineteenth and early twentieth centuries, some critics argue that D'Annunzio's work and life reflect the influence of Aestheticism and Decadence. Others, most recently Paolo Valesio, reject these labels, especially that of gynephobia, as they reevaluate D'Annunzio's continuing influence on Italian culture. Wildly popular during his lifetime for his commercial success, D'Annunzio also was enthusiastically admired by the Italian middle-class for whom, according to Charles Klopp in *Gabriele D'Annunzio,* this "man of action" articulated a social and political ideology. Discussing D'Annunzio's immense popularity, Giuseppe Prezzolini writes that many Italians suffered from "D'Annunzianism," the "Italian disease" of imitating his extravagant lifestyle. They copied his neckwear and goatee, adopted his diction and scorn for creditors, walked dogs with languorous eyes, and associated with ladies with high sounding names.

D'Annunzio began shaping this persona in his teens when, at Cicognini, the Jesuit school near Florence, he exchanged his Abruzzi dialect and manners for the more sophisticated Tuscan; he published his first poetry, *Prima Vere,* at the age of 16. During the 1880s in Rome, D'Annunzio used his role as a society reporter to perfect his metamorphosis into what some have called a "fop" or dandy. Often writing under a pseudonym, a penchant he extended by immediately renaming women acquaintances, D'Annunzio sharpened his writing and shamelessly blended his flamboyant image and experiences into his sensual poetry and stories; the frank depiction of his seduction of wife Maria Hardouin, here named "Yella," in *Intermezzo de rime* (1883), brought accusations of pornography, but boosted sales. In his biographical essay in *European Writers,* Klopp remarks that henceforth, D'Annunzio "treated all that he did in the 'text' of life primarily as material for his writing."

D'Annunzio's literary career flourished in overlapping phases, each dominated by a genre. Following sensual verse and naturalistic short stories, the second phase began with the publication of his first novel, *Il piacere* (1889), an examination of the sexual and sensual pleasures of the facile lover Count Andrea Spinelli, a fictionalized D'Annunzio. His other novels, including the psychological study *L'innocente,* the basis for Luchino Visconti's film (1979), also incorporate autobiographical elements and descriptions of the crumbling urban world of the aristocrats and reflect D'Annunzio's growing interest in Nietzsche's "Superman."

Prior to ending his relationship with Maria Gravina Cruyllas, D'Annunzio met the international actress and diva Eleanora Duse, whom he renamed "Ermione." Like many of D'Annunzio's lovers, she served as his muse. Their tempestuous love affair, detailed in the novel *Il fuoco* (1900), and D'Annunzio's election to Parliament in 1897, mark the beginning of D'Annunzio's writing for the theater. Klopp points out the appropriateness of this inevitable marriage of theater and politics. For the always dramatic D'Annunzio, however, it was politics that would eventually gain supremacy. During this theater phase, D'Annunzio revealed his plan for an Italian national theater. His dramas, many written as starring vehicles for Duse, are noted for their sensational, often mythical, plots with "Superfemmina" or sexually dominant heroines. Klopp ranks Basiliola Faledro, in *La nave* (1908), as D'Annunzio's most outrageously proto-camp "Superfemmina."

In 1910, with Duse already replaced, the ever-extravagant D'Annunzio eluded his creditors by fleeing to France. In 1911, he accepted a commission from Ida Rubenstein, the dancer/mime of the Ballets Russes, to create a role for her. Written in French, *Le Martyre de Saint-Sebastien,* with music by Claude Debussy, profuse costumes and elaborate sets by Leon Bakst, and directed by Michel Fokine, premiered with Rubenstein dancing the title role on 22 May 1911 at the Theater du Chatelet. Several days before the premier, the Archbishop of Paris placed all D'Annunzio's work on the Index; hence most of literary and artistic Paris attended, including an enthusiastic Marcel Proust and Count Robert de Montesquiou, the flamboyant aesthete and wealthy patron of the arts who served as the model for Proust's homosexual Baron de Charlus. Part cantata, part opera, part ballet, *Le Martyre de Saint Sebastien* uses the D'Annunzian mixture of the sacred and the profane as the androgynous protagonist, portrayed by a Jewish woman, represents saint/Christ and Adonis/superman. At the ballet's end, sentenced to death for his Christianity, Sebastian, often regarded as the homosexual's saint, dies in a religious, sadomasochistic ecstasy as he is pierced by his own soldiers' arrows.

While in France, D'Annunzio wrote additional drama and poetry and continued romantic liaisons. Through Ida Rubenstein he met Romaine Brooks, lover and longtime friend of Natalie Barney; Brooks painted several of his portraits, one while he wrote Saint Sebastian and another in Venice. When he returned to Italy in 1915, D'Annunzio's activities became increasingly political. His military exploits—flying over enemy Vienna to drop propaganda leaflets and leading a torpedo boat raid into blockaded Buccari harbor—increased his popularity and, probably, his narcissism. Immediately after the war, D'Annunzio led volunteer troops in the capture of Fiume (Rijeka in present day Croatia); elected the illegal city-state's Comandante, he delivered political speeches and, according to Klopp, "invented much of what became the mottoes and rituals of Mussolini's Fascism." Meanwhile, his writing entered a final phase. In 1916, while convalescing in the Cassetta Rossa in Venice from the loss of his right eye due to an airplane accident, D'Annunzio wrote the successful *Notturno* (1921), a melancholy autobiographical meditation on the sensory world and death, which set the characteristics of future writings.

After Fiume, D'Annunzio retired to his villa Vittoriale degli Italiani on Lake Garda, which he donated to the Italian government in 1923. He continued to write, often sending political letters to newspapers, while editing the 49 volumes of the National Edition of his complete works, financed by Mussolini. The autobiographical *Libro Segreto* (1935), published shortly before his death under the pseudonym Angelo Cocoes, reflects the fears and preoccupations with death of an isolated old man, now writing to examine the meaning of his life.

—Judith C. Kohl

DAVYS, Sarah. *See* **MANNING, Rosemary.**

DELANY, Samuel R.

Nationality: African-American novelist and writer. **Born:** New York City, 1 April 1942. **Education:** Dalton School, Bronx High School of Science; City College of New York, 1960, 1962-63. **Family:** Married poet Marilyn Hacker, 24 August 1961 (divorced, 1980); children: Iva Alyxander. **Career:** Musician, performer, and writer; Butler Professor of English, State University of New York at Buffalo, 1975; Senior Fellow, Center for Twentieth Century Studies, University of Wisconsin, Milwaukee, 1977; Senior Fellow, Society for the Humanities, Cornell University, 1987; professor of Comparative Literature, University of Massachusetts, Amherst, from 1988. **Awards:** Nebula Award, Science Fiction Writers of America, 1966, 1967 (2), 1969; Hugo Award, 1970; American Book Award nomination, 1980; Pilgrim Award, Science Fiction Research Association, 1985. **Address:** c/o Henry Morrison, Inc. P.O. Box 235, Bedford Hills, New York 10507, U.S.A.

WRITINGS

Fiction

The Jewels Of Aptor. New York, Ace Books, 1962; London, Gollancz, 1968; complete edition with introduction by Don Hausdorff, Boston, Gregg Press, 1976.

Captives of the Flame. New York, Ace Books, 1963; revised as *Out of the Dead City,* New York, Sphere Books, 1968.

The Towers of Toron. New York, Ace Books, 1964.

City of a Thousand Suns. New York, Ace Books, 1965.

The Ballad of Beta-2. New York, Ace Books, 1965.

Empire Star. New York, Ace Books, 1966; with introduction by David G. Hartwell, Boston, Gregg Press, 1977.

Babel-17. New York, Ace Books, 1966; with introduction by Robert Scholes, Boston, Gregg Press, 1976.

The Einstein Intersection. New York, Ace Books, 1967; London, Bollancz, 1968; complete edition, New York, Ace Books, 1972.

Nova. Garden City, New York, Doubleday, 1968; with introduction by Algis Budrys, Boston, Gregg Press, 1977.

The Fall of the Towers (contains *Captives of the Flame, The Towers of Toron,* and *City of a Thousand Suns*). New York, Ace Books, 1970; with introduction by Joseph Milicia, Boston, Gregg Press, 1977.

Driftglass: Ten Tales of Speculative Fiction. Garden City, New York, Doubleday, 1971; introduction by Robert Thurston, Boston, Gregg Press, 1977.

The Tides of Lust. New York, Lancer Books, 1973; title restored with restorations of text and "Bibliographical Note" as *Equinox,* New York, Rhinoceros Books, 1994.

Dhalgren. New York, Bantam, 1975; introduction by Jean Mark Gawron, Boston, Gregg Press, 1977; foreword by William Gibson, Hanover, New Hampshire, University Press of New England for Wesleyan University Press, 1996.

The Ballad Of Beta 2. New York, Ace Books, 1975; introduction by David G. Hartwell, Boston, Gregg Press, 1977.

Triton. New York, Bantam Books, 1976; as *Trouble On Triton: An Ambiguous Heterotopia,* with foreword by Kathy Acker, Hanover, University Press of New England for Wesleyan University Press, 1996.

Empire: A Visual Novel, illustrations by Howard V. Chaykin. New York, Berkley Publishing, 1978.

Tales of Nèverÿon. New York, Bantam, 1979; Hanover, University Press of New England for Wesleyan University Press, 1993.

Distant Stars. New York, Bantam, 1981.

Nèverÿona, or, The Tale of Signs and Cities. New York, Bantam Books, 1983; as *Nèverÿona, or, The Tale of Signs and Cities, Some Informal Remarks towards the Modular Calculus, Part Four,* Hanover, University Press of New England, 1993.

Flight from Nèverÿon. New York, Bantam, 1985; Hanover, Wesleyan University Press, published by University Press of New England, 1994.

Stars in My Pocket Like Grains of Sand. New York, Bantam Books, 1984.

The Complete Nebula Award-Winning Fiction. New York, Bantam, 1986.

The Bridge of Lost Desire. New York, Arbor House, 1987; as *Return to Nèverÿon,* Middletown, Connecticut, Wesleyan University, published by University Press of New England, 1994.

The Star Pits. New York, Tor Books, 1989.

They Fly at çiron. New York, Incunabula, 1992.

The Mad Man. New York, Richard Kasak Book, 1994.

Hogg. Normal, Illinois, Black Ice Books, 1994.

Atlantis: Three Tales. Middletown, Wesleyan University, Hanover, Published by University Press of New England, 1995.

Flight From Nèverÿon. New York, Bantam, 1985; Hanover, Wesleyan University Press, published by University Press of New England, 1994.

Nonfiction

The Jewel-Hinged Jaw: Notes on the Language of Science Fiction.
Elizabethtown, New York, Dragon Press, 1977; revised edition,
Berkley Publishing, 1978.

*The American Shore: Meditations on a Tale of Science Fiction by
Thomas M. Disch—"Angouleme."* New York, Dragon Press,
1978.

Heavenly Breakfast: An Essay on the Winter of Love (memoir).
New York, Bantam, 1979.

Starboard Wine: More Notes on the Language of Science Fiction.
New York, Dragon Press, 1984.

*The Motion of Light in Water: Sex and Science Fiction Writing in
The East Village, 1957-1965.* New York, Arbor House/William
Morrow, 1988, 1990; unredacted edition, New York, Richard
Kasak, 1993.

*Wagner/Artaud: A Play of Nineteenth and Twentieth Century Criti-
cal Fictions.* Ansatz Press, 1988.

Straits of Messina (essays). Serconia Press, 1989.

*Silent Interviews: On Language, Race, Sex, Science Fiction, and Some
Comics; A Collection of Written Interviews.* Hanover, Wesleyan
University Press, University Press of New England, 1994.

Longer Views: Extended Essays, introduction by Ken James.
Hanover, University Press of New England, 1996.

*

Biography: *Dictionary of Literary Biography,* Detroit, Gale Research, Vol. 8, *Twentieth-Century American Science Fiction Writers,* 1981, Vol. 33, *Afro-American Fiction Writers after 1955,* 1984;
Samuel R. Delany by Jane Branham Weedman, Starmont House,
1982; *Samuel R. Delany* by Seth McEvoy, Ungar, 1984.

Interviews: *Alive and Writing: Interviews with American Authors
of the 1980s,* edited by Larry McCaffery and Sinda Gregory,
Urbana, University of Illinois Press, 1987.

Bibliography: *Samuel R. Delany: A Primary and Secondary Bibliography, 1962-1979* by Michael W. Peplow and Robert S.
Bravard, G. K. Hall, 1980.

Critical Sources: *The Delany Intersection: Samuel R. Delany
Considered as a Writer of Semi-Precious Words* by George Edgar
Slusser, Borgo, 1977; *Dream Makers: The Uncommon People Who
Write Science Fiction,* edited by Charles Platt, Berkley Books, 1980;
*Science Fiction Writers: Critical Studies of the Major Authors from
the Early Nineteenth Century to the Present Day,* edited by E. F.
Bleiler, Scribner, 1982.

*   *   *

Samuel R. Delany's life and writings bridge several chasms in
contemporary culture: that between African and white America;
that between heterosexual, bisexual, and homosexual; and that between science, science fiction, fantasy, and avant garde writing.
Delany has rigorously refused to accept most of the existing sociological, epistemological, sexual, literary, or political categories.
Indeed he has written to dissolve, displace, even destroy such categories.

His biography abounds in mixtures. Born in Harlem to a father
who was a wealthy funeral director and a mother who worked for
the New York Public Library, he was driven to the exclusive Park
Avenue Dalton Elementary School by a chauffeur. Delany remembers the drive as a "virtually ballistic trip through a
sociopsychological barrier of astonishingly restrained violence."
Later he discovered he differed from the other students not only
by his race but also by his dyslexia, a condition that reaffirmed
for him the completely artificial constructions of society, sexuality, and language.

In 1956 Delany enrolled in Bronx High School of Science. Studying math, physics, music, and literature, he developed his interest
in both science and writing. Delany won prizes for his stories,
wrote for the school magazine, and received a fellowship to the
Bread Loaf Writer's Conference in Vermont during the summer of
1960. In the fall of 1961 Delany enrolled in City College of New
York, where he worked with Marilyn Hacker (also from Dalton
School and Bronx High) on *Prometheus,* the CCNY literary magazine. "In mid-June Marilyn became pregnant with our second
sexual experiment," he recalled in his autobiographical *Motion of
Light.* They went to Michigan, whose laws allowed them to marry,
but the child miscarried.

After the miscarriage in October 1961, Delany began work on
his first novel, *The Jewels of Aptor* (1962), which Hacker's boss
at Ace books promptly published. Novels followed rapidly, as
Delany turned out nine books in as many years, all published by
Ace Books. During the 1960s and later, Hacker and Delany shared
not only a child but also a remarkable New York culture of music,
theater, writing, and liberating sexual habits. In their writings, the
couple blended the boundaries between music, theater, art, sex,
and life. They put on a play at the Coffee House, a gallery and
playhouse in the East Village. In Hacker's *Perseus: An Exercise
for Three Voices* at the Coffee Gallery in April 1961, she read
"Helen," with the closing lines "...the sea is the only lover" while
Delany read his "Silent Monologue for Lefty." The mixture of
races, politics, media forms, and sexual energies informed the lives
of both as Delany and Hacker constantly expanded their repertoire.

In 1971, Delany passed partly beyond the science fiction market into the mainstream when Doubleday published his short stories, *Driftglass: Ten Tales of Speculative Fiction.* Bantam, another
larger press, published *Dhalgren* (1975), *Triton* (1976), *Distant
Stars* (1981), and *Stars in My Pocket Like Grains of Sand* (1984).
Many consider *Dhalgren* his masterpiece. Pioneering the New
Wave in science fiction, Dhalgren brought poetry, linguistics, and
homosexuality into the genre. Critics compared Delany's masterpiece to such models as James Joyce's *Finnegan's Wake,* but
Proust's *Remembrance of Things Past,* deSade's *The Hundred
Twenty Days of Sodom,* and Marilyn Hacker's poetry play all
played an equally important role in empowering Delany's breakthrough.

Delany's sexuality did not immediately appeal to all gay
liberationists, nor did it excite his closeted or straight science fiction readers, who had difficulty with what some called "homosexual pornography." *The Tides of Lust* (also titled Equinox), first
published in a porn series by Lancer Books, went virtually unnoticed by the critical or gay community. Gregory Renault ten years
later found it "a chaos of sexual episodes, a survey of sexual possibilities: hetero- and homosexual couples and foursomes, children
and adults, whites and blacks in various combinations, necrophilia,
incest, rape, sadism, masochism, complete with feathers, sexual
use of excrement and urine, and a sacrilegious orgy...a spectacle
both attractive and disgusting." Delany also explores what some

call sado-masochism in *Hogg,* finished in 1973 but only published in 1994.

Delany examined his own sexuality and society in his autobiographical *The Motion of Light in Water, Sex and Science Fiction Writing in the East Village.* In *Mad Man: A Novel* (1994), Delany mixes the worlds of the academy, homeless street kids, and AIDS. Delany denounces most of the AIDS research and publicity organizers for not pursuing questions of how the disease has spread. Instead, he points out that "vast amounts of hearsay are collected, tabulated, and presented as knowledge and fact."

Delany's theories about sex, race, epistemology, writing, politics, and poetry appear in forms other than his fiction. Wesleyan University Press collected his *Silent Interviews* (1994) and in *Wagner/Artaud: A Play of Nineteenth and Twentieth Century Critical Fictions* (1988) he displays his virtuosity in literary cultural form as he updates Nietzsche with Artaud. Delany describes his own encounters with madness in his autobiography; he seems to have no more interest in being sane than in being white or straight.

In 1993 Delany delivered a keynote address at the Boston Outwrite Lesbian and Gay Writers conference. Here he attempted to summarize the vast unexplored corridors of sexuality that had been swept aside both by the academic establishment and by many conventional gay liberationists. He struggled to recover repressed or repelled knowledge of people like Billy, a Times Square hustler who had died of AIDS. Delany pleaded guilty to trying to put "the sex back into homosexuality." "Sexual experience," he explained, "is still largely outside language" and we must never assume that "everything is ever articulated." The gay experience in particular, "distinct specific and individual for every one of us, has always resided outside language." In his writing, Delany resembles deSade or Gertrude Stein in tapping into the constant flow of words that the writer can use to articulate the unspoken.

—Charley Shively

DELARUE-MARDRUS, Lucie

Nationality: French poet, novelist, playwright, essayist, biographer, and journalist. **Born:** Lucie Delarue in Honfleur, Normandy, 3 November 1874. **Education:** Institut Normal Catholique, Paris. **Family:** Married Dr. Joseph-Charles Mardrus in 1900 (divorced 1915); lover of Natalie Clifford Barney; companion of the singer Germaine de Castro, also referred to as Victoria Gomez, from 1932. **Career:** Self-supporting writer, journalist, and lecturer. Contributed to many periodicals, including *Comoedia, Fantasio, Le Figaro, Gil Blas,* and *Le Journal.* **Died:** Château-Gontier, Mayenne, from crippling rheumatism and pneumonia, 26 April 1945.

Writings

Poetry

Occident. Paris, Editions de la Revue Blanche, 1901.
Ferveur. Paris, Editions de la Revue Blanche, 1902.
Horizons. Paris, Fasquelle, 1904.
Figure de Proue. Paris Fasquelle, 1908

Souffles de Tempête. Paris, Fasquelle, 1918.
A Maman. Paris, Charpentier et Fasquelle, 1920.
Poèmes mignons pour les enfants. Paris, Gédalge, 1929.
Les Sept Douleurs d'octobre. Paris, Ferenczi, 1930.
Mort et printemps. Paris, A. Messein, 1932.
Temps présents. Paris, Cahiers d'Art et d'Amitié, 1939.
Choix de poèmes. Derniers vers inédits. Traductions. Paris, A. Lemerre, 1951.
Nos secrètes amours. Paris, Les Iles, 1957.

Novels

Marie, fille-mère. Paris, Fasquelle, 1908.
Le Roman de six petites filles. Paris, Fasquelle, 1909.
L'Acharnée. Paris, Fasquelle, 1910.
Comme Tout le Monde. Paris, Tallandier, 1910.
Par Vents et marées. Paris, Fasquelle, 1910.
Tout l'amour. Paris, Fasquelle, 1911.
L'Inexpérimentée. Paris, Fasquelle, 1912.
La Monnaie de Singe. Paris, Charpentier, 1912.
Douce Moitié. Paris, Fasquelle, 1912.
Un Cancre. Paris, E. Fasquelle, 1914; juvenile edition, Borrelier, 1931.
Un Roman civil en 1914. Paris, Charpentier, 1916.
Deux Amants. Paris, Charpentier, 1917.
Toutoune et son amour. Paris, Albin Michel, 1919.
L'Ame aux trois visages. Paris, E. Fasquelle, 1919; juvenile edition, Gédalge, 1928.
L'Apparition. Paris, Ferenczi, 1921.
L'Ex-voto. Paris, E. Fasquelle, 1922; second edition, illustrated with photographs from the film *Le Diable au Coeur,* adapted from the novel, Paris, Tallandier, 1929.
Le Pain Blanc. Paris, Ferenczi, 1923
La Mère et le fils. Paris, Ferenczi, 1924.
La Cigale, with 28 original woodcuts by Renefer. Paris, A. Fayard, 1924.
A Côté de l'Amour. Paris, Oeuvres Libres, vol. 12, 1922.
Hortensia dégénéré. Paris, Oeuvres Libres, vol. 50, 1925.
Graine au vent. Paris, L'Illustration, 1925; adapted for the cinema by Maurice Gleize, 1943.
La Petite fille comme ça. Paris, Ferenczi, 1927.
Rédalga. Paris, Ferenczi, 1928.
Amanit. Paris, L'Illustration, 1929.
Le Beau Baiser. Paris, Ferenczi, 1929.
Anatole. Paris, Ferenczi, 1930.
L'Ange et les pervers. Paris, Ferenczi, 1930; as *The Angel and the Perverts,* translated by Anna Livia, New York, NYU Press, 1995.
L'Amour à la mer. Paris, Lemerre, 1931.
L'Autre Enfant. Paris, Ferenczi, 1931.
François et la liberté. Paris, Ferenczi, 1933.
L'Enfant au Coq. Paris, Ferenczi, 1934.
Une Femme mûre et l'amour. Paris, Ferenczi, 1935.
Tout l'Amour. Paris, Ferenczi, 1935.
Chênevieil. Paris, Ferenczi, 1936.
L'Amour Attend. Paris, L'Illustration, 1936.
Roberte no. 10.530. Paris, Ferenczi, 1937.
L'Hermine Passant. Paris, Ferenczi, 1938.
Fleurette, illustrated by L.-P. Pouzargues, Paris, L'Illustration, 1938.
La Girl. Paris, Ferenczi, 1939.

L'Homme du rêve. Paris, Tallandier, 1939.
La Perle magique. Paris, Baudinière, 1940.
Verteil et ses amours. Editions Self, 1943.
Le Roi des reflets. Paris, Ferenczi, 1944.

Short Stories

Le Château tremblant. Paris, Ferenczi, 1920.
Les Trois Lys. Paris, Ferenczi, 1920.
"Ms'ieu Gustave," nouvelle inédite, in Paris, Oeuvres Libres, vol. 4, 1921.
"La Pirane," in Paris, Oeuvres Libres, vol. 117, 1931.
"Other People's Meals," in *Great French Short Stories,* translated by Morris Edmund Speare. Cleveland, World Pub. Co., 1931.
Passions américaines et autres. Paris, Ferenczi, 1934.
Le Coeur sur l'ardoise. 1942

Plays

La Rivale marine (poetic theatre inspired by Maeterlinck). Unpublished, 1901.
Sappho désespérée (performed by the Théâtre Femina, 1917). Upublished, 1904.
La Prêtresse de Tanit; pièce en un acte et en vers (performed in Carthage, Tunisia, 2 April 1907). Unpublished, 1907; with preface by Boz Léveillez, Reims, A l'Ecart, 1993).
La Quatrième Eve. 1932

Biographies

Sainte Thérèse de Lisieux. Paris, Fasquelle, 1926; translated by Helen Younger Chase, London, New York, Longmans and Green, 1929.
Les Amours d'Oscar Wilde. Paris, E. Flammarion, 1929.
Le Bâtard. Guillaume le Conquérant. Paris, Fasquelle, 1931; translated by Colin Shepherd, London, New York, Longmans and Green, 1932.
Eve Lavallière. Paris, Albin Michel, 1935.
La Petite Thérèse de Lisieux. Etude du Révérend Père Ubald d'Alençon. Paris, Fasquelle, 1937.
The Work, Life, and Loves of Edgar Allen Poe, translated by J. H. Hulla. New York, 1941.

Essays

Le Cheval. Paris, Nouvelle Société D'Edition, 1930.
Up to Date. Paris, R. Allou, 1936.

Travel Literature

Le Far-West d'aujourd'hui. Paris, Fasquelle, 1932.
L'Amérique chez elle. Paris, Editions Albert, 1933.
Rouen, illustrated by R.-A. Pichon. Rouen, H. Defontaine, 1935.
El Arab, l'Orient que j'ai connu. Lyon, Editions Lugdunum, 1944.

Other

"Le Cochon d'Inde. Mélodie pour une voix" by Charles la Gourgue, composer. Paris, Herelle et Cie., 1900.
"Les Hibous. Mélodie pour une voix" by Charles la Gourgue, composer. Paris, Herelle et Cie., 1900.
"Les Crabes. Mélodie pour une voix" by Charles la Gourgue, composer. Paris, Herelle et Cie., 1900.
"Essai sur *L'Immoraliste,*" in *Revue Blanche,* 15 July 1902.
"Aurel et le procès des mondains." Paris, J. Povolozky et Cie, 29 April 1921.

Translator, *Six Poèmes: Ulalume, Le Corbeau, La Dormeuse, A Helene, La Cité dans la mer, Lenore* by Edgar Allen Poe. Paris, Dépens des Amateurs, 1922.
Embellissez-vous, illustrated by the author (beauty manual). Paris, Les Editions de France, 1926.
Mes Mémoires (autobiography). Paris, Gallimard, 1938.

*

Adaptations: *La Caravane en folie-Afrique* by Félicien Champsaur (novel based on her life), Paris, Fasquelle, 1920; *Trois Poèmes féminins de Anna de Noailles, Lucie Delarue-Mardrus (et) Marie Noël* by Jacques Pillois (musical score), Paris, Durand, 1935; *Graine au Vent* (film, directed by Maruice Gleize, dialogues by Steve Passeur; showed in Paramount theatres, 1943).

Biography: *Femmes d'aujourd'hui. Colette, Lucie Delarue-Mardrus* by Paul Leroy, Rouen, Eds. Maugard, 1936; *Mon Amie, Lucie Delarue-Mardrus* by Myriam Harry, Paris, Ariane, 1946; "Lucie Delarue-Mardrus" by André Billy, in *L'Epoque 1900,* Paris, Tallandier, 1951, 224-27; "Les Mardrus" by Natalie Clifford Barney, in *Souvenirs indiscrets,* Paris, Flammarion, 1960, 147-85; "Lucie Delarue-Mardrus" by Pauline Newman-Gordon, in *French Women Writers: a Bio-Bibliographical Source Book,* edited by E.M. Sartori and Doroty Wynne Zimmerman, New York, Westport, Connecticut, and London, Greenwood Press, 1991, 108-20; *Lucie Delarue-Mardrus: une femme de lettres des années folles* by Hélène Plat, Paris, B. Grasset, 1994.

Bibliography: "Lucie Delarue-Mardrus" by Emilie Sirieyx de Villers, in *Bibliographie critique,* Paris, Sansot, 1923.

Critical Sources: "Lucie Delarue-Mardrus" by Jean Ernest-Charles, in *Les Samedis Littéraires,* Vol. 4, Paris, Sansot, 1905, 227-90; "Madame Lucie Delarue-Mardrus" by Robert de Montesquiou, in *Professionnelles Beautés,* Paris, Juven, 1905, 51-67; *La Corbeille aux roses ou les dames de lettres* by Jean de Bonnefon, Paris, Bouville, 1909; "Madame Lucie Delarue-Mardrus" by Paul Flat, in *Nos Femmes de lettres,* Paris, Perrin, 1909, 57-97; *Muses d'aujourd'hui* by Jean de Gourmont, Paris, Mercure de France, 1910; "Trois Poétesses, Lucie Delarue-Mardrus, Hélène Picard, Jeanne Perdriel-Vaissière" by Lucien Maury, in *Figures Littéraires,* Paris, Perrin, 1911, 297-308; *Anthologie des poètes français contemporains, 1866-1914,* Vol. 3, by Gérard Walch, Paris, Delagrave, 1914; "Amanit" by Jean Charpentier, in *Mercure de France,* 1 October 1915, 156-57; *L'Avenir de l'Intelligence: Auguste Comte: Le Romantisme féminin: Mademoiselle Monk* by Charles Maurras, Paris, Nouvelle Librairie Nationale, 1917; *La Chaîne des dames* by Gabrielle Réval, Paris, Crès, 1924, 55-68; "Littérature et poudre de riz" by M.-L. Néron, in *La Fronde,* 8 September 1926; *La Conscience embrasée* by Aurel (Aurélie) Mortier, Paris, Radot, 1927; *Honfleur et Madame Lucie Delarue-Mardrus* by Edmond Spalikowski, Rouen, Imprimerie de A. Lainé, 1931; "La Ronde de Lucie Delarue-Mardrus" by Pierre Descaves, in *Visites à mes fantômes,* Paris,

Denoël, 1949, 111-29; "La Dialectique de l'amour et de la haine dans les romans de Lucie Delarue-Mardrus" by Susan E. Clark (master's thesis), University of New Mexico, 1982; "L'Ange et les pervers: Lucie Delarue-Mardrus's Ambivalent Poetic Identity" by Tama Lea Engelking, in *Romance Quarterly,* Vol. 39, No. 4, November 1992, 451-66; "Introduction" by Anna Livia, in *The Angel and the Perverts,* New York, NYU Press, 1995, 1-60; "Lucie et les pervers" by Chantal Bigot, in *Lesbia* (Paris), January 1996, 32.

*   *   *

Lucie Delarue was born on 3 November 1874, to a wealthy middle-class family in Honfleur, Normandy. Her father, a lawyer, was often absent for business—and frequent affairs—so Delarue and her five older sisters grew up surrounded by women: their quietly angry, but gentle mother; "miss," the English governess of the moment, who filled their heads with fairy tales and legends; and their eccentric and creative grandmother. Delarue felt an early calling for the writing of poetry; at 20, recounts Pauline Newman-Gordon, she showed her work to the established poet François Coppée, who suggested that "she take up sewing and housework instead." Not discouraged by this rebuke, Delarue persevered, studied Théodore de Banville's treatise on versification, and began reciting her poems at social gatherings. Having heard her at a dinner, the famous Dr. Mardrus, translator of the *Thousand and One Nights,* pronounced her a genius and asked her to be his wife. The couple was married on 5 June 1900. From then, Delarue always identified herself as Lucie Delarue-Mardrus.

Through her husband's connections, Delarue-Mardrus became gradually active in the literary circle around the *Revue Blanche.* She began a long career as a writer, originally promoted by her ambitious husband, and then on her own. Her first two volumes of poetry were poorly received by critics, but, by the third, more favorable reviews, particularly from Maurras, had made her more creditable. Her first novel, *Marie fille-mère,* was published in serial form in 1906 and appeared as a book in 1908. Once again, intellectuals snubbed her, but her works of fiction became instantly an immense popular success, reaching millions of readers over the years, through publication in serials like *L'Illustration.*

Delarue-Mardrus is best known to those interested in lesbian issues for her novel *The Angel and the Perverts* (translated by Anna Livia in 1995). Writing in *Lesbia,* Chantal Bigot remarks that it has long been deemed proper to dismiss her work as quaint yet obsolete, and see to see *The Angel and the Perverts* as a most unfortunate attempt in the genre and an artistic failure, an opinion shared by her biographer Hélène Plat. It can be argued, however, that Delarue-Mardrus was an intriguing personality—a complex artist who used no medium exclusively because she had talents in so many and whose writing is best looked at as a whole. Her double life—her affection for Mardrus and obvious delight in having admirers—parallel her publicly known and passionate lesbian affections which greatly informed her work. An examination of her life story and her oeuvre suggests that her often hesitant writings on lesbian and homosexual themes were at once consonant with the many social and artistic restrictions placed on women in France at the time, and with the generally subversive, non-mainstream, and non-heteronormative content of her literary work.

Delarue-Mardrus and well-known lesbian writer Natalie Barney met through Renée Vivien, who, in 1902, had sent a volume of hers to the newly recognized poet. Barney and Delarue-Mardrus soon formed an amorous friendship, and while Barney still pined for Renée Vivien, Delarue-Mardrus fell completely in love with her, reciting her passionate poems. These were later published by Barney, after her friend's death, as *Nos Secrètes amours* (1957). The poems belie Barney's claims that this was a mere friendship on her part. Delarue-Mardrus's passion rages, adores, demands, and threatens, with a violence more frequent in her work than is always recognized: "I will set upon you, I will mutilate you! There would be such beauty in the brief flash of a knife's blade!" (translation by Francesca Canadé Sautman). Their affair lasted two years, until Mardrus, concerned by the gossip about his and his wife's relationship with Barney, took his wife to North Africa in 1904.

In North Africa, Mardrus planned to work on a translation of the Qu'ran into French, a project not inimical to French colonial interests in the region. Delarue-Mardrus continued with her writing in her new environs, contributing a play, *La Prêtresse de Tanit,* to a fundraising celebration for an ancient amphitheater in Carthage. In 1909 the Mardrus' were travelling in Turkey, where Delarue-Mardrus conducted investigative reporting on the state of the harems after the secular Revolution in that country, for the Paris-based *Le Journal.* She was able to spend time in the harems of the upper classes. According to her biographer, Hélène Plat, she felt secure and happy amongst all these women who enjoyed themselves immensely together once the men were all sent away and the house became their own.

According to Newman-Gordon and Plat, Delarue-Mardrus' musical ear had enabled her to learn Arabic very fast. Plat's biography indicates that she maintained a profound love for that language, communicating at times with Mardrus and Myriam Harry in it, and taking up the study of Arabic grammar as late as 1940 when she was aged and ill. In Cairo, at the court of princess Nazli, aunt of the Khedive, she witnessed the singing performance of a musician, Sett Oulissa, and stared at her so longingly that the musician had a guest tell her: "Sett Oulissa wants you to know that your eyes are making her die." During her 1910 trip to Egypt, Delarue-Mardrus was invited by prince Fouad to give the inauguration lecture to women of the harems exclusively at the university he founded. She spoke to women, who listened intently behind their veils, of the harems she had visited. She was warmly received by these wealthy ladies. Another memorable encounter was with the African harem singer Sett Bamba, whose voice rivaled only that of Sett Oulissa. Her hair cut short like a man's, in the manner of singers, wearing an old sweater, Sett Bamba sang until daybreak for Delarue-Mardrus, who squatted on the floor in front of her, forgetting the passing of time: "So soon! Isn't time to return...my husband..." the French woman sighed. "If you lived a thousand years, a night like this one, you would never live it again!" retorted the singer. Later in her life, smitten by the singer Germaine de Castro, Delarue-Mardrus would wear an embroidered satin tunic, a gift from Sett Bamba, to officiate in the club she and Germaine de Castro had founded.

In 1910, the Mardrus' settled back in Paris in the Ile St-Louis. At the time, Natalie Barney was making her home at rue Jacob, and the couple introduced her to Rémy de Gourmont, Paul Valéry, André Gide, Marcel Schwob, André Germain, Marguerite Moreno, and the Duchess of Clermont-Tonnerre. Barney has remarked that during that period women admirers formed a procession around Delarue-Mardrus. Delarue-Mardrus was indeed at the apex of her success. Beginning in 1906, the *Journal,* directed by Catulle Mendès, published one of her stories every week. From 1908 on, she was active, with her long time friend Myriam Harry, on the jury of the Prix de la Vie Heureuse, soon to become the Prix Femina. They fought to support such authors as Romain Rolland, Edmond Jaloux, Marguerite Audoux, and, in vain, for Proust's *Swann's Way.* Her play, *Sapho désespérée,* was staged at the Theatre Femina between 1912 and 1914, with Delarue-Mardrus playing Sapho barefoot, which was more scandalous than the role itself. At this point in her life, her husband asked her to accept the cohabitation of an official mistress. Delarue-Mardrus refused and the divorce was settled in 1915. Delarue-Mardrus retained the Normandy estate known as the "Pavillon de la Reine," which she had in fact paid for herself with her author's royalties, no small feat at a time when French women were denied control over their legal and financial lives.

In 1914 the first World War broke out, and Delarue-Mardrus took the Red Cross course, during which she horrified her colleagues by riding horseback, dressing as a man, smoking cigarettes, publishing "risque" novels, and avoiding the Church. As a volunteer nurse in a military hospital near her native Honfleur, she proved extremely competent, caring for ghastly wounds that others could not touch, speaking in Arabic to the Arab soldiers who dubbed her "Madame Arabe," and providing the hospital with an X-ray machine with the fee earned with one of her articles, a measure of the high price her work was fetching at the time. After the war, she returned to Paris, moving near the Ovizes, a couple whom she had befriended. Valentine Ovize, whom she nicknamed "Chattie," soon became Delarue-Mardrus' new passion: "all that you love in me moves towards you, gently, very gently," she wrote.

In 1930 she published her novel *The Angel and the Perverts.* In this work, Marion is born an hermaphrodite, and lives a miserable childhood facing the hatred of her uncomprehending parents. She escapes to Paris where she borrows alternatively a male or female identity and appearance. In these guises, she is witness to a variety of activities among the "perverts" ("inverts," according to the terminology of the time), the lesbians who frequent the American Laurette Wells, and the homosexuals who meet in a friend's basement. The American is a fairly transparent portrait of Natalie Barney, shown here engaged in a struggle to regain the love of Renée Vivien, and indulging in a few escapades on the way. In 1931, Delarue-Mardrus visited her new fling, Miss Trott, in the United States and consigned her impressions in several travel essays.

On 17 November 1932, Delarue-Mardrus met the singer Germaine de Castro at a recital which she attended at Chattie's behest. Completely overcome by the singer's voice, she broke off with Chattie Ovize and put all her resources to work in support of Germaine de Castro, whose material fortunes were, at the least, fluctuating. She wrote songs for her and accompanied her on the piano during recitals, horrifying her high society friends. Hardworking and independent, Delarue-Mardrus increased their finances through an extremely lucrative lecture circuit, first all over Europe to Turkey, then to Portugal and in South America.

A letter written by Delarue-Mardrus to Miss Trott, quoted by Plat, bears witness to the intensity of her passion and the joy it first gave her, in contrast to the gloomy picture of decay and abandon of later years. Delarue-Mardrus wrote: "Now I love—tenderly—a woman—an artist—a musician...and she is Jewish. My tender and wonderful friend, she is music, truth, life. Hard life...the daring and freedom of a woman who lives, who loves. All these things are written on her noble face and in her magnificent eyes."

The disapproval meted out to Delarue-Mardrus for this relationship had racial and social undertones. While her "saphic" ways were by then common knowledge, a "friendship" with someone refined like Valentine Ovize was one thing, but being passionately attached to the "vulgar" Germaine de Castro, who, in the virulently anti-semitic France of the time had the distinct disadvantage of being "openly" Jewish, was quite another. Enthralled with de Castro, Delarue-Mardrus wrote a novel dedicated to her, *Une Femme mûre et l'amour* (1935). It was a barely transposed version of her life, in which Victoria Gomez (de Castro) loomed large indeed, a brilliant, generous figure, oppressed as a woman, a Jew, and an artist: "that extravagant slightly middle aged Jew who rebelled in all her fibers against a society presumptuous enough to try to force her into its mold" (translation by Sautman).

Breaking away from friends and family, Delarue-Mardrus involved herself in de Castro's career, helping her perform in the music-hall. In September 1935, after some financial setbacks, the couple opened a singing cabaret restaurant called rue Treilhard, where large numbers of young writers gathered. The club was successful for a short time. Barney stressed the low points of this experiment—Delarue-Mardrus lost many friends, her connection to papers like the *Figaro,* and her conferences through the *Annales.* Delarue-Mardrus was barely scraping by, and her application for the prix Renée Vivien, which she received despite the fact that it was normally for beginning writers, was a minor scandal and an act of despair. Yet, far from being beaten down, Delarue-Mardrus swallowed her pride and consistently fought for her lover's success, in spite of de Castro's constant bad mood and, later, her habit of blaming Delarue-Mardrus for her own lack of success.

In 1936, Delarue-Mardrus had her first attack of general crippling rheumatism. By 1939, with the outbreak of the war, she was suffering even more seriously. She was then so impoverished that she had to give up her home and seek refuge in Château-Gontier (Mayenne), with de Castro, her new husband, and aging mother, surviving on a small pension accorded by the Société des Gens de Lettres. Her books were being turned down. *Fleurette* was banned by the Nazis and her *Poèmes mignons* removed from school readings, while the fascist periodical *Je Suis Partout* attacked her. Even her typist, tells Plat, refused to type her last novel, *Etoile de David,* because it was "too disrespectful towards God the Father." De Castro had married another performer, Evremond, to hide her Jewish identity under an "Aryan" name. As persecution of Jews intensified in 1940, Delarue-Mardrus refused to desert de Castro and leave the North for the safer zone. In 1943, she arranged for de Castro's flight and hiding in the property of a friend who was hiding his own Jewish lover. Delarue-Mardrus stayed in de Castro's house under the threat of Gestapo intervention. Twice, in fact, the Gestapo raided the house and threatened to arrest the by then completely invalid Delarue-Mardrus. De Castro and Evremond returned after the end of the war. On 26 April 1945, at midnight, Delarue-Mardrus died, having dictated her last lines of improvised poetry for a faithful friend, Laure Renault, present at her side, with de Castro and "Jimmy" the young butch contraband-cigarette vendor they had befriended. "She gave you her most beautiful verse," de Castro cried.

Delarue-Mardrus' writing is hard to classify. As Anna Livia points out in her introduction to *The Angel and the Perverts,* Delarue-Mardrus turned her back on the new literary movements of the time, and continued to write artfully crafted works proceeding from a nineteenth-century, profoundly romantic sensibility. Her poetry is often melancholy, anchored in the landscapes of her native Normandy, at times violent, and filled with lesbian coding. Her fiction is a form of popular, often realistic, literature, addressed to masses of readers in serial form. Delarue-Mardrus entertained strained relations with the feminist movement. André Billy affirms that she was "absolutely not a feminist and bragged about it." While her life was the affirmation of a woman's ability to survive by her talents and to carve herself a place in high society without the support of her famous husband, she stressed her distance from organized feminism and even fell prey to some misogynistic plots, as when Henri de Jouvenel put her up to writing anti-feminist tracts ("Du Chignon au Cerveau") in *Le Matin*.

Furthermore, Delarue-Mardrus' embracing of femininity as the preferred expression of a beloved, erotically charged, female beauty was not that different from views held by other upper class lesbians of the time, for instance, by Barney. In her work it coexisted with more militant stances, where she affirmed the active capabilities of feminine women, and wrote compassionately about prostitutes and battered women. Newman-Gordon quotes this remark of hers in a 1932 article: "Your work must wear a skirt," which illustrates that position well. Indeed, her fictional female characters are far from universally "feminine" in the conventional sense. Most female characters are central actors in Delarue-Mardrus' sometimes sentimental novels, and they share traits of decisiveness and courage—such as the young, naive, but very combative Roberte, (*Roberte no. 10.530,* 1937), who gets into trouble by punching out a boy her age in a fistfight she initiated. This aggressiveness was not unknown to the beautiful, dreamy-eyed Delarue-Mardrus herself, who is known to have crashed her horse into a group of young men who had taunted her and Barney.

Like many women authors of her time who loved women, and, to varying degrees, felt that they should conceal their lesbian life, Delarue-Mardrus often coded her writing by speaking of male homosexuality, or using very abstract formulas, or writing about sexually ambiguous figures. Yet the lesbian content of much of Delarue-Mardrus' poetry was evident enough from the onset; Mardrus elected to ignore it when he read the poems that would become *Occident* (1901), but the critic Maurras, otherwise favorable to her, was "alarmed" at the (lesbian) "perversity" of *Horizons*. Delarue-Mardrus affirmed her refusal of motherhood and reproduction ("Vade Retro" in *Ferveur*), a position reinforced by the atrocities of a war wrought by men. Her poems to Barney burned with unrequited passion and were very explicit. In her *Memoirs,* she freely admits her deep sexual attractions to women at an early age, and the process of this identification is well traced in Anna Livia's introduction. In her novels *L'Acharnée* (1910) and *Le Beau Baiser* (1929) she incorporated memories of her love, at age 21, for Imperia de Heredia, wife of the famous poet, and the passionate kiss she extracted from her.

The Angel and the Perverts is considered the most openly "lesbian" or "gay" of her works, and has received rather negative evaluations. For Chantal Bigot, it is boring to no end and a cheap shot at former lover Natalie Barney. Anna Livia points to her apparent disdain for homosexuals, who merely "act" like those of the opposite sex, and are not, like the true hermaphrodite, biologically both at once. One might suggest, however, that Delarue-Mardrus' life and coded works are more serious testimonies to her lesbian self than works of fiction, filled with fictional conventions—as Anna Livia correctly pointed out, in a very nineteenth-century tradition of the lonely wanderer. The work is a great deal more ambiguous than it seems at first glance. It also extols the beauty, purity, and art-love of homosexuals versus bourgeois mores: "for

dirty perverts, they are decidedly clean-minded" (Ch. VI). Marion's repeated statement that s/he cannot love anyone, of any sex, might be less a negative reflection on homosexuality than one on Delarue-Mardrus' own life, filled with gender ambiguities, and devoid of fulfilled passion. "Love?" she wrote on 6 December 1940, "a few brief fires where imagination replaced the senses, nothing resembling my passionate dreams. A solid reputation of vice, while vice was nothing but a fiasco for me." Even Marion's final choice of maternity—one Delarue-Mardrus strenuously refused herself—may be seen less as compliance with institutions and more as connected to her longstanding theme of neglect, abandonment, and emotional abuse as a child who was desperately in need of love.

From her travels to Tunisia and Egypt, her love of Arabic, her friendships with harem women, and compassion for Arab soldiers, to her Western, orientalist perspective; from her cult, in writing, of strong women, actual or historical, her defense of women stripped of power and means, to her loud professions of anti-feminism; from her love of art and music, culminating in a defiant, and finally, dangerous, relationship transgressing class and racial persecution, to her daring to speaking—however awkwardly—the "love that has no name," Lucie Delarue-Mardrus remains an important figure of lesbian and gay literary history. Ambiguous like one of her own characters, as she played out the contradictions of gender and sexuality, and, as well, her own prejudices, she still offers us a provocative work, filled with questions about the rich, and devastating, relations of identity and cultures.

—Francesca Canadé Sautman

de LAURETIS, Teresa

Nationality: Italian and American essayist, feminist critic, and scholar. **Born:** Italy; maintains dual citizenship in United States and Italy. **Education:** Conservatorio Musicale Giuseppe Verdi, Ravenna, Italy, Fifth Year Diploma 1953; Liceo-Ginnasio Dante Alighieri, Ravenna, Italy, Maturità Classica 1957; Universitá Luigi Bocconi, Milan, Italy, Laurea in Modern Languages and Literature 1963. **Career:** Has held a variety of teaching positions, including instructor in Italian, University of Colorado, Colorado Springs, 1964-65, University of Colorado, Boulder, 1965-66; lecturer in Italian, University of California, Davis, 1966-68; assistant, later associate professor of Italian, 1968-77, associate, later acting director, Center for Twentieth Century Studies, 1977-78, professor of Italian, 1977-85, University of Wisconsin, Milwaukee; professor of the History of Consciousness, University of California, Santa Cruz, from 1985. Visiting professor, University of California, San Diego, 1981-82, University of British Columbia, Canada, 1982, International Summer Institute for Semiotic and Structural Studies, University of Toronto, Canada, 1987, Universiteit van Amsterdam, The Netherlands, 1990, School for Criticism and Theory, Dartmouth College, 1991, Universität Konstanz, Germany, 1993, Institut für Filmwissenschaft, Goethe-Universität, Frankfurt am Main, Germany, 1996; Belle van Zuylen Distinguished Professor, Rikjsuniversiteit te Utrecht, The Netherlands, 1991; Jeannette K. Watson Distinguished Professor in the Humanities, Syracuse University, 1993. Contributor of over 90 articles to scholarly journals, anthologies, and thematic collections. **Member:** Editorial board, *Yale Italian Studies,* 1987-83; general editor, "Theories of Representation and Difference" series, Indiana University Press, from 1985; advisory board member, *differences: A Journal of Feminist Cultural Studies,* from 1987, *Critical Studies,* 1988-91, *Signature: A Journal of Theory and Canadian Literature,* 1989-92, *Revista Estudos Feministas,* from 1992, *Signs: Journal of Women in Culture and Society,* from 1992, *Textual Practice,* from 1994, *Social Semiotics,* 1995, *GLQ: A Journal of Lesbian and Gay Studies, Stanford Italian Review,* and *parallax: a journal of metadiscursive theory and cultural practices*; advisory board member, International Advisory Board of the Graduate School for Advanced Research in Women's Studies, University of Utrecht, The Netherlands, from 1990, and Interdisciplinary Board of Gender Studies, University of Helsinki, Finland, from 1995. **Awards:** National Endowment for the Arts grant in media studies, 1977-78; Humanities Institute fellowship, State University of New York, Stony Brook, 1991; Institute for the Humanities fellowship, University of Michigan, Ann Arbor, 1991; National Endowment for the Humanities fellowship, 1992; Guggenheim fellowship, 1993. **Address:** Board of Studies in History of Consciousness, University of California-Santa Cruz, Santa Cruz, California 95064, U.S.A.

WRITINGS

Nonfiction

La Sintassi del Desiderio: Struttura e Forme del Romanzo Sveviano. Ravenna, Italy, Longo Editore, 1976.
Umberto Eco. Firenze, Italy, La Nuova Italia, 1981.
Alice Doesn't: Feminism, Semiotics, Cinema. Bloomington, Indiana University Press, and London, Macmillan, 1984; translated into Spanish by Silvia Iglesias Recuero, Madrid, Cátedra, 1992.
Technologies of Gender: Essays on Theory, Film, and Fiction. Bloomington, Indiana University Press, 1987; London, Macmillan, 1989.
Differenza e Indifferenza Sessuale. Firenze, Estro Editrice, 1989.
The Practice of Love: Lesbian Sexuality and Perverse Desire. Bloomington, Indiana University Press, 1994; translated into German by Karin Wördemann, Berlin, Berlin Verlag, 1996; translated into Italian by Simona Capelli, Milan, La Tartaruga Edizioni, 1997.
Sui Generis. Scritti di Teoria Femminista, translated by Liliana Losi. Milan, Feltrinelli, 1996.

Editor

With David Allen, "Theoretical Perspectives in Cinema," special issue of *Ciné-Tracts: A Journal of Film and Cultural Studies,* Vol. 1, No. 2, 1977.
With Andreas Huyssen and Kathleen Woodward, *The Technological Imagination: Theories and Fictions.* Madison, Wisconsin, Coda Press, 1980.
With Stephen Heath, *The Cinematic Apparatus.* New York, St. Martin's Press, and London, Macmillan, 1980.
And author of introduction, *Feminist Studies/Critical Studies.* Bloomington, Indiana University Press, 1986; London, Macmillan, 1988.
And author of introduction, "Queer Theory: Lesbian and Gay Sexualities," special issue of *differences: A Journal of Feminist Cultural Studies,* Vol. 3, No. 2, summer 1991.

Selected Essays

"Rebirth in *The Bell Jar,*" in *Women's Studies,* 1976.
"From a Dream of Woman," in *Cinema and Language,* edited by Stephen Heath and Patricia Mellencamp. Frederick, Maryland, University Publications of America and The American Film Institute, 1983.
"The Female Body and Heterosexual Presumption," in *Semiotica,* December 1987.
"Eccentric Subjects: Feminist Theory and Historical Consciousness," in *Feminist Studies,* spring 1990.
"Perverse Desire: The Lure of the Mannish Lesbian," in *Australian Feminist Studies,* autumn 1991.
"Film and the Visible," in *How Do I Look? Queer Film and Video,* edited by Bad Object-Choices. Seattle, Bay Press, 1991.
"Freud, Sexuality, and Perversion," in *Politics, Theory and Contemporary Culture,* edited by Mark Poster. New York, Columbia University Press, 1992.
"Feminist Genealogies: A Personal Itinerary," in *Women's Studies International Forum,* 1993.
"Sexual Indifference and Lesbian Representation," in *The Lesbian and Gay Studies Reader,* edited by Henry Abelove, Michèle Aina Barale, and David Halperin. New York, Routledge, 1993.
"Habit Changes," in *differences: A Journal of Feminist Cultural Studies,* summer-fall 1994.
"On the Subject of Fantasy," in *Feminisms in the Cinema,* edited by Laura Pietropaolo and Ada Testaferri. Bloomington, Indiana University Press, 1995.
"American Freud," in *Amerikastudien/American Studies* (Munich, Germany), Vol. 41, No. 2, 1996.

*

Critical Sources: "Narrative and Theories of Desire" by Jay Clayton, in *Critical Inquiry,* Vol. 16, No. 1, 1989, 33-53; "Seeing Through the Gendered I: Feminist Film Theory" by Paula Rabinowitz, in *Feminist Studies,* Vol. 16, No. 1, 1990, 151-169; "Realizing Love and Justice: Lesbian Ethics in the Upper and Lower Case" by Kathleen Martindale, in *Hypatia,* Vol. 7, No. 4, 1992, 148-171; "(Be)Coming Out: Lesbian Identity and Politics" by Shane Phelan, in *Signs: A Journal of Women in Culture and Society,* Vol. 18, No. 4, 1993, 765-790; "Labors of Love: Analyzing Perverse Desire" by Elizabeth Grosz, in *differences: A Journal of Feminist Cultural Studies,* Vol. 6, No. 2, 1994, 274-313; "The Subversion of Perversion: *The Practice of Love: Lesbian Sexuality and Perverse Desire*" by Ramona Liera-Schwichtenberg, in *Women's Review of Books,* Vol. 12, No. 12, 1995, 24-25.

*   *   *

Teresa de Lauretis' prolific body of writing has helped to shape the current theoretical directions of feminist film theory, feminist literary criticism, and the emerging academic field of gay and lesbian studies. Her numerous essays, articles, and books explore the social and psychic constructions of gender and sexuality against and outside of the dominant heterosexual paradigm. These writings, translated into nine languages, have reached an international audience. Specifically, de Lauretis engages with the problem of the representation of gender and sexual differences across the boundaries of race and class in cinematic, literary, and most recently psychoanalytic texts. Indeed, her work maps out the specificities and mobilities of female and particularly lesbian desire through critical examinations of texts ranging from Fellini films to the novels of Italo Calvino to Adrienne Rich's poetry.

In her second book, *Alice Doesn't: Feminism, Semiotics, Cinema,* de Lauretis began questioning the discursive construction of the tense relation between "woman" as metaphor or image and women as social subjects, the distinction between the woman as ideal and the woman as real; it is a theme to which she consistently returns in later writing. The chapter entitled "Desire in Narrative" crystallizes the key questions and concerns of the entire collection of essays. Here, de Lauretis argues that the "work of cinema as we know it" represents the vicissitudes of the Oedipal narrative or the male protagonist's quest toward "that one true vision that will confirm the truth of his desire." As his narrative quest unfolds in film, "woman" is displayed as a spectacle and object, her desires subsumed to guarantee the vision and subjectivity of the male hero. At the same time, both narrative and cinema "solicit the consent" of the female spectator, hoping to "seduce women into femininity." According to de Lauretis, the project of feminist cinema, then, is to resist Oedipal narratives and represent another context of desire and visibility for a "different social subject," women.

A point of departure for de Lauretis' discussions of film and narrative in *Alice Doesn't* is the idea that spectators—whether female or male, heterosexual or queer—are "historically engendered in social practices, in the real world, and in cinema too." Her next essay collection, *Technologies of Gender,* expands on this theme, with the title essay arguing for the construction of a "view from elsewhere" which would represent the subjectivity of those spectators historically excluded from dominant cinematic and narrative images. To accomplish this task, de Lauretis urges women and feminists "to rewrite cultural narratives" and "create new spaces of discourse" that acknowledge the contradictions and multiplicities of female-gendered subjects positioned "at once inside and outside the ideology of gender" and sexual difference. In the final essay of the collection, "Rethinking Women's Cinema: Aesthetics and Feminist Theory," de Lauretis analyzes specific examples of "women's cinema," focusing on films which inscribe "the difference of women from Woman" as well as the differences among and within women.

De Lauretis expands on the theme of the representation of "difference" in an important essay entitled "Sexual Indifference and Lesbian Representation," a selection which appears in *The Lesbian and Gay Studies Reader* as one "of the best and most significant recent English-language work[s] in the field of gay and lesbian studies." In this essay, de Lauretis argues that the emphasis in feminist theory on definitions of gender as "sexual difference" constitute a "conceptual paradox" in women's lives. Because the concept of "sexual difference" preserves "men" as the marker against which difference is assessed, female desire "for the self same, an other female, cannot be recognized." Subsequently, de Lauretis examines and praises the work of lesbian and feminist artists and writers such as Cherrie Moraga, who attempt to dislodge sex and sexuality from the heterosexualized paradigm of gender and alter the "frame of reference of [lesbian] visibility." By again considering the question of "what can be seen" in current representational practices, de Lauretis underscores the significance of theorizing the differences between and within lesbians in relation to race and its attendant differences of class, generation, and geography. In her introduction for a special "queer theory" issue of the journal *differences,* de Lauretis speculates about the possi-

bilities and limitations of the category "queer" for conceptualizing the myriad differences that constitute all gay and lesbian identities.

While a great deal of de Lauretis' theoretical writing explores the discursive representations of the "difference" of female desire, her latest and most controversial book, *The Practice of Love: Lesbian Sexuality and Perverse Desire,* engages with psychoanalysis in an attempt to develop a theory of sexuality that acknowledges the workings of unconscious processes in the formation of female subjectivity. In particular, *The Practice of Love* reconsiders Freud's theories of sexuality from a lesbian perspective, and in the process, proposes "a model of perverse desire that may account for the representation of lesbianism in texts of fiction, film, poetry and drama, as well as in the interactions and conversations of many years of [her] own life." To develop the idea of "perverse desire," de Lauretis emphasizes Freud's ambivalence regarding the "normality" of heterosexuality and suggests that within this context, "homosexuality is merely another path taken" by an individual. "Perverse desire" is not "pathological" but rather "non-normatively heterosexual," an attraction that eschews a reproductive object choice in favor of other sources of erotic pleasure.

Within the model of "perverse desire," de Lauretis links lesbian desire to the structure of fetishism, a conjoining that proposes an alternative model of sexuality to challenge the standard Freudian concepts of the Oedipus complex and penis-envy as the defining experiences in a subject's psycho-sexual development. From Freud's perspective, the fetishist displaces "his" desire onto an object (or a part of the "other's" body) which acts as a substitute for the "original" but "lost" object of desire, the maternal penis. De Lauretis refers to the structure of fetishism to propose that "what the lesbian desires in a woman is indeed not a penis but a part or perhaps the whole of the female body." In particular, a lesbian fetish is not necessarily an anatomical entity, but rather any object or sign which marks the difference and desire between women lovers. The terms of difference and the signifiers of desire vary from woman to woman in a limitless process or movement toward objects that "conjure up" the "lost female body." De Lauretis refers to her model of lesbian desire as a "passionate fiction" capable of providing, for example, a new explanatory paradigm for "butch" and "femme" sexual positions as well as an interpretive lens for the reconsideration of images of lesbianism in film and literature.

The most controversial aspects of *The Practice of Love* for lesbian and feminist studies are succinctly summarized by Elizabeth Grosz in an extended review of the book. Grosz laments de Lauretis' reliance on Freudian psychoanalysis as "the sole explanatory framework in her account of the structuring of lesbian desire," for it fails to account for the phallic and heterosexist assumptions of a whole range of his concepts. De Lauretis responded to Grosz's criticisms in her 1994 essay "Habit Changes." Here she speculates that one of the potentially liberating effects of her model of "lesbian fetishism" is that "the fetish releases sexuality from its embeddedness in reproduction," thereby demonstrating sexuality and reproduction are not necessarily mutually implicated in one another. If sexuality was freed from its reproductive function, then lesbian desire or, for that matter, all queer desires, could be articulated without reference to heterosexuality as the normative paradigm. From this perspective, de Lauretis' model of "perverse desire" shifts the vantage point of "normalcy" and creates another "view from elsewhere." This conceptual shift conceives of lesbian desire not as a static component of identity, but as a continually changing set of experiences connected to both psychic and social processes. In this regard, *The Practice of Love* partially accomplishes the project de Lauretis maps out in her earlier books—an account of the "difference" of female and, in particular, lesbian desire.

—Annmarie Pinarski

DeLYNN, Jane

Nationality: American novelist and journalist. **Born:** New York, New York, 18 July 1946. **Education:** Barnard College, New York, 1964-68 (Elizabeth Janeway Prize, 1967 and 1968; cum laude), B.A. 1968; University of Iowa, Iowa City, 1968-70 (honors), M.F.A. 1970. **Career:** Teaching assistant, University of Iowa, 1969-70; founder and managing editor, *Fiction,* 1971-72; book reviewer, for *Kirkus Reviews,* 1971-76, Christopher Street, 1976, *Harper's Bazaar,* 1987-88, *New York Times Book Review,* 1988, *Los Angeles Times Book Review,* 1988, *Tikkun,* 1989, *La-Bas,* and *The World*; adjunct assistant professor, 1989-90, substitute assistant professor, 1991-92, Lehman College, City University of New York; freelance writer; contributor of articles and reviews to periodicals, including *Advocate, New York Times Book Review, Rolling Stone,* and others. **Awards:** Elizabeth Janeway Prize, for prose writing, 1967; Book of the Month Club fellowship, 1968; International P.E.N. grant, 1975; New York Foundation for the Arts Award, 1978; MacDowell Foundation Fellowship, 1980; Edward Albee Fondation Award, William Flanagan Memorial Creative Persons Center, 1981; *New York Times* Notable Book award, 1988; Yaddo Fellowship, 1988, 1990. **Address:** 395 Broadway, Apt. 7E, New York, New York 10013-3540.

WRITINGS

Novels

Some Do. Indianapolis, Indiana, Macmillan, 1978.
In Thrall. New York, Clarkson N. Potter, 1982.
Real Estate. New York, Simon and Schuster, 1988; New York, Ballantine Books, 1989.
Don Juan in the Village. New York, Pantheon Books, 1990; New York, Ballantine Books, 1992.

Other

Hoosick Falls (play; produced New York City, 1974).

*

Critical Sources: "Jane DeLynn," in *Contemporary Authors,* edited by Frances Carol Lochen, Vol. 77-80, 1979, 113; review of *In Thrall* by Marcia R. Hoffman, in *Library Journal* (New York), Vol. 107, No. 13, July 1982, 1343; review of *In Thrall* by Richard Keye, in *Nation* (New York), Vol. 235, No. 13-14, 23 October 1982, 411; review of *Real Estate,* in *Publisher's Weekly* (New York), Vol. 232, No. 27, 8 January 1988, 73; review of *Real Estate* by Maria A. Perez Stable, in *Library Journal* (New York), Vol. 113,

No. 4, 1 March 1988, 76; review of *Real Estate* by Ellen Feldman, in *New York Times Book Review* (New York), 20 March 1988, 12; review of *Real Estate* by Thomas M. Disch, in *Playboy* (Chicago, Illinois), Vol. 35, No. 5, May 1988, 26; "The Women Wouldn't Dance with Her" by Bertha Harris, in *New York Times Book Review* (New York), 21 October 1990, 15; "She Takes a Licking and Keeps on Ticking" by Karen Ocamb, in *Advocate* (Los Angeles, California), No. 569, 29 January 1991, 77.

*   *   *

Jane DeLynn is a somewhat controversial figure among her gay and lesbian readers and reviewers. In *Contemporary Authors* she is quoted describing herself as "politically...leftist" and "temperamentally...a skeptic, and lazy." She says, "I consider myself a gay feminist, but I despise the superficiality and smug insularity of most Movement-inspired writings." Perhaps any writer embodying such admittedly contradictory identities and opinions is bound to arouse anger on both sides of her. Perhaps arousing this anger is part of the purpose of her writing.

Some Do, DeLynn's first novel, skewers the counterculture values of the 1960s as it follows a handful of men and women in Berkeley, California, from their hippie years into the 1970s and their efforts to adjust to changing times and priorities. It is a humorously told story, but it is humor with a sting as DeLynn first hones her gift for satire.

In *In Thrall,* DeLynn presents an exploration of lesbianism and adolescent sexual awakening. Published in 1982, the novel is set in the mid 1960s and tells the story of a senior in high school who becomes romantically involved with her female English teacher. DeLynn tells the story in a direct and unemotional way, presenting homosexuality as a simple reality with no judgement or glorification attached. Though some critics find the girl's character unappealing, and Richard Keye writing in the *Nation* wonders humorously why, gender aside, the teacher would be interested in such an obnoxious teenager, the novel does offer a good description of an uneasy and often unattractive time in many people's lives.

Real Estate focuses on heterosexual couples in New York City and the ways in which their lives and relationships are governed and symbolized by their apartments. As a New Yorker, DeLynn has perfectly captured the urban landscape which weaves the reality of lease-dependency with relationships and a sense of home. Her sharp satiric voice is back in this novel. *Real Estate* is thoroughly New York in its identification of the apartment and the self, and the cynical questioning of what is the "real" estate.

Don Juan in the Village is a loosely constructed novel consisting of 14 chapters, each of which is a story in the life of Don Juan, an intellectually and emotionally jaded but sexually athletic butch dyke. Each chapter recounts a separate sexual adventure of the rakish Don Juan, from a scuba seduction in "Night Divings" to a spoof of sadomasochism in "Duchess of LA." Don Juan travels all over the world, taking her readers with her on her erotic journey, but the one constant recurring scene is the lesbian bar. The bar takes on an archetypal role in the novel, as a place for reflection, sadness, and groping, for sex and for wisdom.

The sexuality in *Don Juan in the Village* is explicit. Some parts of the descriptions of s/m sex are so graphic that *Playboy,* a magazine whose content is largely sexual, declined to print it. Some lesbians also have been angered by *Don Juan,* some by its sexual content, but others by the venom DeLynn expresses toward the lesbian community. She had originally intended to attack the straight world in the Don Juan stories, but, as she wrote, she got caught up in describing the painful experience of alienation from one's own kind.

DeLynn herself is critical of lesbians and the lesbian community, stating that she admires gay men more than lesbians, and that they have understood and appreciated her writing more than lesbians have. Don Juan seems to voice DeLynn's own views when she complains about:

> the slowness, the laziness, the inefficiency, the cowardice and hypocrisy of women—so desirous of the amenities of conversation and a nice clean bed. A history for a face that would somehow provide romantic justification for that utterly simple desire to explore...another's body.

Even considering DeLynn's wicked humor and scathing satirical bite, it is not surprising that many reviewers in the lesbian press take exception to her portrayal of their community. *Don Juan* has also been criticized for racism in its depiction of women of color in Don Juan's various exploits.

Also not surprisingly, DeLynn has reacted to her unfavorable reviews in the lesbian press with anger. It is a cycle perhaps not dissimilar to the one Don Juan finds herself in, a longing for community and connection that is frustrated by dissatisfaction with and alienation from the community as it exists. This frustration creates a prickly character who is likely to be rejected by the very community that she herself is rejecting.

—Tina Gianoulis

DEMING, Barbara

Nationality: American essayist, journalist, poet, novelist, and author of short stories. **Born:** New York City, 23 July 1917. **Education:** Friends Seminary, New York City; Bennington College, Bennington, Vermont, B.A. 1938; Western Reserve University (now Case Western Reserve University), Cleveland, Ohio, M.A. in Drama and Theatre 1941. **Family:** Companion of Mary Meigs, 1954-69; companion of Jane Gapen, 1969-84. **Career:** Co-director, Bennington Stock Theatre, summers 1938-39; teaching fellow, Bennington School of the Arts, summers 1940-41; film analyst, Library of Congress film project, Museum of Modern Art, New York City, 1942-44. Regular contributor to *Partisan Review, The Nation,* and other periodicals, c. 1950-69; associate editor, *Liberation,* 1962-69; peace, civil rights, and feminist activist. **Awards:** War Resisters' League Peace Award, 1967. **Died:** Sugarloaf Key, Florida, of stomach cancer, 2 August 1984.

WRITINGS

Essays

"Two Issues or One?," "Poem," "Notes After Birmingham," and "Prison Notes," in *Seeds of Liberation,* edited by Paul Goodman. New York, George Braziller, 1964.

"The Long Walk for Peace: New Mission to Moscow" and "The Peacemakers," in *Peace and Arms: Reports from The Nation,* edited by Henry M. Christman. New York, Sheed and Ward, 1964.
Prison Notes. New York, Grossman, 1966.
With Regis Debray, *Revolution, Violent and Nonviolent.* New York, Liberation, 1968.
Revolution and Equilibrium. New York, Grossman, 1971.
"In Dialogue with Gwenda Blair," in *Remembering Who We Are.* Florida, Pagoda Publications (distributed by Naiad Press), 1981.
Two Essays: On Anger, New Men, New Women. Philadelphia, Pennsylvania, New Society Publishers, 1982.
"A Song for Gorgons," in *Reweaving the Web of Life: Feminism and Nonviolence,* edited by Pam McAllister. Philadelphia, Pennsylvania, New Society Publishers, 1982.
With introduction by Grace Paley and photo essay edited by Joan E. Biren, *Prisons That Could Not Hold.* San Francisco, Spinsters Ink, 1985; reprinted, with a biographical essay by Judith McDaniel and reprint of *Prison Notes,* edited by Sky Vanderlinde, Athens, Georgia, University of Georgia Press, 1995.
"The Challenge of Non-Violence," in *Women On War: Essential Voices for the Nuclear Age,* edited by Daniela Giosetti. New York, Simon and Schuster, 1988.

Other

Running Away From Myself: A Dream Portrait of America Drawn from the Films of the Forties (film criticism). New York, Grossman, 1969.
Wash Us And Comb Us: Stories. New York, Grossman, 1972.
We Cannot Live Without Our Lives (essays, poems, letters, and eulogies). New York, Grossman, 1974.
With a foreword by Barbara Smith, *We Are All Part of One Another: A Barbara Deming Reader,* edited by Jane Meyerding. Philadelphia, Pennsylvania, New Society Publishers, 1984.
A Humming Under My Feet: A Book of Travail (novel). London, The Women's Press, 1985.
With introduction by Judith McDaniel and preface by Grace Paley, *I Change, I Change: Poems,* edited by Judith McDaniel. Norwich, Vermont, New Victoria Publishers, 1996.

*

Manuscript Collections: Schlesinger Library, Radcliffe College, Cambridge, Massachusetts; Oral History Collection, Columbia University, New York City.

Biography: *The Power of the People: Active Nonviolence in the United States,* edited and produced by Robert Cooney and Helen Michalowski, Culver City, California, Peace Press, 1977, updated and enlarged, 1987; "Letter to M" by Andrea Dworkin, in *Lavender Culture,* edited by Karla Jay and Allen Young, New York, Jove/HBJ, 1978, 405-411; *Lily Briscoe, A Self Portrait: An Autobiography* by Mary Meigs, Vancouver, British Columbia, Talonbooks, 1981; "Introduction" by Jane Meyerding, in *We Are All Part of One Another,* Philadelphia, New Society Publishers, 1984, 1-17; "Barbara Deming, 1917-1984" by Joanne Glasgow, in *New Directions for Women* (Dover, New Jersey), Vol. 13, No. 5, September/October 1984, 2; "Dancing Toward Death—Barbara Deming: 1917-1984" by Minnie Bruce Pratt, in *Off Our Backs* (Washington, D.C.), Vol. 14, No. 9, October 1984, 28; "'We Are All Part of One Another'—A Tribute to Barbara Deming" by Leah Fritz, in *Ms* (New York City), Vol. 13, No. 6, December 1984, 41-42; "Deming, Barbara, 1917-1984," in *Contemporary Authors,* New Revision Series, Vol. 15, Detroit, Gale, 1985, 104; "Barbara Deming: 1917-1984" by Mab Segrest, in *Southern Exposure* (Durham, North Carolina), Vol. 13, No. 2/3, March/June 1985, 72-75; "Barbara Deming," in *American Peace Writers, Editors, and Periodicals* by Nancy L. Roberts, New York, Greenwood Press, 1991, 74-75; "The Women She Loved: Poems and Conversations,. An Introduction" by Judith McDaniel, in *I Change, I Change: Poems* by Barbara Deming, Norwich, Vermont, New Victoria Publishers, 1996, 1-25.

Interviews: "Barbara Deming: The Rage of a Pacifist" by Leah Fritz, in *Ms* (New York City), Vol. 7, No. 5, November 1978, 97-98, 101; "Feminism and Disobedience: Conversations with Barbara Deming" by Mab Segrest, in *Reweaving The Web of Life: Feminism and Nonviolence,* Philadelphia, New Society Publishers, 1982, originally published in *Feminary: A Feminist Journal of the South,* Vol. 11, No. 1/2, 1980; "An Interview with Barbara Deming" by Ruthann Robson, in *Kalliope* (Jacksonville, Florida), Vol. 6, No. 1, 1984, 36-45; "Interview with Barbara Deming" by the Boston Women's Video Collection, in *Prisons That Could Not Hold,* San Francisco, Spinsters Ink, 1985, 217-225.

Critical Sources: Review of *Prison Notes,* in *Choice* (Chicago), Vol. 3, No. 10, December 1966, 895; "Stanley Kauffmann on Films," in *New Republic* (Washington, D.C.), Vol. 161, No. 14, 4 October 1969, 22, 33; "Pacifist Guerrillas" by Charles E. Fager, in *Progressive* (Madison), Vol. 36, No. 2, February 1972, 45-46; "Women Writing" by Ann Morrissett Davidon, in *Nation* (New York City), Vol. 217, No. 7, 10 September 1973, 213-215; "A Pacifist Faces Her Anger" by Karen Durbin, in *Ms* (New York City), Vol. 3, No. 5, November 1974, 32, 36-37; *Feminine Forms of Closure: Gilman, Deming, and H.D.* by Katherine Combellick (Ph.D. dissertation), State University of New York at Binghampton, 1983; "Remembering Barbara Deming" by Mary Meigs, in *Women's Review of Books* (Wellesley, Massachusetts), Vol. 2, No. 1, October 1984, 8-9; Review of *We Are All Part of One Another* by Ruthann Robson, in *New Pages* (Grand Blanc, Michigan), No. 9, Spring/Summer 1985, 16-17; "Lesbian Writing: Nonfiction" by Margaret Cruikshank, in *The Oxford Companion to Women's Writing in the United States,* edited by Cathy N. Davidson and others, New York, Oxford, 1995, 510-511.

*   *   *

Pacifist, civil rights, and feminist activist and writer Barbara Deming published work in many genres, but she was best known for essays on political and social issues. Ironically, for many of her productive years, this most personal of political writers believed that crucial elements of her own experience were out of bounds for her writing—except, as she later said, "by analogy." "How can it be that one can both accept one's own nature profoundly—and still tremble at the thought that it will be known?" In *We Cannot Live Without Our Lives,* Deming wrote "I am not black but because I am homosexual I know in my deepest being what it feels like to be despised."

Deming was the only daughter of a prosperous white New York family. She attended Friends Seminary, where she encountered ideas that later appeared in her work, including pacifism, the potential for good within each individual, and the continuing revelation of truth. She discovered her vocation and her sexuality at a young age. "I first became a writer when I was 16," Deming told Ruthann Robson. "I'd just fallen in love for the first time, with an older woman—who then became my lover.... And I don't think it is a coincidence that that's when I began to write."

Deming's first poems sprang from her discovery of her sexuality, but the nature of her sexuality and the extremely personal voice in which she wrote evoked negative responses from early mentors. At Bennington College, Deming told Robson, she learned the "fear [of] becoming the kind of writer who would be called a 'woman writer,'...the fear of being too personal—the fear that it won't be art." After graduation, Deming studied drama, worked at various jobs related to theatre and film, and struggled to establish herself as a writer. Finally, in the 1950s, her poems, stories, and film criticism began to appear in magazines and literary journals. She then entered a long relationship with painter Mary Meigs in 1954.

"'Until I was forty-three years old—which was in 1960,'" Deming told interviewer Leah Fritz, "I was very apolitical...I had the feeling that if I entered the 'political' realm, I would become less truthful, keep less of a grasp on the *complexity* of truth...." Then, in the works of Gandhi, she discovered a way to "cling to a whole complexity of political truths." As a result of her self-discovery, she soon became active in the Committee for Nonviolent Action. Deming travelled to Havana shortly after the Cuban Revolution and an article in *The Nation,* dated 28 May 1960, began her career as a political essayist.

In 1964, Deming joined the interracial Quebec-Washington-Guantanamo Walk for Peace and Freedom. The marchers were arrested in Albany, Georgia, when they insisted on walking together down a major street. Deming spent a month in jail. From this experience, she created *Prison Notes,* her first and most famous book. Written in diary form—first person, present tense, spare, and imaginative—*Prison Notes* juxtaposed political theory with storylike renditions of prisoners' interactions with other prisoners and with their jailers. *Prison Notes* soon gained a reputation as a classic of the 1960s peace and justice movements. Though autobiographical, it made no mention of Deming's life as a lesbian.

Deming's political activism continued with trips to North and South Vietnam (she and four others were deported from Saigon in 1966), an arrest during the 1967 Pentagon action, and work as associate editor of *Liberation,* a pacifist magazine. With the success of *Prison Notes* and Deming's growing fame as an activist, her next three books appeared in short succession. Only one had any gay or lesbian content.

Deming completed *Running Away from Myself: A Dream Portrait of America Drawn From the Films of the Forties,* in 1950. Unable to find a publisher, she laid the work aside until events of the 1960s convinced her that its examination of popular films' reflection of American life was still relevant. *Running Away From Myself* was, perhaps, Deming's least personal and least successful work.

Wash Us and Comb Us contained six short stories Deming wrote during the 1950s. The title story had incidental gay content—an older writer, in the course of her friendship with a young gay male artist, urges him to grab hold of his own life, and assures him his sexual orientation "is no death sentence." The final story, "From 'A Book of Travail'" later reappeared as the first chapter of the lesbian novel, *A Humming Under My Feet.* In this version, the narrator suggests the gender of the loved one only once with an implicit allusion to Penelope in the first paragraph.

Revolution & Equilibrium, Deming's shorter political works from 1960-1970, displayed her development as a pacifist thinker and writer. While not explicitly feminist, these essays—with their inter-connection of different issues and of theory and lived experience, their desanctification of received authority, and confidence in nonviolence as a tactic which defined no one as "Other"—were consistent with her later lesbian feminist writing. *Revolution and Equilibrium* was dedicated to "my sisters in the growing Women's Liberation movement—and especially to Jane."

"Jane" was Deming's partner. During the late 1960s, Deming's relationship with Meigs dissolved and Deming entered another relationship with former college acquaintance Jane Gapen. The couple soon found themselves in an ugly battle to retain custody of Gapen's children, and this demoralizing struggle—they succeeded, through what they felt was bribery—forced Deming to examine her own oppression as a lesbian. Then in 1971, on her way to speak to the War Resisters' League, Deming nearly died in an automobile accident. She never fully recovered.

We Cannot Live Without Our Lives recorded these turning points in Deming's life and writing: the WRL speech she was unable to deliver, in which she called her friends to "confront our own most seemingly personal angers," rather than deal with "anger by analogy," and the 1973 speech in which she publicly came out as a lesbian. Also included was a selection of her poetry, some explicitly lesbian in content, and one previously published poem, "Merrygoround," which now dropped the "Sir" that had appeared in its earlier print incarnation. In a series of letters with an African American comrade of the Quebec-Guantanamo Walk, Deming explained that she had not abandoned, but extended, their struggles for justice: "I have now to face squarely my own particular oppression—never never forgetting—of course—but how could I—that others are oppressed in other ways—and all of us linked."

Deming needed a warmer climate, so she and Gapen moved to south Florida. From Sugarloaf Key, Deming corresponded with allies and opponents in the combative political atmosphere of the 1970s Left. In *Remembering Who We Are,* she self-published her letters on sexuality, patriarchy, and feminist strategy as a series of dialogues—to the extent her correspondents permitted, their articles and letters were also included. Grace Paley described these essay-epistles as "studious, relentless in argument," with a "style which enabled [Deming] to appear to be listening to her correspondent...." Some sections, however, recalled Meigs' description of Deming's style of discussion: "Like an octopus...she would clasp you in her many arms and suck out the counter-arguments until you were bone-dry."

Many of Deming's books were out of print when an anthology made the range of her writings available to a new audience. *We Are All Part of One Another: A Barbara Deming Reader,* published shortly before her death from cancer in 1984, presented a sample of her work in many genres from a 40 year period. Deming and editor Meyerding chose not to edit earlier selections to conform to later usage or insights, so the collection revealed the development of Deming's thinking. As a review by Deming's former companion Mary Meigs noted, the six chapters were "linked by a chain of 18 poems, which sound with quivering intensity the music of a person struggling to be whole." *We Are All Part of One Another* was, the editor observed, "a book about one woman's journey to truth...a glimpse into the 'natural history' of the pacifist-feminist phenomenon" and also a chronicle of Deming's ultimate integration of her struggles as a lesbian with the other justice movements of her era.

Prisons That Could Not Hold appeared posthumously. It included a reprint of her first book, *Prison Notes,* followed by an unfinished essay, "A New Spirit Moves Among Us," about Deming's participation in another peace walk from the 1983 Seneca Women's Peace Encampment and her five days in an improvised jail in upstate New York for acts of civil disobedience. In this essay, addressed to a woman peace activist of the early 1960s, Deming presented a justification for women-only actions and discussed the significance of an open and powerful lesbian presence in the camp. *Prisons That Could Not Hold* thus explicitly linked Deming's later feminist writing with her earlier work about the peace and civil rights movements.

A Humming Under My Feet: A Book of Travail also appeared posthumously, and also explicitly linked Deming's earlier and later writings. Deming began the novel during a trip in the early 1950s, when she was trying to recover from the marriage of a former lover to her brother. In Europe, she fell in love again, with a childhood acquaintance who felt friendship for her but not erotic love. *Humming* fictionalized this year of travel. As the protagonist walks the ruins where the Eleusinian Mysteries (ancient rites celebrating Demeter's reunion with Persephone) were enacted, she feels women's past strength as a humming which still vibrates in the earth. She finds a fragment of a female statue, lays her hands "against the shining ancient breasts," and swears to be the sexual-self that she is, a woman who loves women. "What labour of the spirit have I have been trying to describe?" the narrator asks. "The labour of accepting my sexual self, the labour of guarding it against scorn. My own scorn, of course, as well as that of others."

After Deming wrote the first chapter, "the few friends to whom I submitted those pages couldn't help showing that they were embarrassed for me," she recalled in the foreword; she laid the manuscript aside. Nearly 20 years later, Deming included the chapter in *Wash Us and Comb Us,* but without explicitly lesbian material. Then she began to work on it again. In the final version, the lesbian nature of the story declared itself in the first paragraph, with the loved one named, and the Penelope allusion explicit. A blend of fiction and memoir, poems and polemics, *Humming* showed Deming still pushing at the boundaries of genre, still striving at the end of her life towards a form to contain her personal voice and political struggle as a feminist and lesbian. In *Humming,* she modeled the process of feminist discernment she described to Mab Segrest: "Listening to everything we have to say to ourselves (and also to one another) and trusting that we'll come to see how it all fits together. Not being afraid to seem untidy in the process."

A third posthumous volume, *I Change, I Change,* collected Deming's poetry from her earliest verses written in 1933 when she was involved in her first love affair, to "A Song to Pain," its final lines added a week before her death. Of about 135 poems, only a small portion had been published before. Deming herself planned the volume's organization: eight sections, most named for women she had loved—"Barbara's final uncloseting," noted editor McDaniel. The poems emerged in this collection, in McDaniel's words, as "a small part of [her] legacy, rather than the major expression she hoped for it"—hindered, McDaniel believed, by the layers of "hiddenness" that result from the "closet," and by Deming's ethnic origin in an Anglo-American community which considered social issues unsuitable subjects for poetry.

Esteem for Deming continued to grow after her death, especially among pacifist, feminist, and lesbian activists, for whom she was a model. Since her art and activism were linked, it remained difficult to separate admiration for Deming's living from admiration for her writing. With the posthumous publications, the body of Deming's work brought readers face to face not only with her lifelong development, but also with the implications of the loss to her work because of her lesbian experience. In Grace Paley's words, Deming was "a fine artist who suffered because she was unable to fully use the one unchangeable fact of her life, that she was a woman who loved women."

—Carolynne Myall

DE ROUTISIE, Albert. *See* **ARAGON, Louis.**

DE SAINT ROMAN, Arnaud. *See* **ARAGON, Louis.**

DE VEAUX, Alexis

Nationality: American poet, playwright, and author of short fiction. **Born:** New York City, 24 September 1948. **Education:** State University of New York (SUNY), Empire State College, B.A. 1976; SUNY, Buffalo, M.A. in American Studies 1989, Ph.D. in American Studies 1992. **Career:** Assistant instructor in English, WIN Program of the New York Urban League, 1969; creative writing instructor, Frederick Douglass Creative Arts Center, New York City, 1971; community worker, Bronx Office of Probations, 1972; reading and writing instructor, Project Create, New York, 1973-74; intern, Roundabout Theatre/Stage One, 1974; co-founder and exhibitor, Coeur de l'Unicorne Gallery, New Haven, from 1975; guest lecturer, Livingstone College, Rutgers University, 1975; poetry editor and contributing editor, *Essence* magazine, 1976-90; teacher of creative writing and literature, Sara Lawrence College, New York, 1979-80, Vermont College, 1984-85, Wabash College, Indiana, 1986-87, and SUNY, Buffalo, from 1991. Cultural coordinator, Black Expo for the Black Coalition of Greater New Haven, 1975; co-founder, Flamboyant Ladies Theatre Company, 1977-84; creator, Gap Tooth Girlfriends Writing Workshop, 1980-84. **Awards:** First Prize, Black Creation's National Fiction Contest, 1972; Best Production Award, Westchester Community College Drama Festival, 1973; Art Book for Children Award, Brooklyn Museum, 1974, 1975; Creative Artists in Public Service Grant, New York State Council on the Arts, 1981; National Endowment for the Arts Fellowship, for fiction, 1981; Unity in Media Award, for political reporting, 1982, 1983; Fannie Lou Hammer Award, for excellence in the arts, 1984; MADRE Humanitarian Award, 1984; Coretta Scott King Honor Award, 1988. **Agent:** Charlotte

Sheedy Literary Agency Inc., 65 Bleeker St., New York, New York 10012, U.S.A.

WRITINGS

Fiction

Spirits in the Streets. Doubleday, New York, Anchor Press, 1973.
Li Chen/Second Daughter First Son (prose poem). Ba Tone Press, 1975.

Children's Fiction

Na-ni. New York, Harper & Row, 1973.
An Enchanted Hair Tale. New York, Harper & Row, 1987.

Short Stories

"Remember Him a Outlaw," in *Black Creation,* fall 1972.
"The Riddles of Egypt Brownstone" and "Remember Him a Outlaw," in *Midnight Bird,* edited by Mary Helen Washington. New York, Doubleday, 1980.
"Adventures of the Dread Sisters," in *Memory of Kin, Stories of Family by Black Writers,* edited by Mary Helen Washington. New York, Doubleday, 1991.
"The Ethical Vegetarian," in *The Wild Good: Lesbian Photographs and Writings on Love,* edited by Beatrix Gates. New York, Doubleday, 1996.
"Bird of Paradise," in *Does Your Mama Know,* edited by Lisa Moore. Red Bone Press, 1997.

Poetry

"Poems," in *Hoo-Doo Magazine,* spring 1980.
"Madeline's Dreads," in *Iowa Review,* 1981.
"And do you love me?" in *Open Places,* 1982.
"French Doors: A Vignette," in *Confirmations,* 1983.
"The Sisters," in *Home Girls: A Black Feminist Anthology,* edited by Barbara Smith, Kitchen Table/Women of Color press, 1983; in *Gay and Lesbian Poetry in Our Time: an Anthology,* edited by Carl Morse and Joan Larkin, St. Martins, New York, 1988; in *Love Poems by Women: An Anthology,* edited by Wendy Mulford, 1990.
"Poems," in *Sunbury Magazine,* fall 1984.
Blue Heat: A Portfolio of Poems and Drawings. Brooklyn, Diva Enterprises, 1985.
"Twilight" and "Cuntery," in *Arc of Love: An Anthology of Lesbian Love Poems,* edited by Clare Coss. New York, Scribner, 1996.

Plays

A Little Play and *Whip Cream* (produced the Young People's Workshop of All Soul's Church, Harlem, 1973).
A Season To Unravel (produced St. Mark's Playhouse, New York, 1979).
The Fox Street War (c. 1979).
No (produced New Federal Theatre, New York, 1981).

"The Tapestry" and "Circles," in *Nine Plays by Black Women Playwrights,* edited by Margaret Wilkerson. New York, New American Library, 1986.

Essays

"A Poet's World: Jayne Cortez Discusses Her Life and Her Work," in *Essence,* March 1978.

"Paule Marshall, In Celebration of Our Triumph," *Essence,* May 1979.

"Creating Soul Food: June Jordan," in *Essence,* April 1981.

"Zimbabwe: Women Fire," in *Essence,* July 1981.

"Southern Africa: Listening for the News," in *Essence,* March 1982.

"Sister Love," in *Essence,* October 1983; in *Afrekete: An Anthology of Black Lesbian Writing,* edited by Catherine McKinley and L. Joyce DeLaney, New York, Doubleday, 1995.

"Blood Ties," in *Essence,* January 1983.

"Renegade Spirit: Standing up for Gay Liberation in the Reagan Era," in *Village Voice,* June 1984.

"Going South: Black Women and the Legacies of the Civil Rights Movement," in *Essence,* May 1985.

"New Body, New Life: Dealing with Black Women's Health Issues," in *Essence,* June 1988.

"Alice Walker: Rebel with a Cause," in *Essence,* January 1990.

"Forty Fine: A Writer Reflects on Turning Forty," in *Essence,* January 1990.

"Walking into Freedom with Nelson and Winnie Mandela," in *Essence,* June 1990.

"Remembering Audre (Lorde)," in *Village Voice,* April 1993.

"The Third Degree: Storming the Ivory Tower," in *Essence,* April 1995.

"Indigenous Voice," in *Liberating Memory: An Anthology of Working Class Studies,* edited by Janet Zandy. New Brunswick, New Jersey, Rutgers University Press, 1995.

Other

Don't Explain: A Song of Billie Holiday (biography). New York, Harper & Row, 1980.

Adventures of the Dread Sisters. Independently published comic, 1982.

Motherlands: From Manhattan to Managua, To Africa, Hand To Hand (video documentary).

*

Critical Sources: "Alexis De Veaux" by Priscilla R. Ramsey, in *Dictionary of Literary Biography,* Vol. 38, *Afro-American Writers after 1955: Dramatists and Prose Writers,* edited by Thadious Davis and Trudier Harris, Detroit, Bruccoli Clark, 1985, 92-97; "Alexis De Veaux" by Gerri Bates, in *Black Women in America: An Historical Encyclopedia,* Vol. 1, edited by Darlene Clark Hine, Brooklyn, Calrson, 1993, 333-335; "Alexis De Veaux" by Jewell Gomez, in *Contemporary Lesbian Writers of the United States: A Bio-Bibliographical Sourcebook,* edited by Sandra Pollack and Denise Knight, Westport, Connecticut, Greenwood, 1993, 174-180; "Alexis De Veaux" by Margaret Wilkerson, in *The Oxford Companion to Women's Writing in the United States,* edited by Cathy Davidson and Linda Wagner-Martin, New York, Oxford, 1995, 244.

Alexes De Veaux comments:

The fact that I am a woman who loves women informs all of my work. Whether a particular work is specifically about sexual relationships between women or not. I see the connections between oppressions, not a hierarchical view of them. So I try to balance that seeing.

Over the course of two-and-a-half decades now, I've published in a number of genres: as a writer of children's books, a poet, a playwright, essayist, short fiction writer, and biographer. In all those ways, I was writing from my standpoint as a Black woman working through many things—what it means to be Black and female; how to recognize my own beauty; what it means to be self-defined as an artist; how do, how can, oppressed peoples reconstruct the relationship between the so-called powerful and the so-called powerless; how do I define a female-centered spirituality having grown up in an urban, Black Baptist church as I reject the patriarchal constructs of organized religion; how vegetarianism defines my relationship to and with other life forms; relationship to males and community; an understanding of what homoeroticism means, to me.

Part of what I try to do in my writing about women loving women is to counter traditional and stereotypic images of what that means. Even if that means being at odds with the African American literary "canon." Even if that means being at odds with "acceptable" or "popular" notions of lesbian literature, which tend to privilege issues of sexuality over other issues of difference. The notion that "all lesbians" define ourselves by certain fixed constructs of language and image (butch but not femme; dykes but not "lipstick lesbians"; sexual but not race or class conscious) is confining and false to me. So, in looking for language and images of my own, I try to provide a counter-narrative to what is "politically correct."

The women-identified characters I create, and who become central to my stories, assume lesbianism or lesbian sexuality as a norm, which leaves me far more room, when imagining Black female characters, to talk about the integration of race, sexuality, social status, history, myth-making, and individual expression.

As a writer, I'm trying to imagine the future in the present; a future-present in which the possibilities for love and loving between same-sex partners, especially, are not glossed over, but are as *integrated* as other compelling realities are in the lives of my fictional characters.

*   *   *

For Alexis De Veaux, art is not separate from living: art is life, and life is art. An activist-artist, De Veaux clearly defines her sexual politics in the article "Sister Love" in *Essence* magazine. By rejecting tightly formed categories of lesbian or gay identity, a stand that prefigures the "queer" literary movement of the late 1980s and the 1990s, she declares:

> I am a Daughter of Africa. A Black woman: living in America. At war with the interlocking oppressions of racism and sexism, daily. I celebrate and seek bonds of love and politics with women.

> As I make them, I refuse to wear the stereotypes and labels or fit into categories of dyke/bulldagger/lesbian. Though others use and accept them, these words and

images do not reflect the whole landscape of me. I am more than my sexual expression. I am my race. I am my class. So I must dress myself in my own words. In my conversations and stories. Add the images of my own erotic and everyday and political experiences to those of other/ Black women. To create myself; as valid and positive. My best beautiful. For who will, if I don't.

De Veaux sees sexuality as fluid or flexible, not rigidly determined, but something that can be created and recreated to reflect the individual. In this way, race, class, and gender interact with sexuality, both affecting it and affected by it, which presents both problems and possibilities for each individual. De Veaux believes that if individuals seize control of their own words, stories, and images, they can create and recreate themselves.

Nonetheless, De Veaux understands that there are obstacles to taking control of one's life. Reflecting in "Sister Love" on her own experience as a woman loving woman in the black community, De Veaux confronts the obstacles in her own community:

Now as then; in the revolution and heat of the sixties when I marched to be free; when freedom from racial oppression drew the line at sexual oppression. And certain parts of the Black community did/still does label women with women "incorrect political behavior." To be ashamed of, preferably. Hidden from view. Suppressed.

While reacting to a general environment in both the African-American and the larger society, it is possible that De Veaux is here responding to several reviewers of her play No, staged at the New Federal Theatre in 1981, who were upset about her character Usawa openly showing and discussing her desire for the sculptress Blackberrie. As Jewel Gomez noted in her article on De Veaux in Contemporary Lesbian Writers of the United States: A Bio-Bibliographical Sourcebook, Yusef Salaam, for example, ignored the dramatic quality of the work, dismissed the playwright's anger at the handling of black women by black men, and ended his review "with a flat denial of lesbian existence in African culture."

Though faced with opposition, De Veaux takes a strong stand but looks for a positive solution. As she states in "Sister Love":

But to be silent is to collaborate with my own oppression. To agree—by omission—to generations of negative sexual myths, piled histrionic and solid against me. Against my pussy. And worse: the acceptance of second-class colored/female/leper-status.

But I am not a leper. Something not-to-be discussed; invisible. I live in the light. Iridescent and brazen.

Consequently, for De Veaux, the path that may lead one to "live in the light," to be "iridescent and brazen," is art. Art teaches, yet one might also say that for De Veaux, art is "out," both defiant and enlightening. In art one finds power for oneself and for one's community.

In her anthologized poem "The Sisters," De Veaux, working with strong positive erotic images as well as sensual images of blackness, celebrates the love of woman for woman. The character Selina

muses over the pregnancy of her lover, Ntabuu, and revels in the "summer hot" and their love. With the child as a symbol of their union, Selina agrees to marry Ntabuu, to "Do it proper." The couple agrees to:

Do it voluptuous mornings like this one. In their 4-posted bed. Ntabuu rolls closer. Musk oil and lapis lazuli. Her small hand explores nipple. Selina purrs. Ntabuu fondles the sassy blackness breathing beneath her own. Tongue and tender. Fingers trail her stomach quivers. Ntabuu. Open. Selina. Ntabuu. Way down. Purr Selina.

De Veaux's images meld the erotic to the idea of women bonding, of them forging a long lasting union, but, reflecting a long standing interest, De Veaux concludes the poem with Egyptian imagery:

Purr, Open way down. Slow chant for Isis and Nefertiti. Probe her royal magic. Smell the bold journey. Wait. Flutter. Pulse Ntabuu. Cling Selina. Tangle fingers in hair and slow love sweat. Ancient graffiti hidden on vulva walls.

The use of an ancient Egyptian goddess and an Egyptian queen gives De Veaux's subject of woman loving woman a mythological, almost transhistorical, grounding. The hidden graffiti on vulva walls seems to evoke secret codes of women's sexuality and fertility, a hidden knowledge that binds women lovers together across the ages, that ennobles the love of women. In this way, De Veaux restores power and nobility to women loving women.

In her poem "The Sisters" as well as in her political essays "Sister Love" and "Renegade Spirit: Standing up for Gay Liberation in the Regean Era," De Veaux is "out"; her sexual politics and commitment are clearly asserted. However, in De Veaux's art, the issues of gender, race, and class tend to supersede issues of sexuality. In her writing, woman loving woman sexuality is never relegated to a hidden subtext, but it is often only dealt with in passing—almost as an accepted fact of the text. For example, in Spirits in the Street, the character of Alexis talks with her friend Lynda about her confinement in a girl's home and asks about "the sisters" who ran the home: "how were they with the other girls?" Lynda replies, "ok long as they didn't catch any in bed. it was evil to live without love." Later when Alexis plays a word association game with her friend Michelle, Alexis says, "LOVE," to which Michelle responds, "me. you." In the short story "The Riddles of Egypt Brownstone," the character of Egypt survives being molested as a child and eventually attends college where she is "courted" by her professor, Madame duFer; nonetheless, this potential lesbian affair, which may open new worlds to Egypt, is secondary to the young woman solving the riddle of her family.

Women loving women arises in different contexts and various forms, but it is generally not the central motif for De Veaux's projects. The issues surrounding race, gender, and class are more demanding: the violence, poverty, alienation, and, perhaps most of all, the threat of losing hope are De Veaux's main concerns, the "ailments" she "treats" with her work. In this way, De Veaux clearly demonstrates that issues of sexuality, while present and important, are very much intertwined with other issues, some which can be far more pressing when the survival of the individual and the community are at stake.

—Richard Morris

DONOGHUE, Emma

Nationality: Irish novelist, playwright, and historian. **Born:** Dublin, Ireland, 24 October 1969; daughter of the Irish academic and literary critic Denis Donoghue. **Education:** Muckross Park Dominican Convent, Dublin; University College Dublin, first class degree in English and French; Cambridge University, Ph.D. 1996. **Career:** Co-host, "Book 94" literary television programme, RTE (Irish television), 1994. **Agent:** Caroline Davidson, Caroline Davidson Literary Agency, 5 Queen Anne's Gardens, London W4 1TU, England.

WRITINGS

Novels

Stir-Fry. London, Hamish Hamilton, 1994.
Hood. London, Hamish Hamilton, 1995.

Short Stories

"Words for Things," in *Penguin Anthology of Lesbian Short Fiction,* edited by Margaret Reynolds. London, Hamish Hamilton, 1993; in *Oxford Book of Historical Stories,* edited by Michael Cox and Jack Adrian, London, Oxford University Press, 1994.
"Going Back," in *Ireland in Exile,* edited by Dermot Bolger, Dublin, New Island, 1993; in *Alternative Loves: Irish Gay and Lesbian Stories,* edited by David Marcus, Dublin, Martello, 1994.
"Seven Pictures Not Taken," in *Cimarron Review,* No. 116, July 1996.
Kissing the Witch (fairytales). London, Hamish Hamilton, 1997.

Plays

I Know My Own Heart (produced at Project Arts Centre and Andrews Lane Theatre, Dublin, 1993).
Ladies and Gentlemen (produced at Project Arts Centre, Dublin, 1996).
Trespasses (radio play; produced RTE, 1996).

Other

Passions Between Women: British Lesbian Culture 1668-1801 (history). London, Scarlet Press, 1993.
"Out of Order: Kate O'Brien's Lesbian Fictions," in *Ordinary People Dancing,* edited by Eibhear Walsh. Cork, Ireland, Cork University Press, 1993.
"Noises from Woodsheds: The Muffled Voices of Irish Lesbian Fiction," in *Volcanoes and Pearl Divers,* edited by Suzanne Raitt. London, Onlywomen Press, 1994; revised, in *Lesbian and Gay Visions of Ireland: Towards the Twenty-First Century,* edited by Ide O'Carroll and Eoin Collins. London, Cassell, 1995.
"Liberty in Chains: The Diaries of Anne Lister (1817-24)," in *Breaking the Barriers to Desire.* Nottingham, Five Leaves, 1995.
Editor, *What Sappho Would Have Said: Four Centuries of Love Poems Between Women.* London, Hamish Hamilton, 1997; as *Poems Between Women: Four Centuries of Love, Romantic Friendship and Desire,* New York, Columbia University Press, 1997.

"How Could I Fear and Hold Thee by the Hand? The Poetry of Eva Gore-Booth," in *Sex, Nation and Dissent.* Cork, Ireland, Cork University Press, 1997.
Editor, "Lesbian Encounters," in *The Field Day Anthology of Irish Writing,* Vol. 4, forthcoming.

Recordings: "Expecting" (story), on Radio 4, United Kingdom, 1996.

*

Critical Sources: "Women in Love" by Victoria White, in *Irish Times,* 14 April 1993; "A Sturdy Grip on the Literary Ladder" by Joe O'Connor, in *Sunday Tribune,* 2 January 1994; "New Tastes in a New World" by Eileen Battersby, in *Irish Times,* 22 January 1994; "Take Three Girls" by Michele Roberts, in *Sunday Times,* 13 February 1994; "Stirring Stuff" by Sara Dunn, in *Time Out,* 23 February 1994; "Rhymes with Pariah" by Charlotte Innes, in *Lambda Book Report,* No. 28, 1994; "The Bishop and the Lesbian" by Linda Grant, in *Guardian,* 22 March 1995; "Sect Goddess" by Tilly McAuley, in *Diva,* April 1995; "Emma Donoghue: Love Mourned and Remembered" by E. J. Graff, in *Boston Globe,* 17 March 1996; "Death in Dublin" by Catherine Lockerbie, in *New York Times Book Review,* 24 March 1996.

Emma Donoghue comments:

I write because nothing else gives me such a thrill. I suppose my work has a lot of lesbians in it because (a) so does my life, and (b) very little has been written about lesbians before (relative to heterosexuals), so it's almost virgin territory, which makes it slightly easier to say something new. My first motive is always literary, a matter of what works on the page; my wish to change the world comes a poor second.

I don't have time to worry about the labels used in the publishing business; "lesbian writer" sounds no more limiting than "Irish writer," and neither label narrows the field of what I may write about. I just hope I live long enough to tell all the stories in my head.

*   *   *

In Emma Donoghue's first novel, *Stir-Fry,* Maria, a young student fresh from the country, discovers that she shares the house with a lesbian couple, something which offers her new ways of exploring her own sexuality, after the first confusion has subsided. The book treats the themes of corrupting influences and Irish closeting lightly and humorously. Humour also pervades *Hood,* Donoghue's second novel to date, but the thematics of this book have changed dramatically. It tells of a week in the life of Pen O'Grady, who must come to terms with the death of her lover, Cara, who died in a car crash on her way home from the airport after a holiday in Greece. The routines of Pen's days are interspersed with vivid memories of the ups and downs of their relationship, which began when they were still at convent school. Cara had been a flighty character, whose many flings often upset Pen until they reached a tacit understanding: "'By betrayal,' [Cara] recited, 'I mean promising to be on your side, then being on somebody else's.'...'I'm always on your side, I'm just not always in your bed.'" Pen, steady and monogamous, nevertheless keeps a strong sexual hold over her unpredictable lover: "I always question my motives, my greed for power over the ins and outs of her." For thirteen years they kept "pulling each other's clothes off...when lesbians are meant to hit bed death after two [years]." The graphic descriptions of their active sex life together belie, on a narrative level, the closet life which Pen has kept up—even under the very eye of Cara's father with whom they share the house—and which she now has to confront. The novel brings out most convincingly how the closet prevents the character from releasing her shattering feelings of loss, due to her lack of a recognizable mourning position. Only when she finally opens up to her mother does Pen feel that the tears she has been unable to shed may ground her as the "widow" she actually is.

Beside being a serious—though not heavy—exploration of the nature of loss and love, *Hood* also seems to position itself as a lesbian novel within the context of a male-dominated Irish literary tradition. In the opening scene of the novel Pen crosses half of Dublin's inner city; from the quays along the river Liffey, across College Green, we follow her chasing Cara through Grafton Street and St. Stephen's Green. Inadvertently, the reader is reminded of Leopold Bloom's meandering through Dublin town in James Joyce's *Ulysses,* an association which teasingly keeps emerging when we encounter other aspects of the novel. Like Bloom, Pen suffers from an acute sense of loss caused by death and betrayal. Both characters relive the past through memories they cannot share with others. They each look at themselves through the critical eye of an imaginary observer, and self-irony is for both a means of protection against a seemingly hostile environment. In both novels the characters ultimately search for the immutability of love in a world where everything has changed. Yet, despite these similarities *Hood* seems to go off at its own peculiar tangent. Rather than cow-towing in the wake of Joyce's monolithic novel, Donoghue seems to draw these general comparisons, in order to introduce a world of experiences barely hinted at in *Ulysses.*

The name Donoghue chooses for her protagonist seems a teasing yet indicative allusion to Joyce's Penelope/Molly Bloom character: "...why had my mother given me such a wifey name anyway? The original Penelope should have run off to an island with the wittiest suitor." This is of course precisely what Leopold Bloom is agonizing over when roaming through Dublin. In *Hood,* it is Cara who had left for a Greek isle with her women friends, leaving Pen waiting at home. Like Molly Bloom, Pen gets her period at the end of the novel. But unlike her namesake she does not belong to those women "who slept with men, [and] felt enormous gratitude or grief when the blood came down." For Pen it does not relate to a life-giving force, but is proof "of life surviving in this separate, single body of mine." Whereas Joyce's male fantasy allows for Molly Bloom soliloquizing that she "wouldn't mind being a man and get up on a lovely woman," Pen need not objectify her own body, nor her lover's, as if perceiving it externally through the male gaze. "I want to find her out with the tip of my tongue, going straight to where, though she might expect it, the sensation will startle her most. The reliable surprise of the body saying, oh, that, oh yes that indeed, please that." These words are themselves reminiscent of Molly Bloom's final "yes I said yes I will Yes", yet, in Donoghue's case, firmly anchored in the lesbian experience.

Hood does not show any of the "anxiety of influence" so many Irish novels appear to suffer from in the wake of their monolithic forebear. As a lesbian author, Emma Donoghue, after having settled her score with Joyce, can trace her lineage in the work of Irish writers such as Eva Gore-Booth, Kate O'Brien, and Mary Dorcey, something she has acknowledged in her critical essays. Together with these authors, Donoghue has managed to change the Irish literary landscape once and for all.

—Tonie van Marle

DOTY, Mark (Alan)

Nationality: American poet, memoirist, and educator. **Born:** Maryville, Tennessee, 10 August 1953. **Education:** University of Arizona, 1971-72; Drake University, Des Moines, Iowa, 1974-78, BA in Literature; Goddard College, Plainfield, Vermont, M.F.A. 1980. **Family:** Companion of Wally Roberts, 1951-94. **Career:** Part-time writing and literature instructor, Drake University, Boston University, Suffolk University, and others, 1980-85; writing teacher, Vermont College, 1981-94; faculty member, Goddard College, 1985-90, and Sarah Lawrence College, Bronxville, New York, 1990-94; visiting professor of creative writing, Brandeis University, Waltham, Massachusetts, 1994, Writer's Workshop, University of Iowa, Iowa City, 1995, 1996, Sarah Lawrence College, 1996, and Columbia University, New York City, 1996; professor, Creative Writing Program, University of Utah, from 1997. Regular contributor to *Atlantic Monthly, Boston Globe, Boulevard, Los Angeles Times, Nation, New Yorker, Ploughshares, Poetry,* and *Yale Review.* **Awards:** Massachusetts Artists Foundation Fellowship, 1985; Vermont Council on the Arts Fellowship, 1986; Theodore Roethke Prize, Poetry Northwest, 1986; National Endowment for the Arts fellowship, 1987, 1995; Pushcart Prize, 1987, 1989; James Wright Prize, *Mid-American Review,* 1991; Los Angeles Times Book Award, 1993; National Book Award Finalist, 1993; National Book Critics Circle Award, 1994; Ingram Merrill Foundation Award, 1994; Guggenheim Fellowship, 1994; Whiting Writers Award, 1994; Rockefeller Foundation Fellowship, Bellagio Center, Italy, 1995; American Library Association Notable Book of the Year listing, 1995; Poetry Book Society recommendation, 1995; *New York Times* Notable Book of the Year listing, 1995, 1996; T.S. Eliot Prize, 1996; *Lambda* Literary Award, 1996; Bingham Poetry Prize, 1996; Ambassador Book Award, 1996. **Address:** 19 Pearl Street, Provincetown, Massachusetts 02657-2313, U.S.A.

Writings

Poetry

Turtle, Swan: Poems. Boston, David R. Godine, 1987.
Bethlehem in Broad Daylight: Poems. Boston, David R. Godine, 1991.
My Alexandria: Poems. Urbana and Chicago, University of Illinois Press, 1993.
Atlantis: Poems. New York, HarperCollins, 1995; London, Jonathan Cape, 1996.
Sweet Machine: Poems. New York, HarperCollins, 1998.

Nonfiction

"Reading in the Poetry Garden," in *Design Quarterly* (Minneapolis, Minnesota), No. 160, summer 1994.

"Is There a Future?," in *In the Company of My Solitude: American Writing from the AIDS Pandemic,* edited by Marie Howe and Michael Klein. New York, Persea Books, 1995.

"Sweet Chariot," in *Wrestling with the Angel: Faith and Religion in the Lives of Gay Men,* edited by Brian Bouldrey. New York, Riverhead Books, 1995.

"Poet's Eden," in *New Yorker,* 16 October 1995.

Heaven's Coast: A Memoir. New York, HarperCollins, 1996.

Literary Criticism

"Psalms," in *Parnassus: Poetry in Review* (New York), Vol. 19, No. 2, 1994, 143-150.

"The Brave, Direct, Unflinching Gaze of Paul Monette," in *Boston Globe,* 5 June 1994, B22.

"Horsehair Sofas of the Antarctic: Diane Ackerman's Natural Histories," in *Parnassus: Poetry in Review* (New York), Vol. 20, No. 1-2, 1995, 264-280.

"Places of Memory and Longing," in *Los Angeles Times Book Review,* 22 January 1995, 10.

"City of Angel," in *Los Angeles Times Book Review,* 25 February 1996, 3.

Recordings: "A Display of Mackerel," in *Sixty Years of American Poetry* (videotape), Cambridge, Massachusetts, Harvard University, 1994; *My Alexandria* (audiotape), University of Illinois Press, 1995; *Mark Doty: Readings and Conversations* (videotape), Los Angeles, Lannan Literary Video Series, 1997.

*

Interviews: "That Which Is Left Is Who I Am" by Michael Klein, in *Provincetown Arts* (Provincetown, Maine), Vol. 10, 1994, 19-21, 131-134; "Mark Doty: The Idea of Order on Cape Cod" by Jonathan Bing, in *Publisher's Weekly* (New York), 15 April 1996, 44-45; "Ice and Salt: An Interview with Mark Doty" by Kim Addonizio, in *Poetry Flash* (Berkeley, California), November 1996.

Critical Sources: "Doty Transcendent: Mark Doty's Kind of Heaven on Earth" by Kenny Fries, in *Lambda Book Report* (Washington, D.C.), May 1993, 34; "Book Reviews" by Allen Hoey, in *Southern Humanities Review* (Auburn, Alabama), winter 1993, 99-100; "The Survivor" by David Kirby, in *New York Times Book Review,* 10 March 1996, 10; "How to Live. What to Do: The Poetics and Politics of AIDS" by Deborah Landau, in *American Literature* (Durham, North Carolina), Vol. 68, No. 1, March 1996, 192-225; "Poetry in Review" by Willard Spiegelman, in *Yale Review* (New Haven, Connecticut); "Speak, Gay Memory" by David L. Kirp, in *Nation* (New York), 15-22 July 1996, 33-38.

Mark Doty comments:

For me—as for everyone?—my sexuality is a sort of lens through which I view the world. The queer culture and tradition in which I participate brings with it a number of perspectives, an assortment of gifts: a love of artifice, an interest in surfaces and appearances, in costume and performance, a fascination with the ways we fabricate and fashion ourselves. I believe that it also brings with it a certain attention to the processes and operations of desire, the ways that our longings shape us. And of course, nearly two decades of epidemic have informed contemporary homo culture with a profound sense of transience, too, with a brutally clear view of just how close to the edge we live. We have been reminded of an old fact, which is the inseparability of desire and loss.

Of course these points of view don't have to do with homosexuality per se; they are cultural experiences or perspectives, and are available to anyone. Experiencing oneself as an outsider is both a burden and a sort of privilege, a position of difference from which it is possible to see different things; because I don't belong, perhaps I can know more about what it is I don't belong to. For me, the experiences and perspectives of my decidedly homosexual self are a means of getting at what it is to be human; my wish, as a writer, is to investigate both my difference and my commonality.

*   *   *

In interviews and in his poetry Mark Doty acknowledges the influence of several gay poets, including Constantine Cavafay, James L. White, Elizabeth Bishop, and James Merrill. It is through these poets that Doty developed a poetry of his own that explores gay life, love, and culture with an increasing attention to the effects of the AIDS epidemic. His style has often been called "elegiac" and "transcendent," yet a more evocative description of his work was offered by the poet Philip Levine in his foreword to Doty's *My Alexandria,* where he describes Doty as "a maker of big, risky, fearless poems in which ordinary human experience becomes music."

Mark Doty married at the early age of eighteen, a decision, he remembered in an interview with Jonathan Bing, that was made "in flight from both my family and my sexual orientation which scared me half to death." He worked as a teacher in Des Moines, Iowa, until 1981, when he filed for divorce and moved to New York City "with six hundred dollars to my name, and the kind of energy that springs from knocking down the closet walls and seeing around one a wide and unknown world of possibility," he writes in his memoir *Heaven's Coast.*

Much of Doty's first two books of poetry explores his past, including a childhood growing up in a family in which the effects of alcoholism were evident. The primary movement in this work, however, addresses his growing awareness of himself as gay, as he begins to detail the cultural iconography that this awakening presents. It is through his poetry that Doty was able to reflect upon his turbulent past in order to bring the present into focus. As he relates in an interview with Michael Klein in *Provincetown Arts:*

> Beginning to view your history as a story is a work of interpretation, a way to wield some power over the past, gain authority over it. Rather than be controlled by my own history, I could say, this is how I will understand what memory is, this is how I will understand my life.

In poems such as "Paradise" and "Tiara," both from *Bethlehem in Broad Daylight,* Doty explores the ways in which homosexual desire finds its way into everyday life. This theme finds its way through to his next collection of poetry, *My Alexandria,* which includes the following segment from "Days of 1991":

> After the subway ride,
> he knelt in front of me on the bleachers
> in an empty suburban park, and I reached
> for anything to hold onto, my head thrown back

to blueblack sky rinsed at the rim
with blazing city lights, then down to him:
relentless, dazzling, anyone.

Doty's poetry also brings a sense of dignity and humanity to figures that life might otherwise ignore or revile, such as the drag queen in "Chanteuse" from *My Alexandria*:

Name the color, the one
you've been saving, memory's glimmering
spotlight and sequin: once, upstairs

in a nearly empty room over a crowded bar,
a beautiful black drag queen—perched
on the edge of the piano, under a blue spot,

her legs crossed in front of her
so that the straps of her sparkling ankle shoes
glimmered—sang only to us. The song

was Rodgers and Hart—*My romance
doesn't have to have a moon in the sky*—
and she was perfect.

By 1982 Doty was working as a temp on Park Avenue while teaching in a low-residency M.F.A. program at Vermont College. On a trip to Vermont Doty met Wally Roberts, who was to be his companion for 12 years. Three months later he moved to Boston to live closer to Wally; and in 1985 they both moved to Vermont when Doty joined Goddard College as a full time professor of creative writing. In 1989 both he and Wally took an HIV test, and Wally tested positive. This experience is the subject of "Fog" in *My Alexandria*. In 1990 a new position at Sarah Lawrence College in New York allowed them to move from Vermont to the gay community in Provincetown, Massachusetts, where Wally later died in 1994, and Mark continued to live.

My Alexandria was a finalist for the 1993 National Book Award and stands as a watershed work for Doty. The subject of AIDS is present in all of his work, but it is with Wally's contraction of the HIV virus that it began to take a prominent place in Doty's work, as he relates in these two segments from an interview in *Provincetown Arts*:

An early poem about AIDS, "Turtle, Swan" is about reading these terrible stories in the newspaper and feeling like this could happen in my life, my lover could have AIDS. I wrote that poem in 1984 and now it seems darkly prescient. It was a subject in a sense of something apprehended at a distance. Gradually, it moved closer in, when I found myself writing elegies for friends or acquaintances. The real shift happened when it became not a subject for me, but part of my subjectivity, a part of my daily life.

Sometimes, many times the word is nowhere in sight, the expected details or the expected furniture of a poem about AIDS are nowhere in sight, but that is the dye in which the poem is steeped. It's the condition of my life and I have no choice except to write out of it.

In her study of the poetry of Timothy Liu, Thom Gunn, Paul Monette, and Mark Doty called "The Politics and Poetics of AIDS," Deborah Landau asserts that Doty's approach to the subject of AIDS is unique in "revealing the myths and politics that construct the AIDS epidemic, and by depicting individual acts that defy the pressure of these constructions." The article includes several personal letters that Doty received from readers who thanked him for the "consoling and redemptive power" of his poems. Much of the power of *My Alexandria* and *Atlantis* is derived from his experiences while caring for Wally as his health deteriorated due to the effects of an AIDS related condition known as PML (progressive multifocal leukoencephalopathy).

In *Heaven's Coast* Doty movingly documents Wally's illness, while describing the pain, anger, and sense of loss that accompanied Wally's eventual death in 1994. As Willard Spiegelman commented in the *Yale Review,* "Doty sees beyond death's horror to its luminosity, its beauties." The memoir unflinchingly recounts the process of Wally's and other friends' illness due to AIDS. But Doty does this with an eye that attends to the ways in which this process can be made easier, accepted, and eventually incorporated into one's perception of life.

Heaven's Coast also illuminates *My Alexandria* and *Atlantis* by providing a context for the various landscapes and metaphors that suffuse these collections. It is through his sensual attention to detail that Doty's poetry and prose is able to explore the erotics of life, love, and the significance of death, from a perspective that is at once gay and profoundly universal. Or, as he summarizes in "Description" from *Atlantis,* "What is description, after all, / but encoded desire?"

—Ed Summers

DOWELL, Coleman

Nationality: American novelist, author of short stories, playwright, lyricist, and songwriter. **Born:** Adairville, Kentucky, 29 May 1925. **Education:** Simpson County High in Franklin, Kentucky; University of the Philippines, 1945. **Military Service:** Served in the Army Medical Corps during World War II; Sergeant Major of the 149th Infantry Regiment of the Kentucky National Guard, 1946-50. **Family:** Lived with Dr. Bertram Slaff. **Career:** Songwriter, for the DuMont Television Network show *Once Upon a Tune,* New York, 1950-53; playwright and lyricist, New York, 1953-61. Regular contributor, *Ambit, Conjunctions, New Directions: An International Anthology of Prose & Poetry,* and *Review of Contemporary Fiction;* book reviewer, the *Louisville Courier-Journal,* 1978-85. **Died:** Committed suicide by jumping from the balcony of his 15th-story apartment in New York City, 3 August 1985.

WRITINGS

Novels

The Grass Dies. London, Cassell, 1968; as *One of the Children Is Crying,* New York, Random House, 1968.
Mrs. October Was Here. New York, New Directions, 1974.

Island People. New York, New Directions, 1976.
Too Much Flesh and Jabez. New York, New Directions, 1977.
The Silver Swanne. New York, Grenfell Press, 1983.
White on Black on White. Woodstock, Vermont, Countryman Press, 1983.
Eve of the Green Grass (unpublished manuscript).

Stage Plays

Haymarket. 1949.
Gentle Laurel. 1957.
The Indian Giver. 1959.
The Tattooed Countess (adaptation of novel by Carl Van Vechten; produced New York, 1961). Chappell and Company.
With John LaTouche, *Ah, Wilderness!* (adaptation of play by Eugene O'Neill).
Eve of the Green Grass (produced New York, 1965).

Other

The Houses of Children (collected short stories). New York, Weidenfeld & Nicolson, 1987.
A Star-Bright Lie, introduction by Edmund White (memoir). Normal, Illinois, Dalkey Archive Press, 1993.

*

Manuscript Collections: Coleman Dowell Archives, Fales Collection, Bobst Library, New York University.

Interviews: "An Interview With Coleman Dowell" by John and Linda Kuehl, in *Contemporary Literature,* Vol. 22, No. 3, 1981, 272-91; "Interview with Coleman Dowell" by John O'Brien, in *Review of Contemporary Fiction* (Normal, Illinois), Vol. 2, No. 3, fall 1982, 85-99.

Bibliography: "The Achievement of Coleman Dowell: A Bibliographical Essay" by John and Linda Kuehl, in *Review of Contemporary Fiction* (Normal, Illinois), Vol. 7, No. 3, fall 1987, 227-32.

Critical Sources: "Coleman Dowell's Short Stories" by Miriam Fuchs, in *Review of Contemporary Fiction* (Normal, Illinois), Vol. 2, No. 3, fall 1982, 118-21; "Pushy Jews and Aging Queens: Imaginary People in Two Novels by Coleman Dowell" by Thom Gunn, in *Review of Contemporary Fiction* (Normal, Illinois), Vol. 2, No. 3, fall 1982, 135-45; "Miss Ethel and Mr. Dowell" by John and Linda Kandel Kuehl, in *Review of Contemporary Fiction* (Normal, Illinois), Vol. 2, No. 3, fall 1982, 129-34; "Exorcism and Grace: A Study of Androgyny in *Island People*" by Stephen-Paul Martin, in *Review of Contemporary Fiction* (Normal, Illinois). Vol. 2, No. 3, fall 1982, 124-28; "Some Remarks on *Island People*" by Gilbert Sorrentino, in *Review of Contemporary Fiction* (Normal, Illinois), Vol. 2, No. 3, fall 1982, 122-23; "Thoughts on *White on Black on White*" by Edmund White, in *Review of Contemporary Fiction* (Normal, Illinois), Vol. 2, No. 3, fall 1982, 113-17; "Time Frames—Temporality and Narration in Coleman Dowell's *Island People*" by Ursula K. Heise, in *Journal of Narrative Technique,* Vol. 21, No. 3, 1991, 274-88; "Out with Stars" by Edmund White, in *Lambda Book Report,* Vol. 4, No. 2, January-February 1994, 18-19.

*   *   *

The experimental novels which Coleman Dowell wrote between 1968 and 1983 are preoccupied with the complex ways people use language to conceal their natural inclinations. Narrators take shelter behind other narrators; stories are layered within other stories. Often Dowell's characters begin as stereotypes—bitchy, aging queens, spinster school teachers, ideological revolutionaries. But Dowell quickly strips away their masks. As the characters find a voice for their desires, self-deception makes way for revelation. And what comes to surface is the assurance that we are all composed of opposites: masculine and feminine, moral and immoral, carnal and chaste. In an interview with John and Linda Kuehl, Dowell stated, "...my concern is psychology, the subterranean, the awareness that what's said is not what's meant, and that what we do is not what we would like to do."

Dowell uses sexuality as a mirror to reflect issues of racial and gender inequality. Much of Dowell's preoccupation with sexuality may stem from his childhood fascination with his own father, and from the repeated sexual abuse he experienced at the hands of a teenage boy who worked for his aunt. One of six children, Dowell evoked early family experiences to pen his first novel, *One of the Children Is Crying,* a psychological study of the fictional McChesney family. Dowell acknowledged in his interview with the Kuehls, "I would have gone to bed with my father and sisters in a second." It is partly the horror of incestuous relationships which drives the plot of *One of the Children Is Crying,* in which Erin and Robin, the eldest brother and sister, take on the role of mother and father to protect the other children from their father's abuse. Dowell returns to the theme of incest again in the short story, "My Father Was a River." In this story, according to Meriam Fuchs, "The boy's courtship with the river echoes his parent's relationship. He purposely defers his pleasure, thinking he and his father are slowly seducing each other."

Each of Dowell's novels grows more frank in its exploration of gay themes. While *One of the Children Is Crying* deals with homosexuality only briefly, Dowell's second novel, *Mrs. October Was Here,* is deeply concerned with hatred against gays, blacks, and Jews. The central plot involves the spark of revolution in mythical Tasmania, Ohio, by a woman who hides behind the pseudonym Mrs. October. The citizens have already undergone a sexual revolution, thanks to the central gay character in the novel, Omerie Chad, who lives with his dachshund, Madame Alexis. Omerie has seduced the men of Tasmania (including the police chief) and holds occasional orgies in his home. Through her own revolution, Mrs. October hopes to banish hatred from the town; Omerie is her intended scapegoat. In the *Review of Contemporary Fiction,* Thom Gunn wrote "Omerie has been introduced as the lonely fastidious homosexual exiled in the provinces, sterile and ineffectual—but he isn't ineffectual at all, for he triumphs over Mrs. October, the revolution, and the world, on his own terms."

Dowell continues to explore the theme of homophobia in *Island People.* But now the gay character assumes a primary role. The narrator of this novel is a homosexual, who, like Omerie Chad, lives alone with his dachshund. He hates two things about himself: his feminine nature, and the fact that he is growing old. *Island People* is a work of complex subtlety in which hate is commingled with the need to bring our opposing sides face-to-face. The unnamed narrator, a writer, creates a character named Beatrix whose persona takes possession over him. Through the act of writing as Beatrix, he creates alternating histories for himself. He must make peace with his feminine side before he dies.

In Dowell's fourth novel, *Too Much Flesh and Jabez,* a spinster school teacher, Miss Ethel, reminisces about a former student, Jim, with whom she has been in love. Unsatisfied with the way his life has unfolded, Miss Ethel invents a gay lover for him named Jabez. Like the narrator of *Island People,* who shelters himself behind the character of Beatrix, Miss Ethel hides behind Jabez, inventing an elaborate, erotic seduction of Jim by the fictitious boy. Dowell claimed that this was the first novel he had written which contained homosexual action. As he told John O'Brien, "I had to make Jabez a boy because Miss Ethel could not even face the idea of being penetrated. She could accept homosexuality because it's not a woman, it's not herself."

White on Black on White, Dowell's final novel, examines gay relationships most openly. In this book, a white writer yearns for a black ex-convict named Calvin. The white man feels an unsatisfied lust for Calvin, but also despises him. When the two men see an interracial couple, Calvin rages about whites obsessed by blacks. His companion, ironically, contemplates his own homosexual desire for heterosexual men. The final section of the novel provides the narrator's attempt, through language, to become the black man he and Calvin first viewed with the white woman.

Unfortunately, Dowell's fiction has not yet found a mass audience, and there are few critical studies which discuss these works. The 1993 publication of Dowell's early memoirs, *A Star-Bright Lie,* provides some insight into the man who wrote about gay life with such elaborate cunning. And yet, like his characters, Dowell hides behind his own narrative, concealing key facts. Perhaps the closest we can come to understanding him is through the portrait Dowell painted of himself as Aurelie Angelique, the narrator of *Mrs. October Was Here.* As Dowell told the Keuhls, he rendered himself through this female narrator. "[T]here are people who claim she's not a woman or even a black...So finally I identified myself to the reader." Ultimately Dowell revealed himself, like his characters, not through what he was, but through what he was not.

—Gene Hayworth

DREHER, Sarah

Nationality: American novelist and playwright. **Born:** Sarah Anne Alleman in Hanover, Pennsylvania, 26 March 1937; changed name legally circa 1980. **Education:** Hanover's public schools through grade seven; The Baldwin School, Bryn Mawr, Pennsylvania, through grade 12; Wellesley College, Wellesley, Massachusetts, B.A. in Psychology 1958; Purdue University, West Lafayette, Indiana, M.S. 1961, Ph.D. in Clinical Psychology 1963. **Career:** Clinical psychologist in private practice, specializing in Jungian-oriented dream analysis, Amherst, Massachusetts, from 1963. Co-founder, Women's Community Theater and Theater, Too, a lesbian theater, Amherst/Northampton, Massachusetts; helped to organize Lesbian and Gay pride marches in Northampton, Massachusetts; member, Amherst Town Meeting, 1987-1991, and the Civil Rights Review Commission, co-chair, 1990-1995, secretary, 1995-1996. **Awards:** Reisner Trophy for Short Story Writing, Purdue University, 1959, 1960; Playwriting Fellow, The Artists Foundation, Massachusetts Council for the Arts, 1980; winner, Massachusetts Playwriting Festival, The Artists Foundation, for *Backward, Turn Backward*; winner, First Annual National Lesbian Playwriting Contest, Theatre Rhinoceros, San Francisco, California, for *8x10 Glossy,* 1985; L.A. Weekly Theater Award for outstanding achievement in playwriting, for *8x10 Glossy,* 1986; Alliance for Gay and Lesbian Artists in the Entertainment Industry Media Award, for *8x10 Glossy,* 1987; Jane Chambers Memorial International Gay Playwriting Contest, for *Alumnae News: The Doris Day Years,* 1987; Finalist, Jane Chambers Playwriting Award, for *Open Season,* 1994. **Address:** 21 Valley View Dr., Amherst, Massachusetts 01002, U.S.A.

WRITINGS

Novels

Something Shady. Norwich, Vermont, New Victoria Publishers, 1986; London, Pandora Press, 1988.
Stoner McTavish. Norwich, Vermont, New Victoria Publishers, 1985; and London, Pandora Press, 1987.
Gray Magic. Norwich, Vermont, New Victoria Publishers, 1987.
A Captive in Time. Norwich, Vermont, New Victoria Publishers, 1990.
Otherworld. Norwich, Vermont, New Victoria Publishers, 1993.
Bad Company. Norwich, Vermont, New Victoria Publishers, 1995.

Plays

Ruby Christman and *8x10 Glossy,* in *Places, Please!: The First Anthology of Lesbian Plays,* edited by Kate McDermott. San Francisco, Spinsters, Ink/Aunt Lute Press, 1985.
Lesbian Stages: Collected Works by Sarah Dreher. Norwich, Vermont, New Victoria Publishers, 1988.
Hollandia 45, in *Lesbian Culture: An Anthology,* edited by Julia Penelope and Susan J. Wolfe. Freedom, California, The Crossing Press, 1993.

Other

"Waiting for Stonewall," in *Sexual Practice, Textual Theory,* edited by Susan J. Wolfe and Julia Penelope. Cambridge, Massachusetts, Blackwell Publishers, 1993.
Preface, *Lesbian Culture: An Anthology,* edited by Julia Penelope and Susan J. Wolfe. Freedom, California, The Crossing Press, 1993.
"Stoner McTavish," in "The Gay and Lesbian Detective," *Mystery Readers Journal,* Vol. 9, No. 4, winter, 1993/1994.

*

Critical Sources: *Contemporary Lesbian Writers of the United States,* edited by Sandra Pollack and Denise Knight, Westport, Connecticut, Greenwood Press, 1993; unpublished interview with Sarah Dreher by Andrea L.T. Peterson, 4 August 1995 and September 1996.

*   *   *

Although her love for Snow White—at the tender age of six—did reveal to her the truth about herself at some level, Sarah Dreher still wasn't really out even to herself when, at Wellesley, she was actually outed—and nearly ousted—when a rumor about Dreher and another female student began to make its way around the campus. A few years after the events at Wellesley, she began to write a "coming out" novel which to this day remains unfinished. "Back then it was pretty scary writing as a lesbian," she says. But "as a lesbian" was the only way Dreher knew how to write. She would later say of her plays in particular, that they "are about being a lesbian. Sometimes well-meaning souls suggest that I 'widen my viewpoint, write for a larger audience,' or other variations on the old 'pretend to be like the rest of us' theme. I can't do that, and I won't. I am a lesbian, and I see the world through lesbian eyes."

The loneliest years of her life were those during which she could not accept herself. Writing freely has purged the specters of self-hatred and low self-esteem. She did not come out until 1972 when she became involved in the women's movement. "The women's movement of the 1970s not only created a safe atmosphere in which to 'come out,'" she noted in an interview with *GLL* contributor Andrea L. T. Peterson, but it also "made all of us believe in the strength, power, and value of women and women's work." That realization is the cornerstone of her own work, and passing it on is her gift to another generation of women.

In 1974 she became involved in a revue for International Women's Week, her first theatrical endeavor since high school. She then collaborated on several productions. By 1980 it was clear that her writing was going to be respected; her plays were being performed and her writing was beginning to be published. At this point, when her reputation was being formed, she took her mother's maiden name. "I didn't want my father's family to get the credit," she said of the switch from Alleman to Dreher.

Since 1985, with the publication of Dreher's first novel, *Stoner McTavish,* Dreher has brought back and developed the title character in five additional novels. McTavish, named for Lucy B. Stone who, like the fictional Stoner, frequently found herself knee-deep in someone's else's mess, is an independent, self-motivated lesbian who projects the kind of strength of character, determination, and self-confidence that serves as a model for lesbians raised to believe that women are inferior and lesbians are even more inferior than other women. "Stoner is me with guts," Dreher declared in an interview. Stoner is many lesbians with guts, hence this unassuming travel agent easily engages the imagination of her fans. "She could be me," or "I could be her" is not an unrealistic thought on the part of readers.

As do most writers, Dreher brings to her writing what she knows: lesbianism, the world of therapy and counseling, and a belief in and an interest in things supernatural. Her award-winning play, *Alumnae News: The Doris Day Years,* was inspired by her experience at Wellesley and the invaluable lessons about homophobia it taught her. Although she considers herself "part of a long tradition of lesbian writers, a pretty wonderful tradition," she is, along with heterosexual women mystery writers like Sara Paretsky and Sue Grafton who have paved the way, one of a handful of lesbian mystery writers to be establishing the guidelines and in essence "creating" a new tradition in which women stand alone, often in opposition to those presumed to be more powerful, i.e. men with clout or men with muscle. To this end, for Dreher, the roles of women are central, not subordinated to those of the men in her fiction. Their lesbianism is taken for granted, and her work is not an apologetic for either feminism or gay rights. Her focus is more on women's relationships with each other and with men, good and evil in the universal order of things, as well as in the daily lives of individuals.

Dreher brings an additional dimension to her work, the otherworldly. "I've been told I'm hard to classify because I bring that metaphysical touch [into my work] from time to time," Dreher remarked. That "metaphysical touch" might be anything from intuition and ESP to actual visions, psychic readings, or travel through time that lead to the resolution of McTavish's dilemmas. Her graduate school advisor, Edith Weisskopf-Jeolson, taught her that "there's more than one way to look at everything," and Dreher has expanded that bit of advice beyond the more-than-one-side-to-every-story notion to include many layers of truth and many dimensions of reality. "I have always felt," she says, "there is more to life than it appears."

With more than a dozen plays published and produced and a handful of her novels published in England and translated into German, Dreher's greatest satisfaction "comes from knowing that somewhere in a remote part of the country, there's a young lesbian who feels a little less alone and a little less afraid because something I've written has touched her. If Stoner had been around when I was young," says Dreher, who was young during the 1940s and 1950s, "maybe it would have been a little easier."

Characters like Dreher's Stoner McTavish send a message to all young women, not just lesbians, that they are not alone; that they are not born to be victims; that they are capable of taking control of their own lives and changing the world. In that respect, hers is an invaluable contribution to the ever-growing body of lesbian literature of which it is part. And her self-acceptance and her commitment to being out as well as out there writing as a lesbian is encouragement to others to live free of the closet and to resist the droning pleas of others to conform, to change, to be something they are not.

—Andrea L.T. Peterson

DUNYE, Cheryl

Nationality: American filmmaker and cultural activist. **Born:** Monrovia, Liberia, 13 May 1966; moved with her family to Philadelphia, Pennsylvania, in 1968. **Education:** Merion Mercy Academy for Girls, Merion, Pennsyvlania, 1972-84; Michigan State University, 1984-86; Temple University, B.A. 1990; Rutgers University, M.F.A. 1992. **Family:** Companion of producer Alexandra Juhasz. **Career:** Film writer, producer, and director, from 1991; film instructor, Pitzer College, Claremont, California, from 1996. **Awards:** Art Matters Inc. production fellowship, 1992; Independent Images Fine Cut Winner, WHYY TV 12, 1993; Pew Fellowship for the Arts Discipline Winner, 1993; Rockefeller Foundation Nominee, 1993, 1995; Frameline Completion Grant, 1993, 1995; Whitney Museum of American Art Biennial exhibitor, 1993, 1997; MARMAF Pennsylvania Major Artist Award, 1994; Lesbisch-Schule Filtage Hamburg Ursula Award, for best short film, 1995; New York Lesbian and Gay Film Festival Vito Award, 1995; National Endowment of the Arts Media Production Award, 1995; Los Angeles OUTFEST Audience Award, 1996; Torino (Italy) International Gay and Lesbian Film Festival Audience Award, 1996; Cretiel (France) International Festival of Women's Cinema Audience Award, 1996; Berlin International Film Festival Teddy Award, 1996. **Address:** Pitzer College, Department of Media Studies, Claremont, California 91711, U.S.A.

WRITINGS

Films Written and Directed

And producer, *Janine*. 1990.
And producer, *She Don't Fade*. 1991.
With Pat Branch, and producer, *The Potluck and the Passion*. 1993.
And producer, *An Untitled Portrait*. 1993.
Greetings from Africa. 1994.
And director, *The Watermelon Woman*. 1996.

Essays

"Building Subjects," in *Movement Research Performance Journal* (New York), winter-spring 1992.
"(Re)Position," in *Felix* (New York), spring 1993.
"Possessed," in *Bad Girls*. Cambridge, Massachusetts, MIT Press, 1994.
With Zoe Leonard, "Watermelon Woman: The Fae Richards Photo Archive," in *Parkett* (Zurich, Germany), 1996.
"Vanilla Sex," in *The Wild Good,* edited by Beatrix Gates. New York, Double Day, 1996.
With Zoe Leonard, *The Fae Richards Photo Archive*. San Francisco, Artspace Books, 1997.

*

Critical Sources: "Girl Gets Girl" by Rachel Abramowitz, in *Premiere,* February 1996; "From Phila. Street Vendor to Star of Her Own Small Films" by Carrie Rickey, in *Philadelphia Inquirer,* 7 May 1996, F1; "Black Lesbian Film Likely to Rekindle Arts-funding Furor" by Julia Duin, in *Washington Times,* 14 June 1996; "Cheryl Dunye" by Anne Stockwell, in *Advocate,* 17 September 1996; "Faxu Pas de Deux: *The Watermelon Woman* is the newest NEA whipping boy" by Mark J. Huisman, in *Independent,* October 1996; "Cheryl 2000" by Jennifer Maytorena Taylor, in *FilmMaker,* Vol. 5, No. 1, fall 1996, 31; "Color-corrected Film" by Anne Stockwell, in *Advocate* (San Francisco), 4 March 1997; "Sexin' the Watermelon" by Michele Wallace, in *Village Voice,* 4 March 1997; "A Woman of Independent Mien" by Ernest Hardy, in *LA Weekly,* March 28-April 3 1997; interview with Cheryl Dunye by *GLL* contributor Pamela Green, Boston, Mass, April 1997.

*   *   *

To fully appreciate Cheryl Dunye's films one must place them in the context of contemporary mainstream political views. One must realize the overwhelming absence of the voices of minority women in political discourse, even at the end of the twentieth century. One must ignore politically correct views that sometimes create fearful silence, the silence that Cheryl Dunye works to avoid. Dunye provokes reaction by analyzing the world through the eyes of a black, middle class, educated lesbian who has never found one community in which she truly belongs.

Dunye describes her journey to this outsider's position in the 1994 essay "Possessed": "In the early 1980s...I decided that I was...an anarcho-lesbian feminist separatist—a bad girl. By 1985, the term black was missing from my life so I tried to add it to my anarcho-lesbian feminist separatist label.... And at this time I was a bad girl not because of my race but because of my sexual prefer-

ence. Which brings me to the 1990s and my schizophrenic feelings about identity and politics.... I decided...to be a good girl. A good girl truthfully talks about who she is and how she is." In an interview with *GLL* contributor Pamela Green in 1997 she expanded on this identity metamorphosis: "I'm a bad girl done good. I'm a bad African American because I talk about sexuality. I'm a bad lesbian talking about interracial relationships. But that's not bad. These are just things that have had to be hidden."

Dunye's "bad girl" theme and her quest for identity reoccur throughout her work. She attempts to discuss multiple identities and identity problems which are typical themes for many gays, but especially for minority gays. She pokes at deep-seated stereotypes and articulates some people's deepest darkest secrets. Like filmmaker Spike Lee, Dunye examines the reality of the black community, the reality of being a minority, and the various realities experienced by minorities. But where Spike Lee focuses strictly on race, Dunye broadens her view to include race, gender, sexuality, and all their various interactions. But Dunye's films are not angry diatribes condemning the patriarchy or even the white majority. Instead, Dunye humorously condemns parts of the majority beliefs and also some of the beliefs and ideals of the gay, feminist, and African-American communities.

Dunye commented about her use of humor in "Possessed":

> In the politically correct world of feminist video production, humor tends to clash with things like sexism, racism, and oppression.... There seems to be something too provocative and painful in humor that crosses these personal and political lines, something a bit incorrect. Lately I wonder about these notions of correctness and question their "correctness." Why can't women talk about serious personal and political things in an unserious fashion? Are women artists afraid that humor might weaken the intensity of the issue at hand?"

Dunye told Green that when she began making *The Watermelon Woman* in 1993 she was trying to determine which identity hat she was going to wear: "the black, lesbian hat; the lesbian hat; the feminist hat." Now she has found that it's about wearing all the hats: "Life is about the plurality of identity and being comfortable about that. It's about dealing with cultural baggage and moving on."

The Watermelon Woman, a mock documentary, tells the story of Cheryl, a 25-year-old black lesbian, who wants to make a film about a black lesbian actor from the pre-1950s who was pigeonholed into mammy roles and was known only as the Watermelon Woman. The film depicts the deterioration of Cheryl's relationship with a wealthy white woman as her search for information about her historic "sister" comes together. In *The Watermelon Woman* Dunye proves that lesbians of color are more than the weak stereotypes they've been made out to be by Hollywood, that is, when they are mentioned at all. The characters in all her works—but especially in *The Watermelon Woman* and *The Potluck and the Passion* (a short about a group of friends who congregate over dinner one night and discuss racism, homophobia, and identity through their personal conversations and interactions)—are smart women whose likes have been ignored by mainstream media. Her films are a cry for attention and validity, similar to Virginia Woolf's *A Room of One's Own* in 1929. As Anne Stockwell wrote in the *Advocate*: "This film expands Wolf's message: Lesbian artists have to keep hammering away, Dunye is saying, because we speak for women who will never be heard except through us."

In all of Dunye's works, the lines between stereotypes and real personalities get blurred, as they often do within minority groups in society. She actually uses minority stereotypes as influences. In *Greetings from Africa* she turns the table on a white lesbian who is attracted to black lesbians and travels to Africa with the Peace Corps. In *The Watermelon Woman* Dunye took the black faces that were used solely for humor in the early 1900s and turned them into something complete and realistic. As Dunye told Green: "I take the stereotypes and put something real in their mouth." Dunye's technique of embracing the stereotypes in order to expose the reality of a character creates uncomfortable feelings for some. As the characters in the television shows *All in the Family, The Jeffersons,* and *The Simpsons* make stereotypes obvious and therefore either humorous or humiliating, so do Dunye's characters. Dunye communicates through her films that the time has come for boundaries to be crossed, for the limits and confines of our society to be pushed.

—Pamela Green

DUPLECHAN, Larry

Nationality: African American novelist and short story writer. **Born:** Panorama City, California, 30 December 1956. **Education:** University of California, Los Angeles, B.A. 1978. **Family:** Companion of Greg Harvey, from 1976. **Career:** Pop/jazz vocalist, Los Angeles, 1975-82; librarian's assistant, University of California, Los Angeles, 1976-80; word processor and legal secretary, 1980-90; real estate legal secretary, from 1990. Contributor to periodicals, including *Advocate, Black American Literature Forum, L.A. Style,* and *New York Native.*

WRITINGS

Novels

Eight Days A Week. Boston, Alyson Publications, 1985.
Blackbird. New York, St. Martin's Press, 1986.
Tangled Up in Blue. New York, St. Martin's Press, 1990.
Captain Swing. Boston, Alyson Publications, 1993.

Essays

"She's My Mother" in *A Member of The Family.* New York, Dutton, 1992, 41-52.
"Mar Vista, California" in *Hometowns: Gay Men Write About Where They Belong,* edited by John Preston. Boston, Alyson Publications, 1991, 243-256.

Short Stories

"Presently in the Past" in *Certain Voices: Short Stories About Gay Men,* edited by Darryl Pilcher. Boston, Alyson Publications, 1991, 190-197.

"Peanuts and the Old Spice Kid" in *Black Men/White Men,* edited by Michael Smith. San Francisco, Gay Sunshine Press, 1983, 139-142.
"Zazoo" in *Shade: An Anthology of Fiction By Gay Men of African Descent.* New York, Avon Books, 1996, 165-177.

*

Interviews: "CS Interview with Larry Duplechan" by Christopher Davis, in *Christopher Street,* Vol. 10, 1987, 60-62.

Critical Sources: "Towards a Black Gay Aesthetic: Signifying in Contemporary Black Gay Literature" by Charles I. Nero, in *Brother to Brother: New Writings by Black Gay Men,* Boston, Alyson Publications, 1991, 229-252; "Larry Duplechan" by John H. Pearson, in *Contemporary Gay American Novelists: A Bio-Bibliographical Critical Sourcebook,* Westport, Connecticut, Greenwood Press, 1993, 116-121.

*   *   *

Any movement for change born out of the desire of a social minority to be heard and acknowledged will generate a literature which both articulates political goals and reflects the internal realities of the group. This has been particularly true for the gay and lesbian community, as evidenced by the explosion of works with openly homosexual themes published since 1969. While the content of such politically oriented works as Randy Shilts' *And The Band Played On* and Urvashi Vaid's *Virtual Equality* are accessible to general audiences, much of gay-related poetry and fiction has centered upon the dominant cultural image of the American homosexual as a white male. While the literary tradition of African America had included sporadic daring homosexual voices as far back as the Harlem Renaissance writings of Langston Hughes, Countee Cullen, and the extraordinary pioneering work of Richard Bruce Nugent, it was only during the early 1980s that a substantial number of contemporary works began to be written voicing the lives and concerns of gays and lesbians of color. Short stories and poems were the most popular literary forms initially chosen, leaving the field of longer fiction works vacant of major male characters of color. It is in this context that the contribution of Larry Duplechan's novels must be considered.

The first major anthology of the work of black gay writers, *Black Men/White Men,* appeared in 1983. Among its entries was the short story "Peanuts and the Old Spice Kid," marking the formal beginning of Larry Duplechan's writing career. In an interview for the reference series *Contemporary Authors,* he noted he was motivated to write due to the fact that "there were nearly no black characters in any of the gay books I found." Out of this absence was born the unique being of Johnnie Ray Rousseau, musician, writer, scathing social critic and narrator of three of Duplechan's four novels. He debuted in *Eight Days a Week,* a story of interracial male romance set in Los Angeles which drew upon the author's own experiences as an aspiring pop singer and his personal relationship. The interplay of expectations within an interracial romance and the question of how each partner can and should make demands of the other are dominant themes frankly explored. Challenges raised by the basic question of reconciling the multiple identities of being male, black, and gay are expressed in everything from the collision of musical tastes (girl groups versus Wagner) to the definition of career paths.

The process of exploration continues in Duplechan's second novel, *Blackbird,* an autobiographical work in the tradition of Mildred Taylor's *Roll Of Thunder, Hear My Cry.* Here the scene shifts to analyzing issues of community hypocrisy about sexuality in all forms, racial tensions (both unspoken and overt) and homophobia within the black community through the eyes of one of the few black students in an all-white high school. A younger Johnnie Ray recounts the growth of his awareness of his different sexuality, taking the reader inside the acutely painful choices relating to open expression of any sort of difference which are the essence of adolescent life. Organized religion and its entrenched attitudes on same-sex behaviors are deftly portrayed, culminating in a savagely funny attempt to exorcise the demons possessing the main character. As in *Eight Days a Week,* popular music is used as a powerful omnipresent force, from which the high school students derive their framework of values. An excellent example of this is the work's title, which picks up the theme of isolation from the song lyrics "Blackbird singing in the dead of night...you were only waiting for this moment to arrive."

In *Tangled Up in Blue,* Duplechan shifts focus to consider the complex emotional dynamics of the AIDS pandemic, as expressed among an heterosexual couple and their gay friend. The emphasis in this work is on the creation, development and shattering of networks of trust and intimacy between individuals, and their potential range of sexualities, and capacities for forgiveness and rebirth. This work is in some ways a departure from the familiar first-person voices which narrate the rest of the author's novels and short stories, while stressing the absolute irrelevance of artificial social customs, stereotypes and standards in the face of death.

Captain Swing is perhaps Duplechan's most powerful and harshly frank depiction of the position of homosexuals in African American society. The story brings back an older Johnnie Ray out of the heavily urban setting of Los Angeles where much of his life and past success lies in another world, that of his rural southern kin where his father has returned to die. The hope for final reconciliation over being rejected due to his gay identity (a theme first introduced less directly in the opening pages of *Eight Days a Week*) proves false, a ploy created by his aunt to serve the needs of propriety. Anger over this is used as a vehicle to explore the standards of acceptable conduct and the uses of denial within the Black community on many matters, complicated by the recognition of a younger male relation as gay. Eventually, the unpalatable fact of Johnnie Ray's identity proves too strong for the tight social network of blood kin and the extended family structure created by the church, despite his being valued as a singer. The phenomenon of ageism within the gay community also surfaces through the rejection of an offer of a life in Los Angeles by his cousin, who can accept Johnnie Ray's affection but insists on the chance to create a life on his own terms. In this way, the circle of Duplechan's fiction has come back to its beginning, returning a chagrined older gay man to a life he will never view in quite the same way, watching a younger version of himself heading out into a changed world. Duplechan's willingness to give voice to the often monolithic homophobia, deliberate incomprehension and active rejection faced by openly gay African American men places him firmly with such challenging writers as the poets Essex Hemphill and Assoto Saint and the late Joseph Beam, who have likewise testified to a reality both mainstream American society and the gay and lesbian communities have been reluctant to acknowledge and signify.

—Robert B. Marks Ridinger

DYKEWOMON, Elana

Pseudonyms: Also known as S.P. Wonder and Elana Dykewoman. **Nationality:** Ashkenazi Jewish American novelist, poet, fiction writer, editor, and activist. **Born:** Elana Nachman in New York City, 11 October 1949. **Education:** Studied literature at Reed College, Portland, Oregon; California Institute of Art, B.F.A. in Creative Writing 1971; San Francisco State University, California, M.F.A. in Creative Writing 1997. Editor, *BOX,* Valencia, California, 1971, *Rainbow Grease,* Cummington, Massachusetts, 1971, *The Women's Journal,* Northampton, Massachusetts, 1973-74, *The Women's Film Co-op Catalog,* Northampton, 1973-77, *Bandon Historical Society Press,* Bandon, Oregon, 1980-82, with Dolphin Waletzky, *Diaspora Distribution,* Langlois, Oregon, 1980-85, and *Sinister Wisdom,* 1987-97; printer and typesetter, 1979-94. Performed readings and workshops in U.S.A. and Canada, from 1971; gave day-long workshops in Barcelona, San Francisco, and Michigan Women's Music Festival; Writers' Coordinator, First West Coast Lesbian Festival, 1992; frequent contributor to periodicals, including *Amazon Quarterly, Amazones D'Hier—Lesbiennes D'Aujourd'Hui, Assembling, Big Deal, Black Maria, Bridges: A Journal for Jewish Feminists and Our Friends, Chomo-Uri* (University of Massachusetts), *Common Lives/Lesbian Lives, Diana's BiMonthly, Epoch* (Cornell University), *Fat Girl* (San Francisco), *Feminist Bookstore News, Lynx, Native Dancer* (Reed College, Oregon), *Open Places* (Stephens College), *Shameless Hussy Review, Sinister Wisdom, Transfer* (San Francisco State University), *The Woman's Journal* (Northampton, Massachusetts), and *ZYZZYVA.* **Awards:** Residency, Cummington Community of Art, Cummington, Massachusetts, 1971; residency, Cottages at Hedgebrooke, Langley, Washington, 1993; residency, Helene Wurlitzer Foundation, Taos, New Mexico, 1995; residency, Norcroft Writers' Retreat, Lutsen, Minnesota, 1996. **Address:** 8008 Winthrope St., Oakland, California 94605, U.S.A.

WRITINGS

Novels

Riverfinger Women (as Elana Nachman). Plainfield, Vermont, Daughters, Inc., 1974; Tallahassee, Florida, Naiad Press, 1992; translated into German as *Frauen aus dem Fluss,* West Berlin, Amazonen Frauenverlag, 1977.
Beyond the Pale. Vancouver, British Columbia, Press Gang, 1997.

Poetry

They Will Know Me by My Teeth (short stories and poetry). Northampton, Massachusetts, Megaera, 1976.
Fragments from Lesbos. Langlois, Oregon, Diaspora Distribution, 1981.
"Fifteen Miles from the KKK," in *Nice Jewish Girls,* edited by Evelyn Torton Beck. Watertown, Massachusetts, Persephone, 1982; Boston, Massachusetts, Beacon, 1989.
"learning to breath," in *Shadow on a Tightrope: Writings by Women on Fat Oppression,* edited by Lisa Shoenfielder, Barb Wieser, and Vivian Mayer. San Francisco, California, Aunt Lute Books, 1990.

"I had a dream" and "Even my eyes become mouths," in *Naming the Waves: Contemporary Lesbian Poetry,* edited by Christian McEwen. Freedom, California, Crossing Press, 1990.

"If you were my home" and "Fifteen Miles from the KKK," in *Poetry Readings of the IV International Feminist Bookfair.* Barcelona, Spain, 1990.

"the real fat womon poems," in *Sinister Wisdom* (Berkeley, California), No. 43/44, 1991.

"The Census Taker Interviews the 20th Century" and "The Vilde Chaya and Civilization," in *Bridges: A Journal for Jewish Feminists and Our Friends* (Seattle, Washington), Vol. 3, No. 1, 1992.

"Oakland: February 1991, 1 AM," in *Sinister Wisdom* (Berkeley, California), No. 46, 1992.

"New England Cemetery" and "diving, i kiss," in *Lesbian Culture: An Anthology,* edited by Julia Penelope and Susan Wolfe. Freedom, California, Crossing Press, 1993.

"When to Answer," in *ZYZZYVA,* Vol. 10, No. 2, summer 1994.

"A Law of Physics," in *Bridges: A Journal for Jewish Feminists and Our Friends* (Eugene, Oregon), Vol. 4, No. 1, 1994.

Nothing Will Be as Sweet as the Taste: Selected Poems. London, England, Onlywomen Press, 1995.

Uncollected Short Stories

"The Mezzuzah Maker," in *Common Lives/Lesbian Lives,* No. 8, 1983.

"Staking Claims," in *Common Lives/Lesbian Lives,* No. 17, fall 1985.

"A Train Ride," in *Sinister Wisdom,* No. 28, winter 1985.

"Manna from Heaven," in *The Tribe of Dina,* edited by Melanie Kaye/Kantrowitz and Irena Klepfisz. Boston, Massachusetts, Beacon Press, 1989.

"My Grandmother's Plates," in *Speaking for Ourselves: Short Stories by Jewish Lesbians,* edited by Irene Zahava. Freedom, California, Crossing Press, 1990.

Uncollected Essays

"The Fourth Daughter's 400 Questions," in *Nice Jewish Girls,* edited by Evelyn Torton Beck. Watertown, Massachusetts, Persephone, 1982; Boston, Massachusetts, Beacon, 1989.

"Traveling Fat," in *Out the Other Side: Contemporary Lesbian Writing,* edited by Christian McEwen and Sue O'Sullivan. London, England, Virago Press, 1988; Freedom, California, Crossing Press, 1989.

"Journal Entry," in *For Lesbians Only: A Separatist Anthology,* edited by Sarah Hoagland and Julia Penelope. London, England, Onlywomen Press, 1988.

"The Ex-patriot and Her Name," in *InVersions: Writing by Dykes, Queers & Lesbians.* Vancouver, British Columbia, Press Gang, 1991.

"Introduction," in *Belly Songs,* by Susan Stinson. Northampton, Massachusetts, Orogeny Press, 1993.

"Preface," in *Lesbian Culture: An Anthology,* edited by Julia Penelope and Susan Wolfe. Freedom, California, Crossing Press, 1993.

"A Manifesto, a Genealogy, a Cause—*Found Treasures,*" in *Bridges: A Journal for Jewish Feminists and Our Friends* (Eugene, Oregon), Vol. 5, No. 2, 1995.

Recordings: *Dyke Proud* (tape recording of poetry reading from *Third International Feminist Bookfair in Montreal*). Annor Productions. 1988.

*

Adaptations: Portions of *Beyond the Pale* adapted for the stage by Helen Mintz as part of her one-woman show *Secret Melodies: Jewish Women's Stories,* performed in the U.S.A. and Canada from 1994.

Bibliography: "Elana Dykewomon" by Anna Livia, in *Contemporary Lesbian Writers of the United States: A Bio-Bibliographical Critical Sourcebook,* edited by Sandra Pollack, Denise D. Knight, and Pamella Tucker Farley, Westport, Connecticut, Greenwood Press, 1993, 192-195.

Interviews: "Entrevue avec Elana Dykewomon" by Louise Turcotte, in *Amazones D'Hier—Lesbiennes D'Aujourd'Hui* (Montreal, Canada), No. 21, 1990; "Elana Dykewomon, L'Espoir Radical" by Suzette Triton, Anna Livia, C.G., and B.F., in *Lesbia* (Paris), No. 88, 1990.

Critical Sources: "Riverfinger Womon" by Kayann Short, in *Women's Review of Books,* Vol. 13, No. 4, January 1996; "Reconstructed Selves" by Irena Klepfisz, in *Ms.,* Vol. 3, No. 5, March/April 1993; "Sinister Wisdom" by Bonnie Zimmerman, in *off our backs,* Vol. 22, No. 2, February 1992; *The Safe Sea of Women: Lesbian Fiction, 1969-1989* by Bonnie Zimmerman, Boston, Massachusetts, Beacon Press, 1990; review of *"They Will Know Me By My Teeth"* by Terri Poppe, in *off our backs,* January 1978; review of *"They Will Know Me By My Teeth"* by Marcia Womangold, in *Soujourner,* October 1976.

Elana Dykewomon comments:

I cast my lot with women in my twenties; twenty-five years later it seems to be an irrevocable decision. Words jump through the hoops of self—we make them stand for our presence; they become their own body and walk the earth, sticking their fingers into whatever they can. Once, in a woman's bathhouse in San Francisco, a lesbian told me that reading my first novel made her drop out of college and start jumping freight trains. She seemed to have survived that experience, and I was glad for my words, knowing they'd been hard at work after they'd left me. I hope my words keep finding their way into many wet, rustling places and take root. It is with words, after all, that we begin to create the new worlds we need.

*   *   *

Elana Dykewomon was born Elana Nachman in New York City in October 1949. Raised by Jewish middle-class parents of Russian and Hungarian descent, she is a descendent of the Baal Shem Tov, founder of Hasidim. At the age of eight Dykewomon's family moved to Puerto Rico; at 12 she was placed in a mental hospital. In correspondence with *Gay and Lesbian Literature* contributor tova, Dykewomon states that she "survived psychiatric institutionalization between the ages of 12 and 15 for not knowing a fat Jewish lesbian writer could live in the world—they never told me it was possible during that time, but I eventually decided to 'make it so.'"

After college, Dykewoman attended the Cummington Community of the Arts in Cummington, Massachusetts. While there, she finished her first novel, *Riverfinger Women,* under the name Elana Nachman. *Riverfinger Women* was first published by Daughters Inc. in 1974 when Dykewoman was only 24; the novel was translated into German in 1977, and reprinted in 1992 by Naiad Press. In 1993, Irena Klepfisz described the novel in *Ms. Magazine* as "the first Jewish lesbian work of this era that I know of.... [Dykewomon] has added an afterward to the new edition that describes the politics of lesbian publishing in 1974—a gem and, by itself, worth the price of the book." *Riverfinger Women* was rejected by two mainstream presses, and, at the time, was considered pornographic because of its lesbian content. It was one of the first specifically feminist-oriented lesbian novels and was praised for its poetic nature by many feminist critics.

By the time *They Will Know Me by My Teeth* was published in 1976, Dykewoman was publishing under the name Dykewoman. Her commitment to lesbian feminist writing, publishing, and activism was strong. As Dykewomon told tova in 1997, "I see myself as writing within and for lesbian and womyn's communities." Blossoming in this work are themes—such as honesty, community, and sexuality—and issues—such as fat oppression, Jewish identity, and relationships within the lesbian community—that have continued in all of Dykewomon's work. As Terri Poppe stated in a 1978 *off our backs* review of the short story and poetry collection *They Will Know Me By My Teeth,* the story "Breasts" "is about women, trying to fit into current female standards of size and shape. Lois has a body that doesn't conform." In this work, Poppe continued, "a honed picture emerges: of struggle, honesty, caring among women; a pushing of selves to limits and beyond and becoming stronger; a celebration of our complexity and a challenge to those who dare to look at our Medusas and embrace them."

Some critics of Dykewomon's works have spent more time criticizing Dykewomon's separatist politics than the creative work at hand, at the loss of attention to the most unique elements of her work. Dykewomon's third book, *Fragments from Lesbos,* imprinted with "for lesbians only," was published in 1981 by Diaspora Distribution, a women's distribution and publishing company in Langlois, Oregon, started by Dykewomon and Dolphin Waletzky. At this time, Dykewomon changed the spelling of her name from Dykewoman to Dykewomon, to avoid any association with the word "man." Also about this time, Dykewomon learned the trade of printing, at which she continued to work until 1994, doing everything from letterpress to offset printing and metal to desktop typesetting.

Editing has also always been a major focus of Dykewomon's activist work. She has edited a wide range of works, many of great import to the women's, feminist, and lesbian communities, including *The Women's Film Co-op Catalog* from 1973 to 1977. From 1987 to 1995, Dykewomon edited *Sinister Wisdom,* an international lesbian-feminist journal of arts and politics. Her "Notes for a Magazine," which appeared in almost every issue during her time as editor, would make a fine collection of insightful, creative, and exciting analyses of the directions and theories of the lesbian-feminist movement of those years. When she took over the editorship from Melanie Kay/Kantrowitz and Irena Klepfisz, Dykewomon, as always, concerned herself with power dynamics, ethics, honesty, accountability, and the workings of the lesbian community. She wrote in her first issue:

> I see that although I have power in shaping *SW,* I shape
> first from what comes in the mail. *SW* is a place. A country.

To which lesbians add their own villages, their own geography, issue by issue. Year by year. I worry about singular editorship—about the nature of hierarchy and the ownership of process...I also know the efficiency of primary organizers. And I believe that leadership—strength of idea, purpose, willingness to work—should be encouraged among womyn. I talk about this tension between hierarchy and collectivity—no one has any easy answers. That the editorship of *Sinister Wisdom* changes as it does is part of the solution. That we keep asking questions is another.

Some of the issues addressed in *Sinister Wisdom* ran deep for Dykewomon. As she explained in the issue entitled "Surviving Psychiatric Assault and Creating Emotional Well-Being in Our Communities," published in *Sinister Wisdom* No. 36, "Writing the introduction for this issue has been harder than any other. The material is difficult, painful; the issues are complex.... I have friends and ex-lovers who were locked up; I have friends and ex-lovers who are therapists, ex-therapists and anti-therapists.... It was hard to keep perspective on how personal the political can/should/does get; how politically to interpret personal experience." In an earlier issue, Dykewomon's "the real fat womon" poems were published. These powerful pieces included grief, anger, hope, fear, and strength. In the beginning of the first poem, Dykewomon sets the scene, explaining the "grief at the kitchen sink / womyn's grief / for the life that vanishes / hot water and grease / for the hundred fears / about what we eat / and what size we are / and whether standing, / with soap lining the creases of our hands, / hurts our backs or feet / and if that's our fault."

In 1991, Dykewomon, along with co-editor Caryatis Cardea and the editorial group at *Sinister Wisdom,* put out a 15th anniversary issue. In a 1992 *off our backs* review of this essential part of lesbian history, Bonnie Zimmerman called the special issue a "handsome, thrilling, and memorable double issue" which "aptly illustrates the construction and deconstruction of this notion of lesbian community, and the strategies we have employed during the past 15 years to make a revolution. We can read groundbreaking articles on separatist theory, coming out, lesbian ethics, violence against women, culture and community: all the issues that concerned us as we constructed a sense of what it meant to be a lesbian in the late twentieth century."

After living in Northampton, Massachusetts, for seven years and in Oregon for four, Dykewomon moved to California in 1983 "in the quest for an integrated, dynamic lesbian community," she told tova. In addition to her books and editing, she has written much passionate, amusing, sensuous, and historically-telling fiction and poetry, and numbers of essays of quintessential importance to contemporary lesbian culture. The latter include: "The Ex-patriot and Her Name" in *InVersions: Writing by Dykes, Queers & Lesbians* (1991), a long essay on being a lesbian writer; "The Fourth Daughter's 400 Questions" in *Nice Jewish Girls: A Lesbian Anthology* (1989), concerning Jewish identity and culture and lesbianism; and "Traveling Fat" in *Out the Other Side: Contemporary Lesbian Writing* (1989), dealing with the connections between contemporary dieting and Chinese foot binding. Before lesbian and women's publishing became so prevalent, many of Dykewomon's works were copied and passed around, traveling through the lesbian community on a grassroots level. Her work has been translated into German and French. Her most recent book of poetry, *Nothing Will Be as Sweet as the Taste: Selected Poems, 1995,* was solicited by Onlywomen Press in England. And her newest novel, *Beyond the Pale,* was scheduled to be published in the spring of 1997. *Beyond the Pale* has already won international acclaim as part of Helen Mintz's one-woman show "Secret Melodies: Jewish Women's Stories," performed in the U.S.A. and Canada since 1994.

Throughout the years, Dykewomon has consistently addressed a broad range of issues and themes, while always looking through a lesbian lens. What it "means to be a lesbian in the late twentieth century," has not only shaped all of Dykewomon's writing, editing, lectures, workshops, and activism, but Dykewomon herself has been a substantial figure in shaping that contemporary lesbian history.

—tova

E-F

EDWARDS, Eli. *See* MCKAY, Claude.

————

EFRON, Marina (Ivanovna). *See* TSVETAEVA, Marina.

————

ELIOT, A.C. *See* JEWETT, Sarah Orne.

————

FEINBERG, Leslie

Nationality: American author of fiction and nonfiction. **Born:** Kansas City, Missouri, 1 September 1949; grew up in Buffalo, New York. **Education:** High school education. **Family:** Married to author Minnie Bruce Pratt. **Career:** Writer and lecturer; jobs have included factory worker, security guard, dishwasher, A.S.L. sign language interpreter and typesetter, trade unionist, Worker's World Party activist, and contributing editor to *Worker's World* and *Liberation and Marxism Magazine*. **Awards:** American Library Association Gay and Lesbian Book Award for Literature, 1994; *Lambda* Literary Award, 1994; Trinity Award, International Foundation for Gender Education, 1995; Feinberg Fund for Diversity Training established as a gift from the senior class of Bradford College, 1995; Outreach Award, Outreach Institute of Gender Studies, 1996. **Agent:** Charlotte Sheedy Literary Agency, 65 Bleecker Street, 12th floor, New York, New York 10012, U.S.A.

WRITINGS

Journal of a Transsexual (as Diane Leslie Feinberg; autobiographical pamphlet). New York, World View, 1980.
Transgender Liberation: A Movement Whose Time Has Come (political pamphlet). New York, World View, 1992.
"Butch-to-Butch: A Love Song" and "Letter to a Fifties Femme from a Stone Butch" (autobiographical essays), in *The Persistent Desire: A Femme-Butch Reader,* edited by Joan Nestle. New York and London, Alyson, 1992.
Stone Butch Blues: A Novel. New York, Firebrand, 1993.
Transgender Warriors: Making History from Joan of Arc to Ru Paul (nonfiction). Boston, Beacon Press, 1996.
"One Day at the Mace Factory" (short story), in *Women on Women 3,* edited by Naomi Holoch and Joan Nestle. New York and London, Plume, 1996.

*

Interviews: "Leslie Feinberg and Transgender Liberation" by Victoria Brownworth, in *Deneuve,* July/August 1993; "Politics and Gender: An Interview with Leslie Feinberg" by Kevin Horwitz, in *FTM Newsletter,* 23 May 1993, 1-3; "Leslie Feinberg—Gender Outlaw" by Kevin Horwitz, in *FTM Newsletter,* 24 July 1993, 10-11; "Leslie Feinberg—Stone Butch Blues" by Kevin Horwitz, in *FTM Newsletter,* 26 February 1994, 13-14; "Stone Butch Genius" by Angela Tribelli, in *Paper,* March 1996; "Beyond the (Presumed) Boundaries of Biology: An Interview with Activist/Writer Leslie Feinberg" by Andrea L.T. Peterson, in *Metroline,* 11 April 1996; "Transgender Revolution: An Interview with Activist and Author Leslie Feinberg" by Kore Alexis, in *HX Book Talk,* 12 April 1996; "Across Gender Lines" by Stephen Earley, in *Out Front,* Vol. 21, No. 5, 24 April 1996; "An Interview with Leslie Feinberg about Her 'Life's Work'" by Cris Newport, in *Bay Windows,* 2 May 1996; "PGN Focus: Transgender Warriors" by Harriet L. Schwartz, in *Philadelphia Gay News,* 31 May 1996; "An Interview with Leslie Feinberg: Breaking New Ground for the Trans Community" by Carl M. Szatmary, in *Wisconsin Light,* 6-19 June 1996; "Gender Gap" by Eddie Silva, in *Riverfront Times,* 12-18 June 1996; "Feinberg: Author, Activist, Warrior" by Cynthia White, in *News Telegraph,* Vol. 15, No. 17, 14-27 June 1996; "Transgender Author Chronicles 'History'" by Harriet L. Schwartz, in *Southern Voice,* 25 July 1996.

Critical Sources: *Outlaw* (video) by Alisa Lebow, Women Make Movies, 1994; *S/he* by Minnie Bruce Pratt, Ithaca, New York, Firebrand, 1995; *Lesbians Talk Transgender* by Zachary Nataf, London, Scarlet Press, 1996; "No Place Like Home: The Transgendered Narrative of Leslie Feinberg's *Stone Butch Blues*" by Jay Prosser, in *Modern Fiction Studies* (Baltimore), Vol. 41, Nõs. 3-4, 1995, 483-514; "Stone Butch Celebration: A Transgender-Inspired Revolution in Academia" by Wendy Ormiston, in *Harvard Educational Review,* Vol. 66, No. 2, 1996, 198-215.

Leslie Feinberg comments:

All of my writing—non-fiction and fiction—is an extension of my political activism. I write primarily for working-class readers who have almost been convinced by the educational system that they have no need to read anything "serious." I want to make politics, history, and theory accessible to this vast class of people I am part of, and see as the future movers and shakers who will eventually rebuild this current economic system that is built on the foundations of inequality and injustice. For more than 20 years I have been a socialist journalist, writing on national and international struggles for *Workers World* weekly newspaper. I've written on political prisoners in the United States, battles against racism, protests against Pentagon-led wars, the oppression of disabled people, and in defense of Native Nations' sovereignty, self-determination, and treaty rights. *Transgender Warriors* developed from articles in *Workers World* and *Liberation & Marxism* magazine.

In the early 1990s, a wave of discussion began in lesbian communities across the United States about butch-femme gender expression. About the same time, sympathetic audiences pulled the films *Paris Is Burning* and *The Crying Game* from art houses to Cineplex Odeons. I decided to raise my own voice about transgender oppression through an additional vehicle: fiction. I wrote two short stories for the *Persistent Desire* anthology. The response was so overwhelmingly positive, that I developed the two stories into the novel *Stone Butch Blues*.

I am aware that some people assume *Stone Butch Blues* is fictionalized autobiography. I receive letters addressed to the protagonist and other fictional characters in the novel. *Transgender Warriors* is autobiographical; *Stone Butch Blues* is not. That's important to know.

First, you cannot understand my own life's journey from reading *Stone Butch Blues*. The power of the novel does not derive from the protagonist's experiences, but from the overall consciousness of the author that infuses the narrative. The novel is profoundly political in its essence, not personal. I wrote *Stone Butch Blues* in order to capture and convey the universality of the emotional truths of battling transgender oppression in a particular economic system at particular moments in time. I had read a great deal of gender theory that I felt was so abstracted from human experience that it did not speak to me about my life or the lives of other trans people. I wanted to contribute my voice to the contemporary discussion of gender theory: What is the relationship between sex and gender expression, race, class and desire? What is the relationship between the lesbian, gay and bisexual and the trans communities? I set out to write non-didactic fiction that dealt with these social questions.

It's also important to me as a writer to convey my personal belief that the more independent fictional characters are from the author's life experience, the more compelling the work becomes. I learned during many overhauls of the plot and character development that for fiction writing to live and breath, characters cannot act as stand-ins for the author. I create the characters, yet I must respect that their fictional lives, experiences, decisions, and resulting consciousness are independent of mine.

The revolutionary optimism that runs like a current through this book leads many readers to hope that *Stone Butch Blues* is a "true story" about triumph. It certainly is. Politics are the truth of one person's battles, multiplied by the struggle of millions. Those truths, informed by my consciousness, my heartfelt political beliefs, and my unshakable confidence in the future, are what drives all my writing.

*   *   *

In her—or hir, to use the pronoun s/he prefers—pamphlet on transgender liberation, Leslie Feinberg describes the lesbian/gay and transgender communities as "circles that only partially overlap." More fully than any other twentieth-century author, Feinberg has given voice to this overlap, revealing it to be—though partial—absolutely foundational to both communities. For lesbian and gay literature, hir achievement has been to represent in fiction and nonfiction the ways in which lesbian and gay culture is thoroughly interwoven with cross-gendered threads. In both hir life and hir writing, s/he has made of the crevices between gender and sexual communities, and the crevices within gender and sexuality, a complex, sometimes hazardous but always fertile and enriching home for hirself and for a bi-communal movement.

To understand Feinberg's literary contribution, it helps to know something of the way in which s/he has reshaped hir gender and sexual identity, for reshaped genders and sexualities are key material in hir writing. Feinberg identifies as a transgendered lesbian. S/he is a "stone butch" whose attraction is for "high femme": in

other words, a masculine woman who desires feminine women. As a transgendered lesbian, s/he demonstrates that homosexual desire is not necessarily homo-gender desire (same gender desire). Moreover, Feinberg uniquely embodies hir transgender. S/he has masculinized hir body with the male hormone testosterone and a double mastectomy, and thus passes in the world much of the time as a man—though critically for hir writing and hir politics, s/he continues to locate hirself as a transgendered woman. Hir earliest publication, *Journal of a Transsexual,* provides a detailed account of this twilight zone of gender: the stigmatization, the cultural fear, of any unfixed or in-between identity; the difficulty that results for the subject who traverses borderlands. The "I" in this autobiographical pamphlet literally has no cultural place—"too queer in a men's or women's bathroom: too feminine to be a man, too masculine to be a woman." Beginning from this point of no-place, Feinberg's writing has sought to carve out a definitive transgendered space tied to the lesbian, gay, and bisexual world.

This yoking is performed expertly in hir novel, *Stone Butch Blues,* a book that should be credited both with making transgender a central issue in the lesbian, gay, and bisexual community, and with initiating a specifically transgendered political and cultural movement. *Stone Butch Blues* draws on the gender journey of Feinberg's own life. Like Feinberg, the similarly-named protagonist Jess Goldberg grows up Jewish and differently gendered in Buffalo, New York. Like Feinberg, Goldberg comes out as a young butch lesbian in the pre-Stonewall 1950s, proceeding through male hormones and a double mastectomy when she can no longer find work as a butch woman, a "he-she." And like Feinberg, while she clearly feels more at home in this sexually-reconfigured body, Goldberg comes off the hormones when she realizes that her location is not straight man but transgendered lesbian. Yet Feinberg's decision to write fiction rather than autobiography is important. "I chose fiction," s/he told *Gay and Lesbian Literature* contributor Jay Prosser, "because it was the most flexible vehicle to create an accessible work of gender theory. I also felt that fiction would make it possible for me to draw on emotional truths of oppression that would resonate with the greatest universality." If, as Feinberg continued, "fiction can contain just as much truth as non-fiction," then the fiction of *Stone Butch Blues* spread these truths about gender to a much broader community audience.

Ultimately, Feinberg stressed to Prosser that hir "own life's path has been quite different and much richer" than hir protagonist's. Indeed, the seed of political activism sewn in Jess Goldberg's life has come to fruition in her author's. One of the final scenes in *Stone Butch Blues* is of Goldberg's reemergence from passing as a straight man into the lesbian and gay community. Taking the mike at a rally in the heart of New York's lesbian and gay community, she comes out for what she is, transgendered *and* lesbian—"I am a butch, a he-she." Feinberg has become renowned as much for hir writing as for hir brilliant, impassioned speaking on the political importance of making such links. Through hir presentations and hir writing, s/he has been crucial in moving lesbians, gays, and bisexuals to recognize and connect with transgendered people, and transgendered people to recognize and connect with lesbians, gays and bisexuals. Hir lifework is rooted precisely in hir capacity to build bridges between worlds, to inspire hir audience not only to join their "own" struggle but to recognize that their struggle can only be won in the context of a mass struggle for human freedom.

The cruciality of political affiliation—a tenet surely owing much to Feinberg's involvement with *Workers World* and the trade unions—shapes hir history of transgender in *Transgender War-*

riors. Developed from a pamphlet published with *Workers World* and driven by a politics which insists on struggles in context, *Transgender Warriors* demonstrates that the stigmatization of transgender is enmeshed with other forms of class-structured oppression. Once assigned a place of reverence in pre-patriarchal communalist cultures, transgender has been dislodged to a conceptual non-place in the modern Western world: a result of the ruling-class's division of people against each other into rigid hierarchical categories (sex, sexuality, race, and class) in their attempt to retain power. Because transgendered people disturb the binary-gendered scheme of *either* man *or* woman—and thus the apparently natural order of this power—Western patriarchy has sought to erase transgender. Yet *Transgender Warriors* demonstrates that this erasure has been anything but successful. Building a transhistorical and transcultural narrative of transgender (from Joan of Arc to Ru Paul; from Native American Two-Spirits to Western bodybuilders), Feinberg conveys the richness, the multiplicity, and above all the omnipresence of transgendered lives.

Feinberg's linear and lateral connections lead with inevitable logic to political ones. If transgender has been part of a systematized oppression, then the transgender movement will only achieve its goals if it affiliates with other contemporary movements for the oppressed: with the feminist movement, with antiracism, and with the struggle for lesbian, gay, and bisexual rights: "As trans people, we will not be free until we fight for and win a society in which no class stands to benefit from fomenting hatred and prejudice, where laws restricting sex and gender and human love will be unthinkable."

—Jay Prosser

———————

FLOOD, Lynn. *See* **LYNCH, Lee.**

———————

FRAME, Janet (Paterson)

Pseudonym: Also known as Janet Clutha. **Nationality:** New Zealand novelist and author of short stories, poetry, and essays. **Born:** Dunedin, 28 August 1924; changed surname to Clutha c. 1973, after the river south of Oamaru, her childhood home. **Education:** Oamaru North Primary School, 1934-35; Waitaki Girls' Junior School, 1935-37; Waitaki Girls' High School, 1937-42; Dunedin Teachers' College and University of Otago, 1942-44. **Career:** Teacher, Arthur Street School, Dunedin, 1945; writer, from 1945; lived and wrote on the property of New Zealand writer Frank Sargeson in Takapuna, Auckland, 1954-55; wrote in Spain and England on a New Zealand State Fund Grant, 1956-63; returned to write in New Zealand, from 1963. **Awards:** Hubert Church Award, 1953, 1961, 1973; New Zealand State Fund Grant, 1956; Robert Burns Fellowship, 1964; Yaddo Fellowship, 1967; McDowell Fellowship, 1969; Winn-Menton Scholarship, 1974; C.B.E. on the Queen's Honour List, 1983; Award of the Order of New Zealand; New Zealand Literary Award, for Nonfiction, 1984;

Turnovsky Prize for Outstanding Achievement in the Arts, 1984; Commonwealth Writers' Prize, 1989; honorary doctorate: University of Otago. **Address:** c/o Curtis Brown Ltd., P.O. Box 19, Paddington, N.S.W. 2021, Australia.

WRITINGS

Novels

Owls Do Cry. Christchurch, New Zealand, Pegasus, 1957.
Faces in the Water. Christchurch, New Zealand, Pegasus, 1961.
The Edge of the Alphabet. Christchurch, New Zealand, Pegasus, 1962.
Scented Gardens for the Blind. Christchurch, New Zealand, Pegasus, 1963.
The Adaptable Man. Christchurch, New Zealand, Pegasus, 1965.
A State of Siege. New York, Braziller, 1966.
The Rainbirds. London, W. H. Allen, 1968; as *Yellow Flowers in the Antipodean Room,* New York, Braziller, 1969.
Intensive Care. New York, Braziller, 1970.
Daughter Buffalo. New York, Braziller, 1972.
Living in the Maniototo. New York, Braziller, 1979.
The Carpathians. Auckland, New Zealand, Century Hutchinson, 1988.

Short Stories

The Lagoon: Stories. Christchurch, New Zealand, Caxton, 1951.
The Reservoir: Stories and Sketches. New York, Braziller, 1963.
Snowman, Snowman: Fables and Fantasies. New York, Braziller, 1963.
The Reservoir and Other Stories (contains selections from *The Reservoir: Stories and Sketches* and *Snowman, Snowman: Fables and Fantasies*). Christchurch, New Zealand, Pegasus, 1966.
You Are Now Entering the Human Heart. Wellington, New Zealand, Victoria University Press, 1983.

Uncollected Short Stories and Sketches

"University Entrance," in *New Zealand Listener,* 1946.
"The Gravy Boat" (unpublished radio script), reading broadcast by Radio New Zealand, 1953.
"Lolly-Legs," in *New Zealand Listener,* 1954.
"I Got a Shoes," in *New Zealand Listener,* 1956.
"Face Downwards in the Grass," in *Mate* (New Zealand), 1957.
"The Wind Brother," in *School Journal* (New Zealand), 1957.
"The Friday Night World," in *School Journal* (New Zealand), 1958.
"The Chosen Image," in *Vogue* (London), 1963.
"The Bath," in *Landfall,* 1965.
"A Boy's Will," in *Landfall,* 1966.
"In Alco Hall," in *Harper's Bazaar* (New York), 1966.
"The Birds of the Air," in *Harper's Bazaar* (New York), 1969.
"They Never Looked Back," in *New Zealand Listener,* 1974.
"The Widowers," in *New Zealand Listener,* 1979.
"The Painter," in *New Zealand Listener,* 1975.

Uncollected Nonfiction

"A Letter to Frank Sargeson," in *Landfall,* 1953.
"This Desirable Property," in *New Zealand Listener,* 1964.

"Memory and a Pocketful of Words," in *Times Literary Supplement,* 1964.

"Beginnings," in *Landfall,* 1965.

"The Burns Fellowship," in *Landfall,* 1968.

"Janet Frame on *Tales from Grimm,*" in *Education* (New Zealand), 1975.

"Departures and Returns," in *Writers in East-West Encounter: New Cultural Bearings,* edited by Guy Amirthanayagam. London, Macmillan, 1982.

"A Last Letter to Frank Sargeson," in *Islands* (New Zealand), 1984.

Autobiography

Janet Frame: An Autobiography:

Volume 1, *To the Is-Land.* New York, Braziller, 1982; Auckland, New Zealand, Century Hutchinson, 1989.

Volume 2, *An Angel at My Table.* Auckland, New Zealand, Century Hutchinson, New York, Braziller, and London, Women's Press, 1984; Auckland, New Zealand, Century Hutchinson, 1989.

Volume 3, *The Envoy from Mirror City.* Auckland, New Zealand, Century Hutchinson, New York, Braziller, and London, Women's Press, 1985; Auckland, New Zealand, Century Hutchinson, 1989.

Children's Fiction

Mona Minim and the Smell of the Sun, illustrated by Robin Jacques. New York, Braziller, 1969.

Poetry

"On Paying the Third Instalment," "Timothy," "The Liftman," "Trio Concert," and "The Waitresses," in *New Zealand Listener,* 1954.

"The Transformation," in *New Zealand Listener,* 1955.

"The Ferry," in *New Zealand Listener,* 1956.

"Waiting for Daylight," in *Landfall,* 1956.

"The Dead," in *Landfall,* 1957.

"The Joiner," in *Landfall,* 1964.

"The Road to Takapuna," in *Mate* (New Zealand), 1964.

"Scott's Horse," in *Landfall,* 1964.

"The Senator Had Plans," in *Landfall,* 1964.

"White Turnips: A Timely Monologue," in *New Zealand Monthly Review,* 1966.

The Pocket Mirror: Poems. New York, Braziller, 1967.

"In Mexico City," in *New Zealand Listener,* 1968.

"Jet Flight," in *Landfall,* 1969.

"The Words," in *Mademoiselle,* 1969.

*

Adaptations: *A State of Siege* (drama; produced Dunedin, New Zealand, 1970); *A State of Siege* (film; winner of Golden Hugo Award), Christchurch, New Zealand, School of Canterbury, 1978; *Three Poems of Janet Frame: For High Voice and Twelve Instrumentalists,* Dunedin, New Zealand, University of Otago Press, 1985; *An Angel at My Table* (film; winner of Special Jury Prize, Venice International Film Festival), Hibiscus Films, Auckland, New Zealand, 1990.

Manuscript Collections: Hocken Library, University of Otago, Dunedin, New Zealand; University of Hawaii, Honolulu, Hawaii.

Interviews: "Artists' Retreats," in *New Zealand Listener,* 1970; "Janet Frame: It's Time for France," in *New Zealand Listener,* 1973.

Critical Sources: *Janet Frame* by Patrick Evans, Boston, Twayne, 1977; *The Ring of Fire: Essays on Janet Frame* edited by Jeanne Delbaere, Sydney, Australia, Dangaroo Press, 1992; "Exiles of the Mind: The Fictions of Janet Frame" by Vincent O'Sullivan, in *The Ring of Fire: Essays on Janet Frame* edited by Jeanne Delbaere, Sydney, Australia, Dangaroo Press, 1992, 24-30; *I Have What I Gave: The Fiction of Janet Frame* by Judith Dell Panny, New Zealand, Daphne Brasell, 1992; "Celebrating Janet Frame" by Fiona Farley, in *Social Alternatives,* v. 14 n. 1, January 1995, 63-64; *The Inward Sun: Celebrating the Life and Work of Janet Frame* edited by Barbara Allen; "Janet Frame: The Self as Other/Othering the Self" by Tara Hawes, in *Deep South,* New Zealand, Vol. 1, No. 1, February 1995. *The Unstable Manifold: Janet Frame's Challenge to Determinism* by Karin Hansson, Lund, Sweden, Lund University Press, 1996.

*   *   *

Janet Frame is not only acknowledged as New Zealand's greatest novelist but is internationally famed. Though not easily accessible, her work is complex and infinitely rewarding, imaginatively attacking the issues of memory as fiction, language as deceptive, and women as vehicles for silence in a largely patriarchal world.

For Frame, memory constructs something she calls the "Mirror City," a city of imagination which is explained in volume three of her autobiography. In Mirror City, Frame's reflection is caught and mingled with the reflection/memory of all humankind. This reflection, or memory, becomes a fiction of an irretrievable past. As critics have examined Frame's work and its treatment of memory, they have debated whether her autobiographical work is mostly fiction and whether her fiction is mostly autobiographical, particularly her early fiction.

With typical academic curiosity, critics have attempted to delve further into Frame's personal life, to bring to light the enigma that many find her to be. Frame has refused biographers' advances and has only given a small number of interviews in her career, preferring to let her three volumes of autobiography tell her story. The volumes which were all published in the 1980s, well after her standing as a powerful and prolific master novelist had been established. In conjunction with her understandable reluctance to allow her life to be categorically described and dissected by critics, Frame readily acknowledges that autobiography itself is a fiction. She explains in her autobiography that her memory was affected by the many electroshock therapy treatments that she received during her eight years in mental institutions. Yet even the clearest memory cannot be rendered precisely within the limits of language, as Frame's characters often illustrate.

Frame's work addresses the problem of language as an inept qualifier and mode of communication. Language by itself works as a weak tool to label an individual's life; hence, many of her characters have difficulty relating to others through words. For example, in *Scented Gardens for the Blind,* narrator Vera Glace is tortured by the speechlessness of her daughter, Erlene, whose language contains itself and its varied world in Erlene's mind. Later we discover that language has not only been hidden but also deceptive. Erlene is only Vera's fiction: Vera herself is the mute. In *The Carpathians* New Yorker Mattina Brecon attempts to get to know her neighbors on Kowhai Street, where she has taken up temporary residence in order to research the Memory Flower, for which the town is famous. One night she awakens to find her neighbors screaming without human language, covered by a midnight rain of glittering specks that are the ashes of language: letters and punctuation marks. The townspeople mysteriously disappear, having experienced "the disaster of unbeing," wherein language was the foundation of memory and only memory would keep them alive. Mattina and Kowhai Street are left deserted and no words can explain exactly why.

Language and its many forms—spoken, written, or imagined—occupy much of Frame's prose as equals. The conflicts arise in the ability of a human to communicate self to others, and, on the other hand, in the ability of the others to accept and understand the languages of the one, the individual. This inability to communicate or to be received as communicator divides human population in Frame's novels into two factions. First and most compelling are those who are "speechless" or who struggle with language, along with those who relate as empaths to the speechless and their struggle. Frame most closely identifies with these outsiders in her writing. Their opposites are those who unquestioningly fit themselves within the centripetal stagnation of cultural mores and prescribed language, effectively shunning the outsiders and appearing in Frame's novels as foils to the main characters who wrestle with communication.

Language is never the cure-all that creates a happy ending. In *The Carpathians* the residents of Kowhai Street are dissolved into an existence without language, an existence that Mattina can't fathom. Like her neighbors who become jotted notes in Mattina's research, Mattina finds herself inscribed into the fictions of two other characters. Dinny Wheatstone has written a novel delineating Mattina's life and even her future actions, and Mattina's son John Henry Brecon takes his mother's notes about Kowhai Street and, after her death, writes the novel that she couldn't. This layering of Mattina's story within Dinny Wheatstone's story within John Henry's story creates a dual effect, that of illustrating language as memory-bearer and of language as liar. We can never know the true story of Mattina nor Kowhai Street; we have only Wheatstone's enigmatic account encapsulated in John Henry's hearsay account. The novels insist upon questioning how an individual can be known. Why are we more obsessed with "knowing" than accepting, particularly within the flux of language and memory?

From the viewpoint that language cannot completely reveal the individual, Janet Frame builds characters that are complex and secretive. In "Exiles of the Mind: The Fictions of Janet Frame," Vincent O'Sullivan states, "The reason why Frame's fictions are not novels in any conventional sense is that social relationships in fact mean very little to her. They are simply *us,* who know, whose metaphoric gift is to name the sublime terror of mutes and the exploited, and *them,* which is everybody else who does not." O'Sullivan's concept narrows the dichotomy of human population in Frame's novels to those who "name," or use language to relate to the speechless, and those who don't. Yet while Frame's most sympathetic characters don't always have the capacity to name, they have the capacity to feel. Istina Mavet in *Faces in the Water* cannot voice her feelings, but nonetheless experiences them poignantly. Mattina Brecon isn't able to communicate to her husband nor fully to herself why she must enter into her pilgrimages

which distance her from the comfort of her known world. She can only watch and learn about her Kowhai Street neighbors as an outsider. Yet through her internal and external questioning, the gropings of language toward a metaphoric light that can only blind speech further, the reader can sense the connection or communication between characters and between author and reader through shared experience. Language alone cannot fully delineate an event, but language and feeling or empathy can evoke the similarities of individual experiences within the imagination. It is at this locus of imagination that Frame shows how the individual connects with the "Other."

Frame's work is largely woman-centered. Reflecting the ponderous and woman-negating influences of a patriarchal world, her main characters are usually females who have been silenced or who have protected themselves through silence. Their language moves within this silence and either serves as companion or executioner.

For Erlene in *Scented Gardens for the Blind,* language constructs an internal world that comforts and informs her, through her imaginary conversations with Uncle Black Beetle. Yet outside this world, her mother, Vera Glace, and her father, Edward, believe that she can and must be cured of her muteness, that once she is cured, she will make a statement crucial to humankind. The novel twists in the last chapter to reveal the sustained illusion that Vera Glace herself has been frozen in silence for the last thirty years. It is Vera who struggles to make a first statement, which comes forth as a series of primitive grunts. Like the layers of memory and storytelling in *The Carpathians, Scented Gardens for the Blind* layers the effects of a silence which reaches deep into the psyche, creating new hidden selves within private languages. Vera is a world unto herself, yet to fit actively into the external world, she must evolve beyond her internal world into what is expected of her by the outsiders, the "normal" world. In this breaking of silence, Vera is made most vulnerable. And yet only through the breaking of silence might she evolve into empowerment in both worlds.

The bridging of worlds for the sake of empowerment is central to Frame's work. Though her novels usually stop short of actually empowering her characters, the yearning for communication is apparent, as is the idea of acceptance as potential cure. Society, with its limited language, names as aberrant anyone outside the tight circle of prescribed roles. Frame's characters, chained to society by both language and thought, can only attempt to define their own parameters in society. Despite their frustration and failure at communication, Janet Frame's characters can be thought of as heroic. Through their striving to adjust to the chorus of both their internal realities and the decaying effect of the insistent external reality, they emerge from the complacency of quotidian life into their own unique vitality.

—Susan Swartwout

FREEDMAN, Estelle B(renda)

Nationality: American professor, historian, and writer. **Born:** Harrisburg, Pennsylvania, 2 July 1947. **Education:** Barnard College, New York, B.A. in history 1969 (cum laude); Columbia University, New York (Columbia University Fellow, 1971-74; Woodrow Wilson Dissertation Fellowship in Women's Studies,

1974-75), M.A. in history 1972, Ph.D. 1976. **Family:** Began a committed relationship with Susan Krieger in 1980. **Career:** Instructor, Department of History, Princeton University, 1974-76; assistant professor of history and feminist studies, 1976-83, associate professor, 1983-89, professor, from 1989, Stanford University. Advisory board member, Northern California Lesbian and Gay Historical Society, from 1978, and *Gender and History, National Women's Studies Association Journal,* from 1988; founding co-chair and committee member, Program in Feminist Studies, Stanford University, from 1980; associate editor, *Signs: Journal of Women in Culture and Society,* 1980-85, and *Journal of the History of Sexuality,* 1989-93; consultant for film and television documentaries, including *The Celluloid Closet* and *Common Threads: Stories from the Quilt,* 1989-94; contributor of essays and reviews to periodicals, including *Feminist Studies, Journal of American History,* the *Nation,* and *Women's Review of Books.* **Awards:** Alice and Edith Hamilton Prize, for best scholarly manuscript on women, 1978; National Endowment for the Humanities Fellowship, 1982-83, 1992-93; Pew Foundation Faculty Research Grant, 1984-85; Stanford Humanities Research Center Fellowship, 1985-86; American Association of University Women Founders Fellowship, 1985-86; American Council of Learned Societies Fellowship, 1993. **Address:** Stanford University, History Department, Bldg. 200, Rm. 7, Stanford, California 94305-2024, U.S.A.

WRITINGS

Nonfiction

Their Sisters' Keepers: Women's Prison Reform in America, 1830-1930. Ann Arbor, University of Michigan Press, 1981.
Editor, with others, *The Lesbian Issue: Essays From Signs.* Chicago, University of Chicago Press, 1985.
With John D'Emilio, *Intimate Matters: A History of Sexuality in America.* New York, Harper & Row, 1988.
Maternal Justice: Miriam Van Waters and the Female Reform Tradition. Chicago, Illinois, University of Chicago Press, 1996.

Selected articles

"The New Woman: Changing Views of Women in the 1920s," in *Journal of American History,* September 1974.
"Separatism as Strategy: Female Institution Building and American Feminism, 1870-1930," in *Feminist Studies,* Vol. 5, fall 1979.
"Resources for Lesbian History," in *Lesbian Studies,* edited by Margaret Cruikshank. Old Westbury, New York, Feminist Press, 1982.
"Sexuality in Nineteenth-Century America: Behavior, Ideology and Politics," in *Reviews in American History,* December 1982.
"'Uncontrolled Desires': The Response to the Sexual Psychopath, 1920-1960," in *Journal of American History,* Vol. 74, No. 1, June 1987.
With John D'Emilio, "Problems Encountered in Writing the History of Sexuality: Sources, Theory and Interpretation," in *Journal of Sex Research,* Vol. 27, No. 4, November 1990.
"The Historical Construction of Homosexuality in the United States," in *Socialist Review,* Vol. 25, No. 1, winter 1995.
"The Prison Lesbian: Race, Class, and the Construction of the Aggressive Female Homosexual, 1915-1965," in *Feminist Studies,* Vol. 22, No. 2, summer 1996.

Other

Screenwriter, with others, and producer, with Liz Stevens, *She Even Chewed Tobacco: Passing Women in 19th Century America* (slide and tape presentation). New York, Women Make Movies, 1983; producer of videotape version, 1990.

*

Critical Sources: "'60s Protesters, '80s Professors" by Alvin P. Sanoff, in *U.S. News and World Report,* January 1989, 54-55.

Estelle B. Freedman comments:

I began to explore lesbian and gay history in the 1970s in two different settings: the community-based San Francisco Lesbian and Gay History Project, and through my academic teaching and writing about U.S. women's history. The history project provided an important creative impetus for a number of lesbian and gay writers and filmmakers. (In addition to myself and John D'Emilio, Allan Berube, Eric Garber, Amber Hollibaugh, Jeff Escoffier, Gayle Rubin, Rob Epstein, Liz Stevens, and Frances Reid, among others, were involved in our regular study groups on history and politics). *She Even Chewed Tobacco* originated as a slide lecture by Allan Berube and a group of us turned it into a slide tape, and I later produced the video version.

At the same time my scholarly research interests in women's prisons and the treatment of deviance repeatedly brought to my attention sources for both lesbian and gay history. When I began to integrate lesbian history into my teaching I became more curious about the larger context of sexual history in the United States that helped explain the shifting meanings of love between women. That question partly inspired *Intimate Matters.* It is rewarding to see how much academic scholarship on sexuality in general and lesbian and gay history in particular has emerged in the years since the publication of this synthetic overview. Finally, I am honored to be included in this work along with so many writers whose work I admire.

*   *   *

Historian Estelle Freedman came of age during the campus unrest and protests over the Vietnam war of the late 1960s. These events were "life changing," Freedman told Alvin P. Sanoff of *U.S. News & World Report.* The world of academia that Freedman joined in the early 1970s was contending with feminism and gay liberation, and there was increasing hope among young scholars such as Freedman that the academy could be changed. The work for which Freedman is best known is the ground breaking synthesis of the history of sexuality in the United States, *Intimate Matters: A History of Sexuality in America,* which she co-wrote with John D'Emilio. However, Freedman's contributions to the history of gay and lesbian experience exceed this singular book. Both through her academic work and through community-based history projects, Freedman challenges dualistic theories of sexuality, applies class and gender analysis to the hierarchies in American history, and reveals the rich sources available to expand the historiography of gay and lesbian culture in the United States.

The focus of much of Freedman's work is women in correctional institutions, both the inmates and the staff. It is through this work that Freedman began exploring the sexual and intimate relationships of women prisoners and women professionals, such as Miriam Van Waters, in the first half of the 20th century. Van Waters is the subject of Freedman's fifth book *Maternal Justice: Miriam Van Waters and the Female Reform Tradition.* In speaking about her research for this book, Freedman is passionate about the losses history has suffered due to homophobia. Van Waters burned letters between herself and her partner in an effort to protect herself from political enemies who might try to verify accusations of a lesbian relationship. As a scholar who relies on primary source material as the evidence for her work, Freedman grieves the tremendous loss of historic sources and knowledge about gays and lesbian due to individual censorship, institutional suppression of information, and societal oppression and discrimination.

Informed by her extensive research on women in correctional facilities, Freedman brings to the history of sexuality and specifically the history of the lives of gays and lesbians, class and gender analysis. This contribution is particularly evident in the articles she wrote in the 1980s and 1990s. In "Sexuality in Nineteenth-Century America: Behavior, Ideology and Politics," Freedman challenges the causality of the sexual ideology/sexual behavior paradigm assumed by early scholars of sexuality and argues that such a dichotomy limits the scope of analysis. Freedman asserts that sexual politics must be incorporated as a lens for understanding sexuality. Analysis inclusive of sexual politics is essential, Freedman contends, because sexual politics raises political questions about the power hierarchies in the society—who benefitted and whose interests were served by the dominance of a particular conception of sexual norms. The questions that Freedman raises continue to have meaning for contemporary gay and lesbian activists.

Freedman utilizes the concept of sexual politics in much of her writing. It is especially evident in her book with D'Emilio, *Intimate Matters. Intimate Matters* is the first comprehensive work to survey and to summarize the history of sexuality in America. The book examines the meaning or definition of sexuality, from its linkage to reproduction, to its association with erotic pleasure, to its correlation with identity; the means by which sexuality has been regulated through law, community pressure, proscriptive literature, and other forms of coercion; and the politics of sexuality, such as attempts to articulate a dominant sexual meaning through moral reform efforts, criminalization of certain acts, and sexual liberation movements. A pervading theme throughout *Intimate Matters* is that the history of sexuality in America is not the story of linear progress from repression to liberation. D'Emilio and Freedman's book offers a sweeping history intended to be inclusive of a wide range of source material and experience, but in its omissions *Intimate Matters* serves as a marker of where sources are scarce and where prior research is negligible. Upon the publication of *Intimate Matters* both academic and popular reviewers wrote favorably of its contribution to the understanding of sexuality and its place in American history. Scholars and students of gay and lesbian history were most complimentary of the seamless and natural inclusion of gay and lesbian experiences in the text, which is perhaps the most notable contribution of Freedman and D'Emilio to the history of sexuality.

Freedman's work as a historian and as a professor is influential because it effects the very way in which the history of sexuality, and especially the history of lesbian experience, is written. In both *Intimate Matters* and *The Lesbian Issue* Freedman moves same-sex relationships from the periphery of the discourse to the center of the analysis, without erasing their queerness. In two articles, written eight years apart, "Resources for Lesbian History,"

and "Problems Encountered in Writing the History of Sexuality: Sources, Theory and Interpretation," Freedman challenges historians to grapple with definitions of subject matter, to decode closeted sources, biases, and misinformation, and to uncover and to identify the varied experiences of gay and lesbian Americans of different races and classes. While Freedman incorporates lesbians into mainstream American history and women's history, and demands that they be a part of the story, at the same time she insists upon applying critical analysis to sources which only offer a view of white middle class sexual behavior.

—Jill U. Jackson

FRICKE, Aaron

Nationality: American writer and gay youth activist. **Born:** Pawtucket, Rhode Island, 25 January 1962; moved to Cumberland, Rhode Island, 1964. **Education:** Rhode Island public schools; Cypress College, 1982-85; San Francisco City College, A.A. 1993. **Family:** Companion of Ron Calvillo, from 1991. **Career:** Contributor, *Blueboys, Guys,* and *L.A. Frontiers.* **Awards:** Thespian Award for Outstanding Performance; Key to the Gay Community of San Diego; American Library Association Award, for young adult literature, 1981; *Lambda* Literary Award nominee, 1992; honorable mention, First Annual Gay Men's Erotic Film Fest, 1994. **Address:** c/o Harold Schmidt, 343 W. 12th Street, Apt. 1B, New York, New York 10014.

WRITINGS

Nonfiction

Reflections of A Rock Lobster: A Story About Growing Up Gay. Boston, Alyson Publications, 1981.
With Walter Fricke, *Sudden Strangers: The Story of A Gay Son and His Father.* New York, St. Martin's Press, 1991.

Screenplays

Superfellow (1975).
My Burning Bust (1983).
Dan White: Justice at Last (1984).
Sardonica (1993).

*   *   *

The complex and problematic situation of gay and lesbian youth has come into increasing prominence in recent years, as evidenced by the rise of a wide range of support groups and more open periodical coverage. An important source of the courage necessary to acknowledge one's homosexuality and confront the substantial pressures to conform to heterosexual norms is the knowledge and awareness of successful peer group role models. One of the first role models for adolescent homosexuals in the United States was Aaron Fricke.

Fricke's contribution to the American gay and lesbian movement began in 1980 when he requested permission to take a male date to his high school prom. Upon being denied by the local school district, he initiated legal action and went to the media, resulting in nationwide publicity. Out of this experience, Fricke composed two books. The first, *Reflections of a Rock Lobster* (the title both an indication of his self-image and a reference to a popular song of the day) provides a highly detailed autobiographical account of Fricke's Rhode Island childhood, his encounters with small town ignorance and homophobia, and his gradual growth of awareness that being homosexual was not inevitably a matter of shame. The example of a friend, Paul Guilbert, who in May 1979 was refused permission to take a male date to the senior prom, and his own persecution by classmates, determined Fricke that he, too, would attempt to participate honestly in this traditional rite of passage. Upon making his request in the spring of 1980 and being likewise refused on grounds ranging from concern for personal safety to adverse effects on his classmates, Fricke contacted the National Gay Task Force in Providence and brought suit against the school district in federal court. Following two days of hearings held on May 21 and 22, 1980, Judge Raymond Pettine ruled in his favor, terming the school district's position a violation of the First Amendment right of protection for the social context of an act. This case was widely reported in both gay and mainstream media and served as a major challenge to the invisibility of gay adolescents. *Reflections* was awarded an American Library Association Gay Book Award for 1981.

Sudden Strangers, written a decade after *Reflections,* represents a joint effort by Aaron Fricke and his father to address an even more hidden subject, the powerful emotional pain and turbulence generated within the relationship of a father and son of different sexual orientations as they mutually struggle for comprehension and understanding. It also traces Aaron's continuing inner search, which involved a move to California after graduation and a series of career paths, including writing and producing several films between 1982 and 1995. One of them, *Dan White: Justice at Last* dealt with the murder trial and subsequent fate of the former San Francisco city supervisor involved in the death of Harvey Milk.

—Robert B. Marks Ridinger

FRYE, Marilyn

Nationality: American scholar. **Born:** Tulsa, Oklahoma, in 1941. **Education:** Stanford University, B.A. in philosophy 1963; Cornell University, Ph.D. in philosophy 1969. **Career:** Teaches philosophy and women's studies at Michigan State University. Frequent contributor to feminist journals including *Signs, Lesbian Ethics, Sinister Wisdom,* and *Off Our Backs*; speaker, National Women's Studies Association and the Society for Women in Philosophy conferences; assisted in running a bookstore, a lesbian center, and a small press. **Address:** 516 South Kedzie Hall, East Lansing, Michigan 48824, U.S.A.

WRITINGS

Essays

With Carolyn Shafer, "Rape and Respect," in *Feminism and Philosophy,* edited by Mary Vetterling-Braggin, Frederick Elliston,

and Jane English. Totowa, New Jersey, Littlefield, Adams and Company, 1977.
"On Second Thought...," in *Radical Teacher,* spring 1981.
"Comment on Mother/Nature and Maternal Thinking," in *Philosophy, Children, and the Family,* edited by Albert Cafagna, Richard Peterson, and Craig Staudenbauer. New York, Plenum Press, 1982.
The Politics of Reality: Essays in Feminist Theory. Trumansburg, New York, The Crossing Press, 1983.
"History and Responsibility," in *Hypatia: A Journal of Feminist Philosophy,* Vol. 3, 1985.
"Response to Lesbian Ethics: Why Ethics?" in *Hypatia: A Journal of Feminist Philosophy,* Vol. 5, fall 1990.
"The Body Philosophical," in *Knowledge Explosion,* edited by Dale Spender and Cheris Kramerae. New York, Teachers College Press, 1992.
Willful Virgin: Essays in Feminism. Freedom, California, The Crossing Press, 1992.
"The Necessity of Differences: Constructing a Positive Category of Women," in *Signs,* Vol. 21, No. 4, summer 1996.

*   *   *

Marilyn Frye acknowledges in the introduction to her first book of collected essays her gratitude to the journal *Sinister Wisdom*: "[T]hey cheerfully published what was too feminist (not to mention too lesbian) for philosophy journals and too philosophical for lesbian feminist journals." Rightly confirming the interdisciplinary nature of her scholarship, Frye works at an intersection of various academic and political sites and, depending on where her work is housed, is labeled as either lesbian, feminist, separatist, philosopher, or women's studies essayist.

Most of Frye's essays, first published in lesbian feminist journals like *Off Our Backs* and *Signs* in addition to *Sinister Wisdom,* have been collected in two volumes of essays. The first of these, *The Politics of Reality: Essays in Feminist Theory,* is an indictment of patriarchal culture where Frye privileged gender and gender oppression as the focal points of her investigation. Frye sought to dismantle the normality of patriarchy and reveal its inherent oppression of women, and she asserted that feminism could be successful only to the degree that it did so. "What 'feminist theory' is about, to a great extent, is just identifying those forces [that empower men at the expense of subordinating women]...and displaying the mechanics of their applications to women as a group (or caste) and to individual women. The measure of the success of the theory is just how much sense it makes of what did not make sense before," she noted in the collection.

In her essay "Sexism," Frye attempted to define the term that entitled her essay. She claimed that in a phallocratic culture that seeks to dominate women, the constant demarcation of sex is obligatory; only by constantly declaring, for instance, some characteristics intrinsically male and others female may we then easily distinguish men from women. By so doing, distinctions between men and women seem natural instead of societally constructed. If sexual distinctions are innate, then they are also immutable and perpetual, and the continuance of sexist culture is insured. "It must seem natural that individuals of the one category are dominated by individuals of the other and that as groups, the one dominates the other. To make this seem natural, it will help if it seems...that members of the two groups are very different from each other, and...that within each group, the members are very like one another," she noted. She asserted that this constant sexing maintains a sexist caste system of men as dominant and women as subordinate.

Frye discussed social identities other than gender—specifically race, in "On Being White: Thinking Toward a Feminist Understanding of Race and Race Supremacy," and sexuality, in "Lesbian Feminism and the Gay Rights Movement: Another View of Male Supremacy, Another Separatism"—but returned to and privileged gender as her site of inquiry. In the first of these essays, she claimed that (white) women's pursuit of women's liberation expresses disloyalty to whiteness as (white) feminists' goal should not be equality with white men (which would insure the continuity of racism) but a "disaffiliation from...Whiteness" altogether so that feminism will be a movement that is inclusive of women of color. In the second essay, she found that the experiences of lesbians and gay men are so different in phallocratic culture, gay male politics claiming "maleness and male privilege for gay men" and lesbian feminist politics seeking "the dismantling of male privilege, the erasure of masculinity, and the reversal of the rule of phallic access," that the most the two groups can hope for is occasionally to band together to face homophobic legislative efforts and to coalesce around other infrequent common interests that appear at the only-sporadically overlapping boundaries of lesbians' and gay men's lives.

In her second book, *Willful Virgin: Essays in Feminism*, instead of scrutinizing the power of patriarchy, Frye examined all that feminism enables, particularly as women work together in communities and on feminist initiatives, noting "...the concrete project of construction, as opposed to the analytic project of 'deconstruction,' comes more to the fore." She also explored the self-imposed impediments with which feminism burdens itself, primarily the often contentious relationships between heterosexual and lesbian feminists within the feminist movement.

Examining feminism's attempts to empower women and its own heterosexist presumptions that prevent such empowerment, in her "A Lesbian's Perspective on Women's Studies," Frye declared her mystification at women's studies faculty's refusal to advocate that their female students become lesbians. She notes that such a failure to do so can only result from her colleagues' flawed belief that "...most women are and most women will be heterosexual." She challenged this heterosexist assumption and asked her peers to imagine an entire women's studies program "actively advising women not...to become bonded with any man." When her colleagues respond that many women (often including themselves) simply are not sexually attracted to women, Frye demands to know why: "Why not?...Why aren't you attracted to women?" She demanded that heterosexual women investigate why they desire men, just as lesbians have been forced to examine why they desire women, thus foregrounding lesbian experience and women's studies' subordination of it. She further advanced that lesbians should not work within women's studies programs until heterosexual women engage in such searching exploration.

Frye, however, did remain within women's studies after writing this essay, for she found women's studies a safer space for lesbians than gay and lesbian studies "where lesbians have to struggle almost from scratch for feminist analyses and feminist perspectives, as well as against the sexist perceptions and behavior of the men involved." She continued to influence gay and lesbian studies, however, reminding gay and lesbian studies scholars and activists of the possibilities of enacting sexist oppression as they seek to disband homophobic oppression, just as she reminded her heterosexual women's studies colleagues of the danger of suppressing lesbianism as they move to eradicate sexism.

—Kimberly Gunter

G

GALFORD, Ellen

Nationality: Scottish novelist. **Born:** New Jersey in 1947; moved to Scotland, 1971; attained British citizenship. **Career:** Has held a variety of jobs including book editor, copywriter, TV researcher, restaurant critic, and freelance writer. **Awards:** Lambda Literary Award, for humor, 1995; American Library Association Award finalist, 1995. **Agent:** Curtis Brown, Haymarket House, 28/29 Haymarket, London SW1Y 4SP, England.

WRITINGS

Fiction

Moll Cuttpurse: Her True History. London, Virago, 1984; Ithaca, New York, Firebrand Books, 1985.
The Fires of Bride. London, The Women's Press, 1986; Ithaca, New York, Firebrand Books, 1988.
Queendom Come. London, Virago, 1990.
The Dyke and the Dybbuk. London, Virago, 1993; Seattle, Washington, Seal Press, 1995.

Other

Contributor of fiction and nonfiction to anthologies, including *By the Light of the Silvery Moon,* London, Virago, 1994; *Stonewall 25,* London, Virago, 1994; and *The Slow Mirror,* Nottingham, 5 Leaves Press, 1996.

*

Critical Sources: "Stardust Gets in Your Face-lift" by David Alexander, in *The Times,* 18 October 1990, 22; *Called to Healing: Walking Life's Journey with Women Rooting Self to Self as Earth Stories Them to Wholeness (Truth, Mary Austin, Harriette Arnow, Ellen Galford, Vega Ibis Gomez)* by Jean Troy Smith, The Union Institute, 1993.

* * *

The most outstanding characteristic of Ellen Galford's work is her witty and humorous style of writing and her deep commitment to feminism, to women, and to lesbian history through the ages. In her first novel, *Moll Cutpurse,* she rewrites the "herstory" of Mary Frith, a London pickpocket living in the 1580s under the name Moll Cutpurse. The pickpocket Frith goes to an apothecary with a strange wish: she wants to be a man, no matter the cost. Though the apothecary seems likely only to take her money, his daughter, Bridget (who is also the narrator of the story), aids her in her quest. Bridget takes Frith to her Aunt Mary, a wise healer who is being harassed by an ugly neighbor who is angry because Aunt Mary gave his wife contraceptives. Enter Moll Cutpurse, who helps to trick the wrathful neighbor and lead the women to their escape. From that point on Bridget and Moll are companions for a lifetime. There are more adventures as the pickpocket

Cutpurse deals with Puritans and tricksters, cheating the wealthy of their ill-gotten gains; there is a performance in honour of Moll Cutpurse, and many more stories. Ellen Galford joins two worlds in this novel: that of the woman-loving healer who is very aware of female traditions and works in a woman-centered field of knowledge, and that of the pickpocket Moll Cutpurse, who not only crossdresses but is a wo/man in the world of men.

Galford's second novel, *The Fires of Bride,* tells the story of the women of a far-away island off Scotland, called Cailleach. Lizzie, a feminist within a bunch of sports reporters, is supposed to make a film on Cailleach's culture. Her travels north turn into an adventure, as Lizzie discovers the lesbian topography of Cailleach, beginning with the doctor and leader of a Scottish clan, Catriona MacEochan. Catriona has an encyclopedic knowledge of local history and is deeply into the occult. Lizzie also meets Ina Ibister, one of two bed-and-breakfast ladies who tells Lizzie about the Cailleach Ring, and Maria Milleny, an "incomer" and a Daft artist. Maria finally tells Lizzie the story of how she came to the mythical island. Within this framing story the reader gets to know the difficult relationships between Maria and Catriona, the gossip on Cailleach, and the story of a long-forgotten convent which was once famous for illustrating and writing a new Gospel centered around the tale of Jesus's sister and for worshipping Bride, an old Celtic goddess turned Christian saint.

Queendom Come tells of an incident set in the future in Great Britain. The country is ruled by evil forces; the female Prime Minister tries to cut down expenses and forbids lesbian and gay families by law ("Clause 86, Subsection 33, of the Sexual Normality Act. Corrupting minors by the maintenance of a Pretended Family Relationship."). In these nasty times an ancient chieftainess, Albanna, returns from the grave to save her Queendom. Together with her lesbian High Priestess Gwhyldis, she is fulfilling a promise made to deliver her people in times of trouble. But power soon corrupts and Albanna contemplates taking over the Prime Minister's post. Meanwhile, Gwhyldis not only falls in love with an unemployed doctor named Marion Dillon but also exchanges roles with her, thus becoming the mother of female twins. Albanna, who realizes that she won't be part of herstory if she doesn't go back in time, orders Gwhyldis to send her back, trusting that she will come with her. But Gwhyldis decides to stay with Marion and the twins and lead a life as a fortune-teller and witch for the poor.

In her most recent novel, *The Dyke and the Dybbuk,* Galford describes the life of the London taxi-driver and lesbian film critic Rainbow Rosenbloom. Rainbow—an ambivalent member of a large Jewish family dominated by her five formidable aunts— wakes up one morning and finds that she is possessed by a dybbuk. This executor of vengeance or ancient wrongs, this soul-stealing demon of medieval Jewish folklore and disgruntled employee of Mephisto plc, is called Kokos. The ambivalent spook has hunted Rainbow down through the ages—at considerable cost to her department budget and personal self-esteem—in fulfillment of an 18th-century curse. This curse, spoken long ago by Anya, the lesbian lover of Gittel, after Gittel's marriage, decried that "Gittel should be possessed by a dybbuk; that she should disappoint her husband by bearing only daughters; and the surviving first-borns of the female line should be similarly afflicted unto the thirty-third generation." But Kokos was thwarted in her possession of succeeding generations by a wise Rabbi who locked her up in an old tree. When she is freed she has to deal with a rather tricky situation. Her "victim," Rainbow, is an out and proud lesbian. Kokos must navigate a variety of dilemmas—her troubles fulfilling her mission, her failure to live up to Mephisto plc's motto "Faster, Cheaper, Better," and the declining prestige of even being a dybbuk. Kokos gets herself into a lot of trouble and finally ends up in the film business. And Rainbow falls in mutual love with Anya, who survived the last 200 years or so as an undead.

Galford's novels are deeply ironic and belong to the literary genre of satire. Her inimitable style is a mixture of grotesquery and quick-wittedness, combined with a stunning awareness of lesbian culture and history.

—Birgit Lang

GARBER, Marjorie

Nationality: American educator and author. **Born:** Manhattan, New York, 11 June 1944; grew up in Rockville Centre, Long Island, New York. **Education:** Swarthmore College, Swarthmore, Pennsylvania (Woodrow Wilson Fellow), B.A. 1966; Yale University, New Haven, Connecticut (University Fellowship 1967-69), M. Phil. 1969, Ph.D. 1969. **Family:** Companion of literary critic Barbara Johnson, from 1984. **Career:** Assistant professor of English, 1969-75, associate professor of English, 1975-79, Yale University; professor of English, Haverford College, 1979-81; professor of English, from 1981 (named William R. Kenan, Jr. Professor of English, 1995), director of Graduate Studies, Department of English, 1984-89, and from 1996, director, Harvard Center for Literary and Cultural Studies, from 1986, and Associate Dean for Affirmative Action, Harvard Faculty of Arts and Sciences, from 1990, Harvard University. Trustee, Shakespeare Association of America, 1983-86; director, NEH Summer Seminar for College Teachers, 1983, 1985; director, NEH Summer Seminar for Secondary School Teachers, 1986; chair, The English Institute, 1986; visiting professor of comparative literature, Dartmouth College, summer 1987; executive secretary, The English Institute, 1987-91; editorial board, *Genders,* 1987-89, *Shakespeare Studies,* 1982-88; MLA Division Executive Committee on Shakespeare, 1988-92 (chair, 1991); organizer of conferences on gender and sexuality; contributor to general and academic periodicals, including *College English, New York Times, New Yorker,* and *Shakespeare Quarterly.* **Awards:** Morse Fellowship for Younger Scholars in the Humanities, 1972-73; named one of the ten best teachers at Yale University, 1974; American Council of Learned Societies Fellowship, 1977-78; Petra Shattuck Teaching Award, Harvard Extension School, 1988; American Council of Learned Societies Fellowship, 1989-90; Marta Sutton Weeks Fellow, Stanford Humanities Center, 1989-90. **Address:** c/o Center for Literary and Cultural Studies, 61 Kirkland Street, Cambridge, Massachusetts 02138, U.S.A.

WRITINGS

Literary Criticism

"The Generic Contexts of When We Dead Awaken," in *Dramatic Romance,* edited by Howard Felperin. New York, Harcourt, Brace, Jovanovich, 1973.

Dream in Shakespeare: From Metaphor to Metamorphosis. New Haven, Yale University Press, 1974.

"Fallen Landscape: The Art of Milton and Poussin," in *English Literary Renaissance,* Vol. 5, No. 8, winter 1975.

"Cymbeline and the Languages of Myth," in *Mosaic,* Vol. 10, No. 3, spring 1977.

"Coming of Age in Shakespeare," in *Yale Review,* Vol. 66, No. 4, summer 1977.

"'Infinite Riches in a Little Room': Closure and Enclosure in Marlowe," in *Two Renaissance Mythmakers,* edited by Alvin Kernan. Baltimore, Johns Hopkins University Press, 1977.

"'Vassal Actors': The Role of the Audience in Shakespearean Tragedy," in *Renaissance Drama,* Vol. 9, 1978.

"Marlovian Vision/Shakespearean Revision," in *Research Opportunities in Renaissance Drama,* Vol. 22, 1979.

"The Healer in Shakespeare," in *Medicine and Literature,* edited by Enid Rhodes Peschel. New York, Neal Watson Academic Publications, 1980.

"'Wild Laughter in the Throat of Death': Dark Moments in Shakespearean Comedy," in *Shakespearean Comedy,* edited by Maurice Charney. New York, New York Literary Forum, 1980.

"'The Eye of the Storm': Structure and Myth in Shakespeare's Tempest," in *Hebrew University Studies in Literature,* Vol. 8, No. 1, spring 1980.

Coming of Age in Shakespeare. London, Methuen, 1981.

"'Remember Me': Memento Mori Figures in Shakespeare's Plays," in *Renaissance Drama,* Vol. 12, 1981.

"'The Rest Is Silence': Ineffability and the 'Unscene' in Shakespeare's Plays," in *Ineffability from Dante to Beckett,* edited by Peter S. Hawkins and Anne Howland Schotter. New York, AMS Press, 1984.

"'Here's Nothing Writ': Scribe, Script, and Superscription in Marlowe's Plays," in *Theater Journal,* Vol. 36, No. 3, October 1984.

"'What's Past is Prologue': The Dramatic Role of the Audience in Shakespeare's History Plays," in *Renaissance Genres: Essays on Theory, History, and Interpretation,* edited by Barbara Kiefer Lewalski. Cambridge, Massachusetts, Harvard University Press, 1986.

"The Education of Orlando," in *Comedy from Shakespeare to Sheridan,* edited by A.R. Braunmiller and J.C. Bulman. Newark, University of Delaware Press, 1986.

"Shakespeare's Ghost Writers," in *Cannibals, Witches, and Divorce: Estranging the Renaissance,* edited by Marjorie Garber. Baltimore, Johns Hopkins University Press, 1987.

With Barbara Johnson, "Secret Sharing: Reading Conrad Psychoanalytically," in *College English,* Vol. 49, No. 6, October 1987.

Shakespeare's Ghost Writers: Literature as Uncanny Causality. London, Methuen, 1987.

"Descanting on Deformity: Richard III and the Shape of History," in *The Historical Renaissance: New Essays in Tudor and Stuart Literature and Culture,* edited by Heather Dubrow and Richard Strier. Chicago, University of Chicago Press, 1987.

"Shakespeare as Fetish," in *Shakespeare Quarterly,* Vol. 41, No. 2, summer 1990.

"Fetish Envy," in *October,* Vol. 54, fall 1990.

"The Roaring Girl and the Scandal of Transvestism," in *Staging the Renaissance: Reinterpretations of Elizabethan and Jacobean Drama,* edited by David Scott Kastan and Peter Stallybrass. New York, Routledge, 1990.

"The Transvestite's Progress: Rosalind the Yeshiva Boy," in *The Appropriation of Shakespeare: Post-Renaissance Reconstructions of the Works and the Myth,* edited by Jean Marsden. London, Harvester Wheatsheaf, 1991.

"Overcoming 'Auction Block': Stories Masquerading as Objects," in *Critical Quarterly,* December 1992.

"'Greatness': Philology and the Politics of Mimesis," in *Feminism and Postmodernism* (special issue of *Boundary II*), edited by Margaret Ferguson and Jennifer Wicke. Durham, Duke University Press, 1994.

"The Insincerity of Women," in *Desire in the Renaissance: Psychoanalysis and Literature,* edited by Regina Schwartz. Princeton, Princeton University Press, 1995.

Editor

Cannibals, Witches, and Divorce: Estranging the Renaissance. Baltimore, Johns Hopkins University Press, 1987.

With Jann Matlock and Rebecca L. Walkowitz, *Media Spectacles.* New York, Routledge, 1993.

With Rebecca L. Walkowitz, *Secret Agents: The Rosenberg Case, McCarthyism, and Fifties America.* New York, Routledge, 1995.

With Paul B. Franklin and Rebecca L. Walkowitz, *Field Work: Sites in Literary and Cultural Studies.* New York, Routledge, 1996.

With Nancy J. Vickers, *Don't Look Now: The Medusa Reader.* New York, Routledge, 1997.

Nonfiction

"Spare Parts: The Surgical Construction of Gender," in *differences: A Journal of Feminist Cultural Studies,* Vol. 1, No. 3, fall 1989; reprinted in *The Lesbian and Gay Studies Reader,* edited by Henry Abelove, Michelle Barale, and David Halperin, New York, Routledge, 1993.

"The Occidental Tourist: M. Butterfly and the Scandal of Transvestism," in *Nationalisms and Sexualities,* edited by Andrew Parker, Mary Russo, Doris Sommer, and Patricia Yeager. New York, Routledge, 1992.

"The Chic of Araby: Transvestism and the Erotics of Cultural Exchange," in *Bodyguards,* edited by Julia Epstein and Kristina Straub. New York, Routledge, 1991.

"Joe Camel, an X-Rated Smoke," in *New York Times,* 20 March 1992.

"Read My Lipstick," in *New York Times,* 20 August 1992.

"Strike a Pose," in *Sight and Sound,* September 1992.

Vested Interests: Cross-Dressing and Cultural Anxiety. New York, Routledge, 1992.

"Maximum Exposure," in *New York Times,* 4 December 1993.

"The Bard and the Undead," in *New York Times,* 25 November 1994.

"Back to Whose Basics?," in *New York Times Book Review,* 29 October 1995.

"The Marvel of Peru" (foreword), in *Lieutenant Nun: Memoir of a Basque Transvestite in the New World,* translated by Michele Stepto and Gabriel Stepto. Boston, Beacon Press, 1995.

"Heavy Petting," in *Human, All Too Human,* edited by Diana Fuss. New York, Routledge, 1995.

"Viktor Petrenko's Mother-in-Law," in *Women on Ice,* edited by Cynthia Baughman. New York, Routledge, 1995.

"Bisexuality and Celebrity," in *The Seductions of Biography,* edited by Mary Rhiel and David Suchoff. New York, Routledge, 1995.

"Jello," in *Secret Agents: The Rosenberg Case, McCarthyism, and Fifties America,* co-edited with Rebecca L. Walkowitz. New York, Routledge, 1995.

Vice Versa: Bisexuality and the Eroticism of Everyday Life. New York, Simon & Schuster, 1995.

Dog Love. New York, Simon & Schuster, 1996.

"Why We Love Dogs," in *New Yorker,* 8 July 1996.

"Cinema Scopes: Evolution, Media, and the Law," in *Law and the Domains of Culture,* edited by Austin Sarat. Ann Arbor, University of Michigan Press, 1996.

"What Is Culture? What Are Cultures?," in *Field Work: Sites in Literary and Cultural Studies,* co-edited with Paul B. Franklin and Rebecca L. Walkowitz. New York, Routledge, 1996.

Read My Lipstick and Other Notes on Culture. New York, Routledge, forthcoming.

Home Truths. Under contract with Simon & Schuster, forthcoming.

*

Critical Sources: Review of *Vested Interests* by Martha Vicinus, in *Women's Review of Books,* Vol. 9, No. 4, January 1992; review of *Vested Interests* by Catherine Belsey, in *Shakespeare Quarterly,* Vol. 44, No. 3, fall 1993; review of *Vested Interests* by Elaine Hoffman Baruch, in *Partisan Review,* Vol. 60, No. 1, winter 1993; "Sex: Going Both Ways" by Robert S. Boynton, in *Vogue,* Vol. 185, No. 6, June 1995; "She Dwells on Possibility" by Jan Clausen, in *Women's Review of Books,* Vol. 13, No. 2, November 1995.

*   *   *

Professor of English Marjorie Garber is a Shakespearean by trade, who, early in an extremely prolific career, published mainly in the field of Renaissance literature. Her first three books, *Dream in Shakespeare: From Metaphor to Metamorphosis, Coming of Age in Shakespeare,* and *Shakespeare's Ghost Writers: Literature as Uncanny Causality,* not only place the Bard within his own historical context but consider his larger connection to contemporary life and culture as well. In her introduction to *Ghost Writers* Garber notes that "once again, what interests me is the uncanny extent to which [Shakespearean texts] have mined themselves into our present discourses, whether in literature, history, psychoanalysis, philosophy, or politics." In much the same way, the specter of Shakespeare's ghost "haunts" nearly all of Garber's own writing, from her initial work on Elizabethan drama to her later critiques of the postmodern world. For instance, in a 1993 essay, "Character Assassination," Garber threads Shakespeare, the Clarence Thomas-Anita Hill hearings, and Oliver Stone's epic *JFK* to reveal the political investments embedded in certain popular invocations of the "classics." Similarly, in her 1995 essay, "Viktor Petrenko's Mother-in-Law," Garber calls up not Shakespeare but French philosopher Jacques Derrida to interrogate the Nancy Kerrigan-Tonya Harding spectacle and to support her appeal for same-sex pairs figure skating: "What is a pair, anyway?" Garber ruminates, answering, "Let us again ask Derrida's question: 'What is a pair in this case?'" As these examples attest, Garber's conviction that "high art" (or "high theory") and "real life" are far from separate underpins the entire corpus of her work, although it especially appears in her later writings, which are increasingly directed at a general audience.

Garber's fourth book, *Vested Interests: Cross-Dressing and Cultural Anxiety* (1992), secured her place as a major cultural critic;

as Catherine Belsey, in her review for *Shakespeare Quarterly,* put it: "This is a book that makes a difference." Readers discover in this book not only Garber's characteristic interest in Shakespeare, but much, much more: from Michael Jackson to Madonna, Streisand to Stonewall, Freud to Fliess, the author leaves no stone unturned in her grand tour of transvestism from the sixteenth century through the twentieth. And grand it is indeed—over 400 pages long, *Vested Interests* pulls together an astounding array of evidence to make its central point: that cross-dressing as a cultural phenomena disrupts and confronts society's most cherished (and monolithic) categories of identity, particularly those governing gender. Garber writes, "What this book insists upon...[is that] transvestism is a space of possibility structuring and confounding culture: the disruptive element that intervenes, not just a category crisis of male and female, but the crisis of category itself." Most critics, Garber maintains, have tended to look through rather than at the cross-dresser, "to turn away from a close encounter with the transvestite, and to want instead to subsume that figure within one of the two traditional genders."

Insofar as the book interrogates historical and contemporary manifestations of cross-dressing, and calls attention to the ways in which these manifestations uproot "easy notions of binarity," *Vested Interests* succeeds in looking at this cultural phenomena with a comprehensive and critical eye. Moreover, Garber does not ignore gays and lesbians, whose stories are dialectically and inextricably linked to those of transvestites in western culture. Yet while she returns repeatedly to this connection throughout the book, Garber is quick to point out the fallacy in seeing the two as interchangeable; she writes, "Just as to ignore the role played by homosexuality would be to risk a radical misunderstanding of the social and cultural implications of cross-dressing, so to restrict cross-dressing to the context of an emerging gay and lesbian identity is to risk ignoring, or setting aside, elements and incidents that seem to belong to quite different lexicons of self-definition and political and cultural display." As the preceding aptly suggests, preserving a theoretical space for the complicated and fascinating "display" that is transvestism is precisely what *Vested Interests* aims to do.

Only three years after the publication of *Vested Interests,* Garber put out yet another groundbreaking book of cultural criticism, this time speculating on the unpredictability and fluidity of what modern society broadly terms "sexual orientation." *Vice Versa: Bisexuality and the Eroticism of Everyday Life* seeks to undermine a notion to which many still desperately cling: that people are either attracted to men or women, straight or gay, but never both. This "both" is what *Vice Versa* celebrates—the possibility that human sexuality is far more dynamic, nuanced, and ultimately rich than cast-iron dimorphic categories of identity allow. "Is bisexuality a 'third kind' of sexual identity, between or beyond homosexuality and heterosexuality?," Garber asks. "Or is it something that puts in question the very concept of sexual identity in the first place?" Her response comes in the form of testimony, both from those who admit having been attracted to or actually involved with women and men, and from history, which speaks to the extent to which errant "incidents" of "deviant" desire have been interpellated into one of two permissible norms.

Garber notes that:

> [A]ccording to some definitions, though obviously not those of self-identified bisexuals, a person who used to be straight and is now with a same-sex partner is gay, and

a person who used to be gay and is now with an opposite sex partner is straight. This 'law of the excluded middle' excludes bisexuality, which, in some people's minds, must be concurrent or simultaneous in order to be real.

But invisibility and exclusion are not the only stigmas with which bisexuality has had to contend: thought by straight people to be resolutely non-monogamous because "everyone is a potential partner," perceived by lesbians and gays as "fence sitters" afraid of losing their heterosexual privilege, bisexuals are consistently ghettoized, Garber insists, despite assertions from the popular media to the contrary. Much like her work in *Vested Interests,* Garber maps out an impressively detailed and compelling topography here, and then stakes her claim: in short, that bisexuality is not simply a poor cousin to hetero- and homo-sex, nor is it a flimsy in-between; rather, it is a story unfolding, "an aspect of lived experience, seen in the context of particular relations...Like postmodernism itself, it resists stable referentiality. It performs."

As one might guess after reading the above descriptions of *Vested Interests* and *Vice Versa,* Marjorie Garber's work tends towards the queer. That is, again and again she challenges totalizing and binary categories of identity—gay/straight, male/female, or even man/woman—in favor of a world that is at once far less rigid and infinitely more unstable and complex. Whether discussing the fetishization of Shakespeare in academic circles ("Shakespeare as Fetish," 1990), the anatomy and morphology of the transsexual and transgendered ("Spare Parts," 1989), or Pat Buchanan's appropriation of drag rhetoric at the Republican convention ("Read My Lips," 1992), Garber never fails to incite and engage; as one reviewer remarks, "Garber is never less than interesting and always worth arguing with." Her sixth book, *Dog Love,* is an insightful and incisive meditation on the cultural relevance of humanity's best friend and marks Garber's continued foray into the popular market; excerpts from this book, as well as others of her pieces, have appeared in publications such as *New Yorker* and *New York Times.* Evidently, having established herself as one of the premier Shakespeareans of the twentieth century, Garber feels free to turn her ample energy and attention elsewhere, which—given the scope of her cultural acuity—can't help but fall at some point or another right in one's own backyard. Elaine Hoffman Baruch, writing for the *Partisan Review,* perhaps explains it best: "More than any other writer I can think of, Garber leaps adroitly from high culture to pop culture—from cross-dressing saints of the Middle Ages to Madonna, from the boy actors of the Shakespearean stage to Michael Jackson—and is equally engaging in both worlds." Although referring specifically to *Vested Interests,* Baruch's point is well-taken: theoretically savvy, culturally sophisticated, Marjorie Garber—and her work—will likely be around for a good long time.

—Melissa Tedrowe

GARNER, Helen

Nationality: Australian novelist, playwright, writer of short stories, and journalist. **Born:** Geelong, Victoria, Australia, 7 November 1942. **Education:** Melbourne University, B.A. with honors

1965. **Family:** Married 1) William Garner in 1968 (divorced); one daughter; 2) Jean-Jacques Portail in 1980. **Career:** Teacher at Werribee High School, 1966-67, Upfield High School, 1968-69, and Fitzroy High School, 1971-72, Melbourne, Victoria; freelance journalist, *Digger,* 1973; feature writer, *The Age,* Melbourne, 1981; theatre critic, *National Times,* New South Wales, 1982-83; writer in residence, Griffith University, Nathan, Queensland, 1983, and University of Western Australia, Nedlands, 1984. Member of Australia Council literature board, 1985; has also worked as a songwriter and an actress. **Awards:** National Book Council Award, for *Monkey Grip,* 1978; Australian Council fellowships, 1978, 1979, 1980 and 1983; South Australian Government Biennial Literature Prize, 1986; South Australia Festival Award, 1986; New South Wales Premier's Literary Award, 1986. **Address:** c/o Free Press, 966 3rd Ave., New York, New York 10022, U.S.A.

WRITINGS

Fiction

Monkey Grip. Melbourne, McPhee Gribble Publishers, 1977; London, Virago, 1980; New York, Seaview Books, 1981.
Honour and Other People's Children: Two Stories. Melbourne, McPhee Gribble Publishers, 1980; New York, Seaview Books, 1982.
The Children's Bach. Melbourne, McPhee Gribble Publishers, 1984; Ringwood, Victoria, Australia, New York, Penguin Books, 1985.
Postcards from Surfers: Stories. Ringwood, Victoria, Australia, New York, Penguin Books, 1985; London, Bloomsbury, 1989.
Cosmo Cosmolino. Ringwood, Victoria, Australia, McPhee Gribble Publishers, 1992; London, Bloomsbury, 1993.

Screenplays

With Ken Cameron, *Monkey Grip* (adaptation of novel *Cinecom International*). 1981.
The Last Days of Chez Nous. 1992.
Two Friends. 1995.

Other

With Sarah Clarke, *Our Homes, Ourselves: A Report of an International Conference on Women and Housing.* London, Shelter, 1988.
With Liz Jones and Betty Burstall, *La Mama, The Story of a Theatre.* Fitzroy, Victoria, Australia, McPhee Gribble/ Penguin, 1988.
The First Stone: Some Questions About Sex and Power. New York, Free Press, 1997.

*

Critical Sources: Review of *Monkey Grip* by Paul Ableman, in *Spectator* (London), 26 January 1980; review of *Monkey Grip,* by Galen Strawson, in *Times Literary Supplement* (London), 18 January 1980, 54; "Bits and Pieces" in *New Yorker,* 13 July 1981, 8 March 1982, 29 September 1986, and 2 February 1987; "Of War and Needlework: The Fiction of Helen Garner" by Peter Craven, in *Meanjin* (Parkville, Victoria, Australia), Vol. 44, No. 2, June,

1985, 209-219; "Helen Garner" by Nancy Pate, in *Contemporary Authors,* Vol. 127, Detroit, Gale Research, 1981, 151-152; "Sensual Angels and Exteriority: Helen Garner's *Cosmo Cosmolino*" by Claire Colebrook, in *Journal of Commonwealth Literature,* Vol. 29, No. 1, spring 1994, 55-64.

*   *   *

Raised in southeastern Australia by conservative parents, Helen Garner describes herself as "strictly brought up." Her own conflicts about her background form central themes in most of her work. She has a clear, incisive, and ironic vision of the ways in which identity is formed both by upbringing and by rebellion against that upbringing. Over and over again in her writing her major female characters wrestle with the contradictions between the lives they choose and their ideologies. Often these conflicts revolve around the inherent paradox involved when a feminist and leftist woman chooses to love and live in a relationship with a man.

In her first novels *Monkey Grip* and *Honour, and Other People's Children,* Garner distinctly focuses on a world that has stepped outside the bounds of conservative middle class respectability. Her characters are artists and hippies, commune dwellers and drug users. Even in *The Children's Bach* where the setting is a more conventional normal suburban family, it is the arrival of the rebels, a shoplifting former college friend and her male lover, a rock musician, that sets the story in motion.

Garner herself is familiar with this bohemian world; she has been an actress on stage and in films, a rock music lyricist, and a noted screenwriter. Her grasp of both the differences and the similarities between rebellion and conformity are dead on, and she describes both the desperate dullness of the "cool" life and the underlying passions of "normalcy" with humor and clarity.

It is not only the alternative lifestyles of her characters that make Garner's writing unusual among acknowledged writers, but also her focus on women and children. Her women are often mothers, sometimes single mothers, and she describes their role with depth and affection. In *Postcards from Surfers,* her short story collection, she describes one mother, who plays base in a rock band, "bluntly thumping the heart rhythm."

Her children are also complex characters, and are given alternative lives of their own, not merely attached to parent or family. In the novella *Other People's Children,* which dissects the ramifications of the breakup of a commune, one of the most touching moments is the break between one woman and a child she is close to, the daughter of another woman. In "Two Friends," a screenplay written for Australian television, Garner begins with two very different girlfriends, one conservative and straightlaced, the other a punked-out runaway, and follows them back in time to a place where they were not so very different at all. In the process, she touches all the small and large forces that shape who we become.

Garner's ability to capture the hundreds of forces, huge and tiny, that work to form us characterizes her writing. Her style is both quirky and sincere, much like the lives she describes. She may be telling us her own narrative philosophy in *The Children's Bach* when she has the rock musician give advice to another songwriter, "Make gaps. Don't chew on it. Don't explain everything. Leave holes. The music will do the rest."

Of primary interest to Garner's gay readers are her explorations of feminism and its influence on her characters and her focus on the "other," the outsider in society. The "other" is a central part of Garner's world, and her incisive descriptions strike a chord within the reader that makes it clear that each of us contains an element of the "other." Gay characters do not abound in her stories, but they do occur. *Cosmo Cosmolino* is a collection of three stories where actual sightings of spiritual entities personify the experience of "otherness" or alienation for the characters. In the final story, the sexual connection between two characters, Janet and Maxine, allows them for a time to open to the possibility of reaching beyond their alienation to self knowledge.

In "La Chance Existe," a story in the collection *Postcards from Surfers,* a young gay man describes with poignant sensuality his awakening to his feelings for men. As with Janet and Maxine, this awakening opens him up to a new kind of connection with world and self. At the same time, all of them are tied to the past by their fear of abandoning the familiar. "Now I know exactly what I want," the young man says, "and I also know I'll never get it." This outlook seems bleak for the gays in Garner's writing, but, like all of her characters, there is a kind of ultimate triumph in their questing, feeling humanity.

—Tina Gianoulis

GEARHART, Sally Miller

Pseudonym: Has also written as Sally Sotomayor. **Nationality:** American novelist, educator, and author of short stories and nonfiction. **Born:** Pearisburg, Virginia, 15 April 1931. **Education:** Sweet Briar College, B.A. in English 1952; Bowling Green State University, M.A. in Public Address 1953; University of Illinois, Ph.D. in Theatre 1956. **Career:** Associate professor of Speech and Theatre, Stephen F. Austin State University, Nacogdoches, Texas, 1956-59; associate professor of Speech and Drama and department head, 1960-70, Texas Lutheran College, Seguin, Texas, 1960-70; professor of Speech Communication, 1972-92, head of Speech Communication department, 1981-84, and acting Associate Dean, School of Humanities, San Francisco State University, California, 1984-86. Advisory board, National Center for Lesbian Rights and *Lesbian Review of Books.* **Address:** c/o P.O. Box 1027, Willits, California 95490, U.S.A.

Writings

Novels

The Wanderground. Los Angeles, Alyson Publications, 1979.

Nonfiction

With William R. Johnson, *Loving Women/Loving Men: Gay Liberation and the Church.* San Francisco, California, Glide Publications, 1974.
With Susan Rennie, *A Feminist Tarot.* Los Angeles, Alyson Publications, 1975.

Uncollected Short Stories

"The Chipko," in *Love, Struggle and Change,* edited by Irene Zahava. Freedom, California, Crossing Press, 1988.

"Roxie Raccoon," in *Through Other Eyes: Animal Stories by Women,* edited by Irene Zahava. Freedom, California, Crossing Press, 1988.
"Flossie's Flashes," in *Lesbian Love Stories,* edited by Irene Zahava. Freedom, California, Crossing Press, 1989.
"Roja and Leopold," in *And A Deer's Ear, Eagle's Song, and Bear's Grace: Animals and Women,* edited by Theresa Corrigan and Stephanie Hoppe. San Francisco, California, Cleis Press, 1990.
"Down in the Valley," in *Word of Mouth,* edited by Irene Zahava. Freedom, California, Crossing Press, 1990.
"A Dying Breed," in *The Fourth Womansleuth Anthology: Contemporary Mystery Stories by Women,* edited by Irene Zahava. Freedom, California, Crossing Press, 1991.
With Vivian Sotomayor (under the pseudonym Sally Sotomayor), "Marta's Magic," in *Tomboys! Tales of Dyke Derring-Do,* edited by Lynne Yamaguchi and Karen Barber. Boston, Massachusetts, Alyson Publications, 1994.
"The Pit Bull Opportunity," in *Reality Change: The Global Seth Journal,* summer 1994.
"Wondercrone: Her Humble Origins," in *Sinister Wisdom* (San Francisco, California), Vol. 53, summer/fall 1994.
"Small Town Girl Makes Dyke," in *Testimonies: Lesbian Coming Out Stories,* edited by Karen Barber and Sarah Holmes. Boston, Massachusetts, Alyson Publications, 1994.
"First Love at Sweet Briar," in *The New Our Right to Love: A Lesbian Resource Book,* edited by Ginny Vida. New York, Simon & Schuster, 1996.

Uncollected Essays

"Afterthought: Lesbians as Gays and as Women," in *We'll Do it Ourselves: Combatting Sexism in Education,* edited by David Rosen. Lincoln, Nebraska, University of Nebraska Curriculum Development Center, 1974.
"The Lesbian and God-the-Father," in *Persuasion: Understanding, Practice, and Analysis,* edited by Herbert Simons. San Francisco, California, Addison-Wesley, 1975.
With Peggy Cleveland, "On the Prevalence of Stilps," *Quest,* Vol. 1, No. 4, spring 1975.
"Memoirs of a Hallelujah Dyke," in *Our Right to Love: A Lesbian Resource Book,* edited by Ginny Vida. New York, Prentice Hall, 1978.
"Womanpower: Energy Re-Sourcement," in *Woman-Spirit,* spring, 1979; in *The Politics of Women's Spirituality,* edited by Charlene Spretnak. Garden City, New York, Doubleday, 1982.
"The Womanization of Rhetoric," in *Women's Studies International Quarterly* (Toronto), Vol. 2, summer 1979.
"The Future—If There Is One—Is Female," in *Reweaving the Web of Life: Nonviolence and Women,* edited by Pam McAllister. New York, New Society Publishers, 1982.
"If the Mortarboard Fits . . . Radical Feminism in Academia," in *Learning Our Way: Essays in Feminist Education,* edited by Charlotte Bunch and Sandra Pollack. Trumansburg, New York, Crossing Press, 1983.
"An End to Technology: A Modest Proposal," in *Dea Ex Machina: Women and Technology,* edited by Joan Rothchild. New York, Pergamon Press, 1984.
"Notes from a Recovering Activist," in *Sojourner* (Boston), Vol. 21, No. 1, September 1995.

"The First Time Ever," in *Virgin Territory II,* edited by Shar Rednour. New York, Richard Kasak Books, 1996.

*

Manuscript Collections: University of Oregon Library, Eugene, Oregon.

Critical Sources: "Widening the Dialogue on Feminist Science Fiction" by June Howard, in *Science Fiction Dialogues,* edited by Gary Wolfe, Chicago, Illinois, Academy Chicago, 1982, 155-168; "Lesbian Literature: A Third World Feminist Perspective" by Cherrie Moraga and Barbara Smith, in *Lesbian Studies: Present and Future,* edited by Margaret Cruikshank, Old Westbury, New York, Feminist Press, 1982, 55-65; "World Views in Utopian Novels by Women" by Lucy M. Friebert, in *Women and Utopia: Critical Interpretations,* edited by Marleen Barr and Nicholas D. Smith, Lanham, Maryland, University Press of America, 1983, 67-84; "Can Women Fly?: Vonda McIntyre's *Dreamsnake* and Sally Gearhart's *The Wanderground*" by Inge-Lise Paulsen, *Women's Studies International Forum* (Oxford, England), Vol. 7, No. 2, 1984, 103-110; "Feminist Novel's Approaches to Conflict" by Cheris Kramarae and Jana Kramer, in *Women and Language* (Fairfax, Virginia), Vol. 11, No. 1, winter 1987, 36-39; "The Dream of Elsewhere: Feminist Utopias" by Sarah Lefanu, in *Feminism and Science Fiction,* Bloomington, Indiana, Indiana University Press, 1989, 53-70; *The Safe Sea of Women* by Bonnie Zimmerman, Boston, Massachusetts, Beacon Press, 1990; "Re-Membering Men Dismembered in Sally Miller Gearhart's Ecofeminist Utopia *The Wanderground*" by Mario Klarer, in *Extrapolation: A Journal of Science Fiction and Fantasy* (Kent, Ohio), Vol. 32, No. 4, winter 1991, 319-30; *Radical Imagination: Feminist Conceptions of the Future in Ursula LeGuin, Marge Piercy, and Sally Miller Gearhart* by Margaret Keulen, New York, Peter Lang, 1991; "The Politics of Separatism and Lesbian Utopian Fiction" by Sonya Andermahr, in *New Lesbian Criticism: Literary and Cultural Readings,* edited by Sally Munt, New York, New York University Press, 1992, 133-152; "Gendered Identity and Body Politic: Twentieth Century Transformations of Utopian Form" by Jennifer Burwell (dissertation), Northwestern University, 1993; "Sally Miller Gearhart, 1931—" by Cynthia Secor, in *Contemporary Lesbian Writers of the United States: A Bio-bibliographical Critical Sourcebook,* edited by Sandra Pollack and Denise D. Knight, Westport, Connecticut, Greenwood Press, 1993, 205-212; "Beyond Persuasion: A Proposal for an Invitational Rhetoric" by Sonja K. Foss and Cindy L. Griffin, in *Communication Monographs* (Falls Church, Virginia), Vol. 62, March 1995, 2-18.

Sally Miller Gearhart comments:

There had been so few voices over the centuries, and those precious few had been so soft. Before Stonewall it had been, for most of us, lives of quiet desperation or resignation. So it's not surprising that in the written and oral discourses of the 1970s and 1980s we had a tendency to shout. We had to speak for so many who had gone before—and we had to speak *to* them, wherever they were, to let them know that their lives, however quiet, now had meaning for the world.

And of course we had to speak and write so prolifically and so vigorously because it felt so good at last to say the dreadful words aloud. When I first arrived in San Francisco from my dark Texas closet of twenty-odd years, I accosted strangers on the street and said, "How do you do? I'm Sally Gearhart, and I'm a lesbian!" (I said it so often that I once bolluxed a self-introduction on a panel by saying, "I'm Sally Lesbian, and I'm a Gearhart!") My own writing is still an expression of that newfound freedom and exuberance. Someday lesbians and gay men—and all the rest of us queers—will be an assumption of our society, evident in its every aspect, even in its literature. Though that will be wonderful, the writing will probably be a little less exciting. I, for one, will be happy to pay that price.

*   *   *

Sally Miller Gearhart's *The Wanderground,* variously called a loose novel or a closely linked series of short stories, has gained virtual cult status among lesbian readers since its publication by the pioneering (and now defunct) feminist Persephone Press in 1978. It is generally considered both science fiction and utopia, although most critics feel it inhabits those genres only partially. Gearhart is also known as a public figure in the early "gay liberation" movement, largely through her co-editorship of *Loving Women/Loving Men: Gay Liberation and the Church* (with William R. Johnson) and her performance in the films "Word Is Out" (1977) and the Academy Award-winning "The Life and Times of Harvey Milk" (1984). But it is for *The Wanderground* that she will be best remembered.

The Wanderground posits a postpatriarchal world in which violence and mechanicalness—equated with masculinity and therefore with maleness—have caused life-controlling Nature to revolt and deny male access to Her. Men retain their power only within cities; in the countryside, their machines do not work, their guns will not fire, and they lose their sexual potency. The only people who can live with Nature are the Hill Women, whose retreat to the Wanderground has led them to a more primitive and also more intuitive existence. They live in nests within two major ensconcements; they don't read, manufacture, or form nuclear families, although they do raise girlchildren born through egg transplantations deep underground in sacred cellas. They perceive one another's thoughts and have developed an intricate mental system for gaining privacy, protecting from hurt, and asking for help. Their care for the environment and their belief in the sanctity of all life allows them to achieve mindmelds with animals, plants, and even rivers, allowing all life forms to receive what they need, as illustrated in the story "Krueva and the Pony," in which Krueva bargains with a ravenous mountain lion to delay its attack on a dying pony until Krueva has helped it die. Some of the Hill Women have learned toting—levitating objects so they can be carried easily—and even windriding, in which the body moves effortlessly through space. The science-fiction aspect of the book lies in its postulation of mental capacities developed through respect for Nature.

Into this primitive paradise comes Margaret, a city woman who has been raped, then bound in ancient armor and set loose in the hills. The presence of men outside the city capable of rape, and the newfound telepathic abilities of a small group of Gentle men, threaten an end to the Hill Women's carefully maintained safety. *The Wanderground* is loved because its lesbian readers (and many non-lesbian readers as well) have perceived it as a lesbian-separatist utopia. It embodies many of the ideals of such a utopia: the women are self-sustaining and even self-propagating; they love one another and are able to live in harmony despite differences of belief and temperament; the culture is non-materialistic; and many of the women are lesbians (although this is attributed not merely to the absence of men but to the unassailable superiority of women and, in this work, to the fact that only women are capable of emotional connection and caring). Written during the period now usually referred to as "Lesbian Nation," *The Wanderground* has been seen as separatism's "most comprehensive imaginative shape," according to Bonnie Zimmerman in *The Safe Sea of Women*. Most often grouped with Joanna Russ's *The Female Man*, Marge Piercy's *Woman on the Edge of Time*, and Suzy McKee Charnas's *Motherlines*, it is a near-perfect example of lesbian-separatist imaginings of a return to a simpler, purer, more woman-centered life, one in which the earth and women are fertile even—or especially—in the absence of men.

If it is the book's utopian lesbian ideal which has gained it such a devoted following, it is also what has incurred critics' deepest reservations. It is too often dismissed, as by Inge-Lise Paulsen, as "a not particularly well-written piece of radical feminist propaganda." Gearhart has also been faulted by Sarah Lefanu for offering "no sense of the materiality of the women's lives," and this is true: there are no provisions for shelter from the rain, eradication of cockroaches, or disposal of sewage. Other critics fault the essentialism of her attribution of ecospirituality to women, violence to men. At the same time, as Paulsen has noted in her *Women's Studies International Forum* article, there is something about *The Wanderground* that "fascinate[s]...and provoke[s]." In the decade in which it was written, it represented an ideal so nearly achievable that it was almost palpable to readers. The book continues to sell well—15,000 copies between 1986 and 1992, according to Cynthia Secor— because it nourishes an ongoing lesbian dream of an ideal world.

The political and religious strands of Gearhart's lesbian work interweave in interesting ways with the politics of *The Wanderground*. In an early (1974) piece, "The Miracle of Lesbianism," in *Loving Women/Loving Men*, Gearhart examines the Christian church as a locale for lesbian and feminist sustenance and finds that "whatever rationalizations we muster, however much we hope for the church's renewal, however warm and deep our memories are of 'fellowship' and love, liturgy and song, we are brought to truth with the knowledge that none of it has ever sustained us." Likewise, she sees an urgent need to revise language use away from an emphasis on persuasion (and the violence inherent in that concept) and toward a language of interaction and relation. In *The Wanderground*, "god" has been replaced by deep commitment to the autonomy and sanctity of every other being on the planet, and language created to reconceptualize interrelatedness. These qualities of thought have led to Gearhart's status between 1978 and the present as a spokesperson for lesbian and gay liberation, in such venues as formal television debates with John Briggs about the infamous Proposition Six on the California ballot in 1978, which would have banned gays and lesbians from the classroom, or her leadership of a candlelight march for slain city supervisor Harvey Milk on November 27, 1988. Overall, Gearhart has come as close as any single individual to representing in fiction the lesbian presence in and dreams for our contemporary world.

Gearhart's current work-in-progress extends the two concepts of nonviolence and communication in another speculative fantasy, *Little Blue*, scheduled to be published by Firebrand Press in 1997 or 1998. Gearhart is now retired from San Francisco State University and lives in Northern California.

—Loralee MacPike

GLICKMAN, Gary

Nationality: American novelist, short story writer, and librettist. **Born:** Morristown, New Jersey, 20 March 1959. **Education:** Brown University, B.A. 1981; University of Iowa, M.F.A. 1983. **Career:** Assistant director, Pine Artists Festival, Palenville, New York, 1981-82; writing teacher, University of Iowa, 1982-83, Pace University, 1983-85, private courses, from 1984, Vassar College, 1985-86, Writers Voice, West Side YMCA, New York, 1987, Tufts University, 1990-91, Long Island University, 1993-94, University of Southern California School of Music, Opera Workshop, 1995-96, University of California Los Angeles Writers Program, Extension Division, from 1996; writer-in-residence, University of Mississippi, 1986, Northwestern University, 1990, and State University of New York-Southampton, 1990; manager, University of Southern California Opera, 1995-96; stage manager, University of California Los Angeles Opera, from 1996; script analyst, Catalyst Literary Agency, from 1996; contributor of articles to periodicals, including *Bay Windows* (Boston), *Frontiers, New York Times, Outweek, St. Petersberg Times, U.S.A. Today,* and *Vanity Fair.* Auditor, New York State Council on the Arts, 1993-95; New York cultural correspondent, *Ma'Ariv* (Tel Aviv, Israel), from 1993. **Awards:** New York State Foundation for the Arts fellowship, 1986; National Endowment for the Arts fellowships, 1989, 1991; Helping Hand Fellowship, American Opera Projects, 1995. **Agent:** Elaine Markson Agency, 44 Greenwich Ave., New York, New York 10011, U.S.A.

WRITINGS

Fiction

"Into You," in *Inkling Magazine*, 1983.
"Medal Day at MacDowell," in *Vanity Fair,* December 1986.
"The Triumph of Dora Berensky at the End of the World," in *Mississippi Review,* Spring 1986.
Years from Now (novel). New York, Alfred A. Knopf, 1987.
"Magic," in *Men on Men 2,* edited by George Stambolian. New York, Dutton, 1988.
"Question and Answer," in *Bomb,* March 1990.
"Don't Say It!," in *Frontiers,* 14 February 1992.
"Pride," in *Frontiers,* 26 June 1994.
"Spirit House," in *Men on Men 5,* edited by David Bergman. New York, Plume/Penguin, 1994.
"Buried Treasures," in *Penguin Anthology of Gay Literature.* Penguin/NAL, 1995.

Librettos

Tibetan Dreams (produced Dance Theatre Workshop, New York City, 1989).
Orlando, or Love of a Leg (produced LaMama, New York City, 1992).
Twelfth Night (adaptation of play by William Shakespeare; produced American Opera Projects, New York City, 1995).

*

Critical Sources: "Gary Glickman" by Philip Gambone, in *Contemporary Gay American Novelists: A Bio-Bibliographical Criti-*

cal *Sourcebook,* edited by Emmanuel S. Nelson, Westport, Connecticut, Greenwood Press, 1993, 155-60; unpublished interview with Gary Glickman by Liora Moriel, March 1997.

Gary Glickman comments:

I am interested—a sort of life project—in my identity as a Jew and as a gay person. My writing very much rotates around those two identities, as well—of course—as that of artist.

It's because I'm gay that I see the world so much from the place of women and people who feel excluded from power. I know perfectly well how it feels to perceive oneself as strong and competent and worthy and yet be pre-judged in the world as weak and lesser. When I create women from that point of view they come out clear and credible.

*   *   *

Gary Glickman was born in Morristown, New Jersey, on 20 March 1959, the second of three children. His extended family lived nearby, and both Morristown synagogues were founded by his grandparents, Esse and Milton Schlosser, who came to the town as teenagers and were well known in the community. His father's name was up on the law-firm windows above the town green; his grandfather and uncle and cousin passed the torah down in, as Glickman put it, "a patriarchal show of three generations," and marched through the town at the head of the parade when the synagogue moved to bigger quarters.

"As a result of growing up in such a close and large Jewish family, in a close Jewish community, " Glickman recalled to GLL contributor Liora Moriel, it was only when he reached adolescence that he realized what a minority his community really was. Perhaps that is why he identifies so strongly with his two minority communities, Jewish and gay. "I believe that cultural background and sexuality (not gay/straight but just sexual impulse) are the most important, interesting and illuminating aspects of our experience. So I am very much a gay writer and a Jewish writer. These aspects of my identity influence how I write about all people, not just gay people or Jews. Even so, I believe artists must use everything they have, write as big as they can, and not worry about definitions."

When Glickman was 14 his parents separated (after divorcing they remarried when he was 17). He started writing a novel about a young man "who for some reason can't love the woman who loves him; the virile brother takes her away, and he kills himself," as he described the project to Moriel. His own life as a teenager was more successful: he played a variety of musical instruments (saxophone, bassoon, and piano), sang and played in the high school musicals, wrote poetry, essays, and with two friends wrote and performed the senior class play, 'The Tea,' "a five-person babble-fest about the emptiness and unexpected meanings of polite language" that won the Bucks County Young Artists Prize and was later produced at the Chester Playhouse in New Jersey.

In the late 1970s, Glickman attended Brown University in Rhode Island, majoring in music and English. It was at Brown that he met and befriended another writer, Meg Wolitzer, with whom he lived for several years. Following his graduation from Brown in 1981, Glickman attended the University of Iowa's famous Writers' Workshop, graduating with an M.F.A. in 1983. Returning to New York, Glickman soon met the young gay Jewish writer, David Leavitt, who had just published his first collection of stories, *Family Dancing.*

Upon the death of Leavitt's mother, they bought a dog, Posey, and left Manhattan for a house in East Hampton, where they lived until 1990. Glickman won a literature grant from the New York State Council on the Arts, and taught at Pace University, Vassar College, and the Writer's Voice. Glickman wrote this about Leavitt's contribution to his life: "In terms of writing, he was very influential, and suggested I write more closely about my family life. Also, his celebrity in Europe opened up formative and much beloved European vistas and friendships." In 1987, Gary Glickman published his first novel, *Years From Now,* which was widely reviewed, particularly in the context of his intimate and open association with Leavitt.

While visiting a journalist friend in Tunisia, Glickman realized he had "much still to learn from being away from home"; his experiences showed him the close connection between his Jewish and his gay roots. He told *Contemporary Gay American Novelists* contributor Philip Gambone: "I found that going out into the world as a Jew, I was going out into the world more as a gay person. Each time I went to look for Jews I found gay people; and each time I went to find gay people I found Jews." The experience resulted in an unpublished manuscript entitled "To the Place of Trumpeting: Travels in a Diaspora."

Returning from Tunisia in 1990, Glickman taught at Tufts University in Boston, and soon moved to Provincetown, Massachusetts. There he produced his comic opera, *Orlando, or Love of a Leg,* as a fundraiser for the local AIDS group and began his friendship with singer Deborah Karpel, who was influential in the writing of his (yet unpublished) novel, *Aura. Orlando* was followed in 1993 by his operatic setting of *Twelfth Night,* which he described to Moriel as "a project in un-obscuring the homosexuals!" The opera premiered at American Opera Projects, and was the recipient of their first Helping Hand Fellowship. New York again proved a powerful magnet for creative and personal partnerships for Glickman: he met playwright James Still, with whom he lived for two years before they moved together to Los Angeles.

Glickman managed the USC Opera during the 1995-96 academic year, while putting the finishing touches on the novel *Aura.* In 1996-97 Glickman taught fiction writing at UCLA, stage managed the UCLA opera, and enjoyed "walking the dogs (Posey and Ruby) on the beach with James Still, and working on a novel about the last days of the PLO in Tunisia." Glickman was witness to those days while on one of his many stays in Tunisia. He also visited Israel: "I loved it, but it's reductive to say it was a major influence. I loved feeling like a majority member for the first time in my life, much as gay people feel in Provincetown."

—Liora Moriel

————

GOLD, Ellen. *See* **LYNCH, Lee.**

————

GOOCH, Brad

Nationality: American poet, novelist, and short story author. **Born:** Kingston, Pennsylvania, 31 January 1952. **Education:** Columbia College, New York City, 1969-73 (Phi Beta Kappa, Magna cum laude); Sorbonne, Paris, France, Certificate of French Language and Civilization, 1974; Columbia University, New York City (with honors), M.A. 1977; Columbia University (President's Fellow, 1977-78, 1980-81), M. Phil. 1979, Ph.D. in English and Comparative Literature, 1986. **Family:** Companion of Howard Brookner, 1978-89. **Career:** Held a variety of jobs in modeling, 1978-82; instructor of English, Laguardia Community College, 1979-81; adjunct lecturer in Medieval and Renaissance Humanities, New York School of Continuing Education, 1985; senior preceptor in English, Columbia College, New York City, 1983-86; assistant professor, Columbia University Summer Session, 1986; assistant professor of English, William Paterson College, Wayne, New Jersey, from 1992. Contributor to periodicals, including *Advocate, American Poetry Review, Bomb, Christopher Street, Columbia Review, Elle, Elle Decor, GQ, Harper's Bazaar, Los Angeles Times Book Review, Nation, New Republic, New York Magazine, New Yorker, Out, Oxford Literary Review, Paris Review, Partisan Review, Rohwohlt LiteraturMagazine,* and *Vanity Fair*; member of PEN American Center, from 1993; member of Poetry Society of America, from 1994; judge, short fiction, Scholastic Art and Writing Awards, 1994, 1995; member of The Authors Guild, from 1995; judge, memoir and non-fiction, PEN American Center Prison Writing Awards, 1995, 1996. **Awards:** Woodberry Prize for Poetry, 1972; Academy of American Poets Poetry Prize, 1977; Creative Artists Performance Services, New York State Fiction Grant, 1980; Writer's Choice Award, for fiction, 1985. **Agent:** Joy Harris, The Lantz Harris Literary Agency, 156 Fifth Avenue, Suite 617, New York, New York 10010, U.S.A. **Address:** Department of English, William Paterson College, 300 Pompton Road, Wayne, New Jersey 07470, U.S.A.

WRITINGS

Novels

Scary Kisses. New York, G. P. Putnam's Sons, 1988; London, Pan Books, 1990; Paris, Oliver Orban, 1990; as *Mailand Manhattan,* Frankfurt am Mein, Fischer Taschenbuch Verlag, 1992.
The Golden Age of Promiscuity. New York, Knopf, 1996.

Short Stories

With Gerald Incandella, *Pictures/Stories.* Oakhurst Press, 1981; all stories included in *Jailbait and Other Stories,* New York, Sea Horse Press, 1984.
"Spring," in *Christopher Street* (New York), Vol. 15, No. 9, August 1981.
"Maine," in *Christopher Street,* Vol. 7, No. 10, Issue 83, 1983.
Jailbait and Other Stories. New York, Sea Horse Press, 1984; as *Lockvogel: Storys,* Frankfurt am Mein, Fischer Taschenbuch Verlag, 1992.
"Satan" (originally published in *Between C & D,* 1989), in *Waves: An Anthology of New Gay Fiction,* edited by Ethan Mordden. New York, Vintage, 1994.

Poetry

The Daily News. Calais, Vermont, Z Press, 1977.
With Frank Moore, *Another Country Tune.* Paris, Cité des Arts, 1978.

"Natural High," "Walk," "24," and "X," in *Coming Attraction: An Anthology of American Poets in Their Twenties.* Los Angeles, Little Caesar Press, 1980.
"Frozen Stiff," in *Poets for Life: Seventy-Six Poets Respond to AIDS,* edited by Michael Klein. New York, Crown, 1989.
Poems, in *Neue Amerikanishe Lyrik,* edited by Karin Graf, Martin Ludke, and Delf Schmidt. Hamburg, Rowohlt, 1990.
"Cité des Arts," in *Out of This World: An Anthology of the St. Mark's Poetry Project, 1966-1991,* edited by Anne Waldman. New York, Crown, 1991.
Poems, in *AM LIT: Neue Literatur aus den USA,* edited by Gerhard Falkner and Sylvere Lotringer. Edition Druckhaus III, 1992.

Other

City Poet: The Life and Times of Frank O'Hara (biography). New York, Knopf, 1993.
"A Christian is Someone Who's Met One" (essay), in *Wrestling With the Angel: Faith and Religion in the Lives of Gay Men,* edited by Brian Bouldrey. New York, Riverhead Books, 1995.
Travels in Spiritual America. New York, Knopf, forthcoming.

*

Critical Sources: "Introduction" by Dennis Cooper, in *Jailbait and Other Stories* by Brad Gooch, New York, Sea Horse Press, 1984; "Punk Spunk" by Brendan Lemon, in *New York Native,* 18 June-1 July 1984, 61, 75; review of *Scary Kisses* by Kiki Olson, in *New York Times Book Review,* 13 November 1988, 34-35; "Perfectly Frank" by Joan Acocella, in *New Yorker,* 19 July 1993, 71-78; "Frank O'Hara: Writing on the Run" by Walter Clemons, in *Washington Post Book World,* 29 August 1993, 5, 13; "The Mayakovsky of Macdougal Street" by Geoffrey O'Brien, in *New York Review of Books,* 2 December 1993, 22-24; "I Will Survive" by James Ireland Baker, in *Time Out New York,* 19-26 June 1996, 29.

Brad Gooch comments:

When I was growing up, I didn't know anything about gay fiction. Whatever examples were around were over my young head—Gore Vidal's *The City and the Pillar,* or James Baldwin's *Giovanni's Room.* But I did have moments of gay excitement reading books—the wet, nude men on the submarine in Jules Verne's *Twenty Thousand Leagues Under The Sea,* or the Roman emperor fantasy of either Leopold or Loeb in *Compulsion.* I had moments of gay excitement at the movies—Elvis Presley in *Blue Hawaii.* I had fantasies centered mostly on young criminals in my high school who spent nights in jail where, ideally, their heads were shaved. (I hadn't read Genet yet either!) One of the first writers I found who actually dared to produce some gay product was the poet Frank O'Hara.

So when I finally put "gay" and "literature" together in my head, I already had waiting a post-modernist raw material of word, image, fantasy, poetry, Hollywood movies and prose. Now there was freedom! Gay writing for me was always about freedom. And about what gossip columnists like to call "the mix". Because even though I was at Columbia College in sophisticated New York City in the loose 1970s, I still had to look around if I wanted to find a full bouquet of pleasures that satisfied anything like a gay sensiblity, or longing. My more self-conscious ingredients for hope and arousal and joy in that frontier epoch included: the poems of New York School poets Schuyler and Ashbery; the art films of Fassbinder and Pasolini; the porn films of Halsted and Peter Berlin; the early photographs of Robert Mapplethorpe; the novels of Genet.

Repression is never good. But it can have some surprisingly happy repercussions in art. The stubborn desire for self-satisfaction and freedom are among those repercussions. Once a prisoner, always a dreamer. I still think of my writing as a blank TV set on which I get to watch any program I want. Mostly because in that junior phase I just described, I saw so little that satisfied or excited me. All the channels were straight. The analogy between a blank page and a blank screen and gay life just presented itself. And continues to present itself.

Part of what I usually want to see engraved on the blank screen are scenes of long expressed, delayed, or occasionally even satisfied desire. I want to see things I've never seen there before. I usually like to see things I've repressed. Lately I've been thinking a lot about writing on spirituality. Which I did a bit in my poetry early on. I've been wondering if gay men haven't repressed their inner angel even more powerfully than they have those inner devils we—or at least I—so love to parade.

*   *   *

In "A Christian Is Someone Who's Met One," an essay on his spiritual experience written for *Wrestling with the Angel: Faith and Religion in the Lives of Gay Men*, Brad Gooch writes that "I do feel that gays have particular promise as a group for cultivating a new orchid of spiritual life, as long as it's planted in the black erotic soil they've tilled so generously over the past few decades," adding that "I think my early monastic fantasies were a wish for a community. And perhaps my sexual ones as well." These comments may be said to provide one means of understanding his fiction, the central vision of which is essentially humanistic. For Gooch reminds readers again and again that one's humanity is inextricably linked to community, and that one of the greatest challenges facing gay American culture is the lack of that vital communal connection.

A superficial reading of Gooch's fiction would lead one to believe its point of celebration is the liberating effects of sexuality. Most of his short stories and novels are constructed around sexual encounters, both gay and straight. In the first story collected in *Jailbait,* for instance, two adolescent boys have sex for the first time on a darkened train trestle. In "Airport," from the same volume, Fred, a photographer, meets the stewardess Lucinda while waiting for his bags. They share a cab and end up having sex in his apartment. The subject of *Scary Kisses,* Gooch's first novel, follows the brief modeling career of Todd Eamon (whose two year runway career is about as brief as Gooch's own) as he moves between his desire for girlfriend Lucy and his attraction toward supermodel Frank (and others). And *The Golden Age of Promiscuity* chronicles its central character's explorations of the margins of sexual experience within the underground leather culture in New York City during the decade of the 1970s.

While these various sexual encounters do form the active centers around which his stories coalesce, it is the aftermath of sex—the changes it may bring, for example, in an individual's conception of self—that concerns Gooch the most. In "Spring," the young Brad constructs a sundae on his friend Bobby's "pecker" and then proceeds to eat it. When they hear the "faraway...low tone of the train horn," their different reactions reveal the meaning of their encounter. Bobby reacts by focussing on the need for safety, for he "feels it is up to him to listen so that when the train gets close

enough he can warn Brad and they can scratch their way back down the trestle." For Bobby, this is a fleeting physical act, one which will probably soon fade from immediate memory. For Brad, however, there is an awareness that, because of his desires, he will not be able to remain in his small town for long; the sound of the train begins to awaken within him the understanding that that train must eventually carry him off, most likely to an urban landscape: "Brad feels the train sound means more to him than to anyone else."

In those stories dealing with adult characters, the events that follow sex usually highlight the lack of a strong, continually developing, spiritual communion that sexuality often is seen to initiate. The characters in "Airport," for example, realize their lack of connection, embodied by Lucinda's rewording of a quote from the nineteenth-century American poet, Emily Dickinson. She wonders whether "after a great pleasure comes a formal feeling...." That feeling of formality is the reassertion of the boundaries of self that are dissolved only momentarily during their sexual intercourse. She must re-enter her former life, in which Fred never played a part before, and most likely never will play a part again. So "Lucinda starts thinking about something else," while "Fred feels choked up."

Gooch's first novel, *Scary Kisses,* traces the usually limiting influences sexual partners have on the central character's emotional life. Though attracted to both Frank's good looks (he has sex with him once) and Frank's successful modeling career, Todd realizes that it is only with Lucy that he can find emotional completion. His need for the spiritual connection only she can provide him—though not simply because she fulfill's society's heterosexual norm—is most clearly revealed in a dream he has of a "good-looking girl he doesn't know well, but knows some," with whom he has been sleeping while the world stands on the brink of nuclear annihilation. While missiles bear down upon them, they lie together in that romantic final embrace which dying lovers seek to convey their love, except that "Todd tries to find a comfortable loving position with his partner...but they don't quite fit. She tries his chest but that doesn't work either. They can't quite relax. No one to turn to." From the dream, Todd realizes he must "turn to" Lucy, and does so, leaving New York City for a summer cabin on Long Island. And with them comes Todd's 16-year-old cousin, Robbie. Together they form what the novel's final chapter wittily titles the "Postnuclear Family." Lest the gay reader think that Gooch has bought into the homophobic belief that the only means for enduring spiritual communion is through heterosexuality, Robbie seems to be on the road to a relatively healthy, caring homosexuality, nurtured not so much by a heterosexual example as by the example of love Todd and Lucy show to one another.

Gooch's novel, *The Golden Age of Promiscuity,* takes readers into the maelstrom of gay sexuality that is said to have characterized the high urban culture of the 1970s. This decade has become, in popular gay myth, a "golden age," a time of innocent sexual promiscuity that was untrammeled by the fear of AIDS. The novel's main character, Sean Devlin, arrives in New York City two years after the Stonewall Uprising—two days of rioting by gays, lesbians, and transvestites in response to New York police harassment of the patrons of a bar called Stonewall in 1969. The New York culture of the novel finds expression through anonymous sex in outrageous bars and seedy bathhouses, under the cover of drug-enhanced darkness or beneath bright disco lights, almost always to the flicker of pornographic films or Sean's own porn recording camera.

Readers follow Sean from one seemingly meaningless sexual encounter to another during which he comes closer and closer to that point at which human sexuality becomes purely animal, that point in which the human individual becomes an animal. That point is reached when he feels the desire "to reside in a cage that could be unlocked only from the outside, a cage with only a mat on the floor." After entering this cage—and thereby coming dangerously close to the complete loss of his humanity in a sado-masochistic long distance relationship with "Master Chris," a Washington, D.C.-based insurance underwriter—Sean meets Willie Nichols, opera lover, writer, and one of William S. Burroughs's "acolytes." For the first time, Sean begins "feeling something like love," which does indeed blossom into love, and does so on the very eve of the AIDS epidemic. But while the AIDS epidemic will bring the "golden age" to a tragic close, before it begins Sean has found finally "kindness, knowledge, love, sarcasm, doubt, happiness, incredible idealism," which Gooch juxtaposes against the "unemotional freak show" on the dance floor of the bar in which the novel's final scene unfolds.

As his essay in *Wrestling With the Angel* reveals, Gooch is certain that the joy of gay sex is inseparable from the quest to build gay community, but he seems equally certain that gay sex—or any sex for that matter—that becomes divorced from the very human need for spiritual connection and communion will ultimate lead to the loss of self, the loss of one's humanity. Within one's humanity, then, lies the true meaning of community, and by taking up this theme, and exploring the spaces wherein gay sex and gay community meet, Gooch has firmly placed himself in the forefront of gay American literature in the late twentieth century, and thus within a post-AIDS frontier of gay spirituality that has yet to be fully explored.

—David Peterson

GOODMAN, Melinda

Nationality: American poet. **Born:** New York City, 1 March 1957. **Education:** Hampshire College, B.A. in English 1979; Columbia University, New York City, M.F.A. 1987; New York University, M.A. in English 1992. **Career:** Has held a variety of teaching positions, including teaching assistant in theatre, University of Massachusetts at Amherst, 1979-80; documentary producer and vice president, Relay Productions, Inc., 1980-82; bodywork therapist, Yamuna's Studio, New York City, 1982-87; creator and facilitator of poetry reading series, Knitting Factory, New York City, 1985-87; faculty advisor, Audre Lorde Women's Poetry Center, Hunter College, 1985-88; adjunct lecturer, Department of English, Hunter College of CUNY, New York City, from 1987; director, poetry-theatre production of *STATIONS*, Hunter College Playhouse, New York City, 1988; editor and advertising manager, *Conditions* magazine, 1988-91; faculty advisor, *Quack: a Journal of Tolerance* (student literary magazine), 1989-90; adult basic education teacher, Bronx Community College, New York City, 1989-92; teacher, Spofford Juvenile Detention Center, New York City, 1993-94; conference organizer, *Cultural Diversity and Sexualities: Lesbians, Gays and Bisexuals in the College Curriculum*, Hunter College, April 1994; literacy assistant, Brooklyn Public Library, Grand Army Plaza, 1994-95, and New York Public Library, Branch

Library, Bronx, 1996; G.E.D., literacy, and leadership trainer, Youth Building, Brownsville, New York City, 1996. **Awards:** Columbia University Fellowship Citation, 1986-87; ASTRAEA Foundations Lesbian Poets Award, 1991. **Address:** Department of English, Hunter College of CUNY, 695 Park Ave., New York, New York 10021, U.S.A.

WRITINGS

Poetry

"Count Down" and "Yeah, I'm a Bitch," in *Freshtones: An Anthology of Poetry, Fiction, Essays and Photography by Women*, edited by Patricia Lee. New York, One and One Communications, 1978.
"Hackensack House Warming," in *Common Lives/Lesbian Lives: A Lesbian Quarterly*, No. 14, winter 1984.
"The Wedding Reception," in *Conditions*, No. 11/12, 1985.
"Body Work" and "I Am Married to Myself," in *Early Ripening: American Women's Poetry Now*, edited by Marge Piercy. New York, Pandora/Routledge, and London, Kegan Paul, 1987.
"The Line," in *Sinister Wisdom*, No. 31, winter 1987.
Middle Sister: Poems by Melinda Goodman. Paterson, New Jersey, MSG Press, 1988.
"Just How Crazy Brenda Is" and "Wedding Reception," in *Gay and Lesbian Poetry in Our Time: An Anthology*, edited by Carl Morse and Joan Larkin. New York, St. Martin's Press, 1988.
"Open Poem," in *Outweek*, No. 71, 7 November 1990.
"February Ice Years," in *Conditions*, No. 17, 1990.
"Lullabye for a Butch," in *The Persistent Desire: A Femme-Butch Reader*, edited by Joan Nestle. Boston, Alyson Publications, 1992.
"You Think You're the Butch," in *The Femme Mystique*, edited by Leslea Newman. Boston, Alyson Publications, 1995.
"Who I Am" and "Trouble," in *My Lover Is A Woman*, edited by Leslea Newman. New York, Ballantine Books, 1996.
"New Comers" and "Love All the Time," in *The Arc of Love: An Anthology of Lesbian Love Poems*, edited by Clare Coss. New York, London, Toronto, Scribner, 1996.
"Je me suis mariée avec moi" (translation of "I Am Married to Myself" by Francesca Canadé Sautman), in *Anthologie de la Poésie Contestataire Américaine*, edited by Gilles-Bernard Vachon Simha. Saint-Martin-d'Hères, Maison de la Poésie Rhône-Alpes/le Temps des Cerises, 1996.

Other

"Introducing Audre Lorde," in *Poder: A Journal of Feminist Literary Perspectives* (New York), Vol. 3, No. 2, spring 1989.
"Introduction," in *Standards: An International Journal of Multicultural Studies. Tribute to Audre Lorde* (Stanford University/University of Colorado), Vol. 4, No. 1, 1993-94.

*

Critical Sources: "Checking the Closets" by Donna Masini, in *Conditions*, No. 15, 1988, 148-152; "Opening Your Eyes to Hear" by Nancy Lagomarsino, in *Sojourner*, November 1992, 27; unpublished interview with Melinda Goodman by Francesca Canadé Sautman, November 1996.

Melinda Goodman comments:

(excerpt from "The Line"):

the woman behind the counter is screaming
"This line is closed! This line is closed!"
nobody understands what's going on
most of us don't speak english
I decide to go up to the counter to ask where I should be
as I pass the front of my line
a man shouts at me in a deep voice
"La linea! La linea!"
I can't believe he thinks I'm cutting in
I tell him I'm just going up to ask a question
I'll be right back
"la linea" he grunts
"yeah, yeah . . . la linea la linea" I say
and walk up to the counter
I recognize the woman working there
I am glad to be approaching one of the nicer ones
I wonder if she's gay
she tells me to wait a second
while she finishes with a client
I ask her which line I should be on for the nine fifteen
(by this time it's ten o'clock)
she reaches for my book
"Did you fill it in?" she asks me
"Yes." I say
horrified I realize that she's stamping by book
I want to say No! No! I only wanted to know
what line to go on.
but the words are in my throat
punching each other in the face
she hands me the card to sign and I sign it
in light pencil real fast invisible writing
maybe nobody will notice what has just happened here
I hand back the card she gives me my yellow book
"La Linea!!" I hear as I turn around
"Hey! How did you do that?"
I try not to look at the skinny young man
whose cigarette has burnt out
the one time athlete is standing quietly in the line
I try to explain
"I only wanted to know what line I should be on"
he stares straight ahead
I take my bags
and walk down the stairs
out to the street
the sun
the fucking sun is shining

*   *   *

Poet and teacher Melinda Goodman was born in 1957 in Manhattan, but her family moved when she was one year old to Englewood, New Jersey. She experienced a difficult adolescence. Her family was creative, artistic, and dedicated to leftist politics; it was also unstable and abusive. The Goodmans were the first Jewish family in the neighborhood, and were clearly excluded from numerous social settings in this WASPish and conventional mostly middle class suburb. Goodman thus was rapidly acquainted with discrimination and an inescapable feeling of difference. She went to school in the Bronx from the 5th to the 9th grade, and spent most of her early teen years in Manhattan. Most of her friends were black youth her age and she developed strong emotional bonds with them, leading to a deep sense of identification, built on her admiration for the toughness, self-sufficiency, and pride she found among her schoolmates and their families. Some of these bonds with girls her age became love affairs which left a lasting imprint on her life and writing, the traces of which can be seen in the poem "Just How Crazy Brenda Is." Hers was not a shocking "coming out," for she had been initiated into sex with women at a very early age. In Goodman's poetry, these youthful sexual encounters exude a strong but tender sensuality, mixed with sadness and nostalgia. Such poems stands in stark contrast to the brutal memories expressed in one of her later poems, "February Ice Years." Here, the routine, "ordinary" abuse of a teen by an older woman is depicted with unforgiving directness.

African American culture deeply informed Goodman's sense of self as well as her political views. She rejected her own "whiteness," and was estranged from her white schoolmates. This alienation, coupled with the consciousness that one cannot "unmake" oneself "white" in our society, provided Goodman with a sharp and even confrontational understanding of racism, which appears frequently in her poems, albeit without the rhetorical style of tracts or speeches. A poem like "The Line" captures the shame, confusion, and self-contempt that stem from being caught up unwittingly in the web of "white privilege" and discrimination. Indeed, long years of feeling like a persistent outsider echo throughout her work.

Goodman was a rebellious teen who experimented with drugs—sometimes quite dangerously—and often stayed away from home. These escapades both provided access to precocious sexual discovery and made her vulnerable to damaging experiences beyond the grasp of her own will. Several of her poems express the desperate plea of a child in need of parental affection and understanding, rather than sarcasm and family histrionics.

By the age of 13, Goodman was discovering through books and the radio the poetry of Nikki Giovanni, whose work was one of the earliest and most durable influences on her own writing. Goodman remembers fondly her commanding presence and voice, and Nikki Giovanni was the first in a long line of strong, successful black women who profoundly inspired Goodman's life and poetry. Upon completing her B.A. at Hampshire College in 1979, Goodman moved to Manhattan's Washington Heights. In her mid-twenties, scarred by the end of a long relationship, Goodman met two women who, each in their different ways, were to have a profound and lasting effect on her. At about the same time, she met ST and Audre Lorde.

It was Lorde who took a direct interest in Goodman's poetry, encouraged her to go to graduate school, and helped her get a teaching job at Hunter College of the City University of New York, where she still teaches poetry. A generous mentor, role model, and friend, Audre Lorde gave Goodman guidance and love. Lorde's premature death was an incalculable loss for Goodman, as for so many others, and she has commemorated Lorde's towering presence in prose essays, as well as in one of her most sad and tender poems, "Love All the Time."

Goodman's poetry writing intensified in this part of her life, and became an exacting, daring process of tapping her rawest, most painful emotions, to produce, a few at a time, carefully crafted works. Her book of poems titled *Middle Sister* came out in 1988 and she published actively in lesbian feminist journals like *Conditions,* as well as in publications such as *Heresies: The Poetry Magazine of the Lower East Side, Seditious Delicious,* and *Common Lives/Lesbian Lives.*

Among the poets who have greatly influenced or inspired her work are Lawrence Ferlinghetti, Marge Piercy, Judy Grahn, a group of African American poets called the "Last Poets" who read on the radio when she was listening to Nikki Giovanni, and of course, Audre Lorde. As a teacher of poetry writing at Hunter College, she has become herself a mentor and master craftswoman who inspires and stimulates many young (and not so young) poets of all genders and sexual orientations. But her work is of particular importance to struggling lesbian writers.

In her review of Melinda Goodman's book of poems, *Middle Sister,* Donna Masini commented that she "dares...to speak the unspeakable." In bold, sometimes harrowing images, Goodman's poems indeed speak of discomforting themes: neglect, destructive families, unloved adolescents, abuse, the sinister side of children, coming out, loving women, being misloved by women, sex, butch-femme relations, loss, community, isolation, racism, and social injustice. Goodman admits that she often "goes for the jugular," leaving no hiding place from brutal truths; pain, hardship, and violence have always been an integral part of her life, and, while she bares herself with uncompromising honesty, she expects a certain willingness from those who hear her to be touched in vulnerable places, and even hurt, she told Francesca Canadé Sautman. Her poetry sometimes seems to punch and kick after adopting an insidiously tranquil, anecdotal tone. For instance, Goodman's depiction of sex makes use of very direct language, but combines it with images that take flight from the mundane and the familiar. Even when it appears casual, as in the poems "New Comers," sex in her work is neither sweet nor light: it involves a well acknowledged display of and struggle for power, it is strong and a little threatening, and very effectively erotic.

Masini has aptly identified the poetic process by which Goodman at once startles, charms, and attacks: "continuously peeling back the familiar, she reveals its mysteries, uncovers its ghosts. In clear, unfettered language she ferrets out the strangeness in ordinary life, she creeps up on the mystery until you can't tell where the familiar ends and the extraordinary begins." She adds, "Goodman's approach is narrative, her form anecdotal, her vehicle, intuition. She allows herself to circle the subject slowly, moving closer to the center, until the trapdoor cracks open and we fall with her into the more lyrical associations of the inner life."

—Francesca Canadé Sautman

GOYEN, (Charles) William

Nationality: American novelist, playwright, and author of short stories. **Born:** Trinity, Texas, 24 April 1915. **Education:** Sam Houston High School, Houston, Texas, 1928-32; Rice Institute (later Rice University), Houston, Texas, 1932-39, B.A. in literature 1937, M.A. in comparative literature 1939; University of Iowa, Iowa City, 1939. **Military Service:** Served in the United States Navy, 1939-45. **Family:** Lived with Walter Berns in Taos, New Mexico, 1945-48; had affair with writer Katherine Anne Porter,

c. 1951-52; lived with painter Joseph Glasco in Ottsville, Pennsylvania, c. 1955-60; married actress Doris Roberts in 1963. **Career:** Held a variety of teaching positions including University of Houston, 1939-40, Reed College, Portland, Oregon, 1948, New School for Social Research, New York City, 1955-60, Columbia University, New York City, 1964-65, and University of Houston 1981; script reader for Margo Jones, Dallas, Texas, 1948; Senior Trade Editor, McGraw-Hill, New York City, 1966-71; playwright in residence, Trinity Square Repertory Company, Providence, Rhode Island, 1969; visiting professor, Brown University, Providence, Rhode Island, 1970-74; writer in residence, Princeton University, New Jersey, 1976-78. Reviewer for the *New York Times Book Review,* 1955-56. **Awards:** *Southwest Review* Literary Fellowship, 1948; MacMurray Prize for best first novel by a Texan, 1951; Guggenheim Fellowship, 1952, 1954; Ford Foundation Grant for Theater Writing, 1963; Distinguished Alumni Award, Rice University, 1977. **Died:** Los Angeles, California, 29 August 1983.

WRITINGS

Fiction

The House of Breath (novel). New York, Random House, 1950; twenty-fifth anniversary edition with new preface by author, New York, Random House, and Berkeley, Bookworks, 1975.
Ghost and Flesh: Stories and Tales. New York, Random House, 1952.
In a Farther Country: A Romance. New York, Random House, and London, Peter Owen, 1955.
The Faces of Blood Kindred: A Novella and Ten Short Stories. New York, Random House, 1960.
The Fair Sister (novel). Garden City, Doubleday, 1963; as *Savata, My Fair Sister,* London, Peter Owen, 1963.
Come, the Restorer: A Novel. Garden City, Doubleday, 1974.
Selected Writings of William Goyen. New York, Random House, and Berkeley, California, Bookworks, 1974.
Collected Stories of William Goyen. Garden City, Doubleday, 1975.
Arcadio (novel). New York, Clarkson N. Potter, 1983; Evanston, Illinois, Northwestern University Press, 1994.
Had I a Hundred Mouths: New and Selected Stories 1947-1983 (with an introduction by Joyce Carol Oates). New York, Clarkson N. Potter, 1985.
Half a Look of Cain (novel), edited and with an afterword by Reginald Gibbons. Evanston, Illinois, Northwestern University Press, 1994.

Stage Plays

The House of Breath (adaptation of his novel; produced Off Broadway, 1954; produced Circle in the Square, New York City, 1957).
The Diamond Rattler (produced Boston, 1955, 1960).
Christy (adaptation of his novel *The House of Breath*; produced New York City, 1963).
The House of Breath, Black/White (adaptation of his novel; produced Providence, Rhode Island, 1969).
Aimée! (musical; produced Providence, Rhode Island, 1973).

Television Plays

A Possibility of Oil. CBS-TV, 1961.
The Mind. ABC-TV, 1961.

Literary Criticism

My Antonia. A Critical Commentary, New York, American R.D.M., 1966.

Ralph Ellison's Invisible Man. A Critical Commentary, New York, American R.D.M., 1966.

Other

"Three Poems," in *Le Bayou* (Houston), 1941-42.

Translator, *The Lazy Ones* by Albert Cossery. New York, New Directions, and London, Peter Owen, 1952.

Lyrics, *The Left-Handed Gun* (film). Warner Brothers, 1957.

A Book of Jesus. Garden City, Doubleday, 1973.

Nine Poems by William Goyen. New York, Albondocani Press, 1976.

William Goyen: Selected Letters from a Writer's Life, edited with an introduction by Robert Phillips. Austin, University of Texas Press, 1995.

*

Adaptations: *Whisper to Me* (play adaptation of story "The Letter in the Cedarchest"; produced Dallas and New York, 1955).

Interviews: "An Interview with William Goyen" by Reginald Gibbons, in *Had I a Hundred Mouths: New and Selected Stories 1947-1983,* New York, Clarkson N. Potter, 1985, 251-275.

Critical Sources: *Violence in Recent Southern Fiction* by Louise Y. Gossett, Durham, North Carolina, Duke University Press, 1965; *The Art of Southern Fiction: A Study of Some Modern Novelists* by Frederick J. Hoffman, Carbondale and Edwardsville, Southern Illinois University Press, 1967; *Like a Brother, Like a Lover: Male Homosexuality in the American Novel and Theater from Herman Melville to James Baldwin* by Georges-Michel Sarotte, translated by Richard Miller, Garden City, New York, Anchor Press/Doubleday, 1978; *William Goyen* by Robert Phillips, Boston, Twayne, 1979; *The Gay Novel in America* by James Levin, New York and London, Garland Publishing, 1991; afterword by Reginald Gibbons, in *Half a Look of Cain,* by William Goyen, Evanston, Illinois, Northwestern University Press, 1994, 123-136; afterword by Sir Stephen Spender, in *William Goyen: Selected Letters from a Writer's Life,* edited by Robert Phillips, Austin, University of Texas Press, 1995, 411-413.

* * *

William Goyen is a difficult writer to categorize, since both his work and life defy neat labels. His sexuality, for instance, seems to have been quite fluid. In his afterword to Goyen's letters, Sir Stephen Spender recalls that in the late 1940s and early 1950s Goyen "appeared at this period of his life, to be predominantly homosexual." A few years later, however, he conducted an infamous affair with fellow writer Katherine Anne Porter, which was savagely lampooned by Truman Capote in *Answered Prayers* (1987). Goyen's regional identity was no less stable. Having grown up in eastern Texas, he and his writing seemed of both the South and the Southwest. And yet Goyen resisted assuming either of these regional identities and the burdens of their stereotypes. Af-

ter the publication of his first novel in 1950, he was logically placed within an emerging group of young southern writers, such as Capote, Hubert Creekmore, Thomas Hal Phillips, and Tennessee Williams, who were centrally concerned with same-sex desire between men. Goyen, however, as quoted by Robert Phillips in his introduction to Goyen's letters, heatedly responded, "I am tired of being called a young Southern writer. The themes of my work have no affinity with the eccentricities of Southern personality or Gothic bizarreries, though my work has been attracted into that category by spurious association." He repeatedly maintained this stance, declaring in a 1982 interview with Reginald Gibbons included in *Had I a Hundred Mouths* (1985), "I'm not a 'Texas writer' or a 'regional' one. I'm not interested in that, I never really was."

Goyen's writings comparably resist categorization. From 1950 until his death in 1983, he added to American literature an array of texts that include novels, short stories, plays, and even a retelling of the life of Christ, *A Book of Jesus* (1973). Since his death, even more of his fiction has come into print, and yet surreal, idiosyncratic novels such as *Arcadio* (1983) and *Half a Look of Cain* (1994) have not made classifying Goyen's corpus any easier. A few generalizations nevertheless hold. Influenced by high modernist aesthetics championed by writers of the generation before Goyen, he rarely opted for linear narration and instead often crafted compilations of multiple narrators and framed tales within tales. Readers have both delighted in this complexity and found it maddening. Responses to Goyen's lyrical prose have been similar, as readers and reviewers alike have both praised this lyricism and damned it.

Like Goyen's form and style, his thematic concerns remain fairly consistent. Much like his contemporaries, such as Capote and Carson McCullers, as well as older modernists typified by T. S. Eliot and even Thomas Wolfe, Goyen repeatedly focuses on alienated individuals—outsiders who struggle to understand their identities. These persons' quests usually foreground negotiations of corporeality and eroticism, those densely textured by Goyen with spiritual and emotional significance. Gibbons clarifies in his afterword to *Half a Look of Cain* that for Goyen the "erotic could be a reclaiming of the life of the spirit, deeper than the life of appearance or the material life of the everyday world; but erotic desire could also become ungovernable, could inflict wounds." Goyen typically does not offer graphic realism in these representations of eroticism; rather, as Phillips explains in his study of Goyen, these narratives "are not superficially realistic, but subjective, works of flux and intuition which directly reflect their creator's sensibility." Gibbons concurs that "William Goyen was in no way a realist, in either his aesthetic or the practical sense." In the Gibbons interview, however, Goyen himself implies that the figurative meanings arise only out of representations of physical bodies: "My stories *are* spiritual. And yet there are an awful lot of *genitalia* in them."

Throughout his corpus, Goyen's handling of eroticism includes same-sex desire. Indeed, much of his first critical notice arose from responses to the overtly incestuous homoeroticism between men in *The House of Breath.* Boy Ganchion, the character through whom the novel is largely told, emerges from childhood only to be overwhelmed by the complicated circulations of desire and sexuality within his extended family. His younger uncle, Folner Ganchion, is presumably gay, a flamboyantly effeminate crossdresser who "didn't want to flicker around East Texas" but instead "wanted to *blaze* in the world, to sparkle, to shine, to glisten in the great evil world." In contrast, Christy Ganchion, Boy's older uncle, epitomizes conventional masculinity. When abandoned by Folner, Boy turns to Christy, whose bared body awakens Boy's latent desires: "I found him hairy with a dark down, and nippled, and shafted in an ominous place that I seemed to have so known about always in my memory, not new, although suddenly like a discovery, that I whispered to myself 'Yes!'" Christy returns Boy's erotic investments, and the two metaphorically consummate the relationship in a fateful, violent hunting trip in the woods at the novel's close.

One finds comparably homoerotic representations throughout Goyen's subsequent work, but these depictions perhaps culminate in his posthumously published novels. *Arcadio* features as its eponymous hero a hermaphrodite who spends much of his/her life in a traveling freak show. "I am equipped for lust," Arcadio asserts, "tantalized by my own very body, sometimes itching and burning, sometimes soft open and hard, lip and cod, one part hungering for the other, and it available and welcoming." As in *The House of Breath,* incest is prevalent, since Arcadio's liaisons include ones with his father. *Half a Look of Cain* is equally fantastical in regard to sexuality. In fact, Goyen completed the novella in 1953 but postponed its publication until after his death because of not only the work's formalistic complexity, but also its frank portrayal of both homosexual and heterosexual desire.

—Gary Richards

GOYTISOLO, Juan

Nationality: Spanish novelist, short story writer, literary critic, and editor. **Born:** Barcelona, 5 January 1931; emigrated to Paris, France, 1957. **Education:** University of Barcelona and University of Madrid, 1948-52. **Career:** Editor for Gallimard Publishing Co.; visiting professor at various universities in the United States. **Awards:** Europalia Prize, 1985; Gran Premio Literatura Iberoamericana, Bogotá, 1997. **Address:** Carmen Balcells, Diagonal 580, 08021 Barcelona, Spain.

WRITINGS

Novels

Jugos de Manos. Barcelona, Destino, 1954; translation by John Rust published as *The Young Assassins,* New York, Knopf, 1959.

Duelo in el Paraiso. Barcelona, Planeta, 1955; Barcelona, Destino, 1981; translation by Christine Brooke-Rose published as *Children of Chaos,* London, MacGibbon & Kee, 1958.

Fiestas. Buenos Aires, Editorial Emecé, 1958; Barcelona, Destino, 1981; translation by Herbert Winstock published as *Fiestas,* New York, Knopf, 1960.

La Isla. Barcelona, Seix Barral, 1961, 1982; translation by José Yglesias published as *Island of Women,* New York, Knopf, 1962.

Señas de Identidad. Mexico, Moritz, 1966; translation by Gregory Rabassa published as *Marks of Identity,* New York, Grove, 1969.

Reivindicación del Conde don Julián. Mexico, Mortiz, 1970; translation by Helen R. Lane published as *Count Julian,* New York, Viking, 1974.

Juan sin Tierra. Barcelona, Seix Barral, 1975; translation by Helen R. Lane published as *Juan the Landless,* New York, Viking, 1977.

Makbara. Barcelona, Seix Barral, 1980; translation by Helen R. Lane published as *Makbara,* New York, Seaver Books, 1981.

Paisajes Despuésde la Batalla. Barcelona, Montesinos, 1982; translation by Helen R. Lane published as *Landscapes After the Battle,* New York, Seaver Books, 1987.

Las virtudes del pájaro solitario. Barcelona, Seix Barral, 1988; translation by Helen Lane as *The Virtues of Solitary Bird,* London, Serpents Tail, 1991.

La Cuarentena. Madrid, Mondadori, 1991; translation by Peter Bush as *Quarantine,* Illinois State University Dalkey Archive Press, 1994.

La saga de los Marx. Barcelona, Mondadori, 1993; translation by Peter Bush as *The Marx Family Saga,* London, Faber and Faber, 1996.

El Sitio de los Sitios. Madrid, Santillana, 1995.

Short Stories

Para Vivir Aqui ("To Live Here"). Buenos Aires, Sur, 1960; Barcelona, Bruguera, 1983.

Fin de Fiesta: Tentativas de Interpretación de una Historia Amorosa. Barcelona, Seix Barral, 1962; translation by José Yglesias published as *The Party's Over: Four Attempts to Define a Love Story,* Weidenfeld & Nicolson, 1966, New York, Grove, 1967.

Travel Narratives

Campos de Nijar. Barcelona, Seix Barral, 1960; translation by Luigi Luccarelli published as *The Countryside of Nijar,* Michigan, Alembic Press, 1987.

La Chanca. Paris, Libreria Española, 1962; Barcelona, Seix Barral, 1983; translation by Luigi Luccarelli published as *La Chanca,* Michigan, Alembic Press, 1987.

Aproximaciones a Caudien Capadocia. Barcelona, Mondadori, 1990; translation by Helen Lane as *Space in Motion,* New York, Lumen Books, 1987.

Literary Criticism

El Furgón de Cola ("The Caboose"). Paris, Ruedo Ibérico, 1967; Barcelona, Seix Barral, 1982.

Próloga a la Obra Inglesa de Blanco White. Buenos Aires, Seix Barral, 1977.

Disidencias. Barcelona, Seix Barral, 1978; Madrid, Santillana, 1996.

Contracorrientes. Barcelona, Montesinos, 1985.

El bosque de las letras. Madrid, Santillana, 1995.

Autobiography

Coto vedado. Barcelona, Seix Barral, 1985; translation by Peter Bush published as *Forbidden Territory: The Memoirs of Juan Goytisolo,* San Francisco, North Point Press, 1989.

En los reinos de taifa. Barcelona, Seix Barral, 1986; translation by Peter Bush as *Realms of Strife,* San Francisco, North Point, 1990.

*

Critical Sources: *Juan Goytisolo* by Kessel Schwartz, New York,

Twayne, 1970; review of *Reivindicación del Conde don Julián* by Carlos Fuentes, in *New York Times Book Review,* May 5, 1974; *Contemporary Literary Criticism,* Detroit, Michigan, Gale Research, Vol. 5, 1976, Vol. 10, 1979, Vol. 23, 1983; *Trilogy of Treason: An Intertextual Study of Juan Goytisolo* by Michael Ugarte, Columbia, University of Missouri Press, 1982; *Forbidden Territory* by Juan Goytisolo, San Francisco, North Point Press, 1989; *Understanding Juan Goytisolo* by Randolph Pope, Columbia, University of South Carolina Press, 1995; *Significant Violence* by Brad Epps, Oxford, Clarendon Press, 1996.

*   *   *

Juan Goytisolo's corpus—novels, short stories, travel narratives, literary criticism—places him at the vanguard of twentieth-century Spanish literature. Like other "new wave" writers of his generation, Goytisolo grew up during Francisco Franco's dictatorship (1930-75), an era marked by censorship, oppression, and violence. Goytisolo dedicated himself to writing. From his early social-realist novels written in Spain to his later more experimental work written while living in Paris, he probes the depths of alienation: of being homeless in a world that threatens to destroy family, oppressed through language that reinforces what a dominant group terms "reality," and marginalized because of one's sexual preference.

His family's wealth did little to hold back the nightmares of the civil war. Goytisolo writes in his memoir *Forbidden Territory* that his mother, Julia Gay, "had gone shopping in the center of the city and was caught there by the arrival of the airplanes.... The empty bag: all that remained of her. Her role in life, in our life, had finished abruptly before the end of the first act." With the loss of his mother, his everyday experiences of life were filtered through Franco's propaganda. Though he developed a distaste for the abusive manipulation of language, his developing awareness of the power of language led him to become an author.

The struggle to grow up on the edge of violence was further complicated by his homosexuality. He immersed himself in works of gay writers such as Oscar Wilde and Andre Gide, as well as mainstream novels by the likes of Dos Passos, Orwell, Dostoyevski, and Poe. Reading Gide and Wilde was a dangerous endeavor in Franco's Spain and, more particularly, in Goytisolo's family. He tells us: "The idea of being taken for a member of that guild, an object of universal contempt and hatred, filled me with anguish and fear. My father's pathological horror, daily exacerbated by enforced co-existence with Grandfather, had left a deep impression on me. All my friends, with one or two exceptions, professed equally virulent disgust toward 'perverts.'" During his matriculation at the Universities of Barcelona and Madrid, Goytisolo began consciously to develop a powerful writerly voice that would comment on and resist his socially and sexually oppressive environs.

Goytisolo made his novelistic debut in 1954 with *Juegos de Manos,* a Dos Passos-influenced social-realist tale about a group of students who turn violently on each other. In other novels written during this period—from *El Circo* (1957) through *La Isla* (1961)—Goytisolo stayed with this conventional style, commenting on man's injustice to man via stories of more crazed adolescents who wreak havoc on society. The children are often believed to represent those ideologues, like the fascists, who turn to violence in their desperate attempt to engineer society. He claims to find in children "a sort of microcosm of adult life. Spanish children in particular have a knack of exploiting the world of their

elders." This spate of stark social commentary received mixed critical reviews.

In 1966 Goytisolo entered a more experimental phase, in which he foregrounded issues of national and sexual identity and literary form. As a result of the rereading of classical Spanish literature, his trilogy *Señas de Identidad* (1966), *Reivindicación del Conde don Julián* (1970), and *Juan sin Tierra* (1975) shatters traditional form, interspersing first-, second-, and third-person narrations and moving away from any sense of continuous plot by violently juxtaposing disparate narrative episodes. For example, a series of seemingly random events leads the exiled narrator of *Reivindicación del Conde don Julián* to invade Spain; the language of the story itself becomes increasingly obtuse, turning finally into Arabic. In the *New York Times Book Review* Carlos Fuentes called this novel an "adventure of language, a critical battle against the language appropriated by power in Spain. It is also a search for a new/old language that would offer an alternative for the future."

Among the alternatives Goytisolo sought to explore with this trilogy and its new language were "deviant" modes of existence, including freedom of sexual choice. *Juan sin Tierra* most forcefully assimilates language and life choice. Here the narrator's resistance to conventional storytelling devices—linear plot sequence, lack of punctuation, stream-of-consciousness, and future tense narration—is formally linked to the narrator-as-character's sexual and national "deviancy." Juan floats from one country to another and one body to another, male or female. Juan's sexual and national liminality resists the heterosexual-based nationalism lurking on every street corner. The narrator uses the second person to write of Juan: "exile has turned you into a completely different being, who has nothing to do with the one your fellow countrymen once knew: their law Juan is no longer your law: their justice is no longer your justice." From his marginal position, Juan becomes spokesperson for all "deviants," those who participate in "unproductive love": "the most luminous adjectives of your native tongue flock to your pen in a tumultuous throng and will convert you into a new, noble bard of patrimaternity!" Language functions to liberate Juan from oppressive ideologies that mark him a "renegade," "turncoat," and "sodomite." Juan will rid himself "of the oppressive space-time binomial abandon your ridiculous role of a crusader aspiring to colonize the future in order to share the common lot of those who live as best they can in the precarious and uncertain present."

The heterosexual "Reproductive Couple" are Juan's textual antagonists: "All nations, whatever their ideologies or credos, nourish and foster myth: church and governments, without exception, extol it, the various communications media exploit it to serve promotional and propagandistic ends." Not enjoying Juan's unbounded freedom—he leaps from city to city and bed to bed, language to language—the Reproductive Couple "proceed in the melancholy conditional tenses and slowly and pathetically slip into the imperfect subjunctive...the passive voice and the compound tenses have no place in the nuptial paradigm." Juan finds solace not only in a language that exists outside of heterosexual ideology but also in the tortuous labyrinths of disease-infested cities. Here Juan can "embrace the most vile and ominous attributes of the illegal brotherhood of the body: old age, filth, misery, wretchedness," which "suck [him] up in a violent whirlwind, with the irresistible force of an attack of vertigo: urine, grime, wounds, pus will be the daily nourishment that [he] will consume in lonely pride." Identity exists not just in terms of the mind, but also in terms of the body. Identification in terms of his body becomes especially important for Juan, who is exiled because of his sexuality and his mixed parentage. Although Goytisolo received less favorable reviews for *Juan sin Tierra* because of his obsession with "perverse" sex and scatological imagery, it is precisely Juan's embracing of his body in its entirety that most forcefully resists the Reproductive Couple's denial of the body, which is the basis, for Goytisolo, of Western civilizations' dysfunctionality.

Even after the Franco regime dissipated in the seventies, Goytisolo continued to write novels concerned with sexually "deviant" characters at odds with society. In his plotless novel *Makabara* (1980), Goytisolo's mixture of language, sexuality, and ideology becomes even more bold. The same-sex lovemaking defies any heterosexual romantic illusions:

> I want to ride it like a saddle, pump with my knees and elbows...never mind that they're staring at us, they're jealous of us, they're bored with the pap they get served at home, they'll never know how sweet this molasses is...it's as though you'd deflowered me."

Goytisolo fled Spain for France where he discovered his writerly voice, his identity, outside the suffocating mandates ascribed to by the "Reproductive Couple." Gay Spanish poet Federico Garcia Lorca wasn't so fortunate. For Goytisolo, language and sexuality will continue to strike fear into national ideologues who forcefully deny the presence of their own shadows.

—Frederick Luis Aldama

GREENBERG, David F.

Nationality: American professor of sociology. **Born:** Evanston, Illinois, 6 May 1942. **Education:** University of Chicago, B.A. in Physics 1962; University of Chicago, M.S. in Physics 1963; NATO summer school in Theoretical Physics, Varenna, Italy, 1964; University of Chicago, Ph.D. in Physics, 1969. **Career:** Has held a variety of jobs in academia, including Research Physicist, Physics Department, Carnegie-Mellon University, 1968-70; instructor, Department of Social Sciences, Columbia College, Chicago, 1970-71; senior fellow, Committee for the Study of Incarceration, Washington, D.C., 1971-73; assistant professor, associate professor, later professor, Sociology Department, New York University, New York City, from 1973; academic visitor, London School of Economics, 1986-87; affiliated faculty, New York University Institute for Law and Society, from 1995. Advisory board member, National Development and Research, Inc; editorial board member for academic journals, including *La Questione Criminale: Rivista di Ricerca e Dibattito su Devianza e Controllo Sociale, Social Justice, Journal of Quantitative Criminology, Journal of Homosexuality, Sexuality and Culture: An Interdisciplinary Journal*; advising editor, *Crime, Law and Deviance* book series, Rutgers University Press; former member, National Science Foundation Advisory Panel on Law and the Social/Behavioral Sciences; consultant, for organizations including the Cornell University Center for the Study of Race, Crime, and Social Policy, Hispanic Research Center (Fordham University), New York City Arson Strike Force, KOBA Associates, Inc., and Brooklyn Museum, 1992; contributor of scholarly articles and reviews to periodicals, including *American Journal of Physics, American Sociological Review, Contemporary*

Crisis: Crime, Law and Social Policy, Crime and Delinquency, Journal of Criminal Law and Criminology, Journal of Quantitative Criminology, Journal of Research in Crime and Delinquency, Lettere al Nuovo Cimento, Physical Review, Nuclear Physics, and *Social Forces.* **Awards:** National Science Foundation Fellowship, 1964; Outstanding Scholarship Award, Criminology Section of the American Sociological Association, 1983; fellow, American Society of Criminology, 1994. **Address:** Sociology Department, New York University, 269 Mercer St., Room 402, New York, New York 10003, U.S.A.

WRITINGS

Nonfiction

With Jeremiah A. Cronin and Valentine Telegdi, *University of Chicago Graduate Problems in Physics, with Solutions.* New York, Addison-Wesley, 1967; reprinted, Chicago, University of Chicago Press, 1979.
Struggle for Justice: A Report on Crime and Punishment in America. New York, Hill and Wang, 1971.
Mathematical Criminology. New Brunswick, New Jersey, Rutgers University Press, 1979.
With Ronald C. Kessler, *Linear Panel Analysis: Models of Quantitative Change.* New York, Academic Press, 1981.
"Capitalism, Bureaucracy and Male Homosexuality," in *Contemporary Crises: Crime, Law and Social Policy,* Vol. 8, 1984.
"Why Was the Berdache Ridiculed?" in *Journal of Homosexuality,* Vol. 11, 1985; reprinted in *Anthropology and Homosexual Behavior,* edited by Evelyn Blackwood, New York, Haworth Press, 1986.
The Construction of Homosexuality. Chicago, University of Chicago Press, 1988.
"The Socio-Sexual Milieu of the Love-Letters," in *Journal of Homosexuality,* Vol. 19, 1990.
"The Pleasures of Homosexuality," in *Sexual Nature/Sexual Culture,* edited by Paul R. Abramson and S. D. Pinkerton. Chicago, University of Chicago Press, 1995.
"Transformations of Homosexually-Based Identities," in *The Gender/Sexuality Reader: Culture, History, Political Economy,* edited by Roger N. Lancaster and Nancy Scheper-Hughes. New York, Routledge, 1997.

Editor

And author of introduction, *Corrections and Punishment.* Beverly Hills, California, Sage Publications, 1977.
And author of introduction, *Crime and Capitalism: Essays in Marxist Criminology.* Palo Alto, California, Mayfield, 1981; revised as *Crime and Capitalism: Readings in Marxist Criminology,* 2d edition, Philadelphia, Temple University Press, 1993.
And author of introduction, *Criminal Careers,* 2 Vols. Aldershot, England, Dartmouth Publishing Company, 1996.

Other

Translator, "Gilgamesh Epic, Tablet II (Old Babylonian Version)," in *Queer Spirits,* edited by Will Roscoe. Boston, Beacon, 1995.

*

Critical Sources: "The Construction of Homosexuality" by Nicholas B. Dirks, in *New York Times Book Review,* Vol. 94, 15 January 1989, 9-10; "The Construction of Homosexuality" by K. J. Wininger, in *Contemporary Crises,* Vol. 14, September 1990, 265-266; "The Construction of Homosexuality" by Gary Kinsman, in *Canadian Journal of Sociology,* Vol. 15, winter 1990, 112-15; "The Construction of Homosexuality" by Alanna Mitchell Hutchinson, in *Journal of the History of Sexuality,* Vol. 1, October 1990, 313-316; unpublished interview with David F. Greenberg by contributor David J. Peterson, November 1996.

*   *   *

"There is a bit of a story to my career transition," stated David F. Greenberg when asked by *GLL* contributor David J. Peterson how his career moved from a doctorate in particle physics to research and teaching in the fields of sociology and criminology to work increasingly focused on gay and lesbian studies. "It was a necessity," he explained, one intimately connected with the Civil Rights Movement that began in the late 1950s as well the anti-war protest movement of the 1960s. Greenberg was active in both. In the fall of 1959, during his first term at the University of Chicago, Greenberg joined the campus chapter of the NAACP (National Association for the Advancement of Colored People) and then CORE (Congress of Racial Equality). By 1962, Greenberg, who was then completing his B.S. in physics with a minor in mathematics, had become active in the Council for Abolishing War. Four years later Greenberg worked with the Southern Christian Leadership Conference (a civil rights organization based in Atlanta, Georgia, and led by Martin Luther King, Jr.) and an umbrella organization of civil rights groups to "campaign on behalf of open housing in Chicago, seeking to end widespread practices of racial discrimination in the rental and sale of housing, through a city ordinance barring such discrimination." He also worked in a voter registration campaign in black communities of rural South Carolina.

As the U.S. war-effort in Vietnam escalated in the late 1960s, Greenberg joined a University of Chicago group called "We Won't Go," having signed a pledge to refuse induction into the armed forces as required by the national Selective Service laws. While also attending meetings of the Student Mobilization Committee to End the War, he became one of the founding members of the Chicago Area Draft Resisters (CADRE). He continued his anti-war activities while completing his dissertation on theoretical high-energy physics, and during a two year post-doctorate fellowship at Carnegie-Mellon University in Pittsburgh, Pennsylvania, worked with the Pittsburgh Resistance, another anti-draft organization. In 1970, facing the shrinking job market in physics, as well as the hostile reactions from potential employers for his political activities, Greenberg decided to shift his career path to economics, a decision based in part on having team-taught a course on "Radical Social, Political and Economic Theory" while at Carnegie-Mellon. He was admitted into the graduate economics program at Carnegie-Mellon, with the understanding that he need only take his comprehensive examinations and write a dissertation. But he soon found that, "on orders of the Mellon family," the University had withdrawn his acceptance. However, "without ever having taken a course in sociology," as he told Peterson, he was able to begin teaching in the Social Sciences Department of Chicago's Columbia College.

Greenberg's work in the draft resistance movement stimulated an interest in prison conditions, and thus in criminology. While at Carnegie-Mellon, he had become involved with The American Friends Service Committee, and while at Columbia College founded a prisoner support group call Chicago CONnections. Having lost his position at Columbia College—again for political reasons: he had circulated a petition protesting the firing of a feminist colleague—he became, because of his experience, a senior fellow with the Committee for the Study of Incarceration and moved to Washington, D.C. Finally, in 1973, he took a job as an assistant professor in the Department of Sociology at New York University in New York City, where he eventually became a full professor.

Greenberg's work in gay and lesbian studies sprang from larger developments in sociology. In the 1960s and 1970s the focus of sociological theorizing about deviance shifted from the explanation of deviant behavior to the processes by which some behaviors came to be regarded as deviant. Greenberg took up this question in relation to homosexuality through a comparative and historical investigation that also examined the creation and transformation of the categories used in different societies to classify sexual acts and actors. The result of Greenberg's research in this area is *The Construction of Homosexuality.* Published by the University of Chicago Press in 1988, *The Construction of Homosexuality* provides an important survey of cultural constructions of same-sex desire throughout recorded human history, and does so in language that is accessible to most general readers. Greenberg's study begins with a chapter that focuses on "Homosexual Relations in Kinship-Structured Societies," which argues that "in the study of sexual practices and ideology" within kinship-based societies and their attitudes toward homosexuality, "it is the centrality of kinship to social life that is most relevant." For Greenberg, this translates into a focus on "the relative social statuses of the participants" in same-sex relationships. Greenberg posits four general categories of same-sex relationships: "*transgenerational* (in which the partners are of disparate ages), *transgenderal* (the partners are of different genders), ...*egalitarian* (the partners are socially similar)" and, as he discusses in the book's third chapter, those relationships "in which partners belong to different social classes."

Kinship-structured societies exist, Greenberg argues, in a primarily "stateless" form, and "as such, they lack specialized political bodies with jurisdiction over an extended territory and population." Given Greenberg's Marxist critical stance, it is logical for his focus to turn more toward those societies in which political, religious, and economic power plays a greater role in the construction of homosexuality. Thus, throughout the rest of the book, Greenberg focuses on the construction of homosexuality in such early civilizations as Egypt, Greece, China, the Aztec, the Maya, and so forth, and then to the flowering of Roman culture as well as Christianity. Over half the book is dedicated to tracing the changing cultural perceptions of homosexuality from feudalism down to the late twentieth-century. The significance of such a sweeping survey of societal constructions of homosexuality is that it provides a broader viewpoint from which to understand both homosexuality in cultures radically different from our own as well as those cultures from the past. What his work shows, in essence, is that instead of speaking of homosexuality, we should perhaps best speak of homosexualities; for in each instance of cultural and societal difference, we observe a difference in individual homosexual identity. Such an understanding is vital to any attempt to liberate modern homosexuality from the categories of criminality, deviance, and pathology. While there is, then, a continuity of same-sex desire, Greenberg helps us to understand that such continuity does not extend to a continuity of homosexual identity. Identity categories based on sex and gender are thus seen to be contingent on a society's history, traditions, and values, rather than based on "nature" alone.

—David J. Peterson

GRIMSLEY, Jim

Nationality: American playwright and novelist. **Born:** Rocky Mount, North Carolina in 1955. **Education:** University of North Carolina at Chapel Hill (Honors in Writing, James M. Johnston Scholar), B.A. 1978. **Career:** Founding member, ACME Theatre Company, 1983-87; playwright-in-residence, 7Stages Theater, Atlanta, Georgia, from 1986. Board of directors member, 1988-94, and president, from 1989-94, Celeste Miller & Company; member, and later chairman, Alternate ROOTS Executive Committee, 1986-92; judge, PEN/Hemingway Foundation Award committee, 1997. **Awards:** Rockefeller/NEA Interdisciplinary Program Award, 1988; George Oppenheimer/Newsday Playwriting Award, 1988; Georgia Council for the Arts Grant, 1990; Bryan Prize for Drama, 1993; Prix Charles Brisset, French Academy of Physicians, 1995; Sue Kaufman Prize for First Fiction, 1995; Lambda Award nomination, 1995; American Library Association GLBTF Book Award, for fiction, 1996. **Agent:** Peter Hagen, The Gersh Agency New York, Inc., 130 West 42nd Street, Suite 2400, New York, New York 10036, U.S.A.

WRITINGS

Stage Plays

The Existentialists (produced ACME Theatre, Atlanta, 1983).
The Earthlings (produced 7Stages, Atlanta, 1992).
The Receptionist in Hell (produced Nexus Theatre, Atlanta, 1985).
Estelle & Otto (produced ACME/Nexus Theatre, Atlanta, 1985).
Dead of Winter (produced Dancer's Collective Theatre/ACME, Atlanta, 1986).
On the Appearance of Fire in the West (produced Nexus Theatre, Atlanta, 1987).
Mr. Universe (produced 7Stages, Atlanta, 1987; Off Broadway, 1988).
Math and Aftermath (produced 7Stages, Atlanta, 1988).
Man with a Gun (produced Atlanta Nexus Theatre/SAME, 1989).
White People (produced 7Stages, Atlanta, 1989).
The Lizard of Tarsus (produced 7Stages, Atlanta, 1990).
The Fall of the House of Usher (adaptation of short story by Edgar Allen Poe; produced Theatrical Outlet, Atlanta, 1991).
Bell Ives (produced 7Stages, Atlanta, 1991).
Aurora Be Mine (produced 7Stages, Atlanta, 1992).
The Borderland (produced Currican Theatre, New York, 1994).
The Decline and Fall of the Rest (produced 7Stages, Atlanta, 1996).
A Bird of Prey (produced American Conservatory Theatre, San Francisco, 1996).
The Non (produced 7Stages, Atlanta, 1996).

Novels

Comfort and Joy. Berlin, Germany, Edition Zebra/Dia Books, 1993.

Wintervogel. Berlin, Germany, Edition Zebra/Dia Books, 1993; as *Winter Birds,* Chapel Hill, North Carolina, Algonquin Books, 1994.
Dream Boy. Chapel Hill, North Carolina, Algonquin Books, 1995.
My Drowning. Chapel Hill, North Carolina, Algonquin Books, 1997.

Short Fiction

"City and Park," in *Carolina Quarterly,* fall 1980.
"Silver Bullet," in *Carolina Quarterly,* summer 1981.
"Blood House," in *Carolina Quarterly,* spring 1982.
"We Move in a Rigorous Line," in *Carolina Quarterly,* spring 1983.
"Comfort and Joy," in *Men on Men 6,* edited by David Bergman. New York, Plume/Penguin, 1996.
"New Jerusalem," in *New Virginia Review,* March 1997.
"The Masturbator," in *Flesh and the Word 4.* New York, Penguin/Plume, 1997.
"Free in Asveroth," in *Bending Landscapes.* White Wolf Press/Borealis, 1997.
"Walk Through Birdland," in *The Store of Joys: Writing Celebrate the North Carolina Museum of Art's Fiftieth Anniversary.* John F. Blair Publishing, 1997.

Other

"The Masturbator," "Walk Through Birdland," and "Memo to the Assassin" (performance texts, performed by the author and/or Celeste Miller in *Tales from the Heartland,* 7Stages Theater, Atlanta, 6-8 November 1992).

*

Adaptations: "Beam Angel" (radio play; adaptation of *Dead of Winter* by Berl Boykin), National Public Radio, 1993.

Interviews: "Southern Writer Grimsley Walks Among Old Ghosts" by Kelly McQuain, in *Philadelphia Gay News,* 1 December 1995.

Critical Sources: "Flying South" by Patrick Merla, in *Out,* September 1994; review of *Winter Birds* by Craig Seligman, in *New Yorker,* 24 October 1994; "Breaking The Rules" by John L. Meyers, Lambda Book Report, 1995; review of *Dream Boy,* in *Publisher's Weekly,* 10 July 1995; "Cold Comfort" by Andrew Santella, in *New City's Literary Supplement,* 17 August 1995; "Grimsley's Fairy Tale" by Richard Morrison, in *Independent Reader,* 30 August 1995; "Chances for Survival" by Fred Chappell, in *Raleigh News & Observer,* 3 September 1995; review of *Gay Chicago Magazine,* 3 September 1995; "'Dream Boy' Exceptional" by Ed Madden, in *State* (Columbia, South Carolina), 17 September 1995; by Geoff Manson, in *San Francisco Review of Books,* September/October 1995; review of *Dream Boy* by Tom Beer, in *Out,* October 1995; "He's Leaving Home," in *Detour,* October 1995; "Grim, Graceful 'Dream Boy'" by Renee Graham, in *Boston Globe,* 2 October 1995; "The Awful Beauty, in Grimsley's Fiction" by Michael Skube, in *Atlanta Journal-Constitution,* 29 October 1995; "Reclining against His Savior's Chest" by Robert Reynolds, in *Boston Book Review,* November 1995; "Jim Grimsley" by Kelly McQuain, in *Philadelphia City Paper,* 12 October 1996; "A Hell of a Ride" by Lisa Howorth, in *Reckon Maga-*

zine, winter 1996; "Jim Grimsley's Blood Ties" by Kelly McQuain, in *Art & Understanding,* February 1997.

Jim Grimsley comments:

 I have been writing so long that making any kind of statement about it almost seems superfluous. But it is very important to me to be able to do this work, to talk about all the parts of living that I want to talk about, including gay themes, certainly, but including many other neglected themes as well, including what I know about poverty, racism, gender stuff, and especially the excess of human suffering that I see in the world. For me, the important part of writing is the communication of a story to the reader, and I try to accomplish that in the most compelling terms. As a craftsman, I try to use my craft in a different way each time I sit down to write. As a person, I try to choose stories that will be important to other people.

* * *

With the publication of three critically-acclaimed novels in the mid 1990s, Jim Grimsley has secured a reputation not only as a prodigious playwright, but as one of the finest Southern fiction writers to emerge during the late 20th century.

Grimsley traces his desire to become a writer to his childhood in rural Jones County, North Carolina. Hemophilia, a disease characterized by the inability to stop bleeding, caused him to have to spend weeks at a time in bed. Growing up poor, the cost of Grimsley's treatments often presented a financial hardship for his family, which was not a happy one. When Grimsley was bedridden, a rich imagination was often his only companion. "[W]hen you stay still that long, you develop something inside your head that allows you to imagine some other kind of life for yourself, to daydream or to read books intensely and experience things that way. The stillness of that disease I think helped me a lot as a writer," Grimsley told Kelly McQuain in *Art and Understanding.*

Grimsley's health was further complicated by contaminated blood products that led him to be diagnosed HIV-positive in the mid 1980s. At the time, he notes, "reading about this strange disease that targeted gay men and hemophiliacs [was like] watching a gun being pointed right at me," he told McQuain. As both a gay man and a hemophiliac, he developed a sharp sensitivity to the disparate ways the media viewed these two affected groups. While hemophiliacs where perceived as worthy of public empathy, gays typically were not, a dualism that struck Grimsley as "particularly stupid and inconsistent." It's no wonder then that a sharp sense of irony and a keen sensitivity to troubled outcasts characterize so much of his writing.

Grimsley's award-winning debut novel, *Winter Birds,* provides a gripping account of Danny Crell, an eight year-old hemophiliac trying to survive inside the domestic hurricane of his low-class, rural family—a book so beautifully written that fellow Southerner Dorothy Allison wrote in a letter to Algonquin books that "I wanted to steal it and pretend it was mine."

The novel takes place almost entirely on the Crell family's domestic stage. Their household is ruled over by a tyrannical patriarch, Bobjay, who, like Grimsley's own father, loses an arm in a farm accident. Embittered, unable to provide for his wife and five children, Bobjay Crell violently acts out his frustrations on both his wife and his children. In interviews, Grimsley admits that his first novel, a work 20 years in the making, was inspired by his own upbringing. "Virtually all of the circumstances of my life match

those that I laid out in *Winter Birds,*" he told McQuain. "I am a child of that part of the country, I am a hemophiliac, I am gay—and that's true of Danny, even though he's too young to express it all."

Although well-received by critics, *Winter Birds*' path to publication was not easy; for years its brutally honest subject matter kept it from finding its way into print in the States. Then in 1992, a Berlin publisher impressed by the strength of Grimsley's plays brought the work out in translation. A French version soon followed, winning the prestigious Prix Charles Brisset from the French Academy of Physicians, and making Grimsley the first writer from outside France to carry this distinction. Finally an American edition appeared in 1994 and the acclaim that had so far eluded Grimsley at home was attained at long last when the novel won the Sue Kaufman Prize for First Fiction.

Grimsley's second novel, *Dream Boy,* serves up another chilling dose of domestic dysfunction. Equal parts romance and horror, the story is set against a backdrop of religious fervor, sexual abuse, and the ghosts of the antebellum South. It grew out of a fragment the author eliminated from *Winter Birds.* "I couldn't get it out of my mind," Grimsley confessed to McQuain in an interview, "so I finally took it and made another book out of it."

Told in haunting, pared-down prose, Grimsley brings to life the budding love affair between Nathan, the new boy at school, and Roy, an older, neighboring farm hand. Roy, with his callused hands and slightly large nose, is well-cast as an imperfectly charming object of desire, and when he meets Nathan, it's love at first blush.

As in *Winter Birds, Dream Boy* also depicts a brutalized son; the narrative walks a razor line between romance and terror as Nathan seeks to avoid sexual molestation at the hands of his whiskey-swilling, holy roller father. Nathan's sexual abuse is balanced by his intimacy with Roy, which forces Nathan to acknowledge "the irony that what pleases him with Roy terrifies him with his father"—a remarkable insight for a character who typically avoids self-reflection.

A strategic use of present-tense narration propels the story forward with grim urgency as Nathan seeks to escape adult terrors and find solace in first love. Grimsley's genius for illuminating moments of vulnerability builds to a screaming pitch one dark night as Nathan, Roy, and two other teenagers stumble upon a dilapidated mansion deep in the Carolinian woods. Instead of catching a glimpse of the ghost rumored to haunt the place, Nathan and Roy are visited by their own murderous destiny, a turn of events sparked by betrayal. Whether their love will be enough to overcome such obstacles is the heartfelt crux of the book.

The novel throws into sharp relief themes that have abounded in gay literature for years—ambivalence about "daddy" fantasies, sex with a best friend—achieving, if not verisimilitude, then a work of art that reads like a dream itself, life distilled into poetry. Nathan and Roy's relationship is as much about the redemptive power of love as it is about the rise of dormant passion.

Dream Boy is a worthwhile read for anyone who has ever mourned lost innocence. As critic Geoff Manson notes, "the last 40 pages are some of the best prose one could hope to read." *My Drowning* returns to the milieu of *Winter Birds,* but this time the story centers around Danny's aging mother, Ellen Tote, and concerns, as the author related to McQuain, "the tension between memory and the present." As the days behind Ellen outnumber the days ahead, she sifts through her oldest memories in an effort to understand the course of her life. A death-bed confession by her brother Otis provides the impetus for this self-exploration when he reveals their mother's vain attempt to drown Ellen as an infant. Otis's tale unlocks "something akin to a memory" in his sister, a recurrent dream in which she stands on a riverbank alongside her siblings as their unhappy mother, dressed in nothing but a pale slip, surrenders herself to a dark, winter-swollen river. A mystery emerges. Is this image a fragment of Ellen's memory? Is it mere coincidence that Otis's revelation bears similarity to the dream that has haunted her since childhood? Or is his story a final, wicked barb driven beneath her skin by the last of a family that so often hurt her as a child?

As her past increasingly impinges upon her present, Ellen confronts a torrent of memory. Thus, her drowning becomes something more than the real or imagined attempt toward malice on her mother's part; it symbolizes her own struggle against a deluge of often painful recollections.

The injustices that Ellen endures as a child include the humiliation of having but one dress to wear to school, the ache and shame of hunger, beatings at the hands of her parents, and the lecherous stares of her crippled Uncle Cope. Yet Ellen is a natural survivor, possessing a resilience beyond her years, and a capability to find refuge in joys made all the sweeter by their scarcity: singing hymns in church, finding wonder in the superstitions and folklore of the countryside, communing secretly with the imagined ghost of her sister, and sharing sandwiches offered by a relatively well-off classmate.

Though a hungry, abused child is always an easy mark for reader sympathy, Grimsley avoids sentimentalism by providing Ellen with a simple but poetic voice capable of describing in matter-of-fact terms the hardships of her emotionally and materially impoverished childhood. Like a rush of river water, Ellen's narrative flows into, around, and eventually over the obstacles of her past. Each sentence bristles with equal parts rage and grace.

Although all three of these novels address the theme of children at risk, the ways they do so are significantly different, proving that when it comes to fiction author Grimsley takes risks in form as well as content. For instance, *Winter Birds* is driven by a present-tense, second-person narrative that few writers have mastered so effectively in prose. However, as Grimsley noted in a personal interview, "The second-person is a common point-of-view in poetry, and when I read poetry and saw how it worked there, it seemed to me a very good way to solve some problems in *Winter Birds....* It allowed me to be poetic without seeming to force it."

In *Dream Boy,* a character supersedes his own death by using force of will to rewrite the outcome of the book's plot. Here, present tense is used not only to show the characters' general lack of self-reflection, but to emphasize their power as agents capable of making such bold moves. In *My Drowning,* a confluence of symbolic imagery and formal structure work to show how reminiscence can at once be vivid but imprecise, an arrangement that emphasizes memory's organic structure. While many chapters in the book are nearly as self-contained as short stories, flowing one into the next, they also spiral back on each other as recurrent strands feed into the larger narrative time and again.

Common elements in Grimsley's fiction include child protagonists who often possess what the author has called "an air of fragility." In Danny's case, it comes from his hemophilia and the fact that he has to be physically careful. In Nathan's case, it comes from him being abused by his father. Likewise, the supernatural often figures into the author's work, as evidenced by the appearance of ghosts in both *Dream Boy* and *My Drowning.* Finally, the

'abusive father' is clearly an archetype in Grimsley's fiction, inspired by the violence of his own childhood and often coupled with the author's ambivalent take on the lower-class, conservative Christian environment he so often uses as a backdrop.

In his stage work, Grimsley often addresses themes of religious tension and homosexuality as explicitly as in his fiction, but stresses that his own life does not directly infuse his plays. "My plays don't come out of any kind of autobiographical impulse at all," he told McQuain. "I've got ten full length plays, and they're all over the map." His most notable work to date is *Mr. Universe,* a bloody parable about lust and self-image that centers around two New Orleans drag queens—one a drug dealer, the other a mother hen. Teaming up with a woman friend, they take in a bloodied mute bodybuilder they find on the street one night. This newfound Adonis becomes the catalyst for the main characters acting out struggles that dramatize each one's fractured self-esteem. As the muscle man continually strips down to his posing shorts, author Grimsley simultaneously peels off the sport of body-building's thinly sublimated eroticism. Tension escalates into violence as each character bullies the others, posing the question "Just who is muscling whom?" First performed in 1988 at Atlanta's 7Stages Theatre, where Grimsley has served as playwright-in-residence since 1986, *Mr. Universe* went on to be staged in New Orleans, Los Angeles, New York, and Seattle. A panel of judges that included playwright Edward Albee selected this work as the 1988 winner of the George Oppenheimer/Newsday Playwriting Award for best American play produced in New York.

Other notable plays include *The Lizard of Tarsus* (1990), in which the Messiah is taken political prisoner upon His Second Coming. The play blends science-fiction and dogma as the savior rewrites biblical history to substitute a lower life form in his place on the cross, thereby escaping crucifixion a second time. Another work, *Math and Aftermath* (1988), is an ironic morality play involving porn actors on a desert island film shoot, and is characterized by its self-conscious use of postmodern dramatic techniques to campy effect.

A long-term survivor of HIV, Grimsley carries on his personal fight against AIDS by taking advantage of recent medical advances, and continues to be a productive novelist and playwright.

—Kelly McQuain

GUIBERT, Hervé

Nationality: French novelist, photographer, and filmmaker. **Born:** Paris, 14 December 1955. **Career:** Journalist, *Le Monde,* Paris, 1973-82; writer and photographer, from late 1970 to early 1990s; independent filmmaker. **Died:** Clamart, France, of an overdose of digitalin, 27 December 1991.

WRITINGS

Novels

La Mort Propagande. Paris, France, Deforges, 1977.
Voyage Avec Deux Enfants. Paris, France, Editions de Minuit, 1982.

Des Aveugles. Paris, France, Gallimard, 1985; translated by James Kirkup as *Blindsight,* London, Quartet Books, 1995, New York, G. Braziller, 1996.

Mes Parents. Paris, France, Gallimard, 1986; translated by Liz Heron as *My Parents,* London and New York, Serpent's Tail, 1993.

Les Gangsters. Paris, France, Editions de Minuit, 1988; translated by Iain White as *The Gangsters,* London and New York, Serpent's Tail, 1991.

Fou de Vincent. Paris, France, Editions de Minuit, 1989.

A L'Ami Qui Ne M'a Sauvé la Vie. Paris, France, Gallimard, 1990; translated by Linda Coverdale as *To the Friend Who Did Not Save My Life,* London, Quartet Books, New York, Atheneum, 1991.

Mon Valet et Moi. Paris, France, Editions du Seuil, 1991.

Le Protocole Compassionel. Paris, France, Gallimard, 1991; translated by James Kirkup as *The Compassion Protocol,* London, Quartet Books, 1993, New York, G. Braziller, 1994.

Cytomegalovirus: Journal D'Hospitalisation. Paris, France, Editions du Seuil, 1992; translated by Clara Orban as *Cytomegalovirus,* Lanham, Maryland, University Press of America, 1996.

L'Homme au Chapeau Rouge. Paris, France, Gallimard, 1992; translated by James Kirkup as *The Man in the Red Hat,* London, Quartet Books, 1993.

Le Paradis. Paris, France, Gallimard, 1992; translated by James Kirkup as *Paradise,* London, Quartet Books, 1996.

La Piqure D'Amour et Autres Textes, Suivi de la Chair Fraiche. Paris, France, Gallimard, 1994.

Other

"L'autre journal d'Hervé Guibert," in *L'Autre Journal,* December 1985.

"Les secrets d'un homme," in *Mauve le Vierge.* Paris, 1988.

L'Image Fantome (photography). Paris, France, Editions de Minuit, 1981; translated by Robert Bononno as *Ghost Image,* Los Angeles, Sun & Moon Press, 1996.

Le Seul Visage (photography). Paris, France, Editions de Minuit, 1984.

Vice (photography). Paris, France, J. Bertoin, 1991.

Photographies (photography). Paris, France, Gallimard, 1993.

*

Critical Sources: "Trompe-la-mort" by Raymond Bellour, in *Magazine litteraire,* April 1990, 54-56; "Foucault: The Secrets of a Man" by James Miller, in *Salmagundi,* No. 88/89, fall 1990/ winter 1991; "Hervé Guibert" by Christian Caujolle, in *American Photo* (New York), Vol. 4, No. 2, March-April 1993, 80; "Hervé Guibert" by Juan Vincente Aliaga, in *Artforum* (New York), Vol. 32, No. 7, March 1994, 95; "Flesh Memory/Skin Practice" by Kate Mehuron, in *Research in Phenomenology* (Pittsburgh), Vol. 23, No. 1993, fall 1994, 73; "Hervé Guibert: Writing the Spectral Image" by Donna Wilkerson, in *STCL* (Manhattan, Kansas), Vol. 19, No. 2, summer 1995, 269-88.

*   *   *

Hervé Guibert was born in Paris in 1955, and at age 18 began a journalistic career at *Le Monde* newspaper. During his nine year tenure at *Le Monde,* he not only covered news stories but also served on the photo desk. His scandalous stories were written with remarkable accuracy and together with photographs which depicted the darker side of sadomasochism, they often shocked the paper's readers. In 1977 Guibert published his first book, *Le Mort Propagande.* From the beginning of his writing career Guibert recognized how to utilize words to engage readers in thinking.

Guibert did not hide his sexuality in his work and life. He reviled all forms of hypocrisy and censorship, and laid himself open to attack from self-righteous critics who accused him of paedophilia, perversion, and insanity. His prose took a unique position in contemporary literature, belying a tone of contemptuousness for popular opinion and mediocrity in society. His style, while classical in nature, contained a sharp edge of acidity, outspokenness, and exasperation. Like many of Mapplethorpe's photos, the stories he crafted contained a haunting air about them. French critics saw Guibert as an heir apparent of Jean Genet's literary tradition. At the same time Guibert considered himself the modern protege of Rimbaud, de Sade, Nietzsche, and Thomas Bernhard.

His early works garnered attention due to content rather than literary style. His book *L'Image Fantome* remains one of the best French monographs covering the relationship of person to photography and its negative influences. The book also revealed the relationship between imagery and the homoerotic body. Guibert's first novel *Voyage Avec Deux Enfants* (1982), about two gay sadists who travel and terrorize the world, was followed by *Les Lubies d'Arthur* (1983). His third, *Des Aveugles,* was published in 1985 and later became a play. A year later *Mes Parents* was published, which revealed the darker side of Guibert's life and how his mother attempted to abort him, and screamed during childbirth "let's hope he's born dead." On a personal note, in *Les Chiens* (1982) he described in startling detail his sadomasochist experiences and in *Fou de Vincent* (1989) his love for a boy who parachuted out of a third story window in a dressing gown. Guibert relished shocking mainstream society with his tales of torturing teenage boys, sadomasochism, and with unrepentant sexuality.

In 1988 Guibert was diagnosed as HIV positive and began to describe the ravages of the disease on his body and life in works of auto-fictional biographies. He saw the disease as a modern contrivance which allowed the corpse time to live. Guibert proclaimed he would turn himself into a human fountain pen following the diagnosis, and often wrote while severely debilitated by amnesia. It was the struggle with AIDS which would elevate the prominence of Hervé Guibert to one of the greatest contemporary French authors. AIDS was exposed in its many facets in the last works of Guibert, eloquently detailed in the trilogy *To the Friend Who Did Not Save My Life* (1990), *Compassion Protocol* (1991), and *Man in the Red Hat.* His talent as writer turned AIDS from a source of destruction to one of creativity. Guibert's work was infected by the reality of AIDS, while its imagery connected the real world to fiction. His writing worked like a camera suspending time, immobilizing it, and tempering it to control the fear of death, but the apparition of death was omnipresent in his writings. While Guibert's later books may seem autobiographical in nature, describing his affliction with AIDS and death, the description of his body and objects are always placed outside the realm of reality.

During Guibert's sickness he videotaped countless hours of the everyday and extraordinary in his life. He filmed a rehearsal of his suicide which he detailed in an earlier book. On the eve of his 36th birthday, Guibert took an overdose of digitalin as a self-described radical antidote to the AIDS virus. He succumbed to the overdose, and AIDS, on 27 December 1991 at Antoine-Belere hospital, Clamart, France.

By shedding light on HIV and AIDS Guibert turned the literary world upside down. In his last books he informed readers about his illness in a manner which has never been done before. With humor and candor tinged with sarcasm he wrote about the disease in a clear, unmuted voice that forced many to admire him.

—Michael A. Lutes

H

HACKER, Marilyn

Nationality: American poet and editor. **Born:** The Bronx, New York City, 27 November 1942. **Education:** Bronx High School of Science, Washington Square College of New York University, and Art Students League. **Family:** Married Samuel Delany, 1961 (divorced 1974); one daughter; life partner of Karyn J. London, from 1986. **Career:** Editor, various literary magazines and anthologies, including *City,* 1967-70; editor, with Samuel Delany, of the science fiction series *Quark,* 1970-71; part of editorial collective, *Little Magazine,* 1977-82; editor, *13th Moon,* 1982-86, *Ploughshares,* winter 1989, and *Kenyon Review,* 1990-94; professor of English, Hofstra University, spring 1996; workshop instructor, the Writers Community of the Writers Voice and the Poetry Society of America. **Awards:** Discovery Award, New York 92nd Street YM/YWHA Poetry Center, 1973; Lamont Poetry Selection award, 1973; National Endowment for the Arts grant, 1973, 1984; National Book award, 1975; Guggenheim Fellowship, 1979-81; Creative Artists Public Service Grant, 1980; Ingram-Merrill Foundation fellowship, 1984-85; Coordinating Council of Literary Magazines Editor's fellowship, 1984; Robert Wynner Award, Poetry Society of America, 1987, 1989; Lambda Literary Award, 1991, 1995; John Masefield Memorial Award, 1994; Lenore Marshall Poetry Prize, *Nation,* 1995; Poets' Prize, 1996. **Address:** c/o Frances Collin Literary Agency, P.O. Box 33, Wayne, Pennsylvania 19087-0033, U.S.A.

WRITINGS

Poetry

The Terrible Children. Privately printed, 1967.
With Thomas M. Disch and Charles Platt, *Highway Sandwiches.* Privately printed, 1970.
Presentation Piece. New York, Viking Press, 1974.
Separations. New York, Alfred A. Knopf, 1976.
Taking Notice. New York, Alfred A. Knopf, 1980.
Assumptions. New York, Alfred A. Knopf, 1985.
Love, Death, and the Changing of the Seasons. New York, Arbor House, 1986; New York, Norton, 1995.
Going Back to the River. New York, Random House, 1990.
The Hang-Glider's Daughter: Selected Poems. London, Onlywomen Press, 1990.
Selected Poems: 1965-1990. New York, Norton, 1994.
Winter Numbers. New York, Norton, 1994.

Selected Essays

"Mortal Moralities (Josephine Jacobsen)," in *Nation,* 28 November 1987.
"The Trees Win Every Time: Reading Julia Randall," in *Grand Street,* autumn 1988.
"Begin to Teach (Adrienne Rich)," in *Nation,* 23 October 1989.
"Unauthorized Voices (U.A. Fanthorpe and Elma Mitchell)," in *Grand Street,* summer 1989.

"An Invitation to My Demented Uncle," in *Ploughshares* (Boston), Winter 1989-90.
"Provoking Engagement (June Jordan)," in *Nation,* 29 January, 1990.
"No More Masks," in *Nation,* 27 December 1993.
"A Few Cranky Paragraphs on Form and Content," in *Poetry Pilot,* fall 1995.
"Tectonic Shifts (Alicia Ostriker)," in *Nation,* 5 May 1997.

Other

Translator, *Edge* by Claire Malroux, Winston-Salem, North Carolina, Wake Forest University Press, 1996.

Recordings: The Poetry and Voice of Marilyn Hacker, Caedmon, 1976.

*

Interviews: "Interview with Marilyn Hacker," in *Dispatch,* Vol. 7, No. 1, fall 1988, 16-19; "Marilyn Hacker" by John Weir, in *Advocate,* 20 September 1994; "An Interview with Marilyn Hacker" by Suzanne Gardinier, in *AWP Chronicle,* March/April 1996; "Marilyn Hacker: An Interview of Form" by Annie Finch, in *American Poetry Review,* May/June 1996.

Critical Sources: "Laura, Stella and Ray" by Marilyn French, in *Nation,* 1 November 1986; *The Motion of Light in Water: Sex and Science Fiction Writing in the East Village, 1957-1965* by Samuel R. Delany, New York, Arbor House/Morrow, 1988; "Marilyn Hacker" by Suzanne Gardinier, in *Contemporary Lesbian Writers of the United States,* edited by Sandra Pollack and Denise D. Knight, Westport, Connecticut, Greenwood Press, 258-268, 1993; "Another Jewish Lesbian in France" by Sue Russell, in *Lambda Book Report,* Vol. 4, November 1994, 27; "Chiliastic Sapphic" by Grace Schulman, in *Nation,* 7 November 1994; "Measured Feet 'in Gender-Bender Shoes': The Politics of Form in Marilyn Hacker's *Love, Death, and the Changing of the Seasons*" by Lynn Keller, in *Feminist Measures,* edited by Lynn Keller and Cristianne Miller, East Lansing, Michigan State University Press, 1994; review of *Winter Numbers* by Matthew Rothschild, in *The Progressive,* Vol. 59, January 1995, 43-44; "A Formal Life: Marilyn Hacker's Deep Structure" by Lawrence Joseph, in *Voice Literary Supplement,* February 1995, 25; "The Facts of Death" by Adrian Oktenberg, in *Women's Review of Books,* Vol. 12, No. 7, April 1995, 10-11; review of *Winter Numbers* and *Selected Poems* by George Bradley, in *Yale Review,* Vol. 83, July 1995, 170-181; "Against Elegies: Women's Breast Cancer Poems," in *Beyond Consolation: Death, Sexuality and the Changing Shapes of Elegy,* by Melissa F. Zeiger, Ithaca, New York, Cornell University Press, 1997.

Marilyn Hacker comments:

Poetry has always seemed to me, as reader and writer, to be (among other things) a colloquy extending into the future and the past, whose participants are the poet, her/his readers, and the writers of all the other texts whose musics, assumptions, traditions, are carried forward, countered, or augmented by the poem in question. (I think of "La Compiuta Donzella," writing sonnets, in the 13th century, not on unattainable love, but to protest an arranged marriage; I think of Emily Dickinson writing lyric "codas" to passages from Elizabeth Barrett Browning's verse novel, *Aurora Leigh*.) Thus, one source of my love for "forms," and for juxtapositions of elevated and quotidian language, polysyllables and slang, the Latinate, the Anglo-Saxon, and, why not, an inflection of Yiddish ... it's an acknowledgment of how much language itself, with all its history, is a collaborator in the poem.

"Lesbian writer"? Of course—but only as much as I'm an urban writer, a Jewish-American writer, a materialist-feminist, a writer born in the 1940s, and any number of other possible adjectival self-definitions. "Lesbian"—as concerns my work—is part of a description, not a definition, not a limitation either of what I consider I might one day write, or of whom I imagine my readers to be.

*   *   *

As poet, witness, prankster, storyteller, friend, lover, mother, heir to literary tradition, balladeer, lesbian, and fellow traveler, Marilyn Hacker has emerged as one of a handful of essential poets of the second half of the twentieth century. From its earliest appearance on the poetry scene, her poetry has made readers stand up and "take notice." Hacker's distinctive urban voice and formidable sense of craft, among other qualities, led to an unusual triumph when her first book, *Presentation Piece,* earned her two of the most coveted American literary prizes: the Lamont Poetry Selection for 1973 and the National Book Award for 1975. At age 31, however, Hacker was no mere *enfant terrible* of the literary world. Her flame continued to burn in the series of books that rapidly followed. Even those who might have been uncomfortable with her feminist politics or her explicit sexual content could not help but be impressed with the dazzle of her formal dexterity in the production of villanelles, sestinas, pantoums, and sonnet sequences, among other favored forms.

Hacker's life has so clearly been her art that her readers have had the privilege of observing her autobiography in process, book by book. We have been introduced to her important friends and lovers and watched her daughter, Iva Alyxander, move from babyhood to adolescence and beyond. This does not mean, however, that Hacker can be neatly filed away as a "confessional" poet, for the stories she tells through her poems are also the stories of a generation (post-World War II) and a culture, or more accurately, a meshing of cultures (lesbian—in the later books—, Jewish, American, New York, expatriate, intellectual/literary). They exist within a specific political moment and are informed by the collective history shared by poet and reader alike. Thus, in "Graffiti from the Gare-Saint Manqué," from *Assumptions,* Hacker places herself on a historical continuum as "another Jewish lesbian in France," which is the repeating line in each stanza. Similarly, in "Ballad of Ladies Lost and Found," from the same book, she follows in the footsteps of those "women who, *entre deux guerres...* came out on college-graduation trips."

Hacker was born in the Bronx, the daughter of an industrial chemist and an elementary school teacher. She grew up in a three-room apartment filled with books and attended the famous Bronx High School for Science, where she met her future husband, science fiction writer Samuel (Chip) Delany. She started college at the age of 15 as a student at the Washington Square College of

New York University and married Delany three years later. Theirs was by no means a conventional marriage, as Delany documented in his own memoir, *The Motion of Light in Water: Sex and Science Fiction Writing in the East Village, 1957-1965.* Delany was himself openly gay, and Hacker pursued other relationships as well.

Prominent among poems that establish the milieu of their life together in New York are "Nights of 1962: The River Merchant's Wife" and "Nights of 1964-1966: The Old Reliable." Hacker opens the first of these with a character not unlike herself, "Emigrée from the Bronx, a married child / hit the ghetto-turned barrio, making wild / conjectures and conjunctions, making wrong / turns on lyrics of country-and-western songs." Meanwhile, at the "Old Reliable," the habitués include "Black file clerks with theatrical ambitions" and "White decorators interested in Art" along with other icons of an age in which the music was Motown and the couples going home together were sometimes triples.

Hacker lived on her own in San Francisco from 1967 to 1970 and in London from 1971 to 1976. She served as the editor of the small magazine *City* (where Judy Grahn's "Common Woman" poems were first published) and, together with Delany, edited the science fiction series *Quark* from 1970-71. Their daughter Iva Alyxander was born in 1974, the year in which the couple finally separated. While in London, Hacker worked as an antiquarian bookseller. From there, she first visited Paris on a book-buying trip and later established that city as her second residence. Much of her work from 1980 has France as its setting and the expatriate experience as a major theme.

With the publication of her third book, *Taking Notice,* in 1980, Hacker made public her emerging lesbian identity, aligning herself with the other pre-eminent lesbian poet of her time, Adrienne Rich, with an epigraph to Rich's classic *XXI Love Poems* at the head of her own title sonnet sequence, "Taking Notice": "two women together is a work / nothing in civilization has made simple." Hacker elaborates on those very complexities in the context of her own life:

> Woman I love, as old as new to me
> as any moment of delight risked in
> my lumpy heretofore unbeautiful
> skin, if I lost myself in you I'd be
> no better lost than any other woman.

Since that time Hacker's poems have become essential texts in the growing body of lesbian and gay literature. She has appeared in every important anthology, and her influence has been deeply felt in a younger generation of poets and writers including Robyn Selman, Suzanne Gardinier, and Robin Becker. She won the Lambda Literary Award for *Going Back to the River* in 1991 and again for *Winter Numbers* in 1994. From 1990 to 1994, she edited the prestigious *Kenyon Review,* which, under her leadership, became a model for multi-cultural and gay-friendly editorial policy as well as literary excellence.

Although Hacker loves poetic forms, the word "formalist" hardly begins to encompass her gift. Fellow poet and critic Lawrence Joseph commented in *Voice Literary Supplement* that "the collisions of languages—fast, slangy, switching, sharp, metrically complex— are as much the subject matter...as the thoughts, observations, and feelings expressed by them." Hacker has never subscribed to the aesthetic which dictates that the form of a poem should not call too much attention to itself, although she is certainly capable of creating an easy, unpretentious iambic pentameter line. In fact, she begs the reader to pay attention through a kind of verbal athleticism in which the most unlikely words take on privileged positions, as in "Fifteen to Eighteen" in *Taking Notice.*

> I'd almost know, the nights I snuck in late,
> at two, at three, as soon as I had tucked
> into myself tucked in, to masturbate
> and make happen what hadn't when I fucked.

The audacity of certain rhymes, rhythmic combinations, and split syllables across line breaks reflects the poet's self-consciousness about her own dubious verbal gift. If these "tricks" are indeed easy for her, she wants us to know that she knows it, too, and that she must exert a little control over that impulse. She doesn't let herself get away with empty theatrics for very long. The substance is always there, lurking below the surface, even in the relatively slight "occasional" poems.

This conscious dealing with form as a necessary frame places Hacker into a literary tradition that goes well beyond the confines of contemporary poetry without ever making her work seem elitist or academic. There is something of the Metaphysical poet, blending equal parts sensualist, intellect, and weaver of elaborate conceits, in this selection from her verse novel, *Love, Death, and the Changing of the Seasons*:

> From you will I be absent as the spring
> turns into summer, and the Paris sky
> stays twilit until nearly midnight. I
> don't want to go, wouldn't want to stay, hoping
> the clearer focus of a distancing
> lens will show both of us separately
> comet trails marking your trajectory
> and mine, convergent, or continuing
> asymptotes, toward a human finity
> of works and days. Last night was a white night,
> my arms around you with a burst of words
> compressed between your elbows and your knees.
> There are none here, so, in the graying light,
> I sang you *rossignols* and mockingbirds.

The interplay here is between infinite (though light) sky and finite lovers, the closeness of "now" overshadowed by the distance of "later." That strange mathematical word "asymptotes" serves the same function as Donne's compass or flea, by recasting the love relationship through analogy or abstract principle, which, in turn, enhances or illuminates the expression of that love. Once we take the time to consult a dictionary, a necessary companion for any Hacker book, we learn that "asymptotes" are lines that continually approach but never reach a curve, just as the lovers continually approach each other and then, sadly and inevitably, spin away.

In other Hacker poems, traces of Shakespeare are present, not only in the sonnet form, but also in her comic timing, presentation of character, bawdy wit, and memorable dialogue. All of these elements are at work, again, in *Love, Death, and the Changing of the Seasons,* whose title itself hearkens back to Shakespeare's summary of the customary subject matter for sonnets. Hacker chooses Shakespeare's "Sonnet 73" as one of two epigraphs (the other being to Pound), with its famous ending couplet: "This thou perceivest, which makes thy love more strong, / To love that well which thou must leave ere long." The butch/femme interplay be-

tween the lovers whose story is told in this extended narrative (as in Hacker's now-famous line "I bet you don't wear shoulder pads in bed") in many ways resembles the disguises and complex gender play of Shakespearean comedy and comic opera. But unlike the couples in *Midsummer Night's Dream,* alas, the lovers in this lesbian classic will not marry in the end.

After Auden, another deep influence, Hacker may be our most quotable twentieth century poet, exemplified by these chilling lines that close "Nights of 1964-1966...."

> The file clerks took exams and forged ahead.
> The decorators' kitchens blazed persimmon.
> The secretary started kissing women,
> and so did I, and my three friends are dead.

In some ways, Hacker's *oeuvre* as a whole can be seen as a response to Auden's famous words from his elegy to Yeats, that "poetry makes nothing happen." For Hacker, the words themselves may not change the world, but, if they are well-chosen, they can at least wake us up from a cultural stupor.

With the poems collected in *Winter Numbers,* published simultaneously with *Selected Poems* in 1994, Hacker's vision is augmented by a starkly vivid physical consciousness of aging and disease in the self and others. In the poem "Year's End," dedicated to Audre Lorde and Sonny Wainright, she sees her own experience with breast cancer unflinchingly in the context of a larger societal wound:

> Twice in my quickly disappearing forties
> someone called while someone I loved and I were
> making love to tell me another woman
> had died of cancer.
>
> Seven years apart, and two different lovers:
> underneath the numbers, how lives are braided,
> how those women's deaths and lives, lived and died, were
> interleaved also.

In "Against Elegies," which clearly confronts, with its ironic title and catalog of names and numbers, the impact of deaths from breast cancer, AIDS, and suicide, the personal becomes political in the true feminist sense. The names of friends are joined here with the nameless others woven into the fabric of grief:

> The earth-black woman in the bed beside
> Lidia on the AIDS floor—deaf and blind:
> I want to know if, no, how, she died.
> The husband, who'd stopped visiting, returned?
> He brought the little boy, those nursery-
> school smiles taped on the walls? She traced
> her name on Lidia's face
> when one of them needed something. She learned
> some Braille that week. Most of the time, she slept.
> Nobody knew the baby's HIV
> status. Sleeping, awake, she wept.
> And I left her name behind.

Yet Hacker remains nimble even in this darker vein, still having fun with line breaks when she poses the lyrical question in "Cancer Winter," "Should I tattoo my scar? What would it say? / It could say 'K.J.'s Truck Stop' in plain Eng- / lish, highlighted with a nipple ring...." That combination of mordant wit, intense emotion, and impeccable craft will help to assure that the poetry of Marilyn Hacker is read in years to come by a large and varied audience. Its impact on lesbian and gay readers, in itself, is immense. With her uncompromising intelligence and honest passion, Hacker appeals to the mind as well as the heart, so that even those who respond to poetry with Marianne Moore's adage, "I, too, dislike it," may be wooed by her words in the end.

—Sue Russell

HANSCOMBE, Gillian Eve

Nationality: Australian poet, novelist, and commentator. **Born:** Melbourne, 22 August 1945. **Education:** University of Melbourne, B.A. in English Literature and Music History 1967; Monash University, M.A. in English Literature 1969; St Hugh's College, Oxford University, England, D.Phil. 1979. **Family:** Partner of Indian poet Suniti Namjoshi, from 1985; one son, born 1976. **Career:** Tutor in English, Janet Clarke Hall, University of Melbourne, 1968-69, and Queen's College, London, 1970-73; lecturer in English, Hitchin College of Further Education, Herts, England, 1969-70; part-time tutor in English, Jews' College, London, 1972-75; lecturer, seminar leader, and project advisor, The Experiment in International Living, School for International Training, Academic Studies Abroad, 1974-83; staff reporter, *Gay News,* London, 1981-83; educational consultant, 1983-87; freelance writer, from 1987; Director, Centre for Women's Studies, University of Exeter, England, from 1995. **Awards:** Honorary Research Fellow, Centre for Women's Studies, University of Exeter, from 1995. **Address:** c/o Centre for Women's Studies, University of Exeter, Queen's Building, The Queen's Drive, Exeter, Devon EX4 4QJ, United Kingdom.

WRITINGS

Fiction

Between Friends (novel). Boston, Alyson Press, 1982; London, Sheba Feminist Publishers, 1983; with introduction, London, The Women's Press, 1990.
"Ebbs and Flows," in *The Reach and Other Stories,* edited by Lilian Mohin and Sheila Shulman. London, Onlywomen Press, 1984.
"From the Tory Badlands," in *The Pied Piper and Other Stories,* edited by Lilian Mohin and Anna Livia. London, Onlywomen Press, 1989.
With Suniti Namjoshi, "Hey Diddle Diddle," in *By the Light of the Silvery Moon,* edited by Ruth Petrie. London, Virago Press, 1994.
With Namjoshi, "Longitude 151° 55′ E-Latitude 23° 26′ S," in *Australia for Women: Travel and Culture,* edited by Susan Hawthorne and Renate Klein. Melbourne, Spinifex Press, 1994.
Figments of a Murder. Melbourne, Spinifex Press, 1995.

Poetry

Hecate's Charms. Sydney, Khasmik Poets, 1975; London, Sappho, 1975.

With Namjoshi, *Flesh and Paper.* Canada, Ragweed Press, 1986; United Kingdom, Jezebel Tapes and Books, 1986.
Sybil: The Glide of Her Tongue. Melbourne, Spinifex Press, 1992.
"The Interloper," in *Conversations of Love.* Melbourne, Penguin Australia, 1996.
"Three Poems," "The Invitation," "Hecate's Appearance," "My Appearance," "Hecate the Teacher," "The Charms 1" and "2," in *Mother I'm Rooted: An Anthology of Australian Women Poets,* edited by Kate Jennings. Melbourne, Outback Press, 1975.
"December 1984," in *New Poetry 3: An Anthology,* edited by Alan Brownjohn and Maureen Duffy. London, The Arts Council of Great Britain, 1977.
"Jesus People," in *Bread and Roses: Women's Poetry of the 19th and 20th Centuries,* selected with introduction by Diana Scott. London, Virago Press, 1982.
"The Charms 4" and "8," "Maternity," "An Intentionalist Fallacy," "Plotting," "Ethics," "An Apostrophe to Her Majesty Queen Elizabeth 2," in *Beautiful Barbarians,* edited by Lilian Mohin. London, Onlywomen Press, 1986.
"Fragment," in *Moments of Desire: Feminist Writing About Sex,* edited by Susan Hawthorne and Jenny Pausacker. Melbourne, Penguin Books, 1989.
Poems in *The Oxford Book of Australian Love Poetry,* edited by Jennifer Strauss, Melbourne, O.U.P., 1993.
With Namjoshi, poems in *The Virago Book of Love Letters,* edited by Jill Dawson. London, Virago Press, 1994.
With Namjoshi, "Was It Quite Like That?," "Because of India," "We Can Compose Ourselves," in *Chloe Plus Olivia: An Anthology of Lesbian and Bisexual Literature from the 17th Century to the Present,* edited by Lilian Faderman. New York, Penguin Books, 1994.

Nonfiction

With Jackie Forster, *Rocking the Cradle. Lesbian Mothers: A Challenge in Family Living.* London, Peter Owen 1981; Boston, Alyson Press, 1982; London, Sheba Feminist Publishers, 1982.
The Art of Life: Dorothy Richardson and the Development of Feminist Consciousness. London, Peter Owen, 1982; Miami, Ohio University Press, 1982.
With Andrew Lumsden, *Title Fight: The Battle for Gay News.* London, Brilliance Books, 1983.
"The Right to Lesbian Parenthood," in *Journal of Medical Ethics,* Vol. 9, No. 3, September 1983; in *Intervention and Reflection: Basic Issues in Medical Ethics,* edited by Ronald Munson, 3d edition, Belmont, California, Wadsworth Publishing Company, 1988.
"Reaching the Parts Other Books Can't Reach," in *New Statesman,* Vol. 8, June 1984.
"Not What I Mean By It," in *Girls Next Door,* edited by Jan Bradshaw and Mary Hemming. London, The Women's Press 1985.
Editor and author of preface, with Martin Humphries, *Heterosexuality.* London, GMP Publishers, 1986.
William Golding: Lord of The Flies. Harmondsworth, Middlesex, Penguin Books, 1986.
"Sweating, Thumping, Telling," in *Testimonies,* edited by Sarah Holmes. Boston, Alyson Publications, 1988.
Stan Barstow: Joby. Harmondsworth, Middlesex, Penguin Books, 1988.
"Dorothy Richardson Versus the Novvle," in *Experimental Women Writers,* edited by Ellen G. Friedman and Miriam Fuchs. Princeton, Princeton University Press, 1988.

With Virginia L. Smyers, *Writing for Their Lives: The Modernist Women, 1910-1940.* London, The Women's Press, 1987; Boston, Northeastern University Press, 1988.

"In Among the Market Forces?," in *An Intimate Wilderness,* edited by Judith Barrington, Portland, Oregon, The Eighth Mountain Press, 1991.

With Namjoshi, "Heavenly Enough," in *Trivia,* Vol. 18, fall 1991.

With Namjoshi, "Who Wrongs You, Sappho?," in *Out of the Margins,* edited by Jane Aaron and Sylvia Walby. London, Falmer Press, 1991.

"Katherine Mansfield's Pear Tree," in *What Lesbians Do in Books,* edited by Elaine Hobby and Chris White. London, The Women's Press, 1991.

"Space and Nests and History," in *No Fear of Flying: Women at Home and Abroad,* edited by Jocelynne A. Scutt. Melbourne, Artemis Press, 1994.

Plays

Hecate's Charms (adaptation of her own poetry; music by George French; produced Wigmore Hall, London, June 1978).

With Namjoshi, *Kaliyug Circles of Paradise* (performed Chester Dance Workshop, 1993).

*

Adaptations: *Between Friends* (adaptation by Maggie Antrobus; produced Rose Bruford College of Drama, 1983, and Digby Stuart College, London, 1983).

*   *   *

After a traditional academic education in Australia, Gillian Hanscombe, finding insufficient scope for her lesbianism and gender politics, left for Europe in 1969. Upon arriving in Europe, she continued with an academic career, but found the intellectual ferment of ideas around feminist and gay politics too seductive to ignore. She became involved with alternative educational projects and changed her focus from conventional studies of literature to a consideration of contemporary culture, particularly the role of women in society and the arts. Though a published poet in Australia, her shift in focus spurred her first international recognition as a writer with the publication of *Hecate's Charms* in 1975.

In the introduction to *Sybil: The Glide of Her Tongue,* Hanscombe describes how her life changed as a result of the wave of feminism and gay liberation in the late '60s and '70s.

> When I took courage from the new feminism and began to take this word [lesbian] to myself, I found myself gathered up, welcomed and embraced into a new life.... We lesbians were still shunned, feared, pitied, hated, mocked or threatened by mainstreamers; but we had each other. And the ghetto we shared, we made beautiful with our sounds and scents, our movements and music, our dreams, our plans, our life-histories—but above all with our words."

Like many politically conscious women, Hanscombe joined a consciousness-raising group in London. Her encounter with various feminist perspectives led to her novel *Between Friends* where she examined the relationship among four women: Frances, a heterosexual in a traditional marriage; Meg, a lesbian-feminist, bringing up a son with her partner, Jan; Amy, a heterosexual with a deep commitment to feminism; and Jane, a fierce lesbian-separatist. The story, revealed by letters the women exchange, concerns their attempts to apply feminist principles to their lives and be more honest in their dealings with one another. Although Frances admits to loving Meg, she refuses the change to her marital relationship that feminism would demand. Eventually Frances withdraws from Meg and settles for life with her vain, unfaithful, and abusive husband. Meg breaks with Jan, determined to find a way of living with Jane, though she finds Jane's uncompromising views on the male sex hard to square with her own love for her son. Jane agrees to live in a larger commune that includes Meg, her son Simon, as well as Amy and her New Man, Tim. Jane justifies her compromises thus:

> "I want to say yes to everything—yes to you, yes to Simon, yes to moving to London, yes to life. I won't be cutting off everything here—I'll bring it with me. These women and my life with them here are in my bones, in my heart, in my head—they're part of me. And now you are part of me as well, and I love you."

In the summer of 1978, in the aftermath of an outbreak of tabloid rage against reports of lesbian couples receiving artificial insemination, Hanscombe and Jackie Forster, founder of Sappho, the organisation for lesbians, began a nationwide tour to meet lesbian mothers and their families. The culmination of their tour came in the publication of the book, *Rocking the Cradle.* Amid widespread, mostly hostile publicity concerning the issue of women raising children together, Hanscombe and Forster attempted to present the real lives of lesbian mothers and their children. In the introduction of *Rocking the Cradle,* the two described the impetus for their project as wanting "to talk to them, to see how they lived, and to give them a chance to speak in their own words to the public." They met women from all social classes, white and black women, Catholic and Jewish, non-conformist and atheist. Apart from being lesbians and mothers, there were no ideas, circumstances, nor experiences which all the women had in common. Today, when society is ostensibly more relaxed about single parenthood and homosexuality, these issues would not be considered revolutionary. But in its time it was radical, pioneering research which, as the title suggests, presented a powerful challenge to the notion of the nuclear family as the basis of western society.

As a staff reporter on the London-based newspaper *Gay News* in 1981, Hanscombe was at the centre of gay politics in England. She chronicled the ideological struggles and in-fighting that took place on the newspaper in *Title Fight: The Battle for Gay News.* Her prominence in lesbian-feminist politics led Hanscombe to be invited to chair a panel of lesbian writers in the First International Feminist Book Fair in 1984. One panelist was the Indian poet Suniti Namjoshi, then teaching in Canada. After their meeting, the two corresponded through letters, poems, and story fragments. The correspondence reflected their developing relationship and was later published as *Flesh and Paper.*

In the jointly signed introduction, they made a declaration of the difference between lesbian writing and mainstream writing, the latter dominated by heterosexual men:

> [A] lesbian woman does not inhabit the worlds that make sense to heterosexual men.... [T]he difficulty...is that

all worlds are not equal. The world painted by heterosexual male poets is seen as having more of a bearing on the "real" world; while that painted by lesbian poets is set aside as "personal" and "marginal". But it is our lived experience as lesbians that the "universal truths" of the human heart, which are claimed as knowledge by the male heterosexual literary tradition, are not "universal" at all. For us, love is not the same; sex is not the same; parenting is not the same; work is not the same; safety is not the same; respect is not the same; trust is not the same. Only death might, perhaps, be the same.

There could not be a clearer explanation of the uniqueness of the lesbian sensibility and its effect on writing.

—Anne Hughes

HARRIS, Bertha

Nationality: American novelist. **Born:** Fayetteville, North Carolina, 17 December 1937. **Education:** Women's College of the University of North Carolina, B.A. 1959; University or North Carolina, M.F.A. 1967. **Family:** Married Mr. Wyland in 1963 (divorced 1964); one daughter. **Career:** Worked at clerical jobs, New York, 1959-64; taught literature at East Carolina University and University of North Carolina at Charlotte, where she was also head of the Creative Writing Sequence, 1970-73; Coordinated Women's Studies at the College of Staten Island of the City University of New York; served as part-time editor for Daughters, Inc. **Address:** 300 Riverside Dr., #9A, New York, New York 10025, U.S.A.

WRITINGS

Novels

Catching Saradove. New York, Harcourt Brace, 1969.
Confessions of Cherubino. New York, Harcourt Brace, 1972; New York, Daughters, 1978.
Lover. New York, Daughters, 1976; with new introduction by author, New York, New York University Press, 1993.

Nonfiction

With E. Sisley, *The Joy of Lesbian Sex.* New York, Crown, 1977.
Gertrude Stein. New York, Chelsea House, 1996.

*

Critical Sources: "The Purple Reign of Bertha Harris" by Wayne Koestenbaum, in *Village Voice Literary Supplement,* October 1993, 18-19; "Bertha Harris, A Memoir" by Dorothy Allison, in *Skin: Talking About Sex, Class & Literature,* Ithaca, New York, Firebrand, 1994, 201-208; "Bertha Harris" by Ann Wadsworth, in *The Gay and Lesbian Literary Heritage,* edited by Claude J. Summers, New York, Norton, 1995, 361-362; "Bertha Harris" by L. Tipps, in *Women Writers in the United States,* edited by Cynthia J. Davis and Kathryn West, New York, Oxford, 1996, 250-251; *Following*

Djuna: Women Lovers and the Erotics of Loss, by Carol Allen, Bloomington, Indiana University Press, 1996.

*   *   *

In the writing of Bertha Harris, the world the mind creates exists simultaneously and on an equal plane with the world we think of as "real." As early as her first novel, *Catching Saradove,* Harris expressed this belief in the primacy of the imagination: "Everything is there in my head, the world as I make it. The mask I wear in front of it doesn't matter, but the mask is quite as important as the real thing."

In her next two novels, the masks became more and more elaborate, from the Southern Gothic of *Confessions of Cherubino* to the post-Modern pastiche of *Lover,* as Harris developed the narrative skill and bravado to render her complex vision. It is easy to see how this inclination toward disguise and drama could have developed from the particular background that Harris described in the introduction that accompanies the 1993 edition of *Lover.* Born and raised in rural North Carolina, Harris describes herself as a "child aesthete" misplaced in a family that "didn't own any books." In those post-World War II, pre-television years, the young writer's major cultural influence was, by her own account, the Saturday Metropolitan Opera broadcasts, featuring "a man with a honey of a voice," Milton Cross. Something of that same voice "dispassionately reciting the events of the final scene of Salomé by Richard Strauss" found its way into Harris' own narratives, in which the representation of lust ("natural" or "unnatural"), violence, and dysfunctional families could rival that of any opera, while benefiting from the control of a master prose stylist.

If aesthetic inclination and love of opera are requirements of the gay sensibility, Harris showed these qualities from her earliest writing. But it was not until her groundbreaking third novel, *Lover,* that she concentrated her full powers upon lesbian life as she had seen and lived it. Although lesbian characters appear in both *Saradove* and *Cherubino,* there is an element of ambiguity that leaves the reader in some doubt as to the author's attitude toward them. Saradove, whom we see in chapters that alternate between her North Carolina childhood and her bohemian early adulthood in Manhattan, is obsessed with her female lover, L.E., but plans to enter into a questionable heterosexual marriage. The young female sweethearts in *Cherubino,* ready to graduate from their women's college, may or may not have consummated their relationship, but they also gain "practice" with male partners along the way.

In *Lover,* however, the lesbian perspective is pivotal and clear, though the narrative continually shifts. "*Lover* is the pleasure dome," Harris tells us. "It's a Renaissance heaven I had in mind, where there's sex." With its elaborate cast of characters and layered plot, *Lover* is a certifiable lesbian classic that has been crucial in the creative development of such writers as Dorothy Allison. As Allison notes in her essay, "Bertha Harris: A Memoir": "Lesbian writing that only replicated heterosexual reality was failing to live up to its own potential, getting in the way of that lesbian culture we all needed so badly. This is the standard for greatness, Bertha Harris told us."

Although Harris provides a diagram, complete with family seal ("Lesbia Rhus Typhina"), to help the reader keep track of her richly varied *dramatis personae,* the web of their relationships cannot be so easily contained. Eventually, we accept our own confusion as part of the reading experience and simply let ourselves be entertained. Take, for example Veronica, who "came out of no-where," "began life as a religious poet composing ecstatic meters about drowned nuns," and who can "still, at any moment...render herself again into an exact replica of all the creatures she started as." Likewise, the saints, martyrs, and ecstatics whose stories Harris uses as epigraphs to each chapter, may be genuine or imagined, but as part of the novel's landscape, their existence in the "real" world hardly seems relevant. Time itself becomes a fluid element, freed from the linear confines of pre-conceived notions of history.

It is easy to see in the creator of *Lover* the mark of that young aesthete from Fayetteville, North Carolina, who learned tap dance routines from her father and joined him on the small-time vaudeville circuit. In *Lover,* high and low art, represented, on the one hand by *Der Rosenkavalier,* and on the other by Mr. Bojangles, teaching little Shirley Temple some fancy footwork, converge into a memorable performance piece. It is a hard act to follow.

—Sue Russell

HARTLEY, Marsden

Nationality: American painter, poet, and art critic. **Born:** Edmund Hartley in Lewiston, Maine, 4 January 1877; changed name c. 1906. **Education:** Cleveland School of Art, Ohio, 1898; New York School of Art (Chase school), New York City, 1899; National Academy of Design, New York City, 1900-04. **Career:** Held a variety of jobs including summer work at Green Acre, a utopian community, 1907; Secretary, of Katherine Dreier's Societe Anonyme, 1920; easel painting division, Works Progress Administration (WPA), 1934, 1936. **Awards:** Guggenheim Travel Grant, 1931; Pennsylvania Academy annual exhibit prize; Metropolitan Museum of Art prize, "Artists for Victory" exhibition, 1941. **Died:** Ellsworth, Maine, 2 September 1943.

Writings

Poetry

"Kaleidoscope: 'In The Frail Wood,' 'Spinsters,' 'Her Daughter,' and 'After Battle'," in *Poetry,* July 1918, 195-201.
"Poetic Pieces: 'The Ivory Woman' and 'Sunbather'," in *Little Review,* Vol. 5, December 1918, 26-28.
"Local Boys and Girls," "Small Town Stuff," "Evening Quandary," "Fishmonger," and "The Flatterers," in *Others for 1919: An Anthology of the New Verse,* edited by Alfred Kreymborg. New York, Nicholas L. Brown, 61-68; "Local Boys and Girls" and "Small Town Stuff" reprinted in *Twenty-five Poems,* 1923, 11.
"Two Lily Satires: 'Pernicious Celibates' and 'The Very Wise Virgins'," in *Playboy: Magazine of Art and Satire,* No. 3, 1919, 11.
"The Dowager's Distress," in *Playboy: Magazine of Art and Satire,* Nos. 4-5, 1919, 23.
"Scaramouch," in *Other 5,* February 1919, 16.
"Swallows," in *Others 5,* March 1919, 14.
"Sunlight Persuasions: 'The Festival of the Corn,' 'Español,' 'Girl with the Camelia Smile,' 'The Topaz of the Sixties,' 'The Asses Out-House,' 'To C__,' and 'Saturday'," in *Poetry,* May 1920, 59-70.

"Aperitifs" and "A Portrait," in *Contact,* No. 1, December 1920, 8-9; "A Portrait," reprinted as "Rapture," in *Twenty-five Poems,* Boston Portrait Projections, 1923, 33-34.
"Canticle for October," in *Contact,* No. 3, 1921, 11-12.
"The Crucifixion of Noel," in *Dial,* No. 70, April 1921, 378-80; reprinted in *Twenty-five Poems,* 1923, 2-5, and in *Lyric America: An Anthology of American Poetry 1630-1939,* edited by Alfred Kreymborg, New York, Coward-McCann, Inc., 1930, 460-62; revised edition, with supplement, New York, Tudor Publishing Co., 1935, 460-62.
"Yours with Devotion: trumpets and drums" (unsigned poem), in *New York Dada Globe,* April 1921, 4.
Twenty-five Poems. Paris, Contact Publishing Co., 1923.
"The Woman distorts, with hunger," in *Contact Collection of Contemporary Writers,* edited by Robert McAlmon. Paris, Three Mountain Press, 1925, 87-90.
"The MOUNTAIN and the RECONSTRUCTION," in *Paintings and Watercolors by Marsden Hartley* (exhibition catalogue). Chicago, The Arts Club of Chicago, 1928.
"Four Poems: 'From a Paris window—high,' 'The beautiful rush,' 'Life ahead, life behind,' and '—Corniche, Marseilles,'" in *American Caravan IV,* edited by Alfred Kreymborg, Lewis Mumford, and Paul Rosenfield. New York, The Macaulay Company, 445-47.
"Scenes: 'Brautigam' and 'Window-Washer, Avenue C'," in *Poetry,* No. 40, April 1932, 22-23.
"Return of the Native," in *Contact,* 19 May 1932, 28.
"Signing Family Papers" in *Marsden Hartley: Exhibition of Recent Paintings, 1936* (exhibition catalogue). New York, An American Place, 1936; reprinted in *Androscoggin,* 1940, 35-36.
"An Outline in Portraiture of Self: 'From Letters Never Sent' and 'This portrait of a seadove—dead'," in *Marsden Hartley: First Exhibition in Four years* (exhibition catalogue). New York, An American Place, 1936; "This portrait of a seadove—dead," reprinted in *Androscoggin,* 1940, 32-33, and in *Selected Poems,* 1945, 34-35.
"The Berry House" and "She Went Without Telling," in *The Triad Anthology of New England Verse,* edited by Louise Hall Littlefield. Portland, Maine, Falmouth Book House, 32-33, 48-50; "The Berry House" reprinted in *Androscoggin,* 1940, 49-50, and *Selected Poems,* 1945, 88-89.
Androscoggin. Portland, Maine, Falmouth Publishing House, 1940.
Sea Burial. Portland, Maine, Leon Tebbetts, Editions, 1941.
Selected Poems, edited by Henry W. Wells. New York, The Viking Press, 1945.
Eight Poems and One Essay. Lewiston, Maine, Bates College, 1976.

Nonfiction

Foreword, *Paintings by Marsden Hartley.* New York, Photo-Secession Galleries; reprinted in *Camera Work,* No. 45, January 1914, 16-18.
"What is 291?," in *Camera Work,* No. 47, January 1915, 35-326.
Foreword to exhibition catalogue sponsored by the Munchener Graphik Verlag, Berlin; reprinted in "American Artist Astounds Germans," in *The New York Times,* 9 December 1915.
"A Word," in *The Forum Exhibition of Modern American Painters.* New York, Anderson Galleries, 1916, 53; facsimile reprint, New York, Arno Press, 1968; also reprinted in *Readings in American Art Since 1900,* edited by Barbara Rose, New York, Frederick A. Praeger, 1968, 63-64.

Forward, *Paintings by Marsden Hartley.* New York, Photo-Secession Galleries; reprinted in *Camera Work,* No. 48, October 1916, 12.

"Epitaph for Alfred Stieglitz," in *Camera Work,* No. 48, October 1916, 70.

"Twilight of the Acrobat," in *Seven Arts,* January 1917, 287-91.

"Odilon Redon," in *The New Republic,* No. 9, 20 January 1917, 321-23.

"Albert Pinkham Ryder," in *Seven Arts 2,* May 1917, 93-96.

"A Painter's Faith," in *Seven Arts 2,* August 1917, 502-06.

"John Barrymore's Ibbetson," in *Dial,* Vol. 64, 14 March 1918, 227-29.

"Emily Dickinson," in *Dial,* Vol. 65, 15 August 1918, 95-97.

"The Reader Critic: Divagation's," in *Little Review,* Vol. 5, September 1918, 59-62.

"The Reader Critic: Breakfast Resume," in *Little Review,* Vol. 5, November 1918, 46-50.

"Tribal Esthetics," in *Dial,* Vol. 65, 16 November 1918, 399-401.

"Tribute to Joyce Kilmer: As Friend of an Earlier Time," in *Poetry,* December 1918, 149-54.

"Aesthetic Sincerity," in *El Palacio,* 9 December 1918, 332-33.

"Rex Slinkard: Ranchman and Poet Painter," in *Memorial Exhibition: Rex Slinkard 1887-1918* (exhibition catalogue). Los Angeles, Museum of History, Science, and Art, 1919.

"The Beautiful Neglected Arts: Satire and Seriousness," in *Little Review,* Vol. 5, June 1919, 59-64.

"The Poet of Maine," in *Little Review,* Vol. 5, July 1919, 51-55.

"Art and Wallace Gould," in *Little Review,* Vol. 6, October 1919, 24-29.

"The Business of Poetry," in *Poetry,* December 1919, 152-58.

"Red Man Ceremonials: An American Plea for American Esthetics," in *Art and Archeology,* January 1920, 7-14; as "The Red Man," in *Adventures in the Arts,* 1921, 13-29.

"The Poetry of Arthur B. Davies' Art," in *Touchstone,* February 1920, 277-84; as "Arthur B. Davies," in *Adventures in the Arts,* 1921, 80-86.

"Vaudeville," in *Dial,* March 1920, 335-42.

"Concerning Fairy Tales," in *Touchstone,* December 1920, 172-79; as "Concerning Fairy Tales and Me" (foreword), in *Adventures in the Arts,* 3-10.

Adventures in the Arts: Informal Chapters on Painters, Vaudeville, and Poets. New York, Boni & Liveright, 1921; facsimile reprint, New York, Hacker Books, 1972.

"Dissertation on Modern Painting," in *Nation,* No. 112, February 1921, 235-36.

"The Scientific Esthetic of the Redman": Part 1, "The Great Corn Ceremony at Santo Domingo," in *Art and Archeology,* No. 13, March 1922, 113-19; Part 2, "The Fiesta of San Geronimo at Taos," in *Art and Archeology,* No. 14, September 1922, 137-39.

"Marie Luerencin," in *Der Querschnitt,* No. 2, summer 1922, 102-03.

"A Propos du Dome, etc.," in *Der Querschnitt,* No. 2, Christmas 1922, 235-38.

"Georgia O'Keeffe," in *Alfred Stieglitz Presents One Hundred Pictures Oil, Watercolors, Pastels, Drawings by Georgia O'Keeffe American.* New York, The Anderson Galleries, 1923.

"The Greatest Show on Earth: An Appreciation of the Circus from One of its Grown-up Admirers," in *Vanity Fair,* No. 22, August 1924, 33, 88.

"Recent Paintings by John Marin" (exhibition catalogue). New York, Intimate Gallery, 1928.

"Art—and the Personal Life," in *Creative Art,* No. 2, June 1928, xxxi-xxxvi.

"291—And the Brass Bowl," in *American and Alfred Stieglitz: A Collective Portrait,* edited by Waldo Frank, Lewis Mumford, Dorothy Norman, Paul Rosenfeld, and Harold Rugg. New York, Doubleday Doran & Co., Inc., 1934, 236-42; reprinted, New York, Aperture, Inc., 1979, 119-21.

"George Grosz at An American Place," in *George Grosz: Exhibition of Water Colors (1933-1934* (exhibition catalogue). New York, An American Place, 1935.

"Farewell Charles," in *New Caravan,* 1935, 552-62.

"Albert Pinkham Ryder" in *New Caravan,* edited by Alfred Kreymborg, Lewis Mumford, and Paul Rosenfeld. New York,, W.W. Norton & Co., Inc., 1936, 540-51.

"On the Subject of Nativeness: A Tribute to Main," in *Marsden Hartley: Exhibition of Recent Paintings, 1936* (exhibition catalogue). New York, An American Place, 1936.

"As to John Marin and His Ideas," in *John Marin: Watercolors, Oil Paintings, Etchings* (exhibition catalogue). New York, Museum of Modern Art, 1936, 15-18; facsimile reprint, New York, Arno Press, 1966.

"Georgia O'Keeffe: A Second Outline in Portraiture," in *Georgia O'Keeffe: Exhibitions of Paintings, 1935* (exhibition catalogue). New York, An American Place, 1936.

"Concerning the Work of Richard G," in *Exhibition of Paintings by Richard Guggenheimer* (exhibition catalogue). New York, Lilienfeld Galleries, 1937.

"Seeing the Shows: The Paintings of Harry Watrous," in *Magazine of Art,* No. 30, March 1937, 176.

"The Six Greatest New England Painters," in *Yankee,* No. 3, August 1937, 14-16.

"Three Notes: 'Mary with the Child—of Leonardo in the Pinakotck, Munich,' 'Memling Portraits,' and 'Thinking of Gaston Lachaise,'" in *Twice a Year,* Nos. 3-4, 1939-40, 253-263; excerpt from "Thinking of Gaston Lachise" reprinted in *The Sculpture of Gaston Lachaise,* edited by Hilton Kramer, New York, Easkins Press, 1965, 27-29.

"Commentary," in *Paintings by John Bloomshield* (exhibition catalogue). New York, James St. L. O'Toole Galleries, 1941.

"Spring, 1941," in *Story,* No. 19, September-October 1941, 97-99.

"Pictures," in *Marsden Hartley/Staurt Davis* (exhibition catalogue). Cincinnati, Ohio, Cincinnati Modern Art Society, 1941, 4-6

"Sprinchorn Today," in *Exhibition by Carl Sprinchorn* (exhibition catalogue). Philadelphia, America Swedish Historical Museum, 1942.

Feininger/Hartley (exhibition catalogue). New York, Museum of Modern Art, 1945.

"Letter to Jacques Lipchitz," in *Lipchitz: Early Stone Carvings and Recent Bronzes* (exhibition catalogue). New York, Buchhotz Gallery, 1948, 1-5.

Other

Somehow a Past: The Autobiography of Marsden Hartley, edited by Susan Elizabeth Ryan. Cambridge, Massachusetts, MIT Press, 1997.

*

Manuscript Collections: Beinecke Rare Books and Manuscript Library, Yale University, New Haven, Connecticut.

Biography: *Marsden Hartley* by Elizabeth McCausland, Minneapolis, University of Minnesota Press, 1952; *Marsden Hartley: The Biography of an American Artist* by Townsend Ludington, Boston, Little, Brown, and Company, 1992.

Critical Sources: *Marsden Hartley* by Barbara Haskell, New York, Whitney Museum of American Art (in association with New York University Press), 1980; *On Art,* edited by Gail R. Scott, New York, Horizon Press, 1982; *Marsden Hartley* by Gail R. Scott, New York, Abbeville Press, 1988; *Marsden Hartley* by Bruce Robertson, New York, Abrams (in association with the National Museum of American Art, Smithsonian Institution), 1995.

*   *   *

Marsden Hartley had a long and varied career that did not always receive the critical attention it deserved. While he wrote many essays on art, as well as published three books of poetry, an unpublished autobiography, and left many boxes of unpublished work, Hartley is remembered mainly for his painting. His works of art range from New England landscapes to modernist abstracts, from portraits to still lives. Alfred Stieglitz was an important mentor for Hartley. Stieglitz sponsored Hartley's first one-man show at his studio 291. He had eight more solo shows with Stieglitz, the last one in 1937.

Bruce Robertson writes in *Marsden Hartley* that as a homosexual, Hartley seems to have been too inhibited and insecure to participate in the New York gay subculture. Hartley's sexual orientation acted as a barrier, cutting him out of any complete sympathetic or unconsidered sharing. He always held something back, a pattern which marked his social interactions for all of his life. He could only express his full self, and then very obliquely, in his art.

For Hartley, art and life were inextricably intertwined. He wrote that whatever form he was working in, it was to be read as being connected to his life. As Robertson points out, however, Hartley's insistent claim that art should not be divided from life always ran up against the brick wall of his gay closet. He feared his painting might not be taken as "masculine," and masculinity was a prime force behind art and literature during the first part of the twentieth-century as critics bemoaned the "feminization" of American culture.

As a gay man growing up during the late 1800s and maturing during the first part of the twentieth-century, Hartley went to great lengths to sever his private life from his art. But no matter how hard he tried, his personal emotions seeped into his work. According to Robertson, "as a gay man, Hartley felt that all ordinary expressions of love were forbidden him, especially the life of the home, of domesticity. His private live—his affective life—had to be divided sharply from his public life." Yet, Hartley felt his art expressed his own experience because he was a spectator and he did his best to make an art of observation.

The strain of both hiding and revealing his secret self, and the stratagems he used, lie at the heart of his art and are the source of his power, according to Robertson. Hartley spent his life on the outside, looking with longing and anger at the ordinary world he was shut out of. This alienation was compounded by the death of his mother when he was eight years old. His homosexuality gave him, however, a place of strength beyond the accepted and unanalyzed norms of life where he could observe at a distance and re-create his surroundings in his painting. In Robertson's words, "pushed to the margins, gays and lesbians have been made that much more powerful in their reimaging of the center, as has been true for other disenfranchised communities in America. Playing with, reshaping, and critiquing the culture of the center, they have held up a mirror to mainstream society with a more interesting face in the mirror than may actually stand in front of it."

Although Hartley's landscape paintings have been read as paintings filled with sexual images, it was not until 1935, when he returned to figure painting, that he was able to finally bring together his private life and his art. His paintings of Donny and Alty Mason, two young brothers who drowned, announced the major concerns of his explorations of figure painting: memory, spirituality (both Christian and mystical), and the male figure. These portraits and those that followed were simple and direct. At the same time his landscapes also take on a new spiritual strength. Robertson writes that Hartley's dual aspect emerged forcefully in a series of paintings in which his sexual fantasies began to step forward into clear light. Sailors, athletes, loggers, swimmers, and beautiful men now appeared in his paintings. Hartley made scores of drawings during the last years of his life of men on the beach, luxuriating in their variety of poses and bodies, making do by looking at what he could not touch.

As we take a look at Hartley's work today, it takes on new meanings when it is viewed through the lens of his homosexuality. His paintings become landscapes filled with longing and loneliness.

—Pamelyn Nance Dane

HOFFMAN, William M(oses)

Nationality: American playwright, editor, and critic. **Born:** New York City, 12 April 1939. **Education:** City College (now City College of New York; Phi Beta Kappa, cum laude), 1955-60, B.A. in Latin 1960. **Career:** Editorial assistant, Barnes & Noble publishers, New York, 1960-61; assistant editor, 1961-67, associate editor and drama editor, 1967-68, Hill & Wang publishers, New York; founder and director, Wolf Company, 1968; lecturer, Eugene O'Neill Foundation, 1971; artist-in-residence, Lincoln Center Student Program, 1971-72, and Changing Scene, 1972; visiting lecturer, University of Massachusetts, 1973; playwright-in-residence, American Conservatory Theatre, San Francisco, California, 1978, and La Mama Experimental Theatre Company, New York, 1978-79; star adjunct professor in playwriting, Hofstra University, Hempstead, New York, from 1980. Literary adviser, *Scripts,* 1971-74; drama adviser, Cable Arts Foundation, 1973; member of board of directors, Orion Repertory Company, from 1975; playwriting consultant, CAPS Program of New York State Council on the Arts, 1975-77, and Massachusetts Arts and Humanities Foundation, 1978; founding member, New York Theatre Strategy; contributor to *Dramatics.* **Awards:** MacDowell fellowship, 1971; Colorado Council on the Arts and Humanities grant, 1972; Carnegie Fund for Authors grant, 1972; P.E.N. Center grant, 1972; Guggenheim fellowship, 1974-75; National Endowment for the Arts librettist's grant, 1975-76; National Endowment for the Arts fellowship, 1976-77; Drama Desk Award, for outstanding new play, 1985; Antoinette Perry (Tony) Award nominations (3),

1985; Obie Award, 1985; New York Foundation for the Arts grant, 1985. **Agent:** c/o International Creative Management, 40 West 57th Street, New York, New York, 10011, U.S.A.

WRITINGS

Plays

Thank You, Miss Victoria (produced New York, 1965; London, 1970). In *New American Plays 3,* edited by Hoffman, New York, Hill and Wang, 1970.

Saturday Night at the Movies (produced New York, 1966). In *The Off-Off-Broadway Book,* edited by Albert Poland and Bruce Mailman, Indianapolis, Bobbs Merrill, 1972.

Good Night, I Love You (produced New York, 1966). New York, W. M. Hoffman, 1974.

Spring Play (produced New York, 1967).

Three Masked Dances (produced New York, 1967).

Incantation (produced New York, 1967).

Uptight! (produced New York, 1968).

XXX (produced New York, 1969; as *Nativity Play,* produced London, 1970). In *More Plays from Off-Off Broadway,* edited by Michael T. Smith, Indianapolis, Bobbs Merrill, 1972.

Luna (also director; produced New York, 1970). As *An Excerpt from Buddha,* in *Now: Theater der Erfahrung,* edited by Jens Heilmeyer and Pia Frolich, Cologne, Schauberg, 1971.

A Quick Nut Bread to Make Your Mouth Water (also director; produced New York, 1970). In *Spontaneous Combustion: Eight New American Plays,* edited by Rochelle Owens, New York, Winter House, 1972.

From Fool to Hanged Man (produced New York, 1972). In *Scenarios,* New York, 1982.

The Children's Crusade (produced New York, 1972).

I Love Ya, Ya Big Ape (produced Amherst, Massachusetts, 1973).

Gilles de Rais (also director; produced New York, 1975).

With Roger Englander, *Notes from the New World: Louis Moreau Gottschalk* (televised, 1976).

With Anthony Holland, *Cornbury* (produced New Haven, Connecticut, 1977). In *Gay Plays,* edited by Hoffman, New York, Avon, 1979.

The Last Days of Stephen Foster (televised, 1977). In *Dramatics* (Cincinnati, Ohio), 1978.

A Book of Etiquette, music by John Branden (produced New York, 1978; as *Etiquette,* produced New York, 1983).

Gulliver's Travels, music by John Branden (adaptation of the novel by Swift; produced New York, 1978).

With Anthony Holland, *Shoe Palace Murray* (produced San Francisco, 1978). In *Gay Plays,* edited by Hoffman, New York, Avon, 1979).

Whistler: 5 Portraits (televised, 1978).

With Anthony Holland, *The Cherry Orchard, Part II* (produced New York, 1983).

As Is (produced New York, 1985; London, 1987). New York, Random House, 1985; included in *Best American Plays,* New York, Crown, 1993.

Librettos

The Cloisters: A Song Cycle, music by John Corigliano. New York, Schrimer, 1968.

Wedding Song. New York, Schrimer, 1984.

The Ghosts of Versailles, music by Corigliano. New York, Schrimer, 1993.

Of Rage and Remembrance, music by Corigliano. New York, RCA Victor Red Seal, 1996.

Editor

New American Plays 2, 3, and 4. 3 Vols., New York, Hill and Wang, 1968-71.

Gay Plays: The First Collection. New York, Avon, 1979.

Other

Fine Frenzy (poems). New York, McGraw, 1972.

"AIDS-Involved Drama Syndrome" (essay), in *POZ* (New York), February 1997.

*

Manuscript Collections: University of Wisconsin, Madison; Lincoln Center Library of the Performing Arts, New York.

Interviews: "William M. Hoffman" by John L. DiGaetani, in *A Search for a Postmodern Theatre: Interviews with Contemporary Playwrights,* edited by John DiGaetani, New York, Greenwood, 1991.

Critical Sources: "The Sick Homosexual: AIDS and Gays on the American Stage and Screen" by James W. Jones, in *Confronting AIDS through Literature: The Responsibilities of Representation,* edited by Judith Laurence Pastore, Urbana, Illinois, University of Illinois Press, 1993, 103-123; "Coming Up for Air: Three AIDS Plays" by Gregory D. Gross, in *Journal of American Culture* (Bowling Green, Ohio), Volume 15, Number 2, summer 1992, 63-67; "AIDS and Humor," in *Queer and Loathing: Rants and Raves of a Raging AIDS Clone* by David B. Feinberg, New York, Viking, 1994, 84-89; "Ghostbusters" by K. Robert Schwarz, in *Opera News* (New York), Volume 59, Issue 15, 15 April 1995, 12-13, 44.

*   *   *

A substantial body of literature has grown because of AIDS, and this literature not only shapes our understandings of the disease but impacts upon our conceptions of literature and its purpose. William M. Hoffman asserts in a book review, "Dispatches from Aphrodite's War," that "just as the catastrophes of world war and genocide gave a special urgency to our need for the greater perspective we call art, AIDS is spawning a new vocabulary and a new literature of commitment." Hoffman has been a part of this literary movement since its beginning, and his impact on the literature of AIDS is just one facet of a career that spans years of plays and librettos in the New York theatre and opera scenes.

In a 1997 article in *POZ,* a magazine focused on the impact of AIDS on people's lives, Hoffman writes of the newest infection to hit the American theatre scene, what he calls "AIDS-Involved Drama Syndrome." As he puts it, this form of AIDS "is the prime cause of countless plays, performance pieces, anthologies, and critical works preoccupying some of America's most talented playwrights, sapping them of their ability to write about much else." Hoffman chronicles the progression of AIDS-Involved Drama Syndrome from its beginning in 1984 with Robert Chesley's *Night Sweats* through its growth that included such popular and award-winning plays as Tony Kushner's *Angels in America* and Paul Rudnick's *Jeffrey* toward the time in which the essay was written in 1996 with the explosion of the musical *Rent* by Jonathan Larson. Most of the article focuses on Hoffman's own attitudes and thoughts as he completed his formative contribution to this "syndrome," *As Is,* a play that found favor on Broadway, received three Tony nominations, including one for best play, and has continued to shape understandings of what theatrical representations of AIDS can do and be.

As Is focuses on two lovers, Saul and Rich. As the play begins, they meet for what they think is the last time in their old apartment to divide their belongings. Rich soon tells Saul that he has AIDS, and the play continues. Six other actors, four men and two women, preform various roles throughout the play, including Rich's brother, men in a bar, volunteers on an AIDS information hotline, and a former nun who works at a hospice. In a production note, Marshall W. Mason, the director of the first production, wrote, "I feel it is important that the actors remain on stage as much as possible, to witness as a community the events of the play.... The audience must be kept from feeling 'safe' from the subject, so the actors of the 'chorus' must act as a bridge between the fictional characters and the real theater event." This technique enhances the play's ability to alter traditional conceptions of time and place. Hoffman utilizes flashbacks of earlier moments in Saul and Rich's relationship and shifts between their loft and other sites such as a support group meeting, a bar, and a hospital. These methods allow the play to "move almost exclusively within gay worlds," as James W. Jones noted in "The Sick Homosexual: AIDS and Gays on the American Stage and Screen." Locating the play in such gay places brings them out of the darkness and reveals the locales gay men inhabit, thus emphasizing their importance in the development of gay community and culture.

As Hoffman has articulated, *As Is* relates to other plays in several ways. First, the play "punctuates AIDS with allusions to Nazism," according to Gregory D. Gross, writing in the *Journal of American Culture*. For example, the hospice worker expresses her admiration for David, a Jewish man who had survived the Lodz ghetto in World War II, while Saul refers to Rich's agent as "Dr. Mengele." In the introduction to the play, Hoffman mentions that as he learned more and more about the disease, "stories of the Holocaust came to my mind. Most of my family in Europe had perished during the war. As far as I know they never made it to the concentration camps, but were murdered on the street by their Polish and Latvian neighbors." Using metaphors of the Holocaust in depictions of AIDS has long been a way for many writers to represent the desperation and pain brought about by the disease. Both Larry Kramer in the *Normal Heart* and Tony Kushner in *Angels in America* use similar images in their stories.

The play also connects to debates about the role of humor in literature about AIDS, debates grounded in the writings of David B. Feinberg and Edmund White, who have each addressed this issue with disparate responses. Humor has often been used by gay men to express denial or create a sense of distance from the disease. Hoffman expresses his own use of humor in his introduction, when he relates that when he first heard of the disease he replied, "It must be the combination of quiche and leather." In his work, humor functions variously. Hoffman embraces laughter and

humor in this play, saying in the introduction that he "began to realize that among the people with AIDS that I was meeting, those with a sense of humor were doing better than those without." In the script, a man who volunteers at an AIDS information hotline answers a call from a woman who has called him before; she tells him he has a nice voice and then asks him for a date. The hospice worker relates jokes that her patients tell her and ends her short monologue at the start of the play by saying, "We tell a lot of jokes in my line of work." The lighter moments in the script do not offset the more severe moments, but extend the range of emotions engendered by AIDS. Feinberg considers *As Is* to be an example of the successful use of humor in AIDS literature, a humor that maintains a clear depiction of the horrific realities of this disease.

As Is alludes to Hoffman's other primary project of the time period, an opera commissioned by New York's Metropolitan Opera, *The Ghosts of Versailles,* with libretto by Hoffman and music by John Corigliano. In *As Is,* Lily, a friend of both Rich and Saul, asks Saul to take the head shots she needs to audition for a new production. She is auditioning for the role of Marie Antoinette and remarks how the characters are all dead and come back as ghosts, a reference to the libretto which Hoffman had already begun. The opera took 12 years to complete and opened at the Metropolitan in December, 1991. Though it does not deal with overt gay or lesbian themes, Hoffman's out sexuality has impacted upon some responses to it. One of the newest American operas to open in years, audiences graced performances with standing ovations, and critics generally expressed admiration for it. However, some critics were not so accepting. According to K. Robert Schwarz in *Opera News,* "those who criticized *Ghosts* sometimes employed a strange vocabulary." Some critics referred to the opera's "camp humor," "perversely campy villain," and "Mozartean drag." Schwarz questions whether these words are "coded references" for homophobic reactions, while Hoffman declares his feelings more directly: "Calling it campy is homophobic, absolutely,...knowing the sexual orientation of the artists, they feel they can apply values to us." In a time when drama has tried to embrace diverse perspectives, racist, sexist, and homophobic responses have certainly become less acceptable, at least in some sectors. Such negative reactions still exist, however, for those who cannot get past an author's sexuality and look at the specific, artistic text.

Hoffman has never been one to succumb to the demands of mainstream culture. Early on in his career, he called for changes in dramatic form that would enable the expression of multifarious outlooks. In the late 1960s and early 1970s, he edited three volumes of the anthology series *New American Plays*. In the third volume, he lists several challenges, or projects, to playwrights, including a play for blind people, a play for racists, a play for dogs, a play set in a forest, a pornographic play. These projects were intended to alter our perceptions of what a play should be so that there could then be an innovative "Broadway play using insights gained from performing the nine kinds of plays mentioned above." Volume four's introduction calls for remembering the world in which playwrights live, understanding that "someone is dying the agony of torture in a police state" and that "a cancerous growth is ending life." In his later essay, "AIDS-Involved Drama Syndrome," Hoffman continues this line of thinking, saying "I wasn't thinking of posterity when I wrote *As Is*. I was thinking, 'Wake up, people, wake up!' It woke me up." Throughout his career, Hoffman has expressed that theatre is not just about entertainment or a good story but about variation and connection to political and social realities.

—Nels P. Highberg

HOME, William Douglas

Nationality: British playwright and actor. **Born:** Edinburgh, Scotland, 3 June 1912; son of Charles Cospatrick Archibald, the 13th Earl of Home, and Lilian Lambton Home, daughter of the 4th Earl of Durham; brother of Alec Home, prime minister of the United Kingdom, 1962-63. **Education:** New College, Oxford, B.A. in History 1935; attended Royal Academy of Dramatic Art, 1935-37. **Military Service:** Served in the Royal Armoured Corps, 1940-44; Captain; court-martialed, discharged, and sentenced to one year at hard labor for disobeying orders in World War II. **Family:** Married Rachel Brand on 26 July 1951; three daughters, one son. **Career:** Actor, in stage plays, 1935-60; playwright, from 1937; progressive Independent candidate for Parliament, Cathcart Division, Glasgow, 1942, Windsor Division, Berkshire, 1942, and Clay Cross Division, Derbyshire, 1944. Chairman, Farnham Repertory Theatre Trust, 1971. **Awards:** Playwright of the Year, Variety Club of Great Britain, 1973. **Died:** Winchester, England, of a heart attack, 28 September 1992.

WRITINGS

Stage Plays

Great Possessions (produced London, 1937).
Passing By (produced London, 1940).
Now Barabbas (produced London, 1947). London, Longmans, Green, 1947; included in *The Plays of William Douglas Home,* 1958.
The Chiltern Hundreds (produced London, 1947; as *Yes, M'Lord,* New York, 1949). London and New York, Samuel French, 1949; included in *The Plays of William Douglas Home,* 1958.
Ambassador Extraordinary (produced London, 1948).
The Thistle and the Rose (produced London, 1949). Included in *The Plays of William Douglas Home,* 1958.
Master of Arts (produced Brighton, England, 1949; London, 1949). London and New York, Samuel French, 1950.
The Bad Samaritan (produced Kent, England, 1952; London, 1953). London, Evans Brothers, 1956; included in *The Plays of William Douglas Home,* 1958.
Caro William (produced London, 1952).
The Manor of Northstead (produced London, 1954). London and New York, Samuel French, 1956.
The Reluctant Debutant (produced Brighton, England, 1955; London, 1955; New York, 1956). London, Evans Brothers, 1956; included in *The Plays of William Douglas Home,* 1958.
The Iron Duchess (produced Brighton, England, 1957; London, 1957). London, Evans Brothers, 1958.
The Plays of William Douglas Home (includes *Now Barabbas, The Chiltern Hundreds, The Thistle and the Rose, The Bad Samaritan,* and *The Reluctant Debutante*). London, Heinemann, 1958.

Aunt Edwina (produced Eastbourne, England, 1959; London, 1959). London and New York, Samuel French, 1960.
Up a Gum Tree (produced Ipswich, England, 1960).
The Bad Soldier Smith (produced London, 1961). London, Evans Brothers, 1962.
The Cigarette Girl (produced London, 1962).
The Drawing Room Tragedy (produced Salisbury, England, 1963).
The Reluctant Peer (produced London, 1964). London, Evans Brothers, 1965.
Two Accounts Rendered: The Home Secretary and Lady J.P. (produced London, 1964).
Betzi (produced Salisbury, England, 1965; London, 1975). London and New York, Samuel French, 1977.
A Friend Indeed (produced Windsor, England, 1965; London, 1966). London and New York, Samuel French, 1966.
The Queen's Highland Servant (produced London, 1968).
The Secretary Bird (produced Manchester, England, 1968; London, 1968; Fairfield, Connecticut, 1970). London and New York, Samuel French, 1968.
The Grouse Moor Image (produced London, 1968).
The Jockey Club Stakes (produced London, 1970; New York, 1973). London and New York, Samuel French, 1971.
Uncle Dick's Surprise (produced Salisbury, England, 1970).
The Douglas Cause (produced London, 1971).
Lloyd George Knew My Father (originally produced as *Lady Boothroyd of the By-Pass,* London, 1972; Washington, D.C., 1974). London and New York, Samuel French, 1973.
At the End of the Day (produced London, 1973).
The Dame of Sark (produced London, 1974). London and New York, Samuel French, 1976.
The Lord's Lieutenant (produced Surrey, England, 1974). London and New York, Samuel French, 1978.
In the Red (originally produced as *The Bank Manager,* London, 1975 and 1977). London and New York, Samuel French, 1978.
The Kingfisher (produced London, 1977; New York, 1978). London and New York, Samuel French, 1981.
Rolls Hyphen Royce (produced London, 1977).
The Perch (produced London, 1977).
The Consulting Room (produced London, 1977).
The Editor Regrets (produced London, 1978). London, Evans Plays, 1979.
You're All Right: How Am I? (produced London, 1981).
Four Hearts Doubled (produced London, 1982).
Her Mother Came Too (produced London, 1982).
The Golf Umbrella (produced London, 1983). London, English Theatre Guild, 1984.
David and Jonathan (produced London, 1984).
After the Ball is Over (produced London, 1985). London and New York, Samuel French, 1986.
Portraits (produced London, 1987). London and New York, Samuel French, 1988.
A Christmas Truce (produced London, 1989). London and New York, Samuel French, 1990.

Television Plays

The Bishop and the Actress (BBC, 1968). London and New York, Samuel French, 1969.
The Editor Regrets (BBC, 1970).
On Such a Night (BBC, 1973).

Screenplays

Now Barabbas (adaptation of own play). De Grunwald, 1949.
The Chiltern Hundreds (adaptation of own play). Rank, 1949.
Author of dialogue, The Colditz Story. Republic, 1957.
The Reluctant Debutante (adaptation of own play). Metro-Goldwyn-Mayer, 1958.

Memoirs

Half-Term Report: An Autobiography. London, Longmans, Green, 1954.
Mr. Home Pronounced Hume: An Autobiography. London, Collins, 1979.
Old Men Remember. London, Collins and Brown, 1991.

Other

Home Truths (poetry). London, Lane, 1939.
"The Playwright's Job Is to Write a Good Play, Not a Socially Responsible One" (essay), in *Thalia: Studies in Literary Humor* (Ottawa, Ontario, Canada), fall/winter 1984.
Sins of Commission (letters). London, Michael Russell, 1985.
"The Poor Relation Makes Good" (book review), in *The Spectator* (London), 3 September 1988.
Home and Away (letters/journals). London, Collins and Brown, 1991.

*

Biography: *Will: A Portrait of William Douglas Home* by David Fraser, London, Deutsch, 1995.

Critical Sources: "A Celebration of Friendships" by Jo Grimond, in *The Spectator* (London), Vol. 260, No. 520, 26 October 1991, 30; "The Power of the Individual Will" by Anthony Lambton, in *The Spectator* (London), Vol. 265, No. 736, 16 December 1995, 71.

*   *   *

There seem to be at least two men known as William Douglas Home. First, there is "the king of light comedy," known for numerous plays that depict the lives of aristocratic families on simple yet amusing terms. In 1984, Home wrote an essay, "The Playwright's Job Is to Write a Good Play, Not a Socially Responsible One," where he writes that the purpose of art lies not in politics but in simply telling a good story. There is, however, another William Douglas Home, remembered for his beliefs in individual rights and freedoms, beliefs most clearly expressed in his dishonorable discharge during World War II for disobeying orders. As his friend Jo Grimond wrote in *The Spectator,* "his own good humour and that of his family have made people underestimate him." William Douglas Home is a playwright of interest to gay and lesbian readers not only for his positions on the purpose of literature or his stand on individual liberties, but also for the ways his plays and characters continuously question sexual roles and attitudes.

While overt homosexual themes or fully-defined gay and lesbian characters are never present in Home's work, there are several pieces that question mainstream societal expectations of het-erosexual relationships just as plays in America by Edward Albee and Tennessee Williams were doing in the same general time period. For example, *The Secretary Bird* focuses on a sexually inadequate husband, Hugh Walford, as he tries to secure his relationship with his wife, Liz. Hugh devises a plan that brings together Liz's lover, John, and Hugh's secretary, Molly, in a complicated mating event. The plot unfolds through dialogue laced with sexual innuendo that advances the comedy and amuses the audience. Opening in London in 1968, *The Secretary Bird* became Home's longest-running play. A later play, *The Kingfisher,* features an old bachelor as he attempts to win the hand of a woman who refused him 50 years earlier. After a successful 1978 Broadway run that starred veteran performers Rex Harrison and Claudette Colbert, the play toured the United States and found favor across the country.

Aunt Edwina, an earlier play that highlights sexual transgression more directly, did not find favor as did these other plays, but instead incited protests from London critics; still, Home stood staunchly behind his work to the end. This 1959 comedy tells the story of a mustached, retired military buffer who swallows his horse's hormone pills and "suddenly turned into a woman," as Home's cousin, Anthony Lambton, describes in *The Spectator.* The play has found a position of notoriety within Home's canon both for the aversion expressed by critics and the commitment expressed by Home as he devoted much of his own time and money to keep this comedy running. He even sold his car to keep the play on stage and gave out free tickets at London hotels to increase the audience. After performances, Home would sometimes point to critics in the audience who had panned his work and announce that they were wrong in their assessments. Perhaps the play's critical failure reflects the attitudes of the time, or perhaps, as many critics wrote of *Aunt Edwina* and of other plays by Home from this time period, the playwright had actually hit a dry spell that needed time to resolve. At any rate, Lambton points out, "The play came off after an expensive run but William was happy he had asserted himself."

William Douglas Home is a playwright whose work can certainly be seen differently in a contemporary literary climate. The plays mentioned above, though not overtly gay, can be interpreted in various queer ways for the ways they question relationships and sexuality, ideas that run throughout Home's work as a whole. As another example, one of his first plays, *Now Barabbas,* deals with characters in a men's prison who continuously discuss their wives, girlfriends, and other close relationships. Homosocial situations such as this one in literature, thanks to critics such as Eve Kosofsky Sedgwick, are now being read in ways that highlight the potential for new understandings in a lesbian and gay context. Such analysis and discussion adds to larger debates on the connections between literature and a writer's or reader's lived experience, as well as to extended ponderings on sex and sexuality in general.

—Nels P. Highberg

HUGHES, Holly

Nationality: American performance artist, playwright, painter, and critic. **Born:** 1955 in Saginaw, Michigan; moved to New York City, 1979. **Education:** Kalamazoo College, B.A. in art 1977. **Ca-**

reer: Teacher, Tisch School of the Arts, New York City; teacher, New York University; adjunct professor, Experimental Theatre Wing, New York University; contributor of dramatic works and critical studies, *Drama Review*. **Awards:** Obie award, 1988, 1990; National Endowment for the Arts grant, 1990, 1991; McKnight Fellowship, the Playwright's Center, Minneapolis, Minnesota 1990; Distinguished Alumni Award, Kalamazoo College, 1995. **Address:** Rhode Island School of Design, 2 College St., Providence, Rhode Island 02903-2717, U.S.A.

WRITINGS

Clit Notes: A Sapphic Sampler. New York, Grove Atlantic Press, 1996.
Holding Her Own: The Holly Hughes Story (as Told to Holly Hughes). New York, Grove Atlantic Press, (forthcoming).

Recordings: With Rosalie L. Donlon. *Sexual Harassment: Prevention, Recognition and Correction* (video). Waterford, Connecticut, Prentice Hall, 1995.

*

Interviews: "Holly Hughes Speaks" by Joy Mincey Powell, Minneapolis, Minnesota, London Productions, 1996; "Holly Hughes, Performance Artist" by Rebecca Scheib, in *Utne Reader* (Minneapolis, Minnesota), No. 76, July/August, 1996, 110.

Critical Sources: Review of exhibition by Shellie R. Goldberg, in *ArtNews* (New York), Vol. 86, No. 5, May 1987, 164; "Holly Hughes: Polymorphous Perversity and the Lesbian Scientist" by Rebecca Schneider, in *TDR: The Drama Review* (Cambridge, Massachusetts), Vol. 33, No. 1, spring 1989, 171-183; "Holly Hughes, Playing the Ironies" by Ann Hornaday, in *Ms.* (New York), Vol. 1, No. 3, November/December 1990, 64; "NEA Four Survive a Year of Uproar" by Michael Lassell, in *Advocate* (Los Angeles, California), No. 59, 3 December 1991, 76-78; review of *Clit Notes* by Rob Kendt, in *Back Stage* (New York), Vol. 34, No. 36, 3 September 1993, 11W; review of *Well of Horniness and Clit Notes*, in *Nation* (New York), Vol. 257, No. 8, 20 September 1993, 293; "Holly Hughes: Her Heart Belongs to Daddy" by Laurie Stone, in *Ms.* (New York), Vol. 5, No. 2, September/October, 1994, 88; review of *Clit Notes* by Susan Olcott, in *Library Journal* (New York), Vol. 124, No. 8, 1 May 1996, 94.

*   *   *

Essentially Holly Hughes is a story teller. As a lesbian feminist performance artist, her method of storytelling has often been controversial. Her humor and scathingly sharp perception shape stories that include "Everydyke." Certainly Hughes' past has informed her work. She grew up listening to her father, a jazz musician. And she incorporated what she heard into abstract paintings that mingled geometric and organic shapes in joyous movement. Like her paintings, her plays contain an exuberant movement and marriage of seemingly disparate images. As in jazz, dissonant themes repeat themselves in complex rhythms. In addition, her emigration to join the lesbian experimental theater scene in New York is reflected in her stories. Like her geography, her writing is both brashly playful and satirically sophisticated.

Hughes was drawn to performance art for its freshness, innovation and opportunity. In an interview with Joy Mincey Powell, she said:

> Theater is very intimidating to get into; people think, "I can't do that...I don't have any formal training." Performance art lets in a whole group of folks that normally wouldn't do it. I watch people with training and I think, it would be nice to have some of those skills— and I have studied—but I've stuck with that original idea of having fun.

This sense of openness was fostered by the artists at the Women's One World Cafe (WOW), a lesbian theater group and storefront with whom Hughes worked when she began to do theater in New York, and where she first performed many of her pieces.

Clit Notes: A Sapphic Sampler is a collection of many of her first plays, including *The Well of Horniness, The Lady Dick, World Without End,* and her two Obie award winning pieces, *Dress Suits To Hire,* and *Clit Notes.* The collection also includes an introductory chapter and introductions to each play that are in themselves extremely personal, humorous, and touching. As skillfully written as anything in her plays, the introductions bring the works into the context of the author's life.

Hughes' particular skill lies in her ability to combine satire, silliness, and camp to explore serious issues of late twentieth century American lesbian life as well as to honor that life with all its passion, lust, and contradictions. *Well of Horniness* and *The Lady Dick* are less plays than extended bawdy skits, broad spoofs of film noir that playfully poke at serious themes such as lesbians' mistrust of each other and of bisexual women, butch/femme, and the taboos of women's sexuality. A powerfully written exploration of relationships and the fear and hope that intimacy inspires can be found in *Dress Suits to Hire,* which Hughes wrote for sister WOW Cafe artists, Peggy Shaw and Lois Weaver.

In the collection Hughes has included much of her own life and her intimacy is touching. *World Without End* is a rawly poetic exploration of her mother's death. A sense of the impact of this piece is found in the introduction to the play where Hughes' wrote, "After my mother died...well after my mother died, all of my sentences began with 'after my mother died....'" *Clit Notes* is Hughes' letter to her father. While as lusty and hilarious as the rest of her work, *Clit Notes* is also full of the poignancy and pain of the emerging young lesbian in a straight family in straight American culture. With typical incisiveness and taboo-smashing brashness, Hughes explores her own sexuality, her relationships with her father and mother, and her subsequent attraction to butch lesbians who remind her of her father.

Hughes is perhaps most notorious as one of the "NEA Four," four artists who received grants from the National Endowment for the Arts in 1990. Shortly afterwards the grants were canceled by the NEA on the basis of a clause in the organization's charter requiring that funded art be within "general standards of decency and respect for the diverse beliefs and values of the American public."

Hughes and the other artists of the NEA Four, Karen Finley, John Fleck, and Tim Miller, brought suit against the NEA to have their grants reinstated and to change the wording in the charter, charging that it was too vague and open to political use to abridge the artists' right to freedom of speech. The grants were reinstated, plus damages, but the "decency clause" remains part of the NEA charter. In her conclusion to *Clit Notes: A Sapphic Sampler,* Hughes recounts her experience of being lambasted by right-wing politicians and critics, and calls for her readers not to let their own voices be silenced.

It is not only conservatives who have criticized Hughes' work; she has also received hostile reactions from some members of her lesbian audiences who consider her work pornographic and oppressive to women and who question her identity as a lesbian because she has sometimes related to men. But creating such controversy is obviously the purpose of Hughes' work. She intends to shake up, to titillate, and to agitate. Most of all, she intends to hand herself, her ego, over to the audience with both hands. In the introduction to *Clit Notes: A Sapphic Sampler,* she explains the deeply personal nature of her art this way:

> I want to fill my work with something as clear and necessary as cold water, then I want to give it away. Of course it'll be water from my well, warmed by the heat of my body, and it'll taste like me.

—Tina Gianoulis

HWANG, David Henry

Nationality: American playwright and screenwriter. **Born:** Los Angeles, California, 11 August 1957. **Education:** Harvard Boys School, Hollywood Hills, California; Stanford University, B.A. in English, 1979 (Phi Beta Kappa); attended Padua Hills Writer's Workshop, 1978, and Yale University School of Drama, 1980-81. **Family:** Married Ophelia Y. M. Chong, 21 September 1985; divorced. **Career:** Playwright, director, screenwriter, from 1979; writing instructor in Menlo Park, California, 1979; co-founder, Stanford Asian American Theatre Project; board of directors, Theatre Communications Group, from 1987; board of directors, Dramatists Guild, from 1988; board of trustees, Pitzer College, from 1990; board of directors, P.E.N., from 1990; President's Committee on the Arts and Humanities, from 1994. **Awards:** Drama-Logue Award, 1980, 1983, 1986; Obie Award, for best play, 1981; Drama Desk Award nomination, 1982; CINE Golden Eagle, 1983; Rockefeller playwright in residence award, 1983-84; National Endowment for the Arts fellowship, 1983-84, 1985; New York State Council on the Arts fellowship, 1985; Antoinette Perry ("Tony") Award, 1988; Outer Critics Circle Award, 1988; Drama Desk Award, 1988; John Gassner Award, 1988; Pulitzer Prize nomination, 1989; Guggenheim fellowship. **Agent:** William Craver, Writers and Artists Agency, Inc., 19 West 44th Street, Suite 1000, New York, New York 10036, U.S.A.

Writings

Plays

FOB ("Fresh Off the Boat"; produced Stanford, California, 1979; O'Neill National Playwrights Conference, Waterford, Connecticut, 1979; New York Shakespeare Festival Public Theater, 1980). Included in *FOB and Other Plays,* New York, Plume, 1990.

The Dance and the Railroad (produced Henry Street Settlement's New Federal Theatre, New York, 1981). Included in *FOB and Other Plays,* New York, Plume, 1990.
Family Devotions (produced New York Shakespeare Festival Public Theater, 1981). Included in *FOB and Other Plays,* New York, Plume, 1990.
Sound and Beauty (includes *The House of Sleeping Beauties* and *The Sound of a Voice*; produced New York Shakespeare Festival Public Theatre, 1983). Included in *FOB and Other Plays,* New York, Plume, 1990.
The Dance and the Railroad and Family Devotions. New York, Dramatists Play Service, 1983.
Broken Promises: Four Plays (includes *FOB, The Dance and the Railroad, Family Devotions, The House of Sleeping Beauties*). New York, Avon Books, 1983.
The Sound of a Voice. New York, Dramatists Play Service, 1984.
Rich Relations (produced Second Stage, New York, 1986). Included in *FOB and Other Plays,* New York, Plume, 1990.
As the Crow Flies (produced Los Angeles, 1986).
Broken Promises (includes *The Dance and the Railroad* and *The House of Sleeping Beauties*; produced London, 1987).
M. Butterfly (produced National Theatre, Washington, D.C., 1988; Broadway, 1988; London, 1989). New York, Plume, 1989.
With Philip Glass and Jerome Sirlin, *1000 Airplanes on the Roof* (produced Vienna, 1988; New York, 1988; international tour). Included in *FOB and Other Plays,* New York, Plume, 1990.
FOB and Other Plays. New York, Plume, 1990.
Bondage (produced Actor's Theatre of Louisville, Kentucky, Humana Festival, 1992). New York, Dramatists Play Service, 1996.
Face Value (produced Boston, 1993; revised for Trinity Repertory Theatre, Providence, Rhode Island, 1995).
Trying to Find Chinatown (produced Actor's Theatre of Louisville, Louisville, Kentucky, Humana Festival, 1996). New York, Dramatists Play Service, 1996.

Screenplays

My American Son. Home Box Office, 1987.
M. Butterfly (adaptation of stage play). Geffen Pictures, 1993.
The Dance and the Railroad. Arts and Entertainment Network, 1982.
Also author of *Golden Gate, Possession* (adaptation of A. S. Byatt novel), and *The Idiot* (adaptation of Feodor Dostoevski novel).

Other

"Evolving a Multicultural Tradition," in *Melus,* Vol. 16, No. 3, fall 1989-1990.
With Philip Glass, *The Voyage* (libretto; produced Metropolitan Opera, New York, 1992).
"Facing the Mirror," in *The State of Asian America: Activism and Resistance in the 1990s,* edited by Karin Aguilar-San Juan. Boston, Massachusetts, South End Press, 1994.

*

Interviews: "*M. Butterfly*: An Interview with David Henry Hwang" by John Louis DiGaetani, in *TDR,* Vol. 33, fall 1989, 141-153; "David Henry Hwang," in *The Playwright's Art: Conversations* with *Contemporary Dramatists,* edited by Jackson R. Bryer, New Brunswick, New Jersey, Rutgers University Press, 1995.

Critical Sources: "American Theater Watch, 1987-1988" by Gerald Weales, in *Georgia Review,* Vol. 42, fall 1988, 592-593; "Viewpoint," in *High Performance,* spring 1989, 50-51; "David Henry Hwang's *M. Butterfly* and Philip Kan Gotanda's *Yankee Dawg You Die*: Repositioning Chinese American Marginality on the American Stage" by James S. Moy, in *Theatre Journal,* Vol. 42, No. 1, March 1990, 48-56; "Breaking the Butterfly: The Politics of David Henry Hwang" by Robert Skloot, in *Modern Drama,* Vol. 33, No. 1, March 1990, 60-66; "*M. Butterfly*: Orientalism, Gender, and a Critique of Essentialist Identity" by Dorrine K. Kondo, in *Cultural Critique,* No. 16, 1990, 5-23; "Performative Acts and Gender Construction: An Essay in Phenomenology and Feminist Theory" by Judith Butler, in *Performing Feminisms: Feminist Critical Theory and Theatre,* edited by Sue-Ellen Case, Baltimore, Maryland, John Hopkins University Press, 1990; "Looking for My Penis" by Richard Fung, in *How Do I Look?: Queer Film and Video,* edited by Bad Object-Choices, Seattle, Washington, Bay Press, 1991, 145-169; "The Occidental Tourist: *M. Butterfly* and the Scandal of Transvestism," in *Nationalisms and Sexualities,* edited by A. Parker et al, New York, Routledge, 1992, 133-134; "Glass Plus" by K. Robert Schwarz and "Hwang's World" by Robert Marx, in *Opera News,* October 1992, 10-12, 13-17; "Face Values: The Sexual and Racial Obsessions of David Henry Hwang" by Dinitia Smith, in *New York,* 11 January 1993, 40-45; "'Who's to Say?': Or, Making Space for Gender and Ethnicity in *M. Butterfly*" by Karen Shimakawa, in *Theatre Journal,* Vol. 45, No. 3, October 1993, 349-362; "Of Monkeys and Butterflies: Transformation in M. H. Kingston's *Tripmaster Monkey* and D. H. Hwang's *M. Butterfly*" by John J. Deeney, in *Melus,* Vol. 18, No. 4, winter 1993, 21-39; "The Theatre of Punishment: David Henry Hwang's *M. Butterfly* and Michel Foucault's *Discipline and Punish*" by Kathryn Remen, in *Modern Drama,* Vol. 37, No. 3, fall 1994, 391-400; "William M. Abramowitz Guest Lecture, Massachusetts Institute of Technology" by David Henry Hwang, http://www.mit.edu:8001/afs/athena/user/i/r/irie/www/hdhwang.txt.

*   *   *

Although all of his work examines stereotypes and the powerful ways in which stereotypes are used to continue prejudices and to keep power in place, it is David Henry Hwang's *M. Butterfly* which most directly looks at sexual issues and power issues in ways that are informative to the lesbian, gay, bisexual, and transgender (l/g/b/t) communities. As Gerald Weales notes in the *Georgia Review,* the play was inspired by an incident in which a French diplomat was accused of treason because of his affair with a Chinese opera singer who was a spy. The diplomat claimed that he did not know that his lover was a man. In his imaginative rendering of the incident, Hwang refers to Puccini's opera *Madama Butterfly* to explore the political ramifications of gender and the balances of power between men and women, and between Eastern and Western politics and cultures. In the opera, Butterfly—a woman married to, subservient to, and faithful to the western husband who has deserted her—commits Japanese ritual suicide at the end of the opera, mourning for her lost love. *M. Butterfly* reverses and explores these attitudes in interesting ways, showing the constructed nature of sexuality and attitudes toward gender

politics as, at the close of the play, the diplomat himself takes on the role of Butterfly. As Robert Skloot discusses in *Modern Drama,* "*M. Butterfly* announces the subversion of Puccini's opera while at the same time altering and expanding its gender reference."

M. Butterfly is not a play about homosexuality, but rather about expectations and illusions and the constructions of power that these so often mask. As Hwang notes in an interview with John DiGaetani in *TDR,* "The lines between gay and straight become very blurred in this play, but I think he knows he's having an affair with a man. Therefore, on some level he is gay." Hwang goes on to note, however, that perception and desire to believe the illusion one holds close is very strong:

> If you choose to believe you're heterosexual, then that's your prerogative, to believe in that fantasy. I think this would apply today to people in Chinese, Italian, Spanish, and some other Latin cultures. People in these cultures believe that if you have sex with a man and you do the screwing, you are not gay, but if you're screwed, you're gay.... Gallimard chooses to believe he is heterosexual.

What is so important to, and so telling for, l/g/b/t literature is the constructed nature of social "norms" and mores and political power. Dorrine Kondo points out in her discussion of *M. Butterfly* in *Cultural Critique* that "Asia is gendered, but gender is not understandable without the figurations of race and power that inscribe it." As *How Do I Look?* contributor David Fung discusses in "Looking for My Penis," in the Western imagination, Asian women have been viewed as sexually available and Asian men have been desexed, being either feminized in one of the roles assigned to women, or conceived of as asexual, while masculinity and penetration have been associated with "white" skin and a European background. As Karen Shimakawa indicates in her *Theatre Journal* essay, though, in *M. Butterfly* "both Song and Gallimard move between the seeming poles of male and female genders revealing, in Judith Butler's terms, the *performativity of gender.*"

What this means is that gender expectations, like racism, sexism, and classism, are socially and politically constructed and can therefore be deconstructed and reconstructed. Robert Skloot notes that "we usually behave the way we do because it has been culturally imagined for us already," but, as Kathryn Remen notes in *Modern Drama,* "power is not fixed,...resistance is mobile, and...the rules can and do change." Karen Shimakawa writes that both Song, and at the end of the play, Gallimard, destabilize the existing categories of gender because their gender performances do not meet Western expectations. Such destabilizing of gender identities and reconstruction of varying expectations about gender, sex, race, and class must occur for acceptance of l/g/b/t peoples to increase and for racism to diminish.

All of Hwang's work is an attempt to create a more equitable world. Speaking as Abramowitz Guest Lecturer at the Massachusetts Institute of Technology, Hwang noted that he thinks "it is important to envision futures which are more just and inviting." His early work was concerned with Asian American experience, but his later work has evolved to include a broader spectrum of race relations, prejudices, and power, and what constitutes authenticity of experience. *Face Value* and *Trying to Find Chinatown* both examine expectations of race and culture, and the ways in which these are changing with increasingly mixed and diverse populations. As Hwang notes in "Facing the Mirror," "definitions of race are meaningless, except as a reaction to the meaningless racism of society as a whole."

Bondage illustrates Kondo's statement that "neither race nor gender can be accorded some a priori primacy over the other." The depth of the inter-relatedness of racial and gender constructions is explored in this play. As Hwang notes in an interview with Jackson Bryer in *The Playwright's Art,* "It's too simplistic to say we are all the same and there are no cultural differences at all.... [W]e come from different backgrounds, but the essential universal humanity is ultimately something you can get to from having acknowledged these differences." Also of particular interest to l/g/b/t readers are Hwang's *1000 Airplanes on the Roof,* an exploration of extra-terrestrialism, and the libretto for the opera *The Voyage,* in which the desire for exploration and the subject-in-becoming is explored. As Robert Marx notes in *Opera Notes,* Hwang's recurring themes are explored in this opera: "All that we seek to know / is to know ourselves / To reduce the darkness / By some small degree."

—Patti Capel Swartz

I-J

INGE, William (Motter)

Nationality: American playwright, screenwriter, and novelist. **Born:** Independence, Kansas, 3 May 1913. **Education:** Montgomery County High School, Independence, graduated 1930; University of Kansas, Lawrence, 1930-35, A.B. 1935; Peabody Teachers College, Nashville, Tennessee, 1935-37, M.A. 1938. **Career:** Announcer, radio station KFH, Wichita, Kansas, 1936-37; teacher, Columbus High School, Kansas, 1937-38, Stephens College, Columbia, Missouri, 1938-43, and Washington University, St. Louis, Missouri, 1946-49; humanities critic, *St. Louis Star Times,* 1943-46; lecturer, University of California, Irvine, 1968-69. **Awards:** George Jean Nathan Award, 1951; Pulitzer Prize, 1953; New York Drama Critics Circle Award, 1953; Donaldson Award, 1953; Outer Circle Award, 1953; Motion Picture Academy of Arts and Sciences Award, 1962. **Died:** Committed suicide by carbon monoxide poisoning, in Los Angeles, California, 10 June 1973.

WRITINGS

Full-length Plays

Come Back, Little Sheba (produced Broadway, 1950). New York, Random House, 1950.
Picnic (produced Broadway, 1953). New York, Random House, 1953.
Bus Stop (produced Broadway, 1955). New York, Random House, 1955.
The Dark at the Top of the Stairs (as *Farther Off from Heaven,* produced Dallas, 1947; produced in revised version as *The Dark at the Top of the Stairs,* Broadway, 1957). New York, Random House, 1958.
A Loss of Roses (produced Broadway, 1959). New York, Random House, 1960.
Natural Affection (produced Broadway, 1963). New York, Random House, 1963.
Where's Daddy? (produced Broadway, 1966). New York, Random House, 1966.
Summer Brave (produced Off Broadway, 1973). Included in *Summer Brave and Eleven Short Plays,* 1962.
Four Plays by William Inge (includes *Come Back, Little Sheba, Picnic, Bus Stop,* and *The Dark at the Top of the Stairs*). New York, Random House, 1958; London, Heinemann, 1960.

Shorter Plays

Glory in the Flower. Included in *Twenty-Four Favorite One-Act Plays,* edited by Bennett Cerf and Van H. Cartmell, New York, Doubleday, 1958.
Summer Brave and Eleven Short Plays" (includes "Summer Brave," "The Boy in the Basement," "Riley's Back in Town," "An Incident at the Standish Arms," "The Mail," "Memory of Summer," "People in the Wind," "The Rainy Afternoon," "A Social Event," "The Strains of Triumph," "The Tiny Closet," and "To Bobolink, for Her Spirit"). New York, Random House, 1962.
Caesarian Operation (produced Los Angeles, 1963).

Two Short Plays (includes *The Call* and *A Murder*). New York, Dramatists Play Service, 1968.
Midwestern Manic. Included in *Best Short Plays, 1969,* edited by Stanley Richards, Philadelphia, Chilton, 1969.
The Disposal (produced as *The Last Pad,* Off Broadway, 1970). Included in *Best Short Plays of the World Theatre, 1958-1967,* edited by Stanley Richards, New York, Crown, 1968.
Margaret's Bed. Included in *Best Short Plays of the World Theatre, 1968-1973,* edited by Stanley Richards, New York, Crown, 1973.
Overnight (produced Off Broadway, 1974).
The Love Death (produced Off Broadway, 1975). Published in *Studies in American Drama, 1945-Present,* Vol. 5, Columbus, Ohio State University Press, 1990, 12-22.

Screenplays

Splendor in the Grass. Warner Brothers, 1961; New York, Bantam, 1961.
All Fall Down. Metro-Goldwyn-Mayer, 1962.

Novels

Good Luck, Miss Wykoff. Boston, Little, Brown, 1970; London, Deutsch, 1971.
My Son Is a Splendid Driver. Boston, Little, Brown, 1971.

Other

"More on the Playwright's Mission," in *Theatre Arts,* Vol. 42, No. 8, August 1958, 19.
Out on the Outskirts of Town. NBC-TV, 1964.
"The Taste of Success" and "The Schizophrenic Wonder," in *American Playwrights on Drama,* edited by Horst Frenz. New York, Hill and Wang, 1965.

*

Manuscript Collections: Humanities Research Center, University of Texas, Austin; Independence Community College, Kansas; University of Kansas, Lawrence.

Biography: *William Inge* by R. Baird Shuman, New York, Twayne, 1966, revised, 1989; *A Life of William Inge: The Strains of Triumph* by Ralph F. Voss, Lawrence, University Press of Kansas, 1989.

Interviews: "William Inge" by Roy Newquist, in *Counterpoint,* New York, Simon & Schuster, 1964; "William Inge" by Walter Wager, in *The Playwrights Speak: Interviews with 11 Playwrights,* New York, Delacorte, 1967; "Interview with William Inge" by Digby Diehl, in *Behind the Scenes: Theatre and Film Interviews from the Transatlantic Review,* edited by Joseph McCrindle, New York, Holt Rinehart, & Winston, 1971; "William Inge: The Last Interview" by Lloyd Steele, in *Los Angeles Free Press,* 22 June 1973, 18-22.

Bibliography: *William Inge: A Bibliography* by Arthur F. McClure, New York, Garland, 1982; *A Bibliographical Guide to* *the Works of William Inge* by Arthur F. McClure and C. David Rice, New York, Edwin Mellon, 1991; *William Inge: A Research and Production Sourcebook* by Richard M. Lesson, Westport, Greenwood Press, 1994.

Critical Sources: "The Men-Taming Women of William Inge" by Robert Brustein, in *Seasons of Discontent: Dramatic Opinions 1959-1965,* New York, Simon & Schuster, 1965; "William Inge: 'Homosexual Spite' in Action," in *Like a Brother, like a Lover: Male Homosexuality in the American Novel and Theatre from Herman Melville to James Baldwin* by Georges-Michel Sarotte, translated by Richard Miller, Garden City, Anchor Press/ Doubleday, 1978; "William Inge" by Marten Reilingh, in *American Playwrights Since 1945: A Guide to Scholarship, Criticism, and Performance,* edited by Philip C. Kolin, New York, Greenwood, 1989.

*   *   *

For the student of gay and lesbian literature, examining the work of William Inge is a fascinating, if ultimately frustrating, experience. In his major plays, Inge writes eloquently of the human condition, particularly of repression, loneliness, and compromise. In these dramas, however, there are only veiled allusions to homosexuality, unlike the frequent gay themes in his later work, when his powers had noticeably declined.

With the successful Broadway run of *The Dark at the Top of the Stairs* in 1957-58, Inge as playwright reached a level of critical and popular success matched at the time only by his friend Tennessee Williams. Like Inge's three previous plays—*Picnic, Bus Stop,* and *Come Back, Little Sheba*—*The Dark at the Top of the Stairs* chronicles with great psychological insight the longings and frustrations, particularly sexual, of ordinary women and men playing out their lives in small American towns. As R. Baird Shuman writes in *William Inge,* "Inge was most successful in portraying people of the lower middle class, and he is most convincing when he puts them in the Midwest of the twenties...From 1950 until 1958 [he] rode the crest of a wave that seemed to have no downward trough, a truly remarkable feat."

Although there are no overtly homosexual characters in this quartet of plays, Inge's recurring depiction of an almost stereotypically virile male is worth noting: the bodybuilding milkman as well as the young boyfriend Turk, who poses naked for artists, in *Come Back, Little Sheba;* Hank, whose sexual magnetism wreaks havoc in *Picnic;* Bo, the cowboy in *Bus Stop,* "who wears faded jeans that cling to his legs like shedding skin"; and even Ruben, the philandering father in *The Dark at the Top of the Stairs,* who dresses in western clothes and who, we are told, is "still robust." These characters foreshadow the young men of several of Inge's later works, whose sexuality is often less ambiguous and who are frequently the focus of the attention of older, clearly gay men.

Except for his Academy Award-winning screenplay for *Splendor in the Grass,* Inge's work in the 1960s never achieved the commercial or critical success it had earlier enjoyed. In several of his plays produced in this period, however, a variety of gay relationships are depicted: Tom and Pinky in *Where's Daddy;* Vince and Bernie in *Natural Affection;* and Joker and Spencer (Inge's most "out" gay character) in *The Boy in the Basement,* a one-act play written a decade earlier but not published until 1962.

My Son Is a Splendid Driver, a novel written in 1971, contains a scene that is illustrative of the reticence and ineffectiveness inherent in Inge's gay writing. Structured in the form of a memoir (and reputedly based closely on Inge's own experiences), the novel relates the life of a middle-aged teacher looking back on his early years in Kansas. Almost casually, the narrator recollects an aborted and never-discussed bedroom encounter with his college roommate. The intensity of the narrator's memory of this episode, described in detail, implies a significance for him that warrants further exploration. Instead, Inge writes, "I never asked myself if I was rejecting a love that I might need or enjoy. I never dared tell myself that the possibility of any kind of sexual love could have existed between us. I'll never know whether it could have." The ambiguity of the narrator's feelings on this subject, never again mentioned, is confusing rather than illuminating, and the reader is left with a sense of frustration at Inge's tentative opening and abrupt closing of the closet door.

Inge's difficulty with gay themes is doubtless the result of a variety of factors, including the rigid mores of his time and probably his own personal demons (never comfortable with his homosexuality, he also experienced years of depression and active alcoholism and eventually committed suicide). As a major playwright of mid-twentieth century America, however, he has left a considerable legacy. As his biographer, Ralph F. Voss, writes in *A Life of William Inge,* "ultimately the themes, characters, and conflicts that are found in his works are universal."

—David Garnes

JACOB, Max

Pseudonym: Also known as Cyprien Max Jacob; also wrote as Léon David and Morven le Gaélique. **Nationality:** French poet, painter, critic, and writer. **Born:** Quimper, 12 July 1876. **Education:** La Tour d'Auvergne high school, Quimper, 1887-94 (placed eighth in national Philosophy competition; with a schoolmate, founded two literary reviews presenting their own writing); École Coloniale, Paris, 1894-97; University of Paris, 1894-98, Law degree 1898. **Military Service:** Briefly in 1897; discharged as unsuitable after six weeks. **Family:** Companion of Maurice Sachs and of a man calling himself Sinclair. **Career:** Art critic (as Léon David), for *Le Moniteur des Arts* (later *La Revue d'Art*), 1898-00; held various short-term jobs, including attorney's assistant, secretary, private tutor, and sales-clerk, 1902-07; self-supporting writer and painter, from 1902. **Awards:** Named Chevalier de la Légion d'honneur, 1932; Society of Friends of Max Jacob founded, 1949; Max Jacob Poetry Prize established 1951; Max Jacob Research Centre created, University of St.-Etienne, 1977; pictured on a French postage stamp, 1976; included by the French government in "Célébrations nationales," 1994; streets in St.-Benoît-sur-Loire and in Paris, and high-school in Quimper, named for him. **Died:** In a transit prison at Drancy, near Paris, of bronchial pneumonia, 5 March 1944; train carrying deportees left Drancy two days later for death-camp at Auschwitz.

WRITINGS

Poetry

La Côte. Paris, self-published, 1911; Paris, Crès, 1927.

Les Oeuvres burlesques et mystiques du frère Matorel, illustrated by Derain. Paris, Kahnweiler, 1912.

Le Cornet à dés. Paris, self-published, 1917; Paris, Gallimard, 1945; as *Selected prose poems-Max Jacob,* edited by Michael Brownstein, various translators, New York, SUN, 1979.

La Défense de Tartufe. Paris, Société littéraire de France, 1918; Paris, Gallimard, 1964.

Le Laboratoire central. Paris, Au Sans-Pareil, 1921; Paris, Gallimard, 1960.

Visions infernales. Paris, Gallimard, 1924.

Les Pénitents en maillot rose. Paris, Kra, 1925.

Fond de l'eau. Toulouse, Editions de l'Horloge, 1927.

Sacrifice impérial. Paris, Emile-Paul, 1929.

Rivage. Paris, Les Cahiers Libres, 1931.

Ballades. Paris, Debresse, 1938.

"Ballade de la visite nocturne," in *Le Point,* 14 April 1938, 81-82; in *Ballades,* Gallimard, 1970; as "Ballad of the night visitor," translated by William Kulik, in *The American Poetry Review* (Philadelphia), March-April 1994, 3-4.

Poèmes de Morven le Gaélique (posthumous). Paris, Gallimard, 1953, 1991.

Ballades (collection of six previous works). Paris, Gallimard, 1970.

Poèmes épars - Le Cornet à dés II (une suite). Paris, Orphée/La Différence, 1994.

Actualités éternelles. Paris, La Différence, 1996.

Fiction

Histoire du roi Kaboul 1er et du marmiton Gauwain (children's story). Paris, Picard et Kahn, 1903; Paris, Gallimard, 1971; as *The Story of King Kabul the First and Gawain the Kitchen-Boy,* translated by Moishe Black and Maria Green, Lincoln, Nebraska, University of Nebraska Press, 1991.

Saint-Matorel (novel), illustrated by Pablo Picasso. Paris, Kahnweiler, 1911.

Le Phanérogame (novel). Paris, self-published, 1918.

Cinématoma (collection of narratives). Paris, La Sirène, 1920; Paris, Gallimard, 1929.

Le roi de Béotie (tales and a real-life narrative). Paris, Gallimard, 1921, 1971.

Le Cabinet noir (fictional letters). Paris, Gallimard, 1922; with additions, Gallimard, 1968.

Filibuth (novel). Paris, Gallimard, 1922, 1994.

Le Terrain Bouchaballe (novel). Paris, Emile-Paul, 1923; Paris, Gallimard, 1964.

L'Homme de chair et l'homme reflet (novel). Paris, Gallimard, 1924.

Letters

Correspondance, 2 Vols., edited by François Garnier. Paris, Editions de Paris, Vol. 1, 1953, Vol. 2, 1955.

"Lettres à Marcel Béalu," in *Dernier visage de Max Jacob* by Marcel Béalu. Paris and Lyon, Vitte, 1959.

Lettres à Liane de Pougy (Princess Ghika). Paris, Plon, 1980.

Lettres à un ami (Jean Grenier). Cognac, France, Le Temps qu'il fait, 1988.

Les Propos et les jours, lettres 1904-1944, edited by A. Marcoux and D. Gompel-Netter. Paris, Zodiaque, 1989.

Other

Le Siège de Jérusalem, illustrated by Picasso (play). Paris, Kahnweiler, 1914.

Art poétique (literary theory). Paris, Emile-Paul, 1922; Paris, L'Elocoquent, 1988.

Isabelle et Pantalon, with music by Roland-Manuel (text of an operetta). Paris, Heugel, 1922.

Tableau de la Bourgeoisie, illustrated by Jacob (essay). Paris, Gallimard, 1929.

Conseils à un jeune poète (literary theory). Paris, Gallimard, 1945, 1980; as *Advice to a Young Poet,* translated and edited by John Adlard, London, Ménard Press, 1976.

Méditations and *Méditations religieuses* (religious meditations). Paris, la Table Ronde, 1945; Paris, Gallimard, 1946, 1972; Quimper, Calligrammes, 1982.

Le Miroir d'Astrologie (prose portraits based on astrology). Paris, Gallimard, 1949.

Anthologies

Cahiers Max Jacob, 5 Vols., (journal featuring unpublished pieces by Jacob). Paris, Les Amis de Max Jacob, 1951-61.

Hesitant Fire: Selected Prose of Max Jacob, translated and edited by Moishe Black and Maria Green. Lincoln, Nebraska, and London, University of Nebraska Press, 1991.

L'Echelle de Jacob, edited by N. and J.-E. Cruz (prose and poetry). Paris, Bibliothèque des Arts, 1994.

*

Manuscript Collections: Municipal libraries of Orléans and Quimper, France; Jacques Doucet library, Paris.

Biography: *Alias* by Maurice Sachs, Paris, Gallimard, 1935, 1976; *Max Jacob quotidien,* edited by André Peyre, Paris, José Millas-Martin, 1976; *Max Jacob* by Lina Lachgar, Paris, H. Veyrier, 1981; *Vie et mort de Max Jacob* by Pierre Andreu, Paris, La Table Ronde, 1982.

Bibliography: *Bibliographie et documentation sur Max Jacob* by Maria Green, Paris, Les Amis de Max Jacob, 1988; *Bibliographie des poèmes de Max Jacob parus en revue* by Maria Green and Christine Andreucci, St.-Etienne, France, Université de St.-Etienne, 1991; *Max Jacob et Picasso,* Paris, Réunion des Musées Nationaux, 1994.

Critical Sources: "Sur Max Jacob" by Sinclair, in *Arcadie* (Paris), Vol. 102, 1969, 573-77; *Max Jacob and the Poetics of Cubism* by Gerald Kamber, Baltimore, The Johns Hopkins Press, 1971; *La Revue des Lettres Modernes* (Paris), 1973, 336-39, 1976, 474-78, and 1981, 621-26; "Concealment and Presence—Concealed Emotions in the Poetry of Max Jacob" by Neil Oxenhandler, in *Dada-Surrealism,* Vol. 5, 1975, 53-7; *L'Univers poétique de Max Jacob* by René Plantier, Paris, Klincksieck, 1977; *Clown at the Altar: The Religious Poetry of Max Jacob* by Judith Morgenroth Schneider, Chapel Hill, University of North Carolina, 1978; *Centre de Recherches Max Jacob* (St.-Etienne, France), Vols. 1-10, 1978-87; *The Play of the Text: Max Jacob's Le Cornet à dés* by Sidney Lévy, with selected poems translated by Judith Morgenroth Schneider, Madison, University of Wisconsin Press, 1981; "(Cyprien) Max Jacob," in *Twentieth Century Literary Criticism,* edited by Sharon K. Hall, Vol. 6, Detroit, Gale Research Co., 1982, 189-204; "Présence et tentation du théâtre dans l'oeuvre de Max Jacob" by Hélène Henry, in *Qui (ne) connaît (pas) Max Jacob?,*

Vannes, France, Université du 3e Age et Pour Tous, 1987; *Max Jacob, acrobate absolu* by Christine Van Rogger-Andreucci, Seyssel, France, Champ Vallon, 1993; *Poésie et religion dans l'oeuvre de Max Jacob* by C. Van Rogger-Andreucci, Paris, Champion, 1994; "*Le Cornet à dés*: Au-delà et par delà" by Christian Pelletier, in *Max Jacob, poète et romancier*, Pau, France, University of Pau, 1995, 143-46; *Looking for Heroes in Postwar France: Albert Camus, Max Jacob, Simone Weil* by Neil Oxenhandler, Hanover and London, University Press of New England, 1996.

*   *   *

"There is not just one Max Jacob and you very soon find yourself contending with a number of Max Jacobs," said researcher Hélène Henry, introducing a lecture. "I realize that no man is all of one piece, but Max was a real Proteus," wrote Max's former love-partner Sinclair in the review *Arcadie*, evoking the sea-god who could change form at will. Jacob would have approved both assessments; he claimed in *Le Miroir d'astrologie* that people born, as he was, under the sign of Cancer "don't have a distinct personality; they have a whole bundle of personalities which they assume as need or occasion arises."

Jacob's many faces reinforce and oppose one another. Yet all of them mask his libido, for avowed homosexuality was not acceptable in his generation. (The frankness of André Gide is an exception.) After his death, Jacob was revered variously as poet, Christian, or victim, so that commentators hesitated to "deflower the saints"—so André Peyre puts it in *Max Jacob quotidien*—and in a Max Jacob symposium as late as 1994 it took courage for Christian Pelletier to use the h-word: "From a literary standpoint, Max Jacob's homosexuality is discreet.... Clear references are few."

Discreet, but very much there, once you know, mainly from outside sources. Wrote Sinclair: "It's not easy to talk about a man who's become famous, when for you he was simply a man, a friend, a lover." From a reminiscence, in Peyre's book, by someone who did not succumb, writer and former Orléans mayor R. Secrétain: at their first meeting, "the affection Max showed, which was definitely equivocal, awoke an irresistible stirring in my secret flesh." Or from a wickedly brilliant fictional portrait in the novel *Alias* by another former sexual partner, Maurice Sachs: "He would make love in the evening, go to confession in the morning, take communion, paint, make love, and start over again."

The real Jacob did paint, but he was first and last a poet. To earn that title, one must "suffer much in many ways," he wrote to Marcel Béalu; he himself repeatedly chose poverty, discomfort, and severe artistic self-discipline. And a poet he became; today he is given equal credit with his friend Apollinaire for helping French poetry break from the past, from Symbolism notably, and move into a modernist mode. Jacob wanted poetry to be an "invented dream"—dreams suggest the free association of ideas prized by the moderns, invention the will to shape that association, to select and create.

But this poet often wrote in prose; his best known book, *Le Cornet à dés* (*The Dice Cup*), is a collection featuring the prose poem, a genre he claimed to have invented. Its hallmark is the juxtaposing of unlikely images, with a humorous whimsy that somehow heightens the experience: "Struck by a thunderbolt, the archangel had barely time to loosen his tie." The whimsy extends to wordplay, even outrageous puns, harnessed to the service of poetry: the Sacré-Coeur basilica brings out its artillery to "canonize Paris."

Jacob's poems have an occasional sexually indicative flash. From *The Dice Cup*: "His arms with their whiteness became my whole horizon." But "ses bras" can mean "her arms" or "his arms"; you have to know. In *Le Cornet à dés II*, a collection compiled by others, is the poem "Irregular": "Sodom. The statue of salt has a sign saying Wrong Way!" Clear enough, but it need not refer to the poet. As for a tender love poem, "Ballad of the Night Visitor," it first appeared in an obscure journal and the loved one is disguised as "she."

Max Jacob's prose fiction was not given serious consideration until long after his death. Noteworthy are *Le Terrain Bouchaballe*, a satirical novel of small-town politics, and a collection of imaginary letters called *Le Cabinet noir*. Rare are the explicit homosexual references. One can only speculate as to whether Jacob's sufferings in that respect—rejection by self or family, ill-repressed longings—heightened an exceptional capacity for getting into the skin of each character in turn, in order to express, with words only that person could possibly have uttered, his or her dignity, secret wishes, and frustrations. A frightened unwed mother, a down-and-outer dying in hospital, are made not loveable but very real.

Jacob also wrote for children. His first published volume, *The Story of King Kabul*, served for some years as a book-prize in French schools. He is at his most impressive when writing literary theory in poetic prose: "A giant egg goes slowly down inside me, deep, deep down, and as it goes down it forces up a rising flood of lyric sparks. The sparks are words, word associations," he writes in *Advice to a Young Poet*. A facet of Max Jacob's life that helped create a legend around him was his devotion to younger writers. Legion are those whose early scribblings he read, whom he encouraged to find their individual "pearl," among them André Malraux and the poet Louis Aragon. When these budding talents were not close by, he exchanged innumerable letters with them: with poet René Guy Cadou, even a few with Albert Camus. As of 1996, 26 volumes of his correspondence had been edited and published, with more to come. They afford glimpses of early twentieth-century literary and artistic figures, glimpses into Jacob's theories, his life, and his emotional drives. When he wrote to teacher and critic Jean Grenier, "Some people insist on seeing [homosexuality] as extreme coarseness, others on the contrary as angelic asexuality. I think it's a mixture of the two," he was supposedly discussing Proust, but surely thinking of himself as well. Of interest here are also his friendship and correspondence with lesbian writers Liane de Pougy (Princess Ghika), Natalie Barney, and Gertrude Stein.

Another "contradiction": the poet who wrote in prose lived mainly by the paintbrush. His watercolors, gouaches, and drawings sold well. There have been exhibitions of his work from 1919 onward, including one at the fine-arts museum of Orléans in 1994. Circus scenes, religious and classical subjects, the latter showing more interest in the male than in the female body. His connections with artists, too, form a part of the Max Jacob legend; Modigliani and Braque were his friends, Cocteau and Chagall did drawings of him, Derain and Juan Gris illustrated early editions of his books, and for many months he shared his lodgings with young Pablo Picasso, who had arrived from Spain two years earlier.

Another subject of Jacob's art was his beloved native Brittany. He set stories there, painted the people, captured on paper the way they spoke French, and published a book of pseudo-Breton poems, *La Côte*, "translated" by him. Brittany has always had fervent Catholics and Jacob, in his odd way, was as fervent as any. If poetry is one of the constants in his life, Catholicism is the other. He came to it after two experiences in which, he believed, he saw Christ on the wall of his shabby rented room. "My flesh fell away! I was stripped naked by a bolt of lightning!" we read in *La Défense de Tartufe*. The *Quid* desk encyclopedia lists his among notable religious conversions.

It is in relation to his Catholic beliefs that Max Jacob's homosexuality is most apparent. The Church was far from accepting same-sex orientation, and Jacob far from accepting it in himself but unable to conquer it; indeed his appetite was voracious! Through his poetry, his religious meditations, his letters, and some of his fictional character portraits runs a strong sense of guilt and a yearning to be cleansed. Words such as "sin" or "purity," with a strong awareness of "Satan," typically refer to his own tormented sexuality, and make sense of many writings...once you know.

For explicit statements of this conflict, we are again forced outside the strictly literary works: "This winter I had a terrible experience; I was stricken by a passion which the Church condemns, [caught] between a love that twisted and tore at me till I was reduced to tears and being thrice refused absolution, so that all I could think about was death, since I did not have the right to think about suicide." His confidant on this occasion was a woman who might understand, fellow homosexual Princess Ghika.

Jacob's religious zeal prompted his attempts to convert literally everyone whose path he crossed, and, further contributing to the Max Jacob legend, inspired two sojourns, one of seven years' duration, one of eight, at St.-Benoît-sur-Loire, praying daily in the cold basilica there. St.-Benoît was his attempt to escape the "temptations" of Paris, including homosexual temptations. Instead, the Paris literati—Paul Claudel, Paul Eluard—came to him.

There was a mystic side to Max Jacob's religion, and it took strange forms—an abiding belief in astrology (he kept files of personality traits and vocabulary tics organized by zodiacal signs, and constructed the characters in his books on that basis) and a fascination with Kabala. Last of the many faces, this very Catholic Breton was Jewish, Jewish in his one-to-one dialogues with God, in his genuine humility, in his self-deprecatory sense of humor. "Lucky toad," he apostrophized a wee amphibian in the street (*Derniers poèmes*), "you don't have a yellow star." For a Jew, not a Catholic, was what the Nazi occupant saw, branded (with a star of David), and deported. The lucky toad died before he reached the gas-camps, and a poet-martyr was born.

—Moishe Black and Maria Green

———

JAMES, Mary. *See* **MEAKER, Marijane.**

———

JEWETT, Sarah Orne

Pseudonym: Also wrote as A. C. Eliot. **Nationality:** American author of fiction, short stories, and essays. **Born:** South Berwick, Maine, 3 September 1849. **Education:** Miss Raynes School;

Berwick Academy, graduated 1865. **Family:** Companion of Kate Birckhead, Harriet Waters Preston, and of Annie Fields for 30 years. **Career:** Writer, from 1868 to the early 1900s; regular contributor to periodicals, including *Atlantic Monthly, Century Magazine, Cosmopolitan Magazine, Harper's Bazaar, Harper's Magazine, The Independent, Riverside Companion for Young People, Riverside Magazine, St. Nicholas, Sunday Afternoon,* and *Youth's Companion.* Elected to the Maine Historical Society, 1903; Trustee, Maine Society for the Prevention of Cruelty to Animals, 1908. **Awards:** L.H.D.: Bowdoin College, 1901. **Died:** South Berwick, Maine, of a stroke, 24 June 1909.

Writings

Novels

Deephaven. Boston, James R. Osgood and Co., 1877; South Berwick, Maine, Old Berwick Historical Society, 1993.
A Country Doctor. Boston and New York, Houghton Mifflin and Company, 1884.
A Marsh Island. Boston and New York, Houghton Mifflin and Company, 1885.
Betty Leicester: A Story for Girls. Boston and New York, Houghton Mifflin and Company, 1890.
Betty Leicester's English Xmas, A New Chapter of an Old Story. New York, Dodd, Mead, and Company, 1894; as *Betty Leicester's Christmas,* Boston and New York, Houghton Mifflin and Company, 1899.
The Country of the Pointed Firs. Boston, Houghton Mifflin and Company, 1896; Godine, 1991.
The Tory Lover. Boston and New York, Houghton Mifflin and Company, 1901; South Berwick, Maine, Old Berwick Historical Society, 1975.

Short Stories

Play Days, A Book of Stories for Children. Boston, Houghton Osgood and Company, 1878.
Old Friends and New. Boston, Houghton Osgood and Company, 1879.
Country Byways. Boston, Houghton Mifflin and Company, 1881.
The Mate of Daylight and Friends Ashore. Boston, Houghton Mifflin and Company, 1884.
A White Heron and Other Stories. Boston and New York, Houghton Mifflin and Company, 1886.
The King of Folly Island and Other People. Boston and New York, Houghton Mifflin and Company, 1888.
Strangers and Wayfarers. Boston and New York, Houghton Mifflin and Company, 1890.
Tales of New England. Boston and New York, Houghton Mifflin and Company, 1890.
A Native of Winby and Other Tales. Boston and New York, Houghton Mifflin and Company, 1893.
The Life of Nancy. Boston and New York, Houghton Mifflin and Company, 1895.
The Queens Twin and Other Stories. Boston and New York, Houghton Mifflin and Company, 1899.
An Empty Purse, A Christmas Story. Boston, The Merrymount Press, 1905.

Stories and Tales. Boston and New York, Houghton Mifflin and Company, 1910.

The Uncollected Stories of Sarah Orne Jewett, edited by Richard Cary. Waterville, Maine, Colby College Press, 1971.

Selected Works

The Best Short Stories of Sarah Orne Jewett, 2 Vols., edited by Willa Cather. Boston, Houghton Mifflin, 1925.

The World of Dunnet Landing: A Sarah Orne Jewett Collection. Lincoln, University of Nebraska Press, 1962.

The Country of the Pointed Firs and Other Stories (selected and introduced by Mary Ellen Chase, introduction by Marjorie Pryse). New York, Norton, 1981.

Best Stories of Sarah Orne Jewett. Augusta, Maine, L. Tapley and Company, 1988.

Master Smart Woman: A Portrait of Sarah Orne Jewett (text selected by Cynthia Keyworth). Unity, Maine, North Country Press, 1988.

Sarah Orne Jewett: Novels and Stories: Deephaven, A Country Doctor, The Country of the Pointed Firs, Dunnet Landing Stories, Selected Stories and Sketches, edited by Michael Davitt Bell. New York, Library of America, 1994.

The Irish Stories of Sarah Orne Jewett. Carbondale, Illinois, Southern Illinois University Press, 1996.

Nonfiction

The Story of the Normans, Told Chiefly in Relation to Their Conquest of England. New York and London, G. P. Putnam's Sons, 1887.

"Looking Back on Girlhood," in *Youth's Companion,* 7 January 1892.

Letters

The Letters of Sarah Orne Jewett, edited and introduced by Annie Fields. Boston, Houghton Mifflin, 1911.

Sarah Orne Jewett Letters, edited by Richard Cary. Waterville, Maine, Colby College Press, 1956, revised and enlarged, 1967.

Anthologies

Short Fiction of Sarah Orne Jewett and Mary Wilkins Freeman. New York, New American Library, 1979.

"The Town Poor," in *The Norton Anthology of Literature by Women: The Tradition in English,* edited by Sandra M. Gilbert and Susan Gubar. New York, Norton, 1985.

With notes by Sarah Higginson Begley and Monica L. Kearney, *Four Stories by American Women: Rebecca Harding Davis, Charlotte Perkins Gilman, Sarah Orne Jewett, Edith Wharton,* edited and introduced by Cynthia Griffin Wolff. New York, Penguin Books, 1990.

"Martha's Lady," in *Two Friends and Other Nineteenth-Century Lesbian Stories by American Women Writers,* edited and introduced by Susan Koppelman. New York, Penguin, 1994.

"Together" and "Martha's Lady," in *Chloe Plus Olivia: An Anthology of Lesbian Literature from the Seventeenth Century to the Present,* edited by Lillian Faderman. New York, Viking, 1994.

"A White Heron" (from *Deephaven*), and "The Queen's Twin" and "The Foreigner" (from *The Country of the Pointed Firs*), in *American Women Regionalists: 1850-1910,* edited and introduced by Judith Fetterley and Marjorie Pryse. New York, Norton, 1992.

Uncollected Works

"Jenny Garrow's Lovers" (as A. C. Eliot), in *The Flag of Our Union* (Boston), 18 January 1868.

"The Christmas Ghosts," "The Decay of Churches," "Dr. Theodore Herman Jewett," "For Country Girls," "The Friendship of Women," "A Little Ancestress," "Outgrown Friends," "Recollections of Dr. William Perry of Exeter," and "Thoughts about Housekeeping," in MS.1743.22, Houghton Library, Harvard University.

Other

Editor, *Stories and Poems for Children* by Celia Thaxter. Boston, Houghton, 1895.

Editor, *The Poems of Celia Thaxter.* Boston, Houghton, 1896.

Verses (poetry). Boston, Merrymount Press, 1916.

*

Adaptations: *The White Heron* (film), Jane Morrison, 1978; *Master Smart Woman* (film), Jane Morrison and Peter Namuth, 1984; *The Country of the Pointed Firs,* in Blackstone Audiobooks (audiotape; recorded by Audio Bookshelf); "The Courting of Sister Wisby," in *Great American Short Stories: Vol. 3* (audiotape); "The White Heron," in *Women in Literature: The Short Story* (audiotape); "Editha" by William Dean Howells, "The Courting of Sister Wisby" by Sarah Orne Jewett (audiotape), Commuter's Library; "Miss Tempy's Watchers" (audiotape), Commuter's Library; "The Only Rose" (audiotape), Commuter's Library; "A White Heron and Other New England Tales" (audiotape; recorded by Audio Bookshelf); *Stories of New England: Then and Now,* Vols. 1 & 2, (audiotape; recorded by Audio Bookshelf); *The Country of the Pointed Firs* (play), Pontine Movement Theatre, Portland, Maine, Dartmouth College, Hanover, New Hampshire.

Manuscript Collections: Widner Library, Harvard University; Columbia University Library; University of Michigan; University of New Hampshire; University of Wisconsin at Madison; Boston Anhenæum; Dartmouth University Library; Colby College, Maine.

Biography: *Sarah Orne Jewett* by F. O. Matthiessen, Boston and New York, Houghton Mifflin, 1929; *Sarah Orne Jewett* by Richard Cary, New York, Twayne, 1962; *Sarah Orne Jewett* by Josephine Donovan, New York, Ungar, 1981.

Bibliography: *A Bibliography of the Published Writings of Sarah Orne Jewett* by Clara Carter Weber and Carl J. Weber, Waterville, Maine, Colby College Press, 1949; *Sarah Orne Jewett: A Reference Guide* by Gwen L. Nagel and James Nagel, Boston, G. K. Hall, 1978.

Critical Sources: "Editorial Comment," in *The Letters of Sarah Orne Jewett,* edited by Annie Fields, Boston and New York, Houghton Mifflin and Company, 1911; "Preface" by Willa Cather, to *The Best Short Stories of Sarah Orne Jewett,* 2 Vols., Boston, Houghton Mifflin, 1925; *Appreciation of Sarah Orne Jewett: Twenty Nine Interpretative Essays,* edited by Richard Cary, Waterville, Maine, Colby College Press, 1973; "The Unpublished Love Poems of Sarah Orne Jewett" by Josephine Donovan, in *Fron-*

tiers: A Journal of Women's Studies, Vol. 3, fall 1979, 26-31; "Pure and Passionate: Female Friendship in Sarah Orne Jewett's 'Martha's Lady'" by Glenda Hobbs, in Studies in Short Fiction, Vol. 17, 1980, 21-29; "Sarah Orne Jewett and Her Coast of Maine: An Introduction by Mary Ellen Chase" and "Introduction to the Norton Edition" by Marjorie Pryse, in The Country of the Pointed Firs, New York, Norton, 1981; Critical Essays on Sarah Orne Jewett, edited by Gwen Nagel, Boston, G. K. Hall, 1984; "Biographical Sketch of Sarah Orne Jewett" by Josephine Donovan, in Master Smart Woman: A Portrait of Sarah Orne Jewett, Unity, Maine, North Country Press, 1988; Sarah Orne Jewett, an American Persephone by Sarah Way Sherman, Hanover, New Hampshire, University Press of New England, 1989; Sarah Orne Jewett: Reconstructing Gender by Margaret Roman, University of Alabama Press, 1992; "Introduction" by Judith Fetterley and Marjorie Pryse, in American Woman Regionalists: 1850-1910, New York, Norton, 1992; "Reading Deephaven as a Lesbian Text" by Judith Fetterley and "Perverse Reading: The Lesbian Appropriation of Literature" by Bonnie Zimmerman, in Sexual Theory, Textual Practice: Lesbian Cultural Criticism, Cambridge, Massachusetts and Oxford, U.K., Blackwood, 1993; "Introduction" and "Sarah Orne Jewett" by Lillian Faderman, in Chloe plus Olivia: An Anthology of Lesbian Literature from the Seventeenth Century to the Present, New York, Penguin, 1994; "Preface" and "Introduction" by Susan Koppelman, in Two Friends and Other Nineteenth-Century Lesbian Stories by American Women Writers, New York, Penguin, 1994; "'Not in the Least American': Nineteenth-Century Literary Regionalism" by Judith Fetterley, in College English, Vol. 56, No. 8, December 1994, 877-895; "Sex, Class, and 'Category Crisis': Jewett and the Postmodern Reader" (Keynote Address) by Marjorie Pryse, in Sarah Orne Jewett and Her Contemporaries: The Centennial Conference, Westbrook College, Portland, Maine, 22 June 1996.

*   *   *

In a letter to fledgling writer Willa Cather, who had asked Sarah Orne Jewett for advice, Jewett told Cather to "write to the human heart, the great consciousness that all humanity goes to make up." She further told Cather to "write about life, but never write life itself." Indeed, Jewett's work continues to touch the hearts of readers even today. Jewett's writing is especially important to lesbian readers, critics, and writers who are looking for a caring past. The relationship of Kate and Helen in Jewett's Deephaven, particularly the scene where they dance in the moonlight, has touched deeply the hearts of lesbian readers attempting to find themselves in literature, as do the sparks of desire between the narrator and Mrs. Todd in The Country of the Pointed Firs. Jewett's own long Boston Marriage with Annie Fields, widow of the publisher James Fields, is affirming to lesbians, as is her history with a group of female friends with whom she worked closely to provide a vision through which art and life are intertwined in a world where women can explore the full capabilities that they possess.

Jewett's writing helps to delineate a strong tradition of lesbian, bi-sexual, gay, and trans-writing, a tradition often buried under heterosexual male criticism and canon-formation of the twentieth century. Although Jewett's writing is usually not explicitly sexual, Bonnie Zimmerman pointed out that clues exist within the texts for the lesbian reader, a reader who reads in a specific way from her own experience.

Jewett, a lesbian who had no heterosexual interests in her life, was concerned in her writing with the acceptance of difference. At times, that difference focused on the abilities of country people, lest townspeople should think them slow or having little to offer. She "wanted the world to know their grand, simple lives." In "An Autumn Holiday," Jewett showed her concern with a community's acceptance of gender difference—Dan'el Gunn dresses in his dead sister's clothes, not only at home, but also at church and at the Missionary Circle.

Jewett also wrote about the abilities of women being subsumed into the worlds of marriage and of men. Women's abilities, and the need to realize these abilities without prejudice, is the theme of A Country Doctor and "Tom's Husband." "A White Heron," the story of a young country girl whose circumscribed world is invaded by a male hunter from the larger world in search of a "specimen," is not only the story of Sylvy protecting the natural world, but also, as Judith Fetterley has pointed out, the story of Sylvy's rejection of the economy of heterosexuality. "Martha's Lady," perhaps the most explicitly lesbian of Jewett's published short stories, as Marjorie Pryse notes, looks at class issues and issues of "marriageability" as important to women's ability to live the lives they might choose. Martha need not marry. She can follow from a distance the career of the woman she loves, the woman who allowed her to become herself. Her lady, Miss Helena, however, lives in a social context that demands her marriage and provides her, we are told, a difficult life. It is not until her husband has died and Miss Helena returns to the home of her cousin, Miss Harriet Pyne, that the strong relationship between Martha and her lady can be realized. Then "the long years seemed like days," and Martha lingers over the services she can provide until Miss Helena cries, "Oh, my dear Martha!...won't you kiss me goodnight? Oh, Martha, have you remembered like this, all these long years!"

Like many nineteenth-century American women writers, Jewett was also critical of the heterosexual world that robbed women of opportunity, showing over and over again in her fiction that the modern economy was pathological for women. As Marjorie Pryse pointed out, she disrupts understanding of class and is resistant to categorization of either class or sexuality. Men in her fiction often have feminine understanding, or live in feminized worlds, as in Jewett's most famous book, The Country of the Pointed Firs, often called her masterpiece. The Country of the Pointed Firs centers on women: Almiry Todd, a sibyl and healer with whom the narrator of this book is in wonderful sympathy; Mrs. Blackett, Almiry's mother, whose isolated life on Greene Island with her son William, who is both son and daughter to her, fits her well; Poor Joanna, who, disappointed in love, became a recluse living her days out on Shell Heap Island, representing for the narrator the hermit who lives in all of our lives. The Country of the Pointed Firs is a book in which Jewett takes a close look at what is at hand, just like her father advised her to do when she was young. The close look, however, led beyond what the eye can see, often into other dimensions and other realities than those bounded by the physical world. A sympathetic understanding of the said and the unsaid, of the seen and the unseen, exists among the characters of this text, and gossip and denigration of difference are not privileged by these sympathetic characters.

Jewett has often been labeled a "realist" writer, yet as The Country of the Pointed Firs demonstrates so well, her writing goes beyond realism. As Judith Fetterley points out in her essay in College English, Jewett was a part of a strong tradition of nineteenth-century women writers who might be seen as "a particularly talented practitioner of a long-established tradition" who was critiquing "the self-consciously masculine 'new' realism from a larger historical perspective," and from an entirely different point of view as well, one much more inclusive than that of the male realists. Indeed, Jewett's world of Dunnet Landing described in *The Country of the Pointed Firs*, "The Foreigner," and other Dunnet Landing Stories, critiques the scientific world in which what can be touched and proved is valued over the spiritual and other dimensions which may exist. Her books discuss love and connections that go beyond the physical into the realm of the spiritual, connections like those she felt in her own life to her mother, her sister, her father, her lover, Annie Fields, and friends like Sarah Wyman Whitman and Celia Thaxter. Indeed, a year after Sarah Whitman's death Jewett wrote to Annie Fields of her experience on the day Whitman died: "I remember well that long bright day and the wonderful cloud I watched at evening...It was like a great golden ball or balloon as if it wrapped a golden treasure; her golden string (that Blake writes about) might have made it."

Sarah Orne Jewett's vision was and is a wonderfully kind vision, one in which each individual can recognize her or his potential and one in which difference is cause for celebration. As she told Cather she must do, Jewett dreamed her dreams and went "on to new and more shining ideals." We remain the fortunate beneficiaries of her vision through the legacy of her work.

—Patti Capel Swartz

JORDAN, June

Pseudonym: Also wrote as June Meyer. **Nationality:** American poet, essayist, playwright, and professor of African American Studies and poetry. **Born:** Harlem, New York, 9 July 1936. **Education:** Barnard College, 1953-55, 1956-57; University of Chicago, 1955-56. **Family:** Married to Michael Meyer, 1955, divorced 1965; one son. **Career:** Assistant to the producer, "The Cool World" (movie), 1964; research associate and writer, Mobilization for Youth, Inc., New York, 1965-66; poet-in-residence, Teachers & Writers Collaborative, 1966-68; director, Voice of the Children, 1967-70; teacher of English, City College of the City University of New York, 1967-70, 1972-75, 1977-78, Connecticut College, 1968, Sarah Lawrence College, 1971-75, and Yale University, 1974-75; associate professor of English, 1978-82, professor of English, 1982-89, director of Poetry Center, 1986-89, and director of Creative Writing Program, 1986-89, State University of New York at Stony Brook, New York; visiting poet-in-residence, MacAlester College, 1980; visiting mentor poet, Loft Mentor Series, Minneapolis, 1983; Chancellor's Distinguished Lecturer, University of California, Berkeley, 1986; playwright-in-residence, The New Dramatist, New York, 1987-88; visiting professor of Afro-American Studies, University of Wisconsin, Madison, 1988; professor of African American Studies, University of California, Berkeley, from 1989. Columnist, *Progressive,* from 1989; contributor, *Boston Globe, Essence, Ms., Nation, New Republic, New York Times, San Francisco Bay Guardian, Village Voice,* and *Washington Post.* **Member:** Founder and co-director, Voice of the Children, Inc.; co-founder, Afro-Americans against the Famine; director, Poets and Writers, Inc.; board of directors

member, Teachers and Writers Collaborative, Inc., from 1978, and Center for Constitutional Rights, from 1984; founder and teacher, Poetry for the People, University of California, Berkeley, from 1991; board member, California Poets in the Schools, from 1996. **Awards:** Rockefeller grant for creative writing, 1969; Prix de Rome in Environmental Design, 1970; Nancy Bloch Award, for *The Voice of Children,* 1971; *New York Times* selection as one of the outstanding young adult novels, 1971; National Book Award nomination, 1971; Creative Artists Public Service Program poetry grant, 1978; Yaddo fellowship, 1979-80; National Endowment for the Arts fellowship, 1982; New York Foundation for the Arts fellowship, 1985; National Association of Black Journalists Achievement Award, for international reporting, 1984; Freedom to Write Award, PEN Center U.S.A. West, 1991; Middle East/M.E.R.I.P. Award, 1991; First Founder's Award, National Black Women's Health Project, 1993; Distinguished Service Award, Northfield Mount Hermon School, 1993; Ground Breakers-Dream Makers Award, Women's Foundation, San Francisco, California, 1994; Critics Award and Herald Angel Award, Edinburgh Arts Festival, 1995; Lila Wallace-Reader's Digest Award, 1995-98. **Agent:** Frances Goldin Agency, 305 East 11th Street, New York, New York 10003-7403, U.S.A. **Address:** Department of African American Studies, University of California, Berkeley, 660 Barrows Hall, Berkeley, California 94720-2572, U.S.A.

Writings

Poetry

Things that I Do in the Dark: Selected Poetry. New York, Random House, 1977.
Passion: New Poems, 1977-1980. Boston, Beacon Press, 1980.
Living Room: New Poems, 1980-1985. New York, Thunder's Mouth Press, 1985.
Naming Our Destiny: New and Selected Poems. New York, Thunder's Mouth Press, 1989.
The Haruko/Love Poetry of June Jordan. London, Virago Press, 1993.
I Was Looking at the Ceiling and then I Saw the Sky. New York, Scribner, 1995.
Kissing God Good-bye. New York, Scribner, 1996.

Essays

Civil Wars. Boston, Beacon Press, 1981; with new introductory essay, New York, Scribner, 1996.
On Call: New Political Essays, 1981-1985. Boston, South End Press, 1985.
Lyrical Campaigns: Selected Political Essays. London, Virago Press, 1989.
Moving Towards Home: Selected Political Essays. London, Virago Press, 1989.
Technical Difficulties: New Political Essays. New York, Pantheon Press, 1992.

Plays

In the Spirit of Sojourner Truth (produced New York City Public Theatre, May 1979).

For the Arrow that Flies by Day (produced Shakespeare Festival, New York, April 1981).

Bang Bang Ueber Alles (libretto and lyrics), 1985.

I Was Looking at the Ceiling and then I Saw the Sky: Earthquake Romance, music by John Adams (directed by Peter Sellars; produced Zellerbach Playhouse, Berkeley, California, 1995).

Young Adult

Who Look at Me. New York, T.Y. Crowell, 1969.

His Own Where. New York, T.Y. Crowell, 1971.

Dry Victories. New York, Holt, 1972.

New Room: New Life. New York, T.Y. Crowell, 1975.

Kimako's Story. New York, Houghton Mifflin, 1981.

Editor

Soulscript: Afro-American Poetry. New York, Doubleday, 1970.

With Terri Bush, *The Voice of the Children.* New York, Holt Rinehart, and Winston, 1970.

With Lauren Muller and the Blueprint Collective, *June Jordan's Poetry for the People.* New York and London, Routledge, 1995.

Other

Fannie Lou Hamer (biography). New York, T.Y. Crowell, 1971.

Okay Now. New York, Simon and Schuster, 1977.

High Tide—Marea Alta. Curbstone Press, 1987.

Recordings: *Things I Do in the Dark and Other Poems.* Spoken Arts; *For Somebody to Start Singing,* with music by Bernice Reagon, Watershed, 1979.

*

Critical Sources: "Opinions and Poems" by Darryl Pinckney, in *New York Times Book Review,* 9 August 1981, 8, 26; " . . . The Jumping into It" by Susan McHenry, in *Nation,* Vol. 232, No. 14, 11 April 1981, 437-38; "Chosen Weapons" by Toni Cade Bambera, in *Ms.,* Vol. IX, No. 10, April 1981, 40-42; "Book Reviews: 'Passion: New Poems, 1977-1980'" by Mildred Thompson, in *Black Scholar,* Vol. 12, No. 1, January-February 1981, 96; "From Sea to Shining Sea" by June Jordan, in *Home Girls: A Black Feminist Anthology,* edited by Barbara Smith, New York, Kitchen Table/ Women of Color Press, 1983, 223-229; "Jordan Bio and Speech," http://www.mankato.msus.edu.dept/worldsot/Jordan.htm; "Freedom Time" by June Jordan, in *Progressive,* November 1993, 18-20; "The Hermit's Scream" and "'History Stops for No One'" by Adrienne Rich, in *What Is Found There: Notebooks on Poetry and Politics,* New York, Norton, 1993, 55-71, 128-144; "West Coast Story" by Alisa Solomon, in *The Village Voice,* 26 July 1995, 83-4; "Introduction" by June Jordan, in *June Jordan's Poetry for the People: A Revolutionary Blueprint,* edited by Lauren Muller and the Blueprint Collective, New York and London, Routledge, 1995, 1-12; "New World Consciousness in the Poetry of Ntozake Shange and June Jordan: Two African-American Women's Responses to Expansionism in the Third World" by P. Jane Splawn, in *CLA Journal,* Vol. 20, No. 4, 1996, 417-431.

*   *   *

June Jordan's writing celebrates the revolutionary power of love, as Adrienne Rich pointed out in the foreword to *Haruko/Love Poems.* In the case of the haruko poems, Jordan claims "the love of a woman for a woman as a revolutionary act," according to Rich. In this poetry, Rich noted that "'the motive is driven by desire' and desire is personal, concrete, particular, and sensual;" it is poetry in which it is clear that "fragmentation and self-denial are impediments both to love and to revolutionary life." In *Haruko/Love Poems,* Jordan explores love over a 22 year span, and, as Rich highlighted, she "explores many kinds of love, toward herself and others, male and female," and "the connections between desire and solidarity become palpable in many of these poems."

Jordan "is one of the most musically and lyrically gifted poets of the late twentieth century," according to Rich. Although her language and use of words is often musical and lyrical, her poetry is, as are her essays, concerned with "power: its abuse by those who have it, and the rebellion against that abuse by those who don't," according to *Nation* contributor Susan McHenry. Jordan's *Civil Wars* presents a "chilling but profoundly hopeful vision of living in the U.S.A.," Toni Cade Bambera noted in *Ms.* As in her poetry, "Jordan's vibrant spirit manifests itself throughout this collection of articles, letters, journal entries, and essays. What is fundamental to that spirit is caring, commitment, a deep-rooted belief in the sanctity of life."

The sanctity of all life, and the disregard of those in power for the lives of African Americans or of people of color globally is a recurring theme in all of Jordan's work. As P. Jane Splawn noted in *CLA Journal* of Jordan's and Ntozake Shange's work, both are concerned with the African diaspora and with the conditions of peoples of color. Indeed, in her realization that over three-fifths of the world's population are people of color, Jordan refuses to use the term "third world" to denote the majority of the world's population. Her interests in abuses of power are local, and certainly applicable to the United States in which she lives; but they are also global, as her concerns stretch to encompass the oppression of people worldwide.

Jordan writes against homophobia as a form of oppression. In a column in the *Progressive,* she mourned the death of Tede Matthews, a kind man who died of AIDS as a result of homophobia and the failure to fund medical research. Her anger at deaths from AIDS and deaths as a result of racism is clear in this essay, where she wrote: "I reflected on Tede Matthews's death, and the deaths of thousands upon thousands of young men whom we have loved and lost. And I wanted to rise from my seat in prophetic rage and denounce any scripture/any construct of divinity that does not cherish all of the living people on earth and does not grieve for the cruelties of daily life that afflict every one of us if basic freedom is denied." In "From Sea to Shining Sea," a poem in *Home Girls* that discusses abuses of power toward many Americans, Jordan wrote:

> *This was not a good time to be gay*
> Shortly before midnight a Wednesday
> massacre felled eight homosexual Americans
> and killed two: One man was on his way
> to a delicatessen and the other
> was on his way to a drink. Using an Israeli
> submachine gun the killer fired into the crowd
> later telling police about the serpent in the garden
> of his bloody heart, and so forth.

As she lists the unpopular human conditions of the time, she calls for change, for action to eliminate hate, racism, sexism, ageism, and homophobia. Jordan's essays and her poetry are acts of revolutionary love. The play *I Was Looking at the Ceiling and then I Saw the Sky,* along with its critique of immigration policies, prison "reform" in California, and racism, discusses internalized homophobia as the white, policeman character who gives much time to community service working with boys groups, and who has been extremely homophobic, realizes he is himself gay.

As a teacher of poetry, Jordan has revolutionized the poetry classroom. Her "Poetry for the People" at the University of California, Berkeley has had far reaching effects. Public readings are often standing room only, and student poets have travelled from Berkeley to as far as New York City to provide readings. Student poetry is relevant to life, hopes, and hope for change. In the introduction to *June Jordan's Poetry for the People* she noted, "I would hope that folks throughout the United States would consider the creation of poems as a foundation for true community: a fearless democratic society." A blueprint for her classes and for creating active, political poetry, this book contains valuable bibliographies of gay and lesbian poetry as well as anthologies of the writings of peoples of color, and interviews with poets.

Poetry not only builds community for Jordan, it builds individuals. *New York Times* book reviewer Darryl Pinckney pointed out about *Civil Wars* that "[the] articles form a kind of autobiography of thought and feeling, the story of one individual's activism and search for community." He noted that the poetry in *Passion,* as indeed all her poetry, is "within an oral tradition." And as Adrienne Rich wrote in "History Stops for No One," "African-Americans have had to invent and synthesize a language in which to be both African and American, to 'write...toward the personal truth' of being African-American and create a poetic of that experience." June Jordan's poetry, her work, indeed, all of her life, tells her "personal truth," contributing immeasurably to the voices that tell of the African American experience in this country, and in the world. She is truly a freedom fighter. Her comment in *Progressive* could be a blueprint for her life: "Freedom requires our steady and passionate devotion."

—Patti Capel Swartz

JORDAN, Neil

Nationality: Irish author of short stories, novels, and screen plays, and film director. **Born:** Sligo, 25 February 1950; raised in Dublin. **Education:** University College, Dublin, earning a degree in literature and history. **Family:** Married Vivienne Shields (separated 1980s); two daughters, one son; companion of Brenda Rawn; one son. **Career:** Has worked as a laborer, saxophonist, and theatre staff writer; founder, 1974, chairman of the board, and administrator, Irish Writers Cooperative; script consultant on John Boorman's *Excalibur,* 1981. **Awards:** Art Council bursary 1976; *Guardian* Fiction Prize, for short story collection, 1979; named *Evening Standard's* Most Promising Newcomer, 1982; British Critics Circle Award, Best Director, 1984; Academy Award for Best Original Screenplay, 1992. **Address:** c/o Palace Productions, 16-17 Wardour Mews, London W1, England.

WRITINGS

Novels

The Past. London, Jonathan Cape, 1980.
The Dream of a Beast. London, Chatto & Windus, 1983; New York, Random House, 1989.
Sunrise with Sea Monster. London, Chatto & Windus, 1994; as *Nightlines,* New York, Random House, 1994.

Short Stories

Night in Tunisia and Other Stories. Dublin, Co-Op Books, 1976; Braziller, 1980.
"A Bus, a Bridge, a Beach" and "The Old-Fashioned Lift," in *Paddy No More,* Longship Press, 1978.
"The Artist" and "The Photographer," in *New Writing and Writers* 16, Humanities Press, 1979.
A Neil Jordan Reader. New York, Vintage Books, 1993.

Screenplays

Angel (Motion Picture Company, 1982; released as *Danny Boy,* Triumph Films, 1984.)
With Angela Carter, *The Company of Wolves* (adaptation of story by Carter; Cannon Group, 1984).
With David Leland, *Mona Lisa* (Island Pictures, 1986). Faber & Faber, 1986.
High Spirits (Tri-Star Pictures, 1988).
The Miracle (Channel Four Films, 1991).
The Crying Game (Miramax, 1992).
With Anne Rice, *Interview with a Vampire* (adaptation of novel by Rice; Geffen Pictures, 1994).
Michael Collins (Warner Brothers, 1996).

*

Interviews: "Neil Jordan" by Marlaine Glicksman, in *Film Comment,* Vol. 26, No. 9, January/February 1990; "Neil Jordan" by Lois Gould, in *New York Times Magazine,* 9 January 1994, 22-25; "Neil Jordan" by Fred Schruers, in *Rolling Stone,* 14 November 1996.

Critical Sources: "Here Comes Mr. Jordan" by Allen Barra, in *American Film,* 1 January 1990; "The Cult of *The Crying Game*" by Richard David Story, in *New York,* 25 January 1993; "Racial and Sexual Politics in *The Crying Game*" by Frann Michel, in *Cineaste,* winter 1993; "Genre Conventions and Visual Style in *The Crying Game*" by David Lugowski, in *Cineaste,* winter 1993; "Don't Read This Story" by Richard Corliss, in *Time,* 1 March 1993, 57; "Beyond White and Other: Relationality and Narratives of Race in Feminist Discourse" by Susan Stanford Friedman, in *Signs,* autumn 1995.

*   *   *

Neil Jordan's pursuit of artistic development has taken him on a roller coaster ride from popularity to ostracization to star status. Shunning classifications, both by his example and by his artistic creations, Jordan has broken down arbitrary boundaries in filmmaking and screenwriting. Professionally, Jordan has been primarily a writer and a director, and these two specialties are interrelated. His writing is very visual and cinematic, and his successes in film are largely those he helped to write. Jordan is best known for breaking down the binaries of gender, class, race, and nationality in his analysis of the intricacy of humanity.

A brief summary of Jordan's biography indicates how his fame has ebbed and flowed. The young writer helped to found the Irish Writers Cooperative in 1974, serving as its first chairman and administrator for several years. The organization provided an outlet for Irish writers who often found it hard to publish first works in England, and it was unique in its practice of publishing only paperbacks. Jordan's own first publication, *Night in Tunisia and Other Stories,* was published by the Cooperative in 1976. This book was awarded the *Guardian* Fiction Prize, and Jordan followed it with a novel, *The Past* (1980), which centered on a young man's search for his own history through ancillary narratives and a few old photographs. By 1982 Jordan's writing had been acclaimed sufficiently for him to win the *Evening Standard*'s Most Promising Newcomer award.

Jordan soon joined *Excalibur* director John Boorman as a script consultant, and learned a great deal about filmmaking on the set, eventually producing a documentary on the making of the movie. Jordan wrote a script, called *Angel,* and mentor Boorman helped to convince the Irish film board to fund it. The limited resources went quickly, however, and many were irritated by the large commitment to Jordan's work. The film board collapsed, and Jordan, ostracized, left Ireland.

Jordan's work with Angela Carter on her film adaptation of "The Company of Wolves" (1985) was much more successful, earning him a British Critics Circle award for direction. Also popular was his film *Mona Lisa,* which made a star of Bob Hoskins and also featured Michael Caine. This success was followed by disappointments in Hollywood. Clashing with producers, Jordan eventually walked out on the filming of *High Spirits*; ironically, he is often criticized for elements of the film emphasized by the producers. His next project, *We're No Angels,* also fared poorly, despite starring Robert DeNiro and Sean Penn. Jordan returned to Ireland.

Jordan had some success with *The Miracle* (1991), which features a young Irish man who falls in love with a stranger who turns out to be the mother who abandoned him and his alcoholic father. He followed this up with a film meant for small channel distribution called *The Crying Game,* which eventually earned six Academy Award nominations and one Academy award, for Jordan's screenplay. A combination of a free hand with the production and wise marketing in United States Distribution—including the re-release after nomination to smaller theaters and the mystery surrounding the film's "secret"—allowed Jordan to net $40 million for a film which cost $4.3 million to make. The film was both a financial success and a popular success, despite its status as foreign and artistic. Banking on this achievement, Jordan was hired to adapt Anne Rice's *Interview with a Vampire,* with which he was given fairly free reign, and which yielded more than $100 million.

Despite his fame, Jordan wrote a new novel, *Sunrise with Sea Monster* (called *Nightlines* in the United States), and produced *Michael Collins,* a film script he wrote in 1982 based upon the 1921 Anglo-Irish Treaty which partitioned Ireland. With a large budget—$28 million—Jordan received Hollywood funding but filmed more economically in Ireland. He also economized by getting his stars, Liam Neeson and Julia Roberts, to work for scale.

Throughout his work Jordan has explored the tensions between past and present, male and female, black and white. And he has examined issues of sexuality in *The Miracle,* in which incest is a backdrop as the son makes advances towards the woman whom he doesn't know is his mother, and in *Interview with a Vampire,* with its exploration of the sensuality of blood-sucking rituals and its sexualized child vampire. Yet critics and reviewers have paid little attention to Jordan's nuanced explorations of homosexuality. The short story "Seduction" has received little attention. In *Mona Lisa* the focus of the film is George, and thus the lesbian relationship between Simone and Cathy is barely mentioned, and only in terms of George's disappointment. And in discussions of *The Crying Game,* Jordan's complex treatment of sexuality was subordinated to the marketing plan which aimed to keep the "secret" of Dil's gender silent so viewers could be surprised. The plan helped increase the viewership of the film, but it also prevented discussions of the film's significance until the time when only academics and critics were interested in reading about it.

In an interview with Lois Gould in the *New York Times Magazine,* Neil Jordan mused, "Men never find a way to express their affection, do they? My father thought my first novel was pornographic.... It was about a homosexual relationship. Never got published." From this first, unseen novel, then, homosexuality runs throughout his texts. In *Night in Tunisia and Other Stories,* Jordan explores a variety of sexual adventures, fantasies, and desires. The story "Seduction" focusses upon two teenage boys, the narrator and Jamie, who spend the majority of the story eyeing and discussing an older woman vacationing nearby. As they wait for the woman one night, Jamie breaks down crying, and the two boys plunge into the nearby ocean. As they frolic in the water, Jamie wraps his arms around the narrator, pressing against him. The story ends with the lines: "I heard him say 'this is the way lovers do it' and felt his mouth on my neck but I didn't struggle. I knew that in the water he couldn't see my tears or see my smile" (29). In this way Jordan places the emergence of homosexual desire at the margins of the story, suggesting at once that the boys' mutual attraction has been buried beneath their more acceptable (but unfulfilled) homosexual longings, and yet that their relationship is pleasing, full of promise. Like the boys, Jordan only begins an encounter with homosexuality in the story.

A similar situation occurs in *Mona Lisa,* where the main action is centered upon George, a recently released convict whose boss sets him up as a driver for a prostitute, Simone. George is introduced to a strange new world in which he dresses up and behaves respectably in order to shield Simone's activities, which occur in a subculture full of sadism and bondage. Simone reveals to George her past, her abusive pimp, and her desire to find a friend, Cathy, whom she believes is still with the pimp. As George searches for Cathy he learns more about the seediness of the streets, and he grows to love Simone. George finds Cathy and they flee, pursued by the pimp. Eventually Simone shoots the pimp and his men, and George finds that Simone prefers women, Cathy specifically, to men. The carnage fades into black, and the story resumes with George's life returned to "normalcy"—honest work, stability, and no Simone.

In this story Jordan again uses the margins of his narrative to explore important sexual and social issues. The women in the film are powerless; not only are they dominated sexually but they are also unable to act for themselves, caught up in a world of controlling and intimidating men. Men ensnare them; men free them. Only when Simone shoots the men who are trying to kill her does a woman act with any initiative. George, bumbling his way through the relationship with Simone, asks her if her tricks were good, as if she might be enjoying them. He is jealous of the men, not realizing that the intimacy he has achieved with her—by finding out about her life—far exceeds the merely physical, and he overlooks the many clues to her sexual orientation. Simone is the only black character in the film, and George's attraction to her is therefore taboo, as is her attraction to Cathy, and yet this taboo exists not only on the superficial plane of race, but also on the deeper plane of sexual orientation, complicating the plot further.

Jordan's most significant contribution to the field of gay and lesbian representation is *The Crying Game*. Produced originally for a small-scale audience, Jordan's work was so original and challenging that it surpassed all expectations, and brought homosexual issues to a huge, unsuspecting audience. Because the "secret" of Dil's gender bending was withheld, on the whole, from viewers, most went to see a hostage movie with a surprise twist. They got that: the I.R.A. kidnaps Jodie, a British soldier, and holds him as a hostage trade. When the British refuse to trade, Fergus, who has befriended Jodie, is ordered to kill him, but Jodie runs and a British army truck strikes him dead. Fergus flees and fulfills his promise to find Dil, Jodie's girlfriend. He falls in love with her without realizing that she is a he. The situation is further complicated by the reappearance of his I.R.A. cohorts, including the brutal woman Jude. Dil stands up to the I.R.A. people, shooting them, and Fergus goes to jail for her crimes, but she visits him and they continue their relationship in an enforced platonic manner.

The most shocking scene in *The Crying Game*—and the one in which the secret is revealed—is when Dil undresses before Fergus, revealing her/his flat chest and penis. In this moment the entire film is turned upside down, as are the expectations of the male viewers who have been seduced along with Fergus by the sexual allure of Dil. Fergus must decide whether he is in love with the human being Dil—without regard to his gender—or whether he can only love Dil if she is a woman. Opting for the love that he cannot deny, Fergus continues his relationship with Dil. In the end, Jordan takes what seems to be a traditional story of hetero-

sexual love and twists it to reveal that love may have little to do with such traditional orientations. So much for the hostage thriller.

Perhaps not surprisingly, much of the mainstream press failed to address the issues of homosexuality directly or sympathetically. Dermot Healy, a friend of Jordan's, commented to Gould, "Consider what he's done for the male organ. He's released it," referring to the unique appearance of a penis in an R-rated motion picture. Indeed, the film is often discussed in terms of its maleness and the implications for women. Since Jude is brutal and unsympathetic, the only "positive" image of woman is Dil, a man in drag who bemoans falling for men who show the slightest bit of kindness. Frann Michel commented in *Cineaste*: "[T]he film also implies that the really gay man is a woman. The overtly sexual relationships between men in the film replicate heterosexual paradigms." Yet while many have interpreted this film as being propaganda against women or against gay relationships, the role this film played in bringing the issues to the general public is highly significant.

Neil Jordan commented upon his approach to Allen Barra in *American Film*: "I decided a long time ago to take the most outrageous chances with narration. I refuse to use devices that would let anyone think they were getting to the story too easily—I want to get beneath that level of understanding, stir things up a bit." Jordan told *Film Comment* interviewer Marlaine Glicksman: "I like to choose characters who are surrounded by a life that seems understandable and who slowly find themselves in situations where everything has changed, where no rules exist, and where emotions and realities are brought into play that they are not prepared for." With this desire to discuss the marginalized figure in a challenging environment, it is not unusual that first experiences with homosexuality are prevalent in his work, and it is likely that Jordan will continue to create interesting and arresting work.

—Anne K. Burke Erickson

K

KARLINSKY, Simon

Nationality: American scholar. **Born:** Russian city of Harbin, Manchuria, China, 22 September 1924; arrived in United States, October 1938. **Education:** Kommercheskoe uchilishche, Harbin, 1933-38; Belmont High School, Los Angeles, 1939-41; Los Angeles City College, 1941-42; École Normale de Musique, Paris, 1951-52; Berlin Hochschule für Musik, 1952-58; University of California at Berkeley, 1958-60, B.A. in Slavic Languages and Literatures 1960; Harvard University, 1960-61, M.A. in Slavic Languages and Literatures 1961; University of California at Berkeley, 1961-64, Ph.D. in Slavic Languages and Literatures 1964. **Military Service:** Served in the United States Army, 1943-46; as translator-interpreter (Russian, French, German) in the Control Council for Germany, 1946-48; as liaison interpreter for the U.S. Department of State in Germany, 1948-50; and as liaison officer for the U.S. Command in Berlin, 1952-57. **Family:** Partner of Peter Carleton, from 1974. **Career:** Assistant professor, 1964, associate professor, 1965, professor, 1967-91, professor emeritus, from 1991, Department of Slavic Languages and Literatures, University of California at Berkeley; visiting associate professor of Slavic Languages and Literatures, Harvard University, 1966. Contributing editor, *Christopher Street,* from 1977; contributor of essays and reviews to periodicals, including *Advocate, Christopher Street, Gay Sunshine, Nation, New Yorker, New York Review of Books, New York Times Book Review, Russian Review, Saturday Review, Slavic and East European Review, Slavic Review, Slavonic and East European Review, Times Literary Supplement,* and *Triquarterly.* **Awards:** Woodrow Wilson fellowship, 1960-61; Guggenheim Fellowships, 1969-70, 1978. **Address:** Department of Slavic Languages and Literatures, University of California, Berkeley, California 94720, U.S.A.

WRITINGS

Selected Nonfiction

Marina Cvetaeva: Her Life and Art. Berkeley and Los Angeles, University of California Press, 1966.
The Sexual Labyrinth of Nikolai Gogol. Cambridge, Massachusetts, and London, Harvard University Press, 1976; revised, Chicago and London, University of Chicago Press, 1992.
Marina Tsvetaeva: The Woman, Her World, and Her Poetry. Cambridge and New York, Cambridge University Press, 1985, revised, 1987.
Russian Drama from Its Beginnings to the Age of Pushkin. Berkeley, Los Angeles, and London, University of California Press, 1985.

Selected Edited Works

And translator, with Heim, and author of commentary and introduction, *Anton Chekhov's Life and Thought: Selected Letters and Commentary.* Berkeley, University of California Press, 1973.

With Alfred Appel, Jr., *The Bitter Air of Exile: Russian Writers in the West 1922-1972.* Berkeley, Los Angeles, and London, University of California Press, 1977.
And author of introduction and notes, *The Nabokov-Wilson Letters: Correspondence between Vladimir Nabokov and Edmund Wilson, 1940-1971.* New York, Harper & Row, 1979, revised, 1980; expanded and revised in German as *Briefwechsel mit Edmund Wilson, 1940-1971,* by Vladimir Nabokov, Hamburg, Rowohlt Verlag, 1995.
And author of introduction and notes, *A Difficult Soul: Zinaida Gippius,* by Vladimir Zlobin. Berkeley, University of California Press, 1980.
And author of foreword, *Poèma bez predmeta,* by Valery Pereleshin. Holyoke, Massachusetts, New England Publishing Co., 1989.
With James L. Rice and Barry P. Scherr, *O Rus! Studia literaria slavica in honorem Hugh McLean.* Berkeley, California, Berkeley Slavic Specialties, 1995.

Selected Essays

"Russia's Gay Literature and History (11-20th centuries)," in *Gay Sunshine: A Journal of Gay Liberation* (San Francisco), summer/fall 1976; revised version in *Gay Roots: Twenty Years of Gay Sunshine: an Anthology of Gay History, Sex, Politics, and Culture,* edited by Winston Leyland, San Francisco, Gay Sunshine Press, 1991.
"From Russia, with Love," in *Christopher Street* (New York), March 1977.
"A Hidden Masterpiece: Valery Pereleshin's *Ariel,*" in *Christopher Street* (New York), December 1977.
"Przhevalsky: The Russian Livingstone," in *University Publishing* (Berkeley, California), summer 1978.
"The Case of Gennady Trifonov," in *Christopher Street* (New York), January 1979.
"Death and Resurrection of Mikhail Kuzmin," in *Slavic Review,* March 1979.
"Return to Germany," in *Christopher Street* (New York), September 1979.
"Transformer of the Arts," in *New York Times Book Review,* 7 October 1979.
"Sergei Diaghilev: Public & Private," in *Christopher Street* (New York), March 1980.
"Decadence," in *Christopher Street* (New York), April 1980.
"Gay Life before the Soviets: Revisionism Revised," in *Advocate* (San Mateo, California), 1 April 1982.
"Gay Life in the Age of Two Josephs: McCarthy and Stalin," in *Advocate* (San Mateo, California), 28 April 1983.
"Gennady Trifonov: Update 1986," in *New York Native,* March 1986.
"Should We Retire Tchaikovsky?" in *Christopher Street* (New York), May 1986.
"The Soviet Union vs. Gennady Trifonov," in *Advocate* (Los Angeles), 19 August 1986.
"A Cultural Educator of Genius," in *The Art of Enchantment: Diaghilev's Ballets Russes, 1909-1929,* edited by Nancy Van Norman Baer. San Francisco, Fine Arts Museums of San Francisco, Universe Books, 1988.

"Russia's Gay Literature and Culture: The Impact of the October Revolution," in *Christopher Street* (New York), July 1989; revised version in *Hidden from History: Reclaiming the Gay and Lesbian Past,* edited by Martin Bauml Duberman, Martha Vicinus, and George Chauncey, Jr., New York, New American Library, 1989.

"Tchaikovsky's Loves and Russian Swans," in *San Francisco Performing Arts Library and Museum Journal,* spring 1989.

"Memoirs of Harbin," in *Slavic Review,* summer 1989.

"Kuzmin, Gumilev and Tsvetayeva as Neo-Romantic Playwrights," in *Russian Theatre in the Age of Modernism,* edited by Robert Russell and Andrew Barratt. Houndsmill, Basingstoke, Hampshire, England, Macmillan, New York, St. Martin's Press, 1990.

"Unearthing Russia's Gay Past," in *Advocate* (Los Angeles), 3 December 1991.

"'Vvezen iz-za granitsy...'?: gomoseksualizm v russkoi kul'ture i literature, kratkii obzor" ("'Imported from Abroad...'?: Homosexuality in Russian Culture and Literature, a Brief Survey"), in *Literaturnoe obozrenie* (Moscow), 11, 1991.

"Man or Myth? The Retrieval of the True Tchaikovsky," in *Times Literary Supplement* (London), 17 January 1992.

"Liberating the Sexes: The Freedom that Vanished with the October Revolution," in *Times Literary Supplement* (London), 11 June 1993.

"Nikolai Gogol" and "Russian Literature," in *The Gay and Lesbian Literary Heritage.* New York, H. Holt, 1995.

"Tchaikovsky and the Unholy Alliance," in *Harvard Gay & Lesbian Review* (Boston), fall 1996.

Selected Translations

"Untitled Poem of 1916" by Sergei Esenin; "Untitled Poem of 1924" by Nikolai Klyuev; "At the Party" and "Two Untitled Poems of 1903, 1915" by Mikhail Kuzmin; and "Three Poems from 'Tbilisi by Candlelight'" by Gennady Trifonov, in *Orgasms of Light: The Gay Sunshine Anthology,* edited by Winston Leyland. San Francisco, Gay Sunshine Press, 1977.

Four poems by Valery Pereleshin, in *The Volcano: An Anthology of Latin American Gay Literature,* edited by Winston Leyland. San Francisco, Gay Sunshine Press, 1979.

Three Poems by Gennady Trifonov, in *Gay Sunshine* (San Francisco), summer/fall 1979.

Untitled poem by Gennady Trifonov, in *The Penguin Book of Homosexual Verse,* edited by Stephen Coote. Harmondsworth, Middlesex, England and New York, Penguin, 1983.

With Peter Carleton, "A Ten Minute Drama" by Evgeny Zamiatin, in *Christopher Street* (New York), April 1987.

*

Bibliography: "Simon Karlinsky: A Bibliography" compiled by Molly Molloy with an introduction by Edward Kasinec, in *Russian Review* (Columbus, Ohio), Vol. 49, 1990, 57-76; "Simon Karlinsky: A Bibliography" compiled by Molly Molloy with an introduction by Edward Kasinec, in *For SK: In Celebration of the Life and Career of Simon Karlinsky,* edited by Michael S. Flier and Robert P. Hughes, Berkeley, California, Berkeley Slavic Specialties, 1994, 1-31.

*   *   *

While stationed with the U.S. Army in Germany in late 1945, Simon Karlinsky was assigned to interpret for a group of Soviet Red Army entertainers who were making a tour of American bases around the defeated Nazi state. Having developed a rapport with two gay Soviet performers, the 21-year-old Karlinsky came by their quarters one evening to visit and ended up speaking with them for hours about their lives in Stalinist Russia and his own life as a gay U.S. serviceman. In the course of their meeting, which Karlinsky would describe decades later in *Advocate* as "the most unforgettable conversation of my entire life," the young Russians told him frankly how much they despised the crushingly repressive Soviet regime under which they were forced to live; how they managed, with their fists, to defend themselves against gay-baiters inside their unit; and how their homosexuality, if brought before the authorities, would most certainly condemn them to between five and eight years in a hard-labor camp. They also told him of older gay friends in Moscow who insisted that a rich gay culture had existed in their country before the October Revolution in 1917 and had, for the most part, been tolerated. Although this idea seemed absurd to him at the time, Karlinsky would later learn that these fellows had been absolutely right, and he would eventually become a pioneer in the study of Russian gay and lesbian culture before the Revolution and after.

Karlinsky has never been an exclusively gay-oriented academic. In fact, for well over a decade following the granting of his doctorate and appointment to the faculty of Berkeley's Department of Slavic Languages and Literatures, Karlinsky was more or less silent on gay themes. His dissertation on Marina Tsvetaeva's life and work was published in book form in 1966, but it would be nearly 20 years before he would address her ambiguous sexuality in a second book on the poet. Before widening his net to include gay issues, he published on an enormous variety of topics, from a structural analysis of Vladimir Nabokov's Russian novel *The Gift,* to richly detailed explications of Russian symbolist poetry, to the *Letters of Anton Chekhov.* And since coming out in academe, Karlinsky has published a number of books whose subject matter is far from "gay-oriented," including *The Nabokov-Wilson Letters: Correspondence Between Vladimir Nabokov and Edmund Wilson 1940-1971* and *Russian Drama from Its Beginnings to the Age of Pushkin.*

In 1976 Karlinsky published two works that forthrightly addressed gay issues in Russian literature, and that would forever alter his profile in the field of Slavic Studies: one was an article that appeared in *Gay Sunshine,* "Russia's Gay Literature and History (11-20th centuries)," in which he uncovered gay elements in Russia through the ages, from the earliest medieval hagiography well into the 20th century, drawing readers' attention to the work of a number of gay, lesbian or bisexual Russian cultural figures; the other was a book, *The Sexual Labyrinth of Nikolai Gogol,* in which he presented convincing evidence that Gogol's homosexuality provides important keys to understanding this enigmatic 19th-century writer's life, fiction, and unhappy fate that saw him starve himself to death as the endpoint of a purgative fast ordered by a zealous Orthodox priest.

Sexual Labyrinth is a psychosexual "life and works" of one of Russia's greatest literary innovators, shedding much light on the implications for Gogol's art (and his eventual total repudiation of that art) of his emotional attraction to members of the same sex and concomitant terror of sexually available females. Gogol's biography, all his fiction, much of his non-fiction, his correspondence, and the observations of his friends: all these are examined for what they can reveal of the author's homosexuality. In his introduction, Karlinsky had anticipated his detractors, recognizing that others before him had considered the topic to be "unsuitable for scholarly examination." Nevertheless, as Karlinsky repeatedly insists, scholarship's failure to acknowledge Gogol's sexuality—most likely the result of a combination of academic prudishness and homophobia—has consistently resulted in misreadings of his texts and a failure to understand the "source and the cause of Gogol's personal and literary tragedy."

Following the appearance of *Sexual Labyrinth,* Karlinsky became a frequent contributor to the popular gay press. His contributions throughout the late 1970s and 1980s to *Gay Sunshine, The Advocate,* and *Christopher Street* typically drew on findings from his scholarly research that he felt could be brought to bear in correcting misconceptions held by the at-large gay and lesbian reader. At the risk of making himself unpopular within the left-leaning gay community, Karlinsky worked hard to combat what he described in *Christopher Street* as the "self-imposed brainwashing...in the gay movement." Subjects that he addressed included the virulently homophobic nature of Marxist-Leninist ideology in practice, which many gay liberationists denied, and which, Karlinsky pointed out, had expressed itself in genocidal terror in the Soviet Union and China. In a 1983 *Advocate* article, "Gay Life in the Age of Two Josephs: McCarthy and Stalin," he made an important distinction between the two basic types of "radicals, including gay ones: ...liberators, who seek freedom for themselves and others, and dictatorial authoritarians, whose radical rhetoric is a pretext for controlling or enslaving others."

In a similar spirit, he elsewhere took on the early Soviet voice of sexual liberationism, Aleksandra Kollontai, whom Western feminist scholars had rediscovered and posthumously lionized in the 1970s as an important model for the women's movement. Decrying the sympathetic portrait that certain historians had painted of this early Soviet People's Commissar of Social Welfare—credited with securing women's equality in the Bolshevik state—Karlinsky in *New York Times Book Review* exposed her feminism as resistant to diversity and accused Kollontai of consigning the movement to "men for whom feminist rhetoric was a tool for gaining and extending their own power."

Continuing to debunk myths, Karlinsky has for years attempted to dispel the notion—curiously embraced by both gay and homophobic sources—that Peter Tchaikovsky's death was a suicide, rather than the result of cholera infection from drinking unboiled St. Petersburg water. While some in the gay community cling to the suicide story because it provides them with "a famous gay martyr from the past," homophobic musical historians find it attractive because it supports their image of Tchaikovsky as an unbalanced, unhappy, and guilt-ridden homosexual. The truth is, Karlinsky has argued, Tchaikovsky enjoyed "a reasonably happy and rewarding life until it was cut short by a chance encounter with some cholera bacilli," he writes in *Harvard Gay & Lesbian Review.*

In 1977 Karlinsky became a leading participant in the campaign to assist the Leningrad (now St. Petersburg) poet Gennady Trifonov, who had been sentenced to hard labor for his open homosexuality in Brezhnev's Soviet Union. Rather than live a closeted existence to avoid trial for being gay, Trifonov had been quite open about his homosexuality and privately circulated his gay poems in manuscript; it was this kind of openness that resulted in the state's effort to silence him. Over the next ten years Karlinsky published numerous articles on Trifonov's circumstances, both in the gay press and in more mainstream publications such as *New York Review of Books.* Often accompanied by Karlinsky's own translations of Trifonov's poems, these articles urged readers to write letters to Soviet embassies in Trifonov's behalf, and were

key in establishing for the poet an international profile, which may very well have tempered the authorities' persecution of him.

While Karlinsky was publicizing Trifonov's difficulties, he was also drawing attention to the work of another writer, Valery Pereleshin, one of the most original Russian poetic voices to emerge in this century. In an article published in December 1977, Karlinsky introduced the readers of *Christopher Street* to this poet—Russian-born, but living in Brazil—whose idiosyncratic work (thickly textured, brilliantly layered verse, essentially untranslatable into English) might have denied him all accessibility to an American audience. In particular, Karlinsky discussed Pereleshin's *Ariel,* a collection of sonnets that concern an epistolary romance between the poet and a married male Soviet admirer. In 1989 Karlinsky edited and personally arranged for publication in the U.S. of Pereleshin's autobiographical magnum opus *Poem Without Object* (*Poèma bez predmeta*).

In his second book on Marina Tsvetaeva, *Marina Tsvetaeva: The Woman, Her World, and Her Poetry,* Karlinsky addressed head-on the question of the poet's bisexuality. His earlier book on Tsvetaeva had been written when the poet was all but unknown, without the benefit of many facts that would surface as interest grew in her work and life. In writing the new work on Tsvetaeva, Karlinsky did extensive research on the revolutions of 1905 and 1917, the post-revolutionary emigration to Berlin, Paris, and Prague of the 1920s and 1930s, and the history of the Soviet Union under Stalin, all of which was essential to having his audience understand the fate of one of the most brilliant poets of the 20th century, who, shortly before her suicide, was reduced to applying for, and being denied, a dishwashing job in a provincial Soviet writers' cafeteria. As all the significant events in Tsvetaeva's life, her passionate romantic attachments in the 1910s to the poet Sophia Parnok and the actress Sophia (Sonechka) Holliday are regarded both as facts of the poet's life and, refracted through the prism of her poetry, important sources of artistic inspiration. Tsvetaeva was ambivalent about her sexuality, which likely had something to do with her habit of pursuing unavailable persons, female and male. In late 1940, after returning to the Soviet Union, and several months before her suicide, Tsvetaeva conceived an attraction for a young married schoolmistress Tatiana Kvanina, who was entirely oblivious to Tsvetaeva's amorous feelings. As Karlinsky describes it, "If the love Tsvetaeva needed was possible in the Russia of 1914 or 1920 or in Natalie Clifford Barney's Paris, in Stalin's time it was not even a love that dared not speak its name. It was a love that had no name."

In a 1989 article, "Russia's Gay Literature and Culture: the Impact of the October Revolution," included in the collection *Hidden from History,* Karlinsky chronicled homosexuality in Russia more comprehensively than ever before. While the article tracks centuries of popular and official Russian attitudes toward homosexual love (from the promulgation of the earliest military laws against it under Peter the Great and the establishment of sweeping anti-sodomy legislation by Nicholas I), its emphasis is on the late 19th- and 20th-century history of gay and lesbian Russian culture. Among the celebrated openly gay, lesbian, and bisexual players on the Russian cultural scene of the late 19th and early 20th centuries were the explorer Nikolai Przhevalsky; ballet impresario Sergei Diaghilev; Tchaikovsky; poet and novelist Mikhail Kuzmin, whose novel *Wings* "became the catechism of Russian gay men"; poets Nikolai Kliuev and Sergei Esenin; and writer Lydia Zinovieva-Annibal, whose novel *Thirty-Three Freaks* dealt frankly with lesbian love.

The revolution of 1905, which ushered in a parliamentary system and abolished much censorship, permitted an impressive number of talented and sexually diverse voices to express themselves. The February 1917 revolution forced the tsar's abdication and established a provisional government that promoted democracy, gave the public more freedom than ever before, and, had it not been aborted by events eight months later, would no doubt have resulted in even greater tolerance of homosexuality. What Karlinsky stressed in this article and in many other of his writings is that the October Revolution, rather than continuing the progress of human rights obtained in the revolutions of 1905 and February 1917, actually reversed the advancements that the earlier uprisings had affected. The abolition by the Bolsheviks of the entire pre-revolutionary Criminal Code engendered reports that the Soviet government was pro-gay rights. Nothing could be farther from the truth. Before long the revolutionary government and its press began persecuting (and ignoring the contributions of) openly gay writers. After the October Revolution no new gay or lesbian writers would appear. To be homosexual in the Soviet Union meant being considered irrelevant to the society or a counter-revolutionary or both. As Karlinsky pointed out, homosexuals resorted to the Soviet-prescribed "cure" for their condition: marriage or psychiatric treatment.

Under Stalin, the situation for Soviet homosexuals grew still worse. In 1934 all sexual relations between men became crimes against the state, punishable by between five and eight years of hard labor. The new law became Article 121 of the Soviet Penal Code and it resulted in mass arrests and intensified persecution. Because it was written in 1989, Karlinsky's chronicle ends during the glasnost period, which had begun to relax official intolerance of homosexuality, allowing the discussion of gay topics in the Soviet press.

In a testament to this expansion of public discourse about homosexuality, Karlinsky published an article in 1991 in the Moscow-based *Literary Review* (*Literaturnoe obozrenie*). Titled "'Imported from Abroad...'?" ("'Vvezen iz-za granitsy...'?"), it is a digest of the findings that Karlinsky for years had been sharing with a Western audience and would later treat fully in his 1995 entry on Russian literature in *The Gay and Lesbian Literary Heritage*; its title alluded to a remark that the Russian writer Valentin Rasputin had made in a British television interview: "As far as homosexuals are concerned, let's leave Russia her purity. We have our own traditions. This type of contact between men has been imported from abroad. If they consider their rights infringed upon, then let them leave and live in another country!" Although Rasputin's remark likely reflects the opinion of many Russians, the appearance of Karlinsky's effort—in this leading literary monthly—to not only help restore a name to that love that had none in Stalin's time, but to recover the long-unmentionable history of Russian homosexual culture, was certainly a hopeful sign. (Indeed, in 1993, the post-Soviet Russian government decriminalized homosexuality entirely, although a survey the following year showed the obstinacy of that country's homophobic popular opinion: 23 percent of Russians stated that they would like to see homosexuals killed and 24 percent would advocate isolating them from the rest of the population.) Karlinsky ended this article in a manner that distills the humanistic spirit that has always been at the core of his scholarship: "...what sort of 'purity' of Russia is [Rasputin] fighting for in his interview? For which of 'our own' traditions? For the purity and traditions of Nicholas I, Maxim Gorky, Hitler and Stalin." And, mentioning several straight Russian writers whose tolerance of gay love he had noted, Karlinsky concluded, "Upon reflection, the traditions that proceed from

Pushkin, Przhevalsky, Tchaikovsky, Blok, Gumilev, and Tsvetaeva seem more humane and valuable."

—Christopher Putney

KAYE/KANTROWITZ, Melanie

Nationality: Jewish American essayist, poet, short story writer, editor, professor, and activist. **Born:** Brooklyn, New York, 1945. **Education:** City College, City University of New York, B.A. in English 1966 (Phi Beta Kappa); University of California, Berkeley, California, M.A. 1968, Ph.D. in Comparative Literature 1975. **Career:** Organizer, Remedial Reading Project, Harlem Education Project, New York, New York, 1963-65; instructor, Upward Bound, Richmond, Virginia, 1967, and Berkeley, California, 1968; instructor, Neighborhood Youth Corps, Berkeley, California, 1969, and University of California, Berkeley, California, 1971-72; assistant professor, University Scholars Program, Portland State University, Oregon, 1972-76; community educator, counselor, and organizer, Portland Rape Relief Hotline, Oregon, 1977-78; instructor, Women's Studies, Portland State University, Portland, Oregon, 1977-79; adjunct faculty member, Adult Degree Program, Goddard College, Plainfield, Vermont, 1978-81, Johnson State College, Vermont, 1981, University of New Mexico, Albuquerque, 1981, University of Maine, Rockland Extension, Rockland, 1983; adjunct professor, became associate professor, Adult Degree Program, Vermont College, 1981-88; became associate professor, Graduate Program, Vermont College, Norwich University, Montpelier, Vermont, 1988-90; editor, 1983-87, and contributing editor, 1987-92, *Sinister Wisdom*; editor and publisher, Sinister Wisdom Books, 1984-88; advisory editorial board, *Bridges, A Journal for Jewish Feminists and Our Friends,* from 1989; executive director, Jews for Racial and Economic Justice, New York City, 1992-95; lecturer, Women's Studies, Brooklyn College, City University of New York, 1994; adjunct professor of Women's Studies, University of Washington, Seattle, Washington, 1994-95; Jane Watson Irwin Chair in Women's Studies, Hamilton College, Clinton, New York, 1995-97. **Awards:** New York State Regents Teaching Fellowship, 1966-68; Ford/University of California Special Careers Fellowship, 1967-72; Pushcart Prize nomination, 1977; MacDowell Artists Colony Resident, 1981-82; Millay Artists Colony Resident, 1983, 1985; Basser Arts Foundation Grant, 1984; Writer-in-Residence, New York State Council for the Arts, 1986; Helene Wurlitzer Artists Colony Resident, 1987, 1991; Lambda Literary Award nomination, 1991; YIVO Scholarship, Uriel Weinreich Yiddish Institute at Columbia University, 1991.

WRITINGS

Short Stories

"Jewish Food, Jewish Children," in *The Tribe of Dina,* edited by Melanie Kaye/Kantrowitz and Irena Klepfisz. Montpelier, Vermont, Sinister Wisdom Books, 1986.
"Janey," in *Sinister Wisdom,* No. 31, 1987.
"War Stories, 197-," in *Sinister Wisdom,* No. 33, 1987

"Our First Talk," in *Sojourner,* February 1988.

"For Her," in *Hurricane Alice,* spring 1988.

"Burn," in the *Courier* (Barre-Montpelier, Vermont), 25 March 1988.

"Elements," in *Common Lives/Lesbian Lives,* winter 1988.

"Vacation Pictures," in *Lesbian Love Stories,* edited by Irene Zahava. Freedom, California, The Crossing Press, 1989.

"Some Piece of the Jewish Left," in *Bridges: A Journal for Jewish Feminists and Our Friends* (Eugene, Oregon), spring 1990.

My Jewish Face and Other Stories. San Francisco, California, Aunt Lute Books, 1990.

"The Printer," in *Women on Women 3: Lesbian Fiction,* edited by Joan Nestle and Naomi Holoch. New York, NAL-Penguin, 1996.

Nonfiction

"Lesbians and Literature," in *Sinister Wisdom,* No. 2, 1976.

"On Being a Lesbian Feminist Artist," in *Heresies,* No. 2, fall 1977.

"Culture-Making: Lesbian Classics in the Year 2000?," in *Sinister Wisdom,* No. 13, 1980.

"Sexual Power," in *Sinister Wisdom,* No. 15, 1981.

With Michelle Uccella, "Survival Is an Act of Resistance" and "Women's Capacity for Resistance," in *Fight Back! Feminist Resistance to Male Violence,* edited by Frederique Delacorte and Felice Newman. Pittsburgh, Pennsylvania, San Francisco, California, Cleis Press, 1981.

"Anti-Semitism, Homophobia and the Good White Knight," in *off our backs* (Washington, D.C.), May 1982.

"Some Notes on Jewish Lesbian Identity," in *Nice Jewish Girls,* edited by Evelyn Torton Beck. Watertown, Massachusetts, Persephone, 1982; Boston, Massachusetts, Beacon, 1989.

"To Be a Radical Jew in the Late 20th Century," in *The Tribe of Dina,* edited by Melanie Kaye/Kantrowitz and Irena Klepfisz. Montpelier, Vermont, Sinister Wisdom Books, 1986.

"Seeking a Way Out of the Mire of Israeli-Palestinian Hostilities," in *Times Argus* (Barre-Montpelier, Vermont), 21 January 1988.

"April, a Cruel Month in a Cruel Century," in *Times Argus* (Barre-Montpelier, Vermont), 14 April 1988.

"Ani Mamin, 5749," in *Times Argus* (Barre-Montpelier, Vermont), 22 September 1988.

"Two or Three Points of Light," in *Vermont Women,* December 1988.

"On Education," in *World,* 1 March 1989.

"Courage, Common Sense & Hope in the Territories," in *Times Argus* (Barre-Montpelier, Vermont), 9 March 1989.

"Women in the Intifada," in *Jewish Currents,* May 1989.

"Women, Class and 'The Black-Jewish Question,'" in *Tikkun,* July 1989.

"Women Play Key Role in Opposing the Occupation," in *Utne Reader,* No. 35, September/October 1989.

"Organizing in Vermont for Peace in the Middle East," in *Matrix,* December 1989.

Editor, with Irena Klepfisz, *The Tribe of Dina.* Montpelier, Vermont, Sinister Wisdom Books, 1986; Boston, Beacon Press, 1989.

"The Next Step: Coalition Building in the '90s," in *National Women's Studies Association Journal,* spring 1990.

"The Issue Is Power: Some Notes on Jewish Women and Therapy," in *Women & Therapy,* Vol. 10, No. 4, 1990.

"Hotspots of Anti-Semitism," in *Action and Awareness: Handbook on Anti-Semitism,* edited by Linda Eber, Melanie Kaye/Kantrowitz, and Irena Klepfisz. New York, New Jewish Agenda, 1991.

With Linda Eber and Irena Klepfisz, *Action and Awareness: Handbook on Anti-Semitism.* New York, New Jewish Agenda, 1991.

The Issue Is Power: Essays on Women, Jews, Violence and Resistance. San Francisco, Aunt Lute, 1992.

"Jews in the U.S.: The Rising Costs of Whiteness," in *Names We Call Home: Essays on Racial Identity,* edited by Becky Thompson and Sangeeta Tyagi. New York, Routledge Press, 1995.

"Stayed on Freedom: Jew in the Civil Rights Movement—And After," in *The Narrow Bridge: Jewish Views on Multiculturalism,* edited by Marla Brettschneider. New Brunswick, New Jersey, Rutgers University Press, 1996.

Poetry

"Amazons," in *Conditions,* No. 2, 1977.

"Our Lives Tangle" and "Sign," in *Sinister Wisdom,* No. 5, 1977.

"Carrington" and "My Mother Makes a Mirror," in *Calyx,* Vol. 2, No. 3, 1978.

"Connection," in *Sinister Wisdom,* No. 8, 1979.

We Speak in Code: Poems and Other Writings. Pittsburgh, Pennsylvania, Motherroot Publications, 1980.

"Ritual: We Fight Back," in *Fight Back! Feminist Resistance to Male Violence,* edited by Frederique Delacorte and Felice Newman. Pittsburgh, Pennsylvania, San Francisco, California, Cleis Press, 1981.

"Notes of an Immigrant Daughter: Atlanta," in *Sisterlode,* 1981; in *New America,* Albuquerque, University of New Mexico Press, 1982.

"Farolitos," in *Calyx,* Vol. 7, No. 1, 1982.

"Nagasaki Day," in *IKON,* No. 2, 1983; in *Naming the Waves,* edited by Christian McEwen, London, England, Virago, 1988; Freedom, California, Crossing Press, 1989.

"Kaddish," in *Sinister Wisdom,* No. 25, 1984; in *Naming the Waves,* edited by Christian McEwen, London, England, Virago, 1988; Freedom, California, Crossing Press, 1989.

"Former Friend," in *Sinister Wisdom,* No. 27, 1984.

"Suicide: Jewish, Female, in the 60s," in *Women of Power,* No. 3, 1986.

"Mathematical Model," in *Sinister Wisdom,* No. 31, 1986.

Jerusalem Shadow," in *The Tribe of Dina,* edited by Melanie Kaye/Kantrowitz and Irena Klepfisz. Montpelier, Vermont, Sinister Wisdom Books, 1986.

"Rosh Hashanah" and "Morning Song," in *IKON,* No. 7, 1987.

"eyes," in *An Intimate Wilderness: Lesbian Writers on Sexuality,* edited by Judith Barrington. Portland, Oregon, Eighth Mountain Press, 1991.

"Rosh Hashanah" and "When You Won't Fight Back," in *The Arc of Love: Lesbian Love Poems,* edited by Clare Coss. New York, Scribner, 1996.

"Grogging," in *The Wild Good: Lesbian Photographs and Writings on Love,* edited by Beatrix Gates. New York, Anchor Press, 1996.

*

Critical Sources: Review of *The Tribe of Dina: A Jewish Women's Anthology* by Deborah Gussman, in *Library Journal,* Vol. 114,

No. 14, 1 September 1989, 190; review of *My Jewish Face and Other Stories* by Penny Kaganoff, in *Publishers Weekly,* Vol. 237, No. 27, 6 July 1990, 62; review of *The Tribe of Dina: A Jewish Women's Anthology* by Pamela S. Nadell, in *American Jewish History,* Vol. 80, No. 1, August 1990, 100-108; review of *My Jewish Face and Other Stories* by Molly Abramowitz, in *Library Journal,* Vol. 115, No. 13, August 1990, 143; review of *The Tribe of Dina: A Jewish Women's Anthology* by Kathryn Hellerstein, in *Journal of Religion,* Vol. 7, No. 2, April 1991, 312; review of *The Issue Is Power* by Julia Bard, in *Women's Review of Books,* Vol. 10, No. 8, May 1993, 6-7; "Bold Type: What's in a Name?" by Julie Felner, in *Ms.,* Vol. 4, No. 5, March/April 1994, 75; review of *The Issue is Power* by Michele Dore and Susan Nosov, in *Bridges: A Journal for Jewish Feminists and Our Friends,* Vol. 4 No. 2, spring/summer 1994, 109-114.

*   *   *

Melanie Kaye/Kantrowitz has spent much of her life exploring and interweaving the identities she proudly claims—as a woman, a Jew, a lesbian, a feminist, and an activist. The roots of her identities emerged in the immigrant Jewish community of her youth in Brooklyn, New York and have been evident throughout her career, which has included being an organizer and teacher in the Harlem Education Project in the 1960s, a community educator at Portland, Oregon, Rape Relief Hotline in the 1970s, a Women's Studies teacher and organizer to end the Israeli occupation of the West Bank and Gaza in the 1980s, and an executive director for Jews for Racial and Economic Justice in the 1990s. Her variety of experience is reflected in the content of her work as a writer and an editor.

Her Jewish upbringing influenced not so much her religious identity, but her secular Jewish identity which informs her politics. And it was this background that brought her from her New York home and the civil rights movement to Berkeley in the 1960s. In the early 1970s, Kaye/Kantrowitz moved to Portland, Oregon, where she came out as a lesbian. By the mid-1970s, Kaye/Kantrowitz was already writing for such lesbian feminist publications as *Sinister Wisdom* and *Conditions,* in such varied genres as poetry, with her poem, "Amazons"; essays, including "On Being a Lesbian Feminist Artist"; and reviews, such as on Monique Wittig's *Les Guérillères.* During the end of Kaye/Kantrowitz's stay in Portland, she began to rediscover her Jewish roots and began her quest to integrate her Jewishness with her lesbianism. Kaye/Kantrowitz's first book, *We Speak In Code: poems & other writings,* marked the beginning of her quest to integrate all her identities. In a remark that would also be true of Kaye/Kantrowitz's later works, Tillie Olson noted on the back cover of *We Speak in Code ...* that "these poems are not personal, not political, but insistently both ...." The book mirrors her activism, and celebrates the women's movement, especially the movement against violence, and her Jewish foundations. Her powerful, succinct, yet storytelling poems range from titles such as "Jewish Wives," "Revolutionary in the Late 70s," and "Ritual: for the Portland Women's Night Watch."

During the 1980s, Kaye/Kantrowitz continued writing in many genres for publications, such as *Common Lives/Lesbian Lives, Jewish Currents, The Village Voice,* and *off our backs,* and in anthologies, such as *Lesbian Poetry, Nice Jewish Girls,* and *Fight Back! Feminist Resistance to Male Violence.* At the same time, she taught courses in New Mexico and Vermont with titles like "Heterosexism

and the Oppression of Women," was editor and publisher of the lesbian feminist journal *Sinister Wisdom,* and was part of organizations such as the Advisory Board of the National Women Against Racism Conference. Along with Irena Klepfisz, Kaye/Kantrowitz co-edited, *The Tribe of Dina: A Jewish Women's Anthology,* originally published as a special issue of Sinister Wisdom in 1986, with a second expanded edition by Beacon Press in 1989. This anthology contains essays, artwork, poetry, fiction, and interviews, with translations from Hebrew, Yiddish, and Ladino. Kathryn Hellerstein, in *The Journal of Religion,* hailed the publication as giving "voice to feminists and lesbians who speak from Jewish secular and cultural, rather than religious, perspectives." According to the introduction, part of the motivation for this anthology came from the "June 1982...Israeli invasion of Lebanon, an event which had a profound effect on American Jews, as on Israelis."

In the 1980s and 1990s, the Middle East, class, race, and how they intertwined with lesbianism and Judaism, became more tightly wound into Kaye/Kantrowitz's life and work. She wrote such essays as "Women in the Intifada" and "Women, Class, and 'The Black-Jewish Question,'" reviews of such works as Gloria Anzaldua's *Borderlands/La Frontera* and *Naming the Violence: Speaking Out About Lesbian Battering,* short fiction such as "Some Pieces of the Jewish Left," and co-edited *Action and Awareness: Handbook on Anti-Semitism.* During this time, Kaye/Kantrowitz continued teaching with courses such as "Contemporary Jewish Women" and "Gender/Race/Class/Nation," was executive director for Jews for Racial and Economic Justice, and participated in groups such as the Fellowship of Reconciliation Peace Tour of Israel, the Vermont Women's Action Group, and the Advisory Editorial Board of *Bridges: A Journal for Jewish Feminists and Our Friends.* She gave presentations with the same wide ranging content, such as, "Jewish Queer Radical Politics" for the Lesbian and Gay Writers Conference and "Queer and Jewish in the Age of Newt," at the International Jewish Lesbian and Gay Conference, as well as readings of her work around the United States.

Kaye/Kantrowitz published two major works in the early 1990s: *My Jewish Face & Other Stories* and *The Issue Is Power: Essays on Women, Jews, Violence and Resistance.* Through strong female characters in *My Jewish Face ...,* Kaye/Kantrowitz uses fiction to take the reader through the radical political changes of the 1960s to the 1990s. These stories are serious, impassioned, and humorous, telling fictionalized tales based on her own journeys that become our own, as well as political touchstones for contemporary times.

In *The Issue Is Power,* Kaye/Kantrowitz describes a similar journey to *My Jewish Face,* but this time through forceful, accessible, and sometimes even poetic, essays. Julia Bard noted in the *Women's Review of Books,* that in *The Issue Is Power* "Melanie Kaye/Kantrowitz has grappled with such a variety and range of issues that just to find them between the covers of a single book is challenging." As in *My Jewish Face,* a number of these works have appeared previously, further illustrating the changes in Kaye/Kantrowitz and the world around her. As in all her writing, editing, activist work, and teaching, Kaye/Kantrowitz shows us that the many strands of our identities, our work, and even the many genres writers choose from, can be woven into a fine integrated cloth.

—tova gd stabin

KEENAN, Joe

Nationality: American novelist, lyricist, playwright, and television writer-producer. **Born:** 14 July 1958; raised in Cambridgeport, Massachusetts. **Education:** Attended Columbia University; New York University, M.F.A. **Family:** Companion of Gerry Bernardi, from 1983. **Career:** Copywriter, New York City; writer, executive story consultant, and producer for *Frasier,* NBC-TV; has written plays, books, and lyrics for Off-Off Broadway and workshop productions; has developed and written screenplays and television comedy series. **Awards:** Richard Rodgers Development Award from the American Academy of Arts and Letters, 1991; Kleban Award (for lyrics), 1993. **Address:** c/o Viking Penguin, 375 Hudson St., New York, New York 10014, U.S.A.

WRITINGS

Fiction

Blue Heaven. New York, Penguin, 1988.
"Great Lengths," in *Men on Men 3: Best New Fiction,* edited by George Stambolian. New York, Plume, 1990.
Putting on the Ritz. New York, Viking Penguin, 1991.

Other

The Times (play; produced at the Long Wharf Theatre in New Haven, Connecticut, 1993).
Gloria Vane (television pilot).

*

Critical Sources: "Escapist Fiction of the Cheapest Sort" by Walta Borawski, in *Gay Community News,* 4 September 1988, 12; "An Amateur Sleuth Finds Misadventure" by Frank Bruni, in *Detroit Free Press,* 17 November 1991, 9H; "Lost Horizons" by Felice Picano, in *Advocate,* 21 October 1991, 82-84; review of *Putting on the Ritz* by Michael Bronski, in *Guide,* March 1992, 16-17; "Frolicking with Manhattan's Naughty Hoity-Toity" by Jim Marks, in *Lambda Book Report,* January/February 1992, 28-29; "Joe Keenan" by Michael Schwartz, in *Contemporary Gay American Novelists: A Bio-Bibliographical Sourcebook,* edited by Emmanuel Nelson, Westport, Connecticut, Greenwood, 1993, 226-231; "Laughing Matters" by Rex Poindexter, in *Advocate,* 13 December 1994, 56-58; "Joe Keenan: The Triumph of Arch" by Bob Satuloff, in *Christopher Street,* No. 167, 12-13.

*   *   *

From an early age Joe Keenan's gayness was identified and accepted by his family, including his siblings and his twin brother. Having to make few compromises about his sexuality, Keenan was able to develop a theatrical flare, which his family supported enthusiastically. With a precocious "gay sensibility," Keenan at nine years of age wrote a soap opera parody casting himself as a Gale Sondergaard-type villainess. At 16 he wrote a musical revue called *Going Places,* in which he played a flaming queen director hired to stage a version of *Oedipus Rex* for a Ladies Homeric Society. In an interview for *The Advocate* with Rex Poindexter, Keenan

recalls this production: "As the show unfolds, I end up turning *Oedipus Rex* into a musical loosely inspired by *Gypsy,* with Oedipus as Baby June and Jocasta as Mama Rose. This sort of campiness was applauded and adored by the faculty [of the Jesuit high school he attended], who ate it up like so much catnip." In this way, Keenan demonstrates the type of creativity, wit, and unflinching and irreverent urge to parody that is often identified as "gay sensibility," an attitude most closely associated with the white, middle class construction of being gay.

With such early acceptance of and encouragement for his gay sensibility, it is no surprise that Keenan has been able to convert his humor and intelligence into two successful novels, *Blue Heaven* and *Putting on the Ritz,* and an anthologized short story, "Great Lengths." All three pieces follow the exploits of two gay friends, Philip and Gilbert, whom one reviewer of *Ritz* in *Publisher's Weekly* insightfully likened to Lucy and Ethel, both at their best and their worst. Reviews of Keenan's fiction have generally been favorable, appreciating his wit, his eye for farce, his biting one-liners, and his intricate, dense plotting. He is often compared favorably to P. G. Wodehouse, a literary heritage Keenan himself readily acknowledges. Despite this praise, Keenan is sometimes faulted for creating one-dimensional characters who operate from stereotypes and for lacking social and political consciousness, particularly in the middle of the AIDS epidemic.

Critically, not much work has been done on Keenan's fiction. As noted earlier, reviewers of his fiction have commented on some issues in Keenan's writing, but in general, academics have tended to devalue comedy unless it is satiric, intellectual, or in the realm of the social/political parody; moreover, academic critics are prone to ignore comedy if it derives from the tradition of the "screwball," the "madcap," or the farce. In this way, gay comedy is often relegated to unimportant or "low" cultural status, and thus a large, important aspect of gay life is summarily judged insignificant and finally ignored. Consequently, Keenan's work (like the work of many popular comedians) has been dismissed as "ephemeral" or "light."

However, a more critical assessment of the main characters of Keenan's published fiction, Philip and Gilbert, shows us how their use of madcap exploits and wit gives them some degree of power and control over their lives. Although Philip and Gilbert come from the white middle class, they nonetheless live in a world that is institutionally and economically hostile to them as gay men. In *Blue Heaven,* a stereotypical mafia family with a clear disdain for non-heterosexuals holds economic power. In *Putting on the Ritz,* a Donald Trump-like magnate, Peter Champion, demonstrates his scorn for gays. In Keenan's fiction, both illegal and legal institutions of money and power are rife with homophobia and heterosexism. Keenan aptly illustrates that even if Gilbert decided to give up his get-rich-quick schemes, if Philip left the theatrical world, and if both decided to take "nine to five" jobs, they would still have to adapt to the values and codes of the heterosexual world, a world hostile to deviance from myriad norms, sexual and otherwise. By remaining outside of these institutions, Philip and Gilbert are able to live their lives more to their own choosing.

Yet despite a certain outsider status, the two men must still deal with the institutions steeped in heterosexual values and customs, and they still need money to survive. It is in interacting with these institutions and the people who operate within them that the madcap exploits and wit found in Keenan's fiction (and in so much white, middle class gay fiction and life) become essential. For example, when in *Blue Heaven* Philip helps Gilbert plan and enter into a phony heterosexual marriage just to get the money and presents, the men set into motion a madcap adventure that attempts to exploit this heterosexual ritual but also forces all the heterosexuals to play a game they're not even aware of. For once, Philip, Gilbert, and their compatriots "pull the strings." Even in *Putting on the Ritz,* where the two men seem to be the plaything of battling billionaires, the two friends pursue their own particular goals—mainly the seduction of a beautiful executive, Tommy Parker—manipulating foes and friends alike, drawing them into their improbable schemes. Although it might be noted that their madcap plotting eventually fails in both novels, we realize that Philip and Gilbert have nevertheless been able to defeat the dullness and boredom of routine heterosexual life. In the end, the larger power remains with the rich and elite, but Philip and Gilbert have been able to live their lives on their terms, to pursue their desires and goals in their own particular way, to live through and uphold values that reward them for their sexual orientation instead of opposing or punishing them.

Yet if madcap is a structure that to some degree gets others to "dance a gay tune," the use of wit, which a few reviewers of Keenan's work have sometimes labeled as insensitive or politically incorrect, functions to act as a defense mechanism and help gay men to assess and set appropriate expectations as well as amuse. In *Putting on the Ritz,* Joy Cudgel, the editor-in-chief of billionaire Peter Champion's magazine, is characterized as "Nathan Detroit after a transsexual operation." Peter's wife, Elsa Champion, is described as "a woman who ovulates Fabergé eggs." The use of narrative wit in these cases allows Philip to deal with powerful people who can easily "squash them like flies." It gives him some measure of power—at least on an intellectual plane—and while some of the barbs may seem sexist or classist, no one is exempt from this gay wit. In *Blue Heaven,* Gilbert's social graces are portrayed by Philip as "Josef Mengele touring *Barefoot in the Park*" while Philip assesses his own actions and character flaws with this funny yet morally telling imaginary headline: "GREEDY GAY LYRICIST FOUND DISMEMBERED IN POORLY DECORATED APARTMENT." In passing judgment on his good friend Gilbert and on himself in this funny, deprecating way, Philip critiques both of their character flaws and braces himself against possible failure and disappointment because of those flaws.

While Joe Keenan's humor (as well as the comedy of a legion of popular writers and performers) has not received the critical attention it deserves, at the very least, Keenan must be acknowledged and congratulated for making people, gay and straight, laugh for a little while during the dark days of the AIDS epidemic. Future critical assessments may well venture to look at those aspects of gay humor that some characterize as superficial or insensitive and learn to understand the meaning for and behind the actions and words that establish a gay sensibility.

—Richard Morris

———

KERR, M. E. *See* **MEAKER, Marijane.**

———

KHARITONOV, Evgeny Vladimirovich

Nationality: Russian writer, actor, and theater director. **Born:** Novosibirsk, 1941. **Education:** All-Union State Institute of Cinematography, Candidate of Sciences in Art Studies, 1972. **Career:** Researcher of speech defects, Department of Psychology, Moscow State University; head of a pantomime theater company of deaf-mute actors. **Died:** Moscow, of a heart attack, 29 June 1981.

Writings

Selected Fiction in Russian

"Dukhovka" ("The Oven"), "Zhilets napisal zaiavlenie" ("A Tenant Wrote a Statement"), "Odin takoi, drugoi drugoi" ("One Like This, the Other Different"), and "Nepechatnye pisateli" ("Unpublishable Writers") (short stories), in *Katalog,* edited by Filipp Berman. Ann Arbor, Michigan, Ardis, 1982.
"Vil'boa" (poem), "Alesha Serezha," "Zhiznesposobnyi mladenets" ("A Viable Infant") (short stories), "Slezy na tsvetakh" ("Teardrops on Flowers") (short prose fragments), and "Iz p'esy" ("From a Play"), in *Literaturnyi A-Ia* (Paris), No. 1, 1985.
"Dzyn'" ("Ding"; play), in *Iskusstvo kino* (Moscow), No. 6, 1988.
"Iz stikhov do 1969 goda" ("From Poetry Written before 1969") and "Nepiushchii russkii" ("A Russian Who Does Not Drink") (a cycle of short prose fragments), in *Novoe literaturnoe obozrenie* (Moscow), No. 3, 1993.

Collected Works

Slezy na tsvetakh:
Volume 1, *Pod domashnim arestom* ("Under House Arrest"), edited and with an introduction and comments by Yaroslav Mogutin. Moscow, Glagol, 1993.
Volume 2, *Dopolneniia i prilozheniia* ("Additions and Appendixes"), edited and with an introduction and comments by Yaroslav Mogutin. Moscow, Glagol, 1993.

English Translations

"Teardrops on the Flowers," translated by Arch Tait, in *Glas: New Russian Writing,* No. 4, 1993.
"One Boy's Story: 'How I Got Like That,'" translated by Kevin Moss, in *The Penguin Book of International Gay Writing,* edited by Mark Mitchell. New York, Penguin Books, 1995.
"The Oven," translated by Arch Tait, in *The Penguin Book of New Russian Writing,* edited by Viktor Erofeyev. New York, Penguin Books, 1995.
"The Oven," "One Boy's Story: How I Got Like That," "Alyosha-Seryozha," and "The Leaflet," translated by Kevin Moss, in *Out of the Blue: Russia's Hidden Gay Literature: An Anthology,* edited by Kevin Moss. San Francisco, Gay Sunshine Press, 1996.

*

Bibliography: "Bibliografiia Evgeniia Kharitonova" ("The Evgeny Kharitonov Bibliography"), in *Slezy na tsvetakh,* Vol. 2, 205-06.

Critical Sources: "Svidetel'stva, vospominaniia, kritika" ("Testimonies, Reminiscences, Criticism"), in *Slezy na tsvetakh,* Volume 2, 83-185; "Slezy na tsvetakh" ("Teardrops on Flowers") by Aleksandr Gol'dshtein, in *Novoe literaturnoe obozrenie* (Moscow), No. 3, 1993, 259-65; "'Nevozmozhnoe slovo' i ideia stilia" ("'An Impossible Word' and the Idea of Style") by Kirill Rogov, in *Novoe literaturnoe obozrenie* (Moscow), No. 3, 1993, 265-73; "'Katorzhnik na nive bukvy': 'Drugoi' Kharitonov i ego 'nepechatnoe' tvorchestvo" ("'Prison Laborer in the Field of Letters': The 'Other' Kharitonov and His 'Unpublishable' Writings") by Yaroslav Mogutin, in *Sintaksis* (Paris), No. 35, 1995, 211-20; "The Underground Closet: Political and Sexual Dissidence in East European Culture" by Kevin Moss, in *Post-Communism and the Body Politic,* edited by Ellen E. Berry, New York, New York University Press, 1995; "Preface: Russia's *Fleurs du Mal*" by Viktor Erofeeev, in *The Penguin Book of New Russian Writing,* edited by Viktor Erofeev, New York, Penguin Books, 1995, ix-xxx; "The End of the House Arrest: Gays and Writing in Contemporary Russia" by Vitaly Chernetsky, in *Red Squares, White Nights, Pink Triangles: Gay Russian Writing,* edited by Luc Beaudoin and Tim Scholl, New York, Columbia University Press (forthcoming).

*   *   *

Evgeny Kharitonov, Russia's leading gay writer of the Soviet era, lived in a tragic and paradoxical condition of not being able to publish a single line of his writings in his lifetime, and simultaneously enjoying almost a cult status within the Russian literary underground of the 1970s and 1980s. Belated public recognition of his talent and accomplishments, culminating in the publication in 1993 of the critical edition of Kharitonov's collected writings, and public references to him as "Russia's last literary genius," were combined in his home country with insistent attempts by the cultural establishment to divorce Kharitonov's writing from his homosexuality, while his uniqueness in Russian letters is due not merely to the fact that he never denied his homosexuality. For him, his sexual orientation became the lens for perceiving and representing the world around him.

The prevalent strategy of dealing with the "difficult" subject-matter of homosexuality in Kharitonov's writings among the Russian literati has been to read his works through the prism of those written a good 60 years before Kharitonov's—those of Vasily Rozanov. Looking for strategies for dealing with Kharitonov's gay writings, his Russian critics turned to Rozanov's 1911 book *People of the Moonlight,* the only "theoretical" text on the subject of homosexuality available to them, appropriating Rozanov's images of self-torturing sex-shy homosexuals and projecting them onto Kharitonov. Commentators have been particularly persistent in bringing up Rozanov's name in discussions of Kharitonov's late writings composed as series of fragments—a form favored by Rozanov. However, in difference from Rozanov, Kharitonov's fragments are multi-voiced and playful, each possessing a tone of its own, very loosely identified with the autobiographical narrator. He filtered the text through the intimate, personal experience of himself as a discrete individual, but simultaneously he perceived himself as a spokesperson of an underrepresented (indeed unrepresented) social group: gay people. Kharitonov courageously chose this path, although this made him even more acutely aware that his status was that of unpublishable writer, a subject on which he reflected in one of his texts. Kharitonov's key innovative contribution to Russian literature was his choice of homosexuality as a basis for cognitive universalization. As the writer Vladimir Sorokin notes, in Kharitonov's texts "all reality is saturated with the homosexual sentiment."

According to reminiscences of Kharitonov's friends, he began writing at the age of 20, and throughout the 1960s he was writing poetry imitative of the early twentieth-century Russian modernist school of Acmeism. Approximately in 1969, however, he renounced most of what he had written by then, and embarked on developing a new manner of writing. The manuscript collection of his writings that he prepared shortly before his untimely death (and which was reproduced as the first volume of his collected writings) was structured to showcase his new approach to literature.

"Dukhovka" ("The Oven"), the first work authored by the "new" Kharitonov, and perhaps the best known, is a first person narrative of the acquaintance of a gay man in his late twenties with a 16 year-old boy and of a series of their encounters. It is simultaneously a carefully constructed nostalgic narrative of memory and a testimonial text that introduces the reader to the experience of a member of a culturally and socially oppressed group for whom it is crucial to speak for himself rather than be "spoken for." It is a text situated in a condition of "public intimacy," transgressing the boundaries between literature and life, the public and the private. The story opens with a chance encounter at a small resort town between the unnamed, autobiographically identified protagonist and the boy, Misha; the narrative follows the attempts of the former to get as close as possible to the object of his obsession, to spend as much time as possible in his company. The entire time, however, the narrator is conscious not to provoke the slightest trace of suspicion on behalf of Misha and his friends. At every step, he evaluates his own actions, so that they appear "natural" and logical to Misha and the circle of his straight friends. Like a spy working on an enemy territory, the narrator is constantly engaged in consumption, production, and evaluation of signs. He lovingly collects the smallest signs of Misha's friendliness, and bitterly criticizes himself for slips in his behavior that may result in alienating the object of his desire. For a while he seems to be close to achieving his goal. Then, however, his luck suddenly seems to disappear, and the development of the protagonist's relationship with Misha is reversed. For the rest of the story, he clings to the smallest signs that remind him of his lost object of affection. As critics have remarked, "Dukhovka" is a narrative about the closet, but not a closeted narrative. Although the narrator uses euphemistic vocabulary, he openly shares his thoughts and feelings with the reader from whom he definitely does not conceal his sexuality; in this way, the reader is compelled to identify with the narrative perspective.

The closet does not occupy this central position in Kharitonov's other texts; however, the theme of unrequited desire and failed projects to find "the boy of his dreams" are prominently featured—the hero's passion builds up, but he lets the chance to act on it slip away. It could be, for example, a beautiful dancer whom he sees at a concert, or a particularly well endowed country boy whom he meets at a public bathhouse. Kharitonov's other early prose narratives provide ironic subversions of the narrative of a quest. Instead of acts determined at winning the object of desire, the narrative stages conscious acts leading to disposing of him. In this group of stories, the author/narrator is simultaneously inside and outside the text, directing the action and taking part in it. His is the position of someone who claims he controls the course of his and others' lives, at the same time knowing only too well that that is not the case.

Kharitonov's early quasi-autobiographical narrative works are succeeded by "Roman" ("A Novel"), an experimental text written as an assemblage of mostly brief fragments that combine explorations of the boundaries of text and writing with a strong autobiographical coloring. The pages of "Roman," filled with experiments in spacing, offer sequences of words that become magic formulas, next to "draft" texts with words crossed out—all of them saturated with gay themes and desires. Side by side with these are fragments similar to earlier narratives—stories of the narrator's personal acquaintances, together with personal letters, observations, and reflections.

Upon completing "Roman," Kharitonov experienced a creative crisis that eventually led him to adopt a new writing style, that of the cycles of fragments mixing descriptive sketches with musings on literary, philosophical, and religious topics. "Rozanovian" mode and references to the turn of the century in general are especially prominent in the cycle "Slezy ob ubitom i zadushennom" ("Tears for the Killed and Strangled One")—reflections on Orthodox Christianity, gender roles, the relationship between the artist and the state. Without resorting to the pathos of a Solzhenitsyn, Kharitonov writes with great pain about the repressive totalitarian machine, its cynicism and humiliation—next to descriptions of glory holes, representations of the affected language of "flaming" queens, and moments of high erotic tension. Never in Kharitonov do we find remarks to the extent that he hated himself for being "hopelessly homosexual," as one fellow writer has put it, or that he perceived his homosexuality as a sin, as others suggest. For him, his sexuality was a given, and to apply to it moralizing value judgments would simply be a category mistake. For Kharitonov, sin is not to do what one wants, and for a writer to stray away from his calling. What Kharitonov took up from Rozanov was not the chimeric beliefs concerning aversion to sexuality, but the perception of Christianity as infused with homoeroticism—we find reflections on this topic throughout the late fragments. In his manifesto "Listovka" ("The Leaflet"), Kharitonov takes up Rozanov's assertion that it is gay people who are the ("secret") arbiters of taste and founders of culture.

In the middle of the cycles of fragments the reader encounters an exception: "Rasskaz odnogo mal'chika—'Kak ia stal takim'" ("One Boy's Story: 'How I Got Like That'") is a realistic narrative, an almost documentary, sociological account of the biographies of two gay boys from a provincial town. This text serves as another watershed in the corpus of Kharitonov's writings—the cycles of fragments that follow are much more subdued and introspective. Reflections on the impossibility of producing a narrative text, on the faculty of writing itself, form a thread running through these texts. Kharitonov's late texts still include masterful mini-stories, "scraps" of Proustian detailed remembrances of childhood, but analytical backward glances on life and reflections on death occupy a much more prominent place.

Kharitonov must have had a presentiment of the nearing closure, for in his final days he was primarily preoccupied with carefully assembling his final tome and searching for a definition of his own "gay textuality." Kharitonov asserts that it is homosexuality and its textual representation that provide the transformational momentum for reality, both textual and extra-textual: "if we [gay people] write about them," he insists, "about their monstrous deprived norm, then one should close one's eyes and cry that some final screw has not been placed into them."

The French lesbian writer Monique Wittig has written that to be effective, a text by a minority writer must "make the minority point of view universal." She stresses that this is what enabled the work of such gay writers as Proust and Djuna Barnes to "transform the textual reality of our time." It would not be an overestimation to describe Kharitonov's contribution to contemporary Russian literature in similar terms, thus making the very fact of him being read and discussed in contemporary Russia a significant contribution to the breakdown of the citadel of homophobia in Russian culture.

—Vitaly Chernetsky

KIM, Willyce

Nationality: Asian-American novelist and poet. **Born:** Honolulu, Hawaii, 18 February 1946. **Education:** San Francisco College for Women, Lone Mountain, B.A. in English Literature 1968. **Career:** Supervisor, Graduate Library at the University of California, Berkeley, from 1983. Early member, Women's Press Collective.

WRITINGS

Novels

Dancer Dawkins and the California Kid. Boston, Massachusetts, Alyson Publications, 1985.
Dead Heat. Boston, Alyson Publications, 1988; excerpted in *Women on Women: An Anthology of American Lesbian Fiction,* edited by Joan Nestle and Naomi Holoch. New York, Plume, 1990.

Poetry

Curtains of Light. Albany, California, self-published, 1970.
Eating Artichokes. Oakland, California, Women's Press Collective, 1972.
Under the Rolling Sky. Oakland, Maud Gonne Press, 1976.

Other

"Habits" (short story), in *Bushfire,* edited by Karen Barber. Boston, Alyson Publications, 1991.
"Gardenias" (short story), in *Afterglow,* edited by Karen Barber. Boston, Alyson Publications, 1993.

*

Critical Sources: "Dancer Dawkins/Moll Cutpurse: Two Novels Explore Gender" by Judith Katz, in *Equal Time,* 24 July 1985, 9; "Shy Woman, Bold Poet" by Cathy Cade, in *A Lesbian Photo Album,* Oakland, California, 1987, 21; "Willyce Kim" by Kitty Tsui, in *Contemporary Lesbian Writers of the United States: A Bio-Bibliographical Critical Sourcebook,* edited by Sandra Pollack and Denise D. Knight, Westport, Connecticut, Greenwood Press, 1993, 283-286.

*   *   *

Willyce Kim began her career as a poet in the San Francisco Bay area in the late 1960s. Along with other vocal lesbian poets of the day, such as Pat Parker and Judy Grahn, Kim began publishing her works. She first self-published a volume called *Curtains of Light* (1970). Later, she worked with the Women's Press Collective to put out an edition of her poetry entitled *Eating Artichokes* (1972). As one of the only Asian-American lesbian writers in print, Kim makes an important contribution to our understanding of lesbian literature through her depiction of lesbians as fully functional, multi-faced human beings.

More recently, Kim has turned her attention from poetry to the novel. In her novels, she creates lesbian worlds in which almost all of the characters are lesbian and proud. Her characters are bold, cigar-smoking, fun-loving women who love other women. Although she treats lesbian sexuality frankly, Kim does not focus exclusively on the fact that her characters are lesbian. Unlike earlier lesbian authors such as Radclyffe Hall, who were often caught up in promoting a one-dimensional literary legitimization of the lesbian, Kim's characters are lesbian without apology. For instance, the California Kid, one of Kim's protagonists in her first novel, *Dancer Dawkins and the California Kid,* does not shy away from her lesbianism. Rather, Kid embraces her own sensuality, a fact highlighted in her relationship with Roxie Austin, the owner of the ice cream story at which the Kid works. Lesbian sensuality is removed from the bedroom and thrust into the everyday as the Kid and Roxie trade blatant sexual innuendo over vanilla ice cream cones. For Kim's characters, being lesbian is not shame-worthy.

Harkening back to her poetic roots, Kim's novels break with Western novel tradition to present short scenes instead of chapters. These snippets—perhaps a page long, perhaps just a sentence—control the pace of the novel. Kim masterfully manipulates these snippets to rush the reader through the text, creating in the process a sort of fast-paced, rompingly wild lesbian adventure. Kim's knowledge of poetry also plays a key role in her word choice, particularly in the names she chooses for her characters. The narrator of *Dancer Dawkins and the California Kid* even comments that one of the characters chooses a new name, Fatin Satin Aspen, based on the effectiveness of the rhyme scheme.

In *Dancer Dawkins and the California Kid,* the two protagonists named in the title set out to foil the plans of Fatin Satin Aspen, a.k.a. Morris Minnow, a con artist who is bilking unsuspecting people out of fortunes in the name of sham missionary Viola Vincente. One of the people who has fallen for his nefarious scheme is Jessica Nahale Riggins, girlfriend to Dancer Dawkins. When Dancer sets out to free Jessica from Aspen's clutches, she gets help from a Korean restauranteur named Ta Jan the Korean, a scruffy, bubble-gum chewing kid named Little Willie Gutherie, a.k.a. the California Kid, and a psychic, talking German Shepherd named Killer Shep. Together, these adventurers free Jessica and save the Napa Valley from certain destruction at the hands of Fatin Satin Aspen.

In this novel, Kim manipulates standard Western adventure tropes to comment on the form of the adventure story. The standard Western adventure calls for a manly, John Waynesque hero to save the day; Kim's heros are lesbian, and yet they successfully defeat the forces of evil without using the tools of the patriarchy. In addition, by highlighting the good versus evil dualism, Kim works to undermine it as her reader realizes that no one can be purely good, or purely evil. Kim's novel is so precisely part of the genre of the Western adventure that it becomes a parody, but a parody with a very sharp edge.

In *Dead Heat,* Kim continues her manipulation of the adventure story, creating another escapade in which good is pitted against evil. In this novel, the good comes in the pint-sized package of jockey Cody Roberts who, with the help of the cast from *Dancer Dawkins and the California Kid* and a Hungarian vizsla named Gypsy, defeats the evil forces of Vinny "the Skull" LaRoca, Diamond Jimmy, and Fat Al, small time gangsters trying to make it big by fixing a horse race. Kim adds a complicating character to this novel, however, in the form of a bisexual named Janes Philips Joyce. Janes, the girlfriend of Vinny "the Skull" LaRoca, meets and begins a sexual relationship with the California Kid. Finding herself in the midst of her first lesbian relationship, Janes begins to think about what it might mean to be a lesbian. Kim uses Janes' relationship with the Kid, then, to begin to complicate the unquestioning lesbian world Kim had created in *Dancer Dawkins and the California Kid.* Through their relationship, the heterosexual world creeps more strongly into the somewhat idyllic lesbian world of the novel; all the characters, but particularly the California Kid, must deal with the heterosexist biases of Janes' gangster acquaintances. Although Janes' decision to choose the Kid over Vinny almost gets all of them killed, in the end Kim has returned her world to its lesbian base because Janes has chosen the lesbian community of the California Kid over the heterosexual world of Vinny and his boys.

Kim's novels are fast-paced, colorful, and engaging. She pulls the reader in with a combination of wit and adventure that is hard to resist. In short, these novels are fun to read. Such fun does not preclude the political ramifications of Kim's work, however. By presenting women who are not angst-ridden, but rather are self-aware, fully functioning, heroic, and lesbian, Kim goes a long way toward dismantling the stereotypes which continue to be used to oppress lesbians today.

—Barbara Williamson

KIRKWOOD, James

Nationality: American playwright, novelist, and actor. **Born:** Los Angeles, California, 22 August 1930. **Education:** Attended New York University and University of California, Los Angeles; trained for the stage with Sanford Meisner. **Military Service:** Served in the U.S. Coast Guard Reserve. **Career:** Actor, from 1947; writer, from mid-60s; co-host, *Kirwood-Goodman Show,* WOR Radio, New York City. **Awards:** Tony Award, Drama Desk Award, Drama Critics Circle Award, Theatre World Award, and Pulitzer Prize in Drama, all for *A Chorus Line,* all 1976. **Died:** New York City, of cancer, 21 April 1989.

WRITINGS

Plays

There Must Be a Pony (toured, 1962).
U.T.B.U. (Unhealthy to Be Unpleasant) (produced Helen Hayes Theater, New York City, 1965). New York, Samuel French, 1966.
P.S. Your Cat Is Dead (produced John Golden Theatre, New York City, 1975; produced Off-Broadway, 1978). New York, Samuel French, 1976.

With Nicholas Dante, *A Chorus Line* (produced New York
  Shakespeare Festival, Newman Theatre, later Shubert Theatre,
  New York City, 1975). E.H. Morris, 1977.
Surprise (produced John Drew Theatre, Long Island, New York,
  1981).
Legends (produced Ahmanson Theatre, Los Angeles, 1986).

Screenplays

Good Times/Bad Times. United Artists, 1968.
Some Kind of Hero. Paramount, 1982.
A Chorus Line. Universal, 1985.
Also author of *Witch Story,* United Artists, and *There Must Be a
  Pony!,* Columbia Pictures Televsion.

Novels

There Must Be a Pony! Little, 1960.
Good Times/Bad Times. New York, Fawcett Crest, 1968.
American Grotesque. New York, Simon & Schuster, 1970.
P.S. Your Cat Is Dead, New York, Stein and Day, 1972.
Some Kind Of Hero. New York, Thomas Y. Crowell, 1975.
Hit Me with a Rainbow. New York, Delacorte, 1980.

*

Interviews: "James Kirkwood" by Julian Mark, in *Advocate,* No.
196, 11 August 1976, 41-42; "James Kirkwood: Cultivating Rain-
bows" by William Russo, in *Advocate,* No. 326, 17 September
1981, 40.

*   *   *

The essence of good theater is playing with the minds and hearts
of the audience, a craft which can be carried out in various ways,
among them integrating already present stereotypes, images, and
familiar language to sustain the desired illusion. When a deft actor
decides to turn private experience into public drama (whether on
stage or in print), the results are often powerful. This is particularly true of the writings of the late James Kirkwood. Born to
parents deeply involved with the film industry and acting as both
performers and, in the case of his father, director, it was natural
that Kirkwood would be attracted to the profession as well. His
portfolio ranged from numerous appearances in minor roles, beginning at age 14, through membership in touring companies of
such major shows as *Call Me Madame* to film roles including
Mommie Dearest. While his first published novel, *There Must Be
A Pony!,* draws on his own upbringing in the surreal world of Hollywood, homosexuality is not prominent as a plot theme.

Kirkwood's 1968 novel *Good Times/Bad Times* is a unique contribution to the genre of works set in private schools (most famil-
iarly represented by *Tea and Sympathy*) and is his first work to
address homosexuality directly. The sexually repressive and hypocritical environment of Gilford Academy is reinforced by the
headmaster's deep emotional conflicts over his attraction to young
men, while two of the permitted literary stereotypes of the day
for homosexuals—the effeminate adolescent (in this case, due to
an eventually fatal heart condition) and the overweight furtive—
appear in the cast of students. The growing tension between the
narrator and the headmaster culminating in abuse and murder show
Kirkwood's adoption of the prevalent view that homosexuals were

foredoomed tragic figures whose lives could only end in misery.
Good Times/Bad Times is thus one of the last of this type of literature aimed at the mass market, a genre which would vanish in
1969 in the anger and openness of the gay liberation movement.

Kirkwood's next novel, *Some Kind of Hero,* addresses the painfully mixed world of America during the Viet Nam War from the
perspective of a former P.O.W. The intense same-sex bonding of
the narrator with his unit and, upon capture, his cellmate eventually expands to include sexuality but does not lead to a homosexual relationship, such as that in Manuel Puig's *Kiss of the Spi-
der Woman.*

By the time *P.S. Your Cat Is Dead* appeared on stage in 1976,
Kirkwood's approach had shifted to both presenting less melodramatic homosexual characters and satirizing the newly-visible
gay subculture and its varied norms of behavior. The latter range
from a spoof on bondage (having a bisexual burglar tied up on the
sink) to numerous references to the widespread belief that any
unmarried male actor must be gay, epitomized by the flagrantly
effeminate behavior of two friends who invite themselves to the
hero's apartment for New Years' Eve. Kirkwood's characters re-
visit the theme of how interpersonal male bonding can occur in
the most unlikely conditions, a theme also present in *Good Times/
Bad Times.*

The portrayal of gay people as ordinary individuals sharing their
experiences of such familiar life situations as disappointment in
love and dreams of stardom came to full blossom in the 1975 smash
Broadway hit show which Kirkwood co-authored with Nicholas
Dante, the Pulitzer Prize-wining *A Chorus Line.* Once again, the
world of acting sets the scene, and the play explores the human
dynamics of a casting call for an upcoming production. Of the
group of 17 finalists interviewed by the director, two, Greg and
Paul, are gay. In Greg are lingering echoes of extreme homophobia,
evidenced by his comment that "I thought being gay meant being
a bum all the rest of my life," while Paul had always known he
was gay but "what bothered me was that I didn't know how to
be a boy."

In the preface to Kirkwood's history of the production of his
1986 play *Legends!,* entitled *Diary of a Mad Playwright* and finished shortly before his death in 1989, fellow playwright Terence
Macnally noted that his life was "a lesson in going for broke."
His images of homosexuality are likewise faithful to the changing
spirit of the times when they were crafted and the transformation
of gay men on stage from stereotypes to human beings. In an interview with *The Advocate,* Kirkwood emphasized these elements
of his work when responding to the question whether a "normal"
homosexual character would ever appear on Broadway—"I would
write a play with a homosexual as a central character but it
wouldn't be to crusade for a cause. It would be because I thought
the theme and character were interesting enough to write
about....Gay people come in all shapes and sizes."

—Robert B. Marks Ridinger

KLEPFISZ, Irena

Nationality: American poet, essayist, and translator. **Born:** Poland, 1941; moved to the United States, 1949. **Education:** Edu-

cated in New York City public schools and in Workmen's Circle shules and mitl-shul (high school); City College of New York, B.A. in English 1962; University of Chicago, Ph.D. in English Literature 1970; post-doctoral fellow, Max Weinreich Center for Jewish Studies. YIVO Institute for Jewish Research, New York City, 1974-76. **Career:** Assistant professor of English, Long Island University, Brooklyn, New York, 1969-73; instructor, Yiddish Summer Program, Columbia University, New York, 1976-78, 1988; instructor of Women's Studies, Brooklyn College, New York, 1979; visiting professor of Women's Studies and Judaic Studies, State University of New York at Albany, 1984-85; professor of Creative Writing, Adult Degree Program, Vermont College, Montpellier, 1985-89; visiting professor of English and Women's Studies, University of California at Santa Cruz, California, 1991; professor of Yiddish Women Writers, YIVO's Uriel Weinreich Summer Program in Yiddish Language, Literature, and Culture, Columbia University, New York, 1995; visiting professor in English and Women's Studies, Wake Forest University, Winston-Salem, North Carolina, 1995; adjunct associate professor of Jewish Women's Studies, Barnard College, New York, 1996; visiting professor of Women's Studies, Jewish Studies, and English, Michigan State University, 1997. Founder and editor of *Conditions: A Journal of Women's Writings,* 1976-80; translator in residence, Max Weinreich Center for Jewish Studies, YIVO Institute for Jewish Research, New York, 1989; editorial board, *Bridges: A Journal for Jewish Feminists and Our Friends,* from 1989; executive director, New Jewish Agenda, 1990-92; editorial consultant, *Yiddish Language and Culture, Bridges: A Journal for Jewish Feminists,* and *Our Friends.* **Awards:** National Endowment of the Arts, 1988; New York State CAPS grant, 1976.

WRITINGS

Nonfiction

"Anti-Semitism in the Lesbian/Feminist Movement" and "Resisting and Surviving in America," in *Nice Jewish Girls,* edited by Evelyn Torton Beck. Watertown, Massachusetts, Persephone, 1982; Boston, Massachusetts, Beacon, 1989.
"Secular Jewish Identity: Yidishkayt in America," in *The Tribe of Dina,* edited by Melanie Kaye/Kantrowitz and Irena Klepfisz. Montpelier, Vermont, Sinister Wisdom Books, 1986.
"Women Without Children/Women Without Families/Women Alone," in *Politics of the Heart,* edited by Sandra Pollack and Jeanne Vaughn. Ithaca, New York, Firebrand Books, 1987.
"Jewish Progressives and the Jewish Community," in *Tikkun,* Vol. 4, No. 3, May-June 1989, 83-85.
"The Distance Between Us: Feminism, Consciousness and the Girls at the Office," in *Out the Other Side: Contemporary Lesbian Writing,* edited by Sue O'Sullivan and Christian McEwen. London, England, Virago Press, Freedom, California, The Crossing Press, 1989.
"Yom Hashoah, Yom Yerushalayim: A Meditation," in *Nice Jewish Girls,* 2nd edition, edited by Evelyn Torton Beck. Boston, Massachusetts, Beacon, 1989.

"Forging a Woman's Link in Di Goldene Keyt: Some Possibilities for Jewish American Poetry" in *Conversant Essays: Contemporary Poets on Poetry,* edited by James McCorkle. Detroit, Michigan, Wayne State University Press, 1990.
Dreams of an Insomniac: Jewish Feminist Essays, Speeches, and Diatribes. Portland, Oregon, Eighth Mountain Press, 1990.
"Reconstructed Selves," in *Ms.,* Vol. 3, No. 5, March-April 1993.
"The Politics of Snails," in *Garden Variety Dykes: Lesbian Traditions in Gardening,* edited by Irene Reti and Valeri Jean Chase. Santa Cruz, California, Herbooks, 1994.
"Di mames, dos loshn/The Mothers, the Language: Feminist, Yidishkayt, and the Politics of Memory," in *Bridges: A Journal for Jewish Feminists and Our Friends,* Vol. 4, No. 2, winter/spring 1994, 12-47.
"Queens of Contradiction: A Feminist Introduction to Yiddish Women Writers," in *Found Treasures—Stories by Yiddish Women Writers,* edited by Freida Forman, Ethel Raicus, Sara Silberstien Schwartz, and Margie Wolf. Toronto, Ontario, Second Story Press, 1994.

Poetry

periods of stress. New York, Out & Out Books, 1975.
Keeper of Accounts. Watertown, Massachusetts, Persephone Press, 1982.
Different Enclosures: The Poetry and Prose of Irena Klepfisz. London, England, Onlywomen Press, 1985.
"Warsaw, 1983: Umschlagplatz" and "Der mames shabosim/mother's tongue," in *Bridges: A Journal for Jewish Feminists and Our Friends,* prospectus, 1989.
A Few Words in the Mother Tongue: Poems Selected and New. Portland, Oregon, Eighth Mountain Press, 1990.
"67 Remembered," in *Tikkun,* Vol. 5, No. 3, 1991.
"Bashert," in *Tikkun,* Vol. 5, No. 5, September-October 1991.

Editor

With Melanie Kaye/Kantrowitz, *The Tribe of Dina: A Jewish Women's Anthology.* Montpellier, Vermont, Sinister Wisdom Books, 1986; Boston, Beacon Press, 1989.   •
With Rita Fabel and Danna Nevel, *A Jewish Women's Call for Peace: A Handbook for Jewish Women on the Israeli/Palestinian Conflict.* Ithaca, New York, Firebrand, 1990.
With Linda Eber and Melanie Kaye/Kantrowitz, *Action and Awareness: Handbook on Anti-Semitism.* New York, New Jewish Agenda, 1991.

Other

With Rita Falbel, "Renee Epelbaum: Still Struggling in Argentina" (interview), in *Bridges: A Journal for Jewish Feminists and Our Friends,* Vol. 1, No. 1, Spring 1990, 86-95.
"The Lamp" (parable), in *Bridges: A Journal for Jewish Feminists and Our Friends,* Vol. 1, No. 1, spring 1990, 96-97.
Translator, "From the Archives: Jewish Feminism 1913: Yente Serdatzky's 'Confession' and Vide/Confession," in *Bridges: A Journal for Jewish Feminists and Our Friends,* Vol. 1, No. 2, fall 1990, 77-92.

"Bread and Candy: Songs of the Holocaust" (musical for five voices), in *Bridges: A Journal for Jewish Feminists and Our Friends,* fall 1991, 122-128.

With Judith Helfand, "A Healthy Baby Girl" (video script), 1994.

"Zeyere eygene verter/Their Own Words: Yiddish Women's Voices" (performance piece; produced at the Jewish Museum, New York City).

*

Biography: "Irena Klepfisz: A Life in Print. The Early Years, 1975-1992" by Esther Altshul Helfgott (dissertation), University of Michigan, 1995.

Critical Sources: Review of *Keeper of the Accounts* by Marge Piercy, in *American Book Review,* Vol. 5, September 1983, 12; review of *The Tribe of Dina: A Jewish Women's Anthology* by Genevieve Stuttaford, in *Publishers Weekly,* Vol. 236, No. 2, 14 July 1989, 70; review of *The Tribe of Dina: A Jewish Women's Anthology* by Deborah Gussman in *Library Journal,* Vol. 114, No. 14, 1 September 1989, 190; review of *The Tribe of Dina: A Jewish Women's Anthology* by Pamela S. Nadell, in *American Jewish History,* Vol. 80, No. 1, August 1990, 100-108; review of *A Few Words in the Mother Tongue: Poems Selected and New, 1971-1990* and *Dreams of an Insomniac: Jewish Feminist Essays, Speeches and Diatribes* by Penny Kaganoff, in *Publishers Weekly,* Vol. 237, No. 35, 31 August 1990, 58; "Stepmother Tongues" by Adrienne Rich, in *Tikkun,* Vol. 5, No. 5, September-October 1990, 35-37; review of *A Few Words in the Mother Tongue: Poems Selected and New, 1971-1990* by Molly Abramowitz in *Library Journal,* Vol. 115, No. 16, 1 October 1990, 92; review of *The Tribe of Dina: A Jewish Women's Anthology* by Kathryn Hellerstein, in *Journal of Religion,* Vol. 71, No. 2, April 1991, 312; "Darkness Is the Incubator" by Ellen Stone, in *Bridges: A Journal for Jewish Feminists and Our Friends,* Vol. 2, No. 1, spring 1991, 122-128; review of *A Few Words in the Mother Tongue: Poems Selected and New, 1971-1990* by Adrienne Rich, in *Ms.,* Vol. 2, No. 2, September-October 1991, 75; review of *A Few Words in the Mother Tongue: Poems Selected and New, 1971-1990* by Meryl Altman, in *Women's Review of Books,* Vol. 8, No. 1, October 1991, 16-17; "Contemporary Poetics and History: Pinsky, Klepfisz and Rothenberg" by James McCorkle, in *Kenyon Review,* Vol. 14, No. 1, winter 1992, 171-188; "Irena Klepfisz's 'Fradel Schtok' and the Language of Hyphenated Identity," in *Anglistik & Englischunterricht (A & E)* (Heidelberg, Germany), 1994, 129-139; "Her Face in the Mirror: Jewish Women on Mothers and Daughters" by Henry Carrigan, Jr., in *Library Journal,* Vol. 119, No. 16, 1 October 1994, 86; "Found Treasures: Stories by Yiddish Women Writers" by Sharon Drache in *Canadian-Forum,* Vol. 74, No. 840, June 1995, 44-45.

*   *   *

Irena Klepfisz was born in 1941 in Warsaw, Poland. Her father was killed in 1943 during the Warsaw Ghetto Uprising and, following the war, she and her mother immigrated first to Sweden and then to the United States, arriving in 1949. Throughout her life, Klepfisz has grappled with difficult and complex issues in her writing—passing, immigration, loss, destruction, economics, community, and acts of resistance and courage by "ordinary people." Her Jewish identity was formed not just by der kherbn—

"the destruction," a Yiddish term for the Holocaust—but by the Yiddish speaking progressive Jewish socialist movement. Later, her lesbian identity came out of the contemporary women's movement. Writing in *Ms.* magazine in 1993, Klepfisz speaks of the quintessential importance of both identities: "My coming out was marked by exhilaration—quickly tempered by reality. Heterosexual Jews were appalled and cited social norms and biblical texts; lesbians pointed to the Israeli occupation and to Jewish capitalist tendencies. Each group demanded: give up the other. But even if I had wanted to, I had no idea how to shed either identity."

In her writings and activist work, Klepfisz refuses to compromise or create melodrama. She takes on hard questions and forcefully brings the personal and political together. She de-romanticizes history by speaking of its effect on contemporary issues. As Evelyn Torton Beck writes in the introduction to Klepfisz's *Dreams of an Insomniac,* "The extraordinary power of Irena Klepfisz's work lies in the force of its moral and artistic integrity." Her artistic integrity is pronounced in her careful use of language. By the time Klepfisz was ten she was familiar with four languages. She embraces and sees language as a healer, an obstacle, a tool towards understanding, and a wedge that creates distances. Her poetry and prose have been acclaimed for their dynamic experimental use of language. Much of her work is bilingual, in Yiddish and English—a reflection of the inseparable impact Yiddish and American culture and language have on her life, and her efforts to regain a rich secular Jewish culture.

In over 25 years, Klepfisz has refused to let go of any of her identities, her languages, or the voices of those around her. Her activism, lectures, writing, translations, and research have addressed such varied areas as Jewish identity and "yidishe veltlekhkayt un kultur" (Jewish secularism and culture), feminism, homophobia, lesbian and feminist publishing, class, childlessness, the Holocaust, anti-Semitism, and a two-state solution to the Israeli/Palestinian conflict. She has taught Yiddish, Judaic, and Women's Studies, English literature and creative writing, and worked as a translator for such authors as Kadya Molodowsky, Fradel Schotk, and Blume Lempel. Her poetry and essays have appeared in a variety of journals.

In 1976, Klepfisz became co-founder of the lesbian magazine *Conditions.* Her book of poems, *Periods of Stress,* was published in 1975, followed by *Keeper of the Accounts* in 1982, and *Different Enclosures* in 1985. In these works Klepfisz takes on voices from monkeys caged in a zoo to women workers "caged" in an office. In one of her best known poems, "Bashert," she uses the voices of Holocaust victims and survivors to question the absurdity surrounding either of these outcomes.

In 1986, with Melanie Kaye/Kantrowitz, Klepfisz co-edited *The Tribe of Dina: A Jewish Women's Anthology.* As Kathryn Hellerstein states in the *Journal of Religion,* it "gives voice to feminists and lesbians who speak from Jewish secular and cultural, rather than religious, perspectives." According to the introduction, the anthology was partly motivated by the June 1982 Israeli invasion of Lebanon, "an event which had a profound effect on American Jews, as on Israelis." It was "natural" for Klepfisz to take on Middle East issues and their effects on women. In 1988, she co-founded the Jewish Women's Committee to End the Occupation of the West Bank and Gaza. In 1990, she co-edited *A Jewish Women's Call for Peace: A Handbook for Jewish Women on the Israeli/Palestinian Conflict.*

In 1990, Klepfisz published *A Few Words in the Mother Tongue: Poems Selected and New, 1971-1990* and *Dreams of an Insom-*

niac: Jewish Feminist Essays, Speeches and Diatribes, both of which brought her much critical acclaim. These books brought Klepfisz to the attention of even larger audiences, and Klepfisz seemed to feed off the acclaim by engaging in further activism. She served as Executive Director of New Jewish Agenda from 1990 to 1992; coordinated a major conference for Yiddish women in 1995; and became a member of a newly formed collective, Hemshekh: Feminist Institute for Secular Jewish Cultural Continuity. Klepfisz has insisted on remaining uncompromising about her identity, and her insistence has served as an inspiration to her readers to look directly and honestly into the eyes of any issue; to see loss and to find hope through personal and political searching; and to use history, language and activism to respect our past and look toward the possibilities of the future, while maintaining dignity and power.

—tova gd stabin

KLIUEV, Nikolai Alekseeivich

Nationality: Russian poet. **Born:** The village of Koshtugi, Vytegra District, Volonda Region, 20 October 1887. **Education:** Studied at Petrozavodsk Medical School for one year. **Died:** During internal exile in Siberia in August 1937.

WRITINGS

Sochineniya, edited by Boris Filippov and Gleb Struve. Munich, 1969.
Poems, translated by John Glad. Ann Arbor, Ardis, 1977.
Poems published in *Ogonek,* 1989.

*

Critical Sources: "The Life and Works of Nikolay Klyuyev" by Jesse Davies, in *New Zealand Slavonic Journal,* Vol. 2, 1974, 65-75; "Klyuev, Nikolai Alekseevich (1887-1937)" by John Glad, in *Handbook of Russian Literature,* edited by Victor Terra, New Haven, Yale University Press, 1985, 227; "Nikolai Klyuev (1887-1937)" by Sergei Subbotin, in *Soviet Literature,* Vol. 6, 1988, 142-44.

*   *   *

The voice of homosexuality was seldom heard in the literature of Russia until the beginning of the twentieth-century, during what is colloquially termed the "Silver Age." While several of the major writers such as Mikhail Kuzmin and Marina Tsvetaeva are now familiar to Western audiences, other significant artists are less well known outside their own country. This is particularly true of the colorful and complex figure Nikolai Kliuev. Born in 1887 in a small village near the town of Vytegra in the Russian Far North, he was raised in an isolated and heavily traditional peasant culture which had preserved much of the mythology, folklore, and social structure of ancient rural Russia intact. Though his father was of the Samoyed people, his Russian mother (who passed on to him a wide range of folk tales as well as stories from the Apocrypha)

saw to it that he received an education, first in a village school and later at the Solovetsky Monastery on the White Sea. By the age of 15 his literary talents had been recognized and were employed as a composer of religious songs for the local chapter of the radical underground Khlyst movement, which was opposed to the authority of the Orthodox Church.

Kliuev's first poems appeared in print in 1904, when he was 17, but his emergence as a nationally known poet within Russia began with a letter to the prominent writer Aleksandr Blok, the beginning of a long friendship and a correspondence between them which lasted for six years. Blok was concerned with the gap between the intelligentsia and the mass of Russian peasantry, and regarded Kliuev as one of what would come to be known by the mid 1910s as the "peasant poets." Through his influence, the journal *The Golden Fleece* (devoted to the work of members of the Symbolist group) published two of Kliuev's poems in 1908. By 1916, he had produced four anthologies of verse which were widely read and highly popular.

Once he arrived in St. Petersburg, Kliuev maintained a public identity as a flamboyantly traditional peasant, often appearing in public wearing the full blouse, oiled boots, and trousers of that class. Through his writings, he became acquainted in 1915 with the younger peasant poet Sergei Esenin. His passion for the younger man (who regarded Kliuev as his teacher and mentor) was clearly homosexual, although it is not known if the relationship included physical contact. While in the early period of their careers as poets, Esenin and Kliuev gave joint readings. Critical acclaim for Kliuev's work (and his jealousy of Esenin's relationships with women and the latter's rejection of traditional Russian values in favor of image over content) later drove them apart. Following the Revolution of 1917, Kliuev welcomed the new order but continued to regard it from a peasant viewpoint, an attitude which quickly resulted in his classification by Lev Trotsky as a spokesman for the well-off peasants, or *kulaks,* who were to suffer greatly under the planned collectivization of agriculture. One critic even went so far as to term Kliuev "a *kulak* ideologue."

On 25 December 1925 Esenin (who had become an alcoholic and exhibited aberrant behavior) paid a call on Kliuev and read him his most recent verse, requesting his opinion. Upon being told that a book of such poems would be favored reading for the youth of Russia, Esenin sank into a depression which resulted in his committing suicide on December 28. A stricken Kliuev wept publicly at Esenin's funeral, and later committed his grief to paper in the 1927 work *Lament for Esenin,* crying out "With you I would lie in an honest coffin...I grieve like the bitter grass...I am widowed without you."

Between 1923 and 1931, Kliuev lived in St. Petersburg, returning to Moscow in 1932. Barred from publication after 1928, he supported himself by giving recitations of his works at private dinners. This situation led to his arrest in 1933 on the grounds of spreading "kulak propaganda" and a sentence of internal exile to the Narym region of Siberia. Through the efforts of Maxim Gorky, he was transferred in October 1934 to the city of Tomsk, where he was re-arrested and lived until the summer of 1937. The circumstances of his death later that year remain unclear, although his poetry survived and was reprinted beginning in 1977.

Kliuev's homosexuality shines forth most clearly in those poems dedicated to Nikolai Arkhipov, his lover and director of the Peterhof Museum. His major 1922 work *Mother Sabbath* begins with a description of Arkhipov as "my last joy." In *The Fourth Rome* (Moscow in the theology of the Orthodox Church) Kliuev rejects the modern world (as exemplified by the recently transformed Esenin) and praises "dear Nikolai, Hive of living kisses." Arkhipov received from Kliuev during his exile the second section of a long poem, "Song of the Great Mother" but was himself arrested soon after.

—Robert B. Marks Ridinger

KOTZ, Cappy

Pseudonyms: Has also written as C. Bailey and Crystal Bailey. **Nationality:** American novelist, playwright, and author of short erotic fiction. **Born:** Bozeman, Montana, 18 July 1955. **Education:** Bainbridge High School, Bainbridge Island, Washington; studied theater and dance, Evergreen State College, Olympia, Washington, 1973-74. **Family:** Companion of Betsy Bruce. **Career:** Has worked in the Seattle, Washington, area as a house painter, 1978-84, a firefighter, 1984-87, and a fitness trainer, from 1989. **Address:** 1111 E. Madison, Suite 433, Seattle, Washington 98122, U.S.A.

WRITINGS

Erotic Fiction

"Dykelet May I," in *Sapphic Touch/A Journal of Lesbian Erotica,* Vol. 1. San Francisco, Pamir Productions, 1981.
"How Many More" and "Girl Gang," in *Coming to Power.* Boston, Alyson Publications, 1981.
"My Nympho," in *Backbone 4.* Seattle, Washington, Seal Press, 1982.
"Ride My Bitch II," in *The Leading Edge: An Anthology of Lesbian Sexual Fiction.* Denver, Colorado, Lace Publications (now Alyson Publications), 1988.
The First Stroke. Denver, Lace Publications (now Alyson Publications), 1988.
"Under Cover," in *Dyke Review* (San Francisco), spring 1992.
"Tuesday Night Wild," in *Dyke Review* (San Francisco), summer 1992.

Plays

With Phrin Prickett, *In Search of the Hammer* (produced by Front Room Theater, Seattle, 1983).
With Prickett, *The Return of the Hammer* (produced by Front Room Theater, Seattle, 1985).
With Prickett, *The Grand Fitting* (produced by Front Room Theater, Seattle, 1990).

Recordings: *In Search of the Hammer and Return of the Hammer,* Seattle, Front Room Theater and Gay Community Social Services, 1988.

*

Critical Sources: "Introduction" by Pat Califia, in Cappy Kotz, *The First Stroke,* Denver, Lace Publications (now Alyson Publications), 1988; "Up Close and Personal: An Interview With Cappy Kotz" by Beth Berndt, in *Dyke Review* (San Francisco), summer 1992, 27-29.

Cappy Kotz comments:

Through the course of my childhood the books I read, the movies I saw, and nearly all of the social practices I observed referenced the belief that romance, sex, marriage, family, and home occur when a man and a woman fall in love. When I came out I finally had something I truly believed in to write about. Immediately I launched a frenzy of writing, making up for lost time, and with an inner conviction that fleshing out plots with lesbian dynamics would, eventually, balance out the world. Hadn't I always been told that a writer must write what she knows? I *knew* lesbians, I loved it that we could be real, that we existed, that fiction could be our mirror. However, when I tried to push my stories out of the dark into tales of true love, it became clearer and clearer to me I had no idea how to go there. Something was holding me back, and if I couldn't proceed, my characters certainly couldn't either. At that point the business of writing became a journey deeper into my interior as I sought my own content, the why and wherefore of my early training, and the meaning behind my entrenched silences. Now I understand better: when the male hero is replaced by a female hero, when that female hero loves the woman who is also a hero, the story is different. The form might be the same—for instance, hope leads to love through trials of loss and doubt—but the story is different when the principal characters are women loving women, creating family and home. As a writer it's my job to fine tune this difference, and recently I've begun to think of myself as a "dyke differential." I'm the little gear that helps connect the tried and true plots with lesbian content.

*   *   *

Cappy Kotz likes to say about her multi-faceted career, "I'm a painter by trade, a firefighter by profession, a coach for service, and a writer, by god!" In this way she describes the commitment she has made to keep writing an integral part of her life and her self-definition. It is a commitment and a struggle familiar to all women writers and especially to lesbians who have often found their experiences undervalued and their voices unmarketable.

Growing up in the rural outskirts of Seattle, Kotz began writing as a child. Her poetry and short stories brought her to the attention of family and teachers, who often found her work "odd, but amusing." Her interest in physical activity, a lifelong passion, led Kotz into her studies of drama and theater at Evergreen State College. She felt the need to learn to use her body, and drama provided a new kind of discipline for training the body and mind to work together. In college Kotz also began to discover her lesbianism. Coming out as a lesbian directly affected her work in the theater and her writing in important ways. She soon found the compulsory heterosexuality of many plays restrictive, and she searched for a new and more authentic voice in her writing.

While enrolled in the Theater and Dance department at Evergreen College, Kotz had read and studied plays, and was especially influenced by feminists like Megan Terry. As she became more disenchanted with the limitations of traditional theater, she turned once again to writing, this time writing her own plays. In her body of produced work, written in collaboration with musician/songwriter Phrin Prickett, Kotz has turned her writer's eye unblinkingly on the lesbian community itself. Her plays, while lighthearted and dynamic, focus attention on many serious issues within the lesbian community. In the tradition of the Broadway musical, exemplified by plays like *West Side Story* and *Showboat,* Kotz and Prickett take on central issues of lesbian life and display, dissect, and, quite literally, *sing* them. Fat oppression, non-monogamy, butch-femme roles, and the search for heritage are only a few of the issues engaged in their productions. Such issues, largely drawn from the authors' own lives and sensibilities, require little explanation for lesbian audiences, though they may be unfamiliar to heterosexual society.

When the parents of one character in *In Search of the Hammer,* the first Kotz/Prickett collaboration, respond to their daughter's announcement that she is a lesbian with a long, pregnant pause, then burst into a lively surprise of a song titled "We're So Proud," there is hardly a dry lesbian eye in the house. The subtext for scenes like this exists not in the script but in the audience which is filled with lesbians, many of whom have their own similar stories and unfulfilled longings for such happy endings. It is this need that Kotz has recognized and tapped into: a need to see one's life and concerns reflected in one's culture. Her plays are musical comedies—two of them are archetypal fantasies, and the set for *In Search of the Hammer* was a huge comic book, whose pages turned to change the scene—but most deeply they are true stories of lesbian emotional and cultural life told in a format usually reserved for the display of more traditional values.

Most of Kotz's published writing is in a far less traditional format. Her short erotic fiction generally takes one of two forms, playful and humorous stories of lesbians revelling in sex and their own sexuality, and spare, almost austere tales of sexual power and submission. In the first category are stories like "My Nympho," in which the narrator, an endearingly insecure and lustful lesbian answering an ad in the personals, elicits warm and wry applause from the reader. These stories, though deeply sexual, contain a certain innocence that feels young, brash, and energetic.

The First Stroke is an example of the second type of erotic writing. It is a collection of 13 stories in which the same characters appear. In these and other works, many of the characters appear to be different facets of the author herself and thus remind the reader of the different facets in each of us. These stories, like Kotz's plays, create a world which, though familiar, is tinged with fantasy and magic. Not a rollicking, light sort of magic this time, but a deep and primal one, marked by blood rites and private rituals.

When Kotz's erotic work first began to find publishers, she received much acclaim and support from the sado-masochist (s/m) lesbian community. In the early 1980s s/m was a controversial topic just beginning to be discussed, often hotly, in lesbian circles. Lesbians embracing s/m, like many lesbians a decade earlier, were just beginning to find each other and discuss their lives and their sexuality out loud for the first time. Writing like Kotz's that explored power balances and intentional submission to power was welcomed and devoured.

The next step in Kotz's writing was to move through the dark ritual of s/m into a more holistic approach to sexuality. Complex issues of abuse and healing as well as a return to the appealing lesbian searcher of her earlier work marked her later writings. The late 1990s finds Kotz seeking a publisher for her latest novel, *Lucky Penny.* She compliments her work as a boxing coach and fitness trainer by developing a program of non-competitive boxing, a concept of her own invention for which she is writing a manual.

Throughout her 20 years of writing, Kotz has continued to develop, combining her particular passions for spirituality, sexuality, and the complexities of the physical body. Perhaps the best description of the quality of her work comes from the author herself: "I don't feel there's any topic that comes to me I won't delve into. Even if I feel scared, I'll take the time to confront myself, so I can give it freedom, so it will be a place I can write about."

—Tina Gianoulis

KUREISHI, Hanif

Nationality: British/Pakistani author, director, and playwright. **Born:** Bromley, England, in 1954. **Education:** King's College, London, B.A. in philosophy. **Career:** Worked at a variety of minor jobs in the theatre; writer in residence, Royal Court Theatre, London, 1981, and 1985-86; directed the feature film *London Kills Me,* 1991; contributor of short stories and essays to periodicals, including *Granta, Harpers, London Review of Books,* and *New Yorker.* **Awards:** Thames Television Playwright Award, 1980; George Devine Award, 1981; *Evening Standard* Award, 1985; Most Popular Film Award, Rotterdam Festival, 1986; Best Screenplay Award, New York Film Critics Circle, 1986; Best Screenplay Award, National Society of Film Critics, 1986; Academy Award nomination, for Best Original Screenplay Written Directly for the Screen, 1986; Whitbread Book of the Year Award, First Novel category, 1990; Bookseller Association of Great Britain and Ireland Award, 1990. **Agents:** Stephen Durbridge, The Agency (London) Ltd., 24 Pottery Lane, London W11 4LZ, England; and Deborah Rogers, Rogers Coleridge & White Ltd., 20 Powis Mews, London W11 1JN, England.

WRITINGS

Plays/Screenplays

Soaking Up the Heat (produced in London at the Theatre Upstairs, 1976).

The Mother Country (produced in London at Riverside Studios, 1980).

The King and Me (produced in London at the Soho Poly Theatre, 1980). London, John Calder (Publishers) Ltd., 1983.

Borderline (produced in London at the Royal Court Theatre, 1981). London, Methuen, 1981.

Outskirts (produced in London by the Royal Shakespeare Company at the Royal Shakespeare Company Warehouse, 1981). London, John Calder (Publishers) Ltd., 1983.

Tomorrow—Today! (produced in London, 1981).

Artists and Admirers (adapted from work by Alexander Ostrovsky, translated with David Leveaux; produced in London, 1982; produced in New York City at the City Stage Company Repertory Theatre, 1986).

Birds of Passage (produced in London at the Royal Court Theatre, 1983). London, Amber Lane Press, 1983.

Mother Courage (adapted from a play by Berthold Brecht; produced in London by the Royal Shakespeare Company, 1984).

Cinders (adapted from a play by Janusz Glowacki; produced in London, 1985).

My Beautiful Laundrette (broadcast in England by Channel Four, 1985; distributed in the United States by Orion Classics, 1986). With autobiographical essay "The Rainbow Sign" as *My Beautiful Laundrette and The Rainbow Sign,* London, Faber and Faber Ltd., 1986.

Sammy and Rosie Get Laid (Cinecon, 1987). Published as *Sammy and Rosie Get Laid: The Script and the Diary,* New York, Penguin, 1988.

London Kills Me: Three Screenplays and Four Essays. London, Faber and Faber Ltd., 1991, New York, Penguin, 1992.

My Son the Fanatic. London, Faber and Faber Ltd., 1997.

Fiction

The Buddha of Suburbia (novel). London, Faber and Faber Ltd., and New York, Viking, 1990.

The Black Album (novel). London, Faber and Faber Ltd., and New York, Viking, 1995.

Love in a Blue Time (short stories). London, Faber and Faber Ltd., 1997.

Other

You Can't Go Home (radio play). 1980.

The Trial (radio play; adapted from a novel by Franz Kafka). 1982.

Editor, with Jon Savage, *The Faber Book of Pop* (nonfiction). London, Faber and Faber Ltd., 1995.

*

Biography: "The Rainbow Sign," in *My Beautiful Laundrette and The Rainbow Sign,* London, Faber and Faber, Ltd., 1986.

Critical Sources: "Hanif Kureishi and the Brown Man's Burden" by N. Yousaf, in *Critical Survey,* Vol. 8, No. 1, 1986; "Hanif Kureishi and the Tradition of the Novel" by Alamgir Hashmi, in *Critical Survey,* Vol. 15, No. 1, 1993.

*   *   *

In an early autobiographical essay titled "The Rainbow Sign," Hanif Kureishi identified the kinds of self-hatred he internalized growing up a British-Pakistani. "The word 'Pakistani,'" he wrote, "had been made into an insult. It was a word I didn't want used about me." Such a degree of alienation, particularly for someone born and raised in England—Kureishi's father is Pakistani, his mother English—and for someone so formed by its popular culture, figures repeatedly in his work as a kind of groundlessness. Born in Britain but never accepted as English, his main characters are simultaneously unable to identify fully or unambivalently as either Pakistani or British. Such is the case in *The Buddha of Suburbia,* which begins with its narrator, Karim Amir, identifying himself "as an Englishman born and bred, almost. I am often considered to be a funny kind of Englishman, a new breed as it were, having emerged from two old histories."

Kureishi has never been interested in presenting a vision of a unified or solid Pakistani-British experience. His work has consistently examined the ways the disenfranchised or oppressed unite into factions and, frequently and comically, battle among themselves. In fact, characters who endorse some movement toward Pakistani or Islamic unity are often undercut by their embrace of violence, radical religious conservatism and its corresponding sexual puritanism, sexism, and anti-intellectual censorship, or are exposed as charlatans. Indeed, Kureishi's 1995 novel *The Black Album* takes as one of its major themes the British Islamic reaction to the publication of Salman Rushdie's *The Satanic Verses* and the resultant *fatwah* declared against its author.

If he seems to distrust religion or national sentiment, Kureishi no less rigorously critiques attempts by Pakistanis to assimilate seamlessly into English culture, attempts that usually leave characters rich but broken, lonely, indulgent, and selfish. Such characters have, in embracing western capitalism better than the westerners, abandoned too much and lost sight of community, duty, and family. It is within this series of complex, ambivalent positions that Kureishi stages his fiction and dramas. His characters, like Omar in *My Beautiful Laundrette,* are fully British in ways that make it impossible for them to identify with their parents' nostalgia for Pakistan; at the same time, the color of their skin is used constantly by white Britishers to remind them that they will never be truly English.

Because Kureishi's work is broadly farcical in its focus on the sexual drama between two individuals, but wants at the same time to intervene in current political and social struggles between classes and races, the works often have an oddly abstract quality. Characters in *Sammy and Rosie Get Laid,* for instance, walk serenely through riots that appear to be war zones. It is not that they are self-involved to such a degree that they are oblivious to the outside world, but that, for Kureishi, their lives replay and repeat the same violence and confusion on the streets internally. Violence, even when tragic, has an oddly comic quality that makes it more than somewhat surreal.

Sex is almost always farcically comic, and almost always serves to subvert racial, national, or sexual norms, however provisionally, throughout Kureishi's writing. He has a strong awareness of the ways in which national, racial, and gender politics play out in terms of desire, and he presents sexual encounters as an opportunity for the exploration of differences through curiosity and pleasure rather than violence. His works tend to examine miscegenation—Karim's parents in *The Buddha of Suburbia,* Sammy and Rosie, Omar and Johnny in *My Beautiful Laundrette*—and work toward unity rather than conflict, however tentatively. That some of these relationships are homosexual seems completely unremarkable to Kureishi and his characters; many of his male and female characters are, like Karim, actively and unanxiously bisexual.

Kureishi's world is not without homophobia, though. Characters are driven by their parents or by parental figures to settle down, marry, and grow up, but they often manage to resist the compulsion to assume heterosexuality playfully, cleverly, and on their own terms. And even when they do assume "proper" heterosexuality, like the lesbian Jamila in *The Buddha of Suburbia* who is coerced by her father and her sense of familial duty into an arranged marriage, they can still rewrite that traditional formula in surprisingly non-traditional ways. Kureishi's characters' homosexual relationships also cross racial lines. Such relationships, like Omar and Johnny's, imagine a double-crossing of social constraints that is more fraught and so potentially more radical than heterosexual misceginated relationships. The struggles in a postcolonial state where the established power relations are inverted play themselves out through Omar and Johnny's sexual relationship. Surprisingly funny and subversively sexy, Kureishi's work continuously challenges the ways we have come to think about race, identity, and sex.

—Elliott McEldowney

LA COLÈRE, François. *See* **Aragon, Louis.**

————

LAGERLOF, Selma (Ottiliana Lovisa)

Nationality: Swedish novelist and short story writer. **Born:** Maarbacka, Varmland, 20 November 1858. **Education:** Royal Women's Superior Training College, Stockholm; Upsale University, Ph.D. 1911. **Career:** Teacher, and later mistress, Girls' High School, Landskrona, Sweden, 1880-95. **Awards:** Royal Travelling Scholarship from King Oskar and Prince Eugen, 1895; Gold Medal of Swedish Academy, 1904; Nobel Prize, for literature, 1909; Nils Holgersson Award; awarded membership in Swedish Academy, Sweden's highest honor, 1914. **Died:** Maarbacka, Sweden, of peritonitis, 16 March 1940.

WRITINGS

Novels

Goesta Berlings Saga. Stockholm, 1891; translated by Lillie Tudeer, Chapman & Hall, 1898; translated by Pauline B. Flach as *The Story of Goesta Berling,* Little, Brown, 1898; translated by Robert Bly, New American Library, 1962.
Antikrists Mirakler. A. Bonnier, 1898; translated by P. B. Flach as *The Miracles of Antichrist,* Little, Brown, 1899.
Jerusalem, 2 Vols. A. Bonnier, 1902, 1903; translated by Jessie Broechner, W. Heinemann, 1903; translated by Velma S. Howard, Doubleday, Vol. 1, 1915, Vol. 2, 1918; reprinted, Greenwood Press, 1970.
Liljecronas Hem. A. Bonnier, 1911; translated as *Liliecrona's Home,* by Anna Barwell, Dutton, 1914.
Kejsarn av Portugallien. A. Bonnier, 1914; translated by V. S. Howard as *The Emperor of Portugallia,* Doubleday, 1916.
Bandlyst. Gyldendal, 1918; translated by William Worster as *The Outcast,* Gyldendal, 1920.
Loewenskoeldska Ringen. Stockholm, 1925; translated by V. S. Howard as *The Ring of the Loewenskoelds,* Doubleday, 1931.

Short Stories

Osynliga Laenkar. A. Bonnier, 1894; translated by P. B. Flach as *Invisible Links,* Little, Brown, 1899.
En Herrgaardssaegen. W. Heinemann, 1899; translated by J. Brochner as *From a Swedish Homestead,* McClure, Phillips, 1901; reprinted, Books for Libraries, 1970.
Kristuslegender. Stockholm, 1904; translated by V. S. Howard as *Christ Legends,* Holt, 1908.
Nils Holgersson's Underbara resa Genom Sverige:
Part 1, *The Wonderful Adventures of Nils,* translated by V. S. Howard, Grosset & Dunlap, 1907.

Part 2, *Further Adventures of Nils,* translated by V. S. Howard, illustrated by Astri Heiberg, Doubleday, 1911.

Other

Drottningar i Kungahaella A. Bonnier; translated by C. Field as *The Queens of Kungahaella,* T. W. Laurie, 1917.
Herr Arne's Penningar. Stockholm, 1904; translated by Arthur G. Chater as *Herr Arne's Hoard,* illustrated by Albert Edelfeldt, Gyldendal, 1923; translated by A. G. Chater as *The Treasure,* Doubleday, 1925; reissued, Daughters. Inc., 1973.
En Saga om en Saga. Stockholm, 1908; translated by V. S. Howard as *The Girl from the Marsh Croft,* Little, Brown, 1910.
Astrid Ohlinger. 1910.
Koerkarlen. A. Bonnier, 1912; translated by William F. Harvey as *Thy Soul Shall Bear Witness!,* Odhams Press, 1921.
The Legend of the Sacred Image, translated by V. S. Howard. Holt, 1914.
Troll och Maenniskor. Stockholm, 1915.
Schweden. P. A. Norstedt, 1917.
Toesen Fran Stormyrtorpet. A. Bonnier, 1918.
Maarbacka (autobiography):
Volume 1, *Maarbacka.* A. Bonnier, 1922; translated by V. S. Howard, Doubleday, 1924; reprinted, Gale, 1974.
Volume 2, *Ett Barns Memoarer.* A. Bonnier, 1930; translated by V. S. Howard as *Memories of My Childhood,* Doubleday, 1934; reprinted, Kraus Reprint, 1975.
Volume 3, *Dagbok.* A. Bonnier, 1932; translated by V. S. Howard as *The Diary of Selma Lagerlof,* Doubleday, 1936; reprinted, Kraus Reprint, 1975.
Dunungen. A. Bonnier, 1924.
Hoest. A. Bonnier, 1933; translated by Florence and Naboth Hedin as *Harvest,* Doubleday, 1935.
Julberaettelser (Christmas stories). A. Bonnier, 1938.
Skrifter, 12 volumes. A. Bonnier, 1947-49; reissued, 1961.

*

Adaptations: *The Blizzard* (motion picture), William Fox, 1923; *The Tower of Lies* (motion picture; adaptation of *The Emperor of Portugallia*), Metro-Goldwyn-Mayer, 1925; *The Shepherd's Gift* (color filmstrip with phonodisc and teacher's manual; adaptation of *Silent Night*), Alexark & Norsim.

Critical Sources: *The Treasure* by June Arnold, Daughters Inc., 1973; *Something About the Author,* Vol. 15, edited by Anne Commire, Anne Commire, Gale Research, Detroit, 1979, 160-74; *Twentieth Century Literary Criticism,* Vol. 36, Detroit, Gale Research, 228; "Selma Lagerlof" by Lisbeth Stenberg, in *The Encyclopedia of Homosexuality: Lesbian Histories and Cultures,* Vol. 1, edited by Bonnie Zimmerman, New York, Garland Publishing, forthcoming.

* * *

Although recent scholarship has revealed that she was a lesbian, the writings of Swedish storyteller Selma Lagerlof fall more easily under the rubric of feminist writings than lesbian literature. According to June Arnold, founder and publisher of Daughters Inc., which published *The Treasure* in 1973, Lagerlof has remained a virtual unknown in this country in spite of her being the first woman to win the Nobel Prize for literature in 1909. What little of Lagerlof's writings made it across the Atlantic to the United States—and into English—were stories for children. Her other writings remained Sweden's sole possession for more than five decades.

Critics labeled her a "moralist spinster," but, according to Arnold, Lagerlof's 1911 speech, "Home and State," given to the International Woman Suffrage Alliance Congress, reveals the essential feminist perspective that informed Lagerlof the writer. In that speech, says Arnold, Lagerlof argued that the Home "was the creation of woman and the place where the values of women were nourished and protected. The Home was a community where 'punishment is not for the sake of revenge, but for training and education,' where 'there is a use for all talents, but [she] who is without can make [her]self as much loved as the cleverest....'" For Lagerlof, the home was the "storehouse for the songs and legends of our forefathers"; Lagerlof argued that there is nothing more "mobile, more merciful amongst the creations of [humankind]."

Men, on the other hand, were solely responsible for the creation of the State, which she says, "continually gives cause for discontent and bitterness." No state has ever been able to satisfy all of its members, she argued, but "through the State humankind will reach its highest hopes." These ideas reveal the idealist and the romantic sides of Lagerlof—both personas are also present in her fiction.

According to Lagerlof, the State, the "law and order of men," must be joined by those special virtues, "the God-spirit" of women. *The Treasure* is one particular illustration of this. In this story, the greedy ambitions of men are tempered by the knowing of women. As fairy tales go, this is a rather harsh illustration of how the evil of some men is apparent to women and dogs, but not to other men. It is also an illustration of the painful cost exacted when the greed of ambitious men goes unimpeded.

Her first novel, *The Story of Gosta Berling,* says Lisbeth Stenberg in volume one of *The Encyclopedia of Homosexuality* (to be published in 1999), was "a bold breakthrough with a new type of prose-poetry in a symbolistic, romantic vein." A major influence on romantic literature in Sweden, Lagerlof's writing in *The Treasure,* for example, betrays an awareness on the part of its characters of evil, but the romantic notion of "dying for love" or the "truth" still prevails.

While later work, according to Stenberg, is "more traditional" in its form, Lagerlof wove "deep psychological insights" into her stories which were very symbolically framed. Of particular note is the fact that often in Lagerlof's work "conflicts concerning women's creativity and desire" were skillfully written into male characters—a ploy which since has been used with some success by a number of lesbians not wanting to write explicitly lesbian writings.

Details of Lagerlof's personal life have never really been made public—e.g., her close emotional ties to, and relationships with, other women. Lagerlof did have a close relationship with the widowed Sophie Elkan, but although she was deeply in love with her, in the 25 years their relationship endured she never "lived out the physical side" of the relationship. Likewise, little has been revealed about her relationship with Valborg Olander, her lover and companion of many years, with whom she never lived but on whose support Lagerlof depended in many ways throughout her life.

According to Stenberg, who is also a native of Lagerlof's homeland, thousands of letters written by Lagerlof "to her most intimate friends were sealed until 50 years after her death [in 1940]." Those letters, only recently examined, "reveal a woman full of passion." Her earlier correspondence with Elkan reveals her sexual identity, in spite of the fact that Elkan remained "reluctant" to consummate the relationship. Her relationship with Olander, another teacher whom she met in 1902, was, however, a more complete lesbian relationship.

Clearly, Lagerlof was an early and clear voice for the rights of women. Through her work, she fought for their independence and freedom of thought. Lagerlof's feminist writings, in particular, are an essential component of the body of feminist literature and, by extension, the literature of the later gay, lesbian, and transgender movements.

—Andrea L.T. Peterson

LASSELL, Michael John

Nationality: American poet, essayist, theater critic, and editor. **Born:** New York City, 15 July 1947. **Education:** Great Neck South High School, 1961-1965; Colgate University, A.B. in English 1969 (cum laude, Phi Beta Kappa); California Institute of the Arts, School of Theater, M.F.A. in Acting, 1973; Yale University, School of Drama, M.F.A. in Dramatic Literature and Criticism, 1976 (John Gassner Prize in Criticism). **Career:** Taught in the School of Theater and Division of Critical Studies, California Institute of the Arts, 1976-78; worked as a manager of a script typing service for Hollywood studios, antiques and wall-coverings salesman, and legal secretary 1978-83; theater critic, *Los Angeles Herald Examiner*; theater critic, later managing editor, *L.A. Weekly*; editor/correspondent, *New York Native*; national news editor, *Advocate* (Los Angeles); managing editor, *L.A. Style* (Los Angeles), 1985-90; managing editor, *Interview* (New York), 1990-1991; articles director, *Metropolitan Home* (New York), from 1991. Contributor of articles, fiction, poetry, reviews, personal essays, and humor pieces to periodicals, including *Advocate* (Los Angeles), *City* (France), *Body Politic* (Canada), *City Lights Review* (San Francisco), *Dance, Frontiers* (Los Angeles), *Harvard Gay & Lesbian Review* (Cambridge), *Lambda Book Report* (Washington, D.C.), *L.A. Style, Literary Review* (New York), *Los Angeles Times Magazine, Männer Aktuell* (Germany), *Mid-American Review* (Bowling Green, Ohio), *Metropolitan Home* (New York), *New York Times, ONTHEBUS* (Los Angeles), *Out* (New York), *Outlook* (San Francisco), *Performing Arts* (Los Angeles), *Theater* (New Haven) *Torso* (New York). **Awards:** Amelia's Award, for poetry, 1985 Lambda Literary Award, for poetry, 1990; Gregory Kolovako Award finalist, for writing about AIDS, 1990. **Address:** c/o *Metropolitan Home,* 1633 Broadway, New York, New York 10019 U.S.A.

WRITINGS

Poetry

Poems for Lost and Un-lost Boys. Bakersfield, California, Amelia 1985.

Decade Dance: Poems. Boston, Alyson Publications, 1990.
The Hard Way (poetry, fiction, and essays). New York, A Richard Kasale Book, 1995.

Editor

The Name of Love: Classic Gay Love Poems. New York, St. Martin's Press, 1995.
Eros in Boystown: Contemporary Gay Poems about Sex. New York, Crown Publishers, 1996.
With Lawrence Schimel, *Two Hearts Desire: Gay Couples on Their Love.* New York, St. Martin's Press, 1997.

Other

"How to Watch Your Brother Die," in *Connections,* edited by Sarah Lanier Barber. New York, La Guardia Community College, 1991.
New Worlds of Literature: Writings from America's Many Cultures, 2nd edition, edited by Jerome Beaty and J. Paul Hunter. New York, W.W. Norton, 1994.
Exploring Our Sexuality: An Interactive Text, edited by Patricia Barthalow Koch. Kendall Hunt, 1995.
"Dancing Days," in *Created Writing: Poetry from New Angles,* edited by Paul Agostino. New Jersey, Prentice Hall, 1996.
The Presence of Others, 2nd edition, edited by Andrea Lunsford and John Ruszkiewicz. New York, St. Martin's Press, 1997.

*

Critical Sources: "A Tough Guy's Decade Dance" by Erik Latzky, in *Advocate* (Los Angeles), Vol. 568, January 1991, 70; "To Dance Again Tomorrow" by John-Manuel Andriote, in *Lambda Book Report* (Washington, D.C.), Vol. 2, No. 7, 24; "Dancing in the Mouth of Death" by Philip Gambone, in *Lambda Book Report* (Washington, D.C.), Vol. 4, No. 8, January 1995, 31-32.

Michael Lassell comments:

Being a gay poet is an irrelevancy inside a vacuum. I'd rather be a rock star. Even an old rock star like Mick Jagger. John Baldessari, a conceptual artist, once told me he thought poets were the only pure artists left because poetry has no commercial value. Amen. Poetry is the currency of late nights and lonely afternoons, and of caring why words mean what they do, and why communication is so difficult in this information age. Why do it? How not to? I wrote my first poem when I was eight. I had my first-ever fight with my parents the year before, over a word I loved: Terrarium. They said it didn't exist. I could not demur. If you know you exist, you cannot pretend you do not exist. Nazis taught the world this message: You can kill those you hate, but you cannot make them cease to exist. Had Hitler not killed the millions, they would still be dead, and we would never have known they existed. I do not mean to condone killing. Only to acknowledge certain ironies, even amidst the horror. Adolph Hitler is alive and well in the United States in 1997. Why write? So if the new Hitlers kill us all, there will be a record. A gravestone. So that gay children don't have to go to the library and find only one entry under homosexuality: Psychopathia Sexualis, which was the story of my first encounter with my sexuality. I already knew it in my flesh, when I saw George Bowen take off his clothes in that first sev-

enth-grade gym class in 1960. Who teaches a 13-year old that George Bowen's body is the reason for existence? Who teaches an 8-year old that writing a poem is the best way he can spend his time? Love, sex, death, sadness, politics, anger, the quietest moment in which nothing at all happens, those fleeting memories of people taken so off-guard by incoming death that they failed to leave a trail of their own into the wilderness. What else is poetry? Who are the people who influenced me? Funny people. People I read right from the beginning: A.A. Milne, Dr. Seuss, and later, like Mr. Marlowe, Mr. Shakespeare, and their Elizabethan/Jacobean ilk; writers who opened the world into my heart: Cavafy, Ferlinghetti/Ginsberg (you had to be there); teachers like Richard Howard, Paul Roche, Charles Tomlinson; particular poems, like Shelley's "Sonnet: England in 1819," which give me permission; shards of poetry, like Basil Bunting's "Brag sweet tenor bull/descant on Rawthey's madrigal;" friends like Gavin Geoffrey Dillard, David Trinidad, Paul Monette, Dennis Cooper; friends and writers of courage who may never write poems, like Tim Miller and Jim Pickett both; lovers like my poor lost Roberto and my own dear Ben, whose lives inspire poetry just because they breathe. Poetry is a breath of a kind. And we all need to keep breathing.

*   *   *

While pursuing a career in Los Angeles and New York City as a theater critic, journalist, and editor, Michael Lassell also wrote two books of poetry, published a collection of his essays and poetry, and edited several collections of poetry on the theme of gay love and sexuality. The lengthy list of periodicals that Lassell has contributed to or edited is testament to his unflagging interest in, and support for, gay and lesbian culture.

Lassell became well known as a poet when he published "How to Watch Your Brother Die" in his first book, *Poems for Lost and Un-lost Boys.* This poem explores the meeting between a heterosexual man, his dying brother, and his brother's gay lover. Several educational textbooks have included the poem because of its attempt to bridge heterosexual and homosexual worlds, despite the pressures of homophobia to keep the two apart. Ironically, a gay critic, writing in the *Boston Globe,* mistakenly believed that the author of the poem was heterosexual, an assumption that would be harder to make with Lassell's later work.

Lassell received the *Lambda* Literary Award for *Decade Dance,* which is in part a charting of the staggering effect that AIDS had upon the gay community during the 1980s. Several of the poems found in the "Rendezvous with Death" section explore the ways in which the AIDS virus affected gay life, such as this segment from "How to Visit the Grave of a Friend":

> Read the inscription again. It is his own
> words: "In light of what you see,
> What shadow do I cast?"
> Remember you have never before visited
> the grave of a friend. Remember the day of his
> funeral, the white balloons released
> into a cool, high sky, empty as
> his grandmother's eyes.

Alternatively, the section "Street Meat" investigates the erotic and sometimes violent underworld of gay city life in the shadow of AIDS with poems such as "Claudio":

Claudio has a new tattoo,
a cobra twisting on his
fisting forearm,
echoing
as he dances
the smaller snake that's flicking tongue forks over
loose Jockeys.

and "Casey/jones":

Casey gives nickel blow jobs
in the quarter peeps on Eighth off 42nd
to support his habits:
heroin, humiliation and men.

John-Manuel Andriote perceptively observes that "even in these seedier sides of gay sex, hard as the streets these boys walk, there's a tenderness that comes through." Other poems from *Decade Dance* present political themes with humor and satire, as in "Piss Jesse, or Silence=Death," a take-off on Senator Jesse Helms' public harangues against artists Andres Serrano and Robert Mapplethorpe. This theme can also be found in several of his essays, including "20 Reasons to Hate Heterosexuals" from *The Hard Way*. Occasionally the anger and rage at the marginalization of gays, and the pain of loss due to the AIDS epidemic breaks through, as in "A Modest Proposal" from *Decade Dance*:

...don't tell me not to buy into their hatred!
I've been hating them since before they knew
who or what I am
(my anger is the legacy of their cruelty,
my rage is the birthright of the outcast)—
and all the ex-presidents in mansions in Bel-Air
so layered in latex you couldn't detect a facial twitch
if you rammed his oft-probed ass with a flagpole;
and all the chiefs of police with itchy trigger fingers
choke holds, and Republican aspirations;
all of them up in smoke in the twinkling of an eye.

The Hard Way includes selections of Lassell's poetry and essays published between 1983 and 1993. The section "Poems for Roberto" chronicles Lassell's relationship with his former lover Roberto Muñoz, who died in 1986. Lassell's work as poet, essayist, and journalist reflects his unreserved commitment to writing for a gay audience. The works collected in *The Hard Way* document the impact of AIDS upon his decimated circle of friends and the community at large, while also celebrating the erotics of homosexuality and the joys of gay relationships. Furthermore, through his editorial efforts Lassell has made a significant contribution to the publication and preservation of gay literature.

—Ed Summers

LEYLAND, Winston

Nationality: American publisher, editor, and author of gay literature. **Born:** Atherton, England, 29 August 1940; moved with his family to Providence, Rhode Island, 1952. **Education:** St. Columban's College, Milton, Massachusetts, B.A. 1963, graduate study 1963-66; University of California, Los Angeles, M.A. 1970. **Career:** Ordained Roman Catholic priest, 1966 (resigned 1968); proofreader, *Los Angeles Times,* 1969-70; contributing editor and publisher, *Gay Sunshine Journal,* 1971-82; editor and publisher, Gay Sunshine Press, from 1975; publisher, Leyland Publications, from 1984. **Awards:** Coordinating Council of Literary Magazines grants, from 1974; National Endowment for the Arts grants, 1976, 1978, and 1980; Gay Lesbian, and Bisexual Book Award, American Library Association, 1982; Lambda Literary Award, for best gay book, 1988, 1992; California Arts Council grants, from 1990. **Address:** c/o Gay Sunshine Press, P.O. Box 410690, San Francisco, California 94141, U.S.A.

WRITINGS

Selected Edited Works

Angels of the Lyre: A Gay Poetry Anthology. San Francisco, Gay Sunshine Press and Panjandrum Press, 1975.

Orgasms of Light: The Gay Sunshine Anthology: Poetry, Short Fiction, Graphics. San Francisco, Gay Sunshine Press, 1977.

Gay Sunshine Interviews, Volume 1. San Francisco, Gay Sunshine Press, 1978.

Now the Volcano: An Anthology of Latin American Gay Literature, translated by Erskine Lane, Franklin Blanton, and Simon Karlinsky. San Francisco, Gay Sunshine Press, 1979.

Straight Hearts' Delight: Love Poems and Selected Letters by Allen Ginsberg and Peter Orlovsky. San Francisco, Gay Sunshine Press, 1980.

With Boyd McDonald, *Meat and Flesh: True Homosexual Experiences from S.T.H.,* 2 Vols. San Francisco, Gay Sunshine Press, 1981, 1982.

The Disrobing: Sex and Satire by Royal Murdoch. San Francisco, Gay Sunshine Press, 1982.

Gay Sunshine Interviews, Volume 2. San Francisco, Gay Sunshine Press, 1982.

Physique. San Francisco, Gay Sunshine Press, 1982.

My Deep Dark Pain Is Love: A Collection of Latin American Gay Fiction, translated from Spanish and Portuguese by E.A. Lacey. San Francisco, Gay Sunshine Press, 1983.

Teleny, attributed to Oscar Wilde. San Francisco, Gay Sunshine Press, 1984.

Meatmen: An Anthology of Gay Male Comics, Vols. 1-19. San Francisco, Leyland Publications, 1986-96.

Cruising the South Seas by Charles Stoddard. San Francisco, Gay Sunshine Press, 1987.

The Delight of Hearts, or, What You Will Not Find in Any Book by Ahmad al-Tifashi. San Francisco, Gay Sunshine Press, 1988.

Gay Roots: Twenty Years of Gay Sunshine: An Anthology of Gay History, Sex, Politics, and Culture. San Francisco, Gay Sunshine Press, 1991.

Military Sex series (includes *Enlisted Meat, Warriors and Lovers, Military Sex, Marine Biology,* and *Basic Training*), 5 Vols. San Francisco, Leyland Publications, 1991-95.

Gay Roots, Volume 2: An Anthology of Gay History, Sex, Politics, and Culture. San Francisco, Gay Sunshine Press, 1993.

Queer Dharma: A Buddhist Gay Anthology. San Francisco, Gay Sunshine Press, 1997.

*

Biography: *Gay Sunshine Interviews, Volume 2* edited by Winston Leyland, San Francisco, Gay Sunshine Press, 1982; *Gay Roots: Twenty Years of Gay Sunshine: An Anthology of Gay History, Sex, Politics, and Culture* edited with introduction by Winston Leyland, San Francisco, Gay Sunshine Press, 1991.

Critical Sources: *Unspeakable: The Rise of the Gay and Lesbian Press in America* by Rodger Streitmatter, Boston, Faber and Faber, 1995.

Winston Leyland comments:

Long a believer in the "small is best" approach, I have avoided structuring the counterculture Gay Sunshine Press in imitation of New York corporate publishing. Much work, such as typesetting, cover design, printing, and even a considerable amount of distribution, is "farmed out" to independent contractors. My own energies have been concentrated in the creative field of searching out new projects, making contact with American and Third World gay writers, coordinating production of the books, and keeping the press financially solvent. Publishing requires more than a little gambling and venturing into the unknown.

Throughout the 1980s I strove to publish innovative volumes on various aspects of the gay reality. Third World gay literature has long been among my interests. Among the volumes of Latin American gay literature I have published my favorite is *My Deep Dark Pain Is Love* (1983), which includes fiction (and some nonfiction) by 24 writers from five countries: Brazil, Mexico, Chile, Argentina, and Cuba. Most of this material was gathered by me during several visits I made to Latin American in the 1977-1982 period (a detailed discussion of this will be found in the introduction to the anthology in question.) At this time I also began the book anthologies of true homosexual experiences edited by the inimitable Boyd McDonald. Reader response was massively positive and supportive. Another pioneering volume was Geoff Mains' *Urban Aboriginals: A Celebration of Leathersexuality* (1984). At the end of the decade I published the two ground-breaking books on Walt Whitman (*Drum Beats* and *Calamus Lovers*) edited by Charley Shively. Here Walt Whitman's love affairs were laid bare for the first time, and startling information on an early gay love affair of Abraham Lincoln was unearthed by Charley. The anthology of medieval Arabic stories and poems *The Delight of Hearts* (1988), by Ahmad al-Tifashi, was another such pioneering volume.

Gay Sunshine Press—in existence as a book publisher since 1975, and the oldest independent gay press in the country—is now concentrating more on gay literary material and other nonfiction which falls within the framework of its non-profit status. In 1984 I started Leyland Publications to publish books of gay erotica, fiction, and other pioneering material which needed legally to be done under a separate imprint. There is no value judgment intended by me in such a separation. To date I have published some 70 books under the Leyland imprint.

*   *   *

Winston Leyland was born in Atherton, England, on 29 August 1940, a descendant of a successful farming family. In 1952 the family emigrated to the United States, settling in Providence, Rhode Island, where Leyland continued his education, attending high school and two years of college. In pursuit of a life in the Catholic priesthood he entered St. Columban's College in Milton, Massachusetts.

On 21 December 1966 Leyland was ordained a Roman Catholic priest by Cardinal Cushing. Following ordination, Leyland was assigned to U.C.L.A. to pursue a graduate degree in Medieval History. During his studies at U.C.L.A. Leyland became an outspoken opponent of the Vietnam war in a series of sermons offered at Los Angeles churches. Cardinal McIntyre of Los Angeles, chagrined by Leyland's use of the pulpit, pressured the Society of Saint Columban to invoke an order of silence on Leyland, and the Society placed him under virtual house arrest at their Los Angeles headquarters. The sanction of house arrest and his refusal to lead a hypocritical life as a gay man—he had recently come out—made Leyland's decision to leave the Catholic Church in 1968 a logical step. Leyland never regretted this decision, since he felt he could live without the respect of an institution which persecuted gay and lesbian people.

After leaving the church Leyland worked for several years as a proofreader at the *Los Angeles Times* and resided in Hollywood. In spite of being offered a permanent position on the *Times* staff he moved to northern California. After arriving in Berkeley in 1970 he soon became involved with the new homosexual tabloid *Gay Sunshine,* whose title reflected not only the psychedelic generation but also the new dawn of gay liberation. The paper was a product of the 1960s counter-culture revolution and paralleled many of the beliefs and philosophies of Leyland in sexuality, politics, and literature. Like many of the publications and newsletters which began to spring up around the country following the Stonewall Riot and the birth of the gay liberation movement in New York, *Gay Sunshine* was loosely affiliated with a local gay organization, in this case the Berkeley Gay Liberation Front. The paper hit the streets in August of 1970.

In its infancy *Gay Sunshine* was the product of an independent collective of members who lived communally and had ties to the Berkeley Gay Liberation Front. As a part of this collective, Leyland worked on several of the early issues and attended weekly Gay Liberation Front meetings. The first issues of *Gay Sunshine* were filled primarily with local and national gay news stories. *Gay Sunshine* carried an air of militancy, providing a radical perspective on issues effecting the gay community. The paper attempted to isolate itself from straight society and injected a strong sense of gay nationalism in its editorial content. Believing it was time for gay people to take charge of their lives, *Gay Sunshine* espoused the belief that homosexual separatism was essential. The enemy was straight society, and they should bear the brunt of gay backlash.

The Berkeley Gay Liberation Front disbanded in 1971; the *Gay Sunshine* collective dissolved and the paper suspended publication. The demise of gay and lesbian radicalism not only in Berkeley but also elsewhere was due in part to the lack of progress in securing equal rites for gays and lesbians by the Gay Liberation Front. Leyland decided to resurrect *Gay Sunshine,* however, and resumed publishing with the spring 1971 issue. Several people from the original *Gay Sunshine* collective continued working on the paper while Leyland acted as editor, coordinator, typesetter, and treasurer. The paper moved from focusing primarily on local and national gay news to a mix of news, feature articles on gay oppression and liberation, and gay literature.

Two years and a revised title later, *Gay Sunshine Journal* still appeared in tabloid format but with a dramatic shift in content. The journal discontinued coverage of new stories and became a preeminent gay literary/political quarterly. Leyland began an acclaimed series of in-depth interviews with gay authors and artists. Among those interviewed were Christopher Isherwood, Tennessee Williams, John Rechy, Allen Ginsberg, Jean Genet, Gore Vidal, and many others. The interviews, some running over 25,000 words, came to define gay literature and the gay sensibility more profoundly than any other publication. The *American Book Review* said of the collected interviews: "By drawing together a constellation of 12 stars, each one accompanied by a fine photo, all engaged in naked revelation, Winston Leyland has managed to make hundreds of pieces of definition spark off poetically and dramatically."

Also at this time Leyland took an active interest in seeking out third world gay literature, historical and literary essays, and cutting edge materials. He brought into the field of gay fiction and poetry numerous international authors who soon became noted writers in the genre. For the Fifth Stonewall Anniversary issue of *Gay Sunshine* Leyland collaborated with the Charles Shively of *Fag Rag* in creating the joint issue of *Gay Sunshine/Fag Rag*. The last issue of the *Gay Sunshine Journal* appeared in book format in 1982. The journal was discontinued so that Leyland could concentrate his full attention on book publishing.

During the mid 1970s Leyland had felt the need to publish materials in a more lasting format and started Gay Sunshine Press in 1975. Gay Sunshine Press is now the oldest continuous gay publishing house in the United States. The driving force behind Gay Sunshine Press was Leyland's belief in a "gay cultural renaissance" which would inspire a rediscovery of the gay cultural heritage and its varied forms of expression. Gay Sunshine was a driving force in illuminating the hidden heritage of gay literature. It proved to the literary world that the gay community could produce an intellectual journal of high quality, with influence that extended far beyond the community boundaries.

As editor-in-chief of Gay Sunshine, Leyland received several grants from the NEA which allowed him to publish gay literary landmarks such as Allen Ginsberg and Peter Orlovsky's collection of love poems *Straight Hearts' Delights* (1981), Jean Genet's *Collected Poems,* the Brazilian gay novel *Bom Crioulo,* and the poetry anthology *Orgasms of Light* (1978). He sought out unexplored areas of the gay experience, publishing Geoff Mains' *Urban Aboriginals: A Celebration of Leathersexuality* (1984), two groundbreaking books by Charles Shively—*Drum Beats* and *Calamus Lovers*—detailing homosexuality in the life and writings of Walt Whitman, and Latin and South American contributions to gay literature in the anthologies *Now the Volcano* and *My Deep Dark Pain Is Love.* In collaboration with Boyd McDonald he began the anthology series of true homosexual experiences. In the 1990s he published two groundbreaking collections of literature from other cultures: *Partings at Dawn: An Anthology of Japanese Gay Literature* and *Out of the Blue: Russia's Hidden Gay Literature.* In a review of *Gay Roots Volume 1* published in *Contact II,* poet Kirby Congdon wrote: "The publisher and editor Winston Leyland has, singlehandedly, probably done more for the establishment of sensibility and sensitivity in literature than anyone else I can think of—and I think of the publishers of Joyce's *Ulysses,* D. H. Lawrence, Allen Ginsberg, and William S. Burroughs in this century and of Rimbaud and Housman in the last. Leyland has now capped his career with a compendium that is a monument not only to the man himself, but a whole generation that found itself through its commitments to its own identity in the small-press and the avant-garde."

Leyland's book publishing ventures were expanded with the establishment of Leyland Publications in 1984. While Gay Sunshine Press would remain a non-profit venture focusing on gay literature and non-fiction, Leyland Publications would feature books on gay erotica and fiction. While most people praised the new endeavor several long time supporters withdrew when he began publishing Boyd McDonald's "S.T.H" series. Meanwhile the *Village Voice* described the "S.T.H." books as a radical act in publishing. Leyland was convinced there was no contradiction between the merits of books such as Boyd McDonald's "S.T.H." series and groundbreaking works of gay literature from authors such as Genet, Ginsberg, or Vidal. His unapologetic approach to publishing has been to explore all aspects of gay life, whether gay radical politics, boylove, public sex, S&M, gay erotica, gay literature, etc., as it all fits his depiction of a "gay cultural renaissance" and vividly describes what it means to be gay.

Over the last quarter century Winston Leyland's writings and publications have eloquently depicted the many subtexts of gay life. He has broadened the horizon of gay literature to include internationally renowned gay authors from around the world. Gay Sunshine Press and Leyland Publications have been a major force in the "gay cultural renaissance" and Winston Leyland a pivotal figure.

—Michael A. Lutes

LINCOLN, James. *See* **BATES, Katharine Lee.**

LIVIA, Anna

Pseudonym: Has also written as Faustina Rey. **Nationality:** Irish/British writer and editor. **Born:** Anna Livia Julian Brawn in Dublin, Ireland, 13 November 1955; daughter of Patrick St. John, a writer, and Dympna Brawn, a poet. **Education:** Attended various schools in Africa, including a boys' boarding school in the Swazi Mountains; University of London, B.A. in French Language and Literature 1979, Postgraduate Certificate in Education, 1981; University of California, Berkeley, Ph.D. in French Linguistics, 1995. **Career:** Has held a variety of jobs including catering assistant, dispatch rider, bus conductor, cabaret dresser in London, c. 1970s-80s; member of editorial collective, *Gossip: A Journal of Lesbian Feminist Ethics,* London; teacher of French and English, University of Avignon, France; writer and editor, from 1982; editor, Onlywomen Press, London, 1983-90; editor, *Lesbian Review of Books,* from 1994; assistant professor of French Linguistics, and director of the Commercial French Programme, University of Illinois at Champaign-Urbana, from 1995. **Awards:** Vermont Booksellers Association Special Merit Award, for translation. **Address:** French Department, 2090 Foreign Languages Building, University of Illinois, 707 South Mathews Ave., Urbana, Illinois 61801, U.S.A.

WRITINGS

Fiction

Relatively Norma. London, Onlywomen Press, 1982.
Accommodation Offered. London, Women's Press, 1984.
Bulldozer Rising. London, Onlywomen Press, 1988.
Minimax: A Novel. Portland, Oregon, Eighth Mountain Press, 1991.

Short Stories

"Bedrock Passion," in *Spinster* (London) No. 2, 1983.
"1 Woman = 7 Cups of Tea," in *The Reach,* edited by Lilian Mohin and Sheila Shulman. London, Onlywomen Press, 1984.
"Mind the Gap," in *Everyday Matters Two,* edited by Sheba. London, Sheba, 1984.
"5 1/2 Charlotte Mews," in *Stepping Out: Short Stories on Friendships Between Women.* London, Pandora Press, 1986.
Incidents Involving Warmth. London, Onlywomen Press, 1986.
"Shimmer Hosen," in *Conditions,* Vol. 38, spring 1988.
"Dead Heat," in *Sinister Wisdom* (Berkeley, California), Vol. 34, spring 1988.
"Seekers of Silver Linings," in *Common Lives/Lesbian Lives,* spring 1988.
"Angel Alice," in *The Pied Piper,* edited by Anna Livia and Lilian Mohin. London, Onlywomen Press, 1989.
"Car Spray," in *Lesbian Ethics* (Albuquerque, New Mexico), Vol. 3, No. 3, 1989.
"Spaceship to the Good Planet," in *Sinister Wisdom* (Berkeley, California), Vol. 37, 1989.
Incidents Involving Mirth. Portland, Oregon, Eighth Mountain Press, 1990; as *Saccharin Cyanide,* London, Onlywomen Press, 1990.
"The Promised Land Recedes into a Grey Horizon," in *Finding the Lesbians,* edited by Julia Penelope and Sarah Valentine. Freedom, California, Crossing Press, 1990.
"Saccharin Cyanide," in *In and Out of Time,* edited by Patricia Duncker. London, Onlywomen Press, 1990.
"On Cause, On Cause, C'est Tout Ce Que L'on Sait Faire," in *Lesbia Magazine* (Paris, France), 1991.
"Lust and the Other Half," in *An Intimate Wilderness,* edited by Judith Barrington. Portland, Oregon, Eighth Mountain, 1991.
"Minimax," in *Daughters of Darkness,* edited by Pam Keesey. San Francisco, California, Cleis Press, 1993.
"Bruised Fruit," in *Sinister Wisdom* (Berkeley, California), Vol. 51, winter 1993-94.
"The Boy in the Box," in *Strange Plasma* (Cambridge, Massachusetts), No. 7, 1995.
"A Dildo's Only as Good as the Woman You Use It With," in *Girljock,* No. 14, 1995.
(as Faustina Rey) "The Truth," in *Queer View Mirror,* edited by James Johnstone and Karen Tulchinsky. Vancouver, British Columbia, Arsenal Pulp Press, 1995.
"Lightning Dances across the Prairie Like Lust at a Nightclub," in *Close Call,* edited by Susan Fox Rogers. New York, St. Martin's Press, 1996.

Uncollected Nonfiction

"Love Thy Enemy," in *New Internationalist,* No. 150, August 1985.

"With Gossip Aforethought," in *Gossip* (London), No. 1, 1986.
"You Can Only Be Wrong," in *Women's Review of Books,* Vol. 6, No. 10 and 11, July 1986.
"I Would Rather Have Been Dead than Gone Forever," in *Gossip* (London), No. 5, 1987.
"Lesbian Sexuality: Joining the Dots," in *In Other Words: Writing as a Feminist,* edited by Gail Chester and Sigrid Nielsen. London, Hutchinson, 1987.
"Hippo Cream," in *Lesbian Ethics,* Vol. 3, No. 3, 1989.
"La Mythologie Lesbienne," in *Bulletin des Archives Lesbiennes* (Paris, France), November 1990.
"Lost in Translation," in *Women's Review of Books,* Vol. 9, No. 6, March 1992.
"Look on the Bright Side," in *Unleashing Feminism,* edited by Irene Reti. Santa Cruz, California, HerBooks, 1993.
"Elana Dykewomon and Natalie Clifford Barney," in *Gay and Lesbian Literary Heritage,* edited by Claude Summers. Chester, Connecticut, New England Publishing, 1994.
"The Riddle of the Sphinx: Creating Genderless Characters in French," and "'She Sired Six Children': Pronominal Gender Play in English," in *Cultural Performances: Proceedings of the Third Berkeley Women and Language Conference,* edited by Mary Bucholtz. Berkeley, California, Berkeley Women and Language Group, University of California, 1994, 421-433 434-448.
"Tongues or Fingers," in *Lesbian Erotics.* New York, New York University Press, 1995.
"The Gender Trap," in *Proceedings of Third Kentucky Conference on Narrative,* edited by Joachim Knuf. Lexington, University of Kentucky, 1995.
"Back to the Bare Bones and the Broken Teeth," in *Out of the Class Closet,* edited by Julia Penelope. Freedom, California, Crossing Press, 1995.
"San Francisco Spice Rack," in *Dyke Life: From Growing Up to Growing Old,* edited by Karla Jay. New York, Basic Books, 1995.
"'I Ought to Throw a Buick at You': Fictional Representations of Butch/Femme," in *Gender Articulated: Language and the Socially Constructed Self.* New York, Routledge, 1995.
"Daring to Presume," in *Feminism and Psychology,* Vol. 6, No. 1, 1996, 31-40.
"Disloyal to Masculinity: Linguistic Gender and Liminal Identity in French" and "It's a Girl: Bringing Performativity Back to Linguistics," in *Queerly Phrased: Language, Gender, and Sexuality,* edited by Anna Livia and Kira Hall. New York, Oxford University Press, 1996.
"Natalie Barney, Renee Vivien, Lucie Delarue-Mardrus and Language," in *Encyclopedia of Lesbianism,* edited by Bonnie Zimmerman. New York, Garland Publishing, 1996.

Other

Editor, *The Pied Piper: Lesbian Feminist Fiction.* London, Onlywomen Press, 1989.
Editor, *Queerly Phrased: Language, Gender, and Sexuality.* New York, Oxford University Press, 1997.
Translator, *A Perilous Advantage: The Best of Natalie Clifford Barney.* Norwich, Vermont, New Victoria Pubs, 1992.
Translator, *The Angel and the Perverts* by Lucie Delarue-Mardrus. New York, New York University Press, 1995.

*

Biography: *Contemporary Authors,* Vol. 119, Detroit, Gale Research, 1987; *The Feminist Companion to Literature in English,* New Haven, Connecticut, Yale University Press, 1990; *Science Fiction and Fantasy Literature,* Detroit, Gale Research, 1992; *Encyclopedia of Science Fiction,* London, Orbit, 1993.

Critical Sources: "Relatively Norma," in *British Book News,* June 1983, 389; "Accommodation Offered" by L. Lynch, in *Womens Review of Books,* Vol. 3, February 1986, 8; "Bulldozer Rising" by L. Markowitz, in *Lambda Book Report,* Vol. 1, 1988, 14; "Bulldozer Rising" by A. Johnson, in *Off Our Backs,* Vol. 18, December 1988, 11; review of *Bulldozer Rising* by Mara Math, in *Gay Community News,* Vol. 16, 2 October 1988; "Bulldozer Rising" by Colin Greenland, in *Times Literary Supplement,* No. 4444, 3 June 1988, 622; "Bulldozer Rising" by Josephine Saxton, in *New Statesman,* Vol. 116, No. 2982, 20 May 1988, 26; "Incidents Involving Mirth" by L. Markowitz, in *Lambda Book Review,* Vol. 2, No. 9, March 1991, 32; "Incidents Involving Mirth" by L. Galst, in *Womens Review of Books,* Vol. 8, No. 10, July 1991, 42; "Minimax" by Regan Robinson, in *Library Journal,* Vol. 116, No. 21, December 1991, 197-198; "Minimax" by Louise Rafkin, in *Lambda Book Report,* Vol. 3, No. 3, March-April 1992, 23; "On Genre Fiction" and "Writing Lesbian," in *Sisters and Strangers: An Introduction to Contemporary Feminist Fiction* by Patricia Duncker, Cambridge, Blackwell, 1992, 108-109, 190-193; "A Perilous Advantage: The Best of Natalie Clifford Barney" by Victoria A. Brownworth, in *Lambda Book Report,* Vol. 3, No. 6, September-October 1992, 22; "Genre Fiction: The Comic Novel," in *Contemporary Lesbian Writing: Dreams, Desire, Difference* by Paulina Palmer, Philadelphia, Open University Press, 1993, 83, 87-88, 93-94; "Lesbian Erotics" by Ellen Herman, in *Lambda Book Report,* Vol. 4, No. 11, July-August 1995, 25; "The Angel and the Perverts" by S.A. Inness, in *Choice,* Vol. 33, No. 5, January, 1996, 798.

Anna Livia comments:

I have lived on four continents and called none of them home. I have no sense of national loyalty or patriotism, though I believe a good guest behaves politely. In my fiction, I am not polite and, unlike me, my characters belong where they find themselves. They are Australian, African, Irish, English, American in a way I never can be. I write to create a sense of home, a place where metaphors are played out and situations can reach their own conclusions. My characters are better critics of their society than I can be. They speak from the inside, are enraged, engaged, and amused where I would be distant and cautious, collecting data and creating taxonomies. I write about lesbians and gay men because these are the people I know best; their failings, weaknesses, and triumphs touch me more deeply because I know how much harder they have to work simply to stay in the game.

*   *   *

Anna Livia identifies herself as a "radical feminist lesbian" whose politics were honed by her international wanderings. Born in Ireland in 1955, she spent much of her childhood in Zambia and Swaziland, was educated in London and California, and taught, wrote, and edited in London, France, and the United States. London appears to be the place she formed her lesbian feminist politics, for it was there that she was forced to cope with homophobia,

poverty, being on the "dole," and hostility against the Irish. All of these influences are explored in her novels and short stories. Livia told *GLL* contributor Jacquelyn Marie that these experiences have allowed her to "hear an enormous range of different voices, imagine different characters, and visualize many different settings." Her characters "are not strange to me; their lives were often part of my own."

Anna Livia grew up with a writer father and a poet mother who named their daughter after Anna Livia Plurabelle, the wonderful Dubliner in James Joyce's *Finnegan's Wake.* After such a literary beginning, it is not surprising that Anna Livia went on to become a writer. After graduating from the University of London in languages and education in 1981, she tried to make a living there. She became involved in feminist/lesbian small press, as an editor for *Gossip: A Journal of Lesbian Feminist Ethics* and Onlywomen Press, while working stints as a bus conductor, a dispatch rider, and a cabaret dresser to make ends meet. Livia's long study of languages, which eventuated in receiving a Ph.D. in French linguistics from the University of California, Berkeley, has made her very conscious of words and their meanings. Her Ph.D. dissertation was provocatively titled "Pronoun Envy: Literary Uses of Linguistic Gender."

Her first novel, *Relatively Norma,* was published by Onlywomen Press during her time in London; *British Book News* called it "fast, furious...teeter[ing] agilely on the knife-edge of feminist farce." *Relatively Norma* begins the story, continued in *Minimax,* of a fictionalized family comparable to Livia's, with a mother in Australia and a lesbian daughter in London. The daughter, Minnie, goes to visit the family in Australia with the purpose of coming out to them; instead they are full of their own difficulties, including a sister who is more than interested in the lesbian scene. Paulina Palmer, in *Contemporary Lesbian Writing,* wrote that *Relatively Norma* "questions the significance of lesbianism as the key to personal identity" but also "humorously exposes the excuses heterosexuals employ to avoid confronting and discussing the subject of lesbianism." Patricia Duncker, writing in *Sisters and Strangers,* commented that Livia "combines naturalism with a variety of disruptive alienation devices" but "the disruptive events appear as sudden fissures in the realist text" and are not entirely successful.

Minimax (1991) continues the story of Minnie. The family's characters, especially the sisters, seem changed—they all have male lovers (all humorously named John) and one wonders what happened to the sister who had gone to live with the lesbian in Sydney. In this novel Minnie finds romance with a female vampire named Natalie Barney; their hilarious first night is spent with Natalie talking all night, delighted that she has at last found a listener/muse. The reviewer Regan Robinson, in *Library Journal,* called Livia's writing "bright and funny" and writes that the "story sometimes lifts off and sails through surreal seas but always returns to earth with a bounce." The characters range from lesbian vampires to a parrot who has a love affair with a shopping bag, from a physicist (named John) who plans an extravagant meal to down-and-out Minnie and her alter-ego Milly, who often speaks out as the voice of the Lesbian Nation. Anna Livia, according to John Jacob in *American Book Review,* has written a novel that "James Joyce would have shown an interest in...she has infused her writing with...inventiveness." As Louise Rafkin writes in *Lambda Book Report,* "Livia is adept at social commentary and her comments on lesbiana are half the fun of this wild romp. We are treated to rapid-fire commentary on the ins and outs of lesbian culture."

In 1985, Anna Livia's novel *Accommodation Offered* was published by Women's Press in London. The story centers around Polly, who is reeling from a failed marriage and long-term woman lover relationship and has a house to share. Two younger women rent her space and come to share in an extended family: Sadie, who has been living in South Africa and going mad from trying to balance her love of the country and her dislike of apartheid, and Kim, who is trying to find reasonable work and keep secret that she is a lesbian virgin. Anna Livia has always been concerned with housing, belonging to two London women's housing associations and moving frequently because of a lack of safe lesbian accommodations, so it is not surprising that the desire to have secure housing with supportive and caring housemates is central to this story. Writing in *Women's Review of Books,* Lee Lynch called *Accommodation Offered* a "tale told with tongue in cheek," and hailed the Liberty Boddesses, goddesses who watch over the adventures of the three women, "one of the freshest and most outrageous inventions I've seen recently." But she complained that she was "sometimes lost in the rapid-fire changes of point of view" which are an integral part of Livia's writing style.

Livia's two books of short stories with similar titles, *Incidents involving Warmth* (1986) and *Incidents involving Mirth* (1990), were well-received, particularly the former, with many positive reviews; a good number of the stories have been published separately in anthologies. Many of the stories involve love and women and emotions familiar to us all. "Saccharin Cyanide" tells of a woman who gets a free used car from her brother but finds that the car brings problems, including incidents of violence against women. "5 1/2 Charlotte Mews" uses Livia's experience as a dispatch bike rider, while "Pamelump" is concerned with a young girl and her natural liking for a severely disabled girl she affectionately calls Pamelump. As Liz Galst writes in *Women's Review,* these stories show Livia's "wonderfully acerbic British wit," "dry humor," and "a rare stylistic inventiveness." Laura Markowitz writes in *Lambda Book Review* that her "plots are rich and unpredictable" and "she manages to capture the complexity of our (lesbian) relationships, our lusts and our identity issues, but plays them out in such a way...[that] she caught me off-guard and delivered her wallop." These stories are set in a variety of places—from a London launderette to an alien planet— but are united, in Galst's opinion, by Livia's "fabulous descriptive prose...motivated, always, by her love of women."

Anna Livia has been called a Science Fiction writer, and is listed in *Science Fiction and Fantasy Literature* and *Encyclopedia of Science Fiction.* Her novel *Bulldozer Rising* is a true future dystopia and feminist science fiction tale. *Bulldozer Rising* examines what happens when youth culture with strict gender roles meets "oldwomen" over the age of 40, who are "fair prey for discrimination, humiliation and violence, especially at the hands of youngmen"; *Gay Community News* reviewer Mara Math claimed that the book explored the "logical extreme of youth worship and age hatred." "The hi-tech, low-humanity future of *Bulldozer Rising* is uncomfortably familiar," wrote Math. "Anna Livia has stripped contemporary life to its chilly bones in the incisive satire, in which the imperatives of patriarchal capitalist society are made literal." Reviewer Colin Greenland of the *Times Literary Supplement* called the novel, "syncopated, violent and witty," praising Livia for avoiding "loving women" visions by placing "lesbians in opposition rather than isolation," though finally "isolation is the only solution." However, Patricia Duncker notes that

the "passionate and erotic connection" between all the women is "taken for granted" in this tale. The old and young women do resist in various ways and as Math writes, "these various strands of resistance weave together to form...a quirky wire sculpture, occasionally disjointed but always interesting in its intersections and interstices." Josephine Saxton, in her *New Statesman* review, called the novel "deeply shocking...but completely invigorating" in this age of the "deadening and depressing effect of the backlash against feminism." *Bulldozer Rising,* concluded Math, "will be a feminist classic."

In the 1990s, when Anna Livia came to the United States and started studying linguistics, she began her forays into academic articles on language, particularly lesbian language, and her translations of French feminists, including Natalie Barney and Lucie Delarue-Mardrus. The translations have been universally praised; according to Victoria Brownworth, writing in *Lambda Book Report,* Natalie Barney's "*A Perilous Advantage* is nicely and rather spiritedly translated"; S.A. Inness, in *Choice,* called the first English translation of Delarue-Mardrus's *The Angel and the Perverts* a "notable addition." In *A Perilous Advantage,* Livia looks at all of Natalie Barney's writings (she was born in 1876 and lived to almost 100), autobiographies to poetry to, as Brownworth characterizes them, "bitchy little sketches of contemporaries" such as "Colette, one of her many bedpost notches." However Brownworth finds the collection rather haphazardly constructed with "writings from nearly every period of Barney's life...and in no particular order."

In the translation of *The Angel and the Perverts,* Livia has taken on a lesser-known French writer, Lucie Delarue-Mardrus. Her introduction focuses on the influence of the author's women friends rather than her husband, who has been written by other commentators in the past, and chronicles Delarue-Mardrus's growing affection for and attraction to women. Livia describes this novel as posing a number of questions regarding gender identity and gender roles. In her forward to the book, Karla Jay praises Livia for rereading Lucie Delarue-Mardrus "as a prolific and significant writer...and plac[ing] Delarue-Mardrus's life in a lesbian context for the first time."

Livia's many essays on lesbian language are part of the new writings of "cultural detectives" who are "integrating postmodern theory with lesbian studies," according to Ellen Herman in her review of *Lesbian Erotics* in *Lambda Book Report.* Herman calls Livia's essay "Tongues or Fingers" "a meandering journey through 'the erotic' which considers sensory encounters (with ants, with Indian food, with opera) and then moves beyond them, to a destination that remains necessarily idiosyncratic" and which shows the "more fluid notion of lesbian sexuality".

Livia's "I Ought To Throw A Buick At You," which is included in *Gender Articulated,* another book of essays on language and gender, looks at how butch and femme language is represented in fiction. Livia has written essays in French, such as "La Mythologie Lesbienne," for the French journal *Bulletin des Archives Lesbiennes,* as well as amusing essays on lesbian and working-class life for a variety of journals and anthologies.

Anna Livia continued her exploration into language and gender by editing, with Kira Hall, the 1997 anthology *Queerly Phrased: Language, Gender, and Sexuality,* which includes two of her own essays, "Disloyal to Masculinity: Linguistic Gender and Liminal Identity in French" and "It's a Girl: Bringing Performativity Back to Linguistics." She now teaches sociolinguistics, analysis of francophone African film, and language and gender in the French Linguistics Department at the University of Illinois. A critical thinker and prolific writer, Anna Livia is on the cutting edge of queer theory in linguistics.

—Jacquelyn Marie

LOCKE, Alain L(eRoy)

Nationality: American essayist and editor. **Born:** Philadelphia, Pennsylvania, 13 September 1886. **Education:** Philadelphia School of Pedagogy, Pennsylvania; Harvard University, Cambridge, Massachusetts, B.A. 1908 (magna cum laude; Phi Beta Kappa); Hertford College, Oxford University (Rhodes Scholar), 1907-10; University of Berlin, 1910-11; Harvard University, Ph.D. 1918. **Career:** Assistant Professor of English, 1912-15, professor of philosophy, beginning 1915, then head, Department of Philosophy, from 1918, Howard University, Washington, D.C.; contributor, *Opportunity: Journal of Negro Life,* New York City, from 1923; contributing editor, *Survey Graphic,* New York City, from 1924; visiting professor, Fisk University, Nashville, Tennessee, 1927-28, University of Wisconsin, Madison, 1945-46, New School for Social Research, New York City, 1947, and City College of New York, New York City, from 1948; Inter-American Exchange professor to Haiti, 1943. Editorial board member, *American Scholar;* philosophy editor, *Key Reporter* (Phi Beta Kappa); secretary-editor, Associates in Negro Folk Education, from 1935; president, American Association for Adult Education, 1945; faculty member, Salzburg Seminar in American Studies, 1950; corresponding member, Academie des Sciences Coloniales, Paris; founding member, African Union Society, Oxford; founding member, Conference on Science, Philosophy, and Religion; Honorary Fellow, Sociedad de Estudios Afro-Cubanos; member, American Negro Academy, International Institute of African Languages and Culture, and National Order of Honor and Merit. **Awards:** L.H.D.: Howard University, 1953. **Died:** New York City, of heart failure, 9 June 1954.

WRITINGS

Editor

The New Negro: An Interpretation. New York, Albert and Charles Boni, Inc., 1925; New York, Atheneum, 1969; with introduction by Arnold Rampersad, New York, Macmillan, 1992.
Four Negro Poets. New York, Simon and Schuster, 1927.
With T. Montgomery Gregory, *Plays of Negro Life: A Source-Book of Native American Drama.* New York, Harper, 1927.
The Negro in Art: A Pictorial Record of the Negro Artist and of the Negro Theme in Art. Washington, Associates in Negro Folk Education, 1940.
With Bernhard J. Stern, *When Peoples Meet: A Study in Race and Culture Contacts.* New York, Committee on Workshops, Progressive Education Association, 1942.
World View on Race and Democracy: A Study Guide in Human Group Relations. Chicago, American Library Association, 1943.

Art Criticism

The Negro and His Music. Washington, Associates in Negro Folk Education, 1936.
Negro Art: Past and Present. Washington, Associates in Negro Folk Education, 1936.
Le role du Negre dans la culture americaine. 1943.

Other

A Decade of Negro Self-Expression. Charlottesville, Virginia, 1928.
The Negro in America. Chicago, American Library Association, 1933.
The Critical Temper of Alain Locke: A Selection of His Essays on Art and Culture, edited by Jeffrey C. Stewart. New York, Garland, 1983.

*

Manuscript Collections: Alain L. Locke Papers, Moorland Spingarn Research Center, Howard University, Washington, D.C.

Biography: "A Biography of Alain Locke: Philosopher of the Harlem Renaissance, 1886-1930" by Jeffrey Conrad Stewart (dissertation), Yale University, New Haven, Connecticut; "Locke, Alain LeRoy" by Michael Winston, in *Dictionary of American Negro Biography,* edited by Rayford Logan and Michael Winston, New York, W. W. Norton, 1982.

Bibliography: "A Bio-Bibliography of Alain LeRoy Locke" by Lillian Avon Midgette (master's thesis), Atlanta University, Georgia.

*   *   *

The son and grandson of educators, including one who attended Cambridge in England, Alain Locke was the first Rhodes Scholar of African descent and, at a time when the intellectual capabilities of Africans were under debate among respected social scientists, Locke excelled at Harvard and Berlin, in addition to Oxford. His field was philosophy, with a specialty in value theory; in the late 1920s, most of his work, however, was done in literary criticism. As a literary critic, Locke's work intersected often with others who were, like him, gay, and occurred during a time when he was free of his regular teaching duties at Howard, thanks in part to a byzantine dispute between Howard's faculty and Howard's administration.

He began his career in literary criticism with his guest editing of the March 1925 issue of *Survey Graphic,* titled "Harlem, Mecca of the New Negro." Showcasing the art and writings of Black Americans, this issue ascribed to the art a heightened sense of race on par with the heightened sense of nationhood *Survey Graphic* discussed in its previous articles on Ireland and Russia. "New Negro" was the term Locke coined in this issue, and, because a number of the artists lived and worked in Harlem, the term coined for their artistic movement was "Harlem Renaissance."

"Harlem, Mecca of the New Negro" was expanded and, by December 1925, became *The New Negro.* Part anthology, part criticism, and part social science, *The New Negro* contained the work of established writers and scholars, such as James Weldon Johnson, Kerry Miller, Arthur Schomburg, and W. E. B. DuBois. It also contained the work of younger, then lesser known writers: Claude

McKay, Countee Cullen, Jean Toomer, Zora Neale Hurston, Bruce Nugent, and Langston Hughes.

While the established writers found in *The New Negro* a platform to disseminate their views on race and on the perceived inferiority of Blacks, for the younger writers *The New Negro* launched their careers. Locke had much to do with that. Shortly after the publication of *The New Negro,* Locke met Charlotte Mason, a wealthy widow whose devotion to 1920s primitivism had led her to be a patron of Native Americans. After meeting Locke, "Godmother" became a vital patron to several younger writers.

Locke's relationship with Mason and with the writers she helped proved a curious aspect of his career. An erudite European in almost every respect, Locke nonetheless found a kinship with Mason, who apparently found his personality antithetical to the primitivism she felt in his lectures ón African art. During the 1920s, Locke served as Mason's intermediary with the Harlem Renaissance writers. As her intermediary, Locke functioned with a high degree of trust. Though Mason herself possessed opinions and beliefs common to a woman of her time, age, and station, and though Locke seemed not to mask his homosexuality, there is little evidence that his orientation hindered her trust in him. Rather, she afforded him considerable authority in identifying talent and in dispersing money.

Beyond his role for Mason, as a critic Locke supported younger writers who shared his background and his orientation. From their meeting in the early 1920s, Locke provided critical and emotional support to Countee Cullen, whose preference for the sonnet went against 1920s poetry trends. Locke also boosted Bruce Nugent, a family friend whose avant-garde nature included the writing of gay-themed and homoerotic fiction. Both appeared in *The New Negro.* For two other younger Harlem Renaissance writers, however, Locke's relationship was frosty at best. One was Langston Hughes, represented in both "Harlem, the Mecca of the New Negro," and *The New Negro,* whom Locke attempted to seduce, with Countee Cullen's help and encouragement, in 1923; the other was Wallace Thurman, the novelist and editor, whose bohemianism embraced homosexuality.

The relationship between Hughes and Locke deteriorated throughout the late 1920s; initially warm, by 1930, they were no longer on speaking terms. Locke and Thurman were different entirely. In spite of their commonality (Locke's promotion of the Harlem Renaissance, and Thurman's support of it), the two engaged in a none-too-friendly feud, in which Thurman critiqued negatively *The New Negro* in the Harlem periodical *The Looking Glass* and Locke did the same to the Thurman edited periodical *Fire!!* in *Survey Graphic* in late 1926.

Fire!! was a controversial periodical. Its contributors, Hughes and Hurston among them, touched upon economic as well as socio-political themes. That gave it what critics (including Locke) called "a leftist slant." Interestingly, *Fire!!* also included Nugent's "Smoke, Lilies, and Jade," believed to have been the first published work on gay themes by a Black writer. In his review, Locke did not attack Nugent. Rather, he implies that a journal collected around gay themes would have been more desirable than one collected around leftist themes.

Based upon the body of his work, which remains uncollected, Locke had no comparable opportunity to critique similar lesbian themes in work by women, mostly because such themes were not being presented for publication by Black writers in the 1920s. It is also true that Locke's relationship with women writers lacked the complexities of his relationship with men.

After 1926, and, apparently, at Mason's urging, Locke's attentions turned increasingly toward art criticism. Though he continued reviewing books and working with writers (including Hughes into 1930), art demanded more of his energies. He did publish Nugent's *Sadhji,* with its gay subtext, in *Plays of Negro Life: A Source-Book of Native American Drama* in 1927, but, by 1930, he had left literary criticism almost entirely.

—J. E. Robinson

LOULAN, JoAnn

Nationality: American psychotherapist and lecturer. **Born:** Ohio, c. 1948. **Education:** Educated as a marriage and family counselor, California. **Family:** One son by artificial insemination in 1982. **Career:** Taught health-care professionals, University of California Medical School; counselor to lesbians, California, from 1977; Lesbian Sexuality Workshops, San Francisco, from 1978; contributor, *Out/Look* and *Outweek* magazines; lecturer and workshop provider on lesbian sexuality, United States and Canada. **Address:** 4370 Alpine Rd., #205, Portola Valley, California 94028, U.S.A.

WRITINGS

Nonfiction

Lesbian Sex. Duluth, Minnesota, Spinsters Ink, 1984.
Lesbian Passion: Loving Ourselves and Each Other. Duluth, Minnesota, Spinsters Ink, 1987.
The Lesbian Erotic Dance: Butch, Femme, Androgyny and Other Rhythms. Minneapolis, Spinsters Ink, 1990.
With Bonnie Lopez and Marcia Quackenbush, *Period.* Volcano, California, Volcano Press, 1991.

*

Critical Sources: "The Year of the Lustful Lesbian" by Arlene Stein, in *Sisters, Sexperts, Queers: Beyond the Lesbian Nation,* edited by Arlene Stein, New York, Penguin Books, 1993, 13-34; "The Power and the Pride" by Eloise Salholz, Daniel Glick, Lucille Beachy, Carey Monserrate, Patricia King, Jeanne Gordon, and Todd Barrett, in *Newsweek,* 21 June 1993, 54.

*   *   *

JoAnn Loulan has been called the "Dr. Ruth of lesbian sex." Author of the best-selling book *Lesbian Sex,* she has counseled lesbians since 1977 to be proud of their sexuality and to celebrate diversity in sexual practices. She has also been a strong proponent of safe sex in the lesbian community. She urges lesbians to celebrate their lifestyles and to fight the internal and external homophobia which undermines self-esteem.

Loulan was born and raised in Ohio, but eventually moved to California to study counseling and psychotherapy. She worked in the psychiatric wards of a county hospital for two years, and for a brief time, taught other health-care professionals at the University of California Medical School. In 1975 she took a six-month psychology course which would change her life. It was taught by a variety of liberal therapists and educators—among them Tee Corinne and Pat Califia, who were already prominent in the field of lesbian sex education. This course inspired her to turn her attentions to the dynamics of lesbian sexuality and the ways in which homophobia affects the lesbian community. She soon changed the focus of her private practice to counseling lesbians and in 1978 offered a series of workshops focusing on lesbian sexuality. The workshops were very popular and soon Loulan began to be sought out for speaking engagements throughout the country. She began touring to women's festivals and events giving lectures and workshops on various aspects of lesbian sexuality.

In 1984 Loulan published *Lesbian Sex,* the book for which she is still most widely known. It served to cement her reputation as a leader in the field of lesbian psychotherapy and an expert on the dynamics of lesbian sexuality. In the book, Loulan describes a variety of sexual practices and covers a wide variety of topics associated with sexuality, including: Sex and Aging, Sex and Motherhood, and Sexually Transmitted Diseases and Coming Out. The book does not try to recruit but rather to provide guidance for women who are already self-identified lesbians. As she explains in the introduction, "this book is not aimed at extolling the virtues of lesbian sex; it's aimed at helping you have the sex life that you want." In the final section of the book Loulan includes "Homework Exercises" which "provide a framework within which you can begin to look at your own individual needs around sexuality." The book is an affirmation which reassures lesbians that their sexual practices, in all their diverse forms, are normal and healthy. No subject is taboo and Loulan addresses each with an openness and honesty that is not only refreshing, but empowering. *Lesbian Sex* is still widely read and remains one of the best references available on the subject.

In the mid 1980s Loulan's friend Barbara Austin urged her to give a series of lectures at the Women's Building in San Francisco and to tape these lectures and compile them into a book. Loulan agreed, and this became the basis for her second publication, *Lesbian Passion,* her most interesting and affirming work. The book was ghost-written by Mariah Burton Nelson. In it Loulan focuses on the dynamics of lesbian relationships and self-esteem. In her acknowledgments she notes, "We needed a book that talked about our self-hatred and self-love." Loulan examines the common themes many lesbians struggle with, and the internal homophobia which must be overcome. She urges lesbians to move toward self-love by "healing the little child within." Her warmth, openness, and pride in being an "out" lesbian is apparent throughout the book, and this makes it an invaluable inspiration to those who may feel embarrassed or ashamed about their lesbianism.

In *The Lesbian Erotic Dance* Loulan examines the terms "butch", "femme", and "androgynous" to determine how these labels influence the way in which lesbians interact both socially and sexually. She surveyed 589 lesbians from across the country about their opinions of the use of such labels, what they believe the terms mean, how these labels influence interaction with other lesbians, and where they would place themselves on the butch/femme continuum. She explores how these labels can effect sexual practices and choice of partners and suggests that attitudes surrounding the terms may point to a hidden homophobia present within the lesbian community. Loulan urges a reclaiming of the terms "butch" and "femme" as a first step in creating a language which will speak specifically to lesbians: "I feel it is essential to create a language that we relate to and that speaks to us, beginning with

the words we have had for decades. To ignore or eschew this language is to deny our lesbian history and the part it has played in shaping who we are." She views butch and femme as lesbian archetypes and proposes that a wider, conscious exploration of these terms will help lesbians to connect and to create a language which can deepen communication. She also counters the idea that the terms "butch" and "femme" are rooted in the heterosexual community, and asserts that the use of these terms need not be seen as a desire to mimic heterosexual relationships: "Butch and femme are not male and female. They are uniquely and powerfully our own."

Loulan continues to give workshops and lectures where she counsels lesbians to accept and celebrate themselves. She is a dynamic speaker who combines a highly theatrical presentation style, audience participation, and humor to put audiences at ease, making them more receptive to discussions which might otherwise be difficult. There is no topic Loulan will not take on and her lectures have included discussions of everything from safe sex and masturbation to sex toys and s/m practices. She is unassuming and easy-going and has a style which has been described as "folksy." Her open, honest, "no-holds barred" demeanor allows audiences to consider her views on even the most sensitive topics. As Arlene Stein has noted, "Loulan would gladly assume the role of lesbian sex cheerleader. This folksiness has allowed her to get away with all manner of statements which might otherwise be considered blasphemous."

JoAnn Loulan is a great inspiration to the lesbian community. She is comfortable with her own sexuality and urges others to be comfortable with theirs. Despite her small body of published work, she is well-known and well-respected throughout the American lesbian community. In the 1990s, she was delivering about 20 talks per year and had sold over 100,000 books.

—Beth A. Kattelman

LUCAS, Craig

Nationality: American Playwright, screenwriter, and essayist. **Born:** Atlanta, Georgia, 10 April 1951. **Education:** Boston University, B.F.A. 1974. **Family:** Companion of Patrick Barnes; formerly companion of Timothy Melester (died 1995). **Career:** Playwright and screenwriter; stage actor, appearing in *Shenandoah* (1975), *Rex* (1976), *On the Twentieth Century* (1978), and *Sweeney Todd* (1979); contributing editor, *Bomb* magazine; contributor of articles to periodicals, including *Advocate, American Theater, Bomb,* and *Dramatists Guild Quarterly.* **Awards:** Villager Award, 1981; George and Elizabeth Marton Award, 1984; John Simon Guggenheim Fellowship, 1984; Drama Logue Award, Los Angeles Drama Critics Award, 1985; Burns Mantle, for Best Musical, 1987; Rockefeller Fellowship, 1988; Drama Desk nomination, 1988, 1990, 1995; Rockefeller Bellagio Fellowship, 1988; Antoinette Perry (Tony) nomination, 1990; Obie Award, 1990; Outer Critics Award, 1990; Pulitzer Prize finalist, 1990; Audience Award, Sundance Film Festival, 1990; Yaddo Residency, 1994. **Agent:** Peter Franklin, William Morris Agency, 1350 Avenue of the Americas, New York, New York 10019, U.S.A.

WRITINGS

Stage Plays

With Steven Sondheim and Norman René, *Marry Me a Little* (produced by the Production Company, 1980; produced Off-Broadway, 1981).

Missing Persons (produced by the Production Company, New York, 31 May 1981; revised production, Atlantic Theatre Company, New York, 31 January 1995). New York, Dramatists Play Service, 1996.

Alex Wilder: Clues to a Life (produced Off-Broadway, New York, 1982).

Reckless (produced Off-Broadway, Production Company, New York, 1983; revised production, Off-Broadway, Circle Repertory, 14 September 1988).

Blue Window (produced by the Production Company, New York, 28 May 1984). New York, Samuel French, 1985.

With composer/lyricist Craig Carnelia, *Three Postcards* (produced by South Coast Repertory, Costa Mesa, California, 6 January 1987; revised production, Circle Repertory Company, New York, 16 November 1994). New York, Dramatists Play Service, 1995.

Prelude to a Kiss (produced by South Coast Repertory, Costa Mesa, California, 15 January 1988; revised production, Circle Repertory Company 14 March 1990; produced on Broadway, 1 May 1990). New York, Broadway Play Publishing, 1990.

Reckless [and] *Blue Window: Two Plays by Craig Lucas*. New York, Theatre Communications Group, 1989.

Credo (produced by the Ensemble Studio Theatre Marathon, New York, 1995). Published in *EST Marathon '95: The Complete One Act Plays*, edited by Marisa Smith, Lyme, New Hampshire, Smith and Kraus, 1995.

What I Meant Was (produced by Humana Festival, Actor's Theatre of Louisville, Kentucky, 29 March 1996).

God's Heart (produced by Trinity Repertory, Providence, Rhode Island, spring 1996; produced at Lincoln Center, New York, March 1997).

The Dying Gaul (commissioned by Hartford Stage; production forthcoming).

With David Schulner, *Savage Light* (commissioned for Humana Festival, Actor's Theatre of Louisville).

Screenplays

Blue Window (screenplay; presented as part of "American Playhouse" series). PBS-TV, 1987.

Longtime Companion (screenplay). American Playhouse Theatrical Films, Samuel Goldwyn Company, 1990.

Prelude to a Kiss (screenplay). Twentieth Century Fox, 1992.

Reckless (screenplay). Samuel Goldwyn Company, 1995.

Other

Bad Dream (radio play; produced by Atlantic Theater Company, WBAI Radio, 11 May 1992). Published in *The Actors Book of Gay and Lesbian Plays*, edited by Eric Lane and Nina Shengold, New York, Penguin, 1995.

With composer Gerald Busby, *Orpheus in Love* (opera libretto; produced New York, 1993-94).

"Equality in the Theatre" (criticism), in *Bomb*, New York, fall 1996.

With composer Gerald Busby, *Breedlove* (opera libretto).

*

Critical Sources: "Blue Window" by John Simon, in *New York*, Vol. 17, No. 30, 30 July 1984, 53; "A Christmas Fable of People Who Learn to Know Themselves" by Frank Rich, in *New York Times*, 26 September 1988, C19, C22; "'Prelude to a Kiss': A Fairy Tale of Souls in Love and in Flight," in *New York Times*, 15 March 1990, C15, C18; "What's Art All About? Truth, Beauty, Unruliness," in *New York Times*, 24 June 1990, H1; "Dramatists Guild Letter of Support" by Craig Lucas et al., 3 February 1993, http://users.vnet/phisto/letters.htm; "Getting Their Words' Worth" by Jan Herman, in *Los Angeles Times*, 27 February 1994; "Equality in the Theatre" by Craig Lucas, in *Bomb* (New York), fall 1996; "Eastern Regionals" by Robert L. King, in *North American Review*, March/April 1996, 44-48; "Classics Unillustrated" by Michael Feingold, in *Village Voice*, 24 February 1996, 77; unpublished interview with Craig Lucas by Patti Capel Swartz, October 1996; "Season Highlights Off and Off-Off Broadway," http://www.villagevoice.com/obies/seashigh.htm; "Reckless: Norman René (Director)—Bio," "Reckless: Lindsay Law (Executive Producer)—Bio," and "AIDS-Inspired Film and Video at UNC," http://ils.unc.edu/kparks/aa/film/htm; "Reckless: Craig Lucas (Author)—Bio," http://www.movienet.com/movienet/movinfo/rekren.htm.

Craig Lucas comments:

In the last five years, because of the death of three lovers and dozens of colleagues and friends, including my closest colleague, Norman René, my work has become extremely angry, directly engaging with the larger society in a way my early work did not. My progressive politics manifest themselves more visibly. I believe the work has also grown more visceral and poetic. The persistent struggle is to find voice for the anguish which does not dissolve into nihilism or despair, but rather points the way toward action: "Don't get depressed, *organize*." I do not think that my work's relationship to social responsibility can be separated out from its relationship to personal responsibilities, moral, intellectual, and aesthetic ones; each comes into play simultaneously in the creation, and must be balanced so as not to overwhelm the other goals. All of them are tied to telling the truth, first to oneself, in order to communicate a reflection of that truth in an aesthetically blissful manner. My personal allegiance to the idea of social progress (vis-a-vis the necessity for basic human rights for all individuals from every class, race, sex, nationality, sexual orientation, political belief, religion or lack thereof) compels me to express this ideal in my work, but it is *my own convictions alone* which dictate that very expression and no one else's judgement or reaction or objection or support of these matters concerns me. My work attempts to make the invisible visible: the tragic cost of pursuing material "satisfaction," the quality of living under a panoply of deceptions both personal and societal, and a reverence for the wonder of our spiritual existence.

*   *   *

Craig Lucas's productions read like a who's who in the theatrical world. Through screen adaptations of *Prelude to a Kiss* and

Reckless, and his original screenplay *Longtime Companion,* Lucas's work has also become well known to movie audiences. Lucas is not an artist in isolation from others, nor is his work isolated from political and social contexts. He has collaborated successfully with other writers and with musicians; his long term collaboration with director Norman René until René's death was quite productive.

Lucas has described his early work as essentially comic in tone. In a review of a revival of *Missing Persons,* Michael Feingold commented that this play "could nearly rank with the masters [Moliére] for sparkle." Yet Lucas's plays are funny about serious matters. *Three Postcards,* Lucas notes, depicts three women who "struggle to love one another and continue to grow" despite social prohibitions against women's friendship; *Reckless* narrates "the need to escape from the kind of American idealism which translates into blind denial"; and *Blue Window* examines "the desire for connection in an upper class urban milieu." As critic Frank Rich has pointed out, Lucas demands that the characters of these plays "leav[e] home for the unknown of a starry night and the arduous prospect of selfless love, just as he demands that audiences take the leap out of a literal reality and into the imaginative realm of an adult fable." The underlying seriousness provides comedy that attempts to change the audience through commentary that fractures the boundaries of time, place, and social myth.

Throughout *Reckless,* the character Rachel states that things happen for a reason. Finally, she realizes "things just happen. People die." When Rachel is able to realize this she becomes truly able to help herself and form connections. The search for and lack of security is also evident in Lucas's *Blue Window.* The blue window is associated with the pleasures of free fall in skydiving, and the realities of the free fall in which most of us engage without a chute. Libby, the hostess of a dinner gathering of a mixed group of straight and gay people, lost her ability to believe in security when she and her husband fell from a balcony and she landed on him, killing him, but remaining alive. She longs to be able to float out into a blue with no consequences. As Jana Rivera pointed out in a review of *Blue Window,* "eventually [the characters] find themselves asking the same unanswerable question: How do you stop the ache?"

AIDS has greatly affected Lucas's work and his life, infusing his work with the anguish of loss that comes from the deaths of friends and lovers. His film *Longtime Companion,* about a group of gay men, was the first widely distributed, mainstream film about AIDS. Lucas's *Bad Dream* also speaks directly to AIDS as two lovers, one dying, talk in the middle of the night. The necessity to find intersections of interests for organizing is explored through *God's Heart,* a play Lucas describes as "about extremes in America—rich, poor, black, white, straight, gay, young, old." He describes his *The Dying Gaul* as "about materialism and the cost, both to individuals and to society, of imposing no limits on our passions," and *Savage Light* as discussing "our responsibility to the future." Lucas's *Prelude to a Kiss* has been read by critic Vincent Canby as a metaphor for the AIDS epidemic, and Frank Rich noted that this is "a play that acknowledges even those modern terrors it leaves unmentioned, like AIDS, by forcing its young lovers to test their bond against the threat of imminent physical decay and death." Rich points out that "Lucas's revivifying dream of love, as beautiful as it is miraculous in these precarious nights, hangs on."

In his essay "Equality Issues in the Theatre," Lucas expresses opinions on issues that surround representation, casting, and artistic license, complex concerns which are being widely discussed and debated in almost all aspects of art. In response to debates about interracial casting and writing about groups of which one is not a member, Lucas notes that the milieu of established plays, like opera and ballet, are less problematic than are newer works like *M. Butterfly,* in which casting helps the audience to understand context. He rejects claims that one may not write about what one has not experienced and criticism from gay critics who "would have [him] write predominantly or exclusively gay characters," stating that "the business of artists is to offer what they have seen and to imagine what they cannot truly ever know.... I live in a world filled with straight people; I am more than familiar with their colorful and strange mating rituals, and I believe I can speak sympathetically towards their hopes and fears as well as to the issues facing queer people." As Lucas notes, "homophobia lives in the homosexual community as well as in others, and ghettoizing our experience is not always the same as celebrating it."

Lucas notes that in *Longtime Companion* he showed the ordinary lives of gay men struggling with an epidemic, but that "straight Americans seem much more comfortable with the idea of men dressing up as women...than with the idea of middle-class or working-class characters...choosing to sleep with or make love with members of their own sex." Americans' failure to accept all varieties of people and their underlying Puritanism, Lucas feels, must be resolved if we are to resolve national conflicts. A Buddhist, Lucas aspires to inner calm, but that calm does not preclude committed activity for change. As he notes, "Surely we have learned by now that silence equals death." Lucas has put himself on the line as an openly gay man whose social and political convictions are not separate from his vision as an artist. Critic Peter Keough drew this lesson from Lucas's work: "[T]he only real sins are a blindness to responsibility and a refusal to forgive."

—Patti Capel Swartz

LYNCH, Beverly. *See* **LYNCH, Lee.**

LYNCH, Lee

Pseudonyms: Has also written as Ellen Gold, Carol Lynk, Lynn Flood, Beverly Lynch. **Nationality:** American novelist, author of short stories, columnist, reviewer, and feature writer. **Born:** New York City, 1945. **Education:** University of Bridgeport, Connecticut, B.A. 1967. **Family:** Companion of Akia Woods. **Career:** Has held a variety of jobs including vocational rehabilitation consultant, statistical analyst, Girl Scout field executive, retail food manager and trainer, cab driver, and clerical worker. Author of "The Amazon Trail," syndicated column featured in the *Washington Blade* and other publications; contributor to *Lambda Book Report, Common Lives/Lesbian Lives, Sinister Wisdom, Lesbian Short Fiction,* and *The Ladder.* **Address:** c/o New Victoria Publishers, P.O. Box 27, Norwich, Vermont 05055, U.S.A.

WRITINGS

Novels

Toothpick House. Tallahassee, Florida, Naiad Press, 1983.
The Swashbuckler. Tallahassee, Naiad Press, 1985.
Dusty's Queen of Hearts Diner. Tallahassee, Naiad Press, 1987.
Sue Slate, Private Eye. Tallahassee, Naiad Press, 1989.
That Old Studebaker. Tallahassee, Naiad Press, 1991.
Morton River Valley. Tallahassee, Naiad Press, 1992.

Short Stories

Old Dyke Tales. Tallahassee, Naiad Press, 1984.
Home In Your Hands. Tallahassee, Naiad Press, 1986.
Cactus Love. Tallahassee, Naiad Press, 1994.

Uncollected Short Stories

"At a Bar, In the Morning," in *Common Lives/Lesbian Lives* (Iowa City, Iowa), 1981.
"The Coat," in *Common Lives/Lesbian Lives* (Iowa City, Iowa), 1981.
"The Swashbuckler," in *Sinister Wisdom* (Berkeley, California), No. 24.
"Sy," in *Lesbian Short Fiction,* Vol. 1, No. 1.
"Life Blood," in *The Ladder* (San Francisco, California), August-September 1971.
"The Shade," in *The Ladder* (San Francisco, California), June-July 1972.
"Felicita G.," in *The Lavender Herring,* edited by Barbara Grier and Coletta Reid. Baltimore, Maryland, Diana Press, 1976.
"As Dreams Are Made Of" and "A Hard Row to Hoe," in *The Lesbians Home Journal,* edited by Barbara Grier and Coletta Reid. Baltimore, Maryland, Diana Press, 1976.
"The LoPresto Traveling Magic Show" (as Beverly Lynch), in *Sinister Wisdom* (Berkeley, California), winter 1980.
"Oranges Out of Season," in *Sinister Wisdom* (Berkeley, California), 1981.
"Dutch and Sybil I," in *Common Lives/Lesbian Lives* (Iowa City, Iowa), winter 1983.
"The Ladies," in *Common Lives/Lesbian Lives* (Iowa City, Iowa), winter 1983.
"Marie-Christine II," in *On Our Backs* (San Francisco, California), 1985.
"At A Bar VI: Winter Sun," in *Common Lives/Lesbian Lives* (Iowa City, Iowa), fall 1985.
"Dusty Eats Out," in *On Our Backs* (San Francisco, California), winter 1986.
"The Fires of Winter Solstice," in *Just Out* (Portland, Oregon), January 1987.
"The Big Bad Wolf," in *Common Lives/Lesbian Lives* (Iowa City, Iowa), summer 1988.
"Hanukkah at a Bar," in *Common Lives/Lesbian Lives* (Iowa City, Iowa), winter 1988.
"Cactus Love," in *On Our Backs* (San Francisco, California), March-April 1989.
"New Year's Eve at a Bar," in *Lesbian Love Stories,* edited by Irene Zahava. Freedom, California, Crossing Press, 1989.
"The Wet Night," in *Intricate Passions,* edited by Tee A. Corrine. Austin, Texas, Banned Books, 1989.

"Jacky and Her Mother," "Jacky and the Drag Queens," and "Jacky and the Wedding," in *Word of Mouth,* edited by Irene Zahava. Freedom, California, Crossing Press, 1990.
"Truckstop Woman," in *Lesbian Love Stories 2,* edited by Irene Zahava. Freedom, California, Crossing Press, 1991.
"City Slicker," in *The Erotic Naiad,* edited by Katherine Forrest and Barbara Grier. Tallahassee, Florida, Naiad Press, 1992; in *Diving Deep,* edited by Katherine Forrest and Barbara Grier. Tallahassee, Florida, Naiad Press, 1992; reprinted London, Silver Moon Books, 1992.
"Jacky and the Femme," in *The Persistent Desire,* edited by Joan Nestle. Boston, Massachusetts, Alyson Publications, 1992.
"Inez," in *Out* (Pittsburgh, Pennsylvania), August 1993.
"Jacky and the Psychic," in *Lesbian Culture,* edited by Julia Penelope and Susan Wolfe. Freedom, California, Crossing Press, 1993.
"The Light of Day," in *The Romantic Naiad,* edited by Katherine Forrest and Barbara Grier. Tallahassee, Florida, Naiad Press, 1993.
"Waterfall Falls" (serial), in *Girlfriends* (San Francisco), beginning June-July 1996.

Uncollected Nonfiction

"The Politics of DiPrima," in *Ladder* (San Francisco, California), June-July 1970.
"Gemstones: A Look at Some Minor Works of Djuna Barnes," in *Ladder* (San Francisco, California), October-November 1970.
"Beyond Desire," in *Ladder* (San Francisco, California), April-May 1971.
"Sara Teasdale," "Willa Cather," "Love, Beyond Men and Women: H.D.," and "A Life of Angels: Margaret Fuller," in *Lesbian Lives: Biographies of Women from The Ladder,* edited by Barbara Grier and Coletta Reid. Baltimore, Maryland, Diana Press 1976.
"Mean Norma Jean, a Wave on the Shore," in *Advocate* (Los Angeles, California), 28 February 1989.
"Home, Home on the Grange," in *Advocate* (Los Angeles, California), 20 June 1989.
"Cruising the Libraries," in *Lesbian Texts and Contexts,* edited by Karla Jay. New York, New York University Press, 1990.
"Behind the Scenes at *Common Lives/Lesbian Lives,*" in *Washington Blade* (Washington, D.C.), 17 April 1992.
"Summer Sanctuary," in *Lambda Book Report* (Washington, D.C.), July-August 1993.
"Slogan on a Stick," in *Lambda Book Report* (Washington, D.C.), November-December 1993.

Stage Plays

The Swashbuckler (adapted from original short story; produced New York City, 1984).
Trying To Get Into Life (produced Tucson, Arizona, 1990).

Poetry

"Feast," "Gold," "Luncheonette," and "Summer 2," in *Ladder* (San Francisco, California), June-July 1970.
"Hibernation," "Untitled," "Violinists," and "Waterfall," in *Ladder* (San Francisco, California), April-May 1971.
"Designs," in *Ladder* (San Francisco, California), July 1972.

"Stone Butch," in *The Persistent Desire,* edited by Joan Nestle. Boston, Massachusetts, Alyson Publications, 1992.

Other

The Amazon Trail (collection of syndicated columns). Tallahassee, Florida, Naiad Press, 1988.

Editor, with Akia Woods, *Off the Rag: Lesbians Writing on Menopause.* Norwich, Connecticut, New Victoria Publishers, 1996.

*

Adaptations: *Toothpick House, The Swashbuckler, Dusty's Queen of Hearts Diner, Sue Slate, Private Eye,* and *That Old Studebaker* have all been made into sound recordings by the Womyn's Braille Press.

Lee Lynch comments:

I began to write seriously at age 14. A year later I came out and quickly learned the traditional disguises of the gay writer, such as avoiding gender-specific pronouns. It wasn't until I reached 21 and could subscribe to *The Ladder* (without getting them in trouble for distributing lesbian material to a minor) that I found an outlet where I could write about my real life. Barbara Grier was then editor and a true mentor.

The women's movement, ironically, took away my audience. Publications that supplanted *The Ladder* came from a feminist perspective which, like the political lesbians I knew, shunned 'the life'—from bars to femme/butch. With the birth of the periodicals *Common Lives/Lesbian Lives* and *Sinister Wisdom,* and later, the early publishing companies like Naiad Press, I was once more able to write about lesbian life as I experienced it.

My goal was to write books and stories that would make lesbians feel good about ourselves. My models were Jane Rule and the late Isabel Miller. Although the works of Radclyffe Hall, Valerie Taylor, Ann Bannon, Vin Packer, Claire Morgan, and Ann Aldrich did not always present positive portraits of lesbians and lesbian life, their existence, back in the 1960s, fortified me by acknowledging that I and women like me existed. Today I continue to struggle to document our lives and to enhance the lives of gay readers with characters who look and act and hurt and love and struggle like real-life lesbians.

Once again, irony has overtaken my career. Now that there is a thriving lesbian publishing industry, there is little room for stories of common lives. Mystery, erotica, glamour, top our best seller lists. Yet I hear from individual readers that the characters and stories which miraculously spring from my pen have given these readers hope, strength, courage, and a better understanding of lesbian life. I am grateful to live in an age and a country where I can write about lesbians.

*   *   *

Over the years, Lee Lynch has developed a realm all her own. Her writing strikes a powerful balance between the apolitical and the super-political, the idealistic and the fatalistic. What Lynch does, essentially, is tell a positive story while sneaking in memories, political messages, humor, criticisms, questions, and heartache. She makes the readers want to do something, reminds them of what they're not doing, or tells them what they might be doing wrong. But she is not an outright critic. She also celebrates all of the glorious qualities of queer culture: the diversity, unity, togetherness, perseverance, and strength of the greater gay and lesbian community. All sides of this community are out in the open, holding the same amount of significance and power.

In 1984, Lee Lynch began writing her syndicated column, "The Amazon Trail"; in 1988, these essays were collected into a book by the same title. She writes about gay and lesbian traditions, her life as a lesbian writer, gay and lesbian literature, sobriety, "gay geography", and more. Her perspectives, creativity, and unique sense of humor shine through her uncomplicated words, giving her audience a tangible and genuine taste of gay life in America.

The element of difference is a common thread that runs through much of Lynch's fiction. Differences such as those of class, age, race, appearance, gender identity, and culture among the characters, and between the characters and the society that surrounds them, surface again and again. This use of difference adds to the political undertones of her work as well as a diverse mixture of personas. Lynch frequently sets her stories surrounding periods of great change and political unrest in gay and lesbian history, reflecting both the needs for change and the effects of the changes that take place. One of the unmistakable ways is through plot: she often chronicles an "excerpt" from the gay rights movement, either by telling the story of a faction of the movement or of an individual caught up in it. Such is the case with *The Swashbuckler.* Frenchy is from the "old school" of butch and femme lesbian dynamics, but all around her the times are changing. Influenced by women's liberation, lesbians are becoming more androgynous and the traditional dating rituals are disappearing. Frenchy is therefore caught between what she knows and what she is observing in her community.

Lynch's fiction gives the reader a feeling of familiarity, as if you have met the characters somewhere before, or have visited the places they visit. Many of her characters come back for brief "visits" in her short stories, years after first appearing in a novel, or vice versa. Other characters materialize in the background of one novel and then become heroines in a later novel. Dusty Reilly and Eleanor Hunnicutt are introduced in *Toothpick House;* later they are the central characters of *Dusty's Queen of Hearts Diner.* Frenchy Tonneau, of *The Swashbuckler,* reappears many years later as a minor character in *That Old Studebaker. Toothpick House*'s Annie Heaphy returns in many short stories. Sally and Liz are constants in the "At a Bar" story series, and Henny tells a new tale to her assistant in each installment of the "Fruitstand" series.

Another technique that Lynch frequently employs is the use of groups of protagonists: groups of lesbian characters that are bound together by common needs, friendships, places, hardships, and loves. Her characters do not fall by the wayside—they are central, influential, necessary women. Even when not a main character, each has an important role in the story. Often these groups of women represent a part of the lesbian community, a cluster of one type of lesbian, or a sampling of the diverse cross-section of the culture. And yet each woman is unique; these are lesbian characters that represent a type of "real-life" lesbians. Characters get caught up in a time or situation of sociopolitical strife. They struggle with their own personal politics. They fall in and out of love and friendships. They take on the world that oppresses them. The women in the "At A Bar" series are an excellent example of this technique. The group of characters in these stories are brought together by shared experiences—the bar, holidays, drinking, sadness, joy. Likewise Annie Heaphy, the central character in *Toothpick House,* is surrounded by a loyal group of friends throughout the novel. They do not appear in the shadows as additives to the story, instead they all have their own particular spotlights. The same is true of the people that Andy Blaine encounters on her journey in *That Old Studebaker*—each plays a significant role in her life and in the story.

Lynch's characters share many common qualities. Often they are struggling with their own identities, and their story is one of an inward journey. They are usually at a turning point in their lives, in which self-discovery becomes part of a decision process. They are learning about themselves and how they fit into the world around them. At some point, identity and inner strength are tested. In *Dusty's Queen of Hearts Diner,* Dusty and Eleanor face opposition and discrimination from their small community, and they must decide if they will face the challenge head on or retreat to preserve their safety and sanity. In *Toothpick House,* Annie must come to terms with her friendships, her background, and lifestyle when she falls in love with a young woman of a different social class. Andy Blaine, in *That Old Studebaker,* must decide between an old flame and a new love after a cross-country journey that has changed her thinking and her life. Frenchy is continually struggling with her conflicting worlds and identities—respectful daugh-

ter, suave young butch lesbian, loyal employee—and how to balance them in *The Swashbuckler.* Every character that Lynch creates grows and evolves, learns something about herself, faces her dilemmas, and becomes a wiser woman as a result. In these and other Lynch works, the reader meets new and old friends, and they each represent a small slice of the gay community pie.

In all of her fiction, Lynch presents strong lesbian women who emerge triumphant despite less-than-ideal circumstances (both political and personal). She adds to this combination a small sampling of gay and lesbian culture, a sense of humor, and an awareness that offers her readers a feeling of comfort, belonging, and good company.

—Amy Warner Candela

————

LYNK, Carol. *See* **LYNCH, Lee.**

————

M

MACKAY, John Henry

Pseudonym: Also wrote as Sagitta. **Nationality:** German novelist, poet, author of short stories, and essayist. **Born:** Geenock, Scotland, 6 February 1864; moved with his mother to Germany when 19 months old; became citizen c. 1900. **Education:** Educated in Saarbrücken and a neighboring town; studied philosophy, literature, and the history of art, as an auditor, Universities of Kiel, Leipzig, and Berlin. **Career:** Held a variety of jobs including writer and publisher. **Died:** 16 May 1933.

WRITINGS

Novels

Die Anarchisten. Kulturgemälde aus dem Ende des XIX. Jahrhunderts ("The Anarchists. A Picture of Civilization at the Close of Nineteenth Century"). Zürich, Verlag J. Schabelitz, and Boston, Benjamin R. Tucker, 1891.
Der Schwimmer ("The Swimmer"). 1901.
Fenny Skaller (as Sagitta), in *Die Bücher der namenlosen Liebe* ("The Books of the Nameless Love"). Paris, 1913; second edition, Holland, 1924; as *Fenny Skaller and Other Prose Writings from the Books of the Nameless Love,* translated by Hubert Kennedy, Amsterdam, Southernwood Press, 1988.
Der Freiheitsucher ("The Freedom Seeker"). Berlin-Charlottenburg, 1920.
Der Puppenjunge ("The Hustler"; as Sagitta). Holland, 1926; as *The Hustler: The Story of a Nameless Love from Friedrich Street,* translated by Hubert Kennedy, Boston, Alyson, 1985.

Poetry

Sturm ("Storm"). 1887.
Helene. Zürich, Verlag J. Schabelitz, 1888.
Das starke Jahr ("The Strong Year"). Zürich, Verlag J. Schabelitz, 1890.
Wer sind wir? ("Who are We?"; as Sagitta). Berlin, 1906; in *Die Bücher der namenlosen Liebe* ("The Books of the Nameless Love"), Paris, 1913; second edition, Holland, 1924.
Am Rande des Lebens ("On the edge of life"; as Sagitta). Berlin, 1909; in *Die Bücher der namenlosen Liebe* ("The books of the Nameless Love"), Paris, 1913; second edition, Holland, 1924.

Other

Max Stirner. Sein Leben und sein Werk. ("Max Stirner. His Life and his Work.") Berlin, Schuster und Löffler, 1898.
Die namenlose Liebe. Ein Bekenntnis. ("The Nameless Love. A Creed."; as Sagitta; prose). Berlin, 1906; in *Die Bücher der namenlosen Liebe* ("The Books of the Nameless Love"), Paris, 1913; second edition, Holland, 1924; in *Fenny Skaller and Other Prose Writings from the Books of the Nameless Love,* translated by Hubert Kennedy, Amsterdam, Southernwood Press, 1988.

Gehör!—Nur einen Augenblick! ("Listen! Only a Moment!"; as Sagitta; pamphlet). Berlin, Bernhard Zack, 1908; in *Die Bücher der namenlosen Liebe* ("The Books of the Nameless Love"), Paris, 1913; second edition, Holland, 1924; in *Fenny Skaller and Other Prose Writings from the Books of the Nameless Love,* translated by Hubert Kennedy, Amsterdam, Southernwood Press, 1988.
Gesammelte Werke (collected works), 8 Vols. Berlin-Treptow, Bernhard Zack, 1911.
über die Stufen von Marmor ("Over the Marble Steps"; as Sagitta; play), in *Die Bücher der namenlosen Liebe* ("The Books of the Nameless Love"). Paris, 1913; second edition, Holland, 1924.
Abrechnung. Randbemerkungen zum Leben und Arbeit ("Settlement. Marginal Notes on Life and Work"; autobiography). 1932.

*

Biography: *John Henry Mackay als Mensch* by Friedrich Dobe, Koblenz, Germany, Edition Plato, 1987.

Critical Sources: *Germany's Post-Anarchist John Henry Mackay: A Contribution to the History of German Literature at the Turn of the Century, 1880-1920* by Thomas A. Riley, New York, Revisionist Press, 1972; *Der Bahnbrecher John Henry Mackay: Sein Leben und sein Werk* by Kurt Helmut Zube Solneman, Freiburg/Breisgau, Germany, Verlag der Mackay-Gesellschaft, 1979; "From Propaganda to Literature: Remarks on the Writings of John Henry Mackay" by Edward Mornin, in *Seminar*, Vol. 18, No. 3, 1982, 184-195; *Kunst und Anarchismus: "innere Zusammenhänge" in den Schriften John Henry Mackays* by Edward Mornin, Freiburg/Breisgau, Germany, Verlag der Mackay-Gesellschaft, 1983; "No Good Deed Goes Unpunished: John Henry Mackay's *Helene*" by Hubert Kennedy, in *Germanic Notes* (Bemidji, Minnesota), Vol. 17, No. 1, 1986, 6-8; *Anarchist der Liebe: John Henry Mackay als Sagitta* by Hubert Kennedy, translated into German by Almuth Carstens, Berlin, Edition Aurora, 1988; "Foreword," to John Henry Mackay's *Fenny Skaller and Other Prose Writings from the Books of the Nameless Love* by Hubert Kennedy, Amsterdam, Southernwood Press, 1988, 1-10; "John Henry Mackay" by Hubert Kennedy, in *The Gay and Lesbian Literary Heritage,* edited by Claude J. Summers, New York, Henry Holt and Company, 1995, 456-457.

*   *   *

Born in Scotland of a Scottish father and a German mother, John Henry Mackay lived only 19 months in his homeland before his father died and his mother brought him to Germany, where Mackay grew up speaking German as his first language. The pair settled in Saarbrücken, where his mother remarried. Unfortunately, Mackay did not get along with his stepfather and was anxious to leave home at an early age. After he finished his schooling, he spent many years undecided about his future. He worked as an apprentice at a publishing house, studied at three universities without ever officially enrolling, and traveled widely in Europe. Finally, he decided to become a writer, supported by an allowance from his mother that enabled him to write without worrying about the need to sell his books to a wide audience.

Mackay's first successful publication was *Die Anarchisten,* a propagandistic novel in which he puts forth his individualist anarchistic philosophy appropriated from Max Stirner and Benjamin R. Tucker. In particular, Mackay rejected the authority of State and Church over the individual. Edward Mornin writes in his essay for *Seminar:* "he asserts the fundamental egoism of all men and their absolute right to pursue egoistic goals, to seek happiness and develop as they please according to their own natures." Mackay wanted more than anything for individuals to be able to act out their own desires without any interference from the outside.

Die Anarchisten was a run-away success, and the ensuing decade found Mackay at the height of his fame. But his mother's death in 1902 left him grief-stricken, and the only way he could find to recover from his depression was to take up a new literary campaign for a cause which was greeted with much opposition throughout his lifetime. Under the pseudonym of Sagitta, Mackay took up the "cause of gaining sympathetic recognition of man-boy love," Henry Kennedy writes in his profile of Mackay for *The Gay and Lesbian Literary Heritage.* Mackay referred to this love as a "nameless love," because he felt that no name in existence could adequately describe the love he felt for adolescent boys. Mackay devoted himself to this cause in order to help those who were trying to annul paragraph 175 of the *Reichstrafegesetzbuch,* the code of laws of the German state. Paragraph 175 ordered that all homosexual relations would be severely punished, regardless of whether or not there was mutual consent between the two parties. Mackay entered the debate over paragraph 175 later than many others because he objected to the petition circulated in 1897 that asked for freedom of sexual relations between consensual adults over the age of 16, although it had failed to change the law. Therefore, his Sagitta campaign had two goals, according to Thomas A. Riley, who writes in *Germany's Post-Anarchist John Henry Mackay,* "Mackay had in mind a series of writings that would be art but would nevertheless give the boy-lover a greater respect for his own emotions and disclose to the heterosexual the workings of the mind of the man who is attracted to boys."

In 1906, Mackay published under the name Sagitta 1,000 copies of two introductory books, *Die namenlose Liebe. Ein Bekenntnis* and *Wer sind wir?,* which he issued by subscription, hoping to reach those who would be sympathetic to his cause. At about the same time, the newspapers began to cover the sensational events of a group of the emperor's close advisors who were accused of being homosexuals. The trials of these advisors precipitated a flurry of attention to the question of homosexuality in the German press that encouraged Mackay to publish, again as Sagitta, a pamphlet for the general public called *Gehör!—Nur einen Augenblick!.* Riley writes that this work "endeavored to explain what boys meant to such men and the 'good' to the boy that resulted from such relations." The pamphlet was sent to the heads of boy's schools, clergymen, and members of parliament. Shortly thereafter, all three works by Sagitta were confiscated by the police, and the publisher of *Gehör!,* Bernhard Zack, was arrested for publishing immoral literature. "To Mackay...this failure to recognize his work as pure art and therefore untouchable was the greatest shock of his life," Riley argues. Zack refused to name the author of Sagitta's works, and was fined 600 marks. All of the books were destroyed.

In 1909, Mackay published underground another work by Sagitta, *Am Rande des Lebens.* And in 1913, Mackay published in Paris *Die Bücher der namenlosen Liebe,* which included all of Sagitta's previous writings, in addition to the novel *Fenny Skaller,* the play *über die Stufen von Marmor,* and an introduction on the history of his fight for the nameless love. *Fenny Skaller* is recognized by most critics as largely autobiographical, a depiction of Mackay's early struggle to accept his love for adolescent boys and his many relationships with young boy prostitutes in Berlin. Edward Mornin, in his essay for *Seminar,* argues that the hero of the novel "find[s] in anarchistic individualism the justification for feelings and behavior which seem natural to [him], yet are condemned by custom and the law."

Critics have also detected autobiographical elements in another novel, this one published under his own name: *Der Freiheitsucher,* a depiction of Mackay's early developing anarchistic views. In fact, according to Riley, the novel and *Fenny Skaller* "complement" each other: "The one describes his public life during [his early] years, the other his private life...Those who lead double lives must write double autobiographies." And most Mackay scholars agree that he led a double life, one which caused him a great deal of loneliness. He felt isolated from his society, which judged him as a deviant criminal, although he determined, as his Sagitta writings reveal, to be true to his nature, not letting society's condemnation of men like him turn into self-condemnation.

By 1932, Mackay's identity as Sagitta was an open secret, although modern scholars did not discover the fact until Riley's study was published in 1972. Mackay included a clause in his will that asked that all of the Sagitta writings be published under his own name after his death, although they were not republished until 1979. When he died in 1933, the Nazis had just come into power. During their regime, all action for the emancipation of homosexuals in Germany came to an end, and all of Sagitta's writings were banned. Mackay seems to have anticipated such an outcome when he wrote in 1913 in his introduction to *Die Bücher der namenlosen Liebe* of the repression of his own time and his hope for a freer future:

> I speak no longer to my time, the time in which I have been condemned to live, a time that does not hear me and does not want to hear me because it wants to hear nothing of this love. I speak to that time that is coming after me, a future that will allow itself to be closed off from no question that life poses—to a freer, and hence better and more just time (translated by Hubert Kennedy).

—Anne Boyd

MADDY, Yulisa Amadu (Pat)

Nationality: Sierra Leonean playwright, novelist, and actor. **Born:** Freetown, Sierra Leone, 27 December 1936; emigrated to England in 1960. **Education:** Studied drama and literature in France and England. **Career:** Worked for the Sierra Leone Railways; interviewer/actor, BBC African Service, 1960s; choreographer and trainer, Zambian National Dance Troupe for Expo 70, Zambia, 1970, and Sierra Leonean National Dance Troupe for Festac '77, Lagos, Nigeria, 1977; founder and director, Gbakanda Afrikan Tiata International, Inc., from the late 1970s; visiting professor, University of Iowa, 1992-94; senior lecturer in Performing Arts, University of Ibadan, Nigeria. **Awards:** Arts Fellowship, University of Ibadan; Fringe First Award, Edinburgh, 1979; Fulbright Scholar, University of Maryland, Baltimore County, and Morgan State University, 1985-86; Chevalier de L'Order Republic of Toto Artistic-Cultural Award, 1989; honorary fellow in writing, University of Iowa International Writers program, 1992.

WRITINGS

Novels

No Past, No Present, No Future (novel). London, Heinemann, 1973.
Beasts, Bastards, and Burdens (unpublished).

Plays

Obasai and Other Plays. London, Heinemann, 1971.
Big Berrin (produced 1976).
Big Breeze Blow (produced at University of Ibadan, Nigeria, 1980).
The Amistad Revolt (produced University of Iowa, 1993).

Other

African Images in Juvenile Literature: Commentaries on Neo-Colonialist Fiction. McFarland Publishers, 1996.

*

Critical Sources: "Empathy with the Deprived" by Chris Dunton, in *West Africa,* 30 May 1988, 968-969, 974.

Yulisa Amadu Maddy comments:

Human rights, civil rights, equality, mutuality, justice; these are the necessities of human society and the basis on which homosexuality is included in *No Past, No Present, No Future* and in the play *Big Berrin.* Literature is no less an expression of justice than is law, and both are accountable for their truth-telling and respect-for-life elements. The novel is primarily a rite-of-passage story and traces the sexual as well as intellectual development of three young Africans in the postcolonial era. One of the themes centers on the persistent neocolonialist mentality that influences African nonprogressive underdevelopment and the lives of the people, both young and old. Justice, in this story, is clearly indivisible. It is the umbilical cord that potentially unifies nations, cultures, gender, language groups, people of diverse sexual orientation—in short, the human family in all its great complexity.

*   *   *

The thread of sexuality is deeply interwoven in all types of literary expression, mirroring a wide range of cultural attitudes on subjects from premarital sex to abortion. Forms of sexual expression which are deemed unacceptable are either totally absent or appear as elements in morality tales, serving to reinforce the established social order. Literature as a voice for social criticism more often draws upon voices and images outside the mainstream, utilizing its unique powers to focus the attention of the reader. This is particularly true in the works created as a protest against the experience and legacy of colonialism, some of whose most singularly powerful examples have come from the writers of West Af-

rica. Among them, the works of Yulisa Amadu Maddy of Sierra Leone have been controversial and influential.

In his writing, Maddy has distinguished himself as being willing to use the medium of theater as the venue for posing sharp political and social questions regarding class and postcolonial African life. Maddy has treated homosexuality intermittently in his artistic career, ranging from his novel, *No Past, No Present, No Future* to the 1976 play *Big Berrin,* for which he was briefly jailed. The novel tells the tale of three friends whose common dream is to leave their home for what they imagine will be lives of prosperity in Europe. Maddy creates the most completely human homosexual character yet to appear in modern African fiction in Joe Bengoh. While much of the novel is concerned with the injustices born of race and class status, Joe's homosexuality is introduced quietly, beginning with references to a relationship with a mission priest, proceeding through an affair with a visiting Frenchman, and emerging as a frankly discussed plot theme only after all three men have successfully reached Europe.

Maddy's treatment of the subject (written at a time when the then-new gay liberation movement had made possible increasingly naturalistic depictions of being gay in all forms of performance art) is simple, unapologetic, and direct, with Joe refusing to grant any moral superiority to an uncomprehending and hostile world, whether African or European. From the very beginning, his homosexuality is in the context of coming-of-age conventions and an evolving maturity; ultimately, Joe makes the others uncomfortable as they dissipate (and eventually destroy) themselves through hatred, liquor, and sex. In contrast, Joe Bengoh, by the end of the novel, has attained a balanced integration of his sexuality with the real "other" world, and is the only one of the three to achieve a coherent future. Such a balanced portrayal of the growth of recognition of a gay identity in an African setting is virtually unique. The rarity of homosexual behavior in the public discourse of West Africa is clearly expressed in *Big Berrin,* where the matriarch of the family, upon hearing someone so described, inquires "Homosexuality? Wheyting be dat?" By introducing the subject to a mass audience (albeit at the remove of English), Maddy ranks as one of the pioneers in any African dialogue on the human face of being gay.

—Robert B. Marks Ridinger

MALOUF, David (George Joseph)

Nationality: Australian novelist, poet, librettist, and opera critic. **Born:** Brisbane, Queensland, 20 March 1934. **Education:** Brisbane Grammar School, 1947-50; University of Queensland, Brisbane, B.A. in English 1954 (honors). **Career:** Lecturer in English, University of Queensland, Brisbane, 1955-57; schoolmaster, St. Anselm's College, Birkenhead, Cheshire, England, 1962-68; lecturer, University of Sydney, Australia, 1968-77; full time writer, from 1977, maintaining residences in Australia and Southern Tuscany, Italy. **Awards:** Australian Literature Society Gold Medal, 1974, 1983; Grace Leven Prize, 1975; James Cook Award, 1975; New South Wales Premier's Prize, for fiction, 1979; Melbourne Age Book of the Year award, 1982; Victorian Premier's Award, 1982; New South Wales Premier's Award, for drama, 1987; Miles Franklin prize, 1991; Prix Femina Etranger (France), 1991; Adelaide Festival prize, 1991; Booker Prize nominee, 1993; Los Angeles Times Fiction award, 1994; IMPAC literature prize (Dublin),

1996. **Addresses:** (Agent) Rogers, Coleridge and White, 20 Powis Mews, London, W11 1JN, England; 53 Myrtle St., Chippendale, N.S.W. 2008, Australia.

WRITINGS

Novels

Johnno. St. Lucia, Queensland, University of Queensland Press, 1975.
An Imaginary Life: A Novel. London, Chatto & Windus, 1978.
The Child's Play: The Bread of Time to Come. New York, George Braziller, 1981.
The Child's Play: with Eustace and the Prowler. London, Chatto & Windus, 1982.
Fly Away Peter. London, Chatto & Windus, 1982.
Harland's Half Acre. London, Chatto & Windus, 1984.
The Great World. London, Chatto & Windus, 1990.
Remembering Babylon. London, Chatto & Windus, 1993.
Conversations at Curlow Creek. London, Chatto & Windus, 1996.

Short Stories

Antipodes: Stories. London, Chatto & Windus, 1985.
"The Only Speaker of His Tongue," in *The Oxford Book of Australian Short Stories.* Melbourne and New York, Oxford University Press, 1994.

Poetry

Bicycle and Other Poems. St. Lucia, Queensland, University of Queensland Press, 1970.
Neighbors in a Thicket: Poems. St. Lucia, Queensland, University of Queensland Press, 1974.
Poems, 1975-1976 (limited edition). Sydney, Prism, 1976.
The Year of the Foxes and Other Poems. New York, George Braziller, 1979.
First Things Last: Poems. St. Lucia, Queensland, University of Queensland Press, 1980.
Wild Lemons: Poems. London, Angus & Robertson, 1980.
Selected Poems. Sydney, Angues & Robertson, 1981.
Poems 1959-1989. St. Lucia, Queensland, University of Queensland Press, 1992.
Selected Poems, 1959-1989. London, Chatto & Windus, 1994.

Selected Literary Criticism

"How Does a Poem Mean," in *Teaching in English,* Vol. 20, 1971, 16-22.
"The Dramatist as Critic: John Ford and *The Broken Heart,*" in *Southern Review* (Adelaide), Vol. 5, 1972, 197-206.
"Where in the World Was Kenneth Slessor? A Personal View of the Slessor Tribute at the Adelaide Writer's Week, 1974," in *Southerly* (Sydney), Vol. 34, 1974, 202-206.
"E. M. Forster—A Worthwhile Guide to Life," in *Sydney Morning Herald,* 22 May 1976, 15.
"Other Edens and Lost Horizons," in *Nation Review* (Cremorne Junction), 14-20 May 1976, 764.
"Two Views of the Poetry of John Blight: II," in *Southerly* (Sydney), Vol. 36, 1976, 56-70.

"Christopher and His Kind," in *Quadrant* (Sydney), Vol. 21, No. 6, June 1977, 70-72.
"A Passage From London" and "Passage to America," in *Nation Review* (Cremorne Junction), 26 May/1 June 1977, 16, 20.
"The English Auden," in *Quadrant* (Sydney), Vol. 22, No. 6, 38-40.
"John Manifold: Life and Work," in *Overland* (Melbourne), No. 73, 1978, 47-54.
With R. F. Brissenden and Katherine Brisbane, *New Currents in Australian Literature.* London, Angus & Robertson, 1978.
"A.D. Hope's 'New Cratylus'," in *Meanjin* (Parkville, Victoria), Vol. 39, 1980, 150-162.
"Some Volumes of Selected Poems of the 1970s", in *Australian Literary Studies* (St. Lucia, Queensland), Part 1, Vol. 10, No. 1, 1981, 13-21; Part 2, Vol. 10, No. 3, 1982, 300-310.

Other

Co-editor, *We Took Their Orders and Are Dead: An Anti-War Anthology.* Ure Smith, 1971.
Editor, *Gesture of a Hand* (anthology). New South Wales, Holt, 1975.
12 Edmondstone Street (autobiography). London, Chatto & Windus, 1985.
Blood Relations (drama). Sydney, Currency Press, 1988.
With Michael Berkeley, *Baa Baa Black Sheep: An Opera in Three Acts* (libretto). London, Chatto & Windus, 1993.

Recordings: *An Evening of Australian Poetry: Vincent Buckley, David Malouf, and Les A. Murray Reading Their Poems,* Washington, D.C., Archive of Recorded Poetry and Literature, Library of Congress, 1980; libretto, with Richard Meale, *Voss,* Philips, 1987.

*

Interviews: "With Breath Just Condensing on It: An Interview with David Malouf" by Paul Kavanagh, in *Southerly* (Sydney), September 1986, 247-259; "An Interview with David Malouf" by Richard Tipping, in *Southerly* (Sydney), September 1989, 492-502; "A Conversation with David Malouf" by Ray Wilbanks, in *Antipodes* (Brooklyn, New York), Vol. 4, No. 1, spring 1990, 13-18; "Interview with Jim Davidson," in *Johnno, Short Stories, Poems, Essays and Interview* edited by James Tulip, St. Lucia, Queensland University Press, 1990; "People Get Second Chances" by Barbara Williams, in *Australian and New Zealand Studies in Canada* (London, Ontario), spring 1991, 81-94; "Interview with David Malouf" by Julie Copeland, in *Australian Literary Studies* (St. Lucia, Queensland), Vol. 10, No. 4, October 1992, 429-436; "A Conversation with David Malouf" by Michael Ondaatje, in *Brick* (London, Ontario), winter 1993, 50-58.

Critical Sources: "David Malouf's Fiction" by Peter Pierce, in *Meanjin* (Parkville, Victoria), Vol. 41, No. 4, 1982; "Crooked Versions of Art: The Novels of David Malouf" by C. Craven, in *Scripsi* (Parkville, Victoria), Vol. 3, No. 1, 1985, 99-126; "At the Edge: Geography and the Imagination in the Work of David Malouf" by M. Leer, in *Australian Literary Studies* (St. Lucia, Queensland), Vol. 12, No. 1, 1985, 3-21; "Secret Companions: The Continuity of David Malouf's Fiction" by M. Dever, in *World Literature Written in English* (Arlington), Vol. 26, No. 1, 1986, 62-75; "Homosocial Desire and Homosexual Panic in the Fiction of David

Malouf and Frank Moorhouse" by Stephen Kirby, in *Meanjin* (Parkville, Victoria), Vol. 46, No. 3, 1987, 385-393; "Beyond Language: David Malouf's *An Imaginary Life*" by A. McDonald, in *Ariel* (Calgary), Vol. 19, No. 1, 1988, 45-54; "Body Talk: The Prose of David Malouf" by M. Mansfield, in *Southerly* (Sydney), Vol. 49, Nol. 2, 1989, 230-238; *Imagined Lives: A Study of David Malouf* by P. Nielsen, St. Lucia, University of Queensland Press, 1990.

*   *   *

David Malouf began his literary career as a poet, but established himself as a novelist with the publication of *Johnno* in 1975. Born of Lebanese and English parents in Brisbane, Australia, he has spent significant periods of time abroad in England and Italy. The relationship between the cultures of Australia and Europe is a subject that Malouf explores in a great deal of his poetry, and especially in his novels. This questioning of cultural identity is often accompanied by a corresponding interest in the role that language plays as a mediator of experience. Furthermore, Malouf often recreates historical events in order to draw attention to the ways in which the past and present are interrelated, such as when the poet Ovid tells of his exile from Rome to the wilderness town of Tomis in *An Imaginary Life.*

Malouf's work has been well received and awarded by literary critics around the world. His concern with the themes of personal and cultural identity, language, and nature have been examined in great detail by many literary scholars as he has become a well-known writer of post-colonial fiction. However, the presentation of homosexuality in Malouf's work has received comparatively little attention in literary circles and the press. Stephen Kirby's "Homosocial Desire and Homosexual Panic in the Fiction of David Malouf and Frank Moorhouse" is one of the few essays to analyze the homosexual representations found in Malouf's work. Kirby addresses the lack of critical material on Malouf's interest in homosexuality in the following segment:

> The critics' refusal to discuss the possibility that [the friendship between Johnno and Dante in *Johnno*] might have a sexual dimension obviously reflects a general reluctance to deal with homosexual overtones in fiction.... However, in the case of *Johnno,* this reluctance is partly a result of the ambiguities of the text itself. Peter Pierce pointed out that the text offers the first examples of a theme that is later to dominate Malouf's work, "the sense of incompleteness in the lives of some men who seek intense and dependent relationships with other men."

Homosexuality is not very often a subject that Malouf directly approaches in his fiction; he prefers rather to imbed the possibility of a homosexual relationship into the text, and to hint at its nature.

Malouf's novels consistently involve intense and close relationships between two males, such as Dante and Johnno in *Johnno,* Ovid and the Wild Boy in *An Imaginary Life,* and Gemmy and Lachlan in *Remembering Babylon.* The presentation of these relationships is not overtly sexual, and they often remain unresolved, as in the deaths of Johnno, Ovid, and Gemmy. Asked directly in an interview with Jim Davidson about the possibility of homosexual relationships in *Johnno* and *An Imaginary Life,* Malouf responded:

> For myself the interest of there being other male figures is really that they're all one character. That's the essential part of it. It's obviously a way of externalizing a dialogue or a series of revelations; the things Dante is trying to see about Johnno and the messages he gets back are really all things about the possibilities of himself.

Such an explanation is indicative of the sublimated and abstract approach that Malouf takes to issues of homosexuality in his fiction. Kirby brings light to the complex nature of the homosexual relationships in Malouf's work, and to the fact they are often intertwined with the themes of rebellion and alienation, as well as the concept of "the other." He asserts that the homosexual components of the male relationships in *Johnno* and *An Imaginary Life* serve as acts of rebellion by characters who are outcasts of society.

Malouf's technique is often to guide the reader into making an assessment about the homosexual dimension of his characters, while rarely depicting scenes that would decide the matter. An example of this can be found in *Johnno* when Johnno has left for Africa, leaving his friend Dante behind in Australia. Dante explains how he spends his free time with Johnno gone:

> At weekends I took my bike to the Coast. Nothing extraordinary ever deigned to reveal itself to me. Several times I thought I was in love—once, not so briefly, with a boy from Sarina and we spent a good deal of our time riding suicidally into the darkness off country roads, seeking some sort of romantic dissolution, and skidded often enough for me to be left with half a dozen minor burns.

And just before his death, which is believed to be suicide, Johnno sends a letter to Dante:

> Please please come...Why don't you ever listen to what I say to you? I've spent years writing letters to you and you never answer, even when you write back. I've loved you—and you've never given a fuck for me, except as a character in one of your funny stories. Now for Christ's sake write to me! Answer me you bastard! And please come.

The relationship between Johnno and Dante is one full of tension and possibility, but it is not culminated. The short story "Southern Skies" from *Antipodes* presents a more explicit homosexual encounter. In this story Malouf outlines the relationship between the adolescent narrator and a professor who is a friend of his parents. "Southern Skies" is a coming of age story in which the narrator is involved with his girlfriend, but finds himself one night alone with the Professor, star gazing from his roof:

> Slowly, from far out, I drew back, re-entered the present and was aware again of the close suburban dark—of its moving now in the shape of a hand. I must have known all along that it was there, working from the small of my back to my belly, up the inside of my thigh, but it was of no importance, I was too far off. Too many larger events were unfolding for me to break away and ask, as I might have, "What are you doing?" I must have come immediately...I would look back on that as the real

beginning of my existence, as the entry into a vocation, and nothing could diminish the gratitude I felt for it.

In his later novels Malouf concentrates his efforts more on exploring the themes of language, the natural world, and national/personal identity. However, the theme of homosexuality can be found in places, often deeply imbedded within these other themes, as in *Remembering Babylon*. The central character, Gemmy, was thrown overboard as a boy near the Australian coast, is rescued by a tribe of Aborigines, and re-enters Western society as a man. In a key moment in the novel, Gemmy remembers his earlier life in England, and in particular his relationship with an older boy named Willet:

> Willet provides the only bit of closeness he has ever been offered, and since he has nothing else to love, he loves him with a fierce intensity, a fear too, which is the greatest he knows, that he may get lost, or that Willet one day may abandon him, taking with him the whole world as he conceives it: Ketch, the ferrets, the streets Willett is king of, the razor, the sweet garden smell of his hands, his curses, his kisses...his name, Gemmy, his claim to existence as a boy, as Willet's Boy.

This relationship is one that remains a source of mystery and pain to Gemmy; and in fact, before leaving England as a stowaway, Gemmy burns down the house they live in, with Willet in it. Malouf's fiction consistently presents intimate relationships between men, relationships that are often fraught with tension and ambiguity. His characters are often found on the margins of society, so that the novel can explore the themes of cultural and personal identity. Although the theme of homosexuality is rarely addressed as directly as in "Southern Skies", it is present as an undercurrent in his work, and serves to highlight his other prevailing themes.

—Ed Summers

MANNING, Rosemary Joy

Pseudonyms: Has also written as Mary Voyle and Sarah Davys. **Nationality:** British novelist and children's writer. **Born:** Weymouth, Dorset, 9 December 1911. **Education:** Poltimore College, Devon, 1924-30; Royal Holloway College, University of London, B.A. Honours in Classics 1931. Worked as shop assistant and secretary, 1933-37; school teacher, Sussex, 1938-42, and St. George's, Ascot, 1942-43; joint headmistress of school in Hertfordshire, 1943-50, and St. Christopher's School, Hampstead, 1950-72. **Died:** Tunbridge Wells, Kent, of cancer of the pancreas, 15 April 1988.

WRITINGS

Novels

Look Stranger. London, Jonathan Cape, 1960.

The Chinese Garden. London, Jonathan Cape, 1962; with introduction by Alison Hennegan, London, Brilliance Books, 1984.
Man on a Tower. London, Jonathan Cape, 1965.
Open the Door. London, Jonathan Cape, 1983.

Novels (as Mary Voyle)

Remaining a Stranger. London, William Heinemann, 1953.
A Change of Direction. London, William Heinemann, 1955.

Uncollected Short Stories

"The Fox," in *Horizon* (London), December 1948.
"Alone in the House," in *Transatlantic Review* (London and New York), summer 1962.
"At the House of a Friend," in *Cosmopolitan* (New York), March 1964.
"The Garland of Friendship," in *Homes and Gardens* (London), October 1966.

Autobiographies

A Time and a Time (as Sarah Davys). London, Calder and Boyars, 1971; reissued under Rosemary Manning's own name, with an introduction by the author, London, Marion Boyars, 1981.
A Corridor of Mirrors. London, The Women's Press, 1987.

Children's Fiction

Green Smoke. London, Constable, 1957.
Dragon in Danger. London, Constable, 1959.
The Dragon's Quest. London, Constable, 1961.
Arripay. London, Constable Young Books, 1963.
Boney was a Warrior. London, Hamish Hamilton Antelope Books, 1966.
The Rocking Horse. London, Hamish Hamilton Gazelle Books, 1970.
Dragon in the Harbour. London, Kestrel Books, 1980.

Children's Nonfiction

Heraldry. London, A&C Black, 1966.
Rosemary Manning's Book of Railways and Railwaymen. London, Kestrel Books, 1977.

Other

From Holst to Britten. A Study of Modern Choral Music. London, Workers' Music Association, 1949.
A Grain of Sand, Poems by William Blake Chosen and Introduced for Young Readers by Rosemary Manning. London, Bodley Head, 1967.
"Theodore the Great Neglected" (on T.F. Powys), in *Dorset,* Sherborne, Dorset, 20 July-25 August 1975.
"On being a late starter," in *In Other Words: Writing as a Feminist,* edited by Gail Chester and Sigrid Nielsen. London, Hutchinson, 1987.

*

Interviews: "Gay Life," London Weekend Television, May 1981;

by Beatrix Campbell, in *City Limits,* 16-22 April 1982; "Mavis on 4" by Mavis Nicholson, Channel 4, 1987.

Bibliography: Entry in *The Lesbian in Literature* by Barbara Grier, Talahassee Florida, Naiad Press, 1981, 102.

Critical Sources: *"The Chinese Garden*: A Cautionary Tale" by Gabrielle Griffin, in *What Lesbians Do In Books,* edited by Elaine Hobby and Chris White, London, Women's Press, 1991, 134-54.

*   *   *

Rosemary Manning decided to be a writer when she was 11 years-old and vowed that she would be famous by the time she was 30. She first achieved publication at the age of 38 with a short story called "The Fox," in the last issue of *Horizon* magazine. Encouraged by the novelist and editor David Garnett she began to write novels, publishing two under the pseudonym Mary Voyle in the 1950s. There was no need for her to conceal her identity but, as the Headmistress of a girls' private school—a career which she often claimed to dislike, despite her success and popularity as a teacher—she preferred to keep her writing separate from her public role.

In 1957 Manning published the first of her four children's books about "R Dragon," *Greensmoke.* She often described "R Dragon" as her alter ego. It was as a writer for children that Manning was best known until she acquired a new, and specifically lesbian, audience in the 1980s.

During the 1960s Manning published three novels: *Look Stranger, The Chinese Garden,* and *Man on a Tower,* all of which were well reviewed. She was particularly praised for her elegant style which was likened, by Penelope Mortimer in the *Sunday Times,* to that of Rose Macaulay, and it was this quality in her own writing that Manning valued most. She was widely and deeply read in the canon of English literature and she especially loved the writers of the seventeenth century. All her novels deal with people who feel at odds with society and are often persecuted for their difference, but it is only in *The Chinese Garden* that she explicitly examines this theme in relation to lesbianism. In it she explores the roots of her ambivalence about her own sexuality, and, as she claimed in her 1987 autobiography, *A Corridor of Mirrors,* "it was autobiographical, the most truthful book I have ever written about myself." The novel is set in Bampfield College, a girls' school in the west of England modelled on Poltimore College where Manning herself was educated. All the main characters are closely based on real people and Rachel, the main character, is Rosemary Manning herself. Rachel is an aspiring writer with only two friends, Bisto and Margaret. Margaret is an intelligent rebel against the regime of the school which is designed to turn the girls into English gentlemen by inflicting on them appalling living conditions and a morality based on an Old Testament God who is "just and terrible." It is Rachel's experience of the betrayal of that justice which is the major theme of the novel.

The headmistress, known as Chief, has cropped hair, wears suits and ties, and is sexually involved with various members of her staff, including Miss Burnett, the classics teacher who wears breeches and whom Rachel describes as "irremediably corrupt." It is not her sexuality which makes her corrupt but her world-weary contempt for life and she, like all the other adults, fails Rachel. Despite the lesbian ethos of the school, when Margaret is discovered to be having a sexual relationship with another girl,

Rena, they are both expelled and Rachel is implicated. The rigor with which Margaret and Rena are pursued is partly attributable to the fact that the action occurs in the year of the publication of *The Well of Loneliness.* Rachel finally convinces Chief that she was not involved but, "To myself I was not innocent. I was corrupted with knowledge." Rachel, who has always both despised and been fascinated by Bampfield, feels betrayed by Chief and especially by her housemistress Georgie Murrill, who fails utterly to support or protect her. Manning's own sense of betrayal was heightened by the fact that she was sexually involved with the original of Georgie Murrill—an aspect of the story which is omitted from the novel. In later life she attributed what she saw as her unsatisfactory sexual development to her relationship with her housemistress.

Landscape plays a crucial part in the novel on both a literal and a symbolic level. Much of the novel's eroticism is conveyed through the description of the gardens and parkland surrounding the school. "My attitude to Bampfield was very much that of a lover. I felt possessive and was possessed." The decay of the grounds parallels the moral decay of the school, and the Chinese Garden represents a charmed respite from the harsh life of school. "She entered an exotic world where she breathed pure poetry." The garden too is decaying and after the discovery about Margaret and Rena, Chief had it destroyed. Even before its physical destruction, however, the betrayal of Rachel by Georgie and Chief deprived her of all that the garden represented—"Nothing I read, nothing I witnessed, nothing I experienced, would ever again have for me the radiance, the purity, the perfection which the Chinese garden had symbolized for me. The whole regime was based on a falsehood, in which I was ineluctably involved."

The Chinese Garden was republished in 1984 by a gay publishing house and found a substantial new lesbian and feminist readership. In 1981 the author had 'come out' at the age of 70 on a London Weekend television program, "Gay Life," and in the same year her first autobiography *A Time and a Time* was published under her own name. This led to interviews and personal appearances. Manning very much enjoyed the public recognition and felt a responsibility to explain to a new generation of lesbians what life had been like in the first half of this century when her own attempts to understand her sexuality had been hampered by ignorance and a horror of being abnormal.

A Time and a Time was originally published under the pseudonym Sarah Davys because her business partner feared it would destroy the school they ran together if the identity of the author was known. In the 1960s her fears might well have been justified, since the book deals with Manning's attempted suicide and subsequent recovery, and is quite explicit about the causes of the suicide attempt—the end of her affair with the woman she calls Elizabeth and her great unhappiness at her inability to live what she considered a rewarding life in which her sexuality and her creativity could both take their rightful places. Once Manning had realized, "with almost mystical clarity that I required happiness and that it was my birthright...it was not altogether a matter of searching for an ideal person, but for certain essential qualities." Elizabeth provided these and when the relationship ended Manning saw no point in continuing. Surviving, she tried to find a way to live and the later section of the book celebrates her relationship with "Helen," who was a friend but refused to become a lover. In a book of relationships this is the most enduring.

In *Open the Door,* published in 1982, Manning introduces her only fully developed lesbian character, Gwyneth Morris. In the novel the members of an archaeological team are forced to face their various experiences of loss. The end of Gwyneth's relationship with her lover of five years, Deborah, provides one strand. Travelling back to the dig on a train, she contemplates suicide but is distracted by one of her fellow passengers and dismisses the idea, deciding instead that "I'll give myself a chance to...what? To learn a new code to live by, I suppose, having chosen so deliberately to live." In this she echoes Manning's own decision after her suicide attempt, but Manning writes in *A Corridor of Mirrors* that this was the least autobiographical of her novels and that in it, "pain became for me 'profitable loss.'"

Manning's second autobiography, *A Corridor of Mirrors*, explores aspects of her life not considered in *A Time and a Time*. In this book she writes for the first time without the need for concealment. In it she reflects on her life and highlights what has been most important to her. Writing she says, "is my lifeline," but she also believes that "I have done irreparable damage to myself as a writer by closing my heart. The artist must suffer, has almost a duty to suffer." Relationships have never been easy and "I am sometimes forced to recognize that I have loved certain places more than I have loved people." Nonetheless, the book discusses Manning's many friendships and celebrates a long and happy relationship with her lover January. It ends looking forward to a relationship with the author of this essay which was cut short by Manning's death.

Rosemary Manning always claimed, in *A Corridor of Mirrors* and elsewhere, that she did not write *as* a lesbian and that the habit of secrecy that she cultivated for much of her life did not affect her writing. She was convinced that the freedom to write openly about gay sexuality would not produce better writing. What this argument fails to acknowledge, however, is that she always wrote out of her own pain and frequent loneliness, and that much of that pain and loneliness was a direct consequence of her lesbian identity.

—Lis Whitelaw

MARCUS, Eric

Nationality: American journalist and author. **Born:** New York City, 12 November 1958. **Education:** Public School 99 in Kew Gardens, New York, 1963-70; Russell Sage Junior High School, Forest Hills, New York, 1970-73; Hillcrest High School, Jamaica, New York, 1973-76; Vassar College, Poughkeepsie, New York, B.A. in Urban Studies, 1980; Columbia University Graduate School of Journalism, New York, New York, M.A. in Journalism 1984. **Family:** Companion of Barney M. Karpfinger; commitment ceremony, 8 June 1996. **Career:** Assistant urban planner, Abeles, Schwartz, Haekel, and Silverblatt, New York, 1980-81; architectural assistant, Johnson-Burgee Architects, New York, 1981-82; managing editor, various divisions, Ziff-Davis Publishing Company, New York, 1983-85; associate producer, Good Morning America, American Broadcasting Corporation (ABC), New York, 1987; segment producer, *CBS This Morning*, CBS News, New York, 1988; self-employed writer, from 1988. **Awards:** Gay and Lesbian Task Force Book Award, Gay and Lesbian Task Force of the Social Responsibilities Round Table of the American Librarian Association, for nonfiction, 1993. **Agent:** Joy Harris, Lantz/Harris Literary Agency, 156 Fifth Avenue, New York, New York 10010, U.S.A.

WRITINGS

Nonfiction

Expect the Worst (You Won't be Disappointed). San Francisco, HarperSanFrancisco, 1992.
Is It a Choice? Answers to 300 of the Most Frequently Asked Questions About Gays and Lesbians. San Francisco, HarperSanFrancisco, 1993.
Making History: The Struggle for Gay & Lesbian Equal Rights, 1945 to 1990, An Oral History. New York, HarperCollins, 1992.
The Male Couple's Guide to Living Together: What Gay Men Should Know About Living Together and Coping in a Straight World. New York, Harper and Row, 1988; revised as *The Male Couple's Guide: Finding a Man, Making a Home, Building a Life*, New York, HarperCollins, 1992.
Why Suicide? Answers to 200 of the Most Frequently Asked Questions About Suicide, Attempted Suicide, and Assisted Suicide. HarperSanFrancisco, 1996.

Autobiographies

With Greg Louganis, *Breaking the Surface*. New York, Random House, 1995.
With Rudy Galindo, *Ice Breaker*. New York, Pocket Books, 1997.

Essays

"Ignorance Is Not Bliss," in *Newsweek*, 5 July, 1993.
"They're Not Telling the Truth: An Author's Personal Response to the Attacks from Anti-gay Crusaders," in *Newsweek*, 14 September 1992.
"What a Riot," in *10 percent*, Vol. 2, No. 8, June 1994.
"What's in a Name?" in *10 Percent*, Vol. 1, No. 5, winter 1993.

Other

Contributor, *Out in America*, edited by *OUT* magazine editors. New York, Viking Studio, 1994.
Author of forward, *Family: A Portrait of Gay & Lesbian America* by Nancy Andrews. San Francisco, HarperSanFrancisco, 1994.
Editor, with Lynn Witt and Sherry Thomas, *Out in All Directions: The Almanac of Gay and Lesbian America*. New York, Warner Books, 1995.

*

Eric Marcus comments:

Three things have motivated me in much of my work: a desire to write the books that I wish I could have found at the library when I was growing up; the determination to do good in the world; and the need to pay my mortgage.

*   *   *

Letting the truth speak clearly for itself seems to be the central theme of all the works of Eric Marcus. Marcus has featured prominently in the publishing boom in the area of gay and lesbian literature that started in the late 1980s. His work offers readers materials that have been created or coordinated to help guide the public's understanding of what it is like to have come through an era of tumultuous change often against or in spite of resistance from the general population. Each of his writings attempts to draw a clearer picture for those participating in as well as those observing the movements of the homosexual person in this era.

Marcus has been able to bend his journalistic talents in ways that reach readers through various styles. Oral histories, compilations of possible answers to frequently asked questions, biographical efforts, and "how to" manuals have all become the vehicles that allow this author to help others understand what he and many other gays and lesbians must face on a day to day basis. This body of work has become a veritable reference collection and an oasis of advice that can help anyone who is interested in becoming familiar with the gay experience. With this in mind, it can be posited that Marcus has successfully taken the mystery out of the homosexual as the "other," and has provided avenues for both the homosexual and the non-homosexual to learn to be more comfortable in the discourse of their daily lives together.

With a carefully restrained journalistic tendency, Marcus sets about the task of informing both the homosexual and the non-homosexual populace about the many complex and difficult issues that face members of the homosexual communities. This effort is what comprises the bulk of the material contained in *Is It a Choice?* The book covers questions from "What is a homosexual?" to "Why do gay and lesbian people feel they need laws to protect them from discrimination?" and many topics in between. Topic areas include; AIDS, aging, relationships, religion, sex, the mass media, and the military, among others.

Marcus has also applied the "frequently asked questions" style of this book to a volume dealing with issues surrounding suicide. *Why Suicide?* is sure to be a useful book for people of all orientations who must face issues related to suicide, attempted suicide, and assisted suicide. With these two books Marcus has made an art out of finding answers to the many questions he has asked along the path of his own life and of sharing the answers to those questions for the benefit of all others.

Marcus' personal disposition is well reflected in his essays that have appeared in several national news magazines. Each of the essays address questions regarding the disposition of gay people inside as well as outside the context of the mainstream. In "What's in a Name?" Marcus lets his fellow gays know that he and they should all be careful to allow each individual to define his/her own persona or self-concept. By responding to the military's "don't ask, don't tell" policy forged by the senate at the beginning of President Clinton's term, Marcus informed readers of *Newsweek* magazine that staying in the closet is an unacceptably difficult task that could be put aside if all people would just try to understand the "other" and change their views. Finally, in an effort to debunk the inflammatory rhetoric that is touted by leaders and members of the religious and political right, Marcus again guided *Newsweek* readers with his article "They're Not Telling the Truth" to open up so that they may learn about the homosexual as the "other." With such "popular" and widespread exposure given to Marcus via these news magazine essays, his work and efforts will surely be recognized by a wider audience.

The representation of people, places, and events in the modern gay experience is a specialty for Marcus. This specialty is well demonstrated in his work, *Making History,* an often moving and poignant portrayal of important figures and pivotal events endured during the gay liberation era of the post-World War II decades.

Making History presents the personal stories of various people from all persuasions. The volume is arranged chronologically by decade and deftly highlights people's responses to the social realities concerning homosexuality in the course of the rapid changes of the post war era. Marcus' work brings together the leaders of the gay and lesbian organizations of the 1940s and 1950s. These people, as well as caring non-homosexual people such as Dr. Evelyn Hooker, did much to bring the issue of homosexuality into the public forum. Marcus then moves to circumscribe the decade of the 1960s as one of demands, action, and change on behalf of homosexual people and their rights. Subsequent sections of the book focus on the gay liberation movements of the late 1960s and early 1970s as well as the expansion of and backlash against the gay rights movement throughout the rest of that decade. The final section of *Making History* depicts the development of a cohesive gay and lesbian movement that responded to the devastating AIDS epidemic. Though the epidemic has caused much pain and discrimination to rise in the general population, the phenomenon also has brought issues related to gays and lesbians into the mainstream. The movement embraced this opportunity to help gays and lesbians advance through the epidemic, focusing on making a more solid, honest portrayal of their lives in mainstream America. In *Making History,* Marcus makes sure that those interested in learning the facts about gays and lesbian get all of the facts correct.

Marcus helped draw attention to the need for positive gay role models when he helped write the autobiography of Olympic gold medalist Greg Louganis. Perhaps more than any other of his works, *Breaking the Surface* brought Marcus' name before a wider general audience. With this work, Marcus can be credited with enabling yet one more person to live a full and successful out gay life. The book takes the reader through the life of an adopted child who survived a variety of challenging situations, including a positive HIV status, to come out a winner. Louganis is a good role model for those who admire his golden achievements. And Marcus, along with Greg Louganis, uses Louganis' life as an example of the possibilities for an ever growing plethora of closeted people.

Marcus's process of educating by example spawned many new projects, including his work in co-writing the autobiography of U.S. Figure Skating Champion Rudy Galindo, published in 1997 as *Ice Breaker.* Marcus penned an introduction to the photographic volume by Nancy Andrews entitled *Family: A Portrait of Gay & Lesbian America,* and he co-edited *Out in All Directions,* an almanac that tries to highlight virtually every corner of the homosexual experience. Marcus tries to address all aspects of the homosexual experience in his efforts whenever appropriate. In addition, issues concerning lesbians, bisexuals, and transgendered persons are given substantial treatment.

As an out gay man, success in everyday life is what Marcus would have for himself as well as all gay men. This can be evidenced in his *Male Couple's Guides.* Both the original 1988 edition and the updated and expanded 1992 edition offer thoughts, guidelines, and resources to gay males who choose to make a go of life together. Chapters address issues such as the dating scene, monogamy, living together, family and parenting issues, sex, legalization of relationships, health, and aging. Each section presents the personal experiences of the author as well as various examples drawn from other couples' relationships. Where appropriate, Marcus draws on research and expertise from professionals who work in fields related to the issues at hand. At the end of most of the chapters, Marcus tries to provide a list of resources, including readings, organizations, and professionals that may be of interest should the reader want to pursue the subjects covered in a more extensive and independent manner.

As evidenced by each of his works, Marcus indeed has provided easy access to a wealth of ideas that address the issues involved in the homosexual experience. As situations in life continue to challenge his knowledge and experience, he is sure to share what he learns with any who care to listen.

—Michael J. Miller

————

MARTIN, Violet Florence. *See* **ROSS, Martin.**

————

MASO, Carole

Nationality: American novelist and educator. **Born:** Wycoff, New Jersey, 9 March 1956. **Education:** Vassar College, Poughkeepsie, New York (General Honors, Departmental Honors, Honors for Creative Thesis), A.B. in English 1977. **Family:** Companion of Helen Lang. **Career:** Worked as legal assistant, waitress, artist's model, and fencing instructor; distinguished writer-in-residence, Illinois State University, 1991-92; Jenny McKean Moore writer-in-residence, George Washington University, 1992-93; fiction editor, *Kenyon Review,* 1993, 1994; faculty, Bennington Summer Writing Workshop, 1994, 1995; associate professor of writing, School of the Arts, Columbia University, 1993-94; visiting writer-in-residence, Brown University, 1994; director, Creative Writing Program, and associate professor of English, Brown University, from 1995. **Awards:** Cummington Community of the Arts fellowship, 1982, 1983, 1984, 1987; CAPS Grant for Fiction, 1983; Virginia Center for the Creative Arts fellowship, 1983; Edward Albee Foundation fellowship, 1985; W. K. Rose Fellowship in the Creative Arts, Vassar College, 1985; Provincetown Fine Arts Work Center fellowship, 1986-87, 1990-91; MacDowell Colony fellowship, 1987, 1988, 1989; New York Foundation for the Arts Grant, 1987; National Endowment for the Arts Emerging Artist Reading Grant, 1987; National Endowment for the Arts Literature Grant, 1988; Karolyi Foundation prize, 1988, 1989, 1991; Yaddo fellowship, 1992; Pushcart Prize, 1993; Lannan Literary Fellowship for Fiction, 1993. **Agent:** George Borchardt, 136 East 57 St. New York, New York 10022, U.S.A. **Address:** Creative Writing Program, Brown University, Providence, Rhode Island 02912, U.S.A.

WRITINGS

Novels

Ghost Dance. San Francisco, California, North Point Press, 1986.
The Art Lover. San Francisco, California, North Point Press, 1990.
AVA. Normal, Illinois, Dalkey Archive Press, 1993.
The American Woman in the Chinese Hat. Normal, Illinois, Dalkey Archive Press, 1994.

Aureole. Hopewell, New Jersey, Ecco Press, 1996.
Defiance. New York, Dutton, 1998.

Essays

"One Moment of True Freedom," in *Belles Lettres: A Review of Books by Women,* summer 1993.
"Notes of a Lyric Artist Working in Prose: A Lifelong Conversation with Myself, Entered Midway," in *American Poetry Review,* Vol. 24, No. 2, 1995.
"Frida Etude," in *Fruit,* Vol. 2, 1996.
"not a poem yet," in *Black Ice* (Boulder, Colorado), No. 13, 1996.
"Rupture, Verge and Precipice/Precipice, Verge and Hurt Not," in *Review of Contemporary Fiction,* Vol. 16, No. 1, spring 1996; reprinted in *Tolstoy's Dictaphone, Technology and the Muse,* edited by Sven Birkerts, Saint Paul, Minnesota, Graywolf Press, 1996.
"The Shelter of the Alphabet: Home," in *A Place Called Home,* edited by Mickey Pearlman. New York, St. Martin's Press, 1996.
"Surrender," in *Reclaiming the Heartland: Lesbian and Gay Voices from the Midwest,* edited by Karen Lee Osborne and William J. Spurlin. Minneapolis, Minnesota, University of Minnesota Press, 1996.

*

Interviews: "Carole Maso" by Mickey Pearlman, in *Inter/View: Talks With America's Writing Women* (Lexington, Kentucky), University Press of Kentucky, 1990, republished as *A Voice of One's Own: Conversations with America's Writing Women,* Boston, Houghton Mifflin, 1990; "Carole Maso: An Interview" by Nicole Cooley, in *American Poetry Review,* March-April 1995; "An Interview with Carole Maso" by Steven Moore, in *Review of Contemporary Fiction,* (Normal, Illinois), summer 1995; "Carole Maso," in *The Elms* (Providence, Rhode Island), December 1995; "Carole Maso" by Joyce Hackett, in *Poets & Writers Magazine,* May-June 1996.

Critical Sources: "Review of *Ghost Dance*" by Meredith Sue Willis, in *New York Times Book Review,* 20 July 1986; "Review of *Ghost Dance*" by Cyra McFadden, in *Los Angeles Times Book Review,* 27 July 1986; "Dance of Life" by E. M. Broner, in *Women's Review of Books,* September 1986; "Carole Maso" in *Contemporary Literary Criticism,* Vol. 44, Detroit, Michigan, Gale Research, 1987; review of *AVA* by Lisa Cohen, in *Village Voice Literary Supplement* (New York), May 1993; "Expanding the Boundaries of Fiction" by Patty O'Connell, in *Belles Lettres: A Review of Books by Women,* Summer 1993; review of *AVA* by Wendy Smith, in *New York Times Book Review,* 12 December 1993; review of *The American Woman in the Chinese Hat* by Tom Sleigh, in *New York Times Book Review,* 15 May 1994; "From the Erogenous Zone" by Susan Lasher, in *Parnassus,* Vol. 20, 1994; review of *The American Woman in the Chinese Hat* by Charlotte Innes, in *Lambda Book Report,* September-October 1994; "Women Writers and the Restive Text" by Barbara Page, in *Postmodern Culture,* January 1996.

Carole Maso comments:
I write with great pleasure and awe into the heart of mystery from an insistent feminity and a complex sexuality.

"Language is a woman, a rose, constantly in the process of opening," I once wrote. I still believe that. I believe in works of passion and recklessness and luminosity. I go too far. I want too much. I believe in a literature without limitation. "Language is a rose and the future is still a rose opening."

*   *   *

Although Carole Maso neither studied creative writing at Vassar College nor attended graduate school (she turned down a Helen Deutsch Fellowship at Boston University), she served a seven-year apprenticeship completing self-created writing exercises and assignments; the result was her first novel, *Ghost Dance*. This sensual novel about a family's disintegration through death begins with and then plays and replays the college-age narrator Vanessa's last meeting with her mother, a woman not quite in time. The novel's redemptive ending begins with the union of Vanessa and Sabine, her mother's lesbian lover of 25 years. According to Cyra McFadden in the *Los Angeles Times Book Review*, Vanessa is a "human seismograph, acutely tuned to sensory impressions" which Maso, while "taking enormous risks," fashions with dense, lyrical metaphors; images of snow and fire and indian mythology combine with references to Grace Kelly and Jacqueline Onassis, lethal asbestos, Wounded Knee, and transgressions by American military and businessmen.

This technique, magnified, also gave form to *The Art Lover*, her second novel; photographs of a farmhouse door and a wooden gate, lost pet posters, sign language cards, *New York Times* articles, reproduced details of Giotto's *Noli me tangere*, and Vermeer and Gary Falk paintings augment the story of Caroline, bravely trying to write her family's story, which we read as her world topples. Maso boldly interrupts this double narrative by exposing her own pain in a nonfictive section where she recounts the death from AIDS of good friend, painter Gary Falk, to whom the book is dedicated.

From this novel on, Maso's signature technique, as she described in "Notes of a Lyric Artist Working in Prose: A Lifelong Conversation with Myself, Entered Midway," is "an amalgam of painting, sculpture, theory, film, music, poetry, dance, mathematics—even fiction sometimes." And as she told Nicole Cooley in an interview for *The American Poetry Review*, she uses her life to write from; her third novel, *The American Woman in the Chinese Hat*, is quite autobiographical. She owns the hat featured in the title and she has spent time in France. In an interview with Steven Moore in *Journal of Contemporary Fiction*, she discussed her own state when writing the novel. "Nothing mattered. One day I realized that I could no longer believe in any arrangement of words. I put all my notebooks away." She was also experimenting with whether the events of her "real" life were enough.

In this short, narrative novel filled with French, food, and obsessive, explicit sex, a lesbian writer named Catherine recounts her own mental breakdown, sometimes through writing in her notebook. In flight from her lesbian lover, Lola, whom she has abused for years, Catherine moves from seducing a teenage girl from Arles and other strangers to her final lover, Lucien, a Frenchman, all of whom she uses for her writing and, thus, for her survival. But not even the positive, unconsummated relationship with Sylvia, an older lesbian who knew many of the literary greats, can save her. Calling Maso's novel "shrewd, subtle, unsettling," Tom Sleigh in the *New York Times Book Review* pointed to Maso's repetition and thoughtful exploration of narrative as Caroline moves between

"I" and "she" as she loses control over reality. In "An Essay," Maso noted her "aim...was to dramatize the breakdown of language, and with that carrying off of language, a belief system, a world.... We are forced to witness an entire history: a world is born, evolves, warps and finally breaks."

Lambda reviewer Charlotte Innes placed *The American Woman in The Chinese Hat* squarely in the "What is a lesbian novel" debate. She described the breakdown of Catherine's world as Maso's triumphal point that "the old, (heterosexual male) fictional themes and forms are played out, that lesbians must find their own methods of written communication." Innes noted that this theme of language for women carried into *AVA*. For Maso, the former novel's ending allowed her to understand narrative and, thus, break through into a daring, elegant lyrical style in *AVA*. Here, Maso takes full advantage of the spaciousness the novel form provides. This novel's now familiar pages of acknowledgements and credits include Lorca, Beckett, Virginia Woolf, Eva Hesse, Cixous, Anais Nin, Paul Celan, and Goethe and indicate some of the paths through which Maso filters her own experience to guide her writing.

In "One Moment of True Freedom," Maso described *AVA* as "a living text...it will never be stabilized or fixed." She told Nicole Cooley it is a novel "of bright celebration, of coming together, of all possibilities, of joy, *jouissance*." Inversely, *AVA* recounts literature professor Ava Klein's last day of life; she is dying of a rare blood disease. Yet, Patty O'Connell in her *Belles Lettres* review described the text as hopeful; the short entries and fragments or "abbreviated nuggets" create "an evolving mosaic of Ava's life." The aforementioned sources, to use Maso's words in *AVA*, "flood Ava's mind" and are from "the texts of the world" that Ava has read. In "From the Erogenous Zone," Susan Lasher, critical of the subplots and "banquet" of references, described the Imagist, unrelated sentences as "flotsam and jetsam of remembered words and images [which] float through her [Ava's] consciousness as she lies in bed waiting for death." In "An Essay," Maso wrote that she expected these fragments "to act contrapuntally and trigger through theme, rhythm and other mysterious methods, associations in the reader, as well as the writer." The technique allows the reader freedom to fill the spaces between the fragments, like insertions in electronic writing. Maso's continuing emphasis on language and the body inscribe her debt to linguist Roland Barthes and French feminist theorist and experimental novelist Helene Cixous, particularly Maso's "inability to keep the body out of my writing; it enters the language, transforms the page, imposes its own intelligence," as she noted in "One Moment of True Freedom."

Although Maso, whose first love is poetry, never writes short stories, *Aureole* is a collection of 13 interwoven short pieces whose characters are bound together by desire and by Maso's abandonment to the "trance of language." As she explains in the Preface, "I have tried to slip closer to a language that might function more bodily, more physically, more passionately...to feel the sexual intoxification of the line or page or narrative, to create an open space where pleasures and arousals spread in a lateral radiance, an aureole of desire." Related is a projected literary triptych, *The Bay of Angels*, of which *AVA* is a part. The three novels will resonate from one another. Maso, who often works simultaneously on several projects, interrupted this work to complete *Defiance*, a book about a woman mathematician sentenced to death for murdering two of her students. In preparation she reread Shakespeare's tragedies and all of Dante.

In "Rupture, Verge, and Precipice/Precipice, Verge, and Hurt Not," written in response to novelist David Foster Wallace's query about where she thought literary art was heading, Maso rejects the conservative "yous" who believe that the novel is dying and that hyper-text will kill print fiction. Never one for compromise, in her essay Maso condemns conservative, businessman publishers and wishes for an end to their imposed homogeniety of contemporary fiction. As her novels evidence, she wishes for:

> One wild world.
> Free of categories, free of denominations, dance and fiction and performance and installation and video and poetry and painting—one world—ever hyper—and cyber.

—Judith C. Kohl

McCAULEY, Stephen D(avid)

Nationality: American novelist. **Born:** Boston, Massachusetts, 26 June 1955. **Education:** University of Vermont, Burlington, B.A. in English 1978; Columbia University, M.F.A. 1985 (Phi Beta Kappa). **Career:** Held a variety of jobs, including hotel worker, ice cream vendor, house cleaner, and travel agent; kindergarten teacher, Cambridge, Massachusetts, 1980-81; book review editor and travel tips columnist, *Boston Phoenix,* 1982-86; visiting writer and creative writing teacher, University of Massachusetts, Boston, 1987-1989, Wellesley College, 1989-91, Harvard University, 1991, and Brandeis University, from 1992. Contributor of articles and reviews to periodicals, including *Bay Windows, Boston Magazine, Boston Phoenix, Details, Gay Community News, Harper's, HG, New York Times Book Review, Travel and Leisure,* and *Vogue.* **Awards:** Chevalier des Arts et des Lettres by French Ministry of Culture, 1996. **Agent:** Arlene Donovan, ICM, 40 W. 57th Street, New York, New York 10019, U.S.A. **Address:** Brandeis University, 415 South St., Waltham, Massachusetts 02254, U.S.A.

Writings

Novels

The Object of My Affection. New York, Simon & Schuster, 1987.
The Easy Way Out. New York, Simon & Schuster, 1992.
The Man of the House. New York, Simon & Schuster, 1996.

*

Interviews: Unpublished interviews with Stephen McCauley by Andrea L.T. Peterson, September and February 1996.

Critical Sources: "Stephen D. McCauley," in *Contemporary Literary Criticism,* Vol. 50, Detroit, Gale Research, 1988; "Stephen D. McCauley," in *Contemporary Authors,* Vol. 141, Detroit, Gale Research, 1994; "All in the Dysfunctional Family" by Kevin Allman, in *Washington Post Book World,* 18 February 1996, 6.

*   *   *

"The sometimes unbridgeable gap between parents and their adult children is a hallmark of McCauley's fiction," says reviewer and novelist Kevin Allman. But that borders on understatement. The sometimes unbridgeable gap between any two people seems to be the hallmark of McCauley's fiction—that, and the oftentimes desperately dysfunctionality of all of these relationships, not just those which are familial.

McCauley "became" a writer by taking a route similar to that of his most recent protagonist, Clyde Carmichael of *The Man of the House.* In fact, much the same way as *Man of the House's* Marcus struggles to get his dissertation done and that same book's other characters struggle to get lives—by taking the circuitous route.

McCauley attempted fiction writing, but dropped course after course that would teach him the art. It wasn't until he signed up for a class in writing nonfiction, despite his lack of interest in such writing, that he began to write convincing fiction. "I began writing stories that sounded as if they might have been true (even though they weren't)," he says. That helped him find his voice as a writer.

McCauley's successful attainment of that goal is what makes his fiction so rich, and so important to gay and lesbian literature. "I wanted to write novels," he told *GLL* contributor Andrea L. T. Peterson, "in which the homosexuality of some of the characters was established at the beginning and simply taken for granted. Although the sexuality of the gay characters obviously plays an important role in their lives, a central role, I didn't want the books to be about coming out or dealing with sexuality per se."

Unlike much gay and lesbian literature, homosexuality is not McCauley's focus, and his books are neither apologetics nor sexploits through gay America. McCauley tackles the particularly difficult relationships between adult children and their parents in which there are always challenges, regardless of sexuality. As McCauley attests, however, even in these relationships, the homosexuality of one party—in the case of Clyde, the son—does influence the relationship, but no nearly as much as typical family issues.

With a touch of humor, very tastefully situated, McCauley draws for readers endearing characters with whom it is easy to empathize and for whom it is easy to cheer. Clyde Carmichael is much more entangled in the relationships between friends—college buddy and writer Louise Morris, her adolescent son, Ben, and Ben's real father, Carmichael's roommate Marcus Gladstone—than in his own relationship with any of them. Likewise he is more entwined in the web ensnaring his sister Agnes and her teenage daughter than in his own relationships. As a result, his own relationships—with his ex, Gordon, and with his father, who lives in Agnes's basement and plays the siblings against one another—go unchecked.

The bulk of *The Man of the House,* the inspiration for which McCauley says was his relationship with his own father, nearly masks the fact that the central conflict of the book is between father and son, as well as between Ben and his conflicted father, Gladstone. "Dad and I had a fairly rancorous relationship," he confessed. "I spent a lot of time waiting for us to resolve our differences. It wasn't until shortly after he died that I realized our relationship had been resolved all along. I just hadn't been able to accept the resolution." This is essentially Clyde's relationship with his father. And, while McCauley actually has two brothers, and his fictional character has only one, the only significant difference between the factual and the fictional is that in the latter, the son comes to this realization before his father's death.

The fictional son is spared a considerable amount of grief, literally and figuratively, by not having to resolve the relationship posthumously. These are not gay issues, but universal issues. What McCauley sets out to do, and what he succeeds in doing is to weave "the question of sexuality" into "the whole picture of the characters' lives." In essence, he has made gay people real people in many ways just like everyone else, at least in terms of what makes them human and what makes and breaks their relationships.

McCauley's efforts to portray gay people as people first, gay second, is not peculiar to *The Man of the House.* In his first novel, *The Object of My Affection,* the complicated romantic relationship between a gay man and his straight, pregnant roommate was tackled; in his second, *The Easy Way Out,* he examined life's possibilities and looks at what people all too often simply settle for.

McCauley, like his gay characters, is a man who "just happens to be gay"; a gay man who just happens to be a writer. I think of myself mainly as a storyteller," he says. "I like bringing to life oddball characters and their muddled lives." And in so doing, he reveals to others the normalcy of their seemingly abnormal lives and relationships whether they are peopled with gay or straight characters, whether they are functional, totally dysfunctional, or somewhere in between.

—Andrea L.T. Peterson

MCKAY, Claude (Festus Claudius McKay)

Pseudonym: Also wrote as Eli Edwards. **Nationality:** American poet, novelist, short story writer, essayist, and non-fiction writer. **Born:** Sunny Ville, Jamaica, 15 September 1890 (some sources say 1889); immigrated to the United States in 1912; maintained British citizenship during travels in Russia, Europe, and Africa; naturalized U.S. citizen, 1940. **Education:** Village Schools; Tuskeegee Institute and Kansas State College, 1912-14. **Family:** Married Eulalie Imelda Edwards, 30 June 1914 (separated; no divorce); one child. **Career:** Held a variety of jobs including cabinetmaker's apprentice and wheelwright, constable at Jamaican Constabulary, waiter, porter, bartender, longshoreman, and restauranteur; contributor to periodicals, including *Catholic Worker, Ebony, Epistle, Interracial Review, Izvestia, Jewish Frontier, The Liberator, Nation, Negro World, New York Herald Tribune Books, Pearson's Magazine, Phylon, Seven Arts,* and *Worker's Dreadnought;* associate editor, *The Liberator;* artist's model and actor; shipyard worker; writer, for National Writing Project. **Awards:** Medal and stipend, Jamaican Institute of Arts and Sciences, 1912; Harmon Foundation Award, for *Harlem Shadows* and *Home to Harlem,* National Association of Colored People, 1929; James Weldon Johnson Literary Guild award, 1937. **Died:** Chicago, Illinois, of heart failure, 22 May 1948; buried at Calvary Cemetery, Woodside, New York.

WRITINGS

Poetry

Songs of Jamaica, introduction by Walter Jekyll. London, Gardner, 1912.
Constab Ballads. London, Watts, 1912.

Spring in New Hampshire. London, Richards, 1920.
Harlem Shadows: The Poems of Claude McKay, introduction by Max Eastman. New York, Harcourt, 1922.
Selected Poems, introduction by John Dewey, biographical note by Max Eastman. New York, Bookman, 1953.
The Dialectic Poetry of Claude McKay, edited by Wayne F. Cooper. New York, Books for Libraries Press, 1972.

Novels

Home to Harlem, foreword by Wayne F. Cooper. New York, Harper, 1928; included in *The Northeastern Library of Black Literature,* edited by Richard Yarborough, Boston, Northeastern University Press, 1987.
Banjo, a Story Without a Plot. New York, Harper, 1929.
Banana Bottom. New York, Harper, 1933.

Nonfiction

The Negroes in America. Russian language edition published c. 1922-23; edited by Alan L. McLeod, translated by Robert Winter. Port Washington, New York, and London, Kennikat Press, 1977.
Trial by Lynching: Stories About Negro Life in North America, translated into Russian by A. M. and P. Okhirmenko. Moscow, Ogonek Publishing House, 1925; edited by Alan L. McLeod, translated by Robert Winter, preface by Anniah Gowda, Centre for Commonwealth Literature and Research, University of Mysore, India, 1977.
Harlem: Negro Metropolis. New York, E. P. Dutton & Company, 1940.

Other

"Poems" by Claude McKay, in *The New Negro: Voices of the Harlem Renaissance* (anthology), edited by Alain Locke. New York, Albert and Charles Boni, 1925, 133-136.
Gingertown (short story). New York, Harper, 1932.
A Long Way From Home (autobiography). New York, Lee Furman, 1937.
The Passion of Claude McKay: Selected Poetry and Prose, edited by Wayne F. Cooper. New York, Schocken, 1972.

Recordings: *Anthology of Negro Poets,* Folkways Records, FL9791.

*

Adaptations: *Anthology of Negro Poets in the U. S. A.: 200 Years* (sound recording; read by Arna Bontemps), Folkways Records FL9792; *Spectrum in Black: Poems by 20th Century Black Poets,* Scott, Foresman, and Company, 4149.

Manuscript Collections: The James Weldon Johnson Collection, Beineke Library, Yale University; Papers and Manuscript Collection, Beineke Library, Yale University.

Biography: *Claude McKay: Rebel Sojourner in the Harlem Renaissance* by Wayne F. Cooper, Baton Rouge and London, Louisiana State University Press, 1987.

Critical Sources: *A Long Way From Home* by Claude McKay,

New York, Lee Furman, 1937; *The Negro Novel in America* by Robert A. Bone, New Haven and London, Yale University Press, 1968; "The West Indian Novel in North America" by Lloyd W. Brown, in *Journal of Commonwealth Literature* (Leeds), July 1970, 33-44; *Harlem Renaissance* by Nathan Irvin Huggins, New York and Oxford, Oxford University Press, 1971; *When Harlem Was in Vogue* by David Levering Lewis, New York and Oxford, Oxford University Press, 1981; *Modernism and the Harlem Renaissance* by Houston A. Baker, Jr., Chicago and London, The University of Chicago Press, 1987; "A Spectacle in Color: The Lesbian and Gay Subculture of Jazz Age Harlem" by Eric Garber, in *Hidden From History: Reclaiming the Gay and Lesbian Past,* edited by Martin Duberman, Martha Vicinus, and George Chauncey, Jr., New York, Meridian, 1989, 318-331; "The Unreadable Black Body: 'Conventional' Poetic Form in the Harlem Renaissance" by Amitai F. Avi-Ram, in *Genders,* No. 7, spring 1990, 32-46; *How Do I Look,* edited by Bad Object Choices, Seattle, Bay Press, 1991; "Critical Deviance: Homophobia and the Reception of James Baldwin's Fiction" by Emmanuel Nelson, in *Journal of American Culture,* Vol. 14, No. 3, fall 1991, 91-96; "Banana Bottom" by Marian B. McLeod, "Home to Harlem," and "The Poetry of Claude McKay" by A. L. McLeod, in *Masterpieces of African-American Literature,* edited by Frank N. Magill, New York, HaperCollins, 1992; "Perverse Reading: The Lesbian Appropriation of Literature" by Bonnie Zimmerman, in *Sexual Practice, Textual Theory: Lesbian Cultural Criticism,* edited by Susan J. Wolfe and Julia Penelope, Cambridge, Massachusetts, and Oxford, Blackwell, 1993; "Gay Re-Readings of the Harlem Renaissance Poets" by Gregory Woods, in the *Journal of Homosexuality* (New York), Vol. 26, No. 2/3, 1993, 127-142; "The Social Construction of Gender" by Judith Lorber, in *Race, Class, and Gender in the United States,* edited by Paula S. Rothenberg, New York, St. Martins, 1995; "African Diaspora" by Edward Marx, http://www-engl.cla.umn.edu/visiting/marx/webpage/africa.htm; "The New Negro," http://www.teachersoft.com/Library/nonfict/coombs/chapt09.htm.

*   *   *

The Harlem Renaissance was a time of great creativity for African Americans. W. E. B. DuBois and others hoped that the "talented tenth" of African Americans would be able to prove the intelligence and the creativity of African Americans and thus gain greater acceptance from the white population. During the Harlem Renaissance, writing, music, and art flourished. Harlem was a cultural and artistic center, a mecca for talented writers, artists, musicians, and performers. Claude McKay, although personally peripheral to the creativity of this period, was artistically one of the writers whose work has been considered at its center. McKay's writing has made an important contribution not only to African American writing, but also to gay literature. Despite his absence from Harlem during the 1920s, Claude McKay has been most strongly identified as a Harlem Renaissance writer, helped often by his friend and one of the initiators of the Harlem Renaissance, James Weldon Johnson. Indeed, some date the beginnings of the Harlem Renaissance with McKay's work.

As Eric Garber points out in his essay "A Spectacle in Color: The Lesbian and Gay Subculture of Jazz Age Harlem," during the Harlem Renaissance a gay and lesbian subculture developed in Harlem. Garber points out that although "Claude McKay...spent most of the 1920s in Europe, [he] was active in Parisian gay circles

and pursued relationships with both sexes. Like Bonnie Zimmerman who allows for recovery of and lesbian readings of texts through clues scattered through those texts, Gregory Woods proposes reading strategies to recover the homosexual or bisexual content of the writers of this period." Woods points out that most criticism of the Harlem Renaissance writers by both white and African American scholars, however, has neither noted the gay subculture that existed so strongly in Harlem, nor has it made reference to the gay content of the writers. He quotes Emmanuel Nelson: "Almost all the major figures of the Harlem Renaissance were gay: Alain Locke, Countee Cullen, Langston Hughes, Claude McKay."

Wood proposes reading the content of the poetry of gay or bisexual poets from a gay standpoint as well as from a racial one. He notes that "the degree of...admiration for Alfonso in "Alfonso, Dressing to Wait at Table" leaves more of an impression of [sexual] frission than of [racial] protest," and Wood points out that McKay's "If We Must Die" (one of McKay's own favorite poems because of the protest of oppression that McKay said himself applied to all people) is as related to homosexual oppression as to race oppression. Wood discusses several of McKay's other poems with homosexual as well as racial interpretation: "Courage," "The Barrier," "Adolescence," and "On Broadway." Wayne Cooper noted that "Romance," "The Snow Fairy," "Tormented," and "One Year After" all "celebrated brief affairs with partners whose sex is never explicitly stated."

McKay scatters other clues in his writing as well. Ray, the intellectual character of *Home to Harlem* and *Banjo* who is, perhaps, most closely based on McKay himself, speaks to Jake in *Home to Harlem* of the story of Sappho, the lesbian Greek poet of whom Jake has never heard. Ray says "Her story gave two lovely words to modern language...Sapphic and Lesbian...beautiful words." When Jake replies that "Leshbian" is "what we call bulldyker in Harlem," Ray replies that "Harlem is too savage about some things." Indeed, the men form a fast friendship, one in which Ray does much to educate Jake, and his admiration for Jake's "natural" and rugged body speaks to the reader of desire. In a dream, McKay relates of Ray that "he was a young shining chief in a marble palace; slim, naked...gleaming skinned black boys bearing goblets of wine...Taboos and terrors and penalties were transformed into new pagan delights, orgies of Orient-blue carnival, of rare flowers and red fruits, cherubs and seraphs and fetishes and phalli and all the most-high gods...." Later, when Jake notes that a young prostitute has shown interest in Ray that he does not return, he comments, "Youse awful queer, chappie."

Ray hires on as a worker on a steamer and leaves for Europe before the end of *Home to Harlem.* In *Banjo,* a book set on the waterfront of Marseilles, Ray becomes involved with a man named Banjo, a musician, and the young dockworkers who are a part of his group, admiring the men greatly. For Ray, the bonds with men will always supersede those with women. Like McKay, Ray is not the marrying kind, but rather the vagabond who must always travel on.

Clues to McKay's sexuality are scattered through his non-fiction writing as well, particularly in his autobiography. McKay's early patron, Walter Jekyll, influential in his education and in the publication of his first two books, was not a man who had overnight guests, but McKay often stayed in his home with him. After leaving *The Liberator,* a radical magazine of which McKay was co-editor before an editorial dispute, McKay took a short holiday. He spent much time in the company of a dancer. McKay never mentioned his short, early marriage until his wife walked into his room one night, surprising the two. McKay wrote: "The dancer exclaimed in a shocked tone; 'Why, I never knew that you were *married!*' As if that should have made any difference to *him.*"

McKay moved on, selling autographed copies of his poems to make money to attend the Third International. While in Russia, which had no laws or sanctions against homosexuality at the time, he noted that the poetry of the period he liked best "was that of the peasant poet Yessenin" whose homosexual desire and relationships were clearly evident in his poetry. Zonov, Yessenin's "intimate friend," showed McKay a photograph of Yessenin which startled McKay with its "resemblance to the strange dancer I had known in New York." McKay's writing while in Russia, however, dealt with racial rather than with sexual matters, delineating the condition of African Americans in the United States.

Other incidents from McKay's autobiography bear mention. Frank Harris, who published McKay's early poetry in *Pearson's Magazine,* saw McKay in Nice in the company of a beautiful young woman. Pearson asked McKay to invite her for dinner, and took her home in a cab. When he saw McKay later he asked "why didn't you tell me we were riding to the destination of Lesbos?" McKay answered that he "had warned [Harris] that he [Harris] could be trusted." When McKay developed an interest in a woman named Carmina, his friend Louise Bryant asked, "Why don't you go on living as you always did? Why do you have to go around with a female on your arm, simply because you have written a successful novel?"

McKay's success as a writer of fiction, poetry, and non-fiction seems to stem not only from his racial protest, but also, intertwined with and inseparable from race, his sexuality. While white critics lauded his *Home to Harlem,* African American critics including W. E. B. DuBois and Alain Locke attacked the novel for its sexual content and realism. Robert Bone writes that *Home to Harlem* "bogs down in the secondary contrast between Jake and Ray." If a gay reading of this book is undertaken, however, the sexual difference between the two men, and Ray's sexuality in the subsequent novel *Banjo,* may be seen to be a primary contrast between men, allowing a space for difference and tolerance and for friendship and understanding between heterosexuals and homosexuals. Sexuality and gender are often left vague in McKay's work, with clues left for the reader. As Bad Object Choices points out, like Langston Hughes, McKay lived in a time in which "an artist of the Harlem Renaissance might have felt compelled to be closeted about his homosexuality" except in "safe zones" created within the lesbian, gay, bisexual, and transgendered subculture. Certainly McKay's writing takes note of sexuality. It is often feminine in both feeling and description. A. L. McLeod notes that Jekyll, McKay's mentor, described Jamaican dialect as "a feminine version of masculine English," and McLeod notes that lines in "To Clarendon Hills and H. A. H." suggest "a total male commitment," although the homoerotic content of "The Harlem Dancer" is ignored in McLeod's analysis. In her analysis of *Banana Bottom,* the book that Marian McLeod feels is his most successful, McLeod notes that McKay's earlier books had depicted the world of men. She notes that "twenty years after having left Jamaica, he returned symbolically in the character of Bita Plant...his ideal Caribbean."

As Judith Lorber points out, gender and sexuality are fluid, not fixed. Bita Plant may be Claude McKay's feminine side. Indeed, as Robert Bone points out in his discussion of McKay's *Banana Bottom,* that book is his link with Expressionism, granting him artistic fulfillment. Bone writes "If McKay's spiritual journey carried him 'a long way from home,' in the end he returned to his native island."

Claude McKay's writing during and after the period known as the Harlem Renaissance is valuable because of the complexities of race, class, sexuality, and gender that it contains. His work greatly enriches our legacy of gay and bisexual writing.

—Patti Capel Swartz

———

MEAKER, M. J. *See* **MEAKER, Marijane.**

———

MEAKER, Marijane

Pseudonyms: Has also written as Ann Aldrich, Mary James, M. E. Kerr, M. J. Meaker, and Vin Packer. **Nationality:** American novelist and writer of nonfiction, primarily for young adults and children. **Born:** Auburn, New York, 27 May 1927. **Education:** Vermont Junior College, the New School for Social Research, and the University of Missouri, B.A. 1949. **Career:** Freelance writer, from 1949; held several jobs, including secretarial work for E. P. Dutton and Fawcett, 1949-51. Founding member, Ashawagh Hall Writers' Workshop. **Awards:** Best Book of the Year Award, *School Library Journal,* 1972, 1974, 1977, 1981, 1982, 1987, 1994; Best Book for Young Adults Award, American Library Association, 1972, 1975, 1983, 1985, 1986, 1987, 1995; Children's Spring Book Festival Honor Book, *Book World,* 1973; Children's Books of the Year, Child Study Association of America, 1973; *Media and Methods* Maxi Award, 1974; Outstanding Book of the Year Award, *New York Times,* 1975, 1978; Christopher Award, 1978; New York Public Library's Books for the Teen Age citation, 1979, 1982, 1988, 1990, 1992, 1994, 1995; Golden Kite Award for Fiction, Society of Children's Book Writers, 1981; Book for Youth Editors' Choice Award, American Library Association *Booklist,* 1987, 1991, 1994; Edgar Allan Poe Award Finalist, Mystery Writers of America, 1990; Margaret A. Edwards Award for Lifetime Achievement in Young Adult Literature, 1993; Best Book Honor Award, Michigan Library Association, 1994; Recommended Books for Reluctant Young Adult Readers citation, American Library Association, 1995; Fanfare Honor List, *Horn Book,* 1995. **Agent:** Eugene Winick, McIntosh and Otis, 310 Madison Ave., New York, New York 10017, U.S.A.

WRITINGS

Fiction for Young Adults as M. E. Kerr

Dinky Hocker Shoots Smack!. New York, HarperCollins, 1972.
If I Love You, Am I Trapped Forever?. New York, HarperCollins, 1973.
The Son of Someone Famous. New York, HarperCollins, 1974.

Love is a Missing Person. New York, HarperCollins, 1975.
Is That You, Miss Blue? New York, HarperCollins, 1975.
I'll Love You When You're More Like Me. New York, HarperCollins, 1977.
Gentlehands. New York, HarperCollins, 1978.
Little Little. New York, HarperCollins, 1981.
What I Really Think of You. New York, HarperCollins, 1982.
Him She Loves? New York, HarperCollins, 1984.
I Stay Near You. New York, HarperCollins, 1985.
Night Kites. New York, HarperCollins, 1986.
Fell. New York, HarperCollins, 1987.
Fell Down. New York, HarperCollins, 1989.
Fell Back. New York, HarperCollins, 1989.
Linger. New York, HarperCollins, 1993.
Deliver Us from Evie. New York, HarperCollins, 1994.
Hello, I Lied. New York, HarperCollins, 1997.

Fiction for Children as Mary James

Shoebag. New York, Scholastic, 1990.
The Shut-Eyes. New York, Scholastic, 1993.
Frankenlouse. New York, Scholastic, 1994.
Shoebag's Return. New York, Scholastic, 1996.

Fiction for Adults as Vin Packer

Dark Intruder. New York, Gold Medal Books, 1952.
Spring Fire. New York, Gold Medal Books, 1952.
Look Back to Love. New York, Gold Medal Books, 1953.
Come Destroy Me. New York, Gold Medal Books, 1954.
Whisper His Sins. New York, Gold Medal Books, 1954.
The Thrill Kids. New York, Gold Medal Books, 1955.
The Young and Violent. New York, Gold Medal Books, 1956.
Dark Don't Catch Me. New York, Gold Medal Books, 1956.
Three-Day Terror. New York, Gold Medal Books, 1957.
The Evil Friendship. New York, Gold Medal Books, 1958.
5:45 to Suburbia. New York, Gold Medal Books, 1958.
The Twisted Ones. New York, Gold Medal Books, 1959.
The Girl on the Best Seller List. New York, Gold Medal Books, 1961.
The Damnation of Adam Blessing. New York, Gold Medal Books, 1961.
Something in the Shadows. New York, Gold Medal Books, 1961.
Intimate Victims. New York, Gold Medal Books, 1962.
Alone at Night. New York, Gold Medal Books, 1963.
The Hare in March. New York, New American Library, 1967.
Don't Rely on Gemini. New York, Delacorte Press, 1969.

Fiction for Adults

Game of Survival (as M. J. Meaker). New York, New American Library, 1968.
Shockproof Sydney Skate. New York, Little, Brown, 1972.

Nonfiction for Adults as Ann Aldrich

We Walk Alone. New York, Gold Medal Books, 1955.
We Too Must Love. New York, Gold Medal Books, 1958.
Carol in a Thousand Cities. New York, Gold Medal Books, 1960.
We Two Won't Last. New York, Gold Medal Books, 1963.
Take a Lesbian to Lunch. New York, MacFadden-Bartell, 1972.

Nonfiction for Adults as M. J. Meaker

Sudden Endings. New York, Doubleday, 1964; paperback edition under name Vin Packer, New York, Fawcett, 1964.

Other (for Young Adults)

Me Me Me Me Me, Not a Novel (autobiography, as M. E. Kerr). New York, Harper, 1983.
Foreword (as M. E. Kerr), *Hearing Us Out, Voices from the Gay and Lesbian Community,* by Roger Sutton. New York, Little, Brown and Company, 1994.
"We Might as Well All Be Strangers" (short story), in *Am I Blue?: Coming Out from the Silence,* edited by Marion Dane Bauer. New York, HarperCollins, 1994.

*

Interviews: "An Interview with M. E. Kerr" by Paul Janeczko, in *English Journal,* Vol. 64, December 1975, 75-77; "Her, Her, Her: An Interview with M. E. Kerr" by B. Allison Gray, in *Voice of Youth Advocates,* Vol. 13, February 1991, 337-342; "A Conversation" by Roger Sutton, in *School Library Journal,* Vol. 39, June 1993, 24-29; "An Interview with M. E. Kerr" by Joyce L. Graham, in *Youth in Library Services,* Vol. 7, fall 1993, 31-36; "Marijane Meaker: Happy Endings at Last" by Robin Bernstein, in *Washington Blade,* 14 July 1995, 48-49.

Critical Sources: "Marijane Meaker," in *Something About the Author,* edited by Anne Commire, Vol. 61, Detroit, Gale Research Company, 1989, 117-126; "1993 Margaret A. Edwards Award Acceptance Speech" by M. E. Kerr, in *Youth in Library Services,* Vol. 7, fall 1993, 25-30.

*   *   *

In 1952, *Spring Fire,* a lesbian romance, sold nearly 1.5 million copies. It was Vin Packer's first novel.

In 1964, a woman who used to call herself "Marijane the Spy" inspired the title character of Louise Fitzhugh's classic children's book, *Harriet the Spy.*

In 1972, *Shockproof Sydney Skate,* Marijane Meaker's wildly successful novel about a boy and his mother who fall in love with the same woman, became a Literary Guild alternate and a selection of the Book Find Club.

In 1986, young adult writer M. E. Kerr published *Nightkites,* the world's first young adult book about AIDS.

In 1993, Mary James published *The Shut-Eyes,* an allegory for children about a world in which only ten percent of the population needs to sleep. The nonsleeping majority oppresses the minority, until the shut-eyes fight back with political actions such as night-dress pride parades.

And in 1994, M. E. Kerr's *Deliver Us from Evie* portrayed the first butch lesbian main character in a young adult novel.

All these writers are in fact one person—Marijane Meaker, one of the most respected and celebrated novelists for young adults. Meaker has published over 50 books; won the prestigious Margaret A. Edwards Award for lifetime achievement in young adult literature; and earned wide critical acclaim for her funny, offbeat, truthful characters. She has written positively about gays and lesbians for over 40 years.

Yet incredibly, Marijane Meaker did not come out publicly until 1994, when she wrote the foreword to Roger Sutton's *Hearing*

Us Out: Voices from the Gay and Lesbian Community. In that foreword, Meaker related the story of a woman who asked her how she came to write *Little Little,* a novel about a teenage dwarf. "How do you know so much about denial and intragroup prejudice?" the mother asked. Meaker "told her that growing up homosexual in the late '30s and early '40s had given me all my insights."

Meaker, the daughter of a mayonnaise manufacturer and an avid gossip, was raised in Auburn, New York. As a teenager, the rebellious tomboy dated the local undertaker's son, got suspended from Stuart Hall boarding school in Staunton, Virginia, for throwing darts at photographs of members of the faculty, and wrote with feverish ambition. *Me Me Me Me Me: Not a Novel,* Meaker's autobiography of her teenage years, depicts a predominantly heterosexual young adulthood, except for kissing games played with other girls at boarding school. In a 1995 interview in the *Washington Blade*—the first in which Meaker publicly discussed her lesbianism—Meaker told Robin Bernstein that as a teenager she "enjoyed dating and going steady. I always think that you're informed by your time. I knew that it was wrong to be gay and I was trying not to be, but I was also enjoying myself."

In 1949, at the age of 22, Meaker moved to New York City in search of lesbian life and publishing. She convinced her boyfriends to escort her to lesbian bars, where she felt alienated because she did not identify as either butch or femme. Eventually, however, she found a circle of lesbian friends and discarded her boyfriends.

Meaker worked at Fawcett Publications, where an editor who knew of her lesbianism suggested she write a novel based on her experiences as a college student in a sorority. Meaker wrote *Sorority Girl* (renamed *Spring Fire*), a tortured butch/femme romance, under the name Vin Packer. Gold Medal Books, one of Fawcett's imprints, published *Spring Fire* in 1952; the book sold almost 1.5 million copies. Vin Packer went on to write 18 thrillers, most of which had no lesbian content. And Meaker launched another pseudonym: Ann Aldrich, who wrote nonfiction about lesbian life from the 1950s through the early 1970s.

One day in the mid 1950s, Ann Aldrich received a fan letter from a married woman; Meaker responded with an invitation for the woman to visit her in New York. During their brief affair, Meaker introduced the woman to Dick Carroll, her editor at Gold Medal. The woman and Carroll had a dalliance of their own, and Carroll encouraged her to write a novel for Gold Medal. The woman wrote several under the pseudonym Ann Bannon.

By the 1960s, Meaker became friends with other lesbian writers such as Louise Fitzhugh and Sandra Scoppettone. Fitzhugh, partially inspired by Meaker's childhood adventures as the leader of a gang of child spies, wrote the bestselling novel *Harriet the Spy* in 1964. Fitzhugh introduced Meaker to the genre of young adult literature. Fitzhugh, who wanted to write mysteries like Meaker's, suggested they switch typewriters so Meaker could write a young adult novel and Fitzhugh could write a thriller.

Meaker read a few young adult novels and was unimpressed, until she encountered Paul Zindel's *The Pigman.* Inspired by Zindel's alienated characters (and by her own experience as a volunteer teacher), Meaker adopted the pen name M. E. Kerr and wrote *Dinky Hocker Shoots Smack!,* a 1972 young adult novel about a troubled teenage girl. The book earned numerous accolades and established M. E. Kerr as one of the most important writers in the genre.

Kerr's fourth book, *Is That You, Miss Blue?* (1975), included two minor lesbian characters who were presented as clownish but sympathetic. In 1977, Kerr's sixth book, *I'll Love You When You're*

More Like Me, featured a gay teenager as a secondary character. From the late 1970s through the mid 1980s, Kerr created no gay or lesbian characters, but she continued to concentrate on gay-related themes such as alienation, outsider status, prejudice, and social ostracism.

In 1984, Meaker wrote *Night Kites,* a novel about a boy whose brother contracts the mysterious new disease, GRID (Gay-Related Immune Deficiency). Meaker feared the book would constitute professional suicide: not only would it provoke controversy, but it would also become hopelessly dated when the disease was cured (as Meaker expected it would be within two or three years). Unfortunately, GRID was renamed AIDS, and *Night Kites* became the first of many novels on the subject. Meaker's fears of controversy, however, proved unnecessary; rather than vilify Meaker for touching the subject, teachers soon wrote to her and demanded to know why the book did not mention condoms. Once, according to an interview in the *Washington Blade,* when Meaker spoke in a classroom, a student asked if the characters in *Night Kites* had anal intercourse. Meaker replied, "Certainly that would be an option." The student then asked, "What's an option?" The student was familiar with words "anal intercourse" but not "option."

In 1994, Kerr's *Deliver Us from Evie* introduced the first frankly, positively butch lesbian character to young adult fiction. Meaker told the *Washington Blade* that she created the character because she was "so tired of all these cleaned-up people we see on television—the men all arm-wrestling each other and the women competing as fashion models. I believe very much in the truth of stereotypes. I wanted her to be what I knew of the life when I first came out." Like all of Kerr's novels featuring gay characters, *Deliver Us from Evie* is narrated not by a lesbian but by a heterosexual (in this case, the character's brother). Kerr has published in the voice of a gay character only once: in the short story, "We Might As Well All Be Strangers," in Marion Dane Bauer's *Am I Blue?: Coming Out from the Silence.*

In 1990, Meaker launched a new pseudonym, Mary James, who wrote novels for elementary school readers. James's first novel, *Shoebag,* introduced one of Meaker's typically alienated, Kafkaesque characters—in this instance, a cockroach who woke up one morning to discover, to his horror, that he had been transformed into a boy. James's second novel, *The Shut-Eyes,* embedded a clear gay subtext in its world in which only ten percent of the people needed to sleep, and this minority was hunted down by the non-sleeping majority.

Meaker told the *Washington Blade* in 1995 that she was writing a sequel to *Me Me Me Me Me: Not a Novel.* This second volume of her autobiography, which had not at that time found a publisher, focused on her lesbian life from the 1950s through the 1980s. She took the title, *Remind Me,* from a Mabel Mercer song: "Remind me not to find you too attractive / Remind me that the world is full of men."

—Robin Bernstein

MERRICK, Gordon

Nationality: American novelist. **Born:** Cynwyd, Pennsylvania, 3 August 1916. **Education:** Princeton University, New Jersey, B.A. 1939. **Military Service:** Served in the Office of Strategic Services in France, 1944-45; civilian employee with rank equaling Captain. **Family:** Companion of Charles G. Hulse. Worked as an actor in New York, 1938-41; journalist, with *The Washington Star,*

Baltimore Evening Sun, PM, and *New York Post,* 1941-44. Contributed book reviews and articles to *The New Republic, Ikonos,* and other periodicals. **Died:** Colombo, Sri Lanka, of lung cancer, 27 March 1988.

WRITINGS

Novels

The Strumpet Wind. New York, Morrow, 1947.
The Demon at Noon. New York, Meissner, 1954.
The Vallency Tradition. New York, Meissner, 1955; as *Between Darkness and Day,* London, R. Hale, 1957.
The Hot Season. New York, Morrow, 1958; as *The Eye of One in London,* R. Hale, 1959.
The Lord Won't Mind. New York, Geis, 1970.
One for the Gods. New York, Geis, 1971.
Forth into Light. New York, Avon, 1974.
An Idol for Others. New York, Avon, 1977.
The Quirk. New York, Avon, 1978.
Now Let's Talk About Music. New York, Avon, 1981.
Perfect Freedom. New York, Avon, 1982.
The Great Urge Downward. New York, Avon, 1984.
A Measure of Madness. New York, Warner, 1986.

*

Critical Sources: Review of *The Lord Won't Mind,* in *Publishers Weekly* (New York), Vol. 197, 5 January 1970, 74; "Reader's Report" by Martin Levin, in *New York Times Book Review,* 26 April 1970, 47; review of *The Lord Won't Mind* by D.J.C. Brudnoy, in *National Review,* Vol. 23, 15 July 1971, 663; "Gay is Proud" by Dotson Rader, in *New York Times Book Review,* 3 October 1971, 5; *Playing in the Dark: The Homosexual Novel in America* by Roger Austen, Indianapolis, Bobbs-Merrill Co., 1977; "Homosexuality in the Crucial Decade: Three Novelists' Views" by S. James Elliott, in *The Gay Academic,* edited by Louie Crew, Palm Springs, ETC Publications, 1978, 164-77; "Mappings of Male Desire" by Joseph A. Boone, in *Displacing Homophobia: Gay Male Perspectives in Literature and Culture,* edited by Ronald Butters, John Clum, and Michael Moon, Durham, Duke University Press, 1989, 73-106; *Gaiety Transfigured: Gay Self-Representation in American Literature* by David Bergman, Madison, University of Wisconsin Press, 1991; *The Gay Decades* by Leigh W. Routledge, New York, Plume, 1992; "Richard Labonté's Ten Best and Five Worst Gay Books" by Richard Labonté, in *The Alyson Almanac,* edited by Sasha Alyson, Boston, Alyson Publications, 1993, 103-06; *Gay Men's Literature in the Twentieth Century* by Mark Lilly, New York, New York University Press, 1993; *A Queer Reader,* edited by Patrick Higgins, New York, The New Press, 1993; *The Lesbian and Gay Studies Reader,* edited by Henry Abelove, Michèle Aina Barale, and David M. Halperin, New York, Routledge, 1993; "David Leavitt's Inner Child" by Michael Schwartz, in *The Harvard Gay and Lesbian Review,* Vol 2, No. 1, winter 1995, 40-4; *The Gay and Lesbian Literary Heritage,* edited by Claude J. Summers, New York, Henry Holt, 1995; *The Gay and Lesbian Literary Companion,* edited by Sharon Malinowski and Christa Brelin, Detroit, Visible Ink Press, 1995.

*   *   *

Perhaps the most remarkable fact about the critical response to Gordon Merrick's novels is that there is virtually none. Despite the substantial corpus of 13 novels, one of which (*The Lord Won't Mind*) remained on *The New York Times* best seller list for 16 weeks, critics and reviewers have remained strangely silent about Merrick's work. This could be dismissed as the elitism that has long accompanied the boundary between "high" and "popular" culture, but contemporary theory has sufficiently eroded that boundary so that recent works on gay literature would be expected to deal with Merrick. Such has not been the case. Works such as *The Gay and Lesbian Literary Companion, The Lesbian and Gay Studies Reader, Gaiety Transfigured: Gay Self-Representation in American Literature, Gay Men's Literature in the Twentieth Century, A Queer Reader,* and *The Gay and Lesbian Literary Heritage,* all published in the 1990s, make no reference to him. When Merrick is mentioned at all, it is usually in a dismissive and pejorative fashion.

It is also clear that the commentator often feels somewhat lost when dealing with Merrick. Referring to a different text, for example, Joseph Boone, in "Mappings of Male Desire," states: "Taken out of context, this exchange might seem more the prelude to a soft-porn scene in a gay novel by Gordon Merrick than the encounter of a straight hero with his role model." This seemingly harmless comment actually serves to establish Merrick's writing as a yardstick against which other texts can be favorably compared. In *Playing the Game: The Homosexual Novel in America,* Roger Austen states that "Gordon Merrick has made a splash with his glossy love stories...which are pleasant escape fiction for the Gay and Gray set," but he does not elaborate on this peculiar comment. In *The Gay Decades,* Leigh Rutledge refers to Merrick's "stream of...novels...which become increasingly famous more for their fleshy, suggestive covers than for the quality of the material inside."

Herein lies the crux of the problems involving Merrick's novels. Because his works deal unabashedly and forthrightly with not only gay relationships, but also gay sex, as suggested by the "fleshy, suggestive covers," they have been difficult for critics to categorize. They are certainly romances, and, as such, follow the rules and formulas of the genre, but their unlikely heroes are beautiful and endowed men. Michael Schwartz, in "David Leavitt's Inner Child," defends Merrick's use of formulaic romance when commenting on *The Lord Won't Mind:* "This is a romance, and the heroes and heroines of romance are always beautiful...Readers of romance make a contract with the book, agreeing to see themselves reflected in the characters' beauty..." The dynamics created in Merrick's works thwart any attempt at simple summary, and his novels question many suppositions made by both gay and straight readers about gay men and their lifestyles, needs, relationships, and problems.

Merrick's writing investigates the social roles dictated by gender rules and the representational power of language and other sign systems. Much of what he presents is not attractive, but the trap into which many readers fall is to view his often painful descriptions of gay relationships as prescriptive rather than descriptive. His characters often fight with others and themselves to create some sense of identity in a clearly homophobic and hostile world. They recognize themselves, often gradually, as the Other, or the outsider, and they come to realize the importance of being able to manipulate codes of communication, be they languages, theater performances, or paintings. In this recognition, Merrick was well ahead of his time. His work provides a welcome precursor to contemporary queer theory, which questions the very stability of labels dealing with gender and sexuality, and it lends itself to a reading which emphasizes the impact of gender and language on meaning. One major theme that recurs in Merrick's novels is the necessity of rejecting power, physical and/or ideological, in order to find one's own identity.

In Merrick's first novel, *The Strumpet Wind,* Roger Chandler works in the intelligence field in France during World War II. Although he is an American, his French is fluent, and he is engaged in an assignment in which he must play a role, posing as a friend to a Frenchman who has been caught supplying the Nazis with information about the Allies' movements. Even the communications between the Frenchman and the Nazis are carried out in code, and Chandler becomes heavily involved in the transmission of coded information.

The homosexual presence is minimal in this first novel, but the work touches on themes of individual liberty and freedom from constraint that recur in different guises in later works. Chandler's superior, George Meddling, is a dazzlingly handsome but sadistic bisexual, whose "narcissism led him to find satisfaction in the admiration of both men and women." It would be all too easy to read Chandler's disgust with Meddling as justified and then to dismiss the novel as homophobic. Merrick, however, does not let the reader off so easily, for Chandler himself is no prize. Merrick, therefore, has not presented the reader with a homosexual character to represent evil, but has rather presented a cast of characters, all of whom have various problems and personal situations, highly exacerbated by the surrealism of war, which lead to an inability to deal with the reality outside of themselves.

With *The Lord Won't Mind* Merrick comes into his own, both as a writer and as an observer of the gay male in a straight world. The novel begins in the first person, but the narrator rejects this personal engagement with his story: "'I suppose he's wildly good-looking,' I said. No, not I. *He* said. He. I will not associate myself with the things I have to tell. If I must intrude occasionally, it will be from the distance of time and change. Charlie Mills has nothing to do with me." Merrick then employs this distancing technique at strategic points throughout the novel, using the first person occasionally to weave the reader into and out of the fabric of the narration. Charlie Mills and Peter Martin, both young, strikingly handsome, blond, and well-endowed, meet and fall madly in love. In fact, the book has been criticized for its insistence on beauty in the gay male world. Michael Schwarz, in "David Leavitt's Inner Child," wryly but accurately defends this portrayal:

> Beauty is a part of gay life, an important part—those men aren't spending all those hours at the gym just for the cardiovascular benefits. This 'obsession' has its roots in our core definition: we are gay because we find men beautiful. Beauty has its dangers, of course. That's part of our complex response to it, and it is in fact this complexity that makes beauty a valid and vital subject for our literature.

The main conflict in the story belongs to Charlie. He is internally torn, knowing that he wants Peter desperately, which fills him with fear of his own potential isolation, but also assuming that his grandmother's expectations that he meet the right girl and get married should be fulfilled. He insists on all of the role-playing so prevalent at mid-century, urging discretion to mask the truth. His pursuits, acting and painting, closely parallel his need to put

forth a persona that represents what is not there. It is through Charlie's anguish that the reader catches a glimpse of Merrick's interest in the problems the gay male experiences establishing an identity. Charlie's socially-imposed resistance is contrasted to Peter's childlike innocence. While Charlie vehemently rejects the label "queer," Peter states his feelings openly: "'The thing is, I can't imagine loving anybody who didn't have a cock, so I guess that makes me a queer. I know it's awful and I don't know how it happened and I probably should shoot myself or something, but with you it just seems right.'" When Charlie eventually throws Peter out and marries a woman to protect his reputation, every reader, straight or gay, can detest his duplicity and weakness but must also empathize with the situation that Charlie has had forced upon him by an unaccepting society.

The sham marriage quickly sours and ends with the wife physically mutilating Charlie's penis, and he seeks out Peter for help and comfort. It is only through both mental and physical torment that Charlie finally learns to accept himself and reject his overbearing grandmother's insistence that he distance himself from Peter permanently. Merrick presents this self-isolation as a necessary first step on the road to self-realization. Indeed, after the final showdown with his grandmother, when he states blatantly that he loves Peter, Charlie says to Peter, "'All I can say is I feel as if we were the two most normal people in the world after that.'"

Critics and reviewers were quick to come up with the predictable wordplay on the title. In *Publishers' Weekly,* the reviewer stated: "Maybe the Lord won't mind, but just about everybody else will find something distasteful in this no-holds-barred novel of a homosexual affair." There can be little doubt about the reviewer's discomfort with the subject matter, which robs the review of credibility. D.J.C. Brudnoy, in *The National Review,* similarly asserts, "Maybe the Lord won't mind. Discriminating readers will." With twice the foreboding, Martin Levin, in the *New York Times Book Review,* warns that "It will set homosexuality back at least 20 years." These comments only underscore what Merrick and other authors who chose to portray gay sexuality honestly had to face. They also point up the difficulties critics, both gay and straight, had dealing with a kind of text that was totally new and flew in the face of all convention.

In *One for the Gods,* the second novel of the trilogy, Charlie and Peter have been together for over ten years, and they have had to fend for themselves. The novel provides scenes of infidelity and jealousy, but this need not suggest that Merrick was portraying gay men in a negative light. Rather, he chose to present them in a realistic light, illustrating that men in relationships might experience some of the same insecurities, weaknesses, and lapses of judgment experienced by everyone. In "Gay is Proud," Dotson Rader deems the book "helpful...for it is an honest statement of homosexual romanticism and myth," and while he faults its awkward sentimentality, he finds it "an honest, unembarrassed, oddly defiant romantic novel which makes no apologies to anyone." Because Charlie and Peter have no role models, they are inventing their own rules as they go along. Early in the novel, a character states that fidelity "'is altogether too limiting. Especially for an artist. Even normally married couples don't attempt it.'" Charlie responds, "'But that's just it. We're not a normally married couple so we've made up our own rules.'" When they both become sexually involved with Martha, who becomes pregnant, presumably by Charlie, the reader is left wondering about sexual identity. But this is precisely Merrick's point. While some critics could see this as a statement that gay men cannot live without women and procreation, Merrick is rather suggesting, as he does through all of his later novels, that sexual identity is not necessarily etched in stone just because the power structures of society have attempted to use language to categorize everyone. This does not mean that everyone is bisexual, only that sexual identity is fluid and influenced by the historical and social situations in which we find ourselves.

Charlie makes substantial headway in this novel. "In the unlikely event that somebody organized a campaign to erase the stigma from homosexuality, he would gladly lend a hand. He was what he was..." The satisfaction the reader may experience in Charlie's self-acceptance is tempered only by Merrick's pessimism about society. This emphasizes Merrick's disgust with society, however, and not with gay sexuality. The final scene of the novel, in which Peter finally strikes back (literally, with his fists), may be jarring, but Charlie's reaction while he is being pummeled provides a dark form of comic relief while revealing his dependency on gender roles and labels: "This is a *man,* Charlie thought with wonder as his breath was cut off. I'm in love with a man."

As with many of his works, Merrick uses *An Idol for Others* to explore the awakening of a gay identity and consciousness in the main character, in this case 50 year-old Walter Makin. While he had fooled around with men in his younger years and even now occasionally has an interlude with a man, he meets Tom Jennings and literally runs away from home to be with him. The simple storyline belies the complex issues at stake. Walter is a middle-aged man with a wife, three sons (two with his wife, one illegitimate), and a stunningly successful career in the theater—the world of make-believe, false signification, and role playing. His rejection of the social norms that would bind him to these forces is an enormous move, but a necessary one if he is to finally become one with his inner needs and desires. The story spans approximately 30 years and, at the end, the younger Tom has taught Walter much about the flexibility that gay men have to cultivate if they want to survive in the straight world. Tom helps him to break down his inhibitions about monogamy without feeling as though he had sacrificed fidelity. Merrick makes one of his clearest liberal statements about gay sexuality through Tommy, and it is worth quoting at length:

> "People talk about gays as if we're just like everybody else except that we happen to like our own sex. We're supposed to want what everybody else wants—acceptance in the community, marriage after our fashion and all the rest of it...That's not it at all. We're unique. I'll never be your wife...We're two men. We're rebels...I don't want a model homosexual marriage so that everybody can say we're really nice—considering. I'll break any law if it means getting closer to you. I'm dangerous because I'm bursting with the kind of love that only men can feel for each other."

Despite the schmaltz, the final pages of the book, in which the cancer-ridden Walter dies (from a deliberate overdose of pain medication administered by his wife) and Tom commits suicide, are moving and disturbing. Walter has finally achieved peace with his sexual identity, only to lose everything, and Merrick has created a character who successfully defies the gender norms of society and rejects the categorizing power of language.

The Great Urge Downward, Merrick's second-to-last novel, is one of his most successful works for questioning and challenging the structures of power that delimit sexual and gender identity. Lance Vanderholden, an American, is holed up in a South American country, frittering away the time after having become involved in some legal trouble back home. He meets Robbie, the world-famous painter, and the contest begins. Although not a total stranger to sex with men, Lance resists Robbie because he does not want to spoil what promises to be a splendid friendship by giving in to his baser instincts. Indeed, the very title of the work has provoked criticism along these lines. In "Richard Labonté's Ten Best and Five Worst Gay Books," Labonté states, "Only the self-loathing symbolism of the title makes this particular one of Merrick's too-many sucky romances stand out."

Unfortunately, this comment suggests that the critic read nothing more than the title, as the expression is explained in the novel as a loose translation of the French phrase "la nostalgie de la boue." Lance's pursuer tells him, "'They [the French] know that we've all climbed out of the mud and sometimes wish we could crawl back into it. Somebody called it the great urge downward. You were never allowed anywhere near the mud. Those closed doors.'" Robbie knows that Lance can be reborn only by returning to a primeval existence from which he was always sheltered. Lance is afraid of the animalistic passion he feels during sex with other men. This could be seen as degrading only through puritanical lenses, and Merrick's text clearly does not support such a reading. The fact that Lance finally accepts these passions as part of him suggests that he has successfully made the journey through those doors and away from the binding ties of gender conformity. In stark contrast to *An Idol for Others, The Great Urge Downward* ends on a euphoric note that promises an ongoing attempt to make a relationship work despite the odds. The similarity, of course, is that both main characters had to renounce the ideologies that had controlled their lives before they could move on.

A Measure of Madness was Merrick's last novel, published just over a year before his death. It is a fitting end to his long involvement with the complexities and intricacies of male relationships. Philip Renfield, an American on an extended visit to Greece, becomes involved with men, political intrigue, and consciousness-raising interactions with other vacationing Americans and Greek natives. He is gay from the beginning, and he has a healthy attitude toward sex—"He liked the easy, straightforward friendship that was developing between them, and the easy, straightforward sex that went with it"—but he also needs to go through a series of experiences to make his identity whole. When he engages in a three-way with a married couple, he is amazed at their relaxed attitude. A friend tells him, "'Right and wrong—it all depends on the angle you look from.'"

Once again, this emphasizes Merrick's understanding of the cultural and historical contingency of such issues as gender roles, power structure, and the force of language. This is further underscored in a flashback when a boyhood friend of Phil's starts to perform oral sex on him. "If George was queer, everything he'd been taught to believe about homosexuality was wrong." The key word here is "taught," and the young Phil, like the reader, gay or straight, has much to unlearn before he can reconcile his desires with society's expectations and demands.

Perhaps the greatest blow to socially constructed gender roles, which have strongly influenced understandings of role-playing in sex between men, comes when Manoli, Phil's current bed partner, asks to take the receptive role in anal intercourse. Phil is at first shocked, but he then realizes that they "could be together in the equality of their masculinity." Rather than seeing this as a shamefully feminine surrender on Manoli's part, he finally understands that the gender roles and power structures are created by society and maintained through marginalization and language. Later, Phil discards society's definition of marriage: "Marriage hadn't been invented just so babies could be born. Marriages existed because people wanted mates. Maybe two guys couldn't have a real marriage, but with care and determination they could come close."

The recent reprinting of the trilogy novels by Alyson Publications offers both the reading public and the critics another chance to assess Merrick's works. Because the dynamics of gay interactions and identity have changed so rapidly, some of Merrick's prose is bound to sound quaint. Below the surface, however, lie the seeds of much contemporary queer theory, and the reader would do well to consider Merrick's main points in light of today's cultural and social structures. Merrick vehemently rejected all socially imposed labels, especially those pertaining to gender and sexuality, and, in so doing, he insisted that we all question the social and ideological power structures that covertly run our lives. The only differences between Merrick and other writers who have questioned linguistically determined categories are that he did it mercilessly and he wrote about gay men, who happen to like sex with other gay men, as protagonists. As such, he broke new ground that has only recently become theoretically arable. Deeper probing into Merrick's works will undoubtedly yield richer understandings of the complex social dynamics that construct networks of control over sexuality. I suspect that it will also reveal the carefully crafted prose of a master storyteller.

—Bill McCauley

MEYER, June. *See* **JORDAN, June.**

MINER, Valerie

Nationality: American novelist, author of short stories, and essayist. **Born:** New York City, 28 August 1947. **Education:** University of California, Berkeley, B.A. in English and Journalism 1969, M.J. in journalism 1970; University of Edinburgh, 1968; University of London, 1974. **Family:** Married, 1970-74. **Career:** Freelance journalist and lecturer/instructor in English, journalism, and creative writing departments in Canada and Britain, 1972-76; lecturer in department of mass communication, California State University, Hayward, 1977; lecturer in journalism department, San Francisco State University, 1977-78; lecturer in English, mass communications, humanities, and field studies, 1977-89, and faculty advisory board member, multi-cultural lesbian and gay studies program, 1985-89, University of California, Berkeley; lecturer in department of English, Mills College, Oakland, California, 1980-81; assistant professor of English and core faculty member of women's studies, Arizona State University, Tempe, 1990-92; associate, later full professor of English and creative writing, and affiliated faculty member, Center for Advanced Feminist Studies, University of Minnesota, from 1992. Reporter, *Daily Review,* Hayward, California, 1964; reporter *Castro Valley Vista,* Castro Valley, California, 1965; founding member and member of the steering committee, National Feminist Writers Guild, 1977-79; publications and policies board member, Feminist Press at the City University of New York, from 1988; board of directors, National Book Critics Circle, 1991-96; associate editor, *Signs,* 1992-94; vice president and secretary, National Book Critics Circle, 1992-93; contributor of reviews to periodicals, including *Chicago Sun Times, Feminist Review, Los Angeles Times, Nation, San Francisco Sunday Examiner and Chronicle,* and *Women's Review of Books.* **Awards:** Edna Kinard Award for "Outstanding Woman in Journalism at Berkeley," 1968; Theta Sigma Phi Award, 1969; International Feminist Book Fair citation, London, 1984; PEN Syndicated Fiction Award, 1986; Australia Council Literary Awards Grant, 1988; Rockefeller Foundation Residency, at Bellagio Study Center, Italy, 1994; McKnight Research Fellowship, 1994-97; Jerome Foundation Travel Fellowship, 1995-97; Heinz Foundation Fellowship, Hawthornden Castle, Midlothian, Scotland, 1996; Bush Foundation Sabbatical Supplement Award, 1996-97. **Address:** English Department, University of Minnesota, 207 Lind Hall, 207 Church St. SE, Minneapolis, Minnesota 55455, U.S.A.

WRITINGS

Fiction

With Zoe Fairbairns, Sara Maitland, Michele Roberts, and Michelene Wandor, *Tales I Tell My Mother* (short stories). London, Journeyman Press, 1978; Boston, South End Press, 1980.
Blood Sisters (novel). London, Women's Press, 1981; New York, St. Martin's Press, 1982.
Movement: A Novel in Stories. Trumansburg, New York, Crossing Press, 1982; London, Methuen, 1985.
Murder in the English Department (novel). London, Women's Press, 1982; New York, St. Martin's Press, 1983.
Winter's Edge (novel). London, Methuen, 1984; Trumansburg, New York, Crossing Press, 1985; with afterword by Donna Perry, New York, Feminist Press, 1997.
All Good Women (novel). London, Methuen, 1987; Freedom, California, Crossing Press, 1987.
With Fairbairns, Maitland, Roberts, and Wandor, *More Tales I Tell My Mother* (short stories). London, Journeyman, 1987.
Trespassing and Other Stories. London, Methuen, 1989; Freedom, California, Crossing Press, 1989.
A Walking Fire (novel). Albany, New York, State University of New York Press, 1994.
Range of Light (novel). Cambridge, Zoland Press, 1998.
"Trespassing," in *Lesbian Love Stories,* edited by Irene Zahava. Freedom, California, Crossing Press, 1989; in *American Short Stories,* edited by Chris Brown, Oxford, England, Oxford University Press, 1992.
"Dropping Anchor," in *Dreamers and Desperadoes: Women's Short Fiction of the American West,* edited by Craig Lesley. New York, Dell, 1993.

Nonfiction

With Myrna Kostash, Melinda McCracken, Erna Paris, and Heather Robertson, *Her Own Woman: Profiles of Ten Canadian Women* (essays). Toronto, Macmillan, 1975; Halifax, Formac, 1984.

"Writing Feminist Fiction: Solitary Genius or Collective Criticism?," in *Frontiers: A Journal of Women Studies* (Niwot, Colorado), Vol. 6, October 1981.

"Reading Along the Dyke," in *Out/Look,* Vol. 1, No. 1, spring 1988.

Editor, with Helen E. Longino, *Competition: A Feminist Taboo?* New York, Feminist Press, 1987.

"An Imaginative Collectivity of Writers and Readers," in *Lesbian Texts and Contexts: Radical Revisions,* edited by Karla Jay, Joanne Glasgow, and Catherine R. Stimpson. New York, New York University Press, 1990.

"Spinning Friends: May Sarton's Literary Spinsters," in *Old Maids to Radical Spinsters: Unmarried Women in the Twentieth-Century Novel,* edited by Laura L. Doan. Urbana, University of Illinois Press, 1991.

Rumors from the Cauldron: Selected Essays, Reviews, and Reportage. Ann Arbor, University of Michigan Press, 1991.

"A Walking Fire: Finding Cordelia's Voice as Working-Class Hero," in *Hayden's Ferry Review,* fall/winter 1992.

"Writing and Teaching with Class," in *Working-Class Women in the Academy,* edited by Elizabeth Fay and Michelle Tokarczyk. Amherst, University of Massachusetts Press, 1993.

"Introduction," in *Lavender Mansions,* edited by Irene Zahava. Boulder, Colorado, Westview Press, 1994.

*

Interviews: "Historical Fiction and Fictional History: An Interview with Valerie Miner" by Carole Ferrier, in *Meanjin* (Parkville, Victoria, Australia), Vol. 46, No. 4, 1987, 546-556; "Valerie Miner" by Donna Perry, in *Backtalk: Women Writers Speak Out,* New Brunswick, New Jersey, Rutgers University Press, 1993.

Critical Sources: "Lessing's Influence on Valerie Miner" by Ellen Cronan Rose, in *Doris Lessing Newsletter* (Baltimore County, Maryland), Vol. 6, No. 2, 1982, 15; "Valerie (Jane) Miner," in *Contemporary Literary Criticism,* edited by Daniel G. Marowski, Vol. 40, Detroit, Michigan, Gale Research, 1986, 326-332; *Sisters in Crime,* by Maureen Reddy, New York, Continuum, 1988; *The Safe Sea of Women,* by Bonnie Zimmerman, Boston, Beacon, 1990, 55, 139-140; "Valerie Miner" by Lisa L. Higgins, in *Contemporary Lesbian Writers of the United States: A Bio-Bibliographical Critical Sourcebook,* edited by Sandra Pollack and Denise D. Knight, Westport, Connecticut, Greenwood Press, 1993, 370-374; unpublished interview with Valerie Miner by Anne Boyd, February 1997.

Valerie Miner comments:

I'm interested in playing with a range of styles, subjects, and forms. I aim for a fiction that is lyrically moving and philosophically provocative.

*   *   *

The most consistent element in Valerie Miner's fiction is an exploration of how the political and the personal interact in the lives of everyday people. Miner is widely known as a feminist and lesbian writer whose work is marked by the effort to engage women's concerns across cultural, sexual, and socio-economic boundaries. While some reviewers have criticized Miner for the overt expression of feminist ideals in her work, her strongest writing confronts the difficult task of the individual's search for identity in the context of family, friends, and larger political forces.

Valerie Miner's Scottish and Irish immigrant working-class parents instilled in her a skepticism toward literature that led her to initially pursue a career in journalism. Not only couldn't she recognize herself and her family in the literature by white middle-class males she read in college during the 1960s, but writing literature did not seem like "the sort of thing my people did," she told Donna Perry in an interview for *Backtalk.* After college, Miner moved to Canada as a response to the United States' involvement in Vietnam. While there, she became active in the feminist movement. After she moved to England, Miner began writing fiction, largely due to her involvement with a women's writing group that collaborated on the stories in *Tales I Tell My Mother.* Miner told Perry, "Those collaborative processes were very important to me.... I see my work emerging from some kind of imaginative collectivity, not from solitary genesis."

In "An Imaginative Collectivity of Writers and Readers," the lead essay of her collection, *Rumors from the Cauldron,* Miner explained that the strength a community of women readers and writers can provide for each other is vital to the survival of feminist and lesbian writing. "Although I have 'come out' many times in print and in person, it still feels dangerous," she wrote. "Our books get censored by publishing houses, review journals, bookshops, libraries, schools. Even in liberal environments where people support one's right to perversion, our lesbianism—which for some of us is a political choice—is still only temporarily tolerated. It *is not safe* to be a lesbian writer or reader today; we need our collective wits to survive."

Just as she envisions her writing process as taking place in the midst of a collectivity, her stories about women struggling to understand themselves are told within the context of many women's lives. Her "novel in stories," *Movement,* best exemplifies this technique. A twist on the traditionally individualistic *Bildungsroman, Movement* interweaves the stories of many women's lives, each in movement or transition. At the book's center is the story of Susan's development from housewife to politically active feminist and aspiring writer. Through a series of travels across the globe and across sexual boundaries, Susan discovers her true potential and strength. Susan's journey is, in turn, echoed in the brief, unrelated vignettes of other women's experiences as they, for example, reveal their homosexuality to their faculty colleagues or suddenly disappear from otherwise normal, stable lives as housewives.

Throughout her career, Miner has been interested in the imagery of movement and crossing boundaries, as the title of her collection of stories, *Trespassing,* indicates. Her novel *Range of Light* also addresses this theme. It is about the trip of two friends in the High Sierras of California, exploring boundaries in both the landscape and the imagination. As a result of this interest, Miner has consistently represented a wide range of women in her fiction. "I am particularly engaged by relationships among women which cross cultures, classes, and sexual choices," she wrote in "An Imaginative Collectivity." "It's far more interesting to make connections between lesbians and heterosexual women than simply to write about a particular group all the time."

While Miner's works do contain many lesbian characters and discussions of sexual identity, none of them focuses exclusively or even primarily on the issue of sexual preference. Her stories about the difficulty of coming out as a lesbian are couched within larger narratives such as that in *Blood Sisters,* about women's struggles as members of the Irish Republican Army, or that in *All Good Women,* about the effects of World War II on working-class women in San Francisco. In addition, two of her novels are focused on women whose sexual identity is ambiguous. *Murder in the English Department,* for example, deals with Nan Weaver's attempt to protect a female graduate student who killed her sexist professor as he attempted to rape her. The novel's focus is clearly on the difficulties Nan encounters as she tries to secure tenure, fight sexual harassment on campus, and reconcile with her working-class family. Her sexual identity, about which she has not yet made up her mind, plays a very minor role in the narrative. In *Winter's Edge,* Miner's main characters are two elderly working-class women, one of whom is heterosexual, the other whose sexual preference is never discussed. "Why do some people presume Chrissie MacInnes is a heterosexual?," Miner wrote in "An Imaginative Collectivity." In this novel, again, the focus is not on sexuality but on the intervention of politics into everyday life as the two women clash over a local election.

The theme of working-class families has also been central to Miner's work. Her novel, *A Walking Fire,* is a retelling of Shakespeare's *King Lear,* told from Cordelia's point of view and set in a working-class American family. The novel is a critique of working-class men's involvement in the Vietnam war and a psychological exploration of a family. In her interview with Perry, Miner explained that she has consciously developed "an unapologetic interest in the lives of working-class people." While she felt reluctant at first to focus on them in her fiction, she has felt the necessity of "coming out as someone who grew up in a working-class family." Related to this decision was the desire for honesty that informed her coming out as a lesbian. She told Perry, "for me, being out as a lesbian has to do with honesty and the vitality I get from honesty. It isn't a moral act or a question of conscience so much as it's a way of engaging more fully in the world by being who I am."

It is precisely this honesty about her identity as lesbian and working-class that has been the most difficult, and the most important, issue for her to explore in her fiction. Miner considers her collection of essays, *Rumors from the Cauldron,* to be her most autobiographical work. "Six months before that book came out I wanted to pull it back; I was so embarrassed by the notion of all that self-revelation," she told Perry. The book includes essays that illuminate her origins as a writer, analyses of and interviews with other women writers like Margaret Atwood and Adrienne Rich, and selections from her extensive list of book reviews over the years.

Miner's next project is a cross-genre book called *Capturing Fog* that will be comprised of both fiction and non-fiction. The book is based on her working-class immigrant family and is about "moving across continents and cultures," she said in an interview with *GLL* contributor Anne Boyd. Uniting the threads of her many interests and concerns, this book will explore more overtly the autobiographical themes that have informed her work and made her a sympathetic, honest teller of many women's stories.

—Anne Boyd

MOHR, Richard Drake

Nationality: American philosopher, gay pundit, and social critic. **Born:** Portland, Oregon, 24 October 1950. **Education:** Univer-

sity of Chicago, B.A. 1972; University of Toronto, M.A. in Philosophy, 1973, Ph.D. 1977. **Family:** Companion of Robert W. Switzer, from 1978. **Career:** Professor, University of Illinois-Urbana Champaign, from 1978; founding editor, *Between Men, Between Women: Lesbian and Gay Studies From Columbia University,* 1989-91; editorial board member, *Journal of Gay, Lesbian and Bisexual Identity* and *Journal of Homosexuality.* **Address:** University of Illinois, Department of Philosophy, 105 Gregory Hall, 810 South Wright, Urbana, Illinois 61801.

WRITINGS

Nonfiction

Gays/Justice: A Study of Ethics, Society and Law. New York, Columbia University Press, 1988.
Gay Ideas: Outing and Other Controversies. Boston, Beacon Press, 1992.
A More Perfect Union: Why Straight America Must Stand Up For Gay Rights. Boston, Beacon Press, 1994.

Selected Essays

"Teaching a Gay Issues Class in a Philosophy Department," in *APA Newsletter on Teaching Philosophy,* Vol. 3, No. 1, 1981, 6-7.
"Gay Rights," in *Social Theory and Practice: A Journal of Social Philosophy,* Vol. 8, 1982, 31-41.
"Gay Studies in the Big Ten: A Survivor's Manual," in *Teaching Philosophy,* Vol. 7, 1984, 97-108.
"AIDS, Gay Life, State Coercion," in *Raritan: A Quarterly Review,* Vol. 6, No. 1, 1986, 38-62.
"Policy, Ritual, Purity: Gays and Mandatory AIDS Testing," in *Law, Medicine and Health Care,* Vol. 15, No. 4, winter 1987/88, 178-185.
"AIDS, Gays and the Insurance Industry," in *AIDS, Ethics and Public Policy,* edited by Donald VanDeVeer and Christine Pierce. Wadsworth Publishing, 1988, 138-139.
"Gay Law and the Future for Civil Rights," in *Report from the Institute for Philosophy and Public Policy,* Vol. 12, No. 4, 1992, 12-16.
"The Case for Gay Marriage," in *Notre Dame Journal of Law, Ethics and Public Policy,* Vol. 9, 1994, 219-243.
"The Perils of Postmodernity for Gay Rights," in *Canadian Journal of Law and Jurisprudence,* Vol. 8, No. 1, January 1995, 5-18.

*

Richard Mohr comments:

Before turning my literary attentions to gay issues in the early 1980s, I wrote tangled articles on ancient philosophy. I can barely force myself to look upon those pieces now. The change of subject matter transformed my prose—from artless to crafted, muddy to stylish. Paradoxically, passion and personal engagement enhanced clarity and order.

My first gay article was autobiographical. In the Spring of 1981, I taught my university's first-ever gay studies class—in an Intersession format, three hours a day, five days a week, for three weeks. The students consisted largely of straight women and black football players. The supercharged subject, compressed timing, and tricky demographics combined to make the course one of the most intense and congested experiences of my life. Before getting on with that life, I had to get that class out of my mind, where it just kept spinning around like an all-absorbing black hole. So I wrote about it. And that did the trick. The resulting bittersweet essay, "Gay Studies in the Big Ten: A Survivor's Manual," circulated first within my discipline through the academic journal *Teaching Philosophy*; it reached a wider and gayer audience when it was reprinted in *Christopher Street* and from there by copyright-defying xerox and postal carrier it spread chain-letter fashion across the gay intellectual scene.

This piece cast a mold for my later writing. My gay pieces have frequently played hopscotch along the boundary separating the academic from the popular. An idea that I first bruit about in a law review article can carom into a gay press op-ed that pops up next to an ad for penis enlargers before bouncing from there into a university press anthology.

Further, my gay writings have served me well—well, well enough—as a form of therapy. Not that writing cures anything, but for me it does disperse obsessions. Writing tosses mental knots out beyond thought, breaks up endlessly repeating internal voices, offers release from focusing on things too much.

It does so in part because it induces trances and ecstasies. As in a child's absorption in games, the concentration entailed in writing—just me and the words—and the very mechanics of writing—just me and the screen and the keys—combine to push away the rest of the world with all its luring furies. As in sex, time and space recede from the writer's experience of the world. And writing is ecstatic in another way too. Even as writing seems to push the world away, it also makes one feel thrown beyond the world, indeed beyond oneself. This is "ecstacy" in that term's etymological sense, "a standing outside of (oneself)." As with electroshock therapy, though, it only works if it rattles one into relaxation.

Writing also helps kill habits and fixations by exteriorizing their objects. Getting an obsession, even a pleasant one, out of the mind and onto paper causes me to cease thinking about it. I virtually never return to an old idea with new arguments and insights. This diffidence is not chiefly the result of laziness, dogmatism, or self-love. The function of writing for me has not in the main been to savor or tout an idea, but simply to stop having to think of it anymore. Friends find it perverse that after I wrote a passionate testament of mourning triggered by the initial displays of the NAMES Project's AIDS quilt, I have never made an effort to view the Quilt again. But I didn't write the piece to establish a cult of the Quilt; I wrote the piece so that I could obsess somewhat less about AIDS.

Not that all the killing which writing does is a good thing. For years, my partner and I had a private ritual of scratching our beards together as a substitute or supplement to smooching. I mentioned the ritual in the introduction to my first gay book, *Gays/Justice*, and, whammy, as soon as we'd both read the galleys, we dropped the ritual.

From the outside, writing may look like a miniature version of empire building, an aggrandizing extension of ones' self through the world, but its inner work is that of coring-out—evisceration, excavation, evacuation. A really good writer should be able to combine through his words the best of euthanasia and suicide.

Though writing for me is mostly a self-indulgent, masturbatory activity, it is not simply that. Indeed in the beginning, I had rather high hopes for what my writings might do for others—hopes that even if my repeated efforts failed to have much impact in the world at large, at least they might help steer gay people's energies and politics in the direction of justice. I would accomplish this task, I figured, by sketching out where we ought to be and what we ought to be doing to get there. As far as I can tell, this evangelical project has been a complete bust.

Humbler now, I believe (to steal a metaphor from Annette Baier) that the most a thinker can do for a people is to serve them as the prompter at an opera performance does the dons and divas on stage. Perched out of general sight below the stage's front edge, the prompter helps the overburdened and accident-prone singers to remember their lines. The prompter does not write the lines; the thinker does not generate new values in the world. All he or she can do is to call on, call up, spark recollection of ideas already present in people's minds.

Though modest, this role of the thinker is more important than it may at first appear, especially if one believes, as I do, that people have a better side to their natures, one which is forever losing out to self-interest, or more often to merely hoped-for self-interest, but which remains latent in the soul to be invoked by the right prompter.

In the case of gay folk, my task has been to remind the brethren more times than they care to hear that there are values of dignity and honor which are more important than, and should stand as trumps over, the values of happiness and well-being. This is a message which a downtrodden people tacitly knows but is prone to forget in its struggles for survival. It is a message at which most gays bridle, for deep down they know it is true even as they rationalize their failures to live by its call. Already ill-at-ease in the cosmos, they end up blaming the messenger for their moral dissonance. Those especially resistant to the message are political gays, who think that justice is to be found just around the corner if only we endorse enough candidates who say they love us even as they advance their own interests by degrading us.

Some intellectual friends call me a Jeremiah wannabe; but in this era of objectifying political backlash mounted in response to gays' considerable cultural progress, calling me Cassandra might hit nearer the mark.

Still, for me there's much pleasure to be taken from confecting lines which clatter through the mind like dice tumbling across ceramic tiles—even if the casts almost always come up snake-eyes.

*　　　*　　　*

Perhaps the most severe test of the strength of any movement espousing a particular type of social change is its ability to frame and achieve coherent intellectual dialogue with its opponents and critics on disputed issues of ethics and morality. While the general public may not be widely aware of specific debates, the overall credibility of positions set out by leaders (and hence the willingness of the public to support or deny the legitimacy of claims that change is required) will depend to a great extent on the fit of the logic of movement rhetoric with accepted social values. It is in the area of definition, formulation, and articulation of the philosophy of contemporary gay and lesbian politics that Richard Mohr has made his most significant contributions.

Trained as a philosopher with specializations in Plato, Aristotle, and ethics, Mohr began his involvement as theoretician of the gay movement with the appearance in 1987 of two articles objecting to the then-debated idea of mandatory testing for HIV. The articles stand as forerunners to the appearance in 1988 of a group of 14 essays collectively entitled *Gays/Justice: A Study of Ethics, Society and Law.* His stated intention in this volume was "to inform the general audience of gay experience" and provide the intellectual foundation for necessary social change in a manner similar to Gunnar Myrdal's study of government-sponsored segregation in the United States, *An American Dilemma.* Beginning with the premise that "society at large does not know what to think about gays," Mohr addressed topics ranging from an overview of social attitudes toward homosexuals through discussions of the scope of constitutional immunities against the coercive powers of government (including sodomy laws), arguments for civil rights legislation, and redefinitions of acceptable deployments of state powers occasioned by AIDS, and the growing field of gay studies. The final section explores the evolution of Mohr's own thoughts on the role of reason in creating justice and his endorsement of civil disobedience, based on the ideals of classical liberalism, such as the refusal to abdicate individual dignity.

By 1992, when Mohr's second volume, *Gay Ideas,* appeared, the idea of civil disobedience as an imperative moral act for gay people had been brought to full public development by such organizations as ACT UP and Queer Nation. The essays in this collection both built upon the discussion begun in *Gays/Justice* (expanding it from consideration of specific civil issues to the more general subject of the relationship between a community and its surrounding society) and addressed the broader areas of politics, culture, and identity. One of the more controversial tactics of the new decade was deliberately making public the sexual orientation of an individual without his or her consent, termed "outing." The opening essay of *Gay Ideas* is perhaps the best explication of the place of this action within a moral context, with Mohr strongly challenging opponents of the practice whose arguments are based on privacy, and accepted conventions of secrecy and silence (both within and outside the gay community). The clear explication of the moral framework supporting outing given here was used as the foundation for later writings such as Michelangelo Signorile's 1993 treatise *Queer In America.*

Concern for the definition of and promotion of informed dialogue about the situation of gay people in America was continued in his third book, *A More Perfect Union.* In its preface, Mohr states his belief that "drawing attention to that which is special about gay experience and applying to that experience moral precepts and arguments which Americans as a people have worked through in other areas of national life" will fill a perceptible void in public thought, policy, and discussion relating to gays.

Mohr's works are intended to challenge a plethora of hidden assumptions involved in any discussion of gay rights and the definitions used to address the realities of the lives of gay people prevalent in social policy, and offer a carefully crafted intellectual basis for effective political and philosophical dialogue. His ideas have been widely disseminated both within the academic community and through popular journals and newspapers, serving both the gay and lesbian community and the mainstream society. And his public lectures have become influential in framing discussions of the course of the evolution of a contemporary gay civil presence.

—Robert B. Marks Ridinger

MOLLOY, Sylvia

Nationality: Argentinean literary critic, professor, and novelist. **Born:** Buenos Aires, 29 August 1938. **Education:** Université de Paris, Sorbonne, Licence es Lettres, 1960, Diplome D'Etudes Superieures, 1961, Doctorat, 1967. **Career:** Assistant professor of Spanish, State University of New York, Buffalo, 1967-69, and Vassar College, Poughkeepsie, New York, 1969-70; assistant professor of Spanish, 1970-73, associate professor of Spanish, 1973-81, Emory L. Ford Professor of Spanish, 1981-86, Princeton University, Princeton, New Jersey; professor of Spanish, Yale University, New Haven, Connecticut, 1986-90; Albert Schweitzer Professor of Humanities, New York University, from 1990. **Awards:** American Philosophical Society fellow, 1970; National Endowment for the Humanities fellowship, 1976; Social Science Research Council grant, 1983; Guggenheim Foundation fellowship, 1986-87. **Address:** Spanish and Portuguese Language and Literature, 19 University Place, #406, New York, New York 10003, U.S.A.

WRITINGS

Fiction

En breve cárcel. Barcelona, Seix Barral, 1981; as *Certificate of Absence,* translated by Daniel Balderston and Molloy, Austin, University of Texas Press, 1989.

Literary Criticism

La Diffusion de la littérature hispano-americaine en France au XXe siècle. Paris, Presses Universitaires de France, 1972.
Las letras de Borges. Buenos Aires, Sudamericana, 1979; as *Signs of Borges,* translated by Oscar Montero and Molloy, Durham, North Carolina, Duke University Press, 1994.
At Face Value: Autobiographical Writing in Spanish America. Cambridge, Cambridge University Press, 1991.
With Sara Castro-Klarén and Beatriz Sarlo, *Women's Writing in Latin America.* Boulder, Colorado, Westview Press, 1991.

Selected Essays

"Too Wilde for Comfort: Desire and Ideology in Fin-de-siècle Latin America," in *Social Text,* No. 31/32, 1992, 187-201.
"Decadentismo e Ideologia: Economias de Desejo na América Hispánica Finissecular" (Decadentism and Ideology: Economies of Desire in Fin-de-siècle Spanish America), in *Literatura e Historia na América Latina* (Literature and History in Latin America), edited by Ligia Chiappini and Flávio Wolf de Aguiar. São Paulo, Brazil, Editora da Universidade de São Paulo, 1993.
"Dissecting Autobiography: The Strange Case of Dr. Wilde," in *Journal of Interdisciplinary Studies,* Vol. 5, No. 1, 1993, 119-130.
"His America, Our America: José Marti Reads Walt Whitman," in *Breaking Bounds: Walt Whitman and American Cultural Studies,* edited by Betsy Erkkila and Jay Grossman. Oxford, Oxford University Press, 1995.
"Disappearing Acts: Reading Lesbian in Teresa de la Parra," in *¿Entiendes? Queer Readings, Hispanic Writings,* edited by Emilie Bergmann and Paul Julian Smith. Durham, North Carolina, Duke University Press, 1995.

"Mock Heroics and Personal Markings," in *PMLA*, Vol. 3, No. 5, 1996, 1072-1075.

"From Sappho to Baffo: Diverting the Sexual in Alejandra Pizarnik," in *Sex and Sexuality in Latin America*, edited by Daniel Balderston and Donna Guy. New York, New York University Press, 1997.

*

Interviews: "Sylvia Molloy" by Magdalena Garcia Pinto, in *Women Writers of Latin America: Intimate Histories*, translated by Trudy Balch and Magdalena Garcia Pinto, Austin, University of Texas Press, 1991, 125-143.

Critical Sources: *Gay and Lesbian Themes in Latin American Writing* by David William Foster, Austin, University of Texas Press, 1991, 110-114; "Boundaries Around Identity: Sylvia Molloy's *Certificate of Absence* and the Autobiographical Process" by Virginia Lawreck Muzquiz, in *Monographic Review/Revista Monográfica* (Odessa, Texas), Vol. 9, 1993, 176-188.

*   *   *

Sylvia Molloy's *Certificate of Absence* is one of the first Latin American novels centered on lesbian experiences. Its narrator/protagonist writes the story of her relationship to another woman upon returning to the rented room in which they wrestled through their love. As she writes, she both invokes the lost lover and attempts to free herself from her. The issue of doubleness—the simultaneous evocation and erasure of her past love—forms a central trope in her writing. Significantly, this doubleness is not an endless process. Rather, it serves to enable the construction of some other space, an other identity.

In an interview with Magdalena Garcia Pinto published in *Women Writers of Latin America: Intimate Histories*, Molloy says of her somewhat autobiographical novel:

> My first impulse was to see if I could rid myself of these ghosts.... What stimulated me wasn't just the intuition that I was trying to get something out of myself but that I wanted to distance all this in order to do *something more*. My goal had changed. Now I was composing, actively inserting this material into a fictional context.... And the novel was a way of spying on myself, of spying on the material I'd tried to take out of myself by using third person.

As Molloy herself indicates, her use of third person narration adds a sense of distance and voyeurism to the narrative. It serves as a constant reminder that we as readers are spying on the action of the novel from an outside vantage point, doubly removed from its scene. In part, this sense of voyeurism allows for the normalizing of lesbianism that characterizes the novel.

In *Gay and Lesbian Themes in Latin American Writing*, David William Foster points to the uniqueness of Molloy's treatment of lesbianism in the novel—that is, though emotional relationships are problematized, lesbianism is not. *Certificate of Absence* is clearly focused on the protagonist's connection to the women in her life and to her father. In this way, lesbianism is represented as a fully constituted sexual identity. Upon this identity the rest of the text is layered. Yet the issue of sexual identity, the struggle and conflict over it, does not form a central concern of the narrative. In a similar vein, Molloy has worked toward an understanding and acceptance of gay and lesbian sensibilities in her critical writing.

Given her position as a literary scholar, one could argue that Molloy's recent work on "queering the hispanic canon" (the title of a conference organized by her in New York City) places her at the center of that endeavor. In this sense, she is a critical figure in gay and lesbian studies as both a novelist and a literary critic. The elision of her roles as writer and critic becomes for her a source of vitality. Speaking of the connections between her various writings, Molloy says in her interview with Garcia Pinto, "the practice of criticism strengthens my fiction, and my fiction is made of the threads of all the writers' voices that come together in my own." The efficacy of this convergence is difficult to deny.

The body of Molloy's literary criticism is vast. Significantly, the doubling image of the mask recurs in her works that treat homosexuality. In several of her writings she uses the mask as a tool that dissimulates, that splits the self and other. In *Certificate of Absence* the mask that the protagonist assumes affords her both freedom of expression and a shield against unwanted scrutiny of her relationships. Similarly in her critical writing on the Venezuelan novelist Teresa de la Parra, she reads the mask as an autobiographical tool. In her contribution to *¿Entiendes?: Queer Readings, Hispanic Writings* titled "Disappearing Acts: Reading Lesbian in Teresa de la Parra," Molloy highlights the ways in which de la Parra constructs fictional parallels with her life that afford her a greater freedom of expression than straightforward autobiography. In her use of "oblique autobiography," Molloy believes de la Parra "tempts us with resemblance, only to stress difference." The mask appears again in her *At Face Value: Autobiographical Writing in Spanish America*, where she asserts: "Self-expression is, necessarily, a process of *alteration*: one speaks through the voice of an *other* even if that other...is a simulacrum of oneself."

This doubling and masking works not only to dissimulate sexual identity. It also underscores the distancing of exile that runs across the body of Molloy's work. The protagonist of *Certificate of Absence*, born in Buenos Aires, is in exile. In her critical writings on de la Parra and Gabriela Mistral, Molloy reads their exile as necessary escape from what she calls the "heterosexual regimentation" of Latin American society. Their geo-political exile is presented as parallel to the exile in their writing, the masking they resort to in order to express the self.

Throughout her work we feel the tension of play between the autobiographical drive and the tendency toward masking or doubling. The uses of the personal for Molloy involve performance or, as she says in her essay "Mock Heroics and Personal Markings": "By advocating the use of the personal, by calling it an effect or a pose, I am not thinking of it as a posture of little consequence but respecting it as a calculated move, a political act, the only way at times to draw attention to the necessary duplicity of all texts and discourses." Through this duplicity and doubling, a different and clearer representation of lesbianism and sexual identities emerges on the world stage.

—Elizabeth A. Marchant

MORGAN, Robin

Nationality: American journalist, poet, and essayist. **Born:** Lake Worth, Florida, 29 January 1941. **Education:** Wetter School,

Mount Vernon, New York, graduating with honors in 1956; privately tutored in the U.S. and abroad, 1956-59; attended literature classes at Columbia University in her late teens. **Family:** Married Kenneth Pitchford in 1962; one child. **Career:** Writer, activist, public speaker, and occasional university lecturer; member, Women's Liberation Caucus, CORE (Congress on Racial Equality) and SNCC (Student Nonviolent Coordinating Committee), 1965-66; founder, New York Women's Center, 1969; founding member, WITCH (Women's International Terrorist Conspiracy from Hell); Editor-in-Chief, 1989-93, international consulting editor, from 1993, *Ms.* magazine. Contributor of articles to periodicals, including *Amazon Quarterly, Chrysalis, Everywoman, Los Angeles Times, New York Times, Off Our Backs, Second Wave, Sojourner, Village Voice, Voice of Women,* and others. **Awards:** National Endowment for the Arts Literature Grant in Poetry, 1979-80; Front Page Award, for distinguished journalism, 1981; Wonder Woman Award for International Peace and Understanding, 1982; Ford Foundation Grants, 1982, 1983, 1984; Kentucky Foundation for Women Literature Grant, 1986; "Woman of the Year" Award, Feminist Majority Foundation, 1990; Editorial Excellence citation, *Utne Reader,* 1991; Exceptional Merit in Journalism Award, National Women's Political Caucus, 1991; Warrior Woman Award for Promoting Racial Understanding, Asian American Women's Organization, 1992; Special Achievement Award, Association for Education in Journalism and Communication, 1993; honorary doctorate: University of Connecticut at Storrs, 1992. **Address:** c/o *Ms. Magazine,* 230 Park Avenue, New York, New York 10169-0799, U.S.A.

WRITINGS

Fiction

Dry Your Smile: A Novel. New York, Doubleday, 1987; London, Women's Press, 1988.
The Mer-Child: A Legend for Children and Other Adults. New York, Feminist Press, 1991.

Nonfiction

Going Too Far: The Personal Chronicles of a Feminist (essays). New York, Random House, 1977.
The Anatomy of Freedom. New York, Doubleday/Anchor, and London, Blackwell's/Oxford, 1984.
The Demon Lover: On the Sexuality of Terrorism. New York, W. W. Norton, and London, Methuen, 1989.
The Word of a Woman: Feminist Dispatches (essays). 2nd edition, London, Virago, 1993; New York, W. W. Norton, 1994.

Poetry

Monster: Poems. New York, Random House, 1972.
Lady of the Beasts: Poems. New York, Random House, 1976.
Death Benefits. Port Townsend, Washington, Copper Canyon Press, 1981.
Depth Perception: New Poems and a Masque. New York, Doubleday/Anchor, 1982.
Upstairs in the Garden: Selected and New Poems. New York, W. W. Norton, 1990.

Editor

Sisterhood Is Powerful: An Anthology of Writings from the Women's Liberation Movement. New York, Random House, 1970.
With Joanne Cooke and Charlotte Bunch-Weeks, *The New Woman.* New York, Fawcett, 1970.
Sisterhood Is Global: The International Women's Movement Anthology. New York, Doubleday/Anchor, 1984; London, Penguin, 1985.

*

Critical Sources: *American Women Since 1945* by Robin Gatlin, Jackson, University Press of Mississippi, 1987; "Robin Morgan" by Blanche Wiesen Cook, in *Contemporary Lesbian Writers of the United States: A Bio-Bibliographical Critical Sourcebook,* edited by Sandra Pollack and Denise D. Knight, Connecticut, Greenwood Press, 1993, 384-389; *Gay and Lesbian Rights: A Reference Handbook* by David Newton, California, Instructional Horizons, Inc., 1994.

*   *   *

Robin Morgan made a name for herself as a major figure in the contemporary U.S. feminist movement by editing one of the most influential texts on feminism, *Sisterhood Is Powerful* (1970). Morgan writes in her introduction that the process of editing the book radically changed her position on the Movement. Prior to writing the book, she had believed the Women's Liberation Movement to be an important "wing" of the Left, did not believe that she herself was oppressed, and was hostile toward those women who depended on the Movement for emotional support. But Morgan's views changed as she worked with other women in composing the text and became increasingly aware of the lack of cooperation from the "male" Left. After women writers for the left wing journal *Rat* seized the paper and renamed it *Women's Rat,* Morgan's contribution to the first issue, entitled "Goodbye to All That," announced her "farewell to working with men on the Left."

Several of Morgan's works attempt to put the Movement into perspective. Morgan has argued that the early 1960s Women's Liberation Movement was much more diverse than historians have acknowledged, and that the media helped distort public perception of the Movement by focusing only on white, middle-class feminists, ignoring the Chicano and Black women who were also part of the early Movement. Yet she doesn't hesitate to admit that tensions within the Movement alienated some women. According to Morgan, most women activists were hostile to housewives, many were anti-motherhood, and there was a major split between lesbians and heterosexuals. In *Going Too Far,* she argued that this separatism was encouraged by the media and by gay organizations in an effort to destroy the Women's Liberation Movement:

> They said we were "a lesbian plot," and the carefully implanted and fostered bigotry of many heterosexual feminists rose eagerly to deny that, thereby driving many lesbian women out of the movement, back into the arms of their gay "brothers," who promptly shoved mimeograph machines at them.

Morgan is considered by many to be one of the most influential spokeswomen for both the lesbian and feminist movements.

However, Morgan herself might be disturbed by the distinction made between the two movements. In her much-published 1973 keynote address, "Lesbianism and Feminism," delivered at the West Coast Lesbian Feminist Conference in Los Angeles and included in the collection *Going Too Far,* Morgan berated those lesbians who caved into the lesbian/hetero divisiveness orchestrated by the media and the male Left and gay movements. Although she publicly identified herself as bisexual in the *New York Times,* Morgan was continuously harassed by both lesbians and heterosexuals, either for selling out by marrying a man and having a male child, or for "hating" men. Her speech revealed both her anger and frustration. She began by defining herself as a woman and a feminist who is married to a "faggot-effeminist" (a self-descriptive term used by homosexual men who broke with the Gay Liberation Front for its oppression of women and effeminate men). She pleaded for a recognition that "lesbians are the minority, women the majority," and that only united will they succeed against male oppression. Sardonically, she did not call for unity, but encouraged women to replace the lesbian/straight split with the feminist/collaborator split, arguing that the war is between men and women, not lesbians and straights. She rebuked those lesbians who supported a male in drag who crashed the conference: "We know what's at work when whites wear blackface; the same thing is at work when men wear drag." And she argued that some lesbians were adopting male attitudes that only emphasized their collaboration with the enemy: black leather; contempt for monogamous lesbians; the anti-intellectualism and downward mobility of the male-dominated Left. The speech concluded with a prayer to the Goddess, alluding to the irony that some feminists continue to pray to a male god for relief from male oppression.

Morgan's poetry reveals her early love for women. In her collection *Monster,* "Lesbian Poem" is dedicated to those who open the book to this particular poem first. Other poems detail both the complications and pleasures of women loving women. Although much of her writing, particularly since the late 1970s, is quite personal, including love letters to her husband, Morgan has written very little about her childhood, her parents, or her life before marriage. Yet her 1987 novel *Dry Your Smile* offers a number of insights into the author's early life. The protagonist, Julian Travis, who quotes Mary McCarthy's line "Only in fiction can I tell the truth," is a 45-year-old woman who, as a child, was on a television series called "Family"; Morgan herself was the child star of the 1950s series "Mama." Travis marries at age 18 to escape a suffocating mother, embraces the feminist movement at age 25, and, after her 25-year marriage to a feminist husband ends, falls in love with a possessive woman, Iliana, in a subconscious attempt to exorcise her mother's hold on her.

The lesbian theme of the novel is foreshadowed in the opening quote, a Caribbean proverb: "When a woman loves a woman, it is the blood of the mothers speaking." Iliana, a lesbian who occasionally sleeps with men, has been in love with Julian since they first met at a women's group meeting. At first, in keeping with her emotional denial, Julian defends lesbians in general to her homophobic friends by referring to Iliana, a lesbian who is able to be a close friend with no sexual attachment. Later, she recognizes that Iliana has loved her from the start. Their affair does not begin until Julian's marriage falls apart, and with Iliana, Julian discovers her sexuality for the first time. Julian's (temporary) return to her husband is not unexpected by Iliana or the reader:

> "Oh no, my love. A cliché as tedious as a photograph
> of a baby nose-to-nose with a kitten. The lesbian lover

who infuses her heterosexual beloved with energy—which then gets drained from that relationship and reinvested in the beloved's worn out marriage."

But the marriage ends, and Julian returns to Iliana for mothering before reenacting her childhood escape from her mother's overbearing love. *Dry Your Smile* manages to be both provoking (Julian is too often self-centered and manipulative to be an admirable heroine) and entertaining. Despite being the autobiographical first novel of a feminist activist, a bisexual lesbian, the novel is surprisingly satisfying rather than polemical. It is a brutally honest portrayal of relationships with family, friends and lovers, both male and female.

Morgan has remained a feminist activist since the 1970s, and was involved in the founding of the radical group WITCH (Women's International Terrorist Conspiracy from Hell.) In 1989 she took the high profile position of editor-in-chief of the floundering feminist magazine, *Ms.* The first issue under her charge sold out within a matter of days, and she aided the magazine's turnaround before resigning her post to become an international consulting editor in 1993.

—Stacey Donohue

MORROW, Bruce Shannon

Nationality: American author of nonfiction and fiction. **Born:** Cleveland, Ohio, 12 March 1963. **Education:** Rochester Institute of Technology, New York (R.I.T./Xerox Grant, 1981-85), B.S. in Biology 1985; Columbia University, New York, M.F.A. in Fiction 1992. **Career:** Lab manager and molecular biology research assistant, College of Physicians and Surgeons, Columbia University, New York City, 1986-92; administrator, writer, and curator of contemporary art gallery, Information Gallery, New York City, 1992-93; circulation assistant, Cardozo School of Law, Yeshiva University, New York City, 1993-94; associate director, Teachers and Writers Collaborative, New York City, from 1994. Editorial board member, *Columbia: A Magazine of Poetry and Prose,* Columbia University, 1991-92; contributing editor, *Callaloo: A Journal of African-American and African Arts and Letters,* from 1995; judge, Gregory Kolovakos Seed Grant Awards, for Outstanding New Literary Magazines, 1996; contributor of scientific articles to scholarly periodicals, including *American Journal of Physiology, Circulation,* and *Journal of Bone and Mineral Research.* **Awards:** Pushcart Prize nomination, for short story, 1994; Frederick Douglass Fellowship for Young African-American Fiction Writers, 1995-97; Lambda Literary Award nomination, for best gay and lesbian anthology/fiction, 1996. **Address:** Teachers & Writers Collaborative, 5 Union Square West, New York, New York 10003-3306, U.S.A.

WRITINGS

Fiction

"A Play" (short story), in *Callaloo: A Journal of African-American and African Arts and Letters,* Vol. 16, No. 2, spring 1993; in *Ancestral House: The Black Short Story in the Americas and Europe,* edited by Charles Rowell, Boulder, Colorado, Westview Press, 1995.

Editor, with Charles Rowell, *Shade: An Anthology of Short Fiction by Gay Men of African Descent.* New York, Avon Books,
1996.
"All, Nothing" (short story), in *Shade: An Anthology of Short Fiction by Gay Men of African Descent.* New York, Avon Books,
1996.
"Near the End of the World" (short story), in *Go the Way Your
Blood Beats: An Anthology of Lesbian and Gay Fiction by African-American Writers,* edited by Shawn Stewart Ruff. New York,
Henry Holt, 1996.

Nonfiction

"Black and Gay: A Highwire Act" (essay), in *New York Times,* 6
November 1994.
"Bruce Morrow's Read and Read Again List," in *aRude Maga-
zine,* Vol. 1, No. 1, spring 1995.
"An Interview with Isaac Julien," in *Callaloo,* Vol. 18, No. 2,
spring 1995.
"An Interview with Isaac Julien," in *Fuse Magazine* (Canada), Vol.
18, No. 4, summer 1995.
"Rules of the Bone," in *aRude Magazine,* Vol. 1, No. 2, fall 1995.
"Bruce Morrow's Read and Read Again List," in *aRude Maga-
zine,* Vol. 1, No. 2, fall 1995.
"Things Have Taken a Turn for the Worse" (memoir), in *Speak
My Name: Black Masculinity and the American Dream,* edited
by Don Belton. Boston, Beacon Press, 1995.
"An Interview with Virgie Patton-Ezelle," in *Callaloo,* Vol. 19,
No. 1, winter 1996.

*   *   *

Bruce Morrow's work as a fiction writer and editor has helped
to broaden the view of African-American gay fiction in America
and abroad. Through *Shade: An Anthology of Fiction by Gay Men
of African Descent,* which he co-edited with Charles H. Rowell,
and his own fiction, Morrow highlights a new era in gay literature
and literary studies: one in which African-American, openly-gay
authors, write and are being published, with full recognition of
their dual ethnicity, while not limiting the central issues of their
work to those of race or sexuality. In the introduction to *Shade,*
author Samuel R. Delany wrote, of the anthology, that "[n]ot all
the stories are about being gay—nor even all of them about being
black. But there is an energy evident enough here and common to
most that should...make any writer pleased and proud to be of
such company." As editors of this groundbreaking collection—
the first anthology of African-American gay fiction—Morrow and
Rowell, strove to and succeeded in displaying the diversity of
voices writing within their community.

The publication and success of *Shade* demonstrate just how far
America has come from the homo-repressive days of the Harlem
Renaissance, when Richard Bruce Nugent dared publish his short
story "Smoke, Lilies and Jade" in November 1926 in the pages of
the literary magazine *Fire!!,* and the 1960s when few besides James
Baldwin, with his 1962 novel *Another Country,* treated the subject of being gay within the context of the black community.
Though the 1980s would see the birth of several small literary
magazines and newspapers, including *Blacklight, Habari-Daftari,
Blackheart* and *Moja: Black and Gay,* it was not until 1986 that
black gay writing was anthologized, with the publication of Joseph Beam's *In the Life: A Black Gay Anthology.* Beam wrote in

his introduction, "Together we are making history.... We are bringing into the light the lives which we have led in the shadows." *In
the Life* was, in a sense, a call to arms. Other Countries, the black
gay writers' collective was formed in June of the same year in
New York City. It is from this empowering literary heritage that
Bruce Morrow draws and builds.

Morrow wrote about his experience with Other Countries in
his *New York Times* article, "Black and Gay: A Highwire Act,"
saying, "[t]here are about 10 people at the meeting. Each is a continuum of the possibilities of being black and gay.... I find myself
reveling in their wisdom and generosity, their ability to see that
life is infinitely more complex than any label or category—gay or
straight, black or white, male or female." It is here that Morrow's
work as an editor and writer departs from the tradition of black
gay anthologies like *In the Life, Brother to Brother, Other Countries: Black Gay Voices,* and *Sojourner: Black Gay Voices in the
Age of AIDS*: Morrow's writing is authored by gay African-Americans, but deals with a wide range of subjects, settings, and points
of view aside from those referenced in the titles above. In his memoir, "Things Have Taken A Turn for the Worse," Morrow says to
his stepfather, "I'm gay, and maybe you think that's illegal, but
it's not." As a writer Morrow has owned who he is, and has taken
the freedom to write about other issues that he holds close.

In an interview with G. Winston James, Morrow said, "I am
obsessed with the ideas of powerlessness, being an outsider, race,
and AIDS." It is these themes which are most in evidence in his
work. In his first published short fiction, the 1993 "A Play," which
was nominated for the following year's Pushcart Prize for best
short story, Morrow artfully treats all of these issues. The protagonist is Donald, an African-American who, in the first-person,
recollects his abused youth, muses on his first inter-racial relationship with the son of a wealthy family, and performs a "show"
as a metaphor for his life as a sensitive, gay man who is out to a
public which includes his parents. Donald says, "I close my eyes
often, but I still see everything.... My eyes avoid all ugliness, but
then I look in the mirror and I see myself." This statement ap-
proximates Morrow's own response when asked how he selects
the subject matter for his fiction. "I wish I could choose what I
write about," Morrow told G. Winston James, "but a lot of times
I write about things I don't want to.... This helps me, though, to
discover and learn more about aspects of myself."

It is not surprising then that we find Morrow's protagonists to
be isolated, pondering, and often philosophical gay men. His characters do not, however, so much question their homosexuality,
their race, or their health; rather, Morrow's characters are preoccupied with their relationships, the significance of their pasts, their
sense of belonging to a community (usually ethnic/geographical or
emotional), and themselves. By and large, sexuality and race are
givens with which Morrow's protagonists watch others wrestle.
This is as true of Donald, who reminds his mother, "I told you I
was gay.... Remember?" as it is of Paul, the white main character
in Morrow's "All, Nothing," who "has resigned himself, at the
age of twenty-five, to a life of aloneness."

Morrow's character, Melvin, in "Near the End of the World" is
the most preoccupied with sexuality and AIDS of any of the leads
in his published fiction. Having moved to California, Melvin meets
Tasha, a middle-aged tattoo artist, who helps to relieve his anxiety attacks, the visions of vines binding and smothering him, that
he began having at 16 after the death of his father's lover. Melvin
is carrying his father's ashes in his back-pack and the memories
of having cared for him until his death in his head. While Melvin's

concern is ostensibly his coming to terms with his father's death from AIDS, there is the deeper issue of what his father's once-denied homosexuality did to his family once he no longer wished to live the lie. Tasha stands as an interesting counterpoint to Melvin's worries. With her talk of fluorescents and aliens coming to California because "they've run out of frontiers on their own planets," her character seems to suggest to Melvin that there are other matters that deserve his attention. It is to some of these other matters that Morrow turns in his fiction, and to which a new generation of African-American gay writers are also turning.

—G. Winston James

MUHANJI, Cherry

Nationality: American poet, novelist, and author of short stories. **Education:** Educated at University of Iowa, from 1985. **Family:** Four children and five grandchildren. **Career:** Employed at Detroit, Michigan, phone company, 1968-84.

WRITINGS

Fiction

With Kesho Scott and Egyirba High, *Tight Spaces* (short stories). San Francisco, Spinsters/Aunt Lute, 1987.

Her. San Francisco, Aunt Lute Books, 1990.

*   *   *

In her prose, Cherry Muhanji charts a conflicted territory of identities, carefully investigating the racial, ethnic, and sexual personae of her characters. In the short stories of *Tight Spaces* and in the novel *Her,* Muhanji's female characters are constricted in their development by the roles proscribed to them in a society which devalues women, people of color, and same-sex relationships. Importantly, Muhanji emphasizes the interconnectedness of those identity categories and the impossibility of separating one from the rest.

In the novel *Her,* the main character Sunshine is a young mother-to-be who comes to live with her new husband in his family's home in Detroit. The boy's mother, Charlotte, is a strong-willed woman, and initially the relationship between mother and daughter-in-law is strained. Charlotte had had a female lover many years before when she lived in New Orleans. This ex-lover, named Wintergreen, now owns a lesbian nightclub across the street from Charlotte's house, but the two do not rekindle their romance until far into the novel, when events in Sunshine's life bring them back to each other.

More than a chronicle of these women's history, however, *Her* is about Sunshine's difficulty in forming her ethnic identity as a light-skinned black woman. Her skin color is the barrier that disconnects her from closeness with other black women. As the narrator explains, "Early on, she had despised her milky white skin and viewed it as a shroud—a disgusting thing that separated her from blackness." Sunshine suffers greatly under the stress of her difference, but she has grown able to channel this pain into a fearsome energy. She reaches back into history to carve an identity that represents all her facets, strong and black and resilient. "One day, while her parents were fighting, the child split in two. And became K-a-l-i, the warrior. Kali spoke from the mirror with a vengeance, one that smudged the child's loneliness—blurred it, sent it scrambling." Kali, the Hindu goddess of creation, becomes for her an alter-ego that embodies strength: "Often Sunshine flipped into Kali—sometimes outrageously funny, or clever, or just plain sassy. Anything that worked and made it possible to live in an all-Negro neighborhood as a freak with gray-green eyes, a nose that didn't need pinching, a flat ass and sandy hair with a slow though evident kink to it."

Kali eventually leaves her husband and moves across the street with her baby to live with Wintergreen, who becomes a new surrogate mother figure. One evening, Wintergreen dresses Kali for a night on the town at her club, and Kali emerges with a strikingly attractive boyish look that is irresistible to both sexes. Her powerful, unclassifiable essence makes her the object of the affections of Monkey Dee, a very powerful pimp in the neighborhood. She rejects his claim to her, however, and for her defiance of his power she is brutally assaulted.

Sunshine/Kali comes to personify the distances between black women that are created by racism and misogyny. Wintergreen brings the women of the neighborhood together to plot Kali's revenge, and only in this meeting do they really discover the depth of each other's pain. Chanting together in a circle, the women see Kali in themselves. They recognize how they have failed each other as well as her: "[T]he women began to heave and swear, to call out to all the Kalis in the world. Sister, sister, look what you done to us. House niggahs, mulattoes, creoles, hi-yellahs. Sister, sister, look what you done done."

As Charlotte and Wintergreen reaffirm their place in each other's lives, Kali also admits that despite their differences, she and Charlotte are connected by an unexplainable bond—a "silken cord"—and this bond is worth defending. The connections between women, be they romantic or not, are the source of women's collective power and can enable them to surmount forces of evil, such as Monkey Dee, that threaten to destroy them.

—Caitlin L. Gannon

N-O

NACHMAN, Elana. *See* DYKEWOMON, Elana.

NAMJOSHI, Suniti Manohar

Nationality: Indian poet and fabulist. **Born:** Calcutta, 20 April 1941. **Education:** University of Poona (now spelled Pune), India (Merit Scholarship 1961-63), 1956-63, B.A. in English Literature 1961, M.A. 1963; University of Missouri, M.S. in Public Administration 1969; McGill University, Canada, 1969-72, Ph.D 1972. **Family:** Partner of Australian writer Gillian Hanscombe, from 1984. **Career:** Lecturer in English, Fergusson College, University of Poona, 1963-64; officer, Indian Administrative Service, 1964-69; research assistant, Political Science Department, University of Missouri, 1968-69; teaching assistant, English Department, McGill University, 1969-72; lecturer in English, 1972-73, assistant professor, 1973-78, associate professor, 1978-89, Scarborough College, University of Toronto, Canada; freelance writer, from 1987. **Member:** League of Canadian Poets, Writers' Guild of Great Britain, Appraisal Team of the Poetry Society, Arts Council of Great Britain, 1993, Literature Panel, Arts Council of Great Britain, 1993-94, Women in the Arts Panel, Arts Council of Great Britain, 1994, Literature Panel, Arts Council of England, 1994-96.

WRITINGS

Selected Poetry and Fables

Poems. Calcutta, Writer's Workshop, 1967.
Translator, with Sarojini Namjoshi, *Poems of Govindagraj.* Calcutta, Writer's Workshop, 1968.
More Poems. Calcutta, Writers' Workshop, 1971.
Cyclone in Pakistan. Calcutta, Writers' Workshop, 1971.
The Jackass and the Lady. Calcutta, Writers' Workshop, 1980.
Feminist Fables. London, Sheba Feminist Publishers, 1981; Melbourne, Spinifex, 1993; London, Virago, 1994.
The Authentic Lie. Fredericton, Canada, Fiddlehead, 1982.
From the Bedside Book of Nightmares. Fredericton, Fiddlehead, 1984.
The Conversations of Cow. London, The Women's Press, 1985; New Delhi, Rupa, 1993.
Aditi and the One-Eyed Monkey. London, Sheba Feminist Publishers 1986; Boston, Beacon Press, 1989.
With Gillian Hanscombe, *Flesh and Paper.* United Kingdom, Jezebel Tapes and Books, 1986; Canada, Ragweed, 1986.
The Blue Donkey Fables. London, The Women's Press, 1989.
The Mothers of Maya Diip. London, The Women's Press, 1989.
Because of India (poems). London, Onlywomen Press, 1989.
Saint Suniti and the Dragon. Melbourne, Spinifex Press, 1993; London, Virago, 1994.
Building Babel. Melbourne, Spinifex Press, 1996.

Essays

"Double Landscape: A Study of the Poetry of P.K. Page," in *Canadian Literature,* No. 67, winter 1974.
"Ezra Pound and the Hex Hoax," in *Antigonish Review,* No. 23, autumn 1975.
"In the Whale's Belly: Jay Macpherson's "Welcoming Disaster," in *Canadian Literature,* No. 79, winter 1978.
"Snow White and Rose Green or Some Notes on Sexism, Racism and the Craft of Writing," in *Canadian Woman Studies,* Vol. 4, No. 2, winter 1982.
"Poetry or Propaganda?," in *Canadian Woman Studies,* Vol. 5, No. 1, fall 1983.
"Rose Green Alone," in *Versions,* edited by Betsy Warland. Vancouver, Canada, Press Gang, 1991.
With Gillian Hanscombe, "Heavenly Enough" in *Trivia* (Amherst, Massachusetts), No. 18, fall 1991.
With Gillian Hanscombe, "Who Wrongs You, Sappho?," in *Out of the Margins,* edited by Aaron & Walby. London, Falmer Press, 1991.

*

Critical Sources: Review of *Feminist Fables, The Authentic Lie,* and *The Jackass and the Lady* by Mary Meigs, in *Room of One's Own,* No. 1, February 1984; review of *From the Bedside Book of Nightmares* by M. Travis Lane, in *Fiddlehead,* No. 45, autumn 1985; *Flesh and Paper: The Life and Work of Suniti Namjoshi* (film), directed by Pratibha Parmar, produced by Hyphen Films for Channel 4 Television, first broadcast 3 April 1990; "Female Centered Fables" by Kathleen Jamie, in *Times Literary Supplement,* 14 September 1990; *Reworlding: The Literature of the Indian Diaspora* edited by Emmanuel Nelson, Westport, Connecticut, Greenwood Press, 1992; "Crossing Cultures: Self Identity in the Writing of Suniti Namjoshi" by Margaret Ann Bowers (M.A. Thesis), Department of English, University of Alberta, 1992; *Shakespeare's Queer Children: Sexual Politics and Contemporary Culture* by Kate Chedgzoy, United Kingdom, Manchester University Press, 1995.

*   *   *

Suniti Namjoshi was born in Bombay, India, in 1941. Until the merger of the Princely States which occurred after Independence, her mother's family were rulers of a small Princely State called Phaltan, in Maharashtra. Her grandparents were the Rajah and Rani, and her mother, Sarojini, was the oldest of their children. Sarojini married Manohar Namjoshi, a career test pilot, who was killed in a flying accident when Namjoshi was 12. From the beginning, her education was through the medium of English and she was awarded a B.A. in English literature by the University of Poona in 1961, and completed her M.A. in 1963.

After graduation, Namjoshi successfully competed in the public examinations for entry into the Indian Administrative Service (IAS) as a way of securing some independence from her family. She was posted to Poona, however, where her family had lived for centuries and was viewed by the community as a member of that family and therefore heir to the same groupings, both of friends and enemies. Her family was pleased with her developing career, especially when she was promoted to the post of Magistrate in 1967.

Namjoshi had written verse since adolescence and while in the IAS she met P. Lal, the head of the Calcutta Writers' Workshop. He was preparing to publish the work of Indian poets writing in English and included her poems in the Workshop's 1967 collection. At this time Namjoshi had no feminist awareness, though she hints in an introductory piece of her 1989 work, *Because of India,* that there had been tensions in the family at this time because of her interest in young women rather than young men. She wrote, "...my family was pleased with me. I was no longer fighting them over a particular friend. The word lesbian hadn't been thrown around and it wasn't in my own active vocabulary."

In 1968, Namjoshi applied for a period of study leave, ostensibly to take a master's degree in Public Administration at the University of Missouri, but also convinced that living outside India, beyond the reach of her family, she could achieve a degree of anonymity unavailable in the community where she was born. Unfortunately, the move to America was not the release she had hoped for. Columbia, Missouri, was an example of self-satisfied, inward-looking, small-town America and Namjoshi speaks of her sense of culture-shock and her experience of simultaneously understanding the language but being baffled by the cultural context. A poem she wrote in 1968 from *More Poems* captures her feelings about the town:

> In Columbia, America,
> The little houses grow,
> White, sometimes yellow,
> All in a row.
> The trees are orderly,
> The squirrels discreet,
> And the only jarring note
> Is a bird in bad taste
> Lying dead in the street.
> Accidents will happen.

Despite her disappointment with Columbia, Missouri, she did not wish to return to India and in 1969 resigned from her post at IAS to pursue a Ph.D. from McGill University in Montreal. She found the cosmopolitan atmosphere of McGill congenial, and stimulated by her research on Ezra Pound she began writing poetry again. This time her writing was influenced by her status as outsider and while it was her racial and cultural otherness which gave her poetry its edge, it paved the way for writing from a feminist and lesbian perspective, and grappling with the alienation that those identities create.

In 1972, having been awarded the Ph.D., Namjoshi was appointed Lecturer in English Literature at Scarborough College, University of Toronto. Despite the demands of academic work, she determined to continue writing poetry, and her poems from this time show a mingling of Western and Hindu influences. In the pantheistic Hindu religion all creatures have souls and the ancient Hindu poets, as had the Greek fabulist, Aesop, made full use of a bestiary in their verses and fables. A typical dramatis personae would include an adventuresome prince, a lady, often in some degree of distress, and beasts, variously helpful or dangerous. Unable to be the prince and unwilling to be the damsel, Namjoshi occupied the only vacant post, one of the beasts. The following

1974 poem from *Jackass and the Lady* was originally entitled "The Unicorn" and illustrates her use of the beasts:

> I give her the rose with unfurled petals.
> She smiles
> and crosses her legs.
> I give her the shell with the swollen lip.
> She laughs. I bite
> and nuzzle her breasts.
> tell her, "Feed me on flowers
> with wide open mouths,"
> and slowly,
> she pulls down my head.

The sensuous response of the poet to the woman is here disguised by the adoption of an animal persona. When these poems were eventually published, Namjoshi had been exposed both to feminism and gay liberation and was able to dispense with the mask of the unicorn.

Namjoshi has written that she always knew she was a lesbian, even though the word was not available to her either in English or her mother tongue. In common with most other lesbians in a pre-liberation era, she had no knowledge of the existence of a lesbian sub-culture but as an Asian woman living in the West, albeit one steeped in European elite culture, she had already experienced a certain sense of being marginalized from the mainstream. When finally she was exposed to the strong currents of feminism and gay liberation, she realized that her sense of alienation had as much to do with being a woman and a lesbian as being an Asian in exile.

In 1978 Namjoshi spent a year's sabbatical leave in London and Cambridge and discovered gay women and men who saw themselves as part of a community rather than isolated gay individuals. She made friends with "out" lesbian feminists and, not entirely without resistance, became politicized. Though she considered herself temperamentally unsuited to activism, she admired the bravery of lesbian women academics who refused to deny their affiliations. As she wrote in *Because of India* of her friend Christine Donald:

> "It wasn't just Christine's intellect that was persuasive. It was watching her be brave and get hurt. She wore feminist and gay liberation badges, and sometimes there would be frighteningly aggressive arguments and remarks from men on the street. It shamed me that I was letting other women do the fighting for me. I don't like being an activist...I dislike arguments; but when I returned to Toronto I came out at the University and in print, and together with some women colleagues, I started a Women's Studies Programme at the college."

During her sabbatical, Namjoshi immersed herself in liberation theories, feminist and lesbian. She became conscious of the Christian and patriarchal nature of the English language, not that it was hostile, but that there were gaps which rendered some aspects of female experience almost impossible to express. Like Virginia Woolf before her, she had noticed the difference between the male and the female sentence. As an Indian lesbian feminist writing in English, she realized that she needed to make changes to the language to find her own voice and to communicate with the particular audience that she now realized existed.

Her first work after this Damascene conversion was *Feminist Fables*. She saw the possibility of exploring feminist ideas and their implications through both the Eastern and Western literary traditions. Unlike her earlier work, most of these pieces are written in prose, but this is the prose of fairy tales, rather than the prose of exposition. The following story of the Sleeping Beauty from *Feminist Fables* exemplifies Namjoshi's shift to prose writing. She makes Sleeping Beauty's sister the heroine.

Thorn Rose

Have you heard the story of the little princess, who had a little brother who was going to be king? There were rumours about, the palace was full of them, of how strange she was, not lady like, wore men's clothes. Of this last escapade there are echoes throughout history. When at last she understood that she couldn't ever be king, she challenged her brother to single combat. (She had no army.) The result was defeat. In some versions he lopped off her head. In others, he laughed and sent her to the attic. In the attic there was a spinning wheel, and there she spun out her life for one hundred years and probably died.

No, this is not the story of the Wicked Princess. She was merely anonymous. Perhaps that's why this story seems so unfamiliar?

And yes, she had a sister who didn't like men, preferred women. She clambered to the attic of her own accord, and when she fell asleep, nobody woke her: no women available.

Feminist Fables brought Namjoshi international recognition as a lesbian feminist writer. Other collections followed, including *From the Bedside Book of Nightmares, The Conversations of Cow,* and *Flesh and Paper.* This last was the published record of letters that she and Gillian Hanscombe, an Australian poet, exchanged after they had met in England at the First International Book Fair in 1984, and Namjoshi had gone back to Canada. Here Namjoshi returns to a lyrical mode and her poems reflect the intensity of her feelings as well as the consciousness of writing to another poet.

Well, then let slip the masks
and all the notes we have taken,
let them fall to the ground and turn into petals
to make more luxurious our bed, or let them
turn into leaves and blow into the air, let them
make patterns, let them amuse themselves.
The curve of your breast is like the curve
of a wave: look, held caught, each instant
caught, the wave tipping over and we in our bower,
the two of us sheltered, my hands on your thighs,
your body, your back, my mouth on your mouth
and in the hollows of your jaws and your head
nuzzling my breasts. And the wave above us is
folding over now, folding and laughing. Will you
take to the sea, my darling? Will you let me caress you?
The tips of your feet, your legs, your sex?
Will you let my tongue caress you? Will you
lie in my arms? Will you rest? And if the sun
is too strong, should burn too much, will you
walk with me to where the light is more calm
and be in me where the seas heave and are
serene and heave again and are themselves?

Namjoshi left Canada in 1987 and settled in Devon with Gillian Hanscombe. They have collaborated in many forms of writing: lyric poetry, short fiction, academic articles, drama and literature and creative writing workshops. As well as their joint efforts, Namjoshi maintains her own creative output. She is still interested in melding not only content from both Indian and Western cultures, but also poetic forms, idioms, imagistic associations and styles. Her work is at the same time cultivated and sophisticated, as well as politically charged and utterly contemporary. The satiric drive is always present, focussed on human follies, founded on compassionate ethics and dedicated to celebrating the ancient values of truth, beauty, and justice. When asked by audiences, whether lesbian or straight, feminist or mainstream, how her belief system is construed, or what political values she endorses, her most constant response is "Love is Law."

—Anne Hughes

NAVA, Michael A(ngel)

Nationality: American author of mystery novels and non-fiction. **Born:** Stockton, California, 16 September 1954. **Education:** Attended public schools in Sacramento, California; Colorado College, B.A. 1976; Stanford University, J.D. 1981. **Family:** Companion of Don Romesburg. **Career:** Writer and deputy city attorney, Los Angeles, California, 1981-84; private practice of law, Los Angeles, 1984-86; research attorney, California Court of Appeal, Los Angeles, 1986-95; private practice of law, San Francisco, 1995; full-time writer, from 1995; contributor to *Advocate, LA Style, LA Times,* and *Si.* Member of PEN Center West, California State Bar Association, and Los Angeles Gay and Lesbian Literary Circle. **Awards:** Lambda Literary Awards, for Best Small Press Publication, 1988; Lambda Literary Award, for Best Gay Mystery, 1988, 1990, 1992. **Agent:** Charlotte Sheedy Literary Agency, 65 Bleeker Street, New York, New York 10012.

WRITINGS

Novels

The Little Death. Boston, Alyson Publications, 1986.
Goldenboy. Boston, Alyson Publications, 1988.
How Town. New York, Harper and Row, 1990.
The Hidden Law. New York, HarperCollins, 1992.
The Death of Friends. New York, Putnam, 1966.
The Burning Plain. Forthcoming.

Nonfiction

With Robert Dawidoff, *Created Equal: Why Gay Rights Matter to America.* New York, St. Martin's Press, 1994.
Unlived Lives: The Memoirs of a Misfit. Forthcoming.

Autobiographical Essays

"Gardenland" in *Hometowns,* edited by John Preston. New York, Dutton, 1990; reprinted in *Common Ground: Reading and Writing about America's Cultures,* edited by Laurie G. Kirszner and Stephen R. Mandell, New York, St. Martin's Press, 1994.

"Abuelo" in *A Member of the Family,* edited by John Preston. New York, Dutton, 1992.

"The Marriage of Michael and Bill" in *Friends and Lovers,* edited by John Preston. New York, Dutton, 1994.

"Coming Out and Born Again" in *Wrestling With the Angel,* edited by Brian Bouldrey. New York, Riverhead, 1985.

"Boys Like Us" in *Boys Like Us,* edited by Patrick Merla. New York, Avon Books, 1996.

*

Critical Sources: *Eulogy for a Brown Angel* by Lucha Corpi, Houston, Texas, Arte Publico, 1992; "Introduction" by Joseph Hansen, in *Bohannon's Country,* New York, Penguin, 1993; *Critical Essays: Gay and Lesbian Writers of Color,* edited by Emmanuel S. Nelson, New York, The Haworth Press, 1993; "Murder, They Write" by Adrienne Drell, in *ABA Journal,* June 1994; *Cactus Blood* by Lucha Corpi, Houston, Texas, 1995; "*Wrestling with the Angel:* Faith and Religion in the Lives of Gay Men," in *Riverhead Books,* New York, Riverhead, 1995; "The Death of Friends by Michael Nava," in *News from G. P. Putnam's Sons,* No. 163, New York, Putnam, 1996; "Sexuality Degree Zero: Pleasure and Power in the Novels of John Rechy, Arturo Islas, and Michael Nava" by Ricardo L. Ortiz, in *Journal of Homosexuality,* Vol. 26, No. 2/3, 1996, 111-126; "8 Days a Week" by Jodi Levin, http://www.sfbayguardian.com/AnE/96_04/041796cal.htm; "Quotes on Same Sex Couples—Part 2" by Partners Task Force for Gay & Lesbian Couples, http://eskimo.com/~demian/quotes-2.htm; unpublished interview with Michael Nava by Patti Capel Swartz, October 1996.

Michael Nava comments:

There is an enormous difference for me as to what my work means to me and what it means to my readers. I respect what my readers find in my work, I am often surprised by it, and sometimes feel inadequate to the praise. I began writing mysteries because I identified, as a gay person, with a species of literature in which the protagonist is an outsider who embodies the virtues that society purports to value—like loyalty, decency, and compassion—but seldom demonstrates. For me, coming out as gay required an enormous act of self-compassion after which I could no longer be so intolerant of other kinds of difference or so rigid in my moral certainties. I think that if I were not homosexual, I would be an extremely intolerant person, so perhaps my being gay was a little joke God played on me to teach me tenderness. As for my audience, I write to my 15-year-old self. He is a troubled but precocious boy, lonely, worried that he will never find love and desperately seeking assurance that, his homosexuality notwithstanding, he is a good person. I hope Rios gives him that reassurance.

*   *   *

In his introduction to *Bohannon's Country,* gay mystery writer Joseph Hanson writes that in 1982 he was told that the readers of *Ellery Queen's Mystery Magazine* were not yet ready to accept homosexuality in their stories. Publication of mysteries by gay and lesbian writers at that time was by gay and lesbian presses. However, mainstream publishers have now discovered that a wide audience exists for mysteries not only about gay, lesbian, or bi-sexual protagonists but by mystery writers who are themselves gay, lesbian, bi-sexual, or transgendered. Michael Nava's writing has been at the forefront of the explosion of publication of mysteries with a gay protagonist, and Nava has received several awards for his excellent characterizations and increasing critical recognition for his work.

Like Lucha Corpi's, Nava's writing is infused with Mexican American and Chicano experience. His protagonist, Henry Rios, is a Chicano attorney who does not forget either the difficulties or the joys of growing up as a gay person of color in Paradise Slough, a neighborhood in the fictional town Los Robles. Like Nava, Rio's experiences have taught him tolerance and compassion. As Ricardo Ortiz points out of Nava's *How Town,* "Nava's fictive world is very recognizably contemporary California in all its complexity—sexual, cultural, and political" and that "identity...is fundamentally an effect of the self's troubled relation to memory and desire."

Memory, desire, and movement toward self-understanding pervade Nava's mysteries. In his investigations of murders, Henry Rios also investigates his own inner feelings, his relationships with lovers and with his family, allowing the reader to question his or her own assumptions and to be comforted by Rios' compassion for himself and the characters who join him. Although in *How Town* Rios thinks the setting of his sister's house almost paradisaical, she dispels the idea of ever being able to enter paradise because of past memory, invoking images and words from Primo Levi "to the effect that those who have once been tortured go on being tortured," a reference to the childhood she and Rios knew. Rios himself discusses the social and legal criminalization of poverty. Nava writes of characters, including himself, who have anger because of racial and class discrimination. Gus Peña in *The Hidden Law* "developed a kind of rage" for "having had to work twice as hard for what he deserved on merit alone." Rios notes that his experience was in many ways like Peña's: "The difference was, being homosexual as well as Chicano, I'd had to learn a level of self-acceptance that mitigated my anger. Having to overcome my own self-hatred, I couldn't sustain hatred toward other people very long."

Nava's books provide hope. In *The Hidden Law* Nava writes about courage, about mistaking defiance or fearlessness for courage. "Courage requires hope," he writes, and the courage that comes with hope is abundantly evident in Nava's work. As he points out, there is little violence in his mysteries, and Rios uses "the traditional tools of a lawyer—research and analysis—to find relevant clues out of seemingly irrelevant information." Nava's plots often rise out of his reading about cases. Legal questions are important not only to his writing, but also to Henry Rios's philosophy. In *How Town* Rios muses on the difference between being guided, as a lawyer, by morals or by ethics: "the best lawyers were guided by ethics" which are "boundaries, not judgments; they allow you to be impersonal without becoming inhuman." For Nava, writing is his true work. He considered himself a writer who practiced law "to distract" himself, but he has been writing full time since 1995, and has no plans to return to legal practice. Indeed, as *News from Putnam's* notes, *The Death of Friends* "demonstrates [Nava's] talent for creating intricately-plotted stories peopled by believable characters and resonant with emotional honesty that will appeal to anyone in search of a good novel."

Through believable characters Nava incorporates issues of the gay/lesbian/bi-sexual/transgendered communities. Nava investigates the difficulties of living in the age of AIDS, the difficulty of allowing dignity and choice to a lover who is living with AIDS, of loss of lovers and lovers' dying, as does Rios's lover Josh, a character in several of the Rios books. In "Coming Out and Born Again" Nava talks of issues of religion, warning, as Riverhead's discussion notes, that it is important not to confuse the "political agenda of the Christian Right with the religious impulses of many fundamentalist Christians" as he describes an aunt and uncle who were fundamentalists yet accepting of his sexuality. Nava also writes of building community, of maintaining hope. The Riverhead essay also notes that when Nava realized the love and acceptance of his lover he realized "that my being gay had less to do with sex than with an expression of love that began with the physical but went beyond it" and he could "accept being gay in a way I never had before."

Nava's decision to co-author (with Robert Dawidoff) a book about the need for gay, lesbian, bi-sexual and transgendered rights grew out of his own sense of anger at the removal of protections for gay people in the workplace in California. Geared toward a straight audience, *Created Equal: Why Gay Rights Matter to America* is a carefully written call for the rights all citizens deserve. As Nava and Dawidoff note in the conclusion to this book, "It all comes down to this: Are people equal in this society by virtue of their citizenship or not?" Indeed, this could be said to be the foundation for Nava's writing: the search for love, compassion, and equality without judgment of race, class, or gender issues and the acceptance of people for their positive attributes and acceptance of difference. Nava's writing is rich and full, and moves us forward toward that goal.

—Patti Capel Swartz

NIN, Anais

Nationality: French diarist and writer. **Born:** Angela Anais Juana Antolina Rosa Edelmira Nin y Culmell in Neuilly, 21 February 1903; emigrated to United States, 1914; naturalized. **Education:** Attended Catholic and public schools, New York; self-educated after age 16. **Family:** Married Hugh (Hugo) Parker Guiler, also known as Ian Hugo, 3 March 1923; romantically involved with Henry Miller and possibly June Miller, among others; married Rupert William Pole, c. 1958. **Career:** Held a variety of jobs, including model and Spanish dancer; studied psychoanalysis with Otto Rank, and was, for a time, a psychoanalyst in Europe and briefly in New York in the mid-30s; established Siana Editions with Villa Seurat group (Henry Miller, Alfred Perles, Michael Franekel), France, c. 1935; Society editor, 1937, associate editor, 1937-38, member of editorial board, 1939, *Booster* and *Delta,* Paris; returned to United States to publish own books, 1939-42; general editor, 1959, honorary editor, 1960, *Two Cities;* member of advisory board, *Voyages;* contributor to periodicals, including *Massachusetts Review, New York Times, New York Times Book Review, Ms., Saturday Review,* and the *Village Voice;* lecturer at colleges and universities, including Harvard University, University of Chicago, Dartmouth College, University of Michigan, University of California, Berkeley, and Duke University. Member, National Institute of Arts and Letters, 1974. **Awards:** Prix Sevigne, France, 1971; L.H.D.: Philadelphia College of Art, 1973; Dartmouth College, 1974. **Died:** Los Angeles, California, 14 January 1977.

WRITINGS

Journals

The Diary of Anais Nin, edited by Gunther Stuhlmann, 7 Vols. New York, Harcourt Brace and World, Vol. 1, 1931-34, Vol. 2, 1934-39, Vol. 3, 1939-44, Vol. 4, 1944-47, Vol. 5, 1947-55, Vol. 6, 1955-66, and Vol. 7, 1966-74; Vols. 1-3, co-published with Swallow Press, 1966, 1967, and 1969; Vols. 4-7, co-published with Harcourt Brace Jovanovich, 1971, 1974, 1976, and 1980.
The Early Diary of Anais Nin. New York and London, Harcourt Brace Jovanovich, Vol. 1: *Linotte: The Early Diary of Anais Nin, 1914-1920,* translated by Jean L. Sherman, preface by Joaquin Nin-Culmell, 1980, Vol. 2: *1920-1923,* 1983, Vol. 3: *1923-1927,* Vol. 4: *1927-1931,* 1985.
Henry and June: From the Unexpurgated Diary of Anais Nin. San Diego, Harcourt Brace Jovanovich, 1986.
Incest: From "Journal of Love," The Unexpurgated Diary of Anais Nin. San Diego, Harcourt Brace Jovanovich, 1992.

Fiction

The Winter of Artifice. Paris, The Obelisk Press, 1939; as *Winter of Artifice,* New York, Gemor Press, 1942; Denver, Swallow Press, 1961.
Under a Glass Bell (short story). New York, Gemor Press, 1944; New York, E.P. Dutton, 1948.
The All-Seeing. New York, Gemor Press, 1944.
This Hunger. New York, Gemor Press, 1945.
Ladders to Fire. New York, E.P. Dutton, 1946; Denver, Swallow Press, 1966.
A Child Born Out of the Fog (pamphlet). New York, Gemor Press, 1947
Children of the Albatross. New York, E.P. Dutton, 1947; Denver, Swallow Press, 1966.
The Four-Chambered Heart. New York, Duell, Sloan, and Pearce, 1950; Denver, Swallow Press, 1966.
Solar Baroque. New York, Anais Nin, 1958; enlarged edition published as *Seduction of the Minotaur: A Spy in the House of Love,* Denver, Swallow Press, 1961.
Collages (short story). Denver, Swallow Press, 1964.
Waste of Timelessness and Other Early Stories (short stories). Weston, Connecticut, Magic Circle Press, 1977.

Erotica

Auletris. Carmel, California, Press of the Sunken Eye, 1950.
And author of introduction, *Aphrodisiac: Erotic Drawings by John Boyce for Selected Passages from the Works of Anais Nin.* New York, Crown, 1976.
Delta of Venus: Erotica. New York, Harcourt Brace Jovanovich, 1977; as *The Illustrated Delta of Venus,* London, Allen, 1980.
Little Birds: Erotica. New York, Harcourt Brace Jovanovich, 1979.

Collected Works

Cities of the Interior (includes *Ladders to Fire, Children of the Albatross, The Four-Chambered Heart,* and *Seduction of the Minotaur*), introduction by Sharon Spence. Denver, Swallow Press, 1959; Chicago, Swallow Press, 1974.

The Anais Nin Reader, edited by Philip K. Jason, introduction by Anna Balakian. Chicago, Swallow Press, 1973.

A Woman Speaks: The Lectures, Seminars, and Interviews of Anais Nin, edited by Evelyn Hinz. Chicago, Swallow Press, 1975.

Nonfiction

D.H. Lawrence: An Unprofessional Study. Paris, Edward W. Titus, 1932.

"Alan Swallow," in *Denver Quarterly,* Vol. 2, No. 1, spring 1967, 11-14.

"Dear Djuna Barnes (1937) with a note (1971)," in *A Festschrift for Djuna Barnes on Her 80th Birthday.* Kent, Ohio, Kent State University Libraries, 1972, 16.

In Favor of the Sensitive Man, and Other Essays. New York, Harcourt Brace Jovanovich, 1976.

The White Blackbird and Other Writings. Santa Barbara, California, Capra Press, 1985.

Other

House of Incest (prose poem). Paris, Siana Editions, 1936; New York, Gemor Press, 1947; Denver, Swallow Press, 1961.

A Literate Passion: Letters of Anais Nin and Henry Miller, 1932-1953, edited by Gunther Stuhlmann. San Diego, Harcourt Brace Jovanovich, 1987.

Recordings: *Anais Nin, Contemporary Classics,* issued by Louis and Bebe Barron, Sound Portraits, 1949; *The Diary of Anais Nin, Vol. One: 1931-1934,* Spoken Arts SA995-996, 1968; *An Evening with Anais Nin,* Big Sur Recordings, 1972; *Anais Nin Discusses The Diary of Anais Nin, 1944-1947, Volume IV, "A Journal of Self-Discovery,"* Center for Cassette Studies, 1972; *Craft of Writing,* Big Sur Recordings, 1973; *Anais Nin: The Author Explains the Purpose behind Her Writing,* Center for Cassette Studies, 1975; *Anais Nin in Recital: Diary Excerpts and Comments,* Caedmon, 1979.

*

Interviews: With Duane Schneider, *An Interview with Anais Nin,* Village Press, 1973.

Critical Sources: *Contemporary Authors,* Vols. 13-16, Detroit, Gale Research, 1975; *Contemporary Authors,* Vols. 69-72, Detroit, Gale Research, 1978, 454; *Anais Nin,* Boston, G.K. Hall & Co, 1984; *Anais: The Erotic Life of Anais Nin* by Noel Riley Fitch, New York, Little, Brown, 1993; *Anais Nin and Her Critics* by P.K. Jason, Columbia, South Carolina, Camden House, 1993; *Anais Nin: A Biography* by Deirde Bair, New York, G.P. Putnam, 1995; *Boundary Wars: Intimacy and Distance in Healing Relationships,* edited by Nancy Scholar and Katherine Hancock, Cleveland, Ohio, The Pilgrim Press, 1996.

*   *   *

Placing Anais Nin's work within the context of gay and lesbian literature may be akin to fitting a square peg into a round hole. Her writing is almost exclusively heterosexual, as is her personal sexual experience. Her "affair" with June Miller, wife of Henry Miller—with whom Nin clearly did share a long-term intimate re-

lationship—is alleged by some, including biographer Noel Riley Fitch, to have been only in Nin's head. Her infatuation with women and her deep appreciation for lesbian writers Colette and Djuna Barnes (who snubbed Nin and refused to even share the sidewalk with her, according to Fitch) does not make her a lesbian or a budding bisexual.

Her writing took the road less travelled when she created a body of erotica, presumably for economic reasons rather than for reasons of personal interest. In her work, both homosexuality and heterosexuality are freely and openly depicted.

Nin had a troubled childhood. She was plagued by her inability to win the love of her father before he abandoned the family when she was still a small child. Her chances of winning his love after his departure were even smaller, but Nin idolized Joaquin Nin, the distinguished Spanish composer and concert pianist. Nin spent her life in an endless series of intense affairs, more than likely exclusively with men-artists, musicians, psychoanalysts, and writers (the most notable of which is Henry Miller) in an equally endless effort to reconcile the betrayal of her father. Her aim was to betray men as she has been betrayed, and to somehow make sense of her existence.

Her father is remembered by Nin in her diaries and in her fiction—particularly in *House of Incest,* her first novel—as one who seduced her and violated her. Although the abuse is difficult to prove, the pattern of relationships in her life lend considerable credence to the claim. He frequently told Nin that she was ugly, but then would take pictures of her in the nude.

Conflicted, to say the least, over her relationship with her father, and with men in general, she left a lengthy trail of men in her wake—all major father-figures in her life. Her erotic writings, diaries, and dabbling—at least on paper and in her mind, with lesbianism—led to often believed, but unconfirmed, rumors that she was a nymphomaniac. Her conquests included: Edmund Wilson, Professor John Erskine, Drs. Rene Allendy and Otto Rank, Henry Miller, William Pinckard, Rupert William Pole (who she married while still married to Guiler), and countless others. The patterns of seduction and of betrayal—by Nin of others and by others of Nin—are evident from her earliest encounters with young men for whom she modeled.

Nin, who with her husband Hugo established Gemor Press to publish her own work and to enable her to pursue her own unique path through life, has also been an encouragement to others seeking, but rarely finding, the recognition they deserve without taking an active part in making themselves known.

Diaries comprise a significant portion of Nin's writings (nearly 35,000 pages in 150 volumes) and because "she kept the lengthiest and most complete record of any developing artistic consciousness," she has been called, says biographer Noel Riley Fitch, "the most important psychologist of women." Her diaries have been instructional and inspirational to many young women writers, yet her place in women's culture and literature has not been fully appreciated, says Fitch, in part "because academic feminists are embarrassed by her delicate feminine personae."

Likewise, lesbian culture and literature would not be particularly welcoming to Nin, whose life and work betray an indisputable heterosexuality in practice, in spite of sexual confusion within. Hence, one of her greatest contributions to that culture and literature might be to fuel the debate over just what constitutes gay and lesbian literature/writing.

Perhaps tormented is too strong a word, but Nin was clearly plagued throughout her life by severe self-doubt and an extremely diminished self-esteem. Fortunately, however, she held a very high opinion of herself as an artist and as a writer. Her writings are without a doubt a major influence on women writers of an entire genre—the journal/diary—and on an entire generation.

—Andrea L.T. Peterson

————

NORTON, Eric. *See* **TSUI, Kitty.**

————

NUGENT, Richard Bruce

Pseudonym: Also wrote as Richard Bruce. **Nationality:** American poet, illustrator, playwright, and short story writer. **Born:** Washington, D.C., 2 July 1906 (some sources say 1905). **Education:** Attended Dunbar High School, Washington, D.C. **Career:** Worked as a hellhop, elevator operator, and errand boy, New York City, in his teens; became an illustrator and artist. **Died:** Hoboken, New Jersey, of congestive heart failure, 27 May 1987.

WRITINGS

Fiction

"Sahdji" (short story), in *The New Negro: An Interpretation,* edited by Alain Locke. New York, A. and C. Boni, 1925, 113-114.
"Shadows," in *Opportunity,* Vol. 3, October 1925, 296.
"Smoke, Lilies, and Jade" (as Richard Bruce), in *Fire!!,* No. 1, November 1926, 405-408; in *Go the Way Your Heart Beats: An Anthology of Lesbian and Gay Fiction by African-American Writers,* New York, Henry Holt, 1996, 205-221.
"Cavalier" and "Shadow" (poems; as Richard Bruce), in *Caroling Dusk: An Anthology of Verse By Negro Poets,* edited by Countee Cullen. New York, Harper and Row, 1927.
"Narcissus," in *Trend,* January/March 1933, 127.
"Beyond Where the Stars Stood Still," in *Crisis,* December 1970, 405-408.
Lighting Fire!! Metuchen, New Jersey, *Fire!!* Press, 1982.

Plays

Sadhji, an African Ballet (produced Howard University, Washington, D.C., late 1920s; produced Eastman School of Music, University of Rochester, New York, 1932). In *Plays of Negro Life: A Sourcebook of Native American Drama,* edited by Alain Locke and Motgomery Gregory, New York, Harper, 1927; Rochester, New York, Eastman School of Music, 1961.
With Rose McClendon, *Taxi Fare* (produced by Harlem Players, 135th Street Library Theatre, New York, 1931).

*

Interviews: "Interview with Bruce Nugent," in *Artists and Influences: 1982,* New York, Hatch-Billops Collection, 1982, 81-104.

Critical Sources: *Infants of the Spring* by Wallace Thurman, New York, Macaulay, 1932; "Nugent, Richard Bruce," by Mark Helbling and Bruce Kellner, in *The Harlem Renaissance: A Historical Dictionary for the Era,* Westport, Connecticut, Greenwood Press, 1984, 269; "Richard Bruce Nugent," by Thomas H. Wirth, in *Black American Literature Forum,* Vol. 19, spring 1985, 16-17; "Bruce Nugent: Bohemian of the Harlem Renaissance," by Charles Michael Smith, in *In the Life: A Black Gay Anthology,* edited by Joseph Beam, Boston, Massachusetts, Alyson Press, 1986, 209-21; *Early Black American Playwrights and Dramatic Writers* by Bernard L. Peterson, Jr., Westport, Connecticut, Greenwood Press, 1990, 154-155.

*   *   *

The beginning of a visible homosexual presence in the literature of twentieth-century African Americans lies in the explosion of talent and creativity which took place in New York City during the 1920s, popularly termed the "Harlem Renaissance." Among the writers whose creations set forth new possibilities for their community were some who addressed the joys and problems of being "in the life," as the gay world was termed. Of these, Richard Bruce Nugent was the most direct.

A native of Washington, D.C., he moved to New York at the age of 13, following the death of his father, and abandoned an art apprenticeship to work at a wide range of jobs ranging from errand boy through secretary to ornamental ironworker and designer. A trip to Panama was followed by a costume design class in New York and a visit home to Washington, where he met Langston Hughes, who encouraged his writing. In his 1922 short story "Sahdji," which appeared in Alain Locke's *The New Negro* in 1925 and featured an unsuccessful male love affair as one plot element, he began the trend of discussing this totally forbidden subject. Nugent subsequently collaborated with Locke, expanding the story into a scenario for the choral entertainment *Sahdji, an African Ballet,* first staged in 1932 at the Eastman School of Music. While controversial, it is the 1926 narrative work "Smoke, Lilies and Jade" which is regarded as the most defiantly homosexual text of this era. An unabashed celebration of male beauty, it first appeared in the only issue of *Fire!,* a highly avant-garde journal edited by Langston Hughes, Zora Neale Hurston, and Wallace Thurman for which Nugent served as an associate editor and to which he contributed illustrations of nudes. Its contents were selected with the deliberate intent of shocking mainstream conservative black society. Nugent's piece was widely regarded as a disguised autobiography, with one critic declaring that he had burned the entire issue of the magazine.

While Nugent continued to write poetry all his life, much of his work remained unpublished except as privately printed and illustrated pamphlets. In the mid 1960s, he founded the Harlem Cultural Council and appeared in the 1984 documentary video *Before Stonewall,* becoming recognized as a major resource on the half-forgotten world of his times. His death in 1987 severed one of the few living links with a vibrant era for both the African American and homosexual communities, a significance noted by the inclusion of Nugent's poetry in the 1992 film *A Meditation on Langston Hughes (1902-1967) and the Harlem Renaissance.*

—Robert B. Marks Ridinger

OBEJAS, Achy (Alicia)

Nationality: Cuban-American novelist, short story writer, and journalist. **Born:** Cuba in 1957; moved to the United States in 1963. **Education:** Attended various colleges in Indiana; studied creative writing at Warren Wilson College, North Carolina, M.F.A. **Career:** Has worked as a fine arts painter and as a journalist for the *Chicago Sun-Times, Chicago Magazine, Chicago Tribune, Los Angeles Times, Nation, Reader, Windy City Times,* and others. **Awards:** National Endowment for the Arts Poetry Fellowship, 1986; Peter Lisagor Award, for political reporting, 1989; Studs Terkel Award, for journalism, 1996; Illinois Arts Council Literary Grant; Virginia Center of the Creative Arts fellowship; Ragdale Foundation fellowship. **Address:** c/o Cleis Press, P.O. Box 14684, San Francisco, California 94114, U.S.A.

WRITINGS

We Came All the Way from Cuba So You Could Dress Like This? (short stories). San Francisco, California, Cleis Press, 1995.
Memory Mambo (novel). San Francisco, Cleis Press, 1996.

*

Critical Sources: "Exotica" by Marcia Froelke Coburn, in *Chicago Magazine,* Vol. 44, No 7., July 1995, 25; review of *We Came All the Way from Cuba So You Could Dress Like This?* by Whitney Scott, in *Booklist,* Vol. 91, No. 4, October 15, 1994, 394.

*   *   *

While attending college, Cuban-American author Achy Obejas was sure of two things: that she was a lesbian and that she was a writer. Still certain long after her departure from the ivy halls, and through forays into poetry and painting pictures of Indiana barns, she is now known primarily for her journalism in the *Chicago Tribune,* the *Windy City Times,* and other national publications. Obejas' first full-length work of fiction, a collection of short stories called *We Came All the Way from Cuba so You Could Dress Like This?,* came out in 1994 to acclaim and sold 10,000 copies, unheard of for a debut from a small press.

The book tells the stories of a population of refugees and exiles that includes Cuban boat people, junkies, gays, and lesbians, but *Booklist* reviewer Whitney Scott found the book's strongest pieces to be the "vignettes concerned with parts of Obejas' own life as a Latina lesbian refugee." "These writings of the disenfranchised are for any spiritual immigrant, huddled and yearning to be free," concluded Scott.

"Bill Rickman [president of Kroch's & Brentano's bookstores] told me that I was probably the most cross-indexed writer in the store. Cuban. Gay/Lesbian. Chicago. I told him, 'You know, I'm Jewish too,'" Obejas told *Chicago Magazine.* In these comments lies the secret of her appeal. She writes about a very specific experience—the isolation of being a Spanish-speaking refugee in an English-speaking land, the solitude of being a lesbian in a straight world—in a manner so rich and compelling that even those most removed from the experience can connect to the words. Her refusal to universalize or simplify helped the book find a variety of readers. And it didn't hurt that the *Village Voice* declared that the book contained the best sex scenes of 1994.

For her next work of fiction, Obejas turned her hand to a novel, *Memory Mambo,* and joined what *Vanity Fair* called "The Girlfriends," the top Latina writers including Ana Castillo, Sandra Cisneros, Denise Chavez, and Julia Alverez. The book tells the story of Juani Casas, a Cuban-American lesbian obsessed with memory, counting cousins, violence, desire and the meaning of love. "While it isn't autobiographical in its scope," Obejas told *Chicago Magazine,* "it is in the details." The book is a finely paced piece of work that stands apart from more traditional lesbian pulp fiction romances and stands up next to any work of classic fiction because of its fine writing style.

—Victoria Stagg Elliott

P

PACKER, Vin. *See* MEAKER, Marijane.

PAGLIA, Camille

Nationality: American writer and educator. **Born:** Endicott, New York, in 1947. **Education:** State University of New York, Binghampton (summa cum laude with highest honors), B.A. in English, 1968; Yale University, New Haven, Connecticut, M. Phil. 1971, Ph.D. 1974. **Family:** Companion of artist and curator Allison Maddex. **Career:** Faculty member, Bennington College, Vermont, 1972-80; visiting lecturer, Wesleyan University, 1980, Yale University, 1980-84; professor of humanities, University of the Arts, Philadelphia, from 1984; frequent contributor to periodicals, including *Advocate, Salon* (Web-based), and *Spy.* **Address:** University of the Arts, 320 S. Broad St., Philadelphia, Pennsylvania, 19102-4901, U.S.A.

WRITINGS

Nonfiction

Sexual Personae: Art and Decadence From Nefertiti to Emily Dickinson, New Haven, Yale University Press, 1990, New York, Vintage Books, 1991.
Sex, Art, and American Culture, New York, Vintage Books, 1992.
Vamps & Tramps, New York, Vintage Books, 1994.

*

Interviews: "Hurricane Camille Wreaks Havoc!" in *San Francisco Chronicle Image Magazine,* 27 September 1992; "Camille Anonymous" by Susie Bright, in *San Francisco Review of Books,* January 1993; "An Interview with Camille Paglia" by James Martin, in *America* (New York), Vol. 171, No. 15, 12 November 1994; "Camille Paglia: 'Why Am I So Angry All the Time?'" by Wendy Smith, in *Publishers Weekly* (New York), 28 November 1994; "Camille Paglia" by Emma Taylor, in *Tripod,* 23 January 1996; "In Praise of the Vernacular" by Robin Bernstein, in *Harvard Gay and Lesbian Review* (Cambridge), Vol. 3, No. 2, spring 1996.

Critical Sources: "Of Many Things" by George W. Hunt, in *America,* Vol. 171, No. 15, 12 November 1994.

*   *   *

In 1990 the Freudian anti-feminist Camille Paglia burst onto the cultural criticism scene with *Sexual Personae: Art and Decadence From Nefertiti to Emily Dickinson,* a probing study of the nature of sexual tropes through the ages. This book, along with essays collected into two volumes, caused a stir within the intellectual, feminist, and gay communities. In the early 1990s the *Ad-vocate* attacked her, the *Village Voice* called her an intellectual fraud, and Susie Bright and Pat Califia severely criticized her. Nevertheless, many critics changed their negative opinions and various other critics thought she was brilliant from the start. George W. Hunt, in a 1994 editorial in *America,* described Paglia as "Hurricane Camille," whose style is "like the pelting of a sleet storm, wherein opinions, observations, allusions spatter down at apparent random yet land in concentrated globlets that sting but somehow clear the air." He added that "she seems like an errant offspring of the philosopher Hegel, one who finds in Art the unifying thread that unites the dialectical rhythms of world history, thereby resolving what to the rest of us seem like contradictions. Her interpretive touchstone (or unifying thread) is *pagan* art."

Paglia seems obsessed by the unusual, the untouched analyses. In *Sexual Personae* Paglia offers an analytical critique of art and beauty that starts with mythology and ancient philosophers and writers—Plato, Homer, Sappho—and progresses all the way up to Edgar Allen Poe and Oscar Wilde. She examines the nature of sex and sexuality though a Freudian analysis, and interweaves her views of art and beauty. Rejecting traditional scholarly methodology, she incorporates pop-culture theory, basing all analyses on sex and sexuality. For example, she compares Donatello's David to pedophile pornography and Lord Byron to Elvis Presley. As a Freudian, and possibly partially because of her own homosexuality, she leaves no idea untouched by her Freudian sexual analysis. In her analysis of Coleridge's poetry in *Sexual Personae,* she writes that "We must tour Coleridge's...major poems to demonstrate their eccentric sexual character. Over all of Coleridge's great poems hovers a strange androgyne, a fabricated superself. Coleridge's sexual ambiguities are already evident in 'The Eolian Harp.'" She then goes on to discuss the relationship between Coleridge and Wordsworth:

> Coleridge appeals not to god but to Wordsworth. And what he prays for is more poetry—his own. The universe has become a theater of sex and poetry. Wordsworth, performing, is watched by Coleridge. But Coleridge, seduced and inseminated by Wordsworth, is watched by the rings of eyes.... The erotic ecstasy of a masochistic male heroine is strongly stimulated by a ring of attentive eyes.... Sexual exhibitionism and voyeurism are at the heart of art.

Paglia also realistically analyzes the role of homosexuality in the history of art and literature, a role which has traditionally been ignored by academics. In *Sexual Personae* she discusses what she considers to be the transvestite natures of Dionysus, Athena, and other Greek mythological figures. "[Athena] adds male armor to a female tunic, but [Dionysus] retains nothing male except a beard.... Supermasculine Hercules is enslaved by the Amazon Omphale, who makes him wear women's clothing and spin wool." She mentions Castigliones's open attack on homosexuality in the *Book of Courtier,* and the role of the hermaphrodite in Renaissance art works. She investigates the androgyne's purpose in literature, especially in the works of Virginia Wolf, Jane Austen, Oscar Wilde, and Emily Brönte—"Jane Austen's *Emma* (1816) illustrates the social novel's association of androgyny.... Emma, like Dorian Grey, enchants by a double-sexed charm." She also examines the lesbian undertones in Jane Austin's *Emma* and Virginia Woolf's *Mrs. Dalloway* (320-321), and sexual ambiguities in the works of Emily Dickinson.

Paglia considers the role of homosexuality to be central to our understanding of culture and history. In "Homosexuality at the Fin de Siècle," which originally appeared in *Esquire* and was reprinted in *Sex, Art, and American Culture,* she writes:

> Thinking about sex as the century closes, we must give the question of homosexuality centrality. Modern homosexuality is, in my view, a product of the intolerable pressures and repressions of the affluent, ambitious nuclear family.... I view the modern gay male as occupying the ultimate point on a track of intensifying masculinity shooting away from the mother.... It is more accurate to see men, driven by sexuality anxiety away from their mothers, forming group alliances by male bonding to create the complex structures of society, art, science and technology.

Her argument constructs male homosexuality as the necessary separation from the mother which has become such an intense issue in the twentieth century because of the breakdown of the extended family.

While idealizing the male homosexual in her writings, Paglia ignores or discredits the female homosexual. She analyzes gay men and lesbians through Freudian theory and makes the conclusion that gay men are more valuable because of their rejection of the feminine while lesbians are pathetic creatures because of their embrace of the feminine. "Male homosexuality, pushing outward into risky, alien territory, is progressive and overall, intellectually stimulating. Lesbianism, seeking a lost state of blissful union with the mother, is cozy, regressive, and, I'm sorry to say, too often intellectually enervating, tending toward the inert." She also states in an interview in *Village Voice,* that "When a man becomes gay, he gains 20 IQ points. When a woman becomes gay she loses 20 IQ points."

Such comments have made many critics wonder where she holds her allegiances. Although she is a "feminist" she finds worth only in what the male creates, and she especially values the gay male. "Male concentration and projection are visible everywhere in the aggressive energy of the streets. Fortunately, male homosexuals of every social class have preserved the cult of the masculine, which will never lose its aesthetic legitimacy. Major peaks of western culture have been accompanied by a high incidence of male homosexuality—in classical Athens and Renaissance Florence and London. Male concentration and projection are self-enhancing, leading to supreme achievements," she writes in *Sexual Personae.* She takes the typical masculine intellectual interpretation of history, which accepts that women's roles were lacking in the creation of history, and ignores the achievements of women and the possible inaccuracies in the male-centered telling of history. "My explanation for the male domination of art, science and politics, an indisputable fact of history, is based on an analogy between sexual physiology and aesthetics. I will argue that all cultural achievement is a projection, a swerve into Apollonian transcendence, and that men are anatomically destined to be projectors," she notes in *Sexual Personae.*

Paglia argues throughout her works that anatomy is destiny—in every respect. She tries to explain herself and her seemingly sexist views in *Publishers Weekly:* "What I am saying is that women are more complete, and art and civilization originally began as a flight from women's power. It's through art and technology and externals that man makes himself complete. Women have not made these great breakthroughs because they're not under this compulsion." Such comments have not hindered Paglia from holding her own accomplishments in high esteem, however. In an interview with the *Washington Post* she calls herself a "great scholar" and in a *Boston Globe* interview she says that she has "the power of seeing things: I see the future and I see the past and everything seems alive!"

Such potentially contradictory views have caused some to call Paglia's feminism and her sexuality into question. She rejects the standard feminist arguments of sexism and oppression to explain the lack of inclusion of women in history and instead focuses only on the Freudian interpretation. She glorifies men and especially male homosexuals, yet trivializes women and lesbians. And yet—to the astonishment of many lesbians—she professes in the *San Francisco Chronicle Image Magazine* to be a woman who has "spent hundreds of hours with [my] head between other women's legs. And loves it and is great at it." Paglia addressed these seeming contradictions in a 1991 lecture at M.I.T. (reprinted in *Sex, Art, and American Culture*):

> In terms of my history, you know, for a long while in my life I felt that, well, I have to be gay, because I'm so attracted to women, but then in a way it's living a lie, because then I have to repress my attractions to men. So after a while I thought, well, why do I have to give myself any label? Why can't I just respond from day to day and just go with the flow in the Sixties way? I think that is healthy.... So part of what I want to do is liberate contemporary sexuality from the new rigidity of gay activism, which I think is getting a little too definite in the line it's drawing between gay and straight. Because I don't think that such a sharp line actually exists in real life.

Paglia's paradoxes don't end with her championing the role of the male homosexual while embracing her own contested view of lesbianism. In *Vamps & Tramps* she suggests that homosexuality is at once both abnormal and heroic:

> [H]omosexuality is not normal. On the contrary, it is a challenge to the norm; therein rests its eternally revolutionary character. Note I do not call it a challenge to the idea of the norm. Queer theorists have tried to take the poststructuralist tack of claiming that there is no norm, since everything is relative and contingent. Nature exists, whether academics like it or not. And in nature, procreation is the single, relentless rule. That is the norm. Our sexual bodies were designed for reproduction. Penis fits vagina: no fancy linguistic game-playing can change that basic fact.

Yet she also states that "We have not only the right, but the obligation to defy nature's tyranny. The highest human identity consists precisely in such assertions of freedom against material limitation. Gays are heroes and martyrs who have given their lives in the greatest war of them all."

Paglia amplified her views on the role of the homosexual within culture in an interview in the *Harvard Gay and Lesbian Review:*

I think we have to face the truth that homosexuality is a minority preoccupation. The idea that any minority's agenda should become the primary agenda of any culture is ridiculous. It's far more important for gays to study the larger culture and to understand the larger frame of human life, because...the more gays are in the ghetto, the more they identify overwhelmingly with the gay side of themselves, rather than with all the other human sides of themselves, then the less their artwork will have a general appeal.... Go look at the real world, and try to produce work that has a general perspective that takes in the whole of human achievement in art and literature.

Despite her contradictory views, despite her apathy toward lesbians, despite her rebel brand of feminism, and despite comments that seem to blame the AIDS epidemic on the gay population, Paglia has become a prominent figure in the gay and feminist community. She creates ripples and causes people to choose sides, for or against her. While her arguments may be hard to swallow for many, she draws on history and modern culture and makes her case through logic, albeit Freudian logic. She remains true to her beliefs regardless of the anger they draw from various societal segments. She yells her opinions loud and clear, and never wavers under confrontation. By placing homosexuality at the center of cultural production, even while she argues that homosexuality is peripheral, Paglia has truly become a gay icon.

—Pamela Green

PARMAR, Pratibha

Nationality: Kenyan/Indian/English writer, editor, and filmmaker. **Born:** Kenya, 1960. **Education:** Postgraduate education, Centre for Contemporary Cultural Studies, Birmingham, England. **Career:** Founding member, Black Women Talk publishing house, England. **Awards:** Best Historical Documentary Award, National Black Programming Consortium, 1992; Best Documentary Short, San Francisco International Lesbian and Gay Film Festival. **Address:** c/o Women Make Movies, 462 Broadway, Suite 500-D, New York, New York 10013 U.S.A.

WRITINGS

Film Writer and Director

Emergence. 1986.
Sari Red. 1988.
Memory Pictures. 1989.
Flesh and Paper. New York, Women Make Movies, 1990.
Khush. New York, Women Make Movies, 1991.
A Place of Rage. 1991.
Bhangra Jig (music video). 1991.
Double The Trouble, Twice The Fun. 1992.
Warrior Marks. New York, Women Make Movies, 1993.
Memsahib Rita, in *Siren Spirits* (also featuring films by Ngozi Onwurah, Frances-Anne Solomon, and Dani Williamson). BBC Television, 1994.
Jodie. New York, Women Make Movies, 1996.

Editor

With Pearlie McNeill and Marie McShea, *Through the Break: Women in Personal Crisis.* London, Sheba Feminist Publishers, 1986.
With Martha Gever and John Greyson, and contributor, *Queer Looks: Perspectives on Lesbian and Gay Film and Video.* Routledge, New York, 1993.

Nonfiction

With the Centre for Contemporary Cultural Studies, *The Empire Strikes Back: Race and Colonialsim in 70s Britain.* London, Hutchinson, 1982.
With Valerie Amos, "Challenging Imperial Feminism," in *Feminist Review,* Vol. 17, autumn 1984, 3-19.
"Woman, Native, Other: Pratibha Parmar Interviews Trinh T. Minh-ha," in *Feminist Review,* Vol. 31, spring 1989, 63.
"Black Feminism: The Politics of Articulation," in *Identity, Community, Culture, difference,* edited by Jonathan Rutherford. London, Lawrence and Wishart, 1990.
With Sue O'Sullivan, *Lesbians Talk (Safer) Sex.* 1992.
With Alice Walker, *Warrior Marks: Female Genital Mutilation and the Sexual Blinding of Women.* New York, Harcourt Brace, 1993.

*

Critical Sources: *Now You See It: Studies on Lesbian and Gay Film* by Richard Dyer, London, Routledge, 1990; "New Queer Cinema" by Ruby Rich and Amy Taubin, in *Sight and Sound,* Vol. 2, no. 5, 1 September 1992; "Pratibha Parmar" by Meena Nanjii, in *High Performance,* Vol. 15, summer-fall 1992, 28-29; "Worlds Apart" by Manohla Dargis, in *Village Voice,* Vol. 38, No. 4, 16 November 1993, 68; "Queer Bodies of Knowledge: Constructing Lesbian and Gay Studies" by Lynda Goldstein, in *Postmodern Culture : An Electronic Journal of Interdisciplinary Criticism,* Vol. 4, No. 2, January 1994; *Women Make Movies Catalogue,* New York, Women Make Movies, 1994; *Women Film Directors: An International Bio-Critical Dictionary,* by Gwendolyn Audrey Foster, Westport, Connecticut, Greenwood Press, 1995, 301-303; "True Colours: The Asian Diaspora in Motion" by Pratibha Parmar, in NAATA/CrossCurrent Media, http://www.lib.berkeley.edu/MRC/NAATA.TrueColours.html.

* * *

Pratibha Parmar's small but growing body of work as writer, editor, and filmmaker reflects her ongoing concern for the problematic situation facing women and cultural "others," among them Asian and Indian lesbians and gay men. Born in Kenya to an Indian father and a Kenyan mother who later relocated to Britain, Parmar is well acquainted with the sense of dispossesion and dislocatedness that she seeks to combat in her films. Writing in "True Colours," she commented that "as a woman of colour and as a lesbian, I locate myself not within any community but in the spaces between these different communities."

As far back as 1986, Parmar's work as co-editor of *Through the Break: Women in Personal Crisis* demonstrates her vital concern for women in crisis and the too often limited and/or non-existent support and resources that exist for such women. That same year Parmar "found the courage" to name herself a filmmaker and create her first film, aptly titled *Emergence.* "Nothing excites me more than to be involved in making a film," she writes in "True Colours."

Her continuing interest in women's issues is demonstrated again in the book she co-authored with Alice Walker, *Warrior Marks: Female Genital Mutilation and the Sexual Blinding of Women,* a book Parmar also gave visual form to in her video, *Warrior Marks,* produced in association with England's progressive Channel 4. This documentary about female genital mutilation in Africa includes interviews with the victims, with activists working to halt female circumcision, and with the circumsizers themselves. Parmar's documentation of this gruesome aspect of women's oppression evidences her willingness to bear witness and to demand an end to this inhumane practice. According to *Women Film Directors* author Gwendolyn Audrey Foster, "Parmar and Walker insist that all women rethink racist and misogynist 'cultural practices' that brutalize women on a daily basis."

In addition to her writing and film work about women, Pratibha Parmar has made specifically "queer" films, drawing attention to the situations of lesbian and gay Asians. Parmar's award-winning documentary *Khush* features interviews with lesbian and gay Asians, living both in India—where homosexuality is illegal—and in western countries. Her film documents her interviewees' understanding of their identities, of what it means to be queer and Asian, both in their own country or in countries abroad. *Khush* also chronicles the interviewees' experiences with community and cultural pressures, homophobia, and racism. *Khush* broadens our understanding of the multi-cultural richness of the lesbian and gay life throughout the world, balancing Western views of the lesbian and gay experience.

Parmar's interest in queer life is further documented in her contribution, as co-editor, to *Queer Looks : Perspectives on Lesbian and Gay Film and Video. Queer Looks,* a collection of essays by lesbians and gay men on topics relating to queers in film, continues and expands the discussion of homosexuality in films which began with Vito Russo's groundbreaking book, *The Celluloid Closet.* In Parmar's own essay, titled "That Moment of Emergence," she asserts that reinventing cinema on queer terms offers "the opportunity to use strategies of appropriation as an assault on racism, sexism, and homophobia."

Other distinctly queer films of Parmar's include *Flesh and Paper,* a celebration of lesbian sexuality that centers around the Indian lesbian poet Suniti Namjoshi. "Taken as a whole," writes Foster, Parmar's work "points the way to a new and broader perspective through which the viewer may appreciate the alternative vision posed by Parmar's groundbreaking films and essays."

—David O'Steinberg

PASTRE, Geneviève

Nationality: French poet, philosopher, essayist, publisher, and playwright. **Education:** Educated in the classics; received an "agrégation" of grammar (a prestigious higher education degree awarded to secondary school teachers through a national competition). **Career:** Taught literature in the high school system; contributor, *Masques* journal, 1979-85; president, Fréquence Gaie (radio station), 1982-84; founder, Les Octaviennes, Paris, from 1985

(name changed to Editions Geneviève Pastre (the first specifically lesbian publishing house in France), from 1989); weekly broadcast of "Les affinités électives", Radio-Libertaire, from 1990. Cofounder, Comité d'Urgence Anti-Répression Homosexuelle (CUAHR). **Address:** Editions Geneviève Pastre, 95 Blvd. Voltaire, 75011 Paris, France.

WRITINGS

Nonfiction

Athènes et le Péril Saphique: Homosexualité Féminine en Grèce Antique. Paris, Les Mots à la Bouche/Octaviennes, 1987.
L'Homosexualité dans le Monde Antique. Paris, Les Mots à la Bouche, 1987.
Les Amazones. Du Mythe à L'Histoire. Paris, Editions G. Pastre, 1996.

Essays

With Gisèle Halimi, *Le Programme Commun des Femmes.* Paris, B. Grasset, 1978.
De l'Amour Lesbien. Paris, Pierre Horay, 1980; translated into German, Berlin, SisSi Verlag, 1984.
"Le 'Je' Femme/Homme," in *Revue Cerdic/CNRS Strasbourg,* No. 15, 1985. *L'Homosexuel(le) dans les sociétés civiles et religieuses.*
Le NOUVEAU Manuel d'Orthographe. Paris, Les Octaviennes, 1991.
Le Bien Aimer. Paris, Editions G. Pastre, 1995.

Fiction

"Dialogues d'Octavie et de Fulvie," in *Masques,* No. 1.
L'Espace du Souffle. Paris, C. Bourgeois, 1977.
"Etrange étranger et prochain," in *La Sape: revue d'expression poétique,* No. 3, 1978.
Octavie ou la Deuxième Mort du Minotaure. Paris, Les Octaviennes, 1985.
Fulvie ou le Voyage à Delphes. Paris, Les Mots à la Bouche/Octaviennes, 1986.
"Amélie ou Ondes de choc," translated to German as "Mit Würde und Feuer," Wien, Austria, Frauenverlag, 1993.

Poetry

Pierre Eclatée. Paris, Editions Saint-Germain des Prés, 1972.
Fleur dans le Ventre Vert: 1968-1972, poèmes. Paris, J. Millas-Martin, 1973.
On Gaspille L'Amarre Ici. Paris, Saint-Germain des Prés, 1975.
7 14 17 ou Architecture d'Eros. Rodez, Subervie, Editions G. Pastre, 1978.
Prélude pour un Largo. Paris, Editions G. Pastre, 1988; translated by Marilyn Hacker, in *13th Moon,* Vol. 14, 1996.
Instances d'Eveil. Paris, Octaviennes-G. Pastre, 1994.
Trois Gorgées du Modeste Royaume. Paris, Editions G. Pastre 1995.

Other

"Réflexion pour le Front lesbien," in *Masques,* No. 11, autumn 1981, 73-75.

"Mémoire: Natalie Clifford Barney," in *Masques,* No. 14, summer 1982, No. 14, 23-29.

"Réflexion sur le sexe," in *Masques,* No. 15, autumn 1982, 94-106.

"Le Nouveau *Fréquence Gaie* cuvée 1983-84: Big Brothers," in *Masques,* No. 21, spring 1984, 187-188.

"Une Femme en Colère," in *Actes du colloque, Paroles d'Amour,* Grenoble, 1990.

"De teloorgang van een opelijk verklaard feministich bewustrijn, de plaats van vrouwenliteratuur in frankrijk anno 1992," in *Surplus,* September 1992.

"20th Century Lesbians: Should We Revive Memory or Break with the Past?," in *Journal of Homosexuality: Gay Studies from the French Cultures,* Vol. 25, No. 1-2, 1993, 127-45.

*

Interviews: "Rencontre: Geneviève Pastre, Autour de Son Livre L'Amour Lesbien" by Fidelio and Suzette Triton, in *Masques,* No. 5, summer 1980, 25-35; "Geneviève Pastre," in *Masques,* No. 7, winter 1980-81, 48; "Le Bien Aimer" by Michèle Causse, in *Lesbia Magazine,* January 1996, 33-37; "Geneviève Pastre, êtes-vous une Amazone?" by Christophe Marcq, in *le 3 Keller,* February 1997.

Geneviève Pastre comments:

In order to follow my philosophical thought one has to read the essay "Le 'Je' Femme/Homme," which appeared in *L'Homosexuel/le dans les sociétés civiles et religieuses* in 1985. It recognized me as a philosopher with an original thought. It was at the time, and still is, difficult for such a voice to be heard in France, because of the influence of the materialist-historical thought which imposed its rule at the CNRS and in political groups. (I reject structuralism and the social sciences as essential systems of thought) and I connect, by moving beyond them, with the philosophy of being and of generative anthropology.

It is not hard to imagine that I am still not being heard. The general gender/sex analysis which is currently so successful does not seem to me to stem from sufficiently far-reaching and ontologically founded roots. My position does, in some ways, come close to that analysis, but it absolutely will not be satisfied merely with it. I am presently working to develop my own thinking on this, and although my thesis has not been fundamentally modified, it is becoming more fine-tuned, more explicit, more precise, and richer.

In the deafening desert of social science theories in which I have mediated for a long time, I have written an initial part of this thesis in "De l'amour lesbien," in which I cleared the ground on several points, and, if I seemed "radical," it was because I displaced the focus of the debate and placed myself outside of scientific discourse, something which, again, is merely a tool for me, but must be founded on values, or rather on a philosophy, in the existential domain.

"Le 'Je' Femme/Homme" was a clarification and a broadening of my view of today's mixed world, of the human species and on tomorrow's world. I took up that thesis again in *Le Bien Aimer*'s first sections, as well as in *Les Amazones,* in which, plunging into History, beyond myth and into prehistory, all the way to the upper paleolithic, I set several new markers.

However, in that respect, while I am heard outside of the community, I remain an outsider in the two communities. One journal, *Humoeurs,* gives me my full place. But it is extremely difficult for me to engage the debate with intellectual partners. French intellectuals all have their court and are not too keen on having a new field opened for them. This hurts thinking in general. I thought of creating my own journal, but this is not possible, because of time and health constraints, for me to open up all the fields I would like to. If my thinking is indeed fecund, it will be recognized and heard when the right time comes.

As for my impatience with theorizing that kills life, it stems from the irritation I feel when I see people follow, as a fad and without the slightest critical appraisal, the theory of the moment; but especially, it reflects my conception of a necessary, albeit fragile, balance between poetry and philosophy, as a constant back and forth movement. This impatience also stems from my acute consciousness of temporality and of my need to have my life and my representation of life agree. I am against "ready made" ideas. Need I add that, in France, nobody, except the happy few, understands the basis of my thinking.

The fact that I am a woman, a fortiori, because I am also a lesbian, therefore totally independent from men as males (i.e. Annah Harendt's position towards Heidegger which gives her, ipso facto, a certain stature in the international world of intellectuals), makes my position very difficult. Furthermore, I have never wanted to write a thesis nor enter the university to obtain the much envied title of doctor. Since I was 24 years old, I have always wanted to get away from any form of control or intellectual and poetic dependence. Socially speaking, that position is costly, but it also has no price.

*   *   *

Geneviève Pastre has been a leading force in the modern lesbian and gay movement in France, involved in all its cultural and political battles. She is a firm but non-violent voice in favor of lesbian autonomy, and a tireless advocate for lesbian and gay visibility and power within mainstream society. Trained in Greek and Latin languages and literature, and nurtured by the profound knowledge of the great canonical French writers, poets, and philosophers (Stendhal, Rimbaud, and Montaigne in particular), Pastre has produced an original and versatile body of poetry, fiction, and essays in which her interests as an artist and her advocacy role complement each other.

In the heyday of the post-1968 French feminist movement, Pastre fought for lesbian positions, writing essays and speaking out in favor of a "Lesbian Front," based on radical lesbian positions. She was active within organizations like Choisir ("To Choose") and co-founder of Comité d'Urgence Anti-Répression Homosexuelle (CUARH). She was elected president of the radio station Fréquence Gaie, negotiating with the French government for the attribution of a band to the station. In 1982, the radio station was ranked the fourth free radio of Paris, it had 140 broadcasters, men and women, and functioned 24 hours a day. Pastre left the station in 1984 after a disagreement over what she termed undemocratic, repressive organizational structures. Instead, she has been broadcasting a weekly program entitled "Les Affinités électives" on Radio-Liertaire since 1990. Pastre has consistently taken a position on political issues affecting lesbians and gay men, and valued the role of political action. "The State has the preposterous power to prevent human beings from loving each other. The political fight is therefore crucial," she told interviewer Michèle Causse in January 1996.

Known and respected as a poet for many years, Pastre publicly "came out" in 1980 when she signed her real name to her essay on lesbian love, *De L'Amour Lesbien,* while teaching in a high school. The work was met with a wall of silence from French critics, although it was translated into German in 1984. Her *Athènes et le Péril Saphique,* published in 1987, met the same kind of response. *Athènes et le Péril Saphique* is a polemical scholarly study based on Pastre's knowledge of Greek and Latin texts in the original. Comparing these texts, carefully examining the interpretation of words and concepts, Pastre argues that the rehabilitation of "sapphic love" has not followed that of male Greek love in contemporary studies. This study tries to demystify the idea that Athen's hegemony in the period from the fifth to the fifteenth century B.C. represents the height of Greek civilization. In fact, claims Pastre, the Greek intelligentsia reduced the cultural and sexual freedom of women, and sought to eradicate the expression of lesbian traditions.

In order to give lesbians a stronger voice, Pastre founded the first specifically lesbian publishing house in France, under the title Editions G. Pastre. The house published the series "Les Octaviennes" with a Parisian gay bookstore, "Les Mots à la Bouche". This independent publishing project kicked off with the publication in 1985 of Pastre's *Octavie ou la Deuxième Mort du Minotaure.* In this text, language itself is impugned for its disingenuous claims and murderous effects on women. In a prophetic mode, Pastre incorporates the Greek myth of the Minotaure as a foundation to a book meant to bring about "the end of uncertainties." It calls on women lovers, victims of the Minotaure who "bled so many women to death and to the death of their soul" ("à la mort de l'âme"; translation by contributor), to "undo" old nightmares. This poetic narrative of the power of words becomes a sort of manifesto, stating that to live lesbian desire is to "invent" words, "words touched by our fingers, our teeth, our lips and our knees our palms and our skin," a manifesto in which echoes of Monique Wittig's *Corps Lesbien* resonate.

Several works associated with Pastre's publishing house, written by her or others, have challenged long held assumptions about homosexuality or made taboo subjects highly visible. Since 1989, over 25 titles have been published by Pastre's publishing house, works by Catherine Hubert, Jane Talbot, Michèle Cros, Marie Durenque, and Odette Menteau, including fiction, essays, and poetry. Her publishing house also has a gay male collection, les Gémeaux, which brought the work of Michel Aurouze, Brane Mozetic (translated from the Slovenian), and François Nozières. Pastre's task has been made difficult by a number of obstacles, including indifference and even hostility among a certain number of gay and lesbian journalists. Her works on the Greek past have been studiously ignored by most of the influential periodicals that review books, with the exception of an indepth article on "Athènes et le péril saphique," published in 1988 by Sociétés, under the direction of Michel Maffesoli.

During the spring of 1995, Pastre founded her own political group, the "Politides" or "Lavenders," with a view to forming a full-fledged political party, because she felt that lesbians and gays could not make profound differences in their lives without being in positions of political power. Her group was active in the struggle to get the World Health Organization to remove homosexuality from its list of mental illnesses and to get Amnesty International to recognize the right to political asylum of homosexuals. Pastre presented herself as a candidate for the Presidency, an action "completely free, calculated, symbolic, insolent, argumenta-

tive and foundational; I mediatized this gesture as largely as possible: men made no mistake about it and while many women were afraid, I received many encouragements, gays and lesbians and heterosexuals listened to me." She sees her organization as capable of preparing an autonomous political force "that will wrest respect for us," she told Causse. However, its program is to seek social justice in a global way, rather than organize exclusively for lesbian and gay rights.

Pastre is not merely an activist for the French lesbian community. She is, first and foremost, a poet with seven volumes to her name. While many of these poems celebrate her lover—an act Pastre believes to be fundamentally important—, in interviews and comments on her work, Pastre has pointed out, sometimes with irritation, that her poetry is treated superficially by many critics. She does not, for instance, see herself as an example of "feminine writing," as some publishers have suggested. In fact, she is more likely to make reference to Rimbaud, whose famous "Je est un autre" ("'I' is someone else") bears directly upon Pastre's theories of the visionary inner world of poetry, a meditation which attempts to reach the "unexplored." Yet, it is hard, she told Causse, to be a woman, "devoid of cultural heritage, devoid of intellectual family."

Critics praise Pastre's expression of "feelings" in her poetry, but do not perceive its existential character. Pastre's poetic process is made first of intuitions, then of flashes or surges of completely different writing, such as those producing *L'Espace du Souffle,* for instance. Pastre refuses to give in to the imperative of themes or narrative structures; for her, the substance of poetry is outside of rules. Pastre, in a series of interviews with writers in the journal *Masques,* has affirmed that poetry speaks of that awesome, trembling moment when, in "reciprocal discovery," two women find themselves face to face, a moment she sees as irreducible to analysis and theory, and in fact, precedes "the models."

Pastre thus occupies an ambiguous position with respect to the place of theory in the cultural life and products of lesbians in particular, and gay identity in general. In several essays, Pastre has argued for an independent, autonomous position of lesbians, and as well, has developed a theorization of love which reaches out to all, regardless of gender. *De L'Amour Lesbien* articulated an original theory of lesbian love in its own right, a project not unrelated to Wittig's *Corps Lesbien* or *Dictionnaire des Amantes.* Love as a defining parameter of any homosexual identity is a very strong theme in all of Pastre's work, one she sometimes opposes to discussions of sex and the body, which she views as limiting. For Pastre, lesbians in particular must exult in the act of their love, nurture it, refine it, and celebrate it. In fact, the practice of love and the political praxis cannot be separated.

"Réflexion sur le sexe," published in *Masques* a few years after *L'Amour Lesbien,* raises many crucial theoretical issues about the respective roles of love, sex, and sexuality in the identities of sexual dissidents. Her 1985 essay "Le 'Je' Femme/Homme," marked a clear identification of her work as that of a philosopher with an original thought. Pastre, who has contributed to feminist thinking on gender, often adopts the paradoxical position that theory is something of a waste of time. Less flippantly, she has spoken against a sort tyranny of theory over identity; thus, in *Le Bien Aimer,* she writes: "they trample the delicate garden of desire and pleasure like those old time seigneurs that the peasant called to chase the hare from his vegetable garden, and who would lay his fields to waste." Pastre expresses distrust of the social sciences when they are "raking over" our minds, which they devastate in the process. She suggests that, rather than engaging in endless theorizing, "it would have been better to tend to our love lives, to our respective lovers and to fulfill them to the best of our ability." *Le Bien aimer* ("to love well, the art of loving well") is an essay written clearly in the tradition of Montaigne, an essay that readers are to feel comfortable picking up at any spot and meandering in. As such, it is neither about sex nor about personal confessions: it is a philosophical work that clearly states that love, in particular lesbian/gay love, is always "a founding philosophical act, therefore, an 'outlaw' act."

—Francesca Canadé Sautman

PECK, Dale

Nationality: American novelist. **Born:** Bay Shore, New York, 13 July 1967. **Education:** Drew University, New Jersey, B.A. 1989. **Career:** Worked at *Out Magazine* before moving into full-time creative writing. Former member of AIDS Coalition to Unleash Power (ACT UP). **Awards:** Guggenheim fellow, 1994. **Agent:** Irene Skolnick, 121 West 27th St., Suite 601, New York, New York 10001.

WRITINGS

Novels

Martin and John: A Novel. New York, Farrar, Straus, 1993; published as *Fucking Martin,* London, Chatto & Windus, 1993.
The Law of Enclosures, New York City, Farrar, Straus, 1996.

*

Adaptations: *Fucking Martin* (play), Gay Sweatshop, 1994.

Critical Sources: Review of *Martin and John* by Stuart Klawans, in *Entertainment Weekly,* No. 166, 16 April 1993, 49; review of *Martin and John* by Pamela Wine, in *JAMA: The Journal of the American Medical Association,* Vol. 271, No. 9, 2 March 1994, 717; "Troubles in Mind" by Michael Bronski, in the *Boston Phoenix,* Boston, Massachusetts, December 1995; review of *Law of Enclosures* by John Brenkman, in *Nation,* New York, Vol. 262, No. 4, 29 January 1996, 31; "Silence & Secrets" by James Cary Parkes, in *Gay Times,* London, February 1996, 54-56.

*   *   *

Dale Peck's 1993 first novel, published when he was 25 years old, created a sensation for its depth and delicacy. *Martin and John,* published in the United Kingdom as the more explicitly titled *Fucking Martin,* received mainstream reviews for its complexity and literary style. "[A] book that marks the debut of a remarkably accomplished young writer," wrote Stuart Klawans in *Entertainment Weekly.*

The gay press was equally adoring, and he was compared to gods of the gay literary world, including William Burroughs and Jean Genet. "If Edmund White's *A Boy's Own Story* was the gay novel of the 1980s, then *Fucking Martin* is the ultimate tale of the 1990s," wrote James Carey Parkes in *Gay Times.*

The narrator John is unreliable, and the picture he presents is jumbled but always riveting. "His narratives always have the force of autobiography, yet you never know what's really true," wrote John Brenkman in the *Nation.* Like lesbian author Sarah Shulman, Peck does not rely on the literary conventions of the heterosexual fiction genre to write about the gay experience but experiments wildly with form. In *Martin and John* he favours a patchwork narrative of conflicting stories over linear storytelling.

John is a young man who has escaped from an abusive home into the arms of his lover Martin, who becomes ill with AIDS. Smaller stories, all featuring characters named Martin and John, gay everymen, break up the larger narrative. Martin is a rich man, a security guard in Kansas, a teenage runaway, and a sadistic New York pimp. Stories of John's family life include an abusive, widowed father, a happy long-living mother, and a sickly mother in a nursing home. "Unlike conventional narratives that attempt to capture a life in linear chronology, *Martin and John* follows the psyche's inner logic. Traumatic memories, conflicts and impressions of John's childhood are inexorably mapped onto the fierce connections of adulthood," wrote Pamela Wine in *JAMA.*

Although *Martin and John* was rapidly pigeonholed as an AIDS novel, Peck insists that it was about the death of his mother when he was four years old. "Everybody reads it as an AIDS book but it was about the effects of my mother's death," Peck told the *Gay Times.* "That is the single death that informs all others to me and was the beginning of my morbid fascination with mortality."

Although the book was one of the few gay novels in 1993 to be heavily reviewed in the non-gay press, this does not necessarily mean that it had a straight readership. Peck told the *Boston Phoenix,* "The idea of the so-called gay novel crossing over is a myth. *Martin and John* received enormously positive reviews in the mainstream press, yet, as far as I can tell, my readership was 90 percent white gay men and 10 percent heterosexuals."

A phenomenal first novel is tough to top. Peck's second novel was successful if only because it was so unexpected and hard to handle for the fans of his first novel. *The Law of Enclosures* was two novellas about heterosexual couples. His protagonists were Henry and Beatrice, 20-something newlyweds, and Hank and Bea, 60-somethings in the twilight of their life. Their stories of marriage gone bad are told in alternating chapters interrupted by an autobiographical interlude about Peck's mother and the three stepmothers he acquired as a result of his father's frequent marrying.

Peck makes his home in London in order to concentrate on writing. "In New York, I have so many friends which, as unkind as it might sound, is too distracting," he told *Gay Times.*

—Victoria Stagg Elliott

PENELOPE, Julia

Pseudonyms: Has also written as J. Seeley and, prior to 1980, as Julia Stanley. **Nationality:** American theorist, essayist, editor, and linguist. **Born:** Miami, Florida, 19 June 1941. **Education:** City College of New York, New York City, B.A. 1966; University of Texas at Austin, Ph.D. 1971. **Career:** Instructor and assistant professor of English, University of Georgia, 1968-74; visiting assistant professor, University of South Dakota, 1976; assistant professor, later associate professor, University of Nebraska, Lincoln, 1976-87; visiting associate professor, Washington University, St. Louis, Missouri, 1986-87, and University of Massachusetts, Amherst, 1988; editor and lecturer, from 1987. General editor, *Matrices: Lesbian/Feminist Research Newsletter,* 1974-84; member, Committee on Public Doublespeak, National Council of Teachers of English, 1974-93; publications committee, Gay Caucus for the Modern Languages, 1975-79; member, Commission on Status of Women, Modern Language Association, 1977-78; co-chair, Committee on Lesbian and Gay Male Concerns in the English Profession, National Council of Teachers of English, 1977-80; book review editor, *Sinister Wisdom,* 1979-80. **Awards:** Blanche M. Baker Scholarship Awards, Daughters of Bilitis; National Science Foundation Grant; National Endowment for the Humanities Grant, 1980; Fellow, Schlesinger Library of Women's History, Radcliffe College, 1990-92; Lambda Literary Award nomination, for lesbian anthology, 1993, 1994, 1995. **Address:** 1916 37th Street, Lubbock, Texas 79412, U.S.A.

WRITINGS

Editor

With Susan J. Wolfe, *The Coming Out Stories.* Watertown, Massachusetts, Persephone Press, 1980; as *The Original Coming Out Stories,* Freedom, California, The Crossing Press, 1989.

With Sarah Lucia Hoagland, "Lesbianism: Sexuality and Power/ The Patriarchy: Violence and Pornography," special issue of *Sinister Wisdom,* Vol. 15, fall 1980.

With Hoagland, *For Lesbians Only: A Separatist Anthology.* London, England, Onlywomen Press, 1988, 1992.

With Sarah Valentine, *Finding the Lesbians: Personal Accounts from Around the World.* Freedom, California, The Crossing Press, 1990.

With Valentine, *International Feminist Fiction.* Freedom, California, The Crossing Press, 1992.

With Wolfe, *Sexual Practice/Textual Theory: Lesbian Cultural Criticism.* London, England, Basil Blackwell, 1993.

With Wolfe, *Lesbian Culture: An Anthology.* Freedom, California, The Crossing Press, 1993.

Out of the Class Closet: Lesbians Speak. Freedom, California, The Crossing Press, 1994.

Selected Nonfiction

"Homosexual Slang," in *American Speech,* Vol. 45, spring/summer 1970, 130-134.

"Passive Motivation," in *Foundations of Language,* Vol. 13, 1975, 25-39.

"Uninhabited Angels: Metaphors for Love," in *Margins,* No. 23, 1975, 7-10.

"A Cursory and Precursory History of Language, and the Telling of It," in *Sinister Wisdom,* No. 1, summer 1976, 5-12.

With Susan W. Robbins (later Susan J. Wolfe), "Lesbian Humor," in *Women: A Journal of Liberation,* Vol. 5, No. 1, June 1977, 26-29.

With Robbins, "Truncated Passives: Some of Our Agents Are Missing," in *Linguistic Theory and the Real World,* Vol. 1, No. 2, September 1976, 33-37.

"Lesbian Relationships and the Vision of Community," in *Feminary,* Vol. 9, No. 1, spring 1978, 4-9, 57-59.

With Robbins, "Mother Wit: Tongue in Cheek," in *Lavender Culture,* edited by Karla Jay and Allen Young. New York, Jove Press, 1978, 279-307.

With Wolfe, "Linguistic Problems with Patriarchal Reconstructions of Indo-European Culture: A Little More than Kin, a Little Less than Kind," in *Women's Studies International Quarterly,* Vol. 3, No. 2, 1980, 227-37.

"Mystery and Monster: The Lesbian in Heterosexual Fantasies," in *Sinister Wisdom,* No. 15, fall 1980, 76-91.

"*Whose* Past Are We Reclaiming?," in *Common Lives/Lesbian Lives,* Vol. 13, autumn 1984, 16-36.

"The Lesbian Perspective," in *Lesbian Philosophies and Cultures,* edited by Jeffner Allen. Albany, New York, SUNY Press, 1990, 89-108.

Speaking Freely: Unlearning the Lies of the Fathers' Tongues. Elmsford, New York, Pergamon Press Athene Series, 1990; New York, Teachers' College Press, 1992.

Call Me Lesbian: Lesbian Lives, Lesbian Theory. Freedom, California, The Crossing Press, 1992.

"Learning to Live with My Body," in *Off the Rag,* edited by Lee Lynch and Akia Woods. Norwich, Vermont, New Victoria Publishers, 1996, 126-132.

"Passing Lesbians: The High Cost of Femininity," in *An Intimacy of Equals,* edited by Lilian Mohin. London, England, Onlywomen Press, 1996, 118-152.

Other

With Morgan Gray, *Found Goddesses: From Asphalta to Viscera* (humor). Norwich, Vermont, New Victoria Publishers, 1988.

Crossword Puzzles for Women. Freedom, California, The Crossing Press, 1995.

*

Manuscript Collections: Special Collections, Duke University Library, Durham, North Carolina.

Julia Penelope comments:

Having endured the violence and insult of name-calling from other lesbians for decades, I "retired" as a lesbian activist in January, 1994, after a particularly vicious personal attack at Mama Bear's in Oakland, California. Although a few of the writings mentioned in this entry were published after that date, 1994 was the end, for me, of my dream of a lesbian community. Not I, not anyone, should be expected to go through the pillaging and looting of her soul and then to remain gladly in the charred nightmare of that realm.

From 1973 to 1994, I committed most of my energy to working with other lesbians to create a "land" that we could call our own. I now believe that I have wasted my life, without proper regard for my own health and well-being, and regret the risks I took: No one benefited from them politically, and I lost personally. I would not now make the choices I have made in the past. I am now grateful for that incident at Mama Bear's; the pain of contemplating it forced me to re-evaluate the work I was doing and the choices I was making in order to do it.

I have returned to what was, after all, my first love, language, and to figuring out how and why language can be used at it is, especially by those who wield economic and political power over the rest of us. In this realm, I can do what I love best, and there is no name-calling, no meanness, no pain for me.

*　　　*　　　*

The new lesbian who first finds "others like me" in the pages of *The Coming Out Stories* finds herself in the long line of women who have turned the pages of Julia Penelope's books with sighs of relief, with gasps of recognition, and with chuckles of pleasure. Beginning in the 1960s, this lesbian culture maven has charted the territory that women have been exploring. She first wrote on lesbian and gay literature in the late 1950s and early 1960s under the pseudonym J. Seeley, a part of her career unknown to most of her current readers. These early articles explored the Charlie Johns Investigating Committee on Communism and Homosexuality, the purge of homosexuals at Florida State University in 1959, and other issues.

Trained as a linguist, and early on seeing through patriarchal doublespeak, her early writings focused on unearthing the sexism embedded in the very structure of the language Americans are taught to speak. She uncovered and described the "agentless passive," and in so doing contributed a new and startlingly necessary dimension to linguistic analysis. At the same time she began to more formally note idiosyncratic forms of gay and lesbian speech. As far back as 1970, her article "Homosexual Slang" in *American Speech* suggested intriguing ways to analyze what was being said within the community.

By the end of the decade, Penelope was specifically addressing not only lesbian forms of speech, as in "Mother Wit: Tongue in Cheek," but including and forming lesbian theories of separatism, relationships, and life in a combined humorous/serious vein. Lesbians read and understood, laughed and knew—this lesbian was making a difference.

Over the years, the ability to tell the serious tale in the playful way came to characterize a "Penelope" piece. From "The Articulation of Bias: Hoof in Mouth Disease" to "Fourth and Long: Feminism Stalled in Enemy Territory," societal and cultural icons were felled by her words. And many a lesbian has said out loud or under her breath, "Hail Asphalta, full of grace, help me find a parking place," swearing to friends that the incantation from *Found Goddesses: From Asphalta to Viscera* really works.

But her work is not merely funny; Julia Penelope has presented clear analyses of a patriarchal and heterosexist society. Her books, her collaborated anthologies, her articles, her talks in the community: all point without fear to the real world of the lesbian and to ways to survive within it. She has called lesbians to account, helped the lesbian community to see its severe problems and its rich possibilities.

Of course, taking on such volatile subjects brought controversy. Criticisms about Penelope's positions, from separatism to sadomasochism to choices about her selections in anthologies, often became personal attacks. She met them head on and spoke her truth, a truth that has changed over time as she developed new insights. With characteristic verve, she continued her activist role in her local areas. Wherever Julia Penelope has lived, an activist group thrived. In the national arena, her work, prompted by her principles, influenced the way the lesbian community knew itself and acted.

Finding the Lesbians: Personal Accounts from Around the World (1990) began another focused series of analytical works that brought the international character of lesbian fact and fiction into the spotlight. Then, in 1994, Penelope collected and celebrated the varied textures of specifically lesbian culture. The following year she presented an array of narratives on class with the lesbian community. The last two books, *Lesbian Culture: An Anthology* and *Out of the Class Closet: Lesbians Speak,* were each nominated for a Lambda Literary Award, recognizing her unique contribution to the development and description of these varied lesbian perspectives.

After more than a hundred books and articles and exhausting years of speaking in the lesbian community, Julia Penelope moved back to the Southern part of the country in the 1990s and has turned to editing dictionaries and textbooks. And in an entirely new genre, she devised *Crossword Puzzles for Women,* once again uniting the fun with the serious. She has continued to write, including reflections on her own life as a lesbian as well as theoretical pieces. The more personal "Learning to Live with My Body," published in *Off the Rag,* was a product of this incorporation of the self in the work.

In the decades of her career, Penelope has spanned the range of lesbian possibility, maintaining a clear ethic through the maze of change. From her youngest days as a lesbian outsider in Florida schools to her mature years of clear and careful analysis, she trod the course she set for herself with firm steps. Her integrity and love for lesbians has marked her life and work and made her many strong and loyal friends and supporters. Those women who know her personally and those who have met her through her work have learned the fire of her mind and the gentleness of her heart in ways that changed their lives.

—Krystyna Colburn

PERELESHIN, Valery

Pseudonyms: Valery Frantzevich Salatko-Petryshche; also known as Valério Pereliéchin. **Nationality:** Russian and Brazilian poet, translator of poetry, and memoirist. **Born:** Irkutsk, Siberia, 7 July 1913; taken by his mother to Harbin, Manchuria, in 1920; emigrated to Brazil in 1953. **Education:** Educated in Russian and English at the bilingual Y.M.C.A. High School, Harbin; School of Law, Harbin University, graduated 1935; Russian Orthodox Theological School of St. Vladimir, from 1937. **Career:** Held a variety of jobs in China and Brazil including translator, jeweler's assistant, and Russian and English teacher; poet, writing for various Russian periodicals, Harbin, from 1930; monk, Russian Ecclesiastical Mission in Beijing and Shanghai, 1938-43; librarian, British Council, Brazil, 1957-65. Frequent contributor to periodicals and journals, including *Novoe Russkoe Slovo* ("The New Russian Word"), *Novyi Zhurnal* ("The New Review"), *Vozrozhdenie* ("The Renascence"), *Rubezh* ("The Frontier"), and *Grani* ("Facets"), from 1967. **Died:** Jacaparaguà, Brazil, in 1992.

WRITINGS

Collected Poetry (in Russian)

V puti ("En Route"). Harbin, 1937.
Dobryi ulei ("The Kindly Beehive"). Harbin, 1939.

Zdezda nad morem ("Star over the Sea"). Harbin, 1940.

Zhertva ("Sacrifice"). Harbin, 1944.

Iuzhnyi dom ("Southern Home"). Munich, 1968.

Kachel' ("The Swing"). Munich, Possev-Verlag, 1971.

Zapovednik ("Nature Preserve"). Frankfurt am Main, 1972.

S gory Nevo ("[The View] from Mount Nebo"). Frankfurt am Main, 1975.

Arièl ("Ariel"). Frankfurt am Main, 1976.

Nos odres velhos ("In the Old Wineskins"; in Portuguese). Rio de Janeiro, Achiamé, 1983.

Tri rodiny ("Three Homelands"). Paris, Albatros, 1987.

Iz glubiny vozzvakh. Holyoke, Massachusetts, New England Publishing Co., 1987.

Dvoe—i snova odin? ("Two Men—and Again Alone?"). Holyoke, Massachusetts, New England Publishing Co., 1987.

Vdogonku ("In Hot Pursuit"). Holyoke, Massachusetts, New England Publishing Co., 1988.

Russkii poet v gostiakh u Kitaia, 1920-1952: sbornik stikhotvorenii ("A Russian Poet as a Guest of China, 1920-1952: Selected Poems"), edited in Russian and with an introduction and notes by Jan Paul Hinrichs. The Hague, Leuxenhoff, 1989.

Translator

Skazanie starogo moriaka ("The Rime of the Ancient Mariner") by Samuel Taylor Coleridge. Harbin, 1940.

Stikhi na veere ("Verses Written on a Fan"; an anthology of Chinese classical poetry). Frankfurt am Main, Possev-Verlag, 1970.

Li Sao ("ca. 300 B.C.") by Ch'Y'an. Frankfurt am Main, 1975.

Iuzhnyi krest. Antologia brazil'skoi poèzii ("The Southern Cross. An Anthology of Brazilian Poetry"). Frankfurt am Main, 1978.

Canticos de Alexandria by Mikhail Kuzmin. Rio de Janeiro, 1986.

Other

Russian Poetry and Literary Life in Harbin and Shanghai 1930-1950. The Memoirs of Valery Pereleshin, edited in Russian with an introduction by Jan Paul Hinrichs. Amsterdam, Rodopi, 1987.

Poèma bez predmeta ("Poem Without Object"; book-length autobiography), edited in Russian with an introduction by Simon Karlinsky. Holyoke, Massachusetts, New England Publishing Co., 1989.

*

Manuscript Collections: Valery Pereleshin's archive, in the Library of Leiden University, The Netherlands.

Critical Sources: "A Hidden Masterpiece: Valery Pereleshin's *Arièl*" by Simon Karlinsky, in *Christopher Street,* December 1977, 37-42; preface and introduction by Jan Paul Hinrichs, in *Russian Poetry and Literary Life...,* 1987, 5-23; "Memoirs of Harbin" by Simon Karlinsky, in *Slavic Review,* Vol. 48, No. 2, summer 1989; "Selected Poems" by Winston Leyland, in *Out of the Blue: Russia's Hidden Gay Literature,* edited by Kevin Moss, Gay Sunshine Press, 1997, 183 ff.

*   *   *

From 1922 on, Russian literature published in foreign countries could no longer be imported to the Soviet Union. This led to the somewhat artificial division of modern Russian literature into two separate branches, Soviet and the literature of Russian exiles. This situation remained until around 1989. The centers of Russian literature in exile in the 1920s were Berlin and Prague; in the 1930s this center moved to Paris, and after World War II to New York and Washington, D.C. But between the 1920s and the end of the 1940s there also existed a lively literary scene in the Far East, in Harbin and, to a lesser extent, in Shanghai.

Harbin, the city where Pereleshin grew up and became a poet, was founded by Russians in 1898, in connection with their building of the Chinese Eastern Railroad. It became a boomtown and a major Russian cultural center during the Russo-Japanese War of 1904-05, and even more so after the October Revolution of 1917. By the early 1920s, Harbin's Russian-speaking population rose to 127,000. Novels, collections of stories, and works of nonfiction were regularly published in Harbin, most of which now seem forgettable. The city's literary life manifested itself most intensely and memorably in poetry. There were two recognized older poets in the city, Arseny Nesmelov (1889-1945) and Aleksei Achaïr (1896-1961?), whose work was known and published in the Russian cultural centers in Western Europe. Pereleshin belonged to the group of younger poets who began publishing in the early 1930s. In addition to him, this group comprised Lydia Khaindrova, Larisa Andersen, Nikolai Shchegolev, Harry Satovsky-Rzhevsky, and others. The poets of this generation matured creatively through joining the literary club "Churaevka," organized by Aleksei Achaïr, who steered them toward the poetics of Acmeism, a literary movement in pre-revolutionary Russia which included Anna Akhmatova and Osip Mandelstam.

By the mid 1930s, it became clear that Valery Pereleshin was the most talented and original poet of the "Churaevka" group. In 1935, the notable (and openly gay) Paris critic Georgy Adamovich and Mikhail Kantor invited Pereleshin to make the selection of Far-Eastern poetry for their anthology of exiled poets, *Iakor'* ("The Anchor"), published in Paris the same year. In Pereleshin's personal life, the most significant event in his early twenties was his sojourn at a hospital, where he was placed because of food poisoning. There, the poet shared a private room with Vasily Nesterenko, a young man dying of tuberculosis, with whom Pereleshin fell in love, a love that was reciprocated. Alarmed at the magnitude of his emotions, Pereleshin was attracted to the life of the monks of the Kazan Monastery, who were visible from the hospital window. He switched from the school of law to the school of theology and, a year later, took monastic vows, hoping that this would lessen his homosexual inclinations. On the title page of his second collection of verse, *The Kindly Beehive,* his name was followed by "the Monk Herman."

Within the same year, the newly-minted monk was sent by the ecclesiastical authorities to Beijing, to teach at the Russian parochial school there and to help with services at the local Russian Orthodox church. During his four years in the Chinese capital, Pereleshin made a thorough study of ancient Chinese art and literature and began work on translating ancient Chinese poets, an anthology of which he was to publish three decades later. He gradually came to accept his sexual orientation.

After the scandalous discovery of the poet-monk's affairs with two choirboys, the archbishop in charge of the Beijing mission had him transferred to Shanghai, though, as Pereleshin was later to write in his autobiography in verse, *Poem Without Object,* he found incomprehensible the decision to send "the celibate to Babylon." Thus, after living in rigid Harbin and Beijing, the poet found himself in an international city famed for its licentiousness. In Shanghai, Pereleshin was reunited with many of his literary friends from Harbin. They tried publishing a Russian literary journal, but the cosmopolitan Shanghai did not have the Russian readership that had existed in Harbin. In his personal life, the Shanghai period was notable for his durable liaison with the Chinese bookseller Lü Sin, a relationship that lasted until the victory of Communism in China. With the coming of the new regime, Lü Sin felt obliged to obey the imperatives of the state and the family to marry and procreate. Their painful breakup led Pereleshin to form his theory of spiritual lefthandedness, which consists of emancipating oneself from the imperatives of the species and family, a liberation that is a prerequisite of admitting one's homosexuality to oneself and the world.

In 1950, Pereleshin and his mother tried to join his younger brother Viktor who had fought with the U.S. armed forces during World War II and had settled in America. But upon arrival in San Francisco, Pereleshin was arrested and imprisoned. An anonymous accuser had denounced him as a Soviet agent because he had worked in Shanghai for a brief period as a translator for the Soviet news agency TASS. His duties there entailed nothing more than translating Chinese press clippings into Russian. But the time was the heyday of Senator Joseph McCarthy, when the very fact of accusation was regarded as proof of guilt. He was deported back to China. Pereleshin later learned that he was also charged with helping Soviet emissaries to organize the Chinese Communist Party, an event that occurred when he was seven years old. In 1953, the poet settled in Rio de Janeiro and eventually came to regard himself as a Brazilian poet who happened to write in Russian.

Pereleshin's first four collections of verse, published in Harbin, represent his poetic apprenticeship. In them he follows the example of the Acmeist poet Nikolai Gumiliov (1886-1921) and the exiled Russian poets in Paris, such as Georgy Ivanov, who practiced a restrained and deliberately modest neoromanticism. After the appearance of his fourth volume, *Sacrifice,* there followed an almost quarter-century hiatus, when Pereleshin, while continuing to write poetry and translate Chinese poets, published virtually nothing. Only in 1967 did he resume publishing in Russian literary journals in Paris, New York, and Germany; he also produced his fifth collection of verse, *Southern Home.* In this volume, Pereleshin can be seen as a stronger and more original poet than he was in his work written in China. The book is devoted to the cultures of ancient and modern China and the poet's involvement with both. In the light of his subsequent autobiography, it can be seen that a number of poems in the book are addressed to Lü Sin and reflect the debates between the two lovers prior to their breakup. Pereleshin carefully managed the verbal tenses because in Russian the use of the past tense can reveal the sex of the addressee, so that an uninitiated reader may assume that his lover was a Chinese woman—a stratagem that he was to abandon only in his tenth collection of verse, *Arièl* (1976).

As the late Estonian poet Aleksis Rannit pointed out in his two-part survey of Pereleshin's verse collections (published in *Russian Language Journal* in 1976 and 1978), they tend to alternate between books of religious and mystical poetry, such as *The Swing* and *De Profundis Clamavi* (the original title of this book was not in Russian, but in Old Church Slavic, the liturgical language of the Orthodox Church, so that a Latin rendition seemed appropriate) with volumes of verse on personal and erotic themes: *Arièl* and *Nature Preserve.* Although Pereleshin broke with the Orthodox Church when he gave up his monkhood, metaphysics

and mysticism colored much of his late poetry, most spectacularly in the collection *The Swing,* which includes the virtuosic long poem *Poèma o mirozdanii* ("Poem of the Creation of the World") and the crown of sonnets *Krestnyi put'* ("Stations of the Cross"). Pereleshin's verbal texture in his religious poetry is as assured and sparkling as in his love poetry of the same period.

The two most compelling achievements of the mature Pereleshin are *Arièl* and *Poem Without Object. Arièl* is actually four superimposed books: a narrative sequence of 168 sonnets, both Petrarchan and Spenserian; the poet's personal diary for a three year period; a story of one man's love for another, told in a sort of epistolary novel in verse; and, finally, a survey of celebrated instances of older men loving younger ones in the Western literary tradition (Socrates and Alcibiades, Verlaine and Rimbaud, Stefan George and Maximin, Oscar Wilde and Bosie). The occasion for the book was a three-year correspondence between Pereleshin and the young translator and lover of poetry Yevgeny Vitkovsky, who wrote to the poet from Moscow in February of 1971, expressing his admiration and offering himself as a son, lover, and disciple all in one. The poet's reaction was swift and sweeping: "You willed it so— and you've become my fate / About the twilight of the waning world, / About the flame of Plato and of Shakespeare, / About myself I now converse with you."

Poem Without Object, begun immediately after the completion of *Arièl,* is written in "Onegin stanza," a special strophe, similar to a sonnet but differently rhymed, which Alexander Pushkin devised for his famous novel in verse, *Eugene Onegin.* Also, like Pushkin's novel, Pereleshin's poetic autobiography consists of eight cantos. Finally, still another similarity to Pushkin, the narrative is often interrupted by digressions—literary, personal, and historical. But Pereleshin's long poem is clearly a modern work, despite its outward Pushkinian guise. In a witty, semi-humorous tone, the poet tells of his life in China and Brazil, of his family's historical background, of his own literary career, of his travels, and of his three major loves: Vasily Nesterenko, Lü Sin, and Yevgeny Vitkovsky. A religious perspective is also present, but compared with some of his earlier writings, gay love is now seen as God-given and needed for the soul's path to God.

In present-day Russia, there is much interest in literature produced by exiled writers. There exist now two literary journals in larger Siberian cities devoted to the study of Far Eastern prose and poetry of the 1920s and 1930s. Pereleshin's poetry has appeared in anthologies and collections of twentieth century Russian poets. It is only a matter of time before he is recognized as a major poet of the second half of this century.

—Simon Karlinsky

PERRY, Troy D.

Nationality: American minister, activist, and author of nonfiction. **Born:** Tallahassee, Florida, 27 July 1940. **Education:** Attended public schools in Florida, Georgia, Texas, and Alabama. **Family:** Divorced; two sons. **Military Service:** Served in the United States Army, 1965-67. **Career:** Conducted first Christian worship service for gays and lesbians in Huntington Park, California, 6 October 1968; gay rights activist and political organizer, from 1969; founder and moderator, Universal Fellowship of Metropolitan Community Churches (UFMCC), West Hollywood, California. **Awards:** Honorary Ph.D.: Samaritan College, Los Angeles. **Address:** Universal Fellowship of Metropolitan Community Churches, 8704 Santa Monica Blvd., 2nd Floor, West Hollywood, California 90069, U.S.A.

WRITINGS

Autobiographies

With Charles L. Lucas, *The Lord Is My Shepherd and He Knows I'm Gay: The Autobiography of the Rev. Troy D. Perry.* Los Angeles, Nash, 1972.
With Thomas L.P. Swicegood, *Don't Be Afraid Anymore: The Story of Reverend Troy Perry and the Metropolitan Community Churches.* New York, St. Martin's Press, 1990.

Nonfiction

With Swicegood, *Profiles in Gay and Lesbian Courage.* New York, St. Martin's Press, 1991.

*

Biography: "Perry, Troy D(eroy)" in *Contemporary Authors,* edited by Hal May, Vol. 109, Detroit, Gale, 1983, 372; "Church for Gays Alters Mainline Religion's Views" by John Dart, in *Los Angeles Times* (Los Angeles), 7 June 1991, A1, A36-A37.

Interviews: "Gays and the Gospel: An Interview with Troy Perry," in *Christian Century* (Chicago), Vol. 113, No. 27, 25 September-2 October 1996, 896-899, 901.

Critical Sources: "Out of the Closet" by Charles Whitman, in *Christian Century* (Chicago), Vol. 89, No. 36, 11 October 1972, 1021-1022; review of *The Lord Is My Shepherd and He Knows I'm Gay* by G. Eric Hansen, in *Library Journal* (New York), Vol. 97, No. 20, 15 November 1972, 3702; review of *The Lord Is My Shepherd and He Knows I'm Gay,* in *Choice* (Chicago), Vol. 10, No. 3, May 1973, 541; review of *Don't Be Afraid Anymore,* in *Kirkus Reviews* (New York), Vol. 58, No. 19, 1 October 1990, 1379; review by Mary Deeley of *Don't Be Afraid Anymore,* in *Booklist* (Chicago), Vol. 87, No. 6, 15 November 1990, 581; review of *Profiles in Gay and Lesbian Courage,* in *Kirkus Reviews* (New York), Vol. 59, No. 16, 15 August 1991, 1071; review of *Profiles in Gay and Lesbian Courage* by Marie Kuda, in *Booklist* (Chicago), Vol. 88, No. 3, 1 October 1991, 226; review of *Profiles in Gay and Lesbian Courage* by Jeffry Ingram, in *Library Journal* (New York), Vol. 116, No. 16, 1 October 1991, 112.

Troy Perry comments:

When I wrote *The Lord Is My Shepherd and He Knows I'm Gay* with Charles L. Lucas, there was no book that I knew of that had been published in America by an openly gay male who used his real name and dealt with his spirituality. After founding Metropolitan Community Church in 1968, as the growth of my church progressed and I met more and more individuals who had wrestled, as Jacob did with God, over sexuality and spirituality, I believed with all my heart it was time to "bear my testimony," as a Christian who had "come out" and pastored a Church.

I have always felt that the greatest work that gay and lesbian liberation has in America is *educating* people as to who we are. To me, the most important segment of the American population that I could reach was the religious community in America. I believed that until we changed the minds of individuals who claimed religion or claimed faith and religion as one of the most important parts of their character, we would not be able to get Congress to pass laws that would stop discrimination against the gay/lesbian/bi/transgendered community. I believe that my gut feeling was right as I look back over the last 30 years of my ministry and see the changes that have happened, not only in this country, but worldwide, as all the religious groups in the world now wrestle with the whole subject of how all of our community fits into all of their religious groups.

* * *

Troy D. Perry grew up in a fundamentalist Christian environment in the American South and was licensed to preach at 15. As he explained in his autobiographical book, *Don't Be Afraid Anymore,* "I cannot remember a time when religion did not attract me. Church was like an extended family, with social warmth, emotion, and a strong spiritual magnetism." Perry dropped out of high school after the eleventh grade to become a travelling evangelist. Despite his homosexual tendencies, he married a preacher's daughter when they were both 18. Five years later he was excommunicated from his denomination, the Church of God in Prophecy, and lost his position as a pastor in Santa Ana, California. Shortly thereafter, his wife left him, taking their two young sons with her. Perry moved to nearby Los Angeles and became a Sears, Roebuck and Company employee. His acceptance of his homosexuality accelerated after he was drafted into the U.S. Army, especially because of his close friendship with an openly gay soldier while stationed in West Germany. Following his return to Los Angeles, however, Perry remained troubled by the conflict between his call to Christian ministry and his homosexuality.

Perry resolved this dilemma by instituting weekly Christian worship services aimed at gays and lesbians in the parlor of his Huntington Park, California, home. Perry's first service on 6 October 1968 drew only 12 people, but the congregation grew rapidly thereafter. The Universal Fellowship of Metropolitan Community Churches (UFMCC), the name chosen by Perry for the new denomination, quickly expanded to other American cities during its first decade. Perry travelled constantly in the United States and abroad to build his "gay church," as many commentators called it. He organized not only a structure for his denomination, but also a range of religious and social programs to provide community, social action, and salvation for gays and lesbians. His emphasis on progressive political action to promote gay rights, as well as his acceptance of women and minorities as equal partners in UFMCC, drew adherents to the church. Although the National Council of Churches has rejected both membership and observer status for UFMCC, the success of Perry's denomination increased pressure on mainstream Protestant churches in America to admit openly gay and lesbian members. By 1996 UFMCC had about 46,000 members and 301 congregations in 19 countries. Perry proclaimed in a 1996 *Christian Century* interview: "We continue to expand and grow and carry the good news that Jesus died for our sins, not our sexuality."

With the assistance of two associates, Perry has written three books since the early 1970s. His first effort, *The Lord Is My Shepherd and He Knows I'm Gay,* was written in collaboration with

Charles L. Lucas. The book recounts the minister's life to that point, focusing on his "coming out" as well as the founding, mission, and theology of his church. It ranks with John Murphy's *Homosexual Liberation: A Personal View* (1971) and Arthur Bell's *Dancing the Gay Lib Blues: A Year in the Homosexual Liberation Movement* (1972) as a landmark testimonial to the power of gay liberation after the watershed Stonewall Riots of 1969. *Don't Be Afraid Anymore,* Perry's second book, was co-authored with Thomas L.P. Swicegood. It interweaves the story of Perry's life and his work on behalf of gay rights with the growth of UFMCC. The book also profiles some ministers, particularly women, who have led UFMCC congregations. *Profiles in Gay and Lesbian Courage,* which Perry and Swicegood again co-authored, provides biographical sketches of eight contemporary heroes of the American movement for gay and lesbian rights. Among those featured in *Profiles in Gay and Lesbian Courage* are slain San Francisco supervisor Harvey Milk, lesbian activists Jean O'Leary and Barbara Gittings, and openly gay United States Air Force Sergeant Leonard Matlovich.

—Joseph M. Eagan

PETERS, Fritz

Nationality: American novelist and writer of nonfiction. **Born:** Arthur Anderson Peters in Madison, Wisconsin, 2 March 1913; nephew of editor and author Margaret Anderson. **Education:** Institute for the Harmonious Development of Man, Le Prieuré, France, 1924-29. **Military Service:** Served in the U.S. Army, 1942-46; 2nd Lieutenant. **Family:** Married 1) literary editor of Harper's Bazaar, Mary Louise Aswell, in 1947; 2) Jean Peters in 1951; one son and one daughter; companion of Lloyd Lozes Goff, 1963-67. **Career:** Held numerous temporary jobs as law secretary, New York City and Albuquerque, New Mexico. **Died:** Los Cruces, New Mexico, 19 December 1979.

WRITINGS

Fiction

The World Next Door. New York, Farrar, Straus, 1949; London, Victor Gollancz, 1950.
Finistère. New York, Farrar, Straus, and London, Victor Gollancz, 1951.
The Descent. New York, Farrar, Straus, and Young, 1952.
Blind Flight. London, Victor Gollancz, 1966.

Nonfiction

The Book of the Year. New York, Harper, 1950
Boyhood with Gurdjieff. New York, Dutton, and London, Victor Gollancz, 1964.
Gurdjieff Remembered. London, Victor Gollancz, 1965; New York, Samuel Weiser, 1971.
Balanced Man: A Look at Gurdjieff. London, Wildwood House, 1978.

*

Manuscript Collections: Mugar Library, Boston University, Massachusetts.

Critical Sources: *My Thirty Years' War* by Margaret Anderson, New York, Covici Friede, 1930; letters of Paul Cadmus to Edward Field (in possession of Edward Field); letters of Samuel Steward to Edward Field (in possession of Edward Field); "Obituary," in *The New York Times Biographical Service,* December 1970; "When Not Writing Finistère..." by Edward Field, in *The Harvard Gay & Lesbian Review* (Boston, Massachusetts), Vol. 3, No. 1, winter 1996, 29-33.

*　　*　　*

In 1924, when Fritz Peters was 11, his mother had a mental breakdown. His aunt, Margaret Anderson, editor of *The Little Review,* and her lover Jane Heap adopted Fritz and his brother Tom and enrolled them in the mystic G. I. Gurdjieff's educational center outside Paris, The Institute for the Harmonious Development of Man. Peters' four years with the spiritual master may have been character building, but Gurdjieff was a heavy drinker, and in that respect was not a good influence on the young Fritz, who would later use alcohol to drown his homosexual guilt.

Peters spent most of his life trying to go straight. After an exploratory affair with a woman during World War II in England, he married Mary Louise Aswell, the literary editor of *Harper's Bazaar,* who had published a number of homosexual writers and was certainly sympathetic to her husband's homosexual tendencies. It was this brief marriage that led to his first novel, *The World Next Door* (1949), in which a veteran is committed by his family to a mental hospital after a breakdown and subjected to brutal "therapeutic" procedures, including shock treatment. Peters writes about homosexuality in the book with an openness that must have been startling at the time. The protagonist, clearly Peters himself, admits to a doctor having had a homosexual experience, even that he was in love with the man, but denies that he is a homosexual because the sex "just wasn't any good...It wasn't right, somehow." He even admits that "in the beginning, I was willing to be a fairy...but it didn't turn out that way."

The good reception of the novel encouraged Fritz to take the next step and write *Finistère.* In the novel an adolescent American boy joins his mother in the French provinces with her new husband. She hires a tutor for her son, and the master/pupil relationship blossoms into a love affair. In the context of the era's negative attitudes toward homosexual behavior, it is quite believable that after the affair is discovered the boy becomes suicidal, though his walking into the sea follows the requisite literary formula of that time—e.g., if you are homosexual, the only thing you can do is kill yourself. Peters clearly had decided that it was impossible to live as a homosexual.

A defining moment for Peters occurred in 1949 at one of Gurdjieff's dinner parties in Paris, when someone asked the great teacher who was his heir. With his luminous eyes, Gurdjieff looked around at his eager disciples and announced "Fritz!," pointing to the astonished Peters. "Fritz is my heir!" But after the master's death that year the cult that continued to teach his "system" developed a strict anti-homosexual bias and considered Peters unworthy of the mantle because of his "reputation"—the official line became that the anointing of Fritz as heir was merely one of Gurdjieff's jokes. For the rest of his life he could never escape this contempt.

After getting divorced from Aswell, he tried yet another marriage. Although this time he had children, he was no happier and when drunk he pursued homosexual adventures. Porn writer Samuel Steward, who kept notes on his sex partners, recalled in a letter an episode in 1952 with Fritz, who was "really drunk.... He burst into tears about five minutes after he shot his wad, and began to drink even more...ranting about how he really wasn't gay." Steward concludes that he seemed "afraid of being near or around someone gay or being afraid of being thought gay himself."

By 1963, Peters, now 50, had abandoned family life, and according to the painter Paul Cadmus, was living in New York with Lloyd Lozes Goff, one of Cadmus's models. "Yes, indeed, Lloyd and Fritz were 'lovers,'" Cadmus writes in a letter. "I seem to remember it was to be 'forever' but...I gather Fritz was quite 'unstable.'" The acceptance of his homosexuality, after fleeing it for so long, produced a flurry of books, notably *Boyhood with Gurdjieff,* a vivid account of Peters' teenage years with Gurdjieff, which instantly became a spiritual classic. But the creative streak ended along with the love affair, and after a disastrous, near-farcical attempt to become a teacher of the "work" at a Gurdjieff center in Oregon, Fritz retired to New Mexico, where he died in 1979.

In the postwar decade, *Finistère* is only matched by the other gay classic of the time, Gore Vidal's *The City and the Pillar.* Unfortunately, the two sides of Fritz Peters' nature, represented by *Finistère* and *Boyhood With Gurdjieff,* could never quite be reconciled, resulting, despite his literary achievement, in a strangely unfocused and unresolved life.

—Edward Field

PHILLIPS, Thomas Hal

Nationality: American novelist. **Born:** Near Corinth, Mississippi, 11 October 1922. **Education:** Alcorn Agricultural High School, Kossuth, Mississippi; Mississippi State University, Starkville, B.S. in social science 1943; University of Alabama, Tuscaloosa, M.A. 1948. **Military Service:** Served in the United States Navy, 1943-45; lieutenant (junior grade); saw action in northern Africa and southern Europe. **Career:** Has held a variety of jobs including teacher of creative writing, Southern Methodist University, Dallas, Texas, 1948-50; member, Mississippi Public Service Commission, 1958-63; manager, Republican Rubel Phillips's Mississippi gubernatorial campaign, 1963; businessman, Corinth and Jackson, Mississippi, from c. 1960-70; consultant, actor, and writer for films, including *Ode to Billy Joe, Walking Man II, Roll of Thunder, Hear My Cry, The Autobiography of Miss Jane Pittman,* and *Nashville,* c. 1960-80; head of Mississippi Film Commission. **Awards:** Julius Rosenwald Fellowship, 1947; Eugene F. Saxton Award, 1948; Fulbright Fellowship, 1950; O. Henry Prize, 1951; Guggenheim Fellowship, 1953, 1955. **Address:** Box 8019, Kossuth, Mississippi 38834, U.S.A.

WRITINGS

Novels

The Bitterweed Path. New York and Toronto, Rinehart and Company, 1950; with introduction by John Howard, Chapel Hill and London, University of North Carolina Press, 1996.

The Golden Lie. New York and Toronto, Rinehart and Company, 1951.
Search for a Hero. New York and Toronto, Rinehart and Company, 1952.
Kangaroo Hollow. London, W. Allen, 1954.
The Loved and the Unloved. New York, Harper and Brothers, 1955.

Uncollected Short Stories

"A Touch of Earth," in *Southwest Review* (Dallas, Texas), 1949.
"The Shadow of an Arm," in *Virginia Quarterly Review* (Charlottesville), 1950.
"Love Bridge," in *Southwest Review* (Dallas, Texas), 1951.
"Mostly in the Fields," *Virginia Quarterly Review* (Charlottesville), 1951.

*

Biography: "Thomas Hal Phillips" by Thomas Bonner, Jr., in *Southern Writers: A Biographical Dictionary,* edited by Robert Bain, Joseph M. Flora, and Louis D. Rubin, Jr., Baton Rouge and London, Louisiana State University Press, 1979, 350-351; "Phillips, Thomas Hal" by James M. Davis, Jr., in *Lives of Mississippi Authors, 1817-1967,* edited by James B. Lloyd, Jackson, University Press of Mississippi, 1981, 370-372.

Interviews: "An Interview with Thomas Hal Phillips" by George M. Kelly, in *Notes on Mississippi Writers* (Hattiesburg), Vol. 6, No. 1, 1973, 3-13.

Critical Sources: *Playing the Game: The Homosexual Novel in America* by Roger Austen, Indianapolis and New York, Bobbs-Merrill Company, 1977; *The Gay Novel in America* by James Levin, New York and London, Garland Publishing, 1991; "Introduction" by John Howard, in *The Bitterweed Path* by Thomas Hal Phillips, Chapel Hill and London, University of North Carolina Press, 1996, v-xxi.

Thomas Hal Phillips comments:

Having been brought up in the Bible belt, I always attended church regularly, as well as Sunday School. The David-Jonathan story was always beautiful to me. I still think it is beautiful, and I consider *The Bitterweed Path* to be my best novel. If anything of my work lasts, it will be *The Bitterweed Path.*

*   *   *

Writing in the shadow of the twentieth-century Mississippian writers William Faulkner and Eudora Welty, Thomas Hal Phillips is a novelist concerned with representing his native American South. His attention to detail earned critical praise as he offered fictional depictions of rural Mississippi throughout the 1950s that foregrounded the intricacies of class and race. *The Golden Lie,* for example, focuses on conflicts between blacks and whites, while *The Bitterweed Path* and *The Loved and the Unloved* explore the relations between white landowners and sharecroppers, revealing the anxieties that emerge from economic differences despite the absence of racial tensions.

Phillips's treatment of class and race was not what primarily drew notice when his first novel, *The Bitterweed Path,* appeared in 1950, however. The novel, the published version of his masters thesis, depicts with some frankness—especially to readers of the 1950s—an evolving homoerotic relationship between two boys, Roger Pitt and Darrell Barclay, as they pass through adolescence into adulthood just after the American Civil War. Although there are no graphic sexual images, either hetero- or homosexual, there is an insistent focus on male bodies, their scrutinies by other men, and their eventual physical contact. The novel opens with Roger's first meeting Darrell at a track meet, a scene in which he is captivated by the other boy's nakedness: "Hardly three yards away from him a boy stood smiling; he was very still and naked and the light seemed to bounce away from the pale fullness of his loins. Darrell's gaze measured the body slowly, cautiously; it was almost the size of his own, not quite so heavy or so brown."

As the novel progresses, the boys explore sporadic kisses and other forms of physical contact before adulthood and culturally-determined heterosexuality separate them. Nevertheless, the penultimate chapter offers a crucial scene directly parallel to that which opens the novel. Darrell confesses his love of Roger, kisses him as "in that lost and younger time," and immediately realizes that "the wild tenderness was now upon them." Such a culminating scenario did not go unnoticed by readers. More than a few reviewers were aghast at the images, John Howard explained in his introduction to the 1996 reprint of the novel.

Phillips does not offer an uncomplicated love story in *The Bitterweed Path*. Instead he structured his novel around a plot similar to *Maurice*, E. M. Forster's famous story of same-sex desire between men in Edwardian England, written well before World War I but not published until 1971. Like Forster, Phillips highlighted the anxieties arising in men who love other men within a homophobic culture but also the difficulties of forging and maintaining a same-sex relationship—or any other sort of relationship—across class lines. Roger is the slightly spoiled son of wealthy Malcolm Pitt, while stunningly handsome Darrell is the son of Thad Barclay, a shiftless sharecropper on the Pitts' land. These socio-economic differences are complicated when Malcolm violates the boundaries separating classes, all but adopting Darrell, establishing him in business, and coming to rely on him daily. These actions infuriate Roger, whose love for Darrell is thus tempered by fears that Malcolm prefers Darrell over his biological son.

The boys' jealousy and class differences push them to engage in heterosexual activity; both eventually marry, and Darrell reproduces. It is therefore incorrect to assert that either man displays a gay identity comparable to that crystallizing in urban areas such as New York City when Phillips was writing. Nevertheless, he does characterize Darrell's heterosexual activity as less than gratifying. Darrell is generally unenthusiastic about returning the attention of women such as Miriam Pitt and Nolie Potter, and the gratification offered by his wife's body is largely as the means for the continuation of Darrell's name through his twin sons. Indeed, by the novel's close Phillips has Emily die in childbirth, leaving Darrell not terribly upset at this loss and rather pleased that his household is exclusively male.

Like the content of *The Bitterweed Path*, the structure deserves comment. According to John Howard, Phillips consciously imagined the novel as a reworking of the Old Testament's account of David and Jonathan, the pair of friends who maintained a love "passing the love of women." In such a configuration, Malcolm Pitt and Roger parallel the Israelite King Saul and his son Jonathan, while Darrell stands as David's counterpart. Unlike the biblical account, however, Phillips's novel includes an additional element

of homoeroticism. While Malcolm Pitt is primarily a surrogate father for Darrell, the boy at times wishes the relationship were deeper. Even more dramatic, however, is the suggestion that this desire is reciprocal. When on a business trip Malcolm invites Darrell to share a bed and ostensibly fend off the cold, Phillips's prose becomes erotically charged: "He crossed the room and climbed into bed beside Malcolm and the warmth seemed to swallow him. He turned once and his face was against Malcolm's shoulder and Malcolm pulled him close so that Darrell could feel the great maleness of him, soft and warm and weighty." Malcolm even offers an overt declaration of affection, placing his "lips against his [Darrell's] cheek, partly touching his ear, saying, 'You go to sleep...honey-boy.'" This relationship, understated critic Roger Austen in his *Playing the Game*, "is an unusual one for a Southern gentleman farmer and a hired hand."

Darrell's bond to Malcolm serves as yet another factor complicating the relationship between Darrell and Roger. Darrell's potential displacement of Roger in his father's affections and Malcolm Pitt's sexual intimacy with Darrell haunt Roger. Before Darrell and Roger can consummate their own desire in the final chapters, Roger must resolve this issue: "Did you love Father? I mean *really* love him?" Darrell's affirmative does not greatly upset Roger, however, for he receives both the consolation of Darrell's confession of love and an articulation of their shared understanding that physical interactions between men are not "something ugly."

Although Phillips wrote *The Bitterweed Path* without having read the work of other contemporary southern writers who represented male same-sex desire, the novel clearly belongs in a subset of southern literature that emerged after World War II and included Truman Capote's *Other Voices, Other Rooms* and *The Grass Harp*, Calder Willingham's *End as a Man*, Hubert Creekmore's *The Welcome*, and William Goyen's *The House of Breath*. *The Bitterweed Path* differs significantly from these others in that it does not incorporate conventions of the Southern Gothic, such as isolated settings, macabre occurrences, and other-worldly characters. Moreover, although Phillips's prose is, as reviewers noted, sensitive, it remains far more readable than the often maddening lyricism of Capote and Goyen.

While Phillips's subsequent novels share these stylistics, their focus does not feature overt homoeroticism. And yet these works often include strained relationships between fathers and sons that are reminiscent of those central to *The Bitterweed Path*. About his writing, Phillips offered in a 1972 interview with George M. Kelly that "Yes, the father image is probably the dominant image in my writing." *Search for a Hero*, for example, Phillips's most autobiographical novel, charts a son's struggles to prove himself a hero to a father who dotes upon his other sons who succeed at college football. To become a comparable hero, the protagonist narrator Don Meadows enlists in the navy during World War II and, like Phillips, sees action in northern Africa and Italy.

The Loved and the Unloved, the novel that is apparently Phillips's last, includes a similar tension between the narrator and his father but also returns to Phillips's earlier concerns with class and sexuality. The tension between the poor Maxwell Harper and the wealthy Vance Acroft reminds one of the relationship between Darrell Barclay and Roger Pitt. The outcome in the later novel, however, is far different from the consummation of Darrell's and Roger's desires. Vance's vindictive accusations that Max is the "little sissy" or kept boy of the elegant elderly Mr. Ten Hoor prompt Max to murder Vance. Phillips's final novel thus seems an interesting commentary not so much on homosexuality but on homosexual panic, the often violent response to accusations of same-sex acts and desires.

—Gary Richards

PORTER, Cole (Albert)

Nationality: American composer and lyricist. **Born:** Peru, Indiana, 9 June 1891. **Education:** Studied violin and piano beginning at age 6 at the Marion Conservatory, Indiana; Worcester Academy, Massachusetts (president of mandolin club, editor of school paper), 1906-09, graduated class valedictorian, 1909; Yale University, New Haven, Connecticut (member of glee club, voted "most entertaining man" in class), 1909-13, B.A. 1913; Harvard University Law School, 1914; Harvard School of Music, 1915-16; Schola Cantorum, Paris, 1919 (studied with French composer Vincent d'Indy). **Military Service:** Participated in war relief efforts attached to the French Foreign Legion and the U.S. Embassy, 1918-19. **Family:** Married Linda Lee Thomas in 1919 (died 1954). **Career:** Wrote first work "Song of the Birds" at age 10; published first work, "The Bobolink Waltz," at age 11. Lived in Paris during the 1920s, composing songs for Paris, London, and New York theatre; moved permanent residence to the United States in the 1930s (maintaining residences in New York, Los Angeles, and Williamstown, Massachusetts), and worked as a songwriter primarily for Broadway musicals and films. Member of the American Society of Composers, Authors, and Publishers (ASCAP), from 1931. **Awards:** Tony Award for composer, *Kiss Me, Kate,* 1949; Salute to Cole Porter, presented by ASCAP at the Metropolitan Opera House, New York City, 15 May 1960; D.Mus.: Williams College, 1955; L.H.D.: Yale University, 1960. **Died:** Santa Monica, California, 15 October 1964.

WRITINGS

Complete Scores (Music and Lyrics)

See America First (produced Broadway, 28 March 1916).
Hitchy-Koo of 1919 (produced Broadway, 6 October 1919).
Hitchy-Koo of 1922 (produced Philadelphia, 10 October 1922; closed during pre-Broadway tryout).
Greenwich Village Follies (produced Broadway, 16 September 1924, 127 performances).
Paris (produced Broadway, 8 October 1928, 195 performances).
Fifty Million Frenchmen (produced Broadway, 27 November 1929, 254 performances).
Gay Divorcée (produced Broadway, 29 November 1932, 248 performances; London, 2 November 1933, 180 performances; Off Broadway, March 1979).
Nymph Errant (produced London, 6 October 1933, 154 performances).
Anything Goes (produced Broadway, 21 November 1934, 420 performances; London, 14 June 1935, 261 performances; Off Broadway, 15 May 1962, 239 performances; Lincoln Center Theater, 19 October 1987, 804 performances).
Jubilee (produced Broadway, 12 October 1935, 169 performances).

Red, Hot and Blue! (produced Broadway, 29 October 1936, 183 performances).
Leave It to Me! (produced Broadway, 9 November 1938, 291 performances).
DuBarry Was a Lady (produced Broadway, 6 December 1939, 408 performances; London, 22 October 1942, 178 performances; Off Broadway, 1972).
Panama Hattie (produced Broadway, 30 October 1940, 501 performances; London, 4 November 1943, 308 performances).
Let's Face It! (produced Broadway, 29 October 1941, 547 performances; London, 19 November 1942, 348 performances).
Something for the Boys (produced Broadway, 7 January 1943, 422 performances).
Mexican Hayride (produced Broadway, 28 January 1944, 481 performances).
Around the World in Eighty Days (produced Broadway, 31 May 1946, 75 performances).
Kiss Me, Kate (produced Broadway, 30 December 1948, 1077 performances; London, 8 March 1951, 501 performances; London, 1970).
Out of This World (produced Broadway, 21 December 1950, 157 performances).
Can-Can (produced Broadway, 7 May 1953, 892 performances; London, 14 October 1954, 394 performances).
Silk Stockings (produced Broadway, 24 February 1955, 478 performances).

Contributor of Songs (Musical Theatre)

Hands Up (produced Broadway, 22 July 1915, 52 performances).
Miss Information (produced Broadway, 5 October 1915, 47 performances).
Very Good Eddie (produced London, 18 May 1918, 46 performances).
Telling the Tale (produced London, c. October 1918).
Buddies (produced Broadway, 27 October 1919, 259 performances).
The Eclipse (produced London, 12 November 1919, 117 performances).
As You Were (produced Broadway, 27 January 1920, 143 performances).
A Night Out (produced London, 18 September 1920, 311 performances).
Mayfair and Montmartre (produced London, 9 March 1922, 77 performances).
Phi-Phi (produced London, 16 August 1922, 132 performances).
Up with the Lark (produced London, 25 August 1927).
La Revue Des Ambassadeurs (produced Paris, 10 May 1928).
Wake Up and Dream (produced London, 27 March 1929, 263 performances; Broadway, 30 December 1929, 136 performances).
The New Yorkers (produced Broadway, 8 December 1930, 168 performances).
Hi Diddle Diddle (produced London, 3 October 1934, 198 performances).
O Mistress Mine (produced London, 3 December 1936).
You Never Know (produced Broadway, 21 September 1938, 78 performances).
The Sun Never Sets (produced London, 9 June 1939).
The Man Who Came to Dinner (produced Broadway, 16 October 1939, 739 performances).

Seven Lively Arts (produced Broadway, 7 December 1944, 183 performances).

Contributor of Songs (Films)

The Battle of Paris. Paramount, 1929.
Gay Divorcée. RKO, 1934.
Adios Argentina (unproduced). Fox, 1934-1935.
Anything Goes. Metro-Goldwyn-Mayer, 1936.
Born to Dance. Metro-Goldwyn-Mayer, 1936.
Rosalie. Metro-Goldwyn-Mayer, 1937.
Break the News. Monogram Pictures, England, 1937; released in the United States, 1941.
Broadway Melody of 1940. Metro-Goldwyn-Mayer, 1939.
You'll Never Get Rich. Columbia Pictures, 1941.
Something To Shout About. Columbia Pictures, 1942.
DuBarry Was a Lady. Metro-Goldwyn-Mayer, 1943.
The Pirate. Metro-Goldwyn-Mayer, 1948.
Adam's Rib. Metro-Goldwyn-Mayer, 1949.
Kiss Me, Kate. Metro-Goldwyn-Mayer, 1953.
Anything Goes. Metro-Goldwyn-Mayer, 1956.
High Society. Metro-Goldwyn-Mayer, 1956.
Les Girls. Metro-Goldwyn-Mayer, 1957.
Can-Can. Twentieth Century Fox, 1960.

Collected Works

The Cole Porter Song Album, New York, Harms, Inc., 1935.
103 Lyrics of Cole Porter, with an introduction by Fred Lounseberry. New York, Random House, 1954.
The Cole Porter Songbook: The Complete Words and Music of Forty of Cole Porter's Best-Loved Songs, with a foreword by Moss Hart. New York, Simon & Schuster, 1959.
The Unpublished Cole Porter, edited by Robert Kimball. New York, Simon & Schuster, 1975.
Music and Lyrics by Cole Porter: A Treasury of Cole Porter, with an introduction by Robert Kimball. New York, Chappell & Co., Inc. and Random House, 1991.
Music and Lyrics by Cole Porter: The Sassy, Sophisticated, Sentimental Porter in Song, Vol. II. New York, Chappell Music Company, 1991.

Other

"Bingo Eli Yale" and "Bull Dog" (songs for Yale University, c. 1910-1912).
Within the Quota (score for ballet performed by the Swedish Ballet, Paris and New York City, 1923; revised and performed by the American Ballet Theatre as *Times Past,* 1970).
Aladdin (songs for CBS television special, broadcast on 21 February 1958).

Recordings: *American Songbook Series: Cole Porter,* Smithsonian Collection of Recordings, 1992; *Cole Sings Cole Porter: Rare and Unreleased Songs from Can-Can and Jubilee,* Koch International, 1994.

*

Adaptations: Cole Porter's works have been adapted in various mediums; notable sound recordings include *Kiss Me, Kate* (origi-nal cast recording), Capitol, 1949; *Ella Fitzgerald: The Cole Porter Songbook,* Verve, 1956; *Oscar Peterson Plays the Cole Porter Song Book,* Verve, 1959; *Bobby Short Loves Cole Porter,* Atlantic, 1971; *Classic Cole,* Columbia, 1977; *Blue Porter: Blue Note Plays the Music of Cole Porter,* Blue Note, 1991; *Night and Day: The Cole Porter Songbook,* Verve, 1990; *red hot + blue,* Chrysalis, 1990; *I Get A Kick Out Of You: The Cole Porter Songbook, Vol. II,* Verve, 1991; *You're the Top: Cole Porter in the 1930s,* Koch International Classics, 1992; *Cole Porter in Concert: Just One of Those Live Things,* Verve, 1994. Notable musical revivals and tributes include *The Decline and Fall of the Entire World As Seen Through the Eyes of Cole Porter,* Off Broadway, March 1965; *Ben Brantley's New Cole Porter Revue,* Off Broadway, December 1965; *Words and Music by Cole Porter,* musical tribute telecast on NBC, 25 November 1965; *The Unsung Cole: A Toast to Cole Porter,* Off Broadway, 1977. Notable films and videos include *Night and Day* (film), Warner Brothers, 1946; *You're The Top: The Cole Porter Story,* narrated by Bobby Short (video recording), Island Visual Arts, 1990.

Manuscript Collections: The Cole Porter Collection, Historical Sound Recordings Collection, Yale University.

Biography: *Current Biography: Who's News and Why 1940* edited by Maxine Block, New York, H.W. Wilson Company, 1940, 655-657; *The Cole Porter Story* by Richard G. Hubler, with an introduction by Arthur Schwartz, Cleveland and New York, The World Publishing Company, 1965; *The Life That He Led* by George Eells, New York, G.P. Putnam's Sons, 1967; *Cole* by Robert Kimball and Brendan Gill, New York, Holt, Rinehart & Winston, 1971; *Great Men of American Popular Song,* by David Ewen, revised and enlarged edition, Englewood Cliffs, New Jersey, Prentice Hall, Inc., 1972; *Cole Porter: A Biography* by Charles Schwartz, New York, Da Capo Press, 1977; "Porter, Cole" by Mark White, in *'You Must Remember This...': Popular Songwriters 1900-1980,* New York, Charles Scribner's Sons, 1985, 184-190; *Red, Hot & Rich!* by David Grafton, New York, Stein and Day, 1987; *Travels With Cole Porter* by Jean Howard, New York, Harry N. Abrams, Inc., 1991; *Noel and Cole: The Sophisticates* by Stephen Citron, New York and Oxford, Oxford University Press, 1993.

Bibliography: *Show Tunes, 1905-1991: The Songs, Shows and Careers of Broadway's Major Composers* by Steven Suskin, revised and expanded edition, New York, Limelight Editions, 1992.

Critical Sources: "Cole Porter Is Dead; Songwriter Was 72," in *New York Times,* 16 October 1964, 1, 29; "Reprise to Cole Porter, Revisited" by John Molleson, in *New York Herald Tribune,* 23 December 1965; *American Popular Song: The Great Innovators* by Alec Wilder, London, Oxford and New York, Oxford University Press, 1972; *Encyclopedia of the Musical Theatre* by Stanley Green, New York, Da Capo Press, 1976; "Fringes" by Richard Philp, in *Dance,* September 1977, 92-93; *Broadway Babies: The People Who Made the American Musical* by Ethan Mordden, New York and Oxford, Oxford University Press, 1983; "Theater: 'Gay Divorcée'" by Richard F. Shepard, in *New York Times* 29 May 1983; "Stage: Porter Songs in 'Gay Divorcée'" by Mel Gussow, in *New York Times* 25 February 1987; *The Broadway Musical: A Critical and Musical Guide* by Joseph P. Swain, New York and Oxford, Oxford University Press, 1990; "Block on Rock" by Adam Block, *Advocate,* 4 December 1990, 70; "Rock and Cole" by Ethan Mordden, in *New Yorker,* Vol. 67, No. 36, 28 October 1991, 91-113; "Cole Porter in Britain" by James Ross Moore, in *New Theatre Quarterly,* Vol. 8, No. 30, May 1992, 113-122; "Deluxe Delights" by Brendan Gill, in *New Yorker,* Vol. 69, No. 15, 31 May 1993, 72-73; "Mad About the Boys" by John Mueller, in *New York Times Book Review,* 6 June 1993, 24; *Gay New York: Gender, Urban Culture, and the Making of the Gay Male World, 1890-1940* by George Chauncey, New York, BasicBooks, 1994; "Too Darn Hot: Hollywood, Popular Media and the Construction of Sexuality in the Life of Cole Porter" by George F. Custen, in *Radical History Review,* Vol. 58, winter 1994, 142-171; *The American Popular Ballad of the Golden Era, 1924-1950* by Allen Forte, Princeton, New Jersey, Princeton University Press, 1995; *Genius and Lust: The Creativity and Sexuality of Cole Porter and Noel Coward* by Joseph Morella and George Mattai, New York, Carroll & Graf Publishers, Inc., 1995.

*   *   *

One of the most prolific songwriters of the American musical theatre, Cole Porter wrote nearly 800 songs, provided music for some forty musicals—including seven Broadway shows during the 1930s alone—and contributed songs to several motion pictures. Porter generated most of his work from the 1920s through the 1950s, a time when censorship regulations curtailed discourse on homosexuality, and when other Broadway songwriters maintained a certain innocence and reverence to heterosexual courtship in their lyrics. Porter's unabashedly bold references to sex, his critique and disavowal of heterosexual romance, and the presence of same-sex desire in his lyrics, underscored by his pulsing, aggressively rhythmic music, made his work stand apart from that of his contemporaries. Despite biographers' and other writers' disavowal of Porter's homosexuality and the importance of his songs to gay audiences, Porter and his work have occupied an undeniably queer presence in American popular music that has continued into the 1990s with the ongoing release of contemporary artists' interpretations of his work.

When Porter began achieving success writing for Broadway shows in the late 1920s and early 1930s, new censorship regulations sought to curb the representation of homosexual characters on stage and screen. The padlock bill, passed by the New York State Legislature in 1927, forbade any play from including gay and lesbian characters and from addressing homosexuality. New York City extended this ban to nightclubs in the 1930s and 1940s, while the R-K-O vaudeville circuit issued orders to its theatres nationwide banning the use of the words "fairy" and "pansy" in vaudeville routines, and many states passed laws forbidding female impersonation on stage. Hollywood, too, established a production code in the early 1930s creating industry-wide moral standards and censoring the representation of gay images on film. Gay men and lesbians were able to circumvent the new regulations somewhat by making use of double entendre and codes; but while gay life continued to flourish, it became less visible to outsiders. Porter's songs, in which homosexual desire was often flamboyantly invisible, were part of this culture.

Despite these increasingly repressive legal measures, the environment of American popular music allowed ample space for songwriters to subvert convention and carve out, as Porter did, an iconoclastic or "queer" niche. Songwriters working at the turn of the century, such as George M. Cohan, strove to define the American popular song stylistically. But by the 1920s, the musical genre was well-enough established so that Porter and his contemporaries could take more risks, and incorporate more political satire and commentary on class and sex into their work. Indeed, in his lyrics, Porter talks about sex and homosexuality more explicitly than any songwriter before him. "Love For Sale," first heard in the 1930 show *The New Yorkers,* was banned from radio play for its discussion of prostitution, and his 1941 song "Farming" contained the first blatant allusion to homosexuality in a Broadway show lyric: "Don't inquire of Georgie Raft / Why his cow never calfed / Georgie's bull is beautiful, but he's gay!" It is also significant that Porter produced much of his work before Rodgers & Hammerstein's *Oklahoma!* (1943), the first musical in which music, lyrics, and dramatic content were integrated and interdependent. Porter, who once acknowledged his lack of interest in using his songs to further dramatic plot by saying "I have no book sense," could therefore write songs that were independent of the dramatic content of the musicals in which they appeared. This method of songwriting arguably generated texts that are more conducive to gay and lesbian readings than the post-*Oklahoma!* method, in which songwriters aimed to link lyrics directly to characters in musicals based on traditional heterosexual romance narratives. Many Porter songs were written to accommodate the talents of specific performers ("Night and Day" was written with Fred Astaire's limited vocal range in mind, and "I Get a Kick Out of You" showcased the sheer force of Ethel Merman's voice). Other Porter songs which ultimately became hits, including "Miss Otis Regrets," were initially written for parties attended by Porter's friends, and others were inspired by his extensive travels around the world (a chant heard in Morocco, for example, reportedly sparked "What is This Thing Called Love?").

Porter not only created songs apart from the heterosexualized context in which they were showcased; he infused his work with gay meanings. Like other gay and lesbian writers of his generation, Porter made extensive use of double entendres, producing gay-tinged lyrics that could "pass" for straight when sung in their Broadway context. "I'm a Gigolo" proclaimed: "I should like you all to know, / I'm a famous gigolo / And of lavender, my nature's got just a dash in it...." "Find Me A Primitive Man" asserted boldly: "I've no desire to be alone / With Rudy Vallee's megaphone...The only man who'll ever win me / Has got to wake up the gypsy in me / Find me a primitive man." Porter's lyrics were revolutionary in their critique of heterosexual romance. "Why Marry Them?" cautioned: "As lovers they love you, and as your husbands they snore." "I Hate Men" was even more caustic: "I hate men / I can't abide by 'em even now and then / Than ever marry one of them, I'd rest a virgin rather." Porter delivered a direct invitation to go against the world's sexual conventions with the lyric "We're all alone / No chaperone / Can get our number / The world's in slumber / Let's misbehave," and documented with honesty the temporariness of some sexual relationships with "It was just one of those things / Just one of those crazy flings." Indicative of the censorship-laden era in which he wrote, Porter frequently depicted love as an unnameable, elusive "thing," musing that "you do something to me, something that simply mystifies me," asking "what is this thing called love?" and naming desire as "a hunger, yearning, burning inside of me." Evidence suggests that gay audiences indeed caught onto the expressions of homosexual desire and identity in Porter's songs and embraced his work. As George Chauncey has documented in *Gay New York,* Porter's songs "were mainstays in gay culture" beginning in the 1920s and 1930s.

Porter complemented his practice of pushing lyrical taboos by incorporating musical elements that suggested the arousal of desire, mapping patterns in sound that resemble those of sex. The use of repeated notes, pumping through the verse of "Night and Day," and the swelling and release in the melody of "In the Still of the Night" illustrate this well. Furthermore, Porter's introductory verses are often unusually elaborate in rhythm and melody, and his codas often push a song beyond pop music's traditional format. "Begin the Beguine," for example, is an extraordinary 108 measures long. Thus musically as well as lyrically, Porter's songs celebrate excess, refusing containment. Another recurring theme in Porter's work is his use of chromatic lines in both melody and harmony. In addition, Porter switches back and forth between major and minor keys within a song; most famously, in "Ev'ry Time We Say Goodbye," the musical change is paralleled by the lyric "how strange the change from major to minor." He glides between keys (such as in "Why Shouldn't I?," where he moves from C major to E major to F major and back), and uses triplets in duple meter, creating a sense of shifting rhythm, as in "I Get a Kick Out of You." These musical expressions of constant movement and shifting underscore the themes in Porter's lyrics of love as unnameable and elusive, and constitute a musically "queer" critique of the traditional popular song form. The fact that Porter was an extensively trained musician who wrote musically complex songs tends to be overshadowed by his sophistication as a lyricist; as Alec Wilder pointed out in *American Popular Song,* Porter's music was often "better than it need be" since the outstanding lyrics could "get by with a lot less." The composer Richard Rodgers added in Porter's *New York Times* obituary: "Few people realize how architecturally excellent his music is. There's a foundation, a structure and an embellishment. Then you add the emotion he's put in and the result is Cole Porter."

Porter's life as a gay man arguably contributed to the groundbreaking songs he produced; as Ethan Mordden pointed out in "Rock and Cole," Porter's homosexuality "powered his satire, for it placed him at a certain remove from his favorite subject, the rituals of Western courtship and marriage." Porter's homosexuality was not publicly acknowledged during his lifetime, but writers as early as the 1930s recognized him as "different" from other popular songwriters, and constructed a certain queerness around Porter by conflating him with the unconventional songs he produced. Moss Hart, who collaborated with Porter in writing *Jubilee,* recalled in the introduction to a 1959 songbook when he and Porter first met: "Though I had never seen him before, I knew that the man standing in the doorway was unmistakably Cole Porter; he looks, I thought quickly, exactly like one of his songs." (Hart continued by using the words "gaiety," "impishness," and "audacity" to describe Porter's songs.)

The foreword to the 1935 *Cole Porter Song Album* also fused the idea of "Cole Porter" with his songs, collapsing them into the same queer entity: "The very uniqueness of Cole Porter almost defies any commentary...[His] cleverness and originality in thought and music are spontaneously infectious, sophisticatedly naughty, yet humorously 'different.' He certainly stands alone in his field as a composer and lyricist second to none in trenchant wit and subtlety." As evidenced by publishers' decisions to use such passages in introductions to song albums, Porter's "differentness" was a marketable quality, as long as his homosexuality remained undisclosed.

Many biographers floated in a similar epistomelogical limbo when describing Porter. Richard Hubler wrote in the 1965 biography *The Cole Porter Story,* "Trapping the personality in print is always a most dangerous game...The real characteristics of the subject always evade the right word...," and claimed that "Music was the way to [Porter's] peculiar power...he was always a lonely man who wanted to lose himself in a crowd of glittering notes." The work of Hubler and others effectively accomplished historical erasure, "losing" Porter's homosexuality by displacing it onto his "glittering notes." Some biographers went a step further; trying to reconcile Porter's "good" and "bad" sides in the introduction to a song album, Fred Lounseberry concluded that Porter's "immoral" lyrics must attest to his heterosexual virility: "[W]e respect Porter's ballads more because he has 'been around' in his racy songs. Sentiment, to sum it up, is more impressive in a 'regular guy' than it is in a sap or a softy." And as George Custen has documented, the elimination of gay and lesbian history from the script of Warner Brothers' 1946 biographic film "Night and Day," which starred Cary Grant as Cole Porter (and which Mordden has called "one of the outstanding science-fiction films of the age" because of its hyperbolic distortions of history), presumed heterosexuality as a precondition for and a confirmation of professional accomplishment, implying that Porter's prized work was specifically motivated by heterosexual love. In exchange for the public silencing of his sexuality, Porter was thus able to protect his career image and reap some financial benefit from the film and biographies.

The enduring legacy of Porter's music is a testament to his genius as a songwriter. What makes his accomplishments more remarkable is that he produced such significant work after a horse-riding accident in 1937 broke both his legs and damaged his nervous system. The accident left Porter in constant pain, and he underwent over 30 operations in 20 years before one leg was amputated. Notably, he produced the score for *Kiss Me, Kate,* his most celebrated and world-renowned show, during this time. After a run of over 1,000 performances in New York that began in 1948, *Kate* became the first American musical performed in Vienna, Berlin, Yugoslavia, Hungary, Czechoslovakia, Warsaw, and Iceland. (It also ran in Italy, Belgium, Switzerland, Denmark, Sweden, Israel, Japan, Turkey, Spain, and Brazil.) The success of recordings of Porter's music by dance bands in the 1930s and 1940s, by jazz artists like Ella Fitzgerald, and by rock musicians on the 1990 AIDS benefit album "red hot + blue" has proven that his music is adaptable across styles, and that his lyrics are relevant across generations. More importantly to gay men and lesbians, the continuing popularity of Cole Porter's music ensures a place in the canon of American popular song for work that critiques heterosexual romance and celebrates homosexuality.

—Tara Rodgers

PRICE, Deb

Nationality: American journalist and columnist. **Born:** Lubbock, Texas, 27 February 1958. **Education:** Stanford University, B.A., M.A. in literature 1981. **Family:** Companion of journalist Joyce Murdoch. **Career:** Capital Hill reporter, States News Service, 1983; reporter, *Washington Post,* 1984-89; news editor and Deputy Bureau Chief, 1989-92, columnist, from 1992, *Detroit News.* **Awards:** Outstanding Achievement in Publishing award, Gay and

Lesbian Alliance Against Defamation, 1995; Lambda Literary Award finalist, 1995. **Address:** The Detroit News, 1148 National Press Building, Washington, D.C. 20045, U.S.A.

WRITINGS

With Joyce Murdoch, *And Say Hi to Joyce: America's First Gay Columnist Comes Out.* New York, Doubleday, 1995.

*

Interviews: "Life from a Gay Perspective" by Tony Case, in *Editor & Publisher,* 11 July 1992; "Deb Price: Out in Print" by C.J. Janovy in *Ms.,* September/October 1995; unpublished interview with Deb Price by GLL contributor Pamela Green, May 1997.

*   *   *

On 8 May 1992 Deb Price became the first person to write a weekly column dealing exclusively with gay and lesbian issues for a mainstream publication. Before the column began gay issues were only tackled in various alternative publications, and mainstream newspapers frequently ignored issues concerning gays and lesbians or gave them only minimum consideration. But when Price pitched the idea for the column to her editor at the *Detroit News,* the editor realized that diversity was lacking from the paper and immediately backed the idea. The column was picked up for Gannett syndication from its first appearance, and was soon acquired by the *Los Angeles Times* Syndicate. It now appears in newspapers throughout the United States and Guam.

When Price first started working as a journalist there was a common notion that you could not be both a gay activist and a good journalist. However, Price said in an interview with *GLL* contributor Pamela Green, "I realized that part of my voice was missing when I couldn't use my own life experiences in my work. I wanted to approach [my writing] from a gay perspective." Before Price began the column she realized that a majority of its readers might not know any gays, and especially not any gay couples. Price's goal was to bridge the gap between the gay and heterosexual communities and to open an honest dialogue between and within those communities. Therefore, she opened up her life to the public, introducing herself, along with her partner Joyce, to the readers so that they could get to know the person behind the column.

"For average people just trying to pay the bills, gay issues may look like abstract political issues. I wanted to make it personal, to put a face on it," Price told Green. Therefore, in her first column she wrote about how difficult it was to introduce her partner of six years to her boss because there is no language for the situation. In this column, "Gay Partners Need to Make A Name for Themselves," she wrote:

> There is no confusion when a woman says: "This is my husband." But how do I introduce the woman I've lived with for six years to my boss? Is she my "girlfriend" or my "significant other?" My "longtime companion" or my "lover?" Who says the gay rights movement hasn't made a lot of progress? In just 100 years, we've gone from the love that dare not speak its name to the love that doesn't know its name.

Thus Price introduced to hundreds of thousands of readers the realities of being part of a gay couple. She showed how similar it is to an average heterosexual relationship, yet she also demonstrated how many small problems come with being gay simply because society has not fully accepted homosexuality.

Price tries to give readers a slice of life. She has written about local gay heroes such as a man who started a magazine for Asian gays and a woman who started a pen pal group for older lesbians. She also draws on her own life with Joyce and addresses how the gay and straight communities deal with families and couples. While presenting gay issues in this personal manner she also includes news that affects the gay community and offers news analysis and perspective. Price has written extensively on same-sex marriage, gay parenting, gays in the military, homosexual teenagers dealing with their sexuality, AIDS, and gays in film and television.

—Pamela Green

R

Rachid O.

Nationality: Moroccan author. **Born:** Rabat in 1970.

WRITINGS

Autobiographies

"Rachid," in *L'infini* (Paris), No. 45, Winter 1994, 103–124; as "Amours" in *L'enfant ébloui* (also see below).
L'enfant ébloui (*The Dazzled Child*). Paris, Gallimard, 1996.
Plusieurs vies (*Several Lives*). Paris, Gallimard, 1996.

*

Interviews: "Cinq Questions à Rachid O.," in *Têtu* (Paris), No. 4, June 1996, 54.

Critical Sources: Review of Rachid O.'s *L'enfant ébloui* by Hédi Abdel-Jaouad, in *World Literature Today* (Norman, Oklahoma), Vol. 70, No. 2, Spring 1996.

*   *   *

Since its beginnings after World War II, literature in French from the Maghreb (that part of North Africa colonized by the French, including Morocco, Algeria, and Tunisia) has seldom shied away from sexual matters. Rare indeed are Maghrebian writers who do not discuss same-sex desire or behavior in at least one novel. Some novelists, such as Rachid Boudjedra and Tahar Ben Jelloun, address the topic in many if not most of their works, often to challenge conservative viewpoints concerning sexuality as well as the dominant political classes that attempt to regulate sexuality as a means of maintaining power. In addition, the literary treatment of same-sex love has a long tradition in erotic literature written in Arabic, dating back to the early days of Islam. Abu Nuwas, for example, composed poems in praise of the beauty of young boys as early as the latter part of the eighth century. Yet, as Hédi Abdel-Jaouad writes in a review, "*L'enfant ébloui* is the first Maghrebian book about homosexuality by a self-confessed gay Maghrebian writer. This is not to say that homosexuality has not been treated as a theme by other authors. However, this is the first time, to my knowledge, that an author addresses this question directly and from a personal perspective without provocation, outlandishness, or prudish reserve."

Rachid O. is the author of two collections of *récits*, or narratives or short stories, *L'enfant ébloui* and *Plusieurs vies*, neither of which has yet been translated into English. Rather than being a sequel of the first, the second is more of a parallel set of stories; like the first, it begins with stories from the author's childhood and then describes sexual experiences with boys and men and his understanding of his sexual orientation. *L'enfant ébloui* describes the author's growing up among female relatives, going with them to the women's *hammam* or public bath, listening to their sexual conversations about men, and realizing that he, like the women around him, desires men. The story "My Loves" is about his first relationships with men: his Arabic teacher who—although not gay—was Rachid's first lover; Antoine, the French man living in Morocco with whom Rachid finally decides to live and is still living at the end of the second book; and Julien, another European man whom Rachid cruises in Marrakech.

For Western readers, *L'enfant ébloui* might resemble a coming-out story, wherein a gay or lesbian character comes to terms with his/her sexuality and leaves behind the silence and invisibility of the closet. While the text certainly chronicles sexual discovery, in no way is Rachid's childhood prior to this realization considered unhappy or oppressive. In contrast with many other childhood narratives by Maghrebian men who tend to associate an unhappy childhood with an oppressive father and the supposed oppressiveness of Islam, Rachid O. counters stereotypes of Muslim fathers as tyrants in his descriptions of his own father, who is even supportive of Rachid's sexuality: "He had always understood that I was made for boys, not for girls. We have never talked about it. He's the most understanding person in the family" (translation by contributor). Rachid O. also reconciles his sexuality with a Muslim identity by countering clichés of Muslims as inherently fundamentalist or closed-minded. His cousins who wear the veil are equally understanding with regard to Rachid's homosexuality: "What counted for them, especially for the one I was closest to, was that she was doing what she liked, she practiced 100 percent without bothering anyone in the least by trying to persuade them. She minded her own business. When she found out I was living with Antoine, she didn't make a fuss."

Returning to Rachid's childhood, *Plusieurs vies* begins by describing his amorous, almost sexual relationship with his uncle. The remaining stories in *Plusieurs vies* recount Rachid's cruising as a late adolescent and young adult in the streets of Marrakech, where he moved with Antoine in *L'enfant ébloui,* and his visits to the European countries of Switzerland and France. In these stories, Rachid encounters European racism first-hand and contradicts a number of other European stereotypes about Arab men. Although French literature contains many examples of Europeans who travel to North Africa as sexual tourists looking for cheap fun, *Plusieurs vies* offers an example of a similar trajectory in reverse. Whereas many French gay men believe that any Arab man is willing to have sex with another man (particularly a non-Arab) as long as he is the insertive partner, Rachid meets (and has sex with) several so-called straight European men who would fit the clichés many gay Europeans have of Arab men. Whereas European stereotypes hold that Arabs are thieves, Rachid is the one who ends up getting robbed in a French hotel. Everywhere, he feels the presence of the police who have the right to demand his papers at any time. One police officer even uses his authority to demand Rachid's papers as an excuse to cruise him. In contrast, the Moroccan police in Marrakech, when investigating the murder of a European man by his Moroccan trick, treat his sexual relationship with Antoine with the utmost sensitivity. Again, Rachid O. has reversed stereotypes of the police in so-called "third-world" countries as inevitably corrupt.

As these examples make clear, Rachid O. has made a unique contribution to Maghrebian literature as an openly gay writer. He is far from being the first to discuss the issue of homosexuality, even as a first-person participant in same-sex behavior: Mohamed Choukri describes having sex with men for money in his autobiography *For Bread Alone* (written in Arabic, but translated into both English and French), and the openly gay Algerian poet of European origin, Jean Sénac, wrote homoerotic verse in his later years. (He was also a member of the FLN, which fought for Algerian independence, and a member of the Ben Bella government after independence.) Rachid O. is, however, the first Maghrebian Arab or Berber writer in French to make homosexuality a primary identification and his own homosexuality the major subject of his writing.

—Jarrod Hayes

————

RAMPLING, Anne. *See* **RICE, Anne.**

————

REINIG, Christa

Nationality: German novelist, poet, and author of short stories and radio plays. **Born:** Berlin, Germany, 6 August 1926. **Education:** Studied history of arts and Christian archaeology at the University in East Berlin, 1953-57. Factory worker during World War II; academic assistant at a museum in East-Berlin, 1957-63; stayed in West-Germany after receiving a literary award in 1964; supported by pension after being hurt in an accident, from 1971. **Awards:** Literaturpreis des Kulturbundes Berlin Ost für Junge Autoren, 1948; Literaturpreis der Freien Hansestadt Bremen, 1964; Villa-Massimo-Stipendium, 1965; Hörspielpreis der Kriegsblinden, 1967; Tukan-Preis der Stadt, München, 1969; Ehrengabe der Bayerischen Akademie der Schönen Künste, 1973; Kritikerpreis für Literatur, 1975; Verdienstkreuz am Band des Verdienstordens der Bundesrepublil Deutschland, 1976; Literaturstipendium der Stadt, München, 1980; Jahrespreis des Südwestfunk-Literaturmagazins, 1984. **Agent:** Eremiten-Presse, Postfach 170143, 40082 Düsseldorf, Germany.

WRITINGS

Novels

Die himmlische und die irdische Geometrie. Düsseldorf, Germany, Eremiten-Presse, 1975.
Entmannung. Die Geschichte Ottos und seiner vier Frauen (Castration). Düsseldorf, Eremiten-Presse, 1976.
Die Frau im Brunnen (The woman in the Well). Munich, Germany, Frauenoffensive, 1984.

Short Stories

Drei Schiffe. Prosa. Frankfurt, S. Fischer, 1965; Munich, Stöberlein, 1974; Düsseldorf, Eremiten-Presse, 1978.

Der Traum meiner Verkommenheit. Germany, Fietkau, 1968.
Die Ballade vom blutigen Bomme (The Ballad of Bloody Bomme). Düsseldorf, Eremiten-Presse, 1972.
Der Hund mit dem Schlüssel. Düsseldorf, Eremiten-Presse, 1976.
Der Wolf und die Witwen. Düsseldorf, Eremiten-Presse, 1980.
Mädchen ohne Uniform (Girl without Uniform). Düsseldorf, Eremiten-Presse, 1981.
Die ewige Schule. Erzählungen. Munich, Frauenoffensive, 1982.
Nobody und andere Geschichten. Düsseldorf, Eremiten-Presse, 1989.
Glück und Glas. Düsseldorf, Eremiten-Presse, 1991.

Radio Plays

Die kleine Chronik der Osterwoche. Germany, Süddeutscher Rundfunk, 1962.
Der Teufel, der Stumm bleiben wollte. Germany, RIAS Berlin, 1963.
Tenakeh. Germany, Süddeutscher Rundfunk, 1965.
Das Aquarium. Germany, Süddeutscher Rundfunk, 1967.
Wisper. Germany, Süddeutscher Rundfunk, 1967.
Mädchen in Uniform. Germany, Südwestfunk, 1979.

Poetry

Die Steine von Finisterre. Stierstadt, Eremiten-Presse, 1960.
Gedichte. Frankfurt, S. Fischer, 1963.
Orion trat aus dem Haus: Prosa. Düsseldorf, Eremiten-Presse, 1968.
Schwabinger Marterln. Stierstadt, Eremiten-Presse, 1968.
Schwalbe von Olevano. Stierstadt, Eremiten-Presse, 1969.
Das große Bechterew-Tantra. Exzentrische Anatomie. Stierstadt im Taunus, Germany, Eremiten-Presse, 1970.
Papantscha-Vielerlei. Exotische Produkte Altindiens. Stierstadt im Taunus, Eremiten-Presse, 1971.
Poèmes. Paris, France, Silvaire, 1976.
Müßiggang ist aller Liebe Anfang. Düsseldorf, Germany, Eremiten-Presse, 1979; as *Idleness Is the Root of All Love.* Corvallis, Oregon, Calyx, 1991.
Feuergefährlich. Gedichte und Erzählungen über Frauen und Männer (Inflammatory: Poems and Stories about Men and Women). Berlin, Wagenbach, 1985.
Ein Wogenzug von wilden Schwänen. Ravensburg, Germany, Ravensburger Buchverlag, 1991.
Der Frosch im Glas. Düsseldorf, Eremiten-Presse, 1994.

Collected Works

Die Prüfung des Lächlers. Gesammelte Gedichte. Munich, Deutscher Taschenbuchverlag, 1980.
Sämtlich Gedichte. Düsseldorf, Eremiten-Presse, 1984.
Gesammelte Gedichte 1960-1979. Munich, Luchterhand, 1985.
Gesammelte Erzählungen. Munich, Luchterhand, 1986.

Translator

Marina Zwetajewa: Gedichte. Berlin, Wagenbach, 1968.

*

Interviews: *Mein Herz ist eine gelbe Blume* edited by Ekkehart Rudolph, Düsseldorf, Eremiten-Presse, 1978; *Gespräche mit*

Christa Reinig edited by Marie L. Gansberg, Munich, Frauenoffensive, 1984; *Erkennen, was die Rettung ist* edited by Marie L. Gansberg, Munich, Frauenoffensive, 1986.

Bibliography: "Christa Reinig" in *Kritisches Lexikon zur deutschsprachigen Gegenwartsliteratur,* Munich, Germany, KLG, 1992.

Critical Sources: *Das Bild des Mannes im Frauenroman der siebziger Jahre* by Liselotte Weingant, Urbana-Champaign, University of Illinois Press, 1981; *Deutsche Frauenautoren der Gegenwart* by Manfred Jurgensen, Bern, Switzerland, Francke, 1983; *Hinterlegte Botschaften* by Madleine Marti, Stuttgart, Germany, M und P, 1991; *Frauenliebe und -literatur: (un)gelebte (Vor)Bilder bei Ingeborg Bachmann, Johanna Moosdorf und Christa Reinig* by Cäcilia Ewering, Essen, Germany, Blaue Eule, 1992; *Rotkäppchen erlegt den Wolf: Marieluise Fleißser, Christa Reinig und Elfriede Jelinek als satirische Schriftstellerinnen* by Klaudia Heidemann-Nebelin, Bonn, Germany, Holos, 1994.

*   *   *

Christa Reinig was a well-known author long before her involvement in the Women's Movement and her coming-out as a lesbian. Literary critics divide Reinig's literary work into two parts—that work which came before her coming out and that which comes after—a division which is crucial for all interpretations.

Reinig first went public as lesbian in 1974 on the occasion of the Ihns/Anderson case. In a spectacular trial Marion Ihns and Judy Anderson were sentenced to life in prison because they hired a man to kill Ihns' husband, who was a wife-beater. The boulevard press got hold of the fact that Ihns and Anderson had a lesbian relationship, and soon it was lesbianism that was on trial. Reinig wrote an article in the newspaper *Die Zeit* in October 1974 about the lawsuit and the homophobia of German society, thus using her status as a well-known author to counter the weight of hostile opinion.

In her 1976 novel *Entmannung,* which she later called "her way into the feminist movement," Reinig tells the story of Otto Kyra and of four women, identifying herself with the male Kyra. Although the main figure is a feminist man, the book also includes a character named Wölfi, the first lesbian Reinig ever portrayed. Wölfi is a very depressed figure, an alcoholic who feels oppressed because she can not compete with Otto Kyra. She complains: "Kyra can marry Thea, Wölfi can't. Kyra can make Menni pregnant, Wölfi can't. Kyra is allowed to watch women, Wölfi isn't." In the same novel the author introduced herself as a literary figure, referring to her part in the Ihns/Anderson trial: "Christa Reinig swears: 'I'll abandon all my male friends, I don't want to see them again.'"

From this point on Christa Reinig dedicated her work to the women's movement. Many of her satirical and cynical works have to be seen in this context. But Reinig not only deconstructed patriarchy, she also promoted lesbian culture and identity in novels like *The Woman in the Well,* where she described the relationship of two older dykes. Her writing was—as always—very experimental, and included long poems of Sappho, a woman-centered rewriting of Sappho's life, and a discussion on growing old and dying. "In the temporary doubling of the female narrator and in the specific picturing of the lover Reinig develops a style of writing in which she not only deconstructs patriarchal pictures of

women but also names lesbian existence," wrote Madleine Marti in *Hinterlegte Botschaften.*

Reinig, who was one of the most popular writers of the women's movement, also took part in recapturing lesbian identity and culture. For example, she wrote the foreword to the new publication of Christa Winsloe's *Girls in Uniform,* arguably the most famous lesbian film in Germany, penned several radio plays, and in *Girls without Uniform* engaged in an intense discussion of the work of Christa Winsloe.

Reinig has written many stories on transgender and transexuality which until recently have only been interpreted in feminist and/or lesbian perspectives, never in terms of queer theory. The latest publications of Christa Reinig have not focused on feminist or lesbian issues, drawing connnections instead to her prefeminist work. Nonetheless her aesthetics make her the most interesting contemporary lesbian writer in Germany.

—Birgit Lang

————

REY, Faustina. *See* **LIVIA, Anna.**

————

RICE, Anne

Pseudonyms: Has written as Anne Rampling and A. N. Roquelaure. **Nationality:** American novelist. **Born:** Howard Allen in New Orleans, Louisiana, 4 October 1941; name changed, c. 1947. **Education:** Texas Women's University, 1959-60; San Francisco State College (now University), B.A. 1964, M.A. 1971; graduate study, University of California, Berkeley, 1969-70. **Family:** Married to the poet and painter Stan Rice in 1961; two children. **Career:** Has held a variety of odd jobs; writer. Member, Authors Guild. **Awards:** Honorable mention, Joseph Henry Jackson award, 1970. **Address:** c/o Alfred Knopf Inc., 201 E. 50th St., New York, New York 10022-7703, U.S.A.; 1239 First St., New Orleans, Louisiana 70130, U.S.A.

WRITINGS

Fiction

Interview with the Vampire. New York, Knopf, 1976.
The Feast of All Saints. New York, Simon and Schuster, 1980.
Cry to Heaven. New York, Ballantine, 1976; reissued, New York, Knopf, 1982.
The Claiming of Sleeping Beauty (as A. N. Roquelaure). New York, Dutton, 1983.
Beauty's Punishment (as A. N. Roquelaure). New York, Dutton, 1984.
Beauty's Release (as A. N. Roquelaure). New York, Dutton, 1985.
Exit to Eden (as Anne Rampling). New York, Arbor House, 1985.
The Vampire Lestat. New York, Knopf, 1985.

Belinda: A Novel (as Anne Rampling). New York, Arbor House, 1986.
The Mummy, or Ramses the Damned. New York, Ballantine, 1988.
The Queen of the Damned. New York, Knopf, 1988.
The Witching Hour. New York, Knopf, 1990.
Tale of the Body Thief. New York, Knopf, 1992.
Lasher: A Novel. New York, Knopf, 1993.
Taltos: Lives of the Mayfair Witches. New York, Ballantine, 1994.
Memnoch the Devil. New York, Knopf, 1995.
Servant of the Bones. New York, Knopf, 1996.

*

Adaptations: *Interview with the Vampire* (sound recording; read by F. Murray Abraham), Random House AudioBooks, 1986; *The Queen of the Damned* (sound recording; read by Michael York), 1988; *The Vampire Lestat* (sound recording; read by York), 1989; *The Mummy: Or Ramses the Damned* (sound recording; read by York), 1990; "Vampire Chronicles" (which includes *Interview with the Vampire, The Vampire Lestat,* and *The Queen of the Damned*) have been optioned for film and stage productions.

Biography: *Prism of the Night: A Biography of Anne Rice* by Katherine Ramsland, New York, Dutton, 1991; *Anne Rice* by Bette B. Roberts, New York, Twayne Publishers, 1994.

Bibliography: *Anne Rice: A Critical Companion* by Jennifer Smith, Westport, Connecticut, Greenwood Press, 1996.

Critical Sources: *The Gothic World of Anne Rice,* edited by Ray Broadus Browne and Gary Hoppenstand, Bowling Green, Ohio, Bowling Green State University Popular Press, 1996; *Writing Horror of the Body: The Fiction of Stephen King, Clive Barker, and Anne Rice* by Linda Badley, Westport, Connecticut, Greenwood Press, 1996.

*   *   *

The portrayal of homosexuality in literature has, until recent years, belonged almost exclusively to the depiction of the "other," of a phenomenon beyond the boundaries of the normal heterosexual world of daylight. Even such early sociological works as Jessie Mercer's 1959 study *They Walk In Shadow* perpetuated the image of the homosexual as an inhabitant of a different realm, subject to laws and customs not binding on the majority of the population, a strange being, terrifying because of its boundlessness. Given this thread, it was perhaps inevitable that gay and lesbian characters would appear in various works of Gothic and supernatural literature. This view of gay people as standing at the intersection of the known and the mysterious has been most fully developed in contemporary horror literature by the prolific Anne Rice.

A daughter of the lush and brooding city of New Orleans, Rice gained a familiarity with dual roles when she was christened Howard Allen, the second of four children in an Irish family. Tolerance for imaginative behavior coupled with limitations on some types of intellectual exploration based on her mother's active Catholicism stimulated Rice's creative talents. Her parochial school education also introduced her to the richly evocative powers of ritual which would later be reflected in her writings. The death of her mother in 1956 and her father's remarriage and move to a Dal-

las suburb led to her meeting with her future husband, the poet Stan Rice, as well as hastening her transition into adulthood. Following graduation from high school, she briefly attended Texas Women's University before leaving for San Francisco, and returning to marry in 1961. The newlyweds settled into the raffish world of Haight-Ashbury while Anne completed a bachelor's degree in political science at San Francisco State, finishing in 1964. The birth of her daughter Michele in 1966 was shortly followed by a return to academic life and pursuit of a doctorate in creative writing, acquired in 1972.

Rice's formal writing career begins with the explosive appearance of her first novel, *Interview with the Vampire,* in 1976. The work illustrates her use of literature as a means of exploring sensuality and introduced one of the most unique figures of modern Gothic writing, Lestat de Lioncourt. In addition to beginning what would come to be known as "The Vampire Chronicles," this work also explored the complex emotional patterns of two immortal love/hate relationships, between both Lestat and the young planter Louis (whom he brings into the world of the vampires) and the vampire and their human victims. The powerful dynamics of love and other emotional needs among the undead and their fascination with and need for the deeply sensual aspects of preying on mortals, both for physical sustenance and psychological satisfaction, are themes which Rice would carry forward and elaborate upon throughout all her works in this group of novels. The creation of a child vampire, Claudia, by Lestat, and her bitterly grudging acceptance of the role of daughter to the two males parallels the ideas both of male couples and the issues of gay adoption.

In the second volume of this series, *The Vampire Lestat,* the narrative voice is that of Lestat himself, recounting his birth into the undead during the late eighteenth century in Paris (through a conscious choice analogous to the decision of gays and lesbians to declare their sexuality and "come out") and subsequent career as an immortal. In some ways, in creating Lestat, Rice has embodied many of the best aesthetic qualities traditionally associated with homosexual men—love for, knowledge of, and appreciation for the processes and products of the fine arts and literature, respect for and understanding of possible sensualities, and an ironic humor that pervades his total world view. Lestat is both human and immortal, and rejects the idea that vampires must constitute a hidden secret world of their own, ruled by its own laws, a world he encounters in the catacombs beneath Paris, preferring to live blatantly in the public view. This aspect of his life culminates in his choice in modern times of the career of a rock musician of powerful but ill-defined sexuality, a reference to the frequent rumors in the entertainment community that certain performers might be gay or lesbian. His offering of a challenge to cross over into their world to the audience at his public concert with the cry "How many of you would be vampires?" echoes the calls of activists for gay and lesbian rights that all homosexuals should come out and declare their true natures. The anger of many vampires at Lestat's open flaunting of his secret identity before a mass public, and their call for his destruction, echoes the fear of many closeted homosexuals of the tactics of the gay liberation movement and, most recently, confrontational organizations such as ACT UP and Queer Nation.

Another thread contained in the Vampire Chronicles is the search for an answer to how the undead came into being originally, an intellectual question with clear analogies to the ongoing and contentious search for the causes of homosexuality. Vampires are described in the third volume, *Queen of the Damned* (dedicated in part to the gay writer John Preston), as having been created through the possession of the rulers of Egypt, Akasha and Enkil, by a spirit, a fusion of demonic force and physical actuality from whom all others of their kind had been created. The sister witches whose lives were witnesses to this event, Maharet and Mekare, provide yet another same gender couple, introducing a feminine perspective which serves to balance the male voices of Lestat and Louis. The awakening of the ancients and Akasha's plan to destroy the other vampires mimics the contention of a certain school of psychologists that homosexuals are self-destructive and will inevitably be consumed by their own inner natures.

The second of Rice's early novels, *Cry to Heaven,* takes as its framework the world of the castrati, male singers who were gelded in early childhood to preserve their soprano voices. Their inability to ever function as true heterosexual men places them outside the sexual norm, an inability not chosen but imposed by culture rather than by the matrix of conditioning and genetics considered by many to be the background of attraction to the same gender.

In the early 1990s, Rice shifted the focus of her writing to the beautiful old homes of the Garden District of New Orleans, continuing in *The Witching Hour* and *Lasher and Taltos* themes established in her vampiric works combined with an exploration of her own Celtic heritage. The unfolding of the tale of the Mayfair Witches and their guardian spirit, while utilizing predominantly heterosexual characters, does include the ancestral figure of Julian Mayfair, whose sexuality is seen as ambiguous. The most sharply sexually divergent creation in this trilogy is the being whose name gives the title to the third volume, the *taltos,* a separate ancient species "of searing intelligence and insatiable hungers" whose rebirth is interwoven with the life of one of the leading characters, Dr. Rowan Mayfair. Literary parallels may also be drawn with such other intelligent nonhumans as Marion Zimmer Bradley's *chieri.* The rampantly erotic and overpowering nature of the *taltos'* sexuality also recalls the myth in popular psychology that homosexuals' basic needs were so strong that they would drive them to commit sex crimes to gain satisfaction.

Rice uniquely flavors her exploration of another familiar genre in horror literature, that of tales dealing with the reanimated mummy and its vengeance upon the living. Her presentation in *The Mummy, or Ramses the Damned* echoes the atmosphere of Edwardian society, with its pleasure-seeking and decadent behaviors. In the character of Elliott, Lord Rutherford, the reader is offered a discrete homosexual with an inquiring mind and a willingness to set aside conventional explanations, a mind set which eventually leads to his transformation into an immortal. The work also capitalizes upon the subgenre of pulp fiction dealing with "the mummy's curse," questioning whether immortality must of necessity mean unfulfilled sadness, melancholy, and madness, balancing the dialogue of Lestat with the Parisian vampires in their hidden world beneath the city.

Perhaps the most intricately theological and philosophical of all Rice's novels is the 1995 *Memnoch the Devil.* A supposed offer from the title character provides a unique opportunity for Lestat to continue his journey of self-discovery beyond "beauty, rhythm, symmetry...the only laws I've ever witnessed that seemed natural." Approaching and structuring the universe through purely aesthetic principles is a stereotyped attribute of many gay men, and Lestat's odyssey through cosmic time and realities mirrors the questing of many homosexuals of both genders for their own answers to the riddles of their essential natures.

Picking up the thread of the ancient world first introduced in *Queen of the Damned* and continued in *The Mummy,* Rice's 1996

novel *Servant of the Bones* adds a new character to her array, one who merges aspects of Ramses and Lestat. This figure, Azriel, begins life as a Jew during the Babylonian Captivity, with the uncanny ability to see and converse with Marduk, lord of the city's pantheon. The deep emotional bond between god and mortal echoes that of Lestat for his mortal friend David Talbot of the Talamasca, while his transformation into a genie recalls the birth of Lestat into the dark life. Another exploration of same-gender love is seen in the confrontation between the old Hasidic rabbi and his apostate grandson.

A more subtle appearance of homosexuality is seen in *Exit to Eden,* where a private island resort has been created solely for the purposes of permitting individuals willing to pay to realize their fantasies of dominance and submission in a safe environment. The male protagonist (a photographer from Berkeley) is initially portrayed as preferring male partners, although his sexual history eventually reveals heterosexual experiences as well. One of the administrators of the island is described in terms clearly indicating a homosexual nature. The influence of this work on popular culture stems both from its value as literature and its use as the base for a film which introduced the public to the ideas of the leather world and sexual submission as acceptable and part of the range of normal variations, a position activists within the gay leather community had consistently maintained.

Rice's realistic uses and frank explorations of subtle emotional shadings within same-gender relationships is undoubtedly one of the reasons for her popularity among gay and lesbian readers. Her works also perform another important function, that of familiarizing and educating a mass audience on the realities and potentials of same-gender love. By reversing the expected universe through bringing the marginal to center stage and allowing its articulate and complex voices to be heard, she forces her readers to think about the roots and rationales of social and sexual divisions, categories and boundaries.

—Robert B. Marks Ridinger

————

RICHARDSON, Ethel Florence Lindesay. *See* **RICHARDSON, Henry Handel.**

————

RICHARDSON, Henry Handel

Pseudonyms: Ethel Florence Lindesay Richardson. **Nationality:** Australian novelist and author of short stories. **Born:** East Melbourne, Victoria, 3 January 1870. **Education:** Ladies Presbyterian College, Melbourne (Senior Pianoforte Scholarship, 1886; First Class Honors in Senior English and history, 1887), 1883-87; Leipzig Conservatory, Leipzig, Germany, 1889-92. **Family:** Married John G. Robertson in 1895 (died 1933). Lived in Strasbourg, 1896-03, London, 1903-33, and Sussex, 1933-46. **Career:** Worked briefly as a governess in Australia, C. 1887-88; trained for but did not pursue a career as a concert pianist; essayist, translator, and fiction writer, from 1894. Lifelong member of the Society for Psychical Research. **Awards:** Australian Literature Society gold medal, 1929; Nobel Prize nomination, 1932. **Died:** Sussex, England, 20 March 1946.

WRITINGS

Novels

Maurice Guest. London, Heinemann, and New York, P.R. Reynolds, 1908; with an introduction by Karen McLeod, London, Virago, 1981.
The Getting of Wisdom. London, Heinemann, and New York, Duffield, 1910; revised edition, London, Heinemann, and New York, Norton, 1931; with illustrations by Frederick McCubbin, San Francisco, Mercury House, 1993.
Australia Felix. London, Heinemann, and New York, Norton, 1917; with an introduction by Leonie Kramer, Harmondsworth, Middlesex, and Ringwood, Victoria, Penguin, 1971.
The Way Home. London, Heinemann, 1925; New York, Norton, 1930; with an introduction by Leonie Kramer, Harmondsworth, Middlesex, and Ringwood, Victoria, Penguin, 1971.
Ultima Thule. London, Heinemann, New York, Norton, and Toronto, Doubleday, Doran & Grundy, 1929; with an introduction by Leonie Kramer, Harmondsworth, Middlesex, and Ringwood, Victoria, Penguin, 1971.
The Fortunes of Richard Mahony: Comprising Australia Felix, The Way Home, Ultima Thule. London, Heinemann, 1930, New York, Norton, 1931; as *The Fortunes of Richard Mahony* with foreword by Sinclair Lewis, New York, Press of the Readers Club, 1941.
The Young Cosima. London, Heinemann, and New York, Norton, 1939.

Short Stories

Two Studies. London, Ulysses Press, 1931.
The End of a Childhood and Other Stories. London, Heinemann, 1934; as *The End of a Childhood,* New York, Norton, 1934; as *The End of a Childhood: The Complete Stories of Henry Handel Richardson,* with introduction by Carol Franklin, Pymble, N.S.W., Angus & Robertson, 1992.
Cuffy Mahony and Other Stories. London and Sydney, Angus & Robertson, 1979.

Translator

(As Ethel F. L. Robertson) *Siren Voices,* by Jens Peter Jacobsen. Heinemann's International Library, Vol. 19, London, Heinemann, 1896.
The Fisher Lass, by Bjornsterne Bjornson. London, Heinemann, 1896.

Other

Christkindleins Wiegenlied: An Old German Carol Set to Music. London: Ulysses Press, 1931.
The Bath: An Aquarelle. Sydney, P.R. Stephenson & Co., 1933.
Myself When Young: Together with an Essay on The Art Henry Handel Richardson by I.G. Robertson (unfinished autobiography). London, HeineMann, and New York, Norton, 1948.

Letters of Henry Handel Richardson to Nettie Palmer, edited by Karl-Johan Rossing. Uppsala, Lundequistska, and Cambridge, Harvard University Press, 1953.

*

Adaptations: *The Getting of Wisdom* (children's story adapted by Ida Veirch), Nelson, 1980; *The Getting of Wisdom* (screenplay by Eleanor Whitcombe), Heinemann, 1978; *The Getting of Wisdom* (film), MGM/CBS Home Video, 1980; *The Getting of Wisdom* (soundrecording), Books in Motion, 1992.

Manuscript Collections: National Library, Canberra.

Biography: *Myself When Young: Together with an Essay on the Art of Henry Handel Richardson by I.G. Robertson* by Henry Handel Richardson, New York, Norton, 1948; *Henry Handel Richardson: Some Personal Impressions,* edited by Edna Purdie and Olga M. Roncoroni, Sydney, Angus & Robertson, 1957.

Bibliography: "Henry Handel Richardson" by Maria S. Haynes, in *Bulletin of Bibliography,* Vol. 21, 1955, 130-35; "Henry Handel Richardson: An Annotated Bibliography of Writings About Her" by Verna D. Wittrock, in *English Literature in Transition (1880-1920),* Vol. 7, 1964, 140-87.

Critical Sources: *Henry Handel Richardson: A Study,* by Nettie Palmer, Sydney, Angus & Robertson, 1950; *Henry Handel Richardson and Some of Her Sources* by Leonie J. Gibson, Melbourne, Melbourne University, 1954; *Henry Handel Richardson* by Vincent Buckley, Melbourne, Landsdowne, 1962; "Convention and Freedom: A Study of Maurice Guest" by William H. New, in *English Studies* (Anglo-American Supplement), 1969, lxii-lxviii; *The Georgia Literary Scene, 1910-1935,* revised edition, by Frank Swinnerton, New York, Hutchinson & Co., 1969; *Henry Handel Richardson (Ethel Florence Lindsay Richardson)* by William D. Elliott, Boston, Twayne, 1975; "The Fortunes of Richard Mahony Reconsidered" by A. Norman Jeffares, in *Sewanee Review,* Vol. 87, 1979, 158-64; *The Portrayal of Women in the Fiction of Henry Handel Richardson* by Eva J. Corones, Malmo, Sweden, Liber International, 1983; "Not a Love Story: Henry Handel Richardson's *Maurice Guest*" by Noel Macainsh, in *Westerly: A Quarterly Review,* Vol. 30, 1985, 77-86; "H.H. Richardson's 'Two Hanged Women': Our Own True Selves and Compulsory Heterosexuality" by Carol Franklin, in *Kunapipi,* Vol. 14, 1992, 41-52; "Power-Games in the Novels of Henry Handel Richardson" by Dorothy Green, in *Who is She?,* edited by Shirley Walker, New York, St. Martin's, 84-97; "Some Notes on My Books" by Henry Handel Richardson, in *Virginia Quarterly Review,* Vol. 61, No. 40, 334-47.

*　　*　　*

Australian novelist Henry Handel Richardson, born Ethel Florence Lindsay Richardson, was born in 1870 in East Melbourne, Victoria, Australia, to parents Walter Lindsay Richardson and Mary Bailey Richardson. Her parents had migrated separately to Australia from the British Isles to seek their fortunes, her father from Dublin and her mother from Leicester; they met and married in Australia in 1855. Richardson's father was a medical practitioner who came to Australia during the Australian gold rush; he worked as a storekeeper and then in a general medical practice. On the basis of a small fortune from stock returns, he was able to retire from his general practice in Melbourne in 1869, a successful and prominent citizen. Ethel was born the following year, and a younger sister followed. The Richardsons lived a comfortable life for the next few years, but while on a European tour Walter Richardson's investments failed and the family was forced to return to Australia so that Richardson could rebuild his medical practice; he did not succeed. The family's fortunes continued to decline; they moved around Victoria several times as Walter Richardson's health and mental condition deteriorated, due probably to syphilis. He was institutionalized in asylums and died in 1879 in Koroit, a western village in Victoria where Mary Bailey Richardson had obtained work as a postmistress. Her father's life provided Richardson with the material for her three-volume novel, *The Fortunes of Richard Mahony*.

A year after her husband's death, Mary Richardson moved the family to Maldon, where she continued to rise through the ranks of the postal service. Mary Richardson sent her eldest daughter to board at the Presbyterian Ladies' College in Melbourne. Ethel was there from age 13 to 17; her years there were fictionalized in her bildungsroman, *The Getting of Wisdom*. That novel's hero, Laura Rambotham, is ill-adjusted to the setting of the girls' boarding school and does not make a particular success of her time there. Ethel Richardson herself had better success than her literary character, winning several awards while at school. Laura Rambotham develops a strong and clearly romantic attachment to an older girl, Evelyn, who seems sometimes to return Laura's affection but ultimately denies her. Richardson wrote, in her unfinished autobiography, of this time in her own life and her attachment to Constance Bulteel, an older student at the Presbyterian Ladies' College. She claimed to have "weakened" the strength of the attraction she felt for Bulteel in the novel, but its emotional significance and force is clear, even in the novel.

In *Myself When Young,* Richardson wrote:

> The one episode in the story I deliberately weakened was my headstrong fancy for the girl there called "Evelyn." To have touched this in other than lightly [sic] would have been out of keeping with the tone of the book. The real thing was neither light nor amusing. It stirred me to my depths, rousing feelings I hadn't known I possessed, and leaving behind it a [cruel] heartache.... In those days school-authorities had not begun to look with jaundiced eyes on girlish intimacies. We might indulge them as we chose; and, even when it must have been clear to the blindest where I was heading, the two of us continued to share a room. Some may see in my infatuation merely an overflow of feelings that had been denied a normal outlet. But there was more to it than that. The attraction this girl had for me was so strong that few others have surpassed it. Nor did it exist on my side only. The affinity was mutual.

Richardson's romantic relationship with Bulteel ended after the older girl finished school but both eventually settled in London after marrying and maintained sporadic contact throughout their lives. After Richardson left school and worked briefly as a governess, her mother took her and her sister to Leipzig. Ethel showed great promise as a pianist, so she enrolled in the Leipzig Conservatory and studied there for several years, from 1889 to 1892,

until she eventually decided that she lacked the temperament to be a classical musician, and she quit the conservatory. While living in Leipzig, she met John O. Robertson, a graduate student in German, and they married in 1895. They moved to Strasbourg, where Robertson had an academic appointment, and stayed there until 1903, when they moved to London so that Robertson could chair the German Department at London University. The Robertsons remained in London until J. G. Robertson's death in 1933. After her husband's death, Richardson moved to Sussex, where she remained until her death in 1946. Her companion and secretary for the last several years of her life was Olga Roncoroni. It was Roncoroni who finished the manuscript of Richardson's autobiography, *Myself When Young,* after Richardson died.

Ethel Richardson took the pseudonym Henry Handel Richardson from a Dublin relative from her father's side of the family; she is said to have wanted her novels to appear "masculine." She undertook her writing career after her marriage to Robertson. Her literary style was highly influenced by continental literature and philosophy. Critics variously attribute Richardson's realist style to French, German, or Russian literary influences. She lived a relatively reclusive life, especially after the move to London, and dedicated herself to her writing, The only major travel she undertook after settling in London was a return to Leipzig in 1907 for work on her novel *Maurice Guest,* set in Leipzig; she also spent two months in Australia in 1912 gathering material for her opus, *The Fortunes of Richard Mahony.*

Richardson mined her personal experiences for her literary pieces, and her writings have a gloomy and unsentimental cast. *Maurice Guest* discusses the fate of a young man who is a conservatory student in Leipzig, as Richardson herself was, and focuses on issues of artistic and sexual development, thwarted desires and ambitions, and personal destructiveness. Similar themes appear in Richardson's other works, such as *The Getting of Wisdom* and *The Fortunes of Richard Mahony.* Maurice Guest becomes highly attracted to Louise, a woman he meets in Leipzig. Louise does not sincerely return his affection, though she does keep him hanging on. She is a bisexual character who is variously attracted to a dynamic older male character and another woman. Richardson makes some use of Richard von Kraft-Ebbing's medical model of homosexuality and sexual deviation in *Maurice Guest.*

It is for her trilogy *The Fortunes of Richard Mahony* that Richardson is probably best known, although she was in and out of the public eye as a writer during her own lifetime and remains somewhat obscure today. But *The Getting of Wisdom* and *Maurice Guest* will be more significant texts for readers interested in the lesbian content to Richardson's writings. In both her autobiographical writing and her fictional writing, Richardson is prepared to reveal her sexual interest in women, though her terminology is neither particularly frank nor activist. In her autobiography, she discusses soulfully the physical attractiveness of Bulteel: "her laughing, provocative eyes—dark, velvety eyes under a thatch of sunlit hair—and altogether so lovely that she could pass nowhere unnoticed." She calls *The Getting of Wisdom* "the tombstone [she] had erected to [Bulteel's] memory." A later short story of Richardson's (which is occasionally anthologized) called "Two Hanged Women" seems to harken back to this relationship, and interestingly so. The story, written in 1934, deals with both the need for furtiveness of lesbians in public spaces and the overtness of heterosexual privilege in the public expression of sexual and romantic affection. It also discusses, as does *The Getting of Wisdom,* the relentless personal and social pressure placed on girls and young women to switch their primary emotional bonds from females to males, as a prelude to adult heterosexual bonding, and the grave dilemma this pressure to become heterosexual creates for lesbians.

—Martha Henn

RIGGS, Marlon Troy

Nationality: American film director and teacher. **Born:** Fort Worth, Texas, 1957. **Education:** Harvard University, B.A. 1978; University of California, Berkeley, M.A. in Journalism 1981. **Family:** Companion of Jack Vincent. **Career:** Worked for television station in Texas, 1978-79; worked for various producers and directors of documentary films, mostly in public television, 1981-87; producer and director of original films, from 1986; part-time faculty member, University of California, Berkeley. **Awards:** Emmy Award, for *Ethnic Notions,* 1989; NEA Grant, for *Tongues Untied,* 1989; Black Filmmakers Hall of Fame award, 1989; Atlanta Film Festival award, 1989; Berlin Film Festival award, 1989; Peabody award, for *Color Adjustment,* 1989; Maya Daran Lifetime Achievement Award, American Film Institute, 1991. **Died:** Oakland, California, of complications related to AIDS, 1994.

WRITINGS

Films

And producer and director, *Ethnic Notions.* San Francisco, California Newsreel, 1986.
And producer and director, *Changing Images: Mirrors of Life, Molds of Reality.* 1987.
And director, *Open Window: Innovations from the University of California.* 1988.
And director, *Visions Toward Tomorrow: Ida Louise Jackson.* 1989.
And producer and director, *Color Adjustment.* San Francisco, California Newsreel, 1989.
And producer and director, *Tongues Untied.* San Francisco, Frameline, 1989.
Anthem. 1990.
Black Is ... Black Ain't (completed posthumously by Nichole Atkinson and Christiane Badgely). San Francisco, California Newsreel, 1995.

Other

"Boyz N Hollywood" (essay), in *High Performance,* Vol. 14, No. 4, winter 1991.
"Black Macho Revisited: Reflections of a SNAP! Queen" (essay), in *Black American Literature Forum,* Vol. 25, No. 4, summer 1991.
"Tongues Untied" (poem), in *Brother to Brother: New Writings by Black Gay Men,* edited by Essex Hemphill. Boston, Alyson Publications, and London, GMP Publishers, 1991.

*

Critical Sources: *BLK,* April 1990, 10-19; *Out/look,* spring 1991, 12-19; "New Agendas in Black Filmmaking" by Roy Gerandmann, in *Cineaste,* Vol. XIX, Nos. 2-3, 1992; "Jungle Fever? Black Gay Identity Politics, White Dick, and the Utopian Bedroom" by Darieck Scott, in *GLQ,* Vol. 1, No. 3, 1994; "Marlon Riggs: The Subjective Position of Documentary Video" by Phillip Brian Harper, in *Art Journal,* Vol. 54, No. 4, winter 1995.

*   *   *

Marlon Riggs' major works, his documentary films, are fiercely critical arguments that probe the complex union of racism and homophobia in American history and contemporary popular culture. His films are also, sometimes simultaneously, lyrical celebrations of the communities that have resisted the politics of hate.

His first two films, *Ethnic Notions* and *Color Adjustment,* perform readings of the representation of African Americans in American popular culture. *Ethnic Notions* focuses on the figure of the black, from the Civil War through roughly World War II, in media like blackface minstrel shows, corporate advertising, and film; *Color Adjustment* performs a devastating critique of American television's depictions of blacks from the origins of television through the success of "The Cosby Show." Both documentaries are seamless essays that combine interviews with the creators, insiders, and actors in these media alongside comments by academics, critics, and consumers. Interviews are linked through an unapologetic voice-over narration, film clips, historic documentation, music, art, and text. While the films analyze the effect of white racism on representations of African Americans, they also explore the largely unspoken history of racism within the African American community. The focus is not only on race; Riggs insistently draws attention to the ways that sexism and homophobia form parallel, and sometimes interlocking, systems of oppression. Both films are notable for their investigations not just of the representations of "race," but for Riggs' rigorous inquiry into the politics of representation itself. Riggs insistently wonders how we are to know "good" from "bad" representations, asks who is profiting from the popularity of a representation, racist or non-racist, and demands that we ask ourselves what is at stake in posing the topic of "race" in such simplistic terms.

Riggs came to major national attention, however, for his film *Tongues Untied,* which is a more celebratory, autobiographical, poetic exploration of black gay men. Incorporating poetry by people like Essex Hemphill, memoir, and dance, it is much more of a meditation than his earlier works. Upon its broadcast on the Public Broadcast P.O.V. series, it was attacked by religious and cultural conservatives in the U.S. government as obscene, presumably because of content showing non-pornographic affection between black gay men. That the film—like the Robert Mapplethorpe exhibit—had received funding from the NEA drew attention on a national level to the representation of black men, especially black gay men, in photography, and to the federal government's role in funding the arts. Riggs' film, which even when celebratory continues to examine the differences within black male experience, is remarkable for its unsparing criticism of homophobia and racism in the larger culture and within black communities; he takes on the myth of black macho, Eddie Murphy, and the intolerance of black nationalism.

The film's larger project is to read the logic through which gay black men are shaped by American culture to identify with and desire a white male ideal. "Gay culture" in America, Riggs argues, still means white gay male culture. The film's explorations of gay black male identity are thus a form of revolt and a breaking of silence; the film ends with the appearance of text on the screen accompanied by a chorus of male voices speaking "Black men loving Black men is *the* revolutionary act."

Riggs' final works continued to focus on gay black men. His film, *Black Is...Black Ain't,* which was completed after his death from AIDS in 1994, extends his critique of the politics of representation through his position as a black gay man who is HIV positive. Largely autobiographical and intimately personal, *Black Is...Black Ain't* reflects on the absurdity of simplistic notions of black identity based on terms like skin color, regional origin, or economic status given the complexity of and diversity within the African American community. An exploration and celebration of the differences between black people, *Black Is ... Black Ain't* nevertheless still analyzes the ways in which African-American identity has been formed through an exclusion of the female, the gay, and the lesbian. Riggs repeatedly and powerfully lays claim to his black identity even as he articulates the rhetoric through which he is denied full access to it. In so doing, he contends that the future of the African-American community lies in its ability to embrace contradiction, play on differences, and transcend the history that has shaped it.

—Elliott McEldowney

RILKE, Rainer Maria

Nationality: Austrian poet, novelist, author of short stories, and playwright. **Born:** René Karl Wilhelm Johann Josef Maria Rilke in Prague, Czechoslovakia, 4 December 1875; changed name to the German form in 1897. **Education:** Attended military school at Sankt Pölten, in Lower Austria, 1886-90; at the military upper school at Mährisch-Weißkirchen, in Moravia, 1890-91; at the commercial academy at Linz, 1891-92; received private instruction, 1892-95; studied philosophy at Prague University, 1895. **Military Service:** Served in the Austrian Army, Military Records Office, 1915; discharged. **Family:** Married Clara Westhoff in 1901 (separated 1902); one daughter. **Career:** Wrote for a living and enjoyed the patronage of wealthy friends, from 1896 until his death; secretary to Auguste Rodin, 1905-06. **Died:** Valmont, Switzerland, of leukemia, 29 December 1926.

WRITINGS

Poetry

Advent. Leipzig, Friesenhahn, 1889.
Leben und Lieder: Bilder and Tagebuchbläter. Strassberg and Leipzig, Kattentidt, 1894.
Wegwarten. Prague, Selbstverlag, 1896.
Larenopfer. Prague, Dominicus, 1896.
Todentänze: Zweilicht-Skizzen aus unseren Tagen. Prague, Löwit and Lamberg, 1896.
Tramgekrönt: Neue Gedichte. Leipzig, Friesenhahn, 1897.
Mir zur Feier: Gedichte. Berlin, Meyer, 1899; as *Die frühen Gedichte,* Leipzig, Insel, 1909; New York, Ungar, 1943.

Das Buch der Bilder. Berline, Juncker, 1902; enlarged, 1906; New York, Ungar, 1943.
Das Stunden-Buch enthaltend die drei Bücher: Vom mönchischen Leben; Von der Pilgerschaft; Von der Armuth und vom Tode. Leipzig, Insel, 1905; as *The Book of Hours; Comprising the Three Books: Of the Monastic Life, Of Pilgrimage, Of Poverty and Death,* translated by A.L. Peck, London, Hogarth Press, 1961.
Die Weise von Liebe und Tod des Cornets Chistoph Rilke. Berline, Juncker, 1906; as *The Story of the Love and Death of the Cornet Christopher Rilke,* translated by B.J. Morse, Osnabrück, 1927; as *The Tale of the Love and Death of the Cornet Christoper Rilke,* translated by M.D. Herter Norton, New York, Norton, 1932.
Neue Gedichte, 2 Vols. Leipzig, Insel, 1907-08; as *New Poems,* translated by J.B. Leishman, London, Hogarth Press, 1964; New York, New Directions, 1964.
Requiem. Leipzig, Insel, 1909.
Erste Gedichte. Leipzig, Insel, 1913; New York, Ungar, 1947.
Das Marien-Leben. Leipzig, Insel, 1913; as *The Life of the Virgin Mary,* translated by R.G.L. Barrett, Würzburg, Triltsch, 1921; as *The Life of the Virgin Mary,* translated by C.F. MacIntyre, Berkeley, University of California Press, 1947; as *The Life of the Virgin Mary,* translated by Stephen Spender, London, Vision Press, 1951; New York, Philosophical Library, 1951.
Mitsou: Quarante images par Baltusz. Erlenbach-Zürich and Leipzig, Rotapfel, 1921.
Puppen. Munich, Hyperion, 1921.
Die Sonette an Orpheus: Geschrieben als ein Grab-Mal für Wera Ouckama Knoop. Leipzig, Insel, 1923; as *Sonnets to Orpheus, Written as a Monument for Wera Ouckama Knoop,* translated by J.B. Leishman, London, Hogarth Press, 1936; as *Sonnets to Orpheus,* translated by M.D. Herter Norton, New York, Norton, 1942; New York, Ungar, 1945.
Duineser Elegien. Leipzig, Insel, 1923; as *Duineser Elegien: Elegies from the Castle of Duino,* translated by V. and Edward Sackville-WestLondon, Hogarth Press, 1931; as *Duino Elegies,* translated by J.B. Leishman and Stephen Spender, New York, Norton, 1939.
Vergers suivi des Quatrains Valaisans. Paris, Éditions de la Nouvelle Revue Française, 1926; as *Orchards,* translated by Alfred Poulin, Port Townsend, Washington, Graywolf Press, 1982.
Les Fenêtres: Dix poèms. Paris, Officina Sanctandreana, 1927; as "The Windows," in *The Roses and the Windows,* translated by Alfred Poulin, Port Townsend, Washington, Graywolf Press, 1982.
Les Roses. Bussum, Stols, 1927; as "The Roses," in *The Roses and the Windows,* translated by Alfred Poulin, Port Townsend, Washington, Graywolf Press, 1982.
Visions of Christ: A Posthumous Cycle of Poems, translated by Aaron Kramer, edited by Siegfried Mandel. Boulder, University of Colorado Press, 1967.

Fiction

Am Leben hin: Novellen und Skizzen. Stuttgart, Bonz, 1898.
Zwei Prager Gechichten. Stuttgart, Bonz, 1899.
Vom lieben Gott und Anderes: An Große für Kinder erzählt. Berlin and Leipzig, Schuster and Loeffler, 1900; as *Geschicten vom lieben Gott,* Leipzig, Insel, 1904; as *Stories of God,* translated by Nora Purtscher-Wydenbruck and M.D. Herter Norton, London, Sidgwick and Jackson, 1932.

Die Letzten. Berlin, Juncker, 1902.

Die Aufzeichnungen des Malte Laurids Brigge. Leipzig, Insel, 1910; as *The Notebook of Malte Laurids Brigge,* translated by John Linton, London, Hogarth Press, 1930; as *The Journal of My Other Self,* New York, Norton, 1930.

Ewald Tragy: Erzählung. Munich, Heller, 1929; New York, Johannespresse, 1944; as *Ewald Tragy,* translated by Lola Gruenthal, London, Vision, 1958.

Plays

Im Frühfrost: Ein Stück Dämmerung. Drei Vorgänge. Vienna, Theaterverlag O. F. Eirich, 1897.

Ohne Gegenwart: Drama in zwei Akten. Berlin, Entsch, 1898.

Das tägliche Leben: Drama in zwei Akten. Munich, Langen, 1902.

Nonfiction

Worpswede: Fritz Mackensen, Otto Modersohn, Fritz Overbeck, Hans am Ende, Heinrich Vogeler. Bielefeld and Leipzig, Velhagen and Klasing, 1903.

Auguste Rodin. Berlin, Bard, 1903; translated by Jesse Lemont and Hans Trausil, New York, Sunwise Turn, 1919; as *Rodin,* London, Grey Walls Press, 1946.

Collected Works

Gesammelte Werke, 6 Vols. Leipzig, Insel, 1927.

Gesammelte Gedichte, 4 Vols. Leipzig, Insel, 1930-33.

Aus Rainer Maria Rilkes Nachlaß, 4 Vols. Wiesbaden, Insel, 1950.

Sämtliche Werke, 6 Vols. Wiesbaden and Frankfurt, Insel, 1955-66.

Werke: In 3 Bänden, 3 Vols. Leipzig, Insel, 1978.

Nine Plays, translated by Klaus Phillips and John Locke. New York, Ungar, 1979.

*

Manuscript Collections: Rilke-Archiv, Gernsbach; Rilke-Archiv, Schweizerische Landesbibliothek, Bern, Switzerland; Deutsches Literaturarchiv, Marbach, Germany.

Biography: *René Rilke: Die Jugend Rainer Maria Rilkes* by Carl Sieber, Leipzig, Insel, 1932; *Rainer Maria Rilke* by Eliza M. Butler, Cambridge, Cambridge University Press, New York, Macmillan, 1941; *Rilke: Man and Poet* by Nora Wydenbruck, London, Lehmann, 1949; *Rainer Maria Rilke: Legende und Mythos* by Erich Simenauer, Bern, Haupt, 1953; *Rainer Maria Rilke: The Masks and the Man* by H.F. Peters, Seattle, University of Washington Press, 1960; *Rilke's Last Year* by George C. Schoolfield, Lawrence, University of Kansas Libraries, 1969; *Rilke: Sein Leben, seine Welt, seine Werk* by Wolfgang Leppman, Bern and Munich, Scherz, 1981; *The Sacred Threshold: A Life of Rainer Maria Rilke* by J.F. Hendry, Manchester, England, Carcanet Press, 1983; *Rilke: A Life,* translated by Wolfgang Leppman, Russell S. Stockman, and Richard Exner, New York, Fromm, 1984; *A Ringing Glass: The Life of Rainer Maria Rilke* by Donald Prater, Oxford and New York, Oxford University Press, 1986.

Bibliography: *Rilke-Bibliographie: Erster Teil: Das Werk des Lebenden* by Fritz Adolf Hünlich, Leipzig, Insel, 1935; *Rainer Maria Rilke: Bibliographie* by Walter Ritzer, Vienna, Kerry, 1951.

Critical Sources: *Rainer Maria Rilke* by Lou Andreas-Salomé, Leipzig, Insel, 1928; *Rilke and France: A Study in Poetic Development* by K.A.J. Batterby, London, Oxford University Press, 1966; *Rainer Maria Rilke: The Ring of Forms* by Frank Wood, New York, Farrar, Strauss, and Giroux, 1970; *Rilke in Transition: An Exploration of His Earliest Poetry* by James Rolleston, New Haven, Yale University Press, 1970; *Rainer Maria Rilke: A Centenary Essay* by Timothy J. Casey, London, Macmillan, 1976; *Rainer Maria Rilke and Jugendstil: Affinities, Influences, Adaptations* by Karl E. Webb, Chapel Hill, University of North Carolina Press, 1978; "Homosexual Love in Four Poems by Rilke" by Bernhard Frank, in *The Gay Academic,* edited by Louie Crew, Palm Springs, California, ETC Publications, 1978, 244-51; "Rilke and the Problem of Poetic Inwardness" by Richard Jayne, in *Rilke: The Alchemy of Alienation,* edited by Ernst S. Dick Baron and Warren R. Maurer, Lawrence, Kansas, Regents Press, 1981, 191-222; *Rilke and the Visual Arts,* edited by Frank Baron, Lawrence, Kansas, Coronado, 1982; "Rilke's *Geschichten vom lieben Gott:* The Narrator's Stance toward the Bourgeoisie" by Brigitte L. Bradley, in *Modern Austrian Literature,* Vol. 15, 1982, 1-24; *Russia in the Works of Rainer Maria Rilke* by Patricia Pollock Brodsky, Detroit, Wayne State University Press, 1984; "A Bad Story of Young Rilke" by George C. Schoolfield, in *From Vormärz to Fin de Siècle: Essays in Nineteenth Century Austrian Literature,* edited by Mark G. Ward, Blairgownie, Lochee Publications, 1986, 107-32; *Transcending Angels: Rainer Maria Rilke's Duino Elegies* by Kathleen L. Komar, Lincoln, University of Nebraska Press, 1987; "Paris/ Childhood: The Fragmented Body in Rilke's *Notebooks of Malte Laurids Brigge*" by Andreas Huyssen, in *Modernity and the Text: Revisions of German Modernism,* edited by Andreas Huyssen and David Bathrick, New York, Columbia University Press, 1989, 113-41; "Rainer Maria Rilke," in *Dictionary of Literary Biography,* edited by James Hardin and Donald G. Daviau, Vol. 81, Detroit, Gale, 1989, 244-71; "The Mediating Muse: Of Men, Women, and the Feminine in the Work of Rainer Maria Rilke" by Kathleen L. Komar, in *The Germanic Review,* Vol. 64, 1989, 129-33; "Rilke, Love, and Solitude" by Alan Williamson, in *Michigan Quarterly Review,* Vol. 32, No. 3, 1993, 386-403; *The Beginning of Terror: A Psychological Study of Rainer Maria Rilke's Life and Work* by David Kleinbard, New York, New York University Press, 1993.

*   *   *

Probably the most well-known poet in the German language and certainly one of the premiere poets of the twentieth century in any language, Rainer Maria Rilke has left behind a body of work that has become synonymous with the modern quest for the true self in the face of social disintegration. While his early stories, plays, and poems are generally judged to be mawkish and self-indulgent, they are also admired for their occasional brilliance and insight. His later work, primarily the verse in *New Poems, Duino Elegies,* and *Sonnets to Orpheus,* has been celebrated as some of the most important contributions to modern poetry. Although faulted by many critics for their enigmatic nature, these poems strike at the heart of the modern condition: how to love and find peace in an age in which individuals are alienated from each other, from themselves, and from God.

Rilke's journey as a writer began with the alienation he felt from his bourgeois Catholic background. Many of his early writings reflect his rejection of his mother's religion and Prague, where he had been raised among the socially superior "Prague Germans."

Before he was 20, Rilke left Prague to travel with other European writers and artists all over Europe and Russia, and for the rest of his life he would never feel as if he had a home. While he journeyed outward, though, and moved from one intense relationship to the other, never maintaining any constancy in his life, he pursued a journey inward that was synonymous with his life as an artist.

The quality of inwardness has become the central idea associated with Rilke's work and life. Many have addressed this "problem" in his writing, portrayed as a fear of merging with or becoming lost in the "other." Some read it as a grasping for spirituality, an experience of transcendence that could only be achieved in the depths of the self. Rilke, like the German philosopher Friedrich Nietzsche, believed that God as a manifestation of objective morality and transcendence no longer existed, and that he lived in a time when human beings had to fashion for themselves a replacement for religious belief. Such was the task of the poet, he believed. Richard Jayne, in his essay "Rilke and the Problem of Poetic Inwardness," takes this approach when he writes, "Beneath the dialectical tension between the self and otherness of reality lies Rilke's aesthetic doctrine of art as self-redemption."

Others have read Rilke's withdrawal into the self as an inability to love. Critics cite his failed marriage as evidence; the union lasted only a year before he decided that he was not suited to domestic life. There is also much evidence in his poetry to support such a theory. For example, Rilke begins his poem "Love Song" with "How could I keep my soul so that it might / not touch on yours?" And Alan Williamson, in his article "Rilke, Love, and Solitude" explains, "The (*Duino*) *Elegies* define the problem of love as a problem of innerness." Throughout his poetry Rilke confronts the "problem of love," i.e., the problem of losing oneself and one's creative energies in the act of giving oneself to a beloved. Kathleen L. Komar explains in "The Mediating Muse: Of Men, Women and the Feminine in the Work of Rainer Maria Rilke," that for Rilke, "the poet (male or female) must renounce (or even escape) *being loved* personally in order to create on a larger level of existence."

Due to his large number of relationships with women and his many paeans to women in his poetry, Rilke's critics agree that the author was not homosexual and that "his works evince no particular interest in same-sex behavior," in the words of Bernhard Frank in his essay for *The Gay Academic*. Nonetheless, some critical attention has been paid to the issue of sexuality in his life and works. David Kleinbard, in his psychological study of Rilke, *The Beginning of Terror*, senses a "confusion" of sexual identity in Rilke's life and work, stemming largely from episodes in his childhood that are reproduced in his autobiographical novel, *The Notebooks of Malte Laurids Brigge*. In the novel, the young boy Malte is encouraged by his mother to dress up like a little girl and pretend to be his little sister, who died in infancy, much as Rilke himself had been. Kleinbard speculates that such "games" would lead to "doubt and confusion about one's identity, and in particular one's sexual identity." He goes on to explain that Rilke was torn between identifying with his mother, whose "esteem for poets and poetry ultimately had greater control over his mind and life," and identifying with his father, who "drilled him like a soldier." In Kleinbard's view, the confusion of this dual identification in his early life was dissolved into a "rich integration," a "bisexuality," expressed in the *Duino Elegies* and *Sonnets to Orpheus*. Kleinbard uses the term "bisexuality" to describe Rilke's sense of

the "woman within," a manifestation ultimately of his creative powers and an identification with women that was often bound up in his loving relationships with them.

Kleinbard never explores the possibility that Rilke had loving relationships with men as well, although he does go into much detail about Rilke's emotionally and psychologically intense relationship with the French sculptor, Auguste Rodin, who served as a "father figure" for Rilke, much the same way that many of his female lovers and friends played a maternal role with him. It is clear that Rilke for a while nearly worshipped this "master" with an intensity that rivaled some of his deepest relationships with women, namely Lou Andreas-Salomé and his wife, Clara, although no evidence of a sexual relationship with Rodin has been discovered.

Bernhard Frank has addressed the issue of homosexuality in Rilke's work, namely in four poems from *New Poems*. All four poems deal with the difficulty of loving another human being, similar to the themes of his most famous poems from the *Duino Elegies* and *Sonnets to Orpheus*. Frank points out that the speakers of all four poems are third persons who cannot be identified with the poet himself. Two of the poems are an exchange between Sappho, the poet of Lesbos from the sixth century B.C., and her supposed "favorite," Eranna, a young poet who left her family to join Sappho's community. One has the sense that Rilke took his cues from Sappho's original poems to Eranna, as they dealt with the difficulty these two women had in loving each other. In "Eranna to Sappho," Eranna tells her lover, "I don't know *where* I am. / Me no one can bring back," indicating both her alienation from her kin and her inability to maintain a strong sense of herself in the face of her relationship with Sappho. In "Sappho to Eranna," Sappho revels the volatility of the relationship, as she tells her, "Let me penetrate you like death / and remit you like the grave / unto the All." Frank argues that these two poems reveal the sense that "the moods of love are rarely static."

The other two poems Frank discusses are laments spoken by men who have lost their lovers. The first one is "Lament for Antinous." The young man of the title was the "favorite" of Hadrian, Emperor of the Roman Empire from 110-130 A.D. In this poem, Hadrian believes that his young lover has committed suicide and that he is to blame. "Who then succeeds in loving? Who knows how? As yet, none. / And so I have inflicted endless pain—." The speaker feels that his inability to truly love Antinous has led him to his death. In "Lament for Jonathan," the biblical David laments the loss of his beloved Jonathan, son of King Saul. Frank argues that Rilke probably took his inspiration from 2 Samuel I: 25, 26, in which David tells Jonathan, "your love to me was wonderful, passing the love of women." In Rilke's poem, the author evinces real empathy for the young David, who reflects, "and you who was your intimate does not signify / and must contain himself and hear the news." For fear of persecution from the community, David must hide his feelings for his dead lover. Frank views this poem as evidence of Rilke's understanding and humanization of homosexual lovers. "Although writing in a homophobic age for a homophobic public, he has given his characters complete *laissez-faire,* letting them act out all the foibles and all the grandeur that come with love," Frank writes.

Rilke's most lasting legacy is his poems on the modern person's grasping for and fear of love. And although he was not gay, in his life or his writings, his extension of his central theme to include same-sex relationships is a remarkable one in early twentieth century literature. Although these poems represent a very small fragment of his prodigious output, they deserve recognition due to their uniqueness.

—Anne Boyd

ROBSON, Ruthann

Nationality: American short story writer, novelist, and legal scholar. **Born:** 27 June 1956. **Education:** Ramapo College, Mahwah, New Jersey, 1973-76, B.A. in Philosophy 1976; University of South Carolina, Columbia, 1976-77; Stetson College of Law, St. Petersburg, Florida, 1977-79 (honors), J.D. 1979; University of California at Berkeley School of Law, L.L.M. 1989. **Career:** Has held a number of jobs including waitressing, bartending, factory work, retail sales, working for federal judges, practicing poverty law. and teaching; professor of Law, City University of New York School of Law, New York City, from 1989. **Awards:** Lambda Literary Award nomination, for lesbian debut, 1990; Ferro-Grumley Award for Lesbian Fiction, 1990. **Address:** c/o CUNY Law, Lehman College, Bedford Park Blvd. West, Bronx, New York 10468, U.S.A.

WRITINGS

Short Stories

"Rhea's Daughter," in *Crossing the Mainstream: New Fiction by Women Writers,* edited by Ann E. Larson and Carole A. Carr. Seattle, Washington, Silverleaf Press, 1987.
Eye of a Hurricane. Ithaca, New York, Firebrand Books, 1989.
Cecile. Ithaca, New York, Firebrand Books, 1991.
"The Pool," in *Out for Blood: Tales of Mystery and Suspense by Women,* edited by Victoria A. Brownworth. Chicago, Illinois, Third Side Press, 1995.
"Choices," in *Close Calls: New Lesbian Fiction,* edited by Susan Fox Rogers. New York, St. Martin's Press, 1996.

Novels

Another Mother. New York, St. Martin's Press, 1995.

Nonfiction

Lesbian (Out)law: Survival Under the Rule of Law. Ithaca, New York, Firebrand Books, 1992.
Gay Men, Lesbians, and the Law. New York, Chelsea House Publishers, 1996.

Uncollected Essays

"Mother: The Legal Domestication of Lesbian Existence," in *Adventures in Lesbian Philosophy,* edited by Claudia Card. Bloomington, Indiana University Press, 1994.
"Convictions: Theorizing Lesbians and Criminal Justice," in *Legal Inversions: Lesbians, Gay Men, and the Politics of Law,* edited by Didi Herman and Carl Stychin. Philadelphia, Pennsylvania, Temple University Press, 1995.

"Our Relationships and Their Laws" and "Our Children and Their Laws," in *Dyke Life: From Growing Up to Growing Old, A Celebration of the Lesbian Experience,* edited by Karla Jay. New York, Basic Books, 1995.
"Pedagogy, Jurisprudence, and Finger-Fucking: Lesbian Sex in a Law School Classroom," in *Lesbian Erotica,* edited by Karla Jay. New York City, New York University Press, 1995.

*

Critical Sources: "Ruthann Robson" by Jorjet Harper, in *Contemporary Lesbian Writers of the United States: A Bio-Bibliographical Critical Sourcebook,* edited by Sandra Pollack and Denise D. Knight, Westport, Connecticut, Greenwood Press, 1993, 446-452; "Another Mother" by Kristen Golden, in *Ms.* (New York), Vol. 6, No. 3, November 1995, 89-90; "Gay Men, Lesbians, and the Law" by Akilah Monifa, in *Lambda Book Report* (Washington, D.C.), Vol. 5, No. 3, September, 1996, 23.

*   *   *

The unsuspecting reader should be forgiven for thinking there are two Ruthann Robsons. The first Robson writes fiction, crafting characters that have been defined as quirky, eccentric, or, at the very least, variations on the lesbian characters found in so much other fiction. The other Robson is a noted legal scholar and teacher known for her in-depth interrogations into the impact of legal statutes and systems upon lesbian existence. But these Robsons, it turns out, are one and the same, and the different genres in which she writes represent variations on her overall goal of intensely investigating the complexities of lesbian lives. Whether she uses a short story, an essay, or a legal exploration, Robson focuses first and foremost on the numerous distinct issues and concerns that shape the day-to-day realities of lesbians living in America.

Robson emphasizes the need to explore issues of lesbian survival. In *Lesbian (Out)law,* she defines "survival" in two ways. The first centers on food, shelter, work, protection from violence, and other necessities; the second definition digs a little deeper. Robson highlights the conflict between legal attempts to interpret and explain lesbian reality and the ways lesbians actually discuss and live those same issues. Robson admits that such investigations are complicated and challenging, to say the least. As she puts it, "We each make personal choices about our relationship to the law, based on our own idiosyncrasies and biases. We each make decisions about whether or not to pursue certain legal reforms or denounce them. But we need to confront and consider our choices, and their consequences for lesbianism as we live it, and as we want to live it." Reflecting on these consequences becomes the motivation for Robson's writing in all its forms.

Her novel, *Another Mother,* becomes the fictional equivalent of these legal explorations. The protagonist is Angie Evans, a New York lesbian attorney who defends lesbians with children, including a mother accused of killing her child. Her personal life grows more chaotic as her lover, Rachel, feels more and more neglected, and her legal assistant, Kim, accuses Angie of sexual harassment when she ends their affair. Angie's mother also becomes a primary character, reminding Angie of her painful childhood and their continued strained relationship. Kristen Golden, in *Ms.,* explains how the novel "examines the identity of 'mother' through a kaleidoscope and unflinchingly embraces all kinds of women in their full range of contradictions."

Contradictions abound in Robson's short fiction as well. In *Eye of a Hurricane,* she collects several stories that echo the title by relating the sense of chaos that runs rampant throughout the book. Jorjet Harper notes that Robson's consistent use of the present tense and first person narration creates a sense of "immediacy" and "great emotional suspension." "Lives of a Long-Haired Lesbian: Four Elemental Narrations" represents these feelings and tones. The narrator, who changes her name to Anastasia, is a teenage prostitute. Stacie, her lover, roommate, or—as Anastasia categorizes her—"mirror," commits suicide, sending Anastasia on a journey of growth and change, interacting with women and reflecting on love.

The style of this story also exemplifies Robson's break with traditional conceptions of short story technique. Robson does not concern herself with linear narrative, but constructs her stories in more emotionally evocative ways. *Cecile* is a collection of short stories that can be seen as a novel. All of the stories focus on the same characters and their daily lives. Robson told Harper that she completed this book in this manner "to show people without a big crisis. How people can shape their own lives." She continually writes in sections or interludes, an approach that blurs the lines between poetry and fiction. It also leads to associations that, on the surface, may not clearly relate. Instead, they stay with the reader, gaining more meaning upon reflection.

Even though Robson's stories and books are complete texts, there is the sense that they are still in the process of creation. By depicting lesbian lives as being part of an evolving process, Robson widens common understandings of lesbian lives. She challenges readers and extends our thinking about what it means for lesbians to live and survive in America.

—Nels P. Highberg

ROCHEFORT, Christiane

Nationality: French novelist and essayist. **Born:** Paris, 17 July 1917. **Education:** Lycée Fénelon and, briefly, at the Sorbonne. **Career:** Worked in an office, as a newspaper correspondent covering the Cannes Film Festival, and with Henri Langlois at the Paris Cinémathèque before becoming a full-time writer, from 1958. Political activist in French feminist movement, 1968, and against urban redevelopment and demolition projects. **Awards:** Nouvelle Vague Prize; Roman Populiste prize; Medicis Prize, 1988. **Address:** c/o Editions Bernard Grasset, 61 rue des Saints-Peres, 75006 Paris, France.

WRITINGS

Novels

Le Repos du Guerrier. Paris, Grasset, 1958; translated as *Warrior's Rest* by Lowell Bair, New York, MacKay, 1959.
Les Petits Enfants du Siècle. Paris, Grasset, 1961; translated as *Children of Heaven,* New York, McKay, 1962, and as *Josyane and the Welfare* by Edward Hyams, London, McDonald, 1963.

Les Stances à Sophie. Paris, Grasset, 1963; translated as *Cats Don't Care for Money,* Garden City, New York, Doubleday, 1965.
Une Rose pour Morrison. Paris, Grasset, 1966.
Printemps au Parking. Paris, Grasset, 1969.
Archaos ou le Jardin Étincelant. Paris, Grasset, 1972.
Encore Heureux qu'on Va vers L'Été. Paris, Grasset 1975.
Quand Tu Vas Chez les Femmes. Paris, Grasset, 1982.
La Porte du Fond. Paris, Grasset, 1988.

Short Stories

"Le Démon des Pinceaux," in Les Oeuvres Libres series, Paris, Vol. 313, No. 87, August 1953, 172-224.
"Le Fauve et le Rouge-gorge," in Les Oeuvres Libres series, Paris, Vol. 331, No. 105, February 1955, 120-178.
Pardonnez-Nous Vos Enfances. Paris, Denoël, 1978.

Essays

C'est Bizarre L'Écriture. Paris, Grasset, 1970.
Les Enfants D'Abord. Paris, Grasset, 1976.
Journal de Printemps; Récit d'un Livre. Montréal, Editions l'Etincelle, 1977.
Le Monde est Comme Deux Chevaux. Paris, Grasset, 1984.

Other

Translator, with Rachel Misrahi, *In His Own Write* by John Lennon, as *En Flagrant Délire.* Paris, R. Laffont, 1964.
Ma Vie Revue et Corrigée par L'Auteur (autobiography). Paris, Stock, 1978.
Translator, *Holocauste II* and *La Route d'Ein Harod* by Amos Kenan.

*

Biography: *Twentieth-Century French Women Novelists* by Lucille Frackman Becker, Boston, Twayne Publishers, 1989; "Christiane Rochefort" by Micheline Herz, in *French Women Writers: A Bio-Bibliographical Source Book,* edited by Eva Martin Sartori and Dorothy Wynne Zimmerman, New York, Greenwood, 1991, 369-79; *The Bloomsbury Guide to Women's Literature,* edited by Claire Buck, New York, Prentice Hall, and London, Bloomsbury, 1992.

Interviews: "An Interview with Christiane Rochefort" by Marianne Hirsch, Mary Jean Green, and Lynn Anthony Higgins, in *L'Esprit Créateur,* Vol. 19, No. 2, 1979, 107-20; "The Privilege of Consciousness" by Cécile Arsène, translated by Marilyn Shuster, in *Homosexualities and French Literature: Cultural Contexts/Critical Texts,* edited by George Stambolian and Elaine Marks, Ithaca, New York, Cornell University Press, 1979; "Entretien avec Christiane Rochefort" by Monique Y. Crochet, in *French Review,* Vol. 54, No. 3, February 1981, 428-35; "Christiane Rochefort" by Georgiana Colvile, in *Women Writers Talking,* edited by Janet Todd, New York, Holmes and Meier, 1983; "Christiane Rochefort" by A. Jardine, translated by Carrie Noland, in *Shifting Scenes: Interviews on Women, Writing, and Politics in Post-68 France,* edited by A. Jardine and Anne Menke, New York, Columbia University Press, 1991, 174-91.
Critical Sources: "Rochefort and Godard: Two or Three Things

about Prostitution" by Mary Jean Green, Lynn Higgins, and Marianne Hirsch, in *French Review*, No. 52, 1973, 440-48; *Regards Féminins: Condition Féminine et Création Littéraire: Simone de Beauvoir, Christiane Rochefort, Claire Etcherelli* by Anne Ophir, Paris, Denoël/Gonthier, 1976; "Narration and Metaphor as Ideology in the Works of Christiane Rochefort" by Ailsa Steckel (dissertation), University of Wisconsin, Madison, 1975; "A Portrait of the Sexes: The Masculine and the Feminine in the Novels of Simone de Beauvoir, Marguerite Duras and Christiane Rochefort" by Susan Marie Loffredo (dissertation), Princeton University, 1978; "Le Groupe et l'amour dans l'oeuvre de Christiane Rochefort" by Micheline Herz, in *Perspectives on Contemporary Literature*, Vol. 3, No. 2, 1977, 52-57; "*Le Repos du guerrier*: New Perspectives on Rochefort's Warrior" by Isabelle de Courtivron, in *L'Esprit Créateur*, Vol. 19, No. 2, 1979, 23-35; "The Feminist Rebirth of the Divine Child: Eroticism and Transcendence in Christiane Rochefort's *Encore Heureux qu'On Va vers l'Été*" by Gloria F. Orenstein, in *Journal of Women's Studies in Literature*, No. 1, 1979, 61-73; "Toward a Feminist Eros: Readings in Feminist Utopian Fiction" by Frances Bartkowski (dissertation), University of Iowa, 1982; "French Feminist Re-Visions: Wittig, Rochefort, Bersianik and d'Eaubonne Re-Write Utopia" by Kathryn-Mary Arbour (dissertation), University of Michigan, 1984; "Consuming Women Consumed: Images of Consumer Society in Simone de Beauvoir's *Les Belles Images* and Christiane Rochefort's *Les Stances à Sophie*" by Lynn K. Penrod, in *Simone de Beauvoir Studies*, No. 4, 1987, 159-75; "Effects of Urbanization in the Novels of Christiane Rochefort" by Anne D. Cordero, in *Faith of a (Woman) Writer*, edited by Alice Kessler-Harris and William McBrien, Westport, Connecticut, Greenwood Press, 1988, 83-93; "Realism, Fantasy and Feminist Meaning: The Fiction of Christiane Rochefort" by Diana Holmes, in *Contemporary French Fiction by Women: Feminist Perspectives*, edited by Margaret Atack and Phil Powrie, Manchester and New York, Manchester University Press, 1990; "Christiane Rochefort's *Les Stances à Sophie: From Prescription to Script*" by Carys Owen, in *Romance Studies*, No. 19, winter 1991, 91-103; "Humour e(s)t sagesse: Les Stances à Sophie de Christiane Rochefort" by Lynn K. Penrod, in *Women in French Studies*, 1 July 1993, 55-65; "*Les Petits Enfants du Siècle*, ou la thématique du quotidien" by Claudine Thire, in *French Review*, Vol. 67, No. 4, March 1994, 580-90; "'A la guerre comme à la guerre': A Reappraisal of Christiane Rochefort's *Le Repos du Guerrier*" by Margaret-Anne Hutton, in *Forum for Modern Language Studies*, Vol. 31, No. 3, July 1995, 234-45; "Assuming Responsibility: Christiane Rochefort's Exploration of Child Sexual Abuse in *La Porte du Fond*" by Margaret-Anne Hutton, in *Modern Languages Review*, Vol. 90, No. 2, April 1995, 333-44; "L'Utopie de Christiane Rochefort: le non-principe, une certaine idée du bonheur" by Isabelle Constant, in *French Review*, Vol. 69, April 1996, 739-48; *Archaos ou les Mots Étincelants: Langage de L'Utopie dans L'Oeuvre de Christiane Rochefort* by Isabelle Constant, Amsterdam, Atlanta, Rodopi, 1996.

*   *   *

Christiane Rochefort was born on 17 July 1917, in the fourteenth arrondissement of Paris. She spent the earlier years of her life in Limousin and returned to the capital at the age of five. Her secondary education took place at the Lycée Fénelon; she made a brief stay at the Sorbonne, but was rapidly put off by the type and quality of its education. She did, however, develop a strong

interest and grounding in diverse fields, including ethnology, psychology, and psychiatry. She was also apprenticed to a painter, tried her hand at sculpture, and nurtured a great love of music. Writing, was, however, to become her privileged means of expression. She worked in offices and became a newspaper correspondent, writing a number of articles on film criticism. During this period she worked for Henri Langlois at the Cinémathèque of Paris, an activity she enjoyed, she has said in interviews.

For many years the necessities of earning a living prevented her from publishing full length works of fiction. She did publish two sizeable short stories in 1953 and 1955, in which she explored the world of contemporary painting, giving at once a satirical view of its foibles and her own version of the theme, dear to French literature, of the unsung artist, waiting for recognition while returning to her love of art. The short stories brought her to the attention of publishers.

Her first novel, *Le Repos du Guerrier*, appeared in 1958 and sold 600,000 copies, putting her immediately on the best-seller list. The novel was termed "pornographic" by some, though the book has little to do with sex itself, and rarely speaks of it; rather, she has stated, it is a novel of alienation. Possibly it was, as Georgiana Colvile pointed out in *Women Writers Talking*, the "brutal style of writing" which sexist readers rejected as "unfeminine" that generated that assessment. Rochefort received the Nouvelle Vague prize for this work. She also earned an award, the Roman Populiste prize, for her second novel, *Les Petits Enfants du Siècle* (1961). This work gained immense notoriety, and heralded Rochefort's very dim view of the dehumanizing effects of modern architecture and urbanism. The novel was a scathing attack on the boxed-in life imposed by low income housing, and, in particular, the social programming enacted against young working class women. As someone who was always sensitive to issues of class difference—"I was not exactly born with Suetonius and Livy in my arms," she stated in an interview with Cécile Arsène in *Homosexualities and French Literature*—she was particularly disposed to expose the inequalities inherent in our society. She earned a third prize, the very prestigious Prix Medicis, for *La Porte du Fond*, in 1988.

Rochefort's distinguished writing career includes ten novels, several of which have become classics of contemporary literature, and four essays. The latter play an important role in her oeuvre. *C'Est Bizarre L'Ecriture* (1970) articulated her subtle but exacting questioning of the writing process itself, and her constant project of disrupting and imploding routine formulas, stylistic convention, and narrative canons in the writing of fiction. She has applied these principles with renewed stylistic experimentation in each novel, producing forms of language and narrative syntax that vary from each other and reflect the particular narrative theme; for instance, using archaic, "medievalistic" turns of phrases and intense poetic imagery in her utopian novel, *Archaos*. Writing, she states in that essay, really means "to unwrite" ("écrire consiste vraiment à désécrire"). Rochefort has given particular attention to the relation between the spoken word and the written, creating a thoroughly original texture, in which both compete and complement each other. In that vein, it is probably no coincidence that she lists Raymond Queneau among her favorite writers. Other writers whose influence she has acknowledged include Christine de Pizan, Cervantes, Laclos, Diderot, Faulkner, Kafka, Virginia Woolf, Joyce, Boris Vian, Robert Desnos, and Norman Mailer. But it is hazardous to try to place Rochefort into a niche. For instance, she has recognized the influence Faulkner had on her in early years, only to remark on how much distance separates her from him in her later writing. Rochefort's interest in language is also evidenced in her command of foreign languages; she is fluent in English, has studied and spoken freely Spanish, Italian, German, and Hebrew.

Another famous essay of hers, *Les Enfants D'Abord,* is a true example of "engaged writing," which vehemently and even militantly takes to task the inferior conditions and the social and emotional abuse foisted on children within our contemporary society, all in the name of "family values." The essay brought Rochefort notoriety of a new kind; it was very poorly received by a large portion of the press and public, garnering fierce attacks against her from all participants in a French television debate which was supposed to air balanced views.

While Rochefort is extremely outspoken in her writing, biographers have noted that she is a very private person with respect to personal matters, including politics. She would have described herself as an "anarchist," she told Colvile, but even that was "a label." Many interviews and biographical sketches seem to elude the question of homosexuality in relation to her own writing, although an extensive interview with Cécile Arsène in 1979 made its importance quite clear. Rochefort detests labels, stating that she hates the word "bisexual," even though it probably would be the one used to describe her. She has loved both men and women in her life, but has no difficulty with having been frequently identified as "a lesbian"; in her discussion with Arsène, she offered precise, incisive views of the similarities and differences between her and Monique Wittig.

Rochefort's work exhibits "a common trait, the abhorrence of respected hierarchies and the indiscriminate use of power. Her writing in general is a passionate plea for the right to be different, to deviate from the norm...," Micheline Herz commented in her essay in *Perspectives on Contemporary Literature.* The sometimes homophobic undertone of some critical appraisals of her work—Herz, for example, refers to homosexuals as sexual misfits, and to a character as "condemned to lesbianism"—often decontextualizes the discussion of homosexuality in her work beyond recognition and obscures the extent of the contribution Rochefort has made to the representation of same-sex desire in an already incredibly rich, diverse, and provocative body of work.

Thus, *Les Stances à Sophie* and *Printemps au Parking,* each in their own way, were significant moments in the exploration of same-sex love and desire in modern French literature, imbedded in clear rejection of the patriarchal order in all its forms, particularly its sexual repression and deprivation, its pretensions to beneficial order and "normality." Yet, these are two novels out of ten, and, in a sense, all of Rochefort's work is deeply relevant to a lesbian and gay aesthetic because of its relentless challenge to normativity, and the way that challenge is carried out metaphorically on the sexual plane.

Rochefort was once in her life married—very briefly—and found the institution simply not designed for her. The experience was sufficiently negative to form the basis for the autobiographical element of the *Stances a Sophie,* the one novel Rochefort herself has termed autobiographical. It is the story of a young woman who reluctantly agrees to marry a conventional, bourgeois young man, and then finds herself trapped, until she develops a friendship which turns into a love affair with the wife of one of her husband's business acquaintances. The support and intimacy of the two women stands in stark contrast to the egoistical, power-hungry rapport of men to women. The work had such a strong effect on women readers, many of whom recognized their life story

in it, that Rochefort received numerous supportive letters and was even named in divorce suits. Uncompromising in her developing "intolerance" (her term) of male hegemony, she cut out the actual love scene from the book, so as not to give male readers voyeuristic pleasure. The novel did not hesitate to focus on love between women, however, and made some very fine distinctions in sexual identities; always wary of labels, Rochefort was not writing a "lesbian" novel, nor necessarily showing Céline, the main character, as "exactly a lesbian." At first, both women are terrified by the passage from heterosexual acceptability to being singled as homosexuals, as lesbians, but the narrative leaves Céline more disposed to love women than before, and less tolerant of men.

Printemps au Parking, the author told Arsène, is "the love story of two men written by a woman," a work that is "strictly homosexual in the sense that most people use the term." Here as well, the author carefully eschews labels, and in fact, explores the moment of transition between assumed heterosexuality and the full, passionate, and loving homosexual experience. The story tells of how a student looking for meaning in his life and a young man from the suburbs who has run away from home meet and fall in love. This experience of real love turns one of the characters, Christophe, into a truly free individual, one who is perceived as threatening to the social order, and harbinger of the rebellion that would rock France in May 1968. Rochefort was often challenged for writing about love between two men, and it is apparent that it made quite a few commentators and biographers more uncomfortable than they would admit. For Rochefort, however, the convincing tenderness and eroticism of the rapport between the two adolescents is a measure of her ability to gain enough distance from her material to write about any chosen topic, but also to immerse herself into the plot and the characters, to let the story's own momentum carry it forward, to allow her imagination and her own fantasies to take over. She has detailed, with great honesty, the process of writing this work as the "story" of the book itself; her integrity is apparent in her willingness to change the original plot, a mere friendship, acknowledging to herself "What is this story anyway, they love each other, for Pete's sake."

In a much later novel, *Archaos* (1972), the writer's favorite, Rochefort created an utopia based on characters who are in permanent dialogue, generating a poetic rhythm that constantly destabilizes social and sexual experience. For Isabelle Constant, writing in *Archaos ou les Mots Étincelants,* instead of a structured happiness, *Archaos* presents a liberated sexuality that participates in the disorganization of society. The driving force behind this disorganization is the "Désir Désirant" ("desire in a state of desiring"), a guilt-free desire with infinite possibilities. To achieve the utopia of this desire, Rochefort rejects the habitual masculine/feminine dichotomy and replaces it by androgynous characters and diverse amorous scenarios. In *Archaos,* Rochefort intended to show a world filled, not so much by homosexuality, but rather by what she termed "Polysexuality".

Other works have explored the relationship between sex, abuse, and power, with narrative structures that intrinsically question power and authority. *Quand Tu Vas Chez les Femmes* is a remarkable "descent" into the mind and experience of a man of some power and means who seeks humiliation and pain from the prostitutes he pays to conform to his fantasies, all the while continuing to live unchallenged in his status and material comfort. One woman, Petra, "the maiden of stone," turns things around and wrests his voice from him in the very auditorium where he lectures, while the narration itself is taken away from him by his exploited wife, who begins mid-stream to narrate in his stead. *La Porte du Fond* treats the question of incest and child abuse. Margaret-Anne Hutton, writing in the *Modern Languages Review,* comments that the novel is written from the perspective of the victim, thus denying the reader access to the father's point of view. Rochefort prompts readers to engage with the central issue of responsibility, confronting them with their own prejudices and preconceptions. She attacks institutions like Christianity and Freudian psychoanalysis, but the narrator singles out the nuclear family as a prime facilitator of abuse.

Rochefort is an engaged feminist author, a "contestataire," a subversive mind par excellence, who professes the strongest disdain for theory—particularly literary theory—but offers profoundly insightful views on gender, sexuality, and their relations to writing. Although homosexuality is not the main theme in her work, she has allowed her writing to be moved by its subject matter to powerfully evoke sexual difference and dissidence, to grapple with all stereotypes, no matter how hallowed. Thus, she has consistently offered a confrontational, challenging view of sexual normativity.

—Francesca Canadé Sautman

RODI, Robert

Nationality: American author of novels and short stories. **Born:** Chicago, 28 December 1956. **Education:** Rollins College, B.A. in Philosophy 1979. **Family:** "Espoused" to Jeffrey Smith in 1988. **Career:** Advertising copywriter, Smith, Badofsky & Raffel, Chicago, from 1981; charter member, Pansy Kings gay performance troupe, Chicago. **Agent:** Drake Literary Agency, 314 South Iseminger St., Philadelphia, Pennsylvania 19107-5904, U.S.A.

WRITINGS

Novels

Fag Hag. New York, Dutton, 1992.
Closet Case. New York, Dutton, 1993.
What They Did to Princess Paragon. New York, Dutton, 1994.
Drag Queen. New York, Dutton, 1995.
Kept Boy. New York, Dutton, 1996.
Adaptor, *The Birdcage* (from the movie of the same name). New York, Plume, 1996.

Short Stories

"Twisted," in *Men on Men 5,* edited by David Bergman, New York, Plume, 1994.
"Affairs of the Day," in *His,* edited by Robert Drake and Terry Wolverton, New York, Faber & Faber, 1995.
"The Death of a Young Aesthete," in *Fish Stories Collective I,* edited by Amy G. Davis, Chicago, Fisheye Press, 1995.
"An Extra Smidgen of Eternity," in *Sandman: Book of Dreams,* edited by Neil Gaiman and Edward Kramer. New York, Harper Collins, 1996.

"Mister Kenny: A Memoir," in *Reclaiming the Heartland,* edited by Karen Lee Osborne and William J. Spurlin. University of Minnesota Press, 1996.
Contributor to revue shows *Junk Food* and *Dear Jackie: The Queen of Camelot Remembered,* produced by the Live Bait Theatre Company, Chicago.

*

Critical Sources: Review of *Fag Hay* by Robert Ellsworth, in *Genre,* April 1992; review of *Fag Hag* by Orson Scott Card, in *Magazine of Fantasy and Science Fiction,* Vol. 84, No. 2, February 1993, 23; review of *What They Did to Princess Paragon* by Harmon, in *Booklist,* Vol. 90, No. 14, 15 March 1994, 1328; review of *Drag Queen* by Charles Harmon, in *Booklist,* Vol. 92, No. 6, 15 November 1995, 536; review of *What They did to Princess Paragon* by Ryan Prout, in *Harvard Gay & Lesbian Review,* fall 1995; review of *Kept Boy,* in *Publishers Weekly,* 21 October 1996; review of *Kept Boy* by Tom Steele, in *New York Native,* 2 December 1996.

Robert Rodi comments:

Laughter universalizes the human condition, so laughing at gay people universalizes them in a way that no overt or covert political action can. So I write comic novels about gay people with one eye on entertainment and the other on effecting a subversion of homophobic straight society.

*   *   *

In less than five years, Robert Rodi has gone from first time novelist to top gay writer. His comic novels, praised for their humor and criticized for their less than flattering portrayals of women, are anything but simple. His books subvert the stereotypes within the gay community—fag hags, drag queens, kept boys, and closet cases—and turn them inside out.

Perhaps his most misogynist novel is his first, *Fag Hag,* where he "fashioned a sidesplitting commentary on the bond between gay men and straight women," according to Robert Ellsworth in *Genre.* The story details overweight, straight Natalie Stathis' *Fatal Attraction*-style obsession with her gay male friend, Peter Leland. She is more than a "fag hag" and is determined that if Peter is not going to love her, he will love no one. Peter is not allowed sainthood either, for he is a shallow, superficial party boy. This sharp and witty book earned an unusual review in the *Magazine of Fantasy and Science Fiction.* Reviewer Orson Scott Card wrote, "It's funny. It's good. I don't have the same moral worldview as the author, of course, but then I often don't. What matters to me—and the reason why I'm reviewing this book in a column that...is supposedly devoted to science fiction and fantasy—is that Rodi, with his first novel, has done a marvelous job of introducing readers into an unfamiliar society, giving it depth and detail and attitude until you feel that you've lived there."

Rodi's talent is for farce, pitting the so-called respectable elements of the gay community against the wilder bits, and being unafraid to expose the gay world's foibles to anyone, gay or straight. In *Closet Case* he explored the desperate attempts of a high-powered executive to stay in the closet. In *Drag Queen* a self-proclaimed "normal" gay man discovers that he has a twin brother who he has never met who works as a drag queen in a downtown club. "Camp novelist Rodi's drag romp ends up with

Mitchell not only overcoming his prejudice against drag queens but riding as one in a gay pride parade," wrote Charles Harmon in *Booklist.*

What They Did to Princess Paragon marked a bit of a departure for Rodi. It was still farce but, although the book featured a gay protagonist, it was his most straight book to date. "*Princess Paragon* casts a critical eye over the world of publishing and its power either to cash in on gay characters, bring them to life, or even do both," according to Ryan Prout in *Harvard Gay & Lesbian Review.* The book featured the clash between a gay comic book writer, who is given the task to drag sales of the comic book "Princess Paragon" out of the gutter and turn the character into a lesbian, and a homophobic fan of Princess Paragon, who tries to get rid of the source of the comic heroine's new identity. Charles Harmon wrote in *Booklist,* "Rodi's third romp will most likely appeal to a much larger audience than the first two because its action is much less gay oriented."

Rodi's sixth novel, *Kept Boy,* satirized another aspect of contemporary gay life, and prompted Tom Steele to dub Rodi "the wittiest gay writer of them all" in *New York Native.* The story spins around Dennis Racine, a 31-year-old who looks 23, and 20-year-old Jasper Moran who fight over the affections of Dennis' companion and keeper of 10 years, the weathly theatrical impresario Farleigh Nock. To remain kept and outwit Jasper, Dennis enlists the help of two of his other kept friends. The ensuing romp made a critic in *Publishers Weekly* delight in the "eccentric, wildly exaggerated characters," which made this "completely insubstantial" book a "delightfully juicy distraction."

The reason Rodi's books work, more than anything else, is their sense of fun in a gay literary world filled with serious tomes. "You can switch off your brain at the beginning of the book," wrote Orson Scott Card in *The Magazine of Fantasy and Science Fiction.* "And Rodi will give you several hours of wonderful dumb fun. There aren't enough books that can do that, either."

—Victoria Stagg Elliott

ROQUELAURE, A. N. *See* **RICE, Anne.**

ROSCOE, Will

Nationality: American anthropologist and historian. **Born:** Seattle, Washington, 1955. **Education:** Williams College, Williamstown, Massachusetts, 1973-74; University of Oregon, Eugene, B.S. with honors in Community Service and Public Affairs 1978; University of California, Santa Cruz, Ph.D. in History of Consciousness/Anthropology 1991. **Family:** Companion of Bradley Rose, 1980-96 (died). Educational design consultant, San Francisco, 1980-88; instructor, University of California Extension (Berkeley and Santa Cruz), 1989-90; lecturer, Anthropology Board of Studies, University of California, Santa Cruz, 1991; research associate, Institute for Research on Women and Gender, Stanford

University, 1991-95; lecturer in anthropology, San Francisco State University, 1993-94; lecturer in American Studies, University of California, Berkeley, from 1994. Member, editorial board, *Journal of Homosexuality,* and *Journal of the History of Sexuality* (1994-95); contributor of reviews and essays to *Advocate, San Francisco Chronicle Book Review,* and other periodicals. **Awards:** Crompton-Noll Award, Modern Language Association, 1986; Lambda Literary Award, for nonfiction, 1991; Margaret Mead Award, American Anthropology Association and the Society for Applied Anthropology, for ongoing efforts to interpret anthropology to a broad audience, 1991; Audre Lorde Prize, Committee on Lesbian and Gay History of the American Historical Association, 1994. **Address:** Post Office Box 15154, San Francisco, California 94115, U.S.A.

WRITINGS

Nonfiction

The Zuni Man-Woman. Albuquerque, University of New Mexico Press, 1991.
Queer Spirits: A Gay Men's Myth Book. Boston, Beacon Press, 1995.

Editor

Living the Spirit: A Gay American Indian Anthology. New York, St. Martin's Press, 1988.

With Hay, Harry. *Radically Gay: Gay Liberation in the Words of its Founder.* Boston, Beacon Press, 1996.
With Stephen O. Murray, *Islamic Homosexualities.* New York, New York University Press, 1996.

Essays

"History's Future: Reflections on Lesbian and Gay History in the Community," in *Gay and Lesbian Studies,* edited by Henry L. Minton. Binghamton, New York, Haworth Press, 1992.
"Dreaming the Myth: An Introduction to Mythology for Gay Men," in *Same-Sex Love and the Path to Wholeness,* edited by Robert H. Hopcke, Karin L. Carrington, and Scott Wirth. Boston, Massachusetts, Shambhala Press, 1993.
"How to Become a Berdache: Toward a Unified Analysis of Multiple Genders," in *Third Sex, Third Gender: Beyond Sexual Dimorphism in Culture and History,* edited by Gilbert Herdt. New York, Zone Books, 1994.
"Maurice Kenny" and "Native North American Literature" in *The Gay and Lesbian Literary Heritage: A Reader's Companion to the Writers and Their Works, from Antiquity to the Present,* edited by Claude Summers. New York, Norton, 1995.
"Was We'wha a Homosexual?: Native American Survivance and the Two-Spirit Tradition," *GLQ: A Journal of Lesbian/Gay Studies* (Yverdon, Switzerland), Vol. 2, No. 3, 1995.
"'Strange Craft, Strange History, Strange Folks': Cultural Amnesia and the Case for Lesbian/Gay Studies," *American Anthropologist* (Washington, D.C.), Vol. 97, No. 3, 1995.
"Priests of the Goddess: Gender Transgression in Ancient Religion," *History of Religions* (Chicago), Vol. 35, No. 3, February 1996.

"Writing Queer Cultures: An Impossible Possibility?," in *Out in the Field: Reflections of Lesbian and Gay Anthropologists,* edited by Ellen Lewin and William Leap. Urbana, University of Illinois Press, 1996.

*

Interviews: "On the Future of Lesbian and Gay Studies: A Dialogue with Will Roscoe," in Lawrence D. Moss, *Dialogues of the Sexual Revolution,* New York, Haworth Press, 1990, 234-252; "Breaking the Gender Straitjacket: Anthropological Association Recognizes Will Roscoe for His Studies of the Berdache" by Marv Shaw, in *Bay Area Reporter* (San Francisco), 24 October 1991, 29; "Prances with Wolves: The Search for the Zuni Man-Woman" by Dale Reynolds, in *Frontiers* (Los Angeles), 17 January 1992, 46; "Will Roscoe: The Geography of Gender," in Mark Thompson, *Gay Soul: Finding the Heart of Gay Spirit and Nature with Sixteen Writers, Healers, Teachers, and Visionaries,* San Francisco, HarperSanFrancisco, 1994, 99-115.

Critical Sources: *"The Zuni Man-Woman"* by Evan S. Connell, in *Los Angeles Times Book Review,* 26 May 1991, 1; "Socially Sanctioned Androgyny" by Marv Shaw, in *Bay Area Reporter* (San Francisco), 20 June 1991, 47; "Toward a Third Gender" by Patricia Holt, in *San Francisco Chronicle Book Review,* 30 June 1991, 3, 6; "Wait Till 2050: Native Americans Recovering the Future" by Catherine Rainwater, in *College Literature* (West Chester, Pennsylvania), Vol. 20, No. 2, June 1993, 214-218; "Will Roscoe, *The Zuni Man-Woman*" by Richard O. Clemmer, in *American Indian Quarterly* (Lincoln, Nebraska), Vol. 18, No. 2, Spring 1994, 275; "Books for the Western Library" by Peter MacMillan Booth, in *Journal of the West* (Manhattan, Kansas), Vol. 35, No. 1, January 1996, 102; "Legends of the Third Sex" by Ron J. Juresha, in *Harvard Gay and Lesbian Review* (Cambridge, Massachusetts), Fall 1996, 38-39.

*   *   *

Who are gay people? Where do we come from? What are we here for? Over 40 years ago Harry Hay asked himself and other members of the pioneering gay rights organization the Mattachine Foundation these questions. Anthropologist and historian Will Roscoe, a longtime friend and admirer of Hay, has been trying to provide possible answers to those questions for the past ten years. In research written largely for an academic audience but quite accessible to the larger public, he has excavated some of the "hidden history" of gays and lesbians ignored or suppressed by other scholars. A major theme of his work is the common historic role of gay people as mediators between the genders through social roles which either combined the work of both or encompassed work neither men nor women did. Creative people of all kinds, for example, especially benefitted from the unique perspective gay men and lesbians often possessed.

Until very recently, the dominant Judeo-Christian view of gays and lesbians was as sick or sinful deviants from a heterosexual norm ordained by God for everyone. This view strongly influenced Anglo-American legal and medical systems and is the background against which even contemporary debate about gay issues occurs. Many gay writers and thinkers have disputed the fairness and accuracy of this model without suggesting any replacement

other than the right of free people to do with their bodies and lives as they wish.

Roscoe's study of the berdache role among many American Indian tribes is a fascinating alternative angle through which to view sexuality and gender issues, one which suggests that gay people can play a role in society which neither denigrates nor ignores their differences from the heterosexual majority. In over 130 tribes, certain men (and sometimes women) fulfilled an alternative gender role complementary to male and female but different from both. For instance, a young boy who exhibited behaviors more typical of girls than boys would not necessarily be discouraged from such behavior. His parents and other elders would watch his behavior as he grew older and see where his interests lay. If the traditional male role as defined by that tribe didn't suit him, he would be allowed to combine male and female work assignments. He might dress as the women did, and some tribal traditions prescribed a special ceremonial role for him in religious activities which was distinct from either male or female roles. There was no sense of shame or deviance about the berdache; though statistically not the "norm" it was a respected role for those who embodied it. Roscoe refers to them as a third gender, distinct from men and women but bridging both.

The major work to date in which Roscoe discusses the berdache role is *The Zuni Man-Woman*, a book written before he entered graduate school and accepted in published form as his doctoral dissertation. A biography of a well known Zuni Indian *lhamana* (the Zuni term for berdaches) named We'wha, it also contains a detailed look at the berdache role as a part of Zuni mythology and a history of its encounter with Euro-American homophobia.

We'wha is remembered to this day by the Zunis of New Mexico. Born in 1849, his lifetime coincided with the era in which the Zuni first had extensive contact with Americans, and We'wha was one of the first to interact with whites and learn English. In particular, he befriended Matilda Coxe Stevenson, an early anthropologist who came with her husband to study the Zunis in 1879 and returned several times between then and 1896, the year We'wha died. We'wha was one of her major informants on the Zuni. Amazingly, Stevenson did not discover that "she" was a biological male until after his death! His face in photographs looks quite masculine, yet not only Stevenson but all of Washington, D.C., society when he visited as a cultural ambassador in 1886, believed he was a woman. He gave public demonstrations of textile weaving at the Smithsonian and participated in a public performance at the National Theater. He even met President Grover Cleveland at the White House. We'wha does not appear to have actively deceived Stevenson, but rather to have simply allowed whites to interpret his appearance and manner as they wished.

There is little direct evidence of We'wha's sexual behavior, but other male berdaches were commonly known to have sexual relations with men. Sexual object choice was not the major or defining characteristic of a berdache, though. Roscoe writes, "While Anglos apply the label 'homosexual' primarily on the basis of sexual behavior, the assignment of *lhamana* [berdache] status had always been based on work preference."

The berdache tradition among Native Americans was largely forgotten in this century until the advent of gay liberation in the 1970s prompted gay and lesbian Indians to reexamine their own cultural traditions. Giving them a sense of dignity and connectedness which white conceptions of homosexuality did not offer, the berdache as archetype and inspiration is a major current running through Roscoe's first book, the collection *Living the Spirit: A*

Gay American Indian Anthology. Essays, autobiography, poetry, and myth combine to create a portrait of contemporary gay Indians and some of their historical predecessors.

Queer Spirits: A Gay Men's Myth Book culls widely from disparate cultures and time periods those parts of humankind's legacy most relevant to contemporary gay men. He writes in the preface, "Although they come from faraway and unlikely places, I think that these stories offer insight and inspiration for telling our own stories today. These are not merely documents of same-sex love—its practice, its roles, its presence in other times and places. They are keys to a deeper understanding and appreciation of gayness—the reasons for being gay, the ways of being gay, how we can nurture and foster these ways to discover the deeper meaning of our lives." Written for a broader audience than much of Roscoe's earlier work, *Queer Spirits* brings together a treasure trove of historical material often overlooked in the past.

—Blaine Waterman

ROSS, Martin

Pseudonym: Violet Florence Martin. **Nationality:** Irish novelist, author of short stories, and essayist. **Born:** Ross House, County Galway, Ireland, 11 June 1862. **Education:** Alexandra College, Dublin. **Family:** Companion of Edith Somerville. **Career:** Contributed to *The World,* 1888-89; collaborated with Edith Somerville on novels, stories, travel essays, and political essays, published in book form and for periodicals such as *Badminton Magazine of Sports and Pastimes, Lady's Pictorial,* and *Times Literary Supplement,* 1889-15. Vice president, Munster Women's Franchise League. **Awards:** H.D.: Trinity College, Dublin, 1932. **Died:** Drishane, County Cork, 21 December 1915.

Writings

Fiction, with Somerville

An Irish Cousin. London, Bentley, 1889.
Naboth's Vineyard. London, Spencer, Blackett, 1891.
The Real Charlotte. London, Ward and Downey, 1894.
The Silver Fox. London, Lawrence and Bullen, 1898.
Some Experiences of an Irish R.M. London, Longmans, Green and Co., 1899.
All on the Irish Shore. London, Longmans, Green and Co., 1903.
Further Experiences of an Irish R.M. London, Longmans, Green and Co., 1908.
Dan Russell the Fox. London, Methuen, 1911.
In Mr. Knox's Country. London, Longmans, Green and Co., 1915.

Other, with Somerville

Through Connemara in a Governess Cart (travel book). London, W.H. Allen, 1893.
In the Vine Country (travel book). London, W. H. Allen, 1893.
Beggars on Horseback (travel book). London and Edinburgh, Blackwood, 1895.
A Patrick's Day Hunt (picture book). London, Constable, 1902.

Irish Memories (essays). London, Longmans, Green and Co., 1917.
The Selected Letters of Somerville and Ross, edited by Gifford Lewis. London, Faber and Faber, 1989.

*

Manuscript Collections: Trinity University, Dublin; Queen's University of Belfast Library; Berg Collection, New York Public Library.

Biography: *Somerville and Ross: A Biography* by Maurice Collis, London, Faber and Faber, 1968; *The Irish Cousins* by Violet Powell, London, Heinemann, 1970; *Surpassing the Love of Men: Romantic Friendship and Love Between Women from the Renaissance to the Present* by Lillian Faderman, New York, William Morrow and Company, Inc., 1981; *Somerville and Ross: The World of the Irish R.M.* by Gifford Lewis, New York, Viking, 1986.

Critical Sources: "John Bull's Other Island: A Consideration of *The Real Charlotte* by Somerville and Ross" by Sean McMahon, in *Eire-Ireland,* Vol. 3, 1968, 119-135; *Shadowy Heroes: Irish Literature of the 1890s* by Wayne E. Hall, Syracuse, New York, Syracuse University Press, 1980; *Somerville and Ross: A Critical Appreciation* by Hilary Robinson, New York, St. Martin's Press, 1980; "Edith Somerville and Martin Ross: Women Fighting Back" by Anthony Cronin, in *Heritage Now: Irish Literature in the English Language,* New York, St. Martin's Press, 1983, 75-86; "Some Elements of Truth in the Short Stories of Somerville and Ross" by Harold Orel, in *English Literature in Transition, 1880-1920,* Vol. 30, No. 1, 1987, 17-25; *Irish Women Writers: An Uncharted Tradition* by Ann Owens Weekes, Lexington, University of Kentucky Press, 1990; "'Colliding Stars': Heterosexism in Biographical Representations of Somerville and Ross" by Shawn R. Mooney, in *Canadian Journal of Irish Studies,* Vol. 18, No. 1, 1992, 157-175; "Edith Somerville and Violet Martin" by Margaret Breen, in *The Gay and Lesbian Literary Heritage,* edited by Claude J. Summers, New York, Henry Holt and Company, 1995, 662-663.

*   *   *

Violet Martin, a member of the Anglo-Irish Ascendancy, grew up as a witness to the political and economic decline of the landed class in Ireland. In particular, she was aware of the failure of the men in her family and her class to ensure the continuation of an aristocratic tradition. As Anthony Cronin has written in *Heritage Now: Irish Literature in the English Language,* men, as "defenders of the empire[,] seemed strangely unable to defend their own homes, families, and lands." In fact, Cronin goes on to argue, "[t]o a strong-minded woman with such fierce unionist convictions as Violet Martin cherished it must have seemed as if the men of her caste were under a strange spell."

With the bankruptcy and death of Martin's father in 1872, the family's Ross estate was turned over to her brother, who quickly abandoned it to live in London. As a result, when she was only ten years old, Martin and her mother repaired to Dublin. Sixteen years later, in the absence of any interest on her brother's part to preserve their family's house and lands, Martin herself, after much hard work, reopened the Ross house and restored her family's social position in Ireland. For the rest of her life, she continued to support the upkeep of the house with the income she earned from her literary career, a career she shared with her second cousin and companion, Edith Somerville (1858-1949), who also became solely responsible for her own family's estate in county Drishane by 1898.

Martin and Somerville did not meet until 1886, and the event was one which changed both of their lives. As Somerville wrote in *Irish Memories,* meeting Martin "proved the hinge of my life, the place where my fate, and hers, turned over." Both had been developing their creative talents prior to their first meeting, Martin as a writer and Somerville as an artist. After they became friends, they supported each other in their respective projects, but the two gradually came to recognize the possibility of working together. At first, Martin wrote stories to which Somerville provided the illustrations. But over the next couple of years, although Somerville continued to draw illustrations, the two began to collaborate as writers. Amidst strong opposition from their families, who saw writing for publication as unfeminine and beneath their status as genteel women, Somerville and Martin set out to write a novel that would earn them the money they needed to contribute to their respective estates. The result was *An Irish Cousin,* which appeared under the names of Geilles Herring and Martin Ross, pseudonyms for Somerville and Martin, respectively. Somerville's nom de plume did not survive, although Martin's did, even in private. Somerville had chosen to call Violet by her surname, probably to avoid confusion with another cousin named Violet.

The pair became known as Somerville and Ross, the two names that appeared on all of their subsequent publications. In fact, even after Martin's death in 1915, Somerville continued to include her as co-author on the title page of each successive publication, a practice she carried out until her own death in 1949. She claimed that her collaboration with Martin had not ended with the latter's death; rather, Martin continued to communicate with her as she wrote, resulting in a kind of automatic writing. In addition, Somerville also claimed that many of her publications after Martin's death were the product of collaborative efforts begun during Martin's lifetime. Somerville felt, until her death, that any credit she received was due to Martin as well.

The intimacy of the relationship of these two women writers has received much scrutiny from biographers and has remained of interest to readers. Maurice Collis' biography, *Somerville and Ross,* raised the issue in 1968 when he wrote that Somerville was "not capable of falling in love with a man," while Martin was. According to Collis, Somerville lured Martin into a lesbian relationship, although he found no evidence of sexual consummation. Later scholars, most notably Gifford Lewis and Hilary Robinson, took issue with Collis, claiming, in the words of Robinson, in *Somerville and Ross: A Critical Appreciation,* "Their friendship has been so much misunderstood that it is necessary to say that while their love and respect for each other could hardly have been greater, it never transgressed the bounds set by Christianity." Shawn R. Mooney, in an article for the *Canadian Journal of Irish Studies,* sees these critics' approaches as "heterosexist," arguing that the "attitude that heterosexuality is the moral and psychological norm is pervasive in these biographers' representations of the relationship between Edith Somerville and Violet Martin." Instead, Mooney believes that we should not be concerned with whether or not the two engaged in sexual contact, but should accept Lillian Faderman's definition of love between women in *Surpassing the Love of Men:* "women's strongest emotions and affections are directed toward each other. Sexual contact may be a part of the relationship to a greater or lesser degree, or it may be

entirely absent. By preference the two women spend most of their time together and share most aspects of their lives with each other." Such a definition describes the relationship between Martin and Somerville, and Faderman sees their "romantic friendship" as part of the heritage of nineteenth-century lesbianism.

Martin and Somerville never depicted intimate relationships between women in their fiction, but they did focus on the ineffectuality of heterosexual marriage and love relationships, a theme thoroughly explored in their most well-respected work, the novel *The Real Charlotte.* Wayne E. Hall, in *Shadowy Heroes: Irish Literature of the 1890s,* calls the book "perhaps the greatest Irish novel of the nineteenth century." It reveals, he goes on to say, "a deeply felt regret for the lost way of life." *The Real Charlotte* is about "failure and loss," as Hall writes, but it is also about "the difficulty of achieving mutual love," according to Ann Owens Weekes in *Irish Women Writers: An Uncharted Tradition.* Charlotte Mullen, a middle-aged, plain, and rustic woman, inherits her aunt's estate early on in the novel, suddenly rising from the rank of tenant to landowner. When Charlotte's young cousin, Francie Fitzpatrick, comes to visit, she becomes the center of male attention in Lismoyle. While Francie, a young, beautiful girl with a flirtatious and optimistic air, receives three marriage proposals without lifting a finger, Charlotte remains in the background, plotting to achieve more power and the man she loves, Roderick Lambert. Charlotte hopes to marry Francie to Christopher Dysart, heir to the largest estate in the region, thereby increasing her own status in the community. But Francie is more interested in the romantic fop, Captain Hawkins. In the end, all of the main characters are frustrated in their romantic designs as Francie is thrown from her horse and killed. Charlotte is revealed to be the selfish schemer that she is and so loses Lambert forever to the memory of Francie.

In 1898, during the time that Martin and Somerville began to publish their highly successful hunting stories, Martin experienced a bad fall while hunting. The injury left her badly wounded and in extreme pain for the rest of her life. As a result, the pair concentrated on short story-writing rather than longer writing projects. The outcome was the series of *Irish R.M.* stories centered on Major Yeates, the Resident Magistrate (R.M.), an Anglo-Irishman who brings an English wife to live with him in Ireland. Throughout the series, the couple encounter a variety of characters from the lower classes who provide levity and local color. Later critics have objected to what many see as the stereotypical representation of these characters. Sean McMahon, for example, in an article for *Eire-Ireland* claims that "the jolly, childlike servants of the R.M. stories...smack of white Uncle-Tomism." Nonetheless, these are the stories for which Somerville and Ross are most widely known.

—Anne Boyd

ROZANOV, Vasily Vasilievich

Nationality: Russian essayist, philosopher, and literary critic. **Born:** Vetluga, Kostroma Province, 20 April 1856. **Education:** Graduated from the Historical-Philological faculty of Moscow University, 1882. **Family:** Married Appolinaria Suslova, the former mistress of Fedor Dostoevsky, in 1880 (separated 1886); common-law marriage to Varvara Rudneva; several children. **Career:** Taught at a secondary school in the provinces, 1882-1893;

spent the rest of his life as a professional writer. **Died:** Sergiev Posad, near Moscow, 5 February 1919.

WRITINGS

Nonfiction

O ponimanii ("On Understanding"). Moscow, 1886.

Legenda o Velikom inkvizitore F. M. Dostoevskogo: Opyt kriticheskogo kommentariia ("F.M. Dostoevsky's Legend of the Grand Inquisitor: An Attempt at a Critical Commentary"). St. Petersburg, 1894; as *Dostoevsky and the Legend of the Grand Inquisitor,* translated and with an afterword by Spencer E. Roberts, Ithaca, New York, Cornell University Press, 1972.

Literaturnye ocherki ("Literary Sketches"). St. Petersburg, 1899.

Religiia i kul'tura ("Religion and Culture"). St. Petersburg, 1899.

Priroda i istoriia ("Nature and History"). St. Petersburg, 1900.

V mire neiasnogo i nereshennogo ("In the Realm of the Unclear and the Undetermined"). St. Petersburg, 1901.

Semeinyi vopros v Rossii ("The Family Question in Russia"). St. Petersburg, 1903.

Okolo tserkovnykh sten ("By the Church Walls"). St. Petersburg, 1906.

Russkaia tserkov' i drugie stat'i ("The Russian Church and Other Essays"). Paris, 1906.

Ital'ianskie vpechatleniia ("Italian Impressions"). St. Petersburg, 1909.

Kogda nachal'stvo ushlo ... ("When the Bosses Are Gone ..."). St. Petersburg, 1910.

Liudi lunnogo sveta: Metafizika khristianstva ("People of the Moonlight: Metaphysics of Christianity"). St. Petersburg, 1911; 2nd edition, revised and expanded, St. Petersburg, 1913; as "People of the Moonlight (selections)," translated by Spencer E. Roberts, in *Out of the Blue: Russia's Hidden Gay Literature: An Anthology,* edited by Kevin Moss, San Francisco, Gay Sunshine Press, 1996.

Temnyi lik: Metafizika khristianstva ("The Dark Face: Metaphysics of Christianity"). St. Petersburg, 1911.

Uedinennoe. St. Petersburg, 1912; as *Solitaria,* translated by S.S. Koteliansky, New York, Boni & Liveright, 1927.

Literaturnye izgnanniki ("Literary Exiles"). St. Petersburg, 1913.

Opavshie list'ia. St. Petersburg, 1913; as *Fallen Leaves,* translated by S.S. Koteliansky, London, Mandrake Press, 1929.

Sredi khudozhnikov ("Among Artists"). St. Petersburg, 1914.

Opavshie list'ia, korob vtoroi ("Fallen Leaves, Second Basket"). St. Petersburg, 1915.

Apokalipsis nashego vremeni ("The Apocalypse of Our Time"). Sergiev Posad, 1917-1918.

Essays in Russian Literature: The Conservative View: Leontiev, Rozanov, Shestov, edited, translated, and with an introduction by Spencer E. Roberts. Athens, Ohio University Press, 1968.

The Apocalypse of Our Time, and Other Writings, edited with an introduction by Robert Payne, translated by Robert Payne and Nikita Romanoff. New York, Praeger, 1977.

Four Faces of Rozanov: Christianity, Sex, Jews, and the Russian Revolution, translated and with an introduction by Spencer E. Roberts. New York, Philosophical Library, 1978.

*

Manuscript Collections: Bakhmeteff Archive, Rare Book and Manuscript Library, Columbia University.

Critical Sources: *Rozanov* by Viktor Borisovich Shklovsky, Petrograd, Opoiaz, 1921; *V.V. Rozanov: Zhizn' i tvorchestvo* ("V.V. Rozanov: Life and Work") by Erikh Fedorovich Gollerbakh, Petrograd, Poliarnaia zvezda, 1922; *Rozanov* by Renato Poggioli, New York, Hillary House, 1962; "Vasilii V. Rozanov: Sex, Marriage, and Christianity" by George F. Putnam, in *Canadian Slavic Studies,* Vol. 5, 1971, 301-26; *Rozanov and the End of Literature: Polyphony and the Dissolution of Genre in Solitaria and Fallen Leaves* by Anna Lisa Crone, Würzburg, Jal-Verlag, 1978; *"Opavshie List'ia" V.V. Rozanova* ("V.V. Rozanov's 'Fallen Leaves'") by Andrei Siniavsky, Paris, Sintaksis, 1982; "Rozanov" by Siniavsky, in *Ideology in Russian Literature,* edited by Richard Freeborn and Jane Grayson, New York, St. Martin's Press, 1990, 116-33; "Russia's Gay Literature and History from the Eleventh to the Twentieth Centuries" by Simon Karlinsky, in *Gay Roots: Twenty Years of Gay Sunshine,* Vol. 1, edited by Winston Leyland, San Francisco, Gay Sunshine Press, 1991, 81-104; *The Keys to Happiness: Sex and the Search for Modernity in Fin-de-Siècle Russia* by Laura Engelstein, Ithaca, New York, Cornell University Press, 1992; *V.V. Rozanov: Estetika svobody* ("V.V. Rozanov: Aesthetics of Freedom") by Sergei N. Nosov, St. Petersburg, Logos, 1993; "Constructs of Sin and Sodom in Russian Modernism" by Lindsay F. Watton, in *Journal of the History of Sexuality* (Chicago), Vol. 4, No. 3, January 1994, 369-94; *V.V. Rozanov—pro et contra: Lichnost' i tvorchestvo Vasiliia Rozanova v otsenke russkikh myslitelei i issledovatelei: Antologiia* ("V.V. Rozanov—Pro et Contra: The Personality and Writings of Vasily Rozanov in Evaluations by Russian Thinkers and Researchers: An Anthology"), edited by V.A. Fateev, 2 Vols., St. Petersburg, Russkii khristianskii gumanitarnyi iniversitet, 1995.

*   *   *

A prolific writer of nonfiction texts in a great variety of genres, Vasily Rozanov was one of the brightest and most controversial figures in the turn-of-the-century Russian cultural landscape. Fame came to him with the publication of his ground-breaking study on the role of the Grand Inquisitor figure in Dostoevsky's *Brothers Karamazov* and on the philosophical aspect of Dostoevsky's novels; but arguably his greatest contribution to Russian literature were his texts unprecedented in Russia both in their self-conscious free play with form—in particular in his books of fragments, *Solitaria* and *Fallen Leaves,* that develop an aphoristic style that could be compared to that of Nietzsche—and in paying close attention to matters of sexuality. A seemingly tireless author of numerous books and essays on a wide variety of cultural and social topics, Rozanov was notorious for his often self-contradictory statements, and indiscriminate publication of his writings in both extreme right-wing and left-wing periodicals.

While officially forbidden throughout the Soviet era and not republished until the late 1980s, Rozanov's texts were nevertheless widely read and discussed by the intelligentsia, and exerted significant influence on a number of contemporary Russian writers. His daring views and strong opinions, his habit of never mincing words, and his talent for contradicting himself and making enemies—all these traits carried with them a remarkable freshness and novelty in the stifling years of the Soviet regime. Finally, his last book, *The Apocalypse of Our Time,* also structured as a series of fragments, provided yet another aspect of Rozanov's posthumous fame: in it he recorded his impressions and thoughts about the Russian revolution, remarkable in their sincere tragic tone and visionary perceptiveness.

It is Rozanov's unorthodox views on sexuality, extensively presented in his work, that made him scandalously popular in his lifetime, and served as one of the key reasons for the ban placed on his work. It would be exceedingly difficult to summarize as a consistent theory his extremely self-contradictory pronouncements on the subject; however, it would be safe to say that his was a very affirmative view of sex as such, and he repeatedly attacks those institutions that propagate the ideology of chastity and abstinence. His famous remark that his books are written not with ink or even blood, but with sperm, repeated twice in *Fallen Leaves,* is ample evidence of his valorization of sex. Thus it is with the agenda of critiquing the ideologies that value chastity and abstinence in mind that Rozanov writes his highly speculative volume *People of the Moonlight,* which has remained the only influential book-length study of the topic of homosexuality in Russia.

Simon Karlinsky, in his *Gay Sunshine* article on the history of homosexuality in Russia, remarks that Rozanov did not know personally any homosexuals, and engaged in this book in pure abstract theorizing, as a result of which a number of remarkable insights are continuously mixed with exceedingly bizarre ideas. It is not that Rozanov did not know anyone homosexual personally—he did (the writers Konstantin Leontiev and Dmitry Filosofov, for example); however, it is true that *People of the Moonlight* in its entirety is far removed from Rozanov's personal experiences. Indeed, about half of the book is taken up by lengthy quotes from various (mostly obscure) sources and Rozanov's polemical comments on them, with pure abstraction dominating the other half.

While Rozanov rejects some of the stereotypes about homosexuality—for example, that it is a result of a surfeit of heterosexual experience—he strongly subscribes to another one—the conflation of aversion to sexuality per se with aversion to heterosexual acts. This conviction underlies Rozanov's argument throughout *People of the Moonlight,* and it largely accounts for many of his conclusions. For example, he believed that in nine out of ten cases the actual same-sex copulation does not take place (and lesbian sex is literally unthinkable for him), that homosexuals never masturbate, and that the bottom never ejaculates. He also conflates homosexuality with transsexuality (the cases he quotes from Krafft-Ebing are those of transsexuals, rather than homosexuals), and both of them with androgyny. Finally, he proclaims those who speak out against sex as such "spiritual sodomites," and spends a lot of his ire attacking them.

It takes a great deal of untangling to separate these attacks on "spiritual sodomites," whom he openly wishes to "descend into the grave," from some of his insights remarkable for the time and the context in which they were made. Rozanov emphatically speaks out against the criminal persecution of homosexuals and is fairly skeptical about the possibility of a "cure" for homosexuality. He is also very much against the advice to gays "not to act upon their desires." In addition to that, Rozanov was the first in Russia to emphasize the homoerotic aspect of Christianity, beginning with Jesus himself who is for Rozanov a quintessential "man-maiden," and particularly of the monastic tradition. He was one of the first to assert in print that taking the vows often served as a means for coming to terms with one's own sexuality. While Rozanov admires the fecundity of the Old Testament tradition, he simultaneously asserts that the individual who violates natural laws (including that of procreation) creates the condition of possibility for genius and spirituality, to the point of asserting that it is gays who are to be credited for the birth of civilization. Finally, one of the most remarkable insights of Rozanov, which serves as a direct link to the realm of contemporary Russian gay writing, is his belief that in homosexuality desire saturates the entire being, rather than being confined in a particular organ, that every move, every touch could be sexually charged.

Rozanov's legacy as a writer and thinker is highly controversial. Any discussion of the cultural history of homosexuality in Russia that does not take his work into account, however, would be incomplete, even though his contribution to the discourse on homosexuality is largely limited to merely one of his books and a handful of scattered remarks in his cycles of fragments. Ultimately, it is his iconoclastic spirit and readiness to challenge the most authoritative opinions that could serve as an inspiration for Russian gays and lesbians in their task of confronting the homophobic aspects of contemporary Russian culture and society.

—Vitaly Chernetsky

RUKEYSER, Muriel

Nationality: Jewish-American poet, biographer, translator, literary critic, novelist, and author of children's stories. **Born:** New York City, 13 December 1913. **Education:** New York City Jewish religious schools; Vassar College, Poughkeepsie, New York. **Family:** Married Glynn Collins in 1945 (annulled, 1945); one child. **Career:** Held a variety of jobs including writer, journalist, and film editor; literary editor, Vassar College *Student Review,* 1933; Poster Division, office of War Information, 1943; teacher, California Labor School, 1945; consultant, Exploratorium Museum of Science and Arts, San Francisco, California; teacher, Vassar College, Sarah Lawrence College, 1954-67, teacher, Poetry Workshops, and Poets and Writers Collaborative, c. 1967-76. Frequent contributor to periodicals, including *Accent, American Scholar, Atlantic Monthly, Decision, Harper's Bazaar, Horizon, Kenyon Review, Life and Letters To-Day, New Poems, New Republic, Poetry, Tomorrow, Twice a Year,* and *Yale Review.* **Awards:** Yale Younger Poets Award, 1935; Oscar Blumental Prize, 1940; Harriet Monroe Poetry Award, 1941; American Academy of Arts and Letters prize, 1942; National Institute of Arts and Letters prize, 1942; Guggenheim Fellowship, 1943; Annual Stipend, Anonymous California Woman, 1947-54; Eunice Tietjens Memorial Prize, 1962; Copernicus Prize, 1977; Shelley Prize for Poetry, 1977; L.H.D.: Rutgers University, 1961. **Died:** New York City, 12 February 1980.

WRITINGS

Poetry

Theory of Flight, Vol. 34. New Haven, Connecticut, Yale University Press, 1935.
Mediterranean. Writers and Artists Committee, Medical Bureau to Aid Spanish Democracy, 1938.
U.S. 1. New York, Covici, Friede, 1938.

A Turning Wind: Poems. New York, Viking Press, 1939.
The Soul and Body of John Brown. Private Printing, 1940.
Wake Island. New York, Doubleday, 1942.
Beast in View. New York, Doubleday, 1944.
The Green Wave. New York, Doubleday, 1948.
Elegies. New York, New Directions Press, 1949.
Orpheus. San Francisco, California, Centaur Press, 1949.
Selected Poems. New York, New Directions Press, 1949.
Body of Waking. New York, Harper-Collins Publishers, Inc., 1958.
Waterlily Fire: Poems 1935-1962. New York, Macmillan, 1962.
The Outer Banks. Santa Barbara, California, Unicorn Press, 1967; reprinted, Santa Ana, California, Unicorn Press, 1980.
The Speed of Darkness. New York, Random House, 1968.
Mazes. New York, Simon and Schuster, 1970.
29 Poems. London, England, Rapp and Whiting, 1972.
Breaking Open: New Poems. New York, Random House, 1973.
The Gates: Poems. New York, McGraw-Hill, 1976.
The Collected Poems of Muriel Rukeyser. New York, McGraw-Hill, 1978.
Out of Silence: Selected Poems, edited by Kate Daniels. Evanston, Illinois, TriQuarterly Books, 1992.
"This place in the ways," in *Massachusetts Review,* Vol. 34, No. 2, summer 1993.
A Muriel Rukeyser Reader, edited by Jan Heller Levi, introduction by Adrienne Rich. New York, W.W. Norton & Company, Inc., 1994.

Biographies

Williard Gibbs. New York, Doubleday, 1942; reprinted, Ox Bow Press, Woodbridge, Connecticut, 1988.
One Life. New York, Simon and Schuster, 1957.
The Traces of Thomas Hariot. New York, Random House, 1971.

Children's Fiction

Come Back, Paul. New York, Harper-Collins Publishers, Inc., 1955.
I Go Out. New York, Harper-Collins Publishers, Inc., 1962.
Bubbles, illustrated by Jeri Quinn. New York, Harcourt Brace & Company, HarBrace Juvenile Books, 1967.
More Night, illustrated by Symeon Shimin. New York, Harper-Collins Publishers, Inc., 1981.

Plays

The Middle of the Air (produced Iowa City, Iowa, 1945).
The Colors of the Day (produced Poughkeepsie, New York, 1961).
Houdini (produced Lenox, Massachusetts, 1973).

Translator

Sun Stone by Octavio Paz. New York, New Directions Press, 1963.
Early Poems 1935-1955 by Octavio Paz. Bloomington, Indiana, Indiana University Press, 1963; revised edition, New York, New Directions Press, 1973.
With Leif Sjoberg, *Selected Poems* by Gunnar Ekelöef. New York, Twayne, 1967.
Three Poems by Gunnar Ekelöef. Lawrence, Kansas, T. Williams, 1967.

With Eliot Weinberger, G. Bishop Aroub, Elizabeth Blackburn, Paul Kemp, Denise Levertov Lysander, Mark Strand, Charles Tomlinson, William Carlos Williams, and Monique Wust Fong, *Selected Poems* by Octavio Paz. New York, New Directions, 1984.
With Leif Sjoeberg, *A Molna Elegy: Metamorphoses, 2 Volumes* by Gunnar Ekeloef. New York, Unicorn Press, 1984.

Literary Criticism

The Life of Poetry. New York, Current Books, 1949; reprinted, Germantown, New York, Periodicals Service Company, 1968, New York, New York, William Morrow & Company, Inc., 1974, and with an introduction by Jane Cooper, Paris Press, Inc., 1996.

Other

All The Way Home (film). 1958.
The Orgy (novel). New York, Coward, 1965; reprinted, Paris Press, Inc., 1997.
"The Music of Translation: Papers Delivered at Conference on Literary Translation Held in New York City in May 1970, under Auspices of PEN American Center" (essay), in *The World of Translation,* preface by Gregory Rabassa, introduction by Lewis Galantiere. New York, PEN American Center, 1987.
"Under Forty; From the Archives: Muriel Rukeyser, 1913-1978: 'Poet...woman...America...Jew,'" in *Bridges: A Journal for Jewish Feminists and our Friends,* (Eugene, Oregon), Vol. 1, No. 1, 1990, 23-9.

Recordings: *The Poetry and Voice of Muriel Rukeyser,* New York, Caedmon, 1977.

*

Biography: "Muriel Rukeyser (1913-1980)" by Eloise Klein Healy, in *Contemporary Lesbian Writers of the United States: A Bio-Bibliographical Critical Sourcebook,* edited by Sandra Pollack, Denise D. Knight, and Pamella Tucker Farley, Westport, Connecticut, 1993, 461-467.

Interviews: "Adrienne Rich: 'I happen to think poetry makes a huge difference'" by Matthew Rothschild, in *Progressive,* Vol. 58, No. 1, January 1994, 31-4.

Critical Sources: "Theory of Flight" by W. R. Benet, in *Saturday Review of Literature,* 7 December 1935. "Theory of Flight" by Rachael Roberts, in *Spectator,* 1 May 1936; "Muriel Rukeyser: The Social Poet and the Problem of Communication" by John M. Brinnin, in *Poetry,* Vol. 61, 1943, 554-75; *A History of American Poetry 1900-1940* by Gregory Horace and Marya Zaturenska, New York, Harcourt, Brace, 1946; "Muriel Rukeyser: The Longer Poems" by James Laughlin, in *New Directions in Prose and Poetry,* Vol. 14, 1953, 202-29; *Poetry and the Age* by Randall Jarrell, New York, Knopf-Vintage, 1953, 148; *Selected Criticism: Prose, Poetry,* New York, The Noonday Press, 1955; *Contemporary Poets of the English Language* by Rosalie Murphy, New York, St. Martin's Press, 1970; *American Poetry in the Twentieth Century,* New York, Herder and Herder, 1971; "The Esthetics of Science: Muriel Rukeyser's 'Waterlily Fire'" by Joan F. Adkins, in *Contemporary Poetry: A Journal of Criticism* (Bryn Mawr, Pennsylvania), Vol. 1, No. 2, 1973, 23-27; "Muriel Rukeyser: A Retrospective" by Virginia R. Terris, in *American Poetry Review,* Vol. 3, May/June 1974, 10-15; "The Critique of Consciousness and Myth in Levertov, Rich, and Rukeyser" by Rachel Blau DuPlessis, in *Feminist Studies,* Vol. 3, No. 1, 1975, 199-221; "Lyric Documents: The Critique of Personal Consciousness in Levertov, Rich and Rukeyser" by Rachel Blau Duplessis, in *Myth and Ideology in American Culture,* edited by Regis Durand, Fabre, Michel Universtie de Lille III, Villenueve d'Asca, 1976, 65-80; "Muriel Rukeyser: America Josei Shi Renaissance no Gunzo" by Ikuko Atsumi, in *Eigo Seinen (The Rising Generation)* (Tokyo, Japan), Vol. 122, 1976, 340-341; *The Poetic Use of Womanhood in Five Modern American Poets: Moore, Millay, Rukeyser, Levertov, and Plath* by Bonne Tymorski August (dissertation), in *Dissertation Abstracts International (DAI)* (Ann Arbor, Michigan), Vol. 39, 1978, 3576A-3577A; "Muriel Rukeyser's The Gates" by Robert Coles, in *The American Poetry Review* (Philadelphia, Pennsylvania), Vol. 7, No. 3, May/June 1978, 15; *A Woman of Words: A Study of Muriel Rukeyser's Poetry* by Marsha Hudson (dissertation), in *Dissertation Abstracts International (DAI)* (Ann Arbor, Michigan), Vol. 40, 1979, 257A; *The Poetic Vision of Muriel Rukeyser* by Louise Kertesz, Baton Rouge, Louisiana, Louisiana State University Press, 1980; *Muriel Rukeyser: The Woman Writer Confronts Traditional Mythology and Psychology* by Jane Elizabeth Curtis (dissertation), in *Dissertation Abstracts International (DAI)* (Ann Arbor, Michigan), Vol. 42, No. 9, 1982, 3994A; "Finding Her Voice: Muriel Rukeyser's Poetic Development" by David S. Barber, in *Modern Poetry Studies* (Buffalo, New York), Vol. 11, No. 1, 1982, 127-138; "A Woman's Odyssey: Muriel Rukeyser's 'Searching/Not Searching'" by Kathleen L. Nichols, in *Perspectives on Contemporary Literature* (Lexington, Kentucky), Vol. 8, 1982, 27-33; "'The Poet of Unity': Muriel Ruykeyser's Willard Gibbs" by David S. Barber, in *CLIO: A Journal of Literature, History, and the Philosophy of History* (Fort Wayne, Indiana), Vol. 12, No. 1, fall 1982, 1-15; "Exploring the Human Community: The Poetry of Denise Levertov and Muriel Rukeyser" by Harry Marten, in *Sagetrieb: A Journal Devoted to Poets in the Pound, H. D. Williams Tradition (Sagetrieb)* (Orono, Maine), Vol. 3, No. 3, winter 1984, 51-61; "Muriel Rukeyser" edited by Kate Daniels and Richard Jones, in *Poetry East,* Vols. 16-17, spring/summer 1985; "'Who Is the Double Ghost Whose Head Is Smoke?': Women Poets on Aging" by Diana Hume George, in *Memory and Desire: Aging, Literature, Psychoanalysis,* edited by Kathleen Woodward and Murray M. Schwartz, Bloomington, Indiana, Indiana University Press, 1986, 134-153; *Discoverers of the Not Known: Louise Bogan, Muriel Rukeyser, Sylvia Plath, May Swenson, and Adrienne Rich* by Kim Suzanne Bridgford (dissertation), in *Dissertation Abstracts International (DAI)* (Ann Arbor, Michigan), Vol. 50, No. 2, August 1989, 558; "Barcelona, 1936: A Moment of Proof for Muriel Rukeyser" by Gigliola Sacerdoti Marianai, in *Rivista di Studi Anglo Americani,* Vol. 6, No. 8, 1990, 387-396; "From the Archives: Muriel Rukeyser, 1913-1978: 'Poet...woman...American...Jew,'" in *Bridges: A Journal for Jewish Feminists and our Friends* (Eugene, Oregon), Vol. 1, No. 1, 1990, 23-29; *'New Ways to See Ancestral Lands': Revisionist Myth Making in the Poetry of Sylvia Plath, Muriel Rukeyser, and Adrienne Rich* by Carol Ann Lattimore (dissertation), in *Dissertation Abstracts International (DAI)* (Ann Arbor, Michigan), Vol. 52, No. 4, October 1991, 1330A; "Constructing a Lesbian Poetic for Survival: Broumas, Rukeyser, H. D., Rich, Lourde" by Liz Yorke, in *Sexual Sameness: Textual Differences in Lesbian and Gay Writing,* edited by Joseph Bristow, London, England, Routledge, 1992,

187-209; "Out of Silence: Selected Poems," in *Publishers' Weekly,* Vol. 239, No. 15, 23 March 1992, 65; "Out of Silence: Selected Poems" by Fred Muratori, in *Library Journal,* Vol. 117, No. 8, 1 May 1992, 86; "'A world that will hold all the people': On Muriel Rukeyser" by Suzanne Gardinier, in *Kenyon Review,* Vol. 14, No. 3, summer 1992, 88-105; "Out of Silence: Selected Poems" by Anne Herzog, in *Women's Review of Books,* Vol. 10, No. 1, October 1992, 15-16; *'She Holds Belief in the World': Muriel Rukeyser's Oracular Poetry* by James Michael Brock (dissertation), in *Dissertation Abstracts International (DAI)* (Ann Arbor, Michigan), Vol. 53, No. 6, December 1992, 1905A; *What Is Found There: Notebooks on Poetry and Politics* by Adrienne Rich, New York, W. W. Norton and Company, 1993; "Out of Silence: Selected Poems" by Lee Upton, in *Belles Lettres: A Review of Books by Women,* Vol. 8, No. 3, spring 1993, 30-31; "Opening 'The Gates': Muriel Rukeyser and the Poetry of Witness" by Michele S. Ware, in *Women's Studies,* Vol. 22, No. 3, June 1993, 297-308; "Beginners" by Adrienne Rich, in *Kenyon Review,* Vol. 15, No. 3, summer 1993, 12-19; "Whitman's Multitudinous Poetic Progeny: Particular and Puzzling Instances" by James E. Miller, Jr., in *Walt Whitman: The Centennial Essays,* edited by Ed Folsom, Iowa City, Iowa, University of Iowa Press, 1994, 185-200; "A Muriel Rukeyser Reader" by June Jordan, in *Ms Magazine,* Vol. 4, No. 5, March/April 1994, 70-73; *"Faith and Resistance": Politics and the Poetry of Muriel Rukeyser* by Anne Frances Herzog (dissertation), in *Dissertation Abstracts International (DAI)* (Ann Arbor, Michigan), Vol. 54, No. 11, May 1994, 4093A; "Rukeyser's 'Waking This Morning'" by Alex Clunas, in *Explicator* (Washington, D.C.), Vol. 54, No. 4, summer 1994, 237-239; "A Muriel Rukeyser Reader" by R. Whitman, in *Choice,* Vol. 32, No. 1, September 1994, 109-110; *Social Protest and Poetic Decorum in the Great Depression: A Reading of Kenneth Fearing, Horace Gregory, and Muriel Rukeyser* by Cameron Bardrick (dissertation), in *Dissertation Abstracts International (DAI)* (Ann Arbor, Michigan), Vol. 55, No. 3, September 1994, 563A; "A Muriel Rukeyser Reader" by Florence Howe, in *Women's Review of Books,* Vol. 12, No. 2, November 1994, 12-13; *Reading Muriel Rukeyser: Yes, We Are Looking at Each Other* by Janet Ellen (dissertation), in *Dissertation Abstracts International (DAI)* (Ann Arbor, Michigan), Vol. 55, No.8, February 1995, 2391A; "A Muriel Rukeyser Reader" by M.L. Rosenthal, in *Ploughshares,* Vol. 21, No. 1, Spring 1995, 198-200; "A Muriel Rukeyser Reader" by David Seed, in *Journal of American Studies,* Vol. 29, No. 2, August 1995, 285-86; "A Muriel Rukeyser Reader" by Richard Gray, in *Modern Language Review,* Vol. 90, No. 4, October 1995, 990-91; "A Muriel Rukeyser Reader" by Linda Gregerson, in *Poetry,* Vol. 167, No. 5, February 1996, 292-96; "Meeting Places: on Muriel Rukeyser" by Jane Cooper, in *American Poetry Review,* Vol. 25, No. 5, September/October 1996, 11-16.

*   *   *

Muriel Rukeyser was a third generation Ashkanazi Jew born on Riverside Drive in Manhattan in 1913, the year before the start of World War I. Her parents were upwardly mobile and middle-class. Her mother was a bookkeeper from Yonkers, New York, and was related to the 1st century B.C.E. poet and scholar Akiba; her father was a Wisconsin born concrete salesman who later became a partner in a sand and gravel company. Despite growing up with maids, she related to the working-class and poor neighborhood children and those in gangs, much to her mother's dismay. It was on the streets of Manhattan that Rukeyser first practiced her social analysis and gained a consciousness about the world.

Rukeyser always loved to read. Her parents loved music and opera. She attended private Jewish religious schools, though as a young child her family was not religious. Later when her mother took an interest in religion, she attended Synagogue weekly. She began writing poetry in high school. She attended Vassar college, where she was the literary editor of the leftist journal *Student Review*. She was forced to leave Vassar due to her father's bankruptcy. Despite the educational opportunities her family gave her, she was, in her own words, "expected to grow up and become a golfer...a suburban professional's wife." Later in life, when her political leanings and activities grew more radical, her father disowned her.

Rukeyser left Vassar College in 1933. She traveled as a journalist to Alabama to report on the Scottsboro Case, where nine young Blacks were convicted of raping two white women, a ruling later overturned by the Supreme Court. While covering the case, she was arrested for talking to African American journalists; while in jail, she got Typhoid Fever, which effected her health throughout her life.

In 1935, when Rukeyser was 21 years old, she won the Yale Series of Younger Poets award for her first book of poetry, *Theory of Flight*. The first poem of that collection, "Poem Out of Childhood," begins with the line "Breathe-in experience, breathe-out poetry." This was perhaps a symbol of what Rukeyser would do not only in this collection, but in all of her works. All that Rukeyser "breathed in"—the political and cultural events of an era, the arts, the sciences, her personal experiences as a woman, a Jew, a single mother, and an activist—is integrated within her poetry and other writings. In *Theory of Flight,* she tells of the start of World War I, the Scottsboro case in Alabama, and the influence of both art and science during the time she was writing. The book's title came from a flight manual she used while studying flying at the Roosevelt Aviation School. There are also already signs of the breadth of genre and style that Rukeyser would use and combine in her works, such as poetry side- by-side journalistic writing and long almost epic pieces side-by-side short works.

In 1936, Rukeyser traveled to Gauley Bridge, West Virginia, to report on miners dying of the lung disease silicosis while building a hydroelectric plant. There was much evidence that the new Kanawha Power Company knew beforehand of the dangers of silica mining but expanded the project anyway. The experiences of Gauley Bridge are deeply and innovatively explored in Rukeyser's long piece "The Book of the Dead," contained in her second volume, *U.S. 1.* In *A Muriel Rukeyser Reader,* editor Jan Heller Levi states that the piece is "one of the most original and harrowing documents of American literature...[It] brings together documentary evidence (including testimony from congressional hearings, letters, interviews, even financial printouts from the Stock Exchange) and complex, intertwined poetic explorations to, in effect, develop a new definition of what a poem might be...[it is] an impassioned indictment of capitalist greed and a call for social justice." In the journal *Ploughshares,* M.L. Rosenthal calls this piece a "mixture of modes [creating a]...memorable achievement in poetry dynamics."

In 1936 Rukeyser also traveled to Spain to cover the anti-fascist Olympics; she arrived on the first day the civil war broke out and was evacuated to England. Her companion of the time, Otto Boch, was killed fighting the Spanish Loyalists. In 1939, Rukeyser published *Turning Wind.* Here she reflects on the issue of power swirling around her at the time of the Spanish Civil War and

Hitler's invasion of Poland. In her introduction, she states that "sources of power are obscured again, or vulgarized and locked out," and how in this work, "Using mass material studies in symbolism, studies in individual lives, and the experience to which I have been open, I have hoped to indicate some of the valid sources of power that have come down to us." It is here we first strongly see Rukeyser's interest in biography, a form she would later radicalize. The last section of the book, called "Lives," tells of five New Englanders—the painter Albert Pinkham Ryder, the writer John Jay Chapman, the labor organizer Ann Burlak, the composer Charles Ives, and the scientist Willard Gibbs.

In 1942, Rukeyser published a full length biography of Willard Gibbs, a physicist considered the "father" of thermodynamics. *Willard Gibbs,* however, is not just a biography, but contains poetry, history, science, politics, and culture, all in one. She places Gibbs within a broad context ("...this moment in which we touch life and all the energy of the past and future..."), bringing up issues of the slave trade and the civil war, the labor movement of the 18th century, and the visionary, artistic, and poetic contexts of science. In "Muriel Rukeyser's *Willard Gibbs,*" David S. Barber states that "Central to her poetic aesthetic is the belief that poetry and science are equally valid ways of seeing the world, both needing the other in order to attain their greatest force...Since Gibb's work relates to creativity in any field, the humanist, even the poet, can validly interpret his leading ideas and cultural significance."

In the 1940s, Rukeyser moved to San Francisco, where she taught at the California Labor School. In 1942 Rukeyser published *Beast in View;* in 1944 *Wake Island.* In 1945, she married the painter Glynn Collins; the marriage was annulled 12 weeks later. Her son, William Laurie Rukeyser, was born on September 25, 1947, while she was single; she never revealed who fathered her son. In that same year, an anonymous wealthy woman who admired her work and struggles as a single mom donated to Rukeyser an annual stipend.

In 1948, Rukeyser published *The Green Wave.* Included in this work are translations of six poems by the Mexican poet Octavio Paz and nine "rari's," or love-chants, of the Marquesas by the nineteenth-century poet Mao Tetua, who according to Rukeyser "was a blind leper who could neither read nor write; he was so popular as a composer-poet that 'natives gathered illegally every night outside the leprosarium to listen' to these songs." In 1949, Rukeyser wrote *The Life of Poetry.* The material in this work is mostly a collection of lectures Rukeyser presented on the meaning of poetry and why poetry is met with so much resistance in this culture. In the introduction to this work, Rukeyser states, "In this book, I have tried to track down the resistances to poetry, with every kind of 'boredom' and 'impatience,' the name-calling which says that poetry is 'intellectual and obscure and confused and sexually suspect.' How much of this is true, and how much can be traced to the corruption of consciousness?" Written years before phrases like "multi-culturalism," within this book about poetry is a book about the great diversity in our culture, from jazz and the blues to Native American chants and the voices of women. Rukeyser writes not only about poets and writers, but musicians, scientists, sociologists, labor leaders, and political and spiritual leaders; people as diverse as Walt Whitman, Albert Einstein, Karen Horney, Gene Kelly, Bessie Smith, Emily Dickinson, and Buddha.

In 1954, Rukeyser forfeited her stipend when she began teaching at Sarah Lawrence College. Finances were more difficult to manage, especially as a single mother. Thus, Rukeyser took on some new areas such as children's books and screenplays. Numbers of these projects did not work out, likely due to Rukeyser's political activism. Throughout the 1950s, Rukeyser was investigated by several McCarthyist groups for her political activities. Nonetheless, during this period Rukeyser published two works of poetry, *Selected Poems* (1951), and *Body of Waking* (1958), a collection of poetry and prose called *One Life* (1957), based on the life of Wendell Willkie, the documentary film script "All The Way Home," and her first Children's Book *Come Back, Paul* (1955). When describing *Body of Waking* in *The Muriel Rukeyser Reader*, Jan Heller Levi talks of this work as the first with lesbian illusions, "More and more, we find poems that can be read as evocations of the power and possibility derived from loving another woman. 'King's Mountain' and 'Long Enough,' for example, are richly suggestive lyrics of sexual and political wakening. [Rukeyser] may be writing of her emergence into a country where male fantasies no longer rule her."

During the 1960s, Rukeyser completed *The Orgy* (1965), her "novel" about the lives of a few people in a small village in Ireland, the play "The Colors of the Day (in celebration of the Vassar Centennial)" (1961), two collaborative translations of the work of Octavio Paz and Gunnar Ekelöef, the children's books *I Go Out* (1961) and *Bubbles* (1967), and three books of poetry, *Waterlilly Fire: Poems 1935-1962* (1962), *The Outer Banks* (1967), and *The Speed of Darkness* (1968).

In 1964, at the age of 50, Rukeyser had her first stroke, which affected the right side of her brain and her speech. During this time, as she worked out re-learning language skills, she also began to have a clearer feminist vision. In *The Journal of American Studies*, David Seed calls Rukeyser's *The Speed of Light* "an explicitly feminist rediscovery of language." *The Speed of Light* greatly influenced the then new generation of young feminists. In "The Poem as Mask," is found the well known line "No More Masks! No more mythologies!," used frequently as a feminist rallying cry, and in 1973 as the title of a well-known women's poetry anthology *No More Masks! An Anthology of Poems by Women*, edited by Florence House and Ellen Bass (revised edition, 1993). Also found in *The Speed of Light* is Rukeyser's well known "Käthe Kollwitz." It is here we find the line, "What would happen if one woman told the truth about her life? / The world would split open." From this line came the title of the 1974 anthology *The World Split Open: Four Centuries of Women Poets in England and America, 1552-1950*, edited by Louise Bernikow, with a preface by Rukeyser. Both of these poems have been quoted by many contemporary feminists and poets, such as Adrienne Rich, as well as found on numerous feminist posters and cards of the early 1970s. In the introduction to the 1981 anthology *Lesbian Poetry: An Anthology*, editor Elly Bulkin also speaks of Rukeyser's *The Speed of Light*. After hearing that Rukeyser agreed to speak at a 1978 panel discussion of lesbians in literature, she reassessed *Speed of Light* in relationship to Rukeyser's lesbianism: "the discovery [of her lesbianism] allowed me to understand for the first time that the opening poems...celebrate coming out."

In 1967, Rukeyser resigned from teaching at Sarah Lawrence, but continued to teach poetry workshops around New York City, under the auspices of an organization she helped start, Poets and Writers Collaborative. Rukeyser's activism continued throughout the 1970s. She was active in the anti-Vietnam war movement. She traveled with Denise Levertov and Jane Hart on an unofficial peace mission to Hanoi in 1972. Afterwards, she was arrested in Wash-

ington, D.C., at an anti-war demonstration. In 1975, after learning about the imprisoned South Korean poet and political activist, Kim Chi Ha, she traveled there to protest outside the prison gates of his cell. During this period, her health continued to fail, affected by her past typhoid fever, strokes, and a then diagnosed diabetes. In 1978, Rukeyser agreed to be a part of a Modern Literature Association panel on "Lesbians in Literature." Her health, however, prevented her from attending. She died 12 February 1980.

Throughout her life, Rukeyser not only participated in the political and cultural happenings of the 1970s, but she also wrote of them. During the 1970s Rukeyser's works included *29 Poems* (1972), *Breaking Open* (1973), *The Gates* (1976), and *The Collected Poems of Muriel Rukeyser* (1978). She also wrote a prose book called *The Traces of Thomas Hariot*, the play *Houdini* (1973), and the children's book *Mazes* (1970).

In *The Gates*, Rukeyser explores and explains the situation of South Korean political prisoner Kim Chi Ha. In "Opening 'The Gates': Muriel Rukeyser and the Poetry of Witness," published in *Women's Studies*, Michele S. Ware explains: "[Rukeyser's] identification with the imprisoned poet takes on an increasingly personal dimension when she meets the poet's family, and watches how Kim's son is growing...In poem V, Rukeyser does what Denise Levertov so admired in her work: she 'fuse[s] lyricism and overt social and political concern.'"

In *Breaking Open*, Rukeyser continues her feminist exploration and perspective. In the journal *Perspectives on Contemporary Literature*, Kathleen L. Nichols describes Rukeyser's long poem "Searching/Not Searching," as:

> [S]uccessfully releas[ing] woman from the passive cycle of private identity by sending her out instead on a poetic journey, epic in scope, which takes her imaginatively through her personal and cultural past and present—though history, politics, art, literature, memory, and technology, as well as through Asia, Europe, and modern urban America. Through this journey, Rukeyser reveals woman as both active seeker and receptor of experience—an explorer of both the inner and outer worlds of herself and society—as she searches for feminine role models, new identities, and re-vitalized relationships which will transform both men and women, as well as the political future of the world order.

Additionally, *Breaking Open* contains a series of translated Eskimo poems, which Ruskeyser translated with the anthropologist Paul Radin.

Despite a large body of published literature and a number of awards, critical reception of Rukeyser has been, at best, mixed. She was often criticized for being what at the time was called a "she-poet," for a strong poetic style and political convictions that would have been praised in a man, for being "self-indulgent," and for not going along with the literary "fashion" and theory of the time, no less the "proper" political analysis, even of the left. As Adrienne Rich describes in the *Kenyon Review*:

> In her lifetime she was sometimes the target of extraordinary hostility and ridicule, based on a critic's failure to read her well or even try to understand her methods; often, during the forties and fifties especially, because she was too complicated and independent to follow any political 'line,' or because she would not trim her sails

to a vogue of poetic irony and wit, an aesthetics of the private middle-class life, an idea of what a woman's poetry should look like.

Nonetheless, there have always been those who have praised Rukeyser, even early in her career when the *London Times Literary Supplement* called her "one of America's greatest poets."

With the 1992 publication of Rukeyser's *Out of Silence: Selected Poems* and the 1996 publication of *A Muriel Rukeyser Reader,* Rukeyser is being "rediscovered" and re-evaluated for her rightful place in literary, Jewish, feminist, political, cultural, and lesbian history. Still, we have a long way to go in paying proper homage to this great writer and activist. As Adrienne Rich states in *Bridges: A Journal for Jewish Feminists and Our Friends,* Rukeyser was a "secular and deeply spiritual Jew, sexually independent woman, her work never fitted into the canon of Modernism, and has been largely unexplored by critics. American poetry of the past 60 years will be perceived very differently when Muriel Rukeyser is accorded her rightful place."

—tova

S

————

SAINT, Assotto

Pseudonym: Pen name is a pseudonym of Yves F. Lubin. **Nationality:** Haitian poet, dramatist, and dancer. **Born:** Les Cayes, Haiti, 2 October 1957; immigrated to New York, 1970. **Family:** Companion of Jan Holmgren. **Career:** Founder, Metamorphosis Theatre and Galiens Press. **Awards:** Lambda Literary Award for Poetry, for *The Road Before Us,* 1992. **Died:** New York City, of complications from AIDS, 29 June 1994.

WRITINGS

Risin' to the Love We Need. 1985(?); reprinted in *Spells of a Voodoo Doll,* New York, Masquerade Books, 1996, 323-80.
Black Fag. Reprinted in *Spells of A Voodoo Doll,* New York, Masquerade Books, 1996, 385-405.
New Love Song. 1988; reprinted in *Spells of A Voodoo Doll,* New York, Masquerade Books, 1996, 277-319.
Stations: Poems. New York, Galiens Press, 1989.
Wishing For Wings: Poems. New York, Galiens Press, 1994.
Spells of a Voodoo Doll. New York, Masquerade Books, 1996.

Short Stories

"Risin' to the Love We Need" (excerpt), in *In The Life: A Black Gay Anthology,* edited by Joseph Beam. Boston, Alyson Press, 1986, 243-49.
"Triple Trouble: An Exorcism," in *Gay and Lesbian Poetry In Our Time,* edited by Carl Morse and Joan Larkin. New York, St. Martin's Press, 1988, 352-53.
"Hooked For Life," in *Brother To Brother: New Writings By Black Gay Men,* edited by Essex Hemphill. Boston, Alyson Publications, 1991, 136-41.
"Why I Write," in *Spells of A Voodoo Doll.* New York, Masquerade Books, 1996, 3-8.

Other

Contributor, *Tongues Untied: Poems.* London, Gay Men's Press, 1987.
Editor, *The Road Before Us: 100 Black Gay Poets.* New York, Galiens Press, 1991.
Editor, *Here to Dare: 10 Black Gay Poets.* New York, Galiens Press, 1992.

*   *   *

The situation of black gay men was, until the 1980s, little discussed outside of their own community, while their almost total ex-clusion (along with other persons of color and women) from the national leadership of the gay and lesbian movement left the majority of the gay community unaware of their needs, issues, and gifts. Nowhere was this gap more evident than in the burgeoning field of gay literature, where black characters and writers (with the prominent exception of James Baldwin) were few. This invisibility was shattered in the early 1980s under the influence of Joseph Beam, editor and founder of the journal *Blackheart,* whose seminal work, *In The Life: A Black Gay Anthology* (1986), proudly claimed a place for this genre in both gay and mainstream literary worlds. Among the artists whose work appeared in this pioneering volume was the dancer, poet, and playwright Assotto Saint.

Born in Haiti, Saint immigrated to New York in the summer of 1970 and attended Queens College as a pre-med major before joining the Martha Graham dance company. He did all of this while working at perfecting his own skills as a writer. He became a member of the Blackheart Collective, a New York-based group of writers and artists originally formed in 1981, and founded the Metamorphosis Theatre, which served as a forum for his own explorations synthesizing homosexuality and the vivid Negritude imagery of his home island. His principal works during the 1980s, *Risin' to the Love We Need, Black Fag,* and *New Love Song,* were musical and multimedia pieces for the stage which celebrated the lives of black gay men throughout time. In addition, he contributed 14 poems to the landmark 1987 anthology of black gay poetry *Tongues Untied* and produced a volume of his own works, *Stations.* Marlon Rigg's controversial 1989 filming of *Tongues Untied,* the first work for a mass audience to directly address African-American homosexuality, also featured selected poems by Saint.

Saint's most crucial literary contributions are his filling of the role of editor and advocate for black gay men's writing following the early death of writer and publisher Joseph Beam from AIDS in 1988, and his emergence as one of the most distinctive witnesses to the devastation wrought by AIDS within the African-American community. He founded Galiens Press as a vehicle for the continuing distribution and promotion of this type of writing, publishing the landmark anthologies *The Road Before Us: 100 Gay Black Poets* (1991) and *Here To Dare: 10 Black Gay Poets* (1992). Galiens Press went out of business in late 1994 after posthumously publishing Saint's final collection of poetry, *Wishing For Wings.* He also was a founding member of the New York City black gay writers collective Other Countries, and with his lover Jan Holmgren created the art-rock band Xotika. In 1990, they contributed the song "Forever Gay" to the compact disc *Feeding The Flame: Songs By Men To End AIDS.*

Saint's work received critical acclaim within the gay community, most notably with the selection of *The Road Before Us* as one of the two 1992 Lambda Literary Award winners for poetry. Although his health was failing, he attended the 1993 March On Washington. Memorializing his death in 1994, the editor of the *Lambda Book Report* described him as having possessed "a scarcely believable diligence in searching out and bringing into print talented gay writers." Saint's own view (preserved in the essay "Why I Write") was that "my poems and plays are weapons and blessings that I use to liberate myself, to validate our realities as gay black men, and to elucidate the human struggle."

—Robert B. Marks Ridinger

SARGESON, Frank

Nationality: New Zealand short story writer, novelist, non-fiction writer, and playwright. **Born:** Norris Frank Davey in Hamilton, 23 March 1903; name legally changed, 1946. **Education:** Hamilton High School; Auckland University College, 1921-26. **Family:** Companion of Harry Doyle, 1935-71. **Career:** Admitted as a Solicitor of the Supreme Court of New Zealand, 1926; worked as law clerk, Auckland, 1926-27; estates clerk, New Zealand Public Trust, Wellington, 1928-29; journalist, c. 1931-40. **Awards:** Centennial Literary Competition Prize, 1940; New Zealand Government literary pension, 1947-68; Hubert Church Memorial Prize, 1952, 1968; Katherine Mansfield Award, 1965; L.H.D.: University of Auckland, 1974. **Died:** Auckland, 1 March 1982.

WRITINGS

Short Story Collections

Conversation. Auckland, Unicorn Press, 1936.
A Man and His Wife. Christchurch, Caxton Press, 1940.
That Summer. London, John Lehmann, 1946.
Collected Stories. Auckland, Blackwood & Janet Paul, 1964; with an introduction by E. M. Forster, London, MacGibbon & Kee, 1965; revised edition published as *The Stories of Frank Sargeson,* Auckland, Longman Paul, 1973.

Novels

When the Wind Blows. Christchurch, Caxton Press, 1945.
I Saw in My Dreams. London, John Lehmann, 1949.
I for One.... Christchurch, Caxton Press, 1954.
Memoirs of a Peon. London, MacGibbon & Kee, 1965.
The Hangover. London, MacGibbon & Kee, 1967.
Joy of the Worm. London, MacGibbon & Kee, 1967.
Man of England Now (includes *I for One* . . . and *A Game of Hide and Seek*). Christchurch, Caxton Press, 1972.
Sunset Village. London, Martin Brian & O'Keeffe, 1976.

Plays

A Time for Sowing (produced Auckland, 1961). Published in *Wrestling with the Angel,* 1964.
The Cradle and the Egg (produced Auckland, 1962). Published in *Wrestling with the Angel,* 1964.
Wrestling with the Angel: Two Plays. Christchurch, Caxton Press, 1964.

Other

Editor, *Speaking for Ourselves: A Collection of New Zealand Stories.* Christchurch, Caxton Press, 1945.
Once Is Enough: A Memoir. London, Martin Brian & O'Keeffe, 1973.
More Than Enough: A Memoir. London, Martin Brian & O'Keeffe, 1975.
Never Enough! London, Martin Brian & O'Keeffe, 1977.

Conversation in a Train and Other Critical Writing, edited by Kevin Cunningham. Auckland, Oxford University Press, 1983.

*

Manuscript Collections: Alexander Turnbull Library, Wellington.

Biography: *Frank Sargeson in His Time* by Dennis McEldowney, Dunedin, John McIndoe, 1976; *Frank Sargeson: A Life* by Michael King, New York and London, Penguin Books, 1995.

Interviews: "Conversation with Frank Sargeson" by Michael Beveridge, in *Landfall 93* (Dunedin), Vol. 24, No. 1, March 1970, 4-27, and *Landfall 94* (Dunedin), Vol. 24, No. 2, June 1970, 142-60.

Critical Sources: *Frank Sargeson* by H. Winston Rhodes, New York, Twayne, 1969; *Frank Sargeson* by R. A. Copeland, Wellington, Oxford University Press, 1976; "On the Edge: New Zealanders as Displaced Persons" by Peter C. M. Alcock, in *World Literature Written in English* (Arlington), Vol. 16, No. 1, April 1977, 126-44; *The New English Literatures: Cultural Nationalism in a Changing World* by Bruce King, New York, St. Martin's Press, 1980; "Speaking through the Inarticulate: The Art of Frank Sargeson" by Murray S. Martin, in *JGE: The Journal of General Education* (University Park), Vol. 33, No. 2, summer 1981, 123-34; "Frank Sargeson" by Dan Davin, in *Times* (London), 11 March 1982, 14.

*   *   *

Frank Sargeson occupies a pre-eminent place in New Zealand literature, not only for the quality of his novels and short stories but also for his influence on later generations of New Zealand writers. Sargeson focused exclusively on aspects of New Zealand life, usually the world of the underclass and dispossessed. In the words of Michael King in *Frank Sargeson: A Life,* "he turned his country's literature in a new direction."

Sargeson's choice to remain silent about his homosexuality (he was involved in a relationship for over 30 years with Harry Doyle, an itinerant horse trainer) may have been in part the result of a devastating and well-publicized arrest as a young man in Auckland for indecent assault. It was shortly after this incident that he changed his name, moved from the city, and began his writing career as Frank Sargeson. It is interesting to speculate on the relationship between the coded nature of Sargeson's gay fiction and these key events in his early life.

Although Sargeson's later literary output includes a number of novels and memoirs, some of his best work, particularly that containing a gay subtext, is found in the short stories and novellas he produced during the 1940s and 1950s. Written for the most part in a terse but complex style that makes extensive use of the New Zealand idiom, these stories focus on characters who are often inarticulate, isolated, prone to violence, and sexually alienated. In several of these stories, this alienation is the result of an inability to acknowledge, articulate, or even recognize a homosexual nature.

That Summer, the novella generally acknowledged as Sargeson's finest work, is also the most fully realized in terms of its expression of homosexual love. Billy, the narrator, is typical of Sargeson's wanderers, a guileless out-of-work laborer who makes his way to the city and meets up with Terry, older, somewhat wiser, and similarly rootless. Terry, ill with tuberculosis, moves in with Billy and the two initially share a bed in a scene reminiscent of the Ishmael/Queequeg "marriage" night in *Moby Dick*. After a series of misadventures that reveal each man's loyalty to the other, Billy leaves Terry on his deathbed, unable even then to express his deepest emotional feelings: "Terry, I'd say. But I never could get any further than just saying Terry. I wanted to say something but I didn't know what it was, and I couldn't say it. Terry, I'd say."

In the essay "Speaking through the Inarticulate: The Art of Frank Sargeson" in the journal *JGE,* Murray S. Martin writes: "...indirectness may be the only method available for a writer intensely moved to address his central cares in an alienated and alienating society—certainly a society in which the narrator could not have openly admitted his homosexuality, for example, and survived." Sargeson's point of view in *That Summer,* however, is subtle and skillful in conveying the strong undercurrents of gay sexuality that occur throughout. What is experienced or felt—but not understood—by the hapless Billy becomes in fact the story's dominant motif. When Billy leaves his employment at a restaurant, the burly cook cries and buys him a bunch of flowers. Maggie, another boarder at the house where Terry and Billy room, turns out to be a man, much to Billy's surprise. A stranger Billy meets on a park bench wants to call him—coincidentally—Bill, because Billy reminds him of a long-lost companion of the same name: "A man wants a mate that won't let him down, he said." Sargeson the writer knows exactly what is going on, and so do we, and we grieve for Billy in his isolation and in his lonely search for human connectedness.

In several of Sargeson's stories, unhappy outcomes of a different sort result from the sexual tensions lurking beneath the surface, usually in relationships between working-class men. In "A Pair of Socks," the narrator loses his job because of a gift to his employer that arouses the jealousy of a co-worker. In "A Great Day," Fred, hired by a vacationing acquaintance for whom he has feelings of both physical attraction and envy, capsizes their fishing dingy and abandons his drowning friend. The narrator of "I've Lost My Pal" relates the story of a fellow sheepshearer, George, who professes not to like women and who stands in a tub while washing, "pleased at the things we used to say about the different parts of him." George's relationship with Tom, the narrator's young friend, ends tragically in an outcome heavy with sexual overtones.

Writing as a New Zealander and giving voice to a group of people unique to a particular milieu, Frank Sargeson has at the same time transcended the boundaries of regionalism. His work speaks to a universal audience, and his contributions to the canon of gay literature are significant. As Dan Davin writes in Sargeson's obituary for the *Times* of London, "his words and his work will remain."

—David Garnes

SEGREST, Mab (Mabelle Massey)

Nationality: American essayist, poet, and organizer. **Born:** Birmingham, Alabama, 20 February 1949. **Education:** Attended public schools in Tuskegee, Alabama; Huntingdon College, Montgomery, Alabama (finalist, Woodrow Wilson Fellowship; Danforth Fellowship; summa cum laude), B.A. 1971; Duke University, Durham, North Carolina (Duke University Graduate School Fellow), M.A. 1972, Ph.D 1979. **Family:** Companion of Barbara Culbertson, from 1979; one daughter. **Career:** Graduate tutor, Department of English, Duke University, Durham, North Carolina, 1972-76; instructor, Department of English, Campbell University, Buies Creek, North Carolina, 1976-83; instructor of English as a Second Language, Migrant and Seasonal Farmworkers' Association, summer 1983; instructor of Adult Basic Education, Guess Road Correctional Facility, Durham, North Carolina, 1984; coordinator, 1985-88, director of research and publications, 1989-90, North Carolinians Against Racist and Religious Violence, Durham, North Carolina; freelance writer and consultant, 1991; visiting assistant professor, Department of English, Duke University, spring 1992; coordinator, United States Urban-Rural Mission of the World Council of Churches, Durham, North Carolina, from 1992. Regular contributor to *Southern Exposure,* from 1980; member, editorial collective, *Feminary: A Lesbian-Feminist Journal for the South,* 1977-83; member, board of directors, Center for Democratic Renewal, Atlanta, Georgia; board member, North Coalition for Lesbian and Gay Equality; founding board member, Southerners on New Ground. **Awards:** Wilson Lee Community Service Award, North Carolinians Against Racist and Religious Violence, 1990; North Carolina Pride Service Award, for lesbian-gay activism, 1994; finalist, Best Non-fiction Book Award, Southern Regional Council, 1994; finalist, Lambda Literary Award, for best biography/autobiography, 1994; Lambda Literary Award, Editor's Choice, 1994; Gustavus Myers Center on Human Rights, Outstanding Book on Human Rights in North America, 1994; Humanitarian Service Award, Men of All Colors Together, Winston-Salem, North Carolina chapter, 1996. **Address:** P. O. Box 240, Durham, North Carolina 27702, U.S.A.

WRITINGS

Nonfiction

With Leonard Zeskind, *Quarantines and Death: The Far Right's Homophobic Agenda.* Atlanta, Center for Democratic Renewal, 1991.
"Grassroots Coalition Building: Lessons from North Carolina," in *Fight the Right Action Kit,* edited by Sara Crary Gregory. Portland, Oregon, National Gay and Lesbian Task Force, Fight the Right, 1993.
With Editorial Collective, *We Are the Ones We Are Waiting for: Women of Color Organizing for Transformation.* Durham, North Carolina, Urban-Rural Mission, 1995.

Essays

"Southern Women Writing: Toward a Literature of Wholeness," in *Feminary* (Chapel Hill, North Carolina), Vol. 11, No. 1, 1980.
"Feminism and Disobedience: Conversations with Barbara Deming," in *Feminary,* (Chapel Hill, North Carolina), Vol. 11, No. 1-2, 1980; reprinted in *Reweaving the Web of Life: Feminism and Nonviolence,* edited by Pam McAllister, Philadelphia, New Society Publishers, 1982.
"My Mama's Dead Squirrel and Southern Humor," in *Feminary,* Vol. 11, No. 3, 1981.

"Lines I Dare to Write: Lesbian Writing in the South," in *Southern Exposure* (Durham, North Carolina), summer 1981.

"Delicate Conversations," in *Growing Up Southern: Southern Exposure Looks at Childhood, Then and Now,* edited by Chris Mayfield. New York, Pantheon Books, 1981.

"I Lead Two Lives: Confessions of a Closet Baptist," in *Lesbian Studies: Present and Future,* edited by Margaret Cruikshank. Old Westbury, N.Y. Feminist Press, 1982; reprinted in *Reading for Difference: Texts on Gender, Race, and Class,* edited by Melissa Barth, Thomas McLaughlin, and James Winders, Fort Worth, Texas, Harcourt Brace Jovanovich College Publishers, 1993.

"Gay-Baiting: Anatomy of an Election," in *Southern Exposure,* September/October 1984.

My Mama's Dead Squirrel: Lesbian Essays on Southern Culture. Ithaca, New York, Firebrand Books, 1985.

"Barbara Deming: 1917-1984," in *Southern Exposure,* March/June 1985.

"Homophobia and the University Community," in *Iris* (Charlottesville, Virginia), spring/summer 1989.

"Nothing Can Stop Us Now—But From What?" in *Outlook* (California), winter 1989.

"An Organizer's Memoir," in *Bridges* (Eugene, Oregon), spring/summer 1992.

Memoir of a Race Traitor. Boston, Massachusetts, South End Press, 1994.

"Visibility and Backlash," in *A Question of Equality: Lesbian and Gay Politics in America Since Stonewall,* edited by David Deitcher. New York, Scribner, 1995.

"Fear to Joy: Fighting the Klan," in *Frontline Feminism 1975-1995: Essays from Sojourner's First 20 Years,* edited by Karen Kahn. San Francisco, Aunt Lute Books, 1995.

"The Real Thing? A Look at the Underside of the Atlanta Olympics," in *North Carolina Independent* (Durham, North Carolina), 28 July 1996.

"'Les' Beijing," in *The Wild Good: Lesbian Photographs and Writings on Love,* edited by Beatrix Gates. New York, Doubleday, 1996.

"Dangerously Rising Conservatism in the United States: Racism, Sexism and Homophobia," in *Look at the World through Women's Eyes: Plenary Speeches from the NGO Forum on Women,* edited by Eva Friedlander. New York, NGO Forum on Women, Beijing '95 Inc., 1996.

Other

The Tree of Life in the Poetry of W.B. Yeats (dissertation). Durham, North Caroloina, Duke University, 1980.

Living in a House I Do Not Own (poem). Durham, North Carolina, Night Heron Press, 1982.

With Editorial Team, *When Hate Groups Come to Town* (manual). Atlanta, Center for Democratic Renewal, 1993.

*

Manuscript Collections: Manuscript Collections, Special Collections Library, Duke University, Durham, North Carolina.

Interviews: "Writer/Activist Mab Segrest Confronts Racism: An Interview" by Jean Hardisty, in *Sojourner: The Women's Forum* (Cambridge, Massachusetts), August 1994.

Critical Sources: *My Mama's Dead Squirrel: Lesbian Essays on Southern Culture* by Mab Segrest, Firebrand, 1985; "Writer/Activist Mab Segrest Confronts Racism: An Interview" by Jean Hardisty, in *Sojourner: The Women's Forum* (Cambridge, Massachusetts), August 1994, 1B-2B; *Memoir of a Race Traitor* by Mab Segrest, South End Press, 1994; "Visibility and Backlash" by Mab Segrest, in *A Question of Equality: Lesbian and Gay Politics in America Since Stonewall,* edited by David Deitcher, Scribner, 1995; review of *Memoir of a Race Traitor* by Maryon Gray, in *Race Traitor* (Cambridge, Massachusetts), winter 1995, 90-97; review of *Memoir of a Race Traitor* by E. Broidy, in *Choice* (Chicago), January 1995, 862; unpublished interview with Mab Segrest by Faye A. Chadwell, October 1996.

*   *   *

A well-respected organizer for civil rights, Mab Segrest has striven for social change and justice and has documented acts of racist, religious, and homophobic violence, mostly in North Carolina during the 1980s. Her works represent crucial threads in the larger tapestry of writing by white lesbian activists and authors such as Lillian Smith and Barbara Deming, writing which weaves personal history and experiences with journalistic chronicles of the South's divisive political struggles over racial issues. She told Faye Chadwell in an interview: "I was motivated to become involved in working against the Klan because I saw that what I had run from in Alabama was recurring in North Carolina. I didn't want to keep running. The work I do as an adult is also work I couldn't do as a child. I engage in this work because I want to do what adults of my childhood did not."

Prior to her grassroots organizing, Segrest taught for several years at a small Baptist college in North Carolina. During this time she became involved with the Feminary, a North Carolina-based lesbian-feminist collective, which produced a journal of the same name. *Living in a House I Do Not Own,* a chapbook of verse filled with images of insects, fruits, and flowers, was a product of her experience with Feminary. Part of the small feminist press movement, this editorial collective greatly influenced Segrest's career and writing, helping to launch her investigation of racism as an organizer and a writer. In *Memoir of a Race Traitor,* Segrest writes: "*What did it mean to be lesbians in the South?* we Feminarians asked ourselves and our readers. The query brought us face to face with a potent mixture: the racism of a former slave system, the capitalism that generated it, and the misogyny and homophobia that also held it in place."

In 1983, Segrest began anti-Klan work in North Carolina. By 1985 she was working as the coordinator for North Carolinians Against Racist and Religious Violence (NCARRV). Her first collection of essays, *My Mama's Dead Squirrel: Lesbian Essays on Southern Culture,* is essentially a record of Segrest's literal shift from the world of academia to the realm of activism. In the preface, Segrest herself describes the work as a movement from "literary criticism embedded in autobiography, to pure biography, to journalism that describes an objective reality I intend, with others, to alter." In addition to reminiscing about growing up and living as a lesbian in the South, early essays in this collection reflect Segrest's background as a literary scholar and demonstrate her understanding of Southern literature, especially women writers. The piece, "Lines I Dare: Southern Lesbian Writing" traces the legacy of Southern lesbian writers, from Angelina Weld Grimké, Carson McCullers, and Lillian Smith through to her own contemporaries,

Dorothy Allison and Minnie Bruce Pratt. Poet Adrienne Rich, who introduces this collection, describes the later entries as "bulletins from the front." These bulletins, specifically those under the rubric "Carolina Notebook," are the chrysalis for Segrest's documentation of racism and homophobia in North Carolina and in the United States.

One important piece in *My Mama's Dead Squirrel,* entitled "Gaybaiting: Anatomy of an Election," explains the use of homophobia in conservative North Carolina Senator Jesse Helms' successful bid for a United States Senate seat in 1984 against two-time North Carolina Governor Jim Hunt. While regionally important, this essay proves characteristic of Segrest's later works about homophobia and its threat to gay and lesbian liberation. As an organizer, Segrest has constantly exhorted that violence against gays and lesbians be considered a critical proportion of hate group activity. In the report *Quarantines: The Far Right's Homophobic Agenda,* a collaborative effort with another activist, Leonard Zeskind, she details hate group violence against gays and lesbians and discusses how right wing politicians and proponents such as Lyndon LaRouche, Jerry Falwell, and Paul Cameron have strategically employed homophobia as a tool for maintaining social control not just on a regional, but a national level.

Almost all of Segrest's work on homophobia provides evidence of perhaps her most most significant contribution to gay and lesbian politics and literature. She has consistently initiated the analysis of racism within the gay and lesbian community. She has also promoted resistance to racism, classism, and misogyny, while encouraging coalition building with people of color, feminists, and activists in the labor movement, as a strategy for far-reaching political transformation beyond just civil rights for gays and lesbians. In the essay she contributed to *A Question of Equality,* a companion piece to the similarly titled public TV documentary series on gay and lesbian equality, she urges: "When we are *visibly* racist toward one another, *visibly* sexist, *visibly* leaning ourselves and our organizations toward a power often brutally manifested in U.S. culture, we destroy community and undermine our claims to equality and fair treatment."

Segrest's experiences with NCARRV dominate the pages of *Memoir of a Race Traitor,* her second collection of essays. She painstakingly describes the impact of racist and homophobic murders in various North Carolina locales—specifically Greensboro, Robeson County, and Shelby—and her efforts at bringing the hate violence to public attention. Eventually, the intensity of the work took its toll, and just before she steps down from NCARRV's directorship, she concisely describes her emotional state: "I had become a woman haunted by the dead."

Memoir of a Race Traitor is also an ambitious effort to capture her ancestors' part in a racist history, noteworthy especially in the historical essay "On Being White and Other Lies: A History of Racism in the United States." Reviewer Maryon Gray explains that "Segrest incorporates into this history genealogical material on her own family beginning with their emigration from England in 1613 and placing them very specifically within the context of the development of capitalism and white supremacy in this country." While *My Mama's Dead Squirrel* had presented Segrest's immediate biological family, particularly her mother, for the first time to readers, Segrest's autobiographical elements figure even more importantly in *Memoir of A Race Traitor.* As *Choice* reviewer E. Broidy suggests, she chooses to tell stories about her family that others would not choose to tell, for example, how her relative Marvin Segrest killed black student activist Samuel Younge on Janu-

ary 3, 1966. Besides being an account of racist history, *Memoir of a Race Traitor* recounts Segrest's struggle to deal with this past as a white woman deemed a race traitor and the impact this struggle has on her personally and notably on her relationship to her mother and father. She describes her struggle with some resolution: "It made me a different person—not a *better* person—than either of my parents. To differentiate myself, I have had to accept the gifts they gave me, which paradoxically I could not do until I was sure I am my own person. 'When people have to choose, they go with their own race,' my mother had said, but she was wrong. It is not a matter of choosing one race or family and betraying another. The choice is for *justice? community? humanity? the glimpse that we are all one organism...?*"

Overall, Segrest's work and writing integrate several seemingly contradictory elements. She was trained as an academic, yet has toiled extensively in the field as a grassroots organizer and speaker. A white woman and a lesbian reared in a small Alabama town during the Civil Rights movement during the 1950s and 1960s, she has fought successfully against the re-emergence of the white supremacist movement in the South and for recognition of racism's impact within the gay and lesbian community. In *Memoir of a Race Traitor,* she also has blended a subjective, memoirist's account of her family's role and roots in racism and her participation as a lesbian organizing community response to hate violence with an objective reporting on hate group activities. In an interview with *Sojourner* writer Jean Hardisty, she comments on the primary and inherent tension between her role as a writer and as an organizer, "I think the hardest thing has been reconciling the two, which at times has felt like a kind of schizophrenia, and I've gone in and out of different periods where one or the other role was more predominant." She explains further, "...whatever peculiar strengths I bring as a writer, it's because I try to combine those two things."

—Faye A. Chadwell

SHOWALTER, Elaine

Nationality: American feminist, cultural critic, and educator. **Born:** Elaine Cottler in Cambridge, Massachusetts, 21 January 1941. **Education:** Bryn Mawr College, Pennsylvania, 1958-62, B.A. in English 1962; Brandeis University, Waltham, Massachusetts, M.A. in English 1964; University of California, Davis, Ph.D. in English 1970. **Family:** Married English Showalter in 1963; one daughter and one son. **Career:** Teaching assistant, becoming associate professor of English, University of California, 1964-78; assistant professor of English, Douglass College, New Brunswick, New Jersey, 1970; visiting professor of English and women's studies, University of Delaware, 1976-77; professor of English, Rutgers University, 1978-84; professor of English, from 1984, Avalon Foundation professor of humanities, from 1987, and English Department chairperson, 1990, Princeton University, New Jersey; visiting professor of Scholarly Criticism and Theory, Dartmouth College, 1986; visiting professor Salzburg, Austria, Seminars, 1988; Clarendon lectures, Oxford University, England, 1989; visiting scholar, Phi Beta Kappa, 1993-94. President, Princeton chapter, National Organization for Women, 1969; charter member of the newly formed Modern Language Association Commission on the

Status of Women in the Profession, 1971; reprints committee member, Feminist Press, 1972-75; editor, *Signs,* 1975, and *Women's Studies,* 1992; advisory group member, Virago Press, from 1978. **Awards:** Faculty research council fellow, Rutgers University, 1972-73; Christian and Mary Lindback Foundation Award for Distinguished Teaching at Rutgers University 1976; Guggenheim Fellowship, 1977-78; NEH summer stipend, 1981; John D. Rockefeller Fellowship, 1981-82; Rutgers Research Council Summer Travel Grant to Paris, 1983; NEH fellowship, 1988-89; Howard Behrman humanities award, Princeton University, 1989. **Address:** Princeton University, Department of English, McCosh Hall, Princeton, New Jersey, 08544-1099, U.S.A.

WRITINGS

Nonfiction

A Literature of Their Own: British Women Novelists from Brontë to Lessing. Princeton, Princeton University Press, 1977; London, Virago Press, 1978.

The Female Malady: Women, Madness, and English Culture, 1830-1980. New York, Pantheon Books, 1985; London, Virago Press, 1987.

Sexual Anarchy: Gender and Culture at the Fin de Siècle. New York and Toronto, Canada, Penguin Books, 1990.

Sister's Choice: Tradition and Change in American Women's Writing (Clarendon Lectures, 1989). New York and Oxford, Oxford University Press, 1991.

With Sander L. Gilman, Helen King, Roy Porter, and George Rousseau, *Hysteria Beyond Freud.* Berkeley, University of California Press, 1993.

Hystories: Hysterical Epidemics and Modern Culture. New York, Columbia University Press, 1997.

Editor

Women's Liberation and Literature. New York, Harcourt Brace Jovanovich, 1971.

These Modern Women: Autobiographies of American Women in the 1920s. Old Westbury, New York, Feminist Press. 1978.

The New Feminist Criticism: Essays on Women, Literature, and Theory. New York, Pantheon, Books, 1985.

Alternative Alcott. New Brunswick, New Jersey, and London, Rutgers University Press, 1988.

Speaking of Gender. New Brunswick, New Jersey, Routledge, 1989.

Modern American Women Writers. New York, Scribners, and Toronto, Canada, Collier Macmillan, 1991.

Daughters of Decadence. New Brunswick, New Jersey, Rutgers University Press, 1993.

Scribbling Women: Short Stories by Nineteenth-Century American Women. New York, Bowker, 1996.

Essays

With English Showalter, "Victorian Women and Menstruation," in *Victorian Studies* (Bloomington, Indiana), Vol. 14, 1970.

"Women Writers and Female Consciousness," in *Notes from the Second Year: Women's Liberation, Major Writings of the Radical Feminists.* New York, Radical Feminism, 1970.

"Women and the Literary Curriculum," in *College English* (Urbana, Illinois), May 1971.

"Women Writers and the Double Standard," in *Woman in Sexist Society,* edited by Vivian Gornick and Barbara Moran. New York, Basic Books, 1971.

"Killing the Angel in the House," in *Antioch Review* (Yellow Springs, Ohio), Vol. 32, 1973.

With Jean L'Espérance, "Research on Women in London," in *Women's Studies* (New York), Vol. 1, 1973.

"Dinah Mulock Craik and the Tactics of Sentiment: A Case Study in Victorian Female Authorship," in *Feminist Studies* (College Park, Maryland), Vol. 2, No. 2/3, 1975.

"Literary Criticism," in *Signs: A Journal of Women in Culture and Society* (Chicago, Illinois), Vol. 1, Winter 1975.

"*A Passage to India* as Marriage Fiction," in *Women and Literature,* Vol. 5, 1977.

"Toward a Feminist Poetics," in *Women Writing and Writing About Women,* edited by Mary Jacobus. London, Croom Hulm, and New York, Barnes and Noble, 1979.

"The Unmanning of the Mayor of Casterbridge," in *Critical Approaches to Hardy,* edited by Dale Kramer. London, Macmillan, 1979.

"Feminist Criticism in the Wilderness," in *Critical Inquiry* (Chicago, Illinois), 1981.

Introduction, *The Beth Book* by Sarah Grand. London, Virago Classic Reprints, 1980; New York, Dial, 1981.

"Women and Violence: Rethinking the Seventies," in *Antioch Review* (Yellow Springs, Ohio), Vol. 39, spring 1981.

"Critical Cross-Dressing: Male Feminists and the Woman of the Year," in *Raritan* (New Brunswick, New Jersey), Vol. 3, fall 1983.

Introduction, *The Odd Women* by George Gissing. New York, New American Library, 1983.

"Women's Time, Women's Space: Writing the History of Feminist Criticism," in *Tulsa Studies in Women's Literature* (Oklahoma), fall 1984.

"Women Writers and American Processions: Feminist Criticism 1984," in *Ontario Review* (Princeton, New Jersey), Vol. 21, 1984-85.

With Carol Smith, "A Nurturing Relationship: A Conversation with Maxine Kumin and Anne Sexton," in *No Evil Star: Selected Essays, Interviews and Prose of Anne Sexton,* edited by Steven Colburn. Ann Arbor, University of Michigan Press, 1985.

Introduction, *Red Pottage* by Mary Cholmondeley. London, Virago Press, and New York, Penguin, Viking, 1985.

"Representing Ophelia," in *Shakespeare and the Question of Theory,* edited by Patricia Parker and Geoffrey Hartman. London, Methuen, 1985.

"Piecing and Writing," in *The Poetics of Gender,* edited by Nancy K. Miller. New York, Columbia University Press, 1986.

"Shooting the Rapids: Feminist Criticism in the Mainstream," *Oxford Literary Review* (Stirling, Scotland), Vol. 8, No. 1-2, 1986.

"The Sins of the Fathers: Syphilis, Sexuality, and the Fiction of the Fin-de-Siècle," in *Sex, Politics, and Science in the Nineteenth-Century Novel: Selected Papers for the English Institute, 1983-84,* edited by Ruth Yeazell. Baltimore, Maryland, Johns Hopkins University Press, 1986.

"Women Writers Between the Wars," in *Columbia Literary History,* edited by Emory Elliott et al. New York, Columbia University Press, 1987.

"The Other Bostonians: Gender and Literary Study," in *The Yale Journal of Criticism* (Baltimore, Maryland), spring, 1988.

"A Criticism of Our Own: Autonomy and Assimilation in Afro-American and Feminist Literary Theory," in *The Future of Literary Theory,* edited by Ralph Cohen. New York, Routledge, 1989.

"Feminism and Literature," in *Literary Theory Today.* Ithaca, New York, Cornell University Press, 1990.

"Rethinking the Seventies: Women Writers and Violence," in *Women and Violence in Literature: An Essay Collection,* edited by Katherine-Anne Ackley. New York, Garland, 1990.

"The Death of the Lady Novelist," in *The New American Studies: Essays from Representations,* edited by Philip Fischer. Berkeley, University of California Press, 1991.

"Miranda and Cassandra: The Discourse of the Feminist Intellectual," in *The Tradition and the Talents of Women,* edited by Florence Howe. Urbana, University of Illinois Press, 1991.

"Killing the Angel in the House: The Autonomy of Women Writers," in *Antioch Review* (Yellow Springs, Ohio), Vol. 50, No. 1-2, winter 1992.

"Retrenchments," in *Persuasions: Journal of the Jane Austen Society of North America* (Lancaster, Pennsylvania), Vol. 15, December 1993.

"On Hysterical Narrative" in *Narrative* (Columbus, Ohio), Vol. 1, No. 1, January 1993.

"American Gynocritics" in *American Literary History* (Cary, North Carolina), Vol. 5, No. 1, spring 1993.

*

Interviews: "An Interview With Elaine Showalter" by Susan Fraiman, in *Critical Texts: A Review of Theory and Criticism* (New York), Vol. 4, No. 2, 1987, 7-17.

Critical Sources: "Sander Gilman, Helen King, Roy Porter, George Rousseau, and Elaine Showalter" by Mark S. Micale, in *Bulletin of the History of Medicine* (Baltimore, Maryland), Vol. 68, No. 2, 365-369; "Elaine Showalter" by Marianne DeKoven, in *Dictionary of Literary Biography,* Detroit, Gale, Vol. 67, 1988, 260-67; *Sexual/Textual Politics: Feminist Literary Theory* by Toril Moi, London and New York, Methuen, 1985; "Varieties of Feminist Criticism" by Janet Kaplan, in *Making a Difference: Feminist Literary Criticism,* edited by Coppelia Kahn, London, Methuen, 1985.

*   *   *

Elaine Showalter is best known for her ground-breaking publication *A Literature of Their Own* in which she introduced the concept of a literary tradition for women. She has since made many other contributions not only to feminist criticism of British and American literature, but also to gender and cultural studies. Much of her writing published between 1985 and 1995 analyzed the social construction of gender, particularly in the literature and culture of the fin de siècle.

Upon its publication in 1978, *A Literature of Their Own* was among the first revisionary works which attempted to create a literary history for British women novelists. Showalter divided women authors ranging from Brontë to Lessing into three historical phases: Feminine, Feminist, and Female. The feminine authors of the early nineteenth century imitated male writers and wrote in the sentimental romance tradition while the feminist authors of the late 1800s and early 1900s adopted voices of revolt in an attempt to change standards and values. The writers of our own time were finally able to speak in authentic female voices. A chapter on Woolf rejected her androgynous ideal as a denial of her femininity; the book did not specifically discuss the many significant lesbian relationships of the time period under consideration, but alluded to the "bonds of the female subculture," in Mrs. Humphry Ward's books, for instance.

In two essays written in the 1980s, "Toward a Poetics of Gender" and "Feminist Criticism in the Wilderness," Showalter promoted "gynocritics," originally a French term applied to a woman-centered type of feminist literary criticism, freed from the "linear absolutes of male literary history." Consequently, she rejected more traditional "feminist critiques" as too informed by patriarchal discourse.

Having established "a coherent theory of female literary creativity," as Showalter said in an interview with Susan Fraiman, she developed an interest in the history of psychiatry. *The Female Malady* underscored the association, in the minds of the nineteenth-century English medical profession, between femininity and madness. This book illustrated Showalter's progression in thought as she observed how psychiatrists and patriarchy collaborated in defining womanhood and madness in response to the increasing demands from the so-called New Women, suffragettes and others, who began to make inroads into the male domain. When hysteria, formerly defined as a woman's nervous disorder, began to affect men after World War I, modern psychiatry was born. Showalter speculated that the men's illnesses were due to their victimization and their sudden fear of not being able to fulfill gender role expectations. Her chapter in *Hysteria Beyond Freud* advanced a similar argument.

Speaking of Gender is a collection of essays dealing with various types of gender studies. Showalter's introduction, "The Rise of Gender," demonstrated her transition from a woman-centered feminism to gender studies. She stated that "the introduction to gender into the field of literary studies marks a new phase in feminist criticism" that was largely due to the strides made by African-American, gay, and poststructural criticism.

While Showalter's earlier writing displayed her awareness of the constructedness of femininity, her greater concern for gender in general and lesser emphasis on "gynocritics" has forced her to focus more attention on gay and lesbian issues, as evidenced in a chapter on "Decadence, Homosexuality, and Feminism" in *Sexual Anarchy: Gender and Culture at the Fin de Siècle.* This study examined the fluid borderlines of genres and gender unveiled by the chaos and scandals that mark the end of centuries, particularly those of the nineteenth century as well as of the current one.

She considered *Sexual Anarchy* primarily "a history of sexual change in the late nineteenth century" and detailed the many incidences of overt and covert homosexuality. Showalter thus contributed an important insight into cultural and literary history by drawing attention to the increasing visibility of gays and the fears and resentment this phenomenon evoked. Her review of nineteenth-century medical history shed light on misconceptions about male and female sexuality. New Women, who in public opinion were equated with effeminate decadent artists, sought new fictional forms, and the resulting confusion in literary genres eventually affected gender roles. Writers like Rudyard Kipling, for instance, suddenly began to write in the feminine mode of romance but redefined it with stories of male bonding in exotic, threatening, and feminine places.

According to Showalter, Robert Louis Stevenson's *Dr. Jekyll and Mr. Hyde* illustrated "the fable of fin-de-siècle homosexual panic, the discovery and resistance of the homosexual self." Women's limited possibilities for expression, however, led to frequent neuroses and other nervous disorders. The fear of women's awakening sexuality manifested itself in art and literature through particularly violent scenes or (un-)veiling of the woman's body. In Oscar Wilde's *Salomé,* Showalter perceived a "veiled homosexual desire for the male body" (151). She also pointed out that decadent male writing was often accompanied by a large degree of misogyny, making those who saw homosexuality as the "highest most perfect evolutionary stage of gender differentiation" into supporters of the patriarchy. According to Showalter, similar conflicts persist between some feminists and gay liberationists today even though conservatives view them collectively as destructive elements linked to the spread of AIDS.

In *Daughters of Decadence,* Showalter collected the works of a group of women writers reminiscent of the male aesthetes of the fin de siècle, whose writing was often considered "unmanly and effeminate." For women as well as for men, the end of the century ushered in a time of experimentation and exploration. It is particularly in this often overlooked short fiction that Showalter discerned the authors' attempt to "purge aestheticism and decadence of their misogyny."

The essays collected in *Sister's Choice* expanded the application of gynocritics from British to American women writers. Showalter fully embraced the multiple perspectives of American culture and corrected many of the critical flaws Toril Moi found in *A Literature of Their Own.* Showalter mentioned the close female friendships of the nineteenth century and the "sexual solidarity" which shaped the "homosocial world of women's culture."

Convinced that academic scholarship must remain accessible to a wide audience, Showalter regularly contributes movie and book reviews to *People* magazine and to the *Times Literary Supplement,* popularizing her ideas concerning gender. She has also edited the works of some minor writers, such as Christina Rosetti and Dinah Mulock Craig, Louisa May Alcott and Mary Cholmondeley, and has published these with insightful introductions.

—Susanna Hoeness-Krupsaw

SILVERA, Makeda

Nationality: Jamaican-Canadian short story writer and editor. **Born:** Kingston, Jamaica, 1955; immigrated to Toronto, Canada, 1967. **Family:** Two children. **Career:** Worked as typist-receptionist, freelance journalist, and editorial assistant, *Share* newspaper, Toronto; co-founder, later managing editor, *Sister Vision: Black Women and Women of Colour Press,* Toronto, from 1985. Member of editorial collective, *Fireweed,* Toronto; community activist. **Address:** c/o Sister Vision Press, P.O. Box 217, Station E, Toronto, Ontario M6H 4E2, Canada.

Writings

Short Stories

Remembering G. and Other Stories. Toronto, Sister Vision Press, 1991.

Her Head a Village and Other Stories. Vancouver, Press Gang Publishers, 1994.

Nonfiction (for young adults)

Growing Up Black: A Resource Manual for Black Youth. Toronto, Sister Vision Press, 1989.

Editor

Silenced: Talks with Working-class Caribbean Women about Their Lives and Struggles as Domestic Workers in Canada. Williams Wallace Publishers, 1983; Toronto, Sister Vision Press, 1989.
Fireworks: The Best of Fireweed. Toronto, Women's Press, 1986.
The Issue Is 'Ism: Women of Colour Speak Out. Toronto, Sister Vision Press, 1989.
Piece of My Heart: A Lesbian of Colour Anthology. Toronto, Sister Vision Press, 1991.
The Other Woman: Women of Colour in Contemporary Canadian Literature. Toronto, Sister Vision Press, 1995.

*

Interviews: "All Those Selves and Experiences" by Jeffrey Canton, in *Paragraph* (Stratford, Ontario), Vol. 14, No. 2, 1992, 3-6; "The Characters Would Not Have It" by Interlocutor, in *The Other Woman: Women of Colour in Contemporary Canadian Literature,* edited by Makeda Silvera, Toronto, Sister Vision Press, 1995, 405-420.

*   *   *

An impulse to break silences motivates Makeda Silvera's various endeavors as fiction writer, essayist, interviewer, editor, publisher, and political activist. The silences Silvera targets are those produced by the oppressive forces of racism, homophobia, sexism, and classism; in particular, her work demands that we become alert to the intersection of these "'isms." Refusing to ignore the toll exacted by any one of these pressures, Silvera undertakes the courageous and delicate work of articulating the ways that liberatory projects can be undermined through the enforcement of certain silences *within* oppressed communities. In an issue of *Fireweed* entitled *The Issue Is 'Ism: Women of Colour Speak Out,* Silvera takes on the racism and classism propping up mainstream feminist movements; appearing in the same issue is her essay, "An Open Letter to Rastafarian Sistrens," which addresses the internal sexism of the Rastafarian movement. Raising issues of inequity or hatred internal to movements which are themselves imperiled demands not only acuity of vision, but exceptional bravery. In her introduction to *Piece of My Heart: A Lesbian of Colour Anthology,* for example, Silvera notes that the risk of losing family attendant on coming out is particularly great for women of color: "This is frequently what silences us, because without that home, without family, we often have only that hostile white world."

In the title story of Silvera's collection *Her Head a Village,* a black woman author struggles to write, weighed down by the knowledge that "what made writing dangerous for her was who she was—Black/woman/lesbian/mother/worker." Clearly, as *Her Head a Village* and Silvera's other works demonstrate, these identities render writing at the same time a danger and an imperative. Breaking silences isn't simply an unveiling, but an on-going process; the act of writing is itself an exploration, a way to discover and create realities. In *The Other Woman,* Silvera explains, "I write to understand history and family, I write to make sense out of a world that's full of nonsense, that can be vile and cruel." *Her Head a Village* depicts characters dealing with various injurious oppressions: a lesbian couple facing the enforced closeting and immanent violence produced by homophobia, a woman infantilized and intimidated by a welfare clerk, a domestic worker returning from a Jamaican vacation shamed and interrogated by immigration officers at Toronto's Pearson International Airport.

This last scenario is elaborated in "Caribbean Chameleon," one of the stories in which Silvera employs her Jamaican dialect. In her earlier collection, *Remembering G.,* Silvera reserves patois for dialogue; it inflects the voices in "Out de Candle," for example, a story about adolescent girls exploring their sexuality together. "Caribbean Chameleon," however, conveys the entire narrative through dialect. In her *Other Woman* interview Silvera remarked on the evolution of this narrative voice, recalling: "The woman was angry, and her anger could not be expressed in Standard English—it didn't have the words, and the story would not make sense unless I wrote it in patwah." Another aesthetic/political shift between *Remembering G.* and *Her Head a Village* is evidenced by the lack of a glossary in the latter. While Jamaican terms are explicated for the reader at the conclusion of *Remembering G., Her Head a Village* addresses speakers of the patois first, compelling others to do their own research. Silvera's work demonstrates that the way stories are told is as important as the fact of their telling.

While Silvera's short fiction gives voice to a range of experiences disavowed by the mainstream, it is in her capacity as publisher and editor that she truly gives voice to others. In *Silenced,* for example, she collects the personal narratives of Caribbean domestic workers in Canada and, in *The Other Woman,* she offers a gathering of interviews and essays which reflect the creative, intellectual, spiritual, and political diversity of women who come together (or are at times problematically lumped together) under the rubric "women of color." Perhaps her most significant contribution to gay and lesbian culture is the anthology, *Piece of My Heart,* which is the first collection of writings by lesbians of color living in Canada and the United States. This book is driven by an attention to diversity not only in terms of its representation of identities, but also in terms of genre and motive. Poetry, fiction, drama, letters, journal entries, and articles comprise a volume which offers testimony and critique as well as lustful, loving celebration. Included here is Silvera's own ground-breaking essay, "Man Royals and Sodomites: Some Thoughts on the Invisibility of Afro-Caribbean Lesbians," which investigates the suppressed histories of Afro-Caribbean lesbians in Jamaica and in Canada. This article reflects the ethic propelling all of Silvera's work, an ethic she captions in her introduction to *Piece of My Heart* when she cites Audre Lorde's phrase, "Your silence will not protect you."

—Susan Holbrook

SMITH, Lillian (Eugenia)

Nationality: American novelist and author of nonfiction. **Born:** Jasper, Florida, 12 December 1897. **Education:** Piedmont College, Demorest, Georgia, 1915-16; Peabody Conservatory, Balti-

more, Maryland, 1917-18, 1919-22; Columbia University Teachers College, New York City, 1927-28. **Family:** Companion of Paula Snelling, 1930-66. **Career:** Held a variety of jobs including principal, Dillard, Georgia, 1915, and Tiger, Georgia, 1918; volunteer, Student Nursing Corps, 1918; music teacher, Virginia School, Huckow, China, 1922-25; director of girls' summer camp, Clayton, Georgia, 1925-48; co-editor, with Paula Snelling, and columnist, *South Today* (originally *Pseudopodia,* then *North Georgia Review*), 1936-45; columnist, *Chicago Defender,* 1948-49; representative in India of United States State Department, 1954-55; book reviewer, *Chicago Tribune Books Today,* 1964-66. Member, American Famine Commission, 1946; **Awards:** Julius Rosenwald Fellowship, 1939, 1940; L.H.D.: Howard University, 1950; Oberlin College, 1950; Atlanta University, 1957. **Died:** Atlanta, Georgia, of cancer, 28 September 1966.

Writings

Novels

Strange Fruit. New York, Reynal and Hitchcock, 1944; foreword by Fred Hobson, Athens, University of Georgia Press, 1985.
One Hour. New York, Harcourt, Brace, 1959; introduction by Margaret Rose Gladney, Chapel Hill and London, University of North Carolina Press, 1994.

Nonfiction

Killers of the Dream. New York, Norton, 1949; revised and expanded by the author, New York, Norton, 1961.
The Journey. Cleveland and New York, World Publishing, 1954.
Now Is the Time. New York, Viking, 1955.
Our Faces, Our Words. New York, Norton, 1964.

Other

With Esther Smith, *Strange Fruit* (play; adaptation of her novel; produced Broadway, 1945).
Memory of a Large Christmas (autobiography). New York, Norton, 1962.
From the Mountain: An Anthology of the Magazine Successively Titled Pseudopodia, the North Georgia Review, and South Today, edited with an introduction by Helen White and Redding S. Sugg, Jr. (nonfiction). Memphis, Memphis State University Press, 1972.
The Winner Names the Age: A Collection of Writings by Lillian Smith, edited by Michelle Cliff, preface by Paula Snelling (speeches and essays). New York, Norton, 1978.
How Am I to Be Heard? Letters of Lillian Smith, edited by Margaret Rose Gladney. Chapel Hill and London, University of North Carolina Press, 1993.

*

Manuscript Collections: Lillian Smith Collection, Rare Books and Manuscripts Department, University of Florida Libraries, Gainesville; Lillian Smith Collection, Gargrett Rare Books and Manuscript Library, University of Georgia Libraries, Athens; Lillian Smith Collection, Special Collections, Robert W. Woodruff Library, Emory University, Atlanta, Georgia.

Biography: *Lillian Smith: A Southerner Confronting the South* by Anne C. Loveland, Baton Rouge and London, Louisiana State University Press, 1986.

Critical Sources: *Lillian Smith* by Louise Blackwell and Frances Clay, New York, Twayne, 1971; *Tell About the South: The Southern Rage to Explain* by Fred Hobson, Baton Rouge and London, Louisiana State University Press, 1983; "Foreword" by Fred Hobson, in *Strange Fruit* by Lillian Smith, Athens, University of Georgia Press, 1985, vii-xviii; *How Am I to Be Heard? Letters of Lillian Smith,* edited by Margaret Rose Gladney, Chapel Hill and London, University of North Carolina Press, 1993; *Feminine Sense in Southern Memoir: Smith, Glasgow, Welty, Hellman, Porter, and Hurston* by Will Brantley, Jackson, University Press of Mississippi, 1993; "Introduction" by Margaret Rose Gladney, in *One Hour* by Lillian Smith, Chapel Hill and London, University of North Carolina Press, 1994, vii-xiii.

*   *   *

Lillian Smith was unique among writers of the mid-twentieth century American South for any number of reasons, perhaps the most significant of which was her political activism to combat racism before and during the Civil Rights Movement. In an era in which William Faulkner, arguably the foremost southern author of the day, publicly advocated moderate means to negotiate segregation in the South, Smith stridently condemned the forced separation of races and demanded its immediate end, often much to the irritation of fellow white southerners. As early as the 1930s, in her essays and reviews in *Pseudopodia,* the magazine she edited with her partner Paula Snelling, Smith advocated racial equality, a radical move within the context of the Deep South during the Depression. She continued these assertions throughout her work of the next two decades, rarely shying away from overt political advocacy. Critic Will Brantley rightly maintains that "Smith was a propagandist, a reformer, and a person interested in public affairs, and she could never fully resist the inclination to address her concerns head on."

Indeed, *Now Is the Time* (1955) was her forthright public support of *Brown v. the Board of Education,* the Supreme Court's 1954 ruling that desegregated American public schools, and *Our Faces, Our Words* (1964) was her tribute to the workers of the Civil Rights Movement. For efforts such as these, Smith has come to be considered "a phenomenon: the most courageous, outspoken, and uncompromising white southern liberal of her generation," according to Fred Hobson in his foreword to the 1985 reprint of Smith's first novel, *Strange Fruit.* In her introduction to Smith's letters, Margaret Rose Gladney echoes Hobson, characterizing Smith as "the most liberal and outspoken of white southern writers on issues of social, and especially racial, injustice."

It was Smith's treatment of race in the American South that made *Strange Fruit* such a scandalous success. Her narrative centers around a miscegenistic affair between a white man, Tracy Deen, and a black woman, Nonnie Anderson, that ends with an ill-fated lynching of an innocent black man. As the book swept the nation in the last years of World War II, the city of Boston banned the novel, and it was even briefly prohibited from the United States mail for its frank language and explicit images of interracial sexual interactions. Miscegenation was and is not, however, the only representation of sexuality to disturb readers. The subplot of *Strange*

Fruit features Tracy's sister, Laura, and her homoerotically-charged relationship with Jane Hardy, an older woman who functions as a surrogate mother to Laura since her own mother is cold, calculating, and incessantly preoccupied with social propriety. Smith encodes the eroticism of Jane and Laura's relationship in a clay figurine of a naked woman that Laura sculpts with Jane as her model. Thus, when Alma Deen, Laura's mother, destroys the sculpture, Smith symbolically represents the forces of homophobia and compulsory heterosexuality.

Hurt by negative critical assessments of *Strange Fruit*'s artistry, Smith responded by writing *One Hour* (1959), an often laboriously complex novel and a fictional companion volume to *The Journey* (1954). An attempt to move away from issues of southern race, the novel is, at its broadest, an interrogation of McCarthyism of the 1950s, focusing on a young girl's accusations of sexual assault by a young scientist, Mark Channing. But, like *Strange Fruit, One Hour* also includes marginalized representations of same-sex desire between women. Mark's wife, Grace, confesses to the novel's narrator of a youthful affair with an unnamed camp counselor, designated only as the Woman. It is with horror that Grace eventually realizes that the Woman who taught her "about tenderness and passion" at the camp, "who had seemed to her to have come out of a myth, who did not quite belong in the ordinary world, was nothing but a homosexual." After much struggle with her own sexuality, Grace assumes a heterosexual identity and seemingly exorcises the memory of the Woman. When news of the Woman's suicide reaches Grace, however, she breaks down, forced to admit how much the relationship has meant to her.

A striking characteristic of Smith's representations of lesbians and lesbianism is that they typically arise out of an older woman's education and mentoring of a younger one. This is perhaps not surprising, given Smith's heavy investment in Freudian psychoanalysis. She seems to have accepted Freud's notions of the creation of lesbian sexual identity as an unsuccessful resolution of the child's desire for the mother. Thus, Smith repeatedly focuses on the young girl who must negotiate an estranged mother and find a surrogate in another older woman. This espousal of Freudian doctrine may also have been assisted by Smith's own personal experiences while she directed Laurel Falls Camp, her family's summer camp for girls. Her letters document that she repeatedly witnessed the crushes that younger girls had on the older counselors, women who often facilitated such investments. Smith's own relationship with Paula Snelling was structured similarly. While their difference in age was not dramatic, Smith's letters nevertheless reveal that she thought of herself as the aggressive partner who shaped the relationship while Snelling was somewhat more passively controlled.

Smith rarely wrote of gay men and frankly maintained that there was a significant gulf between gayness and lesbianism. For instance, in a 1962 letter included in Margaret Rose Gladney's recent edition of Smith's correspondences, she asserts that "female homosexuality is, in my opinion, as different as day from night from male homosexuality." In contrast, there is the distinct possibility that Smith wrote even more extensively of lesbianism within both her correspondences and other fiction than her published works reveal; however, thousands of letters as well as unpublished manuscripts of two novels and a novella were destroyed by vandals' fire in November 1955.

—Gary Richards

SOTOMAYOR, Sally. *See* **GEARHART, Sally Miller.**

STAMBOLIAN, George

Nationality: American educator, author, and editor. **Born:** Bridgeport, Connecticut, 10 April 1938. **Education:** Dartmouth College, Amherst, Massachusetts, B.A. 1960; University of Wisconsin, Madison, M.A. 1961, Ph.D. 1969; studied at the Sorbonne, University of Paris, France, 1962-63. **Family:** Companion of Michael Hampton. **Career:** Professor of French and comparative literature, Wellesley College, Massachusetts, 1965-91. Member of the Modern Language Association of America, American Association of University Professors, Societé des Amis de Marcel Proust, Proust Research Association, Beckett Society, Northeast Theater Conference, and Phi Beta Kappa; frequent contributor to periodicals, including *Advocate, Christopher Street,* and *Journal of Popular Culture.* **Died:** New York City, of complications from AIDS, 22 December 1991.

Writings

Nonfiction

Marcel Proust and the Creative Encounter. Chicago, University of Chicago Press, 1972.
Editor, *Twentieth Century Fiction: Essays for Germaine Bree.* New Brunswick, New Jersey, Rutgers University Press, 1975.
Homosexualities and French Literature. Ithaca, New York, Cornell University Press, 1979.
Male Fantasies/Gay Realities. New York, Seahorse Press, 1984.

Editor

Men on Men: Best New Gay Fiction. New York, New American Library, 1986.
Men on Men 2: Best New Gay Fiction. New York, New American Library, 1988.
Men on Men 3: Best New Gay Fiction. New York, Dutton, 1990.
Men on Men 4: Best New Gay Fiction. New York, Dutton, 1992.

*

Critical Sources: "The Art and Politics of the Male Image" by Sam Hardison and George Stambolian, in *Christopher Street* (New York), Vol. 4, No. 7, March 1980, 14-22; "George Stambolian Anthology Editor" (obituary), in *New York Times* (New York), 26 December 1991, D14; "George Stambolian, 54: Wellesley Professor, and Book Editor" (obituary), in *Boston Globe* (Boston), 24 December 1991, 52; "George Stambolian: The Professor of Desire" by Andrew Holleran, in *Christopher Street* (New York), Vol. 14, No. 17, Issue 173, 1992, 3-5; "Remembering George Stambolian" by Jane Troxell, in *Lambda Book Report* (Washington, D.C.), Vol. 3, No. 2, March/April 1992, 4.

*　　　*　　　*

For over 25 years George Stambolian taught French literature and contemporary drama at Wellesley College, retiring in May of 1991. He was an advocate and leader for the recognition of the field of gay literature. He wrote several academic books on French literature, and introduced works of preeminent gay authors such as Edmund White, Felice Picano, and Ethan Mordden in his groundbreaking *Men on Men* series. Articles by Stambolian also frequently appeared in many gay publications such as the *Advocate, New York Native,* and *Christopher Street.*

Stambolian was born and raised in Bridgeport, Connecticut. A child of Armenian heritage, he was filled with stories of the ancestral homeland, some of which he hoped to publish into a book. Fortunately, one of the stories "In My Father's Car," did make it into print and was published in *Men on Men 3.*

After graduating from the University of Wisconsin, Stambolian began teaching at Wellesley College in Massachusetts. His French literature classes were imbued with his deep appreciation of Marcel Proust and titillating tidbits of gay life. Besides teaching French literature he also taught courses on the nude, and gay fiction. He often spoke warmly of his former students, especially Joan Nestle, for whom he defined lesbian lust as "wetness."

Stambolian's first book, *Marcel Proust and the Creative Encounter,* reflected strongly upon his expertise in Proust and French literature. The books which were published later expounded upon his deep appreciation of sex and exultation of the body. He cherished the human form not only in the flesh but in all of its artistic expressions, whether sculpture, canvas, photography, or literature. Stambolian later compiled a series of interviews with an exhibitionist, a voyeur, and a masochist in *Male Fantasies/Gay Realities.* In 1979 he drew together academic literary circles and gay history into the groundbreaking title *Homosexualities and French Literature,* paving the way for future academic studies on gay issues.

An ardent supporter of gay literature, Stambolian believed he could reinvigorate the field of American literature by contesting its underlying social and literary assumptions. He provided the initial link between two unrelated spheres: academia and the gay community. He acted as a catalyst for the development of the field of gay literature, and its exponential growth. Because of Stambolian's work gay studies is now taught in schools, giving access to an ever widening audience, who previously lacked the availability to such materials. Gay fiction opened doors to a diverse community whose identity could no longer be ignored.

In the opening paragraph of *Men on Men* Stambolian waxes philosophically about gay literature, "In matters of gay writing I confess to having the zeal of a missionary for whom nothing is more tempting than a chance to reach new audiences." Or the chance to dispel "the notion so often repeated by hostile critics that gay fiction must inevitably be second rate because homosexuality itself is somehow incomplete."

Under the editorship of Stambolian the *Men on Men* series proved to be a dramatic success. In each of the four volumes in the series AIDS was presented as subject and killer of the writers included. Stambolian emphasized the need for AIDS witnessing in the stories. Through the series he also fought the denial of a gay history and identity along with the conscription of a homosexual identity lacking individuality.

In the wake of the accolades accorded to the *Men on Men* series, Stambolian scouted for new gay writers to complement his publishers repertoire. One of the authors he discovered for his American publisher was British author Neil Barrett, who had just completed *Ready to Catch Him Should He Fall*. In spite of his illness, his boundless enthusiasm and energy in searching for new authors never waned. He managed to attend many of the gay literary conferences along the way, including the Out/Write conferences and the Lambda Awards.

With money left in a trust following the death of authors Michael Grumley and Robert Ferro in the late 1980s, Stambolian and Steve Greco organized and administered the Ferro-Grumley Foundation and awards, the only program to award monetary prizes to gay authors. Looking towards the future of the Ferro-Grumley prize and gay literature, Stambolian left a substantial amount of his inheritance to guarantee the survival of the program. George Stambolian's unwavering devotion to the development of the field of gay studies and literature has left an enduring legacy for both the laymen and the researcher.

—Michael A. Lutes

STEAKLEY, James D.

Nationality: American professor of German language, literature, and culture. **Born:** Miami, Florida, 21 October 1946. **Education:** Attended high schools in suburban Washington, D.C., graduated 1964; University of Chicago, A.B. with general honors and special honors in German, 1968 (Phi Beta Kappa); Goethe Universitat (Frankfurt am Main), exchange scholar, 1968-69; Cornell University, New York, graduate study 1969-73. **Career:** Research assistant, Ontario Institute for Studies in Education, 1973-74; freelance editor, 1974-75; research fellow, Archiv fur sozialistische Literatur, Akademie der DDR, 1976; instructor, Montrose State College, 1977; faculty, University of Wisconsin, from 1977. Member, editorial board, *Journal of Homosexuality*. **Address:** c/o Junior Year in Freiburg, Wallstrasse 15, 79098 Freiburg, Germany.

Writings

Nonfiction

"The Gay Movement In Germany. Part One: 1860-1910," in *The Body Politic*, No. 9, 1973.

"The Gay Movement In Germany. Part Two: 1910-1933," in *The Body Politic*, No. 10, 1973.

"Homosexuality and the Third Reich," in *The Body Politic*, No. 11, 1974.

"The Gay Movement in Germany Today," in *The Body Politic*, No. 13, May/June 1974.

The Homosexual Emancipation Movement in Germany. New York, Arno Press, 1975.

With Gert Hekma and Harry Oosterhuis, "Leftist Sexual Politics and Homosexuality: An Historical Overview," in *Journal of Homosexuality*, Vol. 29, No. 2/3, 1995.

Editor

Documents of the Homosexual Rights Movement in Germany, 1836-1927. New York, Arno, 1975.

Lesbianism and Feminism in Germany, 1895-1910. New York, Arno, 1975.

With Gert Hekma and Harry Oosterhuis, *Gay Men and the Sexual History of the Political Left.* New York: Harrington Park Press, 1995.

With Manfred Herzer, *Von einst bis jetzt. Geschichte einer homosexuellen Bewegung 1897-1922* by Magnus Hirschfeld. West Berlin, Rosa Winkel, 1986.

Other

"Love Between Women and Love Between Men: Interview With Charlotte Wolff," in *New German Critique: An Interdisciplinary Journal of German Studies*, Vol. 23, spring/summer 1981.

The Writings of Dr. Magnus Hirschfeld, Sexologist, Psychiatrist, Homosexual Emancipationist: A Bibliography. Toronto, Canadian Gay Archives, 1985.

*   *   *

The idea that homosexuals possessed equal civil rights with all other citizens has become a familiar (if hotly disputed) feature of the contemporary gay and lesbian movement, along with the long-accepted myth that gay liberation was born on a hot summer night in 1969 outside a seedy bar in New York City. One of the chief casualties of this new radicalism was an almost total break with the older homophile organizations such as The Mattachine Society, some of whose members had remained aware of the past of the European homosexual community and its heritage of political activism. Among the consciousness-raising groups of the early 1970s, a frequently asked question involved the history of gays as part of the process of identity formation as a minority. This inspired a revival of interest in documenting the past of gay people and a rediscovery of the unsuccessful if vibrant German pro-gay movement of the late nineteenth and early twentieth centuries by historians and Germanists, a movement begun by academician James Steakley.

His role as a chronicler for the German movement and its importance for contemporary gay liberation began with a series of four articles which appeared in the Toronto gay newspaper *The Body Politic* in late 1973 and early 1974. Originally begun in 1972 as background research for a doctoral dissertation on the image of male homosexuality in German fiction of the Wilhelmine era, these were the first historical pieces on the subject written for a mass audience since the cessation of Magnus Hirschfeld's journal *Jahrbuch fur sexuelle Zwischenstufen* in 1923. The introduction to the first article briefly reviews the then-contemporary state of gay historical writing, noting that "part of the oppression of gay people lies in the denial of our history.... Now that the Stonewall hysteria has subsided once and for all and a certain retrenching is taking place within the gay movement,...the time has come for broadening our perspective on the present by looking a bit further into the past and beyond our continent."

The series explored the writings of Hanover lawyer Karl Heinrich Ulrichs and reviewed the foundation of the Scientific Humanitarian Committee by Dr. Magnus Hirschfeld and the specific vicious persecutions of homosexuals under the National Socialists (the latter the source of the now-famous pink triangle symbol, originally used as a badge of identification for male homosexual inmates in concentration camps). The final installment examined postwar German gay activism, from the many short-lived groups formed since 1949 (including an unsuccessful attempt to revive the Scientific Humanitarian Committee) to the contrasting situations for homosexuals in East and West Germany and renewed efforts to decriminalize homosexuality. Steakley's writings were used as a source for the first book-length exploration of prewar movement history, John Lauritsen and David Thorstad's *The Early Homosexual Rights Movement (1864-1935)* and were expanded and republished in 1975 under the title *The Homosexual Emancipation Movement in Germany*. In addition, he further expanded the access of the American homosexual community to the history of their German predecessors through the collection and editing of two anthologies of original materials, which appeared in 1975 as *Documents of the Homosexual Rights Movement in Germany, 1836-1927* and *Lesbianism and Feminism in Germany, 1895-1910*.

While diversifying his academic interests into the history of anarchism and labor, Germany's reception of Darwinism, and German music, Steakley remained involved with the retrieval of German gay political and social history through such publications as a bibliography of the writings of Dr. Magnus Hirschfeld (as well as an interview with psychiatrist Charlotte Wolff, Hirschfeld's biographer), the editing and republication of Hirschfeld's own history of the movement, and the relationship of gay men to the ideology of the political left. Steakley's combination of traditional academics with gay studies is further reflected in his roles as contributing editor of *New German Critique* and member of the editorial board of the *Journal of Homosexuality*.

—Robert B. Marks Ridinger

STEFAN, Verena

Nationality: Swiss/German writer, translator, and educator. **Born:** Bern, Switzerland, in 1947; lived in Berlin, Germany, from 1968-77. **Career:** Cofounder of Berlin women's group "Bread and Roses," c. 1969; physical therapist, until 1977; teacher of women's studies; Lives in Munich, Germany. **Awards:** Ehrengabe des Kantons, Bern, 1977. **Address:** c/o Feminist Press at CUNY, 311 E. 94th St., New York, New York 10128, U.S.A.

WRITINGS

Fiction

Es ist reich gewesen: Bericht vom Sterben meiner Mutter. Frankfurt, Fischer Taschenbuchverlag, 1993.
Wortgetreu ich träume: Geschichten und Geschichte. Zürich, Arche, 1987; translated as *Literally Dreaming,* New York, Feminist Press at CUNY, 1994.
Häutungen: Autobiografische Aufzeichnungen, Gedichte, Träume, Analysen. München, Frauenoffensive, 1975; translated as *Shedding,* New York, Daughters Inc., 1978; New York, Feminist Press at CUNY, 1994.

Essays

With "Bread and Roses," *Rauh wild & frei. Mädchengestalten in her Literatur.* Frankfurt, Fischer Taschenbuchverlag, 1997.

Poetry

Mit Füssen mit Flügeln. München, Frauenoffensive, 1980.

Nonfiction

Frauenhandbuch Nr. 1. Berlin, Verlag Frauen im Gerhard Verlag, 1972.

Autobiography

Es ist reich gewesen (Times Have Been Good). Frankfurt am Main, Fischer, 1993.

Other

Translator, with Meixner, *Der Traum einer gemeinsamen Sprache* (Dream of a Common Language), by Adrienne Rich. Munich, Frauenoffensive, 1982.
Translator, with Gabriel Meixner, *Lesbische Völker. Ein Vörterbuch* (Lesbian People. A Dictionary), by Monique Wittig and Sande Sweig. Munich, Frauenoffensive, 1983.

*

Critical Sources: *Political Ideology and Aesthetics in Neo-Feminist Fictions: Verena Stefan, Elfirede Jelinek, Margot Schroeder* by Tobe Levin, Ithaca, Cornell University Press, 1979; "Our Language, Our Selves: Verena Stefan's Critique of Patriarchal Language" by Jeannette Clausen, in *Beyond the Feminine: Critical Essays on Women and German Literature,* edited by Susan L. Cocalis and Kay Goodman, Stuttgart, Heinz, 1982; "Shadowing—Surfacing—Shedding: Contemporary German Writers in Search of a Female Bildungsroman," in *The Voyage In: Fictions of Female Development,* edited by Elizabeth Abel, Marianne Hirsch, and Elizabeth Langland, Hanover, New Hampshire, University Press of New England for Dartmouth College, 1983; "Foreword to Shedding" by Johanna Moore and Beth Weckmueller, in *German Feminism: Readings in Politics and Literature,* Albany, State University of New York Press, 1984; *Frauen Literatur Geschichte,* edited by Hiltrud Gnüg and Renate Möhrmann, Frankfurt, J.B. Metzler, 1985; *Deutsche Literatur von Frauen,* edited by Gisela Brinker-Gabler, Munich, C.H. Beck, 1988; "übergang und Ankunft: Positionen neuerer Frauenliteratur: Zu Anne Dudens 'übergang' und Verena Stefans 'Wortgetreu ich träume,'" in *Jahrbuch fur Internationale Germanistik,* Bern, Switzerland, Vol. 22, No. 2, 1990, 80-94; "Afterword" by Tobe Levin, in *Shedding* [and] *Literally Dreaming,* New York, Feminist Press of CUNY, 1994.

*　　*　　*

Verena Stefan received international attention for her 1975 book *Häutungen* (translated into English as *Shedding*). This groundbreaking novel traces the unfolding of a woman's sexual and individual identity in the 1970s in Germany. The book unexpectedly became a cult phenomenon, consistently going back to press for additional reprints and selling a quarter of a million copies by the 1980s, bringing worldwide recognition to its previously un-known publisher, Frauenoffensive. It also marked the definitive entrance of German feminist literature into the public literary arena.

In *Shedding,* Stefan demonstrates how patriarchal structures of thought and language surround a woman like extra layers of skin. Each layer is imprinted with a "feminine" identity that is not her own, and which impedes her discovery of her true self that is buried beneath the layers. She is made up of a patchwork of these skins: the "gentle, willing-to-compromise skin, the don't-be-so-oversensitive-skin, the I-radiate-peacefulness-skin, the passion-ately-curious skin, the wanting-to-recognize-everything-skin."

The expectation of certain behaviors and attitudes for a woman in contemporary Western society pressures her to attempt to mold herself from the outside in order to conform, rather than from the inside out. Her true self is hidden from even her own view; she loses her identity in the search to become that which her male partners and society expect her to be. Throughout Stefan's short narrative, the main character sheds these artificial layers one by one, discovering along the way how little she understands her own reflexive actions in her relationships. She is forced to recognize that in pursuit of the ideal of a successful sexual relationship with the right man, she has neglected and even undermined her rela-tionships with women. In so doing, she has also neglected herself.

The main character's awakening into her own female selfhood emerges as she learns to live in her own body, getting to know her own physicality for the first time. The act of heterosexual sex distances her from her body. Birth control, for example, requires that she alter her own body in order to have sex: "In order to sleep with a man, I have to become a patient. Birth control has become an unsolvable problem. I am more important to myself than the union with the penis. I am penetrated by me." She de-cides to live in celibacy instead, in order to really get to know herself: "My eyes are directed at me. My lower body begins slowly to grow onto my upper body."

Central to Stefan's criticism of the oppressiveness of patriarchal thinking is her use of language to reveal underlying assumptions about gender and femaleness. Words imbued with misogynistic undertones disembody the woman they describe: "Clitoris has nothing to do with the place on my body that is called clitoris." Stefan replaces male-oriented words for the female body with her own female-centered creations. For example, the German word "Schamlippen" (modesty/shame lips), meaning vulva, becomes "Lippenblüten" (blossoming lips). Reclaiming the language to describe the female body is part of her process of learning to own and appreciate her sexuality.

Lesbianism for Stefan becomes the only acceptable means of expressing sexual love in an environment of equanimity and self-reassurance. Through romantic and sexual involvement with a woman, she is able to shed the suffocating layerings of skin, and experience her femaleness through the reflection of her female lover. For Stefan, the act of love with another woman is simultaneously an act of self-exploration: "I learn something about myself when I am with another woman. With a man I learn only that I am differ-ent." Language fails here too, though, because the language of West-ern society is structured around a heterosexual model. The main character and her lover are exploring new territory, faced with the challenge of creating a new way of loving while avoiding the pit-falls of inequality ingrained in their society: "We found ourselves in an empty field. We didn't want to imitate, but to form new ways and behaviors from within ourselves, from the erotic re-sources between us. The emptiness was confounding." Lesbian-ism in Stefan's narrative is not so much an identity of its own,

but a means by which women can find love while avoiding the power imbalance inherent in heterosexual relationships. The char-acters are able to achieve self-awareness as women through their experience of another woman. In the end, however, this portrayal of lesbianism as a political choice leaves the question open as to whether the choice will always be necessary.

Stefan demonstrates that it takes tremendous strength to de-part from the norm and explore the love of women; the result is a significant step taken towards verbalizing and reclaiming feminine identity. The author's analysis of how structures of language con-tribute to the erasure of the female body and female identity lays the groundwork for feminist critiques of language and aesthetics in later years. *Shedding* has been criticized, however, because of the utopian direction in which the narrative ultimately leads.

Since the groundbreaking publication of *Shedding,* Stefan has written a number of other important works in a variety of genres. Her short story collection *Literally Dreaming* explores the themes of life in harmony with nature. She has also translated the works of noted feminists Monique Wittig, Sande Zweig, and Adrienne Rich into German. Verena Stefan's works represent an important contribution to the development of contemporary feminist and lesbian literary theory.

—Caitlin L. Gannon

STRACHEY, (Giles) Lytton

Nationality: British essayist, critic, biographer, and historian. **Born:** London, 1 March 1880; fifth son of the prominent Indian colonial administrator, Lieutenant General Sir Richard Strachey. **Education:** Hyde Park Kindergarten and School, 1883-84; stud-ied at home, 1884-89; small private school of Henry Forde, Parkstone, 1889-93; New School, Abbotsholme, 1893-94; Leamington College, 1894-97, passed seven subjects in Oxford and Cambridge Lower Certificate Examination; Liverpool University College, 1897-99, passed Intermediate B.A. Examination; Trinity College, Cambridge, 1899-03, Second-Class Honors in History (member and Secretary, Cambridge Conversazione Society, better known as Cambridge Apostles, 1902; Chancellor's Medal, for "Ely: An Ode," an unpublished poem, 1902). **Career:** Worked as re-viewer and drama critic, *Spectator,* 1904-12; regular contributor, *Independent Review, Nation and Athenaeum, New Quarterly,* and *New Statesman,* 1904-32. **Died:** Ham Spray, England, of stomach cancer, 21 January 1932.

WRITINGS

Literary Criticism

Landmarks in French Literature. New York, Henry Holt and Co., and London, Williams and Norgate, 1912.
Books and Characters, French and English. London, Chatto and Windus, and New York, Harcourt, Brace, and Co., 1922.
Characters and Commentaries. London, Chatto and Windus, and New York, Harcourt, Brace, and Co., 1933.

Biographies

Eminent Victorians. London, Chatto and Windus, and Garden City, New York, Garden City Publishing Co., 1918.
Queen Victoria. London, Chatto and Windus, and New York, Harcourt, Brace, and Co., 1921.
Elizabeth and Essex: A Tragic History. London, Chatto and Windus, and New York, Harcourt, Brace, and Co., 1928.

Essays

Portraits in Miniature and Other Essays. London, Chatto and Windus, and New York, Harcourt, Brace, and Co., 1931.
Spectatorial Essays. London, Chatto and Windus, 1964.
The Really Interesting Question and Other Papers. London, Weidenfeld and Nicolson, 1972.
The Shorter Strachey, selected and introduced by Michael Holroyd and Paul Levy. Oxford, Oxford University Press, 1980.

Collected Works

Collected Works, 6 volumes (includes *Eminent Victorians, Queen Victoria, Books and Characters, Elizabeth and Essex, Portraits in Miniature,* and *Characters and Commentaries*). London, Chatto and Windus, 1934.
Collected Works (includes *Landmarks in French Literature, Eminent Victorians, Elizabeth and Essex, Literary Essays,* and *Biographical Essays*). London, Chatto and Windus, 1948.

Other

Virginia Woolf and Lytton Strachey: Letters, edited by Leonard Woolf and James Strachey. London, The Hogarth Press, and Chatto and Windus, 1956.
Ermyntrude and Esmeralda (fiction). New York, Stein and Day, 1969.
Lytton Strachey by Himself: A Self-Portrait (collection of autobiographical essays), edited by Michael Holroyd. London, Heinemann, 1971.

*

Manuscript Collections: British Library; Humanities Research Center, University of Texas at Austin; Duke University, North Carolina; Robert H. Taylor Collection, Princeton University, New Jersey; Sheppard Papers, King's College, Cambridge.

Biography: *Lytton Strachey* by Michael Holroyd, London, Chatto and Windus, 1994.

Critical Sources: *Lytton Strachey: His Mind and Art* by Charles Saunders, New Haven, Yale University Press, 1957; *The Psychological Milieu of Lytton Strachey* by Martin Kallich, New Haven, Yale University Press, 1961; *A Literary-Critical Analysis of the Complete Prose Works of Lytton Strachey: A Re-Assessment of His Achievement and Career* by Barry Spurr, Lewiston, Edwin Mellen Press, 1995.

*   *   *

Lytton Strachey's importance as a gay writer does not lie in his explicit treatment of homosexuality. Rather, it lies in the ethos and tone of his work that are crucially informed by his position as a gay Edwardian/Georgian alienated by the Christian familial values and prudishness of Victorian culture. As Barry Spurr points out, Strachey is extremely circumspect in his "description of the relationship of Beddoes and Degen" in his essay, "The Last Elizabethan," collected in *Literary Essays,* on homosexual Beddoes and equally discreet in his one-sentence description of George III's gay son, the Duke of Cambridge, in *Queen Victoria.* No doubt, he explicitly discusses Francis Bacon's passionate interest in "handsome young men" in *Elizabeth and Essex,* but while his tone in that discussion is non-judgmental, it is also elaborately non-committal, making the issue decidedly marginal to the text.

Even if Strachey does not explicitly discuss homosexuality in his writings, critics like Michael Holroyd and Barry Spurr have made plausible connections between the writer's psychology and texts like *Elizabeth and Essex.* Such connections are to some degree authorized by Strachey's own use of a psychological interpretation of Queen Elizabeth I's political decisions in *Elizabeth and Essex,* a book significantly dedicated to James and Alix Strachey, Freud's English translators, and Strachey's brother and sister-in-law, and by his own analogy of Elizabeth and Essex's relationship to the mythological homoerotic bond between Hercules and Hylas. Further, as Michael Holroyd's biography of Strachey makes clear, in his private correspondence the writer made shrewd psycho-biographical connections between the gayness of figures like Oscar Wilde and E. M. Forster and the subtext of some of their works that did not explicitly seem to represent homosexuality, like Wilde's *The Ideal Husband* and Forster's "The Story of a Panic."

Psycho-biographical accounts of *Elizabeth and Essex* suggest that the empathy Strachey shows in depicting Elizabeth's deep infatuation and ultimately fatal exasperation with the impetuously facile Essex might be connected with the writer's own ambivalent attraction to virile younger men who lacked his intellectual sophistication, like George Mallory. Extending this psycho-biographical interpretation more speculatively, Barry Spurr suggests that Strachey's ambivalent identification with powerful, "androgynous" women like Queen Elizabeth in *Elizabeth and Essex* and the driven Florence Nightingale in *Eminent Victorians,* might be connected with his own challenging of gender conventions as a gay man. Such psychological interpretations should, however, also take into account that Strachey was also highly critical of the repressive way in which psychoanalysis was used by the British medical establishment to "cure" gay men.

Ultimately, Strachey's intellectual and affective experiences at Cambridge may have had a more significant influence in shaping the gay content of his work than his personal idiosyncrasies. At Trinity College, Cambridge, Strachey was a member of the Apostles, a quasi-secret body that was deeply influenced by G. E. Moore's seminal 1903 philosophical text *Principia Ethica.* The importance of the work for Strachey and his friends was that it championed the centrality of personal relationships to an ethically meaningful life. As Michael Holroyd points out, Moore's philosophy became "a moral centre" of the Apostles, "a focus for an alternative sexual code." Scorning and explicitly rebelling against Victorian familial conventions, Strachey and his friends in the Bloomsbury circle, like Keynes, Grant, and Virginia Woolf, often nurtured unorthodox personal relationships which could neither be fit neatly within familial or even conventionally understood heterosexual versus homosexual, conventions. For instance, Strachey shared a strong affective bond with a female artist named Dora Carrington. Carrington loved Strachey and was erotically attracted to him. In fact, after he died she committed suicide. While

tracted to him. In fact, after he died she committed suicide. While Strachey deeply loved Carrington, (Holroyd writes that on his deathbed, Strachey whispered, "Darling Carrington. I love her"), his attachment could hardly be described as conventionally sexual.

Indeed, Strachey was sexually attracted to Carrington's lover, Ralph Partridge. Partridge, however, was not physically attracted to Strachey. Their triangular relationship, while flouting all normative conventions, seemed to have been deeply meaningful for all three individuals, thus fitting Moore's model of the ideal personal relationship. It was precisely his Victorian precursors' obsession with respectable familial conventions, as opposed to meaningful personal relationships, that earned Strachey's derision. The political coerciveness of these conventions became particularly clear at the outbreak of the First World War. In mobilizing an army, Britain appealed to traditional familial as well as national values. Thus, Holroyd writes that when Strachey refused to serve in the military, the tribunal that was examining his motives invoked conventional ideas of a man's responsibility to protect and uphold family respectability by asking Strachey what he would do if he saw a German soldier attack his sister. The writer wittily refused to rise to the bait, declaring that he would attempt to "interpose" himself between them.

The Cambridge Apostles had been formed in part to find ethical alternatives to Christian beliefs with which many educated Victorians and Edwardians were disillusioned. Barry Spurr points out that Strachey combined Moore's emphasis on personal relationships and Hellenistic humanist affirmations of the body to pose an implicitly gay challenge to Christian asceticism in papers that he read to the Apostles, like "Christ and Caliban" in 1902. In his description in *Eminent Victorians* of Thomas Arnold's provincial distaste for sensuality that he rigorously attempted to instill in his young charges at Rugby, and his satirizing of Victorian prudishness in the epistolary novel *Erymentrude and Esmeralda,* Strachey implicitly made the case for more tolerance and affirmation of the body and its desires, even if those desires challenged middle-class Christian norms.

Finally, the tone of Strachey's writings can be said to implicitly advance a sexual politics. Strachey used biting irony in *Eminent Victorians* to undercut self-important Victorian pretensions to high moral seriousness; this tone was what made the work so scandalous to more traditional historians. Since at least the time of Oscar Wilde, such irony was aligned with a "camp" aesthetic and a suspicion of traditional masculine values. Thus, even when not explicitly discussing gay issues, Strachey's writing draws on an aesthetic that is coded as gay in late-Victorian and Edwardian culture.

—Stephen da Silva

SWENSON, May

Nationality: American poet. **Born:** Logan, Utah, 28 May 1913. **Education:** Utah State University. **Family:** Companions included Anca Vrboska, Pearl Schwartz, and Rozanne Knudson. **Career:** Worked as newspaper reporter, Utah; author's assistant, to Anzia Yezierska; writer, Federal Writers' Project; manuscript reader, for New Directions Press. Chancellor, Academy of American Poets, 1980. **Awards:** Rockefeller Writing fellowship; Guggenheim fellowship; Amy Lowell Travelling Scholarship; Bollingen Prize for Poetry, 1981; MacArthur Foundation fellowship, 1987. **Died:** Ocean View, Delaware, 4 December 1989.

WRITINGS

Poetry

Another Animal, in *Poets of Today,* Vol. 1. New York, Scribners, 1954.
A Cage of Spines. New York, Rinehart, 1958.
To Mix with Time: New and Selected Poems. New York, Scribners, 1963.
Half Sun Half Sleep. New York, Scribners, 1967.
Iconographs. New York, Scribners, 1970.
New and Selected Things Taking Place. New York, Atlantic Monthly Press, 1978.
In Other Words: New Poems. New York, Knopf, 1987, 1992.
The Love Poems of May Swenson. Boston, Houghton Mifflin, 1991.
Nature: Poems Old and New. Boston, Houghton Mifflin, 1994.
May Out West. Utah State University Press, 1996.

Poetry (for children and young adults)

Editor, with R.R. Knudson, *American Sports Poems.* New York, Orchard Books, 1988.
The Complete Poems to Solve. New York, Macmillan, 1993.
The Centaur. New York, Simon and Schuster, 1995.

Uncollected Poetry

"My Poems," "Guilty," "Weather," and "Horse," in *Nation,* Vol. 256, 25 January 1993, 96-102.
"Sleeping with Boa" and "Logs in the Grate," in *Yale Review,* Vol. 81, January 1993, 37-9
"What I Did on a Rainy Day," in *Atlantic Monthly,* Vol. 272, November 1993, 124.
"The Most Important" "Statement," "In Progress," "Under the Best of Circumstances," "Beginning Ended," "Overview," and "The Sea," in *Poetry,* Vol. 163, November 1993, 63-9.
"Assuming the Lotus," "The Kiss," and "Something Goes By," in *American Poetry Review,* Vol. 23, September/October 1994, 8, 52.
"Once There Were Glaciers," in *Nation,* Vol. 258, 4 April 1994, 462.

Short Stories

"Appearances," in *New Directions in Prose and Poetry,* No. 13. New York, New Directions, 1951, 69-82.
"Mutterings of a Middlewoman," in *The Poet's Story,* edited by Howard Moss. New York, Macmillan, 1973.

Essays

"The Poet as Anti-Specialist," in *Saturday Review,* 30 January 1965.
"Big My Secret, But It's Bandaged," in *Parnassus: Poetry in Review,* Vol. 12, No. 2, and Vol. 13, No. 1, 1985, 16-44.

Translator

Windows and Stones: Selected Poems of Tomas Transtromer. Pittsburgh, University of Pittsburgh Press, 1972.

Recordings: *The Poetry and Voice of May Swenson,* Caedmon, 1976; *Academy of American Poets Audio Archive: May Swenson,* recorded in New York, 28 October 1985.

*

Manuscript Collections: Washington University, St. Louis, Missouri.

Biography: *The Wonderful Pen of May Swenson* by R. R. Knudson, New York, Macmillan, 1993.

Interviews: "A Conversation with May Swenson" by Lee Hudson, in *Literature in Performance,* Vol. 3, No. 2, April 1983, 55-66.

Critical Sources: Review of *To Mix with Time* by Anthony Hecht, in *New York Review of Books,* Vol. 1, No. 3, 1963, 33; "Turned Back to the Wild by Love" by Richard Howard, in *Alone with America: Essays on the Art of Poetry in the United States since 1950,* New York, Atheneum, 1969, 517-532; "May Swenson and the Shapes of Speculation" by Alicia Ostriker, in *Writing Like a Woman,* Ann Arbor, University of Michigan Press, 1983, 86-101; "A Versatile Dance of the Mind" by Sven Birkerts, in *Parnassus: Poetry in Review,* Vol. 12, No. 2, and Vol. 13, No. 1, 1985, 317-335; "Important Witness to the World" by Mona Van Duyn, in *Parnassus: Poetry in Review,* Vol. 16, No. 1, 1990, 154-156; review of *The Love Poems of May Swenson* by Edward Hirsch, in *New York Times Book Review,* 19 January 1992; review of *The Love Poems of May Swenson* by Alfred Corn, in *Poetry,* February 1993, 295-298; "A Mysterious and Lavish Power: How Things Continue to Take Place in the Work of May Swenson" by Sue Russell, in *Kenyon Review,* Vol. 16, No. 3, spring 1993, 128-139; "Life's Miracles: The Poetry of May Swenson" by Grace Schulman, in *American Poetry Review,* Vol. 23, No. 5, September/October 1994, 9-13; "May Swenson" by Kenneth Pobo, in *The Gay and Lesbian Literary Heritage,* edited by Claude J. Summers, New York, Henry Holt, 1995, 690-91.

*   *   *

May Swenson, the daughter of Swedish immigrants and the oldest child in a family of ten, was born in 1913 and raised in the Mormon faith in Logan, Utah. Her rural childhood seems to have been relatively happy, and she maintained close relationships with her family throughout her life. Still, she knew from an early age that she could not follow the precepts of their religion. After graduating from college and working for a few years as a newspaper reporter in Utah, she made her way to New York City, where she stayed for the rest of her life. There, she worked at a variety of jobs, from ghostwriter to secretary and manuscript reader, until she was eventually able to sustain herself as a poet. Swenson's first book of poetry, *Another Animal,* was published in 1954 and nominated for a National Book Award. Although, at age 41, she might be considered a slow starter, her work would soon take hold in the literary world, garnering her major awards and important publications, including the sought-after *New Yorker* "first" contract, giving the prominent magazine a first reading of all her new

poems.

Swenson belongs to that generation of poets who could not afford to be as open about their lesbian relationships as contemporary readers might like. Nevertheless, she was probably less closeted than most. Straightforward love poems appear even in her earliest books. Although the female gender of the lover is "hidden" behind the pronoun "you" in such poems from the 1950s as "Mornings Innocent," the self-portrait has definite lesbian overtones:

> I wear your smile upon my lips
> arising on mornings innocent
> Your skin is a fleece about me
> With your princely walk I salute the sun
> People say I am handsome.

"People say" she is "handsome," rather than "beautiful," just as the beloved is "princely," so that the two together are characterized by their potential androgyny rather than by a presumed heterosexual relationship. The speaker also seems to enjoy holding on to the secret of her love as if its private nature makes the feeling all the more special, which is certainly one way to contend with the societal stricture against the public display of same-sex affection.

Another early poem, "To F." (the telltale initial obscuring sexual identity), first published posthumously, illustrates the common experience of not being able to kiss one's lover goodbye, though love nevertheless prevails: "Your bus will stop at Christopher / Mine at Abingdon Square / Your hand...'Good luck' and mine 'So long' / The taxi trumpets blare" (*Love Poems*).

The poem "Zambesi and Ranee," from Swenson's second book, *A Cage of Spines* (1958), provides another telling view of lesbian life in the 1950s:

> Bemused at the bars,
> some watchers smile and read
> *Zambesi and Ranee* upon their card;
> They might ring the bell, introduce themselves
> and be welcome. The life these ladies lead,
> upon their stage, repeats itself behind the walls
> of many city streets; silent, or aloud,
> the knowing crowd snickers.

It was Swenson's habit to go out in the morning in search of a poem. Her companion and biographer R. R. Knudson notes that she left herself open to poetic material wherever it might be found. On days when she did not have to go to work, she would set out from her Perry Street apartment in Greenwich Village, destination unknown. It was in such a manner that she found the two feline "ladies" in "Zambesi and Ranee." The poem's epigraph, taken from a plaque on the cage, offers the same information that was given to the poet and the other zoo visitors—that the two cats had been raised together because their mothers refused to nurse them. The strangeness of the animals' situation both attracts and repels their audience.

Acting as participant and observer in this scene, Swenson identifies with the cats while keeping her eyes and ears attuned to the response of the crowd, whose "snickered" comments must include words like "perverse" and "unnatural." The rituals of communication, among both animals and humans, hold her attention. She observes that the two cats "avoid each other's touch; but if, pass-

observes that the two cats "avoid each other's touch; but if, passing, / as much as a whisker of that black-and-orange head / grazes the lion's flank, her topaz eye narrows: irascibly she turns with slugger's paw / to rake the ear of her mate." At that point, the poem, like the cats themselves, takes a slow turn to encompass female homo sapiens along with caged cats.

Given the context of witch hunts and bar raids in the 1950s, we can easily surmise that avoidance of "the other's" (read lover's) touch would be necessary for social survival. Drawing from the same context, the poet as participant/observer would have developed the skill to "read" the response of the crowd, who "tighten their hold on Darling's hand" lest he or she be tempted to stray from the fold. For the poet, as for other "ladies...behind the walls of many city streets," the effort of "passing" in a straight world requires an almost feline agility and grace, but it comes with a cost.

Another poet who understood that cost was Elizabeth Bishop, with whom Swenson developed an important friendship when the two met at the artists' colony, Yaddo, in the early 1950s. Swenson and Bishop kept in touch during the period when Bishop lived in Brazil with her lover, Lota de Macedo Soares. Swenson would write to her from New York with news of the American poetry scene. One of Bishop's letters back became the raw material for the poem, "Dear Elizabeth," which appeared in Swenson's fourth book, *Half Sun Half Sleep* (1967):

> Yes, I'd like a pair of *Bicos de Lacre*—
> meaning beaks of "lacquer or "sealing wax"?
> "...about 3 inches long including the tail,
> red bills and narrow bright red masks..."
> You say the male has a sort of "drooping
> mandarin-mustache—one black stripe"—
> otherwise the sexes are alike.

Once again, Swenson plays with the idea of androgyny within the confines of polite discourse. This poem also illustrates the subject matter the two poets shared. Their keen interest in the natural world allowed for a kind of poem that would be based on observations of flora and fauna but have implications for the human animal as well. The "cover" of nature poetry allowed both poets a level of sensuality that might not otherwise have been possible through conventional narrative. In "Her Early Work," ironically, one of Swenson's later poems, she shows her understanding of this very phenomenon, with most explicit reference to Bishop, who was more reticent than Swenson herself about revealing the intimate details of her life: "Talked to cats and dogs, / to trees, and to strangers. / To one loved, talked through / layers of masks. / To this day we can't know / who was addressed, / or ever undressed" (*In Other Words*).

In Swenson's own later work, she became much more open about her same-sex relationships. In fact, she agreed to have her poems included in one of the early lesbian anthologies, *Amazon Poetry* (1975), though she refused an invitation to appear in a new volume with the less subtle title of *Lesbian Poetry*. Among her later poems, "Poet to Tiger" stands out for its physical specificity and its lively portrait of female lovers at home. This poet, unlike the speaker in "Zambesi and Ranee," gets right in there with the animal rather than standing safely outside the cage in the poem which appeared in *New & Selected Things Taking Place*:

> ...you wake me every hour with sudden
> growled I love-yous

trapping my face between those plushy
shoulders. All my float-dreams turn spins
and never finish. I'm thinner
now. My watch keeps running fast.
But best is when we're riding pillion
my hips within your lap. You let me steer.
Your hand and arm go clear
around my ribs your moist
dream teeth fastened on my nape.

During Swenson's lifetime, her reputation was partially eclipsed by that of Bishop in a male-dominated literary era where it seemed that no more than one woman at a time could be considered "major." Being referred to patronizingly as "woman poet" never sat right with Bishop or Swenson. With the burgeoning of women poets that grew out of the feminist movement in the 1970s, Swenson's poetry gained increasing attention, as her work could begin to be seen in the context of a literary tradition stemming back to Marianne Moore and Emily Dickinson and forward to such poets as Mary Oliver. Her reputation continued to escalate after her death in 1989, and her poetry appears in numerous anthologies that identify her sexual preference. One anthology of love poems by lesbians, *The Key to Everything,* took its title from an early Swenson poem.

Swenson has long been recognized as a formal innovator as well. In *Iconographs* (1970) and other later books, she carefully shaped the poems on the page, letting white space serve a variety of functions to amplify both the message and the strategy of each piece. She always pointed out, however, that the "shaping" or design came after the text. One instance in which lesbian subject matter and formal innovation occur simultaneously is in "A Trellis for R" (formerly titled "Blue"), which functions as a lesbian "Song of Songs," with each of the lover's features appreciated in turn as individual roses in the lattice frame of human touch.

Apart from the poems that concern lesbian love and relationships, Swenson challenged the traditionally "feminine" function of poetry in a number of ways. Although, like many female poets from her era and before, she wrote about the beauty of nature, she was as interested, say, in photosynthesis as a process as in the physical characteristics of wildflowers. She was fascinated with space exploration and with all aspects of modern science, from quantum physics to DNA. She wrote poems about the moon landing and about the re-appearance of Halley's Comet. As poets Grace Schulman and Alicia Ostriker have noted, Swenson accepted the proposition of Renaissance poet John Donne that all knowledge was her province.

Perhaps more than any one other characteristic, the work of May Swenson is unique for the questioning spirit that has been present from the earliest poems, and even within that young girl who was able to separate herself from the stronghold of the Mormon Church. She has grappled in her work with the most difficult metaphysical dilemmas in a voice that maintains an almost childlike clarity and openness. Consider these introductory lines to the poem audaciously titled, "The Universe," from *New and Selected Things Taking Place*: "What / is it about, / the universe, / the universe about us stretching out? / We, within our brains, / within it, / think / we must unspin / the laws that spin it. / We think *why* / because we think / *because*."

Through her ability to turn these questions around, both literally and figuratively, to look at them from every possible angle,

Swenson has revealed major insights about the mysteries of human identity. In her introduction to Swenson's posthumous volume *Nature,* Susan Mitchell notes that Swenson's is "a world looked at through love, through generosity of spirit." It is this spirit that links her openly sexual poems with those that celebrate the expanses of sea, land, and sky. Her conscious acceptance of human appetite in every form makes her an essential poet for any reader, gay or straight.

—Sue Russell

T

TAKAHASHI, Mutsuo

Nationality: Japanese poet, novelist, and critic. **Born:** Yahata, Kyûshû, Japan, 15 December 1937. **Education:** Fukuoka University of Education, B.A. 1962. **Career:** Co-founder and chairman of poetry magazine *Kyôen* (Symposium), from 1976; member, Japan Writers Association and Japan PEN Club; frequent contributor to periodicals, including *Kyôen, Gendai Shi Techô* (Handbook of Modern Poetry), and *Yuriika* (Eureka). **Awards:** Rekitei Prize, for anthology of poetry, 1982; Yamamoto Kenkichi Prize, for adaption of a play, 1987; Takami Jun Prize, for anthology of poetry, 1988; Yomiuri Literature Prize, for anthology of traditional Japanese verse, 1988; Shika Bungakukan Prize, for anthology of poetry, 1996. **Address:** c/o Shueisha, 2-5-10 Hitotsubashi, Chiyoda-ku, Tokyo 101 Japan.

WRITINGS

English Translations

"Christ of the Thieves," translated by Mutsuo Takahashi and James Kirkup, in *Poetry Nippon* (Nagoya), Vol. 13, 1970.
"A Tableau for Sunset; Winter 1955," translated by Harry Guest and Kajima Shozo, in *Post-war Japanese Poetry,* edited by Harry Guest, Lynn Guest, and Kajima Shozo. Harmondworth, Penguin Books, 1972.
"Sleeping Wrestler; A Negro Before He Sings; From Slumber Sin and Fall; End of Summer; Boys; Rose Lover; Dead Boy," translated by James Kirkup, Fumio Miura, and Geoffrey Bownas, in *New Writing in Japan,* edited by Yukio Mishima. New York, Penguin Books, 1972.
Poems of a Penisist, translated by Hiroaki Sato. Chicago, Chicago Review Press, 1975.
"The Finger; Portrait of Myself at the Start; Portrait of Myself as a Baby-Killer; Portrait of Myself in the Final Fire," translated by James Kirkup, in *Modern Japanese Poetry,* edited by A.R. Davis. Milton Keynes, Open University Press, 1978.
"Coming from the Earth and Returning to the Earth," translated by Nahoko Kyogoku, in *Poetry Nippon* (Nagoya), Vol. 7, Nos. 1-2, 1983.
A Bunch of Keys: Selected Poems, translated by Hiroaki Sato. Trumansburg, Crossing Press, 1984.
Sleeping, Sinning, Falling, translated by Hiroaki Sato. San Francisco, City Lights Books, 1992.
"The Searcher; The Rose Lover; The Rose Tree; The Sleeping Wrestler; Myself Departing; Myself with a Motorcycle; Myself with a Glory Hole; Ode; The Hunter," translated by Stephen D. Miller, Hiroaki Sato, and Steven Karpa, in *Partings at Dawn: An Anthology of Japanese Gay Literature,* edited by Stephen D. Miller. San Francisco, Gay Sunshine Press, 1996.

Poetry

Mino, Watashi no Oushi (My Bull, Mino). Self-published, Sabaku Shijin Shûdan, 1959.

Bara no Ki, Nise no Koibito-Tachi (Rose Tree, Fake Lovers). Tokyo, Gendaishi Kôbô, 1964.
Nemuri to Okashi to Rakka to (Sleeping, Sinning, Falling). Tokyo, Shichôsha, 1965.
Yogoretaru Mono wa Sara ni Yogoretaru Koto o Nase (You Dirty Ones, Do Dirtier Things). Tokyo, Shichôsha, 1966.
Homeuta (Ode). Tokyo, Shichôsha, 1971.
Koyomi no ô (King of the Calendar). Tokyo, Shinchôsha, 1972.
Dôshi I (Verbs I). Tokyo, Shinchôsha, 1974.
Watakushi (Self-Portraits). Tokyo, Ringonya, 1976.
Kyojin no Densetsu (Legend of a Giant). Tokyo, Shochi Yamada, 1978.
Dôshi II (Verbs II). Tokyo, Shichôsha, 1979.
Sasurai to iu na no chi nite (In a Place Called Sasurai). Tokyo, Shoshi Yamada, 1979.
Kagitaba (A Bunch of Keys). Tokyo, Shoshi Yamada, 1982.
ôkoku no kôzô (Construction of the Kingdom). Tokyo, Ozawa Shoten, 1982.
Bunkôki (Spectroscope). Tokyo, Shichôsha, 1986.
Usagi no Niwa (Garden of Rabbits). Tokyo, Shoshi Yamada, 1987.
Ane no Shima (The Isle of My Older Sisters). Tokyo, Shûeisha, 1996.

Collected Works

Takahashi Mutsuo Shishû (Anthology of Poetry by Takahashi Mutsuo). Tokyo, Shichôsha, 1969.
Kyûkuchô: Kushû (Notebook of Old Verses: Haiku). Osaka, Yukawa Shobô, 1973.
Kôdôshô: Kushû (Selections from a Wild Youth: Haiku). Tokyo, Shoshi Ringoya, 1977.
Michinoae: Kashû (Road Banquet: Tanka). Tokyo, Shoshi Ringoya, 1978.
Shinsen Takahashi Mutsuo Shishû (New Anthology of Poetry by Takahashi Mutsuo). Tokyo, Shichôsha, 1980.
Keiko Onjiki: Kukashû (Practice/Drinking Eating: Haiku and Tanka). Zushi: Zenzai Kutsu, 1987.
Nihimakura: Kashû (Nihimakura: Tanka). Tokyo: Shichôsha, 1992.
Kanazawa Hyakku: Kushû (100 Verses from Kanazawa: Haiku). Tokyo, Chikuma Shobô, 1993.

Novels

Juni no Enkei (Twelve Perspectives). Tokyo, Chûô Kôronsha, 1970.
Sei Sankakkei (Sacred Triangle). Tokyo, Shinchôsha, 1972.
Zen no Henreki (Zen's Pilgrimage). Tokyo, Shinchôsha, 1974.
(Anonymous) *Mitsuryôsha* (The Hunter). Tokyo, Kawade Shobô Shinsha, 1988.

Literary Criticism

Poeji kara Mugen ni Tôku (Far from Poésie to Infinity). Tokyo, Shinchôsha, 1976.
Shijin no Chi (Blood of a Poet). Tokyo, Ozawa Shoten, 1977.
Kyûtai no Musuko (Son of the Globe). Tokyo, Ozawa Shoten, 1978.
Sei to iu Ba (A Place Called Sacred). Tokyo, Ozawa Shoten, 1978.

Otoko no Kaibôgaku (Male Anatomy). Tokyo, Kadogawa Shoten, 1979.

Jigoku o Yomu (Reading Hell). Osaka, Shinshindô, 1979.

Kotoba no ôkoku e (To the Kingdom of Words). Tokyo, Ozawa Shoten, 1979.

Koi no Hinto (Hints About Eros). Tokyo, Ozawa Shoten, 1990.

Watakushi-Jishin no Tame no Haiku Nyûmon (An Introduction to Haiku for Myself). Tokyo, Shinchôsha, 1992.

Seishun o Yomu, Nihon no Kindai Shi Niju-shichinin (Reading the Springtime of Life, 27 Modern Japanese Poets). Tokyo, Ozawa Shoten, 1992.

Essays

Otoko no Kaibôgaku (Male Anatomy). Tokyo, Kadogawa Shoten, 1979.

Hana Asobi (Playing with Flowers). Tokyo, Ozawa Shoten, 1985.

Shijin no Shokutaku, Mensa Poetae (The Table of a Poet, Mensa Poetae). Tokyo, Heibonsha, 1990.

Kyûtai no Shinwagaku (Global Mythological Studies). Tokyo, Kawade Shobô Shinsha, 1992.

Tomodachi no Tsukurikata (How to Make Friends). Tokyo, Magajin Hausu, 1993.

Other

Editor, *Erosu no Shishû* (Anthology of Erotic Poetry). Tokyo, Ushio Shuppan, 1977.

Oidipusu ô (adaption of *Oedipus Rex* by Sophocles). Tokyo, Ozawa Shoten, 1987.

Iriasu Monogatari (adaption of *The Iliad* by Homer). Tokyo, Sanseidô, 1982.

Odusseia Monogatari (adaption of *The Odyssey* by Homer). Tokyo, Sanseidô, 1982.

ôjo Media (adaption of *Media* by Euripedes). Tokyo, Ozawa Shoten, 1985.

Takanoi (Well of Hawks, Nô and Kyôgen Plays). Tokyo, Chikuma Shobô, 1992.

Tôi Ho (Far Sails: Opera Libretto). Tokyo, Ozawa Shoten, 1995.

Recordings: *Koe no Niwa* (Voice-Garden), 1996.

*

Interviews: "Keizo Aizawa Interviews Mutsuo Takahashi," translated by Hiroaki Sato, *Gay Sunshine Interviews,* Vol. 2, edited by Winston Leyland, San Francisco, Gay Sunshine Press, 1982, 190-206; also included in *Partings at Dawn: An Anthology of Japanese Gay Literature,* edited by Stephen D. Miller, San Francisco, Gay Sunshine Press, 1996, 190-206.

Critical Sources: *Articulate Flesh: Male Homo-eroticism and Modern Poetry* by Gregory Woods, New Haven, Yale University Press, 1987; "Sei Naru Mono no Shinwa" (The Mythology of the Sacred Being) by Shigeo Washisu, in *Gendai Shi Techô* (Tokyo), Vol. 16, No. 9, 1973, 16-42, Vol. 17, No. 2, 1974, 72-89; "Sei Naru Kanata e no Hishô wa Kanô ka" (Is the Flight to the Sacred Far Side Possible?) by Susumu Morita, in *Shikoku Gakuin Daigaku Ronshû* (Zentsuji), Vol. 27, 1973, 55-73.

*   *   *

In an afterward to Mutsuo Takahashi's anthology *You Dirty Ones, Do Dirtier Things,* Tatsuhiko Shibusawa, a well-known Japanese scholar of sexuality and avant-gardism, wrote, "Takahashi appears like a lone elegant beast, an insolent animal dancing out onto the ideologically anemic stage of modern Japanese poetry." Takahashi earned this reputation by featuring poetic expressions of graphic sexuality in his early work and by employing the language of metaphysics to explore the relationship between homosexuality and the divine.

While an adolescent, Takahashi became ill with tuberculosis and spent a year recuperating in a sanatorium. There, under the tutelage of Catholic Brother Joseph Tsukuda, Takahashi read Christian philosophy and Greek literature voraciously, thoroughly absorbing these two subjects which would figure as important influences on his later writing. Many of his poetic works feature Christian symbolism, and a large number of essays examine ancient Greek ideas.

After graduating from the university, Takahashi moved to Tokyo where he became close friends with the novelist Yukio Mishima. Earlier, Takahashi had met Taruho Inagaki, a major voice in the early development of modernist literature in Japan during the 1920s. Both Mishima and Inagaki had explored the philosophical ramifications of homosexuality in their works, and both provided intellectual and literary support to Takahashi in his fledgling years as a poet. Meanwhile, he also became a close friend of the poet Shiego Washisu with whom he shared an interest in Christianity, Greek literature, and the divine. Both writers later dedicated several poems to one another.

Much of Takahashi's earliest poetry consists of rhapsodies for other men and supplications to potential lovers, themes he has gone on to develop throughout his career. In a later book of essays entitled *Hints About Eros,* Takahashi examines the view put forth in Plato's *Symposium* that eros is a means for communing with one's other half or with that part of the whole which has been lost. This thought, perhaps first absorbed during Takahashi's illness, appears in even his earliest anthologies. This idea finds its fullest expression, however, in *Ode* (1971), Takahashi's longest poem to date. The poem, which often verges on the symbolist or surreal, depicts a man who fellates strangers through glory-holes in bath-houses, porno theaters, and restrooms, all the while searching for a connection with the divine. *Ode* opens with the epigraph, "In the name of man, member, and the holy fluid, Amen." This epigraph alone reveals that the object of the protagonist's devotion is the fellated phallus, and the owner of this penis is more than human. He is a faceless god, and the act of oral sex is a means of communicating with all that is sacred.

The glory-hole takes on a symbolic meaning in *Ode.* It is empty by nature, and this emptiness, in turn, mirrors a lack of purpose and divinity in the person who waits beside it. By accepting a penis into one's mouth, the person who figuratively exists as a hole and as a lack of divine fulfillment becomes a hole in a physical sense. As Takahashi writes in the afterword, the fellator accepts into his mouth "the penis as the substance that fills the void innate to man—as the substitute of God." The final pages describe an orgasm with images of flying and the heavens. However, this bliss is cut short once the protagonist's ejaculation subsides, and he is left alone with his longings. Though sex has the ability to bring one closer to the divine, the connection cannot be sustained. Rising to meet the divine inevitably ends with a fall back into the mundane.

The decline of the phallus-god is foreshadowed at the beginning of *Ode* with a series of Daliesque images of decay and ruin.

It is, however, only after the orgasm that the protagonist realizes that the sacred owner of the penis is a mere man, that the god for which the protagonist yearns lives only in the imagination. Takahashi seems to suggest that mankind's desire for divinity and for connection to the eternal sacred cannot be permanently fulfilled through the flesh. Searching for the sacred in man may lead to a connection with the godhead, but such an experience is only temporary. The protagonist is left with the existential emptiness of the glory-hole to exist in a world with only an imagined god.

Other works by Takahashi mirror these themes. The 1974 novel *Zen's Pilgrimage* explores the relationship between homosexuality and divinity in a Buddhist context. The main character travels from Kyûshû to Tokyo, and as part of his sexual pilgrimage he engages in countless sexual encounters with men and Buddhist deities alike. The bodhisattva who becomes his guide teaches him that the penis is a manifestation of the deity known in Sanskrit as Mahavairocana, and sex is thus a means of communion with him. The main character, however, learns that a sustained connection with the divine through the flesh is not possible in this life. In the essay "The Searcher," Takahashi tells of an acquaintance who searches for the ultimate fist-fuck yet finds each partner imperfect. Still, his imagination leads him forward with the delusion that a manifestation of the absolute can be found to fill his void, both literally and figuratively.

During the mid 1970s, Takahashi turned from poetry written in the first-person to works featuring third-person narrative. At the same time he began exploring among a greater diversity of themes and literary genres. He has written several novels, over a dozen volumes of literary criticism and memoirs, a volume of modern nô and kyôgen plays, and a collection of classical Japanese verse. He has even released a CD retrospective of his poetry set to music. Despite the diversity of forms, Takahashi uses his writing as a means to explore the metaphysical essence of a subject and to find truths beyond individual experience. He frequently mentions that it is his goal to write works which transcend individualism and which express universal understandings that will remain true to future generations.

—Jeffrey Angles

TERRY, Megan

Nationality: American playwright and lecturer. **Born:** Josephine Duffy in Seattle, Washington, 22 July 1932; name legally changed. **Education:** Banff School of Fine Arts, Banff, Alberta, Canada, 1950-52, 1956; University of Alberta, 1952-53; University of Seattle, B. Ed. 1956. **Family:** Companion of theatrical director Jo Anne Schmidman. **Career:** Playwright, from the 1950s; toured with Cornish Players of Seattle, 1954-56; founding member, New York Open Theatre, 1963, New York Theatre Strategy, 1971, and Women's Theatre Council, New York, 1971; adjunct Professor of Theatre, University of Nebraska, from 1974; playwright-in-residence, Omaha Magic Theatre, from 1974. **Awards:** Stanley Drama Award, 1965; ABC-Yale University Fellowship, 1966; Rockefeller grant, 1968; National Radio Play Award, 1972; Obie Award, 1970; Guggenheim Fellowship, 1978; Dramatists Guild Annual Award, 1983; Rockefeller Fellowship, 1987; National Endowment for the Arts Fellowship, 1989; elected to College of Fellows, American

Theatre at the Kennedy Center, Washington, D.C., 1995. **Address:** Omaha Magic Theatre, 325 S. 16th St., Omaha, Nebraska 68102, U.S.A.

WRITINGS

Plays

Beach Grass (produced Seattle, 1955).
Seascape (produced Seattle, 1955).
Go Out and Move the Car (produced Seattle, 1955).
The Dirt Boat (television play; produced Seattle, 1955).
New York Comedy: Two (produced Saratoga, New York, 1961).
Ex-Miss Copper Queen on a Set of Pills (produced off-off-Broadway, 1963). Published in *Playwrights for Tomorrow,* edited by Arthur H. Ballet, Vol. 1, Minneapolis, University of Minnesota Press, 1966.
When My Girlfriend Was Still All Flowers (produced off-off-Broadway, 1963).
Eat at Joe's (produced off-off-Broadway, 1964).
The Gloaming, Oh My Darling (produced Minneapolis, 1965). Published in *Viet Rock: Four Plays by Megan Terry,* New York, Simon and Schuster, 1967.
Keep Tightly Closed in a Cool Dry Place (produced off-off-Broadway, 1965). Published in *Tulane Drama Review,* No. 10, summer 1966, 177-200.
Viet Rock (produced off-Broadway, 1966). Published in *Tulane Drama Review,* No. 11, fall 1966, 196-227.
Calm Down Mother (produced off-off-Broadway 1965). Published in New York, French, 1966.
Magic Realists (produced off-Broadway, 1966). Published in *Best One Act Plays of 1968,* edited by Stanley Richards, Radnor, Pennsylvania, Chilton, 1969.
Comings and Goings (produced New York, 1966).
People vs. Ranchman (produced Minneapolis, 1967). Published as *The People vs. Ranchman and Ex-Miss Copper Queen on a Set of Pills: Two Plays,* New York: Dramatists Play Service, 1968.
The Key Is on the Bottom (produced Los Angeles, 1967).
Megan Terry's Home: or Future Soap (television play; produced 1968; as *As Theatre,* London, 1974). New York, French, 1972.
Changes (produced off-Broadway, 1968).
Massachusetts Trust (produced Waltham, Massachusetts, 1968). Published in *The Off-Off Broadway Book,* edited by Albert Poland and Bruce Mailman, Indianapolis, Bobbs-Merrill, 1972.
Jack-Jack (produced Minneapolis, 1968).
Sanibel and Captiva (radio play; 1968). Published in *Three One-Act Plays,* New York, French, 1971.
One More Little Drinkie (television play; produced 1969). Published in *Three One-Act Plays,* New York, French, 1971.
Approaching Simone (produced off-Broadway, 1970). Old Westbury, New York, Feminist Press, 1973.
The Tommy Allen Show (produced Los Angeles, 1969). Published in *Scripts,* No. 2, December 1971, 36-61.
Grooving (produced Brooklyn Academy of Music, 1972).
With Jo Anne Schmidman, *Choose a Spot on the Floor* (produced Omaha, 1972).
Couplings and Groupings. New York, Pantheon, 1973.
Susan Peretz at the Manhattan Theatre Club (produced New York, 1973).

With Sam Shepard and Jean-Claude van Itallie, *Nightwalk* (produced off-Broadway, 1973). Published in *Three Works by the Open Theatre,* New York, Bobbs-Merrill, 1975.

Pioneer (produced off-Broadway, 1974). Published in *Pioneer and Pro-Game,* New York, Ragnarok, 1975.

Pro-Game (produced off-off-Broadway, 1974). Published in *Pioneer and Pro-Game,* New York, Ragnarok, 1975.

Narco Linguini Bust (produced Omaha, 1974).

All Them Women (produced off-Broadway 1974).

Hospital Play (produced Omaha, 1974).

Babes in the Bighouse (produced Omaha, 1974). Published in *High Energy Musicals from the Omaha Magic Theatre,* New York, Broadway Play Publishing, 1983.

Henna for Endurance (produced Omaha 1974).

We Can Feed Everybody Here (produced off-Broadway, 1974).

Hothouse (produced off-off-Broadway, 1975). New York, French, 1975.

100,001 Horror Stories of the Plains (produced Omaha, 1976).

Brazil Fado (produced Omaha, 1977).

Sleazing toward Athens (produced Omaha, 1977).

Lady Rose's Brazil Hide Out (produced Omaha, 1977).

Willa-Willie-Bill's Dope Garden. New York, Ragnarok, 1977.

American King's English for Queens (produced Omaha, 1978). Published in *High Energy Musicals from the Omaha Magic Theatre,* New York, Broadway Play Publishing, 1983.

Fireworks (produced Louisville, Kentucky, 1979).

Attempted Rescue on Avenue B (produced Chicago, 1979).

With Schmidman, *Goona Goona* (produced Omaha, 1979).

Objective Love I (produced Omaha 1980).

Scenes from Maps (produced Omaha 1980).

With Schmidman, *Running Gag* (produced Lake Placid Winter Olympics, 1980). Published in *High Energy Musicals from the Omaha Magic Theatre,* New York, Broadway Play Publishing, 1983.

Objective Love II (produced Omaha 1981).

Mollie Bailey's Traveling Family Circus: Featuring Scenes from the Life of Mother Jones (produced Los Angeles, 1983). New York, Broadway Play Publishing, 1983.

Fifteen Million Fifteen-Year-Olds (produced Omaha 1983).

X-rayed-Late (produced Omaha 1984).

With Schmidman, *Kegger* (produced Omaha, 1985).

Katmandu (produced Omaha, 1985).

Astro-Bride (produced Omaha, 1985).

Family Talk (produced Omaha, 1986).

With Schmidman, *Sea of Forms* (produced Omaha, 1986).

Dinner's in the Blender (produced Omaha, 1987).

With Schmidman, *Walking through Walls* (produced Omaha, 1987).

Retro (produced Omaha, 1988).

Amtrak (produced Omaha, 1988). Published in *Studies in American Drama, 1945-Present,* Vol. 4, 1989, 21-81.

With Schmidman, *Babes Unchained* (produced Omaha, 1988).

Headlights (produced Omaha, 1989).

Cancel That Last Thought (produced Arcata, California, 1989).

Do You See What I'm Saying? (produced Chicago, 1990).

With Schmidman and Sora Kimberlain, *Body Leaks* (produced Omaha, 1989).

Sound Fields: We Are Hear (produced Omaha, 1992).

Remote Control (produced Omaha, 1995).

Star Path Moon Stop (produced Omaha, 1996, and Suwon, South Korea, International Theatre Festival, 1996).

Other

"Cool Is Out! Uptight Is Out!," in *New York Times,* 14 January 1968.

"Who Says Only Words Make Great Drama?," in *New York Times,* 10 November 1968.

"Two Pages a Day," in *Drama Review,* Vol. 21, No. 4, December 1977, 59-64.

Contributor of monologues, *Facing Forward: An Anthology.* New York, Broadway Press, 1995.

*

Manuscript Collections: Omaha Magic Theatre, Omaha, Nebraska.

Interviews: "Interview with Megan Terry" by Dinah L. Leavitt, in *Women in American Theatre,* edited by Helen Krich Chinoy and Linda Walsh Jenkins, New York, Crown Publishers, 1981; "There's a Yuppie Born Every Minute" by Randall Findlay, in *Minnesota Daily,* Vol. 87, No. 38, 15-21 November 1985.

Critical Sources: *Heartwomen: An Urban Feminist's Odyssey Home* by Sandy Boucher, San Francisco, Harper and Row, 1982; *Feminist Theatre* by Helene Keyssar, London, Macmillan, 1984; "Language and Meaning in Megan Terry's 1970s 'Musicals'" by Kathleen Gregory Klein, in *Modern Drama,* Vol. 27, 1984, 574-583; "Omaha Magic Theatre" by Lynn Sanchez, in *High Performance,* Vol. 11, No. 43, fall 1988, 50-53; "Making Magic Public: Megan Terry's Traveling Family Circus" by Jan Breslauer and Helene Keyssar, in *Making a Spectacle: Feminist Essays on Contemporary Women's Theatre,* edited by Lynda Hart, Ann Arbor, University of Michigan Press, 1989, 169-180; "Magic Theater, Leader Expand Their Horizons" by Robert McMorris, in *Omaha World Herald,* 12 October 1996, 33.

*   *   *

Megan Terry has been involved with the theatre for most of her life. At 14, she began hanging around the Seattle Repertory Playhouse, where she learned about the various aspects of theatre—acting, directing, design—and was first introduced to the improvisational techniques that would influence her later work. The theatre was run by Burton and Florence James, and the two inspired her to begin playwriting. She worked on her craft for many years, and finally in 1955 had three of her plays produced by the Cornish Theatre. During the next few years Terry continued to hone her writing skills and eventually moved to New York City. In 1963 she had her first New York production when *Ex-Miss Copper Queen on a Set of Pills* was produced by the Playwright's Unit at the Cherry Lane Theatre. That same year Terry co-founded The Open Theatre with Joseph Chaikin. Her association with the Open Theatre would continue until the company disbanded in 1973. During her New York tenure Terry also had several productions at LaMama, a well-respected off-Broadway theatre company.

In 1970 Terry was invited to do a piece for Boston University's Bicentennial. There she met Jo Anne Schmidman, a student who played the title role in Terry's new play, *Approaching Simone.* She subsequently invited Schmidman to perform the piece at LaMama, winning Terry an Obie Award for Best Play. Schmidman was then invited to work with the Open Theatre and the two have been creating theatre together ever since.

In 1973 Terry returned with Schmidman to Omaha to become the Playwright-in-Residence with the Omaha Magic Theatre (founded by Schmidman in 1968), a position which she still holds. Terry also served as Adjunct Professor of Theatre at the University of Nebraska for a time. She continues to write and produce plays and to lecture internationally.

Terry has been called the "mother of feminist drama" by Helene Keyssar and is credited with developing transformational theatre, a style in which actors transform from one character to another in response to a change in the given circumstances. This technique is used extensively in many of her plays, including *Viet Rock, Keep Tightly Closed in a Cool Dry Place, The Magic Realists,* and *Calm Down Mother.* Keyssar notes in her essay in *Making a Spectacle* that this type of transformational theatre can serve to "free the stage for a fuller, more complex exploration of erotic and social behavior among all human beings and make gender transformations political."

While not overtly lesbian, Terry's works are definitely women-centered. They consistently focus on feminist themes, emphasizing power structures which revolve around gender. Terry's plays frequently feature strong female role-models, showing women who live according to their own dictates, often counter to societal norms. *Approaching Simone* follows the life of Simone Weil, a french philosopher who committed suicide through starvation in 1943. Terry delves into Weil's search for identity and self-knowledge, portraying the philosopher as a martyr who chose suicide as the ultimate way to control her own destiny. In *American King's English for Queens* Terry examines the sexist nature of language and the way it shapes gender roles in society. And in *Mollie Bailey's Traveling Family Circus: Featuring Scenes from the Life of Mother Jones,* Terry presents two very different women who were not afraid to follow their own dreams, despite the odds.

Of particular interest for those interested in gay and lesbian themes is *Babes in the Bighouse,* a play which explores life in a women's prison. While the setting is inherently lesbian, Terry does not emphasize the sexual relationships between the women, but rather uses the setting to explore larger issues of power dynamics and the way in which women are often disenfranchised. Terry highlights the dehumanizing aspects of prison life. In an interview for *High Performance* magazine she explained that, "It was about how one group of people impose their wills on another. We used it as a metaphor for how women are treated in this culture."

Many of Terry's plays are infused with a strong sexual tension between women. The plays, which are formed of a montage of smaller vignettes, often contain moments of lesbian desire. In *Sound Fields: We Are Hear,* for example, a vignette entitled "Magenta" features three actresses who caress and enfold each other while speaking lines of gentle, sensuous poetry. In *Body Leaks* an actress tries to profess her love for another, but the two are unable to make physical connection. An unseen force—self-censorship—causes the object of affection to continually move away. While these two characters are played by females, they are gender-neutral within the context of the play. Because Terry frequently uses cross-gender casting in her pieces, the characters can be seen as male, female, or neutral, no matter the gender of the performer. This technique allows audience members to impose their own views upon the action. In the case of the couple mentioned above, the pair could be read as a lesbian, gay, or heterosexual depending upon the individual audience member. In this way Terry's pieces act as a litmus test for the attitudes of individual audience members.

While Terry does not write openly about gay and lesbian relationships, she does believe that human beings should be allowed to follow their own loves, dreams, and desires. As Terry herself has noted, "my basic concern is that people have the freedom to be who they are." She stands as an important influence in the modern American theatre. Her work serves to raise questions about gender roles and gender identity. It allows audiences and readers to question their own attitudes and to envision alternatives to society's restrictive norms.

—Beth A. Kattelman

THURMAN, Wallace (Henry)

Nationality: American novelist, playwright, essayist, and editor. **Born:** Salt Lake City, Utah, 16 August 1902. **Education:** University of Utah, Salt Lake City, 1919; University of Southern California, Los Angeles, 1922-23. **Family:** Married Louise Thompson in 1928 (separated and divorced shortly afterwards). **Career:** Held various jobs in Los Angeles, including postal worker, columnist for local black newspaper, and editor for own magazine, *Outlet,* 1923-25; reporter and editor, *The Looking Glass,* New York City, 1925; managing editor, *Messenger,* New York City, 1925-26; editor, *Fire!!,* 1926, and *Harlem, A Forum of Negro Life,* 1928; circulation manager, *The World Tomorrow,* New York City, 1926-28; editorial staff, McFadden Publications, New York City, c. 1929; editorial staff, first as reader, then as editor-in-chief, Macaulay Company, New York City, c. 1930. **Died:** New York City, of tuberculosis, 22 December 1934.

WRITINGS

Novels

The Blacker the Berry: A Novel of Negro Life. New York, Macaulay, 1929.
Infants of the Spring. New York, Macaulay, 1932.
With Abraham Furman, *The Interne.* New York, Macaulay, 1932.

Uncollected Short Stories

"You Never Can Tell," in *Outlet* (Los Angeles), 1924.
"You Never Can Tell, Part 2," in *Outlet* (Los Angeles), 1924.
"Grist in the Mill," in *Messenger* (New York), 1926.
"Cordelia the Crude," in *Fire!!* (New York), 1926.

Uncollected Nonfiction

"Eugene O'Neill's 'All God's Chilluns Got Wings,'" in *Outlet* (Los Angeles), 1924.
"Whither Are We Drifting," in *Outlet* (Los Angeles), 1924.
"Christmas: Its Origins and Significance," in *Outlet* (Los Angeles), 1924.
"In the Name of Purity," in *Messenger* (New York), 1926.
"Quoth Brigham Young:—This Is the Place," in *Messenger* (New York), 1926.
"Singers at the Crossroads," in *Greenwich Village Quill* (New York), 1927.

"Harlem: A Vivid Picture of the World's Greatest Negro City," in *American Monthly* (New York), 1927.
"Negro Artists and the Negro," in *New Republic* (New York), 1927.
"Nephews of Uncle Remus," in *Independent* (New York), 1927.
"Harlem Facets," in *World Tomorrow* (New York), 1927.
"Harlem's Place in the Sun," in *Dance Magazine* (New York), 1928.
"Negro Poets and Their Poetry," in *Bookman* (New York), 1928.
With William Jourdan Rapp, "Harlem—as Others See It," in *Negro World* (New York), 1929.

Stage Plays

With William Jourdan Rapp, *Harlem* (produced New York, 1929).
With William Jourdan Rapp, "Jeremiah the Magnificent" (unproduced, c. 1930).

Screenplays

Tomorrow's Children. Bryan Foy, 1934.
High School Girl. Bryan Foy, 1934.

Other

The Negro Life in New York's Harlem. Girard, Kansas, Haldeman-Julius, 1928.

*

Manuscript Collections: Wallace Thurman Folder, James Weldon Johnson Collection, Beinecke Library, Yale University, New Haven, Connecticut; Moorland-Spingarn Research Center, Howard University, Washington, D.C.; William Jourdan Rapp Collection, University of Oregon Library, Eugene.

Biography: "Portrait of Wallace Thurman" by Mae Gwendolyn Henderson, in *The Harlem Renaissance Remembered,* edited by Arna Bontemps, New York, Dutton, Mead, 1972, 147-70; "Thurman, Wallace" by Ernest B. Boynton, Jr., in *Dictionary of American Negro Biography,* edited by Rayford Logan and Michael Winston, New York, Norton, 1982.

Bibliography: "A Study of the Fiction of Wallace Thurman" by Shirley Haynes Wright (dissertation), East Texas State University, 1983; *Wallace Thurman's Harlem Renaissance* by Eleonore van Notten, Amsterdam, Rodopi, 1994.

*   *   *

Wallace Thurman was born in Salt Lake City, Utah, to Oscar and Beulah Thurman. According to *The Dictionary of American Negro Biography,* it was said Thurman's grandmother was a Native American who married a Jewish peddler. Little is known about Thurman's early life in Salt Lake City. At a time when Utah's black population was small and the state's leading institution, the Church of Jesus Christ of Latter-Day Saints, viewed blacks as cursed, Thurman excelled in school and attended the University of Utah as a pre-medical student. He did the same at the University of Southern California. Somewhere between adolescence and early adulthood, Thurman suffered a nervous breakdown. This was the beginning of a period that featured recurrent mental illness and chronic alcoholism. There is some indication that his psychological and drinking problems were related to ambivalence he felt toward his race, toward his dark complexion, and toward his desires.

While in California, Thurman began his writing career, starting with Los Angeles' black newspaper. During that period, Thurman was a supporter of the burgeoning Harlem Renaissance, of its associated New Negro Movement, and of their primary endorser, Alain Locke. His support ended soon after he arrived in New York City in 1925. In his review of *The New Negro,* the anthology of creative work by black Americans edited by Alain Locke and published in late 1925, Thurman was critical of the assumptions he saw beneath it. His criticism proved expensive: when the Thurman-edited *Fire!!* appeared that next year, most writers, including Locke and W. E. B. DuBois, criticized it harshly. Afterwards, Thurman found little support among the older, more established writers. Significantly, he was one of the few artists of the Harlem Renaissance to have had no white patron. Yet, Thurman found his living in publishing, in Broadway theater, and in film. The success he attained in those fields was unprecedented for a black American.

It was during his life in New York that the first hints of his homosexuality are seen. Shortly after arriving, he was arrested on morals charges in a men's room. While editing *Fire!!,* Thurman and Bruce Nugent, a writer becoming known for his homoerotic work, drew lots to determine who would write a short story themed around prostitution, and who would write one themed around homosexuality. Thurman pulled prostitution. Nugent's story, "Smoke, Lilies, and Jade," is considered the first gay-themed work by an African-American.

As Thompson conveyed to Arnold Rampersad during his research for his biography of Langston Hughes, Thurman never admitted to being a homosexual. Aside from "Smoke, Lilies, and Jade," no story touching homosexuality seems associated with him. If he did consider the issue at all, he must have done so via metaphor, using gradations of skin color, his primary theme, as the vehicle. In *Blacker the Berry* and (to a lesser extent) *Infants of the Spring,* Thurman detailed how skin color is used to distill a group, with those more "light" being more acceptable than those more "dark." If this is his metaphor, then it has application to sexuality. Thurman, however, provided no comment on this application. He did, however, include in *Blacker the Berry* an intoxicated embrace between two men. Given his own alcoholism, it is possible that Thurman was one of the characters.

Though they considered him brilliant, Thurman's contemporaries saw his themes and his homosexuality as symbolic of the bohemianism with which he lived out the 1920s and 1930s, and which, it is implied, ended his life. By his death in 1934, Thurman was regarded the *enfant terrible* of the Harlem Renaissance, a role marking him as an obscure figure.

—J. E. Robinson

TRIFONOV, Gennady

Nationality: Russian poet, essayist, and critic. **Born:** Leningrad (St. Petersburg), 3 June 1945. **Education:** Educated in the Soviet state school system.

Writings

Poetry

"Tbilisi pri svechakh," "Dafnis I Khloia," "Kak motylek," "A tot, kotorogo," "Bibleiskii motiv," "Anakreont," "IA, kazhetsia, vyzhil," "IA znaiu," "Kogda iz sna," "Romeo I Dzhul'etta," "Kogda zhivesh," "Novogodnee poslanie druz'iam," "Sentiabr' 1981 goda," in *Blue Lagoon Anthology of Modern Russian Poetry.* Newtonville, Massachusetts, Oriental Research Partners, 1980.

Translated Poetry

"Jailed Gay Soviet's Poem: 'Letter From Prison,'" in *Advocate,* 11 November 1978. Also published in *The Christopher Street Reader,* New York, Perigee Books, 1984.
"For Three Swift Days," in *The Penguin Book of Homosexual Verse.* New York, Penguin, 1983.
"Three Poems From Tbilisi by Candlelight," in *Orgasms of Light: The Gay Sunshine Anthology: Poetry, Short Fiction, Graphics.* San Francisco, Gay Sunshine Press, 1977.
"A Romanza of Farewell," in *Advocate,* 19 August 1986.

Other

The Two Ballets by Balanchine (novel), in *Gay slaviane* (St. Petersburg), 1994.

*

Critical Sources: "About Gennady Trifonov's Poetry" by David Dar, in *Christopher Street,* Vol. 3, No. 6, January 1979, 66-67; "The Case of Gennady Trifonov" by Simon Karlinsky, in *New York Review of Books,* 10 April 1986, 44; "The Soviet Union vs. Gennady Trifonov" by Simon Karlinsky, in *Advocate,* 19 August 1986, 44-49.

*   *   *

The situation of openly gay and lesbian individuals in the society of the Soviet Union has been one of extreme marginality since the days of Joseph Stalin. This condition was a consequence of Article 121 of the criminal code, which went beyond similar legislation (such as Germany's infamous Paragraph 175) by not only prohibiting the committing of any homosexual acts, but defining the condition of being homosexual out of legal existence. One of the sharpest postwar challenges to this condition of enforced invisibility was presented by the poet Gennady Trifonov.

Trifonov was born in Leningrad, a city which under its former name of St. Petersburg had witnessed the florescence of the Silver Age of Russian poetry, among whose most prominent figures were Mikhail Kuzmin and Nikolai Kliuev, whose frankly homosexual writings had been banned by the 1920s. Following a standard education in the Soviet state school system, he was drafted into the Red Army for two years, only to have his sexual orientation discovered by the KGB. Pressure was brought on him to serve as informer against other gay soldiers, which drove him to attempt suicide at least once. After completing his service, Trifonov was hired as a literary secretary

by the prominent novelist and playwright Vera Panova (1905-1973) and her husband David Dar (who later came out following emigration to Israel and wrote one of the few critical evaluations of Trifonov's poetry). During this time, Trifonov was able to travel extensively within the Soviet Union, visiting such remote regions as Georgia and Kazakhstan.

During the 1970s, Trifonov wrote a number of poems and essays which he read at private homes and circulated as *samizdat* copies among his friends, with some copies given to visiting friends and subsequently published abroad. His work first came to the attention of the general Western audience through the December 31, 1976 *New York Times* coverage of the trial of the dissident feminist writer Yulia Voznesenskaya, who was charged with having slandered the Soviet state in three unpublished works, one of which was an introductory essay to Trifonov's autobiography. By the time this trial was held, he had already been held under arrest totally incommunicado for four months in the Kresty Prison, where interrogators eventually succeeded in forcing him to sign a document implicating other dissident writers in a conspiracy against the government, a confession he later repudiated during his appearance as a witness against Voznesenskaya. In November 1976, he was sentenced to four years in a labor camp under the provisions of Article 121, a punishment he served in the northern Ural Mountains.

Reaction to news of his conviction in the West was swift, with publicity on his situation being issued by his friends and translations of several of his poems appearing in the gay press in England and the United States. In the autumn of 1978, his mother petitioned the government for his release. To assist her, Trifonov's poem "Letter From Prison" was simultaneously published by five major gay newspapers and journals in Canada, Great Britain, and the United States. While interned in 1977, he was able to obtain copies of two articles which had appeared in *Ogonyok* and *Literary Gazette,* the former describing his poetry as "miserable homosexual doggerel." In reply, he sent his friends an "Open Letter to the *Literary Gazette*" in which he attacked the depiction of the homosexual in Soviet publications, documented the incarceration and inhumane treatment of homosexuals in labor camps, and called for the convening of a conference of social scientists, physicians, and psychologists to determine what threat (if any) homosexuality posed to the Soviet system.

He returned to Leningrad in 1980 upon completion of his sentence and found work unloading books in a publisher's warehouse and moving furniture, manual labor being the usual type of job available for a convicted homosexual at this time. For the next six years, he shared a small apartment with his mother and resumed his writing. It was in this period that more of his work appeared abroad in such widely-read volumes as *The Penguin Book of Homosexual Verse* and the popular gay literary magazine *Christopher Street.* In January 1986, accusations of "aggravated hooliganism" were made against him but legal proceedings did not materialize, due to extensive publicizing of his situation in the foreign press. Since that time, Trifonov has been allowed to publish works of literary criticism (provided he avoids gay and lesbian subjects) and has abandoned his efforts to secure an exit visa. With the dissolution of the Soviet Union, Trifonov's work began to be more widely circulated, and in 1994 the new St. Petersburg magazine *Gay slaviane* published his novel *The Two Ballets by Balanchine.*

—Robert B. Marks Ridinger

TRINIDAD, David

Nationality: American poet, editor, and educator. **Born:** Los Angeles, California, 20 July 1953. **Education:** California State University at Northridge, B.A. 1979; Brooklyn College, M.F.A. 1990; The New School, New York, New York, M.F.A. in Creative Writing (Poetry), from 1997. **Family:** Companion of Ira Silverberg, from 1989. **Career:** Poetry workshop instructor, Beyond Baroque Literary/Arts Center, Venice, California, 1987-88, The Poetry Project at St. Mark's Church, New York, New York, 1990-91, The Writer's Voice, New York, New York, 1989-96, The New School, New York, New York, 1994-96, The Hudson Valley Writers' Center, Tarrytown, New York, 1996; adjunct lecturer, English Department, Brooklyn College, Brooklyn, New York, 1988-92; instructor, English Department, Rutgers University, New Brunswick, New Jersey, from 1996. Editor/publisher, Sherwood Press, Los Angeles, 1981-84; editor, "15 L.A. Poets" supplement of *B City,* 1988, and *Brooklyn Review,* 1989-90; poetry editor, *OutWeek,* 1990-91, and Amethyst Press, 1992-93. **Awards:** Dorland Mountain Colony Fellowship, 1979; Michael Tuch Foundation Fellowship, 1988; Fund for Poetry Award, 1988, 1996; Lambda Literary Award nomination, for *Hand Over Heart,* 1992; Blue Mountain Center Fellowship, 1992. **Address:** 401 West Broadway, New York, New York 10012, U.S.A.

WRITINGS

Poetry

Pavane. Chatsworth, California, Sherwood Press, 1981.
Monday, Monday. Los Angeles, Cold Calm Press, 1985.
Living Doll. Los Angeles, Illuminati, 1986.
November. New York, Hanuman Books, 1987.
Three Stories (prose poetry). New York, Hanuman Books, 1988.
With Bob Flanagan, *A Taste of Honey.* Los Angeles, Cold Calm Press, 1990.
Hand Over Heart: Poems 1981-1988. New York, Amethyst Press, 1991.
Answer Song. New York, High Risk Books/Serpent's Tail, 1994.
Plush: Selected Poems, edited by Lynn Crosbie and Michael Holmes. Toronto, Coach House, 1995.

Uncollected Poetry

"Something's Got to Give," in *Chelsea,* 1993.
"Accessories," in *Exact Change Yearbook,* 1995.
"Ancient History," in *B City,* 1995.
"Bits 'n Pieces," in *Brooklyn Review,* 1995.
"Fluff," in *The Baffler,* 1995.
"The Game of Life," in *Columbia Poetry Review,* 1995.
"Monster Mash," in *B City,* 1995.
"Chatty Cathy Villanelle," in *American Letters & Commentary,* 1996.
"Pink Poems," in *No Roses Review,* 1996.
"Essay with Moveable Parts," in *Spoon River Poetry Review,* 1997.
"Fortunes," in *Gargoyle,* 1997.

Anthologies

American Poetry Since 1970: Up Late, edited by Andrei Codrescu. New York, Four Walls Eight Windows, 1987.
Under 35: The New Generation of American Poets, edited by Nicholas Christopher. New York, Anchor Books/Doubleday, 1989.
Poets for Life: Seventy-Six Poets Respond to AIDS, edited by Michael Klein. New York, Crown, 1989.
High Risk: An Anthology of Forbidden Writings, edited by Amy Scholder and Ira Silverberg. New York, Dutton/Plume, 1991.
The Best American Poetry 1991, edited by Mark Strand. New York, Scribners/Collier, 1992.
Mondo Barbie, edited by Lucinda Ebersole and Richard Peabody. New York, St. Martin's, 1993.
Sweet Nothings: An Anthology of Rock and Roll in American Poetry, edited by Jim Elledge. Bloomington, Indiana University Press, 1994.
Postmodern American Poetry: A Norton Anthology, edited by Paul Hoover. New York, W.W. Norton, 1994.
American Poets Say Goodbye to the Twentieth Century, edited by Andrei Codrescu and Laura Rosenthal. New York, Four Walls Eight Windows, 1996.

Other

"Introduction," in *Strong Place,* by Tim Dlugos. New York, Amethyst Press, 1992.
"In the Midnight Hour: Helter Skelter Turns Twenty-Five" (essay about the Tate/LaBianca murders), in *Los Angeles Reader Book Supplement,* October 1994.
"Bewitched," in *The Illinois Review,* 1995-96

Editor, *Powerless: Selected Poems, 1973-1990,* by Tim Dlugos. New York, High Risk Books/Serpent's Tail, 1996.

*

Interviews: "Playing with Dolls: Games with David Trinidad" by Joan Larkin, in *Outweek,* 8 May 1991; "A Conversation with David Trinidad: Pop Poet a Go-Go" by Owen Keehan, in *Torso,* July 1995.

Critical Sources: Review of *Pavane* by Peter Clothier, in *Los Angeles Times Book Review,* 6 September 1981; review of *Pavane,* in *Voice Literary Supplement,* November 1981; review of *Pavane* by Kevin Jeffery Clarke, in *Poetry Project Newsletter,* February 1982; review of *Pavane* by Rudy Kikel, in *New York Native,* 15-28 February 1982; review of *Monday, Monday* by Dennis Cooper, in *Poetry Project,* March 1985; review of *Monday, Monday* by Holly Prado, in *Los Angeles Times Book Review,* 25 August 1985; review of *Monday, Monday* by Kevin Killian, in *Poetry Flash,* October 1985; review of *Monday, Monday* by Stan Leventhal, in *Torso,* December 1985; review of *Monday, Monday* by David MacLean, in *The Body Politic,* May 1986; "Personal Best" by Debbie Patino, in *L.A. Weekly,* 4-10 December 1987; review of *A Taste of Honey* by Stan Leventhal, in *Mandate,* April 1991; review of *A Taste of Honey* by John Strausbaugh, in *New York Press,* 6-12 February 1991; review of *A Taste of Honey* by Steve Abbott, in *Poetry Flash,* February 1991; review of *A Taste of Honey* by Reagan Upshaw, in *Onthebus,* No. 8 & 9, 1991; review of *Hand Over Heart*, in *Publishers Weekly,* 12 April 1991; review of *Hand Over Heart* by Dodie Bellamy and Kevin Killian, in *Small Press Traffic,* spring/summer 1991; review of *Hand Over Heart* by Henry Flesh, in *James White Review,* summer 1991; *City Pages,* 7 August 1991; review of *Hand Over Heart* by Robin Selman, in *Voice Literary Supplement,* September 1991; "Subjectivity and Disappointment in Contemporary American Poetry" by David Kaufmann, in *Ploughshares,* winter 1991-92; review of *Hand Over Heart* by Arthur Nersesian, in *East Village Avenues,* February 1992; review of *Hand Over Heart* by Sparrow, in *Poetry Project,* February/March 1993; review of *Hand Over Heart* by David Yezzi, in *Parnassus,* Vol. 18, No. 2/Vol. 19, No. 1, 1993-94; review of *Answer Song* by Gary Sullivan, in *City Pages,* 14 December 1994; review of *Answer Song* by Michael Fitzgerald, in *Gay Community News,* July 1995; review of *Answer Song* by Richard Labonte, in *Feminist Bookstore News,* January/February 1995; review of *Answer Song* by David L. Ulin, in *Los Angeles Reader,* 9 December 1994; *Publishers Weekly,* 26 September 1994; review of *Answer Song* by Christine Cassidy, in *Lambda Book Report,* November/December 1994; review of *Answer Song* by Bruce Hainley, in *Willamette Week,* 6 December 1995; review of *Answer Song* by Lee Hanson, in *Our Own Community Press,* November 1994; *New York Native,* 7 November 1994; review of *Answer Song* by Edmund Miller, in *Bay Windows,* 6 April 1995.

*   *   *

David Trinidad's poetry has developed from the rather mainstream *Pavane,* his first collection, to the experimentation with form and the popular culture icons of *Hand Over Heart* and *Answer Song,* in which he relies to a large extent on various imagery from mostly 1960s rock-and-roll figures and songs; Barbie, Ken, and other dolls; and characters and plots from TV programs and films. While Trinidad believes that popular culture is a facet of "our collective memories," as Owen Keehan, writing in *Torso,* recalled in his interview with the poet, the themes with which he began his career have remained virtually constant whether grounded in the myth of Oedipus or in newspaper accounts of the Tate-LaBianca murders.

Throughout *Pavane,* Trinidad's themes are what one might expect from a young, gay poet: social and familial rejection, failures in personal relationships, a sense of loss. Although he borrows from classical mythology, legends, and fairy tales, he adroitly, at times brilliantly, recasts the old material into a contemporary version of the original. Foremost among Trinidad's borrowings is Oedipus, who becomes the perfect emblem for a contemporary gay man: Oedipus's limp marked him as different, his parents rejected him as a child, he lived in a time of "pestilence," he was doomed as a result of his sexual attraction, and so on. In "The Sphinx," for example, the contemporary monster is homosexuality, and the solution to the riddle she asks the twentieth-century, disco Oedipus is just as contemporary: guilt. "Delphi," also Oedipus-related, reads like the blueprint of a young boy's coping with the realization that he's gay, which may be a surprise to him but to no one else: "My parents first heard it / from the school psychologist. / It stood out in my art work / like a cardboard kitchenette...." Like the ancient Oedipus, this one is also rejected by his parents.

Although *Pavane* investigates the narrator's coming to terms with his sexuality, the moments of eroticism which readers have grown to expect in coming out poetry are brief, spare, and extraordinarily intense. The erotic power of "The Gift of Dionysus,"

for example, is grounded not in what's depicted but what's omitted. "Pavane" rivals Auden's "Lullaby [Lay your sleeping head]" in its ability to delve effortlessly into the heart of love. Teenage angst is the focus of "The Boy." Its narrator is unsure whether or not a neighbor boy actually appeared in the narrator's room or is only a figment of the narrator's imagination, born from his "struggling to outlast / [his] own restlessness." Such "restlessness" informs much of *Pavane.* The present, Trinidad implies, offers nothing positive or meaningful and creates "restlessness," which only the past soothes. In "Warm Winter" or "Scholar," Trinidad's narrators return to the past through memories or construct fantasies in their search for happiness. Escapism is the chief means by which they cope with their lives.

Alcoholism and other substance abuse mark the escapist motif in Trinidad's work, extending from "The Party" to the prose poem "Night and Fog," which focuses on "Christopher N. (an alias)" and his self-destruction. At the beginning, he's "innocent-looking," but Christopher's life and experiences lead the narrator to realize, "No one is ever innocent." In "Nightfall," the narrator's failed life is almost relieved by a moment of grace which is fleeting, and the volume quickly ends with the next poem, "Nightshade," one of utter stasis. Despite its metaphoric darkness, "Nightshade" provides a hint at a new direction in Trinidad's poetics when his narrator refers to life as "leftovers from an old movie or nightmare / in which the pale heroine steps / through the immense halls / of The Count's hilltop castle...." The allusion to Count Dracula is the first of a long litany of pop culture elements which will wind their way into Trinidad's work and become his trademark.

After *Pavane,* Trinidad published four chapbooks of his own work—*Monday, Monday, Living Doll, Three Stories, November*—and a fifth, *A Taste of Honey,* written in collaboration with Bob Flanagan. The contents of all but *A Taste of Honey* are included in *Hand Over Heart,* his second full-length collection, which bridges opposites in his career and life in several ways. It not only marks the end of his years on the West Coast, where he was born and grew into young adulthood, it also signifies transition in his style. On one hand, *Hand Over Heart* offers experiences directly, unadorned, and confessionally in Trinidad's attempt to tell "the truth," according to Joan Larkin in her interview with Trinidad in *Outweek.* Her point is illustrated in Trinidad's poem "Ordinary Things": "I chain-smoked and / drank until I was / numb enough to fall / asleep..." On the other hand, the book reveals Trinidad's shift from poetry as a "lofty, inaccessible thing," according to Larkin, to a more democratic, accessible verse. To achieve both ends, he exchanged classical and other "traditional" allusions for the popular culture landmarks of his time. Oedipus once served to disguise Trinidad, but the figures he employs from popular culture serve to present his self to readers and to underscore themes which surfaced in the earlier volume.

"Dreams" recounts two dreams Trinidad has in one night (they are differentiated by a brief moment, when he wakes at 3:00). Its first half mentions two films suggesting the narrator's life: *The Lost Weekend,* in which Ray Milland plays an alcoholic, and Disney's *In Search of the Castaways,* in which Hayley Mills seeks her missing father. The older, black-and-white movie is unrelenting in its grimy depiction of a life bound in self-destruction; the highly sanitized Disney production is fluff by comparison. Yet, they depict alcoholism and a child's loss of a father, important themes in Trinidad's work, as well as in gay poetry in general. In the second half of the poem, Trinidad relates a dream of his grandfather, admitting in it he hates himself. The confessional intertwines with pop culture, producing a powerful portrait of a young gay man trying to deal with the guilt of his alcoholism and feelings of rejection, but only being able to hate himself.

In "Song," one of Trinidad's most often used popular culture icons, girl groups of the early 1960s and their music, makes its first appearance. He tells us that hearing again the "single by the all-girl group / I worshipped as an adolescent" brings back "teenage emotions" and, more important, that those emotions "survive" into his adulthood and they are just as serious now as then and as "thoughtless as ever." He implies we cannot escape who we were in the past; we can only come to terms with ourselves.

The lengthy "Up & Down" moves from the present to the past and back again, over and over, effortlessly, weaving confession and popular culture tightly together. In the present, Trinidad toys with cocaine and listens to the group Siouxsie and the Banshees, but then he recalls the past, when he listened to "He's So Fine" by The Chiffons, a girl group, as his older brother played baseball with "Paul, a blond neigh- / bor boy I had a secret / crush on...." The Chiffons and the word "crush" imply innocence in sharp contrast to the present, characterized by substance abuse and a group whose lyrics, music, and name—"banshee"—have dark implications. Counterpointing the poet's early crush on Paul is his admission of promiscuity later in the poem. Such behavior is intensified by his "tirades / about suicide and unrequited love."

"Monday, Monday" and "Meet the Supremes" also use 1960s-style music in the same manner for similar results. "Monday, Monday" investigates how pop music influences our concept of love. "Radio's reality," Trinidad warns us, then asks, "Why is it / I've always mistaken /...lyrics for my / true feelings?" He suggests that it's often difficult to differentiate between what should be and what is, while also recognizing, the gap between gay love (his "true feelings") and heterosexual love ("Radio's reality"); because straight love is depicted on the radio and is therefore acceptable, he confuses it for his own. "Meet the Supremes" examines the difference between what appears on the surface and what's beneath it. The happiness conveyed in classic photos of The Supremes—they are "captured forever / ...in an unreal...light" as if "they're in heaven"—contrasts with the betrayal and pain that characterized the group's real life and the relationship of its members to one another. Similarly, the adolescent Trinidad's outer image is tame compared to his inner life, beginning with simple sexual fantasy and developing into an interest in drugs and suicide until "nearly twenty years later I would hit / bottom in an unfurnished Hollywood single, drunk / and stoned and fed up, still spinning those same / old tunes."

Trinidad also employs allusions to a wide variety of TV programs, to titles of books and journals, and to toys (Barbie, in particular) to add humor, to distract, and to distance himself from the depression, pain, loss, and frustration of everyday life. The campy humor in "November," an eleven-part diary poem, is conveyed by such experiences or items as a drag contest, a she/he calendar, listening to an album of TV theme music, etc., and it belies the deadly seriousness of life for the gay male at this century's close. Trinidad only hints at such serious themes, however, among them disenfranchisement from his family, a lack of a permanent love relationship, and AIDS. In "Living Doll," Trinidad takes his particular brand of humor to its extreme, assuming Barbie's persona, and complaining about her and Ken's not-so-perfect relationship—"What went wrong? Why won't he answer my messages?"—echoing his own failed relationships and the camp sincerity of girl-group lyrics.

From its opening poem to its concluding one, *Answer Song* marks the beginning of Trinidad's maturity as a poet. Much of what he so successfully employed in *Hand Over Heart* is continued here, in particular his confessional verse and his reliance on popular culture. Nevertheless, *Answer Song* reveals he's honed his craft and broadened his vision. While Trinidad experimented with form in earlier books, he did so with a little less variety. Here they range from free verse to concrete poetry ("[Doll Not Included]"), prose poems ("The Shower Scene in *Psycho*"), the cross-genre "It's a Wig," and traditional forms (the sonnet "Pacoima, California, 1956" and the villanelle "Invasion"). While the landscape has changed to New York, he includes poems of memory about the West Coast and his days there. In "Song," for example, he again recalls his brother playing ball with neighbor boys as he listens to girl-group songs. Nevertheless, what is most notable is Trinidad's in-your-face confessionalism, which is an extension of his earlier, more-polite version of the genre, and—in very sharp contrast to that genre—poems revealing a happy, healthy love relationship, a first in his work thus far.

The overtly confessional "My Lover," for example, calls into question not only the definition of lover but of love itself. While its title suggests it will be about a single individual, the poem is a Whitman-like catalog of what appears to be tricks, dates, boyfriends, or lovers, each line characterizing a different one. Collectively, they represent Trinidad's, and many other gay men's, experiences with love, most of which appear to be purely physical in nature ("My lover who doesn't know my name / My lover who fucks me standing up"). Only in the last two lines does Trinidad suggest the possibility of a relationship that may be more than simply sex: "My lover who plays 'Killing Me Softly with His Song' / over and over as we make love all afternoon." "Eighteen to Twenty-One," a sequence of seven poems, is as confessional, as blunt, and as focused on sex as "My Lover" is, and it even expands upon some of the situations briefly mentioned in "My Lover." Yet, it tackles "lovers" individually, one to a poem, from the one who, in the first of the seven poems, "said his name was Nick" and later "threatened / to tell [Trinidad's] parents [he] was gay, blackmailed /...and raped [him] at / knifepoint," to an older man, in the last poem, who gave the 21-year-old Trinidad head in a porno theater. Each poem in the sequence is 14 lines long, recalling the sonnet, a form used almost exclusively and traditionally for love poetry. This fact offers the sequence an underlying irony: while the framework (i.e., form) for love is available, the content of love isn't. Outwardly, the couple having sex may seem to be lovers, but there's no emotional involvement, a requirement for real lovers. In short, the outward appearance, or image, doesn't adequately represent the reality.

Offsetting such brutality and squalor are a number of poems focused on Trinidad's relationship with Ira Silverberg, his life partner since 1989, whom he identifies by name in a large number of them. Unlike the "typical" gay love poem, these don't offer snapshots of men as sexual acrobats, but as human beings engaged in a supportive relationship. The first is aptly called "Love Poem," its title as unique in Trinidad's work as it is important. In it, Trinidad "wakes from a nightmare," has a cigarette, and in getting back into bed, wakes Ira. Trinidad admits his nightmare to which Ira replies, "'You're safe now'" and "'Go back to sleep. / You won't have any more bad dreams.'" The poem is about nothing of earth-shattering consequence except the fact that for the first time in several hundred pages of poetry, Trinidad reports that another man has provided him with support, often a major accomplishment in gay life. Their experiences together range from listening to "a tape of Anne Sexton / reading her poems" ("Sunday Evening"), to pushing the snooze button and going back to sleep ("Wednesday Morning"), discussing past experiences ("Dead Flowers"), speaking in one's sleep ("What Ira Said in His Sleep"), planning vacations ("Postcard from Cherry Grove"). Regardless of the topic each recounts, what's important about them is their message, that gay men can find love, love that is at once healthy and supportive. Indeed, the poem "Answer Song" affirms the possibility of love despite the problems imposed upon individuals in their search for it, and it's no accident that the framework for "Answer Song" is, ironically, a girl-group number, Lesley Gore's second hit, "Judy's Turn to Cry."

—Jim Elledge

TSUI, Kitty (Kit Fan)

Pseudonym: Has also written as Eric Norton. **Nationality:** American poet, short story writer, novelist, essayist, and performance artist. **Born:** Hong Kong, 4 September 1952; immigrated to Liverpool, England, at age five; lived in Hong Kong from age ten to fifteen; immigrated to San Francisco, California, 1968. **Education:** Educated in Liverpool, England, and Hong Kong; attended Lowell High School, San Francisco; San Francisco State University, B.A. in Creative Writing 1975; graduate studies in Broadcast Communication Arts. **Family:** Companion of Andrea Pedit. **Career:** Has held a variety of jobs in arts and activism, including freelance writing, performance art, and writing and performing with the collectives *Unbound Feet* and *Unbound Feet Three* from 1979-82. columnist ("Leathertalk Top to Bottom") for *Chicago Nightlines*, 1990-92; member of editorial board, *Lesbian Review of Books*, from 1994; contributor to the *Advocate, Bay Area Reporter, Bay Times, Chicago Outlines, City Arts Magazine, East/West, Lambda Book Report, New Phoenix Rising, off our backs, On Our Backs, Plexus, San Francisco Bay Guardian,* and *Sentinel.* **Awards:** First Place, Friends of the Public Library and Poetry Center, San Francisco State University, for poetry, 1969; National Women's Playwriting Competition finalist, One Act Theater Company, San Francisco, 1980; listed as one of fifty most influential writers of the past decade, *Lambda Book Report,* 1990; Ken Dawson Award, CLAGS (Center for Lesbian and Gay Studies, City University of New York), for research in gay and lesbian history, 1995; Firecracker Alternative Book Award, 1996. **Agent:** Sheryl B. Fullerton, 1010 Church Street, San Francisco, California 94114, U.S.A.

WRITINGS

Poetry

"all your time," "to an old lady," "what i cannot," "to jan," and "for Barry Fong-Torres," in *Third World Women,* co-edited by Kitty Tsui. San Francisco, Third World Communications Press, 1972.

"kapendewa..." and "for my spirit, in love and out of love," in *Time to Greez! Incantations from the Third World,* edited by Janice Mirikitani. San Francisco, Glide Publications, 1975.

"the words of a woman who breathes fire: one," in *Lesbian Poetry,* edited by Elly Bulkin and Joan Larkin. Watertown, Maine, Persephone Press, 1981.

"it's in the name" and "chinatown talking story," in *Breaking Silence: An Anthology of Contemporary Asian American Poets,* edited by Joseph Bruchac. Greenfield Center, New York, Greenfield Review Press, 1983.

The Words of a Woman Who Breathes Fire. San Francisco, California, Spinster's Ink, 1983.

"don't call me sir call me strong," "from red rock canyon, summer, 1977," and "chinatown talking story," in *Early Ripening: American Women's Poetry Now,* edited by Marge Piercy. Winchester, Massachusetts, Pandora Press, 1987.

"a chinatown banquet," in *Gay and Lesbian Poetry in Our Time,* edited by Carl Morse and Joan Larkin. New York, St. Martin's Press, 1988.

"don't let them chip away at our language," in *An Ear to the Ground: An Anthology of Contemporary American Poetry,* edited by Marie Harris and Kathleen Aguero. Athens, Georgia, University of Georgia Press, 1989.

"a chinese banquet," in *Growing Up Gay/Growing Up Lesbian,* edited by Bennett L. Suger. New York, The New Press, 1994.

"a chinese banquet," "how can I show this poem to geraldine?," and "it's in the name," in *Chloe Plus Olivia: An Anthology of Lesbian Literature from the Seventeenth Century to the Present,* edited by Lillian Faderman. New York, Viking, 1994.

"gloriously," in *On a Bed of Rice: An Asian American Erotic Feast,* edited by Geraldine Kudaka. New York, Anchor, 1995.

"gloriously" and "dragon lover," in *My Lover Is a Woman: Contemporary Lesbian Love Poems,* edited by Lesléa Newman. New York, Ballantine Books, 1996.

"sex does not equal death," in *The Second Coming: A Leatherdyke Reader,* edited by Pat Califia and Robin Sweeney. Los Angeles, Alyson, 1996.

"dragon lover," in *Zenith of Desire,* edited by Gerry Gomez Pearlberg. New York, Crown, 1996.

"open heart" and "coming into light," in *Reclaiming the Heartland: Lesbian and Gay Male Voices from the Midwest,* edited by Karen Osbourne and Bill Spurlin. Minneapolis, Minnesota, University of Minnesota Press, 1996.

"suzy wong's been dead a long time," in *The Iowa Review,* Vol. 26, summer 1996, 194-195.

"a dog's poem," in *Queer Dog: Homo/Pup/Poetry,* edited by Gerry Gomez Pearlburgh. Pittsburgh, Cleis Press, 1997.

Short Stories

"Poa Poa Is Living Breathing Light," in *Lesbian Fiction,* edited by Elly Bulkin. Watertown, Maine, Persephone Press, 1981.

"In Training," in *Out from Under, Sober Dykes and Our Friends,* edited by Jean Swallow. San Francisco, Spinster's Ink, 1983.

"Solitary Pleasure," in *Finding Courage: Writings by Women,* edited by Irene Zahava. Freedom, California, Crossing Press, 1989.

"One Night Stand," in *Intricate Passions,* edited by Tee Corinne. Austin, Texas, Banned Books, 1989.

"Why the Milky Way Is Milky," in *Lesbian Love Stories,* edited by Irene Zahava. Freedom, California, Crossing Press, 1989.

"Anita and Auntie" and "a chinese banquet," in *The Very Inside: An Anthology of Writings by Asian and Pacific Islander Lesbian and Bisexual Women,* edited by Sharon Lim-Hing. Toronto, Ontario, Canada, Sister Vision, 1994.

"Vanilla and Strawberries" and "Phonesex," in *Pearls of Passion: A Treasury of Lesbian Erotica,* edited by C. Allyson Lee and Makeda Silvera. Toronto, Ontario, Sister Vision, 1995.

"A Femme, A Daddy, and Their Dyke," in *Queer View Mirror: Lesbian and Gay Short Short Fiction,* edited by James C. Johnstone and Karen X. Tulchinsky. Vancouver, British Columbia, Arsenal Pulp Press, 1995.

"A Femme in Butch Clothing," in *The Femme Mystique,* edited by Lesléa Newman. Los Angeles, Alyson, 1995.

"Special Delivery," in *Heat Wave,* edited by Lucy Jane Bledsoe. Los Angeles, Alyson, 1995.

"Give Joan Chen My Phone Number Anytime," in *Lesbian Erotics,* edited by Karla Jay. New York, New York University Press, 1995.

"The Legend of White Snake," in *Once Upon a Time,* edited by Michael Ford. New York, A Richard Kasak Book, 1996.

"Why the Sea Is Salty," in *The New Worlds of Women,* edited by Cecilia Tan. Cambridge, Massachusetts, Circlet Press, 1996.

With Andrea Pedit, "Step by Step," in *Portraits of Love, lesbians writing about love,* edited by Susan Fox Rogers and Linda Smukler. New York, St. Martin's Press, 1997.

"The Cutting," in *Virgin Territories II,* edited by Shar Rednour. New York, A Richard Kasak Book, 1997.

"D & D," in *Best Lesbian Erotica 1997,* edited by Tristain Taormino. Pittsburgh, Pennsylvania, Cleis Press, 1997.

Novels

Breathless. Ithaca, New York, Firebrand Books, 1996.
Sparks Fly (as Eric Norton). New York, Bad Boy Press, 1997.

Essays

"Breaking Silence, Making Waves and Loving Ourselves: The Politics of Coming Out and Coming Home," in *Lesbian Philosophies and Cultures,* edited by Jeffner Allen. Albany, New York, State University of New York Press, 1990.

"Who Says We Don't Talk about Sex?," in *The Persistent Desire: A Femme-Butch Reader,* edited by Joan Nestle. Boston, Alyson, 1992.

"Lesbian Marriage Ceremonies: I Do" and "A Letter from Anita," in *Dyke Life: From Growing Up to Growing Old, A Celebration of the Lesbian Experience,* edited by Karla Jay. New York, Harper Collins, 1995.

"Asian Pacific Lesbian, aka Dead Girl, China Doll, Dragon Lady or the Invisible Man," in *Our Right to Love: A Lesbian Resource Book,* edited by Ginny Vida. New York, Macmillan, 1996.

Other

Co-editor, *Third World Women* (poems, short stories, and essays). San Francisco, Third World Communications Press, 1972.

With Trinity Ordoña, "Anita and Auntie" (performance art), in *Asian/Pacific Lesbians: Our Identities, Our Movements.* San Francisco, Chicago, New York, Washington D. C., 1987.

"Prelude to Decadence: Dinner for a Date in Under Fifty Minutes," in *Food for Life and Other Dish: A Benefit Book to Help Organizations Providing Meals for People with AIDS,* edited by Lawrence Schimel. Pittsburgh, Pennsylvania, Cleis, 1996.

"Thanksgiving Feast, Chinatown Style," in *Cookin' With Honey,* edited by Amy Scholder. Ithaca, New York, Firebrand Books, 1996.

"Willyce Kim," in *Contemporary Lesbian Writers of the United States: A Bio-Bibliographical Critical Sourcebook,* edited by Denise D. Knight and Sandra Pollack. Westport, Connecticut, Greenwood Press, 1993.

*

Films: Featured or interviewed in *Women of Gold,* directed by Marilyn Abbinck and Eileen Lee, U.S.A., 1990; *Framing Lesbian Fashion,* directed by Karen Everett, U.S.A., 1992; *Cut Sleeve,* directed by N. A. Diaman, U.S.A., 1992; *The Third Sex,* directed by Margaret Wescott, Canada, 1994; also appeared in *Women's Physique,* produced by Male Entertainment Network, and *We Are Here to Stay!!,* produced by Scintilla Productions.

Critical Sources: "don't call me sir call me strong" and "chinatown talking story" by Kitty Tsui, in *Early Ripening: American Women's Poetry Now,* edited by Marge Piercey, Boston, Pandora, 1987, 236-240; "Who Says We Don't Talk about Sex?" by Kitty Tsui and "Flamboyance and Fortitude: An Introduction" by Joan Nestle, in *The Persistent Desire: A Femme-Butch Reader,* edited by Joan Nestle, Boston, Alyson, 1992, 385-387, 13-20; "Premature Gestures: A Speculative Dialogue on Asian Pacific Islander Lesbian and Gay Writing" by Alice Y. Hom and Ming-Yuen S. Ma, in *Critical Essays: Gay and Lesbian Writers of Color,* edited by Emmanuel S. Nelson, New York, London and Norwood, Australia, Haworth Press, 1993, 21-51; "Kitty Tsui" by Ryn L. Edwards, in *Contemporary Lesbian Writers of the United States: A Bio-Bibliographical Critical Sourcebook* edited by Sandra Pollack and Denise D. Knight, Westport, Connecticut, Greenwood Press, 1993; "Anita and Auntie" and "a chinese banquet" by Kitty Tsui, in *The Very Inside: An Anthology of Writing by Asian and Pacific Islander Lesbian and Bisexual Writers,* edited by Sharon Lim-Hing, Toronto, Ontario, Canada, Sister Vision, 1994, 149-155; "Welcome to Dyke Life: An Introduction" by Karla Jay, and "Lesbian Marriage Ceremonies: I Do" and "A Letter from Anita" by Kitty Tsui, in *Dyke Life: From Growing Up to Growing Old, A Celebration of the Lesbian Experience,* edited by Karla Jay, New York, HarperCollins, 1995, 1-18, 111-125, 327; "Introduction" by James C. Johnstone and Karen X. Tulchinsky, in *Queer View Mirror: Lesbian and Gay Short Short Fiction,* edited by James C. Johnstone and Karen X. Tulchinsky, Vancouver, Canada, Arsenal Pulp Press, 1995, 13-15; "A Femme in Butch Clothing" by Kitty Tsui, in *Breathless,* Ithaca, New York, Firebrand, 1996, 33-38; "Breathless" (publicity release) by Nancy K. Bereano, Ithaca, New York, Firebrand, 1996; "Don't Ask, Don't Tell, Don't Know: Sexual Identity and Expression among East Asian-American Lesbians" by Connie S. Chan, in *The New Lesbian Studies: Into the Twenty-First Century,* edited by Bonnie Zimmerman and Toni A. H. McNaron, New York, Feminist Press, 1996, 91-97; "sex does not equal death" by Kitty Tsui, and "Come Soon, Come In, and Come as You Are: An Introduction" and "Safer Sex Guidelines for Leatherdykes" by Pat Califia and Robin Sweeney, in *The Second Coming: A Leatherdyke Reader,* edited by Pat Califia and

Robin Sweeney, Los Angeles, Alyson Publications, 1996, 93-94, XI-XVII, 351-354; "Prelude to Decadence: Dinner for a Date in Under Fifty Minutes" by Kitty Tsui, in *Food for Life and Other Dish: A Benefit Book to Help Organizations Providing Meals for People with AIDS,* edited by Lawrence Schimel, Pittsburgh, Pennsylvania, Cleis Press, 1996, 75-77; unpublished interview with Kitty Tsui by Patti Capel Swartz, January 1997.

Kitty Tsui comments:

I came out when I was 21 into a gay community that was mostly white. It was the mid-seventies in San Francisco. There was a dearth of literature and the faces that surrounded me were white. I began writing to make myself visible, publishing in anthologies. In 1983, my book *The Words of a Woman Who Breathes Fire* was published by Spinsters, Ink, the first by a Chinese-American lesbian. I write in many genres, poetry, short stories, erotica, essays. As an Asian American lesbian I am unrepresented, omitted, silenced, and invisible. I write to fight erasure, to demand a voice, to become visible, to reclaim my history. I write to turn on the light.

*   *   *

Kitty Tsui's writing is as rich and varied as her life, drawing from her varied perspectives as a Chinese daughter who cannot take her lesbian lover to the family banquet (described in "a chinese banquet") to the leatherdyke who writes erotica and everywhere in between. What joins these writings is Tsui's steadfast refusal to wall off segments of her experience as inappropriate or unacceptable; Tsui writes with a full realization of who she is and where she comes from. Coming to write from the full sense of who she is and what she can imagine has not always been easy, however. Overcoming invisibility and gaining a voice, as Kitty Tsui points out, have been difficult for Asian American lesbians.

"For me personally, my writings have been in [over 50] anthologies, but I have always fought to be in them and I feel that I have always been fighting. I fought to be visible. I fought to be heard. I fight to be included," Tsui told Alice Y. Hom's and Ming-Yuen S. Ma, authors of "Premature Gestures: A Speculative Dialogue on Asian Pacific Islander Lesbian and Gay Writing," published in *Critical Essays: Gay and Lesbian Writers of Color.* According to Hom and Ma, visibility has been difficult not only because of the difficulty of getting published—most Asian American and Asian Pacific lesbian writers have been published by women's presses or self-published—but also because lesbians fear disclosing their sexual identity to their families. In "Who Says We Don't Talk about Sex?," an essay condensed from a speech presented at the Horizons Lesbian Conference in Chicago in 1990, Tsui discusses being "raised to be a nice Chinese girl. But nice Chinese girls don't grow up to be dykes or rebels." She notes that her legacy was silence.

Tsui was fortunate to have had a role model close to her life: her grandmother, Kwan Ying Lin, was a Chinese opera star who toured all the Chinatowns in the United States in the 1920s and 1930s, and lived with another actress for ten years. Tsui read widely while growing up, "but none of the books spoke of my own experience. I started writing when I was 11 years old to fill the silence and to turn the years of rejection into affirmation." Tsui claims that "what I write is shaped by my history and experiences, both as a Chinese woman and as a lesbian," and her writing explores Chinese and Chinese American history as well as Tsui's experiences as a lesbian.

In "Who Says We Don't Talk about Sex?," Tsui writes that she did not begin writing about sex until almost ten years after coming out. Even then, writing about sexuality was not easy, not least because of her exploration of sadomasochism (s/m) and leather. In answer to criticism of her sexual politics, Tsui notes: "Some women do not attend my theater or literary events for fear of supporting my sexual politics. I have been accused of recruiting. Never mind that I have a long history of writing, community organizing, and activism. Now I am judged solely for my leather sexuality. It's never been easy being different, but I have always survived. I will continue to speak out, write truths, and make waves." Tsui's writing about sex adds dimension to and provides insight into the questions Joan Nestle asks in her introduction to *The Persistent Desire*: is "the longevity of butch-femme self-expression...a lesbian specific way of deconstructing gender that radically reclaims women's erotic energy?" Tsui's writing, as with other butch-femme and leatherdyke writing, expresses that erotic energy. As Nestle notes, "We [lesbians], of all people, must be able to cherish the woman in the stereotype and the cunning in the transformation of gender restrictions into gender rebellion."

As she has refused to be invisible or silenced as a Chinese American lesbian, so Tsui refuses to deny eroticism or sexuality in her writing. In "A Femme in Butch Clothing" she writes of her fascination with women—"I've been a practicing lesbian for over two decades now, and women still fascinate me"—and of a Chinese femme who "likes to wear leather and lace dresses." The sensuality and sexuality expressed in Tsui's writing is evidenced by the title poem to her 1996 collection of erotic short stories, *Breathless*: "i was born a tough girl/ not many things/ make me gasp for air./ to tell you/ the truth/ your kisses/ make me/ breathless." As Firebrand editor/publisher Nancy K. Bereano notes in publicity material about the collection, "from vanilla sex in a bathroom to S/M in a play space, from raw sex over the phone lines to safe sex by mail, Kitty Tsui's erotic stories invite you to challenge, celebrate, and indulge your senses. *Breathless* sucks you into the hidden worlds of lesbians you know, want to be—or are." Tsui defends the right of each woman to claim her sexuality. In "sex does not equal death" she writes, "i am pro-choice." She advocates that women have full control of their bodies: the right not only to have an abortion, but also of the right of each woman to enjoy sex as she pleases.

Tsui's strong erotic writing is a vibrant contribution to the writings of butch-femme, s/m, and leatherdyke writers who refuse to be erased or silenced by the criticism of those members of a gay and lesbian movement who want to be "cleaned up" and desexualized for mainstream heterosexual acceptance. Her writings celebrate the practices of these communities while acknowledging and promoting the need for safe sex, and they have appeared in anthologies where the need for safe sex is stressed. Indeed, personal politics and safe sex are part of the s/m leatherdyke practice that Tsui details in her writing. Condoms, dental dams, lubricants, gloves—all are eroticized in Tsui's writing. And pleasures do not always depend on physical presence. In "Damn Safe Sex" Tsui writes of the desire for sexual pleasure without protection, the request for such practice. The story climaxes with a request to "let me feel you flesh to flesh" answered with "Yes, you can. In the next letter. As many times as you want. In ink. On paper. As for flesh in real life...you damn well better know the answer to that."

In their introduction to *The Second Coming,* Pat Califia and Robin Sweeney discuss the splits in the lesbian, gay, and bisexual communities that often occur between writers about and practitioners of leather and s/m roleplaying, the "squeamishness" of "mainstream gays who thought we made them look bad and [of] followers of outmoded feminist theories that made no distinction between S/M and violence," and the agenda of the "New Christian Right" which uses s/m practices and leatherdykes as a part of the scare tactics they employ to discredit the lesbian/gay/bisexual/transgender movement. They note "if we don't want to censor ourselves, we still have to do something to confront these antigay bigots and to update the squeamish civil-rights gay activists who ought to be our allies." Writing such as Tsui's, which considers full persons in all of their diversity inseparable from politics, is a step toward understanding, toward doing something.

Kitty Tsui is no stranger to health issues. A former competitive bodybuilder who has been featured in a number of films and has appeared on the covers of *On Our Backs,* the *Advocate,* and *Village Voice,* a woman who has won both bronze (San Francisco, 1986) and gold medals (Vancouver, 1990) at Gay Games II and III, she realizes the importance of physical conditioning. She is aware of the need for safe sex, has worked as an AIDS activist, provided recipes and commentary for *Food for Life...and Other Dish,* which beneffitted organizations who provide meals to people with AIDS, and she is, as well, concerned about and has written about women's health issues, particularly breast cancer in women of color. "Anita and Auntie" is the story of a woman immigrant from China whose mother saved her life by raising her as a man and who masqueraded as a man to avoid deportation and gain acceptance into the Chinese immigrant community, but who later claimed her identity as a woman. "Auntie," as the character is called, established a friendship with another woman who had a daughter, Anita. When this woman marries and she and Anita move away, "Auntie" loses touch with them, until Anita returns years later, after her mother's death, ill because of breast cancer. "Auntie and Anita" is both a story of love and a protest of the treatment of women, of the injustices in the health care system and in traditional Chinese culture. In "A Letter from Anita," Tsui writes of Anita Oñang, her friend of 13 years who died of cancer at 36. Tsui was asked to speak at the memorial service, and she used words from her friend's letters, noting that Anita's "family of friends," butches, femmes, were present, and that she "would have been pleased to see us...gathered together to celebrate her life."

Tsui has also written of the historical Chinese American experience in this country, notably in "chinatown talking story" and in her re-creations of "crane woman" and "dragon woman." She received a grant from Center for Lesbian and Gay Studies at the City University of New York to work on a history of the Asian Pacific lesbian movement in the United States from 1972 to 1992. Other works in progress include a revision of her historical novel, *Bak Sze, White Snake, Breathless Again,* a book of erotica, *Play Dates,* a collection of lesbian erotica, *Nice Chinese Girls Don't,* a collection of poetry, and *We Are Here!: A History of the Asian Pacific Lesbian Movement in America.* She is interested in writing a combination cookbook/memoir which would combine recipes and the memories that are intertwined with them from childhood to the present, combining the importance of food and words to her life. The breadth of her abilities as a writer is shown throughout her work, perhaps most strikingly in *Sparks Fly.* In an interview with Patti Capel Swartz Tsui noted that writing *Sparks Fly* was "very challenging." *Sparks Fly* is the story of the sexual adventures of a gay leatherman in pre-AIDS San Francisco. In undertaking this book, Tsui wanted to test her limits as a writer. She

notes that because of wide reading and talking with gay male friends she was able to successfully complete *Sparks Fly* after being approached at the American Booksellers Convention by publisher Richard Kasak, who asked Tsui why she had not written for him. Tsui told Swartz, "As a writer, I felt I should be—and I was able—to imagine male sexuality."

As she advocates for safe sex and sexual freedom, Tsui is also concerned with issues of lesbian and gay marriage and freedom of choice both to marry and to transform the meaning of marriage and family. Throughout her career, the personal has been intertwined with the political. In 1975, with a group of Asian American writers, Tsui "formed a collective called *Unbound Feet* to write and perform works by and about Asian Americans. Three of us were straight and three were lesbians," she told Swartz. This group toured the West Coast for two years until political differences caused the group to split; three of the women thought that art should be separate from politics while Tsui and two others saw art and politics as intertwined. For another year Tsui, Nellie Wong, and Merle Woo "continued our cultural and political work as *Unbound Feet Three.*"

What James C. Johnstone and Karen X. Tulchinsky say in their introduction to *Queer View Mirror* is true of Tsui's writing in all of its multiplicity: "Our stories, our histories as lesbians and gay men continue to be underrepresented and misrepresented in mainstream commercial media. It is in our own literature that we find true mirrors of our realities as lesbians and gay men claiming our space, surviving, succeeding, and flourishing in a homophobic world." Tsui's work is a part of that fight for recognition. Her life as an activist and a writer can best be described in her poem "don't call me sir call me strong." She is a "strong...spirited... sassy...competent...confident...powerful...proud woman coming into herself."

—Patti Capel Swartz

TSVETAEVA, Marina (Ivanovna)

Given name also transliterated as Maryna and Mariny; surname also transliterated as Tsvetayeva, Cvetaeva, Zwetajewa, Zvetaieva, Cvetajevova, Tzvetaeva, Tzvetayeva, Cwietajewa, and Tsvetaevoi. **Nationality:** Russian writer, poet, essayist, critic, and translator. **Born:** Moscow, 1892; emigrated to Paris, 1925; returned to the Soviet Union, 1939. **Education:** University of Paris (Sorbonne), France. **Family:** Married Sergei Efron (soldier); two daughters. **Died:** Committed suicide in the village of Elabuga, Tatar Republic, 31 August 1941.

WRITINGS

Prose Collections

Proza ("Prose"; essays). Chekhov Publishing House, 1953; as *Proza: Prose of Marina Tsvetaeva,* introduction by Valentina S. Coe, Bradda, 1969.
Izbrannaia v dvukh tomakh: 1917-1937 ("Selected Prose in Two Volumes"). Russica, New York, 1979.
Sochinenia v dvukh tomakh ("Selected Prose in Two Volumes"). Russica, 1979; Khudozhestvennaya Literatura, 1980.

A Captive Spirit: Selected Prose, edited and translated by J. Marin King. Ardis, 1980; reprinted with an introduction by Susan Sontag, Virago, 1983.

Art in the Light of Conscience: Eight Essays on Poetry by Marina Tsvetaeva, translated with an introduction by Angela Livingstone. Cambridge, Harvard University Press, 1992.

Collected Poetry

Vechernii al'bom: Stikhi ("Evening Album"). A.N. Mamonova, 1910.

Volshebnyi fonar': Vtoraia kniga stikhov ("The Magic Lantern"). Ole-Lukoie, 1912; Paris, YMCA-Press, 1979.

Iz dvukh knig ("From Two Books"). Ole-Lukoie, 1913.

Versty II ("Mileposts II"). Kostry, 1921.

Versty I ("Mileposts I"). Gosudarstevnnoe Izdatel'stvo, 1922; facsimile edition, Ardis, 1972; Letchworth, England, Prideaux Press, 1979.

Stikhi k Bloku ("Poems to Blok"). Berlin, Ogon'ki, 1922; Prideaux Press, 1978.

Tsar'-Devitsa ("The King-Maiden"). Epokha, 1922; as *Tsar'-Devitsa: The King Maiden,* Prideaux Press, 1971.

Razluka ("Parting"). Gelikon, 1922.

Psikheia ("Psyche"). Z.I. Grzhebina, 1923.

Remeslo ("Craft"). Gelikon, 1923; reprinted with introduction and notes by Efrim Etkind, W.A. Meeuws, 1981.

Molodets ("The Swain"). Plamia, 1924; as *Molodets: Poems,* Prideaux Press, 1971.

Posle Rossii, 1922-1925 ("After Russia"). Parizh, 1928; YMCA-Press, 1976.

Lebedinyi stan. Originally published in 1957; reprinted, bilingual English and Russian edition with translation, introduction, notes, and commentaries by Robin Kemball, YMCA-Press, 1971; as *The Demons of the Swans,* Ardis, 1980.

Selected Poems of Marina Tsvetaeva, translated by Elaine Feinstein, foreword by Max Hayward. Oxford University Press, 1971; revised and enlarged edition with literal versions by Angela Livingstone and others, Dutton, 1981, 1987.

Stikhotvoreniia i poemy ("Lyric Poems and Longer Poems"). Sovetskii Pisatel', 1979; Russica, 1980.

Stikhotvoreniia i poemy v piati tomakh ("Lyric Poems and Longer Poems in Five Volumes"). Russica, 1980.

Three Russian Women Poets: Anna Akhmatova, Marina Tsvetayeva, Bella Akhmadulina, translated by Mary Maddock, introduction by Edward J. Brown. Crossing Press, 1983.

Selected Poems, translated by David McDuff. Bloodaxe Books, 1987.

Stikhi i poemy (selected poems). Vaga, 1988.

Letters

Pis'ma k A. Teskovoi ("Letters to Teskova"). Academia, 1969; as *Pis'ma k Anne Teskovoi,* with introductory articles by Zdenek Mathauser and Vadim Morkovin, Versty, 1982.

Neizdannye pis'ma ("Unpublished Letters"; includes April 1925 letter to Ariadna Kolbasina), edited by Gleb Struve and Nikita Struve. YMCA-Press, 1972.

Letters, Summer 1926: Boris Pasternak, Marina Tsvetayeva, Rainer Maria Rilke, edited by Yevgeny Pasternak, Yelena Pasternak, and Konstantin M. Azadovky, translated by Margaret Wettlin and Walter Arndt. Harcourt, 1985; Oxford University Press, 1988.

Plays

Metel' ("The Snowstorm"; verse play), also includes *Prikliuchenie* ("An Adventure") and *Ariadna.* Prideaux Press, 1978.

Other

Isbrannoe ("Selected Works"). Goslitizdat, 1961.

Isbrannye proizvedeniia ("Selected Works"). Sovetskii Pisatel', 1965; 'Mastatskaia Literatura, 1984.

Translator, *Prosto serdtse: Stikhi zarubezhnykh poetov v perevode Mariny Tsvetaevoi* ("Simply the Heart: Poems of Foreign Poets in Marina Tsvetaeva's Translations"). Progress, 1967.

Nesobrannye proizvedeniia ("Uncollected Works"). W. Fink, 1971.

Neizdannoe: Stikhi, teatr, proza ("Unpublished Works: Poetry, Drama, Prose"). YMCA-Press, 1976.

Moi Pushkin ("My Pushkin"). Sovetskii Pisatel', 1967; as *Moi Pushkin: My Pushkin,* Prideaux Press, 1977.

*

Critical Sources: *Marina Cvetaeva: Her Life and Art* by Simon Karlinsky, University of California Press, 1966; *Tsvetaeva: A Pictorial Biography,* edited by Ellendea Proffer, translation by Martin King, Ardis, 1980; "With the Grandeur of Homer and the Purity of Sappho..." by Zhanna Ivina, in *Women and Russia: Feminist Writings from the Soviet Union,* edited by Tatyana Mamonova and Sarah Matilsky, Boston, Beacon, 1984, 155-63; *A Handbook of Russian Literature,* edited by Victor Terras, Yale University Press, 1985; *Marina Tsvetaeva: The Woman, Her World and Her Poetry* by Simon Karlinksy, Cambridge University Press, 1985; *A Captive Lion: The Life of Marina Tsvetayeva* by Elaine Feinstein, Dutton, 1987; "After the Ball is Over: Sophia Parnok's Creative Relationship with Marina Tsvetaeva" by Diana Burgin, in *Russian Review,* Vol. 47, 1988; "'I Named Her Ariadna...': The Demeter-Persephone Myth in Tsvetaeva's Poems for Her Daughter" by Laura Weeks, in *Slavic Review* (Stanford), Vol. 49, No. 4, winter 1990, 568-84; *Changing the Subject: Cvetaeva's Revisions of the Female Body* by Joy Stacey Dworkin (dissertation), University of Michigan, April 1992; *The Language of Women? A Study of Three Women Writers: Marina Tsvetaeva, Ingeborg Bachmann, and Monique Wittig* by Irina Kuzminsky (dissertation), University of Oxford, May 1992; "Tsvetaeva and the Two Natal'ia Goncharovas: Dual Life" by Lisa Knapp, in *Cultural Mythologies of Russian Modernism: From the Golden Age to the Silver Age,* edited by Boris Gasparov, Robert P. Hughes, Irina Paperno, and Eric Naiman, Berkeley, University of California Press, 1992, 88-108; "Bells and Cupolas: The Formative Role of the Female Body in Marina Tsvetaeva's Poetry" by Sibelan Forrester, in *Slavic Review* (Stanford), Vol. 51, No. 2, summer 1992, 232-46; *Sophia Parnok: The Life and Work of Russia's Sappho* by Diana Burgin, New York and London, New York University Press, 1994; "The Modernist Poetics of Grief in the Wartime Works of Tsvetaeva, Filonov, and Kollwitz" by Antonia Filonov Gove, in *Russian Narrative and Visual Art: Varieties of Seeing,* edited by Roger Anderson and Paul Debreczeny, Gainesville, University Press of Florida, 1994, 148-72; "Tsvetaeva and the Feminine Tradition in Russian Poetry" by Jane Taubman, in *Marina Tsvetaeva: One Hundred Years/Stoletie Tsvetaevoi,* edited by Viktoria Schweitzer, Jane Taubman, Peter Scotto, and Tatyana Bayonyshev, Berkeley, Berkeley Slavic Specialties, 1994, 77-90; "Chorus and Monologue in Marina Tsvetaeva's *Ariadna:* An Analysis of Their Structure, Versification, and Themes" by Andrew Kahn, in *Marina Tsvetaeva: One Hundred Years/Stoletie Tsvetaevoi,* edited by Viktoria Schweitzer, Jane Taubman, Peter Scotto, and Tatyana Bayonyshev, Berkeley, Berkeley Slavic Specialties, 1994, 162-93; "The Life and Death of a Poet" by Sue Chance, in *Journal of Poetry Therapy,* Vol. 7, No. 3, spring 1994, 137-43; "Letter to an Amazon," translated by Sonja Franeta, in *Harvard Gay and Lesbian Review,* Vol. 1, No. 4, fall 1994, 9-14; "Engaging Sexual Demons in Marina Tsvetaeva's *Devil:* The Body and the Genesis of the Woman Poet" by Pamela Chester, in *Slavic Review* (Stanford), Vol. 53, No. 4, winter 1994, 1025-45; *Marina Tsvetaeva: The Double Beat of Heaven and Hell* by Lily Feiler, Durham and London, Duke University Press, 1994; "Mothers and Daughters: Variations on Family Themes in Tsvetaeva's *The House at Old Pimen*" by Natasha Kolchevska, in *Engendering Slavic Literatures,* edited by Pamela Chester and Sibelan Forrester, Bloomington, University of Indiana Press, 1996, 135-57.

*   *   *

Marina Tsvetaeva is considered today to be one of the four great Russian poets of this century, along with her contemporaries Anna Akhmatova, Osip Mandelstam, and Boris Pasternak. Her prolific career as a poet and writer of prose spanned decades of dramatic political upheaval in Europe and in her native Russia, including the October Revolution and two World Wars. Born in 1892, Tsvetaeva began writing at a very young age and published her first book of poetry at the age of 18 in 1910. This collection, entitled "Evening Album" (Vechernii al'bom), was very well received by critics and marked an auspicious beginning for her literary career. Although Tsvetaeva's next two volumes, "The Magic Lantern" (1912) and "From Two Books" (1913) did not meet with the same level of critical enthusiasm, she had already established strong connections to Russian literary circles which were to have a great influence on her development as a poet.

Following the October Revolution in 1917 and the Civil War that followed, Russia's literary community endured a period of political upheaval and financial insecurity. Tsvetaeva's young husband, Sergei Efron, was a soldier for the White Army and was soon sent to Southern Russia to fight the Bolshevik army. Tsvetaeva was left alone with very little money in Moscow and with two daughters; the youngest died of malnutrition during this time. Her poems of these years, collected in volumes such as "Versty II" (Mileposts II) and "The Craft," display a more urgent and adult tone than her earlier work. In 1922, Tsvetaeva elected to leave Russia with her daughter, Ariadna, to join her husband in Czechoslovakia. This began her long period as a part of the Russian émigré literary community in Europe. She and her family lived in Berlin and Czechoslovakia, and eventually moved to Paris in 1925.

In Paris, Tsvetaeva was hailed as a celebrity by the Russian literary community. However, she distrusted fame, believing that it distracted the artist from the act of creating. She also mistrusted the role of the critic in evaluating art, and explored this topic in her 1926 essay "The Poet to the Critic," written shortly after her arrival in Paris. With this essay, she quickly alienated a large number of her followers by presenting a scathing attack on the most well-known critics of the time, illustrating how little each of them understood the subject on which they claimed the right to pass judg-

ment. In the 1930s, Tsvetaeva began to write more prose than poetry, primarily because the family depended on her earnings at the time, and prose was more likely to sell. At the same time, she grew increasingly unhappy with her awkward position as a poet, in-between and distanced from both her reading audience and the demands of the publishing industry. She explains this sentiment in "The Poet and Time" (translation by Livingstone): "In the order of things here, I am a disorder of things. There [Russia], I wouldn't be published, but I would be read; here, I'm published—and not read."

In 1939, Tsvetaeva made the decision to return to Russia. Her family was unhappy living in France, and her husband, Sergei Efron, had been accused of being an agent of the Soviet secret police. Sergei and their daughter Ariadna returned to Moscow, and Tsvetaeva and their son Georgij joined them in mid-1939. Soon thereafter, Sergei and Ariadna were arrested; Sergei was later executed. Fearing for their safety, in the summer of 1941, Tsvetaeva and 15-year-old Georgij fled with a group of writers to the Tatar Republic, and lived in the small village of Elabuga. There were no opportunities for Tsvetaeva to write or develop her art there; her style differed too greatly from the state-sponsored Socialist Realism paradigm, and she had fallen out of favor with the rest of the Russian literary community. Tsvetaeva hanged herself in August of the same year, and was buried in an unmarked grave.

Much of Tsvetaeva's work was never published during her lifetime, and has only recently been "rediscovered," largely through the efforts of Western scholars. Even today, some of her work has only been published in the West, due to some of the politically controversial aspects of her life. Among the topics that have been de-emphasized with regards to Tsvetaeva, particularly in Soviet scholarship, is her bisexuality and her relationships with women. Lily Feiler writes that when Marina was six years old, she was taken to a performance of *Eugene Onegin,* and she instantly fell in love with both main characters, Onegin and Tatyana; she was in love with love itself, regardless of gender. This was true of her attitude towards love for the rest of her life.

One of the most significant formative experiences of her adult life was her passionate two-year relationship with fellow poet Sophia Parnok, which lasted from 1914 to 1916. Only recently do biographical accounts of Tsvetaeva's life devote significant attention to this affair or its influence on her writing. She and Sophia Parnok met in 1914 at a literary salon at the home of a common friend. Their affair blossomed almost immediately, and continued for two years, despite the fact that Tsvetaeva was married and had a two-year-old daughter. Both Tsvetaeva and Parnok were very open about the nature of their relationship, as homosexuality was an accepted lifestyle in the artistic community of the time. The intensity of feeling and devotion that Tsvetaeva felt for Parnok is evident in the cycle of poems she produced between 1914 and 1916 entitled "Podruga" (translated as "Girlfriend" or "Woman Friend"). This was the only body of Tsvetaeva's poetry written unambiguously to a woman; it remained unpublished during her lifetime, and was not published until 1976 as a part of the *Juvenilia* collection.

Tsvetaeva describes the first meeting with Parnok in a very detailed and evocative poem from the "Podruga" cycle (translation from Mamonova):

> I remember with what sort of face
> you entered,
> Without even the slightest blush,

How you rose, biting your finger,
Barely inclining your head.
Your brow, with love for power
stamped on it
Lies there
Beneath the weight of a reddish
mask,
Neither a woman nor a boy
But something stronger than me.

Thus far, Tsvetaeva's characterization of her woman lover reveals a singular-sided view of her attitude towards gender roles and lesbianism. She was enchanted by Parnok's grace and purpose, and appears to portray Parnok as more "masculine" than herself. The phrases she uses to describe Parnok evoke an image of the lesbian look common in the early decades of the century: sophisticated and poised, with short hair and smoking a cigarette. As the poet continues, however, it is evident that she does not subscribe to such a simplistic view of masculine and feminine roles in a lesbian relationship:

I rose with an unaccustomed movement,
They had surrounded us,
And in a joking tone someone said,
"Let me introduce you, ladies and gentlemen!"
And with a drawn-out movement you placed
your hand in mine,
On my palm there tenderly lingered
A splinter of ice....
You took out a papirosi,
And I extended a match to you,
Not knowing what I should do
Were you to look me
Straight in the face....

Now Tsvetaeva portrays herself as the courting partner; Parnok places her hand in Tsvetaeva's, who offers her a light for her cigarette ("papirosi"). In another poem, Tsvetaeva characterizes herself as the "boy," rather than Parnok (translation in Feiler): "How I brushed over your slender little fingers / With my sleepy cheek. / How you teasingly called me a boy, / How you liked me that way." A third poem depicts Tsvetaeva's admiration of the dual sensual images she admires in her lover; she is attracted to both the feminine and the masculine aspects in Parnok. In the following passage, she sees Parnok as both boyish and womanly (translation in Mamonova):

You act the fool, be it with your fan, or with your
walking stick,
In every fiber and every little bone,
In the shape of every naughty finger,
There's the delicacy of a woman, the impertinence
of a boy.
I parry all your smiles with verse,
I open out the whole world to you,
Everything is in store for us from you,
Unknown woman, with the brow of Beethoven!

As their affair progressed, the strain of Tsvetaeva's marriage to Sergei Efron became too great a burden. Parnok knew that Marina's first obligation was to her husband and daughter, and one can imagine how she must have resented this second-rank status. Tsvetaeva, on the other hand, lamented the impossibility of having a child with the woman she so deeply loved. In 1916, Tsvetaeva and Parnok ended their relationship; it is unknown who exactly initiated the breakup, but it is likely that it was Parnok who recognized that the end had come.

After their breakup, Tsvetaeva remained bitterly conflicted about the significance of Parnok's role in her life. Tsvetaeva had other relationships with women following Parnok, including the actress Sophia (Sonechka) Holliday, but none were of the intensity and depth of that relationship. In 1934, almost two decades after her meeting with Parnok and one year after Parnok's death in 1933, Tsvetaeva wrote a prose piece in French entitled "Lettre a l'amazone" (Letter to an Amazon). The letter was addressed primarily to Natalie Clifford Barney, the "Amazon" lesbian writer living in Paris, whose literary salon had not given Tsvetaeva the reception she felt she deserved. In this letter, Tsvetaeva professes that the main shortcoming of a lesbian relationship is that it cannot produce a child; a younger woman will always leave her woman lover for a man in order to fulfill her desire for a child. However, as Lily Feiler suggests, more than being an attack on Barney and the lesbian literary establishment in Paris, the piece was really a reaction to the unresolved relationship with Sophia Parnok. Feiler comments that Tsvetaeva "needs to ease the pain of having lost Parnok, of having renounced lesbianism—and she finds her justification in her fantasized 'motherhood'." This letter demonstrates, as does Tsvetaeva's early poetry, how deep and lasting Parnok's effect was, in her life and in her work.

As scholarly interest in Marina Tsvetaeva's role in twentieth-century Russian literature grows, in both in the West and in the countries of the former Soviet Union, recognition of her bisexuality and her lesbian relationships is growing as well. One may hope that as we learn more about Tsvetaeva and Parnok, increased attention will also be devoted to the study of lesbianism in literature and the work of lesbian writers on a broader scale. The analysis of Tsvetaeva's life and work certainly contributes a significant first step towards the pursuit of this goal.

—Caitlin L. Gannon

TUSQUETS, Esther (Guillen)

Nationality: Spanish novelist and author of short stories. **Born:** Barcelona, Spain, 30 August 1936. **Education:** Colegio Alemán, Barcelona; studied history, University of Barcelona and University of Madrid. **Family:** One daughter, one son. **Career:** Director, Editorial Lumen, Barcelona, from 1960; contributor of articles to periodicals, including *Destino* and *La Vanguardia*. **Awards:** City of Barcelona Prize, 1979. **Agent:** c/o Editorial Lumen, Ramón Miquel i Planas 10, E 08034 Barcelona, Spain.

Writings

Novels

El mismo mar de todos los veranos. Barcelona, Lumen, 1978; as *The Same Sea as Every Summer,* Lincoln, University Nebraska Press, 1990.

El amor es un juego solitario. Barcelona, Lumen, 1979; as *Love Is a Solitary Game,* London, Calder, 1985.

Varada tras el último naufragio. Barcelona, Lumen, 1980; as *Stranded,* Elmwood Park, Illinois, Dalkey Archive Press, 1991.

Para no volver. Barcelona, Lumen, 1985.

Uncollected Stories

"Juego o el hombre que pintaba mariposas," in *Cuadernos Hispanoamericanos,* No. 347, 1979, 319-27.

"Las inútiles leyes de la simetría," in *Doce relatos de mujeres,* edited by Ymelda Navajo. Madrid, Alianza Editorial, 1982.

"Recuerdo de Safo," in *Los Cuadernos del Norte,* November/December 1982.

"Olivia," in *Litoral Femenino: Literatura Escrita por mujeres en la España contemporánea,* Nos. 169-70, 1986, 365-71.

Other

La conejita Marcela (Marcela, the Little Rabbit; for children). Barcelona, Lumen, 1980.

Siete miradas en un mismo paisaje (short stories). Barcelona, Lumen, 1981.

*

Bibliography: "An Annotated Bibliography of Works by and about Esther Tusquets" by Elizabeth Espadas, in *The Sea of Becoming: Approaches to the Fiction of Esther Tusquets,* edited by Mary S. Vásquez, New York, Greenwood, 1991, 189-226.

Critical Sources: "The Barcelona Group: The Fiction of Alós, Moix, and Tusquets" by Elizabeth Ordóñez, in *Letras femeninas,* Vol. 6, No. 1, spring 1980; "The Language of Eroticism in the Novels of Esther Tusquets" by Catherine G. Bellver, in *Anales de la literatura española contemporánea,* Vol. 9, No. 1-3, 1984, 13-17; *The Quest for Personhood: An Expression of the Female Tradition in the Novels of Moix, Tusquets, Matute, and Alós* by Lucy Lee-Bonanno (dissertation), University of Kentucky, 1985; *Foucault, Feminism, and Power: Reading Esther Tusquets* by Nina Molinaro, Lewisburg, Pennsylvania, Bucknell University Press, 1991; *The Sea of Becoming: Approaches to the Fiction of Esther Tusquets,* edited by Mary S. Vásquez, New York, Greenwood, 1991; *The Apple of Earthly Love: Female Development in Esther Tusquets' Fiction* by Barbara F. Ichiisi, New York, Peter Lang, 1994.

Esther Tusquets comments:

In my novels, where love and death occupy a special place, homosexual and heterosexual relationships are part of the story. I haven't needed any special motivation to write about lesbian love, nor have I perceived any conflict in doing so. I don't write novels to defend any ideological thesis, as I limit myself to telling stories; these stories reflect inevitably my visions of the world, without being vainglorious, cold, nor objective. It's obvious that homosexuality and heterosexuality to me seem valid and equal options.

*   *   *

Esther Tusquets' literary career began in the author's middle years, at age 42, with the publication of *El mismo mar de todos los veranos.* This work explores, among other mature themes, a lesbian relationship involving the novel's main character/narrator, a university professor who has returned to her childhood home in Spain in search of spiritual and emotional refuge. There she discovers alongside her memories new possibilities for love in the form of a young woman named Clara, a student from Colombia. Clara brings radiance and hope to the relationship, where the narrator has experienced heretofore only life's realities and disappointments. Indeed it is Clara's innocence that attracts the older woman; the younger woman is viewed by the narrator at some deeper level as a double, the innocent she once was herself.

As the friendship between the two women develops, the narrator is scarred once more by the news of the death of her grandmother, and turns at this moment of vulnerability to Clara, not only for spiritual sustenance, but also for physical warmth. This climax of their relationship brings a new feeling to the narrator, of completeness and utter security. Barbara Ichiisi, author of *The Apple of Earthly Love: Female Development in Esther Tusquets' Fiction,* says of the scene, "The love act between the two women seems to occur in a pure space outside of time, with the slow floating rhythm of a dream. Their union on the lush Oriental carpets before the hearth fire is for both the experience of pure joy and plenitude which alone can conquer death."

This theme of the healing through love of childhood harms and all the pains of adolescence, even if the healing is only for a moment, recurs throughout Tusquets' fiction. And it is at its most daring in Tusquets' earlier fiction, where the form of that love does not always follow social convention. In later fictional works, Tusquets appears to recommend heterosexual love, but in earlier works like *El mismo mar,* lesbianism sometimes assumes center stage. In *El mismo mar,* the sexual and emotional love between two women can perhaps undo some of the damage done in early years from a troubled mother-daughter relationship. Clara can satisfy the deeper needs of her older lover, the narrator, while the lover in turn provides emotional sustenance.

However, the lesbian relationships in Tusquets' work do not always provide equal benefits for both partners. While Clara in *El mismo mar* can be empowered by the strength of the relationship to look ahead in her life and plan a brighter future, the narrator is left passive in the bliss of the moment. The narrator, with much of her life behind her, cannot envision a truly altered future where she is the initiator of action. The loving relationship is only beneficial as it works for the moment, as if in a dream, and apart from a longer, darker reality.

This inability for the more mature lover to find lasting comfort in a loving relationship persists and develops into bitterness in Tusquets' second novel, *El amor es un juego solitario.* This novel continues what is to be a trilogy, composed of *El mismo mar, El amor,* and the third title, *Varada tras el último naufragio.* The second novel retains a character named Clara, but she is not to be confused with the earlier character: names continue on in Tusquets' novels, but the characters are different in each, representing perhaps different aspects of the psyche, different shades of a personality. In *El amor,* Clara is again a young girl, but this time a player in a much darker drama, the most sordid of the trilogy. She plays victim to the vicissitudes of a married couple, Elia and Ricardo, who selfishly use the young woman, seemingly for sport. Elia, a 30-year-old woman, has lost the ability to connect emotionally with others, and is herself removed from the experience of life. Engaged in a sometimes violent relationship with Ricardo, Elia can easily victimize others, particularly in the arena of sex.

For her, sex allows a pleasurable connection with a life she is otherwise unable to enjoy.

By contrast, Clara enters the scene as a young woman looking for emotional support, and believing she has found it in Elia. She does not like Ricardo, but he is attracted to her, and finds it a curiosity to have Elia make love to Clara, in his mind releasing Elia's "hidden desires." Ultimately Clara becomes the weapon Ricardo and Elia unleash on each other—she is not valued for herself, but as the intermediary of their marriage-long argument. As Ichiisi observes, this relationship is a pure negative of the illumination and freshness of the lesbian encounter in the *El mismo mar.* Where in the first novel, Clara finds rejuvenation and hope, in the second novel, Clara is a complete victim to the sexual whims of more experienced adults. Clara's love operates as a stage for the narcissism of Elia, who betrays Clara several times for her own devices. Where in the first novel, the protagonist may have been disillusioned, in the second, the protagonist Elia has no core concept of self, and so lacks a sense of guidance in her relationship with a younger woman.

The final novel in the trilogy, *Varada tras el último naufragio,* offers an emotional complexity not found in the second novel. Again namesakes are used, here Elia and Clara. Two heterosexual relationships intertwine, one between Jorge and Elia, another between Eva and Pablo, soon to be joined by Eva's adolescent student, Clara. Elia and Eva are best of friends, and have been so for years. While not sexually involved, they are on the most intimate terms with each other, each watching the other curiously through mid-life crises, as husbands distance themselves from wives, and wives explore alternative experiences.

Eva explores a relationship with her young protegé Clara, while Elia quietly observes. More than ever before, Tusquets appears to be making a comment on the homosexual relationships, that they are dark when compared to the mature possibility of heterosexuality. Certainly Eva's relationship with Clara is abusive, not allowing the breath of hope given in Tusquets' first novel.

Unfortunately, the measure of happiness in Tusquets' novels is ever and always love. To not love is to face the reality of death,

without consolation. And for women in Tusquets' novels, the measure of love is heterosexuality; all other successes pale when compared with the love between a man and a woman. It is difficult to discern if this is how Tusquets herself feels, but that is the pattern of the novels: lesbian relationships are but a shadow of a more mature love.

However, the deeper reality of Tusquets' novels may be that no love offers what it seems to promise. This is the paradox of Tusquets' fiction, that love is the only protection from death, but such protection is only temporary and purely psychological; death is always present. Furthermore, her trilogy suggests that no human being can really offer complete consolation: love promises, but never delivers, empathy.

Nevertheless, heterosexual love appears to be the emblem in Tusquets' work of a more complete security, a higher union of mature souls. How is this so? In Tusquets' novels, same-sex relations always involve at least one partner crippled in her ability to mature or to feel deeply, who has sought out another to offset her pain. In the first novel, the older woman cannot achieve from the relationship a lasting security because she has been wounded in love before, and so turns to a younger woman to be reminded of what it is like to be young. In the second novel, sadism and narcissism abound, with the older woman—together with her husband—circumventing the younger woman's chances for happiness. In the third novel, likewise, the older woman uses the younger for her own devices.

If this discussion gives the impression that lesbianism is the focal point of Tusquets' work, that impression may be false, unless lesbianism as a term encompasses all the levels, emotional and sexual, that occur between women, as opposed to the life that places men and their needs at its center. Regardless, Tusquets' work has been called daring and mature for its time, and those commendations point to the sexual core of the writing. Women in Tusquets' pages are exploring a new eroticism probably nonexistent or at least undocumented in all the years of Franco's Spain that preceded her writing.

—Kelly Cannon

U-V

URBANITZKY, Grete von

Nationality: Austrian writer, translator, and journalist. **Born:** Linz, 9 July 1891. **Education:** Attended the village school in Linz; private lessons in Latin and mathematics, Greece; grammar school and A levels in Zürich, Switzerland. **Family:** Married 1) the officer Ludwig Woloszcuk in 1911 (divorced 1913); 2) Petter Passini in 1920 (divorced); 3) companion of Mia Passini, the sister of her second husband, until Passini's marriage in 1945. **Career:** Co-Founder, Austrian P. E. N.-Club, 1923; contributor of reviews and articles to journals, including *Alpenland, Die Bühne, Die Kultur, Die Weg,* and *Literarische Monatshefte.* **Died:** Thonex, Switzerland, 4 November 1974.

WRITINGS

Novels

Wenn die Weiber Menschen werden . . . Gedanken einer Einsamen. Berlin, Silva, 1913.
Des Kaisers junge Soldaten! Vienna, Austria, Der Patriot, 1915.
Das andere Blut. Roman. Leipzig, Germany, Wunderlich, 1920.
Das wilde Meer. Leipzig, Germany, Xenien, 1920.
Die Auswanderer. Vienna, Austria, Wila, 1921.
Die goldene Peitsche. Leipzig, Germany, Haaessel, 1922.
Maria Alborg. Leipzig, Germany, Haaessel, 1923.
Mirijams Sohn. Stuttgart, Germany, 1926.
Der wilde Garten (Wild Garden). Leipzig, Germany, Hesse & Becker, 1927.
Sekretärin Vera. Hannover, Germany, Sponholtz, 1930.
Zwischen den Spiegeln. Stuttgart, Germany, Engelhorn, 1930.
Eine Frau erlebt die Welt. Vienna, Austria, Zsolnay, 1931.
Durch Himmel und Hölle (Through Heaven and Hell). Vienna, Austria, Zsolnay, 1932.
Karin und die Welt der Männer. Vienna, Austria, Zsolnay, 1933.
Ursula und der Kapitän. Vienna, Austria, Zsolnay, 1934.
Nina. Geschichte einer Fünfzehnjährigen. Vienna, Austria, Zsolnay, 1935.
Das Preisausschreiben. Abenteuer zweier Mädels in Dalmatien. Berlin, Weise, 1935.
Heimkehr zur Liebe. Berlin, Vienna, Zsolnay, 1935.
Begegnung in Alassio (Meeting in Alassio). Vienna, Austria, Zsolnay, 1937.
Unsere Liebe Frau von Paris. Roman eines deutsche Steinmetzen. Berlin, Vienna, Zsolnay, 1938.
Das Mädchen Alexa. Berlin, Vienna, Zsolnay, 1939.
Sprung übern Zaun. Zürich, Switzerland, Morgarten, 1940.
Es begann im September . . . Bern, Switzerland, Scherz, 1940.
Miliza. Bern, Switzerland, Scherz, 1941.
Mademoiselle Viviane. Zürich, Switzerland, Bellaria, 1941.
Der große Traum. Bern, Switzerland, Scherz, 1942.
Der Mann Alexander. Bern, Switzerland, Scherz, 1943.

Short Stories

Sehnsucht. Novellen und Märchen. Leipzig, Germany, Xenien, 1911.
Masken der Liebe. Leipzig, Germany, Haaessel, 1922.

Poetry

Ausgewählte Gedichte. Leipzig, Germany, Xenien, 1920.
Der verfolgene Vogel. Vienna, Austria, Wila, 1920.
Das Jahr der Maria. Vienna, Austria, Wila, 1921.

*

Manuscript Collections: Wiener Stadt-und Landesbibliothek, Vienna, Austria.

Bibliography: *'Frau und doch kein Weib.' Zu Grete von Urbanitzky. Monographische Studie zur Frauenliteratur in der österreichischen Zwischenkriegszeit und im Nationalsozialismus* by Ursula Huber, Vienna, University of Vienna, 1990.

Critical Sources: "Eigensinn und Doppelsinn in frauenbezogenen und lesbischen Texten österreichischer Autorinnen 1900-1938" by Hanna Hacker, in *Kulturjahrbuch 2. Wiener Beiträge zur Kulturwissenschaft und Kulturpolitik,* edited by Hubert C. Ehalt, Vienna, 1983, 264-81; *Zum Thema der 'Neuen Frau' in einigen Romanen Grete von Urbanitzkys* by Dela K. Preisinger, Boston, University of Massachusetts, 1989; *'Frau und doch kein Weib'. Zu Grete von Urbanitzky. Monographische Studie zur Frauenliteratur in der österreichischen Zwischenkriegszeit und im Nationalsozialismus* by Ursula Huber, Vienna, University of Vienna, 1990.

*   *   *

Grete von Urbanitzky is a contradictory author. She was one of the few Austrian women who earned her living by writing, a Nazi collaborator, a victim of Nazi politics, and the author of the novel *Wild Garden* (1927), which was "the best-known Austrian lesbian novel" between World Wars I and II, according to Hanna Hacker.

Wild Garden is a novel about Fräulein Dr. Hanna Südekum, a teacher at the local girls school, and her pupil Gertrud 'Gert' Winheim. Südekum, who never married and has lived on her own for several years, is deeply shocked and confused when her pupils begin going through puberty. Even her good friends Mr. and Mrs. Nowotny change because they meet a very attractive sculptor named Alexandra Pseleuditi, who is half-Greek and half-Persian. Both Mrs. and Mr. Nowotny fall in love with her. Hanna Südekum decides to talk to Alexandra Pseleuditi and tells her of her feelings for Gertrud. Alexandra answers "And you really don't know that this is your love, the love you tried to escape your whole life?" Hanna Südekum is utterly confused when Alexandra Pseleuditi tells her that she, Hanna, desires Gertrud. The following dialogue arises—"Südekum asks: 'And you believe that there can be love between two women?' 'Is there not love between prophet and disciple, between men and star, between men and animals, between men and flowers? Isn't it a river that joins us all?', answers Alexandra." Hanna Südekum starts fighting with Alexandra and calls lesbianism disgusting. In the middle of the disagreement the chancellor turns up and tells the two women the story of his friend who finally learns how to love after facing his fear of being alone in old age.

Meanwhile, the girls in school discuss different concepts of living—marriage or not, waiting for true love or not. Gert does not join the discussion; only when she is asked does she answer that she wants to be a dancer and that she does not want to run after her true love because "How can I think of someone else, as long as I am nothing? I will when I am me and free to give what I now don't know."

After the final exams Gert decides to travel south with Alexandra and she tells this to Hanna Südekum. The teacher is silent and leaves. Alexandra and Gert travel to a Greek island, where there are only the two of them. They discover a heathen temple that once belonged to the Goddess of air. Alexandra wants to go back telling Gert that the Christian cross extinguished the old Gods, but Gert refuses to return. She starts to dance and Alexandra undresses and "they dropped down on the mossy and fern covered marble plate. The ancient columns were shaking when a piercing scream of doubled desire penetrated the night." Alexandra and Gert return from their holiday and Alexandra is full of creative energy. Gert becomes a famous dancer.

Wild Garden is an exceptional lesbian novel. The love between Gert and Alexandra is the only 'true' love in the novel and there is a happy ending displaying their lesbian love. Not all of Urbanitzky's lesbian figures were that lucky. "While the lesbians in *Wild Garden* coincide with Urbanitzkys picture of the female artist, and therefore are productive and emancipated women, the lesbian figures of other novels are stereotyped 'happy-go-lucky' young women," writes Ursula Huber. In novels like *Through Heaven and Hell* and *Meeting in Alassio*, lesbians are fashionable and decadent women who try anything "from Lesbos to cocaine." Urbanitzky obviously makes a distinction between "true love" and decadence.

The solution to this contradiction is probably Urbanitzky's specific picture of the position of women, especially of women artists, in society. Many of her female characters are autonomous women who inherit a big content of "masculinity." Urbanitzky was very familiar with the theory of Otto Weininger who, among other things, contrived a theory of an abstract masculinity and femininity which both included certain—very stereotypical—patterns of behavior: femininity as being passive, wanting to be conquered, masculinity as being active, conquering. "Bad" lesbians are connected to decadence, subculture, and big cities—a concept which is picked up by several political parties. Nonetheless, *Wild Garden* is a courageous step, published at a time when female and male homosexuality were still forbidden by law in Austria.

—Birgit Lang

VAID, Urvashi

Nationality: American activist and writer. **Born:** New Delhi, India, 8 October 1958; immigrated to the United States at age seven. **Education:** Attended public schools in Potsdam, New York; Vassar College, B.A. 1979; Northeastern University Law School, 1982. **Family:** Companion of lesbian humorist Kate Clinton. **Career:** Worked as an activist for numerous lesbian, gay, bisexual, and transgender organizations and human rights organizations, including Roadwork, *Gay Community News,* and Lesbians United in Non-Nuclear Action; attorney, National Prison Project of the American Civil Liberties Union, 1983-86; founder, LIPS (lesbian

direct action group), 1984; public information director, 1986-89, executive director, 1989-92, and director, Policy Institute, from 1997, National Gay and Lesbian Task Force. Member, editorial advisory board, *Progressive* magazine, from 1996; contributor to periodicals, including *Out/Look, Ms., Nation,* and the *Advocate.* **Awards:** Named to "Fifty for the Future" list, *Time* magazine, 1993; American Library Association Gay, Lesbian, and Bisexual Book Award, 1996. **Agent:** Jed Mattes, Inc., 2095 Broadway, Room 302, New York, New York 10023-2895, U.S.A.

WRITINGS

Virtual Equality: The Mainstreaming of Gay and Lesbian Liberation. New York, London, Toronto, Sydney, and Auckland, Anchor Books, 1995.

*

Critical Sources: "After Identity" by Urvashi Vaid, in *New Republic,* 10 May 1993, 28; "Let's Get Real about Feminism: The Backlash, the Myths, the Movement" by Gloria Steinem, bell hooks, Naomi Wolf, and Urvashi Vaid, in *Ms.,* Vol. 4, No. 2, September/October 1993; "So Many Ideas, So Little Time" by Todd VerBeek, in *Network News,* January 1994, http://verbeekt.cit.hope.edu/DifferentAngle/So Many Ideas.htm; "50 for the Future: *Time's* Roster of America's Most Promising Leaders Age 40 and Under," in *Time,* 5 December 1994, 64; "Equal but Not Equal" by Chris Thomas, in *OutNOW! The Gay Newspaper of Silicon Valley and the Bay Area,* 19 September 1995; "Vaid, Urvashi. *Virtual Equality: The Mainstreaming of Gay and Lesbian Liberation*" by Jeffery Ingram, in *Library Journal,* 1 October 1995, 107; "Manifesto for the Millennium: Urvashi Vaid on Queer Politics" by Daniel Vaillancourt, in *Seattle Gay News,* 27 October 1995; "Comeback Kid" by Todd Simmons, in *Advocate,* No. 691, 3 October 1995, 36-43; "Urvashi Vaid Speaks Out and Writes Out" by Trudy Ring, in *Outlines Chicago,* November 1995; "Are You Now or Have You Ever Been, a Homosexual?" by David L. Kirp, in *Tikkun,* Vol. 11, January/February 1996, 91-94; "Urvashi Vaid: 'What We Need to Do Is Transform the Mainstream, Not Just Integrate Ourselves into It'" by Anne-Marie Cusac, in *Progressive,* March 1996, 34-38; "Our Queer World; Class Struggle: It's Here. It's Queer. Get Used to It" by Scott Tucker, in *Humanist,* Vol. 56, No. 2, March/April 1996, 44-46; "Urvashi Vaid Charms Audience at F&M BGLAD Days Lecture," in *Lancaster Inqueery,* Vol. 3, No. 2, April/May 1996; "Urvashi Vaid Speaks on Gay and Lesbian Civil Rights" by Joe Anthony Perez, in *Advocate's Forum* (Chicago), Vol. 2, No. 3, May 1996; "Urvashi Vaid Speaks at UK" by David Williams, in *Letter: Kentucky's #1 Gay and Lesbian Newspaper!,* Vol. 7, No. 5, May 1996; "Behind the Scenes," in *Lambda Book Report,* Vol. 5, No. 1, July 1996, 19; "Equality and Respect: An Interview with Urvashi Vaid" by David Barsamian, in *Z Magazine,* September 1996, 47-51; "Where Have All the Radicals Gone?" by J. Jennings Moss, in *Advocate,* No. 722, 10 December 1996, 45-48; "Last Word: Hope versus Hype" by Urvashi Vaid, in *Advocate,* No. 723, 24 December 1996; "Divided We Stand: *Virtual Equality* by Urvashi Vaid" by Sally Owen, in *OTI Online,* http://www.igc.apc.org/onissues/s96vaid.htm.

*   *   *

Activist turned writer Urvashi Vaid chronicles her long career as an activist in the widely discussed book *Virtual Equality: The Mainstreaming of Gay and Lesbian Liberation.* Drawing on her experiences as an attorney for the American Civil Liberties Union, and as public information director and later executive director of the National Gay and Lesbian Task Force (NGTLF), Vaid surveys the progress that lesbian, gay, bisexual, and transgender (l/g/b/t) communities have made in securing greater access to social equality in the United States in the late twentieth century. Vaid stepped down from her prominent post as NGTLF director in 1993 because she was "tired of juggling the pressure of national work with my desire for a personal life" and she was not sure that she fully agreed with the "mainstream civil rights work done by the organization," she writes. Since stepping down, she has since worked actively to promote greater grassroots activism among the communities with which she identifies. She rejoined the organization as director of the Policy Institute in 1997.

In *Virtual Equality,* which *Library Journal* reviewer Jeffery Ingram called "part memoir, part social activist primer," Vaid expresses her concern that single interest campaigns have no real chance of success and are too narrow to meet the needs of the diverse l/g/b/t communities. Further, she notes that a movement that predicates itself only on obtaining civil rights without a contiguous/combined liberation movement is doomed to fail, for the rights gained give the dangerous impression of "virtual equality," or equality in appearance only. She notes that a concentration on civil rights alone often brings with it co-option because of the appearance of acceptance within political circles and the enticements of power-politics that can provide a sense not only of false complacency, but also can deflect a movement from full engagement in issues pertinent to the entire communities—issues of race, class, and social disenfranchisement.

Vaid notes that "the closet" is perhaps the greatest obstacle to both civil rights and liberation movements. "Coming out" of that closet means more visibility to the straight community, which leads to greater acceptance and debate about societal constructions of sexuality and power. Moreover, visibility and numbers are essential for political lobbying. Coming out can also be a transforming and transformative experience, Vaid notes: "it changed [my parents]. It changed our dynamics. It changed the whole understanding my family had about homosexuality. It suddenly got personal." This transformation can also apply societally, for, as Vaid indicates, the fear of people who don't know that they know l/g/b/t people is one of the strongest bolsters of homophobia. As she discusses in an interview with Daniel Vaillancourt in the *Seattle Gay News,* "I think that a lot of the goals of the movement are very much about teaching people the truth about our lives, and assimilating straight culture to who we really are—to get used to us; to deal with the reality of the fact that Gay people are just ordinary people."

Vaid acknowledges the many obstacles to getting members of the l/g/b/t communities working together: closeted middle-class and wealthy gays and lesbians hide behind the screen of "virtual equality," and individuals get too caught up in advocating for the rights of their subgroup. One solution is to articulate broader goals, she explains in an interview with Sally Owen in *OTI Online*: "We must have positions on affirmative action, welfare, and economic justice. Our tendency to see ourselves as an exception, as a special category rather than as one group of many backfires. We lose the respect of those who could be our allies." In the *New Republic,* she writes: "we must

articulate what a post-liberation society looks like, rather than merely reacting to the fears of others."

One of Vaid's greatest concerns is that the NGLTF does not have strong enough grassroots organizing and community support. Since leaving the Task Force she has devoted much of her time to just such issues. She has spoken at numerous l/g/b/t events and conferences, at rallies against the religious right, and at the March on Washington. As she told Anne-Marie Cusac in the *Progressive,* "The way I'm doing my work now is that I work with community groups all over the country, who contact me." She notes that these groups "are sometimes AIDS groups, they are feminist groups, they are student groups, they are South Asian, they are people-of-color groups, gay and lesbian groups. I think clearly there is a need for that kind of organizing assistance, technical assistance." David Williams points out in the *Letter* that Vaid's presence at conferences, even small ones such as that sponsored by University of Kentucky's Lambda student group, inspires student action and validates the experience of l/g/b/t people. As Joe Anthony Perez indicates in *Advocate's Forum,* Vaid includes the audience, brainstorming with them and asking for help with strategizing "about coalition building with other civil rights movements."

As Vaid says in her *Advocate* article, "Hope versus Hype": "I take my hope from the hardworking organizers, the youth activists, the grassroots volunteers, the students, the artists, our progressive allies, the philanthropists—who tackle the political powerlessness, economic barriers, racial prejudice, institutional sexism, and persistent homophobia that make a mockery of our hopes." In her work and through the insights she has provided in *Virtual Equality,* Vaid has provided a vision for transformation. In the *Advocate,* Todd Simmons quotes Vaid: "Civil rights is not an end point for the gay community. Social change and transformation is. The goal of the gay and lesbian movement is to achieve a society in which homosexuality is considered as healthy, natural, and normal as heterosexuality. It's going to require a change in people's attitudes, in people's hearts, and in people's values about what they think is good and bad. It's about morality. And it encompasses much more than legal reform or media visibility." At the end of virtual equality, Vaid presents a guide "for the already political," for "those who are toiling away in the movement." The last of her suggestions is, "Don't despair, no matter what."

—Patti Capel Swartz

VINING, Donald

Nationality: American diarist, columnist, editor, and advocate for older gays and lesbians. **Born:** Benton, Pennsylvania, 20 June 1917. **Education:** Educated in the Department of Drama, Carnegie Tech., 1934-35, West Chester State Teachers College, 1937-39, and Department of Drama, Yale University, 1939-41. **Career:** Sales clerk, Dix Post Exchange, 1941-42, and B. Altman department store, New York City, 1942-43; night desk clerk, Sloane House YMCA, New York City, 1943, 1945-46; janitor, Paramount Pictures Studio, Hollywood, California, 1943-44; clerk and typist, Philippine Desiccated Coconut Co., New York City, 1946-49; office manager, Development Office, Teachers College, Columbia University, 1950-79; publisher, editor, advertising manager, shipping clerk and "everything else," The Pepys Press, from 1979. **Address:** 1270 5th Ave., Apt. 5-G, New York, New York, 10029-3424, U.S.A.

WRITINGS

Short Stories

"Show Me The Way To Go Home," in *Cross Section 1945: A Collection of New American Writing.* New York, L.B. Fischer, 1945.

"The Train To Calais," in *James White Review,* Vol. 1, No. 2, winter 1984, 5-6.

"Menage," in *James White Review,* Vol. 3, No. 4, summer 1986, 13-14.

"D.O.M.," in *James White Review,* Vol. 4, No. 2, winter 1986, 4-5; in *The Gay Nineties; An Anthology of Contemporary Gay Fiction,* Freedom, California, Crossing Press, 1991; in *Lavender Mansions: 40 Contemporary Lesbian and Gay Short Stories,* Boulder, Colorado, Westview Press, 1994.

"Longings & Belongings," in *James White Review,* Vol. 5, No. 1, fall 1987, 11-12.

Cabin Fever And Other Stories. New York, Masquerade Books, 1995.

Nonfiction

A Gay Diary, 5 Vols. New York, Pepys Press, 1979-1993; reprinted as *A Gay Diary, 1933-1946,* New York, Masquerade Books, 1996.

How Can You Come Out If You've Never Been In?: Essays on Gay Life and Relationships. Trumansburg, New York, Crossing Press, 1986.

Essays

"Growing Up and Out with a Lesbian Mother," in *Advocate,* No. 300, 4 September 1980, 14-15, 53.

"Life and Love in the Long Haul," in *Advocate,* No. 308, 25 December 1980, 26-28.

"The Advantage of Age," in *Advocate,* No. 313, 18 March 1981, 22-23.

"Straight Talk," in *Gay Community News,* Vol. 8, No. 36, 4 April 1981, 5.

"On Resisting the Role of Gay Sage," in *Advocate,* No. 330, 12 November 1981, 31-33.

"What's the Good Word?," in *Gay Community News,* Vol. 9, No. 30, 20 February 1982, 10.

"Signs and Shibboleths," in *Advocate,* No. 338, 18 March 1982, 24-27.

"Where Coupledom Begins: Meetings in Likely and Unlikely Places," in *Advocate,* No. 356, 25 November 1982, 23-25.

"A Golden Gay Couple," in *Advocate,* No. 366, 28 April 1983, 18-19, 21.

"Remembering George," in *First Hand,* August 1983.

"Old Is Not a Four Letter Word," in *New York Native,* Vol. 4, No. 4, 16-29 January 1984, 25-26.

"In This Age of Sex Specialization, Is Romance Possible?," in *Advocate,* No. 388, 21 February 1984, 24-25, 52.

"Aging Sagely," in *RFD,* winter 1984.

"Gays and Monogamy," in *Mandala,* March 1984.

"Muscle Bound: Building Bodies Gay Ways," in *Advocate,* No. 92, 17 April 1984, 32-34, 66.

"Gay Pride—Justified?," in *New York Native,* Vol. 4, No. 18, 18 June 18-1 July 1984, 22.

"So He Said No . . . Handling Rejection," in *Advocate,* No. 401, 21 August 1984, 32-33.

"Gay Nesting: The Pleasures and Perils of Living Together," in *Advocate,* No. 404, 2 October 1984, 29-30, 57-58.

"A Spell in the Slammer," in *First Hand,* October 1984.

"Best Foot Forward, March," in *New York Native,* Vol. 5, No. 5, 28 January-10 February 1985, 12.

"Standing Room Only," in *First Hand,* February 1985.

"Stonewall: A Good Symbol but Not the Birth of Gay Lib," in *Advocate,* No. 422, 11 June 1985, 5.

"Where Do We Go from Here? What Does the Future Hold for Gays? Among Other Things, Will Robots Be Doing Our Cruising for Us?," in *New York Native,* Vol. 5, No. 13, 1-14 July 1985, 43-44.

"Gay Ghosts Dispossessed," in *New York Native,* Vol. 5. No. 26, 28 October-3 November 1985, 34-35.

"Happily Ever After: Many Princes May Be Better than One," in *Advocate,* No. 442, 18 March 1986, 9.

"Back to the Gay Future: Master Classes in Subtle Passes?," in *New York Native,* Vol. 6, No. 30, 7 July 1986, 26-27.

"Myths about Gay Men That Even Gay Men Believe," in *Gay Life, Leisure, Love and Living for the Contemporary Gay Male.* New York, Dolphin-Doubleday, 1986.

"American Actives and Passives," in *Gay Community News,* Vol. 14, No. 14, 19-25 October 1986, 5.

"A Living Doll," in *New York Native,* Vol. 7, No. 17, 6 April 1987, 21.

"Rediscovering Our History: Don't Forget the Gay Times," in *Advocate,* No. 489, 5 January 1988, 9.

"Voices of the Gay Past," in *New York Native,* Vol. 9, No. 26, 5 June 1989, 27-29.

"A New Age for Aging Gays," in *Christopher Street,* Vol. 14, No. 12, 29-31.

*

Manuscript Collections: Gay and Lesbian Archives, New York Public Library, New York City.

Donald Vining comments:

I was motivated to publish *A Gay Diary* by my disgust at the downbeat tone of gay literature in the 1950s, which usually ended with the gay man being murdered or committing suicide after a failed pass at a straight man. I wanted to show young gays that it was possible to find reciprocated sexual attraction and even love and to live a life that deserves the description "gay." I thought a novel would be assumed to be fantasy but that my actual diary might convince.

When a major literary agency which had said it would be delighted to see a gay diary returned it saying they were disappointed because it seemed too happy a diary and didn't reflect all the woes they were sure homosexuals endured (straights can be tolerant of us as long as they think we're miserable and unhappy), I decided to invest time and money in publishing it myself. I took early retirement from my job to devote myself to the task.

The stories and articles were motivated by a need to let the gay community know the book was out there, since it was unlikely that reviewers would pay any attention to a self-published book. I noticed that *The Advocate* and *James White Review* used author's blurbs, which said the author of the article or story was also the author of _____. So I started doing fiction and nonfiction for them that had a positive, sometimes joking tone the reader might hope to find also in the diary. When the magazines stopped saying I was the author of *A Gay Diary* and said just that I was a freelance author living in New York I countered by including references to the diary, and even quotations, in the body of the article, so I still got my advertising and got paid for it rather than paying out.

* * *

One of the long-recognized weaknesses of the gay and lesbian community (which has served as a goad for the rise of the burgeoning field of gay and lesbian studies in virtually every humanities and social sciences discipline) is the widespread absence of a coherent sense of history. Until the development of the gay and lesbian archives movement in the 1980s, older members of local gay communities were not recognized as potential sources of living history, their experiences either totally ignored or only marginally recorded, and their social participation sharply limited. Access to accounts of what it meant to live as a self-recognized American homosexual of either gender in the decades prior to gay liberation were thus in scant supply. One writer whose pen has contributed substantially to addressing this need (both through a life diary and later writings for the gay press) is Donald Vining.

Born in the small town of Benton in northeastern Pennsylvania, Vining's life was impacted early on by the separation of his parents and his mother's numerous lesbian relationships with other women. Financial uncertainties are a recurrent theme in the pages of his diary, a habit begun in 1933 which would continue for several decades and culminate in a regular column for *Diarist's Journal*. A lively interest in theater, drama, and literature throughout his secondary education led him to read widely and resulted in the steady production of stories, poems, and plays. After graduation, he pursued his interest in theater for two years at West Chester State Teachers College near Philadelphia, followed by admission to the Yale Drama School in 1939. During his two years there, he wrote approximately one dozen one-act plays for the radio, none of which had any homosexual content. An open declaration of his homosexuality resulted in rejection by the armed forces during mobilization for World War II. Arriving in New York City in 1942, he worked at a variety of jobs and participated extensively in the lively cultural life of the community. In 1950, he joined the development staff of the Teachers College at Columbia University, a position he retained for 29 years.

His contributions to the literature of gay America did not begin in deliberate earnest until after his retirement from Columbia in 1979, and addressed three consistent themes. The first of these is the history of the manners, mores, customs, and foibles of homosexual existence in New York City during the 1940s and 1950s (these writings, along with his detailed diary entries, foreshadowing such later city-specific research as George Chauncey's 1989 dissertation turned book *Gay New York*). These articles re-introduced a new generation of gays and lesbians to such vanished social institutions as the "Bird Circuit" (a popular group of chic bars catering heavily to homosexual clientele) and recounted fashions in dress used to assist gay men in recognizing each other. Even obliterated physical settings of homosexual life such as the old Astor Hotel were memorialized in "Gay Ghosts Dispossessed."

A second theme of Vining's writing is analysis of and commentary on the post-gay liberation society. His wry yet thoughtful pen addressed subjects ranging from coping with being rejected to satire of popular fads and sharp criticism of those many individuals who remained inactive or unwilling to support struggling community institutions.

The third general topic is one almost uniquely absent from the majority of gay non-fiction literature prior to the 1980s, namely the realities, joys, and benefits of life as a senior gay or lesbian. Gay mythology, culture (and, until recently, research) was heavily oriented towards the young, with little or no attention paid to aging members of the community. This situation was recognized in 1977 with the formation of SAGE (Senior Action in a Gay Environment), organized to provide social contact and other support services. Vining affiliated with SAGE, but his essays speak to the causes of the historic invisibility of this segment of the homosexual world and challenge the prevailing mythology that to be old and gay inevitably meant being lonely, unwanted, and ignored. Anticipating later books such as *Long Time Passing: Lives Of Older Lesbians* (1986) and *Quiet Fire: Memoirs of Older Gay Men* (1986), Vining's straightforward accounts of life as one half of a male couple which had endured for four decades provided much-needed perspective for younger generations of openly gay men.

His most significant piece of writing, although not intended to be such, is unquestionably his personal chronicle, which began to appear in print as *A Gay Diary* in 1979 (self-published by Vining under the aegis Pepys Press) and which eventually reached five volumes covering the period 1933-1982. It is virtually the only daily historical account so far known from the United States which permits the tracing of an individual homosexual life through the years of World War II, the immediate post-war era and boom of the 1950s, the rise of gay liberation and the birth of a new public subculture. While as emotionally frank as Ned Rorem's earlier publication *The Paris Diary,* Vining's entries also serve to document a now-vanished species of gay man and the urban New York world he inhabited.

—Robert B. Marks Ridinger

———

VOYLE, Mary. *See* **MANNING, Rosemary.**

———

VRUGT, Johanna Petronella. *See* **BLAMAN, Anna.**

———

WALKER, Alice (Malsenior)

Nationality: American novelist and author of short stories, poetry, and essays. **Born:** Eatonton, Georgia, 9 February 1944. **Education:** Spelman College, Atlanta, Georgia, 1961-63; Sarah Lawrence College, New York, B.A. 1965. **Family:** Married Mel Leventhal in 1967 (divorced 1976); one child, Rebecca; companion of Robert Allen. **Career:** Has held a variety of jobs, including working for New York City's welfare department; worked for civil rights movement, canvassing voters, working with Head Start programs, and campaigning for welfare rights, 1965-68; instructor, Jackson State University, 1968-69, Tougaloo College, 1969-70, Wellesley College, 1972, University of Massachusetts-Boston, 1972, and other universities; contributing editor, *Ms.* magazine, 1974; co-founder, with Robert Allen, Wild Trees Press, 1984. **Awards:** First prize, *American Scholar* essay contest, 1967; Radcliffe Institute Fellowship, Harvard University, 1971-73; Lillian Smith Award, for poetry, 1973; Rosenthal Foundation Award, American Academy of Arts and Letters, 1974; National Endowment for the Arts Award, 1978; MacDowell Colony fellowship, 1979; Radcliffe Institute fellowship, 1979; Guggenheim Foundation fellowship, 1979; American Book Award, 1983; Pulitzer Prize, for fiction, 1983; Townsend Prize, 1984. **Address:** c/o Harcourt Brace, 111 5th Ave., New York, New York 10003, U.S.A.

WRITINGS

Novels

The Third Life of Grange Copeland. New York, Harcourt Brace Jovanovich, 1970.
Meridian. New York, Harcourt Brace Jovanovich, 1976.
The Color Purple. New York, Harcourt Brace Jovanovich, 1982; London, Women's Press, 1983.
The Temple of My Familiar. San Diego, Harcourt Brace Jovanovich, 1989.
Possessing the Secret of Joy. New York, Harcourt Brace Jovanovich, 1992.

Short Stories

In Love and Trouble: Stories of Black Women. San Diego, Harvest/HBJ, 1973.
You Can't Keep a Good Woman Down. San Diego, Harvest/HBJ, 1981; London: Women's Press, 1982.
"Cuddling," in *Essence,* July 1985.
"Kindred Spirit," in *Esquire,* August 1985.
"Olive Oil," in *Ms.,* August 1985.

Poetry

Once: Poems. New York, Harcourt Brace and World, 1968.
Revolutionary Petunias and Other Poems. New York, Harcourt Brace Jovanovich, 1971.

Five Poems. Detroit, Broadside, 1972.
Good Night, Willie Lee, I'll See You in the Morning: Poems. New York, Dial, 1979.
Horses Make a Landscape Look More Beautiful: Poems. New York, Harcourt Brace Jovanovich, 1984.
Her Blue Body Everything We Know: Earthling Poems 1965-1990 Complete. San Diego, Harcourt Brace Jovanovich, 1991.

Other

Langston Hughes: American Poet (biography). New York, Crowell, 1974.
Editor, *I Love Myself When I Am Laughing . . . And Then Again When I Am Looking Mean and Impressive: A Zora Neale Hurston Reader.* Old Westbury, New York, Feminist Press, 1979.
"Porn at Home" (essay), in *Ms.,* February 1980.
In Search of Our Mothers' Gardens: Womanist Prose (essays). San Diego, Harcourt Brace Jovanovich, 1983.
"Not Only Will Your Teachers Appear, They Will Cook New Foods for You" (essay), in *Mendocino Country,* 1 September 1986.
Living by the Word: Selected Writings 1973-1987 (essays). San Diego, Harcourt Brace Jovanovich, 1988.
To Hell with Dying (for children). San Diego, Harcourt Brace Jovanovich, 1988.
With Pratibha Parmar, *Warrior Marks: Female Genital Mutilation and the Sexual Blinding of Women* (nonfiction). New York, Harcourt Brace Jovanovich, 1993; London, Random House, 1993.

Recordings: *Possessing the Secret of Joy,* New York, Simon and Schuster, 1992.

*

Adaptations: *The Color Purple* (film; directed by Steven Spielberg), Warner Brothers, 1985.

Bibliography: "Alice Walker: A Selected Bibliography, 1968-1988" by Keith Byerman and Erma Banks, in *Callaloo,* Vol. 12, No. 2, 1989, 162-163.

Critical Sources: "Alice in the Mainstream" by Loyle Hairston, in *Freedomways,* Vol. 24, summer 1984, 182-190; "No More Buried Lives: The Theme of Lesbianism in Audre Lourde's *Zami,* Gloria Naylor's *The Women of Brewster Place,* Ntozake Shange's *Sassafras, Cypress, and Indigo,* and Alice Walker's *The Color Purple*" by Barbara Christian, in *Black Feminist Criticism: Perspectives on Black Women Writers,* New York, Pergamon Press, 1985, 187-204; "Androgyny as Metaphor in Alice Walker's Novels" by Marie H. Buncombe, in *CLA Journal,* Vol. 30, June 1987, 419-427; "Race, Gender, and Nation in *The Color Purple*" by Lauren Berlant, in *Critical Inquiry,* Vol. 14, summer 1988, 831-859; "Sifting Through the Controversy: Reading *The Color Purple*" by Jacqueline Bobo, in *Callaloo,* Vol. 39, spring 1989, 332-342; "'Don't Tell': Imposed Silences in *The Color Purple* and *The Woman Warrior*" by King-Kok Cheung, and "Womanist Fiction and Male Characters" by George Stade, in *Emerging Voices; A Cross-Cultural Reader: Readings in the American Experience,* edited by Janet and Sara M. Blake Madden-Simpson, Fort Worth, Texas, Holt, Rinehart and Winston, Inc., 1990, 400-421, 379-383; *Alice Walker* by Donna Haisty Winchell, New York, Twayne Publishers, 1992; "African-American Literature, Lesbian" by AnnLouise Keating, in *The Gay and Lesbian Literary Heritage,* edited by Claude J. Summers, New York, Henry Holt and Co., 1995, 12-15.

*   *   *

When Alice Walker was eight years old, one of her brothers shot her in the eye with a BB gun. This event was seminal to Walker's perceptions of the world, as her blinding became metaphoric for other events and relationships. She believed that her brother shot her purposefully and, while he went unpunished, she was wounded and, she felt, fragmented. She attempted to become invisible to the world around her, feeling ugly and ashamed whereas she had once felt attractive, whole, and proud. This event, the resulting reactions to and from the persons involved, and its consequences became, to Walker, emblematic of gender relations. She was female, punished, fragmented, invisible, and ashamed; he was male, unpunished, visible, and whole. She writes in *In Search of Our Mother's Gardens* that it was not until her young daughter said, after watching *The Blue Marble* on television, that she could "see a world in [her mother's] eye" that Walker learned to revise her interpretation of her self, to re-vision it in such a way that she became whole once more. Alice Walker has also revisioned constructions of women, sexuality, relationships, and the family in her writing.

Walker analogizes her visual blinding to what she calls the sexual blinding of women: the practice of genital mutilation, which ranges from nicking the clitoris to excising the clitoris and the labia majora and sewing the remaining tissue almost completely shut. The practice of genital mutilation is explored in Walker's *Possessing the Secret of Joy* and the text she co-wrote with Pratibha Parmar, *Warrior Marks: Female Genital Mutilation and the Sexual Blinding of Women. Possessing the Secret of Joy* is the story of Tashi, an African woman who decides to undergo ritual scarification and genital mutilation in order to bear upon her body the mark of tribal identification. As her tribe dwindles away under the force of external economic, social, and political factors, she utilizes tribal custom as a marker of group identification and solidarity. However, due to the silence which surrounds what, exactly, constitutes this ceremony, Tashi does not realize the full extent of what her choice entails.

Genital mutilation, both in actuality and in Walker's story, is utilized as a means of controlling female agency. The practice, according to Walker, "blinds" women to their own sexual pleasure and desire and binds them within a system of compulsory heterosexuality. Without the clitoris and due to the small size of the opening in the most extreme type of mutilation (clitoridectomy and infibulation or Pharaonic circumcision), women are generally not able to experience clitoral and vaginal pleasure. This helps to ensure that women will not seek sexual pleasure outside of heterosexual marriage—a relationship based not at all on sexual gratification for the woman, but on other factors, such as economics and social mores. In the worst cases, all women can do is endure sexual intercourse. One additional result is that the expression of a full lesbian sexuality is physically prohibited.

Pierre, the product of an extramarital affair between Tashi's husband, Adam, and Lisette, a Frenchwoman, is the source of much of the information on the results and origins of the practice of genital mutilation. He becomes the representative of sexual freedom in the text through his homosexuality, as well as one source of Tashi's psychic liberation through the information he provides. Pierre is able to attain a wholeness and health unavailable to the other characters, who are weighed down by social and sexual constraints. He represents the possibility of happiness.

Walker also uses this work to question the relationship between sexuality and AIDS. In American culture, AIDS has generally been associated with so-called "deviant" sexuality or drug use. When the syndrome first acquired national recognition, through the death of actor Rock Hudson, attention (and blame) was focused on the lesbigay community, linking it with drug culture and painting both as sickly, deviant, and criminal. Within the pages of *Possessing the Secret of Joy,* the character Tashi confronts AIDS when she is imprisoned in a building which also serves those affected with the disease. Through this character Walker reveals a new origin story for the disease, tracing its beginnings to white industrialists who unknowingly process the organs of monkeys carrying the disease in order to create vaccines. Walker thus divorces sexuality—especially homosexuality—from AIDS, and offers a gay character who is representative of the only full health in the story.

Female agency, including sexual desire and fulfillment (or the lack thereof), is at the heart of several of Walker's other texts, including *The Color Purple, Meridian, The Temple of My Familiar,* the short fiction collected in *In Love and Trouble: Stories of Black Women* and *You Can't Keep a Good Woman Down,* and much of her poetry. Walker's representation of race, gender, nationality, and lesbianism in *The Color Purple* has drawn the most attention of any of these texts up until *Possessing the Secret of Joy,* thanks in no small part to its adaptation to film by acclaimed director Steven Spielberg.

Celie is the main character of *The Color Purple,* an epistolary novel which spans the 1920s to the 1940s. Through Celie's letters to God and her reading of her sister Nettie's letters, we learn of Celie's sexual and physical abuse at the hands of her "father" and her husband. Gradually, she falls in love with and is befriended by Shug, a singer in juke joints and her husband's mistress. Shug teaches Celie about her own body and about sexual desire and gratification. Lesbian sexuality becomes the means to Celie's empowerment, and she gradually learns to believe in herself. With Shug's help, she gains the power to leave Mr. _____, her husband, and establish a company based on the pants she sews for family and friends.

Ending with a Fourth of July family reunion and Celie's emotional, spiritual, and economic success, the novel has been accused of being more a fairytale than a realistic treatment of a black woman's life in the South. According to Loyle Hairston and several other critics, mainstream acceptance of the text has followed from its lack of consideration of socio-economic problems faced by blacks. Lauren Berlant joins with Hairston in stating that the text offers an individualistic treatment of the self and society and propagates the notion that all one needs to succeed in America is sexual fulfillment and capitalistic drive. Celie finds herself by finding her vagina and finding economic success; her empowerment is thus limited to the personal sphere, rather than a deconstruction and critique of power relations based on economics, gender, race, or sexuality.

As Jacqueline Bobo documents, several black male critics have found fault with the novel and movie as well—although some of these same critics admit to not having read/seen it themselves—due to what they consider to be the negative portrayal of the black male and the reinstatement of dominant cultural myths about black male behavior, specifically as regards sexuality. George Stade, for instance, cites Walker's definition of womanism, her alternative to the term "feminism," as proof of her attacking and symbolically emasculating the black man. This is in part because she defines womanism, in part, as "a woman who loves other women, sexually and/or nonsexually."

In his discussion of Walker's womanism, however, Stade leaves out the "sometimes loves men" portion of her definition as well as the "[c]ommitted to survival and wholeness of an entire people, male and female" section, emphasizing only Walker's exclusionary parts of her definition. Marie H. Buncombe finds that Walker's work attempts to fashion wholeness, rather than destroy masculinity, through the construction of androgyny in both male and female characters. Rather than offering the male characters salvation by making them into women, as Stade claims, Walker leaves her former husband and her son-in-law "free to be their own men," in King-Kok Cheung's words.

What is ultimately at stake, Bobo writes, is the authority and freedom of black women to delineate the terms of image making. Bobo finds that, unlike many black men, black women have extracted favorable meanings of their own from seeing the film and reading the novel. Celie overcomes sexual and physical abuse, finds the power to control herself and her sexuality, and revises gender, sexual, and spiritual myths.

Writings about and by black lesbians can be traced to the Harlem Renaissance of the early twentieth century, when the verbalization of lesbian desire was camouflaged in song lyrics and in novels. From the 1970s to the 1990s, the number of black lesbian characters and authors has increased and enabled the camouflage to be stripped and the silence broken. Alice Walker's representations of women, men, sexuality, and power relations contributes to this stripping away of coding and silence. At the very least, her writing encourages dialogue about these aspects of our lives and discourages blindness.

—Alyson R. Buckman

WATNEY, Simon

Nationality: British educator, essayist, and AIDS activist. **Born:** England, 13 March 1949. **Education:** University of Sussex, B.A. in History and Theory of Art 1970; Brighton Polytechnic, Post-Graduate Certificate in Education 1971; and Courtauld Institute, University of London, M.Phil. in Art History, 1975. **Career:** Lecturer in art history, Faculty of Art and Design, Brighton Polytechnic, 1971-74; senior lecturer in the history and theory of photography, School of Communication, Polytechnic of Central London, 1976-86; chair, Board of Health Education and Policy Committee, Terence Higgins Trust, 1985-89; founder/director, Red Hot Aids Charitable Trust, United Kingdom, from 1992. Editorial board, *Screen*, 1980-85; columnist, *Gay Times*, 1988-95; founder/trustee, *National AIDS Manual*, 1989; founder/director, Gay Men Fighting Aids, 1991; Contributor of essays on art history and AIDS to periodicals, including *Artforum, Critical Quarterly, New Scientist, differences, Sight-and-Sound, October, Village Voice,* and *Gay Times.* **Awards:** Gregory Kolovakos Prize, U.S. Words Project, 1990. **Address:** c/o Red Hot AIDS Charitable Trust, Suite 32, The Eurolink Centre, 49 Effra Road, London SW2 1BZ, England.

WRITINGS

Nonfiction

Policing Desire: Pornography, AIDS, and the Media. London, Methuen, Minneapolis, University of Minnesota Press, 1987; revised, 1996.

Editor, with Erica Carter, *Taking Liberties: AIDS and Cultural Politics.* London, Serpent's Tail, 1989.

"Missionary Positions: AIDS, 'Africa,' and Race," in *Out There: Marginalization and Contemporary Culture,* New York, MIT/The New Museum of Contemporary Art, 1990.

"Emergent Sexual Identities and HIV/AIDS," in *AIDS: Facing the Second Decade,* edited by Peter Aggleton. London, Falmer Press, 1993.

"Art from the Pit: Memory, Monuments, and AIDS," in *Don't Leave Me This Way,* edited by Ted Gott. London, National Gallery of Australia/Thames and Hudson, 1994.

Practices of Freedom: Selected Writing on HIV/AIDS. London, Rivers Oram Press, and Durham, Duke University Press, 1994.

"Queer Andy," in *Pop Out: The Art of Andy Warhol,* edited by Jennifer Doyle et. al. Durham, North Carolina, Duke University Press, 1996.

Art Criticism

English Post-Impressionism. London, Studiovista, 1980.

"Making Strange: Russian Formalist Photography," in *Thinking Photography,* edited by Victor Burgin. London, Macmillan, 1982.

Editor, with Patricia Holland and Jo Spence, *Photography/Politics—2.* London, Commedia Publishing Group, 1986.

"Gardens of Speculation: Landscape in 'The Draughtsman's Contract,'" in *Picture This: Media Representations of Visual Art and Artists,* edited by Philip Hayward. London, Arts Council, 1988.

The Art of Duncan Grant. London, John Murray Ltd., 1990.

"Ordinary Boys," in *Family Snaps: The Meaning of Domestic Photography,* edited by Jo Spence and Patricia Holland. London, Virago Press, 1991.

"On *House*: Iconoclasm and Iconophobia," in *Rachel Whiteread: House,* edited by James Lingwood. London, Phaidon Press, 1995.

"Painting in the Register of Loss," in *Ross Bleckner,* edited by Lisa Dennison. New York, Solomon R. Guggenheim Museum/Abrams Inc., 1995.

Wolfgang Tillmans. Cologne, Germany, Taschen Publications, 1995.

*

Simon Watney comments:

As a Sixties teenager I was very much involved in CND and pacifist politics before going to the University of Sussex to read History and Theory of Art in 1967. My student years coincided with the emergence of the Gay Liberation Front in London, many of the meetings of which I attended with my then boyfriend. Together in Brighton we formed a local GLF branch, which has a direct line of descent in today's University of Sussex Lesbian and Gay Society. I like such continuities, both politically and culturally. Barthes and Levi-Strauss had lectured at Sussex, and I was fortunate to be taught by Professor Quentin Bell, who brought with him a marvelous model of strong liberalism, and a detestation of fanaticism of all kinds which impressed me deeply. I was also influenced in my late teens and twenties by the artist Duncan Grant, whom I knew well, and who represented a marvelous example of unpretentious creative life, in fact of what it means to be "an artist." For me as an art historian this was not unimportant.

I taught art history at Brighton Poly from 1971 until 1974, when I moved to London to do an M.A. at the Courtauld Institute, supporting myself financially as a Supply Teacher. I was a wretchedly incompetent secondary school teacher, but the following year I started lecturing at a couple of London colleges, and ended up as a Senior Lecturer in the School of Communication of the old Polytechnic of Central London (now swanked up with the preposterous title of the University of Westminster). With Victor Burgin and others I taught film and photography students in a curriculum organized around psychoanalysis, semiotics, and Foucauldian cultural studies. At the same time I was still involved in gay politics, first with Lesbian and Gay Switchboard, and then through the late '70s with Gay Left.

Gay Left consisted of a group of around ten men who meet weekly, year in, year out, as a reading group, as a personal support group, as the organizers of annual Gay Left conferences, and as the writers, editors, and producers of a journal of the same name. Our politics were very much about Gramsci and Freud and Foucault. None of us had been Trotskyites or members of "revolutionary" parties. On the contrary, Gay Left was part of an emergent language of "identity politics" in Britain, and many of the topics we discussed and wrote about in the far-off '70s, e.g. S/M, gay media issues, race, and identity, became central to the political agenda of the '80s and up to today. I also wrote widely in the national gay press, but also began to write in overseas gay publications too. I had close friends in Toronto, associated with *The Body Politic,* an important North American gay publication, and so on. I also developed close friendships in the United States with critics whose work overlapped with mine in photographic studies—Craig Owens, Barbara Kruger, etc. We were all of a generation in the late '70s, regardless of age. We were colleagues and friends. I was invited onto the editorial board of *Screen,* then edited by the excellent Mandy Merck, and my work ranged across a wide field of interests, from anti-censorship issues to early twentieth century British painting, contemporary art, photographic education, and so on.

I gave up my academic career in 1985 to work full-time in HIV/AIDS issues, with which I was increasingly engaged. Since then I've worked in a wide variety of roles and capacities. I wrote a monthly column for seven years in *Gay Times,* helped organize exhibitions, etc. I've worked extensively in the voluntary sector, and have also always written and lectured widely on many aspects of the epidemic, from treatment issues to health promotion for gay men. Much of this work was international, inevitably, since so many of my friends in America were sick many years before their U.K. counterparts. In the meantime I've continued to maintain my work as an art critic. Surrounded by so much death, it is vital to also hold on to the deeper forces of life in our cultures.

Although I've been closely involved in the history of what one might think of as "the politics of the representation of AIDS," this has not for me been the central focus of my work, however important I think such work is.

As an intellectual I have tried to explore and analyze and challenge the complex workings of power within the institutional management of the epidemic, from the pharmaceutical industry to government departments, newspapers, and charities. I've always aimed to stimulate discussion and debate concerning policies and needs, and to provide reliable, up-to-date information, often in somewhat neglected areas. My involvement in politics has always been strictly pragmatic, as in the co-founding with Chris Woods and Keith Alcorn of OutRage in 1990, in response to the wilder excesses of Thatcherism, and in order to pro-actively encourage an activist self-confidence amongst a younger generation of gay men and lesbians.

I've always tended to regard the gay community as my primary constituency, and have little patience for those who loftily trash the gay scene, for whatever reasons. In many ways I am a very English old-fashioned liberal. The intellectuals I most admire are those who always strive to connect theory to practice, who recognize the need to set achievable goals, who stay alive to the present, who are able to change their minds—Stuart Hall, Foucault, Isaiah Berlin, Vaclav Havel, etc. As Hannah Arendt observed: "One can resist only in terms of the identity that is under attack." I have become an itinerant scholar, and I can't now imagine myself going back into teaching. I detest "outing" because it seems to me that if gay identity means anything, it means conscious, voluntary choice. I think activism will always be necessary in a world ruled by politicians and business people whose eyes are only ever fixed on short-term profits and maximum yield. I'm not a Luvvie or a Leftie. I deeply distrust Utopianism. Somehow or other we all have to live together and get along as best we can. This is the great challenge, however unglamorous it may sound to some.

*   *   *

Simon Watney's essays and books have been essential reading for anyone wishing to understand the political, cultural, and personal meanings of AIDS throughout the 1980s and 1990s. His analyses of medicine, the popular media, and the arts decode the many discursive practices that surround AIDS and male homosexuality. Watney's essays frequently feature a strongly articulated, occasionally enraged gay male voice that refuses to allow his reader to forget the personal costs of AIDS. That his arguments are also deftly able to engage with larger theoretical discussions about representation, power, specularity, and identity without losing sight of his personal stake underscores Watney's importance in the field of gay male writings on AIDS.

Watney's first book about AIDS, *Policing Desire: Pornography, AIDS, and the Media,* established many of the topics his later works have continued to examine: the puritanical ideology of the British and American governments that allowed them to perceive AIDS as a sexually transmitted disease rather than a blood disease and so justified their extended inaction; a discourse of pornography that could only see safe sex instruction as obscene; the relative success of gay community support in the face of inaction and ignorance on the part of governmental and medical institutions; and the collusion of the popular media in endorsing and disseminating stereotypic, homophobic misrepresentations of gay men and HIV positive people as interchangeable carriers of plague. Watney, who was trained as an art historian and critic, brings the art critic's perception and theoretical tools to bear on his subjects. The union of those probing analytic skills with the angered voice of the gay activist makes his arguments powerfully persuasive.

Despite the fact that Watney frequently writes in the first person and that many of his essays contain autobiographical material, he has resisted the urge to adopt the tone of righteous activism seen in writing about AIDS from the mid 1980s, such as that by Larry Kramer and David Feinberg. Indeed, at a politicized moment when some suggested that there could be only activism or theory, Watney stressed the necessity of the interarticulation of theory and activism; theory, in Watney's essays, is a crucial form of activism. AIDS, itself already a complex of diseases and not a single, definable thing, thus also marks "a crisis of representation itself, a crisis over the entire framing of knowledge about the human body and its capacities for sexual pleasure," writes Watney in *Policing Desire.* Even given such larger goals, Watney has not lost sight of the local or specific; his early criticisms of Britain's gay community's failure to respond to AIDS as quickly or effectively as New York's is damning, as is his later work which reads the curious de-gaying of AIDS as it has received increased mainstream attention.

Watney's work at its strongest brings together such specific arguments and reads through them the broader cultural issues that define the discourse of AIDS. Many of his early essays might then seem dated; battles have been won or lost and medical information has changed over time. But Watney's project has insisted on the importance of documenting such struggles even as he intervenes in them. His essays argue and persuade and educate, but they also mark sites of resistance and serve as sites of memorials. And his work as the founder and director of the Red Hot AIDS Charitable Trust has raised and distributed funds for community-based HIV/AIDS education in population groups at demonstrably high risk.

—Elliott McEldowney

WEIRAUCH, Anna Elisabet

Nationality: German novelist, playwright, and short story writer. **Born:** Galatz, Romania, 7 August 1887; lived primarily in Berlin, Germany. **Education:** Studied theater and acting with Max Reinhardt, 1906-14; appeared in over 80 Reinhardt productions. **Family:** Lifelong companion of Helena Gaisenhainer. **Died:** Berlin, Germany, 21 December 1970.

WRITINGS

Fiction

Der Tag der Artemis. 1919.
Der Skorpion. 3 Vols. Berlin, Askanisher Verlag, Vol. 1, 1919, Vol. 2, 1930, Vol. 3, 1931; as *The Scorpion,* translated by Whittaker Chambers, Willey Book Co., New York, 1948.
Die kleine Dagmar. 1919.
Sogno: Das Buch der Träume. 1919.
Anja: Die Geschichte einer unglücklichen Liebe. 1919.

Gewissen. 1920.
Die Gläserne Welt. 1921.
Agonie der Leidenschaft. 1922.
Ruth Meyer: Eine fast alltägliche Geschichte. 1922.
Edles Blut. 1923.
Höllenfahrt. 1923.
Nin van't Hell. 1924.
Tina und die Tänzerin. 1927.
Ungleiche Brüder. 1928.
Ein Herr in den besten Jahren. 1929.
Die Farrels. 1929.
Lotte. 1930.
Denken an Sie Oliver. 1931.
Carmen an der Panke. 1931.
Briefe in Bareiros Hand. 1932.
Schlange im Paradies. 1932.
Frau Kern. 1934.
Geheimnis um Petra. 1934.
Das seltsame Testament. 1934.
Ein Mädchen ohne Furcht. 1935.
Das Haus in der Veenestraat. 1935.
Junger Mann mit Motorrad. 1935.
Mijnheer Corremans und seine Töchter. 1936.
Café Edelweiss. 1936.
Der grosse Geiger. 1937.
Iduna auf Urlaub. 1937.
Martina wird mündig. 1937.
Das Rätsel Manuela. 1938.
Donate und die Glückspilze. 1940.
Die entscheidende Stunde. 1940.
Die Geschichte mit Genia. 1941.
Die drei Schwestern Hahnemann. 1941.
Einmal kommt die Stunde. 1942.
Wiedersehen auf Java. 1949.
Schicksale in der Coco-Bar. 1949.
Die letzten Tage vor der Hochzeit. 1955.
Drei Monate, drei Wochen und drei Tage. 1957.
Claudias grosser Fall. 1957.
Der Mann gehört mir. 1958.
Und es begann so zauberhaft. 1959.
Mordprozess Vehsemeyer. 1959.
Mit 21 beginnt das Leben. 1959.
Der sonderbare Herr Sörrensen. 1959.
Tanz um Till. 1960.
Überfall bei Valentin. 1960.
Die geheimnisvolle Erbschaft. 1961.
Bella und Belinda. 1961.
Tante Zinnober und das Wasserschloss. 1961.
Die Flimfanny. 1962.
Ein Leben am Rande. 1965.
Anstatt der angekündigten Vorstellung. 1965.

Plays

Der Garten des Liebenden. 1921.
Falk und die Felsen. 1923.

Children's Books

Das Schiff in der Flasche. 1951.
Karin und Kathi. 1954.

Other

Es Lebe die Liebe (screenplay).
The Scorpion, translated by Whittaker Chambers. Willey Book Co., New York, 1948.
The Outcast, translated by Guy Endore. Willey Book Co., New York, 1948.

*

Manuscript Collections: Spinnboden-Archiv, Berlin, Germany.

Critical Sources: *Sex Variant Women in Literature* by Jeannette Foster, New York, Vantage, 1956; *Lesbianism and Feminism in Germany, 1895-1910,* edited by Jonathan Katz, New York, Arno Press, 1975; *'Der Skorpion': Frauenliebe in der Weimarer Republik* by Claudia Schoppmann, Hamburg, Frühlings Erwachen, 1990; *Lesbians in Germany 1890s-1920s,* edited by Lilian Faderman and Brigitte Ericksson, Tallahassee, Florida, Naiad, 1990; *Eldorado: Homosexuelle Frauen und Männer in Berlin 1850-1950* by Berliner Museum, Berlin, Verlag Rosa Winkel, 1992; "Nachwort" by Michael Fisch, in *Der Skorpion,* Frankfurt, Germany, Ullstein, 1993.

*   *   *

"More even than the men, the women attracted Myra's attention. They ran the whole gamut of types. Some had on dark jackets, with lapels, breast-pockets, and stiff collars. On their mannishly cut hair they wore small men's hats. Others betrayed themselves only by a slight overpainting." Thus Anna Elisabet Weirauch describes a Berlin gay club scene from the 1920s in this passage from her widely read and influential lesbian novel *The Scorpion,* first published in Germany in 1919. Weirauch was a prolific writer of popular fiction throughout her life, but she is best known for the internationally acclaimed *Scorpion* trilogy, which appeared in three volumes in 1919, 1930 and 1931. It is the only one of her works that develops an explicitly lesbian theme.

The title itself is emblematic of the theme of lesbianism in the book. Myra (Mette in the German version) is an aristocratic young woman who is profoundly in love with Olga Rado, an acquaintance of her family. During a visit at Olga's house, Myra admires a cigarette case engraved with a gold scorpion. Olga explains to her that the scorpion is the only animal that will commit suicide if it feels its life is in danger. She was born under the sign of Scorpio, and identifies strongly with the scorpion's myth. The scorpion symbolism surfaces repeatedly in the text, and connects the main characters to each other with an element of suspense, always overshadowed by the implication of death. Myra seems to be in agreement, at least subconsciously, with the commonly-held notion that homosexuality was a disease, incurable and in some cases even fatal. At one point in the story, Myra explains the cause of her "sickness": "I was bitten by a scorpion, and now the poison is all through my blood. And you know, the only thing that will cure a scorpion's bite is scorpion's poison. But there aren't any scorpions here. It's all superstition that [it's] contagious. [...] I believe that people can die of it—but it's not contagious."

This very vague reference to her love for Olga lends itself well to the scorpion analogy. Indeed, Myra's society treated her love for a woman with the same apprehension as they would a scorpion, scared that its sting could infect them. By referring to the sting as not contagious, Myra is supporting the idea that homosexuality could be hereditary; however, she also assumes that it can be deadly.

Weirauch's indictment of homophobia in this novel is very progressive given the prejudice common at the time. The author's depiction of Myra and her female friends and lovers is, however, problematic. Many characters fit the description of the "New Woman" of the 1920s in Germany, wearing short, fashionable "Bubikopf" haircuts that hint at masculinity, yet are effeminized enough to be less threatening. Myra in particular is more feminine and more passive than the others. Here, in the first line of the novel, the narrator introduces her subject: "Frankly, I desired to make Myra's acquaintance because of her evil reputation. [...] As a young girl, she had run around with a remarkable woman, a fashionably dressed sharper, with a decidedly masculine manner. Misled, perhaps, by this friend, she had stolen her father's silver service and pawned it." This initial portrait of Myra reinforces the construct of the passive female; she acts through others and is highly impressionable. Olga, on the other hand, has some distinctly masculine traits: "Olga was very tall and slender. Her face was beautiful and boldly chiseled. Her smooth, rich, dark hair exposed much of her high and admirably modeled forehead. Her thin black brows drew together at the top of her nose, which gave her sharp, metallic-gray eyes an almost threatening expression. Her speech was crisp and hard. But her voice had a deep, soft, cello quality. It made a striking contrast." These characterizations of Olga and Myra betray an assumption that there must be feminine and masculine roles, however subtle, in a lesbian relationship.

When Myra's family finds out about her relationship with Olga, they send her away to an uncle's house for "recovery" and flood her room with anti-homosexual pamphlets, which describe lesbians as women with a "thirst for knowledge and desire for culture, coupled with an abnormal tendency to spendthriftiness, a passionate desire for luxury, and an unnatural predilection for beautiful foot-gear." Several of the secondary characters reinforce this notion, albeit tongue in cheek, that lesbians are all wealthy, cultured, and highly intelligent. Weirauch's lesbian characters conform to many of the lesbian stereotypes and norms of femininity in Weimar society, which made them less threatening to readers, but also less visible as lesbians. This may be read as an indication that the prejudice against the clearly masculine or butch woman was widespread, even in some elite lesbian circles, such as those that Weirauch depicts.

Weirauch offers a realistic and critical portrayal of the difficulties a lesbian in the 1920s had to face. When Myra's parents find out about Olga, they not only send Myra away, but they pursue Olga by paying off her debts and taking financial control of her. Myra's aunt sends Olga threatening letters, and intercepts all mail between Myra and Olga. Eventually, after Myra has been convinced that Olga no longer cares for her, she becomes engaged to a prominent man, and the engagement is announced in the papers. Myra calls off the wedding at the last minute, but it is too late—a friend of Olga's comes to inform her that Olga has shot herself out of despair.

Myra is acutely aware of society's judgment of women like Olga and herself, which construes suicide as proof that lesbians are hysterical and emotionally unstable. Myra vehemently denounces this prejudice: "No, she was not born to kill herself. Decidedly not. There was so terribly much life in her, more life than a single human being can stand, certainly too much for a woman. But it was hate and vulgarity and misunderstanding that systematically hounded her to death!" At the end of the second volume, Myra is exhausted from this fight against society's prejudices, and secludes herself in a country house, surrounded by "a wall which will not let in a single glance, a single word, a single breath."

Anna Elisabet Weirauch's *The Scorpion* is one of very few expressions of the lesbian voice in literary history. Instead of searching for a cure for the "scorpion's sting," Weirauch offers the reader a rare glimpse into the world of those "bitten" by this feared and misunderstood creature. This novel, with all the subtexts and stereotypes it reflects, can be read as a significant chronicle of lesbian lives in the 1910s.

—Caitlin L. Gannon

WESCOTT, Glenway (Gordon)

Nationality: American novelist, essayist, and critic. **Born:** Kewaskum, Wisconsin, 11 April 1901. **Education:** University of Chicago (president, Poetry Club, 1916-17). **Family:** Lifelong companion of art curator Monroe Wheeler. **Career:** Poet, writer, and small journal contributor in the early 1920s; expatriate writer, Villefranche and Paris, 1925-33; writer and lecturer, in New York City and on family farm in western New Jersey, 1933-87. Elected to the American Academy-Institute of Arts and Letters, 1947 (president 1959-61). **Awards:** Numerous honorary degrees. **Died:** At home in Rosemont, New Jersey, 22 February 1987.

WRITINGS

Novels

The Apple of the Eye. New York, Dial Press, 1924; London, T. Butterworth, 1926.
The Grandmothers. New York, Harper and Brothers, 1927; as *A Family Portrait,* London, T. Butterworth, 1927.
The Pilgrim Hawk. New York, Harper and Brothers, 1940; London, Hamish Hamilton, 1946; in *Six Great Modern Short Novels,* New York, Dell, 1954.
Apartment in Athens. New York, Harper and Brothers, 1945; as *Household in Athens,* London, Hamish Hamilton, 1945.

Short Stories

Like A Lover (deluxe edition story). Macon, France, Monroe Wheeler, 1926.
Goodbye, Wisconsin (essay and stories). New York, Harper and Brothers, 1928; London, Jonathan Cape, 1929.
The Babe's Bed (deluxe edition long story). Harrison of Paris, 1930.
A Visit to Priapus (long story), introduction by Jerry Rosco. New York, Jerry Rosco, 1995.

Uncollected Short Stories

"Hurt Feelings," in *North American Review* (New York), September 1932.

"The Sight of a Dead Body," in *Signatures* (New York), Vol. 1, autumn 1936.
"The Rescuer," in *Life and Letters Today* (New York), Vol. 15, autumn 1936.
"Mr. Auerbach in Paris," in *Harpers* (New York), April 1942.
"The Frenchman Six Foot Three," in *Harpers,* July 1942.

Nonfiction

Fear and Trembling. New York, Harper and Brothers, 1932.
A Calendar of Saints for Unbelievers. Harrison of Paris, 1932; New York, Harper and Brothers, 1933.
Continual Lessons: The Journals of Glenway Wescott 1937-55, edited by Robert Phelps and Jerry Rosco. New York, Farrar, Straus, and Giroux, 1990.

Selected Essays

"The First Book of Mary Butts," in *The Dial* (Chicago), Vol. 75, September 1923.
"Concerning Miss Moore's Observations," in *The Dial,* Vol. 78, January 1925.
"Mr. Osbert Sitwell's Fiction," in *The Dial,* Vol. 78, June 1925.
"Elizabeth Madox Roberts: A Personal Note," in *The Bookman* (New York), Vol. 71, March 1930.
"A Sentimental Contribution: Henry James," in *Hound & Horn* (New York), Vol. 7, 1933-34.
"George Platt Lynes: Images of Mythology," in *U.S. Camera* (New York), January-February 1939.
"I Love New York," in *Harper's Bazaar* (New York), Vol. 77, December 1943.
"Paintings of Paris by Camille Pissarro," in *Carstairs Galleries* catalog (New York), April 1944.
"The Moral of F. Scott Fitzgerald," in *The New Republic* (New York), 17 February 1941; in *The Crackup,* edited by Edmund Wilson, New York, New Directions, 1945.
"In Praise of Edith Sitwell," in *Proceedings of the American Academy-Institute of Arts and Letters* (New York), Series 2, Vol. 1, 1951.
"Introduction: Robert Frost," in *Proceedings of the American Academy-Institute of Arts and Letters* (New York), Series 2, Vol. 6, 1956.
"Katherine Anne Porter: The Making of a Novel," in *Atlantic Monthly* (New York), April 1962.
Images of Truth (remembrances and criticism of Katherine Anne Porter, W. Somerset Maugham, Colette, Isak Dinesen, Thomas Mann, Thornton Wilder). New York, Harper and Row, 1962; London, Hamish Hamilton, 1964.
"The Valley Submerged," in *The Southern Review* (Baton Rouge, Louisiana), summer 1965.
"A Dinner, a Talk, a Walk with Forster," in *The New York Times,* 10 October 1971.
"The Breath of Bulls," in *Works in Progress,* Vol. 6, New York, Literary Guild, 1971.
"The Odor of Rosemary," in *Prose* (New York), Vol. 2, spring 1971.
"Memories and Opinions," in *Prose* (New York), Vol. 5, fall 1972.
"Paris 1938 Journal," in *Grand Street* (New York), Vol. 1, fall 1981.
"A Succession of Poets," in *Partisan Review* (Boston), Vol. 50, No. 3, 1984.

"Introduction," to *Four Lives in Paris* by Hugh Ford. San Francisco, North Point Press, 1987.

Poetry

The Bitterns. Evanston, Illinois, Monroe Wheeler, 1920.
"Men Like Birds," in *Contact* (New York), Vol. 5, June 1923.
Natives of Rock. New York, Francesco Bianco, 1925.
"The Summer Ending," in *Poetry* (Chicago), Vol. 56, September 1939.
"Alwyn Tower's Summer Poem," in *Fashion and Travel* (New York), fall 1955.
"Black Art" and other poems, in *Chicago Review,* Vol. 1, No. 37, winter 1990.
"A Memory of Orgasm," in *Amethyst* (Atlanta), No. 7, spring-summer 1991.

Other

Translator, *Carmine* by Prosper Merimee. Harrison of Paris, 1931.
"The Dream of Audubon" (a libretto for a ballet; David Diamond, composer), in *Dance* (New York), December 1940; in *The Best One Act Plays of 1940,* New York, Dodd Mead, 1941.
Narrator, *Twelve Fables of Aesop,* illustrations by Antonio Frasconi. New York, Museum of Modern Art, 1954.

*

Manuscript Collections: Yale University, The Beinecke Library, New Haven, Connecticut; New York Public Library, The Berg Collection, New York.

Interviews: Nine unpublished, recorded interviews with Glenway Wescott by Robert Phelps, 1973-76; seven recorded interviews with Glenway Wescott by Jerry Rosco, 1975-82.

Bibliography: "Glenway Wescott: A Critical and Bibliographical Study" by Sy Myron Kahn, in *Bulletin of Bibliography* (Boston), September-December 1958.

Critical Sources: "Glenway Wescott: Legend Maker" by Dayton Kohler, in *The Bookman* (New York), Vol. 73, April 1931, 142-145; "Thematic Problems of the American Novelist" by Marjorie Brace, in *Accent* (Urbana, Illinois), Vol. 7, 1945, 44-53; *The Exile's Return* by Malcolm Cowley, New York, Viking Press, 1951; "The Whisper of the Devil," in *Craft and Character in Modern Fiction* by Morton Zabel, New York, Viking Press, 1957; *Glenway Wescott* by William H. Rueckert, New York, Twayne, 1965; "Glenway Wescott's Odyssey" by Patricia Kane, in *Critique: Studies in Modern Fiction* (Atlanta), Vol. 8, June 1965, 5-12; "Love Birds of Prey" in *Writing Against Time* by Howard Moss, New York, William Morrow, 1969; *Glenway Wescott: The Paradox of Voice* by Ira D. Johnson, Port Washington, New York, Kennikat Press, 1971; "Remembering Cocteau: Conversations with Glenway Wescott" by Jerry Rosco, in *The Body Politic* (Toronto), No. 128, July 1986, 32-33; "Hemingway and Homophobia" by Jerry Rosco, in *The James White Review* (Minneapolis), Vol. 3, No. 4, summer 1986, 11; "An American Treasure: The Pilgrim Hawk" by Jerry Rosco, in *The Literary Review* (Madison, New Jersey), Vol. 31, No.2, winter 1988, 133-142; "The Poetic Career of a Novelist" by Jerry Rosco, in *Chicago Review,* Vol. 37, No. 1,

winter 1990, 113-129; "Chronology" by Jerry Rosco, in *Continual Lessons: The Journals of Glenway Wescott 1937-55,* New York, Farrar, Straus, and Giroux, 1990; "Dr. Kinsey and Glenway Wescott" by Jerry Rosco, in *The Guide* (Boston), January 1991, 96-99; "Glenway Wescott: Out At Last" by Ralph Pomeroy, in *Bay Area Reporter* (San Francisco), 10 January 1991, 31; "A Heart Laid Bare" by Hortense Calisher, in *Washington Post Book World,* 13 January 1991, 5; "Learning from History" by Stan Leventhal, in *Outweek* (New York), 30 January 1991, 52-53; "Mystery Man" by Ian Young, in *The Advocate* (Los Angeles), 12 February 1991, 79; "Glenway Wescott's Remarkable Candor" by John Litweller, in *Chicago Tribune,* 7 April 1991; "Continual Lessons," in *New Yorker,* 29 April 1991, 104; "Continual Lessons" by Robert Drake, in *Lambda Book Report* (Washington, D.C.), May/June 1991, 34; "Books" by John Gilgun, in *The James White Review* (Minneapolis), Vol. 8, No. 4, summer 1991, 12; "Introduction" by Sargent Bush Jr., in *The Grandmothers* by Glenway Wescott, University of Wisconsin, 1996.

*   *   *

Glenway Wescott's major distinction in American Literature is as a lyrical prose stylist of unsurpassed skill, intelligence, and subtlety. As an author he is associated with the Midwest regional writers, the Paris expatriate writers of the 1920s, and the New York literary scene. And as a public figure, he is a mainstream author whose place in gay literature is part of his legacy, and whose friendship and work with Doctor Alfred C. Kinsey contributed to the breakthrough work of the Institute for Sex Research.

Born on a poor Wisconsin farm in 1901, he made his way in the world as quickly as possible. While boarding in West Bend as a high school student, his best friend was a lesbian student named Virginia Bugbee who smoked cigarettes, drove a fast car, encouraged him to read Whitman aloud at their lakeside hideout, and taught him to rely on himself. As a young teen, he had a three-year affair with an older farmboy, which is captured in his short story "Adolescence," in which the younger of two friends disguises himself as a girl at a Halloween party.

Arriving at the University of Chicago on scholarship at 16, Wescott joined the Poetry Club, which included such future literary stars as novelist Elizabeth Madox Roberts, poet Yvor Winters, and his future wife poet and novelist Janet Lewis. Yet the older students immediately made him president of the club, because of his impressive first poems and his standout ability as a speaker and reader. Although Wescott's professors were astounded by the vast amount of reading he had done on his own, he quit after three semesters in 1919 because of a serious bout with the deadly Spanish Flu. Yet, under the influence of Winters, he made a name for himself among the Imagist poets. And with the guidance of patron Harriet (Mrs. William Vaughan) Moody, and *Poetry* magazine publisher Harriet Monroe, he became known in the finest literary magazines of the era. By then, Glenway had a budding relationship with a distinguished young man from Evansville named Monroe Wheeler, who would become his lifelong lover and a major figure in the art world. "Black Art," an early suppressed poem (published posthumously in 1990), described the balancing act of being gay lovers in a straight world. When Wheeler published Wescott's highly-formal Imagist poems, *The Bitterns* in 1920, Carl Sandburg told him, "It is difficult to make poetry as sophisticated as this fly. But you certainly make it tremble and shake!"

After moving to Greenwich Village in New York, Wescott and Wheeler became friends with Marianne Moore and a wide circle of literary friends. They made several early visits to Europe on a shoestring budget. But after his first novel, *The Apple of the Eye* appeared, they relocated to France in early 1925. On the book's jacket, Sinclair Lewis commented, "It seems to me to have something curiously like genius." And within the lyrical prose of this story of Midwestern farmers is the subplot of a boy, Dan, in love with a worldly, older boy.

Living in the Hotel Welcome in Villefranche for two years, Wescott and Wheeler became close friends with Jean Cocteau as well as a growing circle of British and European artists and writers. On the day of dancer Isadora Duncan's tragic death, they sat with her body through the night. Wescott's second novel, *The Grandmothers,* swept through 26 printings in 1927 and made him one of the best known expatriates. A Midwestern classic, it became a model of the chronicle novel, and Wescott once remarked offhandedly to Jerry Rosco, "I invented the family tree and everyone has been doing it ever since, right down to Alex Haley." Homosexual love between two characters, brothers Leander and Hillary, is recognized by Sargent Bush Jr. in his introduction to the 1996 University of Wisconsin edition of the book. But Wescott himself acknowledged to Jerry Rosco other homosexual characters in *The Grandmothers,* including young protagonist Alwyn Tower (his autobiographical voice) and his new friend at the close of the novel, Orfeo (based on Monroe Wheeler). He also said the sensual character Timothy was modeled after Cocteau's blond boyfriend Jean Bourgoint. The success of the book, meanwhile, annoyed Ernest Hemingway, who made a number of verbal attacks on Wescott, and had portrayed him as a homosexual character, Roger Prentiss, in chapter three of his novel *The Sun Also Rises.*

When they moved to Paris in 1928, new relationships were formed, even as their bond remained secure. Monroe's added lover was photographer George Platt Lynes, who became a permanent part of their family. Glenway's French lover for five years was department store heir and major bibliophile Jacques Guerin. Many years later, when Edmund White was researching his 1993 biography *Genet,* he interviewed Jacques Guerin, who had been a patron of Jean Genet. White noted the Wescott connection in his book, and added that Wescott was "...America's best looking novelist of the 1920s and 1930s." Wescott and Wheeler also developed a permanent friendship with young millionaire Barbara Harrison. Wheeler and Harrison founded Harrison of Paris books, and created 13 of the most extraordinary beaux arts books of the era.

After a 1928 short story collection, *Goodbye, Wisconsin,* Wescott experienced a setback when his 1932 book of prophetic, pre-war essays, *Fear and Trembling,* was badly received. He produced three quality small books, but when he abandoned a large novel-in-progress, he went into a decline—which he blamed partly on reading and speaking French for so long.

Wescott, Wheeler, and George Platt Lynes returned to New York in 1933. Lynes opened a studio and became well-known as a fashion and portrait photographer, and eventually for his male nudes. Wheeler helped build the Museum of Modern Art to its present status. As director of exhibitions and publications, he revolutionized high-quality museum books and catalogs. Throughout his career, he would travel around the world, planning New York exhibits with museums, governments, and directly with many of the leading artists of the century. He became friends with such patrons as the Rockefellers and the Astors, and Wescott and Wheeler were invited as a couple to social events, decades before gay couples were openly acknowledged.

When Barbara Harrison returned to America, she married Wescott's younger brother Lloyd, and the whole clan made a permanent home for themselves on a large western New Jersey farm. Harrison was a major patron of the arts and their friend Katherine Anne Porter dedicated her novel *A Ship of Fools* to her. In New York, the Wheeler-Wescott apartment served as a literary salon for five decades, and Wheeler's dinner parties were always high social events.

Wescott withheld from publication a 1938, 14,000-word homosexual tale called "A Visit to Priapus." When the long story was posthumously, privately printed in 1995, playwright and critic Robert Patrick described it as "classic gay fine-writing" in the *Harvard Gay and Lesbian Review.* Aside from its erotic theme, the story described the dynamics of gay male sexuality with rare honesty and insight. In 1940, Wescott used the same first-person, participating-narrator technique to create a masterpiece. *The Pilgrim Hawk* has been included in anthologies of great modern short novels and appeared in foreign editions. Set in expatriate France, the story takes place in one afternoon and the Wescott character, Alwyn Tower, describes beautifully and achingly the universal joys and sorrows of love, marriage, sex, sexuality, and lust—as well as the creative struggle of the artist. Balancing an external story and internal thoughts, with a trained hawk as symbolic center, and in prose as elegant as dry champagne, Wescott covers a great deal in a simple story. The emotions are universal, but the voice clearly has resonance for the gay reader. Reprint editions carry Christopher Isherwood's bookjacket comment: "Truly a work of art, of the kind so rarely achieved or even attempted nowadays."

Unlike Wescott's other novels, *Apartment in Athens,* 1945, is not autobiographical. The story of a family in Nazi-occupied Greece, this suspenseful, psychological story is held together by skillful narrative. A Book of the Month Club selection, it was a best seller in America and was translated into seven languages. But it was his last experience with celebrity. Over the years, Wescott abandoned four major novel manuscripts, for technical reasons as much as any other. The second half of his career involved literary work for the Academy and Institute of Arts and Letters, essay writing, and lecturing. After E.M. Forster's visit to New York and Wescott's farm in 1949, it was Wescott and Isherwood who created a plan, involving the Academy-Institute, to publish their friend's long-suppressed novel *Maurice* posthumously in America. Wescott's friendship with Dr. Alfred C. Kinsey and his work for the Institute for Sex Research involved a good deal of his time and interest in the 1950s. Imminent biographies, of Wescott by Jerry Rosco, and Kinsey by Jonathan Gathorne-Hardy, cover this period in great detail.

Monroe Wheeler's international work in art agreements and exhibits helped establish New York's Museum of Modern Art and earned him France's Legion of Honor. Wescott left behind a posthumous volume of explicitly gay journals, *Continual Lessons* (1990), and material for a potential second volume. When he died at home in 1987, the 24 February *New York Times* remembered him as "...one of the last of the major expatriate writers," and compared his prose to that of Flaubert. The 27 February *Times of London* suggested that *The Pilgrim Hawk* was as perfect as any work in the English language and stated, "He will be remembered as long as fiction is read."

—Jerry Rosco

WILHELM, Gale

Nationality: American novelist and short story writer. **Born:** Eugene, Oregon, 26 April 1908. **Education:** Attended schools in Oregon, Idaho, and Washington. **Family:** Companion of Helen Hope Rudolph Page, 1938(?)-48(?). **Career:** Associate editor, *Literary America* (New York City), 1935. **Awards:** Honorary membership, International Mark Twain Society, 1942. **Died:** 11 July 1991.

WRITINGS

Novels/Novellas

We Too Are Drifting. New York, Random House, 1935; New York, Arno, 1975; Tallahassee, Florida, Naiad Press, 1984.
No Letters for the Dead. New York, Random House, 1936.
Torchlight to Valhalla. New York, Random House, 1938; as *The Strange Path*, New York, Lion, 1953; New York, Arno, 1975; Tallahassee, Florida, Naiad Press, 1985.
Bring Home the Bride. New York, William Morrow, 1940.
The Time Between. New York, William Morrow, 1942.
Never Let Me Go. New York, William Morrow, 1945.

Uncollected Short Stories

"Under the Leaves," in *Literary America* (New York City), April 1934.
"California Drypoints," in *Literary America* (New York City), January 1935.
"And the Feet Walking," in *Literary America* (New York City), April 1935.
"First Solitude," in *Literary America* (New York City), July 1935.
"Rondo," in *Story* (New York City), August 1935.
"But Not So Final," in *Yale Review* (New Haven, Connecticut), September 1943.
"A Lot of Questions," in *Collier's* (Springfield, Ohio), 11 September 1943.

Uncollected Poetry

"A Group of Sonnets," in *Overland Monthly* (San Francisco, California), December 1930.
"To a Negro Stevedore," in *Contemporary Vision* (Philadelphia, Pennsylvania), winter 1931.
"Strike Leader," in *Nativity* (Delaware, Ohio), 1931.
"Strange Serenade," in *Rebel Poets* (Holt, Minnesota), March 1931.
"Lines for a Lady," in *Rebel Poets* (Holt, Minnesota), May 1931.
"Quest," in *Frontier* (Missoula, Montana), November 1932.
"For What We Lost," in *Literary America* (New York City), June 1935.

Other

Author of introduction, in *Writing for the Experimental Market* by Benjamin Appel and others. New York City, Publications Division [of] Literary America, 1936.

*

Manuscript Collections: Bancroft Library, University of California, Berkeley; University of Illinois Library, Urbana-Champaign.

Biography: *Polk's Eugene and Lane County Directory,* Portland, Oregon, R.L. Polk, 1912, 237, 504; "Quiz: What American Novelist Lives in Quiet Little Town of Oakdale?" by Rossi Reynolds, in *Stockton Record* (Stockton, California), 19 September 1940, 2; *American Novelists of Today* by Harry R. Warfel, New York, American Book Company, 1951, 458; *American Authors and Books: 1640 to the Present Day,* 3rd revised edition by Irving Weiss and Anne Weiss, New York, Crown, 1972, 694; *The Feminist Companion to Literature in English: Women Writers from the Middle Ages to the Present* by Virginia Blain and others, New Haven, Yale University Press, 1990, 1165; "Introduction" by Barbara Grier, in *We Too Are Drifting,* Tallahassee, Florida, Naiad Press, 1984; "Gale Wilhelm Writes" and "Introduction" by Barbara Grier, in *Torchlight to Valhalla,* Tallahassee, Florida, Naiad Press, 1985.

Critical Sources: "Are They Drifting?" by M.L.S., in *Boston Evening Transcript,* 10 August 1935, 4; "Three Women" by Stanley Young, in *New York Times Book Review,* 18 August 1935, 6-7; review by G.G.B., in *Saturday Review of Literature* (New York City), Vol. 12, No. 18, 31 August 1935, 19; review by Mary Ross, in *New York Herald Tribune Books,* 15 September 1935, 13; review, in *Boston Evening Transcript,* 8 August 1936, 6; "A Romantic Woman" by John Cournos, in *New York Times Book Review,* 9 August 1936, 15; "Perverse Romanticism" by Alice Beal Parsons, in *Nation* (New York City), 29 August 1936, 249-50; review by S.H. Dobson, in *Life and Letters* (London, England), Vol. 16, No. 7, spring 1937, 161; "Lesbian Theme," in *Springfield Union and Republican* (Springfield, Massachusetts), 14 August 1938, 73; review by A.B. Tourtellot, in *Boston Transcript,* 27 August 1938, 3; "They Take Time Out for Love" by Mary Ross, in *New York Herald Tribune Books,* 14 February 1943, 3; "Ten-Day Leave" by Margaret Wallace, in *New York Times Book Review,* 14 February 1943, 6; "Ten Days That Shook the Heart" by Bess Jones, in *Saturday Review of Literature* (New York City), Vol. 26, No. 8, 20 February 1943, 11; review by Florence Haxton Bullock, in *New York Herald Tribune Weekly Book Review,* 11 March 1945, 6; review by Nancy Flagg, in *New York Times Book Review,* 11 March 1945, 24; *The Little Magazine: A History and a Bibliography* by Frederick J. Hoffman and others, Princeton, New Jersey, Princeton University Press, 1946; *Sex Variant Women in Literature* by Jeannette Foster, Baltimore, Maryland, Diana Press, 1975, 314-51; *Lesbian Images* by Jane Rule, New York, Pocket Books, 1975, 190-91; "Voice from the Past" by Mary Biggs, in *Women's Review of Books* (Wellesley, Massachusetts), Vol. 3, No. 8, May 1986, 18-19; *Odd Girls and Twilight Lovers: A History of Lesbian Life in Twentieth-Century America* by Lillian Faderman, New York, Columbia University Press, 1991, 102; "Bildungsroman and Kunsterlerroman" by Annis Pratt and "Lesbian Writing: Fiction" by Katie Kent, in *Oxford Companion to Women's Writing in the United States,* edited by Cathy N. Davidson and others, New York, Oxford University Press, 1995, 104-106, 508-510; unpublished interview with Barbara Grier (editor and publisher of Naiad Press) by Carolynne Myall, 29 November 1997.

*   *   *

"Now suppose you are a young writer," began 28 year-old Gale Wilhelm in her introduction to *Writing for the Experimental Market.* "You have something to say and you believe the manner of telling is important...You want to write of something whose appeal is perhaps limited, whose aspect is quite possibly not pretty but whose value to you is indisputable. Then do so."

Wilhelm herself had done so. The year before, in 1935, a major publisher released her first novel, *We Too Are Drifting.* Lean, passionate, and accomplished, it presented its lesbian protagonist's search for a sustaining love without apology or argument. "It is necessary in the beginning to cut away all the surplus flesh...," Wilhelm advised young writers. "There is meaning behind simplicity...a tightness, a swiftness in living. There is no time for cudding an enormous Why?"

Wilhelm's great physical beauty and androgynous presentation of herself shine out from the photographs which accompanied reviews of her first several novels. She was a glamorous and mysterious figure—"shingled and tailored," observed Jeannette Foster—an icon of the lesbian-as-artist. After more than 60 years, her author portraits from the 1930s still seemed contemporary. And while much of Wilhelm's other literary work has dropped from sight, *We Too Are Drifting* and *Torchlight to Valhalla,* her two explicitly lesbian novels, survived in reprint editions.

During much of her life, Wilhelm moved in a wealthy milieu. When her last publisher, Barbara Grier of Naiad Press, met her in 1985, Wilhelm gave an impression of being "to the manor born." Other evidence suggests that Wilhlem came from a less privileged background. She was born in 1908 in Eugene, Oregon. Her parents, Wilson Price and Ethel Brewer Wilhelm, appeared in the Tax List in the 1912 *Polk's Eugene and Lane County Directory* for the unremarkable sum of $800; the *Directory* identified W.P. Wilhelm as a carpenter. It is hard not to speculate that Wilhelm's father was not a routine carpenter, but also—in Wilhelm's eyes—an artist in wood; this might explain the frequent appearance of woodworkers and artists (often the same people) in Wilhelm's work. As a child, Wilhelm lived and attended school in Oregon, Washington, and Idaho; there is no record of her matriculating into any institution of higher education. She moved to San Francisco in 1925, and except for a year in New York City, lived in California the rest of her life, mostly in the San Francisco Bay area. The Berkeley hills and Bay area rain appeared frequently in her work.

"You know that in the experimental magazine you are not obliged to pour your thoughts into definite molds...," Wilhelm wrote to other young writers. "You turn to it quite naturally." This observation reflected Wilhelm's career, which started in small literary journals—so-called "little magazines" which often sponsored innovators and radicals of twentieth-century American writing. Her first publication, "A Group of Sonnets," appeared in a California magazine, *Overland Monthly,* when she was 22 years old, and consisted of 21 free-verse lines divided into three "Arabesques." Spare and delicate, these youthful and unexceptional love poems addressed a lover of unspecified gender. After that, Wilhelm published poetry in a number of "little magazines," including *The Frontier* and *Rebel Poets.* With the sensual and explicitly lesbian "For What We Lost" in 1935—"Cry for.../ the river in the long narrow groove / of its freedom /...Ache for the sweetness swelling to pain / and diminishing on no hollowness like this"—Wilhelm's publication of poetry apparently ceased. It was at just this time that she established her reputation as a fiction writer.

Wilhelm's fiction career began in a "little magazine," the nonpolitical and widely esteemed *Literary America.* "Under the Leaves," appearing in 1934, prefigured *We Too Are Drifting* in style and characters, though its prose had more obviously "experimental" features and its heroine was far less attractive. Wood sculptor Peter Elsasen—born Elsa Petersen—drinks alone in her room. James, a supportive brother-like figure, visits her, along with his friend, Mike, who holds Peter in contempt. Over the course of their conversations, the reader learns that Peter, having abandoned her lover Bernike, has received a cablegram announcing Mike's death. As the story closes, Peter walks out into the San Francisco moonlight with a revolver and, presumably, suicide in mind. So impressed was *Literary America* editor Kenneth Houston with Wilhelm's work that he offered her a position as associate editor.

In 1935, several more stories appeared. Two (perhaps) have lesbian content. "California Drypoints"—a drypoint is a type of print—presents eight vignettes, moments in several individuals' lives. In one, the (presumably female) protagonist remembers her loved one Barbara, a student who prefigures the protagonist's lover in *We Too.* The (gender-unspecified) narrator in "And the Feet Walking" recounts her/his affair with a prostitute, whom s/he "took...because I imagined something in her spoke to something in me."

As *We Too Are Drifting* opens, artist Jan Morale has gained a measure of success for her woodcuts. But she is in mourning for a twin brother who died violently, without friends except for the sculptor Kletkin, and enmeshed in an unfulfilling love relationship with Madeline, a married woman who cannot accept that Jan does not love her. Jan meets a younger woman, Victoria, who admires her work and has the balance and purity of spirit Jan needs. Jan and Victoria become lovers, and Jan can work again—work with "great leanness and simplicity, a pure and definite meaning." But Kletkin dies in an accident, shortly after completing an important work, "Hermaphroditus," for which Jan modeled; Jan breaks with Madeline violently; and Victoria succumbs to pressure to abandon her plans with Jan and spend her vacation with her parents and the young man they hope Victoria will marry. As the novel concludes, Jan watches, hidden, as Victoria's train pulls out. Even critics who were hostile to the work's subject, lack of apology, and stylistic mannerisms (e.g., no quotation marks) recognized the author's talent. "This novel of Lesbian love is written in so perfectly direct a manner and stays so completely within its own little circle that there is no outside comparison or criterion for it," observed the *Saturday Review.* "I know of no novel in this field that has its sureness or artistry," wrote *Herald Tribune* reviewer Mary Ross.

"The young author of a *We Too Are Drifting*...is here concerned with a different theme, yet fully as unsuited to the squeamish reader," sighed the *Boston Evening Transcript* reviewer about Wilhelm's second novel, *No Letters for the Dead.* Paula, the protagonist, is a pianist whose (male) lover Koni is imprisoned on a charge arising from his wife's suicide. Her baby dead, her jobs drying up, Paula moves to San Francisco to be near Koni, even though he will not let her visit him; she writes him letters which reveal little of her outward life as she drifts into prostitution. Just before Koni is scheduled for release, Paula learns he is dead, the incidental victim of a prison break. A review in *Life and Letters Today* declared that Wilhelm "in substituting phrase for symphony has caught the leit-motif of our own generation." But *No Letters* also suffered much praise which damned. In a generally positive *New York Times* review, John Cournos designated Wilhelm's fictional gifts "precious and fragile"; Alice Beal Parsons sniffed that "Miss Wilhelm has pushed her way out of the struggling mass solely because of the nature of the themes she has treated." Though without lesbian content, *No Letters* was consistent in style, tone, and world view with the lesbian-theme novels which preceded and followed it.

As *Torchlight to Valhalla* begins, Morgen, a young writer, lives in happy seclusion with her artist father. Morgen presents him with her first completed manuscript. Her father responds that "all a person has in this life to take with him to his Valhalla is the knowledge of happiness.... My torch, he said, is as bright now as it will ever be," hence the title of this work, about Morgen's search for her own particular happiness. When her father dies, the grieving Morgen succumbs briefly to the courtship of Royal, a sympathetically-portrayed (male) musician. Then Morgen meets a young woman, Toni, whom she immediately recognizes as a twin spirit. Morgen tells Royal she loves Toni; as the novel ends, the young women hope for a happy life together.

Torchlight lacked the tight structure of Wilhelm's first two novels. Its material consisted of three relationships: Morgen and her father, Morgen and Royal, then Morgen and Toni. The romantic triangle is less well developed than in *We Too,* for Toni appears late and is sketchily developed. But Wilhelm may have been seeking a more discursive structure to fit her theme. Certainly the titles of Wilhelm's two lesbian novels indicated their different moods and, perhaps, intentions. *Torchlight*'s reception was mixed, including both praise and distaste for the author's style. Several reviews had an enough-is-enough message about the novel's subject. The *Springfield Union,* for example, called it "a dignified handling of a...now somewhat over-worked subject." "She treated this subject of woman's love for woman adequately and successfully in her first book," opined A.B. Tourtellot in the *Boston Transcript.* "Now she can do nothing but repeat that which she has already said so well."

After *Torchlight,* Wilhelm published no more explicitly lesbian works. "She changed the gender of her characters," reported Barbara Grier, to fit publishing norms. Her next novel, *Bring Home the Bride,* was a heterosexual romance. Carol, a sophisticated and unconventional woman, meets an inexperienced, younger man, the son of one of her former (male) lovers. The two marry and are briefly happy, but Carol dies in an automobile accident. This slight work received a small, mixed reception.

For *The Time Between,* Wilhelm enjoyed the most unequivocally favorable reviews of her career. A wealthy young man who has become a war hero, Dick Hainesford returns to his California home for a ten-day leave. He marries Goby (together, they call themselves GobyDick), reaches a new understanding of his parents, mourns the death of a friend, Goby's brother, and adopts the friend's child when his widow commits suicide. Despite the work's careful structure, Hainesford remains a misty, romanticized figure. While *The Time Between* had no lesbian content, it did contain what may be a personal joke between Wilhelm and her companion Helen Page. Wilhelm dedicated the work to Chico—her name for Page—and included in it a minor character named Chico, a young man who distributes newspapers. Page ran the Oakdale branch of the *Stockton Record.*

During the early 1940s, Wilhelm continued to publish a few short stories, including one each in the *Yale Review* and *Collier's.* Both stories had male protagonists, war themes, conventional punctuation and, ultimately, conventional moral views. "A Lot of Questions"—with the child-protagonist unknowingly shaming his mother, whose husband is away in the Air Corps, out of her liaison with another man—was probably the closest to hack work that Wilhelm ever produced.

In Wilhelm's last novel, *Never Let Me Go,* a wealthy young woman breaks away from her controlling, man-hating mother to become an extraordinarily efficient secretary. She marries the boss, but female relatives on both sides, along with the husband's own jealousy, come between them until they are able to resolve their difficulties. *Never Let Me Go* was negatively reviewed as too conventional. "Emotional cliché...the final effect of shallowness...," stated the *Herald Tribune* review. "'We Too Are Drifting' and 'Twilight (sic) in Valhalla,' though narrowly eclectic in their subject matter...were intensely poetic and sincere." Wilhelm quit writing. She dropped out of sight.

Except for her year as associate editor of *Literary America,* there is no evidence that Wilhelm had any regular employment, apart from writing, at any time of her life. She was successful early, and had published three novels by the time she was 30 years-old. Around that time she also established a relationship with a very wealthy woman, Helen Hope Rudolph Page, with whom she lived for a decade. Because Page was the grand-niece of Stephen Douglas, both she and Wilhelm became correspondents of poet and Lincoln biographer Carl Sandburg; Sandburg wrote "blurbs" for two of Wilhelm's novels. In 1948, Wilhelm returned to the Bay Area; she and Page separated around the time of her move. Wilhelm entered into a relationship with another woman, and lived with her in a Berkeley house overlooking the Bay until Wilhelm's death. She was not aware that Naiad Press had reprinted *We Too* in 1984 until publisher Barbara Grier found her and told her so.

Grier searched for Wilhelm for many years, before an anonymous tip led her to the Berkeley address in 1985. Wilhelm was 77 and in failing health, but she and her companion invited Grier and her partner to their home for tea. "She was the butchiest woman I ever met," Grier recalled, "and the most beautiful. She would have stopped traffic." Wilhelm and her companion were "delightful, reserved, formal, and genteel." They were both very clear that Wilhelm had stopped writing—"stopped dead." "She was shamed at not having been more successful," Grier believed.

But since their original appearance, *We Too* and *Torchlight* have been republished two and three times, respectively. *Torchlight* appeared under a different title during the era of lesbian "pulp" paperbacks in 1953, which may explain why Wilhelm has been listed on some Internet websites as a "pulp writer." During the 1970s, Arno Press released a series entitled "Homosexuality" with both Wilhelm titles. Naiad Press reissued the two in the mid 1980s with author photographs and biographical material; *Torchlight* had a statement by Wilhelm herself.

Critical response since the original publication of Wilhelm's two lesbian-theme novels has varied. Jeannette Foster identified Wilhelm's work as "variant fiction of quality." Jane Rule's *Lesbian Images* described *We Too* as "a novel of resignation, beautifully and economically written," but considered *Torchlight* "remarkable only in the fact of its publication since it stands virtually alone in its unambiguous resolution." In a review of the Naiad editions, Mary Biggs praised Wilhelm's novels in terms of historical importance and literary qualities, and noted that though Wilhelm's style was reminiscent of Hemingway, "she is her own sort of writer." Ultimately, Biggs thought, the novels were old-fashioned in their belief in "romantic longing as both igniter and extinguisher of existential malaise" and in the "magnetic appeal" of a "chain-smoking, hard-drinking" artist (though, of course, some heterosexual novels in the Western canon share these assumptions). Lillian Faderman dropped *We Too* into the category of "depictions of lesbian suicide, self-loathing, hopeless passion..." on the basis of Jan's description of sex with her married lover as "the dirty satisfaction we manage to squeeze out of our bodies." For other readers, the positive presentation of Jan's sexual relationship with Victoria, whom she loves, removed the novel from that category.

—Carolynne Myall

WILLHOITE, Michael

Nationality: American artist and writer. **Born:** Hobart, Oklahoma, 3 July 1946. **Education:** Oklahoma State University, 1964-68, B.F.A. 1968. **Military Service:** Served in the United States Navy, 1968-73. **Career:** Medical illustrator, United States Navy, 1973-81, and United States Army, from 1981. **Awards:** *Lambda* Literary Award, for best gay men's small press book, 1990; James Baldwin Award for Cultural Achievement, Greater Boston Lesbian/Gay Political Alliance, 1993; Community Service Award, Massachusetts Gay and Lesbian Political Caucus, 1995; Flip Foundation Progress Award, Columbus, Ohio, November 1996. **Address:** c/o Alyson Publications, P.O. Box 4371, Los Angeles, California 90078, U.S.A.

WRITINGS

Illustrator (nonfiction)

Out of All Time by Terry Boughner. Boston, Alyson Publications, 1988.
The Alyson Almanac. Boston, Alyson Publications, 1989; reprinted, 1990, 1993.
Gay Men and Women Who Enriched the World by Thomas Cowan. Boston, Alyson Publications, 1992.
HIV+: Working the System by Robert Rimer and Michael Connolly. Boston, Alyson Publications, 1993.
Painting With Words by Sheila Kadra and Patricia Smith. Newton, Massachusetts, Independent School Press, 1994.
Young, Gay, and Proud! (for young adults), edited by Don Romesburg. Boston, Alyson Publications, 1995.

Cartoon and Caricature Collections

Now for My Next Trick. Boston, Alyson Publications, 1986.
The 1990 Gay Desk Calendar. Boston, Alyson Publications, 1989.
Members of the Tribe. Boston, Alyson Publications, 1993.
Willhoite's Hollywood. Boston, Alyson Publications, 1994.

Children's Fiction

(And illustrator) *Daddy's Roommate.* Boston, Alyson Publications, 1990; translated into German by Jan Wandtke as *Papa's Freund*, Berlin, Magnus, 1994.
(And illustrator) *Families: A Coloring Book.* Boston, Alyson Publications, 1991.
Illustrator, *Belinda's Bouquet* by Lesléa Newman. Boston, Alyson Publications, 1991.
(And illustrator) *The Entertainer.* Boston, Alyson Publications, 1992.

(And illustrator) *Uncle What-Is-It Is Coming to Visit!!.* Boston, Alyson Publications, 1993.
(And illustrator) *Daddy's Wedding.* Los Angeles, Alyson Publications, 1996.

*

Adaptations: *Uncle What-Is-It Is Coming to Visit!!* adapted for the stage by Bill Jacob (produced at the Speakeasy Theatre, Boston, spring 1997).

Critical Sources: *Newsweek,* 7 January 1991, 60-61; *U.S. news and World Report,* 17 August 1992, 16; *Time,* 31 August 1992, 14 December 1992, 52-53; "'Daddy's Roommate' Causing Stir in Libraries around Nation" by Ralph Ranalli, in *Boston Herald,* 8 September 1992; "Malice in Wonderland" by Trey Graham, in *Washington Blade,* 18 September 1992; "Teaching about Gays and Tolerance," in *New York Times,* 27 September 1992; *Newsweek,* 21 December 1992, 57; "The Ages of Innocence" by Barbara Kantrowitz, in *Newsweek,* 28 December 1992, 64; *Entertainment Weekly,* 29 January 1993, 66-67; *Home News* (New Brunswick, New Jersey), 25 July 1993, B1-2; *Bay Windows* (Boston), 19-25 August 1993, 1; *Arizona Republic,* 3 September 1993, B3.

Michael Willhoite comments:

When I first started writing for the children of gay parents, it quickly became apparent that I was filling an empty space in children's literature. There had never been books written for this group, except for Lesléa Newman's *Heather Has Two Mommies,* a splendid book which had a very limited exposure until Alyson Publications re-published it. So it became an article of faith that I had sensed this need and rushed to fill the void. I am grateful for the opportunity to have done so, but I must confess it to be largely accidental. My first impulse was simply to write and illustrate for children. Indeed, I think I write simply to have something to illustrate, for I'm an artist by training and very early inclination. I am also gay by early inclination, and it was almost inevitable that this too would be reflected in my work.

My caricatures and cartoons are just as vital to me as my other work, and date back to a time when I had barely a glimmer of my sexual status. I am grateful to be able to publish them in a great gay newspaper, but I feel that these drawings would certainly have seen the light of day in some other venue, even if the subjects of the caricatures had been straight. *The Washington Blade* was simply the wonderful opportunity that happened to present itself.

I am an artist in every atom; my vocation is more an essential part of me than my sexuality, my nationality, or even my gender. But the fact that I am gay is a pungent spice added to the mix. Naturally, it colors my character; so does the fact that my outlook is fundamentally satirical. But an aspect of my art that I've never articulated before is how profoundly my love for literature has informed my artwork. I have an insatiable hunger for art in any form—theatre, architecture, film, music. My art is a lake, and all these are the streams that feed it.

*   *   *

Growing up in Hobart, Oklahoma, in the 1950s and 1960s, Michael Willhoite was raised in part by an aunt who instilled in him a great love of books and writing; at the same time, and for as long as he could remember, Willhoite was considered the class artist. He describes himself as a movie buff from the cradle who spent most of his childhood perched in front of the TV watching every film he could. In high school, turning to the art of caricature, his first subject was British Prime Minister Harold Macmillan.

After graduating from high school in 1964, Willhoite enrolled in Oklahoma State University as an art major, graduating in 1968 with his Bachelor of Fine Arts degree. In order to avoid being drafted for service in Vietnam, he entered the U.S. Navy, where he received orders to Medical Illustration School in Bethesda, Maryland. While there, he enjoyed considerable freedom to develop his artistic talents in design, cartooning, and caricature. His proximity to Washington, D.C., also exposed him to that city's musical and theatrical life, exposure which would find expression in his later work.

Upon his release from the U.S. Navy in 1973, Willhoite's job as a medical illustrator was converted into a civilian position. In 1981, he moved to Massachusetts to take up a similar position as a civilian attached to the U.S. Army, where he remains to this day. Willhoite began a parallel career as a freelance illustrator while living in Bethesda. Until 1990, he indulged his passion for the theater by performing in several plays a year until the early 1990s. It was while appearing in a musical revue in the spring of 1979 that Willhoite met a man whom he found himself tentatively courting: Michael Willhoite had come out of the closet.

By December of that year, his cartoons about gay life were being published on a bi-weekly basis in the *Washington Blade,* the capitol's gay newspaper. Appearing under the title "The Cutting Edge," the cartoons were published over the next two-and-a-half years, and were ultimately collected and published in a book, *Now for My Next Trick,* in 1986.

After moving to Massachusetts, Willhoite continued to draw new cartoons for the *Blade* only briefly before moving onto a new endeavor: caricatures of noteworthy gay men and lesbians. In ten years, Willhoite published 350 caricatures along with brief biographies that were in fact gay history lessons revealing the private as well as the public side of each person profiled. Most of these caricatures have been published in two collections by Alyson Publications: *Members of the Tribe* in 1993, and *Willhoite's Hollywood* in 1994. Willhoite points to Al Hirschfeld, Max Beerbohm, and Mexican artist Miguel Covarrubias, whose work had previously influenced Hirschfeld, as the primary influences on his work as a caricaturist.

Michael Willhoite's career as a writer and illustrator took a dramatic turn in 1989, when his publisher, Sasha Alyson of Boston's Alyson Publications, first proposed to publish a series of children's books with gay and lesbian themes. Alyson was well acquainted with Willhoite's ambition to illustrate children's books, and was most encouraging when Willhoite conceived of *Daddy's Roommate.* Published in the fall of 1989, alongside Lesléa Newman's *Heather Has Two Mommies* as the inaugural titles under the Alyson Wonderland imprint, *Daddy's Roommate*'s initial sales and publicity did little to suggest the tumult that would quickly follow.

In 1990, the two books were included in New York City's Rainbow Curriculum, a decision which sparked a nationwide controversy. Opponents of the book objected to its story about a young boy whose father lives with, and is clearly in love with, another man. The book was subsequently withdrawn from many library collections amidst concerns that exposure to the books might encourage young children to accept or adopt a gay lifestyle. The Dallas Association for Decency said the book promoted sodomy, and suggested that, by including *Daddy's Roommate* in its collec-

tion, the local library was legitimizing gay and lesbian relationships.

In 1993 and 1994, *Daddy's Roommate* was the most-challenged book in the country, according to figures released by the American Library Association's Office of Intellectual Freedom, which has also estimated that it is in fact the most-often banned children's book in American history. At the height of the controversy, *Daddy's Roommate* was the subject of a debate on the floor of the U.S. Senate, where it was a rallying point for social conservatives who supported legislation that would deny federal funding to any school whose programs, books, or teaching materials "encourage or support homosexuality as a positive lifestyle alternative." Ironically, the page of *Daddy's Roommate* which is most often cited by critics is an illustration of the boy's father in bed with his lover as the two are about to go to sleep. Nothing about the text or the illustration suggests that anything besides sleep is imminent, but the simple act of two men sharing the same bed continues to outrage. Challengers of the book in North Carolina went so far as to say that it "promotes a dangerous and ungodly lifestyle from which children must be protected."

During this period, opponents of the book often went so far as to remove it from their libraries' shelves by checking it out and failing to return it. Willhoite's publisher replied to this provocation by donating free copies of the book to librarians requesting them; about 500 took advantage of this offer.

Not all the attention given to *Daddy's Roommate* was negative: the book was read aloud on a memorable edition of ABC's *Nightline.* During the controversy over the Rainbow Curriculum in New York City—during which an openly gay school board member took his oath of office with a hand over two leather-bound volumes of *Daddy's Roommate* and *Heather Has Two Mommies*— the *New York Times* weighed in with an editorial largely supportive of these books, describing them as portraying gay and lesbian "relationships as loving and strong, much as schoolbooks on heterosexual families portray them at their best.... At a time when gay-bashing has become one of the most vicious hate crimes among teen-agers, the need for greater understanding is imperative."

Daddy's Roommate earned for Michael Willhoite the 1990 Lambda Literary Award for best Gay Men's Small Press book. He then collaborated on *Belinda's Bouquet* with Lesléa Newman, for which he provided the illustrations. In the next several years, in addition to the collections of caricatures discussed earlier, Willhoite published three more books under the Alyson Wonderland imprint: *Families, The Entertainer,* and *Uncle What-Is-It is Coming to Visit!!* This last title, published in 1993, stirred up controversy once more, this time within segments of the gay community which objected to his reduction of images of men in dresses and leather to caricature; the Seattle chapter of Queer Nation denounced Willhoite for "making fun of other queers."

—Alistair Williamson

WINANT, Fran (Francine Ellen)

Nationality: American poet, artist, and activist. **Born:** Brooklyn, New York, 28 October 1943. **Education:** Fordham University, New York, New York, B.A. in studio art 1975; studied at the School of Visual Arts, New York, New York, 1975. **Career:**

Has held a variety of what she refers to as "uninteresting" day jobs to support her artistic pursuits. Member, Poetry Society of America. **Awards:** Isaacson Poetry Award, New School for Social Research, New York, 1968; New York State Arts Council CAPS Grant in Poetry, New York Foundation for the Arts, 1978; National Endowment for the Arts, Visual Artists Fellowship, 1989-90. **Address:** c/o Violet Press, P.O. Box 398, New York, New York 10009, U.S.A.

WRITINGS

Stage Plays

Closer since the Shooting (first produced Judson Poets' Theater, New York, 8 February 1969).
Play 1, 2, 3, 4 (first produced Cubiculo Theater, New York, 13 June 1969).

Poetry

Looking at Women. New York, Violet Press, 1971.
Dyke Jacket: Poems and Songs. New York, Violet Press, 1976.
Goddess of Lesbian Dreams. New York, Violet Press, 1980.

Editor

With Judy Grepperd, *We Are All Lesbians.* New York, Violet Press, 1975.

Anthologies

The Lesbian Reader, edited by Gina Covina and Laurel Galana. Oakland, California, The Amazon Press, 1975.
Amazon Poetry: An Anthology of Lesbian Poetry, edited by Elly Bulkin and Joan Larkin. Brooklyn, New York, Out & Out Books, 1975.
The Political Palate, edited by Betsey Beaven. Bridgeport, Connecticut, Sanguinaria Publications, 1980.
Lesbian Poetry: An Anthology, edited by Elly Bulkin and Joan Larkin. Watertown, Massachusetts, Persephone Press, 1981.
The Penguin Book of Homosexual Verse, edited by Stephen Coote. New York, Penguin Books, 1983.
We Become New: Poems by Contemporary American Women, edited by Lucille Iverson and Kathryn Ruby. New York, Bantam, 1986.
New Worlds of Literature, edited by Jerome Beaty and J. Paul Hunter. New York, Norton, 1989.
Out of the Closets: Voices of Gay Liberation, 2nd edition, edited by Karla Jay and Allen Young. New York, New York University Press, 1992.
Lesbian Quotations, edited by Rosemary Silva. Boston, Alyson Publications, 1993.
The Arc of Love: An Anthology of Lesbian Love Poems, edited by Claire Coss. Scribner, New York, 1996.
Queer Dog: Homo/Pup/Poems, edited by Gerry Gomez Pearlberg. San Francisco, Cleis Press, forthcoming 1997.

*

Critical Sources: "Lesbian Art" by John Perreault, in *Soho News,* 2 February 1977; "Lesbian Art: The Colonized Self" by Kay Larsen, in *Village Voice,* 8 March 1977; "A New York City Collective" by Fran Winant et al., in *Heresies Magazine,* Vol. 1, No. 3, fall 1977; "Lesbian Art: Variety is Destiny" by Carrie Rickey and Kay Larson, in *Village Voice,* Vols. 3-9, September 1980; "Lesbian Lessons" and "Is There a Gay Culture?" by John Perreault, in *Soho News,* Vol. 10, September 1980; *112 Workshop/112 Greene Street* by Robyn Brentano with Mark Savitt, New York, New York University Press, 1981; "Lavender: On Homosexuality and Art" by Nicholas A. Moufarrage, in *Arts Magazine,* October 1982; "Redefining What 'Gay Art' Can Express to Everyone" by Marilyn Mizrahi, in *Villager,* Vol. 4, November 1982; "Stonewall Revisited," in *Outweek,* 26 June 1989; "It's Been a Queer Fall" by Arlene Raven, in *Village Voice,* 13 November 1990; *Reweaving the World: The Emergence of Ecofeminism* by Gloria Orenstein and Irene Diamond, San Francisco, California, Sierra Club Books, 1990; "Come Out!! Join the Sisters and Brothers of the Gay Liberation Front," by Fran Winant, paper presented at "Gay Liberation: From Rebellion to Activism" (commemorating the 25th anniversary of Stonewall), New York University, New York, 25 June 1994; *The Sexual Perspective: Homosexuality and Art in the Last 100 Years in the West* by Emmanuel Cooper, New York, Routledge, 1994; "My Life as a Lesbian/My Life as an Artist" by Fran Winant, paper presented at the Women's Caucus for Art Panel at Ceres Gallery, New York, January 1996; "How Many Extinctions?" by Fran Winant, in *Art Journal,* Vol. 55, No. 4, winter 1997.

*   *   *

"Before I made art I was part of a daring work of art," Fran Winant declared, referring to her inclusion in the Gay Liberation Front's now-infamous "Come Out!" poster. The poster, shot in 1970 by Peter Hujar, depicts a group of gays and lesbians (including Winant, who grins from the first row in a polka-dot shirt, her arm around then-partner Judy Grepperd) marching through the streets of New York; some embrace, some raise clenched fists, all share a look of pride, enthusiasm, and—most of all—hope in the nascent activist movement of which they were playing a crucial part. "Although we hardly filled the frame of the poster," Winant recalled, "comparatively few of us were there that day— but in the 25 years that followed, hundreds, thousands, hundreds of thousands of our sisters and brothers came out in gay marches all over the world." As one of the founding members of the Gay Liberation Front (GLF) in 1969, Winant holds a unique vantage point from which to comment on the movement's unfolding: "To me, the most important thing about GLF was its energy," she reflected in a paper given at a panel commemorating the 25th anniversary of Stonewall. "The silence was over. GLF had a new message for the world: 'We're a mass movement, loud, visible, we're everywhere, we're threatening, we're different, we're not like you'...The concept of a mass, activist movement emphasizing visibility and difference was GLF's legacy to our spiritual gay children, all those who would follow us whatever their politics, even those who formed groups meant to 'right' our 'wrongs.'"

When a coalition of women split from the GLF to form RadicaLesbians in 1970, Winant followed. Though she feared that the separation would result in a loss of political efficacy, particularly for the GLF, she saw that "women needed to explore our own identities and bond with as well as challenge the women's liberation movement." As a member of RadicaLesbians, Winant helped launch some of the first all-women's dances and poetry readings, and with Grepperd managed a food co-op called The Lesbian Food Conspiracy. Speaking to members of the Lesbian Herstory Archives in April 1996, Winant described the heated atmosphere of that time as "the mix of culture, self-actualization, and politics" that typified the early gay and lesbian movement— a movement which Winant credits with initiating and sustaining much of her creative drive.

The energies and impulses of the early 1970s gave birth to Winant's poetic muse: in that decade, she and Grepperd started Violet Press, which published three volumes of Winant's poetry— *Looking at Women, Dyke Jacket,* and *Goddess of Lesbian Dreams*— as well as one of the earliest anthologies of lesbian verse, *We Are All Lesbians.* Her oft-quoted poem, "Christopher St. Liberation Day, June 28, 1970," captures the intensity and promise of that first march: "shouting / lifting our arms / we are marching into ourselves.../ it seems we will converge / until we explode / sisters and sisters / brothers and brothers / together." In 1978, Winant received a New York State Arts Council CAPS Grant for her gay liberation poetry, and her poems continue to be reprinted in lesbian, gay, and "mainstream" anthologies, including *The Penguin Book of Homosexual Verse, We Become New,* and *The Arc of Love.* She has authored two plays, both of which were produced in New York City, and continues to write both poetry and fiction.

In 1972, during the height of her political activism, Winant realized that she also wanted to paint. She received a degree in Studio Art from Fordham University, studied at the School of Visual Arts, and has shown her work—which frequently celebrates the beauty and spirit of her dog, Cindy—at exhibitions nationwide. In 1978, Winant was included in the first lesbian art show at an established gallery ("A Lesbian Show," curated by Harmony Hammond), and in 1989 she received a National Endowment for the Arts Visual Artists Fellowship. An "out" lesbian artist long before such an identity became fashionable, Winant warns that "it is still dangerous to be a lesbian despite the fact that open lesbians are occasionally portrayed on sitcoms or posed on covers of magazines. Our biographies are dangerous. And life remains as dangerous as ever for a woman confronting her creative choices."

—Melissa Tedrowe

WINGS, Mary

Nationality: American novelist, author of short stories, sculptor, creator of comic books, and filmmaker. **Born:** Chicago, Illinois, 14 April 1949. **Education:** Shimer College, Waukegan, Illinois; studied ceramics and sculpture, Museum Art School, Portland, Oregon, and art history and technical theatre, San Francisco State University. **Family:** Companions have included Robin Flower, Suzanne Bennett, and Ginger Hellmann. **Career:** Worked as school bus driver; banjo player in feminist musical group "Robin, Woody, and Wings"; graphic designer for the Institute for Policy Studies, Amsterdam; teacher of mystery writing; sculptor; filmmaker. Member of Frameline (the group responsible for organizing and conducting the annual San Francisco International Lesbian and Gay Film Festival), San Francisco Gay and Lesbian History Project, Sisters in Crime, and Mystery Writers of America. **Awards:** Best Novel of the Year Award, *City Limits Magazine,* London, 1987; California Arts Council Grant; Lambda Book

Award, for best lesbian mystery novel, 1994. **Agent:** Charlotte Sheedy, 611 Broadway, Suite 428, New York, New York, 10012.

WRITINGS

Novels

She Came Too Late. London, The Women's Press, 1986; Freedom, California, The Crossing Press, 1987.
She Came in a Flash. London, The Women's Press, 1988; New York, Plume, 1990.
Divine Victim. London, The Women's Press, 1992; New York, Dutton, 1993.
She Came by the Book. London, The Women's Press, 1995; New York, Berkley, 1996.
She Came to the Castro. New York, Berkley, 1997.

Short Stories

"Mars Bar," in *Out/Look,* summer 1990, 32-35.
"Kill the Man for Me," in *A Woman's Eye.* New York, Delacorte, 1991, 235-249.
"Mighty Muff," in *Women on Women 2: An Anthology of American Lesbian Short Fiction.* New York, Plume, 1993, 175-180.
"Reader, I Murdered Him, Too," in *Reader, I Murdered Him, Too.* London, Women's Press, 1995.

Nonfiction

"Shaky City," in *New Statesman and Society,* 3 November 1989.
"Rebecca Redux: Tears on a Lesbian Pillow," in *Daring to Dissent: Lesbian Culture from Margin to Mainstream.* London, Cassell, 1994.
With Dorothy Allison, "Another Country," in *10 Percent,* July 1995.

Other

Come Out Comix (comic book). Portland, Oregon, Portland Women's Resource Center, 1974.
Dyke Shorts (comic book). San Francisco, Last Gasp Publishers, 1980.
Illustrator and designer, *Making a Show of It: A Guide to Concert Promotion* by Ginny Berson. Oakland, California, Redwood Records, 1980.
Are Your Highs Getting You Down? (comic book). Berkeley, Substance Abuse Groups of the Pacific Center, 1981.
And producer, with Eric Garber, "Greta Garbo: A Woman of Affairs" (screenplay).

*

Critical Sources: "Mary Wings" by Sheila Johnston, in *Women's Review,* May 1986, 11; "Body Politic" by Nick Kimberley, in *New Statesman,* 6 June 1986; review of *She Came Too Late,* in *New Directions for Women,* Vol. 17, May 1988, 14; "Writing: *She Came Too Late*" by Jane C. Marlowe, in *Spare Rib,* June 1988, 28; "In a World They Never Made" by Sherri Paris, in *Women's Review of Books,* Vol. 5, July 1988, 20; "A Girl After My Own Heart" by Liz Galst, in *Gay Community News,* 1989, 12-13; review of

She Came in a Flash by Sybil Steinberg, in *Publishers Weekly,* Vol. 235, 3 February 1989, 98; "The Lady Dicks" by R. Ruby Rich, in *Village Voice,* Vol. 9 May 1989, 19; "Genre Bending" by John Howell, in *Elle,* December 1990, 160, 162; "Deadly Delights" by Erika Munk, in *Women's Review of Books,* Vol. 9, February 1992, 8-9; review of *Divine Victim,* in *Belles Lettres,* Vol. 9, winter 1993, 63; review of *Divine Victim,* in *Lambda Book Report,* Vol. 3, July 1993, 37; *Contemporary Lesbian Writers of the United States: A Bio-Bibliographical Critical Sourcebook,* edited by Sandra Pollack and Denise D. Knight, Westport, Connecticut, Greenwood Press, 1993, 572-577; *Great Women Mystery Writers: Classic to Contemporary,* Westport, Connecticut, Greenwood Press, 1994; "The New Avengers" by Marion Shaw, in *The Times of London,* 12 March 1995; review of *She Came by the Book,* in *Publishers Weekly,* Vol. 243, 19 February 1996, 207; review of *She Came by the Book,* in *Booklist,* Vol. 92, 1 March 1996, 1125; "Mary Wings: An Interview" by Adrian Muller, in *Mystery Scene Magazine,* No. 54, fall 1996; "Mary Wings" by Adrian Muller, in *St. James Guide to Crime and Mystery Writers,* 4th edition, edited by Jay P. Pederson, Detroit, Michigan, St. James Press, 1996.

*   *   *

Born in Chicago in 1949 and raised in the Baha'i faith, Mary Wings, preeminent writer of lesbian detective fiction, came on the literary scene just in time to successfully chronicle lesbian cultural history in the late 20th century. Expanding her narrative skills through her own lesbian comics and film ("Greta Garbo, A Woman of Affairs," of which she was co-writer and co-producer), Wings began publishing mystery novels in the late 1980s. From her unique vantage point acquired by having lived in the Netherlands for eight years, Mary Wings has both participated in and observed the shifting lesbian politico-cultural scene in the United States and abroad. Her transculturally informed vision provides especially revealing commentary on contemporary lesbian life in the United States.

Perhaps best known, particularly in Europe, as the author of the mystery series featuring lesbian sleuth Emma Victor, Mary Wings began her series with *She Came Too Late.* Set in Boston and emanating from Victor's job as a crisis counselor for a women's hotline, the novel celebrates lesbian friendship even as it explores the difficulties of initiating and continuing lesbian romantic relationships. As Emma discovers her latent talent for solving mysteries, she also embarks upon a serious relationship—perhaps "the Big One," as Wings terms it—with workaholic Dr. Frances Cohen. Personal and political tensions unfold as Emma unravels the central mystery while attempting to fashion a new life with her lover. Through Emma, Wings expertly explores the delicate balance between work and love, fully demonstrating the danger inherent in allowing either to predominate. In *She Came Too Late* Emma finds out "whodunit" and why, but, more significantly, she learns more about who she is as a lesbian.

From the Boston setting of the first novel, Wings moves Emma to San Francisco, her own home, in *She Came in a Flash,* the second book in the series. Again, Wings provides acute insight into the lesbian community, this time in its Californian incarnation, replete with New Age fascinations. In her newfound capacity as detective, Emma contends with the politics of the women's music scene, as well as with religious fanaticism. Strands of the mystery plot, interspersed with highly charged lesbian love scenes, bring *She Came in a Flash* to a satisfying climax, as Emma herself becomes more fully realized as a character.

Reincarnated as a Californian, Emma continues her exploits in *She Came by the Book.* Here, again, Wings intertwines the personal and political, as Emma exercises her now professional sleuthing skills to solve a series of mysteries besetting the San Francisco gay and lesbian community. The viciousness of relationships gone awry pervades the novel, even as Emma's own relationship with Dr. Frances Cohen frays. Still, as Wings writes, "Certain truths were self-evident...I was sitting in the sun planning next year's flora...I'd had a weekend of heartbreak, murder and mayhem...Frances was, in some way, leaving me...I would get beyond it...And I truly believed that every woman in this dyke life must have a garden." Characteristically, Emma takes heartbreak in stride, knowing that new love will most likely spring from new seeds. Ever the pragmatic optimist, Emma survives and thrives, as indeed she must.

In the Emma Victor books Mary Wings supplies seasoned wisdom concerning lesbian life and love. Unlike some lesbian writers, Wings succeeds in integrating love scenes naturally into the books, so that they emerge spontaneously as a result of character and plot. Honesty and passion, rather than contrivance, dominate the novels. At times, given the *noir* or hardboiled detective tradition in which the books are written, Emma seems to be quite butch, yet she is also soft in all the right places. While Wings sometimes parodies hardboiled detective fiction, she also accommodates it to her heroine. Wings' first person narrative always rings true, creating from language a truly rounded character. This narrative voice—the sense of a real person behind the text—is Wings' true gift, distinguishing her books from those of other writers in the lesbian fiction and mystery genres. Pervading the narrative voice is Wings' wry sense of humor, which renders the books vividly readable.

This humor is particularly evident in *Divine Victim,* Wings' departure from the Emma Victor series. Written after *She Came Too Late* and *She Came in a Flash* following Wings' return to the United States from the Netherlands, *Divine Victim,* like the previous books, is a mystery, but one that is more metaphysical, religious, academic, and gothic in nature. "I had to write *Divine Victim,*" said Wings in an interview, "to cope with the big culture shock of returning to the United States. While the series books were popular, they were really rational, and I needed to write something different." In *Divine Victim,* which won the Lambda Book Award for Best Lesbian Mystery of 1993, Wings displays her erudition about art and sculpture, gleaned from her own career as a graphic artist and sculptor. Also, her international experience comes into play, as portions of the novel transpire in Europe. Richness in language and imagery accompany the unnamed, first person, art historian narrator, as she solves manifold mysteries ultimately resulting in disastrous personal repercussions. Lesbian love affairs, past and present, haunt *Divine Victim,* contributing to its transcendent quality. Even as supernatural gives way to natural in the plot, *Divine Victim* comments on the quality of real lesbian relationships, functional and dysfunctional. From a fantastic perspective, *Divine Victim* portrays ordinary, as well as extraordinary, lesbian/human relationships. Mary Wings' holiday from hardboiled detective fiction has resulted in a memorable gothic novel.

Mary Wings has continued to develop Emma Victor's character in the series books, including *She Came to the Castro.* She has also contributed to the genre of detective fiction by conducting workshops on mystery writing. Entitled the "Mary Wings Magical Mystery Weekends," these workshops have enabled Wings to share her knowledge and love of mystery writing with prospective authors, both gay and straight.

In an interview, Wings observed of her work:

> All the things that I have done have contributed each to the other. Writing is about sculpture, which is about touching things and seeing things. Music has contributed to my prose style. And the Emma Victor novels are like gifts to the readers; they're like sending someone flowers or baking a cake. They strengthen our feelings about who we are as lesbians. I like to create our own lesbian stereotypes.

While her works have touched a large lesbian and feminist audience, they are by no means insular. Along with lesbian mystery writers Sandra Scoppettone and Ellen Hart, Mary Wings has transcended a niche audience to achieve widespread appeal, especially in Europe. Her wit and psychological acumen have rendered her a prominent 20th century writer in the tradition of both lesbian and mystery fiction. She came on time and is here to stay.

—Lynne Maxwell

WOLVERTON, Terry

Nationality: American poet, novelist, short story writer, editor, performance artist, and artist. **Born:** Cape Canaveral, Florida, 23 August 1954. **Education:** University of Detroit, 1972-73, University of Toronto, 1973-74, and Sagaris Institute, 1975; Thomas Jefferson College, B.A. 1977; Feminist Studio Workshop, Certificate 1978; The Grantsmanship Center, Los Angeles, California, Certificate, 1981; The Fundraising School, San Francisco, California, Certificate 1985. **Family:** Companion of artist Susan Silton. **Career:** Newswriter, *Newswest,* 1977-78; co-founder and co-director, Lesbian Art Project, Los Angeles, 1977-80; calendar editor, 1977-81, teacher, adult education and writing workshops, 1977-84, administrative assistant, 1981-84, member of board of directors, 1982-86, development director, 1984-88, executive director, 1988-89, Woman's Building, Los Angeles, California; freelance copywriter and publicist, 1978-80; co-organizer, Incest Awareness Project, Los Angeles, 1979-81; founder, White Women's Anti-Racism Consciousness Raising, 1980; principal, Consult'Her (management consulting firm), from 1982; teacher, Connexus Women's Center/Centro de Mujeres, 1985-87, University of California-Los Angeles Extension, 1987-88, and Los Angeles Gay and Lesbian Community Center; performance artist and writer, 1985-88; founder, Los Angeles Artists Organizations, 1986; founder, "Perspectives Writing Program," Los Angeles Gay and Lesbian Community Center, from 1988. Contributor of articles, stories, reviews, and poems to periodicals, including *Advocate, American Writing, Artweek, ArtWire, Baltimore Alternative, Caprice, Common Lives, CQ: California Quarterly, Chrysalis, Evergreen Chronicles, Frontiers, Glimmer Train, Heresies, High Performance, Jacaranda Review, L. A. Weekly, Lambda Book Report, Lesbian News, Lesbian Lives, Lesbian Tide, Many Mountains Moving, Modern Words, Outweek, Sinister Wisdom, 10 Percent, Tsunami, Women Artists' News,* and *Zyzzyva.* Member, public policy committee, California Confederation of the Arts, 1986-88; member, board of directors, Fringe Festival, Los Angeles, 1987-88; member, ArtTable, 1987-

89; panelist, City of Los Angeles Cultural Affairs Department, 1989, 1992, 1993; member, advisory board, Los Angeles Poetry Festival, from 1990; member, advisory committee, First Impressions Performance, 1991-94; panelist, National/State/County Grants Program, 1991, 1992; panelist, City of Pasadena Cultural Grants Program, 1993; panelist, Grants to Writers with HIV/AIDS, PEN Center West, 1996. **Awards:** New Poets Award, University of Detroit, 1973; Gay and Lesbian Academic Union Award, 1981; Merit Award, JVC Tokyo Video Festival, 1981; Artist in Residence, California Arts Council, from 1984; Lesbian Rights Award, Southern California Women for Understanding, 1986; Los Angeles Cultural Affairs Department grant, 1990-91; Vesta Award in Literature, Woman's Building, 1991; Lambda Book Award nominations, for Best Lesbian Anthology and Best Gay Men's Anthology, 1992, for Best Lesbian Poetry, 1993, and for Best Gay and Lesbian Anthology, 1996; first place winner, *Sheila-Na-Gig* Annual Poetry Contest, 1994; Movers and Shakers Award, Southern California Library for Social Research, 1995; LACE (Lesbian and bisexul women Active in Community Empowerment) Award, Los Angeles Gay and Lesbian Center, for Arts and Entertainment, 1997. **Address:** c/o Faber and Faber, Inc., 53 Shore Road, Winchester, Massachusetts 01890, U.S.A.

Writings

Poetry

Blue Moon (poems and prose). Los Angeles, California, Women's Graphic Center, 1977.
Black Slip (poems). San Diego, California, Clothespin Fever Press, 1992.

Plays and Performance Art Texts

With Norman Fragosa, Chutney Lu Gunderson, Truckie Parts, Jade Satterthwaite, Ann Shannon, and Dyana Silberstein, *FEMINA: An IntraSpace Voyage* (produced at the Woman's Building, Los Angeles, 1978).
With Jerri Allyn, Nancy Angelo, Leslie Belt, Cheri Gaulke, Gunderson, Brook Hallock, Sue Maberry, Louise Moore, Arlene Raven, Catherine Stifter, Cheryl Swannack, and Christine Wong, *An Oral Herstory of Lesbianism* (produced at the Woman's Building, Los Angeles, 1979).
In Silence Secrets Turn to Lies/Secrets Shared Become Sacred Truth (produced at the Woman's Building, Los Angeles, 1979).
With Vicki Stolsen, *Ya Got Class, Real Class* (produced at Los Angeles Contemporary Exhibitions, 1980).
Medium: Memory/Muse (produced at Long Beach Museum of Art, California, 1983).
Me and My Shadow (produced at the University of California, Los Angeles, Woman's Building, Los Angeles, Sushi Gallery, San Diego, California, and ABC No Rio, New York, 1984).
A Merry Little Christmas, (staged reading at Celebration Theatre, Los Angeles, California, 1987).

Editor

With Benjamin Weissman, *Harbinger: Poetry and Fiction by Los Angeles Writers.* Los Angeles, California, Los Angeles Festival and Beyond Baroque, 1990.

With Robert Drake, *Indivisible: New Short Fiction by West Coast Gay and Lesbian Writers.* New York, Plume, 1991.

Blood Whispers: L.A. Writers on AIDS, Los Angeles, Silverton Books and the Gay and Lesbian Community Center, Vol. 1, 1991, Vol. 2, 1992.

Stone Made Flesh: Poems by Michael Niemoeller. Los Angeles, California, Silverton Books, 1995.

With Robert Drake, *Hers: Brilliant New Fiction by Lesbian Writers.* Boston, Faber and Faber, Vol. 1, 1995, Vol. 2, 1997.

With Robert Drake, *His: Brilliant New Fiction by Gay Writers.* Boston, Faber and Faber, Vol. 1, 1995, Vol. 2, 1997.

Anthologies

"In Silence Secrets Turn to Lies/Secrets Shared Become Sacred Truth," in *Voices in the Night: Women Speaking About Incest,* edited by Toni McNaron and Yarrow Morgan. Pittsburgh, Pennsylvania, Cleis Press, 1982; as "Secrets Shared Become Sacred Truth," in *Between Ourselves: Letter Between Mothers and Daughters,* edited by Karen Payne. London, Michael Joseph, Ltd., New York, Houghton Mifflin, 1983.

"Unlearning Complicity, Remembering Resistance," in *Learning Our Way,* edited by Charlotte Bunch and Sandra Pollack. Freedom, California, The Crossing Press, 1983.

"1970," in *Southern California Writers and Artists,* edited by Jacqueline de Angelis and Aleida Rodríguez. Books of a Feather, 1984.

"Water and Earth," in *Women for All Seasons,* edited by Wanda Coleman and Joanne Leedom Ackerman. Los Angeles, California, Woman's Building, 1988.

"Each Poem Is a Fistfight," "For Azul," "She Was Cracking Rocks with a Hammer," "That Poem You Keep Writing in Your Head," "Something about Ice," "I've Been Wondering Why It's so Hard to See You," in *In a Different Light,* edited by Carolyn Weathers and Jenny Wrenn. San Diego, California, Clothespin Fever Press, 1989.

"The Wedding," in *Word of Mouth,* edited by Irene Zahava. Freedom, California, The Crossing Press, 1990.

"Pretty Women," in *Indivisible: New Short Fiction by West Coast Gay and Lesbian Writers,* edited by Terry Wolverton, with Robert Blake. New York, Plume, 1991.

"Things to Do," in *Lesbian Love Stories,* edited by Irene Zahava. Freedom, California, The Crossing Press, 1991.

"Shoes," in *Impediment,* edited by Cheri Gaulke. Women's Studio Workshop, 1991.

"Garage Sale," in *Lovers,* edited by Amber Coverdale Sumrall. The Crossing Press, Freedom, California, 1992.

"Reunification: Changing Relationships Between Lesbians and Gay Men," in *Positively Gay,* edited by Betty Berzon. Celestial Arts, 1992.

"Return to Sender," in *VeriTales,* edited by Helen Wirth. Fall Creek Press, 1993.

"Rites," in *Love's Shadows,* edited by Amber Coverdale Sumrall. Freedom, California, The Crossing Press, 1993.

"Black Slip," in *Stand Up Poetry,* edited by Charles H. Webb. Long Beach, California State University Press, 1994.

"Stories Twist," in *Retouching: The Family Album,* curated by David Humphries. New York, Cone Editions, 1994.

"A Whisper in the Veins," in *Growing Up Gay/Growing Up Lesbian,* edited by Bennett Singer. New York, The New Press, 1994.

"I'm in a Cement Dress," "Rites," and "Black Slip," in *Grand Passion: The Poets of Los Angeles and Beyond.* Red Wind Books, 1995.

"Seduction," in *The Best Lesbian Erotica 1995,* edited by Tristan Taormina and Heather Lewis. Pittsburgh, Pennsylvania, Cleis Press, 1996.

"Requiem," in *The Feminist Art of Community Building,* edited by Betty Ann Brown. New York, Midmarch Press, 1996.

"Crumbs," in *Cookin' with Honey,* edited by Amy Scholder. Ithaca, New York, Firebrand Books, 1996.

"Safe Sex," "Rites," and "Black Slip," in *Between the Cracks,* edited by Gavin Dillard. San Francisco, Daedalus Publishing, 1997.

"Sex Less" (short story), in *Hers: Brilliant New Fiction by Lesbian Writers,* Vol. 2, edited by Terry Wolverton and Robert Drake. Boston, Faber and Faber, 1997.

Media Arts

Equal Time in Equal Space (interactive video installation; directed by Nancy Angelo; produced at the Woman's Building, Los Angeles, California, 1980, and University College Playhouse, Toronto, Canada, 1981).

With Tina Treadwell, *Putting Our Hands to Other Labor: The Women's Art Movement in Southern California* (videotape). Los Angeles, California, Public Access Channel, 1986.

With Catherine Stifter, *Visions and Revisions* (radio play). 1987.

With Pat Cammack, Catherine Cummings, Kathleen Forrest, and Martha Wheelock, *Sweet Fifteen* (videotape). Public Access Channel, Los Angeles, California, 1988.

With Gary Glassman, *Our Voices Will Not Be Silenced* (videotape). California Arts Council, 1990.

With Catherine Stifner, *Violet Ink: Writing by Gays and Lesbians* (radio play). 1991.

With Treadwell, *Me and My Shadow* (videotape). Long Beach Museum of Art Annex, California.

Novels

Bailey's Beads. Boston, Faber and Faber, 1996.

*

Interviews: "Creating a Context of Facades and Feminism" by Samir Hachim, in *Advocate,* 1983; "Theater as Community Ritual" by Bia Lowe, in *Heresies,* 1984; "Power and the Power Over: a Conversation with Terry Wolverton" by Laurel Beckman and Kathleen Sorensen, in *Lucky* (Los Angeles), No. 2, 1989; "Out of the Closet and Into the Community" by Chris Bray, in *Pasadena Weekly,* 7 October 1994; "Knowing You, Knowing Me" by Owen Keehnen, in *OutNow!* (San Jose, California), 15-28 October 1996, *OutLines* (Chicago), September 1996, *Baltimore Alternative,* September 1996.

Critical Sources: "An Oral Herstory of Lesbianism" by Linda Frye Burnham, in *High Performance,* 1979; "Facing a Shadow" by Larry Abrahms, in *Artweek,* 1984; "Totems for Pets" by Nancy Buchanan, in *High Performance,* 1985; "Buried Treasure" by Jeanne Shanin, in *Artweek,* 10 August 1985; "Could Be Verse, Could Be on a Hearse," in *Los Angeles Herald Examiner,* 30 December 1987; "The Function of Art in Culture Today," in *High Performance,* Vol. 11, spring/summer 1988; "Santa Monica Bus

Riders See Poetry in Motion" by Roseanne Keynan, in *Los Angeles Times*, 18 February 1988; "Rites of Passage/Rites of Spring" by Claire Peeps, in *High Performance*, Vol. 12, summer 1989; "Terry Wolverton" by Lynell George, in *L.A. Style*, September 1989; "Introduction" by Terry Wolverton and Robert Drake, in *Indivisible*, New York, Plume, 1990; "Penning Away the Pain" by Vicki P. McConnell, in *Advocate*, August 1991; "California Dreaming" by Nikolaus Merrill, in *Lambda Book Report*, September 1991; "A 'Lucky Accident'" by Tim Coffey, in *Washington Blade*, 1 November 1991; "Woman's Building Lost to a Hitch in 'Herstory'" by Jan Breslauer, in *Los Angeles Times*, 7 January 1992; review of *Blood Whispers* by C.E. Austina-Moore, in *Lambda Book Report*, Vol. 3, No. 2, January/February 1992; review of *Blood Whispers: L.A. Writers on AIDS* by Eleanor J. Bader, in *Utne Reader*, July/August 1992; "Terry Wolverton: Writing to Live" by Deena Rosen, in *High Performance*, Vol. 17, fall 1994; review of *Blood Whispers, Vol. 2* by Jim Marks, in *Lambda Book Report*, November/December 1994; "Universal Lesbian" by Paula Martinac, in *Lambda Book Report*, September 1995; "Their Brilliant Careers" by Bruce Mirken, in *Los Angeles Reader*, 15 September 1995; "*Hers: Brilliant New Fiction By Lesbian Writers*," and "*His: Brilliant New Fiction by Gay Writers*," in Little Sisters New Books, February 1996, "Emphasis on Diversity" by Ross Lipman, in *Harvard Gay and Lesbian Review*, winter 1996; review of *Bailey's Beads* by Rachel Astarte Piccione, in *Lambda Book Report*, August 1996; "Dissolving Memories," in *Washington Blade*, 13 September 1996; http:www.netfinder.com/sisters/newfeb.htm; "Wolverton, Terry. *Bailey's Beads*" by Lisa S. Nussbaum, in *Library Journal*, August 1996; unpublished interview with Terry Wolverton by Patti Capel Swartz, 7 November 1996; "A Look at Books" by Teresa DeCrescenzo, in *The Lesbian News*, November 1997; "Person, Personae" by Kathryn Robyn, in *Harvard Gay and Lesbian Review*, winter 1997; "Passing Along a Passion for the Written Word" by Penelope Moffet, in *Los Angeles Times*, 24 January 1997; "In a Different Light," http://www.uampfa.berkeley.edu/exhibits/idl/interview.htm.

Terry Wolverton comments:

When I came out in 1973, there was no community for lesbian or gay artists. Throughout my career, I've worked not only to improve the craft of my own art, but also to cultivate strong communities in which my work could be contextualized. I don't believe that artists must be solitary geniuses who make their work in isolation; I'm convinced that creativity blossoms in the context of a supportive community that provides encouragement, rigorous feedback, and the impetus to strive for excellence.

*   *   *

Terry Wolverton has been a primary force in creating visibility for artists and writers, and in forging cohesion and creativity within the feminist lesbian, gay, bi-sexual and trans communities. Her own work, writing, and editing, performance and visual art, have been extremely important to creating a space for lesbian and gay artists. She has, in her work and her life, created a space for what curators Lawrence Rinder and Nayland Blake described in an interview about the exhibition "In a Different Light" at Berkeley, as extremely important; she created visibility and connections among creative artists and their works. As Blake indicated, "queer people are the only minority whose culture is really transmitted almost exclusively orally, outside of nuclear/biological family.... In order

for queers to have a history, they have to put these signs out into the world and pull together their tribe from a very dispersed place." Wolverton, through her writing, her performance, and her activism, and her work at Woman's Building in Los Angeles, has contributed to that effort. Wolverton's novel, *Bailey's Beads* illustrates how gays and lesbians develop 'constructed identities,' and how gays and lesbians create 'extended families'—often stronger than biological families," according to Lisa Mincey Farber in *Bailey's Beads: A Novel.*

Wolverton's politics have moved from women's separatism to unity within and for issues pertaining to all of the extended queer communities. As Wolverton and Robert Drake point out in the introduction to *Indivisible*, separation of the lesbian and gay communities "changed in the eighties, when the entire culture of the country seemed to shift.... [T]he values that had guided the sixties and seventies were overturned, [when] it began to seem more necessary to seek allies wherever they could be found, including along lines of race and class and gender." As they point out, the AIDS pandemic increased the necessity for unity. Their jointly edited *Indivisible* attests to that unity as the first literary anthology to include work by both gay and lesbian writers. *Indivisible* also focuses on the work of West Coast writers, writers who had often been notably absent in the east coast centered publishing industry.

Wolverton's and Drake's collections of fiction grew, in part, from Wolverton's work as an activist and teacher in her writing workshops. All of the collections they have completed include both established voices and newer voices speaking to the diversity of the queer communities. These, along with *Blood Whispers*, make an extremely significant contribution to not only gay, lesbian, bisexual, and trans literature, but also to the literature of AIDS. *Blood Whispers* grew directly from Wolverton's work with HIV+ and People With AIDS (PWAs), and a part of the poetry of *Black Slip* refers to this work. Wolverton has also sought to include the writing, art, or performance of lesbian artists in anthologies, as *Hers*, Volumes I and II, attest. Her work within the lesbian community has been productive and prodigious. Working within galleries and performance spaces, like the Barnsdall Gallery Theatre where she performed *Excavations*, her work has examined the diversity of the lesbian community and encouraged that diversity's visibility. As Jeanne Shanin indicated in *Artweek*, *Excavations* began with interviews of 50 lesbians of diverse ages and cultural backgrounds which resulted in a multifaceted performance. Wolverton "has unveiled society's denial of lesbianism and of the contributions made by these women," according to Shanin.

When she moved to Los Angeles in the 1970s, Wolverton was active in the Woman's Building, eventually becoming executive director. Indeed, as Claire Peeps pointed out in *High Performance*, "It amazes me how much real good can be done in the world by a handful of people with relentless energy and clear vision—and Wolverton is one of those whose energy just won't quit." Wolverton went on to establish the Perspectives Writing Program at the Los Angeles Gay and Lesbian Community Center. This program was developed in part because her "interests lie in empowering other lesbian and gay men with the written word," and for "the love of words and to satisfy her strong desire to develop a community of writers around her," according to Deena Rosen in *High Performance*. By including some student writing in her anthologies, Rosen noted that Wolverton "tries to push her students to the next level—out of the literary closet, if you will, and into the larger world." Rosen quotes Wolverton about the Perspectives philosophy: "the simple assumption that 'everybody has a story to tell and everybody has the right to creativity.'" Her workshops, including those for PWAs and caregivers, are, as Wolverton told Rosen, to "create that community and nurture that creative spirit...because I believe when you have that, you can survive any kind of adversity."

Wolverton's work and politics are inseparable. Her life reflects her work, and her work her life. She has never turned away from looking at the issues of the communities in which she works. Discussing what constitutes lesbian work, or what should be included in anthologies, Wolverton writes in the introduction to *Hers,* "Can we conceive of lesbian content that is not about a preoccupation with relationships...or about the pressures of coming out? And if lesbian content is limited to these subjects...doesn't that lead to a narrowing of self-definition, and thus of possibilities, for lesbians?" Rather, Wolverton would like to "see lesbian culture include whatever lesbians create, on any subject, with any content."

Wolverton's work demonstrates a full and diverse spectrum of living and being. Her work, in every form, demonstrates the full range of her humanity. As Rachel Piccione noted in *Lambda Book Report,* "Terry Wolverton successfully enters the complex realm of human relationships and the power of language."

—Patti Capel Swartz

WONG, Norman

Nationality: American short story writer and novelist. **Born:** Honolulu, Hawaii, 9 September 1963. **Education:** University of Chicago, B.A. 1986; Johns Hopkins University, M.A. 1990. **Career:** Membership assistant and volunteer coordinator, Lambda Legal Defense and Education Fund, New York, 1993-95; fiction writing instructor, West Side YMCA, New York, from 1994; development assistant, Public Theater/New York Shakespeare Festival, New York, from 1996; contributor of stories to *Asian/Pacific American Journal of Literature, Bakunin, Kenyon Review,* and *Threepenny Review.*

WRITINGS

Fiction

Cultural Revolution: Stories. New York, Persea Books, 1994.
"Andrew and I," in *Men on Men 6: Best New Gay Fiction,* edited by David Bergman. New York, NAL/Dutton, 1996.
"Disneyland," in *Boys Like Us: Gay Writers Tell Their Coming Out Stories,* edited by Patrick Merla. New York, Avon, 1996.
ABC (novel) New York, Ballantine, in progress.

*

Interviews: "Tall and Lean and Just Turned Thirty" by Christopher Bram, in *Lambda Book Report* (Washington), Vol. 4, No. 3, March/April 1994, 7-9.

Critical Sources: Review of *Cultural Revolution,* in *Publishers Weekly* (New York), Vol. 241, No. 5, 31 January 1994, 75; review

of *Cultural Revolution* by Kevin M. Roddy, in *Library Journal,* Vol. 119, 1 March 1994, 122; review of *Cultural Revolution* by Diane Cole, in *New York Times Book Review,* 27 March 1994, 25; review of *Cultural Revolution* by Tom Howard, in *MultiCultural Review,* Vol. 3, June 1994, 75; review of *Cultural Revolution* by Eric V. Martinez, in *Amerasia Journal,* Vol. 22, spring 1996, 268.

*   *   *

Norman Wong may be the first Chinese-American story writer to interweave the assimilation of successive generations of an immigrant family to post-war America with the definition of a central character's sexual identity. In *Cultural Revolution,* a series of 11 stories, the author traces the history of the Lau family from its origins in China to its acculturation to Hawaii in the 1960s. Representing the third generation of the Lau family, Michael's exploration of his ethnic identity accompanies an exploration of his sexual feelings, especially those toward white men who are attracted to younger men of Asian descent.

Born in Honolulu in 1963 and reared there, Wong came to the mainland of the United States to study English literature at the University of Chicago. He used his experience to contrast the city on the prairie with the comparatively exotic, Asian-dominated environment of Hawaii, providing the metaphoric landscape for the physical differences between Asian men and the white men to whom the central character in *Cultural Revolution* is attracted. Wong's largely autobiographical stories from his youth make *Cultural Revolution* an unconventional, intergenerational bildungsroman.

The stories in which Michael is younger, such as "Fiftieth-State Fair" and "Stitches," evoke with clarity and subtlety the childhood experiences of a gay man, whether through fear of an amusement park ride or identification with his mother's world. In "Ordinary Chinese People," as Michael grows into his adolescent years he develops an infatuation with his after-school track coach, cuts himself in imitation of the despairing Conrad in the motion picture *Ordinary People,* and comes to understand that he is the repository of his father's unfulfilled dreams. In "The Chinese Barber," Michael is approached by an older mainland teenage tourist, who invites him after lunch to his hotel room for a haircut. Despite his attraction to and comfort with Ronnie, when Michael senses the sexual possibilities of the invitation, he abruptly declines.

Written in the spare, unembellished style of short story writers such as Flannery O'Connor, Raymond Carver, and Kazuo Ishiguro, most of the stories in *Cultural Revolution* are told in the past tense by a third-person narrator. The present tense, however, is employed in "Robbed," in which Michael's parents arrive home with his older sister to discover that their apartment has been burglarized, and in "Chinese Movie," in which Michael learns from his older sister Julia to recognize the transvestite prostitutes who populate the area around the motion picture theater his family patronizes. Wong renders personality primarily through accurately shaped dialogue, and often the impatience and subtle cruelties of human interaction are revealed through the domestic situations and events in family life: the harsh exchanges between combative parents, the interruptions of household accidents, the dissonances between hard-working, overprotective, immigrant parents and their new-world children.

—Paul Glassman

WOODSON, Jacqueline

Nationality: American novelist, short story writer, and writer of young adult fiction. **Born:** Columbus, Ohio, 12 February 1963; grew up in Greenville, South Carolina, and Brooklyn, New York. **Education:** Attended schools in Brooklyn; Adelphi University, B.A. in English 1985; studied creative writing at the New School for Social Research. **Career:** Has held a variety of jobs including editorial assistant and drama therapist with runaway and homeless young adults in East Harlem; teacher of writing, Eugene Lang College, 1994, and Goddard College, 1993-95; freelance writer, from 1987; writer-in-residence, National Book Foundation, 1995 and 1996. Contributor to periodicals, including *American Voice, American Identities: Contemporary Multi-Cultural Voices, Common Lives Quarterly, Conditions, Essence, Horn Book, Kenyon Review,* and *Out/Look;* editorial board, Portable Lower East Side/*Queer City.* **Awards:** MacDowell Colony fellowship, 1990, 1994; Fine Arts Works Center fellowship, Provincetown, 1991-92; Best Book Award, American Library Association, 1994; Editor's Choice Award, *Booklist,* 1994; Best Book Award, *Publisher's Weekly,* 1994; Jane Addams Children's Book Award, 1995, 1996; Coretta Scott King Honor Book Award, 1995, 1996; Kenyon Review Award, for Literary Excellence in Fiction, 1996; *Granta* Fifty Best American Authors under 40 Award, 1996; Lambda Literary Award, for Best Fiction and for Best Children's Fiction, 1996; American Film Institute Award. **Agent:** Charlotte Sheedy, 65 Bleecker Street, New York, New York 10012, U.S.A.

WRITINGS

Novels

Last Summer with Maizon. New York, Delacorte, 1990.
The Dear One. New York, Delacorte, 1991.
Maizon at Blue Hill. New York, Delacorte, 1992.
Between Madison and Palmetto. New York, Delacorte, 1993.
The Book Chase. New York, Delacorte, 1993.
I Hadn't Meant to Tell You This. New York, Delacorte, 1994.
From the Notebooks of Melanin Sun. New York, Scholastic, 1995.
Autobiography of a Family Photo. New York, Dutton, 1995.
We Had a Picnic This Sunday Last. New York, Hyperion, 1997.
The House You Pass on the Way. New York, Delacorte, 1997.
Visiting Day. New York, Scholastic, forthcoming.
Sweet, Sweet Memory. New York, Hyperion, forthcoming.

Anthologies and Collections

"Causes" in *Women on Women,* edited by Joan Nestle. New York, New American Library, 1990.
"Slipping Away" in *Am I Blue: Coming Out from the Silence,* edited by Marion Dane Bauer. New York, HarperCollins, 1994.

Editor, *A Way Out of No Way: Writing about Growing Up Black in America.* New York, Holt, 1996.

Uncollected Essays

"The Company of Friends," in *Common Lives Quarterly,* spring 1987.
"Consumption," in *Common Lives Quarterly,* fall 1987.

"Idella's Child, Tyler," in *Conditions,* No. 17, 1990.
"Growing Up Black and Gay among Good Christian Peoples," in *Belle Lettres,* spring 1991.
"The Things He Turns to Gold," "Where My Mother Touches Me," "Slipping Off," and "The Telephone Company," in *Kenyon Review,* Vol. 14, No. 4, fall 1992.
"A Stolen Childhood," in *Essence,* Vol. 24, No. 1, May 1993.
"A Sign of Having Been Here," in *The Horn Book Magazine,* November/December, 1995.

Other

Martin Luther King, Jr. New York, Silver Press, 1990.
With Catherine Saalfield, *Among Good Christian Peoples,* (video), 1991.

*

Critical Sources: "Books from Parallel Cultures: New African American Voices" by Rudine Sims Bishop, in *Horn Book,* September/October 1992, 616-620; "Jacqueline Woodson" by Catherine Saalfield, in *Contemporary Lesbian Writers of the United States: A Bio-Bibliographical Sourcebook,* edited by Sandra Pollack and Denise D. Knight, Westport, Connecticut, Greenwood Press, 1993, 583-586; "Jacqueline Woodson" by Jacqueline Woodson, in *Am I Blue: Coming Out from the Silence,* edited by Marion Dane Bauer, New York, HarperCollins, 1994, 49-61; "I Hadn't Meant to Tell You This" by Joyce A. Litton, *Clip and File Reviews of New Hardcover Fiction,* edited by Gary M. Salver and Virginia R. Monseau, http://scholar.lib.vt.edu/ejournals...//fall94/Clip_and_file.html#Woodson; "Bold Type: Jacqueline Woodson's 'Girl Stories'" by Diane R. Paylor, in *Ms.,* Vol. 5, No. 3, November 1994, 77; "A World Without Childhood" by Catherine Bush, in *New York Times Book Review,* 26 February 1995, 14; "From the Notebooks of Melanin Sun" in *Publisher's Weekly,* 15 May 1995; "Books" by Richard Labonte, in *Q san francisco,* http://www.qsanfrancisco.com/qsf/95summer/books.htm; "Outside Looking in: Representations of Gay and Lesbian Experiences in the Young Adult Novel" by Nancy St. Clair, http://scholar.lib.vt.edu/ejournals/ALAN//fall95/Clair.htm; "A Sign of Having Been Here" by Jacqueline Woodson, in *Horn Book,* November/December 1995, 711-715; "Jacqueline Woodson's *Autobiography of a Family Photo*" by Lee Lawton, *Women's Books Online* http://www.cybergrrl.com/review/gb0469.html#Auto; "Black Lesbian Film and Video Art: Feminist Studies, Performance Studies" by Yvonne Welbon, http://fileroom.aaup.uic.edu/RSG/pform35welbon.htm; unpublished interview with Jacqueline Woodson by Patti Capel Swartz, January 1997.

Jacqueline Woodson comments:

As I wrote in "A Sign of Having Been Here," I don't believe gay writers must always have gay characters. I think we must tell *all* of our stories. Many of my own aren't about gayness, yet are written with an awareness that has arisen from acknowledging who I am. I write about black girls because this world would like to keep us invisible. I write about *all* girls because I know what happens to self-esteem when we turn 12, and I hope to show readers the number of ways in which we are strong. I believe first and foremost that we must write the truth, and this can only be a good thing. These days when I hear the backlash against multiculturalism, I want to scream. How dare people want us to be invisible again, to give up the tiny bit of visibility we've fought so hard for, been arrested for, died for?

*   *   *

"Imagine a tiny room, and in it, the spirits of black writers pointing a Brooklyn girl in the direction of her dream." In her introduction to *A Way Out of No Way* Jacqueline Woodson asked readers to imagine the room, a girl, and her life growing up in the 1970s. The "tiny room" was Woodson's own room as a girl, the room where she discovered the work of black writers. She "read their words hungrily (for until this time I had never read a story by an African American about African Americans), [they were]...making real for me my own dream of becoming a writer." As the title of her essay "A Sign of Having Been Here" indicates, Woodson reads and has read to find herself, "reading the books where I found tiny pieces of myself over and over again." And she writes to help her readers find parts of themselves. In the essay, Woodson noted that even though she is a black gay writer her responsibilities go beyond those two communities "to write beyond the systems of oppression in all communities. As people who exist on the margins, we do have a different view of the world, and it is our responsibility to refocus." Through showing oppressions and redefining world views in writing, Woodson says, "we may help a child who is coming out or struggling with abuse or with family or with health to acquire a clearer vision of the world and thereby grow up stronger."

As Rudine Sims Bishop pointed out in "Books from Parallel Cultures," "Woodson's work features strong, independent black women and girls." However, since Sims appraisal, Woodson has had two books published with prominent male characters: *Between Madison and Palmetto* and *From the Notebooks of Melanin Sun.* Both of the male characters in these books were written with understanding and fullness, and both serve to diminish stereotypical ideas of what constitutes "manhood." One of these characters is Woodson's recurring character of Maizon's father. Maizon, a young black girl living with her grandmother and growing up in Brooklyn has a close friendship with Margaret, who lives down the street, and these books explore a number of issues including death, single parenting, race relationships, and cross-racial friendship. In *Last Summer with Maizon* and *Maizon at Blue Hill* their friendship survives the death of Margaret's father and Maizon's brief enrollment at a private boarding school. In *Between Madison and Palmetto,* this friendship is tested by the inclusion of a white girl into their world, and developing friendships with her, as well as Margaret's failure to accept her changing body and the secretiveness she engenders to hide her eating disorder. Male characters are introduced as Maizon's father, Cooper, who had left her with her grandmother after her mother's death, returns. Cooper is strong because he is able to admit his previous weaknesses and to realize what the world has done to him: "black men aren't just hated, people are afraid of them too. I think that starts making them feel like they're monsters." Of leaving Maizon with her grandmother, he says, "I was young. I was scared. I had just lost the person I loved most in the world. When I felt that helpless bundle in my arms, I knew I wasn't strong enough to give you what you needed to survive. Your grandma was the only woman that could do that."

Melanin Sun is a very different character from Cooper. What he can't say, he writes down. He collects stamps, he keeps notebooks, which he knows can be interpreted as "faggy." In the early part of the book, Melanin notes that there are "two kinds of 'faggy.' There's the kind that I guess if I thought real hard, I kind of was. That's the 'faggy' that really isn't super macho and has notebooks to write stuff down in...The other kind of 'faggy' was the really messed up kind." In *From the Notebooks of Melanin Sun,* Melanin has to come to terms with his homophobia and racism, for his mother tells him she is a lesbian, and her lover Kristin is a white woman. Melanin struggles with himself and his own prejudices and fears (if his mother is lesbian, what does that mean about him?), as well as with the attitudes toward homosexuality that he finds on the streets. He becomes lonely as he withdraws from his mother and friends. He reflects on how the white world pictures him as a black male teen. He reflects about change. He writes in his notebook, "What is this? What makes life so crazy? How come it's her of all the mothers in the world that has to be a dyke?" The portrait of E.C., Melanin's mother, is also carefully drawn through his eyes. The reader feels her pain with the strain of the relationship with her son, but also her need for love, for adult company, and her need to be herself. She asked Melanin to try to see Kristin and herself as people. And, despite his reluctance, Melanin is finally able to do this, and through his love of his mother, his acceptance of who she is, his loneliness is lessened and he can accept himself. As noted in *Notes from the Windowsill,* this novel "is a fascinating portrait of a boy struggling to reconcile many mixed messages as he forms his identity."

As Catherine Saalfield pointed out in her essay about Jacqueline Woodson, "Woodson has maintained the integrity of her characters' complicated lives." Writing of *The Dear One,* Saalfield noted that "Woodson tackles issues like alcoholism, death, divorce, class conflicts in the African-American community, lesbianism, adoption, and mental illness," but "the warm, honest, and loving stories are no less 'realistic' for their complexity, but draw on the most layered influences of each character's experience." Lesbianism is integrated into *The Dear One* as a part of everyday life. Feni, the main character of this book, has a much more difficult time with class issues and morality judgments about Rebecca, the daughter of her mother's college friend who has come to live in her house because of her pregnancy, than she has about her mother's friends Marion and Bernadette, a lesbian couple in a longterm, stable relationship, whose lives are integrated with Feni's own. Despite conflicts and differences in perception, Rebecca and Feni come to understand and appreciate their similarities and their differences, and both grow because of the contact with the other. Feni begins to realize Rebecca's loneliness, the ways in which she misses her friends, and the loss she will face with the adoption of her child. She also begins to understand Rebecca's responsibilities, her need to care for her mother who suffers from depression. Rebecca becomes close with Bernadette, who tutors her, and with Marion, releasing the homophobia that she felt earlier, homophobia fueled by her mother's attitudes despite her earlier friendship with Marion. In the end, Rebecca names her child for Feni, and, in an open adoption, will be able to have some contact with her daughter. *The Dear One* indicates that lessening class conflicts and prejudices is possible through recognizing and respecting difference.

Woodson's writing becomes much more experimental in the interconnected short stories of *Autobiography of a Family Photo.* As Lee Lawton notes in her review of this book, "When you think of the great American novel...you probably wouldn't think of a slender, 113 page volume with prose as spare as poetry and just as descriptive." As Diane Paylor pointed out in *Ms.,* Woodson chose to explore the Vietnam era, the era of her childhood, in these often brutal yet poetic vignettes "because there are so many raw, unexplored feelings about how it affected African Americans." The unnamed narrator, despite her youth, realizes the dysfunction of her family, her community, her country. The realities of life in a house where a brother and a stepfather commit sexual abuse and where homophobia toward a gay son causes the father to say that Vietnam and the army will "make a man of him" (he doesn't return alive) are ironically contrasted with the predominantly white, mythically happy TV families of the time that the children watch. Troy, the oldest brother of five children, loves to dress up in his mother's clothes and heels. He plans to be a queen, and he tells the narrator that she would be a beautiful boy. When he is killed in the war, the entire family mourns, including the brother who denigrated Troy's homosexuality, and who cries under his covers for his loss.

The narrator herself is sexually ambiguous. Young, sexually abused by her brother, and experimenting sexually with her girlfriends, she looks to heterosexual sex as a means of identity, but she is a woman who doesn't like to wear dresses, who walks like her father, who doesn't care about making herself pretty for men. Lesbians will read the female desire in the narrator's question to her friend Marianna about whether or not she remembers their sexual closeness. All readers will recognize the survivor in the narrator, the woman who walks "to get out of some bad story where I'm the pitiful one." As Richard Labonte indicated in "Books," "there is a triumphant powerful girl at the end." As Catherine Bush notes in "A World Without Childhood," *Autobiography of a Family Photo* "is the best kind of survival guide: clear-eyed, gut-true."

Woodson's *I Hadn't Meant to Tell You This* discusses sexual abuse and cross-racial friendships. Like the young girls in *Autobiography of a Family Photo,* the girls know that there are places to go and people to tell, but they do not go to them, nor tell. Instead they go away in their heads, as did Woodson, according to her essay "A Stolen Childhood." Lena, a white child who admits the sexual abuse of her father to Marie, the narrator of this book, makes Marie promise not to tell for she does not want social services to separate her and her younger sister, Dion. *I Hadn't Meant to Tell You This,* like Woodson's "A Stolen Childhood," is a plea for breaking silence and for healing. But it is also much more, as this novel discusses racial and class prejudice, both black and white, interracial friendship, and the hope that people can accept each other simply because all *are* people. As Joyce Litton noted, this book "demonstrates that class and race are not always deterrents to understanding."

Lesbians will recognize themselves in Woodson's books. Maizon and Margaret in *Last Summer with Maizon, Maizon at Blue Hill,* and *Between Madison and Palmetto* are close friends whose differences strengthen their friendship, but as they grow older, Maizon does not express the interest in boys that Margaret is developing. Woodson's short story "Slipping Away" in *Am I Blue* is the story of a young woman who is coming to accept her sexual difference. The tensions in her own life, growing up lesbian and a writer in a family of Jehovah's Witnesses, infuses her writing and the video *Among Good Christian Peoples.* As Nancy St. Clair pointed out in "Outside Looking In," many of the lesbians in her college classes regret that they were not exposed to lesbian or gay literature earlier. Woodson's work is a contribution that can help to fill this void, for whether or not characters are explicitly lesbian or gay, the work is filled with the lesbian sensibility of the writer.

—Patti Capel Swartz

Z

ZAPATA, Luis

Nationality: Mexican novelist, short story writer, playwright, and translator. **Born:** Chilpancingo, Guerrero, 27 April 1951. **Education:** Universidad Nacional Autonoma de México, B.A. in medieval French literature. **Career:** Regular contributor to several Mexican newspapers and journals, including *Punto de Partida* and *Alianza Francesa*. **Awards:** IFAL (French short story prize), 1977; Juan Grijalbo Literary Prize, 1979.

WRITINGS

Novels

Hasta en las Mejores Familias ("Even in the Best of Families"). Mexico City, Organizacion Editorial Novaro, 1975.
Las Aventuras, Desventuras y Sueños de Adonis Garcia, el Vampiro de la Colonia Roma. Mexico City, Editorial Grijalbo, 1979; translated by E. A. Lacey as *Adonis Garcia: A Picaresque Novel.* San Francisco, Gay Sunshine Press, 1981.
De Pétalos Perenes ("Perennial Petals"). Mexico City, Editorial Katún, 1981.
Melodrama. Mexico City, Editorial Posada, 1983.
En Jirones ("In Tatters"). Mexico City, Editorial Posada, 1985.
La Hermana Secreta de Angélica Maria ("Angélica Maria's Secret Sister"). Mexico City, Cal y Arena, 1989.
¿Por Qué Mejor No Nos Vamos? ("Why Don't We Just Leave?"). Mexico City, Cal y Arena, 1992.

Short Stories

De Amor es Mi Negra Pena ("My Deep Dark Pain Is Love"). Mexico City, Panfleto y Pantomima, 1983.
Ese Amor que Hasta Ayer Nos Quemaba ("That Love that Until Yesterday Burned Us"). Mexico City, Editorial Posada, 1987.

Plays

La Fuerza del Amor ("The Power of Love"; first performed in 1989).
With José Joaquin Blanco, *La generosidad de los Axtra–os* ("The Generosity of Strangers"; produced in Mexico City, August 1990).

Other

Translator, with Angelina Martin del Campo, *Renart el zorro* (play; first performed in 1979).
Translator, *Bom-Crioulo* by Adolfo Caminha. Mexico City, Editorial Posada, 1987.
Luis Zapata. *De Cuerpo Entero: Las Cálidas Tardes del Cine Guerrero* (autobiography). Mexico City, UNAM/Corunda, 1990.
Translator, *Tristán e Isolda* (play; first performed in 1990).

*

Adaptations: *Melodrama* was adapted as a film, *Confidencias,* and a play (first performed in 1983).

Interviews: By Reinhard Teichmann, in *De La Onda en Adelante: Conversaciones con 21 Novelistas Mexicanos,* Mexico City, Editorial Posada, 1987.

Critical Sources: *My Deep Dark Pain Is Love: A Collection of Latin American Gay Fiction* edited by Winston Leyland, San Francisco, Gay Sunshine Press, 1983; "La Carne se Sestruye en el Desamor" by José Joaquin Blanco, in *La Jornada,* 9 November 1984, 20; *La Novela Mexicana (1967-1982),* Mexico City, Grijalbo, 1984; "The Poet of Subversive Imagination: Homosexual Utopian Discourse in Contemporary Mexico" by Claudia Shaefer-Rodriguez, in *Latin American Review,* Vol. 33, 1989, 29-41; *Gay and Lesbian Themes in Latin American Writing* by David William Foster, Austin, University of Texas Press, 1991; "Las Joterias de Luis" by Ignacio Trejo Fuentes, in *Unomásuno,* 12 December 1992.

*   *   *

The publication of Luis Zapata's sexually explicit gay novel *Las Aventuras, Desventuras y Sueños de Adonis Garcia, el Vampiro de la Colonia Roma* ("Adonis Garcia: A Picaresque Novel") in 1979 marked the beginning of this author's crusade to revolutionize the Mexican literary scene. Often employing experimental storytelling devices—stream of consciousness, grammatical play, cinematic style—Zapata gives voice to those who inhabit Mexico City's underworld, a sub-culture often represented by sensational tabloids as sexually dangerous and perverse. Zapata populates his novels, short stories, and dramatic productions with characters who struggle to survive in a world that refuses to acknowledge their humanity. Unlike many gay Latin American writers, however, he refuses to "glorify" those who live in the city's underbelly. Rather, he weaves a tapestry that blends together the full range of human possibility; gay characters aren't always free from the trappings of bourgeois idealism, for example. Indeed, his gay fringe-dwelling characters and narrators are just as caught up in the negative dynamics of power and desire as his "straight" middle-class characters. David William Foster writes, "Zapata never intended his fiction to be a plea for the sympathetic understanding of the tensions of a homosexual identity, and, very much in the tradition of John Rechy..., Zapata's principal concern has been to portray unflinchingly the wrenching conflicts of human relationships." Zapata's imagination reaches out to those caught in a middle-class, heterosexual social web that tells people how they must feel and behave; such a system for Zapata ensnares all, straight and queer, leading ultimately to frustrated love and alienation from the world.

In Zapata's first novel, *Hasta en las Mejores Familias* ("Even in the Best of Families"), the first-person narrator, Octavio Rivera, is not so preoccupied with his own sexuality—he's candidly gay—but rather with the meaning of his father's double sexual identity. Octavio's father spends his time masquerading as a macho, boasting at the dinner table of his military achievements. Octavio is shocked when he discovers his father's other life: he is a member of the "Caballeros Rectos," a club for transvestites and gays. Octavio's plight is not so much about coming to terms with his father's covert sexual identity, but about the pressure his father made him feel to grow up a heterosexual macho. The two worlds—supposedly straight and gay—begin to merge, spinning Octavio into a state of deep confusion. His narration (fragmented, grammatically iconoclastic, elliptic) not only reflects his psychic turmoil in a topsy-turvy world but it becomes his true refuge.

Outlawed sexuality, language, and alienation continue to inform Zapata's later novels. His narrator/character Adonis Garcia of *Las Aventuras* also grapples with what it means to exist in the linguistic and sexual margins. Drawing on interviews of gay male prostitutes in Mexico City, Zapata takes his readers into a cityscape filled with sexual "deviants," characters who make a living by offering up their bodies so members of the straight population can live out their same-sex fantasies. Although Adonis uses Mexican slang to give texture to this world, he is by no means uneducated. Rather, he is fully aware of the grand social and sexual hypocrisies, waxing poetic at his struggle to fit into a society that both rejects him by day and accepts him by night. Adonis's spirit is unbroken; he too finds a certain power and sanctuary in language and the telling of his story.

Zapata's other novels, such as *Melodrama* (1983), and *La Hermana Secreta de Angélica Maria* ("Angélica Maria's Secret Sister"; 1989), look at the universally destructive power wielded by the media to restrict behavior and channel sexual energy into buying commodities. In both of these works Zapata juxtaposes the literary style of the popular romance novel with that of the Mexican sentimental film. Such a stylistic pastiche foregrounds how the act of writing can itself function to shape the way people see the world. Zapata's highly self-conscious use of the different styles—hyperbole, cliché upon cliché, jumpcut effects, fade-ins and fade-outs—exposes the heterosexual middle-class lifestyle as an ideological construct. In *La Hermana*, the characters—an aspiring actress, a nightclub singer, and a movie addict—chase dreams of success and sexual fulfillment they have received through the mass media. Frustrated with their lack of success, they turn to makeup like movie-stand popcorn: Alba Maria visits a plastic surgeon who promises to make her into "la mujer de tus sueños" ("the woman of your dreams").

In Zapata's 1985 *En Jirones* ("In Tatters") we follow protagonist and narrator Sebastián's struggle to emotionally disentangle himself from a destructive relationship. Sebastián's lover, "A.", feels such a pressure to be a "productive" member of society that he denies his true love and marries a woman. The net result for both is emotional estrangement. Sebastián cruises bars and streets, identifying the absent "A." in each of the dismembered body parts he encounters; A.'s frustrated love for his wife and his inability to openly love Sebastián lead to violence and destruction, for he returns at the end to rape Sebastián. Fortunately, Sebastián finds strength in recollecting the events. He finds a certain fulfillment and empowerment in writing: "I would like to invent new insults, new ways to drag you through the mud, to demean you.... I would like to be able to invent worse insults...to really wound you in thought, word, and deed."

Zapata's characters—gay and straight—become alienated from themselves and the world when forced to restrict their sexuality to codes of behavior specifically organized for increased biological and material productivity. Their alienation inevitably ensues, for instance, when they are coerced into heterosexual marriage and are deprived of sexual gratification to be able to live out their middle-class dream. By giving voice to these processes of alienation, Zapata seems to be using the creative act of writing as a symbol and a means to explore the realm of infinite possibilities opened by the struggle for a truly human sexual identity.

—Frederick Luis Aldama

ZINOVYEVA-ANNIBAL, Lidiya

Nationality: Russian novelist, playwright, and author of short stories. **Born:** Zagorye, Mogilyov region, February 1866. **Family:** Married Vyacheslav Ivanov (second marriage), c. 1900; three children from previous marriage. **Career:** Hostess of the famous salon of the "Tower" group, 1905-10; contributor, to the illegal journal *Adskaya pochta* ("The Infernal Mail"), 1905-07. **Died:** Zagorye, October 1907.

WRITINGS

Kol'tsa: drama v trekh deystviyakh ("The Rings: A Drama in Three Acts"; stage play). 1904.
Tragichesky zverinets ("Tragic Menagerie"; short stories). 1907.
Tridstat' tri uroda ("Thirty-three Abominations"; novel). 1907.
Nyet! ("No!"; short stories). 1908.

*

Critical Sources: "Lidiya Zinovyeva-Annibal" by Temira Pachmuss, in *Women Writers in Russian Modernism, An Anthology,* translated and edited by Temira Pachmuss, Urbana, University of Illinois Press, 1978; "Lidia Dmitrievna Zinov'eva-Annibal" by Chris Tomei, in *An Encyclopedia of Continental Women Writers,* Vol. 2, edited by Katherina M. Wilson, New York, Garland Publishing, 1991, 1382-83.

*   *   *

Around the turn of the century, Lidiya Zinovyeva-Annibal separated from her first husband and settled in Italy with her three children. Later, in Switzerland, she met and married the Russian symbolist poet, Vyacheslav Ivanov, and returned with him to Russia in 1905, leaving her children behind in Geneva with a governess. The Ivanovs settled in St. Petersburg and there formed the famous literary salon known as the "Tower," which flourished from 1905 to 1910 and became known for its explorations in paganism and eroticism. The intellectual elite gathered at their home every Wednesday night to discuss Oscar Wilde, Friedrich Nietzsche, and neo-Kantian philosophy.

Zinovyeva-Annibal was particularly known for her eccentric and decadent behavior, typical of the Russian Decadents of the time. But as Temira Pachmuss points out in *Women Writers of Russian Modernism,* Zinovyeva-Annibal's eccentricities derived from a different source than many of her contemporaries: "her vagaries stemmed from an intense manifestation of life in all its exuberance; theirs, frequently from the vacuity and lack of vitality of their inner lives." It was this exuberance that formed the core of her writings.

Zinovyeva-Annibal's first publication was the verse play *The Rings* (1904), which was roundly criticized by contemporary reviewers who were preoccupied with the unconventional sensuality it displayed. She had hoped to create a new kind of symbolist theater in which there would be no stage and the actors could improvise their roles, breaking down the barriers associated with conventional theater. The play identifies passion and life itself with death and rebirth, as the heroine goes through a series of Dionysian trials, seeking to experience suffering as the stepping-stone to a realization of true love, which she comes to learn is eternal and cannot be subjected to the earthly circumstance of jealousy.

After the negative reviews of her daring attempt at transforming the theater, Zinovyeva-Annibal turned to fiction writing, producing her first collection of stories, *Tragic Menagerie,* in 1907. The stories, a collection of childhood memories, all feature the narrator, Vera, a young girl who possesses a strong sense of independence and a highly instinctive nature. In these stories, Vera encounters a series of animals and other children in depictions of nature that are barbaric rather than sentimental. The imagery is shocking and the language unusual and gripping, making these stories some of Zinovyeva-Annibal's most unusual but also the most highly praised.

Her next publication, a novel titled *Thirty-Three Abominations* (1907), is the first Russian novel to feature lesbian love. Pachmuss explains that this novel is responding to an outpouring of work by Russian authors that explored the themes of "sensuality and sexual perversion" in many forms. But one can also see that the sensuality of her earlier work here comes into its full fruition. Vera, now a beautiful actress, and her mistress, who is the narrator, are united in their love of an ideal of physical beauty that is woman-centered and not comprehensible by men. After posing in the nude for 33 male artists, Vera's mistress is distressed by their depictions of her. She calls their portraits 33 abominations because they are views of the female body necessarily warped by the male gaze. In contrast, the two women experience a heightened consciousness in their physical love for each other, insisting that the love of the soul is not comprehensible to them. "I do not need your soul, because your body is so beautiful," one of them says.

Her last work, published posthumously in 1908, was another collection of stories, titled *No!* This collection features a critique of the worsening social conditions of the time, a theme hinted at in *Tragic Menagerie,* but here explored in more detail.

—Anne Boyd

CUMULATIVE NAME INDEX

The bold number following each name refers to the volume of *Gay & Lesbian Literature* in which the entry appears; the number following the colon refers to the page on which the entry begins.

L

M

N

CUMULATIVE NATIONALITY INDEX

Authors are listed alphabetically under country of origin and/or their country of citizenship; the number following each name refers to the volume of *Gay & Lesbian Literature* in which the entry is located.

Argentina
Sylvia Molloy *2*
Manuel Puig *1*

Australia
Dennis Altman *1*
Helen Garner *2*
Gillian Eve Hanscombe *2*
David Malouf *2*
Henry Handel Richardson *2*
Patrick White *1*

Austria
Rainer Maria Rilke *2*
Grete von Urbanitzky *2*

Brazil
Adolpho Caminha *2*
Valery Pereleshin *2*

Canada
Nicole Brossard *2*
Emily Carr *2*
Michèle Causse *2*
Katherine V. Forrest *1*
Jane Rule *1*
Makeda Silvera *2*
David Watmough *1*

Cuba
Reinaldo Arenas *2*
Rafael Campo *2*
José Lezama Lima *1*
Achy Obejas *2*

France
Louis Aragon *2*
Natalie Barney *1*
Marie-Claire Blais *1*
Michèle Causse *2*
Hélène Cixous *2*
Jean Cocteau *1*
Colette *1*
Cyril Collard *2*
René Crevel *2*
Lucie Delarue-Mardrus *2*
Michel Foucault *1*
Jean Genet *1*
André Gide *1*
Hervé Guibert *2*
Guy Hocquenghem *1*
Max Jacob *2*
Violette Leduc *1*

Anais Nin *2*
Geneviève Pastre *2*
Marcel Proust *1*
Christiane Rochefort *2*
Michel Tournier *1*
Michel Tremblay *1*
Monique Wittig *1*
Marguerite Yourcenar *1*

Greece
Olga Broumas *2*
C. P. Cavafy *1*

Germany
Adolf Brand *2*
Rainer Werner Fassbinder *1*
Magnus Hirschfeld *1*
John Henry Mackay *2*
Thomas Mann *1*
Christa Reinig *2*
Verena Stefan *2*
Anna Elisabet Weirauch *2*
Christa Winsloe *1*

Haiti
Assotto Saint *2*

India
Suniti Manohar Namjoshi *2*
Pratibha Parmar *2*

Ireland
Elizabeth Bowen *1*
Roger Casement *2*
Emma Donoghue *2*
Neil Jordan *2*
Anna Livia *2*
Martin Ross *2*

Italy
Aldo Busi *1*
Gabriele D'Annunzio *2*
Teresa de Lauretis *2*
Pier Paolo Pasolini *1*
Sandro Penna *1*

Japan
Yukio Mishima *1*
Mutsuo Takahashi *2*

Jamaica
Michelle Cliff *2*
Makeda Silvera *2*

Sholem Asch *2*
John Ashbery *1*
James Baldwin *1*
Ann Bannon *1*
Djuna Barnes *1*
James Barr *2*
Katharine Lee Bates *2*
Joseph Fairchild Beam *2*
Alison Bechdel *2*
Arthur Bell *2*
Allan Bérubé *1*
Becky Birtha *1*
Elizabeth Bishop *2*
Alice Bloch *2*
Francesca Lia Block *2*
SDiane Adams Bogus *2*
John Boswell *1*
Jane Bowles *1*
Paul Bowles *1*
Blanche McCrary Boyd *1*
Malcolm Boyd *1*
Marion Zimmer Bradley *1*
Christopher Bram *1*
Susie Bright *2*
Poppy Z. Brite *2*
Michael Allen Bronski *2*
Romaine Brooks *1*
James Broughton *1*
Rebecca Brown *2*
Rita Mae Brown *1*
Charlotte Bunch *2*
William S. Burroughs *1*
Charles Busch *2*
Judith Butler *2*
Pat Califia *1*
Michael Lane Callen *2*
Peter Cameron *2*
Truman Capote *1*
Michael Cart *2*
Mary Casal *2*
Willa Cather *1*
Jane Chambers *1*
Robert Chesley *1*
Chrystos *2*
Cheryl Clarke *2*
Dennis Cooper *1*
Tee Corinne *1*
Anita Cornwell *2*
Hart Crane *1*
Mart Crowley *1*
Margaret Cruikshank *1*
Countee P. Cullen *2*
Michael Cunningham *2*
Daniel Curzon *1*
Mary Daly *1*
Samuel R. Delany *2*
Jane Delynn *2*
John D'Emilio *1*
Barbara Deming *2*
Alexis De Veaux *2*
Melvin Dixon *1*

Hilda Doolittle *1*
Mark Doty *2*
Coleman Dowell *2*
Sarah Dreher *2*
Martin Bauml Duberman *1*
Robert Duncan *1*
Cheryl Dunye *2*
Larry Duplechan *2*
Christopher Durang *1*
Andrea Dworkin *1*
Elana Dykewomon *2*
Wayne R. Dynes *1*
Lillian Faderman *1*
David B. Feinberg *1*
Leslie Feinberg *2*
Robert Ferro *1*
Harvey Fierstein *1*
Janet Flanner *1*
Charles Henri Ford *1*
Jeannette Howard Foster *1*
Estelle B. Freedman *2*
Aaron Fricke *2*
Marilyn Frye *2*
Marjorie Garber *2*
Sally Miller Gearhart *2*
Allen Ginsberg *1*
Gary Glickman *2*
Jewelle Gomez *1*
Brad Gooch *2*
Melinda Goodman *2*
William Goyen *2*
Judy Grahn *1*
David F. Greenberg *2*
Harlan Greene *1*
Barbara G. Grier *1*
Jim Grimsley *2*
Doris Grumbach *1*
Allan Gurganus *1*
Marilyn Hacker *2*
Richard W. Hall *1*
Joseph Hansen *1*
Bertha Harris *2*
Marsden Hartley *2*
Essex Hemphill *1*
Patricia Highsmith *1*
William M. Hoffman *2*
Andrew Holleran *1*
Holly Hughes *2*
Langston Hughes *1*
David Henry Hwang *2*
William Inge *2*
Christopher Isherwood *1*
Karla Jay *1*
Sarah Orne Jewett *2*
June Jordan *2*
Simon Karlinsky *2*
Jonathan Katz *1*
Melanie Kaye/Kantrowitz *2*
Joe Keenan *2*
Randall Kenan *1*
Jack Kerouac *1*

Willyce Kim *2*
James Kirkwood *2*
Irena Klepfisz *2*
Cappy Kotz *2*
Larry Kramer *1*
Tony Kushner *1*
Michael John Lassell *2*
Teresa de Lauretis *2*
David Leavitt *1*
Ursula K. Le Guin *1*
Winston Leyland *2*
Alain L. Locke *2*
Audre Lorde *1*
JoAnn Loulan *2*
Amy Lowell *1*
Craig Lucas *2*
Lee Lynch *2*
Phyllis Ann Lyon *1*
Eric Marcus *2*
Del Martin *1*
Paula Martinac *1*
Carole Maso *2*
Armistead Maupin *1*
Robert McAlmon *1*
Stephen D. McCauley *2*
Carson McCullers *1*
Claude McKay *2*
Terrence McNally *1*
Marijane Meaker *2*
Gordon Merrick *2*
James Ingram Merrill *1*
Edna St. Vincent Millay *1*
Neil Miller *1*
Kate Millett *1*
Valerie Miner *2*
Richard Drake Mohr *2*
Paul Monette *1*
Cherríe Moraga *1*
Ethan Mordden *1*
Robin Morgan *2*
Bruce Shannon Morrow *2*
Cherry Muhanji *2*
Michael A. Nava *2*
Joan Nestle *1*
Lesléa Newman *1*
Richard Bruce Nugent *2*
Achy Obejas *2*
Frank O'Hara *1*
Camille Paglia *2*
Pat Parker *1*
Robert Patrick *1*
Dale Peck *2*
Julia Penelope *2*
Troy D. Perry *2*
Fritz Peters *2*
Thomas Hal Phillips *2*
Felice Picano *1*
Cole Porter *2*
Minnie Bruce Pratt *1*
John Preston *1*

Deb Price *2*
James Purdy *1*
Lev Raphael *1*
John Rechy *1*
Anne Rice *2*
Adrienne Rich *1*
Marlon Troy Riggs *2*
Ruthann Robson *2*
Robert Rodi *2*
Ned Rorem *1*
Will Roscoe *2*
Alma Routsong *1*
Muriel Rukeyser *2*
Joanna Russ *1*
Vito Russo *1*
Edward Sagarin *1*
May Sarton *1*
Sarah Schulman *1*
Sandra Scoppettone *1*
Mab Segrest *2*
Martin Sherman *1*
Randy Shilts *1*
Ann Allen Shockley *1*
Elaine Showalter *2*
Barbara Smith *1*
Lillian Smith *2*
Jack Spicer *1*
George Stambolian *2*
James D. Steakley *2*
Gertrude Stein *1*
Samuel M. Steward *1*
May Swenson *2*
Sara Teasdale *1*
Megan Terry *2*
Wallace Thurman *2*
Alice B. Toklas *1*
David Trinidad *2*
Kitty Tsui *2*
Parker Tyler *1*
Urvashi Vaid *2*
Gore Vidal *1*
Donald Vining *2*
Alice Walker *2*
Patricia Nell Warren *1*
Glenway Wescott *2*
Edmund White *1*
Gale Wilhelm *2*
Michael Willhoite *2*
Tennessee Williams *1*
Barbara Wilson *1*
Doric Wilson *1*
Lanford Wilson *1*
Fran Winant *2*
Mary Wings *2*
Terry Wolverton *2*
Norman Wong *2*
Jacqueline Woodson *2*
Marguerite Yourcenar *1*
Bonnie Zimmerman *1*

GENERAL SUBJECT AND GENRE INDEX

Abuse or Abusive Relationships
Coleman Dowell
Jim Grimsley
Cherry Muhanji
Dale Peck
Christiane Rochefort
David Trinidad
Jacqueline Woodson

Acceptance
Gerd Brantenberg
Michael Cart
Sarah Orne Jewett
Claude McKay

Activism, Gay and Lesbian
James Barr
Arthur Bell
Adolf Brand
Gerd Brantenberg
Michael Allen Bronski
Nicole Brossard
Charlotte Bunch
Michael Lane Callen
Michèle Causse
Cheryl Dunye
Elana Dykewomon
Leslie Feinberg
Aaron Fricke
Sally Miller Gearhart
David Henry Hwang
Melanie Kaye/Kantrowitz
Geneviève Pastre
Julia Penelope
Troy D. Perry
Urvashi Vaid
Donald Vining
Simon Watney
Fran Winant

Adolescence and Sexuality
Michael Cart
Michael Cunningham
Aaron Fricke
Gary Glickman
Melinda Goodman
David Malouf
Marijane Meaker
Fritz Peters
Deb Price
Glenway Wescott
Norman Wong
Jacqueline Woodson

Ageism/Aging
Donald Vining

AIDS
Reinaldo Arenas
Francesca Lia Block
Poppy Z. Brite

Michael Allen Bronski
Rebecca Brown
Michael Lane Callen
Rafael Campo
Cyril Collard
Michael Cunningham
Mark Doty
Larry Duplechan
Brad Gooch
Hervé Guibert
Marilyn Hacker
William M. Hoffman
June Jordan
Craig Lucas
Carole Maso
Marijane Meaker
Richard Drake Mohr
Dale Peck
Deb Price
George Stambolian
Kitty Tsui
Alice Walker
Simon Watney

Alienation
Paul Bailey
Michael Cunningham
Juan Goytisolo
David Malouf
Rainer Maria Rilke
Christiane Rochefort
Frank Sargeson
Luis Zapata

Androgyny
Gabriele D'Annunzio
Vasily Vasilievich Rozanov
Lytton Strachey
May Swenson

Art Criticism
René Crevel
Marsden Hartley
Alain L. Locke
Simon Watney

Autobiography/Biography
Margaret C. Anderson
Reinaldo Arenas
Charles Busch
Emily Carr
Mary Casal
Michelle Cliff
Gabriele D'Annunzio
Lucie Delarue-Mardrus
Barbara Deming
Larry Duplechan
Leslie Feinberg
Janet Frame
Aaron Fricke
Brad Gooch

Juan Goytisolo
Hervé Guibert
Marilyn Hacker
Marsden Hartley
Simon Karlinsky
Evgeny Vladimirovich Kharitonov
Lee Lynch
John Henry Mackay
David Malouf
Rosemary Joy Manning
Eric Marcus
Carole Maso
Claude McKay
Marijane Meaker
Robin Morgan
Michael A. Nava
Richard Bruce Nugent
Achy Obejas
Dale Peck
Valery Pereleshin
Troy D. Perry
Rachid O.
Henry Handel Richardson
Marlon Troy Riggs
Rainer Maria Rilke
Christiane Rochefort
Muriel Rukeyser
Mab Segrest
Lillian Smith
Lytton Strachey
Wallace Thurman
Alice Walker
Glenway Wescott
Norman Wong

Bisexuality
Francesca Lia Block
Samuel R. Delany
Marjorie Garber
June Jordan
Willyce Kim
Claude McKay
Robin Morgan
Henry Handel Richardson
Christiane Rochefort
Marina Tsvetaeva

Butch/Femme
Leslie Feinberg
Melinda Goodman
Lee Lynch
Marijane Meaker
Kitty Tsui

Children's/Young Adult Literature
Francesca Lia Block
Michael Cart
Alexis De Veaux
Rosemary Joy Manning
Muriel Rukeyser
Makeda Silvera

May Swenson
Michael Willhoite
Jacqueline Woodson

Coming Out
James Barr
Alice Bloch
Michael Cunningham
Aaron Fricke
Eric Marcus
Marijane Meaker
Michael A. Nava
Julia Penelope
Rachid O.
Muriel Rukeyser
Kitty Tsui
Jacqueline Woodson

Death
Margaret C. Anderson
Rebecca Brown
Adolpho Caminha
René Crevel
Countée P. Cullen
Michael Cunningham
Gabriele D'Annunzio
Aaron Fricke
Hervé Guibert
Marilyn Hacker
June Jordan
Nikolai Alekseeivich Kliuev
Michael John Lassell
Rosemary Joy Manning
Carole Maso
Dale Peck
Mab Segrest
Esther Tusquets
Jacqueline Woodson
Lidiya Zinovyeva-Annibal

Diaries
Emily Carr
Roger Casement
Anais Nin
Donald Vining

Drama
Sherwood Anderson
Sholem Asch
Paul Bailey
Jacinto Benavente
SDiane Adams Bogus
Charles Busch
Nancy Cárdenás
Hélène Cixous
Cheryl Clarke
Countee P. Cullen
Gabriele D'Annunzio
Alexis De Veaux
Lucie Delarue-Mardrus
Emma Donoghue

Coleman Dowell
Sarah Dreher
Helen Garner
William Goyen
Jim Grimsley
Gillian Eve Hanscombe
William M. Hoffman
William Douglas Home
Holly Hughes
David Henry Hwang
William Inge
June Jordan
Joe Keenan
Evgeny Vladimirovich Kharitonov
James Kirkwood
Cappy Kotz
Hanif Kureishi
Craig Lucas
Yulisa Amadu Maddy
Richard Bruce Nugent
Geneviève Pastre
Rainer Maria Rilke
Assotto Saint
Frank Sargeson
Lillian Smith
Megan Terry
Wallace Thurman
Anna Elisabet Weirauch
Luis Zapata
Lidiya Zinovyeva-Annibal

Editing
Margaret C. Anderson
Joseph Fairchild Beam
Adolf Brand
Charlotte Bunch
Countee P. Cullen
Juan Goytisolo
Marilyn Hacker
William M. Hoffman
Sarah Orne Jewett
Irena Klepfisz
Winston Leyland
Alain L. Locke
Bruce Shannon Morrow
Pratibha Parmar
Makeda Silvera
George Stambolian
James D. Steakley
Wallace Thurman
Donald Vining
Alice Walker

Education
Melanie Kaye/Kantrowitz

Encoding/Oblique or Masked References
Jacinto Benavente
Roger Casement
Lucie Delarue-Mardrus
William Douglas Home

William Inge
Max Jacob
David Malouf
Richard Bruce Nugent
Henry Handel Richardson
Frank Sargeson
Lillian Smith
May Swenson
Wallace Thurman
Marina Tsvetaeva

Eroticism
Anna Andreyevna Akhmatova
Susie Bright
Olga Broumas
Chrystos
Gabriele D'Annunzio
Lucie Delarue-Mardrus
Alexis De Veaux
Coleman Dowell
Melinda Goodman
William Goyen
Bertha Harris
Cappy Kotz
Winston Leyland
Rosemary Joy Manning
Anais Nin
Valery Pereleshin
Lillian Smith
Lytton Strachey
Mutsuo Takahashi
Terry Wolverton
Lidiya Zinovyeva-Annibal

Essays
Lisa Alther
SDiane Adams Bogus
Karin Boye
Rafael Campo
Roger Casement
Michèle Causse
Chrystos
Hélène Cixous
Cheryl Clarke
Anita Cornwell
Lucie Delarue-Mardrus
Barbara Deming
Larry Duplechan
Elana Dykewomon
Marilyn Frye
Marilyn Hacker
Sarah Orne Jewett
June Jordan
Simon Karlinsky
Melanie Kaye/Kantrowitz
Irena Klepfisz
Michael John Lassell
Teresa de Lauretis
Alain L. Locke
Craig Lucas
John Henry Mackay

Eric Marcus
Claude McKay
Valerie Miner
Robin Morgan
Suniti Manohar Namjoshi
Michael A. Nava
Geneviève Pastre
Julia Penelope
Christiane Rochefort
Martin Ross
Vasily Vasilievich Rozanov
Mab Segrest
Lytton Strachey
May Swenson
Mutsuo Takahashi
Wallace Thurman
Gennady Trifonov
Kitty Tsui
Marina Tsvetaeva
Donald Vining
Simon Watney
Glenway Wescott

Expatriate Community
Sally Miller Gearhart
Glenway Wescott

Family/Societal Relationships
Paul Bailey
Elizabeth Bishop
Anna Blaman
Alice Bloch
Francesca Lia Block
Gerd Brantenberg
Sara Levi Calderon
Peter Cameron
Rafael Campo
Emily Carr
Michael Cart
Chrystos
Countee P. Cullen
Michael Cunningham
Emma Donoghue
Coleman Dowell
Brad Gooch
Melinda Goodman
William Goyen
Juan Goytisolo
Jim Grimsley
Bertha Harris
Holly Hughes
Neil Jordan
James Kirkwood
Irena Klepfisz
JoAnn Loulan
Yulisa Amadu Maddy
Rosemary Joy Manning
Eric Marcus
Carole Maso
Stephen D. McCauley
Gordon Merrick

Valerie Miner
Richard Drake Mohr
Robin Morgan
Bruce Shannon Morrow
Dale Peck
Fritz Peters
Henry Handel Richardson
Rainer Maria Rilke
Ruthann Robson
Christiane Rochefort
Martin Ross
Makeda Silvera
David Trinidad
Esther Tusquets
Urvashi Vaid
Donald Vining
Alice Walker
Michael Willhoite
Norman Wong
Jacqueline Woodson
Luis Zapata

Feminism
Jeffner Allen
Katharine Lee Bates
Nicole Brossard
Charlotte Bunch
Hélène Cixous
Anita Cornwell
Barbara Deming
Marilyn Frye
Ellen Galford
Helen Garner
Marilyn Hacker
Gillian Eve Hanscombe
Holly Hughes
Melanie Kaye/Kantrowitz
Irena Klepfisz
Selma Lagerlof
Teresa de Lauretis
Valerie Miner
Robin Morgan
Pratibha Parmar
Julia Penelope
Christa Reinig
Christiane Rochefort
Muriel Rukeyser
Mab Segrest
Elaine Showalter
Makeda Silvera
James D. Steakley
Verena Stefan
Megan Terry

Fiction (Genre)
Sara Levi Calderon
Alexis De Veaux
Elana Dykewomon
Sarah Orne Jewett
Evgeny Vladimirovich Kharitonov
Winston Leyland

Bruce Shannon Morrow
Michael A. Nava
Verena Stefan

Fiction (Novels)
Lisa Alther
Sherwood Anderson
Louis Aragon
Reinaldo Arenas
Sholem Asch
Paul Bailey
James Barr
Anna Blaman
Alice Bloch
Francesca Lia Block
Karin Boye
Gerd Brantenberg
Nicole Brossard
Rebecca Brown
Charles Busch
Peter Cameron
Adolpho Caminha
Emily Carr
Michael Cart
Michelle Cliff
Cyril Collard
René Crevel
Michael Cunningham
Gabriele D'Annunzio
Samuel R. Delany
Lucie Delarue-Mardrus
Jane Delynn
Barbara Deming
Emma Donoghue
Coleman Dowell
Sarah Dreher
Larry Duplechan
Elana Dykewomon
Leslie Feinberg
Janet Frame
Ellen Galford
Helen Garner
Sally Miller Gearhart
Gary Glickman
Brad Gooch
William Goyen
Juan Goytisolo
Jim Grimsley
Hervé Guibert
Gillian Eve Hanscombe
Bertha Harris
William Inge
Max Jacob
Neil Jordan
Joe Keenan
Willyce Kim
James Kirkwood
Cappy Kotz
Hanif Kureishi
Selma Lagerlof
Anna Livia

Lee Lynch
John Henry Mackay
Yulisa Amadu Maddy
David Malouf
Rosemary Joy Manning
Carole Maso
Stephen D. McCauley
Marijane Meaker
Gordon Merrick
Valerie Miner
Sylvia Molloy
Cherry Muhanji
Anais Nin
Dale Peck
Fritz Peters
Thomas Hal Phillips
Christa Reinig
Anne Rice
Henry Handel Richardson
Rainer Maria Rilke
Ruthann Robson
Christiane Rochefort
Robert Rodi
Martin Ross
Frank Sargeson
Lillian Smith
Mutsuo Takahashi
Wallace Thurman
Kitty Tsui
Esther Tusquets
Grete von Urbanitzky
Alice Walker
Anna Elisabet Weirauch
Glenway Wescott
Gale Wilhelm
Mary Wings
Terry Wolverton
Norman Wong
Jacqueline Woodson
Luis Zapata
Lidiya Zinovyeva-Annibal

Fiction (Short Stories)
Lisa Alther
Sherwood Anderson
James Barr
Anna Blaman
Francesca Lia Block
SDiane Adams Bogus
Poppy Z. Brite
Rebecca Brown
Peter Cameron
Emily Carr
Chrystos
Cheryl Clarke
Michelle Cliff
Anita Cornwell
Michael Cunningham
Gabriele D'Annunzio
Barbara Deming
Coleman Dowell

Joe Keenan
James Kirkwood
Irena Klepfisz
Hanif Kureishi
Anna Livia
JoAnn Loulan
Craig Lucas
Marijane Meaker
Gordon Merrick
Christa Reinig
Marlon Troy Riggs
Robert Rodi
Mab Segrest
Makeda Silvera
Lillian Smith
Urvashi Vaid
Anna Elisabet Weirauch
Jacqueline Woodson

Horror
Poppy Z. Brite
Jim Grimsley
Anne Rice

Humor/Satire
Lisa Alther
Alison Bechdel
Jacinto Benavente
Charles Busch
Jane Delynn
Ellen Galford
Helen Garner
Neil Jordan
Joe Keenan
James Kirkwood
Robert Rodi
Donald Vining
Michael Willhoite
Mary Wings

Institutional Repression/Oppression
Reinaldo Arenas
Jacinto Benavente
Adolf Brand
Gerd Brantenberg
Charlotte Bunch
Roger Casement
Chrystos
Michelle Cliff
Anita Cornwell
Alexis De Veaux
Neil Jordan
Joe Keenan
Teresa de Lauretis
Yulisa Amadu Maddy
Eric Marcus
Claude McKay
Robin Morgan
Christa Reinig
Christiane Rochefort
Makeda Silvera

Verena Stefan
Alice Walker
Jacqueline Woodson

Journalism—Print/Broadcast
Sherwood Anderson
Louis Aragon
Reinaldo Arenas
Arthur Bell
Michael Cart
Gabriele D'Annunzio
Lucie Delarue-Mardrus
Jane Delynn
Barbara Deming
Helen Garner
Hervé Guibert
Valerie Miner
Robin Morgan
Achy Obejas
Deb Price
Muriel Rukeyser
Grete von Urbanitzky
Simon Watney

Laws/ Legislation
Adolf Brand
Ruthann Robson

Lesbianism
Margaret C. Anderson
Louis Aragon
Sholem Asch
Katharine Lee Bates
Alison Bechdel
Elizabeth Bishop
Anna Blaman
Alice Bloch
Francesca Lia Block
SDiane Adams Bogus
Karin Boye
Susie Bright
Nicole Brossard
Olga Broumas
Rebecca Brown
Charlotte Bunch
Sara Levi Calderon
Nancy Cárdenas
Mary Casal
Michèle Causse
Chrystos
Hélène Cixous
Cheryl Clarke
Anita Cornwell
Lucie Delarue-Mardrus
Jane Delynn
Alexis De Veaux
Emma Donoghue
Sarah Dreher
Cheryl Dunye
Elana Dykewomon
Leslie Feinberg
Estelle B. Freedman

Marilyn Frye
Ellen Galford
Sally Miller Gearhart
Melinda Goodman
Marilyn Hacker
Gillian Eve Hanscombe
Bertha Harris
Holly Hughes
Sarah Orne Jewett
June Jordan
Melanie Kaye/Kantrowitz
Willyce Kim
Irena Klepfisz
Cappy Kotz
Teresa de Lauretis
Anna Livia
JoAnn Loulan
Lee Lynch
Rosemary Joy Manning
Carole Maso
Marijane Meaker
Valerie Miner
Sylvia Molloy
Robin Morgan
Cherry Muhanji
Suniti Manohar Namjoshi
Achy Obejas
Pratibha Parmar
Geneviève Pastre
Julia Penelope
Christa Reinig
Henry Handel Richardson
Ruthann Robson
Christiane Rochefort
Mab Segrest
Makeda Silvera
James D. Steakley
Verena Stefan
May Swenson
Kitty Tsui
Marina Tsvetaeva
Esther Tusquets
Grete von Urbanitzky
Alice Walker
Anna Elisabet Weirauch
Gale Wilhelm
Fran Winant
Mary Wings
Terry Wolverton
Jacqueline Woodson

Letters/Correspondence
Max Jacob
Sarah Orne Jewett
Selma Lagerlof
Suniti Manohar Namjoshi
Gennady Trifonov
Marina Tsvetaeva

Linguistics
Anna Livia
Christiane Rochefort

Literary Criticism
Hélène Cixous
Cheryl Clarke
Mark Doty
Marjorie Garber
Juan Goytisolo
Bertha Harris
Alain L. Locke
David Malouf
Sylvia Molloy
Vasily Vasilievich Rozanov
Muriel Rukeyser
Elaine Showalter
Lytton Strachey

Literature/Literary Movements
Michael Cart
Mutsuo Takahashi

Marginality
Reinaldo Arenas
Paul Bailey
James Barr
Joseph Fairchild Beam
SDiane Adams Bogus
Adolpho Caminha
Rafael Campo
Emily Carr
Cheryl Clarke
Mark Doty
Helen Garner
Juan Goytisolo
Jim Grimsley
Gillian Eve Hanscombe
Neil Jordan
James Kirkwood
Hanif Kureishi
Rosemary Joy Manning
Marijane Meaker
Achy Obejas
Julia Penelope
Christiane Rochefort
Frank Sargeson
David Trinidad
Alice Walker
Simon Watney
Anna Elisabet Weirauch
Jacqueline Woodson
Luis Zapata

Mateship
Michael Cunningham
Deb Price
David Trinidad
Kitty Tsui
Donald Vining

Medicine/Science/Technology
James Barr

Memoirs
Paul Bailey

Katharine Lee Bates
Jacinto Benavente
Elizabeth Bishop
Anna Blaman
Alice Bloch
Francesca Lia Block
SDiane Adams Bogus
Karin Boye
Rupert Brooke
Nicole Brossard
Olga Broumas
Adolpho Caminha
Rafael Campo
Nancy Cárdenas
Roger Casement
Michèle Causse
Chrystos
Cheryl Clarke
Michelle Cliff
René Crevel
Countee P. Cullen
Gabriele D'Annunzio
Lucie Delarue-Mardrus
Barbara Deming
Alexis De Veaux
Mark Doty
Elana Dykewomon
Janet Frame
Brad Gooch
Melinda Goodman
Marilyn Hacker
Gillian Eve Hanscombe
Marsden Hartley
Max Jacob
June Jordan
Melanie Kaye/Kantrowitz
Willyce Kim
Irena Klepfisz
Nikolai Alekseeivich Kliuev
Michael John Lassell
John Henry Mackay
David Malouf
Claude McKay
Robin Morgan
Cherry Muhanji
Suniti Manohar Namjoshi
Richard Bruce Nugent
Geneviève Pastre
Valery Pereleshin
Christa Reinig
Rainer Maria Rilke
Muriel Rukeyser
Assotto Saint
Verena Stefan
May Swenson
Mutsuo Takahashi
Gennady Trifonov
David Trinidad
Kitty Tsui
Marina Tsvetaeva
Grete von Urbanitzky

Fran Winant
Terry Wolverton

Politics/Political and Social History
Jeffner Allen
Louis Aragon
Alison Bechdel
Alice Bloch
SDiane Adams Bogus
Adolf Brand
Michael Allen Bronski
Nicole Brossard
Olga Broumas
Charlotte Bunch
Judith Butler
Roger Casement
Cheryl Clarke
Anita Cornwell
Jane Delynn
Barbara Deming
Larry Duplechan
Elana Dykewomon
Leslie Feinberg
Estelle B. Freedman
Helen Garner
Sally Miller Gearhart
David F. Greenberg
Marilyn Hacker
Gillian Eve Hanscombe
David Henry Hwang
June Jordan
Melanie Kaye/Kantrowitz
Irena Klepfisz
Hanif Kureishi
Craig Lucas
John Henry Mackay
Valerie Miner
Richard Drake Mohr
Pratibha Parmar
Muriel Rukeyser
Mab Segrest
James D. Steakley
Verena Stefan
Kitty Tsui
Urvashi Vaid
Simon Watney

Pornography
Gabriele D'Annunzio
Christiane Rochefort

Prostitution
Sholem Asch
Christiane Rochefort

Psychology
Louis Aragon
Karin Boye
Teresa de Lauretis
Lytton Strachey

Race Relations/Multiculturalism
Joseph Fairchild Beam
SDiane Adams Bogus
Olga Broumas
Adolpho Caminha
Emily Carr
Chrystos
Cheryl Clarke
Michelle Cliff
Anita Cornwell
Countee P. Cullen
Michael Cunningham
Samuel R. Delany
Alexis De Veaux
Emma Donoghue
Coleman Dowell
Cheryl Dunye
Larry Duplechan
Estelle B. Freedman
Melinda Goodman
Marilyn Hacker
David Henry Hwang
June Jordan
Neil Jordan
Melanie Kaye/Kantrowitz
Irena Klepfisz
Hanif Kureishi
Teresa de Lauretis
Winston Leyland
Alain L. Locke
Claude McKay
Robin Morgan
Bruce Shannon Morrow
Cherry Muhanji
Suniti Manohar Namjoshi
Richard Bruce Nugent
Thomas Hal Phillips
Marlon Troy Riggs
Muriel Rukeyser
Assotto Saint
Mab Segrest
Makeda Silvera
Lillian Smith
Wallace Thurman
Kitty Tsui
Alice Walker
Norman Wong
Jacqueline Woodson
Luis Zapata

Radio
Hanif Kureishi
Christa Reinig
Terry Wolverton

Recordings
Anna Blaman
Francesca Lia Block
SDiane Adams Bogus
Susie Bright
Rebecca Brown

Cheryl Clarke
Emma Donoghue
Mark Doty
Elana Dykewomon
Marilyn Hacker
Holly Hughes
June Jordan
Cappy Kotz
David Malouf
Claude McKay
Muriel Rukeyser
May Swenson
Alice Walker

Religion/Spirituality
Sholem Asch
Karin Boye
Nicole Brossard
Chrystos
Countee P. Cullen
Larry Duplechan
Gary Glickman
Brad Gooch
William Goyen
Jim Grimsley
Marilyn Hacker
Max Jacob
Melanie Kaye/Kantrowitz
Irena Klepfisz
Winston Leyland
Craig Lucas
Camille Paglia
Valery Pereleshin
Troy D. Perry
Fritz Peters
Rainer Maria Rilke
Will Roscoe
Vasily Vasilievich Rozanov
Mutsuo Takahashi
Esther Tusquets

Sadism/Sadomasochism
Gabriele D'Annunzio
Hervé Guibert
Esther Tusquets

Science Fiction
Samuel R. Delany

Sexual Ambiguity/Ambivalence
Jacinto Benavente
Rupert Brooke
Peter Cameron
René Crevel
Lucie Delarue-Mardrus
Teresa de Lauretis
David Malouf

Sexual Health/Safety/Education
Michael Lane Callen
Rafael Campo

JoAnn Loulan
Terry Wolverton

Sexual Identity
Sherwood Anderson
James Barr
Francesca Lia Block
Judith Butler
Rafael Campo
Nancy Cárdenas
Michael Cart
Mary Casal
Michèle Causse
Michelle Cliff
Cyril Collard
Michael Cunningham
Emma Donoghue
Sarah Dreher
Larry Duplechan
Helen Garner
Gary Glickman
Brad Gooch
Juan Goytisolo
David F. Greenberg
Evgeny Vladimirovich Kharitonov
Nikolai Alekseeivich Kliuev
Hanif Kureishi
Selma Lagerlof
Michael John Lassell
Anna Livia
JoAnn Loulan
Craig Lucas
Eric Marcus
Gordon Merrick
Sylvia Molloy
Camille Paglia
Geneviève Pastre
Thomas Hal Phillips
Christa Reinig
Rainer Maria Rilke
Christiane Rochefort
Lillian Smith
Mutsuo Takahashi
Megan Terry
Gennady Trifonov
David Trinidad
Norman Wong
Luis Zapata

Sexuality/Gender Roles
Jeffner Allen
Sherwood Anderson
Louis Aragon
Francesca Lia Block
Gerd Brantenberg
Poppy Z. Brite
Nicole Brossard
Adolpho Caminha
Nancy Cárdenas
Mary Casal
Michèle Causse

Hélène Cixous
Michael Cunningham
Jane Delynn
Barbara Deming
Alexis De Veaux
Coleman Dowell
Larry Duplechan
Estelle B. Freedman
Marjorie Garber
William Goyen
Juan Goytisolo
David F. Greenberg
Hervé Guibert
William Douglas Home
David Henry Hwang
William Inge
Sarah Orne Jewett
June Jordan
Neil Jordan
Melanie Kaye/Kantrowitz
James Kirkwood
Hanif Kureishi
Michael John Lassell
Yulisa Amadu Maddy
Rosemary Joy Manning
Claude McKay
Gordon Merrick
Robin Morgan
Camille Paglia
Pratibha Parmar
Cole Porter
Deb Price
Rachid O.
Martin Ross
Vasily Vasilievich Rozanov
Mab Segrest
Elaine Showalter
Makeda Silvera
Lillian Smith
George Stambolian
Verena Stefan
Megan Terry
Marina Tsvetaeva
Lidiya Zinovyeva-Annibal

Social Commentary
Louis Aragon
Reinaldo Arenas
James Barr
Arthur Bell
Jacinto Benavente
Adolf Brand
Gerd Brantenberg
Michael Allen Bronski
Nicole Brossard
Adolpho Caminha
Roger Casement
Cheryl Clarke
Jane Delynn
Alexis De Veaux
Cheryl Dunye

Larry Duplechan
Marjorie Garber
Hervé Guibert
Gillian Eve Hanscombe
Holly Hughes
Simon Karlinsky
Melanie Kaye/Kantrowitz
Anna Livia
Craig Lucas
Yulisa Amadu Maddy
Valerie Miner
Richard Drake Mohr
Bruce Shannon Morrow
Geneviève Pastre
Julia Penelope
Deb Price
Rainer Maria Rilke
Robert Rodi
Mab Segrest
Elaine Showalter
Verena Stefan
Mutsuo Takahashi
David Trinidad
Lidiya Zinovyeva-Annibal

Stereotypes
Michael Lane Callen
Alexis De Veaux
Coleman Dowell
Larry Duplechan
David Henry Hwang
Neil Jordan
Joe Keenan
Rachid O.
Martin Ross
Vasily Vasilievich Rozanov
Grete von Urbanitzky

Stonewall Rebellion, 1969
Arthur Bell
Brad Gooch

Teaching/Academia
Katharine Lee Bates
Judith Butler
Mark Doty
Estelle B. Freedman
Marilyn Frye
Marjorie Garber
Sally Miller Gearhart
Melinda Goodman
David F. Greenberg
June Jordan
Simon Karlinsky
JoAnn Loulan
Carole Maso
Richard Drake Mohr
Camille Paglia
Julia Penelope
Marlon Troy Riggs
Elaine Showalter

George Stambolian
James D. Steakley
David Trinidad

Television
William Douglas Home
Joe Keenan

Third Sex
Will Roscoe

Translations
Anna Andreyevna Akhmatova
Gerd Brantenberg
Nicole Brossard
Olga Broumas
Michèle Causse
Marilyn Hacker
Irena Klepfisz
Teresa de Lauretis
Henry Handel Richardson
Christiane Rochefort
Muriel Rukeyser
May Swenson
Marina Tsvetaeva
Grete von Urbanitzky
Luis Zapata

Transgenderism
Francesca Lia Block
Leslie Feinberg
Marjorie Garber
Christa Reinig
Vasily Vasilievich Rozanov

Travel Writing
Juan Goytisolo

Violence
Arthur Bell
Charlotte Bunch
Cyril Collard
Lucie Delarue-Mardrus
Barbara Deming
Alexis De Veaux
William Goyen
Jim Grimsley
Bertha Harris
Melanie Kaye/Kantrowitz
James Kirkwood
Achy Obejas
Frank Sargeson
Makeda Silvera
Gennady Trifonov
Esther Tusquets
Luis Zapata

Visual Arts
Marsden Hartley
Michael Willhoite
Fran Winant
Terry Wolverton

War
James Barr
Rupert Brooke
James Kirkwood

Western Adventure
Willyce Kim

Women's Studies
Olga Broumas
Estelle B. Freedman
Marilyn Frye
Valerie Miner

GAY AND LESBIAN LITERARY AWARDS

American Library Association Gay/Lesbian Book Award

1997   **Nonfiction**
Geography of the Heart: A Memoir, Fenton Johnson

Literature
Hood, Emma Donoghue

1996   **Nonfiction**
Virtual Equality: The Mainstreaming of Gay and Lesbian Liberation, Urvashi Vaid

Literature
Dream Boy, Jim Grimsley

1995   **Nonfiction**
Skin: Talking about Sex, Class & Literature, Dorothy Allison

Literature
Uncommon Heroes: A Celebration of Heroes and Role Models for Gay and Lesbian Americans, Phillip Sherman and Samuel Bernstein

1994   **Nonfiction**
Family Values: Two Moms and Their Son, Phyllis Burke

Literature
Stone Butch Blues, Leslie Feinberg

1993   **Nonfiction**
Making History: The Struggle for Gay and Lesbian Equal Rights, 1945-1990, An Oral History, Eric Marcus

Literature
Ceremonies: Prose and Poetry, Essex Hemphill

1992   **Nonfiction**
Odd Girls and Twilight Lovers: A History of Lesbian Life in Twentieth Century America, Lillian Faderman

Literature
Halfway Home, Paul Monette

1991   **Nonfiction**
Encyclopedia of Homosexuality, Wayne Dynes, Editor

Literature
Crime Against Nature, Minnie Bruce Pratt

1990   **Nonfiction**
In Search of Gay America: Women and Men in a Time of Change, Neil Miller

Literature
Eighty-Sixed, David B. Feinberg

Exceptional Achievement
Armistead Maupin, "Tales of the City" Series

1989   *After Delores*, Sarah Schulman

The Swimming-Pool Library, Alan Hollinghurst

1988   *And the Band Played On: Politics, People, and the AIDS Epidemic*, Randy Shilts

A Restricted Country, Joan Nestle

1987   *The Spirit and the Flesh: Sexual Diversity in American Indian Culture*, Walter Williams

1986   *Sex and Germs: The Politics of AIDS*, Cindy Patton

1985   *Another Mother Tongue: Gay Words, Gay Worlds*, Judy Grahn

1984   *Sexual Politics/Sexual Communities: The Making of a Homosexual Minority in the United States, 1940-1970*, John D'Emilio

1983   No Award

1982   *Surpassing the Love of Men: Romantic Friendship and Love between Women from the Renaissance to the Present*, Lillian Faderman

Black Lesbians: An Annotated Bibliography, J. R. Roberts, Compiler

The Celluloid Closet: Homosexuality in the Movies, Vito Russo

1981   *Christianity, Social Tolerance, and Homosexuality: Gay People in Western Europe from the Beginning of the Christian Era to the Fourteenth Century*, John Boswell

1980   *Now the Volcano: An Anthology of Latin American Gay Literature*, Winston Leyland, Editor

1979   *Now That You Know: What Every Parent Should Know About Homosexuality*, Betty Fairchild and Nancy Hayward

1978   *Our Right to Love: A Lesbian Resource Book*, Ginny Vida, Editor

1977   *Familiar Faces, Hidden Lives: The Story of Homosexual Men in America Today*, Howard Brown

1976   No Award

1975   *Homosexuality: Lesbians and Gay Men in Society, History, and Literature*, Jonathan Katz, Editor

1974 *Sex Variant Women in Literature: A Historical and Quantitative Survey,* Jeannette Foster

1973 No Award

1972 *The Gay Mystique: The Myth and Reality of Male Homosexuality,* Peter Fisher

Lesbian/Woman, Del Martin and Phyllis Lyon

1971 *Patience and Sarah,* Isabel Miller

Lambda Literary Awards

1996 **Lesbian Fiction**
Autobiography of a Family Photo, Jacqueline Woodson

Gay Men's Fiction
Flesh and Blood, Michael Cunningham

Lesbian Biography/Autobiography
Aimee and Jaguar, Erica Fischer

Gay Men's Biography/Autobiography
Tom: The Unknown Tennessee Williams, Lyle Leverich

Lesbian Studies
Dyke Life, edited by Karla Jay

Gay Men's Studies
De Los Otros, Joseph Carrier

Lesbian Poetry
Dark Fields of the Republic, Adrienne Rich

Gay Men's Poetry
Atlantis, Mark Doty

Lesbian Mystery
Intersection of Law and Desire, J.M. Redmann

Gay Men's Mystery
Closet, R.D. Zimmerman

Lesbian and Gay Science Fiction/Fantasy
Shadow Man, Melissa Scott

Slow River, Nicola Griffith

Lesbian and Gay Anthologies/Nonfiction
Gay and Lesbian Literary Heritage, edited by Claude J. Summers

Lesbian and Gay Anthologies/Fiction
Tasting Life Twice, edited by E.J. Levy

Lesbian and Gay Drama
Thinking About the Longstanding Problems of Virtue and Happiness (Slavs!), Tony Kushner

Go Fish, Guinevere Turner and Rose Troche

Gay and Lesbian Humor
The Butches of Madison County, Ellen Orleans

Lesbian and Gay Children's/Young Adult Literature
From the Notebooks of Melanin Sun, Jacqueline Woodson

Photography/Visual Arts
Paris Was a Woman, Andrea Weiss

Lesbian and Gay Spirituality
Wrestling with the Angel, edited by Brian Bouldrey

Editors' Choice
Forbidden Passages, introduction by Pat Califia and Janine Fuller

Restricted Entry, Janine Fuller and Stuart Blackley

Publisher's Service Award
Nancy Bereano, Publisher, Firebrand Press

Lambda Literary Foundation Pioneer Award
L. Page "Deacon" Maccubbin, president and CEO of Lambda Rising Inc.

1995 **Lesbian Fiction**
The Folding Star, Alan Hollinghurst

Gay Men's Fiction
Gifts of the Body, Rebecca Brown

Lesbian Biography/Autobiography
Gertrude Stein in Words and Pictures, Renate Stendahl

Gay Men's Biography/Autobiography
My Own Country, Abraham Verghese

Lesbian Studies
Skin, Dorothy Allsion

Gay Men's Studies
Gay New York, George Chauncey

Lesbian Poetry
Winter Numbers, Marilyn Hacker

Gay Men's Poetry
Collected Poems, Thom Gunn

Lesbian Mystery
Small Sacrifice, Ellen Hart

Gay Men's Mystery
Midnight in the Garden of Good and Evil, John Berendt

Lesbian and Gay Science Fiction/Fantasy
Trouble and Her Friends, Melissa Scott

Lesbian and Gay Anthologies/Nonfiction
Sister and Brother, edited by Joan Nestle and John Preston

Lesbian and Gay Anthologies/Fiction
Chole Plus Olivia, edited by Lillian Faderman

Lesbian and Gay Drama
Angels in America, Part 2: Perestroika, Tony Kushner

Lesbian and Gay Humor
The Dyke and the Dybbuk, Ellen Galford

Lesbian and Gay Children's/Young Adult Literature
Am I Blue?, edited by Marion Dane Bauer

Lesbian and Gay Photography/Visual Arts
Family, Nancy Andrews

Lesbian and Gay Small Press Book Award
Her Tongue on My Theory by Kiss & Tell, Press Gang

Editors' Choice
Memoir of a Race Traitor, Mab Segrest

Publisher's Service Award
Barbara Smith, Kitchen Table/Women of Color Press

1994　**Lesbian Fiction**
Written on the Body, Jeanette Winterson

Gay Men's Fiction
Living Upstairs, Joseph Hansen

Lesbian Biography/Autobiography
Marguerite Yourcenar, Josyanne Savigneau

Gay Men's Biography/Autobiography
Genet, Edmund White

Lesbian Studies
Boots of Leather, Slippers of Gold, Elizabeth Kennedy
　and Madeline Davis

Gay Men's Studies
Conduct Unbecoming, Randy Shilts

Lesbian Poetry
The Marvelous Arithmetics of Distance, Audre Lorde

Gay Men's Poetry
Collected Poems, James Schuyler

1990, Michael Klein

Lesbian Mystery
Divine Victim, Mary Wings

Gay Men's Mystery
Catilina's Riddle, Steven Saylor

Lesbian and Gay Science Fiction/Fantasy
The 5th Sacred Thing, Starhawk Bantam

Lesbian and Gay Anthologies
Lesbian and Gay Studies Reader, Henry Abelove,
　Michele Aina Barale, and David Halperin

Lesbian and Gay Drama
Angels in America: Millenium Approaches, Tony
　Kushner

Lesbian and Gay Humor
Spawn of Dykes to Watch Out For, Alison Bechdel

Children's/Young Adult Literature
Tbe Cat Came Back, Hilary Mullins

Lesbian and Gay Small Press Book Award
Stone Butch Blues, Leslie Feinberg

Sojourner, edited by B. Michael Hunter

Editors' Choice
A Star-Bright Lie, Coleman Dowell

Publisher's Service Award
Michael Denneny, St. Martin's Press

1993　**Fiction**
Running Fiercely toward a High Thin Sound, Judith Katz

Let the Dead Bury the Dead, Randall Kenan

Nonfiction
Eleanor Roosevelt, Blanche Wiesen Cook

Becoming a Man, Paul Monette

Poetry
Counting Myself Lucky, Edward Field

Undersong, Audre Lorde

Humor
Dykes to Watch Out For (The Sequel), Alison Bechdel

Mystery
Crazy for Loving, Jaye Maiman

The Two-Bit Tango, Elizabeth Pincus

The Hidden Law, Michael Nava

Science Fiction/Fantasy
Ammonlite, Nicola Griffith

China Mountain Zhang, Maureen F. McHugh

Anthologies
A Member of the Family, John Preston, Editor

Persistent Desire, Joan Nestle, Editor

Young Adult Literature
When Heroes Die, Penny Raife Durant

Editor's Choice
Gay Ideas, Richard Mohr

Publisher's Service Award
Craig Fodwell, Founder

Oscar Wilde Memorial

1992   **Fiction**
What the Dead Remember, Harlan Greene

The Gilda Stories, Jewelle Gomez

The Revolution of Little Girls, Blanche McCrary Boyd

Nonfiction
The Zuni Man-Woman, Will Roscoe

Cancer in Two Voices, Sandra Butler and Barbara Rosenblum

Poetry
The Road Before Us: 100 Black Gay Poets, Assoto Saint, Editor

Atlas of the Difficult World: Poems 1988-1991, Adrienne Rich

Humor
Putting On the Ritz, Joe Keenan

Mystery
A Country of Old Men, Joseph Hansen

Murder Tradition, Katherine V. Forrest

Science Fiction/Fantasy
The Dark Beyond the Stars, Frank M. Robinson

The Gilda Stories, Jewelle Gomez

Anthologies
Brother to Brother, Essex Hemphill, Editor

Chicana Lesbians: The Girls Our Mothers Warned Us About, Carla Trujillo, Editor

Children's/Young Adult Literature
The Duke Who Outlawed Jelly Beans, Johnny Valentine

Editor's Choice
Odd Girls and Twilight Lovers: A History of Lesbian Life in Twentieth-Century America, Lillian Faderman

Lesbian/Gay Small Press Book Award
Gay Roots: Twenty Years of Gay Sunshine, Winston Leyland, Editor

Publisher's Service Award
Barbara Grier and Donna McBride of Naiad Press

1991   **Fiction**
The Body and Its Dangers, Allen Barnett

Out of Time, Paula Martinac

Nonfiction
Coming Out Under Fire, Allan Bérubé

The Safe Sea of Women, Bonnie Zimmerman

Poetry
Decade Dance, Michael Lassell

Going Back to the River, Marilyn Hacker

Humor
New, Improved Dykes to Watch Out For, Alison Bechdel

Mystery
Gaudi Afternoon, Barbara Wilson

Ninth Life, Lauren Wright Douglas

Howtown, Michael Nava

Science Fiction/Fantasy
Gossamer Axe, Gael Baudino

Magic's Price, Mercedes Lackey

Secret Matter, To Johnson

Anthologies
Men on Men 3, George Stambolian, Editor

Women on Women, Joan Nestle and Naomi Holoch, Editors

AIDS
The Way We Live Now, Elizabeth Osbourn, Editor

Debut
Her, Cherry Muhanji

Dancing on Tisha B'av, Lev Raphael

Editor's Choice
The Encyclopedia of Homosexuality, Wayne Dynes, Editor

Gay Men's Small Press Book Award
Daddy's Roommate, Michael Wilhoite

Lesbian Small Press Book Award
Different Mothers, Louise Rafkin, Editor

Making Face/Making Soul, Gloria Anzaldua

Publisher's Service Award
Phil Wilkie and Greg Baysans

The James White Review

1990   **Fiction**
Eighty-Sixed, David B. Feinberg

The Bar Stories, Nisa Donnelly

Nonfiction
In Search of Gay America, Neil Miller

Really Reading Gertrude Stein, Judy Grahn, Editor

Poetry
Poets for Life, Michael Klein, Editor

Humor
Gay Comics, Robert Triptow, Editor

Mystery
The Beverly Malibu, Katherine V. Forrest

Simple Suburban Murder, Mark Zubro

Science Fiction/Fantasy
What Did Miss Darrington See?, Jessica Amanda Salmonson, Editor

Somewhere in the Night, Jeffrey N. McMahan

Anthologies
Hidden from History: Reclaiming the Gay and Lesbian Past, Martin Bauml Duberman, Martha Vicinus, and George Chauncey, Jr., Editors

Intricate Passions, Tee A. Corinne, Editor

Out the Other Side, Cristian McEwen and Sue O'Sullivan, Editors

Young Adult/Children's
Losing Uncle Tim, MaryKate Jordan

AIDS
Reports from the Holocaust, Larry Kramer

Debut
The Names of the Moons of Mars, Patrica Roth Schwartz

The Irreversible Decline of Eddie Socket, John Weir

Editor's Choice
Lifting Belly by Gertrude Stein, Rebecca Mark, Editor

Gay and Lesbian Small Press Book Award
My Life as a Mole, Larry Mitchell

Publisher's Service Award
Carol Seajay

Feminist Bookstore News

1989   **Fiction**
The Beautiful Room Is Empty, Edmund White

Trash, Dorothy Allison

Nonfiction
Borrowed Time, Paul Monette

Lesbian Ethics, Sarah Hoagland

Poetry
Gay and Lesbian Poetry in Our Time, Carl Morse and Joan Larkin, Editors

Mystery/Science Fiction
Skiptrace, Antoinette Azolakov

Goldenboy, Michael Nava

AIDS
Borrowed Time, Paul Monette

Debut
Bird-Eyes, Madelyn Arnold

The Swimming-Pool Library, Alan Hollinghurst

Editor's Choice
Why Can't Sharon Kowalski Come Home?, Karen Thompson and Julie Andrzejewski

Gay Men's Small Press Book Award
Goldenboy, Michael Nava

The Delight of Hearts, Almad al-Tifashi

Lesbian Small Press Book Award
Trash, Dorothy Allison

Publisher's Service Award
Sasha Alyson

Publishing Triangle Awards

1996   **Bill Whitehead Award for Lifetime Achievement**
Joan Nestle

Robert Chesley Gay and Lesbian Playwriting Awards
Susan Miller, Robert Patrick (both for lifetime achievement)

Ferro-Grumley Awards for Literary Excellence
Felice Picano, Sarah Schulman

1995 **Bill Whitehead Award for Lifetime Achievement**
Jonathan Ned Katz

Ferro-Grumley Awards for Literary Excellence
Heather Lewis, Mark Merlis

Robert Chesley Gay and Lesbian Playwriting Awards
Doric Wilson (for lifetime achievement), Victor Lodata

1994 **Bill Whitehead Award for Lifetime Achievement**
Judy Grahn

Ferro-Grumley Awards
Jeanette Winterson, John Berendt

Robert Chesley Gay and Lesbian Playwriting Awards
Lisa Kron

1993 **Bill Whitehead Award for Lifetime Achievement**
Samuel Delany

Ferro-Grumley Awards
None

Gregory Kolovakos Award for AIDS Writing
The Man with Night Sweats, Thom Gunn

1992 **Bill Whitehead Award for Lifetime Achievement**
Adrienne Rich

Ferro-Grumley Awards
Dorothy Allison, Randall Keenan

Gregory Kolovakos Award for AIDS Writing
To the Friend Who Did Not Save My Life, Hervé Guibert

1991 **Bill Whitehead Award for Lifetime Achievement**
James Purdy

Ferro-Grumley Awards
Melvin Dixon, Blanche McCrary Boyd

1990 **Bill Whitehead Award for Lifetime Achievement**
Audre Lord

Ferro-Grumley Awards
Allen Barnett, Cherry Muhanji

1989 **Bill Whitehead Award for Lifetime Achievement**
Edmund White

Ferro-Grumley Awards
Dennis Cooper, Ruthann Robson

SELECTED ANTHOLOGIES AND
CRITICAL STUDIES

This bibliography is meant to provide the reader with a number of resources that may be usefully consulted in the search for more information about the works and literary movements discussed throughout this book. The editors make no claims for the comprehensiveness of this bibliography, for the explosion of gay, lesbian, bisexual, and transgender studies in the last several years has produced vast amounts of material on nearly every facet of queer culture.

Culture and History

About Time: Exploring the Gay Past, Martin Bauml Duberman, New York, Gay Press of New York, 1986.

AIDS: Cultural Analysis/Cultural Activism, edited by Douglas Crimp, Cambridge, Massachusetts, MIT Press, 1987.

An American Seafarer in the Age of Sail: The Erotic Diaries of Philip C. Van Buskirk, 1851-1870, B. R. Burg, New Haven, Yale University Press, 1994.

And the Band Played On: Politics, People, and the AIDS Epidemic, Randy Shilts, New York, St. Martin's Press, 1987.

The Apparitional Lesbian: Female Homosexuality and Modern Culture, Terry Castle, New York, Columbia University Press, 1993.

The Arena of Masculinity: Sports, Homosexuality, and the Meaning of Sex, Brian Pronger, Toronto, University of Toronto Press, 1992

Bike Boys, Drag Queens & Superstars: Avant-garde, Mass Culture, and Gay Identities in the 1960s Underground Cinema, Juan Antonio Suarez, Bloomington, Indiana University Press, 1996.

Boots of Leather, Slippers of Gold: The History of a Lesbian Community, Elizabeth Lapovsky Kennedy and Madeline D. Davis, New York, Routledge, 1993.

Borderlands/La Frontera: The New Mestiza, Gloria Anzaldua, San Francisco, Spinsters/Aunt Lute, 1987.

Camp Grounds: Style and Homosexuality, edited by David Bergman, Amherst, University of Massachusetts Press, 1993.

Charles T. Griffes: A Life in Music, Donna K. Anderson, Washington, Smithsonian Inst. Press, 1993.

Contested Closets: The Politics and Ethics of Outing, Larry Gross, Minneapolis, University of Minnesota Press, 1993.

The Cultural Construction of Sexuality, edited by Pat Caplan, Routledge, London, 1987.

Cultural Politics/Queer Reading, Alan Sinfield, Philadelphia, University of Pennsylvania Press, 1994.

Danger Zones: Homosexuality, National Identity, and Mexican Culture, Claudia Schaefer, Tucson, University of Arizona Press, 1996.

Daring to Dissent: Lesbian Culture from Margin to Mainstream, edited by Liz Gibbs, London, Cassell, 1994.

Displacing Homophobia: Gay Male Perspectives in Literature and Culture, edited by Ronald Butters, John Clum Ronald, and Michael Moon, Durham, North Carolina, Duke University Press, 1989.

Een Stilzwijgende Samenzwering, Lesbische Vrouwen in Nederland, 1920-1970, Judith Schuyf, IISG, Amsterdam, 1994.

Families We Choose: Lesbians, Gays, Kinship, Kath Weston, New York, Columbia University Press, 1991.

Fear of a Queer Planet: Queer Politics and Social Theory, edited by Michael Warner, Minneapolis, University of Minnesota Press, 1993.

Gay and Gray: The Older Homosexual Man, Raymond H. Berger, Urbana, University of Illinois Press, 1982.

Gay New York: Gender, Urban Culture, and the Making of the Gay Male World, 1890-1940, George Chauncey, New York, Basic Books, 1994.

Gayspeak: Gay Male and Lesbian Communication, edited by James W. Chesebro, New York, Pilgrim, 1981.

Gender Reversals and Gender Cultures: Anthropological and Historical Perspectives, edited by Sabrina Press Ramet, London, New York, Routledge, 1996.

Generation Q: Gays, Lesbians, and BiSexuals Born Around 1969's Stonewall Riots Tell Their Stories of Growing Up in the Age of Information, edited by Robin Bernstein and Seth Clark Silberman, Los Angeles, Alyson Publications, 1996.

Gertrude and Alice, Diana Souhami, New York, HarperCollins, 1991.

Hidden from History: Reclaiming the Gay and Lesbian Past, edited by Martin Bauml Duberman, Martha Vicinus, and George Chauncey, Jr. , New York, New American Library, 1989.

The History of Sexuality: Volume One, Michel Foucault, New York, Vintage, 1978.

Homosexuality in Cold War America: Resistance and the Crisis of Masculinity, Robert J. Corber, Durham, North Carolina, Duke University Press, 1997.

Homosexuality in History, Colin Spencer, San Diego, Harcourt Brace, 1996.

The Invention of Heterosexuality, Jonathan Katz, New York, New York, Dutton, 1995.

Lesbian and Gay Visions of Ireland, Towards the Twenty-first Century, Ide O'Carroll and Eoin Collins, Cassell, London, 1995.

The Lesbian Menace, Sherrie A. Inness, Amherst, University of Massachusetts Press, 1997.

Lesbian Philosophies and Cultures, Jeffner Allen, Albany, State University of New York Press, 1990.

Lesbisch zijn in Nederland, Carla Jonker, Theo Sandfort, and Desirée Schyns, Utrecht, Homostudies/ISOR, 1994.

Making History: The Struggle for Gay and Lesbian Equal Rights, 1945-1990, an Oral History, Eric Marcus, New York, HarperCollins, 1992.

Making Things Perfectly Queer: Interpreting Mass Culture, Alexander Doty, Minneapolis, University of Minnesota Press, 1993.

Making Trouble: Essays on Gay History, Politics, and the University, John D'Emilio, New York, Routledge, 1992.

The Material Queer: A LesBiGay Cultural Studies Reader, edited by Donald Morton, Boulder, Colorado, Westview Press, 1996.

More Man Than You'll Ever Be: Gay Folklore and Acculturation in Middle America, Joseph Press Goodwin, Bloomington, Indiana University Press, 1989.

Muses from Chaos and Ash: AIDS, Artists, and Art, Andrea R. Vaucher, New York, Grove Press, 1993.

My Country, My Right to Serve: Experiences of Gay Men and Women in the Military, World War II to the Present, Mary Ann Humphrey, New York, HarperCollins, 1990.

A Not So Gay World: Homosexuality in Canada, Marion Foster and Kent Murray, Toronto, McClelland and Stewart, 1972.

Out in Culture: Gay, Lesbian, and Queer Essays on Popular Culture, edited by Cory K. Creekmur and Alexander Doty, Durham, North Carolina, Duke University Press, 1995.

Out of the Past: Gay and Lesbian History from 1869 to the Present, Neil Miller, New York, Vintage Books, 1995.

Outing Goethe and His Age, edited by Alice A. Kuzniar, Stanford, California, Stanford University Press, 1996.

Passions between Women: British Lesbian Culture, 1668-1801, Emma Donoghue, Scarlet Press, London, 1993.

The Politics and Poetics of Camp, edited by Moe Meyer, New York, Routledge, 1994.

The Queering of America: Gay Culture in Straight Society, David Van Leer, New York, Routledge, 1995.

Queering the Renaissance, edited by Jonathan Goldberg, Durham, North Carolina, Duke University Press, 1994.

A Queer Romance: Lesbians, Gay Men, and Popular Culture, edited by Paul Burston and Colin Richardson, New York, Routledge, 1995.

The Regulation of Desire: Sexuality in Canada, Gary Kinsman, Montreal, Black Rose Books, 1987.

Resist: Essays Against a Homophobic Culture, edited by Mona Okkawa, Dionne Falconer, and Ann Dector, Toronto, Canada, Women's Press, 1994.

Rights of Passage: Struggles for Lesbian and Gay Legal Equality, Didi Herman, Toronto, University of Toronto Press, 1994.

The Rise and Fall of Gay Culture, Daniel Harris, New York, Hyperion, 1997.

The Rise of a Gay and Lesbian Movement, Barry D. Adam, Boston, Twayne, 1987.

A Road to Stonewall: Male Homosexuality and Homophobia in English and American Literature, 1750-1969, Byrne R. S. Fone, New York, Twayne, 1995.

The Ruling Passion: British Colonial Allegory and the Paradox of Homosexual Desire, Christopher Lane, Durham, North Carolina, Duke University Press, 1995.

The Sacred Hoop: Recovering the Feminine in American Indian Traditions, Paula Gunn Allen, Boston, Beacon, 1986.

Sex and Conquest: Gendered Violence, Political Order, and the European Conquest of the Americas, Richard C. Trexler, Ithaca, New York, Cornell University Press, 1995.

Sex, Drugs, Death, and the Law: An Essay on Human Rights and Overcriminalization, David A. J. Richards, Totowa, New Jersey, Rowman & Littlefield, 1982.

Sex, Nation, and Dissent in Irish Writing, edited by Eibhear Walshe, New York, St. Martin's Press, 1997.

Sexual Artifice: Persons, Images, Politics, edited by Ann Kibbey, Kayann Short, and Abouali Farmanfarmaian, New York, New York University Press, 1994

Sexual Dissidence: Augustine to Wilde, Freud to Foucault, Jonathan Dollimore, Oxford, Clarendon Press, 1991.

The Sexual Perspective: Homosexuality and Art in the Last 100 Years in the West, 2nd ed., Emmanuel Cooper, London and New York, Routledge, 1994.

The Social Construction of Lesbianism, Celia Kitzinger, London and Newbury Park, California, Sage Publications, 1987.

Sophia Parnok: The Life and Work of Russia's Sappho, Diana Lewis Burgin, New York, New York University Press, 1994.

The Spirit and the Flesh: Sexual Diversity in American Indian Culture, Walter L. Williams, Boston, Beacon, 1986.

The Stonewall Experiment: A Gay Psychohistory, Ian Young, London and New York, Cassell, 1995.

Surpassing the Love of Men: Romantic Friendship and Love Between Women from the Renaissance to the Present, Lillian Faderman, New York, William Morrow and Company, 1981.

Taking Liberties: Gay Men's Essays on Politics, Culture, and Sex, edited by Michael Bronski, New York, Masquerade Books, 1996.

Textual Orientations: Lesbian and Gay Students and the Making of Discourse Communities, Harriet Malinowitz, Portsmouth, New Hampshire, Heinemann, 1995.

Un/popular Culture, Kathleen Martindale, Albany, State University of New York Press, 1997.

"We of the Third Sex": Literary Representations of Homosexuality in Wilhelmine Germany, James W. Jones, New York, Peter Lang, 1990.

The Wilde Century: Effeminacy, Oscar Wilde, and the Queer Movement, New York, Columbia University Press, 1994.

Yours in Struggle: Three Feminist Perspectives on Anti-Semitism and Racism, Elly Bulkin, Minnie Bruce Pratt, and Barbara Smith, Ithaca, Firebrand, 1984.

The Zuni Man-Woman, Will Roscoe, Albuquerque, University of New Mexico Press, 1991.

Fiction

AIDS Narratives: Gender and Sexuality, Fiction and Science, Steven F. Kruger, New York, Garland Publications, 1996.

Alcibiades at the Door: Gay Discourses in French Literature, Lawrence R. Schehr, Stanford, California, Stanford University Press, 1995.

American Women Short Story Writers: A Collection of Critical Essays, edited by Julie Brown, New York, Garland, 1995.

Between Men: English Literature and Male Homosocial Desire, Eve K. Sedgwick, New York, Columbia University Press, 1985.

Come As You Are: Sexuality and Narrative, Judith Roof, New York, Columbia University Press, 1996.

Confronting AIDS Through Literature: The Responsibilities of Representation, edited by Judith Laurence Pastore, Urbana, University of Illinois Press, 1993.

Critical Essays: Gay and Lesbian Writers of Color, edited by Emmanuel S. Nelson, New York, Haworth, 1993.

Dayneford's Library: American Homosexual Writing, 1900-1913, James Gifford, Amherst, University of Massachusetts Press, 1995.

Double Talk: The Erotics of Male Literary Collaboration, Wayne Koestenbaum, New York, Routledge, 1989.

Embracing a Gay identity: Gay Novels as Guides, Wilfrid R. Koponen, Westport, Bergin & Garvey, 1993.

Erotic Universe: Sexuality and Fantastic Literature, edited by David Palumbo, Westport, Connecticut, Greenwood Press, 1986.

Essays on Gay Literature, edited by Stuart Kellogg, New York, Harrington Park Press, 1985.

Fictions of Sappho, 1546-1937, Joan E. DeJean, Chicago, University of Chicago Press, 1989.

Following Djuna, Carolyn Allen, Bloomington, Indiana University Press, 1996.

Gaiety Transfigured: Gay Self-Representation in American Literature, David Bergman, Madison, University of Wisconsin Press, 1991.

Gay and Lesbian Themes in Latin American Writing, David William Foster, Austin, University of Texas Press, 1991.

Gay Fictions Wilde to Stonewall: Studies in a Male Homosexual Literary Tradition, Claude J. Summers, New York, Continuum, 1990.

Gay Men's Literature in the Twentieth Century, Mark Lilly, New York, New York University Press, 1993.

The Gay Novel in America, James Levin, New York, Garland, 1991.

Heavenly Love?: Lesbian Images in Twentieth-century Women's Writing, Gabriele Griffin, Manchester, Manchester University Press, New York, St. Martin's Press, 1993.

Henry James and Masculinity: The Man at the Margins, Kelly Cannon, New York, St. Martin's Press, 1994.

Hero, Captain, and Stranger: Male Friendship, Social Critique, and Literary Form in the Sea Novels of Herman Melville, Robert K. Martin, Chapel Hill, University of North Carolina Press, 1986.

Heterosexual Plots and Lesbian Narratives, Marilyn R. Farwell, New York, New York University Press, 1996.

The Homosexual as Hero in Contemporary Fiction, Stephen D. Adams, London, Vision, 1980.

Homosexual Characters in Young Adult Novels: A Literary Analysis, 1969-1982, Allan A. Cuseo, Metuchen, New Jersey, Scarecrow Press, 1992.

Homosexual Themes in Literary Studies, edited by Wayne R. Dynes and Stephen Donaldson, New York, Garland, 1992.

Homosexualities and French Literature: Cultural Contexts/Critical Texts, edited by George Stambolian and Elaine Marks, Ithaca, Cornell University Press, 1979.

Homosexuality in Renaissance and Enlightenment England: Literary Representations in Historical Context, edited by Claude J. Summers, New York, Harrington Park, 1992.

Laws of Desire: Questions of Homosexuality in Spanish Writing and Film, 1960-1990, Paul Julian Smith, New York, Oxford University Press, 1992.

Lesbian and Gay Writing: An Anthology of Critical Essays, edited by Mark Lilly, Philadelphia, Temple University Press, 1990.

The Lesbian in Literature, 3rd ed., Barbara Grier, Tallahassee, Fla., Naiad Press, 1981.

Literary Visions of Homosexuality, edited by Stuart Kellogg, New York, Haworth, 1983.

Love between Men in English Literature, Paul Hammond, New York, St. Martin's Press, 1996.

Love's Litany: The Writing of Modern Homoerotics, Kevin Kopelson, Stanford, California, Stanford University Press, 1994.

Mannerliebe: Homosexualitat und Literatur, Wolfgang Popp, Stuttgart, J.B. Metzler, 1992.

Nice Jewish Girls: A Lesbian Anthology, edited by Evelyn Torton Beck, Boston, Beacon Press, 1989.

Ontmoeting met Djuna Barnes, Michele Causse, Amsterdam, Furie, 1989.

Romance Revisited, edited by Jackie Stacey and Lynne Pearce, New York, New York University Press, 1995.

The Sadomasochistic Homotext: Readings in Sade, Balzac, and Proust, Douglas B. Saylor, New York, Peter Lang, 1993.

The Safe Sea of Women: Lesbian Fiction, 1969-1989, Bonnie Zimmerman, Boston, Beacon, 1990.

Scandal in the Ink: Male and Female Homosexuality in Twentieth-century French Literature, Christopher Robinson, London and New York, Cassell, 1995.

Sex Scandal: The Private Parts of Victorian Fiction, William A. Cohen, Durham, North Carolina, Duke University Press, 1996.

The Sexual Dimension in Literature, edited by Alan Bold, London and Totowa, New Jersey, Vision, 1982.

Sexual Sameness: Textual Differences in Lesbian and Gay Writing, edited by Joseph Bristow, London, Routledge, 1992.

Sex Variant Women in Literature, 2nd ed., Jeannette H. Foster, Baltimore, Maryland, Diana Press, 1975.

The Shock of Men: Homosexual Hermeneutics in French Writing, Lawrence R. Schehr, Stanford, California, Stanford University Press, 1995.

Sisters & Strangers: An Introduction to Contemporary Feminist Fiction, Patricia Duncker, Oxford, Blackwell, 1992.

Skin: Talking about Sex, Class, and Literature, Dorothy Allison, Ithaca, Firebrand, 1994.

Sodometries: Renaissance Texts, Modern Sexualities, Jonathan Goldberg, Stanford, California, Stanford University Press, 1992.

Strategies of Deviance: Studies in Gay Male Representation, Earl Jackson, Bloomington, Indiana University Press, 1995.

Sweet Dreams: Sexuality, Gender and Popular Fiction, edited by Susannah Radstone, London, Lawrence & Wishart, 1988.

Uma tema crucial: Aspetos do homossexualismo na literatura, Paulo Hecker Filho, Porto Alegre, RS, Editora Sulina, 1989.

Uranian Worlds: A Guide to Alternative Sexuality in Science Fiction, Fantasy, and Horror, 2nd ed., Eric Garber, with Lyn Paleo, Boston, Massachusetts, G.K. Hall, 1990.

Willa Cather, Sharon O'Brien, New York, Chelsea House, 1995.

Writing AIDS: Gay Literature, Language and Analysis, edited by Timothy Murphy and Suzanne Poirier, New York, Columbia University Press, 1993.

Writing as Witness: Essay and Talk, Beth Brant, Toronto, Canada, Women's Press, 1994.

Poetry

Hart Crane and the Homosexual Text: New Thresholds, New Anatomies, Thomas E. Yingling, Chicago, University of Chicago Press, 1990.

Lesbian Desire in the Lyrics of Sappho, Jane McIntosh Snyder, New York, Columbia University Press, 1997.

The Highest Apple: Sappho and the Lesbian Poetic Tradition, Judy Grahn, San Francisco, Spinsters Ink, 1985.

The Homosexual Tradition in American Poetry, Robert K. Martin, Austin, University of Texas Press, 1979.

Theatre

Acting Gay: Male Homosexuality in Modern Drama, John M. Clum, New York, Columbia University Press, 1992.

Communists, Cowboys, and Queers: The Politics of Masculinity in the Work of Arthur Miller and Tennessee Williams, David Savran, Minneapolis, University of Minnesota Press, 1992.

Drama, Sex and Politics, edited by James Redmond, Cambridge, Massachusetts, Cambridge University Press, 1985.

En Travesti: Women, Gender Subversion, Opera, edited by Corinne E. Blackmer and Patricia Juliana Smith, New York, Columbia University Press, 1995.

Erotic Politics: Desire on the Renaissance Stage, edited by Susan Zimmerman, New York, Routledge, 1992.

Feminism and Theatre, Sue-Ellen Case, New York, Methuen, 1988.

Gay and Lesbian American Plays: An Annotated Bibliography, Ken Furtado and Nancy Hellner, Metuchen, New Jersey, Scarecrow, 1993.

Homosexualities in the English Theatre: From Lyly to Wilde, John Charles Franceschina, Westport, Connecticut, Greenwood Press, 1997.

Stages of Desire: Gay Theatre's Hidden History, Carl Miller, London and New York, Cassell, 1996.

Staging Gay Lives: An Anthology of Contemporary Gay Theater, edited by John M. Clum, Boulder, Colorado, Westview Press, 1995.

Straight Acting: Popular Gay Drama from Wilde to Rattigan, Sean O'Connor, Washington, D.C., Cassell, 1997.

"We Can Always Call Them Bulgarians": The Emergence of Lesbians and Gay Men on the American Stage, Kaier Curtin, Boston, Alyson Publications, 1987.

Women Playwrights of Diversity, Jane T. Peterson, Westport, Connecticut, Greenwood Press, 1997.

Film

Deviant Eyes, Deviant Bodies: Sexual Re-orientations in Film and Video, Chris Straayer, New York, Columbia University Press, 1996.

Gay Hollywood Film & Video Guide: 75 Years of Gay & Lesbian Images in the Movies, 2nd ed., Stephen Stewart, Laguna Hills, California, Companion Publications, 1994.

Gays and Lesbians in Mainstream Cinema: Plots, Critiques, Casts and Credits for 272 Theatrical and Made-for-television Hollywood Releases, James Robert Parish, Jefferson, North Carolina, McFarland & Co., 1993.

Hitchcock and Homosexuality: His 50-year Obsession with Jack the Ripper and the Superbitch Prostitute, a Psychoanalytic View, Theodore Price, Metuchen, New Jersey, Scarecrow Press, 1992.

Immortal, Invisible: Lesbians and the Moving Image, edited by Tamsin Wilton, London, Routledge, 1995.

In the Name of National Security: Hitchcock, Homophobia, and the Political Construction of Gender in Postwar America, Robert J. Corber, Durham, North Carolina, Duke University Press, 1993.

Jump Cut: Hollywood, Politics, and Counter Cinema, Peter Steven, New York, Praeger, 1985.

Now You See It: Studies on Lesbian and Gay Film, Richard Dyer, London and New York, Routledge, 1990.

Queer Looks: Perspectives on Lesbian and Gay Film and Video, edited by Martha Gever, John Greyson, and Pratibha Parmar, New York, Routledge, 1993.

What Are You Looking At?: Queer Sex, Style, and Cinema, Paul Burston, London and New York, Cassell, 1995.

Bibliography and Reference

An Annotated Bibliography of Homosexuality, Vern L. Bullough, New York, Garland Publications, 1976.

Contemporary Lesbian Writing, Paulina Palmer, Buckingham and Philadelphia, Open University Press, 1993.

Contemporary Lesbian Writers of the United States: A Bio-Bibliographical Critical Sourcebook, edited by Sandra Pollack and Denise D. Knight, Westport, Connecticut, Greenwood Press, 1993.

Gay and Lesbian Characters and Themes in Mystery Novels: A Critical Guide to over 500 Works in English, Anthony Slide, Jefferson, North Carolina, McFarland & Company, 1993.

The Gay and Lesbian Literary Heritage: A Reader's Companion to the Writers and Their Works, from Antiquity to the Present, edited by Claude J. Summers, New York, Holt, 1995.

A Gay Bibliography: Eight Bibliographies on Lesbian and Male Homosexuality, New York, Arno Press, 1975.

A Guide to Gay and Lesbian Writing in Australia, Michael Hurley, St. Leonards, N.S.W., Allen & Unwin, 1996.

The Homosexual and Society: An Annotated Bibliography, Robert B. Marks Ridinger, New York, Greenwood Press, 1990.

Homosexuality Bibliography, William Parker, Metuchen, New Jersey, Scarecrow Press, 1985.

Homosexuality: A Research Guide, Wayne R. Dynes, New York, Garland Publications, 1987.

Homosexuality: A Selective Bibliography of Over 3,000 Items, William Parker, Metuchen, New Jersey, Scarecrow Press, 1971.

International Directory of Gay and Lesbian Periodicals, H. Robert Malinowsky, Phoenix, Oryx Press, 1987.

Latin American Writers on Gay and Lesbian Themes: A Bio-Critical Sourcebook, edited by David William Foster and Emmanuel S. Nelson, Westport, Connecticut, Greenwood Press, 1994.

Lesbian in Literature: A Bibliography, 1st ed., Barbara Grier, San Francisco, Daughters of Bilitis, 1967; 2nd ed., Reno, Nevada, The Ladder, 1975.

Lesbians in Print, Margaret Gillon, Irvine, California, Bluestocking Books, 1995.

The Male Homosexual in Literature: A Bibliography, 2nd ed., Ian Young, Metuchen, New Jersey, Scarecrow Press, 1982.

Out on the Shelves: Lesbian Books into Libraries, Jane Allen, Newcastle-under-Lyme, AAL Publishing, 1989.

Proust, Cole Porter, Michelangelo, Marc Almond and Me: Writings by Gay Men on Their Lives and Lifestyles from the Archives of the National Gay and Lesbian Survey, foreword by Kenneth Barrow, introduction by Kerry Sutton-Spence, New York, Routledge, 1993.

Queer Studies and Theory

Academic Outlaws: Queer Theory and Cultural Studies in the Academy, William G. Tierney, Thousand Oaks, California, Sage Publications, 1997.

Bodies that Matter: On the Discursive Limits of "Sex," Judith Butler, New York and London, Routledge, 1993.

Classics in Lesbian Studies, edited by Esther D. Rothblum, New York, Harrington Park Press, 1997.

Cruising the Performative: Interventions into the Representation of Ethnicity, Nationality, and Sexuality, edited by Sue-Ellen Case, Philip Brett, and Susan Leigh Foster, Bloomington, University of Indiana Press, 1995.

Dazzling Dialectics, Sally Bishop Shigley, New York, Peter Lang, 1997.

Difference Troubles: Queering Social Theory and Sexual Politics, Steven Seidman, New York, Cambridge University Press, 1997.

The Ethics of Marginality: A New Approach to Gay Studies, John Champagne, Minneapolis, University of Minnesota Press, 1995.

Excitable Speech: A Politics of Performance, Judith Butler, New York and London, Routledge, 1997.

The Gay Academic, Louie Crew, Palm Springs, ETC Pubs., 1978.

Gay and Lesbian Studies in Art History, edited by Whitney Davis, New York, Haworth Press, 1994.

Gender Trouble: Feminism and the Subversion of Identity, Judith Butler, New York and London, Routledge, 1990.

Homographesis: Essays in Gay Literary and Cultural Theory, Lee Edelman, New York, Routledge, 1994.

Homophile Studies in Theory and Practice, W. Dorr Legg, San Francisco, California, GLB Publishers, 1994.

Inside/Out: Lesbian Theories, Gay Theories, edited by Diana Fuss, New York, Routledge, 1991.

The Lesbian and Gay Studies Reader, edited by Henry Abelove, Michèle Aina Barale, and David M. Halperin, New York, Routledge, 1993.

The Lesbian Postmodern, edited by Laura Doan, New York, Columbia University Press, 1994.

Lesbian Studies: Present and Future, edited by Margaret Cruikshank, Old Westbury, New York, Feminist Press, 1982.

Lesbian Studies: Setting an Agenda, Tamsin Wilton, London and New York, Routledge, 1995.

Lesbian Subjects: A Feminist Studies Reader, edited by Martha Vicinus, Bloomington, Indiana University Press, 1996.

Lesbian Texts and Contexts: Radical Revisions, edited by Karla Jay, Joanne Glasgow, and Catharine R. Stimpson, New York, New York University Press, 1990.

A Lure of Knowledge: Lesbian Sexuality and Theory, Judith Roof, New York, Columbia University Press, 1991.

Men Writing the Feminine: Literature, Theory, and the Question of Genders, edited by Thais E. Morgan, Albany, State University of New York Press, 1994.

New Lesbian Criticism: Literary and Cultural Readings, edited by Sally Munt, New York, Columbia University Press, 1992.

The New Lesbian Studies: Into the Twenty-first Century, edited by Bonnie Zimmerman and Toni A. H. McNaron, New York, Feminist Press at the City University of New York, 1996.

Perversions: Deviant Readings, Mandy Merck, New York, Routledge, 1993.

Professions of Desire: Lesbian and Gay Studies in Literature, edited by George E. Haggerty and Bonnie Zimmerman, New York, Modern Language Association of America, 1995.

A Queer Reader, edited by Patrick Higgins, New York, New Press, 1993.

Queer Studies: A Lesbian, Gay, BiSexual, & Transgender Anthology, edited by Brett Beemyn and Mickey Elianon, New York, New Yourk University Press, 1996.

Queer Words, Queer Images: Communication and the Construction of Homosexuality, edited by R. Jeffrey Ringer, New York, New York University Press, 1994.

(Sem)erotics: Theorizing Lesbian Writing, Elizabeth A. Meese, New York, New York University Press, 1992.

Sexual Practice, Textual Theory: Lesbian Cultural Criticism, edited by Susan J. Wolfe and Julia Penelope, Cambridge, Massachusetts, Blackwell, 1993.

Sisters, Sexperts, Queers, edited by Arlene Stein, Plume, 1993.

Social Perspectives in Lesbian and Gay Studies: A Reader, edited by Peter M. Nardi and Beth E. Schneider, New York, Routledge, 1997.

Straight Studies Modified: Lesbian Interventions in the Academy, edited by Gabriele Griffin and Sonya Andermahr, London and Washington, D.C., Cassell, 1997.

Teaching What You're Not: Identity Politics in Higher Education, edited by Katherine J. Mayberry, New York, New York University Press, 1996.

Tilting the Tower: Lesbians, Teaching, Queer Subjects, edited by Linda Garber, New York, Routledge, 1994.

Music

Queer Noises: Male and Female Homosexuality in Twentieth Century Music, John Gill, Minneapolis, University of Minnesota Press, 1995.

Queering the Pitch: The New Gay and Lesbian Musicology, edited by Philip Brett, Elizabeth Wood, and Gary C. Thomas, New York, Routledge, 1994.

Seduced and Abandoned: Essays on Gay Men and Popular Music, Richard Smith, London and New York, Cassell, 1995.

Transgender Issues

Sex Changes, Pat Califia, 1997 San Francisco, California, Cleis Press, 1997.

Sex/Gender in a Transsexual Perspective, Ines Orobio de Castro, Amsterdam, Het Spinhuis, 1993.

Transgender Liberation: A Movement Whose Time Has Come, Leslie Feinberg, New York, New York, World View Forum, 1992.

Transgender Nation: Transsexual Ideology, Transgenderism, and the Gender Movement in America, Gordene Olga MacKenzie, Bowling Green, Ohio, Bowling Green State University Popular Press, 1994.

Transgender Warriors: Making History from Joan of Arc to RuPaul, Leslie Feinberg, Boston, Beacon Press, 1996.

Transsexuals, Gerald Ramsey, Freedom, California, Crossing Press, 1996.

Other

The Aerial Letter, Nicole Brossard, Toronto, Canada, Women's Press, 1988.

Are Girls Necessary?, Julie Abraham, New York, Routledge, 1996.

Body Alchemy, Loren Cameron, Pittsburgh, Pennsylvania, Cleis Press, 1996.

Crossing the Stage: Controversies on Cross-Dressing, edited by Lesley Ferris, London, Routledge, 1993.

Cures: A Gay Man's Odyssey, Martin Duberman, New York, Dutton, 1991.

Dangerous Intimacies, Lisa Lynne Moore, Durham, North Carolina, Duke University Press, 1997.

Entiendes?: Queer Readings, Hispanic Writings, edited by Emilie L. Bergmann and Paul Julian Smith, Durham, North Carolina, Duke University Press, 1995.

Epistemology of the Closet, Eve Kosofsky Sedgwick, Berkeley, University of California Press, 1990.

Gender Blending, Amherst, New York, Prometheus Books, 1997.

Haciendo Caras: Making Face, Making Soul, edited by Gloria Anzaldua, San Francisco, Aunt Lute, 1990.

Homos, Leo Bersani, Cambridge, Massachusetts, Harvard University Press, 1995.

The Issue Is Power, Melanie Kaye/Kantrowitz, San Francisco, Aunt Lute Books, 1992.

Lesbian Configurations, Renee C. Hoogland, New York, Columbia University Press, 1997.

Lesbian Panic, Patricia Juliana Smith, New York, Columbia University Press, 1997.

Male Impersonators, Mark Simpson, New York, Routledge, 1994.

Massacre of the Dreamers: Essays on Xicanisma, Ana Castillo, Albuquerque, University of New Mexico Press, 1994.

The Matter of Images, Richard Dyer, New York, Routledge, 1993.

Myths and Mysteries of Same-sex Love, Christine Downing, New York, Continuum, 1989.

Negotiating Lesbian and Gay Subjects, edited by Monica Dorenkamp and Richard Henke, New York, Routledge, 1995.

Oceanic Homosexualities, edited by Stephen O. Murray, New York, Garland, 1992.

Passion and Penance, Dawn B. Sova, Boston, Massachusetts, Faber and Faber, 1997.

The Persistent Desire: A Femme-Butch Reader, edited by Joan Nestle, Boston, Alyson Publications, 1992.

Rebellion: Essays 1980-1991, Minnie Bruce Pratt, Ithaca, Firebrand, 1991.

A Restricted Country, Joan Nestle, Ithaca, New York, Firebrand Books, 1987.

The Search for a Woman-centered Spirituality, Annette Joy Van Dyke, New York, New York University Press, 1992.

Tendencies, Eve Kosofsky Sedgwick, Durham, North Carolina, Duke University Press, 1993.

This Bridge Called My Back: Writings by Radical Women of Color, edited by Gloria Anzaldua and Cherrie Moraga, New York, Kitchen Table Press, 1981.

Where the Meanings Are, Catharine R. Stimpson, New York, Routledge, 1990.

NOTES ON ADVISERS AND CONTRIBUTORS

ALDAMA, Frederick Luis. Graduate student, Stanford University English department; he has published an article that investigates the intersection of colonialism and gay identity formation in Latin American fiction and poetry. **Essays:** Campo; Cardenas; Goytisolo; Zapata.

ALFONSO, Rita. Graduate student in continental philosophy and feminisms, University of Memphis, Tennessee. **Essay:** Allen.

ANGLES, Jeffrey. Graduate student, Ohio State University, Columbus; writing thesis on the early works of Mutsuo Takahashi. **Essays:** Takahashi.

BELL, Julia. Tutor of creative writing, University of East Anglia, Norwich; completing a volume of short stories to be published in spring 1998. **Essay:** Brite.

BENEMANN, William. Head of technical services, Boalt Hall Law Library, University of California, Berkeley. **Essay:** Brooke.

BERNSTEIN, Robin. Co-editor of *Generation Q* (Alyson Publications, 1996); contributor to reference books and anthologies, including *Best Lesbian Erotica 1997* and *Eating Our Hearts Out*; member of core editorial group, *Bridges: A Journal for Jewish Feminists and Our Friends*. **Essays:** Asch; Bechdel; Meaker.

BLACK, Moishe. Professor Emeritus of French, University of Saskatchewan, Canada; co-translator, *Hesitant Fire: Selected Prose of Max Jacob* (1991), *The Story of King Kabul* by Max Jacob (1994); author of articles on Jacob, Camus, Montaigne, Voltaire, Flaubert, and Corneille. **Essay:** Jacob.

BOYD, Anne. Ph.D. student in American studies at Purdue University, West Lafayette, Indiana; writing dissertation on nineteenth-century American women writers; contributor to *Contemporary Popular Writers,* published by St. James Press. **Essays:** Mackay; Rilke; Ross; Zinovyeva-Annibal.

BUCKMAN, Alyson R. Graduate student, Purdue University, West Lafayette, Indiana; writing dissertation on the construction of monstrosity in the works of four contemporary American women writers, including Alice Walker; author of "The Body as a Site of Colonization: Alice Walker's *Possessing the Secret of Joy*" in *Journal of American Culture.* **Essay:** Walker.

CANDELA, Amy Warner. Graduate student, University of Kentucky, Lexington; contributor to *The Femme Mystique,* 1995. **Essay:** Lynch.

CANNON, Kelly. Humanities reference librarian, Muhlenberg College, Allentown, Pennsylvania; author of *Henry James and Masculinity: The Man at the Margins,* St. Martin's Press, 1992; contributor to the forthcoming *Robert Frost Encyclopedia* and *American National Biography.* **Essay:** Tusquets.

CARON, David. Assistant professor of French, University of Michigan, Ann Arbor; author of "Playing Doctors: Refiguring the Doctor-Patient Relationship in Herve Guibert's AIDS novels," *Literature and Medicine,* 1995; finishing a book entitled *Social Ills, Literary Cures.* **Essay:** Collard.

CHADWELL, Faye A. Head of collection development, University of Oregon Library system, Eugene, Oregon; regular reviewer for *Library Journal* and author of the bibliographic essay on feminism and science in *Biology and Women: A Dynamic Interaction* by Sue V. Rosser, New York, Twayne, 1992. **Essay:** Segrest.

CHERNETSKY, Vitaly. Assistant professor, department of Slavic languages, Columbia University; author of articles on Russian literature and art in *Postmodern Culture, Slavic and East European Journal, Slavic Review* and several collected volumes; translator of Russian literary texts. **Essays:** Kharitonov; Rozanov.

COLBURN, Krystyna. Active lesbian feminist; coordinator of W.I.T.C.H. Feminist Lecture Series; articles on lesbian readings of Virginia Woolf. **Essay:** Penelope.

DANE, Pamelyn Nance. Ph.D., University of Oregon; teaches writing and literature at Lane Community College, Eugene, Oregon. **Essay:** Hartley.

da SILVA, Stephen. Graduate student, Rice University; completing dissertation on late-Victorian and Modernist British gay male writers' uses of mythologies of primitivism and Hellenism in challenging the stereotype of the psychically arrested homosexual. Has published on Eve Kosofsky Sedgwick, literary critic and gay/lesbian theorist. **Essay:** Strachey.

DILLON, Sioban. Essay: Akhmatova.

DONOHUE, Stacey. Assistant professor of English, Central Oregon Community College, Bend, Oregon; has published essays on Mary McCarthy and Mary Lavin, and is writing a book on Irish American women writers. **Essay:** Morgan.

DOUGLAS, C. Steven. Graduate student, Purdue University, West Lafayette, Indiana; studying American cultural constructions of race and sexuality. **Essay:** Busch.

EAGAN, Joseph M. Head, government reference service, Enoch Pratt Free Library, Baltimore, Maryland; contributor to *Gay & Lesbian Biography,* 1996. **Essays:** Beam; Bell; Cunningham; Perry.

ELLEDGE, Jim. Professor of English, Illinois State University, Normal; author of four books of poetry--*Into the Arms of the Universe,* 1995; *Earth as It Is,* 1994; *Various Envies,* 1989; and *Nothing Nice,* 1987--and of six other books: *Sweet Nothings: An Anthology of Rock and Roll in American Poetry,* 1994; *The Little Magazine in Illinois: A Directory,* 1993; *Standing "Between the Dead and the Living:" The Elegiac Technique of Wilfred Owen's War Poems,* 1992; *Frank O'Hara: To Be True to a City,* 1990; *Weldon Kees: A Critical Introduction,* 1985; and *James Dickey: A Bibliography, 1947-1974,* 1979. **Essay:** Trinidad.

ELLIOTT, Victoria Stagg. Deputy editor, *New Moon Magazine*; regular contributor to *Gay Times* and *Diva Magazine.* **Essays:** Obejas; Peck; Rodi.

ERICKSON, Anne. Graduate instructor, Purdue University, West Lafayette, Indiana; writing dissertation on Irish short stories; active in composition pedagogy and publication. **Essay:** Neil Jordan.

FARMER, Ellen. Senior academic editor, University of California, Santa Cruz; co-editor, with Deborah Abbott, of the Crossing Press anthology *From Wedded Wife to Lesbian Life: Stories of Transformation,* 1995. **Essay:** Brown.

FIELD, Edward. Poet; author of *Counting Myself Lucky: Selected Poems, 1963-1992* (1992); editor, *Head of a Sad Angel: Stories, 1953-1966* by Alfred Chester. **Essay:** Peters.

GANNON, Caitlin. Editor and publisher, Javelina Press, Tucson, Arizona; freelance writer and German translator; editor, *Southwestern Women: New Voices,* 1997. **Essays:** Calderon; Muhanji; Stefan; Tsvetaeva; Wierauch.

GARNES, David. Reference librarian, University of Connecticut, Storrs; contributor to *Liberating Minds: The Stories and Professional Lives of Gay, Lesbian and Bisexual Librarians*; *Connecticut Poets on AIDS: A Cross Culture Collection*; *Gay and Lesbian Biography*; and *A Testimony: Remembering Loved Ones Lost to AIDS.* **Essays:** Inge; Sargeson.

GIANOULIS, Tina. General handywoman, political worker, and sometime writer; published in *Sinister Wisdom* and *Common Lives, Lesbian Lives.* **Essays:** Bogus; Broumas; Carr; Cornwell; DeLynn; Garner; Hughes; Kotz.

GILLON, Margaret. Editor, *Lesbians in Print: A Bibliography of 1,500 Books with Synopses,* 1995; web master, "Lesbians in Print," 1996-97; programmer/analyst 1985-1997; publisher, Bluestocking Books, a feminist/lesbian press, from 1995.

GLASSMAN, Paul. Art and architecture librarian and assistant professor, Pratt Institute, Brooklyn, New York; contributor to *Inland Architect,* 1990-92, and *International Dictionary of Architects and Architecture,* 1993. **Essays:** Cameron; Wong.

GREEN, Maria. Professor Emeritus, University of Saskatchewan, Canada; author of *Bibliographie des poemes de Max Jacob Parus en Revue* (1991), *Bibliographie et documentation sur Max Jacob*; co-translator, *The Hesitant Fire: A Prose Anthology of Max Jacob*; contributor of scholarly essays to periodicals. **Essay:** Jacob.

GREEN, Pamela. New York City-based freelance writer; frequent contributor to various feminist and gay publications. **Essays:** Dunye; Paglia; Price.

GREENBLATT, Ellen. Coordinator of cataloging services and special collections, Auraria Library, Denver, Colorado; former chair, American Library Association Gay, Lesbian, and Bisexual Book Awards Committee; former co-chair, American Library Association, Gay, Lesbian, and Bisexual Task Force; co-editor, *Gay and Lesbian Library Service* (1990); creator, Library Q world-wide web site for queer librarians.

GUNTER, Kimberly. Doctoral student, University of Illinois, Urbana; focusing on lesbian language issues. **Essay:** Frye.

HAYES, Jarrod. Assistant professor of French and francophone studies, University of Michigan, Ann Arbor; author of "Proust in the Tearoom," *PMLA,* 1995; currently working on a book entitled *Something Queer about the Nation: Sexual Subversions of National Identity in Maghrebian Literature in French.* **Essay:** Rachid O.

HAYWORTH, Gene. Working on his first novel, *True Curiosity News,* from his home in Boulder, Colorado. **Essays:** Aragon; Dowell.

HENN, Martha. Reference librarian for arts and humanities, Sterne Library, University of Alabama-Birmingham. **Essay:** Richardson.

HIGHBERG, Nels P. Writer, Columbus, Ohio. **Essays:** Home; Hoffman; Robson.

HOENESS-KRUPSAW, Susanna. Assistant professor of English, University of Southern Indiana, Evansville, Indiana; wrote dissertation on the role of the family in the novels of E. L. Doctorow; contributor to *Feminist Writers.* **Essay:** Showalter.

HOKENSON, Jan. Professor of French and comparative literature, Florida Atlantic University; editor of *Forms of the Fantastic* (1986); author of numerous essays, including "Proust's Japonisme" (forthcoming in *Modern Language Studies,* 1998), "Intercultural Autobiography" in *a/b Auto/Biography Studies* (1995), and "The Breeches of Authority: The Monologue and Its Relation to Ideologies of Gender" in *Romance Languages Journal* (1993). **Essay:** Alther.

HOLBROOK, Susan. Graduate student, University of Calgary, Alberta, Canada; writing dissertation on twentieth-century poetics. **Essay:** Brossard; Silvera.

HUGHES, Anne. Lecturer in education and women's studies, University of Hong Kong (retired); active in feminist and gay politics in Hong Kong and the United Kingdom. **Essays:** Hanscombe; Namjoshi.

IMHOF, Robin. Reference librarian, Burlingame, California. **Essay:** Boye.

JACKSON, Jill U. Archivist, Archives for Research on Women and Gender, University of Texas at San Antonio. **Essay:** Freedman.

JAMES, G. Winston. Executive director, Other Countries: Black Gay Expression artists collective; member, John Oliver Killens Writers Workshop Inc.; anthologized in *Waves: An Anthology of New Gay Fiction,* 1994, *Shade: An Anthology of Short Fiction by Gay Men of African Descent,* 1996, and *HIS: Brilliant New Gay Fiction,* 1997. **Essay:** Morrow.

JENSON, Deborah. Assistant professor of French at the University of New Mexico; editor of Hélène Cixous's *"Coming to Writing" and Other Essays*; published articles on nineteenth-century French literature and culture. **Essay:** Cixous.

KARLINSKY, Simon. Professor Emeritus of Slavic languages and literatures, University of California, Berkeley; author of *The Sexual Labyrinth of Nikolai Gogol; Marina Tsvetaeva: The Woman, Her World and Her Poetry*; and *Russian Drama from its Beginnings to the Age of Pushkin*; editor of *Anton Chekhov's Life and Thought* and *The Nabokov-Wilson Letters.* **Essay:** Pereleshin.

KATTELMAN, Beth A. Graduate student, Ohio State University; writing dissertation on female hard-boiled detective characters in the plays of Holly Hughes and Joan Schirle; contributor to *The Gay and Lesbian Literary Heritage,* 1995, *The American National Biographical Dictionary,* and the *Oxford Dictionary of National Biography.* **Essays:** Loulan; Terry.

KENDALL, Gillian. Contributor of short stories to periodicals, including *Girlfriends, Thirteenth Moon,* and *The Sun;* co-writing a biography, *How I Became a Human Being* (Kodansha Press, 1997). **Essays:** Bloch; Cooper.

KOHL, Judith C. Professor Emeritus of English and humanities, Dutchess Community College, Poughkeepsie, New York; contributor to *Dictionary of Women Writers, British Women Writers, Contemporary Authors, Contemporary Popular Writers, Gay and Lesbian Biography,* and *Lesbian Histories and Cultures.* **Essays:** D'Annunzio; Maso.

LANG, Birgit. Essays: Galford; Reinig; Urbanitzky.

LUTES, Michael A. Reference and government documents librarian, University of Notre Dame; contributor to *Gay and Lesbian Literature,* (1994), and *Gay and Lesbian Literary Companion* (1995); reviewer for *Library Journal* and *Choice.* **Essays:** Arenas; Guibert; Leyland; Stambolian.

MacPIKE, Loralee. Professor of English, California State University, San Bernardino; founder and editor of *The Lesbian Review of Books;* author of *There's Something I've Been Meaning to Tell You* (1989), *Dostoevsky's Dickens* (1981), and several essays. **Essays:** Casal; Chrystos; Gearhart.

MALINOWSKY, H. Robert. Manager of collections development and reference, University of Illinois at Chicago; member of ALA Gay and Lesbian Task Force; member of SLA Caucus on Gay and Lesbian Issues; member of the University of Illinois at Chicago's Chancellor's Committee on the Status of Lesbian and Gay Issues; editor of the *International Directory of Gay and Lesbian Periodicals,* 1987; editor, *AIDS Book Review Journal: An Electronic Journal,* from 1993.

MARCHANT, Elizabeth A. Assistant professor of Latin American literature and culture, University of California, Santa Barbara; author of "The Critical Discourse of Lucia Miguel Pereira" (1992); writing a book on Latin American women and cultural criticism, 1920-1950. **Essays:** Caminha; Molloy.

MARIE, Jacquelyn. Reference/womens studies librarian, University of California, Santa Cruz, California; contributor to *Gay and Lesbian Literature, Feminist Writers,* and *Gay and Lesbian Biography.* **Essay:** Livia.

MARKS, Jim. Publisher, Lambda Book Report; contributor of criticism to the *Advocate,* the *Washington Blade,* the *Washington Post,* and numerous other publications; author of "We Three," in *Friends and Lovers,* edited by John Preston.

MAXWELL, Lynne. English instructor, law librarian, writer on social science issues, and literary critic; contributor to *Lambda Book Report, College Composition and Communication,* and *Is-*

sues: The Newsletter of the Adoptive Family Rights Council. **Essay:** Wings.

McCAULEY, Bill. Teaches English at the German School, Washington; working on Ph.D. in English literature and criticism at Indiana University of Pennsylvania. **Essay:** Merrick.

McELDOWNEY, Elliott. Graduate student, Tufts University, Medford, Massachusetts; writing dissertation on addiction and homosexuality in twentieth-century American fiction. **Essays:** Kureishi; Riggs; Watney.

McQUAIN, Kelly. English instructor, Temple University, Philadelphia, Pennsylvania; essays and fiction have appeared in the *Philadelphia Inquirer Magazine, Kansas Quarterly/Arkansas Review, James White Review,* and the anthologies *Certain Voices, Generation Q,* and *Best Gay Erotica 1997.* **Essay:** Grimsley.

MILLER, Michael J. Social work librarian and coordinator, social science electronic information resources, Whitney M. Young, Jr. Memorial Library of Social Work, Columbia University, New York. **Essay:** Marcus.

MORIEL, Liora. Doctoral student, comparative literature program, University of Maryland, College Park. **Essays:** Glickman; DeHaan.

MORRIS, Richard. Visiting professor, Valparaiso University, Valparaiso, Indiana; co-author of *Networks of Writing: On-line Culture in the Information Age.* **Essays:** de Veaux; Keenan.

MYALL, Carolynne. Head of collection services, Eastern Washington University Library, Cheney, Washington; co-author, *Women and the Values of American Librarianship* (1994); contributor to library and Quaker publications. **Essays:** Deming; Wilhelm.

OLSON, Tanya. Doctoral student in English, University of North Carolina, Greensboro; writing dissertation on the uses of queer sexuality in Irish literature. **Essay:** Casement.

O'STEINBERG, David. Irish/Jewish/American poet, short story, fiction, and nonfiction writer; author of "Kafka's Nightmare," *Disgruntled* (http://www.disgruntled.com); "Not Me Either," *Evergreen Chronicles,* 1997; "Heaven" and "Another Day," *The Chiron Review,* 1997; "Gingko Trees, Eureka Street," *A Loving Testimony: Remembering Loves Ones Lost to AIDS,* 1996. **Essay:** Parmar.

PETERSON, Andrea L. T. Freelance writer. **Essays:** Bailey; Bronski; Callen; Dreher; Lagerlof; McCauley; Nin.

PETERSON, David J. Graduate student, University of Georgia, Athens; currently completing a dissertation on Walt Whitman and the construction of homosexuality in his poetry. **Essays:** Anderson; Gooch; Greenberg.

PINARSKI, Annmarie. Instructor, English and women's studies, Bowling Green State University, Bowling Green, Ohio. **Essays:** Cliff; DeLauretis.

PROSSER, Jay. Author of *Second Skins: The Body Narratives of Transsexuality,* forthcoming. **Essay:** Feinberg.

PUTNEY, Christopher. Assistant professor of Slavic languages and literatures, University of North Carolina at Chapel Hill. **Essay:** Karlinsky.

RICHARDS, Gary. Lecturer, Vanderbilt University, Nashville, Tennessee; completed dissertation on same-sex desire in mid-twentieth-century Southern fiction. **Essays:** Goyen; Smith; Phillips.

RIDINGER, Robert B. Marks. Essays: Barr; Brand; Duplechan; Fricke; Kirkwood; Kliuev; Maddy; Mohr; Nugent; Rice; Saint; Steakley; Trifonov; Vining.

ROBINSON, J.E. Short story writer. **Essays:** Locke; Thurman.

RODGERS, Tara. Graduate of Brown University, 1995; musician and freelancer in publishing, New York City. **Essay:** Porter.

ROMERO, Alberto, Jr. Student of English literature, University of Illinois, Urbana-Champaign. **Essay:** Benavente.

ROSCO, Jerry. Co-editor of *Continual Lessons: The Journals of Glenway Wescott,* and author of biography, *Glenway Wescott Personally;* contributor of articles and stories to periodicals and anthologies. **Essay:** Wescott.

RUSSELL, Sue. Poet and critic; contributor to *Kenyon Review, Lambda Book Report, VLS,* and *Women's Review of Books;* co-editor of anthology of writing by individuals with bipolar disorder. **Essays:** Bishop; Hacker; Harris; Swenson.

SAUTMAN, Francesca Canadé. Professor of French, women's studies, and medieval studies at Hunter College and the graduate school of CUNY; author of *La Religion du quotidien: Rites et croyances populaires de la fin du moyen age* (Firenze, Leo S. Olschki, 1995); co-editor, with Pamela Sheingorn, *Women and Same-Sex Desire in the Middle Ages* (forthcoming); writing a book entitled *Invisible Women: Lesbian Working Class Culture in France, 1880-1930.* **Essays:** Causse; Crevel; Delarue-Mardrus; Goodman; Pastre; Rochefort.

SCHIFF, Adam L. Principal cataloger, University of Washington libraries, Seattle; member, ALA Gay, Lesbian, and Bisexual Task Force; former chair, ALA Gay and Lesbian Book Award Committee; director, Biological Sciences Division, Special Libraries Association; former editor, *Biofeedback.*

SHIVELY, Charley. Essay: Delany.

STONE, Martha E. Coordinator for reference services, Treadwell Library, Massachusetts General Hospital, Boston; book reviewer for numerous publications; associate editor at *The Harvard Gay and Lesbian Review.* **Essay:** Katharine Lee Bates.

SUMMERS, Edward. Social sciences librarian, University of Illinois, Champaign-Urbana. **Essays:** Doty; Lassell; Malouf.

SWARTWOUT, Susan. Assistant professor of English, Southeast Missouri State University, Cape Girardeau, Missouri; author of *Freaks: A Collection of Poetry,* 1995, and *Uncommon Ground,* 1996; small press editor for Amazon.com and regular contributor to *American Book Review.* **Essay:** Frame.

SWARTZ, Patti Capel. Instructor in English, Morehead State University, Morehead, Kentucky; author of manuscript *Tongues Afire,* discussing women's writing and pedagogy; working on a book detailing the lesbian content of nineteenth-century writer Constance Fenimore Woolson. **Essays:** Block; Brantenberg; Hwang; Jewett; June Jordan; Lucas; McKay; Nava; Tsui; Vaid; Wolverton; Woodson.

TEDROWE, Melissa. Graduate student, University of Illinois at Urbana-Champaign. **Essay:** Garber.

THOMAS, Wendy. Public service librarian, Schlesinger Library on the History of Women in America, Radcliffe College, Cambridge, Massachusetts; coordinator, Social Responsibilities Round Table, American Library Association, from 1996; co-chair, Gay, Lesbian & Bisexual Task Force, American Library Association, 1993-96.

TOVA. Editor and author of poetry, fiction, essays, and journalistic pieces; published in *Queerly Classed, Nice Jewish Girls, Growing Up in America,* and *Bridges: A Journal for Jewish Feminists and Our Friends;* environmental research librarian; vegetarian columnist for online travel journal; core editorial group member of *Bridges: A Journal for Jewish Feminists and Our Friends.* **Essays:** Dykewomon; Kaye/Kantrowitz; Klepfisz; Rukeyser.

TURNER, Deborah. Multicultural outreach librarian, University of California, Santa Cruz; contributor to the anthologies *Liberating Minds: The Stories and Professional Lives of Gay, Lesbian and Bisexual Librarians,* 1997, and *Testimony: Young African-Americans on Self-Discovery and Black Identity,* 1995. **Essays:** Clark; Cullen.

VAN GESSEL, Nina. Lecturer; dissertation examined autobiographies of modernist women publishers and editors; author of forthcoming articles about Margaret Anderson. **Essay:** Anderson.

VAN MARLE, Toni. Essays: Blaman; Donoghue.

WALTER, Virginia. Associate professor of library and information science, Graduate School of Education and Information Studies, University of California, Los Angeles; author of *War and Peace Literature for Children and Young Adults: A Resource Guide to Significant Issues,* 1993, and *HIV/AIDS Information for Children: A Guide to Resources and Issues,* with Melissa Gross, 1997. **Essay:** Cart.

WATERMAN, Blaine. Reference librarian, San Francisco Public Library. **Essay:** Roscoe.

WEST, Gabriella. Writer and book reviewer; regular contributor to *San Francisco Review of Books,* 1990-95; contributor to anthologies, including *Early Embraces* and *Hot Ticket.* **Essay:** Bright.

WHITELAW, Lis. Lecturer in literature, University of Birmingham School of Continuing Studies; associate lecturer, Open University; author of *The Life and Rebellious Times of Cicely Hamilton,* 1990, and of short fiction published in various anthologies by Onlywomen Press. **Essay:** Manning.

WILLIAMSON, Alistair. Associate editor, *The Harvard Gay & Lesbian Review;* former director of Alyson Publications. **Essay:** Willhoite.

WILLIAMSON, Barbara. Graduate student, University of Nebraska, Lincoln; writing dissertation on the transforming images of women in twentieth-century American literature and popular film. **Essay:** Kim.

WRAY, B.J. Ph.D. student, department of English, University of Calgary, Alberta, Canada; writing dissertation on contemporary Canadian lesbian performance art, fiction, poetry, and film entitled *An Aesthetics of Lack: Reading Canadian Lesbian Texts.* **Essay:** Butler.

ZIMMERMAN, Bonnie. Professor of women's studies, San Diego State University; author of *The Safe Sea of Women: Lesbian Fiction 1969-1989* (1990); co-editor of *Professions of Desire: Lesbian and Gay Studies in Literature* (1995), and *The New Lesbian Studies: Into the 21st Century* (1996); editor of *The Encyclopedia of Homosexuality, Volume I: Lesbian Histories and Cultures* (1999).